DOMESDAY GAZETTEER

DOMESDAY GAZETTEER

BY

H. C. DARBY, Litt.D., F.B.A.

AND

G. R. VERSEY, M.A.

CAMBRIDGE UNIVERSITY PRESS

CAMBRIDGE

LONDON · NEW YORK · MELBOURNE

Published by the Syndics of the Cambridge University Press
The Pitt Building, Trumpington Street, Cambridge CB2 1RP
Bentley House, 200 Euston Road, London NW1 2DP
32 East 57th Street, New York, NY 10022, USA
296 Beaconsfield Parade, Middle Park, Melbourne 3206, Australia

Library of Congress catalogue card number: 75-19532

ISBN: 0 521 20666 9

First published 1975

Printed in Great Britain
at the
University Printing House, Cambridge
(Euan Phillips, University Printer)

CONTENTS

The map section is at the end of the volume.

PREFACE

The maps in the other volumes of *The Domesday Geography of England* rarely show place-names because of the limitation imposed by their scales. It is with this in mind that the present volume has been prepared. The Index includes both the Domesday place-names and their modern equivalents, and so indicates how the various Domesday place-names have been identified and allocated. The Maps show the distribution of Domesday vills against a background of relief and rivers. An Introductory Note explains the method of both Index and Maps.

Although designed for readers of the 'Domesday Geographies', it is hoped that the *Gazetteer* will also be of use to others who work in the field of English medieval history and geography.

CAMBRIDGE
St Tibb's Day, 1975

H. C. DARBY
G. R. VERSEY

LIST OF ABBREVIATIONS

Beds.	Bedfordshire
Berks.	Berkshire
Bucks.	Buckinghamshire
Cambs.	Cambridgeshire
Ches.	Cheshire
Corn.	Cornwall
D.B.	Domesday Book
Derby.	Derbyshire
Devon	Devonshire
Do.	Dorset
E.R.	East Riding of Yorkshire
Ess.	Essex
Exch. D.B.	Exchequer Domesday Book
Exon D.B.	Exeter Domesday Book
Gloucs.	Gloucestershire
Hants.	Hampshire
hd	hundred
Heref.	Herefordshire
Herts.	Hertfordshire
Hunts.	Huntingdonshire
I.O.W.	Isle of Wight
Lancs.	Lancashire
Leics.	Leicestershire
Lincs.	Lincolnshire
L.D.B.	Little Domesday Book
Mdlx.	Middlesex
Norf.	Norfolk
N'hants.	Northamptonshire
N.R.	North Riding of Yorkshire
Notts.	Nottinghamshire
Oxon.	Oxfordshire
Salop.	Shropshire
Som.	Somerset
Staffs.	Staffordshire
Suff.	Suffolk
Sx.	Sussex
T.R.E.	*Tempore regis Edwardi*
Unid.	Unidentified
Warw.	Warwickshire
W.R.	West Riding of Yorkshire
Wilts.	Wiltshire
Worcs.	Worcestershire
Yorks.	Yorkshire

INTRODUCTORY NOTE

Over 13,000 separate places are named in Domesday Book – 13,278 in Domesday England itself, and about 140 (it is impossible to be precise) in districts now within Wales. These totals include 111 boroughs in England and one (Rhuddlan) in North Wales. As many as 175 places out of the grand total of 13,418 cannot be precisely located but they can be assigned to particular parishes; these 'lost' names are shown in italics on the maps. As a result of coastal changes some places have disappeared under the sea – sixteen along the coast of the East Riding and two (including the borough of Dunwich) along that of Suffolk. Furthermore, 386 names out of the total (just under 3%) have not been identified.

A place is often mentioned more than once in Domesday Book with different spellings, and each variant has been included in the Index. For the place-names of Essex, Norfolk and Suffolk, the folio references are those of the Little Domesday Book. A further range of variant spellings appears in the Exeter Domesday Book which surveys the counties of Cornwall and Somerset, almost the whole of Devonshire, about one-third that of Dorset and a solitary Wiltshire manor. These Exeter names and their folio references are given in brackets, but when an Exeter name is the same as that in the main, or so-called Exchequer, Domesday Book, the fact is indicated by an asterisk wherever convenient. These are examples of the variants in the Index for Devonshire:

Orcartone(*-tona*)	See Orcheton
Orcheton	*Orcartone* 105b(*-tona* 217b)
(*Estotdona*)	See Staddon
Staddon	*Stotdone* 110 (*Estotdona* 331)
Stotdone	See Staddon
Badgworthy	*Bicheordin* 110b(*402b, 499)
*Bicheordin**	See Badgworthy

Many Domesday place-names are represented today only by hamlets, by individual houses and farms, or by minor topographical features such as fields. The parishes in which these lie have not been indicated except where it has been necessary to distinguish between different places bearing the same name. The names of over 2,300 modern parishes are not mentioned in Domesday Book. Although they cannot appear on the maps, they have been included in the Index and described as 'Not in D.B.'. The result of these various complications is that the number of entries in the Index greatly exceeds the total of Domesday places and amounts to some 36,000.

The total number of settlements in 1086 must have been far greater than the 13,400 or so named places. In the first place, the constituent vills of a large number of manors were not separately named. These components included *berewichae*, *appendicii*, *membrae*, *pertinentes* and sub-tenancies; their resources were often contained within the totals for a manor as a whole, and Domesday Book does not enable us to say whether or not they were at places mentioned in other entries. Even when there is no reference to such dependencies we may strongly suspect their existence on many manors with very large totals for hides, men, teams and other resources. Furthermore, we hear of holdings that had been added to (*addita*) or taken away from (*ablata*) manors; some of these holdings were at named places, others were not. The latter are included in the Index under the names of their parent manors.

Secondly, some adjoining places may have been described under one name. A number of these came to be represented in later times by groups of two or more places with distinguishing appellations such as Great and Little or East and West. The folios for such places are given in the Index under their basic names, e.g. Shelford in Cambridgeshire; but Great and Little Shelford are also indexed with cross-references to Shelford. On the maps of the other volumes of this series each of such groups is indicated by a single symbol. The larger scale of the present maps, on the other hand, enables all the places in such groups to be shown separately. This has been done by means of open circles, e.g. an open circle each for Great and Little Shelford; but it must be pointed out that we cannot be sure that two separate settlements were already in existence here by 1086. Occasionally, however, Domesday Book does reveal the fact that more than one settlement did exist by speaking, for example, of *Cocheswelle* and *alia Cocheswelle*, that is Great and Little Coxwell in Berkshire, of *Bedefunt* and *Westbedefund*, that is East and West Bedfont in Middlesex, or, again, of *Nortstoches* and *Sudstoches*, that is North and South Stoke in Lincolnshire. Some adjoining places bearing the same name were described under different hundreds; thus in Suffolk, *Saham* (Hoxne hundred) and *Saham* (Loes hundred) have become Monk and Earl Soham respectively; such places have likewise been counted as separate settlements. These names (with their folio references) have been entered separately in the Index, e.g. East Bedfont and West Bedfont but not Bedfont itself. They appear on the maps each with a solid symbol in the usual manner.

Then, thirdly, we know of yet other places in 1086 that were not named in Domesday Book. They are mentioned in contemporary or near-contemporary documents that may have been associated with the Domesday Inquest – the *Inquisitio Comitatus Cantabrigiensis*, the *Inquisitio Eliensis*, the Domesday Monachorum, the Excerpta and the Exeter Geld Rolls. Still more places can be identified from other documents such as pre-Domesday charters and post-Domesday cartularies and surveys. But in view of the uneven nature of the evidence and of the varying degree of certainty involved, no use has been made of these latter documents. To this there is one exception. A transcript of the Herefordshire folios (Balliol MS 350), made probably between 1160 and 1170, has marginal annotations, and these include a number of place-names that do not appear in Domesday Book itself. Altogether, these associated documents add a further 26 names to the Domesday total of settlements. Twenty-two appear in brackets on the maps, and the remaining four are unidentified.

Furthermore, there are some other unnamed Domesday holdings which cannot be identified; and we cannot tell whether they were at places named in other entries or whether they were at places entirely unrecorded in Domesday Book. All anonymous Domesday holdings, identified and unidentified, are set out at the end of the Index for each county in the order in which they occur. They appear in Domesday Book in a variety of contexts and it is impossible to summarize them in a uniform manner. When available, the following information is given for each: name of tenant and tenant-in-chief; assessment; name of hundred; folio; identification.

The Index is arranged by counties as they were in the years around 1900. In thinking of the relation of these to the Domesday counties, the following points must be borne in mind:

1. Northumberland, Durham, Cumberland and Westmorland were not described in Domesday Book except that four places now in Cumberland and 24 now in Westmorland were named in the Yorkshire folios.

2. There is no Domesday account of Lancashire as such, and the name did not appear until towards the end of the twelfth century. The places in the area to the north of the Ribble were named in the Yorkshire folios. The area to the south of the Ribble was described in a kind of appendix to the account of Cheshire, under the heading *Inter Ripam et Mersham*.

3. Rutland did not appear as a separate county until the thirteenth century. Its eastern part was in Domesday Northamptonshire, and its western part formed an anomalous unit called *Roteland* which was described after Nottinghamshire.

4. The boundary with Wales was in a very fluid condition in the eleventh century. As many as 40 places now in Wales were described in the folios for Shropshire, Herefordshire and Gloucestershire and another 100 in, or at the end of, the Cheshire folios. The Domesday forms of these names have been included in the Index under their respective county headings with cross-references to a separate list of places now in Wales. The 114 places that can be identified have been marked on the relevant county maps.

5. Finally, there have been various changes in boundaries between counties, and some places described in the folios for one county have been transferred to other counties at various dates. A few places were described partly under one county and partly under another; and, furthermore, a number of places were mentioned or described in the folios of a Domesday county in which they were never geographically situated.

The Index for each county includes:

(*a*) All modern place-names together with their Domesday forms and folio references, including any references from other Domesday counties. In the latter case, the county is indicated. After each modern name a grid reference indicates its position on the relevant map. The following are characteristic entries for Bedfordshire:

Biscot, C. 7	*Bissopescote* 209b
Harrowden, C. 4	*Hergentone* 217
	Herghetone 211b, 214b
Barwythe, C. 8	*Bereuuorde* 138, Herts.
Podington, B. 2	*Podintone* 215b, 216
	Potintone 225b, N'hants.

(*b*) All the Domesday names that appear in the folios for a county, with cross-references to their modern names, normally in the same county but sometimes in another. The following are characteristic entries, again for Bedfordshire:

Chaisot	See Keysoe
Chenebaltone	See Kimbolton, Hunts.

This arrangement is intended to be useful to those who approach the Gazetteer either from the point of view of modern names or from that of Domesday names.

BEDFORDSHIRE—*BEDEFORDSCIRE*

Folios 209–218b

MAP 2

Achelei(a)	See Oakley
Ai(ss)euuorde	See Eyeworth
Alricesei(a), -eie	See Arlesey
Ammetelle	See Ampthill
Ampthill, C. 5	*Ammetelle* 214
Arlesey, E. 5	*Alricesei(a), -eie* 210b, 212, 214b, 218
Aspeleia	See Aspley Guise
Aspley Guise, B. 5	*Aspeleia* 213
Astwick, E. 5	*Estuuiche* 213b, 215b
Badelesdone, -estone	See Battlesden
Barton in the Clay, D. 6	*Bertone* 210b
Barwythe, C. 8	*Bereuuorde* 138, Herts.
Battlesden, B. 6	*Badelesdone, -estone* 211, 216, 218
Bedeford	See Bedford
Bedford, C. 4	*Bedeford* 209, 210b
Beeston, E. 4	*Bistone* 212b, 215, 216b, 218, 218b
Bereforde	See Great Barford, Little Barford
Bertone	See Barton in the Clay
Bichelesuuade	See Biggleswade
Biddenham, C. 4	*Bide(n)ham* 210, 210b, 211, 213b, 214b, 218
Bide(n)ham	See Biddenham
Biggleswade, E. 4	*Bichelesuuade* 217 *bis* *Pichelesuuade* 217
Billington	Not in D.B.
Biscot, C. 7	*Bissopescote* 209b
Bissopescote	See Biscot
Bistone	See Beeston
Blach-, Blecheshou	See Bletsoe
Bledone	See Bleadon, Som.
Bletsoe, C. 3	*Blach-, Blecheshou* 213, 217

Blun(e)ham	See Blunham
Blunham, D. 4	*Blun(e)ham* 210b, 212b, 217b
Bolehestre	See Bolnhurst
Bolnhurst, D. 3	*Bole-, Bulehestre* 209b, 210, 211, 217
Brimeham	See Bromham
Bromham, C. 4	*Brimeham* 218b *Bruneham* 211, 213b, 217
Broom, E. 5	*Brume* 214
Brume	See Broom
Bruneham	See Bromham
Bulehestre	See Bolnhurst
Caddington, C. 7	*Cadendone* 211, Beds.; 136, Herts.
Cadendone	See Caddington
Cainhoe, D. 5	*Cainou* 218 *Chainehou* 214
Cainoe	See Cainhoe
Caisot	See Keysoe
Calnestorne	See Chawston
Cameston(e)	See Kempston
Campton, D. 5	*Chambeltone* 211b, 212, 216b
Cardington, D. 4	*Chernetone* 212b, 217b
Carlentone	See Carlton
Carlton, B. 3	*Carlentone* 209b, 214b, 216b, 218b
Celgrave	See Chalgrave
Cerlentone	See Chalton
Chainehou	See Cainhoe
Chainhalle	See Channell's End
Chaisot	See Keysoe
Chalgrave, C. 6	*Celgrave* 212, 216b
Chalton, D. 4	*Cerlentone* 217b
Chambeltone	See Campton
Channell's End, D. 3	*Chainhalle* 212b
Chauelestorne	See Chawston

Chawston, D. 3	*Calnestorne* 213b *Chauelestorne* 212, 215
Chellington	Not in D.B.
Chenebaltone	See Kimbolton, Hunts.
Chenemondewiche	See Kinwick
Chenotinga	See Knotting
Chernetone	See Cardington
Chichesana, *-sane*	See Chicksands
Chicksands, D. 5	*Chichesana*, *-sane* 210b, 218
Chochepol	See Cople
Clapham, C. 3	*Clopeham* 212 *bis*
Clifton, D. 5	*Cliftone* 210b *Clistone* 210b, 212b, 214b, 217b
Cliftone, *Clistone*	See Clifton
Clopeham	See Clapham
Clopelle	See Clophill
Clophill, D. 5	*Clopelle* 214
Cochepol	See Cople
Cockayne Hatley, F. 4	*Hatelai* 217b, 218
Coldentone	See Goldington
Colmeborde, *-eworde*	See Colmworth
Colmworth, D. 3	*Colmeborde* 211b *Colmeworde* 213b *Culmeuuorde* 213
Cople, D. 4	*C(h)ochepol* 213b *bis*, 214, 217b
Cranfelle	See Cranfield
Cranfield, B. 5	*Cranfelle* 210b
Crauelai	See Husborne Crawley
Crauenhest	See Gravenhurst
Crawelai	See Husborne Crawley
Cudessane	Unid., 211b, 214
Culmeuuorde	See Colmworth
Danitone	See Dunton
Dean, Lower and Upper, C. 2	*Dena* 209b *Dene* 210, 211b, 218b
Dena, *Dene*	See Dean
Dodintone	See Toddington
Donitone	See Dunton

Dunstable	Not in D.B.
Dunton, E. 4	*Danitone* 216 *Donitone* 211b
Eastcotts	Not in D.B.
Eaton Bray, B. 7	*Eitone* 209b
Eaton Socon, E. 3	*Etone* 212
Echam	See Higham Gobion
Edeuuorde	See Edworth
Edingeberge	See Edlesborough, Bucks.
Edworth, E. 5	*Edeuuorde* 212, 218b
Egginton	Not in D.B.
Eitone	See Eaton Bray
Elnestou	See Elstow
Elstow, C. 4	*Elnestou* 217
Eluendone	See Elvedon
Elvedon, C. 2	*Eluendone* 216b
Eseltone	See Shelton (in Marston Moretaine), Shelton (near Swineshead)
Esseltone	See Shelton (in Marston Moretaine)
Estodham	See Studham
Estone	See Little Staughton
Estuuiche	See Astwick
Etone	See Eaton Socon
Eversholt, C. 6	*Evres(h)ot* 209b, 213, 218b
Everton, E. 4	*Evretone* 217b
Evres(h)ot	See Eversholt
Evretone	See Everton
Eyeworth, E. 4	*Ai(ss)euuorde* 215, 218
Falmeresham	See Felmersham
Farndish, B. 2	*Fernadis* 216, 216b *Farnedis* 225b, N'hants.
Felmersham, C. 3	*Falmeresham* 217 *Flammeresham* 216b
Fernadis	See Farndish

Flammeresham	See Felmersham
Flicteuuiche	See Flitwick
Flictha	See Flitton
Flitton, C. 5	*Flictha* 215
Flitwick, C. 6	*Flicteuuiche* 216
Giveldene	See Yelden
Gledelai	See Nares Gladley
Goldentone	See Goldington
Goldington, C. 4	*Coldentone* 218b *Goldentone* 210, 212b, 213b
Gravenhurst, D. 5	*Crauenhest* 213
Great Barford, D. 4	*Bereforde* 213b *bis*
Hagenes	See Haynes
Hanefeld(e)	Unid., 211b, 218b
Haneslau(ue)	See Henlow
Haneuuic(h)	See Hinwick
Hanslau(e)	See Henlow
Hareuuelle	See Harrold
Harlington, C. 6	*Herlingdone* 214
Harrold, B. 3	*Hareuuelle* 217
Harrowden, C. 4	*Hergentone* 217b *Herghetone* 211, 214b
Hatelai	See Cockayne Hatley
Haynes, D. 5	*Hagenes* 213
Heath	Not in D.B.
Heneuuic(h)	See Hinwick
Henlow, E. 5	*Haneslau(ue)* 214b, 218 *Hanslau(e)* 215b, 218
Hergentone, *Herghetone*	See Harrowden
Herlingdone	See Harlington
Higham Gobion, D. 6	*Echam* 213
Hinwick, B. 3	*Haneuuic(h)* 216 *bis* *Heneuuic(h)* 210, 214b, 216b, 218
Hocheleia	See Hockliffe
Hockliffe, B. 6	*Hocheleia* 218
Holcot, B. 5	*Holecote* 214b
Holecote	See Holcot

Holewella, *-welle*	See Holwell, Herts.
Holma, *Holme*	See Holme
Holme, E. 5	*Holma* 213b *Holme* 212, 214b, 215b, 217, 217b, 218b
Houghton Conquest, C. 5	*Houstone* 213, 217 *Oustone* 217b
Houghton Regis, C. 7	*Houstone* 209b *bis*
Houstone	See Houghton Conquest, Houghton Regis
Husborne Crawley, B. 5	*Crauelai* 216 *Crawelai* 214
Hyde	Not in D.B.
Kempston, C. 4	*Cameston(e)* 217 *ter*, 217b
Kensworth, C. 7	*Canesworde* 136, Herts.
Keysoe, C. 2	*C(h)aisot* 212b *bis*, 216b *Caissot* 205b, 207b, Hunts.
Kinwick, E. 4	*Chenemondewiche* 210b
Knotting, C. 2	*Chenotinga* 209b
Lalega	See Thurleigh
Langeford	See Langford
Langford, E. 5	*Langeford* 215b *bis*
Leagrave	Not in D.B.
Leighton Buzzard, B. 7	*Lestone* 209, 210b
Lestone	See Leighton Buzzard
Lidlington, C. 5	*Litincletone* 211
Limbury	Not in D.B.
Lintone	See Luton
Litincletone	See Lidlington
Little Barford, E. 3	*Bereforde* 210b, 216b
Little Staughton, D. 2	*Estone* 210 *bis*, 211b, 213, 216 *bis*, 216b
Loitone	See Luton

Lower Dean	See Dean
Luton, D. 7	*Lintone* 216, 218b *Loitone* 209, 209b
Malpertesselle	See Meppershall
Marston Moretaine, C. 5	*Mer(e)stone* 211b, 214
Maulden, C. 5	*Meldone* 211b, 213, 214, 217, 218b
Melceburne	See Melchbourne
Melchbourne, C. 2	*Melceburne* 209b
Meldone	See Maulden
Melebroc	See Millbrook
Melehou	See Millow
Meppershall, D. 5	*Malpertesselle* 216b *Maperteshale* 142, Herts.
Mer(e)stone	See Marston Moretaine
Middeltone, *Mildentone*	See Milton Bryant, Milton Ernest
Millbrook, C. 5	*Melebroc* 214
Millow, E. 5	*Melehou* 210b, 211b, 212
Milton Bryant B. 6	*Middletone* 213 1st entry *Mildentone* 209b
Milton Ernest, C. 3	*Middletone* 212, 213 2nd entry *Mildentone* 214b, 215b, 218, 218b
Moggerhanger	Not in D.B.
Nares Gladley, B. 6	*Gledelai* 217
Neuuentone	See Newton Bromswold, N'hants.
Nortgible, *Nortgiue(le)*	See Northill
Northill, D. 4	*Nortgible* 214 *Nortgiue(le)* 212b, 215
Oakley, C. 3	*Achelei(a)* 215, 217
Odell, B. 3	*Wad(eh)elle* 211, 215b
Otone	See Wootton

Oustone	See Houghton Conquest
Pabeneham	See Pavenham
Partenhale	See Pertenhall
Pavenham, C. 3	*Pabeneham* 211, 215, 216b
Pechesdone	See Pegsdon
Pegsdon, D. 6	*Pechesdone* 210b
Pertenhall, D. 2	*Partenhale* 208, Beds.; 203b, Hunts.
Pichelesuuade	See Biggleswade
Pileworde	See Tilsworth
Podington, B. 2	*Podintone* 215b, 216 *Potintone* 225b, N'hants.
Podintone	See Podington
Polehanger, D. 5	*Polehangre* 137b, Herts.
Polochessele	See Pulloxhill
Potesgrava, *-grave*	See Potsgrove
Potone	See Potton
Potsgrove, B. 6	*Potesgrava*, *-grave* 216, 217, 218b *bis*
Potton, E. 4	*Potone* 217b *bis*
Prestelai	See Priestley
Priestley, C. 6	*Prestelai* 214, 218b
Pulloxhill, C. 6	*Polochessele* 214
Putenehou	See Putnoe
Putnoe, C. 4	*Putenehou* 212b *ter*
Radeuuelle	See Radwell
Radwell, C. 3	*Radeuuelle* 214b, 217
Ravensden	Not in D.B.
Renhold	Not in D.B.
Ridgmont	Not in D.B.
Risedene	See Rushden, N'hants.
Riselai	See Riseley
Riseley, C. 2	*Riselai* 210 *bis*, 212b, 213, 216b *bis*
Rochesdone, *-estone*	See Roxton
Roxton, D. 3	*Rochesdone*, *-estone* 213b, 215

Salchou	See Salph End
Saleford	See Salford
Salford, B. 5	*Saleford* 213
Salph End, D. 3	*Salchou* 213
Sandeia	See Sandy
Sandy, E. 4	*Sandeia* 212
Scernebroc	See Sharnbrook
Segenehou	See Segenhoe
Segenhoe, B. 5	*Segenehou* 216
Segresdone	See Shirdon
Sernebroc, *Serneburg*	See Sharnbrook
Sethlindone	See Shillington
Sewell, C. 7	*Sewelle* 209b
Sewelle	See Sewell
Sewilessou	See Silsoe
Sharnbrook, C. 3	*S(c)ernebroc* 210, 213b, 216, 216b *bis*, 217, 218 *Serneburg* 211
Shefford	Not in D.B.
Shelton (in Marston Moretaine), C. 5	*Es(s)eltone* 214, 216b, 217b
Shelton (near Swineshead), C. 2	*Eseltone* 210
Shillington, D. 6	*Sethlindone* 210b
Shirdon, D. 2	*Segresdone* 216
Silsoe, D. 5	*Sewilessou* 216 *Siuuilessou* 214
Siuuilessou	See Silsoe
Sonedone	See Sundon
Souldrop	Not in D.B.
Southill, D. 5	*Sudgible* 212b *Sudgiuele* 212, 215, 215b, 216, 217b
Stachedene	See Stagsden
Stagsden, B. 4	*Stachesdene* 209b, 211, 212b, 217
Stanbridge	Not in D.B.
Standone	See Stondon
Stanewiga	See Stanwick, N'hants.
Stanford, D. 5	*Stanford(e)* 212b *bis*, 213b, 215, 218, 218b
Stanford(e)	See Stanford
Stepigelai	See Steppingley
Steppingley, C. 5	*Stepigelai* 214b

Stevington, C. 3	*Stiuentone* 211
Stiuentone	See Stevington
Stodfald	See Stotfold
Stondon, D. 5	*Standone* 210b, 218
Stopsley	Not in D.B.
Stotfalt	See Stotfold
Stotfold, E. 5	*Stodfald* 218 *Stotfalt* 213
Stradl(e)i, *Straillei*	See Streatley
Stratone	See Stratton
Stratton, E. 4	*Stratone* 211b, 215b, 217, 217b
Streatley, C. 6	*Stradl(e)i* 212, 214b *bis*, 218b *Straillei* 213
Studham, C. 8	*Estodham* 215
Subberie	See Sudbury
Sudbury, E. 3	*Subberie* 216
Sudgible, *Sudgiuele*	See Southill
Sudtone	See Sutton
Suineshefet	See Swineshead
Sundon, C. 6	*Sonedone* 211b
Sutton, E. 4	*Sudtone* 217b *ter*, 218b *bis* *Suttone* 212
Suttone	See Sutton
Swineshead, C. 2	*Suineshefet* 205b, 206, 208, Hunts.
Tamiseforde	See Tempsford
Tempsford, D. 3	*Tamiseforde* 210, 212, 216, 218b
Thurleigh, C. 3	*Lalega* 212, 213b, 215, 215b
Tilebroc	See Tilbrook, Hunts.
Tilsworth, B. 7	*Pileworde* 212b
Tingrei	See Tingrith
Tingrith, C. 6	*Tingrei* 214
Toddington, C. 6	*Dodintone* 212 *Totingedone* 214b *bis*
Tornai, *-nei(a)*, *Toruei(e)*	See Turvey
Totenehou	See Totternhoe
Totingedone	See Toddington
Totternhoe, C. 7	*Totenehou* 215b, 216

Turvey, B. 3	*Tornai*, *nei(a)* 210, 214b, 215b *Toruei(e)* 209b, 211, 213b, 215, 218b
Upper Dean	See Dean
Wad(eh)elle	See Odell
Warden, D. 4	*Wardone* 215, 217, 218
Wardone	See Warden
War(r)es	See Ware, Herts.
Wel(i)tone	See Willington
Wescota, *-cote*	See Wilshamstead Cotton End
Westoning, C. 6	*Westone* 132b, Herts.
Whipsnade	Not in D.B.
Wiboldestone, *-tune*	See Wyboston
Wilden, D. 3	*Wildene* 209b
Wildene	See Wilden
Willington, D. 4	*Wel(i)tone* 213, 214
Wilshamstead, C. 5	*Winessamestede* 217
Wilshamstead Cotton End, D. 5	*Wescota*, *-cote* 214, 218b
Wimentone	See Wymington
Winessamestede	See Wilshamstead
Woberne	See Woburn
Woburn, B. 6	*Woberne* 218b *Woburne* 211
Woburne	See Woburn
Wootton, C. 4	*Otone* 216b *bis*
Wrestlingworth	Not in D.B.
Wyboston, D. 3	*Wiboldestone*, *-tune* 210b, 212, 213b, 214b, 216, 218
Wymington, B. 2	*Wimentone* 214b, 215b *bis*, 218b *bis*
Yelden, C. 2	*Giveldene* 210

ANONYMOUS HOLDINGS

No place-names appear in the following six entries, and it is possible that some (or even all) of these refer to holdings at places not named elsewhere in Domesday Book:

Geoffrey of Trailly (from bishop of Coutances), 4 hides in Willey hd, 210.
Turgis (from Nigel of Albini), one hide in Manshead hd, 214.
Fulcher of Paris (from Nigel of Albini), half a hide in Biggleswade hd, 214b.
Osbern (from Countess Judith), 2 hides and 3 virgates in Barford hd, 217b.
Turgot and his mother (from the king), half a hide in Stodden hd, 218b.
Osiet (from the king), half a hide in Willey hd, 218b.

BERKSHIRE—*BERROCHESCIRE*

Folios 56–63b

MAP 3

Abendone	See Abingdon
Abingdon, D. 2	*Abendone* 59
Acenge	Unid., 63b
Ældremanestone	See Aldermaston
Aldermaston, E. 6	*Ældremanestone* 56b *Eldremanestune* 58 *Heldremanestune* 58
Aldworth, D. 4	*Elleorde* 63
Alia Cocheswelle	See Little Coxwell
Aneborne	See Enborne
Apleford	See Appleford
Apletone, *-tune*	See Appleton
Appleford, D. 2	*Apleford* 59
Appleton, C. 2	*Apletone*, *-tune* 61b, 63b
Arborfield	Not in D.B.

Ardington, C. 3	*Ardintone* 62 *bis*
Ardintone	See Ardington
Ashbury, A. 3	*Eissesberie* 59b
Ashridge, D. 4	*Assedone* 60
Assedone	See Ashridge
Aston Tirrold, E. 3	*Estone* 56b, 60, 63
Auuilma, *-ilme*	See Ewelme, Oxon.
Avington, B. 5	*Avintone* 62b
Avintone	See Avington
Bagenore	See Bagnor
Bagley Wood	Not in D.B.
Bagnor, C. 5	*Bagenore* 63
Baiorde	See Bayworth
Balking	Not in D.B.
Barkham, G. 6	*Bercheham* 57
Barton, D. 2	*Bertune* 58b *ter*
Basildon, E. 4	*Bastedene* 57
Bastedene	See Basildon
Bayworth, D. 2	*Baiorde* 58b
Bechesgete	See Bagshot, Wilts.
Beckett, A. 3	*Becote* 60
Becote	See Beckett
Bedene	See Beedon
Bedretone	See Betterton
Beech Hill	Not in D.B.
Beedon, D. 4	*Bedene* 58b
Beenham	Not in D.B.
Ben(e)ham	See Benham
Benham, C. 5	*Ben(e)ham* 58b, 63
	Benneham 63b
Benneham	See Benham
Bercheham	See Barkham
Bertune	See Barton
Besentone	See Benson, Oxon.
Bessels Leigh, C. 2	*Leie* 58b
Betterton, C. 3	*Bedretone* 57, 61b
Binfield	Not in D.B.
Bisham, H. 3	*Bistesham* 60b
Bistesham	See Bisham
Blewbury, D. 3	*Blidberie* 56
	Blitberie 56b, 60
Blidberie, *Blitberie*	See Blewbury
Bocheland(e)	See Buckland
Bochentone	See Bockhampton
Bochesorne	See Boxford
Bockhampton, B. 4	*Bochentone* 62b, 63b

Borche(l)deberie, *Borgedeberie*	See Bucklebury
Borgefel(le)	See Burghfield
Borgeldeberie	See Bucklebury
Boroardescote	See Buscot
Bourton	Not in D.B.
Bovsore	See Boxford
Boxford, C. 5	*Bochesorne* 63
	Bovsore 58b
Bradefelt	See Bradfield
Bradfield, E. 5	*Bradefelt* 60b
Brai(o), *Bras*	See Bray
Bray, H. 4	*Brai(o)* 56, 57
	Bras 63b
Bricsteuuelle	See Brightwell
Brightwalton, C. 4	*Bristoldestone* 59b
Brightwell, E. 3	*Bricsteuuelle* 56
	Bristowelle 58
Brimpton, E. 6	*Brintone* 62, 62b
Brintone	See Brimpton
Bristoldestone	See Brightwalton
Bristowelle	See Brightwell
Buckland, B. 2	*Bocheland(e)* 58b, 59b
Bucklebury, D. 5	*Boche(l)deberie* 57, 61b
	Borge(l)deberie 60, 63
Burghfield, F. 5	*Borgefel(le)* 60b, 62b
Burlei	Unid., 60b, 63b *bis*
Buscot, A. 2	*Boroardescote* 60
Calcot, B. 5	*Colecote* 60
Carswell, B. 2	*Chersvelle* 63b
Catmere	See Catmore
Catmore, C. 4	*Catmere* 60
Caueresham	See Caversham
Caversham, F. 5	*Caueresham* 56b
	Cavesham 157b, Oxon.
Cedeledorde, *Cedeneord*	See Chaddleworth
Celgraue	See Chalgrove, Oxon.
Celrea	See Childrey
Celsea, *-sei*	See Cholsey
Cerletone	See Charlton (near Wantage)

Cernei	See Charney Bassett
Ceveslane	See Challow
Chaddleworth, C. 4	*Cedeledorde* 62 *Cedeneord* 59b
Challow, East and West, B. 3	*Ceveslane* 60
Charlton (near Hungerford), B. 5	*Cerletone* 71b, Wilts.
Charlton (near Wantage), C. 3	*Cerletone* 57, 60, 60b, 61, 62b
Charney Bassett, C. 2	*Cernei* 59b
Cheneteberie	See Kintbury
Chenitun	See Kennington
Chersvelle	See Carswell
Chieveley, D. 5	*Civelei* 58b
Childrey, B. 3	*Celrea* 61, 62b, 63
Chilton, D. 3	*Cil(le)tone* 59, 61b
Chingestune	See Kingston Bagpuize
Cholsey, E. 3	*Celsea, -sei* 56b, 62b
Cil(le)tone	See Chilton
Civelei	See Chieveley
Clapcot, E. 3	*Clopecote* 61b *bis*
Clewer, I. 4	*Clivore* 62b
Clivore	See Clewer
Clopecote	See Clapcot
Cocheham	See Cookham
Cocheswelle	See Great Coxwell
Cocheswelle, Alia	See Little Coxwell
Cold Ash	Not in D.B.
Colecote	See Calcot
Coleselle, Coleshalle	See Coleshill
Coleshill, A. 2	*Coleselle* 59b, 63 *Coleshalle* 61 *Coleselle* 72b, Wilts.
Combe, B. 6	*Cumbe* 46b, Hants.
Comenore	See Cumnor
Compton (near Aldworth), D. 4	*Contone* 57b, 58b
Compton Beauchamp, A. 3	*Contone* 61
Contone	See Compton (near Aldworth), Compton Beauchamp

Cookham, H. 3	*Cocheham* 56b, Berks.; 146, Bucks.
Coserige	See Curridge
Crem	See Crowmarsh Gifford and Preston Crowmarsh, Oxon.
Crocheham	See Crookham
Crochestrope	Unid., 60
Crookham, D. 6	*Crocheham* 63b
Crowthorne	Not in D.B.
Cumnor, C. 1	*Comenore* 58b *ter*
Curridge, D. 5	*Coserige* 59b, 62b, 63b
Daneford	See Denford
Dedworth, I. 4	*Dideorde* 63
Dencheswordе	See Denchworth
Denchworth, B. 3	*Dencheswordе* 60b, 61, 62
Denford, B. 5	*Daneford* 61
Deritone	See Donnington
Dideorde	See Dedworth
Donnington, C. 5	*Deritone* 61
Dorkecestre	See Dorchester, Oxon.
Draicote	See Draycott
Draitone, -tune	See Drayton
Draycott, C. 2	*Draicote* 59
Drayton, D. 2	*Draitone, -tune* 60, 61b
Dry Sandford, C. 2	*Sanford* 58b
Dudochesforde	See Duxford
Duxford, B. 2	*Dudochesforde* 63b
Earley, G. 5	*Erlei* 58 *Herlei* 57, 62 2nd entry *Hurlei* 62b
East Challow	See Challow
East Garston	Not in D.B.
East Hagbourne	See Hagbourne
Easthampstead, H. 5	*Lachenestede* 59b
East Hanney	See Hanney
East Hendred	See Hendred
East Ilsley	See Ilsley

East Lockinge	See Lockinge
East Shefford	See Shefford
Eaton (in Appleton), C. 1	*Edtune* 61b *Eltune* 61b
Eaton Hastings, A. 2	*Etone* 61
Ebrige	Unid., 63
Eddevetone	See Eddington
Eddington, B. 5	*Eddevetone* 57b
Edtune	See Eaton (in Appleton)
Eissesberie	See Ashbury
Eldeberie	See Albury, Oxon.
Eldeslei	See Ilsley
Eldremanestune	See Aldermaston
Elentone	See Maidenhead
Eling, D. 5	*Elinge* 62b
Elinge	See Eling
Elleorde	See Aldworth
Eltune	See Eaton (in Appleton)
Enborne, C. 6	*Aneborne* 61, 61b *Taneburne* 61, 62b
Englefel	See Englefield
Englefield, E. 5	*Englefel* 60b *Inglefelle* 60b
Enrede	See Hendred
Erlei	See Earley
Eseldeborne	See Shalbourne, Wilts.
Essages	See Shaw
Estoche	See Stoke, Little, North and South, Oxon.
Estone	See Aston Tirrold
Estralei	See Streatley
Etingedene	See Yattendon
Etone	See Eaton Hastings
Faleslei, *Farellei*	See Fawley
Farnborough, C. 4	*Fermeberge* 59
Fawley, C. 4	*Faleslei* 57b *Farellei* 60
Ferendone	See Great Faringdon
Fermeberge	See Farnborough
Fernham	Not in D.B.
Finchamestede	See Finchampstead
Finchampstead, G. 6	*Finchamestede* 57

Fivehide	See Fyfield
Follescote	See Fulscot
Frieliford	See Frilford
Frilesham	See Frilsham
Frilford, C. 2	*Frieliford* 58b
Frilsham, D. 5	*Frilesham* 60
Fulscot, D. 3	*Follescote* 62b
Fyfield, C. 2	*Fivehide* 60b *bis*
Gainz	See Ginge
Garford, C. 2	*Wareford* 59
Genetune	See Kennington
Ginge, C. 3	*Gainz* 59b
Goosey, B. 3	*Gosei* 59
Gosei	See Goosey
Gratentun	See Gatehampton, Oxon.
Grazeley	Not in D.B.
Great Coxwell, A. 2	*Cocheswelle* 57b
Great Faringdon, A. 2	*Ferendone* 57b
Greenham, D. 6	*Greneham* 60b
Greneham	See Greenham
Grove	Not in D.B.
Hacheborne	See Hagbourne
Hagbourne, East and West, D. 3	*Hacheborne* 61b, 63
Hamesteda, *-stede*	See Hampstead Marshall
Hampstead Marshall, C. 6	*Hamesteda*, *-stede* 63 *bis*
Hampstead Norris, D. 4	*Hanstede* 63
Hanlei, *Hannei*	See Hanney
Hanney, East and West, C. 3	*Hanlei* 59, 60 *Hannei* 60 *bis*, 61b
Harewelle, *Harowelle*	See Harwell
Hartridge, E. 4	*Hurterige* 60b
Haruuelle	See Harwell
Harwell, D. 3	*Harewelle* 62b *bis* *Harowelle* 62b *Haruuelle* 58
Haselie	See Haseley, Oxon.
Hastinges	See Hastings, Sx.
Hatford, B. 2	*Hevaford* 62
Heldremanestune	See Aldermaston

Hendred, East and West, C. 2	*Enrede* 62b *Henret* 57b, 59b, 60, 60b, 63, 63b
Henret	See Hendred
Henstede	See Hampstead Norris
Hentone	See Hinton Waldrist
Herlei	See Earley, Hurley
Hevaford	See Hatford
Hildeslei	See Ilsley
Hingepene	See Inkpen
Hinton Waldrist, B. 2	*Hentone* 63b
Hislelei, *-leu*	See Ilsley
Hocfelle	See Wokefield
Hodcott, D. 4	*Hodicote* 61, 62b
Hodicote	See Hodcott
Hungerford	Not in D.B.
Hurlei	See Earley
Hurley, H. 4	*Herlei* 62, 1st entry
Hurst	Not in D.B.
Hurterige	See Hartridge
Ilsley, East and West, D. 4	*Eldeslei* 56 *Hildeslei* 58, 62 *bis* *Hislelei*, *-leu* 60, 61
Ingepene	See Inkpen
Ingheflot	See Inglewood
Inglefelle	See Englefield
Ingleflot, *-fol*	See Inglewood
Inglewood, B. 6	*Ingheflot* 63b *Ingleflot*, *-fol* 62, 63b
Inkpen, B. 6	*Hingepene* 61 *Ingepene* 63b
Kennington, D. 1	*Chenitun* 58b *Genetune* 58b
Kingston Bagpuize, C. 2	*Chingestune* 60b, 61
Kingston Lisle	Not in D.B.
Kintbury, C. 6	*Cheneteberie* 57b, 60, 61b
Knighton, A. 3	*Nisteton* 63b
Lachenestede	See Easthampstead
Lachinge(s)	See Lockinge

Lamborne	See Lambourn
Lambourn, B. 4	*Lamborne* 57b, 62, 63 *Lanborne* 61b
Lanborne	See Lambourn
Lecanestede	See Leckhampstead
Leckhampstead, C. 4	*Lecanestede* 58b
Lede(n)cumbe	See Letcombe
Leie	See Bessels Leigh
Letcombe Bassett and Regis, B. 3, B. 4	*Lede(n)cumbe* 57b, 62
Leverton, B. 5	*Lewartone* 59
Lewartone	See Leverton
Lierecote	Unid., 63b
Linford	See Lyford
Little Coxwell, A. 3	*Alia Cocheswelle* 57b
Little Wittenham	See Wittenham
Littleworth, B. 2	*Ordia* 58
Lockinge, East and West, C. 3	*Lachinge(s)* 59b, 60b
Lolindone	See Lollingdon
Lollingdon, E. 3	*Lolindone* 62
Lonchelei	Unid., 61b
Longcot	Not in D.B.
Long Wittenham	See Wittenham
Longworth, C. 2	*Ordam* 59
Losfelle	See Losfield
Losfield, I. 4	*Losfelle* 61b
Lyford, C. 2	*Linford* 59
Maidenhead, H. 4	*Elentone* 61b
Marcham, C. 2	*Merceham* 58b
Merceham	See Marcham
Middeltune	See Milton
Midgham, E. 5	*Migeham* 61b
Migeham	See Midgham
Milton, D. 3	*Middeltune* 59
Moreton, North and South, D. 3, E. 3	*Mortune* 61 *bis*, 63
Mortune	See Moreton
Moulsford	Not in D.B.
Nachededorne	Unid., 57b
Neuueham	See Newnham Murren, Oxon.

Newbury, D. 6	*Ulvritone* 62b
Newland	Not in D.B.
Newton, B. 2	*Niwetone* 62
Nisteton	See Knighton
Niwetone	See Newton
Niwetune	See Newington, Oxon.
North Hinksey	Not in D.B.
North Moreton	See Moreton
Odstone, A. 3	*Ordegeston* 61
Offelle	See Wokefield
Offentone	See Uffington
Offetune	See Ufton Nervet
Ollavintone	See Woolhampton
Olvelei	See Woolley
Olvricestone	See Woolstone
Optone	See Upton
Ordam	See Longworth
Ordegeston	See Odstone
Ordia	See Littleworth
Ortone	Unid., 61b
Oxene-, *Oxineford*	See Oxford, Oxon.
Padworth, E. 6	*Peteorde* 61, 63b
Pande-, *Pangeborne*	See Pangbourne
Pangbourne, E. 4	*Pande-*, *Pangeborne* 58, 61b
Peasemore, C. 4	*Praxemere* 60, 62, 62b
Peise	See Pusey
Perie	See Waterperry, Oxon.
Pesei	See Pusey
Peteorde	See Padworth
Piritune	See Pyrton, Oxon.
Porlaa, *-lei*	See Purley
Praxemere	See Peasemore
Purley, F. 4	*Porlaa*, *-lei* 62b, 63
Pusey, B. 2	*Peise* 59b, 60b *Pesei* 59b, 62b
Radinges	See Reading
Radley	Not in D.B.
Rameham	See Remenham
Reading, F. 5	*Radinges* 57 *bis* *Red(d)inges* 56, 58 *bis*, 60
Red(d)inges	See Reading
Remenham, G. 4	*Rameham* 57
Ruscombe	Not in D.B.
Sandhurst	Not in D.B.
Sandleford	Not in D.B.
Sanford	See Dry Sandford
Seacourt, D. 1	*Seuacoorde* 58b
Selingefelle	See Shinfield
Serengeford	See Shellingford
Seriveham	See Shrivenham
Seuacoorde	See Seacourt
Sewelle	See Sheffield
Shaw, D. 5	*Essages* 62b
Sheffield, F. 5	*Sewelle* 60
Shefford, East and West, C. 5	*Siford* 62, 62b *bis*, 63
Shellingford, B. 3	*Serengeford* 59b
Shinfield, F. 5	*Selingefelle* 57
Shippon, D. 2	*Sipene* 58b
Shottesbrook, H. 4	*Sotesbroc* 63b
Shrivenham, A. 3	*Seriveham* 57b
Siford	See Shefford
Sipene	See Shippon
Sireburne	See Shirburn, Oxon.
Soanesfelt	See Swallowfield
Sogoorde	See Sugworth
Solafel	See Swallowfield
Soleham	See Sulham
Soninges	See Sonning
Soningeuuel	See Sunningwell
Sonning, G. 5	*Soninges* 58
Sotesbroc	See Shottesbrook
Sotwell, E. 3	*Sotwelle* 59b
Sotwelle	See Sotwell
Southcot, F. 5	*Sudcote* 61
South Hinksey	Not in D.B.
South Moreton	See Moreton
Sparsholt, B. 3	*Spersold*, *-solt* 57, 57b, 59, 60b, 61b, 63
Speen, C. 5	*Spone* 63
Spersold, *-solt*	See Sparsholt
Spone	See Speen
Standen, B. 5	*Standene* 72, Wilts.
Stanford	See Stanford in the Vale

Place	D.B. form
Stanford Dingley, E. 5	*Stanworde* 61
Stanford in the Vale, B. 2	*Stanford* 60b
Stanworde	See Stanford Dingley
Steventon, D. 3	*Stivetune* 57b
Stivetune	See Steventon
Stradfeld	See Stratfield Mortimer
Stratfield Mortimer, F. 6	*Stradfeld* 62b *Stradfelle* 47, Hants.
Streatley, E. 4	*Estralei* 62
Sudcote	See Southcot
Sudton(e), -tune	See Sutton Courtenay
Sugworth, D. 2	*Sogoorde* 58b
Sulham, F. 5	*Soleham* 61, 61b, 63
Sulhamstead Abbots and Bannister	Not in D.B.
Sunninghill	Not in D.B.
Sunningwell, D. 2	*Soningeuuel* 58b
Sutton Courtenay, D. 2	*Sudton(e), -tune* 56, 57 *bis*, 57b, 59 *Suttone* 56
Suttone	See Sutton Courtenay
Swallowfield, F. 6	*Soanesfelt* 57 *Solafel* 58 *bis*, 63b *Sualefelle* 48 *bis*, Hants.
Taceham	See Thatcham
Taneburne	See Enborne
Thatcham, D. 5	*Taceham* 56b
Tidmarsh	Not in D.B.
Tilehurst	Not in D.B.
Tobenie	See Tubney
Tubney, C. 2	*Tobenie* 58b
Twyford	Not in D.B.
Uffington, B. 3	*Offentone* 59
Ufton Nervet, E. 5	*Offetune* 61, 61b
Ulvritone	See Newbury
Upton, D. 3	*Optone* 63
Wachenesfeld	See Watchfield
Walengeford, -fort	See Wallingford
Waliford	See Welford
Walingeford	See Wallingford
Wallingford, E. 3	*Walengeford, -fort* 56, 58 *bis*, 59b *bis*, 61 *Walingeford* 56, 56b, 57, 57b, 58 *Warengeford* 60, 61b
Walsince	See Wasing
Waltham	See Waltham St Lawrence, White Waltham
Waltham St Lawrence, H. 4	*Waltham* 56b
Wanetinz	See Wantage
Wantage, C. 3	*Wanetinz* 57 *bis*
Wareford	See Garford
Warengeford	See Wallingford
Warfield, H. 5	*Warwelt* 57
Wargrave, G. 4	*Weregrave* 57
Warwelt	See Warfield
Wasing, E. 6	*Walsince* 63
Watchfield, A. 3	*Wachenesfeld* 59
Watecumbe	See Whatcombe
Watelintune	See Watlington, Oxon.
Welford, C. 5	*Waliford* 58b
Wellhouse, D. 5	*Wille* 61b
Wenesfelle	See Winkfield
Weregrave	See Wargrave
West Challow	See Challow
West Hagbourne	See Hagbourne
West Hanney	See Hanney
West Hendred	See Hendred
West Ilsley	See Ilsley
West Lockinge	See Lockinge
Weston, C. 5	*Westun* 58b
West Shefford	See Shefford
Westun	See Weston
Westune	See South Weston, Oxon.
West Woodhay	Not in D.B.
Whatcombe, C. 4	*Watecumbe* 62
Whistley, G. 5	*Wiselei* 59
White Waltham, H. 4	*Waltham* 58, 59b

Whitley, F. 5	*Witelei* 63
Wibalditone	See Willington
Wille	See Wellhouse
Willington, D. 3	*Wibalditone* 60b
Windesores	See Windsor
Windsor, I. 5	*Windesores* 56b *bis*, 62, 62b, Berks.; 32, Surrey; 151b, Bucks.
Winkfield, H. 5	*Wenesfelle* 59
Winnersh	Not in D.B.
Winteham	See Wytham
Winterbourne, C. 5	*Wintreborne*, *-burne* 58 *bis*, 61b
Wintreborne, *-burne*	See Winterbourne
Wiselei	See Whistley
Witeham	See Wittenham
Witelei	See Whitley
Wittenham, Little and Long, D. 2	*Witeham* 56, 59, 60
Wokefield, F. 6	*Hocfelle* 58 *bis* *Offelle* 61b
Wokingham	Not in D.B.
Woolhampton, E. 5	*Ollavintone* 60b
Woolley, C. 4	*Olvelei* 61
Woolstone, B. 3	*Olvricestone* 58
Wootton	Not in D.B.
Wytham, D. 1	*Winteham* 58b
Yattendon, E. 5	*Etingedene* 61

ANONYMOUS HOLDINGS

No place-names appear in the following sixteen entries, and it is possible that some (or even all) of these refer to holdings at places not named elsewhere in Domesday Book:

The king, one hide in Reading hd (appraised with Swallowfield in Charlton hd), 58.
Tori (from bishop of Salisbury), $1\frac{1}{2}$ hides in Wantage hd, 58.
Warin (from Abingdon abbey), half a hide in Ganfield hd, 59b.
Rainald (from Abingdon abbey), 2 hides in Wantage hd, 59b.
Count of Evreux, 5 hides in Wantage hd, 60.
Count of Evreux, one hide in Wantage hd, 60.
Count of Evreux, one hide, 3 virgates and 2 acres in Ganfield hd, 60.
Count of Evreux, 2 hides and 2 acres in Ganfield hd, 60.
Henry de Ferrers, 3 hides and one virgate in Wantage hd, 60b.
Gilbert de Breteville, half a hide in Bucklebury hd, 62.
Robert (from Gilbert of Ghent), 6 hides in *Roeberg* hd, 62.
Robert of Ouilly, one hide in Wantage hd, 62.
Roger de Laci, 2 hides in Wantage hd, 62b.
Alsi of Faringdon (from the king), half a hide in Wantage hd, 63b.
A certain woman, Eddid (from the king), one virgate in Ganfield hd, 63b.
A certain woman, Eldit (from the king), one virgate in Ganfield hd, 63b.

BUCKINGHAMSHIRE—*BOCHINGEHAMSCIRE*

Folios 143–153

MAP 4

Achecote	See Edgcott
Achelei	See Akeley, Oakley
Addingrove, A. 5	*Eddingrave* 147
Addington, B. 3	*Ed(d)intone* 145, 150b
Adstock, B. 3	*Edestocha* 148
Akeley, B. 2	*Achelei* 147b

Ambretone, *Ambritone*	See Emberton
Amersham, E. 7	*Elmodesham* 144, 146, 150b, 151b *bis*, 152 *Elnodesham* 149b
Ashendon, B. 5	*Assedone*, *-dune* 147, 150
Ashley Green	Not in D.B.
Assedone, *-dune*	See Ashendon
Aston Abbots, C. 4	*Estone* 145b
Aston Clinton, D. 5	*Estone* 150b
Aston Sandford, C. 6	*Estone* 144b, 150, 152
Astwood	Not in D.B.
Aylesbury, C. 5	*Eilesberia* 143 *Elesberie* 143b
Barton Hartshorn, A. 3	*Bertone* 145
Beachampton, C. 2	*Bec(h)entone* 147b, 151b, 153
Beachendon, C. 5	*Bichedone* 144b, 150
Beaconsfield	Not in D.B.
Bec(h)entone	See Beachampton
Bechesdene	See Biddlesden
Bedgrove, C. 5	*Begraue* 144
Begraue	See Bedgrove
Berlaue	See Marlow
Bertone	See Barton Hartshorn
Betesdene	See Biddlesden
Bichedone	See Beachendon
Biddlesden, A. 2	*Bechesdene* 143b *Betesdene* 146b
Bierton, C. 5	*Bortone* 144
Bledelai	See Bledlow
Bledlow, C. 6	*Bledelai* 146
Bledone	See Bleadon, Som.
Bletchley	Not in D.B.
Boarstall	Not in D.B.
Bocheland	See Buckland
Bochingeham	See Buckingham
Bortone	See Bierton, Bourton
Botolph Claydon	See Claydon
Boueni(a)e	See Boveney
Bourton, B. 3	*Bortone* 143 *Burtone* 147b
Boveney, E. 9	*Boueni(a)e* 146, 152b
Bow Brickhill	See Brickhill
Boycott, A. 2	*Boicote* 160, Oxon.
Bradeham	See Bradenham
Bradenham, C. 7	*Bradeham* 153
Bradeuuelle	See Bradwell
Bradwell, C. 2	*Brade-*, *Brodeuuelle* 148, 148b, 150b
Brichella(e), *-helle*	See Brickhill
Brickhill, Bow, Great and Little, D. 3	*Brichella(e)* 145, 145b, 147 *Brichelle* 145, 148
Bricstoch	See Burston
Brill, A. 5	*Brunhelle* 143b
Broch	See Brook
Brodeuuelle	See Bradwell
Brook, C. 8	*Broch* 150b
Brotone	See Broughton (near Aylesbury), Broughton (near Moulsoe)
Broughton (near Aylesbury), C. 5	*Brotone* 148 2nd entry
Broughton (near Moulsoe), D. 2	*Brotone* 148 1st entry, 152b
Brunhelle	See Brill
Buckingham, B. 3	*Bochingeham* 143
Buckland, D. 5	*Bocheland* 144
Burneham	See Burnham
Burnham, D. 9	*Burneham* 151
Burston, C. 4	*Bricstoch* 146, 147, 150, 151
Burtone	See Bourton
Caldecote, D. 2	*Caldecote* 146b, 148b, 153
Calverton, C. 2	*Calvretone* 150b
Calvretone	See Calverton
Castle Thorpe	Not in D.B.
Cavrefelle	See Caversfield, Oxon.
Caldestane, *-stone*	See Shalstone
Celfunde, *-funte*	See Chalfont
Cerdeslai, *Cerleslai*	See Chearsley
Cestreham	See Chesham

Cetedene, *Cete(n)done*	See Cheddington
Ceteode	See Chetwode
Chalfont St Giles, St Peter, E. 7, E. 8	*Celfunde*, *-funte* 144, 151b
Charndon, A. 4	*Credendone* 151b
Chauescote	See Gawcott
Chearsley, B. 5	*Cerdeslai* 150 *Cerleslai* 147
Cheddington, D. 5	*Cetedene* 148b *Cete(n)done* 146b, 149, 149b, 150b, 153
Chenebella	See Great Kimble
Chenebelle, *Parva*	See Little Kimble
Chenies	Not in D.B.
Chentone	See Quainton
Chesham, E. 7	*Cestreham* 144 *bis*, 150b, 151b, 153
Chetwode, A. 3	*Ceteode* 145
Chicheley, D. 1	*Cicelai* 149
Chilton, B. 5	*Ciltone* 147
Chipping Wycombe	See Wycombe
Cholesbury	Not in D.B.
Cicelai	See Chicheley
Ciltone	See Chilton
Claidone	See Claydon, Botolph etc.
Claindone	See Claydon, Botolph etc.; Steeple Claydon
Claydon, Botolph, East and Middle, B. 4	*Claidone* 150 *bis* *Claindone* 148 *bis*, 149b
Cliftone	See Clifton Reynes
Clifton Reynes, D. 1	*Cliftone* 152b *Clis-*, *Clystone* 145b, 149 *bis*
Clis-, *Clystone*	See Clifton Reynes
Coblincote	See Cublington
Cocheham	See Cookham, Berks.
Cold Brayfield	Not in D.B.
Coleshill	Not in D.B.
Crafton, D. 4	*Croustone* 145b, 146
Crauelai	See North Crawley
Credendone	See Charndon, Long Crendon
Creslow, C. 4	*Cresselai* 150b
Cresselai	See Creslow
Croustone	See Crafton
Cublington, C. 4	*Coblincote* 152
Cuddington	Not in D.B.
Daceta	See Datchet
Dadford, A. 2	*Dodeforde* 151b, 153
Daneham	See Denham
Danitone	See Dinton
Datchet, E. 9	*Daceta* 152b
Denham, F. 8	*Daneham* 145b
Dileherst, D. 9	Lost in Taplow, 144
Dinton, C. 5	*Danitone* 144
Ditone	See Ditton
Ditton, E. 9	*Ditone* 148b
Dodeforde	See Dadford
Dodintone	See Dunton
Dornei	See Dorney
Dorney, D. 9	*Dornei* 149b
Dorton, B. 5	*Dortone* 147
Dortone	See Dorton
Draintone	See Drayton Parslow
Draitone	See Drayton Beauchamp, Drayton Parslow
Drayton Beauchamp, D. 5	*Draitone* 146, 152
Drayton Parslow, C. 3	*Drai(n)tone* 144b, 151b
Duchitorp	See Tythorp
Dunton, C. 4	*Dodintone* 144b
Easington, B. 6	*Hesintone* 147
East Burnham, E. 9	*Esburneham* 145b
East Claydon	See Claydon, Botolph etc.
Eddinberge	See Edlesborough
Eddingrave	See Addingrove
Eddintone	See Addington
Edestocha	See Adstock
Edgcott, B. 4	*Achecote* 147b
Edingeberge	See Lenborough
Edintone	See Addington

Edlesborough, E. 4	*Eddinberge* 149b *Edingeberge* 215, Beds.
Eie	See Towersey, Oxon.
Eilesberia, *Elesberie*	See Aylesbury
Ellesborough, C. 6	*Esenberga*, *-berge* 148b, 151b
Elmodesham, *Elnodesham*	See Amersham
Emberton, D. 1	*Ambretone* 145b *Ambritone* 152b
Esburneham	See East Burnham
Esenberga, *-berge*	See Ellesborough
Estone	See Aston Abbots, Aston Clinton, Aston Sandford, Ivinghoe Aston
Eton, E. 9	*Ettone* 151
Etone	See Water Eaton
Ettone	See Eton
Euresel	See Evershaw
Evershaw, A. 2	*Euresel* 153
Evinghehou	See Ivinghoe
Evreham	See Iver
Falelie	See Fawley
Farnham, E. 9	*Ferneham* 151b
Fawley, B. 8	*Falelie* 147
Fenny Stratford	Not in D.B.
Ferneham	See Farnham
Fingest	Not in D.B.
Fleet Marston	See Marston
Foxcote, B. 3	*Foxescote* 144b
Foxescote	See Foxcote
Fulmer	Not in D.B.
Gateherst	See Gayhurst
Gawcott, B. 3	*Chauescote* 144
Gayhurst, C. 1	*Gateherst* 145
Gerrard's Cross	Not in D.B.
Grandborough, C. 4	*Grenesberga* 145b
Great Brickhill	See Brickhill
Great Hampden	See Hampden
Great Horwood	See Horwood
Great Kimble, C. 6	*Chenebella* 147
Great Linford, D. 2	*Linforde* 146b, 148, 148b, 150b

Great Marlow	See Marlow
Great Missenden	See Missenden
Great Woolstone	See Woolstone
Grendon Underwood, B. 4	*Grennedone* 151
Grenesberga	See Grandborough
Grennedone	See Grendon Underwood
Grove, D. 4	*Langraue* 152
Haddenham, B. 6	*Nedreham* 143b
Halton, D. 6	*Haltone* 143b
Haltone	See Halton
Hambleden, C. 8	*Hanbledene* 152b
Hamdena	See Hampden
Hamescle	See Hanslope
Hampden, Great and Little, D. 6	*Hamdena* 148b
Hanbledene	See Hambleden
Hanechedene	See Radnage
Hanslope, C. 1	*Hamescle* 152
Hardmead, D. 1	*Herouldmede* 149 *Herulfmede* 150b, 152b *Horelmede* 148
Harduic(h)	See Hardwick
Hardwick, C. 4	*Harduic(h)* 146, 150, 151
Hartwell, C. 5	*Herdeuuelle*, *Herdewelle* 144, 147, 148, 151 *bis*
Haseleie, C. 3	Lost in Thornton, 151b
Haversham, C. 2	*Havresham* 148
Havresham	See Haversham
Hawridge	Not in D.B.
Hedgerley	Not in D.B.
Hedsor	Not in D.B.
Helpestorp, *-trope*	See Helsthorpe
Helsthorpe, D. 4	*Helpestorp*, *-trope* 146, 152
Herdeuuelle, *Herdewelle*	See Hartwell
Hereworde	See Horwood
Herouldmede, *Herulfmede*	See Hardmead
Hesintone	See Easington
Hibestanes	See Ibstone
High Wycombe	See Wycombe

Hillesden, B. 3	*Ilesdone* 146b *Ulesdone* 147b
Hitcham, D. 9	*Hucheham* 149b
Hochestone	See Hoggeston
Hocsaga	See Hogshaw
Hoggeston, C. 4	*Hochestone* 148b
Hogshaw, B. 4	*Hocsaga* 148
Holedene, *Holendone*	See Hollingdon
Hollingdon, D. 4	*Holedene* 152b *Holendone* 148b, 150
Horelmede	See Hardmead
Horsedene, *-dune*	See Horsenden
Horsenden, C. 6	*Horsedene*, *-dune* 144, 146, 153
Horton (in Ivinghoe), D. 4	*Hortone* 146b, 149b, 150
Horton (near Slough), F. 9	*Hortune* 151
Hortone	See Horton (in Ivinghoe)
Hortune	See Horton (near Slough)
Horwood, Great and Little, C. 3	*Hereworde* 147b
Huchedene	See Hughenden
Hucheham	See Hitcham
Hughenden, D. 7	*Huchedene* 144b
Hulcott	Not in D.B.
Ibstone, C. 7	*Hibestanes* 152b *Ebestan*, *Ypestan* 160b *bis*, Oxon.
Ickford, A. 6	*Iforde* 146, 150
Iforde	See Ickford
Ilesdone	See Hillesden
Ilmer, C. 6	*Imere* 144b
Imere	See Ilmer
Iver, F. 9	*Evreham* 149
Ivinghoe, E. 5	*Evinghehou* 143b
Ivinghoe Aston, E. 5	*Estone* 146b, 149b
Lamport, B. 2	*Lan(d)port* 147b, 152
Landport	See Lamport
Langley	Not in D.B.
Langraue	See Grove
Lanport	See Lamport
Late(s)berie	See Lathbury
Lathbury, D. 1	*Late(s)berie* 145 *bis*, 150b
Lauendene, *Lauue(n)dene*	See Lavendon
Lavendon, D. 1	*Lauendene* 152b *Lauue(n)dene* 145b, 146b, 148, 153
Lecham(e)stede	See Leckhampstead
Leckhampstead, B. 2	*Lecham(e)stede* 144b, 147b, 149b
Lede	See Lude
Ledingberge	See Lenborough
Lee	Not in D.B.
Lelinchestane	See Lillingstone Dayrell
Lenborough, B. 3	*Edingeberge* 147b *Ledingberge* 144b
Lesa	See Nashway
Lillingstone Dayrell, B. 2	*Lelinchestane* 147b
Lillingstone Lovell, B. 2	*Lillingestan* 160, 160b, Oxon.
Lincelada	See Linslade
Linforde	See Great Linford, Little Linford
Linslade, D. 4	*Lincelada* 150b
Litecota, *-cote*	See Littlecote
Little Brickhill	See Brickhill
Littlecote, C. 4	*Litecota*, *-cote* 147, 148b, 150
Little Kimble, C. 6	*Parva Chenebelle* 151
Little Hampden	See Hampden
Little Horwood	See Horwood
Little Linford, C. 2	*Linforde* 145
Little Marlow	See Marlow
Little Missenden	See Missenden
Little Woolstone	See Woolstone
Lochintone	See Loughton
Long Crendon, B. 6	*Credendone* 147
Lotegarser	See Ludgershall
Loughton, C. 2	*Lochintone* 146b, 147b, 152
Lower Wichendon	See Wichendon
Lude, D. 8	*Lede* 144

Ludgershall, A. 5	*Lotegarser* 145, 151
Luffield	Not in D.B.
Maids Moreton, B. 3	*Mortone* 147b, 153
Marlow, Great and Little, D. 8	*Berlaue* 144b, 151 *Merlaue* 150, 152b
Marsh Gibbon, A. 4	*Mersa*, *Merse* 146b, 148b
Marston, Fleet and North, C. 4, C. 5	*Merstone* 144b, 145, 148b, 150, 151
Marsworth, D. 5	*Misseuorde* 149b
Medemeham	See Medmenham
Medmenham, C. 8	*Medemeham* 150b
Mentemore	See Mentmore
Mentmore, D. 4	*Mentemore* 146b
Merlaue	See Marlow
Mersa, *Merse*	See Marsh Gibbon
Merstone	See Marston
Mid(d)eltone	See Milton Keynes
Middle Claydon	See Claydon, Botolph etc.
Midueltone	See Milton Keynes
Milton Keynes, D. 2	*Mid(d)eltone* 148, 153 *Midueltone* 149
Missedene	See Missenden
Missenden, Great and Little, D. 7	*Missedene* 146, 147, 150b, 151b
Misseuorde	See Marsworth
Moleshou	See Moulsoe
Monks Risborough	See Risborough
Mortone	See Maids Moreton
Moulsoe, D. 2	*Moleshou* 148
Mursley, C. 3	*Muselai* 146b, 147b, 153
Muselai	See Mursley
Nash	Not in D.B.
Nashway, A. 5	*Lesa* 151b
Nedreham	See Haddenham
Neuport	See Newport Pagnell
Neutone	See Newton Longville
Newport Pagnell, D. 2	*Neuport* 148b
Newton Blossomville	Not in D.B.
Newton Longville, C. 3	*Neutone* 147b
North Crawley, D. 2	*Crauelai* 149
North Marston	See Marston
Oakley, A. 5	*Achelei* 149
Olnei	See Olney
Olney, D. 1	*Olnei* 145b
Oltone	See Wotton Underwood
Olvonge	See Oving
Opetone	See Upton (in Dinton), Upton (in Slough)
Oving, C. 4	*Olvonge* 145
Oxeneford	See Oxford, Oxon.
Padbury, B. 3	*Pateberie* 149, 152
Parva Chenebelle	See Little Kimble
Pateberie	See Padbury
Penn	Not in D.B.
Petsoe	Not in D.B.
Pincelestorne, *Pincenestorne*	See Pitstone
Pitchcott	Not in D.B.
Pitstone, E. 5	*Pincelestorne* 146, 146b, 150 *Pincenestorne* 147
Policote	See Pollicott
Pollicott, B. 5	*Policote* 147
Poundon	Not in D.B.
Preston Bissett, A. 3	*Prestone* 144b
Prestone	See Preston Bissett
Princes Risborough	See Risborough
Quainton, B. 4	*Chentone* 150, 152b
Quarrendon, C. 5	*Querendone* 149b
Querendone	See Quarrendon
Radclive, B. 3	*Radeclive* 151b
Radeclive	See Radclive
Radnage, C. 7	*Hanechedene* 144b
Raveneston	See Ravenstone
Ravenstone, C. 1	*Raveneston* 148

Risborough, Monks and Princes, C. 6	*Riseberge* 143b *bis* *Risenberga* 148b *Riseberge* 154, Oxon.
Riseberge, *Risenberga*	See Risborough
Salden, C. 3	*Sceldene* 146b, 153
Santesdone, *-dune*	See Saunderton
Saunderton, C. 6	*Santesdone*, *-dune* 144b, 150
Sceldene	See Salden
Seer Green	Not in D.B.
Senelai	See Shenley Brook End, Shenley Church End
Senlai	See Shenley Brook End
Serintone	See Sherington
Sevinestone	See Simpson
Shabbington, A. 6	*Sobintone* 150
Shalstone, A. 2	*Celdestane*, *-stone* 144b, 149b
Shenley Brook End, C. 3	*Sen(e)lai* 151b, 152
Shenley Church End, C. 2	*Senelai* 146b, 147
Sherington, D. 1	*Serintone* 145b
Shipton Lee, B. 4	*Sibdone* 148, 151, 153
Sibdone	See Shipton Lee
Simpson, D. 3	*Sevinestone* 145 *Siuuinestone* 153
Sincleberia	See Singleborough
Singleborough, C. 3	*Sincleberia* 147b
Siuuinestone	See Simpson
Slapetone	See Slapton
Slapton, D. 4	*Slapetone* 146
Slough	Not in D.B.
Sobintone	See Shabbington
Soeneberno	See Swanbourne
Soleberie	See Soulbury
Sortelai, B. 4	Lost in Quainton, 150, 153
Soulbury, D. 4	*Soleberie* 148b, 150, 150b, 152, 153 *bis*
Stanes	See Stone. See also Staines, Mdlx.

Stantonbury, C. 2	*Stantone* 150b
Stantone	See Stantonbury
Steeple Claydon, B. 4	*Claindone* 153
Stewkley, D. 4	*Stiuelai* 145, 150b
Stiuelai	See Stewkley
Stoches	See Stoke Goldington, Stoke Hammond, Stoke Mandeville, Stoke Poges
Stoke Goldington, C. 1	*Stoches* 145b, 148
Stoke Hammond, D. 3	*Stoches* 152
Stoke Mandeville, C. 6	*Stoches* 143b
Stokenchurch	Not in D.B.
Stoke Poges, E. 9	*Stoches* 148b
Stone, C. 5	*Stanes* 144, 149
Stou	See Stowe
Stowe, A. 2	*Stou* 144b
Stradford	See Water Stratford
Sudcote, C. 5	Lost in Stone, 151
Sueneberie, *-berne*, *-borne*	See Swanbourne
Swanbourne, C. 4	*Soeneberno* 147 *Sueneberie* 148b, 149b *Sueneberne*, *-borne* 143b, 146b
Taplow, D. 9	*Thapeslau* 144
Tattenhoe	Not in D.B.
Tedinwiche	See Tingewick
Te(d)lingham	See Tyringham
Ternitone	See Thornton
Tetchwick, B. 4	*Tochingeuuiche* 148
Thapeslau	See Taplow
Thornborough, B. 3	*Torneberge* 152
Thornton, B. 3	*Ternitone* 151b
Ticheforde	See Tickford
Tickford, D. 2	*Ticheforde* 149
Tilleberie	See Turville
Tingewick, A. 3	*Tedinwiche* 145
Tochingeuuiche	See Tetchwick

Torneberge	See Thornborough
Tueverde	See Twyford
Turvestone	See Turweston
Turville, C. 8	*Tilleberie* 151b
Turweston, A. 2	*Turvestone* 151
Twyford, A. 4	*Tueverde* 151b *Tuiforde* 154, Oxon.
Tyringham, D. 1	*Te(d)lingham* 145, 148b
Tythorp, B. 6	*Duchitorp* 155b, Oxon.
Ulchetone	See Woughton on the Green
Ulesdone	See Hillesden
Ulsiestone	See Woolstone
Upetone	See Upton (in Dinton)
Upper Wichenden	See Wichenden
Upton (in Dinton), C. 5	*Opetone* 149b *Upetone* 148
Upton (in Slough), E. 9	*Opetone* 143b
Votesdone	See Waddesdon
Waborne	See Wooburn
Waddesdon, B. 5	*Votesdone* 150
Wadone	See Whaddon (near Bletchley), Whaddon (in Slapton)
Wadruge	See Waldridge
Waldridge, C. 6	*Wa(l)druge* 144b, 149b
Waldruge	See Waldridge
Walton	Not in D.B.
Wandene	See Wendover Dean
Wandoure	See Wendover
Warrington	Not in D.B.
Water Eaton, D. 3	*Etone* 145
Water Stratford, A. 3	*Stradford* 149b
Wau(u)endone	See Wavendon
Wavendon, D. 2	*Wau(u)endone* 146b, 150b, 153 *bis*

Wendover, D. 6	*Wandoure* 153 *ter* *Wendovre* 143b
Wendover Dean, D. 6	*Wandene* 153
Wendovre	See Wendover
Weneslai	See Winslow
Wermelle	See Worminghall
Westberie	See Westbury
Westbury, A. 3	*Westberie* 144b, 151b
Westcott	Not in D.B.
Westone	See Weston Turville, Weston Underwood
Weston Turville, D. 5	*Westone* 144 *bis*
Weston Underwood, D. 1	*Westone* 145b, 146b, 152b
West Wycombe	See Wycombe
Wexham	Not in D.B.
Whaddon (near Bletchley), C. 3	*Wadone* 147b
Whaddon (in Slapton), D. 4	*Wadone* 144b, 150b
Whitchurch, C. 4	*Wicherce* 147
Wicg	See Droitwich, Worcs.
Wichendon, Lower and Upper, B. 5	*Wichendone* 147 *Witchende* 146
Wichendone	See Wichendon
Wicherce	See Whitchurch
Wicumbe	See Wycombe
Willen	Not in D.B.
Windesores	See Windsor, Berks.
Wing, D. 4	*Witehunge* 146
Wingrave, D. 4	*Wit(h)ungraue* 146, 150, 152b
Winslow, C. 4	*Weneslai* 146
Wirecesberie	See Wraysbury
Witchende	See Wichendon
Witehunge	See Wing
Wit(h)ungraue	See Wingrave
Wlsiestone	See Woolstone
Wluerintone	See Wolverton
Wolverton, C. 2	*Wluerintone* 152
Wooburn, D. 8	*Waborne* 144
Woodham	Not in D.B.

Woolstone, Great and Little, D. 2	*Ulsiestone* 147b, 148b *Wlsiestone* 147b
Worminghall, A. 6	*Wermelle* 145
Wotton Underwood, B. 5	*Oltone* 147
Woughton on the Green, D. 2	*Ulchetone* 146b, 152
Wraysbury or Wyrardisbury, E. 9	*Wirecesberie* 149b
Wycombe, Chipping, High and West, C. 7, D. 7, D. 8	*Wicumbe* 143b, 144b *bis*, 146, 149

ANONYMOUS HOLDINGS

No place-names appear in the following thirteen entries, and it is possible that some (or even all) of these refer to holdings at places not named elsewhere in Domesday Book:

Walter (from bishop of Lincoln), half a hide in Burnham hd, 144.
Bishop of Bayeux, 3 hides and 3 virgates in Lamua hd, 145.
Two Englishmen (from Walter Gifard), one virgate in Cottesloe hd, 147.
A certain Englishman (from William son of Ansculf), half a hide in Stone hd, 148b.
Baldwin (from William son of Ansculf), 2 hides in Lamua hd, 148b.
Wibert (from William son of Ansculf), 4 hides in Moulsoe hd, 149.
William de Cahaignes (from Geoffrey de Mandeville), 3½ hides in Lamua hd, 149b.
Alma de Odona (from Miles Crispin), one hide in Moulsoe hd, 150b.
Rannulf (from Edward of Salisbury), one hide and 1½ virgates in Waddesdon hd, 150b.
Ralf (from Walter son of Other), 4 hides in Moulsoe hd, 151.
Fulcuin (from Walter the Fleming), one hide and one virgate in Moulsoe hd, 151.
Ralf (from Gozelin the Breton), 1½ hides in Yardley hd, 152.
Alvred of Thame (from Gilo brother of Ansculf), one hide and 3 virgates in Ixhill hd, 152b.

CAMBRIDGESHIRE — *GRENTEBR'SCIRE*

Folios 189–202b

MAP 5

Abington, Great and Little, D. 8	*Abintone* 190, 4th entry, 194, 199b *bis*
Abington Pigotts, B. 9	*Abintone* 190 *ter* 1st to 3rd entries, 193, 198, 200b
Abintone	See Abington, Great and Little; Abington Pigotts
Alia Lintone	See Little Linton
Alia Mordune	See Guilden Morden
Arrington, B. 8	*Erningtone*, *-tune* 193b, 194b
Ashley, F. 7	*Esselie* 199b
Atelai	See East Hatley
Au(e)resdone	See Eversden
Babraham, D. 8	*Badburgh* 194 *Badbur(g)ham* 190, 191, 197b, 199, 199b, 201b, 202
Badburgh, *Badbur(g)ham*	See Babraham
Badlingham, F. 6	*Bellingeham* 195b
Balsham, E. 8	*Beles(s)ham* 190b, 195b, 199

Barenton(e)	See Barrington
Barham, E. 9	*Bercheham* 191, 193b
Barrington, C. 8	*Barenton(e)* 193, 194b, 196, 196b, 200b
Bartlow	Not in D.B.
Barton, C. 7	*Bertone* 193, 200, 201b 2nd entry
Basingborne	See Bassingbourn
Bassingbourn, B. 9	*Basingborne* 190, 194, 198b
Bece, *Bech*	See Landbeach
Beles(s)ham	See Balsham
Bellingeham	See Badlingham
Benwick	Not in D.B.
Bercheham	See Barham
Bertone	See Barton, Comberton
Bochesuuorde	See Boxworth
Bodichessham	See Bottisham
Bottisham, E. 7	*Bodichessham* 196
Bourn, B. 7	*Brone* 192b, 201b *Bruna*, *Brune* 195, 200b
Boxworth, B. 6	*Bochesuuorde* 192b, 195, 197, 197b, 199
Brinkley	Not in D.B.
Brone, *Bruna*, *Brune*	See Bourn
Burch	See Burrough Green
Burewelle	See Burwell
Burrough Green, F. 7	*Burch* 195b
Buruuella, *Buruuelle*	See Burwell
Burwell, E. 6	*Burewelle* 192b *Buruuella*, *Buruuelle* 193, 195b See also anon. holdings on p. 31
Caldecote, B. 7	*Caldecote* 195, 198b, 202
Cambridge, D. 7	*Grante-*, *Grentebrige* 189, 190, 194

Camps, Castle and Shudy, F. 9	*Canpas* 196b, 199b
Canpas	See Camps
Carle(n)tone	See Carlton
Carlton, F. 8	*Carle(n)tone* 195b, 196, 197b, 202
Castle Camps	See Camps
Caustone	See Caxton
Caxton, B. 7	*Caustone* 198b
Cestreforde	See Chesterford, Ess.
Cestretone	See Chesterton
Cetriz	See Chatteris
Chatteris, C. 4	*Cetriz* 191b, 192b
Chavelai	See Cheveley
Chenepewelle	See Knapwell
Chenet	See Kennett
Cherry Hinton, D. 7	*Hintone* 193b *bis*
Chertelinge	See Kirtling
Chesterton, D. 7	*Cestretone* 189b
Cheveley, F. 7	*Chavelai* 189b, 195
Childerley, C. 7	*Cilderlai* 201b, 202b *Cildrelai* 190b, 201b
Chingestone	See Kingston
Chipeham	See Chippenham
Chippenham, F. 6	*Chipeham* 197
Chishill, Great and Little, C. 9	*Cishella*, *-helle*, L.D.B., 33b *bis*, 52b, 62b, 100b, Ess.
Cilderlai, *Cildrelai*	See Childerley
Clopton, B. 8	*Cloptune* 190, 197b, 200b
Cloptune	See Clopton
Coeia	See Quy
Comberton, C. 7	*Bertone* 201b 1st entry *Cumbertone* 189b, 200b, 202b
Connington, B. 6	*Contone* 197 *Cunitone* 197b, 199
Contone	See Connington
Coteham	See Cottenham
Coton	Not in D.B.
Cottenham, D. 6	*Coteham* 191b, 192b, 201b *ter*

Coveney	Not in D.B.
Crauuedene	See Croydon
Crochestone	See Croxton
Croxton, A. 7	*Crochestone* 199, 202
Croydon, B. 8	*Crauuedene* 193, 194, 197b, 198, 200b
Cumbertone	See Comberton
Cunitone	See Connington
Ditone	See Woodditton
Dochesuuorde	See Duxford
Doddington, C. 3	*Dodinton* 191b
Dodesuuorde	See Duxford
Dodinton	See Doddington
Downham, D. 4	*Duneham* 192
Draitone	See Dry Drayton, Fen Drayton
Dry Drayton, C. 7	*Draitone* 193, 195 2nd entry, 199, 202, 202b
Dulingham, *Dulling(e)ham*	See Dullingham
Dullingham, F. 7	*Dulingham* 195b *Dulling(e)ham* 193, 197b, 202
Duneham	See Downham
Duxford, D. 8	*Dochesuuorde* 196, 196b *bis*, 198 *Dodesuuorde* 194
East Hatley, B. 8	*Atelai* 194 *Hatelai* 197b 1st entry, 200b
Einuluesberie	See Eynesbury, Hunts.
Elesuuorde, *Elesworde*	See Elsworth
Elm	Not in D.B.
Elsworth, B. 6	*Elesuuorde*, *Elesworde* 192b, 197, 199
Eltisley, B. 7	*Hecteslei* 196
Ely, E. 5	*Ely* 191b, 192 *Eli*, L.D.B., 392, Suff.
Epintone	See Impington
Erningtone, *-tune*	See Arrington

Escelford(e)	See Shelford
Esceprid(e)	See Shepreth
Esselie	See Ashley
Essel(l)inge	See Exning, Suff.
Euresdone	See Eversden
Eversden, Great and Little, C. 8	*Au(e)resdone* 194b, 198b *Euresdone* 199, 200
Fen Ditton	Not in D.B.
Fen Drayton, B. 6	*Draitone* 190, 192b, 195 1st entry, 197b, 201
Fordeham	See Fordham
Fordham, F. 6	*Fordeham* 189b *Forham* 195b, 197
Forham	See Fordham
Fowlmere, C. 9	*Fugelesmara* 194 *Fuglemære* 196b
Foxetune	See Foxton
Foxton, C. 8	*Foxetune* 193, 197
Fugelesmara, *Fuglemære*	See Fowlmere
Fulbourn, D. 7	*Fuleberne* 190, 191, 193b, 197, 201b
Fuleberne	See Fulbourn
Gamelinge(i)	See Gamlingay
Gamlingay, A. 8	*Gamelinge(i)* 197b, 201b, 202
Girton, C. 7	*Gretone* 192b, 193 *bis*, 201
Gisleham	See Isleham
Grantchester, C. 7	*Granteseta*, *-sete* 193, 194b, 196, 200, 200b, 202
Grantebrige	See Cambridge
Grantedene	See Little Gransden
Granteseta, *-sete*	See Grantchester
Gratedene	See Little Gransden
Gravelei	See Graveley
Graveley, A. 6	*Gravelei* 192b
Great Abington	See Abington
Great Chishill	See Chishill
Great Eversden	See Eversden
Great Shelford	See Shelford
Great Wilbraham	See Wilbraham
Grentebrige	See Cambridge

Gretone	See Girton
Guilden Morden, B. 9	*Alia Mordune* 193 *Mordune* 197, 198, 200, 200b *ter*
Haddenham, D. 5	*Hadreham* 192
Hadreham	See Haddenham
Haneia	See Henny
Harduic	See Hardwick
Hardwick, C. 7	*Harduic* 191b
Harlton, C. 8	*Herletone* 196 *bis*, 200b
Harston, C. 8	*Herlestone* 191, 194, 196b, 200
Haslingefeld(e)	See Haslingfield
Haslingfield, C. 8	*Haslingefeld(e)* 189b, 194, 197, 200b
Hatelai	See East Hatley, Hatley St George
Hatley St George, B. 8	*Hatelai* 195, 197b 2nd entry, 201
Hauochestone, *-tun*	See Hauxton
Hauxton, C. 8	*Hauochestone*, *-tun* 191, 198
Hecteslei	See Eltisley
Helle	See Hill
Henny, E. 5	*Haneia* 192
Herlestone	See Harston
Herletone	See Harlton
Hestitone	See Hinxton
Heydon, C. 9	*Hai(n)dena*, L.D.B., 19b, 97, Ess.
Hichelintone	See Ickleton
Hildersham, E. 8	*Hildricesham* 199b
Hildricesham	See Hildersham
Hill, C. 5	*Helle* 192
Hintone	See Cherry Hinton
Hinxton, D. 9	*Hestitone* 200 *Histetone* 189b, 190, 198
Histetone	See Hinxton
Histon, C. 6	*Histone* 190, 191b, 193
Histone	See Histon
Hochinton(e)	See Oakington
Horningesie	See Horningsea
Horningsea, D. 7	*Horningesie* 191
Horseheath, E. 8	*Horsei* 193b, 196b, 198, 199b
Horsei	See Horseheath
Ichelintone	See Ickleton
Ickleton, D. 9	*Hichelintone* 196 *Ichelintone* 190 *Inchelintone* 198 *bis*
Impington, D. 7	*Epintone* 191b *bis*, 201
Inchelintone	See Ickleton
Isleham, E. 5	*Gisleham* 189b, 190b, 195b, 199
Kennett, F. 6	*Chenet* 196b
Kingston, B. 7	*Chingestone* 189b, 193b, 194b, 197b, 198b, 200b
Kirtling, F. 7	*Chertelinge* 202
Knapwell, B. 7	*Chenepewelle* 192b
Kneesworth	Not in D.B.
Landbeach, D. 6	*Bece*, *Bech* 195, 201b
Landwade	Not in D.B.
Leverington	Not in D.B.
Lidlin(g)tone, *Lidtingtone*	See Litlington
Linden, D. 5	*Lindone* 192
Lindone	See Linden
Linton, E. 8	*Lintone* 194
Lintone	See Linton
Lintone, *Alia*	See Little Linton
Litelport	See Littleport
Liteltedford	See Little Thetford
Litingtone	See Litlington
Litlington, B. 9	*Lidlin(g)tone* 190 *bis* *Li(d)tingtone* 198 *bis*
Little Abington	See Abington
Little Chishill	See Chishill
Little Eversden	See Eversden
Little Gransden, B. 8	*Gra(n)tedene* 191b, 197b
Little Linton, E. 8	*Alia Lintone* 194
Littleport, E. 4	*Litelport* 191b
Little Shelford	See Shelford
Little Thetford, D. 5	*Liteltedford* 191b
Little Wilbraham	See Wilbraham
Lode	Not in D.B.

Place	Domesday form
Lolesuuorde	See Lolworth
Lolworth, C. 6	*Lolosuuorde* 201, 201b
Long Stanton All Saints, St Michael, C. 6	*Stantone*, *-tune* 195, 197, 197b *bis*, 201, 201b
Long Stowe, B. 7	*Stou* 192b *bis*, 195, 198b
Mading(e)lei	See Madingley
Madingley, C. 7	*Mading(e)lei* 190, 201
Manea	Not in D.B.
March, C. 3	*Mercha*, *Merche* 191b, 192
Melbourn, C. 9	*Melleborne*, *-burne* 191b, 193b, 194b, 198b
Meldreth, C. 8	*Melrede* 191, 193b, 194b, 198b, 199b
Melleborne, *-burne*	See Melbourn
Melrede	See Meldreth
Mepal	Not in D.B.
Mercha, *Merche*	See March
Middeltone	See Milton
Milton, D. 7	*Middeltone* 201b
Mordune	See Guilden Morden, Steeple Morden
Mordune, *Alia*	See Guilden Morden
Neuport	See Newport, Ess.
Newton (near Cambridge)	Not in D.B.
Newton (near Wisbech)	Not in D.B.
Oakington, C. 6	*Hochinton(e)* 191b, 192b, 201, 202b *bis*
Ord(e)uuelle, *Ore(d)uuelle*	See Orwell
Orwell, C. 8	*Ord(e)uuelle* 193b, 196, 197 *bis*, 198b, 200; *Ore(d)uuelle* 193, 194b
Oure	See Over
Outwell	Not in D.B.

Place	Domesday form
Over, C. 6	*Oure* 192b, 193, 199, 201, 202b
Pampesuuorde	See Pampisford
Pampisford, D. 8	*Pampesuuorde* 191, 194, 197b, 198, 199, 200, 202
Papeuuorde, *Papeworde*	See Papworth
Papworth Everard and St Agnes, A. 6, B. 7	*Papeuuorde*, *Papeworde* 195, 196b, 197, 199, 199b, 201, Cambs.; 206b, Hunts.
Parson Drove	Not in D.B.
Quy, D. 7	*Coeia* 190b, 200. See also anon. holdings on p. 31
Rampton, C. 6	*Rantone* 201
Rantone	See Rampton
Risedene	See Rushden, Herts.
Saham	See Soham
Salsiton(e)	See Sawston
Sawston, D. 8	*Salsiton(e)* 193, 197, 197b
Saxon Street, F. 7	*Sextone* 199b
Scelgei	See Shingay
Severlai	See Silverley
Sextone	See Saxon Street
Shelford, Great and Little, D. 8	*Escelford(e)* 190, 191, 194, 198; *Scelfort*, L.D.B., 7, Ess.
Shepreth, C. 8	*Esceprid(e)* 191b, 193, 194b, 197, 198b *bis*
Shingay, B. 8	*Scelgei* 193
Shudy Camps	See Camps
Silverley, F. 7	*Severlai* 199b
Snailwell, F. 6	*Snellewelle* 199
Snellewelle	See Snailwell
Soham, E. 5	*Saham* 189, 189b, 190b, 192, 195b *ter*
Stantone, *-tune*	See Long Stanton
Stapleford, D. 8	*Stapleforde* 191

Stapleforde	See Stapleford
Steeple Morden, B. 9	*Mordune* 190, 193, 198
Stetchworth, F. 7	*Sti(ui)cesuuorde* 195b, 199 *Stuuicesworde* 190b
Sti(ui)cesuuorde	See Stetchworth
Stou	See Long Stowe
Stow, D. 7	Not in D.B., but see anon. holdings on p. 31
Stradham	See Stretham
Streetly, E. 8	Not in D.B., but see anon. holdings on p. 31
Stretham, D. 5	*Stradham* 191b
Stuntenei	See Stuntney
Stuntney, E. 5	*Stuntenei* 191b
Stuuicesworde	See Stetchworth
Suaf(h)am	See Swaffham
Suavesy(e)	See Swavesey
Sudtone	See Sutton
Sutton, C. 5	*Sudtone* 192
Swaffham Bulbeck and Prior, E. 6, E. 7	*Suaf(h)am* 190b, 195, 196, 197b, 199, 199b
Swavesey, C. 6	*Suavesy(e)* 194b *bis*, 195, 197, 197b
Tadelai	See Tadlow
Tadlow, B. 8	*Tadelai* 200, 202, 202b
Teuersham, *Teuresham*	See Teversham
Teversham, D. 7	*Teuersham* 191, 201b *Teuresham* 193b
Thorney, D. 2	*Torny* 192b
Thriplow, C. 8	*Trepeslai*, *-lau* 191, 197, 199
Toft, C. 7	*Tofth* 194b, 200b, 202b
Tofth	See Toft
Torny	See Thorney
Trepeslai, *-lau*	See Thriplow
Trumpington, D. 7	*Trumpinton(e)* 196, 196b, 200, 202 *bis*
Trumpinton(e)	See Trumpington
Tydd St Giles	Not in D.B.
Upwell	Not in D.B.
Vtbech	See Waterbeach
Wadone, *Wadune*	See Whaddon
Wandei, *Wandrie*	See Wendy
Warateuuorde	See Wratworth
Waratinge	See West Wratting
Waterbeach, D. 6	*Vtbech* 201b, 202
Wateuuelle	See Whitwell
Wendy, B. 8	*Wandei* 198 *Wandrie* 194
Wentworth, D. 5	*Winteworde* 192
Werateuuorde	See Wratworth
Weslai	See Westley Waterless
Westley Waterless, F. 7	*Weslai* 190b, 195b, 197b, 202
Weston Colville, F. 8	*Westone* 196, 198 *Westuna*, L.D.B., 292b, Suff. See also anon. holdings on p. 31
Westone	See Weston Colville
Westuuiche	See Westwick
Westwick, C. 6	*Westuuiche* 201b, 202
West Wickham, E. 8	*Wicheham* 191, 193b, 196b *bis*, 198
West Wratting, E. 8	*Waratinge* 190b, 195b, 196b, 198, 199
Whaddon, B. 8	*Wadone* 191, 198b *bis* *Wadune* 194b, 196b
Whittlesey, A. 3	*Witesie* 191b, 192b
Whittlesford, D. 8	*Witelesforde* 194, 198 *bis*, 202
Whitwell, C. 7	*Wateuuelle* 198b *Witeuuella*, *-uuelle* 193b, 194b, 200b
Wiborgham	See Wilbraham
Wiceford(e)	See Witchford
Wiceham	See Witcham
Wicha	See Wicken
Wicheham	See West Wickham
Wicken, E. 6	*Wicha* 195b

Place	Domesday form
Wilbertone	See Wilburton
Wilbraham, Great and Little, E. 7	*Wiborgham* 199b *Witborham* 189b See also anon. holdings below
Wilburton, D. 5	*Wilbertone* 192
Willingham, C. 6	*Wiuelingham* 191b, 195, 201
Wimblington	Not in D.B.
Wimpole, B. 8	*Winepol(e)* 194b, 197b
Winepol(e)	See Wimpole
Winteworde	See Wentworth
Wisbech, D. 1	*Wisbece* 192 *bis*, 192b, 193, 196b
Wisbece	See Wisbech
Witborham	See Wilbraham
Witcham, D. 5	*Wiceham* 192
Witchford, D. 5	*Wiceford(e)* 191b, 192
Witelesforde	See Whittlesford
Witesie	See Whittlesey
Witeuuella, -uuelle	See Whitwell
Wiuelingham	See Willingham
Woodditton, F. 7	*Ditone* 189b, 195
Wratworth, B. 8	*Warateuuorde* 194b, 198b, 200, 200b *Werateuuorde* 193b

ANONYMOUS HOLDINGS

The following eleven entries involve anonymous holdings. The *Inquisitio Comitatus Cantabrigiensis* and the *Inquisitio Eliensis*, however, enable us to assign eight of the entries to their respective localities; they also show that two pairs of adjoining places were each separately in existence in 1086 – see N. E. S. A. Hamilton, *Inquisitio Comitatus Cantabrigiensis subjicitur Inquisitio Eliensis* (London, 1876); the pages given below refer to this edition.

It is possible that some (or even all) of the other three holdings refer to places not named elsewhere in Domesday Book:

Picot (from abbot of Ely), 3 hides and 3 virgates in Quy in Staine hd, 190b. *I.C.C.* (pp. 15–16) shows that this included Stow.

Abbot of Ely, 1½ hides in West Wickham in Chilford hd, 191. *I.E.* (p. 103) shows that this included Streetly.

Odo (from Count Alan), 4 hides in Staine hd, 195b. *I.C.C.* (p. 15) shows this was at Wilbraham.

Odo (from Count Alan), one hide in Staine hd, 195b. *I.C.C.* (p. 15) shows this was at Quy and Stow.

Wihomarc (from Count Alan), 1½ hides in Radfield hd, 195b. *I.C.C.* (p. 22) shows this was at Weston Colville.

Harduin de Scalers (from the king), half a hide in Staple hd, 197b. *I.C.C.* (p. 6) shows this was at Burwell.

Reinald (from Albert de Vere), half a hide in Staine hd, 199b. D.B. attributes this to Wilbraham (*In eadem villa*), but *I.C.C.* (p. 15) shows it was at Quy and Stow.

Picot of Cambridge, 4½ hides and 10 acres in Quy in Staine hd, 200. *I.C.C.* (pp. 15–16) shows that this included Stow.

Picot (from Countess Judith), 3 virgates in Longstow hd, 202.

Picot (from Countess Judith), one hide in Papworth hd, 202.

Picot (from Countess Judith), 3 hides in Northstow hd, 202.

D.B. makes no distinction between Great and Little Wilbraham, but the *I.C.C.* (p. 15) speaks of *ii Wilburgeham.*

D.B. makes no distinction between Swaffham Bulbeck and Swaffham Prior, but one of the documents appended to the *I.E.* (p. 192) mentions *Suuafham* and *altera Suuafham.*

CHESHIRE — *CESTRESCIRE*

Folios 262b–269

MAPS 6–7

Name	Domesday form
Acatone	See Acton (near Nantwich)
Acton (near Nantwich), G. 7	*Acatone* 268 *Actune* 265b
Acton (near Northwich)	Not in D.B.
Actune	See Acton (near Nantwich)
Aculvestune	See Occleston
Adlington, J. 4	*Edulvintune* 264
Agden (near Altrincham)	Not in D.B.
Agden (near Malpas)	Not in D.B.
Alburgham	See Alpraham
Alchene	See Halkyn, Wales
Aldelime	See Audlem
Alderley, Nether and Over, I. 4, J. 4	*Aldredelie* 266, 266b
Aldersey	Not in D.B.
Aldford	Not in D.B.
Aldredelie (*Hamstan* hd)	See Alderley
Aldredelie (*Roelau* hd)	Unid., 263b
Alentune	See Allington, Wales
Allostock	Not in D.B.
Alpraham, G. 6	*Alburgham* 267
Alretone	See Oulton
Alretune	See Ollerton
Alsager, I. 6	*Eleacier* 264
Altetone	See Oulton Lowe
Altrincham	Not in D.B.
Alvanley, F. 4	*Elveldelie* 267b
Alvaston	Not in D.B.
Anderton	Not in D.B.
Antrobus, G. 4	*Entrebus* 263b, 264
Appleton, G. 3	*Epletune* 267b
Arrowe	Not in D.B.
Ascelie	See Ashley
Ashley, I. 3	*Ascelie* 266b
Ashton (near Tarvin), F. 5	*Estone* 265
Ashton upon Mersey	Not in D.B.
Asketone	See Axton, Wales
Aston (near Budworth), H. 4	*Estone* 266 3rd entry
Aston (in Newhall), G. 7	*Estune* 265b
Aston (near Sutton), F. 4	*Estone* 266 2nd entry
Aston juxta Mondrum, G. 6	*Estone* 266 1st entry
Audlem, H. 8	*Aldelime* 265
Austerson, H. 7	*Essetune* 265b
Bache	Not in D.B.
Bachelie	See Bagilt, Wales
Backford	Not in D.B.
Baddiley, G. 7	*Bedelei* 265b
Baddington	Not in D.B.
Bagelei	See Baguley, Lancs.
Barnshaw	Not in D.B.
Barnston, C. 3	*Bernestone* 266
Barrow, E. 5	*Bero* 266
Barthomley, I. 7	*Bertemeleu* 265b
Bartington, G. 4	*Bertintune* 267b *bis*
Barton	Not in D.B.
Basford, H. 7	*Berchesford* 265b
Batherton, H. 7	*Berdeltune* 265b
Bebington	Not in D.B.
Bed(d)esfeld	See Bettisfield, Wales
Bedelei	See Baddiley
Beeston, F. 6	*Buistane* 264b
Berchesford	See Basford
Berdeltune	See Batherton
Bernestone	See Barnston
Bero	See Barrow
Bertemeleu	See Bathomley
Bertintune	See Bartington
Betchton	Not in D.B.
Bevelei	See Byley
Bexton	Not in D.B.

Bichelei	See Bickley
Bickerton, F. 7	*Bicretone* 264b
Bickley, F. 7	*Bichelei* 264b
Bicretone	See Bickerton
Bidston	Not in D.B.
Birkenhead	Not in D.B.
Birtles	Not in D.B.
Biscopestreu	See Bistre, Wales
Blachehol	See Blacon
Blachenhale	See Blackenhall
Blackden	Not in D.B.
Blacon, E. 5	*Blachehol* 267
Blakenhall, H. 7	*Blachenhale* 267
Blorat	See Blorant, Wales
Bocstone	See Boughton
Bodeurde	See Little Budworth
Bodugan	See Bodeugan, Wales
Bogedone	See Bowdon
Boleberie	See Bunbury
Bollinfee	Not in D.B.
Bollington (near Altrincham)	Not in D.B.
Bollington (near Macclesfield)	Not in D.B.
Bosden	Not in D.B.
Boselega	See Bosley
Bosley, J. 5	*Boselega* 266b
Bostock, H. 5	*Botestoch* 265
Botelege	See Butley
Botestoch	See Bostock
Boteuuarul	Unid., Wales
Boughton, E. 5	*Bocstone* 263
Bowdon, I. 3	*Bogedone* 266b
Bradley	Not in D.B.
Bradwall	Not in D.B.
Bramale	See Bramhall
Bramhall, J. 3	*Bramale* 266b
Bredbury, J. 2	*Bretberie* 265
Bren	See Bryn, Wales
Brennehedui	See Bryn-hedydd, Wales
Brenuuen	See Bryngwyn, Wales
Brereton, I. 5	*Bretone* 267
Bretberie	See Bredbury
Bretone	See Brereton
Bridgemere	Not in D.B.
Bridge Trafford	See Trafford, Bridge and Wimbolds
Brimstage	Not in D.B.
Brindley	Not in D.B.
Brinnington	Not in D.B.
Brochetone, *-tune*	See Broughton, Wales
Bromborough	Not in D.B.
Broomhall, G. 7	*Brunhala* 265b
Brosse	See Broxton
Broxton, F. 7	*Brosse* 264b
Bruen Stapleford	See Stapleford
Bruge	See Handbridge
Bruncot	See Broncoed, Wales
Brunfor(d)	See Brynford, Wales
Brunhala	See Broomhall
Budewrde	See Great Budworth
Buerton (near Audlem), H. 8	*Burtune* 265b
Buerton (near Chester)	Not in D.B.
Buglawton	Not in D.B.
Buistane	See Beeston
Bulkeley	Not in D.B.
Bunbury, G. 6	*Boleberie* 264b
Burland	Not in D.B.
Burton (near Neston)	Not in D.B.
Burton (near Tarvin), F. 6	*Burtone* 263
Burtone	See Burton (near Tarvin)
Burtune	See Buerton (near Audlem)
Burwardeslei	See Burwardsley
Burwardestone	See Iscoyd, Wales
Burwardsley, F. 6	*Burwardeslei* 264b
Butelege	See Butley
Butley, J. 4	*Bote-*, *Butelege* 264b, 267b
Byley, H. 5	*Bevelei* 266b
Cairos	See Caerwys, Wales

Caldecote	See Caldecott. See also Calcot, Wales
Caldecott, E. 7	*Caldecote* 266b
Calders	See Caldy
Caldy and Lower Caldy, C. 3	*Calders* 264b, 266b
Calmundelei	See Cholmondeley
Calstan	See Kelston, Wales
Calveley	Not in D.B.
Calvintone	Unid., 265
Cancarnacan	See Carn-y-chain, Wales
Capeles	See Capenhurst
Capenhurst, D. 4	*Capeles* 266
Capesthorne, J. 4	*Copestor* 264
Carden	Not in D.B.
Carrington	Not in D.B.
Castretone	See Llys Edwin, Wales
Cauber	See Cwybr, Wales
Cauber, Parva	See Cwybr-bach, Wales
Caughall	Not in D.B.
Cavelea	See Cheveley
Cedde	See Cheadle
Celeford	See Chelford
Celelea	See Chowley
Cepmundewiche, I. 4	Lost in Peover Superior, 267
Cerdingham	See Kermincham
Cerlere	See Chorley (near Nantwich)
Cerletune	See Chorlton (near Nantwich)
Cestre	See Chester
Charcan	See Cyrchynan, Wales
Cheadle, J. 3	*Cedde* 267b
Checkley	Not in D.B.
Chelford, I. 4	*Celeford* 264
Chelmundestone	See Cholmondeston
Chenoterie	See Noctorum
Cheslilaued	See Gellilyfdy, Wales
Chespuic	Unid., Wales
Chester, E. 5	*Cestre* 262b, 263
Cheveley, E. 6	*Cavelea* 263
Chidlow	Not in D.B.
Chiluen	See Cilowen, Wales
Chingeslie	See Kingsley
Cholmondeley, F. 7	*Calmundelei* 264
Cholmondeston, G. 6	*Chelmundestone* 266
Chorley (near Macclesfield)	Not in D.B.
Chorley (near Nantwich), G. 7	*Cerlere* 265b
Chorlton (near Chester)	Not in D.B.
Chorlton (near Malpas)	Not in D.B.
Chorlton (near Nantwich), H. 7	*Cerletune* 265b
Chowley, F. 6	*Celelea* 264b
Christleton, E. 5	*Cristetone* 264
Church Coppenhall	See Coppenhall
Church Hulme	Not in D.B.
Church Lawton, I. 6	*Lautune* 266b *bis*
Church Minshull	See Minshull
Churton by Aldford	Not in D.B.
Churton by Farndon	Not in D.B.
Cinbretune	See Kinderton
Claitone	Unid., Wales
Claventone	See Claverton
Claverton, E. 6	*Claventone* 268b
Clifton, F. 4	*Clistune* 263
Clistune	See Clifton
Clive, H. 5	*Clive* 264
Clotone	See Clotton
Clotton, F. 6	*Clotone* 267b
Clutone	See Clutton
Clutton, E. 7	*Clutone* 266
Cocheshalle	See Cogshall
Cocle	Unid., 266b
Coddington, E. 6	*Cotintone* 263b
Cogeltone	See Congleton
Cogshall, G. 4	*Cocheshalle* 265, 267
Coiwen	Unid., Wales
Colborne, -burne	See Golborne
Coleselt	See Coleshill, Wales

Comberbach	Not in D.B.
Congleton, J. 6	*Cogeltone* 266b
Coole	Not in D.B.
Copehale	See Coppenhall
Copestor	See Capesthorne
Coppenhall, Church and Monks, H. 6	*Copehale* 265b
Cotintone	See Coddington
Cotton	Not in D.B.
Crabwall	Not in D.B.
Cranage, I. 5	*Croeneche* 264b
Creu	See Crewe (by Nantwich)
Creuhalle	See Crewe (near Farndon)
Crewe (near Farndon), E. 7	*Creuhalle* 264b
Crewe (by Nantwich), H. 7	*Creu* 265
Cristetone	See Christleton
Croeneche	See Cranage
Crostone	See Croughton
Crostune	See Croxton
Croughton, E. 5	*Crostone* 263
Crowton	Not in D.B.
Croxton, H. 5	*Crostune* 267
Cuddington (near Malpas), E. 7	*Cuntitone* 264b
Cuddington (near Northwich)	Not in D.B.
Cunetesford	See Knutsford
Cuntitone	See Cuddington (near Malpas)
Danfrond	Unid., Wales
Daresbury	Not in D.B.
Darnhall	Not in D.B.
Davenham, H. 5	*Deveneham* 265
Davenport, I. 5	*Deneport* 267
Delamere	Not in D.B.
Deneport	See Davenport
Depenbech	See Malpas
Deveneham	See Davenham
Dicolin	See Dincolyn, Wales
Dinmersch	See Tremeirchion, Wales
Disley	Not in D.B.

Dissard	See Dyserth, Wales
Dissaren	Unid., Wales
Dochintone	See Duckington
Dodcott	Not in D.B.
Doddington	Not in D.B.
Dodestune	See Dodleston
Dodleston, D. 6	*Dodestune* 268b
Done	Unid., 263b
Doneham	See Dunham Massey, Dunham on the Hill
Duckington, F. 7	*Dochintone* 264b
Duddon	Not in D.B.
Dukinfield	Not in D.B.
Dunham Massey, H. 3	*Doneham* 266b
Dunham on the Hill, E. 4	*Doneham* 263b
Duntune	See Dutton
Dutton, G. 4	*Duntune* 266, 267b *bis*
Eastham, D. 4	*Estham* 263b
Eaton (near Chester), E. 6	*Etone* 263b
Eaton (near Congleton)	Not in D.B.
Eaton (near Northwich)	Not in D.B.
Eaton (near Tarporley)	Not in D.B.
Eccleston, E. 6	*Eclestone* 267
Eclestone	See Eccleston
Eddisbury, F. 5	*Edesberie* 263b
Edelaue	See Hadlow
Edesberie	See Eddisbury
Edge, F. 7	*Eghe* 264, 264b
Edleston	Not in D.B.
Edritone	Unid., Wales
Edulvintune	See Adlington
Egerton	Not in D.B.
Eghe	See Edge
Eitune	See Eyton, Wales
Eleacier	See Alsager
Elton (near Frodsham), E. 4	*Eltone* 263b
Elton (near Sandbach)	Not in D.B.

Eltone	See Elton (near Frodsham)
Elveldelie	See Alvanley
Enelelei	See Enley
Enley, F. 4	*Enelelei* 266
Entrebus	See Antrobus
Epletune	See Appleton
Erpestoch	See Erbistock, Wales
Essetune	See Austerson
Estham	See Eastham
Estone	See Ashton (near Tarvin), Aston (near Budworth), Aston (near Sutton), Aston juxta Mondrum. See also Aston, Wales
Estune	See Aston (in Newhall)
Eswelle	See Heswall
Eteshale	See Hassall
Etingehalle	See Iddinshall
Etone	See Eaton (near Chester), Hatton (near Chester)
Faddiley	Not in D.B.
Fallibroome	Not in D.B.
Farndon, E. 7	*Ferentone* 263, 266b
Ferentone	See Farndon
Folebroc	See Fulbrook, Wales
Frankby	Not in D.B.
Frith, G. 7	*Tereth* 265b
Frodsham, F. 4	*Frotesham* 263b
Frotesham	See Frodsham
Fulk Stapleford	See Stapleford
Gaitone	See Gayton
Gawsworth, J. 5	*Gouesurde* 264
Gayton, C. 4	*Gaitone* 264b
Godley	Not in D.B.
Golborne Bellow and David, E. 6	*Colborne*, *-burne* 265, 267b
Goostrey, I. 5	*Gostrel* 266, 266b
Gostrel	See Goostrey
Gouesurde	See Gawsworth
Grafton	Not in D.B.
Grappenhall, G. 3	*Gropenhale* 267b
Gravesberie	See Greasby
Greasby, C. 3	*Gravesberie* 267b
Great Budworth, H. 4	*Budewrde* 266
Great Meols	See Meols
Great Mollington	See Mollington
Great Saughall	See Saughall
Great Stanney	See Stanney
Great Sutton	See Sutton
Gretford	See Gresford, Wales
Gronant	See Gronant, Wales
Gropenhale	See Grappenhall
Guilden Sutton, E. 5	*Sudtone* 263 1st entry, 264b
Hadlow, D. 4	*Edelaue* 263b
Hale, I. 3	*Hale* 266b
Halton, F. 3	*Heletune* 266
Hamede-, *Hameteberie*	See Henbury
Hampton, F. 7	*Hantone* 264
Handbridge, E. 5	*Bruge* 266, 266b *bis*
Handforth	Not in D.B.
Handley, E. 6	*Hanlei* 267b
Hankelow	Not in D.B.
Hanlei	See Handley
Hantone	See Hampton
Haordine	See Harwarden, Wales
Hapsford	Not in D.B.
Haregrave	See Hargrave
Haretone	See Hatherton
Hargrave, D. 4	*Haregrave* 264b
Hartford, G. 5	*Herford* 267
Harthill	Not in D.B.
Haslington	Not in D.B.
Hassall, I. 6	*Eteshale* 265 *bis*
Hatherton, H. 7	*Haretone* 265b
Hattersley	Not in D.B.
Hatton (near Chester), E. 6	*Etone* 267b
Hatton (near Runcorn)	Not in D.B.

Liscard	Not in D.B.
Little Budworth, G. 5	*Bodeurde* 263b
Little Leigh, G. 4	*Lege* 266
Little Meols	See Meols
Little Mollington	See Mollington
Little Neston	See Neston
Little Saughall	See Saughall
Little Stanney	See Stanney
Little Sutton	See Sutton
Lostock Gralam	Not in D.B.
Lower Caldy	See Caldy
Lower Kinnerton	Not in D.B.
Lower Peover	See Peover
Lower Tabley	See Tabley
Ludworth, K. 2	*Lodeuorde* 273, Derby.
Lymm, H. 3	*Lime* 267, 267b
Macclesfield, J. 4	*Maclesfeld* 263b
Macefen	Not in D.B.
Maclesfeld	See Macclesfield
Maineual	See Maen-Efa, Wales
Malpas, F. 7	*Depenbech* 264
Maneshale, Manessele	See Minshull
Manley, F. 5	*Menlie* 263b
Marbury (near Nantwich), F. 7	*Merberie* 265b
Marbury (near Northwich)	Not in D.B.
Marlston, D. 6	*Merlestone* 268b
Marple	Not in D.B.
Marston	Not in D.B.
Marton (near Congleton), J. 5	*Meretone* 266b *Merutune* 264
Marton (near Northwich)	Not in D.B.
Meincatis	Unid., Wales
Melas	See Meols
Melchanestone	Unid., Wales
Melor	Not in D.B.
Menlie	See Manley
Meols, Great and Little, C. 3	*Melas* 264b *bis*
Mera	See Mere
Merberie	See Marbury (near Nantwich)
Mere, H. 3	*Mera* 267
Meretone	See Marton (near Congleton). See also Mertyn, Wales
Merlestone	See Marlston
Merutune	See Marton (near Congleton)
Mickle Trafford, E. 5	*Traford* 263b
Middleton, F. 4	*Midestune* 263
Middlewich, H. 5	*Wich* 268
Midestune	See Middleton
Millington, H. 3	*Mulintune* 266
Minshull Vernon and Church Minshull, H. 6	*Maneshale* 265b *Manessele* 265b
Mobberley, I. 4	*Motburlege* 266b
Moclitone	See Mechlas, Wales
Moletune	See Moulton
Molintone	See Mollington
Mollington, Great and Little, E. 5	*Molintone* 264b *bis*
Monks Coppenhall	See Coppenhall
Moore	Not in D.B.
Moreton (near Birkenhead)	Not in D.B.
Moreton (near Congleton)	Not in D.B.
Moston (near Chester)	Not in D.B.
Moston (near Middlewich)	Not in D.B.
Mostone	See Mostyn, Wales
Motburlege	See Mobberley
Motre	See Mottram
Mottram, J. 4	*Motre* 267b
Moulton, G. 5	*Moletune* 265
Mulintone	Unid., Wales
Mulintune	See Millington
Munentone	Unid., Wales
Nantwich, G. 7	*Wich* 263b *bis*, 265b, 268
Ness, D. 4	*Nesse* 265
Nesse	See Ness
Neston and Little Neston, C. 4, D. 4	*Nestone* 263, 264b, 266
Nestone	See Neston

Nether Alderley	See Alderley
Netherleigh and Overleigh, E. 5	*Lee* 266, 266b
Netherpool and Overpool, D. 4	*Pol* 265
Neubold	See Newbold Astbury
Neutone	See Newton (in Middlewich), Newton by Chester
Newbold	Not in D.B., see Lea cum Newbold
Newbold Astbury, J. 6	*Neubold* 267
Newentone	See Newton by Chester
Newhall	Not in D.B.
Newton (in Middlewich), H. 5	*Neutone* 267
Newton (near Stalybridge)	Not in D.B.
Newton by Chester, E. 5	*Neutone* 262b *Newentone* 266
Newton by Daresbury	Not in D.B.
Noctorum, C. 3	*Chenoterie* 265
Norberie	See Norbury (near Malpas)
Norbury (near Hazelgrove), K. 3	*Nordberie* 266b
Norbury (near Malpas), F. 8	*Norberie* 265b
Nordberie	See Norbury (near Hazelgrove)
Norley	Not in D.B.
North Rode, J. 5	*Rodo* 266b
Northwich, H. 4	*Norwich* 268, 268b *Wich* 266, 267 *ter*
Norton, F. 3	*Nortune* 266
Nortune	See Norton
Norwich	See Northwich
Norwordine	See Northenden, Lancs.
Oakmere	Not in D.B.
Occleston, H. 6	*Aculvestune* 264
Odd Rode, I. 6	*Rode* 268
Odeslei	See Hoseley, Wales
Offerton	Not in D.B.
Oldcastle	Not in D.B.
Ollerton, I. 4	*Alretune* 263b, 266b, 267, 267b
Opetone	See Upton (near Chester)
Optone	See Upton (near Birkenhead), Upton (near Chester)
Oulton, G. 5	*Alretone* 263b
Oulton Lowe, G. 6	*Altetone* 267b
Over, G. 5	*Ovre* 263b
Over Alderley	See Alderley
Overleigh	See Netherleigh
Over Peover	See Peover
Overpool	See Netherpool
Over Tabley	See Tabley
Overton, E. 7	*Ovretone* 264b
Ovre	See Over
Ovretone	See Overton
Partington	Not in D.B.
Parva Cauber	See Cwybr-bach, Wales
Peckforton, F. 6	*Pevretone* 264b
Peintret	See Pentre, Wales
Penegors	Unid., Wales
Pengdeslion	Unid., Wales
Pensby	Not in D.B.
Peover, Lower and Over, H. 4, I. 4	*Pevre* 266, 267 *ter*
Pevre	See Peover
Pevretone	See Peckforton
Pexall	Not in D.B.
Pichetone	See Picton. See also Picton, Wales
Pickmere	Not in D.B.
Picton, E. 5	*Pichetone* 265
Plumley	Not in D.B.
Pol	See Netherpool, Poole
Pontone	See Poulton (near Birkenhead), Poulton (near Chester)
Poole, G. 6	*Pol* 265b, 266
Potitone	See Puddington

Pott Shrigley	Not in D.B.
Poulton (near Birkenhead), D. 3	*Pontone* 267b
Poulton (near Chester), E. 6	*Pontone* 265
Poynton	Not in D.B.
Prenton, D. 3	*Prestune* 265
Prestbury	Not in D.B.
Prestetone	See Prestatyn, Wales
Preston on the Hill	Not in D.B.
Prestune	See Prenton
Puddington, D. 4	*Potitone* 266b
Pulford, D. 6	*Pulford* 263b, 266b
Putecain	See Bychton, Wales
Quisnan	See Gwysaney, Wales
Rabie	See Raby
Raby, D. 4	*Rabie* 263, 266
Radeclive	See Redcliff
Radenoure	See Radnor (near Gresford), Wales
Radintone	See Radington, Wales
Raduch	See Hiraddug, Wales
Rahop	See Gop, Wales
Rainow	Not in D.B.
Redcliff, E. 5	*Rade-*, *Redeclive* 262b, 263, 266b
Redeclive	See Redcliff
Reuuordui	See Rhydorddwy, Wales
Ridley	Not in D.B.
Risteselle	See Rhos Ithel, Wales
Riuelenoit	See Trelawnyd, Wales
Rode	See Odd Rode
Rodestorne	See Rostherne
Rodo	See North Rode
Roelend, *-lent*	See Rhuddlan, Wales
Romiley, K. 2	*Rumelie* 264
Rope	Not in D.B.
Rostherne, I. 3	*Rodestorne* 267
Rowton	Not in D.B.
Ruargor	Unid., Wales
Rudheath	Not in D.B.
Ruestoch	See Meliden, Wales
Rumelie	See Romiley
Runcorn	Not in D.B.
Rushton, G. 5	*Rusitone* 263b
Rusitone	See Rushton
Saighton, E. 6	*Saltone* 263
Salhale, *Salhare*	See Saughall
Saltone	See Saighton
Sanbec(o)	See Sandbach
Sandbach, I. 6	*Sanbec(o)* 264, 266b
Santune	See Shavington
Saughall, D. 5	*Salhale* 265 *Salhare* 263
Saughall Massie	Not in D.B.
Schiuian	See Ysceifiog, Wales
Senelestune	See Snelson
Shavington, H. 7	*Santune* 265b
Shipbrook, H. 5	*Sibroc* 265
Shocklach, E. 7	*Socheliche* 264b
Shotwick, D. 5	*Sotowiche* 263
Shurlach, H. 4	*Survelec* 265
Sibroc	See Shipbrook
Siddington, J. 5	*Sudendune* 266b
Smallwood	Not in D.B.
Smethwick	Not in D.B.
Snelson, I. 4	*Senelestune* 267
Socheliche	See Shocklach
Somerford and Somerford Booths, I. 5	*Sumreford* 266b, 267b
Sotowiche	See Shotwick
Sound	Not in D.B.
Sproston, H. 5	*Sprostune* 265b
Sprostune	See Sproston
Spuretone	See Spurstow
Spurstow, F. 6	*Spuretone* 264b
Stab(e)lei	See Tabley
Stalybridge	Not in D.B.
Stanei	See Stanney
Stanleu	See Stoneley
Stanlow	Not in D.B.
Stanney, E. 4	*Stanei* 264

Turstanetone	See Thurstaston
Tushingham, F. 8	*Tusigeham* 264b
Tusigeham	See Tushingham
Twemlow	Not in D.B.
Tytherington	Not in D.B.
Ulchenol	Unid., Wales
Ulfemiltone	See Golftyn, Wales
Uluesgraue	See Golden Grove, Wales
Ulure	Unid., 265
Upton (near Birkenhead), C. 3	*Optone* 265
Upton (near Chester), E. 5	*Op(e)tone* 263b, 264
Upton (near Macclesfield)	Not in D.B.
Utkinton	Not in D.B.
Walcretune	See Walgherton
Walea	See Wallasey
Walgherton, H. 7	*Walcretune* 265b
Wallasey, D. 2	*Walea* 264b
Walton	Not in D.B.
Wanetune	See Wharton
Warburgetone	See Warburton
Warburton, H. 3	*Warburgetone* 267b *Wareburgetune* 266
Wardle, G. 6	*Warhelle* 266b
Wareburgetune	See Warburton
Wareford	See Warford
Wareneberie	See Wrenbury
Warford, I. 4	*Wareford* 267
Warhelle	See Wardle
Warmingham	Not in D.B.
Warnet	See Werneth
Watenhale	See Wettenhall
Waverton, E. 6	*Wavretone* 267b
Wavretone	See Waverton
Weaver, H. 5	*Wevre* 264 *bis*, 266b
Weaverham, G. 4	*Wivreham* 263b
Weltune	Unid., Wales
Wenescol	See Gwaenysgor, Wales
Wenfesne	Unid., Wales
Wenitone	See Winnington
Wepre	See Wepre, Wales
Werelestune	See Worleston
Werneth, K. 2	*Warnet* 264 *bis*
Wervin, E. 5	*Wivevrene* 263 *Wivrevene* 265
Wesberie	See Gwespyr, Wales
Weston (near Crewe)	Not in D.B.
Weston (near Runcorn), F. 4	*Westone* 266
Westone	See Weston (near Runcorn). See also Whitchurch, Salop.
Wettenhall, G. 6	*Watenhale* 267
Wevre	See Weaver
Wharton, H. 5	*Wanetune* 265
Wheelock, I. 6	*Hoiloch* 267
Whitby	Not in D.B.
Whitley, G. 4	*Witelei* 266
Wibaldelai	See Wimboldsley
Wice	See Leftwich
Wich	See Middlewich, Nantwich, Northwich
Widford	See Whitford, Wales
Widhulde	Unid., Wales
Wigland	Not in D.B.
Wilavestune	See Willaston (near Nantwich)
Wilkesley, G. 8	*Wivelesde* 265b
Willaston (near Chester)	Not in D.B.
Willaston (near Nantwich), H. 7	*Wilavestune* 265b
Willington, F. 5	*Winfletone* 265
Wilmslow	Not in D.B.
Wimboldsley, H. 6	*Wibaldelai* 264 *bis*, 266b
Wimbolds Trafford	See Trafford
Wimeberie	See Wybunbury
Wimundisham	See Wincham
Wincham, H. 4	*Wimundisham* 267
Wincle	Not in D.B.
Winfletone	See Willington
Winnington, G. 4	*Wenitone* 267, 267b

Wiresuelle, -swelle	See Wirswall
Wirswall, F. 8	*Wiresuelle, -swelle* 265b *bis*
Wisdelea	See Lea by Backford
Wiselei	Unid., Wales
Wistanestune	See Wistaston
Wistaston, H. 7	*Wistanestune* 265b
Wisterson, H. 7	*Wistetestune* 265b
Wistetestune	See Wisterson
Witelei	See Whitley
Witestan	Unid., Wales
Withington, I. 5	*Hungrewenitune* 264
Witton, H. 4	*Witune* 267
Witune	See Witton
Wivelesde	See Wilkesley
Wivevrene	See Wervin
Wivreham	See Weaverham
Wivrevene	See Wervin
Woodchurch	Not in D.B.
Woodcott	Not in D.B.
Woodford	Not in D.B.
Woolstanwood	Not in D.B.
Worleston, H. 6	*Werelestune* 265b
Wrenbury, G. 7	*Wareneberie* 265b
Wybunbury, H. 7	*Wimeberie* 263

ANONYMOUS HOLDINGS

No place-name appears in the following entry, and it is impossible to say whether or not it refers to a place named elsewhere in Domesday Book:

Unus serviens comitis [Earl Hugh] *tenet unam terram in hoc hundreto Tunendune*, 267b.

CORNWALL
CORNVALGIE (CORNUGALLIA)

Exchequer Domesday Book, folios 120–25
Exeter Domesday Book, folios 99–102b, 111b–12, 180b–81b, 199–208b, 224–65, 334b, 397b, 507–8
Exeter Domesday names and folio references are given in brackets. An asterisk * indicates that the names in the Exeter D.B. and the Exchequer D.B. are the same.

MAPS 8–9

Advent	Not in D.B.
Aissetone (-tona)	See Ashton
Altarnun	Not in D.B.
Alvacott, D. 3	*Alvevacote* 123b (*-cota* 239b)
Alverton, B. 7	*Alwaretone* 121b (*Alwartona* 255)
Alvevacote (-cota)	See Alvacott
Alwaretone (Alwartona)	See Alverton
*Amal**	See Amble
Amble, H. 2	*Amal* 122b (*239)
Antone (-tona)	See Antony
Antony, L. 4	*Antone* 121 (*-tona* 180b)
Appledore, K. 3	*Pedeleford* 122 (*-forda* 258)
*Arganlis**	See Arrallas
*Argentel**	See Tregantle
Arrallas, F. 4	*Arganlis* 123 (*249b)
Ashton, L. 3	*Aissetone* 122 (*-tona* 258b)
Avalde (Avalda)	See Havet

Balsdon, C. 3	*Bellesdone* 123b (*-dona* 237b)
Bellesdone (*-dona*)	See Balsdon
Bennacott, C. 4	*Betnecote* 123 (*-cota* 264b)
Bennartone (*-tona*)	See Binnerton
*Bentewoin**	See Pentewan
*Bernel**	See Brannel
Bernerh (*Berner*)	See Burniere
Betnecote (*-cota*)	See Bennacott
Beveshoc (*Bevesehoc*)	See Bissick
Bewintone	See Towan
Bichetone (*-tona*)	See Bicton
Bicton, K. 3	*Bichetone* 122 (*-tona* 258)
Binnerton, C. 7	*Bennartone* 120b (*-tona* 111b)
Bissick, F. 5	*Beveshoc* 124b (*Bevesehoc* 254)
Blisland, I. 2	*Glustone* 120 (*-tona* 101b, 507)
(*Bocent*)	See Bosent
Bochenod	See Boconnoc
Boconnoc, I. 4	*Bochenod* 124 (*Botchonod* 229b)
Bodardle, I. 4	*Botharder* 123 (*249b)
*Bodbran**	See Bodbrane
Bodbrane, J. 4	*Bodbran* 124 (*229)
Boden, E. 8	*Boten* 120 (*99b, 226b)
*Bodewitghi**	See Bodiggo
Bodeworgoin	See Bodrugan
Bodeworwei (*Bodeworuei*)	See Bojorrow
(*Bodewrgoin*)	See Bodrugan
Bodigga, K. 4	*Botchatwo* 120 (*Botchatuwo* 101b)
Bodiggo, H. 4	*Bodewitghi* 122b (*247)
Bodmin, H. 3	*Bodmine* 120b (*202)
*Bodmine**	See Bodmin
(*Bodowrueu*)	See Bojorrow
Bodrugan, H. 6	*Bodeworgoin* 122b (*Bodewrgoin* 247b)

Boduel, J. 3	*Botiual* 125 (*231)
Boietone (*Boiatona*, *Boietona*)	See Boyton
Bojorrow, D. 8	*Bodeworwei* 120 (*Bodeworuei* 100, *Bodowrueu* 227)
Bonyalva, K. 4	*Pennadelwan* 120 (*101b)
*Borge**	See Borough, Devon
Bosent, J. 3	*Buchent* 122 (*Bocent* 228b)
Bossiney, A. 4	*Botcinnii* 121 (*-cinnu* 203b)
Botchatwo (*Botchatuwo*)	See Bodigga
(*Botchonoam*)	See Bucklawren
(*Botchonod*)	See Boconnoc
Botcinnii (*-cinnu*)	See Bossiney
Botconoan	See Bucklawren
Botelet, J. 4	*Botiled* 124 (*230b)
*Boten**	See Boden
*Botharder**	See Bodardle
*Botiled**	See Botelet
*Botiual**	See Boduel
Botus Fleming	Not in D.B.
*Bowidoc**	See Bowithick
Bowithick, J. 1	*Bowidoc* 124 (*243b)
Boyton, D. 4	*Boietone* 121b, 123 (*Boiatona*, *Boietona* 181b, 232b, 508)
Braddock, I. 3	*Brodehoc* 122 (*236)
Brannel, G. 5	*Bernel* 121b (*249)
Brea, A. 7	*Bret* 124 (*255b)
Breage	Not in D.B.
Brecelesbeorge	See Buttsbear
*Bret**	See Brea
(*Bretelesbeorge*)	See Buttsbear
*Brethei**	See Burthy
*Brodehoc**	See Braddock
Buchent	See Bosent
Bucklawren, K. 4	*Botconoan* 120 (*Botchonoam* 101b)
Buddock	Not in D.B.

Burniere, G. 2	_Bernerh_ 120b (_Berner_ 199b)
Burthy, G. 4	_Brethei_ 122b (*248b)
Buttsbear, C. 2	_Brecelesbeorge_ 124 (_Bretelesbeorge_ 244)
Cabilla, I. 3	_Cabulian_ 124b (*231b)
_Cabulian_*	See Cabilla
_Caer_*	See Gear
(_Calestoc_)	See Callestock
Calestoch	See Callestock, Calstock
Callestock, E. 5	_Calestoch_ 121 (-_stoc_ 202b)
Callington, L. 3	_Calwetone_ 120 (-_witona_ 102)
Calstock, L. 3	_Calestoch_ 122 (_Kalestoc_ 256)
Calwetone (-_witona_)	See Callington
Camborne	Not in D.B.
Cann Orchard, C. 2	_Orcet_ 124 (*244)
Caradon, K. 2	_Carneton_, -_tone_ 120, 123 (_Carnatona_, -_etona_ 102, 245)
_Carbihan_*, G. 2	Lost in St Minver, 125 (237b)
Cardinham	Not in D.B.
Carewrge (-_euurga_, -_eurga_)	See Carworgie
_Cargau_*	See Cargoll
Cargoll, F. 4	_Cargau_ 121 (*203)
_Cariahoil_*, _Cariorgel_*	See Crawle
Carneton, -_tone_ (_Carnatona_, -_etona_)	See Caradon
Carsella, G. 4	_Karsalan_ 124b (*254)
Cartuther, J. 3	_Croftededor_ 122b (_Croutededor_ 228b)
Carworgie, G. 4	_Carewrge_ 120b (-_euurga_, -_eurga_ 112, 507b)
Chelenoch (-_noc_)	See Kelynack
Chenmerch	See Kilmarth
_Chenowen_*	See Trenewan
(_Chienmerc_)	See Kilmarth
Chilchetone	See Kilkhampton
_Chilcoit_*	See Colquite
_Chilorgoret_*	See Killigorrick
_Chori_*	See West Curry
Climsom, L. 2	_Clismestone_ 120 (-_tona_ 102)
Clinnick, I. 3	_Clunewic_ 123 (_Gluinwit_ 231b)
Clismestone (-_tona_)	See Climsom
Clunewic	See Clinnick
Colan	Not in D.B.
Colquite, H. 2	_Chilcoit_ 122b (*259b)
Conarditone (-_tona_)	See Connerton
Connerton, C. 6	_Conarditone_ 120 (-_tona_ 111b)
Constantine, E. 7	_Sanctus Constantinus_ 121 (*207)
Cornelly	Not in D.B.
Cosawes, E. 6	_Cudawoid_ 122 (-_woit_ 224b)
Coswarth, F. 4	_Cudiford_ 121 (-_fort_ 205, 507b) _Gudiford_ 120b (-_forda_ 111b, 507b)
Crachenwe (_Crachemua_)	See Crackinton Haven
Crackington Haven, B. 3	_Crachenwe_ 123b (_Crachemua_ 240)
Crantock, E. 4	_Langoroch_ 121 (-_gorroc_ 206)
Crawle, C. 7	_Cariahoil_ 120 (*99b) _Cariorgel_ 123 (*224b)
Creed	Not in D.B.
Croftededor (_Croutededor_)	See Cartuther
Crowan	Not in D.B.
Cubert	Not in D.B.
Cuby	Not in D.B.
Cudawoid (-_woit_)	See Cosawes
Cudiford (-_fort_)	See Coswarth
Cury	Not in D.B.

Dannonchapel, H. 1	*Duuenant* 125 (*263)
Davidstow	Not in D.B.
Dawna, I. 4	*Douenot* 123 (*235)
Delabole, H. 1	*Deliau*, *-iou* 125 *bis* (*Delio* 261, 263)
Deliau, *-iou* (*Delio*)	See Delabole
(*Dewintona*)	See Towan
*Dimelihoc**	See Domellick
*Disart**	See Dizzard
Dizzard and Old Dizzard, B. 4	*Disart* 124b (*243) *Lisart* 123b (*238b)
Domellick, D. 4	*Dimelihoc* 124b (*254b)
Donecheniv (*Domnechenif*)	See Downinney
*Douenot**	See Dawna
Downinney, B. 4	*Donecheniv* 122b (*Domnechenif* 259)
*Drainos**	See Draynes
Draynes, Great and West, J. 3	*Drainos* 124b *bis* (*231, 232)
Duloe	Not in D.B.
Dunhevet (*-heved*)	See Launceston
*Duuenant**	See Dannonchapel
East Looe	Not in D.B.
(*Ecglosberria*)	See St Buryan
(*Ecglostudic*)	See St Tudy
*Edelet**	See Idless
Egleshos	See Philleigh
Eglosberrie	See St Buryan
Egloshayle	Not in D.B.
Egloskerry	Not in D.B.
(*Eglossos*)	See Philleigh
*Elent**	See Illand
*Elerchi**	See Veryan
*Elhil**, *Elil**	See Ellenglaze
Ellbridge, L. 3	*Telbrig* 122 (*-bricg* 245b)
Ellenglaze, E. 4	*Elhil*, *Elil* 121 *bis* (*202b, 213b)
Ermenheu	See Halvana
(*Eschewit*)	See Skewes
Falmouth	Not in D.B.
Fawintone (*Fawitona*)	See Fawton
Fawton, I. 3	*Fawintone* 121b (*Fawitona* 228)
Feock	Not in D.B.
Forchetestane (*-tana*)	See Froxton
Forrabury	Not in D.B.
*Fosnewit**	See Fursnewth
Fowey	Not in D.B.
Froxton, C. 3	*Forchetestane* 125 (*-tana* 334b)
Fursnewth, J. 3	*Fosnewit* 121 (*204b)
Galowras, H. 6	*Gloeret* 123b (*252b)
Garah, D. 8	*Garuerot* 120 (*99b, *Garuro* 226)
Garalle (*-alla*)	See Tregarland
*Garuerot** (*Garuro*)	See Garah
Gear, E. 8	*Caer* 122 (*225b)
Germoe	Not in D.B.
Gerrans	Not in D.B.
Ghivaile (*-aili*)	See Goviley
*Glin**	See Glynn
*Gloerot**	See Galowras
(*Gluinwit*)	See Clinnick
Glustone (*-tona*)	See Blisland
Glynn, I. 3	*Glin* 124 (*230)
Goodern, E. 6	*Woderon* 122b (*Uderon* 248)
Gothers, G. 4	*Widewot* 124b (*254b)
Goviley, G. 6	*Ghivaile* 122b (*-aili* 247b)
Grade	Not in D.B.
Grampound	Not in D.B.
Great Draynes	See Draynes
Gudiford (*-forda*)	See Coswarth
Guerdevalan	See Worthyvale
Gulval, B. 7	*Landicle* 120b (*-icla* 200b)
Gunwalloe	Not in D.B.
(*Gurdavalan*)	See Worthyvale
Gurlyn, C. 7	*Woreslin* 123 (*255b)

Landewednack	Not in D.B.
Landicle (*-icla*)	See Gulval
*Landighe**	See Kea
*Landiner**	See Landinner
Landinner, J. 1	*Landiner* 121b (*261b) *Lanliner* 100b Devon (*Laniliner* 93, *Lanliner* 495b Devon)
Landmanuel	See Lamellan
Landrake, L. 4	*Lander* 122 (*Landrei* 261b)
(*Landrei*)	See Landrake
*Landseu**	See Launcells
Landulph, L. 4	*Landelech* 122b (*260)
Laneast	Not in D.B.
Lanehoc	See Lanow
Lanescot, H. 4	*Lisnestoch* 122b (*248b)
Langenewit	See Langunnett
Langoroch (*-gorroc*)	See Crantock
*Languer**	See Lancare
*Languer**	Unid., 122 (257b)
(*Languihenoc*)	See Padstow
Languitetone (*-tona*)	See Lawhitton
(*Langunuit*)	See Langunnett
Langunnett, I. 4	*Langenewit* 122 (*Langunuit* 229b)
Lanhadron, H. 5	*Lanlaron* 122 (*252)
Lanher	See Lannear
Lanherne, F. 3	*Lanherweu* 120b (*-herueu* 200)
Lanherweu (*-herueu*)	See Lanherne
Lanhydrock	Not in D.B.
Lanivet	Not in D.B.
*Lanlaron**	See Lanhadron
*Lanlawernec**	See Lanwarnick
Lanlivery	Not in D.B.
*Lannachebran**	See St Keverne
(*Lannahoo*)	See Lanow
Lannear, J. 5	*Lanher* 122 (*Lanner* 235b)
(*Lanner*)	See Lannear
(*Lannohoi*, *-hoo*)	See Lanow

Lanow, H. 2	*Lanehoc* 120 (*Lannohoo* 101, *Lannahoo* 507b) *Lantloho* 123b (*238, *Lannohoi* 507b *bis*)
*Lanpiran**	See Perranzabuloe
Lanreath, J. 4	*Lauredoch* 122b (*Lanredoch* 229)
(*Lanredoch*)	See Lanreath
Lansallos, I. 5	*Lansalhus* 122b (*-saluus* 229)
Lansalhus (*-saluus*)	See Lansallos
Lanscauestone (*-tona*)	See St Stephens by Launceston
Lanteglos (near Camelford)	Not in D.B.
Lanteglos (near Fowey)	Not in D.B.
Lanthien	See Lantyan
Lantien	See Lancallen
(*Lantien*)	See Lancallen, Lantyan
Lantivet, I. 5	*Nantuat* 122b (*Namtiuat* 236b)
*Lantloho**	See Lanow
(*Lantmanuel*)	See Lamellan
*Lantmatin**	See Lametton
Lantyan, I. 4	*Lanthien* 124 (*Lantien* 252)
Lanwarnick, J. 4	*Lanawernec* 124b (*231)
Lanwenehoc	See Padstow
Launcells, C. 2	*Landseu* 124 (*244)
Launceston, K. 1	*Dunhevet* 121b (*-heved* 264b)
Lauredoch	See Lanreath
Lawhitton, K. 1	*Languitetone* 120b (*-tona* 200b)
Lee, C. 1	*Lege* 123 (*Lega* 232b)
Lege (*Lega*)	See Lee
*Legea**	See Leigh
Leigh, K. 3	*Legea* 125 (*261)
Lesnewth, B. 4	*Lisniwen* 124b (*242)
Lewannick	Not in D.B.
Lezant	Not in D.B.
Linkinhorne	Not in D.B.

Lisart	See Dizzard
(*Lisart*)	See Dizzard, Lizard
*Liscarret**	See Liskeard
Liskeard, J. 3	*Liscarret* 121b (*228)
*Lisnestoch**	See Lanescot
*Lisniwen**	See Lesnewth
Little Petherick	Not in D.B.
Lizard, D. 9	*Lusart* 120 (*99b, *Lisart* 226)
Lostwithiel	Not in D.B.
Lower Polscoe	See Polscoe
Ludgvan, B. 7	*Luduham* 122b (*Luduam* 260)
Luduham (*Luduam*)	See Ludgvan
*Lusart**	See Lizard
Luxulian	Not in D.B.
Mabe	Not in D.B.
Macretone (*-tona*)	See Maker
Madron	Not in D.B.
(*Maiuian*)	See Mawgan in Meneage
Maker, L. 5	*Macretone* 122, Corn.; 100b, Devon (*-tona* 256b, 505, Corn.; 87, Devon)
Manaccan	Not in D.B.
Manely, I. 4	*Mingeli* 124 (*229b)
Marazion	Not in D.B.
Marhamchurch, C. 2	*Maronecirche* 123 (*Maronacirca* 232b)
Maronecirche (*Maronacirca*)	See Marhamchurch
Matele (*-ela*, *Mathela*)	See Methleigh
Mawan (*Mawant*)	See Mawgan in Meneage
Mawgan in Meneage, D. 8	*Mawan* 120 (*Maiuian* 99b, *Mawant* 226)
Mawgan in Pyder	Not in D.B.
Mawnan	Not in D.B.
Melledham (*-dam*)	See Trevalga

Menheniot	Not in D.B.
Merther	Not in D.B.
Methleigh, C. 8	*Matele* 120b (*-ela* 199, *Mathela* 507b)
Mevagissey	Not in D.B.
Michaelstow	Not in D.B.
Mideltone (*Middeltona*)	See Milton
Millbrook	Not in D.B.
Milton, C. 1	*Mideltone* 123 (*Middeltona* 232)
*Mingeli**	See Manely
Minster, A. 4	*Talcar* 122b (*239)
*Moireis**	See Moresk
Moresk, F. 6	*Moireis* 121b (*249)
Moreton, C. 2	*Mortune* 123b (*-tuna* 237b)
Mortune (*-tuna*)	See Moreton
Morwenstow	Not in D.B.
Morvah	Not in D.B.
Morval	Not in D.B.
Mullion	Not in D.B.
Mylor	Not in D.B.
(*Namtiuet*)	See Lantivet
Nancekuke, D. 5	*Lanchehoc* 120b (*Lancichuc* 202b)
*Nanchert** (*Nantchert*)	See Lancarffe
Nantuat	See Lantivet
Neotestou	See St Neot
Neweton	See Newton Ferrers
Newlyn	Not in D.B.
Newquay	Not in D.B.
*Nietestou** (*Nietessou*)	See St Neot
Newton Ferrers, K. 3	*Neweton*, *Niwetone* 122 *bis* (*Niwetona* 258, 258b)
Niwetone (*-tona*)	See Newton Ferrers
North Hill	Not in D.B.
North Tamerton	Not in D.B.
Norton, C. 2	*Nortone* 123b (*-tona* 237)
Nortone (*-tona*)	See Norton

*Odenol**	See Perranuthnoe
Old Dizzard	See Dizzard
*Orcert**	See Week Orchard
*Orcet**	See Cann Orchard
Otrham	See Otterham
Otterham, B. 4	*Otrham* 122b (*Ottram* 259b)
(*Ottram*)	See Otterham
Padstow, G. 2	*Lanwenehoc* 120b (*Languienoc* 202)
Paenpau	See Penpoll
*Paindran** (*Paindram*)	See Pendrim
*Panguol**	See Pengold
Patrieda, K. 2	*Peret* 121b (*Pedret* 262)
Paul	Not in D.B.
Pautone (*-tona*)	See Pawton
Pawton, G. 3	*Pautone* 120b (*-tona* 199b)
(*Pedret*)	See Patrieda
Pelynt, J. 4	*Plunent* 124b (*230b)
Pencarrow, H. 2	*Penguare* 122b (*Penquaro* 233)
*Pendavid**	See Pendavy
Pendavy, H. 2	*Pendavid* 120 (*101b, 507)
Pendrim, J. 4	*Paindran* 120 (*101b, *Paindram* 507)
*Penfontenio**	See Penventinue
*Penfou**	See Penfound
Penfound, C. 3	*Penfou* 124 (*242)
Pengelle (*-gelli*)	See Pengelly
Pengelly, K. 2	*Pengelle* 124b (*-gelli* 245)
Pengold, B. 3	*Panguol* 125 (*238b)
Penguare	See Pencarrow
Penhallam, B. 3	*Penhalun* 122b (*Pennalum* 259)
Penhalt, B. 3	*Pennalt* 124 (*243b)
Penhalun	See Penhallam
Penharget, K. 3	*Pennehalgar* 121b (*181)

Penhawger, K. 3	*Pennhalgar* 122 (*Pennahalgar* 256)
Penheale, K. 1	*Pennehel* 120 (*102b)
Penhole, K. 2	*Polhal* 124b (*261b)
*Pennadelwan**	See Bonyalva
(*Pennahalgar*)	See Penhawger
*Pennalt**	See Penhalt
(*Pennalum*)	See Penhallam
*Pennehalgar**	See Penharget
*Pennehel**	See Penheale
Pennhalgar	See Penhawger
(*Penpau*)	See Penpoll
*Penpel**	See Penpell
Penpell, G. 5	*Penpel* 123 (*250b)
Penpoll, K. 3	*Paenpau* 122 (*Penpau* 257b)
Penpont, J. 1	*Penponte* 124 (*-ponta* 243b)
Penponte (*-ponta*)	See Penpont
(*Penquaro*)	See Pencarrow
Penryn	Not in D.B.
Penzance	Not in D.B.
Peret	See Patrieda
Pentewan, H. 5	*Bentewoin* 124b (*253b)
Penventinue, I. 4	*Penfontenio* 123 (*251b)
Pepeleford (*-forda*)	See Appledore
Perranarworthal	Not in D.B.
Perranuthnoe, B. 7	*Odenol* 124b (*255)
Perranzabuloe, E. 4	*Lanpiran* 121 (*206b)
Phillack	Not in D.B.
Philleigh, F. 6	*Egleshos* 123 (*Eglossos* 250b)
Pigesdone (*Pighesdona*)	See Pigsdon
Pigsdon, C. 3	*Pigesdone* 125 (*Pighesdona* 397b)
Piletone (*Pilatona*)	See Pillaton
Pillaton, L. 3	*Piletone* 122 (*Pilatona* 257)
*Plunent**	See Pelynt

Pochehelle (*Poccahetilla*)	See Poughill
*Podestot**	See Poundstock
Polduh (*Poldu*)	See Polsue
Polefand	See Polyphant
Polescat (*-schat*)	See Polscoe
*Polhal**	See Penhole
(*Polofant*)	See Polyphant
Polrode (*-roda*)	See Polrode
Polrode, H. 2	*Polrode* 121 (*-roda* 204)
*Polscat**	See Polscoe
Polscoe, Higher and Lower, I. 4	*Polescat* 122 (*-schat* 228) *Polscat* 125 (*230b)
Polsue, F. 5	*Polduh* 122b (*Poldu* 248)
Polyphant, J. 1	*Polefand* 123b (*Polofant* 243)
*Pondestoch** (*Pondestoca*)	See Poundstock
*Portatlant**	See Porthallow
Porthallow, J. 5	*Portatlant* 124b (*264b)
Poughill, C. 2	*Pochehelle* 124 (*Poccahetilla* 233b)
Poundstock, B. 3	*Podestot* 120 (*101, 507) *Pondestoch* 123b (*Pondestoca*, *-stoch* 238, 507b)
Probus, F. 5	*Lanbrebois* 121 (*Lanbrabois* 206)
Quethiock	Not in D.B.
Rame, L. 5	*Rame* 121 (*181)
Raphael, J. 5	*Raswale* 122 (*-wala* 236)
Raswale (*-wala*)	See Raphael
Recharedoc	See Rosecraddock
Redruth	Not in D.B.
(*Rekaradoc*)	See Rosecraddock
*Renti**, *Rentin** (*Rentis*)	See Rinsey
Rialton, F. 3	*Rieltone* 120b (*-tona* 202)
Richan (*Ricann*)	See Trecan

Rieltone (*-tona*)	See Rialton
*Riguen**	See Tredwen
Rillaton, K. 2	*Risleston* 121b (*Rislestona* 264)
Rinsey, C. 7	*Renti* 120 *bis* (*Renti*, *-tis* 99, 100, 225b) *Rentin* 124b (*262b)
Risleston (*Rislestona*)	See Rillaton
Ritwore (*-wori*)	See Roseworthy
Roche	Not in D.B.
Roscaret	See Roscarrock, Tregarrick
(*Roscaret*)	See Roscarrock
*Roscarnan**	See Roscarnon
Roscarnon, E. 8	*Roscarnan* 120, 123b (*100, 224b)
Roscarrock, G. 1	*Roscaret* 123b (*241b)
*Roschel**	See Rosecare
Rosebenault, J. 1	*Rosminuet* 123b (*241)
Rosecare, B. 3	*Roschel* 123b (*240)
Rosecraddock, K. 3	*Recharedoc* 123 (*Rekaradoc* 234)
Roseworthy, C. 6	*Ritwore* 120 (*-wori* 102b)
Roslech (*-let*)	See Treslay
*Rosminuet**	See Rosebenault
Rosperuet (*-paruet*)	See Tresparrett
Ruan Lanihorne	Not in D.B.
Ruan Major and Minor	Not in D.B.
(*Sainguilant*)	See St Juliot
*Sainguinas**	See St Gennys
St Agnes	Not in D.B.
St Allen	Not in D.B.
St Anthony in Meneage	Not in D.B.
St Anthony in Roseland	Not in D.B.
St Austell	Not in D.B.
St Blazey	Not in D.B.
St Breock	Not in D.B.
St Breward	Not in D.B.
St Buryan, A. 8	*Eglosberrie* 121 (*Ecglosberria* 207)

St Cleer	Not in D.B.
St Clement	Not in D.B.
St Clether	Not in D.B.
St Columb Major and Minor	Not in D.B.
St Dennis	Not in D.B.
St Dominick	Not in D.B.
St Endellion	Not in D.B.
St Enoder, F. 4	*Heglosenuder* 121 (*Hecglosenuda* 203)
St Erme	Not in D.B.
St Erth	Not in D.B.
St Ervan	Not in D.B.
St Eval	Not in D.B.
St Ewe	Not in D.B.
St Gennys, B. 3	*Sainguinas* 120 (*101) *Sanwinas* 123b (*Sanguinas* 238b, 507, 507b)
St Germans, K. 4	*S' Germani* 120b (*Sc̄s German* 199b, 507)
St Gluvias	Not in D.B.
St Goran, H. 6	*Tregauran* 123 (*251b)
St Hillary	Not in D.B.
St Issey	Not in D.B.
St Ive	Not in D.B.
St Ives	Not in D.B.
St John	Not in D.B.
St Juliot, B. 4	*Sanguiland* 122b (*Sainguilant* 238b)
St Just	Not in D.B.
St Just in Roseland	Not in D.B.
St Keverne, E. 8	*Lannachebran* 121 (*205b)
St Kew	Not in D.B.
St Keyne	Not in D.B.
St Levan	Not in D.B.
St Mabyn	Not in D.B.
St Martin	Not in D.B.
St Martin in Meneage	Not in D.B.
St Mary	Not in D.B.
St Mary Magdalene	Not in D.B.
St Mellion	Not in D.B.
St Merryn	Not in D.B.
St Mewan	Not in D.B.
St Michael Caerhays	Not in D.B.
St Michael Penkevil	Not in D.B.
St Michael's Mount, B. 7	*Sc̄s Michael* 120b (*Sc̄s Michahel* 208b)
St Minver	Not in D.B.
St Neot, J. 3	*Neot-*, *Nietestou* 121, 124 (*Nietesstou*, *-testou* 207, 230b)
St Pinnock	Not in D.B.
St Sampson	Not in D.B.
St Stephen in Brannel	Not in D.B.
St Stephens	Not in D.B.
St Stephens by Launceston, K. 1	*Lanscauestone* 120b (*-tona* 206b)
St Teath	Not in D.B.
St Tudy, H. 2	(*Ecglos-*, *Hecglostudic* 204b, 507b). Not in Exch. D.B.
St Veep	Not in D.B.
St Weun	Not in D.B.
St Winnow, I. 4	*Sanwinuec* 120b (*San Winnuc* 201)
Saltash	Not in D.B.
Sancreed	Not in D.B.
*Sanctus Constantinus**	See Constantine
S' Germani (*Sc̄s German*)	See St Germans
Sc̄s Michael (*Sc̄s Michahel*)	See St Michael's Mount
Sanguiland	See St Juliot
Sanwinas (*Sanguinas*)	See St Gennys
Sanwinuec (*San Winnuc*)	See St Winnow
*Savioch**	See Sheviock
Schewit	See Skewes
Sennen	Not in D.B.
Sheviock, L. 4	*Savioch* 121 (*180b)
Sithney	Not in D.B.

Skewes, D. 8	*Schewit* 120 (*Eschewit* 99, 225b)
South Hill, K. 2	*Hela* 121b (*261b)
South Petherwin	Not in D.B.
Stithians	Not in D.B.
Stoke Climsland	Not in D.B.
Stratone (*-tona*)	See Stratton
Stratton, C. 2	*Stratone* 121b (*-tona* 237)
Tacabere (*-beara*)	See Tackbear, Devon
*Talcar**	See Minster
*Talcarn**	See Tolcarne (in Newquay)
*Talgar**	See Tolcarne (in North Hill)
Talgolle (*-gollo*)	See Tolgullow
Talland	Not in D.B.
(*Tarcharn*)	See Tolcarne (in Newquay)
Tedintone (*Tedentona*)	See Tehidy
Teglaston	See Treglasta
Tehidy, D. 6	*Tedintone* 121b (*Tedentona* 255)
Telbrig (*-bricg*)	See Ellbridge
Temple	Not in D.B.
*Tewardevi**	See Trethevey
*Thersent**	See Trezance
Thinten (*Tinten*)	See Tinten
Thorne, C. 3	*Torne* 123 (*Torna* 233)
Thurlibeer, C. 2	*Tirlebere* 124 (*-bera* 233b)
*Tibesteu**	See Tybesta
Ticoith (*Ticoit*)	See Tucoyse (in St Ewe)
Tintagel	Not in D.B.
Tinten, H. 2	*Thinten* 120b (*Tinten* 200b)
Tirlebere (*-bera*)	See Thurlibeer
*Tiwardrai**	See Tywardreath
*Tiwarthel**	See Tywarnhayle
Tolcarne (in Newquay), F. 4	*Talcarn* 121 (*205, *Tarcharn* 508)
Tolcarne (in North Hill), J. 2	*Talgar* 121b (*181b)
Tolgullow, E. 6	*Talgolle* 124b (*-gollo* 225)
Torne (*Torna*)	See Thorne
Torpoint	Not in D.B.
Torwednack	Not in D.B.
Torwell, J. 4	*Trewelle* 112 (*-wella* 235b)
Towan, H. 5	*Bewintone* 120 (*Dewintona* 100b)
*Tragaraduc**	See Tregardock
*Tragol**	See Treal
*Travider**	See Trevedor
(*Traviscoit*)	See Trevisquite
*Trawint**	See Trewint
Trawiscoit	See Trevisquite
Treal, D. 9	*Tragol* 120 (*100)
Trebarfoot, B. 3	*Treuerbet* 122b (*239)
Trebartha, J. 2	*Tribertha'* 123 (*-bertan* 264)
Trebeigh, K. 3	*Trebichen* 121b (*Tre-*, *Tribicen* 181b, 508), Corn. *Trebihan* 121b (*-bihau* 262), Corn. *Trebichen* 100b (93, *Tribichen* 495b), Devon
Trebichen (*-bicen*)	See Trebeigh
Trebihan (*-hau*)	See Trebeigh
*Trebleri**	See Tremblary
Trecan, I. 4	*Richan* 122 (*Ricann* 229)
(*Trecut*)	See Tregoose
*Tredaual**	See Tredaule
Tredaule, J. 1	*Tredaual* 123b (*242b)
(*Tredeoworch*)	See Tredower
Tredhac	See Trethake
Tredinnick, L. 4	*Trehinoch* 122 (*-hynoc* 256b)
Tredower, E. 8	*Tretdeword* 120 (*-wort* 100, *Tredeoworch* 227b)
Tredwen, J. 1	*Riguen* 125 (*262b)
*Trefilies**	See Trevillis

*Trefitent**	See Trewithen
*Trefornoc** (*Trefoznohc*)	See Trevornick
Trefreock (in St Endellion), H. 1	*Trefrioc* 125 (*263)
Trefreock (in St Gennys), B. 3	*Trerihoc* 123b (*240)
*Trefrioc**	See Trefreock (in St Endellion)
Trefrize, K. 2	*Treverim* 122 (*257b)
*Tregal**	See Tregole
*Treganmedan**	See Tregavethan
Tregantle, L. 5	*Argentel* 122 (*256b)
Tregardock, H. 1	*Tragaraduc* 124b (*263b)
Tregarland, J. 4	*Gargalle* 112 (-*galla* 235b)
Tregarrick, K. 3	*Roscaret* 124 (*Hroscarec* 245)
*Tregauran**	See St Goran
Tregavethan, E. 5	*Treganmedan* 123 (*251)
Tregeagle, F. 5	*Tregingale* 124b (*Treghingala* 253)
Tregear, F. 6	*Tregel* 120b (*Trigel* 199)
Tregel	See Tregear
Tregemelin (*Treghemelin*)	See Trigamelling
Tregingale (*Treghingala*)	See Tregeagle
Treglasta, J. 1	*Teglaston* 121b (*Treglastan* 237)
(*Treglastan*)	See Treglasta
*Tregoin**	See Trewoon
Tregolds, F. 2	*Turgoil* 121 (*204b)
Tregole, B. 3	*Tregal* 124b (*242b)
Tregon (*Tregona'*)	See Tregona
Tregona, F. 3	*Tregon* 121 (-*gona'* 204b, 507b)
Tregoney	Not in D.B.
Tregoose, D. 8	*Tricoi* 120 (*99b, *Trecut* 226)
*Tregrebri**	Unid., 123b (240b)

Tregrenon (-*nou*)	See Trewornan
*Tregril**	See Tregrill
Tregrill, K. 3	*Tregril* 124 (*263b)
(*Treguin*)	See Trewen
*Trehauoc**	See Trehawke
Trehawke, K. 4	*Trehauoc* 122 (*257b)
Trehinoch (-*hynoc*)	See Tredinnick
*Treiswantel**	See Trewanta
*Treiwal**	See Truthwall
Treknow, H. 1	*Tretdeno* 121 (*203b)
*Trelamar**	See Tremar
Trelan and Trelanvean, E. 8	*Treland* 122b (-*lant* 244) *Tretland* 120 (-*lant* 100, 227)
Treland (-*lant*)	See Trelan
Trelaske, K. 1	*Trelosch* 124 (-*losca* 263b)
Trelawne, J. 4	*Trewellogan* 122 (*Trevelloien* 235b)
Treliever, E. 7	*Trewel* 120b (*Trelivel* 199)
Trelingan (-*ligani*)	See Treluggan (in Gerrans)
(*Trelivel*)	See Treliever
*Trellewaret**	See Trelowarren
*Trelloi**	See Treloy
*Treloen**	See Trelowia
Trelosch (-*losca*)	See Trelaske
Trelowarren, D. 8	*Trellewaret* 120 (*99b, *Trelweren* 226b)
Trelowia, K. 4	*Treloen* 123 (*234b)
Trelowth, H. 5	*Trelwi* 123 (-*luwi* 250)
Treloy, F. 3	*Trelloi* 121 (*203)
Treluge (-*luga*)	See Treluggan (in Landrake)
Treluggan (in Gerrans), F. 6	*Trelingen* 125 (-*ligani* 253)
Treluggan (in Landrake), L. 4	*Treluge* 124 (-*luga* 244b)
(*Treluwi*)	See Trelowth
(*Trelweren*)	See Trelowarren
Trelwi	See Trelowth

Tremadart, J. 4	*Tremeteret* 124 (*Tremethereht* 230)
Tremail, I. 1	*Tremail* 121 (*204)
Tremaine	Not in D.B.
Tremar, J. 3	*Trelamar* 124b (*234)
Tremarustel (*Tremarwstel*)	See Trenance (in St Austell)
Trematon, L. 4	*Tremetone* 122 (*-tona* 256)
Tremblary, I. 1	*Trebleri* 123b (*238)
Trembraze, E. 8	*Trenbras* 120 (*99b, 226)
Tremeteret (*Tremethereht*)	See Tremadart
Tremetone (*-tona*)	See Trematon
Tremhor	See Tremore
Tremoan, L. 3	*Tremor* 122 (*257)
Tremoddrett, H. 4	*Tremodret* 123 (*250b)
*Tremodret**	See Tremoddrett
Tremor	See Tremoan
(*Tremor*)	See Tremoan, Tremore
Tremore, H. 3	*Tremhor* 121 (*Tremor* 205, 508)
Trenance (in Mullion), D. 8	*Trenant* 120 (*99, 225b)
Trenance (in St Austell), H. 4	*Tremarustel* 125 (*Tremarwstel* 245b)
Trenance (in St Keverne), E. 8	*Trenant* 124b (*224)
Trenand (*Trenant*)	See Trenant (in Duloe)
*Trenant**	See Trenance (in Mullion), Trenance (in St Keverne), Trenant (in Fowey)
Trenant (in Duloe), J. 4	*Trenand* 124 (*Trenant* 230)
Trenant (in Fowey), I. 5	*Trenant* 123, 124 (*251b, 252b)
*Trenbras**	See Trembraze
Trenderway, J. 4	*Trewinedoi* 122b (*Treuiunadoi* 236b)
Treneglos	Not in D.B.
Trenewan, I. 4	*Chenowen* 122b (*234)
*Trenhal**	See Trenhale
Trenhale, F. 4	*Trenhal* 121 (*205, 507b)
(*Trenidered*)	See *Trewderet*
Treninnick, F. 4	*Trinnonec* 121 (*Trincnonet* 205, *Trinnonech* 508)
Trenowth, G. 5	*Trenwit* 121b (*Trenuwit* 249)
Trenuth, I. 1	*Trevoet* 123b (*241)
Trenwit (*Trenuwit*)	See Trenowth
Trerice, G. 4	*Treuret* 123b (*253)
Trerihoc	See Trefreock (in St Gennys)
*Trescau**	See Trescowe
Trescowe, C. 7	*Trescau* 124b (*225)
Treslay, B. 4	*Roslech* 123b (*-let* 240)
Tresmeer	Not in D.B.
Tresparrett, B. 4	*Rosperuet* 123b (*-paruet* 238)
*Tretdeno**	See Treknow
Tretdeword (*-wort*)	See Tredower
*Trethac**	See Tretheake
(*Trethac*)	See Trethake, Tretheake
Trethake, I. 5	*Tredhac* 123 (*Trethac* 235)
Tretheake, G. 6	*Trethac* 123 (*250)
Trethevey, H. 2	*Tewardevi* 122b (*260)
Tretland (*-lant*)	See Trelan
*Tretweret**	See Treverres
*Treuerbet**	See Trebarfoot
*Treuret**	See Trerice
(*Treuithal*)	See Truthall
(*Treuiunadoi*)	See Trenderway
Treurgen (*Treurghen*)	Unid., 123b (264b)
*Treurnivet**	See Trewarnevas
*Treuthal**	See Truthwall
Trevagau (*-gan*)	See Trevague

Trevague, J. 1	*Trevagau* 123b (*-gan* 242b)
Trevalga, A. 4	*Melledham* 120b (*-dam* 112)
(*Trevalla*)	See Trevallack
Trevallack, K. 3	*Trewale* 124b (*Trevalla* 245)
Trevedor, E. 8	*Travider* 120 (*100b)
Trevego, I. 4	*Trevocarwinoc* 125 (*-winnoc* 231b)
Treveheret	See Trewethart
*Trevelien**	See Trevellion
Trevell, J. 1	*Trewille* 121b (*Trevilla* 262)
Trevellion, H. 4	*Trevelien* 124 (*252)
(*Trevelloien*)	See Trelawne
Trevelyan, I. 4	*Trewillen* 122 (*Trevillein* 229b)
Treveniel, J. 2	*Treviniel* 124 (*244b)
*Treverbin**	See Treverbyn
Treverbyn, H. 4	*Treverbin* 122b (*248)
*Treverim**	See Trefrize
Treverres, F. 6	*Tretweret* 124b (*254)
*Treviliud**	See Trewidland
(*Trevilla*)	See Trevell
(*Trevillein*)	See Trevelyan
Trevillis, J. 4	*Trefilies* 125 (*231b)
*Treviniel**	See Treveniel
Trevisquite, H. 2	*Trawiscoit* 122b (*Trauiscoit* 260)
Trevocarwinoc (*-winnoc*)	See Trevego
*Trevoet**	See Trenuth
Trevornick, G. 3	*Trefornoc* 121 (*205, *Trefoȝnohc* 507b)
Trewale	See Trevallack
Trewallen (*-lem*)	See Trewolland
*Trewant**	See Trewanta
Trewanta, J. 1	*Treiswantel* 121b (*261b)
	Trewant 121b (*181b, 508)
Trewarnevas, E. 8	*Treurnivet* 120 (*100, *Trewrnivet* 227)
(*Trewda*)	See Treworder
Trewderet (*Trenidered*)	Unid., 124b (245b)
(*Treweheret*)	See Trewethart
Trewel	See Treliever
Trewelle (*-wella*)	See Torwell
Trewellogen	See Trelawne
Trewen, H. 2	*Trewin* 123b (*Treguin* 240b)
*Trewent**	See Trewince
Trewethart, H. 1	*Treveheret* 125 (*Treweheret* 263)
Trewidland, J. 4	*Treviliud* 124b (*232)
Trewille	See Trevell
Trewillen	See Trevelyan
Trewin	See Trewen
Trewince, E. 8	*Trewent* 124b (*224)
Trewinedoi	See Trenderway
Trewint, J. 1	*Trawint* 125 (*260b)
Trewirgie, F. 5	*Trewitghi* 121b (*249b)
*Trewitghi**	See Trewirgie
Trewithen, G. 5	*Trefitent* 124b (*253b)
Trewode	See Treworder
Trewolland, K. 3	*Trewallen* 123 (*-lem* 234b)
Trewoon, H. 5	*Tregoin* 123 (*251)
Treworder, D. 9	*Trewode* 120 (*-wda* 100)
Trewornan, G. 2	*Tregrenon* 121b (*-nou* 181)
*Treworoc**	See Treworrick
Treworrick, G. 5	*Treworoc* 123 (*250)
(*Trewrnivet*)	See Trewarnevas
Trezance, I. 3	*Thersent* 122 (*228b)
Triberthan (*-tan*)	See Trebartha
(*Tribicen*)	See Trebeigh
*Tricoi**	See Tregoose
Trigamelling, J. 5	*Tregemelin* 123 (*Treghemelin* 234b)

(*Trigel*)	See Tregear
Trinnonec (*-ech*, *Trincnonet*)	See Treninnick
*Trouthel**	See Truthal
Truthal, D. 7	*Trouthel* 120 (*100, *Treuithal* 227)
Truthwall, B. 7	*Treiwal* 120b (*208b, 508) *Treuthal* 125 (*258b)
*Tucowit**	See Tucoyse (in Constantine)
Tucoyse (in Constantine), D. 7	*Tucowit* 125 (*225)
Tucoyse (in St Ewe), G. 5	*Ticoith* 122b (*Ticoit* 247b)
*Turgoil**	See Tregolds
Tybesta, G. 5	*Tibesteu* 121b (*247)
Tywardreath, H. 4	*Tiwardrai* 122b (*247)
Tywarnhayle, E. 4	*Tiwarthel* 121 (*202b)
(*Uderon*)	See Goodern
(*Uingetona*, *Uinnetona*)	See Winnianton
Ullavestone (*Ullovastona*)	See Woolston (in St Ive)
Ulnodestone (*Ulnotestona*)	See Woolston (in Poundstock)
Uny Lelant	Not in D.B.
Veryan, G. 6	*Elerchi* 124b (*253)
Wadebridge	Not in D.B.
Wadefeste (*Wadafeste*)	See Wadfast
Wadfast, C. 3	*Wadefeste* 123 (*Wadafeste* 233)
*Walesbrau**	See Whalesborough
Warbstow	Not in D.B.
Warleggan	Not in D.B.
Week Orchard, C. 3	*Orcert* 123 (*232b)
Week St Mary, C. 3	*Wich* 122b (*Wihc* 259)
Wendron	Not in D.B.
Wescote (*-cota*)	See Westcott
Westcott, C. 3	*Wescote* 123b (*-cota* 239b)
West Curry, C. 3	*Chori* 123b (*264b)
West Draynes	See Draynes
West Looe	Not in D.B.
Whalesborough, B. 2	*Walesbrau* 124 (*242)
Whitstone, C. 3	*Witestan* 125 (*255b)
Wich	See Week St Mary
Widemouth, B. 2	*Widemot* 124 (*241b)
*Widewot**	See Gothers
*Widie**	See Withiel
(*Wihc*)	See Week St Mary
Wilewrde (*-eurda*)	See Wilsworthy
Wilsworthy, C. 3	*Wilewrde* 122b (*-eurda* 239)
Winetone (*Wine-*, *Winnetona*)	See Winnianton
Winnianton, D. 8	*Winetone* 120 (*Uingetona*, *Uinnetona* 225b *ter*, 226, 226b, 227b, *Wine-*, *Winnetona* 99, 226b *quater*, 227 *ter*, 508b)
*Witemot**	See Widemouth
*Witestan**	See Whitstone
Withiel, H. 3	*Widie* 121 (*203b)
Woderon	See Goodern
Woolston (in Poundstock), C. 2	*Ulnodestone* 123 (*Ulnotestona* 240b)
Woolston (in St Ive), K. 3	*Ullavestone* 124b (*Ullovastona* 263b)
*Woreslin**	See Gurlyn
Worthyvale, I. 1	*Guerdevalan* 123 (*Gurdavalan* 241)
Zennor	Not in D.B.

ANONYMOUS HOLDINGS

No place-names appear in the following five entries, and it is possible that some (or even all) of these refer to holdings at places not named elsewhere in Domesday Book:

Walter de Claville (from the king), one virgate, 120b (112).

From the church of St German . . . one hide of land . . . And Reginald de Valletort now holds it of the Count of Mortain, 120b (201, 507).

From the church of St German . . . one acre of land . . . Reginald de Valletort now holds this of the count, 120b (201, 507).

From the church of St German . . . one virgate of land . . ., and now Hamelin holds this of the count, 120b (201, 507).

Of 2 manors (taken away from Perranzabuloe) Berner holds one of the count. And from the other hide . . . the count has taken away all the stock, 121 (206b).

CUMBERLAND

Yorkshire folio 301b

MAP 65

Bodele	See Bootle
Bootle, B. 3	*Bodele* 301b
Hougenai, *Hougun*	See Millom
Kirksanton, C. 3	*Santacherche* 301b
Millom, C. 3	*Hougenai*, *Hougun* 301b *ter*
Santacherche	See Kirksanton
Whicham, C. 3	*Witingham* 301b
Witingham	See Whicham

DERBYSHIRE—*DERBYSCIRE*

Folios 272–278

MAPS 10–11

Abney, D. 4	*Habenai* 276
Achetorp	See Oakthorpe, Leics.
Adelardestreu	See Allestree
Æstun	See Aston upon Trent
Aidele	See Edale
Aisseford	See Ashford
Aitone	See Long Eaton
Aitun	See Eaton Dovedale
Aiune	See Eyam
Alchementune	See Alkmonkton
Alderwasley	Not in D.B.
Aldwark	Not in D.B.
Aleuuoldestune	See Alvaston
Alfreton, F. 6	*Elstretune* 278
Alia Heorteshorne	See Hartshorne Hall
Alia Stratune	See Stretton Hall
Alia Summersale	See Potter Somersall
Alkmonkton, D. 8	*Alchementune* 274b
Allestree, F. 8	*Adelardestreu* 273b
Alsop le Dale, D. 6	*Elleshope* 272b

Place	Domesday form
Alton	Not in D.B.
Aluuoldestun	See Elvaston
Alvaston, F. 9	*Aleuuoldestune* 276b
Ambaston, G. 9	*Emboldestune* 276b
Aneise	See One Ash
Apleby	See Appleby, Leics.
Arleston, F. 9	*Erlestune* 275b
Ash, E. 9	*Eisse* 274b
Ashbourne, D. 7	*Esseburne* 272b *bis*
Ashford, D. 5	*Aisseford* 272b
Ashleyhay	Not in D.B.
Ashover, F. 5	*Essovre* 277
Aston (near Hope), D. 3	*Estune* 272b
Aston (near Sudbury), D. 9	*Estune* 274b
Aston upon Trent, F. 9	*Æstun* 273 *Estune* 275b
Atlow, D. 7	*Etelauue* 274
Ault Hucknall	Not in D.B.
Badequella	See Bakewell
Bakewell, D. 5	*Badequella* 272b
Ballidon, D. 6	*Belidene* 277
Bamford, D. 3	*Banford* 277
Banford	See Bamford
Barcovere	See Birchover
Barctune	See Barton Blount
Bareuue	See Barrow upon Trent
Barlborough, G. 4	*Barleburg* 277
Barleburg	See Barlborough
Barleie	See Barlow
Barlow, F. 4	*Barleie* 277b, 278b
Barrow upon Trent, F. 9	*Bar(e)uue* 272b, 275b, 277b
Barton Blount, D. 9	*Barctune* 274b
Baruue	See Barrow upon Trent
Baslow, E. 5	*Basselau* 272b
Basselau	See Baslow
Bearwardcote, E. 9	*Bereuuardescote* 275b *Beruerdescote* 273
Bectune	See Beighton
Beeley, E. 5	*Begelie* 273
Begelie	See Beeley
Beighton, G. 3	*Bectune* 273b, 277, 278
Belesovre	See Bolsover
Belidene	See Ballidon
Belper	Not in D.B.
Benedlege	See Fenny Bentley
Beneleie	See Hungry Bentley
Berceles	See Birchill
Bereuuardescote	See Bearwardcote
Berleie	See Burley
Beruerdescote	See Bearwardcote
Biggin	Not in D.B.
Birchill, D. 5	*Berceles* 272b
Birchover, D. 6	*Barcovere* 275b
Blacheuuelle	See Blackwell (near Tideswell)
Blackwell (near Alfreton)	Not in D.B.
Blackwell (near Tideswell), C. 5	*Blacheuuelle* 272b
Blanghesbi	See Blingsby
Blingsby, G. 5	*Blanghesbi* 273b
Boilestun	See Boyleston
Boletune	See Boulton
Bolsover, G. 5	*Belesovre* 276
Bolun	Unid., 274
Bonsall, E. 6	*Bunteshale* 272
Boulton, F. 9	*Boletune* 277
Boyleston, D. 9	*Boilestun* 275
Boythorpe, F. 5	*Buitorp* 272
Brackenfield	Not in D.B.
Bradbourne, D. 7	*Bradeburne* 274
Bradeburne	See Bradbourne
Bradelei	See Bradley (in Belper)
Bradestune	See Breaston
Bradewelle	See Bradwell
Bradley (near Ashbourne), D. 7	*Braidelei* 274b
Bradley (in Belper), F. 7	*Bradelei* 275
Bradwell, D. 4	*Bradewelle* 276
Braidelei	See Bradley (near Ashbourne)
Braideshale	See Breadsall
Braidestone, -tune	See Breaston
Brailesford	See Brailsford

Brailsford, E. 8	*Brailesford* 274b
Bramley, G. 5	*Branlege* 278
Brampton, F. 5	*Brandune* 276b
	Brantune 277b *bis*
Brandune	See Brampton
Branlege	See Bramley
Brantune	See Brampton
Branzinctun	See Brassington
Brassington, D. 6	*Branzinctun* 274
Breadsall, F. 8	*Braideshale* 275b
Breaston, G. 9	*Bradestune* 275
	Braidestone, *-tune* 276b, 277b, 278
Bredelauue	See Broadlowash
Bretby, E. 10	*Bretebi* 272b
Bretebi	See Bretby
Brimington, F. 4	*Brimintune* 272
Brimintune	See Brimington
Broadlowash, D. 7	*Bredelauue* 272b
Broctune	See Church Broughton
Brough	Not in D.B.
Brushfield	Not in D.B.
Bubedene, *-dune*	See Bupton
Bubenenli	See Bubnell
Bubnell, E. 5	*Bubenenli* 272b
Buitorp	See Boythorpe
Bunteshale	See Bonsall
Bupton, D. 8	*Bubedene*, *-dune* 273, 275 *bis*
Burbage	Not in D.B.
Burley, E. 5	*Berleie* 272
Burnaston, E. 9	*Burnulfestune* 275b
Burnulfestune	See Burnaston
Burton, D. 5	*Burtune* 272b
Burtune	See Burton
Buxton	Not in D.B.
Caldecotes	See Owlcotes
Caldelauue	See Callow
Caldewelle	See Caldwell
Caldwell, E. 11	*Caldewelle* 273
Calehale	See Calow
Calke	Not in D.B.
Callow, E. 7	*Caldelauue* 272b
Calow, F. 5	*Calehale* 278b
Caluoure	See Calver
Calver, D. 4	*Caluoure* 272b

Carsington, E. 7	*Ghersintune* 272b
Castle Gresley	Not in D.B.
Castleton	Not in D.B.
Catton, D. 11	*Chetun* 274
Cedesdene	See Chaddesden
Celard-, *Celerdestune*	See Chellaston
Cellesdene	See Chelton
Ceolhal	See Chunal
Cestre	See Little Chester
Cestrefeld	See Chesterfield
Chaddesden, F. 8	*Cedesdene* 275
Chapel en le Frith	Not in D.B.
Charlesworth, B. 2	*Cheuenesuurde* 273
Chatsworth, E. 5	*Chetesuorde* 273
Chellaston, F. 9	*Celardestune* 275b
	Celerdestune 272b
Chelmorton	Not in D.B.
Chelton, F. 9	*Cellesdene* 278b
Chendre	See Kinder
Cheniuetun	See Kniveton
Chesterfield, F. 5	*Cestrefeld* 272
Chetelestune	See Kedleston
Chetesuorde	See Chatsworth
Chetun	See Catton
Cheuenesuurde	See Charlesworth
Chinewoldemaresc	See Killamarsh
Chinley	Not in D.B.
Chiseuurde	See Chisworth
Chisworth, B. 2	*Chiseuurde* 273
Chiteslei	See Kidsley
Chunal, B. 2	*Ceolhal* 273
Church Broughton, D. 9	*Broctune* 274b
Church Gresley	Not in D.B.
Cildecote	See Chilcote, Leics.
Clifton, D. 8	*Cliptune* 277b
Cliftune	See Clifton Campville, Staffs.
Cliptune	See Clifton
Clowne, G. 4	*Clune* 277, 278b
Clune	See Clowne
Coal Aston, F. 4	*Estune* 278b
Cobelei	See Cubley
Codetune	See Cottons
Codnor, F. 7	*Cotenoure* 276
Coldeaton, C. 6	*Eitune* 272b
Collei	See Cowley
Conkesbury, D. 5	*Cranchesberie* 272b

Cornun	See Quarndon
Cotenoure	See Codnor
Cotes	See Cotes (in Darley), Coton in the Elms
Cotes (in Darley), E. 5	*Cotes* 272
Coton in the Elms, E. 11	*Cotes*, superscribed above *Cotune*, 273
Cottons, F. 9	*Codetune* 272b, 275b *bis*
Cotune	See Coton in the Elms
Cowley, E. 6	*Collei* 274
Coxbench, F. 8	*Herdebi* 275 *bis*, 277b
Cranchesberie	See Conkesbury
Crice	See Crich
Crich, F. 6	*Crice* 277 *quater*
Crocheshalle	See Croxall, Staffs.
Cromford, E. 6	*Crunforde* 272b
Crunforde	See Cromford
Cubley, D. 8	*Cobelei* 275
Curbar	Not in D.B.
Dalbury, E. 9	*Delbebi* 276
	Dellingeberie 273
Darley, E. 6	*Derelei(e)* 272, 272b
Delbebi, *Dellingeberie*	See Dalbury
Denby, F. 7	*Denebi* 277b
Denebi	See Denby
Dentinc	See Dinting
Derby, F. 8	*Derby* 280 *bis*, Notts.
Derelei(e)	See Darley
Derwent	Not in D.B.
Detton	See Little Eaton
Dinting, B. 2	*Dentinc* 273
Dochemanestun	See Duckmanton
Dore	See Dore, W.R.
Doveridge, C. 9	*Dubrige* 274
Drachelauue	See Drakelow
Draicot	See Draycott
Drakelow, D. 10	*Drachelauue* 278
Dranefeld	See Dronfield
Draycott, G. 9	*Draicot* 273
Dronfield, F. 4	*Dranefeld* 272
Dubrige	See Doveridge
Duckmanton, G. 5	*Dochemanestun* 277
Duffield, F. 8	*Duuelle* 275
Duluestune	See Edlaston
Dunston	Not in D.B.
Durandestorp	See Donisthorpe, Leics.
Duuelle	See Duffield
Eaton Dovedale, C. 8	*Aitun* 275
Echintune	See Eckington
Eckington, G. 4	*Echintune* 272, 277
Edale, C. 3	*Aidele* 272b
Edensor, D. 5	*Ednesoure* 273, 276
Edlaston, D. 8	*Duluestune* 275
Ednaston, D. 8	*Ednodestun(e)* 273b, 276b
Ednesoure	See Edensor
Ednodestun(e)	See Ednaston
Ednunghal(l)e	See Edingale, Staffs.
Egginton, E. 9	*Eghintune* 276b
Eghintune	See Egginton
Egstow, F. 5	*Tegestou* 277
Eisse	See Ash
Eitune	See Coldeaton
Elleshope	See Alsop le Dale
Elmton, H. 4	*Helmetune* 276b
Elstretune	See Alfreton
Elton, D. 6	*Eltune* 274
Eltune	See Elton
Elvaston, G. 9	*Aluuoldestun* 276b
Emboldestune	See Ambaston
Englebi	See Ingleby
Erlestune	See Arleston
Esnotrewic	See Snodswick
Esseburne	See Ashbourne
Essovre	See Ashover
Estune	See Aston (near Hope), Aston (near Sudbury), Aston upon Trent, Coal Aston
Etelauue	See Atlow
Etewelle	See Etwall
Etwall, E. 9	*Etewelle* 276, 276b
Eyam, D. 4	*Aiune* 273

Fairfield	Not in D.B.
Faitune	See Fenton
Farleie	See Farley
Farley, E. 6	*Farleie* 272
Faruluestun	See Foston
Fenny Bentley, D. 7	*Benedlege* 272b
Fenton, D. 7	*Faitune* 275
Fernilee	Not in D.B.
Findern, E. 9	*Findre* 273
Findre	See Findern
Flagg, C. 5	*Flagun* 272b
Flagun	See Flagg
Foolow	Not in D.B.
Foremark, F. 10	*Forneuuerche* 278
Forneuuerche	See Foremark
Foston, D. 9	*Faruluestun* 274b
Froggatt	Not in D.B.
Geldeslei	See Yeldersley
Ghersintune	See Carsington
Gheveli	See Yeaveley
Giolgrave	See Youlgreave
Glapewelle	See Glapwell
Glapwell, G. 5	*Glapewelle* 276
Glosop	See Glossop
Glossop, B. 2	*Glosop* 273
Gratton, D. 6	*Gratune* 275b
Gratune	See Gratton
Great Hucklow	See Hucklow
Great Longstone	See Longstone
Greherst	See Greyhurst
Greyhurst, F. 5	*Greherst* 272
Grindlow	Not in D.B.
Habenai	See Abney
Haddon, Nether and Over, D. 5	*Hadun(a)*, *Hadune* 272b *ter*
Hadfield, B. 2	*Hetfelt* 273
Hadun(a), *Hadune*	See Haddon
Hainoure	See Heanor
Halen	See Hallam
Hallam, Kirk and West, G. 8	*Halen* 277b *Halun* 277b
Halun	See Hallam
Handley (in Staveley), F. 4	*Henleie* 278b
Handley (in Stretton), F. 6	*Henlege* 277
Hanson, C. 6	*Hanzedone* 272b

Hanzedone	See Hanson
Hardstoft, G. 6	*Hertestaf* 273b
Harthill, D. 5	*Hortel* 275b *Hortil* 277
Hartington, C. 6	*Hortedun* 274
Hartshorne, E. 10	*Heorteshorne* 274
Hartshorne Hall, E. 10	*Alia Heorteshorne* 274
Hasland	Not in D.B.
Hassop, D. 5	*Hetesope* 272b
Hathersage, D. 3	*Hereseige* 277
Hatton, D. 9	*Hatun(e)* 274b, 275
Hatun(e)	See Hatton
Hayfield, B. 3	*Hedfelt* 273
Hazelbadge, D. 4	*Hegelebec* 276
Hazelwood	Not in D.B.
Heage	Not in D.B.
Heanor, G. 7	*Hainoure* 276
Hearthcote, E. 10	*Hedcote* 278
Heath, G. 5	*in Duobus Lunt* 273b
Hedcote	See Hearthcote
Hedfelt	See Hayfield
Hegelebec	See Hazelbadge
Helmetune	See Elmton
Henlege	See Handley (in Stretton)
Henleie	See Handley (in Staveley)
Heorteshorne	See Hartshorne
Heorteshorne, *Alia*	See Hartshorne Hall
Herct	See Hurst
Herdebi	See Coxbench
Hereseige	See Hathersage
Hertestaf	See Hardstoft
Hetesope	See Hassop
Hetfelt	See Hadfield
Higham	Not in D.B.
Highlow	Not in D.B.
Hilton, D. 9	*Hiltune* 273, 274b
Hiltune	See Hilton
Hiretune	See Kirk Ireton
Hochelai	See Hucklow
Hoge	See Hough
Hognaston, D. 7	*Ochenauestun* 272b
Hoilant	See Hulland
Holbrook, F. 7	*Holebroc* 275
Holebroc	See Holbrook

Lullitune	See Lullington
Lunt (*Duobus* superscribed above)	See Heath, Lowne
Machenie	See Mackeney
Macheuorde	See Mackworth
Mackeney, F. 8	*Machenie* 275
Mackworth, E. 8	*Macheuorde* 273b
Maneis	See Monyash
Maperlie	See Mapperley
Mapletune	See Mappleton
Mapperley, G. 8	*Maperlie* 273
Mappleton, D. 7	*Mapletune* 272b
Marchetone	See Markeaton
Markeaton, E. 8	*Marchetone* 273b *Merchetune* 275
Marsh, F. 9	*Mers* 278b
Marston Montgomery	Not in D.B.
Marston on Dove, D. 9	*Merstun* 274
Matlock, E. 6	*Meslach* 272
Matlock Bridge, E. 6	*Mestesforde* 272, 272b
Melbourne, F. 10	*Mileburne* 272b *bis*, 277b
Mercaston, E. 8	*Merchenestune* 276
Merchenestune	See Mercaston
Merchetune	See Markeaton
Mers	See Marsh
Merstun	See Marston on Dove
Meslach	See Matlock
Messeham	See Measham, Leics.
Mestesforde	See Matlock Bridge
Mickleover, E. 9	*Overe* 275 *Ufre* 273
Middeltone	See Stony Middleton
Middeltune	See Middleton by Wirksworth, Middleton by Youlgreave, Milton, Stony Middleton
Middleton by Wirksworth, E. 6	*Middeltune* 272b 1st entry
Middleton by Youlgreave, D. 6	*Middeltune* 275b
Mileburne	See Melbourne
Milford, F. 8	*Muleforde* 275
Milton, E. 10	*Middeltune* 272b 2nd entry
Mogintun	See Mugginton
Monyash, C. 5	*Maneis* 272b
Morelei	See Morley
Moresburg	See Mosborough
Morleia	See Morley
Morley, F. 8	*Morelei* 276 *Morleia* 275b
Morton, F. 6	*Mortune* 276b
Mortune	See Morton
Mosborough, G. 4	*Moresburg* 277
Muchedesuuelle, C. 4	Lost in Wormhill, 272b, 275b
Mugginton, E. 8	*Mogintun* 275b
Muleforde	See Milford
Nether Haddon	See Haddon
Nether Padley	Not in D.B.
Nether Seal	See Seal
Neutone	See Newton (in Blackwell)
Neutune	See Newton Grange
Neuuebold	See Newbold
Newbold, F. 4	*Neuuebold* 272
Newetun	See Newton Solney
New Mills	Not in D.B.
Newton (in Blackwell), G. 6	*Neutone* 277
Newton Grange, C. 7	*Neutune* 274
Newton Solney, E. 10	*Newetun* 272b
Norbury, C. 8	*Nordberie*, *Nortberie* 275 *bis*
Nordberie	See Norbury
Normanestune	See Normanton by Derby
Normanton by Derby, F. 9	*Norman(es)tune* 272b, 275b
Normantune	See Normanton by Derby, Temple Normanton

Normentune	See South Normanton
Northerie	See Norbury
North Wingfield, F. 5	*Winnefelt* 276b
Nortun(e)	See Norton, W.R.
Ochebroc	See Ockbrook
Ochenauestun	See Hognaston
Ockbrook, G. 8	*Ochebroc* 276b
Offcote, D. 7	*Ophidecotes* 272b
Offerton, D. 3	*Offretune* 272b, 277
Offretune	See Offerton
Ogston, F. 6	*Ougedestun* 277 *Oughedestune* 276b
One Ash, C. 5	*Aneise* 272b
Onestune	See Unstone
Opetune	See Hopton
Opeuuelle	See Hopwell
Ophidecotes	See Offcote
Oslavestune	See Osleston
Osleston, E. 8	*Oswardestune* with *laves* superscribed, i.e. *Oslavestune* 275
Osmaston (near Ashbourne), D. 8	*Osmundestune* 275 *bis*
Osmaston by Derby, F. 9	*Osmundestune* 272b, 275b *bis*
Osmundestune	See Osmaston (near Ashbourne), Osmaston by Derby
Oswardestune	See Osleston
Ougedestun, *Oughedestune*	See Ogston
Overe	See Mickleover
Over Haddon	See Haddon
Over Seal	See Seal
Owlcotes, G. 5	*Caldecotes* 276b
Padefeld	See Padfield
Padfield, B. 2	*Padefeld* 273
Padinc	See Padleywood
Padleywood, F. 6	*Padinc* 272
Palterton, G. 5	*Paltretune* 277
Paltretune	See Palterton
Parva Ufra	See Littleover
Parwich, D. 6	*Pevrewic* 272b *bis*
Peak Cavern, C. 3	*Pechefers* 276
Pechefers	See Peak Cavern
Pentric	See Pentrich
Pentrich, F. 7	*Pentric* 277, 277b
Pevrewic	See Parwich
Pilesberie	See Pilsbury
Pilsbury, C. 5	*Pilesberie* 274
Pilsley (near Bakewell), D. 5	*Pirelaie* 275b
Pilsley (near Clay Cross), G. 6	*Pinneslei* 276b
Pinneslei	See Pilsley (near Clay Cross)
Pinxton	Not in D.B.
Pirelaie	See Pilsley (near Bakewell)
Pleasley	Not in D.B.
Potlac	See Potlock
Potlock, E. 9	*Potlac* 273
Potter Somersall, C. 9	*Alia Summersale* 274b
Presteclive	See Priestcliff
Priestcliff, C. 5	*Presteclive* 272b
Quarndon, F. 8	*Cornun* 280, Notts.
Rabburne	See Radbourne
Radbourne, E. 8	*Rabburne* 276 *Radburne* 276
Radburne	See Radbourne
Ralunt	See Rowland
Ramshaw, F. 4	*Rauenes . . . n* 272
Rapendun(e)	See Repton
Rauenes . . . n	See Ramshaw
Ravensdale Park	Not in D.B.
Ravenestun	See Ravenstone, Leics.
Redeslei	See Rodsley
Redlauestun	See Rosliston
Redlesleie	See Rodsley
Repton, E. 10	*Rapendun(e)* 272b *bis*, 273, 278
Reuslege	See Rowsley
Ripelie	See Ripley
Ripley, F. 7	*Ripelie* 277b
Riselei(a)	See Risley
Risley, G. 9	*Riselei(a)* 278, 278b
Rodsley, D. 8	*Redeslei* 275 *Redlesleie* 273
Roschintone, *-tun*	See Roston

Rosliston, D. 11	*Redlauestun* 272b
Roston, C. 8	*Roschintone*, *-tun* 275 *bis*
Rouecestre	See Rocester, Staffs.
Rowland, D. 4	*Ralunt* 272b
Rowsley, E. 5	*Reuslege* 272b
Rowthorne, G. 5	*Rugetorn* 278 *bis*
Rugetorn	See Rowthorne
Salham	See Soham
Salle	See Sawley
Sandiacre, G. 8	*Sandiacre* 278b *bis* *Sandiriaca* 291b, Notts.
Sapertune	See Sapperton
Sapperton, D. 9	*Sapertune* 274b
Sawley, G. 9	*Salle* 273
Scarcliffe, G. 5	*Scardeclif* 277
Scardeclif	See Scarcliffe
Scelhadun	See Sheldon
Scetune	See Shatton
Scipelie	See Shipley
Scochetorp	See Shuckstonefield
Scroftun	See Scropton
Scropton, D. 9	*Scroftun* 274b *Scrotun(e)* 274b *bis*
Scrotun(e)	See Scropton
Seal, Nether and Over, E. 11	*Scella* 233b, Leics. *Alia Scela* 233b, Leics. *Sela* 236, Leics.
Sedenefeld	See Sinfin
Sedsall, C. 8	*Segessale* 275
Segessale	See Sedsall
Serdelau	See Shardlow
Shardlow, G. 9	*Serdelau* 273
Shatton, D. 4	*Scetune* 272b
Sheldon, D. 5	*Scelhadun* 272b
Shipley, G. 8	*Scipelie* 277b
Shirebrook	Not in D.B.
Shirland, F. 6	*Sirelunt* 276
Shirley, D. 8	*Sirelei(e)* 274b *bis*
Shottle, E. 7	*Sothelle* 274
Shuckstonefield, F. 6	*Scochetorp* 277
Sinfin, F. 9	*Sedenefeld* 275b
Sinitretone	See Snitterton
Sirelei(e)	See Shirley
Sirelunt	See Shirland
Sivardingescotes	See Swadlincote
Smalei	See Smalley
Smalley, F. 8	*Smalei* 272b
Smerrill	Not in D.B.
Smidesbi	See Smisby
Smisby, F. 10	*Smidesbi* 278
Smitecote	See Smithycote
Smithycote, G. 7	*Smitecote* 276
Snellestune	See Snelston
Snelston, C. 8	*Snellestune* 273, 275
Snitterton, E. 6	*Sinitretone* 272
Snodswick, F. 6	*Esnotrewic* 276
Soham, C. 5	*Salham* 274
Somersall Herbert, C. 9	*Summersale* 274b
Sorchestun	See Swarkeston
Sothelle	See Shottle
South Normanton, G. 6	*Normentune* 276
South Wingfield, F. 6	*Winefeld* 273b
Spondon, F. 9	*Spondune* 273, 275
Spondune	See Spondon
Stainsby, G. 5	*Steinesbi* 273b
Stanlei	See Stanley
Stanley, F. 8	*Stanlei* 278
Stanton by Bridge, F. 10	*Stantun* 278b *bis*
Stanton by Dale, G. 8	*Stantone* 277b
Stanton by Newhall, E. 10	*Stantun* 274
Stanton in the Peak, E. 5	*Stantune* 275b
Stantone	See Stanton by Dale
Stantun	See Stanton by Bridge, Stanton by Newhall
Stantune	See Stanton in the Peak
Stapenhille	See Stapenhill, Staffs.
Stavelie	See Staveley
Staveley, G. 4	*Stavelie* 277b

Steinesbi	See Stainsby
Steintune	See Stenson
Stenson, E. 9	*Steintune* 275b
Stertune	See Sturston
Stoche	See Stoke
Stoke, D. 4	*Stoche* 272b
Stony Houghton, G. 5	*Holtune* 276b
Stony Middleton, D. 4	*Middeltone*, *-tune* 273, 277 *bis*
Stratune	See Stretton
Stratune, *Alia*	See Stretton Hall
Streitun	See Stretton en le Field, Leics.
Stretton, F. 6	*Stratune* 277
Stretton Hall, F. 6	*Alia Stratune* 277
Sturston, D. 7	*Stertune* 275
Sudberie	See Sudbury
Sudbury, C. 9	*Sudberie* 273, 274b
Sudtun	See Sutton on the Hill
Sudtune	See Sutton on the Hill, Sutton Scarsdale
Suerchestune	See Swarkeston
Summersale	See Somersall Herbert
Summersale, *Alia*	See Potter Somersall
Sutton on the Hill, D. 9	*Sudtun(e)* 273, 274b
Sutton Scarsdale, G. 5	*Sudtune* 273b
Swadlincote, E. 10	*Sivardingescotes* 278
Swarkeston, F. 9	*Sorchestun* 275b *Suerchestune* 272b
Taddington, C. 5	*Tadintune* 272b
Tadintune	See Taddington
Taneslege	See Tansley
Tansley, E. 6	*Taneslege* 277 *Teneslege* 272
Tapetune	See Tapton
Tapton, F. 4	*Tapetune* 272, 278b
Taxal	Not in D.B.
Tegestou	See Egstow
Temple Normanton, F. 5	*Normantune* 272 *bis*

Teneslege	See Tansley
Thornhill	Not in D.B.
Thornsett, B. 3	*Tornesete* 273
Thorpe, D. 7	*Torp* 272b
Thulston, F. 9	*Torulfestune* 276b *Torulvestun* 275b
Thurvaston, D. 8	*Tor-*, *Turverdestune* 275 *bis*
Tibecel	See Tibshelf
Tibshelf, G. 6	*Tibecel* 273
Tichenhalle	See Ticknall
Ticknall, F. 10	*Tichenhalle* 272b *bis*, 273, 278
Tidesuuelle	See Tideswell
Tideswell, C. 4	*Tidesuuelle* 272b
Tilchestune	See Ilkeston
Tissington, D. 7	*Tiʒinctun* 274
Tiʒinctun	See Tissington
Top(e)tune	See Tupton
Tornesete	See Thornsett
Torp	See Thorpe
Torulfestune	See Thulston
Torverdestune	See Thurvaston
Totingelei	See Totley, W.R.
Toxenai	See Trusley
Trangesbi, *-by*	See Thringstone, Leics.
Trusley, E. 9	*Toxenai* 274b
Tuiforde	See Twyford
Tunestal(le)	Unid., 273b, 277
Tupton, F. 5	*Top(e)tune* 272, 276b, 278b
Turnditch	Not in D.B.
Torulvestun	See Thulston
Turverdestune	See Thurvaston
Twyford, E. 9	*Tuiforde* 275b *bis*
Uffentune	See Uftonfields
Ufra, *Parva*	See Littleover
Ufre	See Mickleover
Uftonfields, F. 6	*Uffentune* 277 *Uftune* 276
Uftune	See Uftonfields
Ulvritune, G. 8	Lost in Sandiacre, 278b
Unstone, F. 4	*Honestune* 272 *Onestune* 272
Upetun	See Upton
Upton, F. 4	*Upetun* 272

Wadescel	See Wadshelf
Wadshelf, E. 5	*Wadescel* 276b, 277b *bis*
Walestune	See Wallstone
Waletune	See Walton (near Chesterfield), Walton upon Trent
Wallstone, E. 7	*Walestune* 274
Walton (near Chesterfield), F. 5	*Waletune* 272
Walton upon Trent, D. 10	*Waletune* 272b
Wardlow	Not in D.B.
Warrington, E. 7	*Werredune* 277b
Waterfield, D. 4	*Watrefeld* 276
Watrefeld	See Waterfield
Welledene	Unid., 272b
Wensley, E. 6	*Wodnesleie* 272
Werchesu(u)orde	See Wirksworth
Werredune	See Warrington
Wessington, F. 6	*Wistanestune* 276b, 277
West Hallam	See Hallam
Westone	See Weston upon Trent
Weston Underwood, E. 8	*Westune* 277b
Weston upon Trent, F. 9	*Westone* 272b *Westune* 273
Westune	See Weston Underwood, Weston upon Trent
Whaley	Not in D.B.
Wheston	Not in D.B.
Whitfield, B. 2	*Witfeld* 273
Whittington, F. 4	*Witintune* 272
Whitwell, H. 4	*Witeuuelle* 277

Widerdestune	See Wyaston
Wilelmestorp	See Williamthorpe
Willetune	See Willington
Williamthorpe, G. 5	*Wilelmestorp* 276b
Willington, E. 9	*Willetune* 277
Wilne	Not in D.B.
Wilsthorpe	Not in D.B.
Winbroc	See Ivonbrook
Windley	Not in D.B.
Winefeld	See South Wingfield
Wineshalle	See Winshill, Staffs.
Wingerworth, F. 5	*Wingreurde* 272
Wingreurde	See Wingerworth
Winnefelt	See North Wingfield
Winster, D. 6	*Winsterne* 274
Winsterne	See Winster
Wirksworth, E. 7	*Werchesu(u)orde* 272b *bis*, 277
Wistanestune	See Wessington
Witeuuelle	See Whitwell
Witfeld	See Whitfield
Witintune	See Whittington
Wiuleslei(e)	See Willesley, Leics.
Wodnesleie	See Wensley
Woodthorpe	Not in D.B.
Wormhill, C. 4	*Wruenele* 275b
Wruenele	See Wormhill
Wyaston, D. 8	*Widerdestune* 275
Yeardsley	Not in D.B.
Yeaveley, D. 8	*Gheveli* 275
Yeldersley, D. 8	*Geldeslei* 274b
Youlgreave, D. 5	*Giolgrave* 275b

ANONYMOUS HOLDINGS

None.

DEVONSHIRE

DEVENESCIRE (*DEVENESCIRA*, *-SIRA*)

Exchequer Domesday Book, folios 100–18b
Exeter Domesday Book, folios 83–8, 93–8, 108–11, 117–36, 161–73, 177–80b, 182–84b, 194–6, 210–23, 286, 288–315, 316–44, 345–49b, 356, 366–68b, 371, 376–79b, 382, 388–97, 398–421b, 456–62b, 468–73, 475–76b, 481–90, 495–508
Exeter Domesday names and folio references are given in brackets. An asterisk * indicates that the names in the Exeter D.B. and the Exchequer D.B. are the same.

MAPS 12–13, 14

Abbots Bickington, C. 6	*Bichetone* 117 (*Bicatona* 456)
Abbotsham, C. 4	*Hame* 103b (*Hama* 178b)
Abbotskerswell, H. 11	*Carsuelle* 104 (*-ella* 184)
*Acha**	See Oak
Achie (*Achia*)	See Hacche
Addeberie (*-beria*)	See Yedbury
*Adonebovi**	See Little Bovey
Adrelie	See Hatherleigh (near Okehampton)
Adworthy, G. 5	*Odeordi* 114b (*341)
Aedelstan (*Aeidestan*)	See Yowlestone
(*Aexeministra*)	See Exminster
Afetone (*-tona*, *Afretona*)	See Afton
Afton, H. 11	*Afetone* 114b (*-tona* 342b, *Afretona* 503b)
(*Ailavesfort*)	See Elsford
(*Ailesberga*)	See Aylesbeare
(*Ailesuescota*, *Aileuescota*)	See Aylescott
Ainech-, *Ainichesdone* (*Ainechesdona*)	See Ingsdon
*Aisa**	See Ash Thomas
Aisbertone (*-tona*)	See Ashprington
(*Aiscirewilla*)	See Shirwell
(*Aiseforda*)	See Ashford (near Barnstaple), Ayshford
Aiserstone	See Sherberton
Aisse (*Aissa*)	See Ash (in Bradworthy), Ash (in Petrockstow), Ash (in South Tawton), Ashford (in Aveton Gifford), Ashreigney, Ashwater, Rose Ash
Aissecome (*-coma*)	See Ashcombe
Aisseford	See Ashford (near Barnstaple), Ayshford
Aisselie	See Ashleigh
Aisseminstre (*Aixeministra*)	See Exminster
Alesland (*-lant*)	See Allisland
Alestou	See Halstow (in Dunsford)
Alfelmestone	See Yealmpstone
Alferdintone (*-tona*)	See Arlington
Alfintone (*-tona*)	See Alphington
Alforde (*-forda*)	See Oakford
Alfreincome (*-coma*)	See Ilfracombe
(*Alintona*)	See South Allington
Alintone	See East Allington, South Allington
Aller (in Abbotskerswell, H. 11)	*Alre* 117b (*Alra* 473)
Aller and Bulealler (in Kentisbeare),	*Alre* 113b (*Alra* 458b)

/over

Aller and Bullealler (in Kentisbeare) cont., J. 6, J. 7	*Avra* 107 (*Avrra* 303b)
Aller (in South Molton), F. 4	*Alre* 102b, 116b (*Alra* 130, 377b, 499b)
Aller (in Upottery), L. 6	*Alreford* 108b (*Alraforda* 313b)
Allisland, D. 6	*Alesland* 118 (*-lant* 482)
Almerescote (*-cota*)	See Almiston
Almiston, B. 5	*Almerescote* 116b (*-cota* 376)
Alphington, I. 8	*Alfintone* 101 (*-tona* 95b)
(*Alraforda*)	See Aller (in Upottery)
Alre (*Alra*)	See Aller (in Abbotskerswell), Aller (in Kentisbeare), Aller (in South Molton)
Alreford	See Aller (in Upottery)
Alsbretone	See Halberton
Alseminstre (*Alsemenistra*, *-ministra*)	See Axminster
Alsemude (*-muda*)	See Axmouth
Alston, F. 14	*Alwinestone* 109 (*-tona* 322b)
Alverdiscott, D. 4	*Alveredescote* 105 (*-cota* 212b)
Alveredescote (*-cota*)	See Alverdiscott
Alvintone (*-tona*)	See West Alvington
Alwineclancavele	See East Youlstone
Alwinestone (*-tona*)	See Alston
Alwinestone (*-tona*)	Unid., 105 (213b, 499b)
Alwinetone (*-tona*)	See Alwington
Alwington, C. 4	*Alwinetone* 104b (*-tona* 210)
(*Alwynelancavele*)	See East Youlstone
Anestige, *-inge* (*Anestiga*, *-inga*, *-inghes*)	See Anstey
Anstey, East and West, H. 4	*Anestige*, *-inge* 103, 104b *bis*, 107 (*Anestiga*, *-inga*, *-inghes* 130b, 286 *bis*, 300, 499b)
Apledore (*-dora*)	See Appledore (in Clannaborough)
Appledore (in Burlescombe), J. 5	*Suraple* 112 (*-apla* 395)
Appledore (in Clannaborough), G. 7	*Apledore* 106b (*-dora* 295b)
Arlington, E. 2	*Alferdintone* 115b (*-tona* 371, 499)
(*Asaberga*)	See Oussaborough
Ascerewelle	See Shirwell
Aseberge	See Oussaborough
Ash (in Bradworthy), B. 5	*Aisse* 114 (*Aissa*, *Eissa* 335b, 497)
Ash (in Petrockstow), D. 6	*Aisse* 103b (*Aissa* 182)
Ash (in South Tawton), F. 8	*Aisse* 100b (*Aissa* 93b, 498)
Ash Barton (in Braunton), D. 3	*Essa* 110b (*401b)
Ashburton, G. 11	*Essebretone* 102 (*-tona* 119)
Ashbury, D. 7	*Esseberie* 116 (not in Exon D.B.)
Ashclyst	See Clyst Gerred
Ashcombe, H. 9	*Aissecome* 114 (*-coma* 336, 498)
Ashford (in Aveton Gifford), F. 13	*Aisse* 104 (*Aissa* 182b)
Ashford (near Barnstaple), D. 3	*Aisseford* 106b (*Aiseforda* 298) *Esforde* 107 (*Efforda* 301)
Ashleigh, C. 9	*Aisselie* 108b (*Assileia* 317)
Ashmansworthy, B. 5	*Essemundehord* 106 (*-horda* 293)
Ashprington, G. 12	*Aisbertone* 101b (*-tona* 111)
Ashreigney, E. 6	*Aisse* 101b (*Aissa* 109b)
Ash Thomas, I. 6	*Aisa* 112b (*394b)

Ashton, H. 9	*Essestone* 117 (*Essetona* 498b)
Ashwater, C. 8	*Aisse* 102 (*Aissa* 121b)
Assecote (*Assacota*)	Unid., 111 *bis* (416b *bis*, 502)
(*Assileia*)	See Ashleigh
Atherington	Not in D.B.
Aulescome (*-coma*)	See Awliscombe
Aunk, J. 7	*Hanc*, *Hanche* 114, 114b (*Hanc*, *Hanca* 337b, 340, 501)
Ause (*Ausa*)	See Tapps
(*Avetona*)	See Blackawton
Avetone	See Aveton Gifford, Blackawton
Aveton Gifford, F. 13	*Avetone* 115 (not in Exon. D.B.)
(*Avrra*)	See Aller and Bulealler
Awliscombe, K. 7	*Aulescome* 110b *bis*, 112b (*-coma* 391b, 400b *bis*)
(*Axeministra*, *-tre*)	See Axminster, Exminster
Axeminstre	See Exminster
Axminster, K. 2	*Alseminstre* 100, 100b, 111 (*-menistra*, *-ministra*, *Axeministra*, *-tre* 84b *quater*, 405b, 503 *ter*, 503b *quin*)
Axmouth, L. 8	*Alsemude* 100b (*-muda* 85)
Aylesbeare, J. 8	*Eilesberge* 108 (*Ailesberga* 308b)
Aylescott, D. 2	*Eileuescote* 102b (*Ailesues-*, *Aileuescota* 127b, 500)
Ayshford, J. 5	*Aisseford* 112 (*Aiseforda* 395)
Baccamoor, E. 12	*Bachemore* 110 *bis* (*-mora* 331 *bis*, 505b *bis*)
(*Bacetesberia*)	See Battisborough
Bachedone (*-dona*)	See Bagton
Bacheleford	See Battleford
Bachemore (*-mora*)	See Baccamoor
(*Bacheslac*)	See Backslade
Bachestane	See Backstone
Bachetesberia	See Battisborough
Backstone, H. 5	*Bachestane* 113 (not in Exon D.B.)
*Badentone** (*Badendone*)	See Bampton
Badestane (*-tana*)	See Batson
Badgworthy, G. 2	*Bicheordin* 110b (*402b, 499)
Baentone (*-tona*)	See Bampton
Bagatore (*Bagathora*)	See Bagtor
Bagton, F. 14	*Bachedone* 109 (*-dona* 321b)
Bagtor, G. 10	*Bagetore* 117 (*Bagathora* 470)
Baldrintone (*-tona*)	See Barlington
Bampton, I. 5	*Baden-*, *Baen-*, *Bentone* 100b, 111b (*Badendone*, *-entone*, *Baentona* 85b *bis*, 345b)
(*Bardestapla*)	See Barnstaple
Barlington, E. 5	*Baldrintone* 102 (*-tona* 124b, 500)
*Barnestapla** *-staple* (*-stabla*)	See Barnstaple
Barnstaple, E. 3	*Barnestapla*, *-staple* 100 *ter*, 102 *bis*, 102b, 105b, 106b, 108b, 113 (*Bardestapla*, *Barnestabla*, *-stapla* 87b *bis*, 88, 123b, 128b, 136, 298, 315, 334b
(*Batesilla*)	See Battishill
Batson, F. 14	*Badestane* 105b (*-tana* 222)
Battisborough, E. 13	*Bachetesberia* 116 (*Bacetesberia* 504b)

Battisford, E. 12	*Botesforde* 111b (*-forda* 417)
Battishill, D. 9	Unnamed, held with Bridestowe 105b (*Batesilla* 289, 495)
Battleford, H. 11	*Bacheleford* 116 (not in Exon D.B.)
Baverdone (*-dona*)	See Beaford
Beaford, D. 5	*Baverdone* 101 (*-dona* 94)
Beaworthy, D. 7	*Begeurde* 111 (*-eurda* 415b)
Bechetone (*Bechatona*)	See Bicton
Bedendone (*-dona*)	See Bittadon
Bedeford (*Bediforda*)	See Bideford
Bedricestan (*Bretricestan*), I. 8	Lost in Clyst Honiton, 102 (119)
Beenleigh, G. 12	*Beuleie* 113 (*Benleia* 421)
Beer, L. 8	*Bera* 104 (*184, 1 ferling of the abbot of Horton, 503b)
Beera, F. 5	*Bere* 111 (*Bera* 366b)
Beer Charter Barton, D. 3	*Bera* 102b (*126b)
Beetor, F. 9	*Begatore* 106b (*-tora* 297)
Begatore (*-tora*)	See Beetor
Begeurde (*-eurda*)	See Beaworthy
Beldrendiland (*-lant*)	See Brandize
Belestham (*Bellestam*)	See Belstone
Belstone, E. 8	*Belestham* 106 (*Bellestam* 290)
Benedone (*Beneadona*)	See Neadon
(*Benleia*)	See Beenleigh
Benton, F. 3	*Botintone* 101b (*-tona*, *Bontintona* 117b, 499b)
Bentone	See Bampton
*Bera**, *Bere*	See Beer, Beera, Beer Charter Barton, Cherubeer, Netherton
Bere Ferrers, C. 11	*Birland* 105 (*-landa* 222b)
(*Beri*)	See Berry Pomeroy
(*Beria*)	See Bury
Berie	See Berry Pomeroy, Bury
Berlescome (*-coma*)	See Burlescombe
(*Berna*)	See Burntown
Bernardesmore (*-mora*)	Unid., 107b (303b)
Bernintone (*-intona*, *Bernurtona*)	See Burrington (near Chulmleigh)
Berrynarbor, E. 2	*Hurtesberie* 111b (*-beria* 345)
Berry Pomeroy, H. 12	*Berie* 114b (*Beri* 342)
Besley, J. 5	*Lege* 116 (*Lega* 461b)
Betunie (*-ia*)	See Twinyeo
Beuleie	See Beenleigh
(*Bicatona*)	See Abbots Bickington
Bicheberie (*-beria*)	See Bigbury
Bichecome (*-coma*)	See Bickham
Bicheford (*-forda*)	See Bickford
Bichelie (*-leia*)	See Bickleigh (near Plymouth)
Bichelie (*-lia*)	See Bickleigh (near Silverton)
Bichenelie (*-leia*, *-lia*)	See Langley formerly Bickingleigh
Bichentone (*-tona*)	See High Bickington
*Bicheordin**	See Badgworthy
Bichetone	See Abbots Bickington
Bickford, E. 12	*Bicheford* 113b, 118 (*-forda* 488b)
Bickham, H. 5	*Bichecome* 113 (*-coma* 420b)
Bickington (near Ashburton)	Not in D.B.

Bickleigh (near Plymouth), D. 11	*Bichelie* 111b (*-leia* 417b)
Bickleigh (near Silverton), I. 6	*Bichelie* 105b (*-lia* 214)
Bickleton, D. 4	*Picaltone* 115b (*-tona* 407b)
Bicton, J. 9	*Bechetone* 117b (*Bechatona* 472)
Bideford, C. 4	*Bedeford* 101 (*Bediforda* 108b)
Bigbury, F. 13	*Bicheberie* 105 (*-beria* 218)
Bihede (*-heda*)	See Boehill
*Birige**	See Swimbridge
Birland (*-landa*)	See Bere Ferrers
Bishop's Nympton, G. 4	*Nimetone* 102 (*-tona* 119b)
Bishop's Tawton, E. 4	*Tautone* 101b (*-tona* 118)
Bishopsteignton, H. 10	*Tantone* 101b (*Taintona* 117)
Bittadon, D. 2	*Bededone* 103 (*-dona* 130b)
Biude (*Biuda*)	See Bywood
(*Blacaberga*)	See Blackborough
(*Blacagrava*)	See Blagrove
(*Blacapola*)	See Blackpool
(*Blachagava*)	See Blagrove
Blacheberge	See Blackborough
Blacheberie (*-beria*)	See Blackborough
Blachegrave	See Blagrove
Blacheurde (*-eorde*)	See Blachford
Blachepole	See Blackpool
Blachestach (*-tac*)	See Blackslade
Blachestane	See Blaxton
Blachewelle (*-willa*)	See Blakewell
Blachford, E. 12	*Blacheurde* 109b, 113b (*-eorde* 327)
Blackawton, G. 13	*Avetone* 100b (*-tona* 85b)
Blackborough, J. 6	*Blacheberge*, *-berie* 107, 114, 117b (*Blacaberga*, *Blacheberia* 303, 337b, 475b)
Blackpool, F. 4	*Blachepole* 101 (*Blacapola* 95, 499)

Blackslade, F. 10	*Blachestach* 114b (*-tac*, *Bacheslac* 342, 502b)
Black Torrington, D. 6	*Torintone* 101 (*-tona* 93b, 497)
Blagrove, G. 5	*Blachegrave* 111 *bis* (*Blacagrava*, *Blachagava* 416, 416b, 502)
Blakewell, E. 3	*Blachewelle* 107 (*-willa* 299b)
Blaxton, D. 11	*Blachestane* 116 (not in Exon D.B.)
Bluehayes, I. 8	*Herstanhaia* 113 (*-anahaia* 398)
Boasley, D. 8	*Boslie* 105b (*-leia* 288b)
(*Bocchelanda*)	See Buckland (in Dolton)
(*Bochelan*)	See Buckland Filleigh
Bocheland	See Buckland (in Braunton), Buckland (in Dolton), Buckland (in Haccombe), Buckland (in Thurlestone), Buckland, East and West, Buckland Brewer, Buckland Filleigh, Buckland Monachorum, Buckland-Tout-Saints, Egg Buckland
(*Bochelanda*)	See Buckland (in Haccombe), Buckland (in Thurlestone), Buckland, East and West, Buckland Brewer, Buckland in the Moor, Buckland Monachorum,

(*Bochlanda*) cont.	Buckland-Tout-Saints, Egg Buckland
Bochelande	See Buckland in the Moor, Buckland-Tout-Saints
(*Bochelant*)	See Buckland (in Braunton), Buckland, East and West
(*Bochesorda*, -*surda*)	See Bulkworthy
Bochewis (-*ewys*, *Bochiywis*)	See Buck's Cross
Bodelie (-*leia*)	See East Budleigh
Boehill, J. 5	*Bihede* 112 *bis* (-*heda* 395 *bis*)
(*Boeurda*)	See Boode
Bolberry, F. 14	*Boltesberie*, *Boteberie* 105, 105b (*Boltesberia*, *Botestesberia* 219b, 220, 505)
(*Boldesworda*)	See Ebsworthy
Boleborde	See Bulworthy
*Boleham**	See Bolham, Bolham Water
(*Bolehorda*)	See Bulworthy
Bolenei (-*neia*)	See Bondleigh
*Bolewis**	See Bowlish
Bolham (in Tiverton), I. 5	*Boleham* 117b (*476)
Bolham Water (in Clayhidon), K. 6	*Boleham* 107b (*306)
Boltesberie (-*beria*)	See Bolberry
Bondleigh, F. 7	*Bolenei* 102 (-*neia* 124b)
(*Bontintona*)	See Benton
Boode, D. 3	Unnamed, 1 virgate in Braunton, *T.R.E.* 102b (*Boeurda* 126b)
(*Borna*)	See Burn (in Silverton)
Borough, A. 7	*Borge* 124 (*244), Corn.
Boslie (-*leia*)	See Boasley

Boteberie (-*beria*)	See Bolberry
Botesforde (-*forda*)	See Battisford
(*Botestesberia*)	See Bolberry
Botintone (-*tona*)	See Benton
Botreforde (-*forda*)	See Butterford
Bottor, G. 9	*Brungarstone* 102 (-*tona* 135b)
Bovelie (-*lia*)	See Bowley
Bovey Tracey, G. 9	*Bovi* 102 *bis* (*135 *bis*, 504b)
*Bovi**	See Bovey Tracey, North Bovey
Bowcombe, F. 12	*Cume* 105b (*Coma* 220b)
Bowley, H. 7	*Bovelie* 111 (-*lia* 416)
Bowlish, H. 8	*Bolewis* 114 (*336b)
Bracton (-*tona*)	See Braunton
Bradaford, C. 8	*Bradeforde* 108b (-*forda* 317b, 500b)
(*Bradaleia*)	See West Bradley
Bradeford	See Bradford (near Cookbury), Bradford (in Pyworthy), Bradford (in Witheridge), Broadaford
(*Bradeforda*)	See Bradaford, Bradford (in Witheridge), Broadaford
Bradeforde	See Bradaford
(*Bradefort*)	See Bradford (near Cookbury), Bradford (in Pyworthy)
Bradehode (-*hoda*)	See Broadwood Kelly
Bradelie	See Broadley, Great Bradley, West Bradley
(*Bradeleia*)	See Broadley, Great Bradley
Bradenese (-*esa*)	See Bradninch
(*Bradeoda*)	See Broadwoodwidger
Bradestone (-*tana*)	See Bradstone

Bradewelle (*Bradeuilla*)	See Bradwell
Bradewode (*-woda*)	See Broadwoodwidger
Bradford (near Cookbury), C. 6	*Bradeford* 106 (*-fort* 291)
Bradford (in Pyworthy), B. 7	*Bradeford* 109 (*-fort* 319)
Bradford (in Witheridge), G. 5	*Bradeford* 110b, 111 (*-forda* 367, 404b, 502)
Bradninch, I. 7	*Bradenese* 101b (*-nesa* 403b)
Bradstone, C. 9	*Bradestone* 101 (*-tana* 93)
Bradwell, D. 2	*Bradewelle* 113b (*Bradeuilla* 457b)
Bradworthy, B. 6	*Brawordine* 114 (*Braor-*, *Bravordina* 335b, 496b)
*Brai**, *Braia**	See Bray, High and Little; South Bray
Bramblecombe, E. 6	*Bremelcome* 116 (*-coma* 456b, 498b)
Bramford Speke, I. 7	*Branford*, *-fortune* 103, 112 (*-fort*, *-fortuna* 131b, 392) *Brenford* 107b *bis* (*-fort* 306b, 307b)
Branchescome (*-coma*)	See Branscombe
Brandize, D. 6	*Beldrendiland* 106 (*-lant* 123b)
Brandone (*-dona*)	See Brendon
Branford, *-fortune* (*-fort*, *-fortuna*)	See Bramford Speke
Branscombe, L. 8	*Branchescome* 102 (*-coma* 120)
*Brantone** (*-tona*)	See Braunton
(*Braordina*)	See Bradworthy
Bratone (*-tona*)	See Bratton Clovelly, Bratton Fleming
Bratton Clovelly, D. 8	*Bratone* 105b (*-tona* 288b, 495)
Bratton Fleming, E. 3	*Bratone*, *Brotone* 101b *bis*, 105 (*Bratona*, *-tone* 117b *bis*, 213, 499)
Braunton, D. 3	*Bracton* 107 (*-tona* 83b, 299b) *Brantone* 100, 102b, 104, 107 (*-tona*, *-tone* 83b, 126b, 194b, 300b, 498b *bis*)
Brawordine (*Bravordina*)	See Bradworthy
Bray, High and Little, F. 3	*Brai*, *Braia* 102b *bis* (*126b, 128, 499)
Brayley, F. 4	*Bredelie* 116b (*-lia* 378)
Breadwick, E. 2	*Breduiche* 102b (*-uica* 128b)
Bredeford (*-fort*)	See Bridford
Bredelie (*-lia*)	See Brayley
Breduiche (*-uica*)	See Breadwick
Bremelcome (*-coma*)	See Bramblecombe
*Bremerige**	See Bremridge
Bremridge, F. 4	*Bremerige* 102b (*129b)
Brendon, G. 2	*Brandone* 114 (*-dona* 337, 499)
Brenford (*-fort*)	See Bramford Speke
*Brenta**, *Brente*	See South Brent
Brentor	Not in D.B.
(*Bretricestan*)	See *Bedricestan*
Brexworthy, B. 6	*Bristelesworde* 118 (*-shorda* 481b)
Brictricestone	See Brixton (in Shaugh Prior)
Brideford (*-forda*)	See Bridford
*Bridestou**	See Bridestowe
Bridestowe, D. 8	*Bridestou* 105b (*288b, 495)
Bridford, G. 9	*Bredford* 107b (*-fort*, 307) *Brideford* 109 (*-forda* 319b)
Bridgerule, B. 7	*Brige* 114b (*411)

*Brige**	See Bridgerule
Brigeford (*-forda*)	See Brushford
Brimley	See Northleigh
*Briseham**	See Brixham
Brisestone (*-tona*)	See Brixton (near Yealmpton)
Brisforde (*-forda*)	See Brushford
Bristanestone (*-tona*)	See Brixton (in Broadwood Kelly)
Bristelesworde (*-shorda*)	See Brexworthy
(*Bristrichestona*)	See Brixton (in Shaugh Prior)
Brixham, I. 12	*Briseham* 109 (*321)
Brixton (in Broadwood Kelly), E. 7	*Bristanestone* 106 (*-tona* 292b)
Brixton (in Shaugh Prior), D. 12	*Brictricestone* 110 (*Bristrichestona* 331)
Brixton (near Yealmpton), D. 13	*Brisestone* 109b *bis* (*-tona* 330, 330b)
Broadaford, F. 12	*Bradeford* 100b, 105b (*-forda* 85b, 219, 504b)
Broad Clyst, I. 7	*Clistone* 101 (*-tona* 95)
Broadhembury and Payhembury, J. 7, K. 7	*Ham-*, *Han-*, *Henberie* 107, 112, 116b, 118 (*Hain-*, *Ham-*, *Han-*, *Hemberia* 302, 348b, 378, 486b, 500, 503b)
Broadhempston and Little Hempston, G. 11	*Hamestone*, *Hamistone* 101, 105, 109 (*Hamistona* 96b, 217, 320b)
Broadley, F. 12	*Bradelie* 109 (*-leia* 323b)
Broadnymet	See Nymet, Broadnymet etc.
Broadwood Kelly, E. 6	*Bradehode* 106 (*-hoda* 292)
Broadwoodwidger, C. 8	*Bradewode* 108b (*-eoda*, *-ewoda* 316, 496)
Brocheland, *-lande** (*-landa*)	See Bruckland
Brotone	See Bratton Fleming
Bruckland, K. 3	*Brocheland*, *-lande* 114b *bis* (*-landa*, *-lande* 343, 411b, 497)
Brungarstone (*-tona*)	See Bottor
Brushford, F. 6	*Brigeford* 106 *bis*, 112b (*-forda* 296 *bis*, 389) *Brisforde* 117 (*-forda* 468)
Bucfestra	See Buckfast
Bucheside	See Budshead
Bucheswrde (*-surda*)	See Bulkworthy
Buckerell, K. 7	*Orescome* 110b, 114 *bis* (*-coma*, *-comma*, *-comme* 338b *bis*, 404, 501b) *Holescome*, *-cumbe* 110b, 114b (*-coma*, *-comba* 342, 405, 502b *bis*) *Horescome* 110b (*-coma* 403b)
Buckfast, G. 11	*Bucfestra* 104 (*Bulfestra* 183)
Buckland and North Buckland (in Braunton), D. 3	*Bocheland* 110, 110b 1st entry (*-lant* 401, 401b)
Buckland (in Dolton), E. 6	*Bocheland* 116b (*Bocchelanda* 377)
Buckland (in Haccombe), H. 10	*Bocheland* 110b 2nd entry (*-landa* 405)
Buckland (in Thurlestone), F. 14	*Bocheland* 105 (*-landa* 220, 505)

Buckland, East and West, F. 3, F. 4	*Bocheland* 102b *bis*, 103, 106b (*-landa*, *-lant* 129b *bis*, 131, 299)
Buckland Brewer, C. 5	*Bocheland* 104b (*-landa* 210b, 497)
Buckland Filleigh, D. 6	*Bocheland* 106 (*-lan* 123)
Buckland in the Moor, F. 10	*Bochelande* 117b (*-landa* 472b)
Buckland Monachorum, D. 11	*Bocheland* 111b (*-landa* 417b)
Buckland-Tout-Saints, G. 13	*Bocheland*, *-lande* 112, 113 (*-landa* 396, 396b, 504 *bis*)
Buck's Cross, B. 5	*Bochewis* 115 (*Bochewys*, *Bochiywis* 407, 497)
Budshead, C. 12	*Bucheside* 116 (not in Exon D.B.)
Bulealler	See Aller (in Kentisbeare)
(*Bulfestra*)	See Buckfast
Bulkworthy, C. 5	*Buchesworde* 104b (*-surda* 211, *Bochesorda*, *-surda* 497b, 506)
Bulworthy, H. 5	*Boleborde* 118 (*Bolehorda* 487b)
Buretone (*-tona*)	See Burrington (in Weston Peverel)
Burietescome (*Buriestescoma*)	See Buscombe
Burlescombe, J. 5	*Berlescome* 112b (*-coma* 391)
Burn (in Silverton), I. 7	*Burne* 117 (*Borna* 469b)
Burne	See Burn (in Silverton)
Burn Town, D. 10	Unnamed, held with Marytavy 108b (*Berna* 318, 495)
Burrington (near Chulmleigh), E. 5	*Bernintone* 103b (*-intona*, *Bernurtona* 179, 497b)
Burrington (in Weston Peverel), D. 12	*Buretone* 109b (*-tona* 328b)
Burston	See Nymet, Broadnymet etc.
Bury, F. 6	*Berie* 101b (*Beria* 117)
Buscombe, F. 3	*Burietescome* 102b (*Buriestescoma* 127)
Buterlei (*-leia*)	See Butterleigh
Butreforde	See Butterford
Butterford, F. 12	*Botre-*, *Butreforde* 109b *bis* (*Botreforda* 326b *bis*)
Butterleigh, I. 6	*Buterlei* 118b (*-leia* 483b)
Bywood, K. 6	*Biude* 112 (*Biuda* 392)
Cacheberge (*-berga*)	See Cookbury
(*Cadabira*)	See Cadbury
Cadbury, H. 6	*Cadebirie* 111 (*Cadabiria* 415b)
Cadebirie	See Cadbury
Cadeledone	See Cheldon
Cadeleigh, H. 6	*Cadelie* 110b, 117b (*-lia* 400, 475)
Cadelie (*-lia*)	See Cadeleigh
Cadewile (*-wila*)	See Kidwell
Caffins Heanton, F. 2	*Hantone* 114 (*-tona* 337)
Cageford (*-fort*)	See Chagford
Calmonleuge	See Chulmleigh
Calodelie (*-leia*)	See Calverleigh
Calvelie (*-leia*)	See Chawleigh
Calverleigh, I. 6	*Calodelie* 118 (*-leia* 488)
Canonsleigh, J. 5	*Leige* 112 (*Leiga* 395b)
Canonteign, H. 9	*Teigne* 103b (*Teigna* 135)
*Carmes**	See Charles
(*Carseuilla*)	See Kerswell (in Broadhembury)
Carsewelle	See Abbotskerswell, Kerswell (in Broadhembury)

Chettiscombe, I. 5	*Chetelescome* 108 (*Chetellescoma* 312b)
Cheveletone (*-tona*)	See Chivelstone
(*Chevetorna*)	See Chevithorne
Chevithorne, I. 5	*Chenetorne* 114b (*Chevetorna* 341b, 502b) *Chiveorne* 108 (*-orna* 312)
Chichacott, E. 7	*Cicecote* 105b (*-cota* 288)
Chichelesberie (*-beria*)	See Chittleburn
Chiderleia	See Gidleigh
Chiderlie	See Chitterley
Chieflowman and Craze Loman, I. 5, I. 6	*Lonmele* 112 (*-mela*, *Lonnela* 393, 502b) *Lonmine* 112b (*-mina* 394)
(*Chiempabera*)	See Kimber
(*Chienemetona*)	See Kilmington
Chillington, G. 14	*Cedelintone* 100b (*-tona* 97, 503b)
Chilsworthy, B. 6	*Chelesworde* 118 (*-sorda* 481)
Chilton, H. 7	*Cilletone* 116b (*-tona* 379) *Cillitone* 117 (not in Exon D.B.)
Chinnesford (*-fort*)	See Kingsford
Chisewic	See Clyst St George
Chitterley, I. 7	*Chiderlie* 105b (*Chederlia* 214)
Chittleburn, D. 12	*Chichelesberie* 109b (*-beria* 330)
Chittlehampton, E. 4	*Curem'tone* 118 (*Citremetona* 484)
Chivelstone, G. 14	*Cheveletone* 109b (*-tona* 325b)
Chiveorne (*-orna*)	See Chevithorne
Chiwartiwis (*-thiwis*)	See Great Huish
(*Chochintona*)	See Cockington
(*Chrietona*)	See Crediton
Christow	Not in D.B.
(*Chritetona*)	See Crediton

Chudleigh	Not in D.B.
Chudleigh Knighton, H. 10	*Chenistetone* 102 (*-tona* 119b)
Chulmleigh, F. 5	*Calmonleuge* 108 (*Chalmonleuga* 309b)
Churchill, E. 2	*Cercelle* 111 (*Cercilla* 366b)
Churchstow	Not in D.B.
Churston Ferrers, H. 12	*Cercetone* 109 (*Cercitona* 321)
Cicecote (*-cota*)	See Chichacott
Ciclet	Unid., 112b (391b)
Cilletone, *Cillitone* (*Cilletona*)	See Chilton
Ciretone (*-tona*)	See Cheriton (in Brendon)
(*Citremetona*)	See Chittlehampton
Clannaborough, G. 7	*Cloenesberg* 106b (*-berga* 295b)
Clavetone (*-tona*)	See Clawton
Clawton, B. 7	*Clavetone* 108b (*-tona* 318b)
Clayhanger, J. 5	*Clehangre* 110 (*-hangra* 356)
Clayhidon, K. 5	*Hidone* 107b (*-dona* 304b)
Clehangre (*-hangra*)	See Clayhanger
Clifford, G. 8	*Cliford*, *-forde* 107b, 117 (*-forda*, *fort* 304b, 470)
Cliford, *-forde* (*-forda*, *-fort*)	See Clifford
*Clis**	See Sowton formerly Clyst Formison
(*Clisewic*)	See Clyst St George
*Clist**	See Clyst Gerred etc., Clyst Hydon, Clyst William
Cliste (*Clista*)	See Clyst St Mary, West Clyst
Clistone (*-tona*)	See Broad Clyst
Cloenesberg (*-berga*)	See Clannaborough
Clovelie (*-leia*)	See Clovelly
Clovelly, B. 4	*Clovelie* 101 (*-leia* 108)

Clyst Gerred, St Lawrence and Ashclyst, J. 7	*Clist* 105, 107 2nd entry, 116b (*213b, 301b 2nd entry, 457b)
Clyst Honiton	Not in D.B.
Clyst Hydon, J. 7	*Clist* 107 1st entry (*301b 1st entry)
Clyst St George, I. 8	*Chisewic* 114 (*Clisewic* 339b)
Clyst St Lawrence	See Clyst Gerred etc.
Clyst St Mary, I. 8	*Cliste* 102 (*Clista* 132b)
Clyst William, J. 7	*Clist* 118b (*487)
Cobecume	See Shapcombe
Cochalescome (*-coma*)	See Curscombe
Cochintone	See Cockington
Cockington, H. 11	*Cochintone* 111 (*Chochintona* 367b, 502b)
(*Codaforda*)	See Coddiford
Coddiford, H. 6	*Codeford* 118 (*-aforda* 486b)
Codeford	See Coddiford
Coffinswell, H. 11	*Welle* 103b (*Willa* 180)
*Coic**	See Cowick
(*Colacoma*)	See Collacombe
Colaton Raleigh, J. 9	*Coletone* 101 (*-tona* 96b, 502)
Coldridge, F. 6	*Colrige* 102b (*-riga* 125, 498)
Coldstone, D. 12	*Coltrestan* 110 (*332)
Colebroch, *-broche* (*-broca*)	See Colebrook
Colebrook, I. 6	*Colebroch*, *-broche* 104b, 110b (*-broca* 216, 400, 501)
Colebrooke	Not in D.B.
Colecome	See Collacombe
Colelie (*-leia*)	See Culleigh
Coleridge (in Egg Buckland), D. 12	*Colrige* 109b (*329)
Coleridge (in Stokenham), G. 13	*Colrige* 112 *bis* (*-riga*, *-rige* 349, 349b, 504)
Coleton, H. 13	*Coletone* 109 (*-tona* 321)

Coletone (*-tona*)	See Colaton Raleigh, Coleton, Collaton, Shiphay Collaton
Colewille (*-willa*)	See Colwell
Colitone (*-tona*)	See Cullompton
(*Collabera*)	See Culbeer
Collacombe, C. 10	*Colecome* 113 (*Colacoma* 419)
Collaton, F. 14	*Coletone* 109 (*-tona* 322)
Collebere	See Culbeer
(*Colriga*)	See Coleridge (in Stokenham)
*Colrige**	See Coldridge, Coleridge (in Egg Buckland), Coleridge (in Stokenham)
Colscott, B. 5	*Colsovenescote* 118 (*-cota* 481)
Colsovenescote (*-cota*)	See Colscott
Colston, H. 5	*Celvertesberie* 103 (*-beria* 133, *Chelverstesberia* 502)
Coltesworde (*-shorda*)	See Culsworthy
*Coltrestan**	See Coldstone
Colum	See Colunbjohn
(*Colum*)	See Columbjohn, Combe Sackville, Culm Vale
Columbjohn, I. 7	*Colum* 117b (*469)
Colun	See Combe Sackville, Culm Pyne, Culm Vale
(*Culun*)	See Culm Pyne
(*Colunp*)	See Combe Sackville
Colwell, L. 7	*Colewille* 108b (*-willa*) 314
Colyton, L. 8	*Culitone* 100b (*-tone* 85)
(*Coma*)	See Bowcombe, Combpyne, Coombe (in Templeton),

(*Coma*) cont.	Coombe (in Uplowman)
(*Comba*)	See Combebow, Combe Fishacre, Combeinteignhead, Combe Martin, Coombe (in Cheriton Fitzpaine), Culm Davy, Longcombe, Spriddlescombe
Combe	See Spriddlescombe
Combe (in South Pool), G. 14	*Cumbe* 109 3rd entry (*Conba* 324b)
Combebow, D. 8	Unnamed, held with Bridestowe 105b (*Comba* 289, 495)
Combe Fishacre, H. 11	*Cumbe* 109 2nd entry (*Comba* 320 2nd entry)
Combeinteignhead, H. 10	*Cumbe* 110b (*Comba* 403)
Combe Martin, E. 2	*Cumbe* 111 (*Comba* 366)
Combe Raleigh	See Ottery, Mohuns etc.
Combe Royal, F. 13	*Cumbe* 113b (not in Exon D.B.)
Combe Sackville, I. 7	*Colun* 107, 118 (*Colum*, *Colunp* 303b, 486b)
Combpyne, K. 3	*Come* 108b (*Coma* 314)
Come	See Combpyne, Coombe (in Templeton), Coombe (in Uplowman)
Compton, D. 12	*Contone* 109b (*-tona* 329)
(*Conba*)	See Combe (in South Pool), Coombe (in Cruwys Morchard)
(*Conma*)	See Coombe (in Uplowman)
Contesberie (*-beria*)	See Countisbury
Contone (*-tona*)	See Compton
Cookbury, C. 6	*Cacheberge* 106 (*-berga* 291b)
Cookbury Wick, C. 6	*Wiche* 113 (*Wicha* 419b)
Coombe (in Cheriton Fitzpaine), H. 6	*Cumbe* 115b (*Comba* 409b)
Coombe (in Cruwys Morchard), H. 6	*Cumbe* 117b (*Conba* 471b)
Coombe (in Drewsteignton), G. 8	*Cume* 118 (*Cuma* 484b)
Coombe (in Templeton), H. 5	*Come* 103 *ter* (*Coma* 133, 133b *bis*)
Coombe (in Uplowman), I. 5	*Come* 112, 112b (*Coma*, *Conma* 393b, 394)
Coriton (*-tona*)	See Coryton
Cornehode (*-huda*)	See Cornwood
(*Corneorda*)	See Cornworthy, Curworthy
Corneorde	See Cornworthy
Corneurde	See Curworthy
Cornwood, E. 12	*Cornehode* 105 (*-huda* 218b)
Cornworthy, H. 12	*Corneorde* 109 (*-orda* 323b)
Cortescanole (*-ola*)	See Curtisknowle
Coryton, C. 9	*Coriton* 102 (*-tona* 121)
Cotelie (*-leia*)	See Cotleigh
Cotleigh, L. 7	*Cotelie* 105 (*-leia* 217b)
Countisbury, G. 1	*Contesberie* 110b (*-beria* 401b)
Cowick, H. 8	*Coic* 107b (*303b)
(*Crabecoma*, *Crahecome*)	See Creacombe (near Witheridge)
Cravelech (*-lec*)	See Creely
Crawecome (*-coma*)	See Creacombe (in Newton Ferrers), Creacombe (near Witheridge)
Craze Loman	See Chieflowman

Creacombe (in Newton Ferrers), E. 13	*Crawecome* 116 (*Crawecoma* 504b)
Creacombe (near Witheridge), G. 5	*Crawecome* 108 *bis* (*Crabecoma*, *Crahecome*, *Crawecoma* 310, 310b, 506b *bis*)
Credie (*Creda*)	See Lower Credy
Crediton, H. 7	*Critetone* 101b (*Chrietona*, *Chritetona* 177, 499)
Creely, I. 8	*Cravelech* 103 (*-lec* 132b)
Cressewalde (*-walla*)	See Kerswell (in Hockworthy)
Crideholde (*-holda*)	See Croyde
Cridie (*-ia*)	See Lower Credy
Crintone	See Ilkerton
Critetone	See Crediton
Crochewelle (*-wella*)	See Crockernwell
Crockernwell, G. 8	*Crochewelle* 115 (*-wella* 414)
Crooke, F. 7	*Cruc* 117b (*475)
Croyde, C. 3	*Crideholde* 105 (*-holda* 213)
*Cruc**	See Crooke
Cruwys Morchard, H. 6	*Morceth* 103 *bis* (*-cet*, *-ceta* 132b *bis*, 501b) *Morchet* 110b (*404)
Culbeer, L. 7	*Collebere* 108b (*Collabera* 314b)
Culitone (*-tona*)	See Colyton
Culleigh, C. 5	*Colelie* 104b (*-leia* 210b, 497)
Cullompton, J. 6	*Colitone* 104 (*-tona* 195)
Culm Davy, K. 5	*Cumbe* 115b (*Comba* 409 *bis*, 500b)
Culmestoche (*-stocha*)	See Culmstock
Culm Pyne, K. 5	*Colun* 107b (*306)
Culmstock, K. 6	*Culmestoche* 101b (*-stocha* 118)
Culm Vale, I. 7	*Colun* 117b (*Colum* 470)
Culsworthy, B. 6	*Colteswor de* 118 (*-shorda* 481b)
(*Cuma*)	See Coombe (in Drewsteignton)
Cumbe	See Combe (in South Pool), Combe Fishacre, Combeinteignhead, Combe Martin, Combe Royal, Coombe (in Cheriton Fitzpaine), Coombe (in Cruwys Morchard), Culm Davy, Longcombe
Cume	See Bowcombe, Coombe (in Drewsteignton)
Curem'tone	See Chittlehampton
Curscombe, K. 7	*Cochalescome* 105b (*-coma* 214b)
Curtisknowle, F. 12	*Cortescanole* 169 (*-ola* 323)
Curworthy, E. 7	*Corneurde* 116 (*Corneorda* 496)
Dalilei (*-lea*)	See Delley
Dalwood	Not in D.B.
Danescome (*-coma*)	See Dunscombe
Dart (in Cadeleigh), H. 6	*Derte* 111 (*Derta* 415b)
Dartington, G. 11	*Dertrintone* 111 (*-tona* 368b)
Dartmouth	Not in D.B.
Dart Raffe, G. 5	*Derte* 111b, 116b (*Derta* 378b, 416b)
Dawlish, I. 10	*Doules* 101b (*Douelis* 117b)
Dean Prior, F. 11	*Dene* 111 (*Dena* 368)
Deer Park	See Waringstone
Delley, D. 4	*Dalilei* 116b (*-lea* 376)

(*Dena*)	See Dean Prior
Denbury, G. 11	*Deveneberie* 103b (*Devenaberia* 180)
Dene	See Dean Prior
*Deneord**, K. 2	Lost in Membury, 100b (84b, 503)
Denesberge (*-berga*)	See Dunsbear
(*Denewynesdone*)	See Dunsdon
Dennington, L. 6	*Donitone* 104 (*-tona* 195b)
Densham, G. 6	*Dimewoldesham* 111 (*367) *Donevoldehame* 104b (*-hamma* 216b, 501)
(*Depdona*)	See *Deptone*
(*Depeforda*)	See Diptford
Depeforde	See Dipford, Diptford
(*Deppaforda*)	See Dipford
Deptone (*Depdona*), F. 10	Lost in Widecombe in the Moor, 111 (367b, 502b)
Derte (*Derta*)	See Dart (in Cadeleigh), Dart Raffe
Dertre (*Dertera*)	See Queen Dart
Dertrintone (*-tona*)	See Dartington
Deveneberie (*Devenaberia*)	See Denbury
Didasham (*-sam*)	See Dittisham
*Dimewoldesham**	See Densham
(*Dinintona*)	See Dinnaton
Dinnaton, E. 12	*Dunintone* 105b (*Dinintona* 219) *Dunitone* 100b *bis* (*-tona* 85b *bis*, 504 *bis*)
Dipford, I. 4	*Depeforde* 111b (*Deppaforda* 346)
Diptford, F. 12	*Depeforde* 100b (*-forda* 85b, 504)
Dittesham, H. 12	*Didasham* 102 (*-sam* 120b)
Docheorde (*Dochorda*)	See Dockworthy
Dockworthy, F. 6	*Docheorde* 115 (*Dochorda* 414b)
Dodbrooke, G. 13	*Dodebroch* 118b (*-broca* 489b)
Doddiscombsleigh, H. 9	*Leuge* 117 (*Leuga* 468b)
Dodebroch (*-broca*)	See Dodbrooke
Dodecote (*-cota*)	See Dodscott
Dodscott, D. 5	*Dodecote* 112b (*-cota* 388b)
Doducheswelle (*Doduceswilla*)	See Dunkeswell
Dolton, E. 6	*Duveltone* 116 (*-tona* 462, 503b) *Oueltone* 106b (*Dueltona* 295)
(*Dona*)	See Down St Mary, Down Thomas, Rousdon
Dondritone (*-tona*)	See Dunterton
Dune	See Down St Mary, Down Thomas, Rousdon
Donesland (*-landa*)	See Dunsland
Donestanestone (*-stanstona*)	See Dunstone (in Yealmpton)
Donevoldehame (*-hamma*)	See Densham
Donicestone (*-tona*)	See Donningstone
Donitone (*-tona*)	See Dennington
Donningstone, J. 4	*Donicestone* 105 (*-tona* 213b, 499b)
(*Donsedoc*)	See Dunchideock
Dotton, J. 8	*Otrit* 107b (*308b)
Doules (*Douelis*)	See Dawlish
Dowland, E. 6	*Duvelande* 112b *bis* (*-landa* 390 *bis*, 498 *bis*)
Downacarey, C. 8	*Kari* 108b (*316b)
Down Ralph	See Rousdon
Down St Mary, G. 7	*Done* 103b (*Dona* 182)
Down Thomas, D. 13	*Done* 109b (*Dona* 330b)
Draheford (*-forda*)	See Drayford
Drayford, G. 6	*Draheford* 112 (*-forda* 393)
Drewsteignton, G. 8	*Taintone* 107b (*-tona* 304)
(*Dueltona*)	See Dolton

(*Duna*)	See East Down, Rousdon, West Down
Dunchideock, H. 9	*Dunsedoc* 113b (*Donsedoc* 457)
Dune	See East Down, Rousdon, West Down
Dunesford (*-forda*)	See Dunsford
*Dunestal**	See Townstal
(*Dunestanaetuna*)	See Dunstone (in Widecombe in the Moor)
Dunestanetone	See Dunstone (in Stokenham)
Dunestanetune (*-tuna*)	See Dunstone (in Widecombe in the Moor)
Dunewinesdone (*-winnusdona*)	See Dunsdon
Dunintone	See Dinnaton
Dunitone (*-tona*)	See Dinnaton
Dunkeswell, K. 6	*Doducheswelle* 114 (*Duduceswilla* 338b)
Dunsbear, D. 6	*Denesberge* 118 (*-berga* 482)
Dunscombe, H. 6	*Danescome* 114b (*-coma* 340)
Dunsdon, B. 6	*Dunewinesdone* 114 (*-winnusdona* 335, *Denewynesdone* 496b)
Dunsedoc	See Dunchideock
Dunsford, G. 8	*Dunesford* 111b, 118b (*-forda* 347, 490)
Dunsland, C. 7	*Donesland* 106 (*-landa* 290b)
Dunstone (in Stokenham), G. 14	*Dunestanetone* 113b (not in Exon D.B.)
Dunstone (in Widecombe in the Moor), F. 10	*Dunestanetune* 114b (*-tuna* 342, *Dunestanaetuna* 502b)
Dunstone (in Yealmpton), E. 13	*Donestanestone* 118b (*-stanstona* 489b)
Dunterton, C. 9	*Dondritone* 106 (*-tona* 289b)
Duvelande (*-landa*)	See Dowland
Duveltone (*-tona*)	See Dolton
East Allington, G. 13	*Alintone* 113b (not in Exon D.B.)
Eastanton, F. 2	*Standone* 114 (*Estandona* 337b)
East Buckland	See Buckland, East and West
East Budleigh, J. 9	*Bodelie* 100 (*-leia* 84)
East Down, E. 2	*Dune* 113b (*Duna* 457)
Eastleigh, D. 4	*Lei* 110 (*Leia* 399b, 506)
East Ogwell	See Ogwell
East Portlemouth	Not in D.B.
East Prawle, G. 14	*Prenla* 108b (*314b)
East Putford, B. 5	*Potiforde* 104b (*-forda* 211)
East Worlington	See Worlington, East and West
East Youlstone, A. 5	*Alwineclancavele* 114 (*Alwynelancavele* 335b)
Ebsworthy, D. 8	Unnamed, held with Bridestowe 105b (*Etboldus Wrda*, *Boldesworda* 289, 495)
*Ecclesia Sanctae Mariae**	See St Mary Church
Echeburne	See Exbourne
Eddetone	See Ilton
Edeslege (*-lega*)	See Iddesleigh
(*Edetona*)	See Ilton
Edginswell, H. 11	*Wille* 113b (*Willa* 461b)
Efford, D. 12	*Elforde* 113b (not in Exon D.B.)
(*Efforda*)	See Ashford (near Barnstaple)
Eggbear, G. 8	*Eigebere* 107b (*Eighebera* 307b)

Egg Buckland, D. 12	*Bocheland* 109b (*-landa* 327b)
Eggesford	Not in D.B.
Eigebere (*Eighebera*)	See Eggbear
Eilasesford	See Elsford
Eilesberge	See Aylesbeare
Eileuescote	See Aylescott
(*Eissa*)	See Ash (in Bradworthy)
(*Ela*)	See Hele (in Buckland Brewer)
Elforde	See Efford
Elfordleigh, D. 12	*Lege* 110 (*Lega* 333)
Elintone (*-tona*)	See Yealmpton
Elsford, G. 9	*Eilavesford* 102 (*Ailavesfort* 135b)
Eltemetone (*-tona*)	Unid., 108 (311)
Embury, D. 6	*Hame* 118 (*Hama* 482b)
Engestecote (*-cota*)	See Henscott
Engleborne (*-borna*)	See Englebourne
Englebourne, G. 12	*Engleborne* 108b, 111 (*-borna* 314b, 368b)
Erberneforde	See Harbourneford
Ermentone (*-tona*)	See Ermington
Ermington, E. 12	*Ermentone* 100b, 105b (*-tona*, *-tone* 85b *ter*, 218, 504b *bis Hermentona* 85b, 504)
Ertacomestoche (*-stoca*)	See Stockland
(*Erticoma*)	See Yarcombe
Eruescome (*-coma*)	See Irishcombe
(*Esastapla*)	See Instaple
(*Escaga*)	See Shaugh Prior
(*Escapeleia*)	See Shapley (in Chagford), Shapley (in North Bovey)
(*Eschipabroca*, *-pebrocha*)	See Shobrooke (in Morchard Bishop)
(*Escobecoma*)	See Shapcombe
(*Esestapla*)	See Instaple
(*Eslapaforda*)	See Lapford
Esforde	See Ashford (near Barnstaple)
(*Esmarige*, *Esmaurige*)	See Smallridge
(*Esmiteham*, *Esmitteham*)	See Smytham
(*Esnideleia*)	See Snydles
(*Espicewita*)	See Spitchwick
(*Esprecoma*)	See Spreacombe
(*Espredelestona*, *-eletona*)	See Spriddlestone
(*Espreitona*)	See Spreyton
Esprewei (*Espreuweia*)	See Spurway
*Essa**	See Ash Barton
Essaple (*-apla*)	See Shapley (in North Bovey)
Essastaple	See Instaple
Essebeer, G. 5	*Labere* 116 (*-bera* 378b)
Esseberie	See Ashbury
Essebretone (*-tona*)	See Ashburton
(*Essecestra*, *-tre*)	See Exeter
Esselingeforde (*-gaforda*)	See Shillingford
Esseminstre (*-ministra*)	See Exminster
Essemundehord (*-horda*)	See Ashmansworthy
(*Esseorda*)	See Exworthy
Essestone (*Essetona*)	See Ashton
*Essoic**	See Exwick
(*Estaforda*)	See Stowford (in Colaton Raleigh)
(*Estandona*)	See Eastanton
(*Estantona*)	See Churchstanton, Som.
(*Estapeleia*)	See Staplehill
(*Estatforda*)	See Stowford (near Lifton)
(*Estaveforda*)	See Stowford (in West Down)
(*Estocha*)	See Stoke (in Holne), Stoke Rivers
(*Estocheleia*)	See Stockleigh (in Highampton), Stockleigh (in

(*Estocheleia*) cont.	Meeth), Stockleigh English, Stockleigh Pomeroy
(*Estochelia*)	See Leigh (in Silverton), Stockleigh (in Meeth)
(*Estodleia*, *Estolleia*)	See Stoodleigh (near Oakford)
(*Estotacoma*)	See Stedcombe
(*Estotdona*)	See Staddon
(*Estotleia*)	See Stoodleigh (in West Buckland)
Estrete (*-eta*)	See Strete Raleigh
(*Etboldus Wrda*)	See Ebsworthy
(*Etcheborna*)	See Exbourne
Exbourne, E. 7	*Echeburne* 106 (*Etcheborna* 290b) *Hechesburne* 116 (not in Exon D.B.)
Execestre	See Exeter
Exeter, I. 8	*Execestre* 101b *bis*, 102, 104, 104b, 105b, 108b, 110, 112, 113b *bis*, 114b, 115, 116, 117 *bis* (*Essecestra*, *-tre* 88, 94b, 117, 120b, 136 *bis*, 180b, 196, 222b, 315, 334b, 344, 349b, 406, 460, 462b, 473) *Exonia* 100, 101, 103b, 106b, 108b (*297, 334, 505b *quater*, 506 *sexiens*, 506b)
Exminster, I. 8	*Aise-*, *Axe-*, *Esseminstre* 100, 110, 111b (*Aexe-*, *Aixe-*, *Axe-*, *Esseministra* 83, 399b, 457, 498, 498b)

*Exonia**	See Exeter
Exwick, H. 8	*Essoic* 107b (*304)
Exworthy, I. 6	(*Esseorda* 501b) not in Exch. D.B.
Fallei (*-lea*)	See Varley
Fardel, E. 12	*Ferdendel*, *-delle* 100b, 105b (*-del*, *-della* 85b, 218, 504)
Farewei (*-weia*)	See Farway
Farleigh, G. 12	*Ferlie* 100b (*-leia* 85b, 504)
Farringdon, J. 8	*Ferentone* 104b (*-tona* 216, 501) *Ferhendone* 117b (*-dona* 471b)
Farway, K. 8	*Farewei* 103, 113 (*-weia* 135, 396)
Farwood, L. 8	*Forhode* 111b (*Forohoda* 417)
*Fedaven**	See Villavin
*Fen**	See Venn
Fenacre, J. 5	*Wennacre* 112b (*Vennacra* 391b)
Feniton, K. 7	*Finetone* 105 (*Finatona* 214b)
*Ferdendel**, *-delle* (*-della*)	See Fardel
Ferding	Unid., 115b (not in Exon D.B.)
Ferentone (*-tona*)	See Farringdon
*Fereordin**	See Virworthy
Fereurde (*-urdi*)	See Virworthy
Ferhendone (*-dona*)	See Farringdon
Ferlie (*-leia*)	See Farleigh, Varleys
Fernehalle (*-halla*)	See Fernhill
(*Ferneurda*, *-ewrda*)	See Fernworthy
Fernhill, E. 12	*Fernehelle* 110 (*-hella* 332)
Fernworthy, D. 9	Unnamed, held with Bridestowe 105b (*Ferneurda*, *-ewrda* 289, 495)
Ferse (*Fersa*)	See Furzehill
*Fierseham**	See Fursham
Filelei (*-leia*, *Filileia*)	See Filleigh

Filleigh, F. 4	*Filelei* 107 (*-leia* 300b, *Fileleia* 498b)
Finetone (*Finatona*)	See Feniton
Flete Damarel, E. 13	*Flutes* 113 (*421)
Flueta (*Fluta*)	See Seaton
*Flutes**	See Flete Damarel
Foleford (*-fort*)	See Fulford
Foletone (*-tona*)	See Follaton
Follaton, G. 12	*Foletone* 109b (*-tona* 325b)
Ford (in Chivelstone), G. 14	*Forde* 109b (*Forda* 325b)
Forde (*Forda*)	See Ford (in Chivelstone)
Forde (*Forda*), K. 2	Lost in Musbury, 108 (313b)
Forhode (*Forohoda*)	See Farwood
Framintone (*-tona*)	See Fremington
Fredelestoch (*-eletestoc*)	See Frithelstock
Fremington, D. 3	*Framintone* 102 (*-tona* 123b)
*Friseham**	See Frizenham
Frithelstock, D. 5	*Fredelestoch* 104b (*Fredeletestoc* 210b)
Frizenham, D. 5	*Friseham* 105 (*211b)
Fulford, G. 8	*Foleford* 107b (*-fort* 308)
Fursham, F. 8	*Fierseham* 107 (*307)
Furzehill, F. 2	*Ferse* 111 (*Fersa* 366)
Galeshore (*-hora*)	See Galsworthy
Galmentone (*-tona*)	See Galmpton (in Churston Ferrers)
Galmpton (in Churston Ferrers), H. 12	*Galmentone* 113b (*-tona* 462)
Galmpton (in South Huish), F. 14	*Walementone* 109 (*Walenimtona* 322)
Galsworthy, C. 5	*Galeshore* 104b (*-hora* 211, 497)

Gappah, H. 10	*Gatepade* 114b (*-pada* 341b, 502b)
Gatcombe, L. 8	*Gatecumbe* 117b (*Gatcumba* 476b)
Gatecumbe (*Gatcumba*)	See Gatcumbe
Gatepade (*-pada*)	See Gappah
Genelie	See Ingleigh
Georgeham, D. 3	*Hame* 115b (*Hama* 408)
George Nympton, F. 5	*Limet* 116b (*377, 499b) *Nimete* 101 (*Nimet*, *Nimeta* 95, 499b)
George Teign, H. 9	*Teigne* 106b (*Teigna* 297)
Germansweek and Southweek, C. 8	*Wiche* 106, 113b (*Wica*, *Wyca* 289, 335)
Gerwille	See Gorwell
Gherneslete (*-leta*)	See Greenslade
(*Ghiderleia*)	See Gidleigh
Gidcott, C. 6	*Gildescote* 113 (*-cota* 419b)
Gidesham (*-sam*)	See Gittisham
Gidleigh, F. 8	*Chiderleia* 104b (*Ghiderleia* 210)
Gildescote (*-cota*)	See Gidcott
Gillscott, F. 6	*Chetelescote* 112b (*Chetellescota* 390b)
Gittisham, K. 7	*Gidesham* 112b (*-sam* 392)
Godelege (*-lega*)	See Goodleigh
Godescote (*-cota*)	See Guscott
Godevecote (*-vacota*)	See Goodcott
Godrintone (*-tona*)	See Goodrington
*Gohewis**	See Gorhuish
Goodcott, E. 6	*Godevecote* 112b (*-vacota* 391)
Goodleigh, E. 3	*Godelege* 113 (*-lega* 420)
Goodrington, H. 12	*Godrintone* 112 (*-tona* 347b)
Goosewell, D. 13	*Gosewelle* 111b (*-wella* 417)
Gorhuish, D. 7	*Gohewis* 106 (*292)

Gorwell, K. 6	*Gerwille* 115b (name defective 409, *Gorwilla* 500b)
(*Gorwilla*)	See Gorwell
Gosewelle (*-wella*)	See Goosewell
Gratton, F. 3	*Gretedone* 102b (*-dona* 128)
Great Bradley, H. 6	*Bradelie* 103, 117b (*-leia* 134b, 472b)
Great Huish, H. 8	*Chiwartiwis* 117b (*-thiwis* 471, 500)
Great Torrington, D. 5	*Toritone* 116, 116b *bis* (*-tona* 376b *bis*, 456b)
Greenslade, F. 7	*Gherneslete* 106b (*-leta* 296b)
Greenslinch, I. 7	*Grenneliʒe* 117 (*-liʒa* 469b)
Greenway, K. 6	*Grenowei* 112 (*-weia* 348, 503b)
Grenneliʒe (*-liʒa*)	See Greenslinch
Grenowei (*-weia*)	See Greenway
Gretedone (*-dona*)	See Gratton
Grimpstonleigh, G. 13	*Lege* 116 *bis* (*Lega* 504b)
Grimston, G. 13	*Grismetone* 116 (not in Exon D.B.)
Grismetone	See Grimston
Guscott, D. 8	*Godescote* 106 (*-cota* 290)
Hacche, F. 4	*Achie* 116b (*Achia* 377b)
Haccombe (in Exeter St Thomas), H. 8	*Hacome* 110 (*-coma* 401)
Haccombe (near Newton Abbot), H. 11	*Hacome* 108 (*-coma* 311b)
Hacheurde	See Hackworthy
Hackworthy, G. 8	*Hacheurde* 117 (not in Exon D.B.)
Hacome (*-coma*)	See Haccombe (in Exeter St Thomas),
Hacome (*-coma*) cont.	Haccombe (near Newton Abbot)
(*Hadreleia*)	See Hatherleigh (near Okehampton)
(*Hagawila*)	See Halwell (in Brixton)
Hagetone	See Hagginton
Hagewile	See Halwell (in Brixton)
Hagginton, D. 2	*Haintone* 106b (*Hagintona* 298b) *Hagetone* 111b (*Hagitona* 345, 498b)
(*Hagintona*)	See Hagginton, Kingsheanton
Hagintone	See Kingsheanton
(*Hagitona*)	See Hagginton
(*Hainberia*)	See Broadhembury
Hainemardun	See Hemerdon
(*Hainghestecota*)	See Henscott
(*Hainoc*)	See Hennock
Haintone	See Hagginton
(*Haiserstona*)	See Sherberton
Halberton, I. 6	*Als-*, *Halsbretone* 101b (*-tona* 110b, 502b)
Haldeword (*-eurdi*)	See Holsworthy
(*Halestou*)	See Halstow (in Dunsford)
Haletreu (*-trou*), G. 13	Lost in Woodleigh, 113 (421b)
Halgewelle (*-willa*)	See Halwill
Halsbretone (*-tona*)	See Halberton
Halse, F. 7	*Hax* 106b (*295b)
Halstow (in Dunsford), G. 8	*Alestou* 117 (*Halestou* 470)
Halwell (in Brixton), D. 13	*Hagewile* 110 (*Hagawila* 334)
Halwell (near Moreleigh)	Not in D.B.
Halwill, C. 7	*Halgewelle* 101 (*-willa* 108)
(*Hama*)	See Abbotsham, Embury, Georgeham

Hamberie (*-beria*)	See Broadhembury
Hame	See Abbotsham, Embury, Georgeham
Hamestone	See Broadhempston
Hamihoch (*-hoc*)	See Hemyock
Hamistone (*-tona*)	See Broadhempston
Hampson	See Nymet, Broadnymet etc.
Hamsworthy, B. 6	*Hermodesword* 102 (*Hermondesworda* 122)
Hanberie (*-beria*)	See Broadhembury
*Hanc**, *Hanche* (*Hanca*)	See Aunk
Hancheford (*Hanecheforda*)	See Hankford
Hanechelole (*Hanenchelola*)	See Honicknowle
Hanitone	See Highampton
Hankford, C. 5	*Hancheford* 115 (*Hanecheforda* 414)
Hanoch	See Hennock
Hantone (*-tona*)	See Caffins Heanton, Heanton Punchardon, Heanton Satchville, Highampton, West Heanton
Harberton	Not in D.B.
Harbourneford, F. 11	*Erberneforde* 111 (*Herberneforda* 368b)
(*Hareoda*)	See Horwood
Harestane (*-tana*)	See Hareston
Hareston, E. 12	*Harestane* 104b, 105 (*-tana* 221b *bis*, 505 *bis*)
Harford, F. 12	*Hereford* 105 (*-forda* 218b)
Harlei (*-leia*)	See Hatherleigh (in Bovey Tracey)
Haroldesore	See Hazard
Harpford	Not in D.B.
Hartland, A. 4	*Hertitone* 100b (*-tona* 93b)

Hartleigh, D. 6	*Herlege* 102 (*Hierlega* 123b)
Hatherleigh (in Bovey Tracey), G. 9	*Harlei* 102 (*-leia* 135b)
Hatherleigh (near Okehampton), D. 7	*Adrelie* 103b (*Hadreleia* 178)
Hauocmore (*-mora*)	See Hawkmoor
Haustone (*-tona*)	See Haxton
Hawkchurch	Not in D.B.
Hawkmoor, G. 9	*Hauocmore* 102 (*-mora* 135b)
*Hax**	See Halse
Haxton, F. 3	*Haustone* 101b (*-tona* 117b, 499b)
Hays Park, J. 6	*Hewise* 110b (*-isa* 400)
Hazard, G. 12	*Haroldesore* 113 (not in Exon D.B.)
Heanton Punchardon, D. 3	*Hantone* 106b (*-tona* 298b)
Heanton Satchville, D. 6	*Hantone* 106 (*-tona* 293b)
Heathfield (in Aveton Gifford), F. 13	*Hetfeld* 104 (*-felt* 182b)
Heathfield (in Honiton), K. 7	*Hetfelle* 112 (*-fella* 347b)
Heavitree, I. 8	*Hevetrove* 114b (*-trowa* 343b)
Hechesburne	See Exbourne
Heierde (*-erda*)	See Yard (in Silverton)
*Hela**, *Hele*	See Hele (in Buckland Brewer), Hele (in Ilfracombe), Hele (in Petrockstow)
Hele (in Bradninch), I. 7	*Hiele* 116 (not in Exon D.B.)
Hele (in Buckland Brewer), C. 5	*Hele* 105 (*Ela*, *Hela* 212, 497b)
Hele (in Ilfracombe), D. 2	*Hela* 102b (*128)
Hele (in Meeth), D. 6	*Helescaue* 106b (*Helecaue* 294b)

Hele (in Petrockstow), D. 6	*Hela* 117 (*468)
Helescaue (*Helecaue*)	See Hele (in Meeth)
(*Hemberia*)	See Broadhembury
Hembury Fort, K. 7	*Otri* 110b, 114b (*Otri*, *Otria* 342, 405)
Hemerdon, E. 12	*Hainemardun* 115 (not in Exon D.B.)
Hemyock, K. 6	*Hamihoch* 100 (*-hoc* 84)
Henberie	See Broadhembury
Henford, B. 8	*Hindeford* 109 (*-fort* 319b)
Henlei (*-leia*)	See Highleigh
Hennock, H. 9	*Hanoch* 108 (*Hainoc* 312)
Henscott, C. 6	*Engestecote* 102 (*-cota* 122b, *Hainghestecota* 497)
Heppastebe (*-steba*)	Unid., 114b (340, 501)
(*Herberneforda*)	See Harbourneford
Hereford (*-forda*)	See Harford
Herlege	See Hartleigh
Herlescome (*-coma*)	See Yarnscombe
(*Hermentona*)	See Ermington
Hermodesword (*Hermondesworda*)	See Hamsworthy
Hernescome (*-coma*)	See Yarnscombe
Herstanhaia (*-anahaia*)	See Blue Hayes
Herticome	See Yarcombe
Hertitone (*-tona*)	See Hartland
(*Hesmalacoma*)	See Smallicombe
Hetfeld	See Heathfield (in Aveton Gifford)
Hetfelle (*-fella*)	See Heathfield (in Honiton)
(*Hetfelt*)	See Heathfield (in Aveton Gifford)
(*Heuis*)	See South Huish
Hevetrove (*-trowa*)	See Heavitree
*Hewis**	See North Huish, South Huish
Hewise (*-isa*)	See Hays Park
Hidone (*-dona*)	See Clayhidon
Hiele	See Hele (in Bradninch)
Hierde (*-erda*)	See Yard (in Rose Ash)
(*Hierlega*)	See Hartleigh
Highampton, D. 7	*Hanitone* 106 (*Hantona* 291)
High Bickington, E. 5	*Bichentone* 101, 101b (*-tona* 94b, 110, 499)
High Bray	See Bray
Highleigh, H. 4	*Henlei* 114b (*-leia* 341)
Highweek	Not in D.B.
Hilesdone	See Hillersdon
Hill (in Cruwys Morchard), H. 6	*Hille* 117b (*Hilla* 471b)
Hille (*Hilla*)	See Hill
Hillersdon, I. 6	*Hilesdone* 116b (*Hillesdona* 378b)
(*Hillesdona*)	See Hillersdon
Hindeford (*-fort*)	See Henford
Hiteneslei (*-leia*)	See Hittisleigh
Hittisleigh, F. 8	*Hiteneslei* 107b (*-leia* 305)
Hiwis	See Huish (near Dolton)
*Ho**	See Hooe
Hocha (*Hoca*)	See Hook
Hocheorde (*Hochaorda*)	See Hockford Waters
Hochesham (*-sam*)	See Huxham
Hochesile (*-ila*)	See Huxhill
Hockford Waters, J. 5	*Hocheorde* 111b (*Hochaorda* 346)
Hockworthy, J. 5	*Hocoorde* 107 (*-rda* 300)
Hocoorde (*-rda*)	See Hockworthy
Hola	See Hole (in Hartland)
(*Hola*)	See Hole (in Georgeham), Hole (in Hartland)
Holbeam, G. 10	*Holebeme* 117 (*-bema* 471)
Holbeton	Not in D.B.

Holbrook, I. 8	*Holebroch* 118 (*-broca* 487b)
Holcombe (in East Dawlish), I. 10	*Holecome* 114 (*Holcomma* 336b)
Holcombe Burnell, H. 8	*Holecumbe* 101b (*-cumba* 110b)
Holcombe Rogus, J. 5	*Holecome* 107 (*-coma* 299b)
(*Holcomma*)	See Holcombe (in East Dawlish), Hollowcombe (in Fremington)
Hole	See Hole (in Georgeham)
Hole (in Clayhidon), K. 6	*Holne* 107b (*Holna* 306b)
Hole (in Georgeham), C. 3	*Hole* 115b (*Hola* 408)
Hole (in Hartland), A. 5	*Hola* 115 (*407)
Holebeme (*-bema*)	See Holbeam
Holebroch (*-broca*)	See Holbrook
(*Holecoma*)	See Holcombe Rogus, Hollacombe (near Holsworthy), Hollacombe (in Kentisbury)
Holecome	See Holcombe (in East Dawlish), Holcombe Rogus, Hollacombe (near Holsworthy), Hollacombe (in Kentisbury), Hollowcombe (in Fremington)
Holecumbe (*-cumba*)	See Holcombe Burnell
Holescome (*-coma*)	See Buckerell, Hollowcombe (in Ermington)
Holescumbe (*-cumba*)	See Buckerell
(*Holla*)	See Holne
Hollacombe (near Holsworthy), C. 7	*Holecome* 117b (*-coma* 481b)
Hollacombe (in Kentisbury), F. 2	*Holecome* 111b (*-coma* 345)

Hollam, D. 5	*Holnham* 115 (*413)
Holland, E. 12	*Hovelande* 110 (*Honelanda* 331b)
Holle	See Holne
Hollowcombe (in Ermington), E. 13	*Holescome* 105b (*-coma* 218)
Hollowcombe (in Fremington), D. 3	*Holecome* 115b (*Holcomma* 408)
Holne (*Holna*)	See Hole (in Clayhidon)
Holne, F. 11	*Holle* 111 (*Holla* 367b)
*Holnham**	See Hollam
Holsworthy, B. 7	*Haldeword* 101 (*-eurdi* 93b)
Honecherde (*-chercha*)	See Honeychurch
(*Honelanda*)	See Holland
Honesham (*-ssam*)	See Huntsham
Honetone (*-tona*)	See Honiton (near Axminster)
Honeychurch, E. 7	*Honecherde* 106 (*-chercha* 292)
Honicknowle, D. 12	*Hanechelole* 105b (*Hanenchelola* 222)
Honiton (near Axminster), K. 7	*Honetone* 100, 104b (*-tona* 84b, 216b, 503, 503b)
Honiton (in South Molton), F. 4	*Hunitone* 116b (*-tona* 377b)
Hooe, D. 13	*Ho* 110 (*334)
Hook, E. 5	*Hocha* 117 (*Hoca* 468)
(*Horeoda*)	See Horwood
Horescome (*-coma*)	See Buckerell
Horewod, *-wode** (*Horewda*, *-woda*)	See Horwood
Horton, B. 5	*Hortone* 102 (*-tona* 122b, 496b, 505)
Hortone (*-tona*)	See Horton
Horwood, D. 4	*Horewod*, *-wode* 102 *bis*, 114 (*Horewda*, *-woda*, *-wode* 122b, 124,

Horwood cont.	336, *Hareoda*, *Horeoda* 496b, 505)
Houndtor, G. 9	*Hundatore* 103b (*-tora* 179b)
Hovelande	See Holland
Huish (near Dolton), D. 6	*Hiwis* 112b (*Hywis* 388b) *Iwis* 116b (*Ywis* 376b, 497)
Huish (in Instow), D. 4	*Torsewis* 102 (*124)
Hundatore (*-tora*)	See Houndtor
Huneseue (*-eua*)	See Huntshaw
Hunitone (*-tona*)	See Honiton (in South Molton)
Huntsham, I. 5	*Honesham* 116b (*-ssam* 379b)
Huntshaw, D. 4	*Huneseue* 110 (*-eua* 399)
Hurtesberie (*-beria*)	See Berrynarbor
Huxham, I. 7	*Hochesham* 114 (*-sam* 339b)
Huxhill, D. 4	*Hochesile* 115 (*-sila* 412b)
(*Hywis*)	See Huish (near Dolton)
(*Ida*)	See Ide
Iddesleigh, E. 6	*Edeslege* 101b (*-lega* 109) *Iweslei* 112b (*Ywesleia* 388)
Ide, H. 8	*Ide* 101b (*Ida* 117b)
Ideford, H. 10	*Yudeford* 117 (*Yudaforda* 472)
Ilesham (*-sam*)	See Ilsham
(*Ilestintona*)	See Islington
Ilfracombe, D. 2	*Alfreincome* 107 (*-coma* 301)
Ilkerton, F. 2	*Crintone* 110b (*Incrintona* 402, 498b)
Ilsham, I. 11	*Ilesham* 117b (*-sam* 476)
Ilsington, G. 10	*Lestintone* 113b (*Ilestintona* 460)
Ilton, F. 14	*Eddetone* 109 (*Edetona* 322b)
(*Incrintona*)	See Ilkerton
Ingleigh, E. 6	*Genelie* 116 (not in Exon D.B.)
Ingsdon, G. 10	*Ainech-*, *Ainichesdone* 113b, 117 (*Ainechesdona* 460 *bis*)
Instaple, B. 6	*Essastaple* 110 (*Esas-*, *Esestapla* 399, 496b)
Instow, D. 4	*Johannestou* 112b (*-sto* 390b)
Inwardleigh, E. 7	*Lege* 106 (*Lega* 291b)
Iplepene (*-pena*)	See Ipplepen
Ipplepen, H. 11	*Iplepene* 113b (*-pena* 462, 462b)
Irishcombe, G. 5	*Eruescome* 101b (*-coma* 109b)
Ivelie (*-leia*), J. 7	Lost in Broad Clyst, 117b (469)
Iweslei	See Iddesleigh
Iwis	See Huish (near Dolton)
Jacobescherche (*-cherca*)	See St James's Church
Jacobstowe	Not in D.B.
Johannestou (*-sto*)	See Instow
(*Kagefort*)	See Chagford
*Kari**	See Downacarey
Kelly, C. 9	*Chenleie* 106 (*-leia* 289b)
Kenn, I. 9	*Chent* 105b, 106b (*297, 315)
Kennerleigh	Not in D.B.
Kentisbeare, J. 6	*Chentesbere* 107 *bis* (*-bera* 303 *bis*)
Kentisbury, E. 2	*Chentesberie* 107 (*-beria* 299b)
Kenton, I. 9	*Chentone* 100b (*-tona* 94b)
Kersford, D. 9	Unnamed, held with Bridestowe 105b (*Cars-*,

Kersford cont.	*Casforda* 289, 495)
Kerswell (in Broadhembury), J. 6	*Carsewelle* 113b (*-euilla* 458b)
Kerswell (in Hockworthy), J. 5	*Cressewalde* 111b (*-walla* 346)
Keynedon, G. 14	*Chenigedone* 114b (*Chenighedona*, *-inghedona* 343b, 504)
Kidwell, J. 5	*Cadewile* 112 (*-wila* 393, *Chadewilla* 502b)
Killington, F. 2	*Cheneoltone* 102b (*-tona* 127)
Kilmington, L. 7	*Chenemetone* 101 (*Chienemetona* 97)
Kimber, D. 7	*Chempebere* 115 (*Chiempabera* 412, 496)
Kimworthy, B. 6	*Chemeworde* 103 (*-worda* 122)
Kingsbridge	Not in D.B.
Kingsford, J. 6	*Chinnesford* 107 (*-fort* 303)
Kingsheanton, E. 3	*Hagintone* 102b (*-tona* 126)
Kingskerswell, H. 11	*Carsewelle* 100b (*-willa* 85)
King's Nympton, F. 5	*Nimetone* 101 (*-tona* 98, 502)
King's Tamerton, C. 12	*Tanbretone* 100b (*-tona* 87)
Kingsteignton, H. 10	*Teintone* 100 (*-tona* 84)
Kingston	Not in D.B.
Kingswear	Not in D.B.
(*Kluperiga*)	See Lupridge
Knowstone, H. 4	*Chenudestane* 118b *bis* (*Chenutdestana* 487 *bis*) *Chenuestan* 111b *bis* (*346b *bis*)
Labere (*-bera*)	See Essebeer
(*Lachebroc*)	See Lashbrook
Lacome	See Lank Combe
*Laierda**	See Yard (in Ilfracombe)
Laira Green, D. 12	*Leuricestone* 109b (*Lieurichestona* 328)
Lambert, G. 8	*Lanford* 117, 118 (*-forda*, *Lantfort* 458, 484)
Lambretone	See Lamerton
Lambside, E. 13	*Lamesete* 109b (*Lammeseta* 327b)
Lamerton, C. 10	*Lambretone* 114b (*Lanbretona* 411)
Lamesete (*Lammeseta*)	See Lambside
(*Lanbretona*)	See Lamerton
*Lanchers**	See Landcross
(*Lancoma*)	See Lank Combe
Landcross, D. 4	*Lanchers* 106b (*294)
Landesherg (*-hers*)	Unid., 104b (286)
Landkey	Not in D.B.
Lanford (*-forda*)	See Lambert
(*Langadona*)	See Langdon
(*Langafort*)	See Langford (in Cullompton)
Langage, E. 12	*Langehewis* 103b (*135b)
Langdon, D. 13	*Langedone* 110 *bis* (*-gadona* 331b, 332)
Langedone	See Langdon
Langeford	See Langford (in Cullompton), Langford (in Ugborough)
(*Langeforda*)	See Langford (in Ugborough)
*Langehewis**	See Langage
Langestan	See Langstone
Langetreu (*-trewa*)	See Langtree
Langford (in Cullompton), J. 7	*Langeford* 107 (*-gafort* 302b)
Langford (in Ugborough), F. 12	*Langeford* 101 (*-forda* 97b)
(*Langhestan*)	See Langstone
Langley formerly Bickingleigh, E. 4	*Bichenelie* 101, 101b (*-leia*, *-lia* 94b, 110, 499)

Langstone, G. 9	*Langestan* 108 (*Langhestan* 311b)
Langtree, C. 5	*Langetreu* 101 (*-trewa* 108b)
(*Laniliner*)	See Landinner, Corn.
Lank Combe, G. 2	*Lacome* 114 (*Lancoma* 337, 499)
*Lanliner**	See Landinner, Corn.
*Lannor**	See Leonard
(*Lantfort*)	See Lambert
Lapford, F. 6	*Slapeford* 101b (*Eslapa-*, *Slapeforda* 109b, 497b)
Larkbeare, J. 7	*Laurochebere* 107, 116 (*-bera* 302, 499b)
Lashbrook, C. 6	*Lochebroc* 106 (*Lachebroc* 291)
Laurochebere (*-bera*)	See Larkbeare
Lege (*Lega*)	See Besley, Challonsleigh, Elfordleigh, Grimpstonleigh, Inwardleigh, Leigh (in Churchstow), Leigh (in Harberton), Leigh (in Loxbeare), Leigh (in Milton Abbot), Leigh (in Modbury), Mariansleigh, Monkleigh, Northleigh
Lei (*Leia*)	See Eastleigh
(*Leiga*)	See Canonsleigh, Mariansleigh
Leige	See Canonsleigh
Leigh (in Churchstow), F. 13	*Lege* 112b (*Lega* 397)
Leigh (in Harberton), G. 12	*Lege* 109 (*Lega* 324)
Leigh (in Loxbeare), H. 5	*Lege* 117b (*Lega* 473)
Leigh (in Milton Abbot), C. 10	*Lege* 103b (*Lega* 177b)
Leigh (in Modbury), F. 13	*Lege* 109b (*Lega* 326)
Leigh (in Silverton), I. 6	*Stochelie* 104b 1st entry (*Estochelia* 214)
Leonard, I. 6	*Lannor* 112 (*395b) *Limor* 117b (*Linor* 461b)
Lestintone	See Ilsington
Leuge (*Leuga*)	See Doddiscombsleigh
*Leuia**	See Northlew
Leuricestone	See Laira Green
(*Leuya*)	See Lewtrenchard
Levelege (*Levaliga*)	See Lowley
Levestone (*-tona*)	See Lympstone
Lewe	See Lewtrenchard
Lewendone (*-dona*)	See Lowton
Lewtrenchard, C. 9	*Lewe* 106 (*Leuya* 289, 495)
(*Liclemora*)	See *Lidemore*
Liddaton, C. 9	*Lidel-*, *Liteltone* 103b *bis* (*Lideltona* 177b *bis*)
Lideford, *-forde* (*-forda*, *-fort*)	See Lydford
Lideltone (*-tona*)	See Liddaton
Lidemore (*Liclemora*)	Unid., 109 (319)
Liege (*Liega*)	See Mariansleigh, Rashleigh
(*Lieurichestona*)	See Laira Green
Lifton, C. 9	*Listone* 100b (*-tona* 93, 495b, 496)
*Lim**	See Uplyme
*Limet**	See George Nympton; Nymet, Broadnymet etc.; Nymet Rowland
Limete (*Limeta*)	See Nymet, Broadnymet etc.; Nymet Rowland

Limor	See Leonard
(*Lina*)	See Lyn
(*Lincoma*)	See Lincombe
Lincombe, D. 2	*Lincome* 107 (*-coma* 301, 499b)
Lincome	See Lincombe
Line	See Lyn
(*Linor*)	See Leonard
Lintone (*-tona*)	See Lynton
Lipson, D. 12	*Lisistone* 105b (*-tona* 222, *Lisitona* 505b)
Lisistone (*-tona*, *Lisitona*)	See Lipson
Listone (*-tona*)	See Lifton
*Liteham**	See Littleham (near Bideford), Littleham (near Exmouth)
Litel Racheneford (*-forda*)	See Little Rackenford
Liteltone	See Liddaton
Liteltorelande (*-trorilanda*)	See Woodland
Litelwere (*-wera*)	See Little Weare
Little Bovey, H. 10	*Adonebovi* 102 (*135b)
Little Bray	See Bray
Littleham (near Bideford), C. 4	*Liteham* 101 (*108b)
Littleham (near Exmouth), J. 9	*Liteham* 104 (*184)
Little Hempston	See Broadhempston
Littleland, H. 6	*Loteland* 112b (*-landa* 394)
Little Marland	See Marland
Little Rackenford, H. 5	*Litel Racheneford* 111b (*-forda* 347)
Little Torrington, D. 5	*Torintone*, *Toritone* 100b, 106 (*-tona* 94, 293)
Little Weare, D. 4	*Litelwere* 116b (*-wera* 376b)
*Loba**	See Lobb
Lobb, D. 3	*Loba*, *Lobe* 107, 115 (*Loba* 300b, 414)

Lobe	See Lobb
*Lochebroc**	See Lashbrook
Lochesbere (*-bera*)	See Loxbeare
Locheshore, *-sore* (*Lochesora*, *-ssora*)	See Loxhore
Lochetone (*-tona*)	See Lupton
Lochetore (*-tora*)	See Loughtor
Loddiswell, F. 13	*Lodeswille* 109 (*-willa* 321)
Lodebroc	See Ludbrook
Lodeswille (*-willa*)	See Loddiswell
(*Lodrebroc*)	See Ludbrook
Lollardesdone, *-estone* (*-esdona*)	See Loosedon
Longcombe, H. 12	*Cumbe* 109 1st entry (*Comba* 320 1st entry)
Lonmele, *-mine* (*-mela*, *-mina*, *Lonnela*)	See Chieflowman
Loosebeare, F. 6	*Losbere* 104 (*-bera* 194)
Loosedon, E. 6	*Lollardesdone*, *-estone* 112b *bis* (*-esdona* 389, 390, 498)
*Loperige**	See Lupridge
Losbere (*-bera*)	See Loosebeare
Loscume (*-cumma*)	See Luscombe
Loteland (*-landa*)	See Littleland
Loughtor, D. 12	*Lochetore* 110 (*-tora* 333)
Lovacott, C. 6	*Lovecote* 115 (*-cota* 413b)
*Lovapit**	See Luppitt
Lovecote (*-cota*)	See Lovacott
Lovenetorne (*-torna*)	See Loventor
Loventor, H. 11	*Lovenetorne* 109 (*-torna* 320b)
Lower Credy, H. 7	*Credie*, *Cridie* 103, 114b *bis* (*Creda*, *Cridia* 132b, 340, 340b, 506)
Lowley, H. 8	*Levelege* 117 (*Levaliga* 468b)
Lowton, G. 8	*Lewendone* 117 (*-dona* 472, 502)

Loxbeare, H. 5	*Lochesbere* 103 (*-bera* 134b)
Loxhore, E. 3	*Locheshore*, *-sore* 106b *bis* (*-sora*, *-ssora* 298, 298b)
Ludbrook, F. 12	*Lodebroc* 104b, 105b (*219, 219b, *Lodrebroc* 505) *Ludebroch* 100b (*-broca* 85b, 504b)
Ludebroch (*-broca*)	See Ludbrook
Luffincott	Not in D.B.
Luperige (*-riga*)	See Lupridge
Luppitt, K. 6	*Lovapit* 112 (*348)
Lupridge, F. 12	*Loperige* 104b (*219b, *Olperiga* 505) *Luperige* 112b, 113 (*-riga* 397, *Kluperiga* 397)
Lupton, H. 12	*Lochetone* 109 (*-tona* 320b)
Luscombe, G. 11	*Loscume* 111 (*-cumma* 368b)
Lustleigh	Not in D.B.
Lydford, D. 9	*Lideford*, *-forde*, *Tideford* 100 *bis*, 108b, 114 (*Lideforda*, *-fort* 87b, 88, 334, 335)
Lympstone, I. 9	*Levestone* 113 (*-tona* 460)
Lyn, F. 2	*Line* 110b *bis* (*Lina* 402, 499)
Lynton, F. 1	*Lintone* 110b (*-tona* 402, 498b)
(*Maaberia*)	See Membury
Macheswelle	Unid., 115 (not in Exon D.B.)
Madescame (*-cama*)	Unid., 110b (404, 501b)
Madford (*-fort*)	See Matford
Madone (*-dona*)	See Meddon
Magnelege (*-lega*)	See Manley
Magnetone (*-tona*)	Unid., 108 (312b)
Maiberie	See Membury
Maidencombe, I. 11	*Medenecome* 107b (*-coma* 306b)

(*Malacota*)	See Mullacott
Malborough	Not in D.B.
Malston, G. 13	*Mellestone* 109b (*-tona* 325)
Mameorde (*-orda*)	See Wembworthy
Mamhead, I. 9	*Mammeheua* 106b (*-hetua* 297b) *Manneheua* 118b (*490)
Mammehua (*-hetua*)	See Mamhead
Manadon, D. 12	*Manedone* 109b (*-dona* 328b)
Manaton, G. 9	*Manitone* 118 (*-tona* 488b)
Maneberie (*Manberia*)	See Membury
Manedone (*-dona*)	See Manadon
Manelie (*-lia*)	See Manley
Manitone (*-tona*)	See Manaton
Manley, I. 6	*Magnelege* 113 (*-lega* 394b) *Manelie* 117 (*-lia* 459)
*Manneheua**	See Mamhead
Mariansleigh and Romansleigh, F. 5, G. 5	*Lege*, *Liege* 103b, 117b (*Leiga*, *Liega* 179b, 475b)
Marland, Little and Peters, D. 6	*Mer-*, *Mirland* 115, 115b (*-landa* 407b, 413)
Marldon	Not in D.B.
Martin, F. 8	*Mertone* 107b (*-tona* 305)
Martinhoe, F. 2	*Matingeho* 102b (*125)
Marwood, D. 3	*Merehode* 115b (*-hoda* 408b) *Mereude* 113 (*-uda* 420) *Merode* 107 (*-oda* 301b)
Marystowe	Not in D.B.
Marytavy, D. 9	*Tavi* 108b (*317b, 495)
Matford, I. 8	*Madford* 105 (*-fort* 212b) *Matford* 110 (*-forda* 401)

Matford (-forda)	See Matford
*Matingeho**	See Martinhoe
*Mauessart**	See Meshaw
Meavy, D. 11	*Mewi* 109b *quater* (*329b *quater*)
*Meda**	See Meeth
Meddon, A. 5	*Madone* 118 (*-dona* 482)
Medenecome (-coma)	See Maidencombe
Medland, G. 8	*Mideland* 118 (*-landa* 484b)
Meeth, D. 6	*Meda* 106b (*294)
Melbury, D. 8	*Meleberie* 111 (*-beria* 415b)
Meleberie (-beria)	See Melbury
Meleford	See Milford (in Stowford)
Meleforde (-forda)	See Milford (in Hartland)
(*Melefort*)	See Milford (in Stowford)
*Melewis**	See Melhuish
Melhuish, G. 8	*Melewis* 107b (*305)
Mellestone (-tona)	See Malston
Membland, E. 13	*Mimidlande* 109b (*-landa* 327b)
Membury, L. 7	*Maiberie* 110b (*Maaberia* 405b) *Maneberie* 100 (*Manberia* 84, 503b)
Merehode (-hoda)	See Marwood
Mereude (-uda)	See Marwood
Merland (-landa)	See Marland
Merode (-oda)	See Marwood
Merton, D. 6	*Mertone* 102 (*-tona* 123)
Mertone (-tona)	See Martin, Merton
Meshaw, G. 5	*Mauessart* 108 (*309b)
(*Metcoma*)	See Metcombe
Metcombe, D. 3	*Metcome* 102b (*-coma* 126)
Metcome	See Metcombe
Metwi	Unid., 113b (not in Exon D.B.)
*Mewi**	See Meavy
Middeltone	See Middleton, Milton Abbot
Middlecott (in Broadwood Kelly), E. 6	*Mildecote*, *Mildelcote* 106 *bis* (*Mildelcota* 292b *bis*)
Middlecott (in Chagford), F. 9	*Midelcote* 118b (*-cota* 483b)
Middleton, F. 2	*Middeltone* 102b (*Mideltona* 129)
Middlewick, G. 5	*Wiche* 103 (*Wica*, *Wicca* 134, 506)
Middle Yeo	See Nymet, Broadnymet etc.
Mideland (-landa)	See Medland
Midelcote (-cota)	See Middlecott (in Chagford)
(*Mideltona*)	See Middleton, Milton Abbot, Milton Damerel
Mideltone	See Milton Damerel, South Milton
Milchewis	See Mowlish
Mildecote	See Middlecott (in Broadwood Kelly)
Mildedone (-dona)	See Mildon
Mildelcote (-cota)	See Middlecott (in Broadwood Kelly)
(*Mildeltona*)	See Milton Abbot
Mildon, H. 5	*Mildedone* 110b (*-dona* 404b, 502)
(*Milehyuis*)	See Mowlish
Milford (in Hartland), A. 5	*Meleforde* 115 (*-forda* 407)
Milford (in Stowford), C. 9	*Meleford* 103 (*-fort* 121b)
(*Miltitona*)	See South Milton
Milton Abbot, C. 9	*Middeltone* 103b (*Midel-*, *Mildeltona* 177b, 495b)
Milton Damerel, C. 6	*Mideltone* 113 (*-tona* 419)
Mimidlande (-landa)	See Membland

Mirland (*-landa*)	See Marland
Mochelesberie (*-beria*)	See Muxbere
Mockham, F. 3	*Mogescome* 106b (*-coma* 299)
Modbury, F. 13	*Mortberie* 105 (*Motberia* 221, 505) *Motbilie* 105b (*-lia* 217b)
Modlei (*-leia*)	See Mutley
Mogescome (*-coma*)	See Mockham
Mohun's Ottery	See Ottery, Mohun's etc.
Molecote (*Molacota*)	See Mullacott
Molland (in North Molton), F. 3	*Molland* 115b (*-landa* 409)
Molland (in West Anstey), G. 4	*Mollande* 101, 103 (*-landa* 95 *bis*, 130b, 499, 499b *bis*)
Molland, *-lande* (*-landa*)	See Molland (in North Molton), Molland (in West Anstey)
(*Monacochamentona*)	See Monk Okehampton
Monkleigh, C. 5	*Lege* 104b (*Lega* 210)
Monk Okehampton, E. 6	*Monuchementone* 106 (*Monacochamentona* 290b)
Monkton	Not in D.B.
Monuchementone	See Monk Okehampton
Moor, C. 8	*More* 108b (*Mora* 317)
(*Mora*)	See Moor
Morbade (*-batha*)	See Morebath
Morceth (*-cet*, *-ceta*)	See Cruwys Morchard
Morchard Bishop, G. 6	*Morchet* 101b (*110)
*Morchet**	See Cruwys Morchard, Morchard Bishop
More	See Moor
Morebath, I. 4	*Morbade* 101 (*-batha* 95)
Moreleigh, G. 13	*Morlei* 116 (*Morleia* 504b)
Moretonhampstead, G. 9	*Mortone* 101 *bis* (*-tona* 96)
Morlei (*-leia*)	See Moreleigh, Murley
Mortberie	See Modbury
(*Morteho*)	See Mortehoe
Mortehoe, C. 2	*Mortehou* 113b (*-ho* 458)
Mortehou	See Mortehoe
Mortone (*-tona*)	See Moretonhampstead
Motbilie (*-lia*, *Motberia*)	See Modbury
Mowlish, I. 9	*Milchewis* 118b (*Milehyuis* 490)
Mullacott, D. 2	*Molecote* 117 (*Molacota* 469, 498b)
Murley, J. 5	*Morlei* 112 (*-leia* 393b)
Musberie (*-beria*)	See Musbury
Musbury, L. 8	*Musberie* 108 (*-beria* 313)
Mutley, D. 12	*Modlei* 109b *bis* (*-leia* 328 *bis*)
Muxbere, J. 6	*Mochelesberie* 116 (*-beria* 461, 502b)
Natson	See Nymet, Broadnymet etc.
Natsworthy, F. 9	*Noteswrde* 113b (not in Exon D.B.)
Neadon, G. 9	*Benedone* 108 (*Beneadona* 312)
Nether Exe, I. 7	*Niresse* 103 (*-essa* 132)
Netherton, K. 8	*Bere* 112 (*Bera* 395b)
Neutone (*Neuetona*)	See Newton (in Chittlehampton)
(*Newentona*)	See Newton (in Zeal Monachorum), Newton St Cyres, Newton Tracey

Newentone	See Newton (in Zeal Monachorum), Newton Tracey
Newetone	See Newton St Petrock
Newton (in Chittlehampton), F. 4	*Neutone* 107 (*Neuetona* 300b)
Newton (in Zeal Monachorum), F. 7	*Newentone* 117 (*-tona* 468) *Niwetone* 112b (*Niuetona* 389b)
Newton Ferrers, D. 13	*Niwetone* 105 (*-tona* 218b)
Newton St Cyres, H. 7	*Niwetone* 101b, 118 (*Newen-*, *Niwentona* 117, 483)
Newton St Petrock, C. 6	*Newetone* 117b (*Nietona* 483)
Newton Tracey, D. 4	*Newentone* 112b (*-tona* 388b)
Nichol's Nymet	See Nymet, Broadnymet etc.
(*Nietona*)	See Newton St Petrock
Nimet	See Nymet, Broadnymet etc.
(*Nimet*)	See George Nympton; Nymet, Broadnymet etc.
Nimete (*Nimeta*)	See George Nympton
(*Nimeth*)	See Nymet, Broadnymet etc.
Nimetone (*-tona*)	See Bishop's Nympton, King's Nympton
Niresse (*-essa*)	See Nether Exe
Nistenestoch (*-stoc*)	See Stoke St Nectan
(*Niuetona*)	See Newton (in Zeal Monachorum)
(*Niwentona*)	See Newton St Cyres
(*Niwetona*)	See Newton Ferrers

Niwetone	See Newton (in Zeal Monachorum), Newton Ferrers, Newton St Cyres
Nochecote (*-cota*)	Unid., 117 (459b)
Norcote (*-cota*)	See Northcote
Northam, C. 4	*Northam* 104 (*194)
North Bovey, G. 9	*Bovi* 109 (*320)
North Buckland	See Buckland (in Braunton)
Northcote, E. 2	*Norcote* 102b *bis* (*-cota* 128b, 129)
Northcott	Not in D.B.
North Huish, F. 12	*Hewis* 104b (*220b, 505)
Northleigh, Southleigh and Brimley, K. 7, L. 8	*Lege* 104b, 111, 117b (*Lega* 217, 405b, 473, 503)
Northlew, D. 7	*Leuia* 101 (*108)
North Molton, G. 4	*Nortmoltone* 100b (*-tona* 94b)
North Petherwin	Not in D.B.
North Pool	See Pool
North Tawton, F. 7	*Taue-*, *Tawetone* 100, 106b (*-tona* 83, 296b)
Northwick, C. 6	*Wiche* 118 (*Wica* 481)
Nortmoltone (*-tona*)	See North Molton
Norton (in Broadwood-widger), C. 8	*Nortone* 108b (*-tona* 316b)
Norton (in Churchstow), F. 13	*Notone* 104 (*-tona* 183)
Nortone (*-tona*)	See Norton (in Broadwood-widger)
Noteswille (*-willa*)	See Nutwell
Noteswrde	See Natsworthy
Notone (*-tona*)	See Norton (in Churchstow)
Nutwell, I. 9	*Noteswille* 118 (*-willa* 487b)
Nymet, Broadnymet, Nichol's Nymet,	*Limet*, *Limete* 102b, 103b, 106b *ter*, 118 (*Limet*,

Nymet cont. Nymet Tracey, Burston, Hampson, Middle Yeo, Natson, Walson and Zeal Monachorum, F. 7	*Limeta* 125, 182, 295b, 296, 296b, 483) *Nimet* 112b *ter* (*389b *bis*, 390b, *Nimeth* 498)
Nymet Rowland, F. 6	*Limet* 106b (*295)
Nymet Tracey	See Nymet, Broadnymet etc.
Oak, D. 7	*Acha* 106 (*291b)
Oakford, H. 5	*Alforde* 110b (-*forda* 404, 502)
Ochementone	See Okehampton
Ocheneberie (-*beria*)	See Okenbury
(*Ochenemitona*)	See Okehampton
Odeburne (-*borna*)	See Woodburn
Odeford (-*forda*)	See Woodford
Odehiwis	See Woodhuish
Odelie (-*lea*)	See Woodleigh
*Odeordi**	See Adworthy
Odesclive (-*cliva*)	See Undercleave
*Odetreu** (-*trewa*)	See Ottery (in Lamerton)
(*Offawilla*)	See Offwell
Offecome (-*coma*)	See Uffcumbe
Offewille	See Offwell
Offwell, L. 7	*Offewille* 108b (*Offawilla* 314)
Ogewille (*Oghawilla*)	See Ogwell
Ogwell, East and West, G. 11, H. 11	*Ogewille* 114 *bis* (*Oghawilla* 339 *bis*) *Wogewille*, *Wogwel* 117, 118 (*Wogewil*, *Woguwel* 470b, 484b)
Okehampton, E. 8	*Ochementone* 105b (*Ochenemitona* 288)
Okenbury, E. 13	*Ocheneberie* 109b (-*beria* 327)
Oladone (-*dona*)	See Woolladon
Oldridge, H. 8	*Walderige* 107b (*305b)

Olecumbe	See Owlacombe
(*Olfaldeshodes*)	See Woolfardisworthy (near Witheridge)
(*Olfereordi*)	See Woolfardisworthy (near Hartland)
(*Olperiga*)	See Lupridge
(*Olpessa*)	See Up Exc
(*Oluardesdona*)	See Woolfin
Olurintone (-*tona*, *Oluridintona*)	See Worlington, East and West
(*Olveberia*)	See Wolborough
(*Olveleia*)	See Woolley
(*Olvelia*)	See Woolleigh
Olvereword	See Woolfardisworthy (near Hartland)
(*Olvietetona*)	See Wollaton
(*Olwritona*)	See Werrington
Opecote (-*cota*)	See Upcott
Oplomie (-*ia*)	See Uplowman
Oppelaume (*Oppaluma*)	See Uplowman
Orcartone (-*tona*)	See Orcheton
Orcheton, E. 13	*Orcartone* 105b (-*tona* 217b)
Ordie (-*ia*)	See Worthy
Ordihelle (-*hella*)	See Worthele
Orescome (-*coma*, -*comma*, -*comme*)	See Buckerell
Orrewai (*Orrawia*)	See Orway
Orway, J. 6	*Orrewai* 115b (*Orrawia* 371)
(*Oteri*)	See Rapshays, Waringstone
Otrei	See Ottery St Mary, Waringstone
Otri	See Hembury Fort; Ottery, Mohun's etc.; Rapshays; Waringstone
(*Otri*)	See Hembury Fort; Ottery, Mohun's etc.; Ottery St Mary
(*Otria*)	See Hembury Fort, Waringstone

*Otrit**	See Dotton
Otritone (*-tona*)	See Otterton
Otterton, J. 9	*Otritone* 104 (*-tona* 194b)
Ottery, Mohun's; Upottery; Combe Raleigh, K. 7, L. 6	*Otri* 112 *bis*, 114b (*342b, 348, 348b)
Ottery (in Lamerton), C. 10	*Odetreu* 113 (*419, *-trewa* 495)
Ottery St Mary, J. 8	*Otrei* 104 (*Otri* 195)
Oueltone	See Dolton
Oussaborough, D. 2	*Aseberge* 115b (*Asaberga* 408b)
Owlacombe, E. 5	*Olecumbe* 115b (*Ulacumba* 407b)
Paignton, H. 12	*Peintone* 102 (*-tona* 119)
Pancrasweek	Not in D.B.
*Panestan**	See Panson
Panson, B. 8	*Panestan* 114b (*411b, 497)
Pantesford (*-fort*)	See Ponsford
Paorde (*-orda*)	See Pyworthy
Parford, F. 8	*Patford* 116b (*-forda* 456, 496)
Parkham, C. 5	*Percheham* 106, 118 (*293, 293b, 483)
Parracombe, F. 2	*Pedrecumbe* 111 (*Pedracomba* 366)
Patchole, E. 2	*Patsole* 102b (*-sola* 127)
Patcott, I. 6	*Petecote* 108 (*-cota* 309)
Patford (*-forda*)	See Parford
Patsole (*-sola*)	See Patchole
Payhembury	See Broadhembury
Peadhill, I. 5	*Pedehel* 103 (*-hael* 134b)
Peamore, H. 8	*Peumere* 114 (*-mera* 336b)
*Pech**	See Peek (in Luffincott), Peek (in Ugborough)
Pedehel (*-hael*)	See Peadhill
(*Pedicchesw ella*)	See Pickwell
Pedley, G. 6	*Pidelige* 111 *bis* (*Peideliga*, *Pidaliga*, *Piedelege* 416, 416b, 502)
Pedrecumbe (*Pedracomba*)	See Parracombe
Peek (in Luffincott), B. 8	*Pech* 115 (*412, 496)
Peek (in Ugborough), F. 12	*Pech* 105b (*219)
(*Peideliga*)	See Pedley
Peintone (*-tona*)	See Paignton
*Percheham**	See Parkham
Petecote (*-cota*)	See Patcott
Peters Marland	See Marland
Petertavy, D. 10	*Tawi* 116 (not in Exon D.B.)
Pethill, D. 12	*Pidehel* 110 (*332b)
Petrochestou (*-cestoua*)	See Petrockstow
Petrockstow, D. 6	*Petrochestou* 103b (*Petrocestoua* 182)
Peumere (*-mera*)	See Peamore
Picaltone (*-tona*)	See Bickleton
Pickwell, C. 2	*Wedicheswelle* 102b (*Pedicchesw ella* 127b)
(*Pidaliga*)	See Pedley
*Pidehel**	See Pethill
Pidelige (*Piedelega*)	See Pedley
Pilland, D. 3	*Pillande*, *Welland* 102b *bis* (*Pillanda* 125b, 127b)
Pillande (*-landa*)	See Pilland
Pilton, E. 3	*Wiltone* 102b (*Pi[lto]na* 125b)
(*Pi[lto]na*)	See Pilton
Pinhoe, I. 8	*Pinnoch* 101 (*Pinnoc* 95b)
Pinnoch (*Pinnoc*)	See Pinhoe
Pirzwell, J. 6	*Pissewelle* 110b (*-willa* 400)
Pissewelle (*-willa*)	See Pirzwell
Plaistow, E. 3	*Pleistou* 102b (*Pleiestou* 130)
Plantelie (*-leia*, *Plateleia*)	See Praunsley

Pleistou (*Pleiestou*)	See Plaistow
Plemestoch (*-stocha*)	See Plymstock
Plintone (*-tona*)	See Plympton St Mary
*Plumtrei**	See Plymtree
Plymouth	Not in D.B.
Plympton St Mary, D. 12	*Plintone* 100b (*-tona* 86)
Plymstock, D. 13	*Plemestoch* 103b (*-stocha* 180)
Plymtree, J. 7	*Plumtrei* 116b (*378b)
Pocheelle (*-eella*)	See Poughill
Pochehille (*-hilla*)	See Poughill
Podiford (*-forda*)	See West Putford
(*Pola*)	See Pool
*Poldreham**	See Powderham
Pole	See Pool
Polebroch (*-broc*)	See Pullabrook
Polesleuge, *-lewe* (*-leuga*, *-leuia*)	See Polsloe
*Polham**	See Pulham
Polochestone (*-tona*)	See Poulston
Polsloe, I. 8	*Polesleuge*, *-lewe* 103b, 107 (*-leuga*, *-leuia* 135b, 307b)
Poltimore, I. 7	*Pontimore* 107 *bis* (*-mora* 307b, 309, 500b) *Pultimore* 117b (*-mora* 469b, 500)
Ponsford, I. 6	*Pantesford* 107 *bis* (*-fort* 302b *bis*)
Pontimore (*-mora*)	See Poltimore
Pool, North and South, G. 14	*Pole* 109, 112b, 114b (*Pola* 324b, 343b, 396b, 504)
Porlemute (*Porlamuta*)	See West Portlemouth
Porrige (*-iga*)	See Potheridge
(*Potaforda*)	See West Putford
Poteford, *-forde* (*-forda*, *-fort*)	See West Putford
Potheridge, D. 6	*Porrige* 106 (*-iga* 293b)
Potiforde (*-forda*)	See East Putford
Potitone (*-tona*)	See Puddington
Poughill, H. 6	*Pocheelle* 104b (*-eella* 215, 500b) *Pochehille* 115 (*-hilla* 414b)
Poulston, G. 12	*Polochestone* 109 (*-tona* 323)
Powderham, I. 9	*Poldreham* 111b (*457)
Praunsley, G. 4	*Plantelie* 115 (*-leia* 414b, *Plateleia* 499b)
*Prenla**	See East Prawle
Puddington, H. 6	*Potitone* 110b (*-tona* 404b)
Pudeforde (*-forda*)	See West Putford
Pulham, G. 4	*Polham* 115 (*414b, 499b)
Pullabrook, G. 9	*Polebroch* 102 (*-broc* 135b)
Pultimore (*-mora*)	See Poltimore
(*Puteforda*)	See West Putford
Pyworthy, B. 7	*Paorde* 108b (*Paorda* 318b)
Queen Dart, H. 5	*Dertre* 115b (*Dertera* 410)
Rachenefode (*-foda*)	See Rackenford
Rachun	See Rocombe
Rackenford, H. 5	*Rachenefode* 108 (*-foda* 311)
Racome, *-cumbe* (*-coma*, *conba*, *-cum*)	See Rocombe
Raddon (in Marystowe), C. 9	*Ratdone* 108b (*-dona* 316)
Raddon (in Thorverton), I. 7	*Radone*, *Redone* 103b, 117b (*Radona*, *Raddona*, *Reddona* 179b, 475b, 500)
(*Raddona*)	See Raddon (in Thorverton)
Radeclive (*-cliva*)	See Rutleigh
Radehide (*-hida*)	See Roadway
Radelie (*-leia*)	See Raleigh
Radeode (*-euda*)	See Radworthy (in Challacombe)

Radewei	See Rudway
Radish, K. 8	*Redic*, *Redix* 114b *bis* (*Radix*, *Radiʒ*, *Reddix* 343b, 411b, 497)
(*Radix*, *Radiʒ*)	See Radish
Radone (*-dona*)	See Raddon (in Thorverton)
Radworthy (in Challacombe), F. 2	*Radeode* 111 (*-euda* 415)
Radworthy (in North Molton), G. 3	*Raordin* 110b (*402b)
Raleigh, E. 3	*Radelie* 102b (*-leia* 126)
*Raordin**	See Radworthy (in North Molton)
Rapshays, K. 7	*Otri* 110b, 114 (*Oteri* 340, 403b)
Rashleigh, F. 6	*Liege* 106b (*Liega* 295)
Ratdone (*-dona*)	See Raddon (in Marystowe), West Raddon
*Ratreu**	See Rattery
Rattery, G. 12	*Ratreu* 111 (*368)
Raweberge (*-berga*)	See Roborough
Rawridge, L. 6	*Rouerige* 100 (*84b, 503b) *Rourige* 104 (*195)
(*Reddix*)	See Radish
(*Reddona*)	See Raddon (in Thorverton)
Redic, *Redix*	See Radish
Redone	See Raddon (in Thorverton)
Reimore (*-mora*)	See Ringmore (near Bigbury)
Restone (*-tona*)	See Rifton
(*Reuwa*)	See Rewe
Revelstoke	Not in D.B.
Rewe	See Rewe
Rewe, I. 7	*Rewe* 103 (*Reuwa* 131b)
Riddlecombe, E. 5	*Ridelcome* 112b (*-coma* 389)
Ridelcome (*-coma*)	See Riddlecombe
Rifton, H. 5	*Restone* 115b (*-tona* 410, 501b)
(*Righendona*)	See Ringdon (in West Anstey)
Rinestanedone (*-dona*)	See Ruston
Ringdon (in George Nympton), F. 4	*Ringedone* 100 (*-dona* 83b, *Ringhedona* 499b)
Ringdon (in West Anstey), H. 4	*Ringedone* 107 (*Righendona*, *Ringhendona* 300, 499b)
(*Ringedona*)	See Ringdon (in George Nympton)
Ringedone	See Ringdon (in George Nympton), Ringdon (in West Anstey)
(*Ringhedona*)	See Ringdon (in George Nympton)
(*Ringhendona*)	See Ringdon (in West Anstey)
Ringmore (near Bigbury), F. 13	*Reimore* 109b (*-mora* 327)
Ringmore (in St Nicholas), I. 10	*Rumor* 107b (*304b)
Risford (*-fort*)	See Rushford
Roadway, D. 2	*Radehide* 113b (*-hida* 457b)
Roborough, E. 5	*Raweberge* 102 (*-berga* 124b, 500)
Rochebere (*-bera*, *Rocebera*)	See Rockbeare
Rockbeare, J. 8	*Rochebere* 104b, 107b *bis*, 108 (*Roce-*, *Rochebera* 216, 308, 308b, 309, 501)
Rocombe, H. 11	*Rachun* 117 (*Racum* 470b) *Racome* 107b (*Racoma* 307) *Racumbe* 110b (*Raconba* 403)
Rodelie (*-leia*)	See Rowley
Romansleigh	See Mariansleigh
Rose Ash, G. 5	*Aisse* 108 (*Aissa* 310)
Rouecome (*-coma*)	See Ruckham

*Rouerige**, *Rourige**	See Rawridge
Rousdon and Down Ralph, K. 3	*Done*, *Dune* 118 *bis* (*Dona*, *Duna* 489 *bis*)
Rowley, F. 2	*Rodelie* 103 (*-leia* 131)
Ruckham, H. 6	*Rouecome* 117b (*-coma* 471b)
Rudway, I. 7	*Radewei* 116 (not in Exon D.B.)
*Rumor**	See Ringmore (in St Nicholas)
Rushford, F. 8	*Risford* 107b (*-fort* 305)
Ruston, G. 6	*Rinestanedone* 103b (*-dona* 134b)
Rutleigh, D. 7	*Radeclive* 115 (*-cliva* 412, 496)
St Giles in the Wood	Not in D.B.
St Giles on the Heath	Not in D.B.
St James's Church, I. 8	*Jacobescherche* 118b (*-cherca* 487)
St Mary Church, H. 11	*Ecclesia Sanctae Mariae* 101b (*120) *Sanctae Mariae Cerce* 105 (*– – Cherche* 216b)
Salcombe	Not in D.B.
Salcombe Regis, K. 8	*Selcome* 102 (*-coma* 118b)
Sampford Courtenay, E. 7	*Sanford* 106 (*-fort* 290)
Sampford Peverell, J. 6	*Sanforde* 113 (*-forda* 460b)
Sampford Spiney, D. 10	*Sanford* 111b (*-forda* 417b)
Sanctae Mariae Cerce (*– – Cherche*)	See St Mary Church
Sancti Petri de Plintone	See Sutton Prior
Sandford	Not in D.B.
Sanford	See Sampford Courtenay, Sampford Spiney
(*Sanforda*)	See Sampford Peverell, Sampford Spiney
Sanforde	See Sampford Peverell
(*Sanfort*)	See Sampford Courtenay
Santone (*-tona*)	See Saunton
Saterlei (*-leia*)	See Satterleigh
Satterleigh, F. 5	*Saterlei* 117 (*-leia* 469)
Saunton, C. 3	*Santone* 115b (*-tona* 408)
Scabatore (*-tora*)	See Scobitor
Scage	See Shaugh Prior
Scapelie	See Shapley (in Chagford), Shapley (in North Bovey)
Schipebroc	See Shobrooke (in Morchard Bishop)
Scobecome (*Scobacoma*)	See Shapcombe
Scobitor, F. 10	*Scabatore* 102 (*-tora* 135b)
Seaton, L. 8	*Flueta* 104 (*Fluta* 184)
Sedborough, B. 5	*Sedeborge* 118 *bis* (*-borga* 482b, 483) *Seteberge* 106 (*Setleberga* 293b)
Sedeborge (*-borga*)	See Sedborough
Sedemude (*-muda*)	See Sidmouth
*Selac**	See Sellake
Selcome (*-coma*)	See Salcombe Regis
Selineforde (*-forda*)	See Shillingford
Sellake, I. 6	*Selac* 108 (*312b)
*Selvestan**	See Shilstone
Sepesberie (*-beria*)	See Shebbear
Seteberge (*Setleberga*)	See Sedborough
Shapcombe, K. 7	*Cobecume* 116b (*Scobacoma* 378, 500) *Scobecome* 112 (*Escobecoma* 348b, 503b)

Shapley (in Chagford), F. 9	*Scapelie* 106b *ter* (*Escapeleia* 297b *ter*)
Shapley (in North Bovey), F. 9	*Essaple* 118b (*-apla* 488) *Scapelie* 117 (*Escapeleia* 456, 496)
Shaugh Prior, D. 11	*Scage* 110 *bis* (*Escaga* 332b *bis*)
Shebbear, C. 6	*Sepesberie* 101 (*-beria* 94)
Sheepstor	Not in D.B.
Sheepwash	Not in D.B.
Sheldon, K. 6	*Sildene* 114 (*-denna* 337b)
Sherberton, F. 10	*Aiserstone* 104 (*Haiserstona* 182b)
Sherford (in Brixton), D. 12	*Sireford* 109b (*-fort* 329b)
Sherford (near Kingsbridge), G. 13	*Sireford* 100b (*-forda*, *-fort* 97b, 503b)
Shillingford, H. 8	*Esselingeforde* 117b (*-aforda* 468b) *Selingeforde* 110 (*-forda* 399b)
Shilston, F. 12	*Silvestene* 105b (*Silfestana* 220b)
Shilstone, F. 8	*Selvestan* 116b (*458, 500)
Shiphay Collaton, H. 11	*Coletone* 109 (*-tona* 320b)
Shirwell, E. 3	*Ascerewelle* 106b (*Aiscirewilla* 298) *Sirewelle* 111, 116b (*-willa* 377, 415)
Shobrooke (near Crediton), H. 7	*Sotebroch* 104b (*-broca* 215b)
Shobrooke (in Morchard Bishop), G. 7	*Schipebroc* 112b (*Eschipabroca*, *-pebrocha* 391, 498)
Shute	Not in D.B.
Shyttenbrook, I. 8	(*Sotrebroc* 459) not in Exch. D.B.
Sidbury, K. 8	*Sideberie* 102 (*-beria* 118b, 506)
Sideberie (*-beria*)	See Sidbury
*Sideham**	See Sydeham
*Sidelham**	See Sydenham Damerel
*Sidreham**	See Sydenham (in Marystowe), Sydenham Damerel
Sidmouth, K. 8	*Sedemude* 104 (*-muda* 195)
Sigeford (*-forda*)	See Sigford
Sigford, G. 10	*Sigeford* 115 (*-forda* 414b)
Sildene (*-denna*)	See Sheldon
(*Silfestana*)	See Shilston
Silverton, I. 7	*Sulfretone* 100 (*-tona* 83b, *Suffertona* 501b)
Silvestene	See Shilston
Siredone (*-dona*)	See Skerraton
Sireford (*-forda*, *-fort*)	See Sherford (in Brixton), Sherford (near Kingsbridge)
Sirewelle (*-willa*)	See Shirwell
Skerraton, F. 11	*Siredone* 118b (*-dona* 489b)
Sladone (*-dona*)	See Slapton
Slapeford (*-forda*)	See Lapton
Slapton, G. 13	*Sladone* 102 (*-dona* 120b)
Smallicombe, L. 7	*Smelecome* 108b (*Hesmalacoma* 313b)
Smallridge, K. 2	*Smarige*, *Smaurige* 100, 114b (*Esmarige*, *Esmaurige* 84b, 343, 503b)
Smarige, *Smaurige*	See Smallridge
Smelecome	See Smallicombe
Smidelie	See Snydles
Smitheham	See Smytham
Smytham, D. 5	*Smitheham* 104b (*Esmite-*, *Esmitteham* 211b, 497b)
Snydles, F. 5	*Smidelie* 107 (*Esnideleia* 302)

Soar, F. 14	*Sure* 109 (*Sura* 322b)
Sorley, F. 13	*Surlei* 109 (*-leia* 323)
Sotebroch (*-broca*)	See Shobrooke (near Crediton)
(*Sotrebroc*)	See Shyttenbrook
Sourton, D. 8	*Surintone* 103 (*-tona* 121)
South Allington, G. 14	*Alintone* 109 (*-tona* 324b)
South Bray, F. 4	*Brai* 118 (*Braia* 483b)
South Brent, F. 12	*Brenta*, *Brente* 104 *bis* (*Brenta* 183b *bis*)
Southbrook, G. 9	*Sutreworde* 111b (*-worda* 347)
South Huish, F. 14	*Hewis* 109 *bis* (*323b, *Heuis* 322)
Southleigh	See Northleigh
South Milton, F. 14	*Mideltone* 116 (*Miltitona* 504b)
South Molton, F. 4	*Sudmoltone* 100, 104 (*Sut Moltona* 83b, 194b, 499b)
South Pool	See Pool
South Tawton, F. 8	*Tauestone*, *-etone* 100b, 116b, 117, 117b (*Tauetona* 93, 456 *bis*, 475, 495b, 496 *bis*, 498)
Southweek	See Germansweek
Sovretone	See Staverton
Sowton formerly Clyst Fomison, I. 8	*Clis* 103 (*131b)
Sparkwell, G. 11	*Sperchewelle* 108 (*-willa* 312b)
Speccott, D. 5	*Spececote* 115 (*-cota* 407b)
Spececote (*-cota*)	See Speccott
Sperchewelle (*-willa*)	See Sparkwell
Spicewite	See Spitchwick
Spitchwick, F. 10	*Spicewite* 101 (*Espicewita* 97)
Spreacombe, D. 2	*Sprecome* 115b (*Esprecoma* 408)
Sprecome	See Spreacombe
Spredelestone	See Spriddlestone
Sprei	See Sprytown
Spreitone	See Spreyton
Sprewe (*Sprewea*)	See Spurway
Spreyton, F. 7	*Spreitone* 107b (*Espreitona* 304)
Spriddlescombe, F. 13	*Combe* 105b (*Comba* 220b)
Spriddlestone, D. 13	*Spredelestone* 105 (*Espredelestona*, *-eletona* 222, 505b)
Sprytown, C. 9	*Sprei* 115b (not in Exon D.B.)
Spurway, H. 5	*Esprewei* 111b (*Espreuweia* 347) *Sprewe* 103 (*Sprewea* 133)
Stadbury, F. 13	*Stotberie* 109b (*-beria* 326b)
Staddiscombe, D. 13	*Stotescome* 109b (*-coma* 330b)
Staddon, D. 13	*Stotdone* 110 (*Estotdona* 331)
(*Stadforda*)	See Stafford
Stafford, E. 6	*Staford* 116 (*-fort* 456b, *Stadforda* 498b)
Staford	See Stafford, Stowford (in Colaton Raleigh), Stowford (near Lifton)
(*Stafort*)	See Stafford
Stallenge, J. 5	*Stanlinȝ* 116b (*378)
(*Stancoma*)	See Stancombe
Stancombe, G. 13	*Stancome* 109b (*-coma* 325)
Stancome	See Stancombe
Standone	See Eastanton
Stanehus	See Stonehouse
Stanlinȝ *	See Stallenge
Stantone	See Churchstanton, Som.
Stapelie	See Staplehill
Staplehill, G. 10	*Stapelie* 117b (*Estapeleia* 472)

Staveford	See Stowford (in West Down)
Staverton, G. 11	*Sovretone* 101b (*Stovretona* 120)
Stedcombe, L. 8	*Stotecome* 108b (*Estotacoma* 313b)
Stoch (*Stoc*)	See Stoke Fleming
(*Stocha*)	See Stoke Canon
Stoche	See Stoke (in Holme), Stoke Canon, Stoke Rivers
Stochelie	See Leigh (in Silverton), Stockleigh (in Highampton), Stockleigh (in Meeth), Stockleigh English, Stockleigh Pomeroy
*Stoches**	See Stoke Damerel, Stokeinteignhead
Stockland, L. 7	*Ertacomestoche* 78 (*-stoca* 44b), Do.
Stockleigh (in Highampton), D. 7	*Stochelie* 104b 2nd entry (*Estocheleia* 210)
Stockleigh (in Meeth), D. 6	*Stochelie* 105 2nd entry, 106 (*Estocheleia*, *-lia* 212, 294)
Stockleigh English, H. 6	*Stochelie* 104b 4th entry, 105 1st entry (*Estocheleia* 215 2nd entry, 215b, 500, 500b)
Stockleigh Pomeroy, H. 7	*Stochelie* 104b 3rd entry, 114 (*Estocheleia* 215 1st entry, 339b, 500b)
Stodlei	See Stoodleigh (near Oakford), Stoodleigh (in West Buckland)
Stoke (in Holne), F. 10	*Stoche* 111 1st entry (*Estocha* 367b)
Stoke Canon, I. 7	*Stoche* 101b (*Stocha* 118)
Stoke Damerel, D. 12	*Stoches* 113 (*421b)
Stoke Fleming, H. 13	*Stoch* 112 (*Stoc* 348b)
Stoke Gabriel	Not in D.B.
Stokeinteignhead, H. 11	*Stoches* 117 (*470b)
Stokenham	Not in D.B.
Stoke Rivers, E. 3	*Stoche* 111 2nd entry (*Estocha* 415)
Stoke St Nectan, A. 4	*Nistenestoch* 117 (*Nistenestoc* 456)
Stollei	See Stoodleigh (near Oakford)
Stonehouse, D. 12	*Stanehus* 113b (not in Exon D.B.)
Stoodleigh (near Oakford), I. 5	*Stodlei* 114b (*Estodleia* 341) *Stollei* 103 (*Estolleia* 133b)
Stoodleigh (in West Buckland), F. 3	*Stodlei* 102b (*Estotleia* 129b) *Stotlege* 111b (*-lega* 345b)
Stotberie (*-beria*)	See Stadbury
Stotdone	See Staddon
Stotecome	See Stedcombe
Stotescome (*-coma*)	See Staddiscombe
Stotlege (*-lega*)	See Stoodleigh (in West Buckland)
(*Stovretona*)	See Staverton
Stowford (in Colaton Raleigh), J. 9	*Staford* 104b (*Estaforda* 286)
Stowford (near Lifton), C. 9	*Staford* 116b (*Estatforda* 376)
Stowford (in West Down), D. 2	*Staveford* 102b (*Estaveforda* 127b)
Strete Raleigh, J. 8	*Estrete* 114b (*-eta* 340b)
Sudmoltone	See South Molton

Sudtone	See Sutton (in Plymouth)
Suetetone (*Suetatona*, *Suetetona*)	See Sutton (in Halberton)
Sufretone (*-tona*, *Suffertona*)	See Silverton
(*Sura*)	See Soar
Suraple (*-apla*)	See Appledore (in Burlescombe)
Sure	See Soar
Surintone (*-tona*)	See Sourton
Surlei (*-leia*)	See Sorley
Sutcombe, B. 6	*Sutecome* 103 (*-coma* 121b)
Sutecome (*-coma*)	See Sutcombe
(*Sut Moltona*)	See South Molton
(*Sutona*)	See Sutton (in Plymouth)
Sutone	See Sutton (in Widworthy)
Sutreworde (*-worda*)	See Southbrook
Sutton (in Halberton), J. 6	*Suetetone* 116 *bis* (*Suetatona*, *Suetetona* 461 *bis*, 502b)
Sutton (in Plymouth), D. 12	*Sudtone* 100b (*Sutona* 86b)
Sutton (in Widworthy), L. 7	*Sutone* 117b (*Sutuna* 476b)
Sutton Prior, D. 12	*Sancti Petri de Plintone* 113b (not in Exon D.B.)
(*Sutuna*)	See Sutton (in Widworthy)
Swimbridge, E. 4	*Birige* 104 (*194b, 498)
Sydeham, H. 5	*Sideham* 112 (*393)
Sydenham (in Marystowe), C. 9	*Sidreham* 108b (*317)
Sydenham Damerel, C. 10	*Sidelham* 108b (*318, *Sidreham* 495b)
Tackbear, A. 7	*Tacabere* 125 (*-beara* 244b), Corn.

(*Taigna*)	See Teigngrace, Teignharvey
Taigne	See Teigngrace
Taincome (*-coma*)	See Teigncombe
Taine	See Teignharvey
(*Taintona*)	See Bishopsteignton, Drewsteignton
Taintone	See Drewsteignton
(*Tala*)	See Tale
Talaton, J. 7	*Taletone* 102 (*-tona* 118b)
Tale	See Tale
Tale, J. 7	*Tale* 114 *bis* (*Tala* 338 *bis*)
Talebrige (*-breia*, *-brua*)	See Thelbridge
Taletone (*-tona*)	See Talaton
Tambretone	See Tamerton Foliot
Tamerlande (*-landa*), B. 8	Lost in Luffincott, 114b (411b, 496)
Tamerton Foliot, D. 12	*Tambretone* 116 (not in Exon D.B.)
Tanbretone (*-tona*)	See King's Tamerton
Tantone	See Bishopsteignton
Tapelie (*-leia*)	See Tapeley
Tapeley, D. 4	*Tapelie* 103 (*-leia* 124, 500)
Tapps, H. 4	*Ause* 108 (*Ausa* 311)
Tattiscombe, E. 2	*Totescome* 105 (*-coma* 212b)
Tauestoch, *-stoche* (*-stoca*, *-stocha*)	See Tawstock
Tauestone	See South Tawton
Tauetone (*-tona*)	See North Tawton, South Tawton
Tautone (*-tona*)	See Bishop's Tawton
Tavelande (*-landa*)	See Taw Green
Tavestoc (*-stocha*)	See Tavistock
*Tavi**	See Marytavy
Tavistock, D. 10	*Tavestoc* 103b (*-stocha* 177)
Tawetone (*-tona*)	See North Tawton

Taw Green, F. 7	*Tavelande* 117b (*-landa* 475, 495b)
Tawi	See Petertavy
Tawstock, E. 4	*Tauestoch*, *-stoche* 101, 101b (*-stoca*, *-stocha* 94b *bis*, 110, 499)
Tedburn St Mary, G. 8	*Teteborne*, *-burne* 107b *bis*, 110b (*-borna* 305b, 306, 403)
(*Teigna*)	See Canonteign, George Teign
Teigncombe, F. 9	*Taincome* 103 (*-coma* 131)
Teigne	See Canonteign, George Teign
Teigngrace, H. 10	*Taigne* 108 (*Taigna* 311b)
Teignharvey, H. 10	*Taine* 107b (*Taigna* 305b)
Teignmouth	Not in D.B.
Teintone (*-tona*)	See Kingsteignton
Templeton	Not in D.B.
Tetcott, B. 7	*Tetecote* 108b (*-cota* 319, 495b)
Teteborne, *-burne* (*-borna*)	See Tedburn St Mary
Tetecote (*-cota*)	See Tetcott
Teweberie (*-beria*)	See Thuborough
Thelbridge, G. 6	*Talebrige* 103 (*-breia*, *brua* 134, 506)
Thorn, H. 5	*Toredone* 110b (*-dona* 405, 502)
Thornbury (in Drewsteignton), F. 8	*Torneberie* 105b (*-beria* 214)
Thornbury (near Holsworthy), C. 6	*Torneberie* 103b (*-beria* 178b)
Thorne, B. 6	*Torne* 103 (*Torna* 122)
Thorverton	Not in D.B.
(*Thotonensium*)	See Totnes
Throwleigh, F. 8	*Trule* 113b (*Trula* 458b)
Thrushelton, C. 8	*Tresetone* 108b (*316)
Thuborough, B. 6	*Teweberie* 113 (*-beria* 419b)
Thurlestone, F. 14	*Torlestan* 109 (*321b)
Tideford	See Lydford
Tilleslow, C. 8	*Tornelowe* 108b (*-lowa* 317b, 500b)
Tiverton, I. 6	*Tovretone* 100b, 113b (*-tona* 98, 110b, 460b)
*Topeshant**	See Topsham
Topsham, I. 8	*Topeshant* 101 (*95b)
Torbryan, G. 11	*Torre* 118b (*Torra* 488b)
Toredone (*-dona*)	See Thorn
*Tori**	See Torridge
Torilande (*-landa*)	Unid., 114 (336)
Torintone (*-tona*)	See Black Torrington, Little Torrington
Toritone (*-tona*)	See Great Torrington, Little Torrington
*Torix**	See Torridge
*Torlestan**	See Thurlestone
Tormoham, H. 11	*Torre* 117b (*Torra* 476)
Torne (*Torna*)	See Thorne
Torneberie (*-beria*)	See Thornbury (in Drewsteignton), Thornbury (near Holsworthy)
Tornecome (*-coma*)	See Thorncombe (near Seaborough), Do.
Tornelowe (*-lowa*)	See Tilleslow
Torre (*Torra*)	See Torbryan, Tormoham
Torridge, D. 12	*Tori* 105 (*221, 505) *Torix* 110 (*333)
*Torsewis**	See Huish (in Instow)
*Totenais** (*Toteneis*)	See Totnes
Totescome (*-coma*)	See Tattiscombe
Totheneis	See Totnes

Totnes, G. 12	*Totenais* 100 *bis*, 108b (*-nais*, *-neis* 87b, 88, 334) *Totheneis* 101 (*Thotonensium* 97b)
Tovretone (*-tona*)	See Tiverton
Townstal, H. 13	*Dunestal* 112 (*349b)
Trebichen	See Trebeigh, Corn.
*Trendesholt**	See Trentishoe
Trentishoe, F. 2	*Trendesholt* 102b (*128b)
*Tresetone**	See Thrushelton
(*Tribichen*)	See Trebeigh, Corn.
*Trisma**	See Trusham
Trule (*Trula*)	See Throwleigh
Trusham, H. 9	*Trisma* 104 (*182b)
Tuchebere (*Tucabera*)	See Twigbear
(*Tuchel*)	See Twitchen (in Arlington)
Tuichebere (*Tuicabera*)	See Twigbear
Tuichel	See Twitchen (in Arlington)
Twigbear, D. 6	*Tuche-*, *Tuichebere* 115 *bis* (*Tuca-*, *Tuicabera* 413, 413b)
Twinyeo, H. 10	*Betunie* 118b (*Betunia* 488b)
Twitchen (in Arlington), E. 3	*Tuichel* 115b (*Tuchel* 371)
Twitchen (near North Molton)	Not in D.B.
(*Udeborda*)	See Widworthy
Uffculme, J. 6	*Offecome* 111b (*-coma* 346b)
Ugborough, F. 12	*Ulgeberge* 116 (not in Exon D.B.)
(*Ulacumba*)	See Owlacombe
Ulestanecote	See Woolston (in Staverton)
Ulfeldeshodes	See Woolfardisworthy (near Witheridge)
Ulgeberge	See Ugborough
Ulpesse	See Up Exe
Ulsistone (*-tona*)	See Woolston (in West Alvington)
Uluredintone (*-tona*)	See Werrington
Uluredintune, *Ulurintone*, (*Uluurintona*)	See Worlington, East and West
Ulveberie	See Wolborough
Ulvelei	See Woolley
Ulvelie	See Woolleigh
Ulvevetone	See Wollaton
Ulvretone	See Worlington (in Instow)
Ulwardesdone	See Woolfin
(*Ulwritona*)	See Worlington (in Instow)
Umberlei (*-leia*)	See Umberleigh
Umberleigh, E. 4	*Umberlei* 104 (*-leia* 194)
Undercleave, K. 2	*Odesclive* 100b (*-cliva* 84b, 503)
Upcott, G. 8	*Opecote* 107b (*-cota* 308)
Up Exe, I. 7	*Ulpesse* 103 (*Olpessa* 132)
Uplowman, J. 5	*Oplomie* 112b (*-ia* 394) *Oppelaume* 114b (*Oppaluma* 341b, 502b)
Uplyme, K. 3	*Lim* 103b (*161)
Upottery	See Ottery, Mohun's etc.
Upton Hellions	Not in D.B.
Upton Pyne	Not in D.B.
Varley, D. 3	*Fallei* 102b (*Falleia* 130)
Varleys, D. 6	*Ferlie* 118 (*-leia* 482b)
Venn, F. 12	*Fen* 105b (*218b)
(*Vennacra*)	See Fenacre
Villavin, E. 5	*Fedaven* 112b (*388)
Virginstow	Not in D.B.

Virworthy, B. 6	*Fereodin* 112b (*388) *Fereurde* 110 (*-urdi* 399)
Wachetone (*-tona*)	See Walkhampton
Waddlestone, D. 9	*Wadelescote* 106 (*-cota* 289b, 495)
*Wadeham**	See Wadham
Wadelescote (*-cota*)	See Waddlestone
*Wadestan**	See Whitestone (in Chittlehampton)
Wadham, G. 4	*Wadeham* 118b (*486b)
Waford (*-fort*, *Wafforda*)	See Washford Pyne
(*Wagesfella*)	See Warne
Walcome (*-coma*)	See Welcombe
*Walderige**	See Oldridge
(*Waleforda*)	See *Waliforde*
Walementone (*Walenimtona*)	See Galmpton (in South Huish)
Waleurde (*-urda*)	See Wallover
Waliforde (*Waleforda*), E. 12	Lost in Plympton St Mary, 110 (331b)
Walkhampton, D. 11	*Wachetone* 100b *bis* (*-tona* 86b, 87 *ter*, 505)
Wallover, F. 3	*Waleurde* 102b (*-urda* 129)
Walson	See Nymet, Broadnymet etc.
Warbrightsleigh, H. 5	*Wasberlege* 118b (*Wirlbesliga* 488)
(*Warcoma*)	See Warcombe
Warcombe, D. 2	*Warcome* 102b (*-coma* 129)
Warcome	See Warcombe
Waringstone and Deer Park, K. 7	*Otri*, *Otrie* 110b *bis*, 114, 114b (*Oteri*, *Otria* 338b, 342, 400b, 405, 502b *bis*)
Warmhill, H. 9	*Wermehel* 102 (*135b)
Warne, D. 9	Unnamed, held with Marytavy 108b (*Wagesfella* 318, 495)
Wasberlege	See Warbrightsleigh
Waseborne (*-borna*)	See Washbourne
Wasfelle, *-felte* (*-fella*, *-felta*)	See Washfield
Wasforde (*-forda*)	See Washford Pyne
Washbourne, G. 12	*Waseborne* 113 (*-borna* 396)
Washfield, I. 5	*Wasfelle*, *-felte* 113b, 114b (*-fella*, *-felta* 341, 460b)
Washford Pyne, G. 6	*Waford* 111 (*-fort* 367) *Wasforde* 112 (*Wafforda*, *Wasforda* 392b, 501b) *Wesford* 115b *ter* (*-forda*, *-fort* 409b *ter*, 501b *quater*)
Way (in Bridestowe), D. 8	Unnamed, held with Bridestowe 105b (*Weia* 289, 495)
Weare Gifford, D. 5	*Were* 115 (*Wera* 412b, 505b)
Webbery, D. 4	*Wiberie* 117 (*Wibeberia* 468)
Wederige (*Wedreriga*)	Unid., 105 (222b, 505b)
Wedfield, B. 5	*Widefelle* 105 (*-fella* 211b)
Wedicheswelle	See Pickwell
(*Wedreriga*)	See *Wederige*
(*Weia*)	See Way
Welcombe, A. 5	*Walcome* 103 (*-coma* 122b)
Welingedinge (*Welisedinga*)	See Wilson
Welland	See Pilland
Welle	See Coffinswell
Wellecome (*-coma*)	See Woolacombe
Wembury	Not in D.B.
Wembworthy, F. 6	*Mameorde* 106b (*-orda* 296b)

Wenford	See Wonford (in Heavitree), Wonford (in Thornbury)
(*Wenforda*)	See Wonford (in Thornbury)
(*Wenfort*)	See Wonford (in Heavitree)
Wennacre	See Fenacre
*Wenneham**	See Winsham
Were (*Wera*)	See Weare Gifford
(*Wereia*)	See Wray
(*Wereingeurda*)	See Wringworthy
Wergi	See Wray
(*Weringheorda*)	See Wringworthy
*Wermehel**	See Warmhill
Werrington, B. 8	*Uluredintone* 101 (*-tona* 98 Devon, 508 Corn.) (*Olwritona* 178b) not in Exch. D.B.
Wesford (*-forda*, *-fort*)	See Washford Pyne
Weslege (*-lega*)	See Westleigh
West Alvington, F. 14	*Alvintone* 100b (*-tona* 86)
West Bradley, H. 6	*Bradelie* 103 (*Bradaleia* 133b)
West Buckland	See Buckland, East and West
West Clyst, I. 8	*Cliste* 107 (*Clista* 309, 500b)
West Down, D. 2	*Dune* 102b (*Duna* 125b, 499)
West Heanton, D. 6	*Hantone* 118 (*-tona* 482b)
Westleigh, D. 4	*Weslege* 113 (*-lega* 420)
West Ogwell	See Ogwell
Westone (*-tona*)	See Weston Peverel
Weston Peverel, C. 12	*Westone* 109b (*-tona* 328)
West Portlemouth, F. 14	*Porlemute* 109 (*Porlamuta* 322b)
West Putford, B. 5	*Podiford* 101 (*-forda* 93b) *Poteford*, *-forde*

West Putford cont.	110, 115 (*Potaforda*, *-fort*, *Peteforda* 399, 412b, 496b *bis*) *Pudeforde* 114 (*-forda* 336, 497)
West Raddon, H. 7	*Ratdone* 104b, 112 (*-dona* 215b, 392b)
West Worlington	See Worlington, East and West
Weycroft, K. 2	*Wigegroste* 114b (*Wigacrosta* 343) *Willecroste* 114b (*-crosta*, *-crostra* 343b, 505b)
Whiddon, D. 3	*Willedene* 116b (*-denna* 377)
Whimple, J. 7	*Winple* 107 *bis*, 110b, 116 (*Winpla* 302, 402b, 499b)
Whipton, I. 8	*Wipletone* 110b (*-tona* 404b)
Whitchurch, D. 10	*Wicerce* 115 (not in Exon D.B.)
Whitefield (in Challacombe), F. 2	*Witefelle* 102b 2nd entry (*-fella* 127)
Whitefield (in High Bray), F. 3	*Witefelle* 102b 1st entry (*-fella* 126b)
Whitefield (in Marwood), E. 3	*Witefelle* 113 (*-fella* 420b)
Whitestone (in Chittlehampton), F. 4	*Wadestan* 107 (*300b)
Whitestone (near Exeter), H. 8	*Witestan* 107b, 108, 111b (*306b, 308b, *-tani* 459)
Whiteway, H. 10	*Witewei* 108 (*-weia* 312)
Whitford, L. 8	*Witeford* 101 (*-fort* 97)
Whitleigh, D. 12	*Witelie* 109b, 113 (*-leia* 328b, 505)
Whitley, K. 7	(*Witeleia* 503) not in Exch. D.B.
Whitnage, J. 5	*Witenes* 113 (*394b)

Whitnole, H. 5	*Withechenolle* 117 (*Witechenolla* 471b)
Wiberie (*Wibeberia*)	See Webbery
Wiburde (*-borda*), L. 7	Lost in Cotleigh, 104b (217, 503)
(*Wica*)	See Germansweek, Middlewick, Northwick, Wyke (in Shobrooke)
(*Wicca*)	See Middlewick, Wyke (in Axminster)
Wicerce	See Whitchurch
(*Wicha*)	See Cookbury Wick
Wiche	See Cookbury Wick, Germansweek, Middlewick, Northwick, Wyke (in Axminster), Wyke (in Shobrooke)
(*Wida*)	See Widey
Widdicombe, G. 14	*Wodicome* 112 (*Wodiacoma*, *-comma* 349, 504)
Wide	See Widey
Widebere (*-bera*)	See Woodbeer
(*Widecoma*)	See Withycombe Raleigh
Widecombe in the Moor	Not in D.B.
Widecome	See Withycombe Raleigh
Widefelle (*-fella*)	See Wedfield
Widefield, D. 7	(*Witefelda* 499) not in Exch. D.B.
Wideworde (*-worda*)	See Widworthy
Widey, D. 12	*Wide* 113 (*Wida* 421b, 505)
Widworthy, L. 7	*Wideworde* 115b (*-worda* 410, *Udeborda* 503)
Wifleswille	See Winswell
Wifleurde	See Willsworthy

Wigegroste (*Wigacrosta*)	See Weycroft
*Wilavestreu**	See Willestrew
Wilelmitone (*-tona*)	See Wilmington
(*Willa*)	See Coffinswell, Edginswell
Willand, J. 6	*Willelande* 116b (*-landa* 379b)
Wille	See Edginswell
Willecroste (*-crosta*, *-crostra*)	See Weycroft
Willedene (*-denna*)	See Whiddon
Willelande (*-landa*)	See Willand
Willelmetone (*-matona*, *Willemitona*)	See Wilmington
Willestrew, C. 10	*Wilavestreu* 113 (*419)
Willsworthy, D. 9	*Wifleurde* 115b (not in Exon D.B.)
Wilmington, L. 7	*Wilelmitone* 108b (*-tona* 314b) *Willelmetone* 115b (*-matona* 410b, *Willemitona* 503)
Wilson, G. 5	*Welingedinge* 108 (*Welisedinga* 310b)
Wiltone	See Pilton
Wincheleie (*-leia*)	See Winkleigh
Winescote (*-cota*)	See Winscott
Winestane (*-tona*)	See Winston
Winkleigh, E. 6	*Wincheleie* 101b (*-leia* 109)
Winple (*Winpla*)	See Whimple
Winscott, D. 6	*Winescote* 115 (*-cota* 413b)
Winsham, D. 3	*Wenneham* 102b (*128)
Winston, E. 13	*Winestane* 104b (*-tona* 221b, 505)
Winswell, D. 6	*Wifleswille* 115 (*Wivleswilla* 413b)
Wipletone (*-tona*)	See Whipton
Wirige (*-riga*)	See Witheridge
(*Wirlbesliga*)	See Warbrightsleigh

(*Witechenolla*)	See Whitnole
(*Witefelda*)	See Widefield
Witefelle (*-fella*)	See Whitefield (in Challacombe), Whitefield (in High Bray), Whitefield (in Marwood)
Witeford (*-fort*)	See Whitford
(*Witeleia*)	See Whitleigh, Whitley
Witelie	See Whitleigh
*Witenes**	See Whitnage
Witestan *Witestan** (*-tani*)	See Whitestone (near Exeter)
Witewei (*-weia*)	See Whiteway
Withechenolle	See Whitnole
Witheridge, G. 5	*Wirige* 100b (*-riga* 96)
Withycombe Raleigh, J. 9	*Widecome* 112 (*-coma* 392b)
(*Wivleswilla*)	See Winswell
Wodeberie (*-beria*)	See Woodbury
Wodicome (*Wodiacoma*, *-comma*)	See Widdicombe
Wogewille (*-wil*)	See Ogwell
Wogwel (*Woguwel*)	See Ogwell
Wolborough, H. 11	*Ulveberie* 108 (*Olveberia* 313)
(*Wolestanecota*)	See Woolston (in Staverton)
Wollaton, E. 13	*Ulvevetone* 109b (*Olvievetona* 330)
Wolnecome (*-coma*)	See Woolacombe
Wonford (in Heavitree), I. 8	*Wenford* 100b (*-fort* 95b)
Wonford (in Thornbury), C. 6	*Wenford* 114b (*-forda* 411b)
Woodbeer, J. 7	*Widebere* 112b (*-bera* 391b)
Woodburn, H. 5	*Odeburne* 108 (*-borna* 311)
Woodbury, J. 9	*Wodeberie* 100b (*-beria* 96b)
Woodford, D. 12	*Odeford* 110 *bis* (*-forda* 333b *bis*, 505b *bis*)
Woodhuish, H. 12	*Odehiwis* 113b (not in Exon D.B.)
Woodland (in Little Torrington), D. 5	*Liteltorelande* 104b (*-trorilanda* 212, 497b)
Woodleigh, F. 13	*Odelie* 113 (*-lea* 421)
Woolacombe, C. 2	*Wellecome* 115b (*-coma* 408b) *Wolnecome* 110 (*-coma* 401)
Woolfardisworthy (near Hartland), B. 5	*Olvereword* 118 (*Olfereordi* 481b)
Woolfardisworthy (near Witheridge), H. 6	*Ulfaldeshodes* 111b (*Olfaldeshodes* 416b)
Woolfin, G. 7	*Ulwardesdone* 101b (*Oluardesdona* 109b)
Woolladon, D. 6	*Oladone* 106 (*-dona* 294)
Woolleigh, D. 5	*Ulvelie* 106b (*Olvelia* 294b)
Woolley, G. 9	*Ulvelie* 102 (*Olveleia* 135b *bis*)
Woolston (in West Alvington), F. 14	*Ulsistone* 109 (*-tona* 323b)
Woolston (in Staverton), G. 11	*Ulestanecote* 113 (*Wolestanecota* 397)
Worde	See Worth
Worlington (in Instow), D. 4	*Ulvretone* 102 (*Ulwritona* 124b)
Worlington, East and West, G. 6	*Olurintone* 111 (*Uluurintona* 367) *Uluredintune* 103 (*Oluridintona* 134) *Ulurintone* 116b (*Olurintona* 379, 501, 501b)
Worth, I. 5	*Worde* 111b (*Wrda* 416b)
Worthele, E. 12	*Ordihelle* 109b (*-hella* 326)

Worthy, H. 5	*Ordie* 108 (*Ordia* 310b)
Worthygate, B. 4	*Wrdiete* 103b (*-ieta* 178b)
Wray, G. 9	*Wergi* 118 (*Wereia* 485)
(*Wrda*)	See Worth
Wrdiete (*-ieta*)	See Worthygate
Wringworthy, D. 10	Unnamed, held with Marytavy 108b (*Wereingeurda* 318, *Weringheorda* 495)
(*Wyca*)	See Germansweek
Wyke (in Axminster), K. 2	*Wiche* 118 (*Wicca* 489)
Wyke (in Shobrooke), H. 7	*Wiche* 104b (*Wica* 215b)
Yarcombe, L. 6	*Herticome* 104 (*Erticoma* 195b)
Yard (in Ilfracombe), D. 2	*Laierda* 107 (*301)
Yard (in Rose Ash), G. 5	*Hierde* 108 (*Hierda* 310)
Yard (in Silverton), I. 7	*Heierde* 117 (*Heierda* 469b)
Yarnscombe, E. 4	*Herlescome* 115 (*-coma* 407) *Hernescome* 106 (*-coma* 293)
Yealmpstone, E. 12	*Alfelmestone* 115 (not in Exon D.B.)
Yealmpton, E. 13	*Elintone* 100b (*-tona* 86b)
Yedbury, H. 6	*Addeberie* 114b (*-beria* 340b)
Yowlestone, H. 6	*Aedelstan* 111 (*Aeidestan* 403b)
Yudeford (*Yudaforda*)	See Ideford
(*Ywesleia*)	See Iddesleigh
(*Ywis*)	See Huish (near Dolton)
Zeal Monachorum	See Nymet, Broadnymet, etc.

ANONYMOUS HOLDINGS

The following seven entries involve anonymous holdings. The Exon D.B., however, enables us to assign the ten holdings mentioned in three of the entries to their respective localities. It is possible that some (or even all) of the others refer to holdings at places not named elsewhere in Domesday Book:

St Peter of Plympton (from the king), 2 hides, 100b (86).

Bishop of Coutances, one virgate in Braunton, 102b. Exon D.B. shows this was at Boode (126b).

Bishop of Coutances, one hide, 103 (132).

Baldwin the sheriff, with this manor (i.e. Bridestowe) half a hide and 1½ ferlings formerly held by six thegns, 105b. Exon D.B. shows that these lands were at Kersford, Battishill, Combebow, Ebsworthy, Fernworthy and Way (289, 495).

Nigel (from Juhel of Totnes), with this manor (i.e. Marytavy) one virgate formerly held by three thegns, 108b. Exon D.B. shows that these lands were at Warne, Burntown and Wringworthy (318, 495).

Ralf (from William the usher), one virgate, 117b (475).

Alward Mert, half a virgate, 118 (483).

DORSET
DORSETE (DORSETA)

Exchequer Domesday Book, folios 75–85
Exeter Domesday Book, folios 11b–12b, 25–45, 47–62b
Exeter Domesday names and folio references are given in brackets. An asterisk * indicates that the names in the Exeter D.B. and the Exchequer D.B. are the same.

MAP 15

Abbotsbury, C. 5	*Abedesberie* 78 *Abodesberie* 79
Abbott's Wootton	See Wootton Fitzpaine
Abedes-, Abodesberie	See Abbotsbury
Abristetone (*Abristentona*)	See Ibberton
Acford (*-forda*)	See Child Okeford
Acton, H. 6	*Tacatone* 84 (*-tona* 61)
Adber, D. 1	*Ateberie* 95b (*-beria* 355b), Som. *Etesberie* 93 (*-beria* 279), Som. *Ettebere* 99 (*Eattebera* 493b), Som.
Adelingtone	See Allington
Adford	See Okeford Fitzpaine
*Aelfatune**	See Hethfelton
Affapidele (*-pidela*)	See Affpuddle
Afflington, H. 5	*Alfrunetone* 85 (*-tona* 62) *Alveronetune* 82b *Alvretone* 80, 82 *Alvronetone* 80
Affpuddle, F. 4	*Affapidele* 77b (*-pidela* 36b)
Ailwood, H. 5	*Aleoude* 84b
Aisemare (*-mara*)	See Ashmore
Aisse	See Ash
Alcester	Not in D.B.
Aldershot	Not in D.B.
Aleoude	See Ailwood
Aleurde	See Elworth
Alford	See Okeford Fitzpaine
Alfrunetone (*-tona*)	See Afflington
All Hallows Farm, H. 2	*Opewinburne* 75 (*Obpewinborna* 27)
Allington, B. 4	*Adelingtone* 80b
Almer	Not in D.B.
Altone	See Alton Pancras
Alton Pancras, E. 3	*Altone* 75b
Alveronetune, Alvretone, Alvronetone	See Afflington
Amedesham	See Edmondsham
Anderson	See Winterborne Clenston etc.
Arne	Not in D.B.
Ash, G. 2	*Aisse* 82
Ashmore, G. 1	*Aisemare* 75b (*-mara* 29b)
Askerswell, C. 2	*Oscherwille* 78b (*-wlla* 42)
Athelhampton	See Tolpuddle etc.
Atrem	See Atrim
Atrim, B. 4	*Atrem* 78b (*Atrum* 40)
(*Atrum*)	See Atrim
Bardolfeston	See Tolpuddle etc.
Batcombe	Not in D.B.
Beaminster, B. 3	*Beiminstre* 77
Beastewelle	See Bestwall
Beer Hackett	Not in D.B.
Beiminstre	See Beaminster
Beincome	See Bincombe

Bere (*Bera*)	See Bere Regis
Bere Regis, G. 4	*Bere* 75, 79, 83b (*Bera* 27, 27b, 56b)
Bessintone (*-tona*)	See Bexington
Bestwall, G. 5	*Beastewelle* 79b
Bettiscombe	Not in D.B.
Bexington, C. 5	*Bessintone* 82b (*-tona* 50b)
Bincombe, E. 5	*Beincome* 78b
Bishop's Caundle	See Caundle, Bishop's etc.
Blachemanestone	See Blackmanston
Blackmanston, G. 5	*Blachemanestone* 84b *bis*
(*Blaeneford*)	See Langton Long Blandford
Blandford St Mary, G. 3	*Blaneford*, *-forde* 79b 1st entry, 82b *Bleneford*, *-forde* 79b, 80b, 84
Blaneford, *-forde*	See Blandford St Mary, Bryanston
Bleneford, *-forde*	See Blandford St Mary, Langton Long Blandford
Blocheshorde (*-esborda*)	See Bloxworth
Bloxworth, G. 4	*Blocheshorde* 77b (*-esborda* 36b)
Bochehamtone (*-tona*)	See Bockhampton
Bocheland	See Buckland Ripers
Bochelande	See Buckland Newton
(*Bochelant*)	See Buckland Ripers
Bochenham	See Buckham
Bockhampton, E. 4	*Bochehamtone* 85 (*-tona* 33)
Bothenhampton	Not in D.B.
Bourton	Not in D.B.
Bourtone (*-tona*)	See Burcombe
Bovehric	See Boveridge
Boveridge, I. 2	*Bovehric* 77b
Bovewode	See Bowood
Bovington, F. 4	*Bovintone* 84b
Bovintone	See Bovington

Bowood, B. 3	*Bovewode* 77
Bradeford	See Bradford Abbas, Bradford Peverell
Bradelege	See Bradle
Bradford Abbas, D. 2	*Bradeford* 77
Bradford Peverell, D. 4	*Bradeford* 80b
Bradle, G. 5	*Bradelege* 83
Bradpole, B. 4	*Bratepolle* 75 (*-polla* 27)
Branksome	Not in D.B.
Bratepolle (*-polla*)	See Bradpole
Bredy (in Burton Bradstock), C. 4	*Bridie* 82b
Brenscombe, H. 5	*Brunescume* 84 (*61b)
Briants Puddle	See Puddle
Brideport (*-porta*)	See Bridport
Bridetone (*-tona*)	See Burton Bradstock
Bridge, D. 6	*Briga*, *Brige* 83, 83b, 84b (*Briga* 57)
Bridie	See Bredy (in Burton Bradstock)
Bridport, B. 4	*Brideport* 75, 77, 78b (*-porta* 12, 28)
*Briga**, *Brige*	See Bridge
Broadmayne, E. 5	*Maine* 80 *bis*
Broadwey, Upwey, Weymouth, D. 5, E. 6	*Wai*, *Waia* 75b, 79 *ter*, 83, 83b *bis*, 84 (*Waia* 31, 54b, 55)
Broadwindsor, B. 3	*Windesore* 85
Brochemtune	See Brockington
Brocheshale (*-essala*)	See Wraxall
Brockington, H. 2	*Brochemtune* 79b
*Brunescume**	See Brenscombe
Bryanston, G. 2	*Blaneford* 79b 2nd entry
Buckham, B. 3	*Bochenham* 77
Buckhorn Weston, A. 2	*Westone* 79
Buckland Newton, E. 3	*Bochelande* 77b

Buckland Ripers, D. 5	*Bocheland* 83b (*-lant* 54b)
Burcombe, C. 3	*Bourtone* 78b (*-tona* 40)
Bureuuinestoch	See Burstock
Burstock, B. 3	*Bureuuinestoch* 80
Burton Bradstock, B.4	*Bridetone* 75 *bis*, 78 (*-tona* 27, 28)
Calvedone (*-dona*)	See Chaldon Herring
*Cameric**	See Kimmeridge
*Candel**, *-dele*, *-delle*	See Caundle, Bishop's etc.; Caundle Marsh
Canford Magna, I. 3	*Cheneford* 80b
Cann	Not in D.B.
(*Canolla*)	See Church Knowle
Castellum Warham	See Corfe Castle
Castleton	Not in D.B.
Catesclive	See Catsley
Catherston Leweston, A. 4	*Cerneli* 80
Catsley, C. 3	*Catesclive* 80
Catistock, D. 3	*Stoche* 78 (*Estocha* 43)
Caundle, Bishop's, Purse, Stourton and Caundle Wake, E. 1, E. 2	*Candel* 78b, 80 *bis*, 82, 83 Do.; 93 Som.; (*41 Do.; 280b Som.) *Candele*, *-delle* 82 *bis*, 84b 1st entry
Caundle Marsh, E. 2	*Candele* 84b 2nd entry
Caundle Wake	See Caundle, Bishop's etc.
(*Cealvaduna*)	See Chaldon Herring
Celberge (*-berga*)	See Chelborough
Celvedune	See Chaldon Herring
Ceoselburne (*-burna*)	See Little Cheselbourne
Ceotel	See Chettle
Cerdestoche	See Chardstock, Devon
Cereberie (*-beria*)	See Charborough

Cerletone (*-tona*)	See Charlton Marshall
Cerminstre	See Charminster
(*Cerna*)	See Godmanstone
Cerne	See Forston etc., Godmanstone
Cerne Abbas, D. 3	*Cerneli* 77b (*-elium* 36)
Cernel	See Forston etc., Godmanstone
Cerneli	See Catherston Leweston, Cerne Abbas
(*Cernelium*)	See Cerne Abbas
Cernemude	See Charmouth
Ceseburne	See Cheselbourne
Chalbury	Not in D.B.
Chaldon Herring and West Chaldon, F. 5	*Calvedone* 75b, 79 (*-dona* 26b, 28) *Celvedune* 83b (*Cealvaduna* 59b)
Charborough, G. 3	*Cereberie* 75 (*-beria* 25b)
Charlton Marshall, G. 3	*Cerletone* 75 (*-tona* 27b)
Charminster, E. 4	*Cerminstre* 75b
Charmouth, A. 4	*Cernemude* 80
Cheddington	Not in D.B.
Chelborough, East and West, C. 2, C. 3	*Celberge* 81b, 82b (*-berga* 49, 50)
Cheneford	See Canford Magna
Chenistetone	See West Knighton
Chenolle	See Church Knowle
Chenoltone, *-tune* (*-tona*)	See Knowlton
Cheselbourne, F. 3	*Ceseburne* 78b
Chetnole	Not in D.B.
Chettle, H. 2	*Ceotel* 83
Chickerell, D. 5	*Cicherelle* 84
Chideock, B. 4	*Cidihoc* 75 (*Cidiohoc* 27)
Child Okeford, F. 2	*Acford* 75, 79 (*-forda* 25)
Chilcombe, C. 4	*Ciltecome* 84b

Chilfrome and Frome Vauchurch, D. 3	*Frome* 75, 80b, 81b *bis* (*Froma*, *Fromma* 27b, 48b *bis*)
Chimedecome	See Higher Kingcombe, Lower Kingcombe
Chinestanestone	See Kinson, Hants.
Chingestone	See Kingston (in Corfe Castle)
Chintone	See Kington Magna
*Chirce**	See Crichel
Church Knowle, H. 5	*Chenolle* 82 *Cnolle* 82, 82b (*Canolla* 62)
Cicherelle	See Chickerell
Cidihoc (*Cidiohoc*)	See Chideock
Ciltecome	See Chilcombe
Circel	See Crichel
Clifton Maybank, C. 2	*Clistone* 80
Clistone	See Clifton Maybank
*Clive**	See Clyffe
Clyffe, F. 4	*Clive* 78 (*43b)
Cnolle	See Church Knowle
Colber, F. 1	*Colesberie* 75 (-*breia* 27)
Colehill	Not in D.B.
Colesberie (-*breia*)	See Colber
Come	See Coombe (in Langton Matravers), Coombe Keynes
Compton, Nether and Over, D. 1	*Contone* 77
Compton Abbas (near Bridport), C. 4	*Contone* 78 (-*tona* 43)
Compton Abbas (near Shaftesbury), G. 1	*Cuntone* 78b
Compton Valence, D. 4	*Contone* 83
(*Contona*)	See Compton Abbas (near Bridport)
Contone	See Compton, Nether and Over; Compton Abbas (near Bridport); Compton Valence
Coombe (in Langton Matravers), H. 6	*Come* 84b
Coombe Keynes, F. 5	*Come* 77b, 82b (*Cume* 62b)
Corf	See Corfe Mullen
Corfe Castle, H. 5	*Castellum Warham* 78b
Corfe Mullen, H. 3	*Corf* 80b
Corfetone	See Corton
Cories-, *Coriscumbe*	See Corscombe
Corscombe, C. 3	*Cories-*, *Coriscumbe* 80, 84b *Corscumbe* 77
Corscumbe	See Corscombe
Corton, D. 5	*Corfetone* 80
Cranborne, I. 2	*Creneburne* 75b (-*borna* 29)
Craveford	See Crawford
Crawford, G. 3	*Craveford* 84
Creech, East and West, G. 5	*Cric* 82 *Crist* 79b *Criʒ* 80, 84 (*60b)
Creneburne (-*borna*)	See Cranborne
Cric	See Creech
Crichel, Long and More, H. 2	*Chirce* 75, 83 (*27) *Circel* 80b
Crist, *Criʒ**	See Creech
(*Cume*)	See Coombe Keynes
Cuneliʒ	See Kimmeridge
Cuntone	See Compton Abbas (near Shaftesbury)
Dedilintone	See Didlington
Dervinestone (-*tona*)	See Durweston
Derwinestone	See Durweston
Devenis	See Dewlish
Dewlish, F. 3	*Devenis* 79
Didlington, H. 2	*Dedilintone* 79
Dodesberie	See Dudsbury

Dorchester, E. 4	*Dorecestre* 75 *bis*, 75b, 79 (*-cestra* 11b, 27b *bis*)
Dorecestre (*-cestra*)	See Dorchester
Dudsbury, I. 3	*Dodesberie* 82
Durweston, G. 2	*Dervinestone* 79b, 83b (*-tona* 58b)
	Derwinestone 83
East Chelborough	See Chelborough
East Creech	See Creech
East Hemsworth	See Hemsworth
East Holme, G. 5	*Holne* 82b, 84b (*Holna* 62)
East Lulworth	See Lulworth
East Orchard	Not in D.B.
East Pulham, E. 2	*Poleham* 81b (*48)
East Stafford, E. 4	*Stanford* 79
East Stoke, G. 5	*Stoches* 79b
East Stour	See Stour, East etc.
Edmondsham, I. 2	*Amedesham* 83
	Medesham 75b, 83 (*-essan* 29b)
Elsangtone	See Ilsington
Eltone	See Hilton
Elworth, D. 5	*Aleurde* 80b
Ertacomestoche (*-stoca*)	See Stockland, Devon
(*Escapewich*)	See Shapwick
(*Estocha*)	See Cattistock
Etiminstre	See Yetminster
Euneminstre	See Iwerne Minster
Eversholt	Not in D.B.
Farnham, H. 1	*Ferneham* 78b (*57b)
	Fernham 83 *ter*, 83b
*Ferneham**, *Fernham*	See Farnham
Fifehead Magdalen, F. 1	*Fifhide* 80
Fifehead Neville, F. 2	*Fifhide* 82
Fifehead St Quinton, F. 2	*Fifhide* 78b
Fifhide	See Fifehead Magdalen,

Fifhide cont.	Fifehead Neville, Fifehead St Quinton
Fleet, D. 5	*Flete* 75b (*Fleta* 26)
	Flote 79 (*Flota* 28)
Flete (*Fleta*)	See Fleet
Flote (*Flota*)	See Fleet
Folke	Not in D.B.
Fontemale	See Fontmell Magna
Fontmell Magna, G. 1	*Fontemale* 78b
Fordington, D. 4	*Fortitone* 75 (*-tona* 27b)
Forston, Herrison and Pulston, D. 4, E. 4	*Cerne* 79 *quater*
	Cernel 77, 79 2nd entry, 83
Fortitone (*-tona*)	See Fordington
Frampton, D. 4	*Frantone* 75, 78b
Frantone	See Frampton
Frome (*Froma*)	See Chilfrome, Frome Billet
Frome Billet and Whitfield, E. 4	*Frome* 79 *bis*, 83b, 84b (*Froma* 54)
Frome St Quinton, D. 3	*Litelfrome* 75b (*-froma* 29)
Frome Vauchurch	See Chilfrome
Frome Whitfield	See Frome Billet
(*Fromma*)	See Chilfrome
Galton, F. 5	*Galtone* 85
	Gaveltone 84b
Galtone, *Gaveltone*	See Galton
Gelingeham, *Gelingham*, (*Gelingeha*)	See Gillingham
Gessic	See Gussage All Saints
Gillingham, B. 1	*Gelingeham*, *Gelingham* 75, 77b, 78b, 80b, 84 *ter*, 84b (*Gelingeha* 27b)
	Gelingeham 73b Wilts.
Glanville Wootton, E. 2	*Widetone* 82
Glole	See Lutton Gwyle

Goathill, E. 1	*Gatelme* 92b (*-elma* 278b), Som.
Godmanstone, D. 3	*Cerne* 78 (*Cerna* 45)
	Cernel 79 1st entry
Gorewood	Not in D.B.
Graston, C. 4	*Graustan* 83b (*57b)
*Graustan**	See Graston
Gussage All Saints, H. 2	*Gessic* 79b
Gussage St Michael, H. 2	*Gessic* 69, Wilts.
Hafeltone	See Hethfelton
Haintone	See Hinton St Mary
Halegewelle	See Holwell (in Radipole)
Halstock	Not in D.B.
(*Ham*)	See Hammoon
(*Hama*, *Hame*)	See Hampreston
Hame	See Hammoon, Hampreston
Hammoon, F. 2	*Hame* 81b (*Ham* 48)
Hampreston, I. 3	*Hame* 75b, 82b, 83b, 84 (*Hama*, *Hame* 30, 56b)
Hamworthy	Not in D.B.
Handley, H. 1	*Hanlege* 78b
Hanford, G. 2	*Hanford* 79
Hanlege	See Handley
(*Harpera*)	See Hurpston
Haselbury Bryan	Not in D.B.
Havocumbe (*-cumba*)	See Hawcombe
Hawcombe, C. 4	*Havocumbe* 75 (*-cumba* 27)
Haydon	Not in D.B.
(*Heltona*)	See Hilton
Hemedesworde, *-wrde*	See Hemsworth
Hemsworth, East and West, H. 3	*Hemedesworde*, *-wrde* 79b, 83
Herestone (*-tona*)	See Herston
Hermitage	Not in D.B.
Herpere	See Hurpston
Herrison	See Forston etc.

Herston, H. 6	*Herestone* 82b (*-tona* 52)
	Herstune 85
Herstune	See Herston
Hethfelton, G. 5	*Aelfatune* 78 (*37)
	Hafeltone 82, 83
Higher Kingcombe, C. 3	*Chimedecome* 80b
Hill, G. 2	*Hille* 82b
Hille	See Hill
Hillfield	Not in D.B.
Hilton, F. 3	*Eltone* 78b (*Heltona* 39)
Hinetone	See Hinton Martell
Hinton Martell, H. 3	*Hinetone* 76
Hinton St Mary, F. 1	*Haintone* 78b
Hiwes	Unid., 80b
Holne (*Holna*)	See East Holme
Holnest	Not in D.B.
Holt	Not in D.B.
Holton, H. 4	*Holtone* 82
Holtone	See Holton
Holverde (*-verda*)	See Holworth
Holwell (near Bishop's Caundle)	Not in D.B.
Holwell (in Radipole), D. 5	*Halegewelle* 79
Holworth, F. 5	*Holverde* 78 (*-verda* 44b)
Hooke, C. 3	*Lahoc* 79b
*Horcerd**	See Orchard
Horton, I. 2	*Hortune* 78b
Hortune	See Horton
Hurpston, G. 5	*Herpere* 84 (*Harpera* 60b)
Ibberton, F. 2	*Abristetone* 75b (*-tentona* 25b)
Iland	See Nyland
Ilsington, F. 4	*Elsangtone* 80
Inlande	See Nyland
(*Iwerna*)	See Stepleton Iwerne
Iwerne	See Ranston
Iwerne Courtney, G. 2	*Werne* 81

Iwerne Minster, G. 2	*Euneminstre* 78b
Kimmeridge, G. 6	*Cameric* 78 (*38b) *Cuneliz* 82
Kingston (in Corfe Castle), H. 6	*Chingestone* 78b *bis*
Kingston Russell	Not in D.B.
Kington Magna, F. 1	*Chintone* 80b, 82, 84
Knowlton, I. 2	*Chenoltone*, *-tune* 75, 79b (*-tona* 28)
Lahoc	See Hooke
(*Langatona*)	See Langton Herring
Langebride (*-bridia*)	See Long Bredy
Langeford	Unid., 77b
Langetone	See Langton Herring
Langton Herring, D. 5	*Langetone* 75b, 83b (*Langatona*, *Languetona* 31, 59)
Langton Long Blandford, G. 3	*Bleneford* 82b, 84, 84b (*Blaeneford* 50b)
Langton Matravers	Not in D.B.
(*Languetona*)	See Langton Herring
Lazerton, G. 2	*Werne* 84
Leftisford, I. 2	*Levetesford* 77b
Lege	See Leigh (in Colehill)
Leigh (in Colehill), I. 3	*Lege* 80b
Leigh (near Yetminster)	Not in D.B.
Levetesford	See Leftisford
Lewell, E. 5	*Lewelle* 84 *Liwelle* 84b
Lewelle	See Lewell
Leweston	Not in D.B.
Lichet	See Lytchett Matravers
Lillington	Not in D.B.
Lime	See Lyme Regis
Liscome (*-coma*)	See Lyscombe
Litelbride (*-brida*)	See Littlebredy
Litelfrome (*-froma*)	See Frome St Quinton
Litelpidele, *-pidre* (*-pidel*, *-pidra*)	See Little Puddle
Liteltone	See Littleton
Littlebredy, D. 4	*Litelbride* 78 (*-brida* 37)
Little Cheselbourne, E. 3	*Ceoselburne* 83b (*-burna* 54)
Little Puddle, E. 4	*Litelpidele* 75b (*-pidel* 25b) *Litelpidre* 77b (*-pidra* 36)
Littleton, G. 3	*Liteltone* 79b
Littlewindsor, B. 3	*Windresorie* 81b (*-soria* 49b)
Litton Cheney	Not in D.B.
Liwelle	See Lewell
Loders, C. 4	*Lodres* 75b (*26b)
Loders Matravers, C. 4	*Lodre* 79b 3rd entry, 84b
*Lodra**	See Uploders
Lodre	See Loders Matravers, Uploders
*Lodres**	See Loders
Loloworde	See Lulworth
Long Bredy, C. 4	*Langebride* 78 (*-bridia* 37b)
Longburton	Not in D.B.
Long Crichel	See Crichel
Longfleet	Not in D.B.
Lower Kingcombe, C. 3	*Chimedecome* 84b
Luluorde (*Luluurda*)	See Lulworth
Lulworth, East and West, F. 5, G. 5	*Loloworde* 79b *Luluorde* 75, 83 (*Luluurda* 28)
Lutton Gwyle, G. 5	*Glole* 80
Lydlinch	Not in D.B.
Lym	See Lyme Regis
Lyme Regis, A. 4	*Lime* 85 *Lym* 75b, 77b
Lyscombe, E. 3	*Liscome* 78 (*-coma* 44)
Lytchett Matravers, H. 4	*Lichet* 80b

Maiden Newton, D. 3	*Newetone* 82b
Maine	See Broadmayne
Malperetone (*Malperretona*)	See Mapperton (near Beaminster)
Manestone	See Manston
Manitone	See Mannington
Mannington, I. 3	*Manitone* 79b
Manston, F. 1	*Manestone* 82
Maperetone, *Mapertune* (*Mapertona*)	See Mapperton (near Beaminster)
Mapledre	See Mappowder
Mapledretone	See Mapperton (in Almer)
Mapperton (in Almer), G. 3	*Mapledretone* 78b
Mapperton (near Beaminster), C. 3	*Malperetone* 81b (*Malperretona* 49b) *Maperetone* 80b *Mapertune* 75 (*-tona* 25)
Mappowder, E. 3	*Mapledre* 79b, 80b, 84
Margaret Marsh	Not in D.B.
Marnhull	Not in D.B.
Marshwood	Not in D.B.
Medesham (*Medessan*)	See Edmondsham
Melbury Abbas, G. 1	*Meleberie* 78b
Melbury Bubb, Osmund and Sampford, C. 2, D. 2	*Meleberie* 82b, 84 (*-beria* 50) *Melesberie* 79b, 80b
Melcombe Bingham and Horsey, E. 3, F. 3	*Melcome*, *Melecome* 75b, 78b
Melcombe Regis	Not in D.B.
Melcome	See Melcombe Bingham
(*Meleberia*)	See Melbury Bubb etc.
Meleberie	See Melbury Abbas, Melbury Bubb etc.
Meleborne	See Milborne Stileham
Meleburne	See Milborne St Andrew, Milborne Stileham. See also Milborne Port, Som.
Melecome	See Melcombe Bingham
Melesberie	See Melbury Bubb etc.
Metmore	See Smedmore
(*Mideltona*)	See West Milton
Mideltone	See Milton on Stour, West Milton
Mideltune	See Milton Abbas
Milborne St Andrew, F. 3	*Meleburne* 82b
Milborne Stileham, F. 4	*Meleborne*, *-burne* 83, 84b
Miltetone	See Milton on Stour
Milton Abbas, F. 3	*Mideltune* 78 (*Miteltona* 43b)
Milton on Stour, B. 1	*Mideltone* 84 *Miltetone* 82
Minterne Magna	Not in D.B.
(*Miteltona*)	See Milton Abbas
Moleham	See Moulham
Monkton Up Wimborne, H. 2	*Winburne* 79
Moorbath, B. 4	*Mordaat* 83
Mordaat	See Moorbath
Morden, G. 4	*Mordone* 79b, 83b, 84 (*-dona* 56, 62b) *Mordune* 82b *bis*
Mordone, *-dune* (*-dona*)	See Morden
More Crichel	See Crichel
Moreton, F. 4	*Mortune* 79b, 84b
Mortestorne	See Mosterton
Mortune	See Moreton
Mosterton, B. 3	*Mortestorne* 83
Motcombe	Not in D.B.
Moulham, H. 5	*Moleham* 85
Netelcome (*-coma*)	See Nettlecombe
Netherbury, B. 3	*Niderberie* 77
Nettlecombe, C. 4	*Netelcome* 78 (*-coma* 38)

Newetone	See Maiden Newton
Newentone	See Sturminster Newton
Niderberie	See Netherbury
Nodford, *Nortforde*	See Nutford
North Poorton	See Poorton
North Wootton	Not in D.B.
(*Notforda*)	See Nutford
Nutford, G. 2	*Nodford* 85 *Nortforde* 75b (*Notforda* 31b)
Nyland, E. 1	*Iland* 79 *Inlande* 80b
Obcerne	See Up Cerne
Oborne, D. 1	*Wocburne* 77
(*Obpewinborna*)	See All Hallows Farm
Odeham	Unid., 77b
Odetun	See Wootton Fitzpaine
Odiete	See Woodyates
Ogre	See Owermoigne
Okeford Fitzpaine and Shillingstone, F. 2	*Adford* 77b *Alford* 83
Opewinburne	See All Hallows Farm
*Ora**	See Ower
Orchard (in Church Knowle), H. 5	*Horcerd* 84 (*61b)
Orde (*Orda*)	See Worth Matravers
Orgarestone	See Woolgarston
Oscherwille (*-wlla*)	See Askerswell
Osmentone (*-tona*)	See Osmington
Osmington, E. 5	*Osmentone* 78 (*-tona* 43b)
Ower, H. 5	*Ora* 78 (*44b)
Owermoigne, F. 5	*Ogre* 82b
Pamphill	Not in D.B.
Parkstone	Not in D.B.
Pedret	See South Perrott
Pentric	See Pentridge
Pentridge, I. 1	*Pentric* 77b

Perlai	See West Parley
Petersham, H. 3	*Petrishesham* 83 *Pitrichesham* 84
Petrishesham	See Petersham
Piddlehinton	See Tolpuddle etc.
Piddletrenthide, E. 3	*Pidrie* 77b
Pidele (*Pidela*)	See Puddle; Tolpuddle etc.
Pidere	See Tolpuddle etc.
(*Pidra*)	See Puddle; Tolpuddle etc.
Pidre	See Puddle
(*Pidredone*)	See Puddletown
Pidrie	See Piddletrenthide
Pilesdone	See Pilsdon
Pilsdon, B. 3	*Pilesdone* 84b
Pimperne, G. 2	*Pinpre* 75 (*Pinpra* 27b)
Pinpre (*Pinpra*)	See Pimperne
Piretone (*-tona*, *-tune*)	See Puddletown
Pitretone	See Puddletown
Pitrichesham	See Petersham
Plumber, F. 2	*Plumbere* 84
Plumbere	See Plumber
Pocheswelle (*-wella*)	See Poxwell
*Poleham**	See East Pulham, West Pulham
Pomacanole (*-nola*)	See Puncknowle
Poole St James	Not in D.B.
Poorton, North and South, C. 3	*Povertone* 80b, 82b (*-tona* 51) *Povrtone* 83 *Powrtone* 78b (*-tona* 42)
Porland (*-landa*)	See Portland
Portesham (*-esam*)	See Portisham
Portisham, D. 5	*Portesham* 78b (*-esam* 39b)
Portland, E. 6	*Porland* 75 (*-landa* 26)
Povertone (*-tona*)	See Poorton
Povington, G. 5	*Povintone* 80b
Povintone	See Povington
Povrestoch (*-stoca*)	See Powerstock
Povrtone	See Poorton
Powerstock, C. 4	*Povrestoch* 82b (*-stoca* 50b)

Powrtone (*-tona*)	See Poorton
Poxwell, E. 5	*Pocheswelle* 78 (*-wella* 37)
Poyntington, D. 1	*Ponditone* 93 (*-tona* 279), Som.
Prestetune	See Preston (in Tarrant Rushton)
Preston (in Tarrant Rushton), H. 3	*Prestetune* 77b
Preston (near Weymouth)	Not in D.B.
Puddle, Briants and Turners, F. 4	*Pidele* 83b, 84b (*Pidela* 56b) *Pidre* 78 (*Pidra* 44b)
Puddletown, E. 4	*Piretone* 75 *bis* (*-tona*, *-tune* 25 *bis*) *Pitretone* 79 (*Pidredone* 28)
Pulston	See Forston etc.
Puncknowle, C. 4	*Pomacanole* 83b (*-nola* 58)
Purse Caundle	See Caundle, Bishop's etc.
Radipole, D. 5	*Retpole* 77b (*-pola* 36b)
Ragintone (*-tona*)	See Rollington
Ramesham	See Rampisham
Rampisham, C. 3	*Ramesham* 77
Ranston, G. 2	*Iwerne* 80b
Renscombe, H. 6	*Romescumbe* 78 (*-cumba* 38b)
Retpole (*-pola*)	See Radipole
Ringestede (*Ringhestede*, *-steta*)	See Ringstead
Ringstead, E. 5	*Ringestede* 83, 83b *bis*, 84b (*Ringhestede*, *-steta* 60 *bis*)
Ristone (*-tona*)	See Rushton
Rollington, H. 5	*Ragintone* 82b (*-tona* 51b)
Romescumbe (*-cumba*)	See Renscombe

Rushton, G. 5	*Ristone* 82, 83, 83b, 84, 84b (*-tona* 59b)
Ryme Intrinseca	Not in D.B.
Sandford Orcas, D. 1	*Sanford* 99 (*-forda* 466b, 521b), Som.
Scapeuuic	See Shapwick
Sceptesberie	See Shaftesbury
Scetre (*Scetra*)	Unid., 75b (31b)
Scilfemetune	See Shilvinghampton
Scireburne	See Sherborne
Seaborough, B. 3	*Seveberge* 87b *bis* (*-berga* 154 *bis*, *Sewebeorga*, *Sewoberga* 513 *bis*), Som.
(*Sefemetona*)	See Shilvinghampton
Selavestune	Unid., 82b
Seltone	See Silton
Sepetone (*-tona*)	See Shipton Gorge
Sevemetone	See Shilvinghampton
Shaftesbury, G. 1	*Sceptesberie* 75
Shapwick, H. 3	*Scapeuuic* 75 (*Escapewich* 27)
Sherborne, D. 1	*Scireburne* 77 *ter*, 82
Shillingstone	See Okeford Fitzpaine
Shilvinghampton, D. 5	*Scilfemetone* 80 *Sevemetone* 78b (*Sefemetona* 39b) *Silfemetone* 84b
Shipton Gorge, C. 4	*Sepetone* 75 (*-tona* 27)
Sidelince	See Sydling Fifehead, Sydling St Nicholas
(*Sidelincea*)	See Sydling St Nicholas
Silfemetone	See Shilvinghampton
Silton, A. 1	*Seltone* 82
Simondesberge (*-berga*)	See Symondsbury

Slitlege	Unid., 84b
Smedmore, G. 6	*Metmore* 82
Sonwic (*Sonuich*)	See Swanage
South Perrott, B. 2	*Pedret* 80
South Poorton	See Poorton
Spehtesberie, *Spesteberie* (*Spestesberia*)	See Spettisbury
Spettisbury, G. 3	*Spehtesberie* 82 (*Spestesberia* 47b) *Spesteberie* 79b
Staford (*-fort*)	See West Stafford
Stalbridge, E. 1	*Staplebrige* 77
Stalbridge Weston, E. 1	*Westone* 77
Stanberge	See Stoborough
Stanford	See East Stafford
Stantone	See Stanton St Gabriel
Stanton St Gabriel, A. 4	*Stantone* 80
Staplebrige	See Stalbridge
Steeple, G. 5	*Stiple* 80
Stepleton Iwerne, G. 2	*Werne* 81b (*Iwerna* 49)
Sterte (*Sterta*)	See Sturthill
Stibemetune	See Stubhampton
Stincteford	See Stinsford
Stinsford, E. 4	*Stincteford* 84b *Stiteford* 83
Stiple	See Steeple
Stiteford	See Stinsford
Stoborough, G. 5	*Stanberge* 79b
Stoche	See Cattistock, Stoke Abbott, Stoke Wake, Stoke Wallis
Stoches	See East Stoke, Stock Gaylard, Stoke Wallis
Stock Gaylard, E. 2	*Stoches* 82
Stockwood	Not in D.B.
Stodlege	See Studley
Stoke Abbott, B. 3	*Stoche* 77
Stoke Wake, F. 2	*Stoche* 78b
Stoke Wallis, A. 4	*Stoche*, *Stoches* 80b *bis*, 84b
Stollant	See Studland
Stour, East and West and Stour Provost, F. 1	*Stur*, *Sture* 78b *bis*, 80
Stourpaine, G. 2	*Sture* 83, 85
Stourton Caundle	See Caundle, Bishop's etc.
Stratton	Not in D.B.
Stubhampton, G. 2	*Stibemetune* 82b
Studland, I. 5	*Stollant* 79b
Studley, B. 4	*Stodlege* 84b
Stur	See Stour, East etc.
Sture	See Stour, East etc., Stourpaine
Sturminster Marshall, H. 3	*Sturminstre* 80
Sturminster Newton, F. 2	*Newentone* 77b
Sturminstre	See Sturminster Marshall
Sturthill, C. 4	*Sterte* 83b (*Sterta* 57b)
Sudtone	See Sutton Waldron
Sutone (*-tona*)	See Sutton Poyntz
Sutton Poyntz, E. 5	*Sutone* 75 (*-tona* 27b)
Sutton Waldron, G. 1	*Sudtone* 82
Svere	See Swyre
Swanage, I. 6	*Sonwic* 85 (*Sonuich* 33) *Swanwic* 84 (*61)
*Swanwic**	See Swanage
Swyre, C. 4	*Svere* 80b
Sydling Fifehead, D. 3	*Sidelince* 79b 1st entry
Sydling St Nicholas, D. 3	*Sidelince* 78, 79b 2nd entry (*Sidelincea* 43)
Symondsbury, B. 4	*Simondesberge* 78 (*-berga* 38b)
Tacatone (*-tona*)	See Acton
(*Taerenta*, *Tarenta*)	See Tarrant Gunville etc.
Tarente	See Tarrant Crawford; Tarrant Gunville etc.

Tarrant Crawford, G. 3	*Tarente* 77b 1st entry
Tarrant Gunville, Hinton, Keyneston, Launceston, Monkton, Rawston and Rushton, G. 2, G. 3, H. 2, H. 3	*Tarente* 75b *ter*, 76, 77b *bis* 2nd and 3rd entries, 78b, 79, 83, 83b *ter* (*Taerenta*, *Tarenta* 31, 31b, 32, 58, 59 *bis*) *Terente* 80b, 82b
*Tatentone**, *Tatetun*	See Tatton
Tatton, D. 5	*Tatentone* 83b (*58) *Tatetun* 83
Terente	See Tarrant Gunville etc.
Thorncombe (in Blandford St Mary), G. 3	*Tornecome* 84
Thorncombe (near Seaborough), A. 3	*Tornecome* 108 (*-coma* 313), Devon
Thornford, D. 2	*Torneford* 77
Thornham, G. 5	*Torne* 84 *bis* (*Torna* 61, 61b)
Thornhill, I. 3	*Tornehelle* 84
Thorton, F. 1	*Torentone* 80b
Tigeham	See Tyneham
Tincladene	See Tincleton
Tincleton, F. 4	*Tincladene* 80
Tingeham	See Tyneham
Todber, F. 1	*Todeberie* 82 (*-beria* 47)
Todeberie (*-beria*)	See Todber
Toller Fratrum and Porcorum, C. 3	*Tolre* 82b
Toller Whelme, C. 3	*Tolre* 80
Tolpuddle, Piddlehinton, Athelhampton and Bardolfeston, E. 3, F. 4	*Pidele* 77 *bis*, 78, 78b *bis*, 79 *bis*, 79b (*Pidela* 39, 43b) *Pidere* 82b (*Pidra* 53)
Tolre	See Toller Fratrum, Toller Whelme
Torentone	See Thorton
Torne (*Torna*)	See Thornham
Tornecome	See Thorncombe (in Blandford St Mary)
Torneford	See Thornford
Tornehelle	See Thornhill
Torneworde	See Turnworth
Trelle	See Trill
Trent, D. 1	*Trente* 93 (*Trenta* 279), Som.
Trill, D. 2	*Trelle* 80
Turners Puddle	See Puddle
Turnworth, F. 2	*Torneworde* 82b
Tyneham, G. 5	*Tigeham* 79b, 84b *Tingeham* 80, 83
Up Cerne, D. 3	*Obcerne* 75b
Uploders, C. 4	*Lodra* 83b (*58) *Lodre* 79b *bis* 1st and 2nd entries
Upwey	See Broadwey, etc.
(*Urda*)	See Worth Matravers
*Vergroh**	See Worgret
Verwood	Not in D.B.
Waddon, D. 5	*Wadone* 79, 84b
Wadone	See Waddon
Wai, *Waia**	See Broadwey etc.
Waldic	See Walditch
Walditch, B. 4	*Waldic* 85
Walford, H. 3	*Walteford* 84
Walteford	See Walford
Wardesford	See Woodsford
Wareham, G. 5	*Warham* 75, 75b, 78b *bis*, 79b, 80, 80b *bis* (*12b, 28b, 48)
*Warham**	See Wareham
Warmemoille, *Warmewelle* (*-wella*)	See Warmwell
Warmwell, E. 5	*Warmemoille* 80 *Warmewelle* 83b (*-wella* 60) *Warmwelle* 79b
Warmwelle	See Warmwell

Watercombe, E. 5	*Watrecome* 75b (-*coma* 31b)
Watrecome (-*coma*)	See Watercombe
Weathergrove, D. 1	*Weregrave* 89 (-*grava* 152, *Werregrave* 522b), Som.
Wedechesworde	See Wilksworth
Wellacome	See Woolcombe (in Toller Porcorum)
Welle	See Wellwood, Wool
Wellecome	See Woolcombe (in Melbury Bubb)
Wellwood, B. 3	*Welle* 77
Wenfrot	See Wynford Eagle
Werdesford (-*fort*)	See Woodsford
Weregrote	See Worgret
Werne	See Iwerne Courtney; Lazerton; Stepleton Iwerne
West Chelborough	See Chelborough
West Creech	See Creech
West Hemsworth	See Hemsworth
West Knighton, E. 5	*Chenistetone* 82
West Lulworth	See Lulworth
West Milton, C. 4	*Mideltone* 78 (-*tona* 38)
Westone	See Buckhorn Weston, Stalbridge Weston
West Orchard	Not in D.B.
West Parley, I. 3	*Perlai* 83
West Pulham, E. 2	*Poleham* 79
West Stafford, E. 4	*Staford* 83b (-*fort* 55b)
West Stour	See Stour, East etc.
Weymouth	See Broadwey etc.
Whitchurch Canonicorum, A. 4	*Witcerce* 78b (*28)
Whitcombe, E. 5	*Widecome* 78 (-*coma* 43b)
Whitecliff, I. 5	*Witeclive* 82b (-*cliva* 53)
Wichemetune (*Wichamatuna*)	See Witchampton
Widecome (-*coma*)	See Whitcombe
(*Widetona*)	See Wootton Fitzpaine
Widetone	See Glanville Wootton, Wootton Fitzpaine
Wilceswde (-*wda*)	See Wilkswood
Wilchesode (-*oda*)	See Wilkswood
Wilecome	See Woolcombe (in Toller Porcorum)
Wilkswood, H. 6	*Wilceswde* 84 (-*wda* 60b) *Wilchesode* 84 (-*oda* 61b)
Wilksworth, H. 3	*Wedechesworde* 84 *bis*
Wille	See Wool
Wimborne Minster, H. 3	*Winborne* 75 (-*borna* 27) *Winburne* 75b *bis*, 76 *bis*, 78b *bis*, 79b, 80b (*30b)
Wimborne St Giles, I. 2	*Winburne* 77b, 83b, 84, 85 (-*burna* 56)
Winborne (-*borna*)	See Wimborne Minster
(*Winburna*)	See Wimborne St Giles
Winburne	See Monkton Up Wimborne, Wimborne Minster, Wimborne St Giles
(*Winburne*)	See Wimborne Minster
*Windelham**	See Wyndlam
Windesore	See Broadwindsor
Windestorte	See Woodstreet
Windresorie (-*soria*)	See Littlewindsor
Winfrith Newburgh, F. 5	*Winfrode* 75, 79 (-*froda* 28 *bis*)
Winfrode (-*froda*)	See Winfrith Newburgh

Wraxall, C. 3	*Brocheshale* 82b (*-essala* 51)
Wrde	See Worth Matravers
Wyke Regis	Not in D.B.
Wyndlam, B. 1	*Windelham* 82b (*50)
Wynford Eagle, C. 4	*Wenfrot* 80b
Yetminster, D. 2	*Etiminstre* 75b

ANONYMOUS HOLDINGS

No place-names appear in the following eleven entries, and it is possible that some (or even all) of these refer to holdings at places not named elsewhere in Domesday Book:

Richard (from William de Braiose), 7 hides less half a virgate in Purbeck hd, 82.
Hugh de Boscherbert, 10 hides, 83.
Ralf (from Hugh d'Ivry), *in tribus locis* for 5 hides, 83.
William (from wife of Hugh son of Grip), 1½ virgates, 83b (56b).
Dodo, half a hide, 84.
Alward, third of a virgate, 84.
Godwin the huntsman, one virgate and 4 acres, 84.
Ulric the huntsman (from the king), one hide, 84.
Two bordars, quarter of a virgate, 84b.
William d'Aumery, 3 hides and 2½ virgates, 84b.
Hugh Gosbert, one virgate, 84b.

ESSEX — *EXSESSA*

Little Domesday Book, folios 1–107b

MAPS 16–17

Abberton, H. 4	*Edburg(h)etuna* 28, 46b, 73b
Abbess Roding	See Roding, Abbess and Beauchamp
Accleia	See Oakley
Acleta	Unid., 49b
Adem (?*Acle*)	See Oakley
Ælduluesnasa	See Sokens
Aldeham	See Aldham
Alderford, F. 3	*Alreforda* 39b
Alderton, B. 7	*Aluertuna* 16
Aldham, G. 3	*Aldeham* 24
Aleforda	See Alresford
Alfelmestuna	See Alphamstone
Alferestuna	See Bigods formerly Alfriston
Alia Molesham	See Moulsham (in Great Leighs)
Alia Nessetocha	See Navestock
Almesteda	See Elmstead
Alphamstone, G. 2	*Alfelmestuna* 20, 40, 102
Alreforda	See Alderford
Alresford, I. 4	*Aleforda* 40b *E(i)lesforda* 11b, 25b, 32b
Alsenham	See Elsenham
Altenai	See Iltney
Altera Fifhida	See Fyfield
Althorne	Not in D.B.
Aluertuna	See Alderton
Alui(th)elea	See Aveley
Amberdana	See Amberden

Amberden, C. 3	*Amberdana* 73b
Angra	See Onger
Archesdana	See Arkesden
Ardleigh, I. 3	*Erlega* 83b *Erleia* 59b, 67b, 89b *Erliga* 106b *Herlega* 83b
Arkesden, C. 2	*Archesdana* 51b, 52, 68, 100b
Asce	See Ashen
Ascenduna	See Ashdon
Ashdon, D. 2	*Ascenduna* 71
Asheldham, H. 6	*Hain(c)tuna* 46, 47
Ashen, F. 2	*Asce* 39b
Ashingdon, G. 7	*Nesenduna* 45b
Ashwell, E. 3	*Asseuuella* 95
Asseuuella	See Ashwell
Astoca	See Navestock
Atahou	See Hutton
Ateleia	Unid., 54b
Auileia	See Aveley
Aveley, D. 9	*Aluielea* 97 *Aluithelea* 24b *Auileia* 84b
Aythorpe Roding	See Roding, Aythorpe etc.
Babiterna	See Baythorn
Bacheneia	See Beckney
Baddow, Great and Little, E. 6, F. 5	*Baduuen* 21b, 31, 70, 96b
Baduuen	See Baddow
Banhunta	See Bonhunt
Bardfield, Great and Little, E. 3	*Berdefelda* 41b *Birdefelda* 34, 41 *Byrdefelda* 102b
Bardfield Saling	See Saling
Barking, B. 8	*Berchingas*, *-ingu* 17b *bis*
Barlea	See Borley
Barling, H. 8	*Berlinga* 13b, 23b
Barn Hall, H. 5	*Borooldituna* 69b
Barnston, D. 4	*Bernestuna* 60b
Barrow, G. 8	*Berreuuera* 41b
Barstable, E. 8	*Berdestestapla* 22b
Basildon, E. 8	*Be(r)lesduna* 42b *bis*
Bassetts, F. 5	*Mildemet* 12b
Baythorn, E. 2	*Babiterna* 81

Beauchamp Roding	See Roding, Abbess and Beauchamp
Beaumont, J. 4	*Fulepet* 77b
Bebenhers	See Pebmarsh
Becangra	See Birchanger
Beckney, G. 7	*Bacheneia* 23b
Bedenesteda	See Bensted
Belcamp, *Belcham*	See Belchamp
Belchamp Otten, St Paul and Walter, F. 2	*Belcamp* 77 *Belcham* 12b, 28b, 29, 87b
Belesduna	See Basildon
Belesteda	See Belstead
Belindune	See Ballingdon, Suff.
Belstead, E. 5	*Belesteda* 37b, 97b
Bendysh, D. 2	*Benedisc* 34, 102b
Benedfelda	See Bentfield
Benedisc	See Bendysh
Benetle(i)a	See Bentley
Benfleet, North and South, F. 8	*Benflet* 1b, 4, 14, 43
Benflet	See Benfleet
Bensted, F. 6	*Bedenesteda* 54, 85b
Bentfield, C. 3	*Benedfelda* 65
Bentley, Great and Little, I. 4, J. 4	*Benetle(i)a* 35b, 77b *Menetlea* 40b
Benton, F. 5	*Breddinchou* 19b
Berchingas, *-ingu*	See Barking
Bercolt(a)	See West Bergholt
Berdane	See Berden
Berden, B. 3	*Berdane* 47
Berdestestapla	See Barstable
Berewic	Unid., 25
Berlesduna	See Basildon
Berlinga	See Barling
Berners Roding	See Roding, Aythorpe etc.
Bernestuna	See Barnston
Berreuuera	See Barrow
Bertuna	See Byrton
(Barstable hd)	
Bertuna (Clavering hd)	Unid., 101
Bigods formerly Alfriston, D. 4	*Alferestuna* 61

Bilichangra	See Birchanger
Billericay	Not in D.B.
Bineslea	See Binsley
Binsley, G. 2	*Bineslea* 39b, 79
Birch (in Kirby-le-Soken), K. 4	*Birichou* 32b
Birch, Great and Little, H. 4	*Bricceia* 30 *Bricia* 66 *Parva Bricceia* 93b
Birchanger, C. 4	*Becangra* 3b *Bilichangra* 21 *Blichangra* 62b
Birdbrook, E. 2	*Bridebroc* 80b
Birdefelda	See Bardfield
Birichou	See Birch (in Kirby-le-Soken)
Blacham	See Blatchams
Blackmore	Not in D.B.
Black Notley	See Notley
Blatchams, G. 5	*Blacham* 32
Blichangra	See Birchanger
Blundeshala	See Blunt's Hall
Blunt's Hall, F. 5	*Blundeshala* 27, 72
Bobbingworth, C. 6	*Bubingeorda* 81
Bocchesteda	See Boxted
Bochinges	See Bocking
Bocking, F. 4	*Bochinges* 8
Bockingham, H. 4	*Botingham* 100
Boituna	See Boyton
Boli(n)tuna	See Bollington
Bollington, C. 3	*Boli(n)tuna* 65b, 101 *bis*
Bonhunt, C. 3	*Banhunta* 93
Boreham, F. 5	*Borham* 31b, 37b, 47b
Borham	See Boreham
Borley, G. 1	*Barlea* 91b, 101b, 102
Borooldituna	See Barn Hall
Botingham	See Bockingham
Bowers Gifford, F. 8	*Bura* 14, 71b, 86, 98
Boxted, H. 3	*Bocche-*, *Bucchesteda* 29b, 50b *Bocstede*, Exch. D.B. 208, Hunts.
Boyton, E. 3	*Boituna* 40, 40b

Brac(c)hesteda, *Bracteda*	See Braxted
Bradefelda	See Bradfield
Bradfield, J. 3	*Bradefelda* 83b, 89 *bis*
Bradwell juxta Coggeshall	Not in D.B.
Bradwell on Sea	Not in D.B.
Bradwell Quay formerly Hackfleet, H. 6	*Hacflet* 24
Braintree, F. 4	*Branchetreu* 101b, 103
Branchetreu	See Braintree
Branduna	See Brundon, Suff.
Braxted, Great and Little, G. 5	*Brac(c)hesteda* 49, 55 *Bracteda* 12
Breddinchou	See Benton
Brentwood	Not in D.B.
Bricceia, *Bricia*, *Parva Bricceia*	See Birch, Great and Little
Brictriceseia	See Brightlingsea
Bridebroc	See Birdbrook
Brightlingsea, I. 4	*Brictriceseia* 6 *bis* *Brictesceseia* 286b, Suff.
Broc(c)hesheuot	See Broxted
Bromley, Great and Little, I. 3	*Brumbeleia* 97 *Brumle(i)a* 40b, 87
Broomfield, E. 5	*Brumfelda* 58b
Broxted, D. 3	*Broc(c)hesheuot* 18b, 50
Brumbeleia	See Bromley
Brumduna	See Brundon, Suff.
Brumfelda	See Broomfield
Brumle(i)a	See Bromley
Bubingeorda	See Bobbingworth
Buckhurst Hill	Not in D.B.
Bulenemera	See Bulmer
Bulgeuen	See Bulphan
Bulmer, G. 2	*Bulenemera* 39b
Bulphan, D. 8	*Bulgeuen* 17b
Bumesteda	See Helions Bumpstead, Steeple Bumpstead
Bummesteda	See Steeple Bumpstead

Bunsteda	See Helions Bumpstead
Bura	See Bowers Gifford, Bures, Mount Bures
Bures, G. 3	*Bura* 40b, 84b *Buro* 39b, 40b
Burghesteda	See Burstead
Burna	Unid., 32b
Burn(e)ham	See Burnham
Burnham, H. 7	*Burn(e)ham* 70, 99b
Buro	See Bures
Burstead, Great and Little, E. 7	*Burghesteda* 11b, 22b
Buttsbury, E. 7	*Cinga* 57
Byrdefelda	See Bardfield
Byrton, H. 4	*Bertuna* 94
Cadenhou	See Hadstock
Cane(d)felda	See Canfield
Canewdon, G. 7	*Carenduna* 44
Canfield, Great and Little, D. 4	*Cane(d)felda* 35, 36b, 76, 100 *Chenefelda* 61b
Canvey	Not in D.B.
Carenduna	See Canewdon
Car(e)seia	See Northey Island
Castle Hedingham	See Hedingham
Ceauride	See Chaureth
Celdeforda	See Shalford
Celdewella	See Chadwell
Celmeresfort	See Chelmsford
Celuestuna	See Coupals formerly Chelveston
Ceseuuic	See Chiswick
Cestreforda, *-fort*	See Chesterford
Cetham	See Chatham
Chadwell, D. 9	*Celdewella* 12, 23, 98
Chappel	Not in D.B.
Chardwell formerly Ainsworth, B. 2	*Einesuurda* 38
Chatham, E. 5	*Cetham* 58
Chaureth, D. 3	*Ceauride* 103
Chelleuadana, *-euedana*	See Kelvedon
Chelmsford, E. 6	*Celmeresfort* 10b

Cheneboltuna	Unid., 40
Chenefelda	See Canfield
Chesterford, Great and Little, C. 2	*Cestreforda*, *-fort* 3b, 87 *Cestreforde*, Exch. D.B., 189b, 190, Cambs.
Chickney, D. 3	*Cicchenai* 72b
Chignall, E. 5	*Cingehala* 58b *bis*, 59 *Cinguehella* 67
Chigwell, B. 7	*Cingheuuella* 90b *bis*
Childerditch, D. 8	*Ciltedic* 42, 92b *Ciltendis* 5
Chingford, A. 7	*Cing(h)efort* 12b, 64
Chipping Ongar	See Ongar
Chiswick, B. 2	*Ceseuuic* 90b
Chrishall, B. 2	*Cristeshala* 33
Cicchenai	See Chickney
Cice	See St Osyth
Ciltedic, *Ciltendis*	See Childerditch
Cinga	See Buttsbury
Cingefort	See Chingford
Cingehala	See Chignall
Cinghefort	See Chingford
Cingheuuella	See Chigwell
Cinguehella	See Chignall
Cishella, *-helle*	See Chishill, Cambs.
Cita	See St Osyth
Clachintuna	See Clacton
Clacton, Great and Little, J. 4	*Clachintuna* 11
Clare	See Claret
Claret, F. 1	*Clare* 28b
Clauelinga	See Clavering
Clavering, C. 3	*Clauelinga* 46b, 47
Cliff, J. 3	*Cliua* 83b
Cliua	See Cliff
Coggeshall, Great and Little, G. 4	*Cogheshala*, *-essala* 8, 26b, 96, 99b
Cogheshala, *-essala*	See Coggeshall
Colchester, H. 3	*Colecastro* 14b, 18, 27, 30 *Colecestra* 11, 22, 29b, 72b, 104 *bis*, 107, 107b

Cold Norton, G. 6	*Nortuna* 69
Colecastro, *-cestra*	See Colchester
Coles	See Colne, Earls etc.
Colne, Earls, Wakes and White, G. 3	*Coles* 77 *Colun* 20, 30, 40b, 86b, 88b, 102b *bis*, 103
Colne Engaine, G. 3	*Parva Colun* 88b
Colun	See Colne, Earls etc.
Colun, *Parva*	See Colne Engaine
Copeforda	See Copford
Copford, H. 4	*Copeforda* 10b
Cornish Hall formerly Norton, E. 2	*Nortuna* 102
Corringham, E. 8	*Currincham* 11b
Coupals formerly Chelveston, E. 1	*Celuestuna* 40, 101
Cowbridge, D. 7	*Cubrigea* 81b
Cranham formerly Bishop's Ockenden, D. 8	*Craohu* 24b
Craohu	See Cranham
Crauuelaea	See Crawley
Crawley, B. 2	*Crauuelaea* 34
Cray's Hill, E. 7	*Winthelle* 92b
Creeksea, H. 7	*Criccheseia* 23b *bis*, 95
Crepinga, *-inges*	See Crepping
Crepping, G. 3	*Crepinga*, *-inges* 95b, 102b
Cressing	Not in D.B.
Criccheseia	See Creeksea
Cristeshala	See Chrishall
Cubrigea	See Cowbridge
Cuica	See Quickbury
Culverts, F. 5	*Richeham* 67
Curlai	See Curling Tye Green
Curling Tye Green, F. 6	*Curlai* 69
Currincham	See Corringham
Cuton, E. 5	*Keuentuna* 59
Dagenham	Not in D.B.
Danbury, F. 6	*Danengeberia* 59

Danengeberia	See Danbury
Daneseia	See Dengie
Dantuna	See Dunton
Debden (in Loughton), B. 7	*Tippedana* 16
Debden (near Newport), C. 3	*Deppedana* 73b
Dedham, I. 3	*Delham* 83
Delham	See Dedham
Dengie, H. 6	*Daneseia* 21, 24
Deppedana	See Debden (near Newport)
Der(e)leia	See Derleigh
Derleigh, I. 3	*Der(e)leia* 81b, 95b
Dicheleia	See Dickley
Dickley, J. 3	*Dicheleia* 67b
Doddenhenc	See Doddinghurst
Doddinghurst, D. 7	*Doddenhenc* 85
Dommauua	See Dunmow
Dona	See Down
Dorseda	See Orsett
Dovercourt, K. 3	*Druvrecurt* 77b
Down, H. 6	*Dona* 49b *Duna* 74b *bis*
Druvrecurt	See Dovercourt
Duna	See Down
Dunilanda	See East Donyland
Dunmow, Great and Little, D. 4	*Dommauua* 27b, 36b, 38b, 46b, 50, 55, 61, 61b, 62, 69
Dunton, D. 8	*Dantuna* 22b, 99
Dunulanda	See East Donyland
Earls Colne	See Colne, Earls etc.
East Donyland, I. 4	*Dunilanda* 30, 95b, 96 *bis* *Dunulanda* 30
Easter, Good and High, D. 5	*Estra* 20b, 60
East Ham	See Ham
East Hanningfield	See Hanningfield
East Horndon	See Horndon
Easthorpe, G. 4	*Estorp* 30
East Mersea	See Mersea
Easton, Great and Little, D. 3, D. 4	*E(i)stanes* 36, 61b, 86b, 91b
East Tilbury	See Tilbury

Eastwood, G. 8	*Estuuda* 43b *Nestuda* 45b
Edburg(h)etuna	See Abberton
Effecestra, *-cestre*	See St Peter's Chapel
Eiland, H. 3	*Eiland* 47
Eilesforda	See Alresford
Einesuurda	See Chardwell formerly Ainsworth
Eistanes	See Easton
Elesforda	See Alresford
Elmdon, B. 2	*Elmerduna* 33b
Elmdon Lee formerly Leebury, C. 2	*Lea* 33b
Elmerduna	See Elmdon
Elmesteda	See Elmstead
Elmstead, I. 3	*Almesteda* 48 *Elmesteda* 106b
Elsenham, C. 3	*Alsenham* 94b *Elsenham* 68
Eltenai	See Iltney
Emanuel Wood, C. 2	*Monehala* 35b *Munehala* 62b
Emwella	See Amwell, Herts.
Epinga	See Epping
Epping, B. 6	*Ep(p)inga*, *-inges* 15b, 35, 80b *ter*
Eppinga, *-inges*	See Epping
Erlega, *-leia*, *-liga*	See Ardleigh
Ersham	See Horseham
Esceldeforde	See Shalford
Essoberia	See Shoebury
Estanes	See Easton
Estinfort	See Stifford
Estoleia	See Studly
Estorp	See Easthorpe
Estra	See Easter
Estuuda	See Eastwood
Eurewic	See York, N.R.
Fairstead, F. 4	*Fairsteda* 72b
Fairsteda	See Fairstead
Falcheburna	See Faulkbourne
Fanbruge	See North Fambridge
Fanton, F. 7	*Fantuna* 17b *Phantuna* 14 *bis*

Fantuna	See Fanton
Farnham, C. 4	*Phern(e)ham* 55b, 65b, 100b, 101
Faulkbourne, F. 4	*Falcheburna* 54b
Feering, G. 4	*Ferigens* 106b *Feringas* 100 *Pheringas* 14b
Felesteda	See Felsted
Felsted, E. 4	*Felesteda* 97 *Felstede* 96 *Phensteda* 21b
Felstede	See Felsted
Fenna, *Fenne*	See Stow Maries
Ferigens, *Feringas*	See Feering
Festinges	See Fristling
Fifhida, *Altera Fifhida*	See Fyfield
Finchingfield, E. 3	*Fincing(h)efelda* 39b *bis* *Phincing(h)efelda* 4, 29 *bis*, 35, 35b, 39, 40, 101b
Fincing(h)efelda	See Finchingfield
Fingrinhoe	Not in D.B.
Fingrith, D. 6	*Phingheria* 5 *bis*
Fobbing, E. 8	*Phobinge* 26
Fordeham	See Fordham
Fordham, H. 3	*For(de)ham* 38, 41, 89b, 102b
Forham	See Fordham
Foscearde	See Foxearth
Fouchers, D. 7	*Ginga* 81b
Foulness	Not in D.B.
Foulton, K. 3	*Fuletuna* 48, 85b
Foxearth, F. 1	*Foscearde* 40
Frating, I. 4	*Frat-*, *Fretinga* 32b, 75b
Frat-, *Fretinga*	See Frating
Frie(n)tuna	See Frinton
Frinton, K. 4	*Frie(n)tuna* 32b, 59b
Fristling, E. 6	*Festinges* 18
Froruuica	See Frowick
Frowick, J. 4	*Froruuica* 32b
Fryerning and Ingatestone, D. 6	*Inga* 18, 66b, 67 *bis*
Fulepet	See Beaumont
Fuletuna	See Foulton
Fyfield, D. 6	*Altera Fifhida* 84b *Fifhida* 31 *bis*, 84b

Geddesduna	Unid., 15
Geld(e)ham	See Yeldham
Gerdelai	See Yardley
Gerham	See Yeldham
Gernesteda	See Greensted
Gestingthorpe, F. 2	*Ghestingetorp* 39 *Glestingethorp* 98
Ghestingetorp	See Gestingthorpe
Ginga	See Fouchers; Margaretting
Glestingethorp	See Gestingthorpe
Goldhanger, G. 5	*Goldhangra* 32, 54, 76
Goldhangra	See Goldhanger
Goldingham, F. 2	*Goldingham* 88
Good Easter	See Easter
Gosfield	Not in D.B.
Gravesanda, E. 9	Lost in Tilbury, 26b
Grays Thurrock	See Thurrock
Great Baddow	See Baddow
Great Bardfield	See Bardfield
Great Bentley	See Bentley
Great Birch	See Birch
Great Braxted	See Braxted
Great Bromley	See Bromley
Great Burstead	See Burstead
Great Canfield	See Canfield
Great Chesterford	See Chesterford
Great Clacton	See Clacton
Great Coggeshall	See Coggeshall
Great Dunmow	See Dunmow
Great Easton	See Easton
Great Hallingbury	See Hallingbury
Great Henny	See Henny
Great Holland	See Holland
Great Horkesley	Not in D.B.
Great Leighs	See Leighs
Great Maplestead	See Maplestead
Great Oakley	See Oakley
Great Parndon	See Parndon
Great Saling	See Saling
Great Sampford	See Sampford
Great Slamseys, E. 4	*Slamonesheia* 9b
Great Stambridge	See Stambridge
Great Tey	See Tey
Great Totham	See Totham
Great Wakering	See Wakering
Great Waltham	See Waltham

Great Warley	See Warley
Great Whitmans, F. 6	*Witham* 64b
Great Wigborough	See Wigborough
Great Yeldham	See Yeldham
Greenstead, H. 4	*Grenesteda* 104
Greensted, C. 6	*Gernesteda* 56
Grenesteda	See Greenstead
Hacflet	See Bradwell Quay formerly Hackfleet
Hacheleia	See Hockley
Hac(he)uuella	See Hawkwell
Hadfelda	See Hatfield Broad Oak, Hatfield Peverel
Hadleigh	Not in D.B.
Hadstock, C. 1	*Cadenhou* 19
Hafelda	See Hatfield Peverel
Hainctuna	See Asheldham
Haindena	See Heydon, Cambs.
Haingheham	See Hedingham
Haintuna	See Asheldham
Halesduna	Unid., 53b
Halesheia, *-leia*	See Hazeleigh
Halingeb(er)ia, *Halingheberia*	See Hallingbury
Hallingbury, Great and Little, C. 4	*Halingeb(er)ia* 46, 52, 60 *Halingheberia* 12b *Hallingeberia* 60
Hallingeberia	See Hallingbury
Halstead, F. 3	*Hal(te)steda* 37, 40, 101b, 103
Hal(te)steda	See Halstead
Ham, East and West, B. 8	*Hame* 14b, 64 *bis*, 72b
Hame	See Ham
Hamsteda	See Hempstead
Haneghefelda	See Hanningfield
Hanies	See Henny
Haningefelda	See Hanningfield
Hanningfield, East, South and West, E. 6, E. 7, F. 6	*Haneghefelda* 25 *Haningefelda* 37b *bis*, 70b, 85b
Harlow, B. 5	*Herlaua* 19b, 27b, 49, 80

Place	Domesday form and folio
Harwich	Not in D.B.
Hasing(h)ebroc	See Hassenbrook
Hasingham	Unid., 102b
Hassenbrook, E. 8	*Hasing(h)ebroc* 23, 42b
Hatfelde	See Hatfield Broad Oak
Hatfield Broad Oak, C. 4	*Hadfelda* 2 *Hatfelde* 55
Hatfield Peverel, F. 5	*Ha(d)felda* 23b, 72
Hauelingas, *Haueringas*	See Havering-atte-Bower
Havering-atte-Bower, C. 7	*Hauelingas* 53, 85, 100 *bis* *Haueringas* 2b
Hawkwell, G. 7	*Hac(he)uuella* 45b, 51b *Hechuuella* 50
Hazeleigh, F. 6	*Halesheia* 73 *Halesleia* 73b
Hecham	See Higham
Hechuuella	See Hawkwell
Hedingham, Castle and Sible, F. 2	*Haingheham* 76b *Hedingham* 83 *Hidingham* 87b
Helions Bumpstead, D. 2	*Bumesteda* 77b, 103 *Bunsteda* 82
Helituna	See Kenningtons
Hempstead, D. 2	*Hamsteda* 41b
Henham, C. 3	*Henham* 71, 101
Heni(es)	See Henny
Henny, Great and Little, G. 2	*Hanies* 101 *Heni(es)* 74, 84, 87b, 99b, 101b
Herchesteda	See Harkstead, Suff.
Herefort	See Hertford, Herts.
Herlaua	See Harlow
Herlega	See Ardleigh
Hers(h)am	See Horseham
Heybridge formerly Tidwoldington, G. 5	*Tidwolditυna* 13b
Hidingham	See Hedingham
Higham, A. 7	*Hecham* 78b
High Easter	See Easter
High Laver	See Laver
High Ongar	See Ongar
High Roding	See Roding, Aythorpe etc.
Hobruge	See Howbridge
Hocheleia	See Hockley
Hockley, F. 7	*Hacheleia* 45 *Hocheleia* 18b, 43b
Hocsenga	Unid., 102b
Hodesduna	See Hoddesdon, Herts.
Ho(i)landa	See Holland
Holland, Great and Little, K. 4	*Ho(i)landa* 33, 91
Hornchurch	Not in D.B.
Horndon, East and West, D. 8	*Tor(n)induna* 23b, 42, 90
Horndon on the Hill, E. 8	*Horninduna* 12, 26, 42, 93, 93b, 99
Horninduna	See Horndon on the Hill
Horseham, E. 1	*Ersham* 101b *Hers(h)am* 20b, 77, 103
Horstedafort	See Stebbingford
Housham, C. 5	*Ouesham* 36, 91
Howbridge, F. 5	*Hobruge* 12, 63b
Howe, E. 3	*Weninchou* 39b *Weninghou* 101b
Hunt's Hall formerly Pooley, G. 3	*Polheia* 37
Hutton, D. 7	*Atahou* 20b
Ilefort	See Ilford
Ilford, B. 8	*Ilefort* 94
Iltney, G. 6	*Altenai* 45b *Eltenai* 27b
Inga	See Fryerning, Ingrave
Ingatestone	See Fryerning
Ingrave, D. 7	*Inga* 22b, 72, 79b
Inworth	Not in D.B.
Jacques Hall formerly Manston, J. 3	*Manestuna* 83b

Kal-, *Kelenduna*	See Kelvedon Hatch
Kelituna	See Kenningtons
Keluenduna	See Kelvedon Hatch
Kelvedon, G. 4	*Chelleuadana*, *-euedana* 14, 52b
Kelvedon Hatch, D. 6	*Kal-*, *Kelenduna* 24, 56 *Keluenduna* 14b
Kenningtons, D. 8	*Helituna* 48 *Kelituna* 37b
Keuentuna	See Cuton
Kirby-le-Soken	See Sokens
Kuenaduna	See Quendon
Lacelea	See Lashley
Lac(h)enduna, *Lachentuna*	See Latchingdon
Lagafara, *Laghefara*	See Laver
Laghenberia	See Lawn Hall
Laindon, E. 8	*Legenduna* 9b *Leienduna* 12
Laingaham	See Langham
Laleforda	See Lawford
Lalinga, *-inge*	See Lawling
Lamarsh, G. 2	*Lamers* 74, 74b, 99b, 101b
Lambourne, C. 7	*Lamburna* 31
Lamburna	See Lambourne
Lamers	See Lamarsh
Landuna	Unid., 49b
Langdon, E. 8	*Langenduna* 42
Langefort	See Langford
Langenduna	See Langdon
Langenhoe, H. 4	*Langhou* 27b
Langford, F. 5	*Langefort* 68b *Langheforda* 71
Langham, I. 3	*Laingaham* 41
Langheforda	See Langford
Langhou	See Langenhoe
Langley	Not in D.B.
Lashley, D. 3	*Lacelea* 101b
Latchingdon, G. 7	*Lac(h)enduna* 3, 8, 98b *Lachentuna* 53 *Lessenduna* 3
Latton, B. 5	*Lattuna* 19b, 27, 78
Lattuna	See Latton
Laver, High, Little and Magdalen, C. 5	*Lagafara* 30b *Laghefara* 31, 91
Lawford, I. 3	*Laleforda* 6, 40b, 70b, 81b *Leleforda* 33
Lawling, G. 6	*Lalinga*, *-inge* 8, 49b, 74b, 85, 103
Lawn Hall, D. 4	*Laghenberia* 25
Layer Breton, de la Haye and Marney, G. 4, H. 4	*Legra* 4b, 10 *bis*, 22, 28, 53b, 73b, 92b, 95, 99b
Lea	See Elmdon Lea formerly Leebury, Lee Chapel
Leaden Roding	See Roding, Aythorpe etc.
Lee Chapel, E. 8	*Lea* 12b
Lega (Chelmsford hd)	See Leighs
Lega (Winstree hd)	Unid., 64b
Legenduna	See Laindon
Legra	See Layer; Leigh; Leighs
Leienduna	See Laindon
Leigh, G. 8	*Legra* 75b
Leighs, Great and Little, E. 4, E. 5	*Leg(r)a* 51, 59
Lei(n)tuna	See Leyton
Leleforda	See Lawford
Lessendena	See Lexden
Lessenduna	See Latchingdon
Lexden, H. 4	*Lessendena* 4b *Lexsendena* 104
Lexsendena	See Lexden
Leyton, A. 8	*Lei(n)tuna* 14b, 52b, 64b, 78b, 85 *bis*
Liffildeuuella	Unid., 101
Limpwella	Unid., 25
Lindesela, *-seles*	See Lindsell
Lindsell, D. 3	*Lindesela*, *-seles* 20b, 49
Liston, G. 1	*Listuna* 89b, 95b
Listuna	See Liston
Litelbyria	See Littlebury
Little Baddow	See Baddow
Little Bardfield	See Bardfield

Little Bentley	See Bentley
Little Birch	See Birch
Little Braxted	See Braxted
Little Bromley	See Bromley
Little Burstead	See Burstead
Littlebury, C. 2	*Litelbyria* 19
Little Canfield	See Canfield
Little Chesterford	See Chesterford
Little Clacton	See Clacton
Little Coggeshall	See Coggeshall
Little Dunmow	See Dunmow
Little Easton	See Easton
Little Hallingbury	See Hallingbury
Little Henny	See Henny
Little Holland	See Holland
Little Horkesley	Not in D.B.
Little Laver	See Laver
Little Leighs	See Leighs
Little Maplestead	See Maplestead
Little Oakley	See Oakley
Little Parndon	See Parndon
Little Sampford	See Sampford
Little Stambridge	See Stambridge
Little Tey	See Tey
Littlethorpe, G. 8	*Torpeia* 44b
Little Thurrock, D. 9	*T(h)urrucca* 11b, 99
Little Totham	See Totham
Little Wakering	See Wakering
Little Waltham	See Waltham
Little Warley	See Warley
Little Wigborough	See Wigborough
Little Yeldham	See Yeldham
Lochetuna, *Lochintuna*	See Loughton
Lohou	Unid., 94
Londonia	See London, Mdlx.
Loughton, B. 7	*Lochetuna* 3, 64b, 79 *Lochintuna* 16 *bis*, 79
Magdalen Laver	See Laver
Magellana, *Magghedana*	See Manuden
Maldon, G. 6	*Malduna* 5b *Meldona* 73 *Melduna* 4b, 29, 48, 75, 107b
Malduna	See Maldon

Manestuna	See Jacques Hall formerly Manston
Manningtree	Not in D.B.
Manuden, C. 2	*Magellana* 69b *Magghedana* 65, 101 *Menghedana* 65b
Maplesteda	See Maplestead
Maplestead, Great and Little, F. 2	*Maplesteda* 65b, 84 *Mappesteda* 101
Mappesteda	See Maplestead
Margaret Roding	See Roding, Aythorpe etc.
Margaretting and Mountnessing, D. 7, E. 6	*Ginga* 5, 81, 91b
Markshall, G. 3	*Mercheshala* 53b
Marks Tey	See Tey
Masceberia	See Mashbury
Mashbury, D. 5	*Masceberia* 100 *Massebirig* 58b
Massebirig	See Mashbury
Matching, C. 5	*Matcinga*, *-inge* 60, 64, 93b *Metcinga* 20b
Matcinga, *-inge*	See Matching
Mayland	Not in D.B.
Meldona, *-duna*	See Maldon
Melesham	See Moulsham (in Great Leighs)
Menetlea	See Bentley
Menghedana	See Manuden
Mercheshala	See Markshall
Meresai(a)	See Mersea
Mersea, East and West, H. 5, I. 5	*Meresai(a)* 8, 22, 46b
Messing, G. 4	*Metcinges* 69b, 83
Metcinga	See Matching
Metcinges	See Messing
Michaelstow, K. 3	*Michelestou* 70b
Michelestou	See Michaelstow
Middleton, G. 2	*Milde(l)tuna* 40, 98, 103b
Midebroc	Unid., 99b
Mildeltuna	See Middleton
Mildemet	See Bassetts
Mildentuna	See Milton
Mildetuna	See Middleton
Milton, G. 8	*Mildentuna* 8b

Ouituna	See Ovington
Ovington, F. 2	*O(l)uituna* 87b, 102
Pachenhou	See Peyton
Pachesham	See Paglesham
Pacingas, *-inges*	See Patching
Paglesham, G. 7	*Pachesham* 15, 38, 71, 86, 99b
Panfield, E. 3	*Penfelda* 22, 39
Parndon, Great and Little, B. 5	*Perenduna* 17b, 27, 80 *ter*
	Perinduna 78b
Parva Bricceia	See Birch
Parva Colun	See Colne Engaine
Parva Stanfort	See Stanford Rivers
Paslow, D. 6	*Passefelda* 16
Passefelda	See Paslow
Patching, E. 9	*Pacingas*, *-inges* 25b, 58b, 67
Pattiswick	Not in D.B.
Peben(h)ers	See Pebmarsh
Pebmarsh, G. 3	*Bebenhers* 102
	Peben(h)ers 40, 87b, 101
Peldon, H. 4	*Peltenduna* 46b, 94b
Peltenduna	See Peldon
Penfelda	See Panfield
Pentelauua	See Pentlow
Pentlow, F. 1	*Pentelauua* 69b
Perenduna	See Parndon
Peresteda	See Prested
Perinduna	See Parndon
Peyton, C. 3	*Pachenhou* 37
Phantuna	See Fanton
Phenbruge	See South Fambridge
Phenge	See Vange
Phenna	See Stow Maries
Phensteda	See Felsted
Pheringas	See Feering
Phern(e)ham	See Farnham
Phincing(h)efelda	See Finchingfield
Phingheria	See Fingrith
Phobinge	See Fobbing
Piceseia	See Pitsea
Pincepo	See Pinchpools

Pinchpools, C. 3	*Pincepo* 92b
Pitsea, E. 8	*Piceseia* 98
Pledgdon, C. 3	*Plicedana* 50b, 62b
Pleshey	Not in D.B.
Plesinchou	See Plesingho
Plesingho, D. 5	*Plesinchou* 27b, 100b
Plicedana	See Pledgdon
Plumberga	See Plumberow
Plumberow, G. 7	*Plumberga* 38, 45
Plumtuna	See Plunker's Green
Plunker's Green, D. 7	*Plumtuna* 75
Polheia	See Hunt's Hall formerly Pooley
Prested, G. 4	*Peresteda* 74b
Pritteuuella	See Prittlewell
Prittlewell, G. 8	*Pritteuuella* 44
Pudsey, G. 7	*Puteseia* 45, 45b *ter*
Purlai	See Purleigh
Purleigh, G. 6	*Purlai* 27b, 53 *ter*, 64b, 86b *bis*
Puteseia	See Pudsey
Quendon, C. 3	*Kuenadana* 51
Quickbury, C. 5	*Cuica* 36
Radenduna	See Rettendon
Radwinter, D. 2	*Redeuuintra* 51b, 78, 82, 92
Rageneia, *Ragheleia*	See Rayleigh
Raineham	See Rainham
Raines	See Rayne
Raines	Unid., 55
Rainham, C. 8	*Raineham* 96
	Reineham 91
	Renaham 66b
	Reneham 24b
Ramesdana, *-duna*	See Ramsden
Rameseia	See Ramsey
Ramsden Bellhouse and Crays, E. 7	*Ramesdana* 9b, 12, 23, 52b, 63b, 79b
	Ramesduna 63b

Ramsey, K. 3	*Rameseia* 70b
Ratenduna	See Rettendon
Rawreth	Not in D.B.
Rayleigh, F. 7	*Rageneia* 43b *Ragheleia* 43b
Rayne, E. 4	*Raines* 10, 53b, 82b, 83
Redeuuintra	See Radwinter
Reineham, *Renaham*, *Reneham*	See Rainham
Retleia	See Ridley
Rettendon, F. 7	*Radenduna*, *Ratenduna* 19, 51, 75
Richeham	See Culverts
Richelinga	See Rickling
Rickling, C. 3	*Richelinga* 7
Rideuuella	See Ridgewell
Ridgewell, E. 2	*Rideuuella* 28
Ridley, F. 5	*Retleia* 60
Riuuehala	See Rivenhall
Rivenhall, F. 4	*Riuuehala* 63b *Ruenhala*, *-hale* 27 *bis*, 96b *Ruuuenhala* 46
Rochefort	See Rochford
Rochford, G. 7	*Rochefort* 44b
Rockells formerly Wyggepet, B. 2	*Wicgepet* 100b *Wigghepet* 100
Roda	See Rothend
Roding, Abbess and Beauchamp, D. 5	*Roinges* 35b, 50b, 57b
Roding, Aythorpe, Berners, High, Leaden, Margaret and White, C. 5, D. 4, D. 5	*Rodinges*, *-ingis* 3, 19, 36b *bis*, 49, 52, 55, 60b, 61b *bis*, 62 *ter* *Roinges* 40b, 61b *Rochinges* 262, Norf.
Rodinges, *-ingis*	See Roding, Aythorpe etc.
Roinges	See Roding, Abbess and Beauchamp; Roding, Aythorpe etc.
Romford	Not in D.B.
Rothend, D. 2	*Roda* 35b
Roxwell	Not in D.B.
Roydon, B. 5	*Ruindune* 80
Ruenhala, *-hale*	See Rivenhall
Ruindune	See Roydon
Runewella	See Runwell
Runwell, F. 7	*Runewella* 13b, 31b *bis*
Ruuuenhala	See Rivenhall
Ryes, C. 4	*Siriceslea* 55
Saffron Walden, C. 2	*Waledana* 62
St Lawrence formerly Newland, H. 6	*Niuuelanda* 81 *Niwelant* 8
St Osyth, J. 5	*Cice* 11, 75b *Cita* 32b
St Peter's Chapel, I. 5	*Effecestra*, *-cestre* 21, 53b
Salcota	See Virley
Salcott	Not in D.B.
Saling, Bardfield and Great, E. 3	*Salinges* 84, 102
Salinges	See Saling
Samantuna	See Sampsons
Sampford, Great and Little, D. 2, D. 3	*Sanforda* 41 *Sanfort* 7b
Sampsons, H. 5	*Samantuna* 24
Sandon	Not in D.B.
Sanforda, *-fort*	See Sampford
Scaldefort	See Shalford
Scelda	See Shellow Bowells
Scelfort	See Shelford, Cambs.
Scelga	See Shellow Bowells
Scenefelda	See Shenfield
Sceringa	See Sheering
Sciddeham	Unid., 103
Sciddinchou	See Old Hall formerly Sheldon or Sharing
Scilcheham	Unid., 93
Scopelanda	See Shopland
Scortegrava	See Shortgrove
Senleia	See Shelley

Shalford, E. 3	*Celdeforda* 3b *Esceldeforde* 106b *Scaldefort* 94b, 95
Sheering, C. 5	*Sceringa* 78
Shelley, C. 6	*Senleia* 57b
Shellow Bowells, D. 6	*Scelda* 3 *Scelga* 50, 61 *bis*, 62
Shenfield, D. 7	*Scenefelda* 26b
Shoebury, North and South, H. 8	*Essoberia* 44, 44b *Soberia* 23b
Shopland, G. 8	*Scopelanda* 34b
Shortgrove, C. 2	*Scortegrava* 68 *Sortegraua* 28, 28b
Sible Hedingham	See Hedingham
Sireceslea	See Ryes
Slamondesheia	See Great Slamseys
Smalelant	See Smallands
Smallands, F. 5	*Smalelant* 85
Smalton, F. 2	*Smaltuna* 101
Smaltuna	See Smalton
Smedetuna	See Smeetham
Smeetham, G. 2	*Smedetuna* 29
Soberia	See Shoebury
Sokens, The: Kirby-le-Soken, Thorpe-le-Soken and Walton-le-Soken, J. 4, K. 4	*Aelduluesnasa* 13b
Sortegraua	See Shortgrove
South Benfleet	See Benfleet
Southchurch, G. 8	*Sudcerca* 8b
South Fambridge, G. 7	*Phenbruge* 97b
South Hanningfield	See Hanningfield
Southminster, H. 6	*Sudmunstra* 10
South Ockendon	See Ockendon
South Shoebury	See Shoebury
South Weald, D. 7	*Walda* 66b *Welda* 16b
Springafelda	See Springfield
Springfield, E. 5	*Springafelda* 75 *Springinghefelda* 67
Springinghefelda	See Springfield
Stabinga	See Stebbing
Stambourne, E. 2	*Stanburna* 55b *bis*, 100b *bis*
Stambridge, Great and Little, G. 7	*Stanbruge* 8b, 23b, 44b, 99b

Stanbruge	See Stambridge
Stanburna	See Stambourne
Stanesgata	See Stanesgate
Stanesgate, H. 6	*Stanesgata* 74b, 99b
Stanesteda	See Stanstead, Stansted Mountfitchet
Stanewega	See Stanway
Stanford Rivers, C. 6	*Parva Stanfort* 30b *Stanfort* 30b
Stanfort, *Parva Stanfort*	See Stanford Rivers
Stanmer, E. 7	*Stantmere* 92b
Stanstead, F. 3	*Stanesteda* 88, 88b
Stansted Mountfitchet, C. 4	*Stanesteda* 65
Stantmere	See Stanmer
Stanway, H. 4	*Stanewega* 4b
Stapleford Abbots and Tawney, C. 7	*Stapleforda*, *-fort* 20, 47b, 66b
Stapleforda, *-fort*	See Stapleford
Stauintuna	See Stevington
Staumtuna	See Stevington
Stebbing, E. 4	*Stab-*, *Stibinga* 56b, 74
Stebbingford, E. 4	*Horstedafort* 94
Steeple, H. 6	*Stepla* 4b, 49b, 57, 103
Steeple Bumpstead, E. 2	*Bum(m)esteda* 28b, 35, 37, 40, 82, 102
Steintuna	See Stevington
Stepla	See Steeple
Stevington, D. 2	*Stauintuna* 35b, 78 *Staumtuna* 103b *Steintuna* 82
Stibinga	See Stebbing
Stiesteda	See Stisted
Stifford, D. 9	*Estinfort* 24b *bis* *Stiforda*, *-fort* 18, 97
Stiforda, *-fort*	See Stifford
Stisted, F. 4	*Stiesteda* 8
Stock	Not in D.B.
Stondon Massey	Not in D.B.
Stow Maries, F. 6	*Fenna* 86b *Fenne* 62 *Phenna* 63
Strathala	See Strethall

Ulinghehala	See Willingale
Ulting, F. 5	*Ultinga* 68b
Ultinga	See Ulting
Ulwinescherham	Unid., 4b
Upham	Unid., 36
Upminster, D. 8	*Upmonstra* 16b *Upmunstra*, *-tre* 24b, 91
Upmonstra, *Upmunstra*, *-tre*	See Upminster
Vange, E. 8	*Phenge* 22b, 71b
Virley, H. 5	*Salcota* 65
Vueseia	See Osea Island
Wachelinga, *Wacheringa*	See Wakering
Wakering, Great and Little, H. 8	*Wachelinga* 44 *Wacheringa* 45
Wakes Colne	See Colne, Earls etc.
Walcfara	See Walter
Walda	See North Weald Bassett, South Weald
Waldham	See Waltham
Waledana	See Saffron Walden
Walfara	See Walter
Walham	See Waltham Holy Cross
Walla	See North Weald Bassett, Wallbury
Wallbury, C. 4	*Walla* 38b
Walter, E. 5	*Wal(c)fara* 16b, 25b, 98b
Waltham, Great and Little, E. 5	*Waldham* 58 *Waltham* 20, 31b, 58, 85b
Waltham Holy Cross, B. 6	*Wal(t)ham* 15b, 64, 80b
Walthamstow, A. 8	*Wilcumestou* 92
Walton-le-Soken	See Sokens
Wanstead, B. 8	*Wenesteda* 9b
War(e)leia	See Warley, Great and Little
Warley, Great and Little, D. 7, D. 8	*War(e)leia* 10b, 18, 47b, 92b

Watele(i)a	See Wheatley
Wdefort	See Woodford
Wdeham	See Woodham Mortimer and Walter
Welda	See South Weald
Weeley, J. 4	*Wileia* 51
Well, E. 7	*Wella* 11b
Wella	See Well
Wemtuna	See Wennington
Wendena	See Wendens
Wendens Ambo and Lofts, B. 2, C. 2	*Wendena* 38, 65, 71, 100b
Wenesteda	See Wanstead
Wenesuuic, *Wesuunic*	Unid., 63, 100b
Weninchou, *Weninghou*	See Howe
Wennington, C. 9	*Wemtuna* 15
West Bergholt, H. 3	*Bercolt(a)* 41, 89, 102 *bis*
Westend, G. 1	*Westuna* 29, 88
West Ham	See Ham
West Hanningfield	See Hanningfield
West Horndon	See Horndon
West Mersea	See Mersea
Westnanetuna	Unid., 97
Westrefelda	See Wethersfield
West Thurrock	See Thurrock
West Tilbury	See Tilbury
Westuna	See Westend
Wesuunic	See *Wenesuuic*
Wethersfield, E. 3	*Westrefelda* 4, 40 *Witheresfelda* 98b
Wheatley, F. 8	*Watele(i)a* 23, 43 *bis*
White Colne	See Colne, Earls etc.
White Notley	See Notley
White Roding	See Roding, Aythorpe etc.
Wica	See Wicken (in Wicken Bonhunt), Wickham St Pauls, Wix
Wicfort	See Wickford

Wicgepet	See Rockells formerly Wyggepet
Wicgheberga	See Wigborough
Wicham	See Wickham Bishops, Wickham St Pauls
Wicken (in Wicken Bonhunt), C. 3	*Wica* 93
Wickford, F. 7	*Wi(n)cfort* 23 *ter*, 42b *bis*, 43 *bis*, 95, 95b
Wickham Bishops, G. 5	*Wicham* 10b
Wickham St Pauls, F. 2	*Wica* 39 *Wicham* 13
Widdington, C. 3	*Widi(n)tuna* 21, 68, 99b
Widemondefort	See Wormingford
Widi(n)tuna	See Widdington
Wigborough, Great and Little, H. 5	*Wi(c)gheberga* 18, 55b, 73b, 93, 100b
Wigghepet	See Rockells formerly Wyggepet
Wigheberga	See Wigborough
Wilcumestou	See Walthamstow
Wileia	See Weeley
Willingale Doe and Spain, D. 6	*Ulinghehala* 35 *Willing(h)ehala* 46b, 73, 94
Willing(h)ehala	See Willingale
Wimbeis	See Wimbish
Wimbish, D. 2	*Wimbeis* 69b
Wincfort	See Wickford
Winthelle	See Cray's Hill
Wiretela, *Wiritela*	See Writtle
Witelebroc	Unid., 70b
Witesuuorda	Unid., 41
Witham, F. 5	*Witham* 1b, 27, 63b, 95
Witham	See Great Whitmans, Witham
Witheresfelda	See Wethersfield
Wiunhou	See Wivenhoe
Wivenhoe, I. 4	*Wiunhou* 66
Wix, J. 3	*Wica* 54, 87
Wochaduna, *Woche(n)duna*	See Ockendon
Woodford, B. 7	*Wdefort* 16
Woodham Ferrers, F. 6	*Udeham* 57
Woodham Mortimer and Walter, F. 6	*Odeham* 73 *Wdeham* 69
Woolston, B. 7	*Ulfelmestuna* 5
Wormingford, H. 3	*Widemondefort* 66
Wrabenasa	See Wrabness
Wrabness, J. 3	*Wrabenasa* 20
Wringehala	Unid., 49b
Writa, *Writela*	See Writtle
Writtle, E. 6	*Wiretela* 31 *Wiritela* 5b *Writa* 26 *Writela* 5
Yardley, D. 3	*Gerdelai* 81b
Yeldham, Great and Little, F. 2	*Geld(e)ham* 28b, 39, 81, 102 *Gerham* 35

ANONYMOUS HOLDINGS

No place-names appear in the following nineteen entries, and it is possible that some (or even all) of these refer to holdings at places not named elsewhere in Domesday Book:

Grim the reeve (from the king), 10 acres in Rochford hd, 4b.
The king, 4 salt-pans and 10 acres in Thurstable hd, 7b.
Barking abbey, 2 hides and 50 acres in Barstable hd, 17b.
Count Eustace, one berewick of half a hide and 20 acres in Chelmsford hd, 20b.
Eight sokemen (abbey of St Ouen, Rouen), 107 acres in Winstree hd, 22.
Two sokemen (abbey of St Ouen, Rouen), half a hide and 30 acres in Winstree hd, 22.

ANONYMOUS HOLDINGS (continued)

Geoffrey de Mandeville, 12 hides in Barstable hd, 59b.
Edeva, half a hide in Chelmsford hd, 98b.
Quidam famulus, 8 acres in Chelmsford hd, 98b.
Godwin the deacon, 9 acres, 98b.
One man (from William son of Grossa), 2 acres, 98b.
Seven freemen (from the king), half a hide in Lexden hd, 99.
One freeman (from the king), 3½ acres in Lexden hd, 99.
One freeman (from the king), 13 acres in Lexden hd, 99.
One freeman (from Hugh de Montfort) and ten freemen (from William son of Grossa), 3 hides and 9 acres, 100.
Four freemen (from Hugh de Montfort), 2 hides and 20 acres, 100.
Three freemen (from Hugh de Montfort), one hide and 30 acres in Lexden hd, 100.
One freeman (from Westminster abbey), 40 acres in Chalford hd, 100.
Berenger (from Count Eustace), 15 acres in Rochford hd, 103b.

GLOUCESTERSHIRE — *GLOWECESTRESCIRE*

Folios 162–170b

MAPS 18–19

Abinghall	Not in D.B.
Abson	Not in D.B.
Achelie	See Oakley
Achetone	See Acton Turville
Acton Turville, F. 8	*Achetone* 169
Actune	See Iron Acton
Adlestrop, K. 3	*Tedestrop* 165b
Ætone	See Natton
Aicote	See Eycot
Aiforde	See Eyford
Ailewrde	See Aylworth
Alcrintone	See Alkerton
Aldeberie (*Grimboldestou* hd)	See Oldbury on the Hill
Aldeberie (*Respiget* hd)	Unid., 168b
Aldelande	See Oldland
Alderley, E. 7	*Alrelie* 169b
Alderton, H. 2	*Aldritone* 163b, 165b
Aldesorde, *Aldeswrde*	See Aldsworth
Aldritone	See Alderton
Aldsworth, J. 5	*Aldesorde* 165b *Aldeswrde* 170b
Alkerton, E. 5	*Alcrintone* 170b
Alkington, E. 6	*Almintune* 163
Allaston, D. 5	*Alvredestone* 166b
Almintune	See Alkington
Almondesberie	See Almondsbury
Almondsbury, D. 8	*Almondesberie* 163
Almundestan	See Elmstone
Alrelie	See Alderley
Alstone	Not in D.B.
Alveston, D. 7	*Alwestan* 163
Alvestone	See Olveston
Alvington, D. 6	*Alwintune* 185b, Heref.
Alvredestone	See Allaston
Alvredintune	See Arlington
Alwestan	See Alveston
Ampney Crucis, St Mary, St Peter and Down Ampney, I. 6	*Omenel* 164 *Omenie* 165b, 166b, 168, 169, 169b, 170 *bis*
Arlingham, E. 5	*Erlingeham* 163
Arlington, I. 5	*Alvredintune* 164

Ashbrook, I. 5	*Esbroc* 168b *Estbroce* 170
Ashchurch	Not in D.B.
Ashleworth, F. 3	*Esceleuuorde* 163
Ashley, G. 6	*Esselie* 71b, Wilts.
Aston Blank, I. 3	*Estone* 165
Aston on Carrant, G. 2	*Estone* 163, 163b
Aston Subedge, I. 1	*Estune* 166b
Athelai	See Down Hatherley
Aust, C. 7	*Austrecliue* 164b
Austrecliue	See Aust
Avening, G. 6	*Aveninge* 163b
Aveninge	See Avening
Avre	See Awre
Awre, E. 5	*Avre* 163
Aylburton	Not in D.B.
Aylworth, I. 3	*Ailewrde* 167 *Elewrde* 168b
Badgeworth, G. 4	*Beiewrde* 167
Bagendon, H. 5	*Benwedene* 169
Barnsley, I. 5	*Bernesleis* 164b
Barnwood, F. 4	*Berneuude* 165b
Barrington, Great and Little, J. 4	*Berni(n)tone* 164 *bis*, 167, 169
Barton (in Bristol), D. 9	*Bertune* 163
Barton (near Gloucester), F. 4	*Bertune* 162b, 165b
Batsford, J. 2	*Beceshore* 169b
Baudintone, *-tune*	See Baunton
Baunton, H. 5	*Baudintone*, *-tune* 168b, 170b
Beceford	See Beckford, Worcs.
Beceshore	See Batsford
Becheberie	See Bibury
Bedminster, C. 9	*Beiminstre* 86b, Som. (*Betministra*, *-tre*, Exon D.B. 90b, 525, Som.)
Begeberie	See Bibury
Beiewrde	See Badgeworth
Benwedene	See Bagendon
Berchelai	See Berkeley
Berkeley, D. 6	*Berchelai* 163 *quin*, 164
Bernesleis	See Barnsley
Berneuurde	See Barnwood
Berni(n)tone	See Barrington
Bertune	See Barton (in Bristol), Barton (near Gloucester)
Betone	See Bitton
Beurestane	See Beverstone
Beverstone, F. 6	*Beurestane* 163
Bibury, I. 5	*Becheberie* 164b *Begeberie* 164b
Bicanofre	See English Bicknor
Bichemerse	See Bickmarsh, Worcs.
Biselege	See Bisley
Bishop's Cleeve, H. 3	*Clive* 165
Bisley, G. 5	*Biselege* 166b
Bitton, D. 9	*Betone* 170b
Bladintun	See Bledington
Blaisdon	Not in D.B.
Bledington, K. 3	*Bladintun* 165b
Bledisloe, D. 5	*Bliteslau* 163 *bis*
Bliteslau	See Bledisloe
Blockley, J. 2	*Blochelei* 173, Worcs.
Bochelande	See Buckland
Boddington, G. 3	*Botingtune* 166 *bis* *Botintone* 163b
Bortune	See Bourton on the Hill, Bourton on the Water
Botingtune, *Botintone*	See Boddington
Bourton on the Hill, J. 2	*Bortune* 166 *bis*
Bourton on the Water, J. 3	*Bortune* 165b
Boxewelle	See Boxwell
Boxwell, F. 7	*Boxewelle* 165b
Bradewelle	See Broadwell
Brawn, F. 3	*Brewere* 162b *Bruurne* 169b
Breadstone	Not in D.B.
Brewere	See Brawn
Brimesfelde	See Brimpsfield

Brimpsfield, G. 4	*Brimesfelde* 168b
Bristentune	See Ebrington
Bristol, C. 9	*Bristou* 163 *bis*, 164b, Gloucs.; 88, Som.; Exon D.B., 141b, Som.
Bristou	See Bristol
Broadwell, J. 2	*Bradewelle* 166
Brockhampton	Not in D.B.
Brockworth, G. 4	*Brocowardinge* 169
Brocowardinge	See Brockworth
Bromsberrow, E. 2	*Brunmeberge* 168
Brookthorpe, F. 4	*Brostorp* 162b
Brostorp	See Brookthorpe
Brunmeberge	See Bromsberrow
Bruurne	See Brawn
Buckland, I. 2	*Bochelande* 165b
Bulelege	See Bulley
Bulley, E. 4	*Bulelege* 169
Cainscross	Not in D.B.
Calcot, I. 5	*Caldecot* 166
Caldecot	See Calcot
Caldecote	See Caldicot, Wales
Callicote	See Westfield
Cam, E. 6	*Camma* 163
Camma	See Cam
Campedene	See Chipping Campden
Caneberton	See Kemerton, Worcs.
Canole	See Knowle
Carleion	See Caerleon, Wales
Caroen	See Caerwent, Wales
Carswall, E. 3	*Crasowel* 167b
Castlett, I. 3	*Cateslat* 167
Cateslat	See Castlett
Cedeorde	See Chedworth
Cerintone	See Cherington
Cerletone	See Charlton Abbots
Cernei	See North Cerney, South Cerney
Chalford	Not in D.B.
Charfield, E. 7	*Cirvelde* 170
Charingworth, J. 1	*Cheuringaurde* 168

Charlton Abbots, H. 3	*Cerletone* 165b
Charlton Kings	Not in D.B.
Chedworth, H. 4	*Cedeorde* 164
Cheisnecot(e)	See Sezincote
Cheltenham, G. 3	*Chinteneham* 162b
Chenemeresforde	See Kempsford
Chenemertone, *-tune*	See Kemerton, Worcs.
Chenepelei	See Kempley
Cherington, G. 6	*Cerintone* 169b
Chesnecote	See Sezincote
Cheuringaurde	See Charingworth
Chiesnecote	See Sezincote
Chilecot	See Kilcot
Chinemertune	See Kemerton, Worcs.
Chingescote	See Kingscote
Chingestune	Unid., 163
Chinteneham	See Cheltenham
Chipping Campden, J. 1	*Campedene* 166b
Chipping Sodbury	See Sodbury
Chire	Unid., 163
Chitiford	See Ketford
Churcham, E. 4	*Hamme* 165b 2nd entry
Churchdown, G. 4	*Circesdune* 164b
Church Icomb, J. 3	*Iacumbe* 173, Worcs.
Circesdune	See Churchdown
Cirecestre	See Cirencester
Cirencester, H. 6	*Cirecestre* 162b, 167 See also anon. holdings on p. 159
Cirvelde	See Charfield
Claenhangare	See Clingre
Clapton, J. 4	*Lechetone* 170
Clifort	See Clifford Chambers, Warw.
Clifton, C. 9	*Clistone* 170
Cliftone	Unid., 163b
Clingre, E. 6	*Claenhangare* 163
Clistone	See Clifton
Clive	See Bishop's Cleeve
Cloptune	See Clopton (in Quinton), Warw.

Coaley, E. 6	*Couelege* 163	Daglingworth	Not in D.B.
Coates	Not in D.B.	*Dantesborne*	See Duntisbourne
Coberleie	See Coberley	Daylesford, K. 3	*Eilesford* 173, Worcs.
Coberley, H. 4	*Coberleie* 168 *Culberlege* 164b *bis*	*Dedmertone*	See Didmarton
Codrington	Not in D.B.	Deerhurst, G. 2	*Derheste* 166
Cold Ashton, E. 9	*Escetone* 165	*Dene*	See Mitcheldean
Coleford	Not in D.B.	*Derheste*	See Deerhurst
Colesborne, H. 4	*Colesborne*, *-burne* 164b, 165, 169b *bis*	*Dersilege*	See Dursley
		Didintone	See Doynton
		Didmarton, F. 7	*Dedmertone* 168b
Colesborne, *-burne*	See Colesborne	*Dimoch*	See Dymock
Colne	See Coln St Dennis	*Dinan*	See Dinham, Wales
Coln St Aldwyn, J. 5	*Culne* 165b	*Dirham*	See Dyrham
Coln St Dennis, I. 5	*Colne* 166	Ditchford, J. 2	*Dicford* 173, Worcs.
Compton Abdale, I. 4	*Contone* 165 *Cuntune* 164b	Dixton, H. 2	*Dricledone* 163b
		Dodesuuelle	See Dowdeswell
Compton Greenfield, C. 8	*Contone* 164b	Dodington, E. 8	*Dodintone* 165, 168
		Dodintone	See Dodington
Condicote	See Condicott	Donnington	Not in D.B.
Condicott, J. 3	*Condicote* 164b, 165, 168b *Connicote* 167b	*Dorsintune*	See Dorsington, Warw.
		Dowdeswell, H. 3	*Dodesuuelle* 165
Connicote	See Condicott	Down Ampney	See Ampney Crucis etc.
Contone	See Compton Abdale, Compton Greenfield. See also Little Compton, Warw.	Down Hatherley, F. 3	*Athelai* 162b
		Doynton, E. 9	*Didintone* 165
		Dricledone	See Dixton
Corse	Not in D.B.	*Drifelle*	See Driffield
Couelege	See Coaley	Driffield, I. 6	*Drifelle* 166b
Cowley, H. 4	*Kulege* 166	*Dubentone*	See Dumbleton
Cranham	Not in D.B.	Dumbleton, H. 2	*Dubentone* 166 *Dunbentune* 167
Crasowel	See Carswall		
Cromale, *Cromhal*	See Cromhall	*Dunbentune*	See Dumbleton
Cromhall, E. 7	*Cromale* 163 *Cromhal* 163	*Duntesborne*	See Duntisbourne
		Duntisbourne Abbots and Rouse, H. 5	*Dantesborne* 169b, 170b *Duntesborne* 165b, 166b, 167, 168b *Tantesborne* 166, 167b, 169b, 170
Culberlege	See Coberley		
Culcorto(r)ne	See Culkerton		
Culkerton, G. 6	*Culcorto(r)ne* 167, 168, 168b		
Culne	See Coln St Aldwyn	Dursley, E. 6	*Dersilege* 163
Cuntune	See Compton Abdale	Dymock, E. 2	*Dimoch* 164
		Dyrham, E. 9	*Dirham* 167
Cutsdean, I. 2	*Codestune* 173, Worcs.	Earthcott, D. 8	*Herdicote* 165

Eastington (near Northleach)	Not in D.B.
Eastington (near Stroud)	Not in D.B.
Eastleach Martin and Turville, J. 5	*Lec(c)e* 167b, 168b *bis*
Ebrington, J. 1	*Bristentune* 167
Edelmintone	See Admington, Warw.
Edgeworth, G. 5	*Egeisuurde* 166b *Egesworde* 167b
Eduuardestou	See Stow on the Wold
Egeisuurde, *Egesworde*	See Edgeworth
Elberton, D. 7	*Eldbertone* 163
Elchestane	See Elkstone
Eldbertone	See Elberton
Elewrde	See Aylworth
Elkstone, H. 4	*Elchestane* 169b
Elmore	Not in D.B.
Elmstone, G. 3	*Almundestan* 166
English Bicknor, C. 4	*Bicanofre* 167b
Erlingeham	See Arlingham
Esbroc	See Ashbrook
Esceleuuorde	See Ashleworth
Escetone	See Cold Ashton
Essetone	See Ashton under Hill, Worcs.
Estbroce	See Ashbrook
Estoch	See Stoke Gifford
Estone	See Aston Blank, Aston on Carrant. See also Ashton under Hill, Worcs.
Estrighoiel	See Chepstow, Wales
Estune	See Aston Subedge. See also Aston Somerville, Worcs.
Ete(s)lau	See Etloe
Etherope	See Hatherop
Etloe, D. 5	*Ete(s)lau* 163 *bis*
Euuelege	See Uley
Evenlode, J. 2	*Eunilade* 173, Worcs.
Evington, G. 3	*Giuingtune* 166
Eycot, H. 5	*Aicote* 164b
Eyford, J. 3	*Aiforde* 169b
Fairford, J. 6	*Fareforde* 163b
Falfield	Not in D.B.
Fareforde	See Fairford
Farmcote, I. 2	*Fernecote* 167
Farmington, I. 4	*Tormentone* 164b
Fernecote	See Farmcote
Fiddington, G. 2	*Fitentone* 163, 163b *bis*
Filton	Not in D.B.
Fitentone	See Fiddington
Flaxley	Not in D.B.
Fortemeltone	See Forthampton
Forthampton, F. 2	*Fortemeltone* 163b *Forhelmentone* 180b, Heref.
Foxcote, H. 4	*Fuscote* 165
Frampton (in Toddington), H. 2	*Freolintune* 165b
Frampton Cotterell, D. 8	*Frantone* 169
Frampton Mansell, G. 5	*Frantone* 168
Frampton on Severn, E. 5	*Frantone* 168b
Frantone	See Frampton Cotterell, Frampton Mansell, Frampton on Severn
Freolintune	See Frampton (in Toddington)
Fretherne, E. 5	*Fridorne* 169b
Fridorne	See Fretherne
Frocester, F. 5	*Frowecestre* 165b
Frowecestre	See Frocester
Fuscote	See Foxcote
Getinge	See Guiting
Giete	See Yate
Giuingtune	See Evington
Gloucester, F. 4	*Glouuecestre* 162, 163, 163b, 165 *bis*, 165b, 166 *bis*, 166b *bis*, 167b *ter*,

Gloucester cont.	168, 168b *bis*, 169 *ter*, 170b, Gloucs.; 172b, Worcs. *juxta ciuitatem* 162b
Glouuecestre	See Gloucester
Godrinton	See Gotherington
Gosintune	See Gossington
Gossington, E. 6	*Gosintune* 163
Gotherington, H. 2	*Godrinton* 165
Great Badminton, F. 8	*Madmintune* 169
Great Barrington	See Barrington
Great Rissington	See Rissington
Great Washbourne, H. 2	*Waseburne* 163b
Grenhamstede	See Miserden
Guiting Power and Temple Guiting, I. 3	*Getinge* 167, 167b, 170
Hagenepene, *Hagepine*	See Hampen
Hailes, H. 2	*Heile* 167b
Hallinge	See Hawling
Ham	Not in D.B.
Hambrook, D. 8	*Hanbroc* 165
Hamme	See Churcham, Highnam
Hampen, I. 3	*Hagenepene* 167 *Hagepine* 164b
Hampnett, I. 4	*Hantone* 168
Hanbroc	See Hambrook
Hanham, D. 9	*Hanun* 169
Hanlege	See Hanley Castle, Worcs.
Hantone	See Hampnett, Meysey Hampton, Minchinhampton
Hanun	See Hanham
Hardwick, G. 3	*Herdeuuic* 166
Hardwicke	Not in D.B.
Harehille	See Harnhill
Harescombe, F. 4	*Hersecome* 162b
Haresfield, F. 5	*Hersefel(d)* 162b, 168b
Harford, I. 3	*Hurford* 168b
Harnhill, I. 6	*Harehille* 168

Hartpury	Not in D.B.
Hasedene	See Hazleton (near Northleach), Hazleton (in Rodmarton)
Hasfelde	See Hasfield
Hasfield, F. 3	*Hasfelde* 166
Hatherop, J. 5	*Etherope* 169 *Hetrope* 167b
Havochesberie	See Hawksbury
Hawksbury, E. 7	*Havochesberie* 166
Hawling, I. 3	*Hallinge* 170
Hayes, E. 3	*Hege* 170
Hazleton (near Northleach), I. 4	*Hasedene* 170
Hazleton (in Rodmarton), G. 6	*Hasedene* 168
Hechanestede	See Hempsted
Hedecote	See Hidcote Bartrim
Hege	See Hayes
Heile	See Hailes
Hempsted, F. 4	*Hechanestede* 164
Henberie	See Henbury
Henbury, C. 8	*Henberie* 164b
Heniberge	See Cow Honeybourne, Worcs.
Herdeuuic	See Hardwick
Herdicote	See Earthcott
Hereford	See Hereford, Heref.
Hersecome	See Harescombe
Hersefel(d)	See Haresfield
Heslinbruge	See Slimbridge
Hetrope	See Hatherop
Hewelsfield, C. 6	*Hiwoldestone* 167
Hidcote Bartrim, J. 1	*Hedecote* 166 *Hidicote* 165b
Hidicote	See Hidcote Bartrim
Highnam, F. 3	*Hamme* 165b 1st entry
Hilcote, H. 4	*Willecote* 165
Hildeslei	See Hillsley
Hill, D. 6	*Hilla* 163
Hilla	See Hill
Hillsley, E. 7	*Hildeslei* 169b
Hinetune	See Hinton. See also Hinton on

Hinetune cont.	the Green, Worcs.
Hinton, D. 5	*Hinetune* 163
Hirslege	See Hurst
Hiwoldestone	See Hewelsfield
Hochilicote	See Hucclecote
Hochinton	See Uckington
Hope	See Longhope
Horedone	See Horton
Horefelle	See Horfield
Horfield, C. 8	*Horefelle* 163
Horselei	See Horsley
Horsenehal	See Oxenhall
Horsley, F. 6	*Horselei* 166b
Horton, E. 7	*Horedone* 168
Hucclecote, G. 4	*Hochilicote* 164b
Huesberie	See Westbury on Trym
Hullasey, H. 6	*Hunlafesed* 163
Hundeuuic	Unid., 163b
Hunlafesed	See Hullasey
Huntelei	See Huntley
Huntley, E. 4	*Huntelei* 167
Hurford	See Harford
Hurst, E. 5	*Hirslege* 163
Iccomb, J. 3	*Ic(c)umbe* 167b, 168, 168b
Iccumbe	See Iccomb
Icetune	See Itchington
Icumbe	See Iccomb
Idleberg, J. 2	*Ildeberga* 175b, Worcs.
Iron Acton, D. 8	*Actune* 165, 170 *bis*
Itchington, D. 7	*Icetune* 164b
Kemble, H. 6	*Chemele* 67, Wilts.
Kempley, D. 2	*Chenepelei* 167b
Kempsford, J. 6	*Chenemeresforde* 169
Ketford, E. 2	*Chitiford* 170
Kilcot, E. 3	*Chilecot* 170
Kingscote, F. 6	*Chingescote* 163
King's Stanley, F. 5	*Stantone* 169b
Kingswood (near Bristol)	Not in D.B.
Kingswood (near Wotton under Edge)	Not in D.B.

Knowle, D. 9	*Canole* 98, Som. (*Canola*, Exon D.B., 447, Som.)
Kulege	See Cowley
Ladeuent	Unid., 163
Lalege	See Leigh
Lamecare	See Llanvair-Discoed, Wales
Langeberge	See Longborough
Langenei	See Longney
Lasborough, F. 6	*Lesseberge* 166b
Lassington, F. 3	*Lessedune* 164b
Lecce	See Eastleach, Northleach
Lece	See Eastleach
Lecelade	See Lechlade
Lechametone, *Lechantone*	See Leckhampton
Lechetone	See Clapton
Lechlade, J. 6	*Lecelade* 169
Leckhampton, G. 4	*Lechametone* 170b *Lechantone* 167b
Ledene	See Upleadon
Ledenei	See St Briavels
Lega	Unid., 165
Leigh, F. 3	*Lalege* 166
Leighterton	Not in D.B.
Lemington, J. 2	*Leminingtune* 166 *Limentone* 163b
Leminingtune	See Lemington
Leonard Stanley, F. 5	*Stanlege* 168
Lesseberge	See Lasborough
Lessedune	See Lassington
Limentone	See Lemington
Lindenee	See Lydney
Liteltone	See Littleton upon Severn
Lite(n)tune	See Littleworth
Little Barrington	See Barrington
Little Rissington	See Rissington
Little Sodbury	See Sodbury
Littleton upon Severn, D. 7	*Liteltone* 165
Little Washbourne, H. 2	*Waseburne* 173, Worcs.
Littleworth, H. 2	*Lite(n)tune* 167b, 168b

Longborough, J. 2	*Langeberge* 163, 166b, 170
Longhope, D. 4	*Hope* 167
Long Newnton, G. 7	*Newentone* 67, Wilts.
Longney, E. 4	*Langenei* 170b
Lower Slaughter	See Slaughter
Lower Swell	See Swell
Lydney, D. 5	*Lindenee* 164
	Lidenegie 181b, Heref.
Lypiatt	Not in D.B.
Madmintune	See Great Badminton
Maisemore, F. 3	*Merwen* 162b
Malgeresberiae	See Maugersbury
Manegodesfelle	See Mangotsfield
Mangotsfield, D. 8	*Manegodesfelle* 163
Marshfield, F. 9	*Meresfelde* 163
Matson	Not in D.B.
Maugersbury, J. 3	*Malgeresberiae* 165b
Mene	See Meon, Warw.
Meresfelde	See Marshfield
Merestone	See Long Marston, Warw.
Merestune	See Broad Marston, Worcs.
Mereuuent	See Morwent
Merwen	See Maisemore
Meysey Hampton, I. 6	*Hantone* 166b 2nd entry
Mickleton, J. 1	*Muceltude* 166
Minchinhampton, G. 6	*Hantone* 166b 1st entry
Minsterworth	Not in D.B.
Miserden, G. 5	*Grenhamstede* 169b
Mitcheldean, D. 4	*Dene* 167b
Modesgate, C. 6	*Modiete* 164, 167b
Modiete	See Modesgate
Morcote	See Murcott
Moreton in Marsh, J. 2	*Mortune* 166
Moreton Valence, E. 5	*Mortune* 168b
Morton, F. 4	*Mortune* 165b

Mortune	See Moreton in Marsh, Moreton Valence, Morton
Morwent, F. 3	*Mereuuent* 165b
Muceltude	See Mickleton
Murcott, F. 4	*Morcote* 167b
Nailsworth	Not in D.B.
Nass, D. 6	*Nest* 164
Nategraue	See Notgrove
Natone	See Natton
Natton, G. 2	*Ætone* 163b
	Natone 163
Naunton (near Northleach), I. 3	*Niwetone* 168b, 170b
Naunton (in Toddington), H. 2	*Niwetone* 165b
Nesse	See Sharpness
Nest	See Nass
Neueton	See Newington Bagpath
Neuneham	See Newnham
Newent, E. 3	*Noent* 163, 166
Newerne, D. 5	*Niware* 181, Heref.
Newington Bagpath, F. 6	*Neueton* 163
Newland	Not in D.B.
Newnham, D. 4	*Neuneham* 167
Nimdesfelle	See Nympsfield
Niwetone	See Naunton (near Northleach), Naunton (in Toddington)
Noent	See Newent
Norcote	See Norcott
Norcott, H. 5	*Nor(t)cote* 166b, 170
Nortcote	See Norcott
North Cerney, H. 5	*Cernei* 164b, 168b
Northleach, I. 4	*Lecce* 164b
North Nibley	Not in D.B.
Norton (near Gloucester), F. 3	*Nortune* 164b
Norton (in Weston Subedge), I. 1	*Nortune* 169b

Place	Domesday form
Nortune	See Norton (near Gloucester), Norton (in Weston Subedge)
Notgrove, I. 3	*Nategraue* 165
Nympsfield, F. 6	*Nimdesfelle* 163
Oakley, H. 6	*Achelie* 168, 168b, 169b
Oddington, J. 3	*Otintune* 164b
Odelaveston	See Woolaston
Oldbury on the Hill, F. 7	*Aldeberie* 169
Oldbury upon Severn	Not in D.B.
Oldland, D. 9	*Aldelande* 165
Old Sodbury	See Sodbury
Olsendone	See Woolstone
Olveston, D. 7	*Alvestone* 165
Omenel, *Omenie*	See Ampney Crucis etc.
Optune	See Upton St Leonards
Oridge Street, F. 3	*Tereige* 166
Osleuuorde	See Ozleworth
Otintune	See Oddington
Oxendone	See Oxenton
Oxenhall, E. 3	*Horsenehal* 167b
Oxenton, G. 2	*Oxendone* 163b
Ozleworth, F. 7	*Osleuuorde* 163
Painswick, F. 5	*Wiche* 167b
Pamington, G. 2	*Pamintonie* 163
Pamintonie	See Pamington
Pantelie	See Pauntley
Pauntley, E. 2	*Pantelie* 170
Pebeworde	See Pebwoth, Worcs.
Peclesurde	See Pegglesworth
Pegglesworth, H. 4	*Peclesurde* 165
Penneberie	See Pinbury
Peritone, *-tune*	See Purton
Pignocsire	See Pinnock
Pinbury, G. 5	*Penneberie* 166b
Pinnock, I. 3	*Pignocsire* 170b
Pitchcombe	Not in D.B.
Pontune	See Poulton (in Awre)
Poole Keynes, H. 6	*Pole* 69b, Wilts.
Postlip, H. 3	*Poteslepe* 169b
Poteschiuet	See Portskewett, Wales
Poteslepe	See Postlip
Poulton (near Ampney St Peter), I. 6	*Poltone* 68b, Wilts.
Poulton (in Awre), E. 5	*Pontune* 164
Prescott	Not in D.B.
Prestbury, H. 3	*Presteberie* 165
Presteberie	See Prestbury
Prestetune	See Preston (near Cirencester), Preston (near Ledbury)
Prestitune	See Preston (near Cirencester)
Preston	See Preston on Stour, Warw.
Preston (near Cirencester), H. 6	*Prestetune* 166b *Prestitune* 170
Preston (near Ledbury), D. 2	*Prestetune* 165b
Prinknash	Not in D.B.
Pucklechurch, E. 8	*Pulcrecerce* 165
Pulcrecerce	See Pucklechurch
Purton, D. 5	*Peritone*, *-tune* 163 *bis*, 164
Quedgeley	Not in D.B.
Quenington, J. 5	*Quenintone* 167b
Quenintone	See Quenington
Quenintune	See Quinton, Warw.
Rangeworthy	Not in D.B.
Ranwick	Not in D.B.
Rawelle	See Roel
Redeuuiche	See Redwick
Redmarley D'Abitot, E. 2	*Ridmerlege* 173, Worcs.
Redmertone	See Rodmarton
Redwick, C. 7	*Redeuuiche* 164b
Rendcomb, H. 5	*Rindecome*, *-cumbe* 168b *bis*
Rindecome, *-cumbe*	See Rendcomb
Risedune, *Risendone*, *-dune*	See Rissington

Rissington, Great, Little and Wyck, J. 3, J. 4	*Risedune* 167b *Risendone*, *-dune* 168, 168b
Rochemtune	See Rockhampton
Rockhampton, D. 7	*Rochemtune* 168b
Rodborough	Not in D.B.
Rodele	See Rodley
Rodley, E. 4	*Rodele* 169
Rodmarton, G. 6	*Redmertone* 166b, 170b
Roel, I. 3	*Rawelle* 166b
Ruardean, D. 4	*Ruuirdin* 185, Heref.
Rudeford	See Rudford
Rudford, E. 3	*Rudeford* 170b
Saberton, H. 2	*Sapletone* 165
St Briavels, C. 5	*Ledenei* 167
Saintbury, I. 1	*Suineberie* 169b
Salperton, I. 4	*Salpretune* 169
Salpretune	See Salperton
Sandhurst, F. 3	*Sanher* 162b
Sanher	See Sandhurst
Sapletone	See Saberton
Sapletorne	See Sapperton
Sapperton, G. 5	*Sapletorne* 168
Scipetone	See Shipton Moyne
Scipetune	See Shipton Oliffe and Solars
Sciptone	See Shipton Moyne
Sciptune	See Shipton Oliffe and Solars
Scireburne	See Sherborne
Sclostre	See Slaughter
Senendone	See Shenington, Oxon.
Sevenhampton, H. 3	*Sevenhamtone* 165
Sevenhamtone	See Sevenhampton
Sezincote, J. 2	*Cheisnecot(e)* 169b *bis*, 170 *Ch(i)esnecote* 168b, 169
Sharpness, D. 5	*Nesse* 163
Sherborne, J. 4	*Scireburne* 165b
Shipton Moyne, G. 7	*Scip(e)tone* 167, 170 *bis*
Shipton Oliffe and Solars, H. 4	*Scip(e)tune* 164b, 167b, 168b, 169, 169b
Shorncote, H. 6	*Schernecote* 73, Wilts.
Shurdington	Not in D.B.
Siddington, H. 6	*Sudi(n)tone* 167, 169b, 170 *Suintone* 168
Side	See Syde
Simondeshale	See Symond's Hall
Siston, D. 9	*Sistone* 168
Sistone	See Siston
Slaughter, Lower and Upper, J. 3	*Sclostre* 162b, 168
Slimbridge, E. 5	*Heslinbruge* 163
Snawesille	See Snowshill
Snowshill, I. 2	*Snawesille* 165b
Sodbury, Chipping, Little and Old, E. 8	*Sopeberie* 163b, 166b
Somerford Keynes, H. 6	*Summreford* 66, Wilts.
Sopeberie	See Sodbury
Southam, H. 3	*Surham* 165
South Cerney, H. 6	*Cernei* 168, 169
Southrop	Not in D.B.
Southwick, G. 2	*Sudwicham* 163
Standish, F. 5	*Stanedis* 164b
Stanedis	See Standish
Stanhus	See Stonehouse
Stanlege	See Leonard Stanley, Stanley Pontlarge
Stanley Pontlarge, H. 2	*Stanlege* 163b
Stanton, I. 2	*Stantone* 165b
Stantone	See King's Stanley, Stanton
Stanuuelle	See Stowell
Stanway, I. 2	*Stanwege* 163b
Stanwege	See Stanway
Staruenton	See Staverton
Staunton, C. 4	*Stantun* 181, Heref.
Staure	See Stears
Staverton, G. 3	*Staruenton* 166
Stears, D. 4	*Staure* 167

Stinchcombe	Not in D.B.
Stoch	See Lark Stoke, Warw.
Stoche	See Stoke Bishop, Stoke Gifford
Stoches	See Stoke Orchard
Stoke Bishop, C. 8	*Stoche* 164b
Stoke Gifford, D. 8	*Estoch* 165 *Stoche* 168b
Stoke Orchard, G. 3	*Stoches* 163b, 165
Stone	Not in D.B.
Stonehouse, F. 5	*Stanhus* 166b
Stowell, I. 4	*Stanuuelle* 164b
Stow on the Wold, J. 3	*Eduuardestou* 165b
Stratone	See Stratton
Stratton, H. 5	*Stratone* 168
Strigoielg	See Chepstow, Wales
Sudeley, H. 3	*Sudlege* 169
Sudi(n)tone	See Siddington
Sudlege	See Sudeley
Sudtune	See Sutton under Brailes, Warw.
Sudwicham	See Southwick
Suelle	See Swell
Suindone	See Swindon
Suineberie	See Saintbury
Suintone	See Siddington
Surham	See Southam
Suuelle	See Swell
Swell, Lower and Upper, J. 3	*Su(u)elle* 166, 167, 168
Swindon, G. 3	*Suindone* 164b
Syde, G. 5	*Side* 169b
Symond's Hall, F. 6	*Simondeshale* 163
Taddington, I. 2	*Tatintone* 163b
Tantesborne	See Duntisbourne
Tarlton, H. 6	*Torentune* 168 *Tornentone* 166b
Tatinton	See Taynton
Tatintone	See Taddington
Taynton, E. 3	*Tatinton* 167b *Tetinton* 167
Tebriston	See Tibberton
Teddington, H. 2	*Teotintune* 173, Worcs.

Tedechesberie	See Tewkesbury
Tedeham	See Tidenham
Tedekesberie	See Tewkesbury
Tedeneham	See Tidenham
Tedestrop	See Adlestrop
Telinge, F. 2	Lost in Tirley, 166
Temple Guiting	See Guiting
Teneurde	See Yanworth
Teodechesberie	See Tewkesbury
Teodeham	See Todenham
Teodekesberie	See Tewkesbury
Tereige	See Oridge Street
Tetbury, G. 7	*Teteberie* 168
Tetbury Upton, G. 6	*Uptone* 168
Teteberie	See Tetbury
Tetinton	See Taynton
Tewkesbury, G. 2	*Tedechesberie* 163b *Tedekesberie* 163b *bis* *Teodechesberie* 163 *bis* *Teodekesberie* 163b *ter*
Thornbury, D. 7	*Turneberie* 163b
Througham, G. 5	*Troham* 166b
Thrupp	Not in D.B.
Tibberton, E. 3	*Tebriston* 167
Tideham	See Tidenham
Tidenham, C. 6	*Tede(ne)ham* 164, 167b *Tideham* 166b
Tidrentune	See Tytherington
Tirley, F. 3	*Trinleie* 166 *bis*
Tochintune	See Tockington
Tockington, D. 7	*Tochintune* 164
Toddington, H. 2	*Todintun* 169
Todenham, K. 2	*Teodeham* 166 *Toteham* 166
Todintun	See Toddington
Torentune	See Tarlton
Tormarton, E. 8	*Tormentone* 168b
Tormentone	See Farmington, Tormarton
Tornentone	See Tarlton
Tortworth, E. 7	*Torteword* 169b
Torteword	See Tortworth
Toteham	See Todenham
Tredington, G. 2	*Trotintune* 163

Trewsbury, H. 6	*Tursberie* 168b
Trinleie	See Tirley
Troham	See Througham
Trotintune	See Tredington
Tueninge	See Twining
Tuffelege	See Tuffley
Tuffley, F. 4	*Tuffelege* 165b
Tuninge	See Twining
Turchedene, *Turghedene*	See Turkdean
Turkdean, I. 4	*Turchedene* 168b *Turghedene* 167b
Turneberie	See Thornbury
Tursberie	See Trewsbury
Twigworth	Not in D.B.
Twining, G. 2	*Tu(e)ninge* 163b, 165b
Tytherington, D. 7	*Tidrentune* 165
Uckington, G. 3	*Hochinton* 166
Udecestre	See Woodchester
Uletone	Unid., 167b
Uley, F. 6	*Euuelege* 163
Upleaden, E. 3	*Ledene* 165b
Upper Slaughter	See Slaughter
Upper Swell	See Swell
Uptone	See Tetbury Upton
Upton St Leonards, F. 4	*Optune* 162b
Utone	See Wotton (in Gloucester)
Valton	See Walton (in Deerhurst)
Vutune	See Wotton under Edge
Wadune	See Whaddon
Walton (in Deerhurst), G. 2	*Valton* 166
Walton Cardiff, G. 2	*Waltone* 163, 163b
Waltone	See Walton Cardiff
Wapelei, -lie	See Wapley
Wapley, E. 8	*Wapelei, -lie* 162b, 165, 168
Waseburne	See Great Washbourne

Welleford	See Welford on Avon, Warw.
Wenecote	See Wincot, Warw.
Wenitone	See Ullington, Worcs.
Wenric	See Windrush
Wermetun	See Wormington
Wes(t)berie	See Westbury on Severn
Westbury on Severn, E. 4	*Wes(t)berie* 163 *bis*, 167 *bis*
Westbury on Trym, C. 8	*Huesberie* 164b
Westerleigh	Not in D.B.
Westfield, I. 3	*Callicote* 167
West Littleton	Not in D.B.
Weston (in Henbury), C. 8	*Westone* 163
Weston Birt, F. 7	*Westone* 166b, 167
Westone	See Weston (in Henbury), Weston Birt, Weston Subedge. See also Weston on Avon, Warw.
Weston Subedge, I. 1	*Westone* 169b
Westune	See Weston on Avon, Warw.
Whaddon, F. 4	*Wadune* 168b
Wheatenhurst, E. 5	*Witenhert* 170b
Whiteshill	Not in D.B.
Whittington (near Cheltenham), H. 3	*Witetune* 167b
Whittington (in Staunton), C. 4	*Wiboldingtune* 182, Heref.
Wicecombe, *Wicelcombe*, *-cumbe*	See Winchcomb
Wicfeld	See Wightfield
Wich(am)	See Droitwich, Worcs.
Wiche	See Painswick. See also Droitwich, Worcs.
Wichen	See Wickwar
Wick	Not in D.B.

Wickwar, E. 7	*Wichen* 170 *bis*
Wicuene	See Child's Wickham, Worcs.
Widecestre	See Woodchester
Widiforde	See Widford, Oxon.
Widindune	See Withington
Wigheiete	See Wyegate
Wightfield, F. 2	*Wicfeld* 166
Wilcote	See Willicote, Warw.
Willecote	See Hilcote
Willersei	See Willersey
Willersey, I. 1	*Willersei* 166
Wincelcumbe	See Winchcomb
Winchcomb, H. 2	*Wicecombe* 163b *bis* *Wicelcombe*, *-cumbe* 165 *bis*, 166 *ter*, 167 *bis*, 169, 170b *Wincelcumbe* 162b, 167b, 168 *bis*
Windrush, J. 4	*Wenric* 165b, 167b, 170b *bis*
Winestan(e)	See Winstone
Winestune	See Winson
Winson, I. 5	*Winestune* 169b
Winstone, H. 5	*Winestan(e)* 169b, 170
Winterbourne, D. 8	*Wintreborne* 162b
Wintreborne	See Winterbourne
Wiquenna	See Child's Wickham, Worcs.
Witcombe	Not in D.B.
Witenhert	See Wheatenhurst
Witetune	See Whittington (near Cheltenham)
Withington, H. 4	*Widindune* 164b
Woodchester, F. 5	*Udecestre* 164 *Widecestre* 170b
Woodmancote	Not in D.B.
Woolaston, C. 6	*Odelaveston* 166b
Woolstone, H. 2	*Olsendone* 166
Wormington, H. 2	*Wermetun* 168
Wotton (in Gloucester), F. 4	*Utone* 170
Wotton under Edge, E. 6	*Vatune* 163
Wyck Rissington	See Rissington
Wyegate, C. 5	*Wigheiete* 166b
Yanworth, I. 4	*Teneurde* 170
Yate, E. 8	*Giete* 164b

ANONYMOUS HOLDINGS

No place-names appear in the following sixteen entries, and it is possible that some (or even all) of these refer to holdings at places not named elsewhere in Domesday Book:

The king, half a hide *juxta ciuitatem* in Dudstone hd, 162b. Counted with Gloucester.
The king, 5 hides in Cirencester hd, 162b. Counted as part of Cirencester.
Roger (from the king), 5 hides in Berkeley hd, 163.
The king, 10 hides in Bradley hd, 163.
Bishop of Coutances, one hide in Swineshead hd, 165.
Two men (from Earl Hugh), 4 hides in Longtree hd, 166b.
Church of Cirencester, 2 hides in Cirencester hd, 166b. Counted with Cirencester.
William son of Baderon, 2½ virgates in Westbury hd, 167.
William Goizenboded, half a hide in Westbury hd, 167.
William son of Norman, one hide and half a virgate in Blidsloe hd, 167b.
Ralf Pagenel, 1½ virgates (*tenebat* Roger d'Ivry) in Longtree hd, 168.
Durand of Gloucester, 3 hides in Westbury hd, 168b.
Walter the crossbowman, half a hide in Blidsloe hd, 169.
Roger son of Ralf, one hide in Swineshead hd, 170.
Walter (from Roger son of Ralf), one virgate in Swineshead hd, 170.
Edward (from the king), half a hide in Dudstone hd, 170b.

HAMPSHIRE — *HANTESCIRE*

Folios 37b–54

For Isle of Wight see p. 171 below

MAPS 20–21

Abbot's Barton	Not in D.B.
Abbotstone, F. 5	*Abedestune* 40b
Abbot's Worthy	See Worthy
Abbotts Ann	See Ann
Abedestune	See Abbotstone
Abedric	See Awbridge
Acangre	See Oakhanger
Achelie (*Bovre* hd)	Unid., 51b
Achelie (*Rodbrige* hd)	Unid., 51
Aclei	See Church Oakley
Adelingeham	See Ellingham
Aldershot	Not in D.B.
Alia Tiderlege	See Tytherley
Alia Wallope	See Nether Wallop
Allington, E. 7	*Ellatune* 48b
Alresford, F. 5	*Alresforde* 40
Alresforde	See Alresford
Alton, H. 5	*Aultone* 43 *bis*
Alverstoke, G. 9	*Alwarestoch* 41b
Alwarestoch	See Alverstoke
Alwinetune	Unid., 51
Ambledune	See Hambledon
Ambresberie	See Amesbury, Wilts.
Ampfield	Not in D.B.
Amport	See Ann
Andover, D. 4	*Andovere* 39
Andovere	See Andover
Andwell	Not in D.B.
Ann: Abbots Ann, Amport, Ann Savage, Monxton and Thruxton, C. 4	*Anna* 43 *Anne* 39, 45b, 47, 49
Anna, *Anne*	See Ann, Little Ann
Ann Savage	See Ann
Anstey, H. 5	*Hanstige* 38
Aoltone	See Upton Grey

Aplestede	Unid., 45b
Appleshaw	Not in D.B.
Arnewood, C. 9	*Ernemude* 50b
Ashe, F. 4	*Esse* 47
Ashley (in Milton), C. 10	*Esselei*, *-lie* 51, 51b
Ashley (near Winchester)	Not in D.B.
Ashmansworth	Not in D.B.
Aultone	See Alton
Avere	See Avon
Avington, F. 6	*Avintune* 41
Avintune	See Avington
Avon, A. 9	*Avere* 44b, 46
Awbridge, C. 6	*Abedric* 45, 47b
Baddesley (in Boldre), D. 9	*Bedeslei* 51
Badley, now Clare Park, I. 4	*Beddeleie* 41
Bailocheslei	See Bashley
Bartley, H. 3	*Berchelei* 49b
Barton (in Milton), B. 10	*Ber-*, *Burmintune* 51 *bis*
Barton Stacey, E. 5	*Bertune* 38b, 46b, 48b
Bashley, C. 9	*Bailocheslei* 44
Basing, G. 3	*Basinges* 45
Basinges	See Basing
Basingestoches	See Basingstoke
Basingstoke, G. 3	*Basingestoches* 39 *ter*, 43
Battramsley, C. 9	*Betramelei* 51b
Baughurst	Not in D.B.
Beaulieu	Not in D.B.
Beauworth	Not in D.B.
Beceslei	See Beckley (in Ringwood)
Beckley (in Christchurch), B. 10	*Bichelei* 51

Beckley (in Ringwood), B. 9	*Beceslei* 51
Beddeleie	See Badley
Bedecote	Unid., 39
Bedeslei	See Baddesley (in Boldre), North Baddesley
Bedhampton, H. 8	*Betametone* 43
Beneclege, *-lei*	See Bentley (in Mottisfont)
Benedlei	See Bentley (near Crondall)
Benestede	See Binsted
Bentley (near Crondall), I. 4	*Benedlei* 40b
Bentley (in Mottisfont), C. 6	*Beneclege*, *-lei* 48b, 50
Bentworth	Not in D.B.
Berchelei	See Bartley
Bermintune	See Barton (in Milton)
Bertune	See Barton Stacey
Bessete	See Bradshott
Betametone	See Bedhampton
Betestre	See Bisterne
Betramelei	See Battramsley
Bichelei	See Beckley (in Christchurch)
Bichetone	See Bickton
Bickton, A. 8	*Bichetone* 44b
Bieforde	Unid., 40
Bighetone	See Bighton
Bighton, G. 5	*Bighetone* 43
Bile	Unid., 51
Binsted, H. 5	*Benestede* 41b, 46
Biondene	See Bramdean
Bishop's Sutton, G. 6	*Sudtone* 44b *bis*
Bishopstoke, E. 7	*Stoches* 40
Bishop's Waltham, F. 7	*Waltham* 40
Bisterne, A. 9	*Betestre* 51b
Bitterne	Not in D.B.
Blendworth	Not in D.B.
Boarhunt, G. 8	*Bor(e)hunte* 41b, 44b, 45b
Bocheland	See Buckland
Bocolt	See Buckholt (in Colbury)
Bolderford, C. 9	*Bovreford* 51b
Boldre, C. 9	*Bovre* 51b
Bolende	See Bullington
Bor(e)hunte	See Boarhunt
Borgate	See Burgate
Bortel	See Burton
Boseham	See Bosham, Sx.
Bosintone	See Bossington
Bossington, D. 6	*Bosintone* 46b
Botelie	See Botley
Botley, F. 8	*Botelie* 46b
Bournemouth	Not in D.B.
Boviete	See Boyatt
Bovre	See Boldre
Bovreford	See Bolderford
Boyatt, E. 7	*Boviete* 49
Bradelie	See Bradley
Bradewatre	See Broadwater, Sx.
Bradley, G. 5	*Bradelie* 40
Bradshott, H. 5	*Bessete* 47b
Bramdean, G. 6	*Biondene* 49b *Brondene* 49b
Bramley, G. 3	*Brumelai* 45
Bramshaw, C. 7	*Bramessage* 74 *bis*, Wilts.
Bramshill, H. 2	*Bromeselle* 45b, 48
Bramshott, I. 5	*Brenbresete* 46b
Brandesberee	See Bransbury
Bransbury, E. 4	*Brandesberee* 41b
Breamore, A. 7	*Brumore* 39 *bis*
Brenbresete	See Bramshott
Brestone	See Broughton
Broceste	See Brockenhurst
Brochelie	See Brookley
Brochem(a)tune	See Brockhampton
Brocheseve	See Brockham
Brockenhurst, C. 9	*Broceste* 51b
Brockham, H. 4	*Brocheseve* 49
Brockhampton, H. 9	*Brochem(a)tune* 43, 45b
Bromeselle	See Bramshill
Brondene	See Bramdean
Brookley, C. 9	*Brochelie* 51b
Broughton, C. 5	*Brestone* 38b, 39, 42
Brown Candover	See Candover
Brownwich, F. 9	*Burnewic* 40b
Brumelai	See Bramley

Brumore	See Breamore
Buckholt (near Broughton)	Not in D.B.
Buckholt (in Colbury), D. 8	*Bocolt* 51b
Buckland, G. 9	*Bocheland* 45b
Bullington, E. 5	*Bolende* 44
Burgate, A. 7	*Borgate* 39 *bis*, 50b
Burghclere and Highclere, E. 3	*Clere* 41
Buriton	Not in D.B.
Burmintune	See Barton (in Milton)
Burnewic	See Brownwich
Bursledon	Not in D.B.
Burton, B. 10	*Bortel* 44
Campessete	See Kempshott
Candevre	See Candover, Brown and Chilton; Preston Candover
Candover, Brown and Chilton, F. 5	*Candevre* 40b, 42
Candovre	See Preston Candover
Canterton, C. 8	*Cantortun* 50b
Cantortun	See Canterton
Catherington	Not in D.B.
Celeorde	See Chilworth
Celtone	See Chawton
Ceptune	See Chalton
Cerdeford, *Cerdifort*	See Charford
Cerewartone	See Cholderton
Chalton, H. 7	*Ceptune* 38, 44b *ter*
Charford, North and South, B. 7	*Cerdeford* 44b *bis*, 46, 46b, 48 *Cerdifort* 50
Chawton, H. 5	*Celtone* 45b *bis*
Chelmestune	See Kilmeston
Chementune	See Kimpton
Chenep	See Knapp
Chenol	See Knowle
Cheriton	Not in D.B.
Chilbolton, D. 5	*Cilbode(n)tune* 41, 48
Chilcomb, F. 6	*Ciltecumbe* 41
Chiltley, I. 5	*Ciltelei* 38
Chilton Candover	See Candover
Chilworth, D. 7	*Celeorde* 47b
Chineham, G. 3	*Chineham* 45
Chingescamp	Unid., 40b
Cholderton, C. 4	*Cerewartone* 45b, 48, 48b, 49b
Church Oakley, F. 4	*Aclei* 45b, 46b, 48
Cilbode(n)tune	See Chilbolton
Cildeest	Unid., 51b
Ciltecumbe	See Chilcomb
Ciltelei	See Chiltley
Cladford	See Upper Clatford
Clanfield	Not in D.B.
Clanville, C. 4	*Clavesfelle* 46
Clatinges	Unid., 44b, 46
Clavesfelle	See Clanville
Clere	See Burghclere and Highclere; Kingsclere
Cleresden	See Cliddesden
Cliddesden, G. 4	*Cleresden* 47b
Cocherlei	Unid., 51b
Colbury	Not in D.B.
Coldrey	Not in D.B.
Colemere	See Colemore
Colemore, G. 5	*Colemere* 49
Compton, D. 6	*Cuntune* 48b
Copenore	See Copnor
Copnor, G. 9	*Copenore* 46b
Copythorne	Not in D.B.
Corhampton, G. 7	*Quedementune* 45
Coseham	See Cosham
Cosham, G. 9	*Cos(s)eham* 38, 46, 49b
Cosseham	See Cosham
Cove, I. 3	*Cove* 41
Cranbourne, E. 4	*Gramborne* 42b
Crauuelie	See Crawley
Crawley, E. 5	*Crauuelie* 40
Crofton, F. 9	*Croftone*, *-tune* 44 *bis*
Croftone, *-tune*	See Crofton
Crondall, I. 4	*Crundele* 41
Crone	See Crow
Crookham	Not in D.B.
Crow, B. 9	*Crone* 51b
Crundele	See Crondall

Crux Easton, E. 3	*Estune* 49
Cumbe	See Combe, Berks.
Cuntune	See Compton
Curdbridge	Not in D.B.
Damerham, A. 7	*Dobreham* 66b, 67b, Wilts.
Deane, F. 4	*Dene* 47 *bis*
Dena	See East Dean
Dene	See Deane, East Dean
Denebrige	See Dunbridge
Depedene	See Dibden
Derleie	See Durley (in Colbury)
Dibden, D. 8	*Depedene* 51b
Dodintune	See Totton
Dogmersfield, I. 3	*Ormeresfelt* 49b
Draitone	See Drayton
Drayton, E. 4	*Draitone* 42b
Drocheneford	See Droxford
Droxford, G. 7	*Drocheneford* 41b
Dummer, F. 4	*Dummere* 45b, 49b
Dummere	See Dummer
Dunbridge, C. 6	*Denebrige* 48
Dunwood	Not in D.B.
Durley (near Bishop's Waltham)	Not in D.B.
Durley (in Colbury), D. 8	*Derleie* 50b
East Dean, C. 6	*Dena*, *Dene* 38b, 42, 48, 48b *bis*
Eastleigh, E. 7	*Estleie* 49
East Meon, G. 7	*Mene(s)* 38, 40b 2nd entry
Easton, F. 6	*Estune* 40
Eastrop, G. 3	*Estrope* 47b
East Tytherley	See Tytherley
East Wellow, C. 7	*Weleue* 50
East Woodhay	Not in D.B.
East Worldham	See Worldham
Ebintune	See Ovington
Eccleswelle	See Itchingswell
Edintune	See Ovington
Edlinges	See Eling
Effelle	See Yateley
Efford, C. 10	*Einforde* 51b
Einforde	See Efford
Eisseburne	See Hurstbourne Priors
Eling, D. 8	*Edlinges* 38b
Ellatune	See Allington
Ellingham, A. 8	*Adelingeham* 50
Ellisfield, G. 4	*Esewelle* 46
Elveteham	See Elvetham
Elvetham, I. 3	*Elveteham* 43b
Embley, C. 7	*Emelei* 47b
Emelei	See Embley
Empshott, H. 6	*Hibesete* 49
Ernemude	See Arnewood
Eschetune	Unid., 48
Esewelle	See Ellisfield
Esse	See Ashe
Esseborne	See Hurstbourne Tarrant
Esseham	See Lasham
Esselei, *-lie*	See Ashley
Essessentune	See Exton
Estleie	See Eastleigh
Estrope	See Eastrop
Estune	See Crux Easton; Easton
Etham	See Knight's Enham
Eversley, I. 2	*Evreslei* 43b
Evreslei	See Eversley
Ewhurst, F. 3	*Werste* 45
Exbury	Not in D.B.
Exton, G. 7	*Essessentune* 41b
Eyeworth, B. 8	*Jvare* 39
Faccombe, D. 3	*Facumbe* 39b
Facumbe	See Faccombe
Falegia, *Falelie*	See Fawley
Fareham, F. 8	*Fernham* 40b
Faringdon, H. 5	*Ferendone* 43
Farleigh Wallop, G. 4	*Ferlege* 50
Farley Chamberlain, D. 6	*Ferlege* 48b *bis*
Farlington	Not in D.B.
Farnborough, I. 3	*Ferneberga* 41b
Fawley, E. 9	*Falegia* 41b *Falelie* 51
Ferendone	See Faringdon

Ferlege	See Farleigh Wallop, Farley Chamberlain
Ferlei	See Quarley
Ferneberga	See Farnborough
Fernehelle	See Fernhill
Fernham	See Fareham
Fernhill, C. 10	*Fernehelle* 51
Fifhide	See Fyfield
Finlei	Unid., 49
Fleet	Not in D.B.
Forde	See Fordingbridge
Fordingbridge, A. 8	*Forde* 46b
Foxcott, D. 4	*Fulsescote* 48
Fratton, G. 9	*Frodintone* 47
Freefolk, E. 4	*Frigefole* 41
Frenchmoor	Not in D.B.
Frigefole	See Freefolk
Fritham	Not in D.B.
Frodintone	See Fratton
Froli	See Froyle
Froxfield	Not in D.B.
Froyle, H. 4	*Froli* 43b
Fugelerestune	See Fullerton
Fullerton, D. 5	*Fugelerestune* 42
Fulsescote	See Foxcott
Funtelei	See Funtley
Funtley, F. 8	*Funtelei* 44, 46b, 49
Fyfield, C. 4	*Fifhide* 47b
Gatewood, E. 9	*Gatingeorde* 51b
Gatingeorde	See Gatewood
Gerlei (Chutely hd)	Unid., 46b, 47, 48b
Gerlei (Fordingbridge hd)	See Gorley
Godesmanescamp	Unid., 51b
Godorde	See Goodworth Clatford
Goodworth Clatford, D. 4	*Godorde* 44
Gorley, B. 8	*Gerlei* 49b
Gramborne	See Cranbourne
Grateley	Not in D.B.
Grayshott	Not in D.B.
Greatham, I. 6	*Greteham* 38
Greteham	See Greatham, Gritnam
Greywell	Not in D.B.
Gritnam, C. 8	*Greteham* 51b
Hale	Not in D.B.
Haliborne	See Holybourne
Halingei	See Hayling Island
Hallege	See Headley
Hamble	Not in D.B.
Hambledon, G. 7	*Ambledune* 46b *Hamledune* 44b
Hamledune	See Hambledon
Hanger, D. 8	*Hangre* 50b
Hangre	See Hanger
Hanitune	See Hannington
Hannington, F. 3	*Hanitune* 41b, 50b
Hanstige	See Anstey
Hantone, *-tune*	See Southampton
Harbridge, A. 8	*Herdebrige* 51b
Hardelie	See Hardley
Hardley, E. 9	*Hardelie* 51b
Hariforde	See Hartford
Harlege	See Hartley Mauditt
Harlei	See Hartley Wespall
Hartford, D. 9	*Hariforde* 51
Hartley Mauditt, H. 5	*Har-*, *Herlege* 46b, 47b
Hartley Wespall, H. 3	*Har-*, *Herlei* 49b, 50
Hartley Wintney	Not in D.B.
Hatch Warren, G. 4	*Heche* 49
Havant, H. 8	*Havehunte* 43
Havehunte	See Havant
Hawkley	Not in D.B.
Hawley	Not in D.B.
Hayling Island, H. 9	*Halingei* 38 *Helingey* 43b *Helinghei* 43
Headbourne Worthy, E. 6	*Ordie* 46b *bis*, 47b
Headley, I. 5	*Hallege* 44b
Heckfield	Not in D.B.
Heche	See Hatch Warren
Helingey, *-ghei*	See Hayling Island
Henert	See Herriard
Hentune	See Hinton Admiral, Hinton Ampner

Herdebrige	See Harbridge
Herdel	See Hordle
Herlege	See Hartley Mauditt
Herlei	See Hartley Wespall
Herne	See Hurn
Herriard, G. 4	*Henert* 45b
Hibesete	See Empshott
Highclere	See Burghclere
Highcliffe	Not in D.B.
Hincelveslei	See Hincheslea
Hincheslea, C. 9	*Hincelveslei* 51b
Hinton Admiral, B. 10	*Hentune* 51 *bis*
Hinton Ampner, G. 6	*Hentune* 41b
Hoburne, B. 10	*Hoburne* 51b
Hoddington, H. 4	*Odingetone* 41b
Hoe, G. 7	*Hou* 45
Holdenhurst, A. 10	*Hole(h)est* 39, 44
Hole(h)est	See Holdenhurst
Holstune	See Houghton
Holybourne, H. 5	*Haliborne* 38, 50b
Hook, E. 9	*Houch* 45
Hordle, C. 10	*Herdel* 51
Hore	See Ower
Hotlop	Unid., 50
Hou	See Hoe
Houch	See Hook
Houghton, D. 6	*Holstune* 44b, 45, 48, 49b *Houstun* 40b
Hound, E. 8	*Hune* 45
Houston	See Houghton
Hune	See Hound
Hunton	Not in D.B.
Hurn, A. 9	*Herne* 46
Hursley	Not in D.B.
Hurstbourne Priors, E. 4	*Eisseburne* 41
Hurstbourne Tarrant, D. 3	*Esseborne* 39 *bis*
Ibsley, A. 8	*Tibeslei* 46
Icene	See Itchen Abbess
Idsworth	Not in D.B.
Itchell, I. 4	*Ticelle* 41
Itchen Abbess, F. 5	*Icene* 48
Itchen Stoke, F. 6	*Stoche* 43b
Itchingswell, E. 3	*Eccleswelle* 41b
Jvare	See Eyeworth
Kempshott, G. 4	*Campessete* 45
Kilmeston, F. 6	*Chelmestune* 40 *bis*
Kimpton, C. 4	*Chementune* 46
Kingsclere, F. 3	*Clere* 39 *bis*, 43, 45, 48b, 50b *bis*
Kingsley	Not in D.B.
King's Somborne	See Somborne
King's Worthy	See Worthy
Kinson, A. 9	*Chinestanestone* 80b, Do.
Knapp, A. 10	*Chenep* 46
Knight's Enham, D. 4	*Etham* 50 *bis*
Knowle, F. 3	*Chenol* 45, 47
Lainston	Not in D.B.
Lammere	See Lomer
Langelie	See Langley
Langley, E. 9	*Langelie* 50b *bis*
Langrish	Not in D.B.
Larode	See Lyewood
Lasham, G. 4	*Esseham* 38b
Latelie	See Netley
Laverstoke, E. 4	*Lavrochestoche* 43
Lavrochestoche	See Laverstoke
Lec(ht)ford	See Leckford
Leckford, D. 5	*Lec(ht)ford* 42, 43b
Lentune	See Lymington
Lesborne	See Selborne
Lesteorde	Unid., 51
Lestred	See Testwood
Lichepet	See Lickpit
Lickpit, G. 3	*Lichepet* 43
Lidessete	See Ludshott
Linchehou	See Linkenholt
Linhest	See Lyndhurst
Linkenholt, D. 3	*Linchehou* 43
Lis	See Liss
Liss, H. 6	*Lis* 43b
Litchfield, E. 3	*Liveselle* 45b
Liteltone	See Littleton (in Kimpton)
Little Ann, D. 4	*Anna* 44
Little Somborne	See Somborne

Littleton (in Kimpton), C. 4	*Liteltone* 45b
Littleton (near Winchester)	Not in D.B.
Liveselle	See Litchfield
Locherlega, *Locher(s)lei*	See Lockerley
Lockerley, C. 6	*Locherlega* 45b *Locher(s)lei* 42, 50 *bis*
Lomer, G. 7	*Lammere* 43
Longstock, D. 5	*Stoches* 43b
Long Sutton, H. 4	*Sudtune* 41b
Ludshott, I. 6	*Lidessete* 45b
Lyewood, G. 6	*Larode* 48b
Lymington, C. 10	*Lentune* 51
Lyndhurst, C. 8	*Linhest* 39
Malpedresham	See Mapledurham
Mapledrewelle	See Mapledurwell
Mapledurham, H. 7	*Malpedresham* 38
Mapledurwell, H. 3	*Mapledrewelle* 46b
Mapleham	Unid., 51b
Marchwood, D. 8	*Merceode* 50b
Martin	Not in D.B.
Martyr Worthy	See Worthy
Matingelege	See Mattingley
Mattingley, H. 3	*Matingelege* 49b
Medstead	Not in D.B.
Melchet Park	Not in D.B.
Melebroc	See Millbrook
Melleford	See Milford
Mene	See East Meon, Meon (in Titchfield)
Menes	See East Meon, West Meon
Menestoche(s)	See Meonstoke
Meon (in Titchfield), F. 9	*Mene* 40b 3rd entry
Meonstoke, G. 7	*Menestoche(s)* 38, 39, 40b
Merceode	See Marchwood
Miceldevre	See Micheldever
Micheldever, F. 5	*Miceldevre* 42b
Michelmersh	Not in D.B.
Middeltune	See Middleton
Middleton, E. 4	*Middletune* 44

Midgham, A. 8	*Mingeham* 50, 50b
Mildeltune	See Milton
Milford, C. 10	*Melleford* 51b *bis*
Millbrook, D. 8	*Melebroc* 41b
Milton, B. 10	*Mildeltune* 50b
Mindeslei	See Minley
Mingeham	See Midgham
Minley, I. 3	*Mindeslei* 49b
Minstead, C. 8	*Mintestede* 51b
Mintestede	See Minstead
Monk Sherborne, G. 3	*Sireborne* 46
Monxton	See Ann
Morestead	Not in D.B.
Mortelhunte, *Mortesfunde*	See Mottisfont
Mottisfont, C. 6	*Mortelhunte* 50 *Mortesfunde* 42
Mulceltone	Unid., 50
Nataleie	See Nately
Nately, H. 3	*Nataleie* 45
Neatham, H. 5	*Neteham* 38
Neteham	See Neatham
Nether Wallop, C. 5	*Alia Wallope* 38b
Netley, E. 8	*Latelie* 48
Netley Marsh, C. 8	*Nutlei* 51b 1st entry
Neutibrige	See Newtimber
Newentone	See Newton Valence
Newtimber, H. 8	*Neutibrige* 44b
Newton Stacey, D. 5	*Niwetone* 48b
Newton Valence, H. 5	*Newentone* 47b
Newtown	Not in D.B.
Niwetone	See Newton Stacey
Noclei	See Nutley
Northam, E. 8	*Northam* 49b
North Baddesley, D. 7	*Bedeslei* 47
North Charford	See Charford
Northington	Not in D.B.
North Stoneham	See Stoneham
North Waltham	Not in D.B.
Norton (in Selborne), H. 5	*Nortone* 46, 47

Norton (in Wonston), E. 5	*Nortune* 49b
Nortone	See Norton (in Selborne)
Nortune	See Norton (in Wonston)
Notesselinge	See Nursling
Nursling, D. 7	*Notesselinge* 41
Nutlei (*Bovre* hd)	Unid., 51b
Nutlei (*Rodbrige* hd)	See Netley Marsh
Nutley, G. 4	*Noclei* 49
Oakhanger, H. 5	*Acangre* 49b
Odecote	See Woodcott
Odetone	See Wootton St Lawrence
Odetune	See Wootton (in Milton)
Odiham, H. 4	*Odiham* 38, 49b *Hodiham*, L.D.B. 450b, Suff.
Odingetone	See Hoddington
Olvestune	See Woolston
Optune	See Upton (in Hurstbourne Tarrant)
Ordie	See Headbourne Worthy; Worthy, Abbot's etc.
Ormeresfelt	See Dogmersfield
Oselei	Unid., 51 *bis*
Otoiche	See Outwick
Otreburne	See Otterbourne
Otreorde	See Otterwood
Otterbourne, E. 7	*Otreburne* 46b
Otterwood, D. 9	*Otreorde* 51b *bis*
Outwick, A. 7	*Otoiche* 48
Overton, F. 4	*Ovretune* 40
Over Wallop, C. 5	*Wallop*(*e*) 38b *bis*, 45b *ter*, 50 *bis*
Ovington, F. 6	*Ebintune* 43b *Edintune* 40b
Ovretune	See Overton
Ower, C. 7	*Hore* 43b
Oxelei	Unid., 51b
Pamber	Not in D.B.
Penitone	See Penton

Penton Grafton and Mewsey, C. 4	*Penitone* 43b, 44b
Petersfield	Not in D.B.
Pilley, D. 9	*Pistelei* 51b *Pisteslai*, *-lei* 51, 51b
Pistelei, *Pisteslai*, *-lei*	See Pilley
Pittleworth, C. 6	*Put*(*el*)*eorde* 42, 49
Plaitford, C. 7	*Pleiteford* 74, Wilts.
Polemetune	See Polhampton
Polhampton, F. 4	*Polemetune* 41b, 47
Popeham	See Popham
Popham, F. 4	*Popeham* 42b
Porcestre	See Porchester
Porchester, G. 9	*Por*(*t*)*cestre* 38, 47b
Portcestre	See Porchester
Portsmouth	Not in D.B.
Portswood	Not in D.B.
Preston Candover, G. 5	*Candevre* 45b, 47b, 49b *bis* *Candovre* 44b, 47
Priors Dean	Not in D.B.
Privett	Not in D.B.
Put(*el*)*eorde*	See Pittleworth
Quarley, C. 4	*Ferlei* 39
Quedementune	See Corhampton
Redbridge, D. 8	*Rodbrige* 46
Rincvede	See Ringwood
Ringwood, A. 9	*Rincvede* 39
Riple	See Ripley
Ripley, B. 9	*Riple* 46, 50b
Rocheborne	See Rockbourne
Rocheford	See Rockford
Rochesire	See Rockstead
Rockbourne, A. 7	*Rocheborne* 39 *bis*, 50 *bis*
Rockford, B. 8	*Rocheford* 46
Rockstead, A. 7	*Rochesire* 46
Rodbrige	See Redbridge
Rollstone, E. 9	*Roweste* 51b
Romesy	See Romsey
Romsey, D. 7	*Romesy* 43b
Ropley	Not in D.B.

Rotherwick	Not in D.B.
Roweste	See Rollstone
Rowner, F. 9	*Ruenore* 47b
Rownhams	Not in D.B.
Ruenore	See Rowner
St Mary Bourne	Not in D.B.
Sanhest	Unid., 51b
Sarisbury	Not in D.B.
Sarson, C. 4	*Soresdene* 48
Sceptone, *-tune*	See Shipton Bellinger
Sclive	Unid., 51
Segensworth, F. 8	*Sugion* 45
Selborne, H. 5	*Lesborne* 48b *Selesburne* 38
Seldene	See Shalden
Selesburne	See Selborne
Seneorde	See Sunwood
Shalden, H. 4	*Seldene* 47b
Shedfield	Not in D.B.
Sheet	Not in D.B.
Sherborne St John, G. 3	*Sireburne* 45
Sherfield English, C. 7	*Sirefelle* 45b
Sherfield upon Loddon	Not in D.B.
Shipton Bellinger, B. 4	*Sceptone*, *-tune* 46b, 47b
Shirley, D. 8	*Sirelei* 46b
Shoddesden, C. 4	*Sotesdene* 50
Sidemanestone	See Sidmonton
Sidmonton, E. 3	*Sidemanestone* 44
Silcestre	See Silchester
Silchester, G. 2	*Silcestre* 47 *bis*
Sireborne	See Monk Sherborne
Sireburne	See Sherborne St John
Sirefelle	See Sherfield English
Sirelei	See Shirley
Slacham	Unid., 39
Snoddington, C. 4	*Snodintone* 45b
Snodintone	See Snoddington
Soberton, G. 7	*Sudbertune* 38 *bis*, 40, 48b, 49
Somborne, King's and Little, D. 5, D. 6	*Sumburne* 39b, 47, 47b, 48b *bis*
Sopelie	See Sopley
Sopley, B. 9	*Sopelie* 48b
Soresdene	See Sarson
Sotesdene	See Shoddesden
Southampton, D. 8	*Hantone*, *-tune* 41b, 46b, 47b, 52 *bis*
South Charford	See Charford
South Stoneham	See Stoneham
South Tidworth, B. 4	*Tedorde* 46b *Todeorde* 46b, 49
South Warnborough, H. 4	*Wergeborne* 48
Southwick	Not in D.B.
Sparsholt	Not in D.B.
Staneham	See Stoneham
Stanes	See Stone
Staneude	See Stanswood
Stanham	See Stoneham
Stanpeta	See Stanpit
Stanpit, B. 10	*Stanpeta* 46 *bis*
Stanswood, E. 9	*Staneude* 38b
Steep	Not in D.B.
Steventon, F. 4	*Stivetune* 50b
Stivetune	See Steventon
Stoche	See Itchen Stoke, Stockbridge
Stoches	See Bishopstoke, Longstoke, Stoke Charity
Stockbridge, D. 5	*Stoche* 49b
Stoke Charity, E. 5	*Stoches* 40b
Stone, E. 9	*Stanes* 50b
Stoneham, North and South, E. 7	*Stan(e)ham* 41b, 43
Stradfelle	See Stratfield Saye and Turgis. See also Stratfield Mortimer, Berks.
Stratfield Saye and Turgis, H. 2, H. 3	*Stradfelle* 45b, 48 *bis*, 49b
Stratune	See West Stratton
Stubbington, F. 9	*Stubitone* 45
Stubitone	See Stubbington

Sualefelle	See Swallowfield, Berks.
Suantune	See Swampton
Sudberie	Unid., 50
Sudbertune	See Soberton
Sudtone	See Bishop's Sutton
Sudtune	See Long Sutton, Sutton Scotney
Suei(a)	See Sway
Sugion	See Segensworth
Sumburne	See Somborne
Sunwood, H. 7	*Seneorde* 44b *ter*
Sutton Scotney, E. 5	*Sudtune* 46b, 49b
Swampton, E. 4	*Suantune* 47
Swanmore	Not in D.B.
Swarraton	Not in D.B.
Sway, C. 9	*Suei(a)* 44, 51 *bis*, 51b
Taceberie	See Tatchbury
Tadley	Not in D.B.
Tangley	Not in D.B.
Tatchbury, C. 8	*Taceberie* 43 *Teocreberie* 51b
Tederleg	See Tytherley
Tedorde	See South Tidworth
Teocreberie	See Tatchbury
Testwood, D. 8	*Lestred* 46
Thruxton	See Ann
Thuinam	See Twynham
Tibeslei	See Ibsley
Ticefelle	See Titchfield
Ticelle	See Itchell
Tichborne	Not in D.B.
Tiderlege, -lei, Alia Tiderlege	See Tytherley
Tidgrove, F. 3	*Titegrave* 46b
Timbreberie	See Timsbury
Timsbury, D. 6	*Timbreberie* 43b
Tisted, G. 6	*Tistede* 40b
Tistede	See Tisted
Titchfield, F. 9	*Ticefelle* 39
Titegrave	See Tidgrove
Tochiton	See Tufton
Todeorde	See South Tidworth
Totintone	See Totton
Totton, D. 8	*Dodintune* 44 *Totintone* 50b
Tru(c)ham	Unid., 51 *ter*, 51b *bis*
Tufton, E. 4	*Tochiton* 44
Tuiforde	See Twyford
Tuinam	See Twynham
Tuneworde	See Tunworth
Tunworth, G. 4	*Tuneworde* 45
Twyford, E. 6	*Tuiforde* 40 *bis*
Twynham, B. 10	*T(h)uinam* 38b *bis*, 44 *ter*
Tytherley, East and West, C. 6	*Alia Tiderlege* 42 *Tederleg* 50 *bis* *Tiderlege, -lei* 42, 48, 48b *Tuderlege* 74, Wilts.
Udemanecote	See Woodmancote
Ulvretune	See Wolverton
Upham	Not in D.B.
Upper Clatford, D. 4	*Cladford* 38b
Upton (in Hurstbourne Tarrant), D. 3	*Optune* 38b
Upton Grey, H. 4	*Aoltone* 45b
Utefel	Unid., 51b
Vernham Dean	Not in D.B.
Walde	See Wield
Walhampton, D. 10	*Wolnetune* 51
Wallop(e)	See Over Wallop
Wallope, Alia	See Nether Wallop
Waltham	See Bishop's Waltham
Warblington, H. 9	*Warblitetone* 23b, Sx.
Wardham	See Worldham
Warneford	See Warnford
Warnford, G. 7	*Warneford* 43, 45 *bis*
Warwelle	See Wherwell
Waterloo	Not in D.B.
Weleue	See East Wellow
Welle	See West Wellow

Wenesistune	See Wonston
Wergeborne	See South Warnborough
Werildeham	See Worldham
Weringetone	See Winkton
Werste	See Ewhurst
Wesberie	See Westbury
Westbury, G. 7	*Wesberie* 45
West Meon, G. 6	*Menes* 40b 1st entry
Westone	See Weston Patrick
Weston Patrick, H. 4	*Westone* 47b
West Stratton, F. 5	*Stratune* 42b
West Tytherley	See Tytherley
West Wellow, C. 7	*Welle* 48
West Worldham	See Worldham
Weyhill	Not in D.B.
Wherwell, D. 5	*Warwelle* 44
Whitchurch, E. 4	*Witcerce* 41
Whitsbury	Not in D.B.
Wicheham	See Wickham
Wickham, F. 8	*Wicheham* 45
Wield, H. 6	*Walde* 40b
Wigarestun	Unid., 51b
Wildehel	See Will Hall
Will Hall, H. 5	*Wildehel* 48b
Wimeringes	See Wymering
Wincestre	See Winchester
Winchester, E. 6	*Wincestre* 38b *bis*, 39, 40b, 42, 43b, 44, 44b, 45, 46b, 47b, 48, 49b *bis*, 51b
Winchester cont.	*Wintonia* 39b, 43b, 44, Hants.; 100, Devon; Exon D.B., 88, Devon
Winchfield, H. 3	*Winesflet* 43b
Windenaie	See Witnal
Winesflet	See Winchfield
Winesflot	See Winslade
Winkton, B. 10	*Weringetone* 48
Winslade, G. 4	*Winesflot* 45
Wintonia	See Winchester
Witcerce	See Whitchurch
Witnal, E. 3	*Windenaie* 41
Wolnetune	See Walhampton
Wolverton, F. 3	*Ulvretune* 49 *bis*
Wonston, E. 5	*Wenesistune* 41b
Woodcott, E. 3	*Odecote* 48b
Woodmancote, F. 4	*Udemanecote* 42
Woolston, E. 8	*Olvestune* 49
Wootton (in Milton), C. 9	*Odetune* 51b
Wootton St Lawrence, F. 3	*Odetone* 41b, 46
Worldham, East and West, H. 5	*Wardham* 50b *Werildeham* 49
Worthy, Abbot's, King's and Martyr, E. 5, E. 6, F. 5	*Ordie* 38b, 41b, 42b
Worting, G. 3	*Wortinges* 43
Wortinges	See Worting
Wymering, G. 9	*Wimeringes* 38
Yateley, I. 2	*Effelle* 45b

ANONYMOUS HOLDINGS

No place-names appear in the following thirty-five entries, and it is possible that some (or even all) of these refer to holdings at places not named elsewhere in Domesday Book:

The king, one virgate in Fordingbridge hd. Mainly in the forest, 39.
Mauger (from bishop of Winchester), one hide in *Evingare* hd, 41.
Alvric the priest (from bishop of Winchester), one hide in *Evingare* hd, 41.
Alsi (from Winchester abbey), *in uno alio loco*, one hide in Micheldever hd, 42b.
Edward the sheriff (from Milton abbey), 12 acres in *Egheiete* hd, 43b.
Canons of Twynham, 8 acres in Boldre hd. In the forest, 44.
Count Alan, 5 hides in Titchfield hd, 44.

ANONYMOUS HOLDINGS (continued)

Count of Mortain, 4 hides in Somborne hd, 44b.
Troarn abbey (from Earl Roger), 5 hides in *Boseberg* hd, 44b.
Ralf de Mortemer, one virgate in Titchfield hd, 47.
Ralf de Mortemer, 2 hides in Somborne hd, 47.
Ricoard (from William de Braiose), half a hide in Neatham hd, 47.
Fulcold (from William Malduith), one hide in Portsdown hd, 47b.
William Malduith, 2 hides less one virgate in Portsdown hd, 47b.
Gilbert de Breteville, one hide in Somborne hd, 48.
Hugh (from William son of Stur), one hide in Somborne hd, 48b.
Henry the treasurer, one hide in *Bermesplet* hd, 49.
Alvred the priest, one hide in Titchfield hd, 49.
Durand the barber, one hide in Titchfield hd, 49.
Anschitil son of Osmund (from the king), half a hide in Portsdown hd, 49b.
Milo the porter (from the king), 2½ virgates in *Bermesplet* hd, 49b.
Alric (from the king), half a hide in Redbridge hd, 50b.
Alwin Wit (from the king), 2 hides in Clere hd, 50b.
Edwin the huntsman (from the king), 2 hides in Clere hd, 50b.
Eldred brother of Odo (from the king), half a hide in Somborne hd, 50b.
Almer (from the king), half a hide in Somborne hd, 50b.
Ulvric the huntsman (from the king), 1½ hides in Somborne hd, 50b.
Godwin the falconer (from the king), half a hide in Basingstoke hd, 50b.
Alvric Petit (from the king), one virgate in Redbridge hd. In the forest, 50b.
Bernard (from William of Eu), 2 hides in *Rodedic* hd. Partly in the forest, 51.
Willac, 4 acres of meadow in *Egeiete* hd, 51b.
Alvric the physician, 4 acres of meadow in *Egeiete* hd, 51b.
Sawin, one virgate in Boldre hd. Mainly in the forest, 51b.
Hunta and Pagen, 2½ virgates in Boldre hd. Mainly in the forest, 51b.
Alwold (from Alvric), 3 virgates in *Rodedic* hd. Partly in the forest, 51b.

ISLE OF WIGHT
INSULA DE WIT

Folios 39b–40, 52–54

Abaginge	Unid., 53b
Abedestone	See Adgestone
Abla	Unid., 40
Adgestone, F. 11	*Abedestone* 39b
Adrintone	See Arreton
Affetune	See Afton
Afton, D. 11	*Affetune* 52
Alalei	See Lea
Alia Witesfel	See Little Whitefield
Alvington, E. 10	*Alwinestune* 52b
Alvrestone	Unid., 53
Alwinestune	See Alvington
Apledeforde, *Apleford*	See Appleford
Appleford, E. 11	*Apledeforde* 53b *Apleford* 52b, 54
Arreton, F. 11	*Adrintone* 39b
Atehalle	See Hale
Atherfield, E. 11	*Avrefel* 52b *Egrafel* 52b
Avicestone	See Aviston

Aviston, G. 11	*Avicestone* 53, 53b
Avrefel	See Atherfield
Barnsley, G. 10	*Benverdeslei* 39b *Benveslei* 53
Bathingbourne, F. 11	*Bedingeborne* 39b
Bedingeborne	See Bathingbourne
Bembridge	Not in D.B.
Benestede	See Binstead
Benv(erd)eslei	See Barnsley
Berardinz	See Brading
Binstead, F. 10	*Benestede* 53
Blackpan, F. 11	*Bochepone* 53
Bochepone	See Blackpan
Bonchurch, F. 11	*Bonecerce* 53
Bonecerce	See Bonchurch
Bordourde	See Borthwood
Borthwood, F. 11	*Bordourde* 53
Bouecome	See Bowcombe
Bowcombe, E. 11	*Bouecome* 52, Hants.; 64b, Wilts.
Brading, G. 11	*Berardinz* 53
Brandestone	See Branstone
Branstone, F. 11	*Brandestone* 53
Breilesforde	See Briddlesford
Briddlesford, F. 10	*Breilesforde* 53
Brighstone	Not in D.B.
Broc	See Brook
Brook, D. 11	*Broc* 52
Calbourne, E. 11	*Cauborne* 52b *bis*
Cantune	See Compton
Carisbrooke	Not in D.B.
Cauborne	See Calbourne
Cela	See Chale
Celatune	See Chilton
Celertune	See Chillerton
Celvecrote	Unid., 53b
Cevredone	See Cheverton
Chale, E. 12	*Cela* 52b, 54
Chenistone	See Knighton
Cheverton, E. 11	*Cevredone* 52b
Chillerton, E. 11	*Celertune* 53b *bis*
Chilton, D. 11	*Celatune* 53b *bis*
Chingestune	See Kingston
Chochepon	See Puckpool
Compton, D. 11	*Cantune* 52

Coombe, E. 11	*Seutecome* 53b
Done	See Down (near Knighton)
Down (near Bathingbourne), F. 11	*Ladone* 39b
Down (near Knighton), F. 11	*Done* 39b
Drodintone	Unid., 54
Dungewood, E. 11	*Dunniorde* 52b
Dunniorde	See Dungewood
Eddington, G. 10	*Etharin* 39b
Egrafel	See Atherfield
Ermud	See Yarmouth
Eseldecome	See Shalcombe
Essuete	See Sheat
Etharin	See Eddington
Everelant, Evreland	See Yaverland
Frescewatre	See Freshwater
Freshwater, D. 11	*Frescewatre* 52, 53b
Gadetune	See Gotten
Gatcombe, E. 11	*Gatecome* 52b
Gatecome	See Gatcombe
Godshill	Not in D.B.
Gotten, E. 11	*Gadetune* 52b
Great Pan, E. 10	*Lepene* 53b
Haldley, E. 10	*Heldelie* 52
Hale, F. 11	*Atehalle* 53
Hamestede	See Hamstead
Hamstead, D. 10	*Hamestede* 53b *bis*
Hardelei	See Hardley
Hardley, G. 11	*Hardelei* 52b
Haselie	See Heasley
Heasley, F. 11	*Haselie* 39b
Heldelie	See Haldley
Heceford	Unid., 54
Horringford, F. 11	*Ovingefort* 54
Hoteleston(e)	See Nettlestone
Huffingford, F. 11	*Huncheford* 54
Huncheford	See Huffingford
Idlecombe, E. 11	*Ulwarcumbe* 52b

Kern, F. 11	*Lacherne* 39b
Kingston, E. 11	*Chingestune* 52b
Knighton, F. 11	*Chenistone* 39b, 54
Lacherne	See Kern
Ladone	See Down (near Bathingbourne)
Lamore	See Moor
Lea, F. 11	*Alalei* 53b
Lenimcode	See Ningwood
Lepene	See Great Pan
Lessland, F. 11	*Liscelande* 39b
	Litesland 53
Levegarestun	Unid., 53
Levintun(e)	See Limerstone
Limerstone, E. 11	*Levintun(e)* 52b, 54
Liscelande, *Litesland*	See Lessland
Little Whitefield, F. 10	*Alia Witesfel* 53
Lovecumbe	See Luccombe
Luccombe, F. 11	*Lovecumbe* 39b
Melevsford	See Milford
Merestone	See Merstone
Merstone, F. 11	*Merestone* 53
	Messetone 53
Messetone	See Merstone
Milford, D. 10	*Melevsford* 53b
Modrestan	See Mottistone
Moor, F. 11	*Lamore* 53
Mottistone, D. 11	*Modrestan* 53b
Neeton	See Niton
Nettlestone, G. 10	*Hoteleston(e)* 39b, 53b *bis*
Newchurch	Not in D.B.
Newport	Not in D.B.
Ningwood, D. 10	*Lenimcode* 54
Niton, F. 12	*Neeton* 40
Nonoelle	See Nunwell
Northwood	Not in D.B.
Nunwell, F. 10	*Nonoelle* 39b
Odetone	See Wootton
Orham, G. 10	*Orham* 53
Ovingefort	See Horringford
Perreton, F. 11	*Prestetone* 53

Prestetone	See Perreton
Puckpool, G. 10	*Chochepon* 39b
Rode	See Roud
Rodeberge	See Rowborough
Roud, F. 11	*Rode* 53
Rowborough, G. 10	*Rodeberge* 53
Ryde	Not in D.B.
St Helens	Not in D.B.
Sande	See Sandown
Sandford, F. 11	*Sandford* 39b
Sandown, G. 11	*Sande* 39b
Scaldeford	See Scottlesford
Scottlesford, F. 11	*Scaldeford* 39b, 53 *bis*
Seldeflet	See Shalfleet
Selins	See Sullens
Sencliz	See Shanklin
Seutecome	See Coombe
Shalcombe, D. 11	*Eseldecome* 52b
Shalfleet, D. 10	*Seldeflet* 53b
Shanklin, F. 11	*Sencliz* 53
Sheat, E. 11	*Essuete* 53b
	Soete 54
Shide, E. 10	*Sida*, *Side* 52b, 53b *bis*
Shorwell, E. 11	*Sorewelle* 52b, 53b
Sida, *Side*	See Shide
Soete	See Sheat
Sofleet, F. 10	*Soflet* 40
Soflet	See Sofleet
Sorewelle	See Shorwell
Standen, F. 10	*Standone* 53 *bis*
Standone	See Standen
Staneberie	See Stenbury
Stenbury, F. 11	*Staneberie* 39b
Sullens, F. 11	*Selins* 53
Thorley, D. 10	*Torlei* 53b
Torlei	See Thorley
Totland	Not in D.B.
Ulvredestune	See Woolverton
Ulwarcumbe	See Idlecombe
Ulwartone	See Wolverton
Valpenne	See Walpen
Ventnor	Not in D.B.

Walpen, E. 12	*Valpenne* 52b
Warochesselle	See Wroxall
Watchingwell, E. 10	*Watingewelle* 52b
Watingewelle	See Watchingwell
Week, F. 12	*Wica* 39b
Welige	See Wellow
Wellow, D. 10	*Welige* 52
Wenechetone	Unid., 39b
Weristetone	Unid., 53b
Whippingham, F. 10	*Wipingeham* 39b, 53
Whitcombe, E. 11	*Witecome* 52b
Whitefield, F. 10	*Witesfel* 53
Whitwell	Not in D.B.
Wica	See Week
Wilmingeham	See Wilmingham
Wilmingham, D. 10	*Wilmingeham* 52
Wipingeham	See Whippingham
Witecome	See Whitcombe
Witesfel	See Whitefield
Witesfel, Alia	See Little Whitefield
Witestone	Unid., 53
Witingeham	Unid., 53b
Wolverton, G. 10	*Ulwartone* 39b
Woolverton, E. 11	*Ulvredestune* 53b
Wootton, F. 10	*Odetone* 40
Wroxall, F. 11	*Warochesselle* 39b
Yarmouth, D. 10	*Ermud* 54
Yaverland, G. 11	*Everelant* 39b *Evreland* 53

ANONYMOUS HOLDINGS

No place-names appear in the following two entries, and it is possible that either (or even both) of these refer to holdings at places not named elsewhere in Domesday Book:

St Mary of Lyre, 2 hides and 2½ virgates, 52b.
Ulnod (from the king), half a virgate in Bowcombe hd, 54.

HEREFORDSHIRE—*HEREFORDSCIRE*

Folios 179–187b

MAP 22

Abbey Dore	Not in D.B.
Ach	Unid., 181b
Achel	See Yarkhill
Acle	See Ocle Pychard
Aconbury	Not in D.B.
Acton Beauchamp, F. 4	*Actune* 176, Worcs.
Adforton, B. 2	*Alfertintune* 260, Salop.
Adley, B. 2	*Adelestune* 260b, Salop. *Edelactune* 258b, 260b, Salop.
Ailey, B. 5	*Walelege* 187
Alac	Unid., 179b, 180b
Alcamestune	Unid., 187
Almeley, A. 4	*Elmelie* 182b
Almundestune	Unid., 187
Alretune	See Orleton
Alwintune	See Alvington, Gloucs.
Amberley, D. 5	*Amburlege* 186
Amburlege	See Amberley
Ardeshope	See Yarsop
Ascis	See Ash Ingen
Ash Ingen, D. 7	*Ascis* 180, 181
Ashperton, E. 5	*Spertune* 183b, 185b, 186b, 187b
Ashton, D. 3	*Estune* 180
Astenofre	See Eastnor
Aston (near Wigmore), C. 2	*Hesintune* 183b

Aston Ingham, F. 8	*Estune* 186
Auretone	See Richards Castle
Avenbury, E. 4	*Aweneburi* 183
Aweneburi	See Avenbury
Aylton, E. 6	Not in D.B., but see anon. holdings on p. 185
Aymestry, C. 3	*Elmodestreu* 180 *ter*
Bach, A. 5	*Becce* 187
Bachetune	See Bacton
Backbury, D. 6	*Bageberge* 182
Bacton, B. 6	*Bachetune* 184
Bageberge	See Backbury
Baissan	See Baysham
Baldehalle	Lost in Hanley Castle, Worcs.
Ballingham, D. 7	Not in D.B., but see anon. holdings on p. 185
Bartestree, D. 5	*Bertoldestreu* 183
Barton, A. 4	*Beuretune* 181
Baysham, D. 7	*Baissan* 181
Becce	See Bach
Beltrov	Unid., 187
Berchelincope	See Burlingjobb, Wales
Bernoldune	Unid., 187
Bertoldestreu	See Bartestree
Bertune	See Burton
Beuretune	See Barton
Bickerton, E. 7	*Bicretune* 185b
Bicretune	See Bickerton
Birley, C. 4	*Burlei* 183b *bis*, 184b
Biselie	See Bushley, Worcs.
Bishop's Frome, E. 5	*Frome* 181b, 185 1st entry
Blakemere	Not in D.B.
Bodeham	See Bodenham
Bodenham, D. 4	*Bodeham* 184, 186b
Boitune	See Byton
Bolelei	See Bowley
Bollingham, A. 4	*Burardestune* 181
Bolstone	Not in D.B.
Boninhope, *Boniniope*	See Bullingham formerly Bullinghope

Boritune	See Burrington
Bosbury, F. 5	*Boseberge* 182
Boseberge	See Bosbury
Bowley, D. 4	*Bolelei* 183
Bradefelde	See Broadfield
Bradeford	See Broadward
Bradelege	See Bradley
Bradley, A. 3	*Bradelege* 186b
Brampton Abbotts, E. 7	*Bruntune* 182b *bis*
Brampton Bryan, B. 2	*Brantune* 260b, Salop.
Breadward, A. 4	*Brudeford* 181
Bredenbury, E. 4	*Brideneberie* 185
Bredwardine, B. 5	*Brocheurdie* 186
Breinton	Not in D.B.
Bretlege	See Brierley
Bricge	See Bridge Sollers
Brideneberie	See Bredenbury
Bridge Sollers, C. 5	*Bricge* 182b *Brigge* 182b
Bridstow	Not in D.B.
Brierley, C. 4	*Bretlege* 180
Brigge	See Bridge Sollers
Brilley	Not in D.B.
Brimfield, D. 2	*Brome-*, *Brumefelde* 180 *bis*
Brinsop, C. 5	*Hope* 186 1st entry
Brismerfrum	See Castle Frome
Broadfield, D. 4	*Bradefelde* 180
Broadward, C. 4	*Bradeford* 180, 185b
Brobury, B. 5	*Brocheberie* 184b
Brocheberie	See Brobury
Brochementone	See Brockmanton
Brocheurdie	See Bredwardine
Brockhampton (near Bromyard)	Not in D.B.
Brockhampton (near Ross), E. 7	*Caplefore* 181b
Brockmanton, D. 3	*Brochementone* 180
Brocote	Unid., 181
Bromefelde	See Brimfield
Bromgerbe	See Bromyard
Bromyard, E. 4	*Bromgerbe* 182b
Brudeford	See Breadward
Brumefelde	See Brimfield

Bruntune	See Brampton Abbotts, Little Brampton
Buckton, B. 2	*Buctone* 260b, Salop.
Buiford	See Byford
Bullingham formerly Bullinghope, D. 6	*Boninhope* 186, 186b *Boniniope* 184
Bunesulle	See Bunshill
Bunshill, C. 5	*Bunesulle* 187b
Burardestune	See Bollingham
Burcstanestune	Unid., 186b
Burgelle	See Burghill
Burghill, C. 5	*Burgelle* 186
Burlei	See Birley
Burrington, C. 2	*Boritune* 183b
Burton, D. 6	*Bertune* 181b
Buterlei, *Butrelie*	See Butterley
Butterley, E. 3	*Buterlei* 180 *Butrelie* 185
Byford, B. 5	*Buiford* 185
Byton, B. 3	*Boitune* 186b
Calcheberge	See Coldborough
Callow	Not in D.B.
Camehop	See Covenhope
Canon Frome, E. 5	*Frome* 184b
Canon Pyon	See Pyon
Cape	See King's Caple
Capel	See How Caple
Caplefore	See Brockhampton (near Ross)
Carlion	See Caerleon, Wales
Cascope	See Cascob, Wales
Castle Frome, E. 5	*Brismerfrum* 184
Cerlestreu	See Cholstrey
Chabenore	See Chadnor
Chadnor, C. 4	*Chabenore* 183
Chenecestre	See Kenchester
Chenille	See Knill
Chetestor	Unid., 187
Cheweshope	See Cusop
Chickward, A. 4	*Cicwrdine* 181, 187 *Stiuingeurdin* 181
Chingestone	See Kingstone (near Hereford)
Chingestune	See Kingstone (in Weston under Penyard)
Chingtune	See Kington
Chipeete	See Kilpeck
Chipelai	Unid., 185
Cholstrey, C. 3	*Cerlestreu* 180
Chonhelme	See Queenhill, Worcs.
Cicwrdine	See Chickward
Clatretune	See Clatterbrune, Wales
Cleeve, E. 7	*Clive* 179b
Clehonger, C. 6	*Cleunge* 186b, 187
Cleunge	See Clehonger
Clifford, A. 5	*Cliford* 183, 184
Cliford	See Clifford
Clive	See Cleeve
Cobewelle	See Cobhall
Cobhall, C. 6	*Cobewelle* 184
Coddington, F. 5	*Cotingtune* 182
Coldborough, E. 7	*Calcheberge* 186b
Colewelle	See Colwall
Colgre	See Little Cowarne
Colintune	See Collington
Collington, E. 3	*Col(l)intune* 182b, 185
Collintune	See Collington
Colwall, F. 5	*Colewelle* 182
Combe	Not in D.B.
Cotingtune	See Coddington
Covenhope, B. 3	*Camehop* 183b
Cradenhille	See Credenhill
Cradley, F. 5	*Credelaie* 182 *bis*
Craswall	Not in D.B.
Credelaie	See Cradley
Credenelle	See Credenhill
Credenhill, C. 5	*Cradenhille* 182b *Credenelle* 187
Croft, C. 3	*Crofta* 185b
Crofta	See Croft
Curdeslege	Unid., 187b
Cusop, A. 5	*Cheweshope* 179b
Cuure	See Much Cowarne
Dermentune	See Dormington
Dewsall, C. 6	Not in D.B., but see anon. holdings on p. 185

Didley, C. 6	*Dodelegie*, *-lige* 181b *bis*
Dilge, *Dilven*	See Dilwyn
Dilwyn, B. 4	*Dilge* 180 *bis* *Dilven* 185b
Dinedor, D. 6	*Dunre* 183
Dinmore	Not in D.B.
Discote	See Discoed, Wales
Docklow	Not in D.B.
Dodelegie, *-lige*	See Didley
Dodintune	See Dorstone
Donnington, F. 6	*Dunninctune* 181b
Dormington, D. 6	*Dermentune* 182b See also anon. holdings on p. 185
Dorstone, A. 5	*Dodintune* 186b
Downton, C. 2	*Duntune* 183b
Dulas	Not in D.B.
Dunninctune	See Donnington
Dunre	See Dinedor
Duntune	See Downton
Eardisland, C. 3	*Lene* 179b 2nd entry
Eardisley, A. 5	*Herdeslege* 181, 184b, 187
Eastnor, F. 6	*Astenofre* 182
Eaton (in Foy), E. 7	*Edtune* 186
Eaton (near Leominster), D. 3	*Etone* 180
Eaton Bishop, C. 6	*Etune* 181b
Edresfelle	See Eldersfield, Worcs.
Edreshope	See Yarsop
Edtune	See Eaton (in Foy)
Edvin Loach, E. 3	*Edevent* 176b, Worcs.
Edwardestune	Unid., 184
Edwyn Ralph, E. 4	*Gedeuen* 180 *bis*
Egleton	Not in D.B.
Elburgelega	See Kinnersley
Elintune	See Elton
Elmelie	See Almeley
Elmodestreu	See Aymestry
Elnodestune	See Elston Bridge
Elston Bridge, B. 7	*Elnodestune* 184
Elton, C. 2	*Elintune* 183b

Elvastone, D. 7	*Elwistone* 181
Elwistone	See Elvastone
Erdeshop, *-sope*	See Yarsop
Estune	See Ashton, Aston Ingham
Etone	See Eaton (near Leominster)
Etone (*Sulcet* hd)	Unid., 187
Ettone	See Eyton
Etune	See Eaton Bisop
Evesbatch, F. 5	*Sbech* 184b
Ewias	See Ewias Harold, Longtown formerly Ewias Lacy
Ewias Harold, B. 7	*Ewias* 181b, 184 1st entry, 185, 186
Exton	Not in D.B.
Eyton, C. 3	*Ettone* 180
Fec(c)heham	See Feckenham, Worcs.
Felton, D. 5	*Feltone* 182b
Feltone	See Felton
Fencote, E. 3	*Fencote* 180
Fenne	See Venn
Ferne	See Vern
Fernehalle	See Fernhill
Fernelau	See Farlow, Salop.
Fernhill, B. 4	*Fernehalle* 184b
Ford, D. 4	*Forne* 180
Forhelmentone	See Forthampton, Gloucs.
Forne	See Ford
Fownhope and Sollers Hope, D. 6, E. 6	*Hope* 186 2nd entry, 187
Foy	Not in D.B.
Frome	See Bishop's Frome, Canon Frome, Priors Frome
Gadredehope	See Gattertop
Ganarew	Not in D.B.
Garway, C. 8	*Lagademar* 181
Gattertop, C. 4	*Gadredehope* 180
Gedeuen	See Edwyn Ralph
Getune	See Yatton
Goodrich	Not in D.B.

Grafton	Not in D.B.
Grendon Bishop, E. 4	*Grenedene* 185
Grenedene	See Grendon Bishop
Halmond's Frome, E. 5	*Nerefrum* 184
Haloede	See Hollow Court, Worcs.
Hamenes	See Hamnish
Hamme	See Holme Lacy
Hamnish, D. 3	*Hamenes* 180
Hampton (in Hope under Dinmore), D. 4	*Hantone* 180 *bis* 2nd and 3rd entries
Hampton Bishop, D. 6	*Hantune* 182
Hampton Wafer, D. 4	*Hantone* 180 1st entry
Hanlei	See Hanley
Hanley, F. 5	*Hanlei* 185
Hanlie	See Hanley Castle, Worcs.
Hanlie (*Wimstrui* hd)	Unid., 186b
Hantinetune	See Huntington (near Kington)
Hantone	See Hampton (in Hope under Dinmore), Hampton Wafer
Hantune	See Hampton Bishop
Harewde	See Harewood (in Clifford)
Harewood (in Clifford), A. 5	*Harewde* 187
Harewood (near Ross), D. 7	Not in D.B., but see anon. holdings on p. 185
Hasles	See Hazle
Hatfield, D. 3	*Hetfelde* 180 *bis*
Haywood	Not in D.B.
Hazle, F. 6	*Hasles* 182
Heath, D. 3	*Hed* 184
Hech	See Nash
Hed	See Heath
Hentland	Not in D.B.

Hercope	See Lower Harpton
Herdeslege	See Eardisley
Hereford, D. 6	*Hereford* 179b, 180b *ter*, 181b, 184, 186, Heref.; 163b, Gloucs.; 172, 176b Worcs. *Herefordie* 182b, Heref.
Herefordie	See Hereford
Hergest, A. 4	*Hergest*(*h*) 181 *bis*
Hergest(*h*)	See Hergest
Hertune	See Harpton, Wales
Hesintune	See Aston (near Wigmore)
Hetfelde	See Hatfield
Hide	See Westhide
Hinetune	See Hinton
Hinton, B. 6	*Hinetune* 182b
Holemere	See Holmer
Holme Lacy, D. 6	*Hamme* 181b
Holmer, D. 5	*Holemere* 182
Hope	See Brinsop, Fownhope and Sollers Hope, Hope Mansell, Hope under Dinmore, Hopley's Green, Miles Hope, Woolhope
Hope Mansell, E. 8	*Hope* 185b
Hopetune	See Hopton Sollers
Hope under Dinmore, D. 4	*Hope* 182b
Hopley's Green, B. 4	*Hope* 179b, 184b
Hopton Sollers, E. 4	*Hopetune* 185b
How Caple, E. 7	*Capel* 181b
Howle, E. 8	*Hulla* 181
Huilech	See Whyle
Hulla	See Howle
Humber, D. 4	*Humbre* 180
Humbre	See Humber

Hungerstone, C. 6	Not in D.B., but see anon. holdings on p. 185
Huntenetune	See Huntington (near Hereford)
Huntington (near Hereford), C. 5	*Huntenetune* 182
Huntington (near Kington), A. 4	*Hantinetune* 181
Iarpol(e)	See Yarpole
Iavesoure	See Yazor
Ivington, C. 4	*Ivintune* 180
Ivintune	See Ivington
Kenchester, C. 5	*Chenecestre* 187
Kenderchurch	Not in D.B.
Kentchurch	Not in D.B.
Kilpeck, C. 7	*Chipeete* 181
Kimbolton	Not in D.B.
King's Caple, D. 7	*Cape* 181 See also anon. holdings on p. 185
Kingsland, C. 3	*Lene* 179b 1st entry
King's Pyon	See Pyon
Kingstone (near Hereford), C. 6	*Chingestone* 179b
Kingstone (in Weston under Penyard), E. 7	*Chingestune* 182b
Kington, A. 4	*Chingtune* 181
Kinnersley, B. 4	*Elburgelega* 183b
Kinsham	Not in D.B.
Knill, A. 3	*Chenille* 186b
Lacre	Unid., 187b
Ladgvern	See Llanwarne
Lagademar	See Garway
Langedune	See Longdon, Worcs.
Lapule	See Pull Court, Worcs.
Last	See Laysters
Lautone, *-tune*	See Lawton
Lawton, C. 3	*Lautone*, *-tune* 179b, 184b
Laysters, D. 3	*Last* 185, 186b, 187b
Lea, E. 8	*Lecce* 182b
Lecce	See Lea
Lecwe	See Lye
Ledbury, F. 6	*Liedeberge* 182
Lede(ne)	See Upleadon
Ledicot, B. 3	*L(e)idecote* 183b, 184b
Lega, *Lege*	See Lye
Lege (*Elsedune* hd)	Unid., 187
Leidecote	See Ledicot
Leine	See Monkland
Leinthall Earls and Starkes, C. 2	*Lenhale* 183b *Le(n)tehale* 180 *ter* *Lintehale* 183b
Leintwardine, B. 2	*Lenteurde* 252, 258, 260, Salop.
Lene	See Eardisland, Kingsland
Lenehalle	See Lyonshall
Lenhale, *Lentehalle*	See Leinthall
Leode	See Lyde
Leofminstre	See Leominster
Leominster, C. 3	*Leo(f)minstre* 180 *bis*, 180b, 181, Heref.; 259b, Salop.
Leominstre	See Leominster
Lestret	See Street
Letehale	See Leinthall
Letton (near Clifford), B. 5	*Letune* 184b
Letton (near Wigmore), B. 2	*Lectune* 260, Salop.
Letune	See Letton (near Clifford)
Lidecote	See Ledicot
Lidenegie	See Lydney, Gloucs.
Liedeberge	See Ledbury
Lincumbe, E. 5	*Lincumbe* 187
Lingen, B. 2	*Lingham* 260, Salop.
Lintehalle	See Leinthall
Linton (near Bromyard)	Not in D.B.
Linton (near Ross), E. 7	*Lintone*, *-tune* 179b, 185b
Lintone, *-tune*	See Linton (near Ross)
Litley, D. 6	*Lutelei* 186b

Little Birch	Not in D.B.
Little Brampton, A. 3	*Bruntune* 186b
Little Cowarne, E. 4	*Colgre* 183
Little Dewchurch	Not in D.B.
Little Hereford, D. 2	*Lutelonhereford* 182b
Little Marcle, E. 6	*Merchelai* 184b, 185b
Livers Ocle	See Ocle
Llancillo	Not in D.B.
Llandinabo	Not in D.B.
Llangarren	Not in D.B.
Llanrothal	Not in D.B.
Llanveynoe	Not in D.B.
Llanwarne, D. 7	*Ladgvern* 181b
Longtown formerly Ewias Lacy, A. 7	*Ewias* 184 2nd entry
Longworth, D. 6	Not in D.B., but see anon. holdings on p. 185
Lower Harpton, A. 3	*Hercope* 186b
Lower Lye	See Lye
Lucton	Not in D.B.
Lucuordne	See Lugwardine
Lude	See Lyde
Ludeford	See Ludford, Salop.
Lugwardine, D. 5	*Lucuordne* 179b
Lulham, C. 5	*Lulleham* 181b
Lulleham	See Lulham
Luntley, B. 4	*Lutelei* 180b
Luston, C. 3	*Lustone* 180
Lustone	See Luston
Lutelei	See Litley, Luntley
Lutelonhereford	See Little Hereford
Lyde, D. 5	*Leode* 182b *Lude* 184 *bis*, 186b
Lye, Lower and Upper, B. 2	*Lecwe* 183b *Lega*, *Lege* 180, 183b, 186b, 187b, Heref.; 260, Salop.
Lyonshall, A. 4	*Lenehalle* 184b

Madley, C. 6	*Medelagie* 181b
Mage(ne), *Magga*, *Magge*	See Maund
Mainaure, D. 6	Lost in Birch, 181
Malfelle	See Mawfield
Malveselle, *Malveshille*	See Mansell
Manetune, *Manitone*	See Monnington (in Vowchurch)
Manitune	See Monnington on Wye
Mansell Gamage and Lacy, B. 5, C. 5	*Malveselle* 184b, 187b *bis* *Malveshille* 182b
Marden, D. 5	*Maurdine* 179, 179b, 184, 185b, 187b
Marston (in Pembridge), B. 3	*Merstune* 185b
Marston Stannett, D. 4	*Merstune* 185
Marstow	Not in D.B.
Mateurdin	Unid., 181, 187b
Mathon, F. 5	*Matma*, *Matme* 184b, 186b, Heref.; 175b, Worcs.
Matma, *Matme*	See Mathon
Maund Bryan and Rose Maund, D. 4	*Mage(ne)* 183, 184 *Magga*, *Magge* 184, 185b
Maurdine	See Marden
Mawfield, C. 6	*Malfelle* 184
Medelagie	See Madley
Merchelai	See Little Marcle, Much Marcle
Mereston, *-tun*	Site of Wigmore Castle, 179b, 183b
Merlie	See Martley, Worcs.
Mersetone	Unid., 180
Merstone	Unid., 187
Merstune (*Plegeliet* hd)	Unid., 187b
Merstune (*Stepleset* hd)	See Marston (in Pembridge), Marston Stannett
Miceltune	See Middleton on the Hill

Place	D.B.
Michaelchurch	Not in D.B.
Michaelchurch Escley	Not in D.B.
Middleton on the Hill, D. 3	*Miceltune* 180
Middlewood (in Clifford), A. 5	*Midewde* 187
Middlewood (in Winforton), A. 5	*Mideurde* 182b
Mideurde	See Middlewood (in Winforton)
Midewde	See Middlewood (in Clifford)
Mildetune	See Milton
Miles Hope, D. 3	*Hope* 180
Milton, B. 3	*Mildetune* 183b, 186b
Moccas, B. 5	*Moches* 182b, 183
Moches	See Moccas
Monemude	See Monmouth, Wales
Moneslai	See Munsley
Monkland, C. 3	*Leine* 183
Monnington (in Vowchurch), B. 6	*Manetune* 186 *Manitone* 186
Monnington on Wye, B. 5	*Manitune* 183
Moor, A. 5	*More* 182b
Mordiford	Not in D.B.
More	See Moor
Moreton Jeffreys, E. 5	*Mortune* 181b
Moreton on Lugg, D. 5	*Mortune* 182
Mortune	See Moreton Jeffreys, Moreton on Lugg
Much Birch	Not in D.B.
Much Cowarne, E. 5	*Cuure* 186
Much Dewchurch	Not in D.B.
Much Marcle, E. 6	*Merchelai* 179b, 180, 182b
Muleslage, *Muneslai*	See Munsley
Munsley, E. 5	*Moneslai* 185b *Muleslage* 185b, 187 *Muneslai* 184b
Nash, A. 3	*Hech* 186b
Nerefrum	See Halmond's Frome
Neutone	See Newton (near Clifford)
Newentone	See Newton (near Leominster)
Newton (near Clifford), A. 5	*Neutone* 186b
Newton (near Ewias Harold)	Not in D.B.
Newton (near Leominster), D. 4	*Newentone* 180 *Niwetune* 185b
Niware	See Newerne, Gloucs.
Niwetune	See Newton (near Leominster)
Norton (near Bromyard)	Not in D.B.
Norton Canon, B. 5	*Nortune* 182b
Nortune	See Norton Canon
Ocle Pychard and Livers Ocle, D. 5, E. 5	*Acle* 184 See also anon. holdings on p. 186
Orcop	Not in D.B.
Orleton, C. 2	*Alretune* 183b
Ortune	See Harpton, Wales
Panchille	See Pontshill
Pedwardine, B. 2	*Pedewrde* 260b *ter*, Salop.
Pelelei	See Pilleth on Lugg, Wales
Pembridge (near Leominster), B. 3	*Penebruge* 186 *bis*
Pencombe, E. 4	Not in D.B., but see anon. holdings on p. 185
Pencoyd	Not in D.B.
Penebecdoc	Unid., 181
Penebruge	See Pembridge (near Leominster)
Peterchurch	Not in D.B.
Peterstow	Not in D.B.
Peune	See Pyon
Picheslei	See Pixley

Pillesdune	See Puddleston
Pionie	See Pyon
Pipe, D. 5	*Pipe* 182b
Pixley, E. 6	*Picheslei* 186, 187
Pletune	Unid., 184b
Pontshill, E. 8	*Panchille* 186b
Poscetenetune	See Poston
Poston, B. 6	*Poscetenetune* 185b
Poteslepe	See Putley
Prestetune	See Preston Wynne
Preston on Wye, B. 5	*Prestretune* 181b
Preston Wynne, D. 5	*Prestetune* 181b
Prestretune	See Preston on Wye
Priors Frome, D. 6	*Frome* 182b, 185 2nd entry, 187
Puddleston, D. 3	*Pillesdune* 184
Putley, E. 6	*Poteslepe* 184
Pyon, Canon and King's, C. 4	*Peune* 182 *Pionie* 184b
Querentune	Lost in Presteigne, Wales
Raddrenoue	See Old Radnor, Wales
Recesford	See Rochford, Worcs.
Retrowas	See Rotherwas
Richards Castle, C. 2	*Auretone* 185, 186b
Risbury, D. 4	*Riseberie* 180
Riseberie	See Risbury
Rose Maund	See Maund
Ross, E. 7	*Rosse* 182
Rosse	See Ross
Rotherwas, D. 6	*Retrowas* 186b
Rowden, E. 4	*Ruedene* 181, 187b
Rowlstone	Not in D.B.
Ruedene	See Rowden
Ruiscop	See Rushock
Rushock, A. 3	*Ruiscop* 181 *bis*, 185b
Ruuenore	Unid., 186b
Ruuirdin	See Ruardean, Gloucs.

St Devereux	Not in D.B.
St Margarets	Not in D.B.
St Weonards	Not in D.B.
Salberga, *Sargeberie*	See Sawbury
Sarnesfelde	See Sarnesfield
Sarnesfield, B. 4	*Sarnesfelde* 180 *bis*
Sawbury, E. 4	*Salberga* 181b *Sargeberie* 185
Sbech	See Evesbatch
Scelwiche	See Shelwick
Scepedune	See Shobdon
Sellack	Not in D.B.
Shelwick, D. 5	*Scelwiche* 182 *bis*
Shirley, B. 3	*Sirelei* 260, Salop.
Shobdon, B. 3	*Scepedune* 183b
Sollers Hope	See Fownhope
Spertune	See Ashperton
Standune	See Staunton on Wye
Stane	Unid., 181b
Stanford	See Stanford Bishop
Stanford Bishop, F. 4	*Stanford* 180 *bis*, 185
Stantun	See Staunton, Gloucs.
Stantune	See Staunton on Arrow; Staunton on Wye
Stanway, B. 2	*Stanewei* 260, Salop.
Stapleton	Not in D.B.
Staunton on Arrow, B. 3	*Stantune* 183b
Staunton on Wye, B. 5	*Standune*, *Stantune* 184b *bis*, 186b
Stiuingeurdin	See Chickward
Stoca	See Stoke Prior
Stoch	See Stoke Bliss, Worcs.
Stoches	See Stoke Edith, Stoke Lacy
Stockton, D. 3	*Stoctune* 180
Stoctune	See Stockton
Stoke Edith, E. 5	*Stoches* 183b
Stoke Lacy, E. 4	*Stoches* 185
Stoke Prior, D. 4	*Stoca* 180
Stratford	See Stretford

Stratone	See Stretton (in Stretton Sugwas)
Stratune	See Stretton Grandison
Street, C. 3	*Lestret* 184b *Strete* 179b
Strete	See Street
Stretford, C. 4	*Stratford* 186
Stretton (in Stretton Sugwas), C. 5	*Stratone* 184, 187
Stretton Grandison, E. 5	*Stratune* 185b
Suchelie	See Suckley, Worcs.
Sucwessen	See Sugwas (in Stretton Sugwas)
Sudtune	See Sutton
Suenestun	See Swanstone
Sugwas (in Stretton Sugwas), C. 5	*Sucwessen* 182
Sutton St Michael, St Nicholas, D. 5	*Su(d)tune* 183 *bis*, 187
Sutune	See Sutton
Swanstone, C. 4	*Suenestun* 184b
Tarrington, E. 5	*Tatintune* 184b, 186
Tatintune	See Tarrington
Tedesthorne	See Tedstone
Tedstone Delamere and Wafer, F. 3	*Tedesthorne* 181b *Tetistorp* 185
Tetistorp	See Tedstone
Thinghill, D. 5	*Tingehalle*, *-hele* 182b, 183
Thornbury, E. 3	*Torneberie* 186
Thruxton, C. 6	*Torchestone* 186b
Tibrintintune	See Tyberton
Tingehalle, *-hele*	See Thinghill
Titel(l)ege	See Titley
Titley, A. 3	*Titel(l)ege* 186b *bis*
Topeslage	See Tupsley
Torchestone	See Thruxton
Torneberie	See Thornbury
Tretire	Not in D.B.
Treville, C. 6	*Trieueline* 179b
Trieueline	See Treville
Tupsley, D. 5	*Topeslage* 182
Turlestane, E. 6	Lost in Much Marcle, 179b
Turnastone	Not in D.B.
Tyberton, B. 6	*Tibrintintune* 181b
Ulfelmestune	See Welson
Ulferlau	See Wolferlow
Ullingswick, E. 4	*Ullingwic* 181b
Ullingwic	See Ullingswick
Underley, E. 3	Not in D.B., but see anon. holdings on p. 185
Upcott, A. 4	Not in D.B., but see anon. holdings on p. 185
Upetone	See Upton (in Brimfield)
Upleadon, E. 5	*Lede(ne)* 184b *bis*, 186
Upper Lye	See Lye
Upper Sapey	Not in D.B.
Upton (in Brimfield), D. 3	*Up(e)tone* 180, 185
Upton Bishop, E. 7	*Uptune* 182
Uptone	See Upton (in Brimfield)
Uptune	See Upton Bishop
Urmelauia	See Wormelow
Venn, D. 5	*Fenne* 185b
Vern, D. 4	*Ferne* 185b
Vowchurch	Not in D.B.
Wadetune	Unid., 184
Walecford	See Walford (near Ross)
Walelege	See Ailey
Walesapeldor	See Walsopthorne
Walford (near Leintwardine), B. 2	*Waliford(e)* 260, 260b, Salop.
Walford (near Ross), D. 8	*Walecford* 182
Walintone	See Wellington
Walsopthorne, E. 5	*Walesapeldor* 185b
Walterstone	Not in D.B.

Wapleford	Unid., 179b
Wapletone	See Wapley
Wapley, B. 3	*Wapletone* 180
Warham, C. 6	*Werham* 182
Wavertune	See Wharton
Webetone	See Webton
Webton, C. 6	*Webetone* 184 *bis*
Wellington, C. 5	*Walintone* 187 *bis*
Welsh Bicknor	Not in D.B.
Welsh Newton	Not in D.B.
Welson, A. 4	*Ulfelmestune* 181
Wenetone	See Woonton (in Laysters)
Wennetune	See Woonton (in Almeley)
Weobley, B. 4	*Wibelai* 184b
Werham	See Warham
Wermeslai	See Wormsley
Westelet	Unid., 182b
Westeude	See *Westuode*
Westhide, D. 5	*Hide* 183, 184b
Weston (in Pembridge), B. 4	*Westune* 183b
Weston Beggard, D. 5	*Westune* 184
Weston under Penyard, E. 7	*Westune* 186b
Westune	See Weston (in Pembridge), Weston Beggard, Weston under Penyard
Westuode, *Westeude*, C. 6	Lost in Llanwarne, 181 *bis*
Wharton, D. 4	*Wavertune* 180
Whitbourne	Not in D.B.
Whitchurch	Not in D.B.
Whitney, A. 5	*Witenie* 181, 182b
Whitwick, E. 5	*Witewiche* 185b
Whyle, D. 3	*Huilech* 186b
Wibelai	See Weobley
Wiboldingtune	See Whittington (in Staunton), Gloucs.
Wich	See Droitwich, Worcs.
Wickton, D. 4	*Wigetune* 187b
Widferdestune	See Winforton
Widingtune	See Withington
Wigemore	See Wigmore
Wigetune	See Wickton
Wighemore	See Wigmore
Wigmore, B. 2	*Wig(h)emore* 180 *bis*, 183b
Wilehalle	See Winnall
Willaveslege	See Willersley
Willersley, A. 5	*Willaveslege* 183
Willey	Not in D.B.
Wilmastone, B. 5	*Wilmestune* 187
Wilmestune	See Wilmastone
Wilton, D. 7	*Wiltone* 179b See also anon. holdings on p. 185
Wiltone	See Wilton
Winetune	Unid., 182b
Winforton, A. 5	*Widferdestune* 183
Winnall, C. 6	*Wilehalle* 187
Wirecestre	See Worcester, Worcs.
Witenie	See Whitney
Witewiche	See Whitwick
Withington, D. 5	*Widingtune* 181b
Wluetone, B. 6	Lost in Lyonshall, 187
Wolferlow, E. 3	*Ulferlau* 183b, 185
Woolhope, E. 6	*Hope* 181b
Woonton (in Almeley), B. 4	*Wennetune* 181, 184b
Woonton (in Laysters), D. 3	*Wenetone* 184
Wormbridge	Not in D.B.
Wormelow, C. 7	*Urmelauia* 179
Wormsley, C. 5	*Wermeslai* 185 *bis* *Wrmesleu* 182b
Wrmenton, *Wrmoton*	Not in D.B., but see anon. holdings on p. 185
Wrmesleu	See Wormsley
Yarkhill, E. 5	*Achel* 184
Yarpole, C. 3	*Iarpol(e)* 180, 180b, 185
Yarsop, B. 5	*Ardeshope* 181b *Edreshope* 185 *Erdeshop* 185b *Erdesope* 187b
Yatton, E. 7	*Getune* 181
Yazor, B. 5	*Iavesoure* 185

ANONYMOUS HOLDINGS

The following twenty-seven entries involve anonymous holdings. A transcript of the Herefordshire folios (Balliol MS 350), however, enables us to assign fifteen of the entries to their respective localities – see V. H. Galbraith and J. Tait, *Herefordshire Domesday, circa 1160–1170* (Pipe Roll Society, London, 1950); the pages given below refer to this.

It is possible that some (or even all) of the others refer to holdings at places not named elsewhere in Domesday Book:

The king, one of these 4 hides (of Lugwardine) was and is reveland, 179b. Balliol MS pp. 5 and 83 show this was at Longworth.

Ilbert son of Torold (from the king), 2 hides, 179b. Balliol MS pp. 6 and 83 show this was at Hungerstone.

Roger de Laci (from the king), half a hide, 179b.

The king, of this manor (Cleeve) there is *in foresta ...*, 179b. Balliol MS pp. 9 and 84 show this was at King's Caple.

William son of Baderon (from the king), one hide and 3 virgates (of manor of Cleeve), 179b. Balliol MS pp. 9 and 84 show this was at Wilton.

Elward (from Grifin), half a hide, 180b.

The king, in Archenfield 100 men less 4, etc., 181.

Gilbert son of Torold, one manor in Archenfield, 181. Balliol MS pp. 19 and 87 show this was at Ballingham.

Werestan, one vill in Archenfield, 181. Balliol MS pp. 19 and 87 show this was at Harewood.

Odo (from Roger de Laci), part of manor of *Westuode*, 181. Balliol MS pp. 20 and 88 show this was at *Wrmenton*, unid.

Ralf de Saucey, part of manor of *Westuode*, 181. Balliol MS pp. 21 and 88 show this was at *Wrmoton*, unid.

William and Ilbert (from Ralf de Todeni), one hide in *Westeude*, 181. Balliol MS pp. 21 and 88 show this was at Dewsall.

One radman (from church of Hereford), one hide in *Stradford* hd, 181b.

Two freemen (from church of Hereford), 4 hides in *Stradford* hd, 181b.

The church of Hereford, 4 hides in *Stradel* hd, 182b.

The church of Hereford, one hide of Welsh land in *Stradel* hd, 182b.

Roger de Laci (from church of St Guthlac), 4 hides in Almeley. *Alterius villae homines laborant in hac villa*, 182b. Balliol MS pp. 32 and 92 show that the vill from which the men came was Upcott.

Nigel the physician, one berewick of Bartestree, 183. Balliol MS pp. 32 and 92 show this was part of Dormington.

Ralf de Mortemer, 2 hides in Wolferlow, 183b. Balliol MS pp. 39 and 95 show this was at Underley.

Roger de Laci, a fishery in the Wye, 184.

Herbert (from Roger de Laci), one virgate in *Tornelaus* hd, 184.

Elwin (from Roger de Laci), 1½ hides in *Ulfei* hd, 184.

Another Turstin (from Turstin son of Rolf), 3 hides in Marcle, 185b. Balliol MS pp. 57 and 110 show this was at Aylton.

Alvred de Merleberge, 15 hides in *Tornelaus* hd, 186. Balliol MS pp. 59 and 112 show this was at Pencombe.

ANONYMOUS HOLDINGS (continued)

Hugh Lasne, one hide in *Tornelaus* hd, 187. Balliol MS pp. 69 and 120 show this was part of Ocle.

Hugh Lasne, 3 virgates in *Tornelaus* hd, 187.

Elmer (from the king), half a hide in *Ulfei* hd, 187b.

HERTFORDSHIRE—*HERFORDSCIRE*

Folios 132–142b

MAP 23

Abbots Langley, D. 5	*Langelai* 135b
Absa	See Napsbury
Absesdene	See Aspenden
Aiete	See Ayot
Albury, C. 4	*Eldeberie* 133b
Aldbury, H. 3	*Aldeberie* 136b
Aldeberie	See Aldbury
Aldenham, E. 6	*Eldeham* 135, 136
Alfledauuicha	See Beauchamps formerly Affledwick
Almeshou	See Almshoe
Almshoe, E. 3	*Almeshou* 134
Alsieswiche	See Alswick
Alswick, G. 2	*Alsieswiche* 138
Altera Offelei	See Little Offley
Amwell, Great and Little, G. 4	*Emmewelle* 138, 140
	Emwella, L.D.B. 2b, Ess.
Anestei, *-tige*	See Anstey
Anstey, G. 2	*Anestei* 142
	Anestige 137
Ardeley, F. 3	*Erdelei* 136
Asceuuelle	See Ashwell
Ashwell, F. 1	*Asceuuelle* 139b
	Escewelle 135, 141 *bis*, 141b
Aspenden, G. 2	*Absesdene* 139
Aston, F. 3	*Estone* 134
Ayot St Lawrence, St Peter, E. 4	*Aiete* 135, 137b, 142b
Baldock	Not in D.B.
Barkway, G. 2	*Bercheuuei(g)* 139, 139b, 141b, 142
Barley, G. 1	*Berlai* 134b, 136, 139 *bis*, 140, 141b
Bayford, F. 5	*Begesford* 133
Beauchamps formerly Affledwick, G. 2	*Alfledauuicha* 137b
Begesford	See Bayford
Belingehou	See Bengeo
Belintone	See Bennington
Bendish, E. 3	*Benedis* 136
Benedis	See Bendish
Bengeo, G. 4	*Belingehou* 137, 138b, 139b, 140b, 141
Bennington, F. 3	*Belintone* 141
Berchamstede	See Berkhamsted
Berchedene	See Berkesdon
Berchehamstede	See Berkhamsted, Little Berkhamsted
Bercheuuei(g)	See Barkway
Bereuuorde	See Barwythe, Beds.
Berkesdon, G. 2	*Berchedene* 137, 141b
Berkhamsted, C. 5	*Berch(eh)amstede* 136b *ter*
Berlai	See Barley
Bigrave	See Bygrave
Bishops Hatfield, F. 5	*Hetfelle* 135

Bishop's Stortford, H. 3	*Storteford* 134	Chaldean, H. 3	*Celgdene* 133b
Bissei	See Bushey	Charlton, E. 2	*Cerletone* 132b
Blachemene	See Blackmore	*Cheleselle*	See Kelshall
Blackmore, F. 4	*Blachemene* 140b	Chells, F. 3	*Escelueia* 141 *Scelua*, *Scelue* 137b, 140
Bochelande	See Buckland	*Chenepeworde*	See Knebworth
Boorscroft, B. 4	*Bure* 136b	Cheshunt, G. 5	*Cestrehont*, *-hunt* 137 *ter*
Bordesdene	See Bozen	Chipping Barnet	Not in D.B.
Bovingdon	Not in D.B.	*Chodrei*	See Cottered
Boxbury, F. 3	*Boxe* 134, 138b, 141	*Cladhele*	See Clothall
Boxe	See Boxbury	Clothall, F. 2	*Cladhele* 134b, 137, 138b, 141b
Bozen, H. 3	*Bordesdene* 137b, 138, 139b	*Cochehammestede*	See Cockhampstead
Brachinges	See Braughing	*Cochenac*	See Cokenach
Bradefella, *-felle*	See Broadfield	Cockhampstead, H. 3	*Cochehammestede* 137b
Bramfield, F. 4	*Brandefelle* 142	Codicote, E. 3	*Codicote* 135b
Brandefelle	See Bramfield	Cokenach, G. 1	*Cochenac* 140
Braughing, G. 3	*Brachinges* 137b	Cornbury, G. 2	*Cornei* 137
Brent Pelham	See Pelham	*Cornei*	See Cornbury
Briceuuold(e)	Unid., 142 *bis*	Cottered, G. 2	*Chodrei* 133
Briche(n)done	See Brickendon	*Daceuuorde*	See Datchworth
Brickendon, G. 4	*Briche(n)done* 136b, 139b, 140b, 142	*Daneslai*	See Dunsley
Broadfield, G. 2	*Bradefella*, *-felle* 135, 137b, 141b, 142	Datchworth, F. 3	*Daceuuorde* 133, 135, 140, 140b
Brochesborne	See Broxbourne	*Deneslai*	See Dunsley, Temple Dinsley
Broxbourne, G. 5	*Brochesborne* 142b	*Dereuelde*	See Therfield
Bublecote	See Gubblecote	*Dichelesuuelle*	See Digswell
Buckland, G. 2	*Bochelande* 134b	Digswell, F. 4	*Dichelesuuelle* 139b, 141
Buntingford	Not in D.B.	*Dodesdone*	See Hoddesdon
Bure	See Boorscroft	Dunsley, B. 4	*Dan-*, *Deneslai* 136b, 142
Bushey, D. 6	*Bissei* 139b *bis*	East Barnet	Not in D.B.
Bygrave, F. 1	*Bigrave* 135 *bis*	Eastwick, H. 4	*Esteuuiche* 140b
Cadendone	See Caddington, Beds.	Eckington, G. 2	*Ichetone* 134b, 137, 139, 141, 141b
Caissou	See Cassio	*Eia*	See Rye
Caldecota	See Caldecote	*Eldeberie*	See Albury
Caldecote, F. 1	*Caldecota* 138	*Eldeham*	See Aldenham
Canesworde	See Kensworth, Beds.	Elstree	Not in D.B.
Cassio, D. 6	*C(h)aissou* 136, 139b	*Emmewelle*	See Amwell
Celgdene	See Chaldean		
Cerletone	See Charlton		
Cestrehont, *-hunt*	See Cheshunt		
Chaissou	See Cassio		

Epcombs, F. 4	*Thepecampe* 142
Erdelei	See Ardeley
Escelueia	See Chells
Escepehala, *-hale*	See Shephall
Escewelle	See Ashwell
Essendon	Not in D.B.
Esteuuiche	See Eastwick
Estone	See Aston
Flammestede	See Flamstead
Flamstead, D. 4	*Flammestede* 138
Flaunden	Not in D.B.
Flesmere, *Flexmere*	See Flexmore
Flexmore, E. 3	*Flesmere*, *Flexmere* 133, 141
Furneaux Pelham	See Pelham
Furreuuelde	See Therfield
Gatesdene	See Great Gaddesden, Little Gaddesden
Gilston	Not in D.B.
Grauelai	See Graveley
Graveley, F. 2	*Grauelai* 134, 137b, 138b, 140b, 141
Great Amwell	See Amwell
Great Gaddesden, C. 4	*Gatesdene* 139
Great Hormead	See Hormead
Great Munden	See Munden
Great Offley, E. 2	*Offelei* 132b, 133, 139
Great Wymondley	See Wymondley
Gubblecote, B. 4	*Bublecote* 136b
Hadam	See Much Hadham
Hadam, *Parva*	See Little Hadham
Hailet	See Hailey
Hailey, G. 4	*Hailet* 140
Hain(ge)steuuorde	See Hinxworth
Hainstone	Unid., 138, 139b
Hamelamestede	See Hemel Hempstead
Hamsteuuorde	See Hinxworth
Hanstead, E. 5	*Henammesteda* 135b
Hare Street formerly Langport, G. 2	*Langeport* 137, 139b

Harpenden	Not in D.B.
Haslehangra, *Helsangre*	Unid., 134b, 141b
Heg(a)estanestone	See Hexton
Helsangre	See *Haslehangra*
Hemel Hempstead, D. 5	*Hamelamestede* 136b
Henammesteda	See Hanstead
Herefordingberie	See Hertingfordbury
Hertford, G. 4	*Hertforde* 132 *Herefort*, L.D.B. 2b, Ess.
Hertforde	See Hertford
Hertingfordbury, F. 4	*Herefordingberie* 138b
Hetfelle	See Bishops Hatfield
Hexton, D. 2	*Heg(a)estanestone* 133, 136, 140
Hinxworth, F. 1	*Hain(ge)steuuorde* 141, 141b *Hamsteuuorde* 138b
Hitchen, E. 2	*Hiȝ* 132, 132b *deciens*, 133 *septiens*, 140 *bis*
Hixham, H. 2	*Tedricesham* 134
Hiȝ	See Hitchen
Hoddesdon, G. 5	*Dodesdone* 142 *Hodesdone* 137, 137b, 139b *Odesdone* 139 *Hodesduna*, L.D.B. 2b, Ess.
Hodenhoe, G. 2	*Odenhou* 134b, 141b
Hodesdone	See Hoddesdon, Hunsdon
Holwell, E. 2	*Holewella*, *-welle* 210b, 211, Beds.
Honesdone	See Hunsdon
Horemede	See Hormead
Hormead, Great and Little, G. 2, H. 2	*Horemede* 137b, 138b, 142
Hunsdon, H. 4	*Hodesdone* 142b *Honesdone* 138b
Hyde Hall formerly Somersale, G. 2	*Summersele* 138

Ichetone	See Eckington
Ickleford	Not in D.B.
Ippollitts	Not in D.B.
Kamintone	See Kimpton
Kelshall, G. 1	*Cheleselle* 135
Kimpton, E. 3	*Kamintone* 134b
Kings Langley, D. 5	*Langelei* 136b
King's Walden, E. 2	*Waldenei* 132b
Knebworth, F. 3	*Chenepeworde* 139
Lampeth	Unid., 134
Langelai	See Abbots Langley
Langelei	See Kings Langley, Langley (near Stevenage)
Langeport	See Hare Street formerly Langport
Langley (near Stevenage), E. 3	*Langelei* 140
Layston	Not in D.B.
Leceworde	See Letchworth
Leglega	See Leygreen
Letchworth, E. 2	*Leceworde* 137b
Leuuareuuiche	Unid., 133b
Leygreen, E. 3	*Leglega* 133
Libury, G. 3	*Stuterehela*, *-hele* 133, 141 *bis*, 142 *Sutrehella* 139 *Sutreshele* 134
Lilley, D. 3	*Linlei(a)* 133, 140
Linlei(a)	See Lilley
Little Amwell	See Amwell
Little Berkhamsted, F. 5	*Berchehamstede* 142
Little Gaddesden, C. 4	*Gatesdene* 136b
Little Hadham, H. 3	*Parva Hadam* 133b
Little Hormead	See Hormead
Little Munden	See Munden
Little Offley, D. 2	*Altera Offelei* 132b
Little Wymondley	See Wymondley
Lufenel(le), *Lufenhate*	See Luffenhall
Luffenhall, F. 2	*Lufenel(le)* 136, 141b *Lufenhate* 134b
Maperteshale	See Meppershall, Beds.
Mardleybury, F. 3	*Merdelai* 137b
Markyate	Not in D.B.
Mascewelle	See Miswell
Meesden, H. 2	*Mesdone* 133b
Menlesdene	See Minsden
Merdelai	See Mardleybury
Mesdone	See Meesden
Mimmine	See North Mimms
Minsden, E. 3	*Menlesdene* 132
Misseuuelle	See Miswell
Miswell, B. 4	*Mascewelle* 138 *Misseuuelle* 136b
Monken Hadley	Not in D.B.
Much Hadham, H. 3	*Hadam* 133b *ter*, 134, 135
Mundane	See Munden
Munden, Great and Little, G. 3	*Mundane*, *-dena*, *-dene* 137 *bis*, 139 *bis*
Mundena, *-dene*	See Munden
Napsbury, E. 5	*Absa* 135b
Nettleden	Not in D.B.
Neuham	See Newnham
Neusela	See Newsells
Newnham, F. 1	*Neuham* 136
Newsells, G. 1	*Neusela* 139 *bis* *Nuesselle* 139
Northaw	Not in D.B.
Northchurch	Not in D.B.
North Mimms, E. 5	*Mimmine* 135
Norton, F. 2	*Nortone* 135b
Nortone	See Norton
Nuesselle	See Newsells
Nuthampstead	Not in D.B.
Odenhou	See Hodenhoe
Odesdone	See Hoddesdon
Offelei	See Great Offley
Offelei, *Altera*	See Little Offley
Orduuelle	See Orwell
Orwell, G. 2	*Orduuelle* 134b, 141b
Oxewiche	See Oxwick
Oxwick, E. 4	*Oxewiche* 135b

Parva Hadam	See Little Hadham
Patemere	See Patmore
Patmore, H. 3	*Patemere* 133b
Peleham	See Pelham
Pelham, Brent, Furneaux and Stocking, H. 2	*Peleham* 133b *quin*, 134 *bis*
Pendley, B. 4	*Pentlai* 136b
Pentlai	See Pendley
Peritone	See Pirton
Pirton, E. 2	*Peritone* 138
Polehangre	See Polehanger, Beds.
Preston	Not in D.B.
Prichemareworde	See Rickmansworth
Puteham	See Puttenham
Puttenham, B. 4	*Puteham* 134
Radeuuelle	See Radwell
Radwell, F. 1	*Radeuuelle* 134b, 141
Redborne	See Redbourn
Redbourn, D. 4	*Redborne* 134b, 135b, 136, 136b
Reed, G. 1	*Rete* 137
	Retth 134b, 137 *bis*, 139, 141b
Rete, *Retth*	See Reed
Rickmansworth, D. 6	*Prichemareworde* 136
Ridge	Not in D.B.
Risendene	See Rushden
Rochesforde	See Roxford
Rode(ne)hangre	Unid., 140, 142b
Roxford, F. 4	*Rochesforde* 140b
Royston	Not in D.B.
Rushden, F. 2	*Risendene* 142
	Risedene 200b, 201, Cambs.
Rye, G. 4	*Eia* 134b
Sabrixteworde	See Sawbridgeworth
Sacombe, G. 3	*Seuechampe* 141
	Stuochampa 133
	Sueuecampe, *-champ* 141b, 142, 142b
St Albans, E. 5	*Villa Sancti Albani* 135b
St Paul's Walden, E. 3	*Waldene* 135b
Sancti Albani, Villa	See St Albans
Sandon, G. 2	*Sandone* 136
Sandone	See Sandon
Sandridge, E. 4	*Sandrige* 135b
Sandrige	See Sandridge
Sapeham	Unid., 138
Sarratt	Not in D.B.
Sawbridgeworth, H. 4	*Sabrixteworde* 139b
Scelua, *Scelue*	See Chells
Scenlai, *-lei*	See Shenley
Sela	See Sele
Sele, F. 4	*Sela* 140b
Senlai	See Shenley
Seuechampe	See Sacombe
Shenley, E. 6	*Scenlai*, *-lei* 135b, 136b
	Senlai 139b
Shephall, F. 3	*Escepehala*, *-hale* 133, 135b
Stagenhoe, E. 3	*Stagnehou* 138b
Stagnehou	See Stagenhoe
Standon, G. 3	*Standone* 142b
Standone	See Standon
Stanes	See Stonebury
Stanestede	See Stanstead Abbots
Stanstead Abbots, G. 4	*Stanestede* 138b, 139b, 140b, 142b
Stapleford	Not in D.B.
Stevenage, F. 3	*Stigenace* 135 *bis*
Stigenace	See Stevenage
Stiuicesuuorde	Unid., 139b
Stocking Pelham	See Pelham
Stonebury, G. 2	*Stanes* 141
Storteford	See Bishop's Stortford
Stuochampa	See Sacombe
Stuterehela, *-hele*	See Libury
Sueuecampe, *-champ*	See Sacombe
Summersele	See Hyde Hall formerly Somersale

Wodtone	See Watton
Woolwicks, F. 3	*Wluueneuuiche* 137b, 141
Wormley, G. 5	*Wermelai* 136b, 137, 142
Wyddial, G. 2	*Widihale* 141b
Wymondley, Great and Little, E. 2	*Wimunde(s)lai* 132, 134, 137b, 140b

ANONYMOUS HOLDINGS

No place-name appears in the following entry, and it is impossible to say whether or not it refers to a place named elsewhere in Domesday Book:

Humfrey (from Eudo the steward), half a hide in Hertford hd, 139.

HUNTINGDONSHIRE—*HUNTEDUNSCIRE*

Folios 203–208b

MAP 24

Abbotsley	Not in D.B.
Abbots Ripton	See Ripton
Acumesberie	See Alconbury
Adelintune	See Elton
Adone	See Haddon
Alia Cateworde	See Little Catworth
Alia Emingeforde	See Hemingford Grey
Alconbury, C. 5	*Acumesberie* 203b, 204, 206 *quin* *Almundeberie* 208
Alconbury Weston, C. 4	*Westune* 206
Almundeberie	See Alconbury
Alwalton, C. 2	*Alwoltune* 205
Alwoltune	See Alwalton
Barham, C. 5	Not in D.B., but see anon. holdings on p. 195
Bierne	See Bythorn
Bluntesham	See Bluntisham
Bluntisham, E. 5	*Bluntesham* 204, 204b
Bocstede	See Boxted, Ess.
Botolph Bridge (in Huntingdon), D. 5	*Botulvesbrige* 206
Botolph Bridge (in Orton Longueville), C. 2	*Botulvesbrige* 203b
Botulvesbrige	See Botolph Bridge (in Huntingdon), Botolph Bridge (in Orton Longueville)
Boughton, C. 6	*Buchetone* 206b
Brampton, D. 5	*Brantune* 203b, 207b, 208
Brantune	See Brampton
Breninctune	See Brington
Brington, B. 5	*Breninctune* 204b
Broctone, -*tune*	See Broughton
Broughton, D. 4	*Broctone*, -*tune* 203, 204, 208
Buchesworde	See Buckworth
Buchetone	See Boughton
Buckden, C. 6	*Bugedene* 203b
Buckworth, C. 5	*Buchesworde* 205b, 208
Bugedene	See Buckden
Bury	Not in D.B.
Bythorn, B. 5	*Bierne* 204b
Caissot	See Keysoe, Beds.
Caldecote, C. 3	*Caldecote* 206

Cateworde	See Catworth
Cateworde, *Alia*, *Parva*	See Little Catworth
Catworth, B. 5	*Cateworde* 205b, 206, 206b, 207b, 208, Hunts.; 222, N'hants.
Cestretune	See Chesterton
Chenebaltone	See Kimbolton
Chesterton, C. 2	*Cestretune* 205, 206
Chetelestan	See Keyston
Cilvelai	See Woolley
Colne, E. 5	*Colne* 204
Coninctune	See Conington
Conington, C. 4	*Coninctune* 206b, 208
Copemaneforde	See Coppingford
Coppingford, C. 4	*Copemaneforde* 205b
Cotes	See Cotton
Cotton, D. 6	*Cotes* 203b, 206b
Covington, B. 5	*Covintune* 205b
Covintune	See Covington
Dellinctune	See Dillington
Denton, C. 3	*Dentone* 203b
Dentone	See Denton
Diddington, C. 6	*Dodinctun* 207 *Dodintone* 203b
Dillington, C. 6	*Dellinctune* 204b
Dodinctun, *Dodintone*	See Diddington
Easton, C. 5	*Estone* 208 See also anon. holdings on p. 195
Einuluesberia, *-berie*	See Eynesbury
Elintune	See Ellington
Ellington, C. 5	*Elintune* 204b
Elton, B. 3	*Adelintune* 204b *Adelintone* 221, 222, N'hants.
Emingeforde	See Hemingford Abbots
Emingeforde, *Alia*	See Hemingford Grey
Eregrave	See Hargrave, N'hants.
Estone	See Easton

Everton, C. 7	*Evretune* 207
Evretune	See Everton
Eynesbury, C. 7	*Einuluesberia*, *-berie* 206b *ter*, 207, Hunts.; 200b, Cambs.
Eynesbury Hardwick	Not in D.B.
Farcet	Not in D.B.
Fen Stanton, E. 6	*Stantone* 207
Fenton	Not in D.B.
Fletone	See Fletton
Fletton, C. 2	*Fletone*, *-tun* 205, 208b
Fletun	See Fletton
Folchesworde	See Folksworth
Folksworth, C. 3	*Folchesworde* 205b
Geddinge, *Gedelinge*	See Gidding
Gel(l)inge, *Ghellinge*	See Yelling
Gidding, Great, Little and Steeple, B. 4, C. 4	*Geddinge* 203b *Gedelinge* 208 *Redinges* 204b *bis*, 206, 207
Glatton, C. 4	*Glatune* 205
Glatune	See Glatton
Godmanchester, D. 5	*Godmundcestre* 203b
Godmundcestre	See Godmanchester
Grafham, C. 5	*Grafham* 203b, 206, 208
Gransden, D. 7	*Grantesdene* 203b
Grantesdene	See Gransden
Great Gidding	See Gidding
Great Paxton	See Paxton
Great Raveley	Not in D.B.
Great Staughton, C. 6	*Tochestone* 203b
Great Stukeley	See Stukeley
Haddon, C. 3	*Adone* 205
Hail Weston, C. 6	*Westone*, *-tune* 206b, 207, 208 *bis*
Haliewelle	See Holywell
Hambertune	See Hamerton
Hamerton, C. 4	*Hambertune* 205b

Hartford, D. 5	*Hereforde* 203b
Hemingford Abbots, D. 5	*Emingeforde* 204b *bis*, 206, 207 *bis*, 208 *bis*
Hemingford Grey, D. 5	*Alia Emingeforde* 204b
Hereforde	See Hartford
Heregrave	See Hargrave, N'hants.
Hilton	Not in D.B.
Hoctune	See Houghton
Holywell, E. 5	*Haliewelle* 204
Houghton, D. 5	*Hoctune* 204b
Holme	Not in D.B.
Huntedone, *-dun*	See Huntingdon
Huntingdon, D. 5	*Huntedone*, *-dun* 203 *bis*
Iacheslei	See Yaxley
Kenebaltone	See Kimbolton
Ketelestan	See Keyston
Keyston, B. 5	*Chetelestan* 203b *Ketelestan* 208
Kimbolton, B. 6	*Chenebaltone* 205b, Hunts.; 211b, Beds. *Kenebaltone* 205b, 208
Kings Ripton	See Ripton
Lectone	See Leighton Bromswold
Leighton Bromswold, B. 5	*Lectone* 203b
Little Catworth, B. 5	*Alia Cateworde*, *Parva Cateworde* 204, 205b, 208
Little Gidding	See Gidding
Little Paxton	See Paxton
Little Raveley	Not in D.B.
Little Stukeley	See Stukeley
Lodintune	See Lutton, N'hants.
Lolinctune	See Luddington, N'hants.
Long Stow, B. 5	Not in D.B., but see anon. holdings on p. 195
Midloe	Not in D.B.
Molesworde	See Molesworth
Molesworth, B. 5	*Molesworde* 206b
Morborne, C. 3	*Morburne* 204
Morburne	See Morborne
Newetone	See Water Newton
Offord Cluny and D'Arcy, D. 6	*Opeforde* 206b *bis* *Upeforde* 204b, 205b
Old Hurst	Not in D.B.
Old Weston, B. 4	*Westune* 204b
Opeforde	See Offord
Opetune	See Upton
Orton Longueville and Waterville, C. 2	*Ovretone*, *-tune* 203b *bis*, 205 *bis*, 206 *bis*
Ovretone, *-tune*	See Orton
Pachstone	See Paxton
Papeuuorde	See Papworth, Cambs.
Parchestune	See Paxton
Partenhale	See Pertenhall, Beds.
Parva Cateworde	See Little Catworth
Paxton, Great and Little, C. 6	*Pachstone* 207, 208 *Parchestune* 205b
Perry, C. 6	*Pirie* 206b
Pidley	Not in D.B.
Pirie	See Perry
Ramesy	See Ramsey
Ramsey, D. 4	*Ramesy* 204b
Redinges	See Gidding
Ripton, Abbots and Kings, D. 4, D. 5	*Riptune* 204
Riptune	See Ripton
St Ives	Not in D.B.
St Neots	Not in D.B.
Saltrede	See Sawtry
Sawtry, C. 4	*Saltrede* 204b, 206, 206b, 207b, 208b
Sibestune	See Sibson
Sibson, B. 2	*Sibestune* 205 *quater*

Slepe, E. 5	*Slepe* 204
Somersham, E. 4	*Summersham* 204
Southoe, C. 6	*Sutham* 206b, 207
Spalduic(e)	See Spaldwick
Spaldwick, C. 5	*Spalduic(e)* 204 *bis*, 208
Stanground, C. 2	*Stangrun* 205
Stangrun	See Stanground
Stantone	See Fen Stanton
Stebintone, -tune	See Stibbington
Steeple Gidding	See Gidding
Stibbington, B. 2	*Stebintone, -tune* 205 *bis* *Stabintone* 229, N'hants.
Stic(h)iltone	See Stilton
Stilton, C. 3	*Stic(h)iltone* 203b *bis*, 206
Stivecle	See Stukeley
Stukeley, Great and Little, D. 5	*Stivecle* 204, 206, 206b
Suineshefet	See Swineshead, Beds.
Summersham	See Somersham
Sutham	See Southoe
Tetworth	Not in D.B.
Tilbrook, B. 5	*Tilebroc* 211b, Beds.
Tochestone	See Great Staughton
Torninge	See Thurning, N'hants.
Toseland	Not in D.B.
Upeforde	See Offord
Upehude	See Upwood
Upton, C. 4	*Opetune* 205b
Upwood, D. 4	*Upehude* 204
Waltune	See Wood Walton
Warboys, E. 4	*Wardebusc* 204b
Wardebusc	See Warboys
Waresley, D. 7	*Wederesle* 206b *Wedreslei(e)* 205b, 207
Washingley, C. 3	*Wasingelei(a)* 206, 207b
Wasingelei(a)	See Washingley
Water Newton, B. 2	*Newetone* 205
Wederesle, Wedreslei(e)	See Waresley
Westone	See Hail Weston
Westune	See Alconbury Weston, Hail Weston, Old Weston
Winewiche	See Winwick
Winwick, B. 4	*Winewiche* 206 *Winewiche, -wincle* 221b, 228, N'hants.
Wistou	See Wistow
Wistow, D. 4	*Wistou* 204
Witune	See Wyton
Wodestun	See Woodstone
Woodhurst	Not in D.B.
Woodstone, C. 2	*Wodestun* 205
Wood Walton, D. 4	*Waltune* 205b
Woolley, C. 5	*Cilvelai* 206, 207b
Wyton, D. 5	*Witune* 204b
Yaxley, C. 3	*Iacheslei* 205
Yelling, D. 6	*Gel(l)inge* 207, 208 *Ghellinge* 204b

ANONYMOUS HOLDINGS

One entry involves three anonymous holdings. The *Inquisitio Comitatus Cantabrigiensis*, however, enables us to assign these to their respective localities – see N. E. S. A. Hamilton, *Inquisitio Comitatus Cantabrigiensis subjicitur Inquisitio Eliensis* (London, 1876); the page given below refers to this edition:

Abbot of Ely, 15 hides in Spaldwick, 204. *I.C.C.* p. 166 shows that this included the berewicks of Barham, Long Stow and Easton; the first two were unnamed in D.B. and the third only incidentally in the appendix on Disputes, 208.

KENT — *CHENTH*

Folios 1–14b

MAPS 26–27

Acol	Not in D.B.
Acres	See Acrise
Acrise, J. 6	*Acres* 11b
Addela	See Deal
Addington, D. 4	*Eddintune* 7
Adisham, J. 4	*Edesham* 5
Ælvetone	See Elmstone
Afettune	Unid., 10b
Aia	Unid., 13b
Aiglessa	See Eccles
Aimolde	See Hammil
Aisiholte	Unid., 1b
Aldelose	See Aldglose
Aldglose, I. 5	*Aldelose* 10b
Aldington (near Hythe), I. 6	*Aldinton(e)* 4 *ter*
Aldington (in Thurnham), F. 4	*Audintone* 7b
Aldinton(e)	See Aldington (near Hythe)
Alham	See Elham
Alia Craie	See St Pauls Cray
Alia Essetesford	See Ashford
Alia Piria	See Perry (in Faversham)
Alius Bocheland	See Buckland (in Luddenham)
Alkham	Not in D.B.
Allington (in Hollingbourne), F. 4	*Alnoitone* 7b
Allington (near Maidstone), E. 4	*Elentun* 7
Alnoitone	See Allington (in Hollingbourne)
Alteham	See Eltham
Apeldres	See Appledore
Apletone	See Appleton
Appledore, G. 7	*Apledres* 5
Appleton, L. 5	*Apletone* 11
Arclei	See Oakleigh
Arnolton, H. 4	*Ernoltun* 10
	Ernulfitone 1
Ash, D. 3	*Eisse* 6

Ashenfield, I. 5	*Esmerefel* 12
Ashford, H. 6	*Alia Essetesford* 13
Ashurst	Not in D.B.
Asmeslant	See Gammons
Atterton, K. 6	*Etretone* 13
Audintone	See Aldington (in Thurnham)
Aylesford, E. 4	*Elesford* 2b
Bacheham	See Beckenham
Badelesmere	See Badlesmere
Badlesmere, H. 4	*Badelesmere* 10
	Bedenesmere 12b
Bapchild	Not in D.B.
Barfreston, K. 5	*Berfrestone* 9b
Barham, J. 5	*Berham* 9b
	See also anon. holdings on p. 208
Barming, East and West, E. 4	*Bermelie* 8b
	Bermelinge 14
Beamonston, H. 5	*Betmontestun* 10b
Bearsted	Not in D.B.
Beauxfield, K. 5	*Bevesfel* 12b
Beckenham, A. 3	*Bacheham* 7
Beckley, E. 2	*Bichelei* 9
Bedenesmere	See Badlesmere
Bedesham	See Betteshanger
Bekesbourne	See Bourne
Belice	Unid., 9b, 13
Benedestede	See Bensted
Benenden, F. 7	*Benindene* 11
Benindene	See Benenden
Bensted, E. 5	*Benedestede* 8b
Berchuelle	See Buckwell
Berewic	See Berwick
Berfrestone	See Barfreston
Berham	See Barham
Berlinge	See Birling
Bermelie, -linge	See Barming
Berwick, I. 6	*Berewic* 4b
Bethersden	Not in D.B.
Betmontestun	See Beamonston
Betteshanger, K. 5	*Bedesham* 11
Bevesfel	See Beauxfield

Bexley, B. 2	*Bix* 3
Bichelei	See Beckley
Bicknor	Not in D.B.
Bidborough	Not in D.B.
Biddenden	Not in D.B.
Bilsington, H. 7	*Bilsuitone* 10b
Bilsuitone	See Bilsington
Birchington	Not in D.B.
Bircholt	Not in D.B.
Birling, D. 4	*Berlinge* 7b
Bishopsbourne, J. 5	*Burnes* 3b
Bix	See Bexley
Blachemenestone	See Blackmanstone
Blackmanstone, I. 7	*Blachemenestone* 13
Blean, I. 4	*Bleham* 14
Bleham	See Blean
Bobbing	Not in D.B.
Bocheland, *Alius*, *Tercius*	See Buckland (in Luddenham)
Bocheland(e)	See Buckland (near Dover), Buckland (in Luddenham)
Bochelande (Stowting hd)	Unid., 9b
Bocoland	See Buckland (in Woodnesborough)
Bodesham	See Bodsham
Bodsham, I. 5	*Bodesham* 12b
Bogelei	See Bowley
Boltone	See Boughton Malherbe
Boltune	See Boughton Aluph, Boughton under Blean
Bonintone	See Bonnington
Bonnington, I. 7	*Bonintone* 13b
Borchemeres	See Burmarsh
Borchetelle, *Borcstele*	See Borstal
Borden	Not in D.B.
Borham	See Burham
Borne	See Bourne
Borstal, E. 3	*Borchetelle* 5b *Borcstele* 5b
Boseleu	See Boxley
Boswell Banks, K. 6	*Brochestele* 11, 11b
Boughton Aluph, H. 5	*Boltune* 14
Boughton Malherbe, G. 5	*Boltone* 4, 8
Boughton Monchelsea	Not in D.B.
Boughton under Blean, H. 4	*Boltune* 3b
Bourne: Bekesbourne and Patrixbourne, J. 4	*Borne* 9, 12 *Burnes* 9
Bowley, G. 5	*Bogelei* 8
Boxley, E. 4	*Boseleu* 8b
Brabourne, I. 6	*Br(ad)eburne* 10b, 13b
Bradeburne	See Brabourne
Brand(et)	See Brenzett
Brasted, B. 4	*Briestede* 4
Breburne	See Brabourne
Bredgar	Not in D.B.
Bredhurst	Not in D.B.
Brenchley	Not in D.B.
Brensete	See Brenzett
Brenzett, H. 7	*Brand(et)* 2 *bis* *Brensete* 2
Bridge	Not in D.B.
Briestede	See Brasted
Briseuuei	Unid., 1
Broadstairs	Not in D.B.
Brochestele	See Boswell Banks
Bromley, A. 3	*Bronlei* 5b
Bronlei	See Bromley
Brook, I. 5	Not in D.B., but see anon. holdings on p. 208
Brookland	Not in D.B.
Broomfield, F. 5	*Brunfelle* 8
Broteham	See Wrotham
Brulege	See Throwley
Brunfelle	See Broomfield
Buckland (near Dover), K. 6	*Bocheland(e)* 1b *bis*, 11b
Buckland (in Luddenham), H. 3	*Alius Bocheland* 1 *Bocheland(e)* 1, 10, 10b *Tercius Bocheland* 1

Buckland (in Woodnesborough), K. 4	*Bocoland* 4b
Buckwell, H. 5	*Berchuelle* 10b
Burham, E. 3	*Borham* 7b
Burmarsh, I. 7	*Borchemeres* 12b *Burwarmaresc* 12b
Burnes	See Bishopsbourne; Bourne
Burwarmaresc	See Burmarsh
Canterbury, J. 4	*Cantuaria* 1 *bis*, 2 *bis*, 2b, 3, 4, 5, 8 *ter*, 9, 9b, 10 *ter*, 10b, 11b, 12 *bis*, 14b *Cantuariensis* 9b
Cantuaria, *-iensis*	See Canterbury
Capel (near Tonbridge)	Not in D.B.
Capel le Ferne	Not in D.B.
Celca	See Chalk
Cerce	See Upchurch
Cerlentone	See Charlton (near Dover)
Cerletone	See Charlton (near Greenwich)
Certeham	See Chartham
Certh	See Chart Sutton, Great Chart
Ceteham	See Chatham
Chalk, D. 2	*Celca* 8b
Challock	Not in D.B.
Charing, G. 5	*Cheringes* 3b
Charlton (near Dover), K. 6	*Cerlentone* 1b
Charlton (near Greenwich), A. 2	*Cerletone* 6b
Chartham, I. 4	*Certeham* 5
Chart Sutton, F. 5	*Certh* 8
Chatham, E. 3	*Ceteham* 8b
Chelsfield, B. 3	*Ciresfel* 6b
Chenetone	See Kennington
Chenoltone	See Knowlton
Cherinchehelle	See Shillingham
Cheringes	See Charing
Cheriton	Not in D.B.
Chestan	See Keston
Chevening	Not in D.B.

Chiddingstone	Not in D.B.
Chilham, I. 4	*Cilleham* 10
Chillenden, K. 4	*Cilledene* 11b
Chislehurst	Not in D.B.
Chislet, J. 3	*Cistelet* 12
Cildresham, *Schildricheham*	Unid., 1, 10
Cilledene	See Chillenden
Cilleham	See Chilham
Ciresfel	See Chelsfield
Cistelet	See Chislet
Cliffe, E. 2	*Clive* 4b, 9
Clive	See Cliffe
Cobham	Not in D.B.
Coclestane	See Cuxton
Codeham	See Cudham
Coldred, K. 5	*Colret* 11
Colinge(s)	See Cooling
Colret	See Coldred
Cooling, E. 2	*Colinge(s)* 9 *bis*
Coombegrove, I. 5	*Cumbe* 10b
Court-at-Street, I. 7	*Estraites* 13b
Cowden	Not in D.B.
Crai(e)	See Foots Cray
Craie, *Alia*	See St Pauls Cray
Cranbrook	Not in D.B.
Crayford formerly Eard, C. 2	*Erhede* 3
Croctune	See Crofton
Crofton, B. 3	*Croctune* 7
Crundale	Not in D.B.
Cudham, B. 4	*Codeham* 7
Cumbe	See Coombegrove
Cuxton, E. 3	*Coclestane* 5b
Danetone	See Denton (near Barham)
Danitone	See Denton (near Gravesend)
Darenden	See Dernedale
Darenth, C. 2	*Tarent* 3, 6
Dartford, C. 2	*Tarentefort* 2b
Davington	Not in D.B.
Deal, L. 5	*Addela* 1b *quin*
Dean, H. 5	*Dena*, *Dene* 1, 10b
Delce, E. 3	*Delce* 8b *bis*
Dena, *Dene*	See Dean
Dengemarsh, H. 8	*Maresc* 10b, 11

Denton (near Barham), J. 5	*Danetone* 11b
Denton (near Gravesend), D. 2	*Danitone* 5b
Dernedale, I. 5	*Darenden* 12
Detling	Not in D.B.
Dictune	See Ditton
Didele	See Idleigh
Ditton, E. 4	*Dictune* 7
Doddington	Not in D.B.
Dodeham	See Luddenham
Dover, K. 6	*Dovera* 2 *Dov(e)re* 1 *bis*, 1b, 2, 3, 11, 11b, 13
Dovera, *Dov(e)re*	See Dover
Downe	Not in D.B.
Dymchurch	Not in D.B.
Each, K. 4	*Ece* 11b *bis*
Easole, K. 5	*Essewelle* 11b *Eswalt* 9b
East Barming	See Barming
Eastbridge, I. 7	*Estbrige* 13
Eastchurch	Not in D.B.
East Farleigh, E. 4	*Ferlaga* 4b
East Langdon	Not in D.B.
East Lenham	See Lenham
Eastling, H. 4	*Eslinges* 10b *bis*
East Malling	See Malling
East Peckham	See Peckham
Eastry, K. 4	*Estrei* 5
East Sutton	See Sutton Valence
Eastwell, H. 5	*Estwelle* 13
Eccles, E. 4	*Aiglessa* 7
Ece	See Each
Eddintone	Unid., 6
Eddintune	See Addington
Edenbridge	Not in D.B.
Edesham	See Adisham
Egerton	Not in D.B.
Eisse	See Ash
Elentun	See Allington (near Maidstone)
Elesford	See Aylesford, Eynsford
Elham, J. 6	*Alham* 9b
Elmley	Not in D.B.
Elmsted	Not in D.B.
Elmstone, K. 4	*Ælvetone* 12b

Elmton, K. 5	*Esmetone* 11b
Eltham, B. 2	*Alteham* 6b
Erclei	See Hartley
Erhede	See Crayford formerly Eard
Erith	Not in D.B.
Ernoltun, *Ernulfitone*	See Arnolton
Esledes	See Leeds
Eslinges	See Eastling
Esmerefel	See Ashenfield
Esmetone	See Elmton
Esnoiland	See Snodland
Essamelesford	See Shalmsford
Essedene	See Nashenden
Essella	Unid., 13
Essetesford, *Alia*	See Ashford
Essewelle	See Easole
Estanes	See Stone (near Dartford)
Estbrige	See Eastbridge
Estefort	See South Ashford
Estenberge	See Statenborough
Estoches	See Stoke
Estochingeberge	See Stocking
Estotinghes	See Stowting
Estraites	See Court-at-Street
Estrei	See Eastry
Estselve	See Old Shelve
Esturai	See Sturry
Estursete	See Westgate (in Canterbury)
Estwelle	See Eastwell
Eswalt	See Easole
Etretone	See Atterton
Etwelle	See Temple Ewell
Evegate, I. 6	*Tevegate* 14
Ewelle	See Temple Ewell
Eynsford, C. 3	*Elesford* 4
Eythorne, K. 5	Not in D.B., but see anon. holdings on p. 208
Fachesham	See Fawkham
Fairbourne, F. 5	*Fereburne* 7b, 8
Fairfield	Not in D.B.
Fan(n)e	See Fanscombe
Fanscombe, I. 5	*Fan(n)e* 10b, 14
Farnborough	Not in D.B.

Farningham, C. 3	*Ferlingeham* 6 *Ferningeham* 6 *bis* *Forningeham* 4
Farthingloe, K. 6	*Ferlingelai* 1b
Faversham, H. 4	*Favreshant* 2b
Favreshant	See Faversham
Fawkham, C. 3	*Fachesham* 5b
Fereburne	See Fairbourne
Ferlaga	See East Farleigh, West Farleigh
Ferlingeham	See Farningham
Ferlingelai	See Farthingloe
Ferningeham	See Farningham
Finglesham, L. 4	*Flenguessam* 4b
Fleet, K. 4	*Fletes* 3b
Flenguessam	See Finglesham
Fletes	See Fleet
Folkestone, J. 6	*Fulchestan* 9b
Foots Cray and North Cray, B. 2	*Crai(e)* 6b *bis*
Fordwich, J. 4	*Forewic* 12
Forewic	See Fordwich
Forningeham	See Farningham
Frandesberie	See Frindsbury
Fredenestede	See Frinsted
Frindsbury, E. 3	*Frandesberie* 5b *bis*
Frinsted, G. 4	*Fredenestede* 7b
Frittenden	Not in D.B.
Fulchestan	See Folkestone
Gammons, I. 7	*Asmeslant* 5
Gara	Unid., 1
Garlinge	Not in D.B.
Garrington, G. 4	*Warwintone* 12
Gecham	See Ickham
Gelingeham	See Gillingham
Getinge	See Giddinge
Giddinge, K. 5	*Getinge* 5
Gillingham, F. 3	*Gelingeham* 3b, 8
Gocistone	See Guston
Godeselle	See Wormshill
Godmersham, I. 5	*Gomersham* 5
Gollesberge	See Woodnesborough
Gomersham	See Godmersham
Goodnestone	Not in D.B.
Goslaches	Unid., 1
Goudhurst	Not in D.B.

Gravenel	See Graveney
Graveney, H. 3	*Gravenel* 4
Gravesend, D. 2	*Gravesham* 7b
Gravesham	See Gravesend
Great Chart, H. 6	*Certh* 5
Greenwich, A. 2	*Grenviz* 6b
Grenviz	See Greenwich
Guston, K. 5	*Gocistone* 1b
Hackington	Not in D.B.
Hadlow, D. 5	*Haslow* 7b
Hadone	See Haven
Hagelei	See Hawley
Haintone	See Hampton
Halling, E. 3	*Hallinges* 5b
Hallinges	See Halling, Yalding
Halstead	Not in D.B.
Ham, L. 4	*Hama* 11b
Hama	See Ham
Hamestede	See Hemsted
Hammil, K. 4	*Aimolde* 11 *Hamolde* 11
Hamolde	See Hammil
Hampton, I. 6	*Haintone* 13
Hanehest	See Henhurst
Harbiton, F. 5	*Herbretitou* 8
Harbledown	Not in D.B.
Hardes	See Hardres
Hardres, Lower and Upper, J. 4, J. 5	*Hardes* 9 *bis*, 9b
Hariardesham	See Harrietsham
Harrietsham, G. 4	*Hariardesham* 7b
Hartanger, K. 5	*Hertange* 11
Hartley, D. 3	*Erelei* 6
Hartlip	Not in D.B.
Harty, H. 3	*Herte* 1
Haslow	See Hadlow
Hastingelai, -lie	See Hastingleigh
Hastingleigh, I. 5	*Hastingelai, -lie* 11b, 14
Hauochesten	See Hawkhurst
Haven, E. 7	*Hadone* 9 *bis*
Hawkhurst, E. 7	*Hauochesten* 2
Hawkinge	Not in D.B.
Hawley, C. 2	*Hagelei* 2b, 6
Hayes	Not in D.B.
Headcorn	Not in D.B.

Hecham	See Higham
Hed(*a*)*e*	See Hythe
Hemsted, I. 6	*Hamestede* 11b
Henhurst, D. 3	*Hanehest* 9
Herbretitou	See Harbiton
Herne	Not in D.B.
Hernehill	Not in D.B.
Herste	See Hurst (in Chilham)
Hertange	See Hartanger
Herte	See Harty
Hever	Not in D.B.
Hicham	See Hougham
Higham, E. 2	*Hecham* 9
High Halden	Not in D.B.
High Halstow	Not in D.B.
Hildenborough	Not in D.B.
Hinxhill	Not in D.B.
Hoath	Not in D.B.
Hoilingeborde, *Holingeborne*	See Hollingbourne
Hollingbourne, F. 4	*Hoilingeborde* 4b *Holingeborne* 4
Hoo, F. 2	*Hou* 8b
Hope All Saints	Not in D.B.
Horsmonden	Not in D.B.
Horton (in Chartham), I. 4	*Hortone* 1, 10b
Hortone	See Horton (in Chartham), Monks Horton
Horton Kirby, C. 3	*Hortune* 6
Hortun	See Monks Horton
Hortune	See Horton Kirby
Hothfield	Not in D.B.
Hou	See Hoo, Howbury
Hougham, K. 6	*Hicham* 1b *Hu*(*c*)*ham* 9b *bis*
Howbury, C. 2	*Hou* 6b
Hucham	See Hougham
Hucking	Not in D.B.
Huham	See Hougham
Hulviz	See Woolwich
Hunton, E. 5	Not in D.B., but see anon. holdings on p. 208
Hurst (near Ashford)	Not in D.B.
Hurst (in Chilham), I. 5	*Herste* 1, 10
Hythe, J. 7	*Hed*(*a*)*e* 4, 4b
Ickham, J. 4	*Gecham* 5
Idleigh, D. 3	*Didele* 6
Ifield	Not in D.B.
Ightham	Not in D.B.
Isle of Grain	Not in D.B.
Isle of Sheppey	See anon. holdings on p. 207
Ivychurch	Not in D.B.
Iwade	Not in D.B.
Jaonei	Unid., 13b
Kemsing	Not in D.B.
Kenardington	Not in D.B.
Kennington, H. 5	*Chenetone* 12b
Keston, A. 3	*Chestan* 7
Kidbrook	Not in D.B.
Kingsdown (near Dartford)	Not in D.B.
Kingsdown (near Faversham)	Not in D.B.
Kingsnorth	Not in D.B.
Kingston	Not in D.B.
Knockholt	Not in D.B.
Knowlton, K. 4	*Chenoltone* 11
Lamberhurst	Not in D.B.
Lamport	See Langport (near Romney)
Langafel	See Longfield
Langley, F. 5	*Languelei* 8
Langport (near Romney), H. 8	*Lamport* 4b
Languelei	See Langley
Lanport (Bridge hd)	See Longport (in Canterbury)
Lanport (Stowting hd)	Unid., 12b
Lasela	See Seal
Latintone	See Nackington
Leaveland, H. 4	*Levelant* 4
Ledesdune	See Luddesdown
Lee, A. 2	*Lee* 6b
Leeds, F. 4	*Esledes* 7b
Leigh	Not in D.B.

Leleburne	See Leybourne
Leminges	See Lyminge
Lenham and East Lenham, G. 5	*Ler(t)ham* 4b, 12
Ler(t)ham	See Lenham
Lessness, B. 2	*Loisnes* 6b
Leueberge	Unid., 11 *bis*
Levelant	See Leaveland
Levesham	See Lewisham
Lewisham, A. 2	*Levesham* 12b
Leybourne, D. 4	*Leleburne* 7
Leysdown	Not in D.B.
Limes	See Lympne
Linsted	Not in D.B.
Linton	Not in D.B.
Liteburne	See Littlebourne
Litelbroteham	See Wrotham Heath
Litelcert	See Little Chart
Littlebourne, J. 4	*Liteburne* 12
Little Chart, G. 5	*Litelcert* 5
Loisnes	See Lessness
Lolingeston(e)	See Lullingstone
Longfield, D. 3	*Langafel* 5b
Longport (in Canterbury), J. 4	*Lanport* 12
Loose, E. 5	Not in D.B., but see anon. holdings on p. 208
Lower Halstow	Not in D.B.
Lower Hardres	See Hardres
Luddenham, H. 3	*Dodeham* 10b
Luddesdown, D. 3	*Ledesdune* 7b
Lullingstone, C. 3	*Lolingeston(e)* 6 *ter*
Lydd	Not in D.B.
Lydden	Not in D.B.
Lyminge, J. 6	*Leminges* 4
Lympne, I. 7	*Limes* 4
Macebroc	Not in D.B., but see anon. holdings on p. 207
Macheheve(t)	See Macknade
Macknade, H. 4	*Macheheve(t)* 1, 10
Maidstone, E. 4	*Meddestane* 3
Malling, East and West, D. 4, E. 4	*Mellingetes* 5b *Metlinges* 3
Malplescamp, *Mapledescam*	See Maplescombe
Maplescombe, C. 3	*Malplescamp* 6 *Mapledescam* 6
Marden	Not in D.B.
Maresc	See Dengemarsh
Margate, L. 2	Not in D.B., but see anon. holdings on p. 208
Marley, G. 4	*Merlea* 8
Marourde	See Mereworth
Marshborough, K. 4	*Masseberge* 11b
Masseberge	See Marshborough
Meddestane	See Maidstone
Mederclive, K. 6	*Medredive* 2
Medredive	See Mederclive
Melestun	See Merston
Meletune	See Milton (near Gravesend)
Mellingetes	See Malling
Meopham, D. 3	*Mepeham* 4b
Mepeham	See Meopham
Merclesham	Unid., 2
Mereworth, D. 4	*Marourde* 14
Merlea	See Marley
Merseham	See Mersham
Mersham, H. 6	*Merseham* 3b
Merston, E. 2	*Melestun* 9
Metlinges	See Malling
Middeltone, *-tun(e)*	See Milton Regis
Midelea	See Midley
Midley, H. 8	*Midelea* 11b
Milde(n)tone	See Milton Regis
Milsted	Not in D.B.
Milton (near Canterbury)	Not in D.B.
Milton (near Gravesend), D. 2	*Meletune* 7b
Milton Regis, G. 3	*Middeltone* 14b *Middeltun(e)* 2b *bis* *Milde(n)tone* 14b *bis*
Minster (in Sheppey)	Not in D.B.
Minster (in Thanet), K. 3	*Tanet* 12 See also anon. holdings on p. 207
Molash	Not in D.B.

Mongeham, L. 5	*Mundingeham* 12b
Monks Horton, I. 6	*Hortone*, *-tun* 13b *bis*
Monkton, K. 3	*Monocstune* 4b
Monocstune	See Monkton
Mottingham	Not in D.B.
Mundingeham	See Mongeham
Murston	Not in D.B.
Nackington, J. 4	*Latintone* 9b See also anon. holdings on p. 207
Nashenden, E. 3	*Essedene* 7
Nedestede	See Nettlestead
Nettlestead, E. 5	*Nedestede* 8b
Neuentone	See Newington (near Folkestone)
Neutone	See Newington (near Milton Regis)
Newchurch	Not in D.B.
Newedene	See Newenden
Newenden, F. 7	*Newedene* 4
Newetone	See Newington (near Milton Regis)
Newington (near Folkestone), J. 6	*Neuentone* 11b, 13b
Newington (near Milton Regis), F. 3	*Neutone* 14b *Newetone* 14b
Newnham	Not in D.B.
New Shelve, G. 5	*Westselve* 8
Nonington	Not in D.B.
Norborne	See Northbourne
Nordeslinge	See North Eastling
Nordeude	See Northgate, Northwood
Nordeuuode	See Northwood
Norfluet	See Northfleet
Northbourne, L. 5	*Norborne* 12b
Northburg	Unid., 1
North Cray	See Foots Cray
North Eastling, H. 4	*Nordeslinge* 10
Northfleet, D. 2	*Norfluet* 3
Northgate, J. 4	*Norduede* 5
Northwood, H. 7	*Nordeu(uo)de* 2 *bis*
Norton, H. 4	*Nortone* 10
Nortone	See Norton, Whitstable formerly Norton
Notestede	See Nurstead
Nurstead, D. 3	*Notestede* 7b
Oakleigh, E. 2	*Arclei* 9
Oare, H. 3	*Ora*, *Ore* 1, 10 *bis*
Obtrepole	See Otterpool
Ofeham	See Offham
Offham, D. 4	*Ofeham* 7, 7b
Oistreham	See Westerham
Oldeham	See Wouldham
Old Shelve, G. 5	*Estselve* 8 *bis*
Olecumbe	See Ulcombe
Ora, *Ore*	See Oare
Orgarswick	Not in D.B.
Orlavestone	See Orlestone
Orlestone, H. 7	*Orlavestone* 13b
Orpington, B. 3	*Orpinton*, *-tun* 4, 4b
Orpinton, *-tun*	See Orpington
Oslachintone	Unid., 1
Ospringe, H. 4	*Ospringes* 1, 10
Ospringes	See Ospringe
Otefort	See Otford
Oteham	See Otham
Otford, C. 4	*Otefort* 3
Otham, F. 4	*Oteham* 8
Otrin(ge)berge	See Wateringbury
Otringedene	See Otterden
Otterden, G. 4	*Otringedene* 8
Otterpool, I. 6	*Obtrepole* 14
Oxney	Not in D.B.
Paddlesworth (near Dover)	Not in D.B.
Paddlesworth (in Snodland), D. 3	*Pellesorde* 7
Palestrei	See Palstre
Palstre, G. 7	*Palestrei* 10b
Patrixbourne	See Bourne
Pecheham	See Peckham
Peckham, East and West, D. 5	*Pecheham* 4b, 7b
Pellesorde	See Paddlesworth (in Snodland)
Pembury	Not in D.B.

Penenden, E. 4	*Pinnedenna* 1
Penge	Not in D.B.
Penhurst	Not in D.B.
Perie	See Perry (in Faversham), Perry (in Selling)
Perry (in Faversham), H. 4	*Alia Piria* 1 *Perie* 10 2nd entry
Perry (in Selling), H. 4	*Perie* 10 1st entry *Piria* 1
Pesinges	See Pising
Petham, I. 5	*Piteham* 3b
Pett, H. 5	Not in D.B., but see anon. holdings on p. 208
Piham	See Pineham
Pimp's Court, E. 5	*Pinpa*, *Pinpe* 8b *bis*
Pinden, C. 3	*Pinnedene* 6
Pineham, K. 5	*Piham* 10b
Pinnedene	See Pinden
Pinnedenna	See Penenden
Pinpa, *Pinpe*	See Pimp's Court
Piria	See Perry (in Selling)
Piria, *Alia*	See Perry (in Faversham)
Pising, K. 5	*Pesinges* 10b
Pistinges	See Postling
Piteham	See Petham
Piventone	See Pivington
Pivington, G. 5	*Piventone* 10b
Platenout	See Wadholt
Pluchelei	See Pluckley
Pluckley, G. 5	*Pluchelei* 3b
Plumestede	See Plumstead
Plumstead, B. 2	*Plum(e)stede* 6b, 12
Plumstede	See Plumstead
Poltone	See Poulton
Ponshall, K. 5	*Popeselle* 9b *Popessale* 9b
Popeselle, *-ssale*	See Ponshall
Postinges	See Postling
Postling, I. 6	*Pistinges* 10b *Postinges* 13
Poulton, K. 6	*Poltone* 13b
Prestetone	See Preston (in Faversham)
Prestetune	See Preston (near Fordwich)
Preston (in Faversham), H. 4	*Prestetone* 5
Preston (near Fordwich), K. 4	*Prestetune* 12b
Queenborough	Not in D.B.
Rainham	Not in D.B.
Ramsgate	Not in D.B.
Rapentone	See Ripton
Reculver, J. 3	*Roculf* 3b
Redlege	See Ridley
Ridley, D. 3	*Redlege* 6
Riesce	See Ryarsh
Ringetone	See Ringleton
Ringlestone, G. 4	*Rongostone* 10b
Ringleton, K. 4	*Ringetone* 11
Ringwould	Not in D.B.
Ripa, *Ripe*	See Ripe
Ripe, H. 8	*Ripa*, *Ripe* 2 *bis*
Ripple	Not in D.B.
Ripton, H. 6	*Rapentone* 12
River	Not in D.B.
Riverhead	Not in D.B.
Rochelei	See Ruxley
Rochester, E. 3	*Rou(e)cestre* 2, 2b, 3, 5b, 7, 7b *bis*, 8, 8b, 9, 14b
Rochinges	See Ruckinge
Roculf	See Reculver
Rodmersham	Not in D.B.
Rolvenden	Not in D.B.
Romenel	See Romney
Romney, H. 8	*Romenel* 4, 4b, 10b
Rongostone	See Ringlestone
Rooting, G. 5	*Rotinge* 12
Rotinge	See Rooting
Rou(e)cestre	See Rochester
Ruckinge, H. 7	*Rochinges* 13b
Ruxley, B. 3	*Rochelei* 6b
Ryarsh, D. 4	*Riesce* 7
St Margaret's at Cliffe, L. 5	*Sancta Margarita* 1b *ter*, 2
St Martin's, J. 4	*Sanctus Martinus* 4 *bis*
St Mary Cray, B. 3	*Sudcrai* 6b

St Mary in the Marsh	Not in D.B.
St Nicholas at Wade	Not in D.B.
St Pauls Cray, B. 3	*Alia Craie* 6b
Salteode	See Saltwood
Saltwood, J. 6	*Salteode* 4b
Sancta Margarita	See St Margaret's at Cliffe
Sanctus Martinus	See St Martin's
Sandgate	Not in D.B.
Sandhurst	Not in D.B.
Sandlings, B. 3	*Sentlinge* 7
Sandwic(e)	See Sandwich
Sandwich, L. 4	*Sandwic(e)* 3, 5, 11 *Sanwic* 1 *bis*, 3
Sanwic	See Sandwich
Sarre	Not in D.B.
Schildresheham	See *Cildresham*
Scortebroc	Unid., 2
Seal, C. 4	*Lasela* 6b
Seasalter, I. 3	*Seseltre* 5
Sedlinges	See Sellindge
Seievetone	See Sevington
Selesburne	See Shelborough
Selinge(s)	See Shelving
Sellindge, I. 6	*Sedlinges* 13b
Selling, H. 4	*Setlinges* 12
Sentlinge	See Sandlings
Seseltre	See Seasalter
Setlinge	See Selling
Sevenoaks	Not in D.B.
Sevington, H. 6	*Seivetone* 13
Shadoxhurst	Not in D.B.
Shalmsford, I. 4	*Essamelesford* 10b
Sheerness	Not in D.B.
Shelborough, G. 5	*Selesburne* 7b
Sheldwich	Not in D.B.
Shelving, K. 4	*Selinge(s)* 9b, 11b
Shillingham, I. 4	*Cherinchehelle* 12b
Shipbourne	Not in D.B.
Sholden	Not in D.B.
Shoreham	Not in D.B.
Shorne	Not in D.B.
Sibertesuuald, -uualt	See Sibertswold
Sibertswold, K. 5	*Sibertesuuald, -uualt* 1b *ter*, 2, 12b

Siborne	Unid., 13b
Siffleton, E. 4	*Sifletone* 7
Sifletone	See Siffleton
Sittingbourne	Not in D.B.
Smarden	Not in D.B.
Snargate	Not in D.B.
Snave	Not in D.B.
Snodland, E. 3	*Esnoiland* 5b
Soaneclive	See Swalecliffe
Soles, K. 5	*Soles* 11
Solton, L. 5	*Soltone* 11
Soltone	See Solton
Sondresse	See Sundridge
Soninges	Unid., 6
South Ashford, H. 6	*Estefort* 13
Southborough	Not in D.B.
Southfleet, D. 2	*Sudfleta* 5b
Speldhurst	Not in D.B.
Stalisfield, H. 5	*Stanefelle* 10
Stanefelle	See Stalisfield
Stanestede, Stanetdeste	See Stansted
Stanford	Not in D.B.
Stansted, I. 6	*Stanestede* 2 *Stanetdeste* 2
Staple	Not in D.B.
Staplehurst	Not in D.B.
Statenborough, K. 4	*Estenberge* 4b
Stelling, J. 5	*Stellinges* 9
Stellinges	See Stelling
Stepedone	See Stuppington
Stoches	See Stoke
Stochingeberge	See Stockbury
Stockbury, F. 4	*Stochingeberge* 7b
Stocking, E. 5	*Estochingeberge* 7b
Stodmarsh	Not in D.B.
Stoke, F. 2	*Estoches* 5b *Stoches* 8b
Stonar	Not in D.B.
Stone (near Dartford), C. 2	*Estanes* 5b
Stone (near Faversham)	Not in D.B.
Stone-cum-Ebony	Not in D.B.
Stourmouth, K. 3	Not in D.B., but see anon. holdings on p. 207
Stowting, I. 6	*Estotinghes* 4

Strood	Not in D.B.
Stuppington, H. 4	*Stepedone* 9
Sturry, J. 4	*Esturai* 12
Sturtune	Not in D.B., but see anon. holdings on p. 208
Sudcrai	See St Mary Cray
Sudfleta	See Southfleet
Sudtone	See Sutton Valence
Suanetone	See Swanton (in Bilsington), Swanton (in Lydden)
Suestone	See Swetton
Suinescamp	See Swanscombe
Sundridge, B. 4	*Sondresse* 3
Sutton (near Deal)	Not in D.B.
Sutton Valence and East Sutton, F. 5	*Sudtone* 8 *bis*
Swalecliffe, I. 3	*Soaneclive* 10
Swanscombe, D. 2	*Suinescamp* 6
Swanton (in Bilsington), H. 6	*Suanetone* 13b
Swanton (in Lydden), K. 5	*Suanetone* 11
Swarling, I. 4	Not in D.B., but see anon. holdings on p. 207
Swetton, J. 7	*Suestone* 14
Swingfield	Not in D.B.
Tanet	See Minster (in Thanet)
Tangas	See Tonge
Tarent	See Darenth
Tarentefort	See Dartford
Temple Ewell, K. 6	*E(t)welle* 11 *bis*, 13b *bis*
Tenterden	Not in D.B.
Tercius Bocheland	See Buckland (in Luddenham)
Testan	See Teston
Teston, E. 4	*Testan* 8b
Tevegate	See Evegate
Teynham	Not in D.B.
Thanington, I. 4	Not in D.B., but see anon. holdings on p. 207
Throwley, H. 4	*Brulege* 1

Throwley cont.	*Treuelai* 10
Thurnham, F. 4	*Turneham* 8
Ticheteste	See Tickenhurst
Tickenhurst, K. 4	*Ticheteste* 11b
Tiffenden, G. 6	*Tipindene* 13b
Tilemanestone	See Tilmanstone
Tilmanstone, K. 5	*Tilemanestone* 4b
Tintentone	See Tinton
Tinton, H. 7	*Ti(n)tentone* 13 *bis*
Tipindene	See Tiffenden
Titentone	See Tinton
Tivedele	See Tudeley
Tonbridge, C. 5	*Tonebrige* 5b
Tonebrige	See Tonbridge
Tonge, G. 3	*Tangas* 9
Totesclive	See Trottiscliffe
Totintune	See Tottington
Tottington, E. 4	*Totintune* 7 *bis*
Treuelai	See Throwley
Trottiscliffe, D. 4	*Totesclive* 5b
Tudeley, D. 5	*Tivedele* 7b
Tunestelle	See Tunstall
Tunstall, G. 3	*Tunestelle* 9
Turneham	See Thurnham
Ulcombe, F. 5	*Olecumbe* 4
Upchurch, F. 3	*Cerce* 9
Upper Hardres	See Hardres
Wadholt, K. 5	*Platenout* 12b
Waldershare, K. 5	*Walwalesere* 11b
Walmer	Not in D.B.
Waltham	Not in D.B.
Walwalesere	See Waldershare
Wanesberge	See Woodnesborough
Warden	Not in D.B.
Warehorne, H. 7	*Werahorne* 5
Warwintone	See Garrington
Wateringbury, D. 4	*Otrin(ge)berge* 8b *bis*
Welle	See Westwell
Werahorne	See Warehorne
Wesclive	See Westcliffe
West Barming	See Barming
Westbere	Not in D.B.
Westcliffe, L. 5	*Wesclive* 11
Westerham, B. 4	*Oistreham* 14
West Farleigh, E. 4	*Ferlaga* 8b

Westgate (in Canterbury), I. 4	*Estursete* 3b, 4
Westgate on Sea	Not in D.B.
West Langdon	Not in D.B.
West Malling	See Malling
West Peckham	See Peckham
Westselve	See New Shelve
Westwell, H. 5	*Welle* 5
West Wickham, A. 3	*Wicheham* 6b
Whitfield	Not in D.B.
Whitstable formerly Norton, I. 3	*Nortone* 3b
Wi	See Wye
Wic	Not in D.B., but see anon. holdings below
Wicheham	See West Wickham, Wickhambreaux
Wichling, G. 4	*Winchelesmere* 8
Wickhambreaux, J. 4	*Wicheham* 9
Wilderton, H. 4	*Wirentone* 12
Willsborough	Not in D.B.
Wilmington	Not in D.B.
Winchelesmere	See Wichling
Wingham, K. 4	*Wingheham* 3b
Wingheham	See Wingham
Wirentone	See Wilderton
Witenemers	See Wricklesmarsh
Wittersham	Not in D.B.
Womenswold	Not in D.B.
Woodchurch	Not in D.B.
Woodnesborough, K. 4	*Gollesberge* 11 *Wanesberge* 11b
Woolwich, B. 2	*Hulviʒ* 14
Wootton	Not in D.B.
Wormshill, G. 4	*Godeselle* 8
Worth	Not in D.B.
Wouldham, E. 3	*Oldeham* 5b
Wricklesmarsh, A. 2	*Witenemers* 6b
Wrotham, D. 4	*Broteham* 3
Wrotham Heath, D. 4	*Litelbroteham* 8b
Wye, H. 5	*Wi* 1, 11b
Yalding, E. 5	*Hallinges* 14

ANONYMOUS HOLDINGS

The following forty-two entries involve anonymous holdings. The Domesday Monachorum and the Excerpta, however, enable us to assign 16 holdings in 11 entries to their respective localities – see (i) D. C. Douglas, *The Domesday Monachorum of Christ Church, Canterbury* (Royal Historical Society, London, 1944); (ii) A. Ballard, *An Eleventh-Century Inquisition of St Augustine's, Canterbury* (British Academy, London, 1920); the pages given below refer to these.

It is possible that some (or even all) of the others refer to holdings at places not named elsewhere in Domesday Book:

The king, *Terra Sophis*, 1.

St Martin of Dover, one sulung in Blackburn hd, 2.

Vitalis (from archbishop of Canterbury), 3 sulungs, one yoke and 12 acres belonging to manor of Whitstable, 3b. D.M. p. 84 shows this was at 3 places, *Tanet* (? Minster in Thanet), *Macebroc* (unid.) and Stourmouth (*Eʒilamerth*).

Godfrey and Nigel (from archbishop of Canterbury), 1½ sulungs and one yoke belonging to manor of Petham, 3b. D.M. pp. 83 and 95 shows that Godfrey held half a sulung at Swarling.

Five men (from archbishop of Canterbury), one sulung and 6 yokes belonging to manor of Westgate, 3b. D.M. pp. 81–82 shows that 3 of the 5 men held at Thanington, *Wic* (unid.) and Nackington.

Godfrey the steward (from archbishop of Canterbury), half a sulung in *Scape* (? Isle of Sheppey), 4b.

ANONYMOUS HOLDINGS (continued)

Godfrey (from archbishop of Canterbury), half a sulung belonging to manor of East Farleigh, 4b. D.M. p. 95 shows this was at Hunton.
Abel (from archbishop of Canterbury), holding worth £6 belonging to manor of East Farleigh, 4b. D.M. p. 95 shows this was at Loose.
William (from archbishop of Canterbury), half a sulung belonging to manor of Little Chart, 5. D.M. p. 90 shows this was at Pett.
Two knights (from archbishop of Canterbury), 3 sulungs belonging to manor of Adisham, 5. D.M. pp. 89–90 shows that 2 sulungs were at Eythorne and one was at Barham.
Archbishop of Canterbury, one sulung in Wye hd, 5. D.M. p. 92 shows this was at Brook.
William Folet (from archbishop of Canterbury), one yoke belonging to Gammons, 5. D.M. p. 84 shows this was at *Sturtune* (unid.).
Adam son of Hubert (from bishop of Bayeux), half a yoke in Rolvenden hd, 9b.
Vitalis (from bishop of Bayeux), one yoke in Whitstable hd, 10.
Osbern Paisfor (from bishop of Bayeux), 12 acres in Bewsborough hd, 10b.
Robert of Romney (from bishop of Bayeux), half a yoke in Aloesbridge hd, 11.
Osbern (from bishop of Bayeux), 1½ yokes in Eastry hd, 11.
Wibert (from bishop of Bayeux), half a yoke in Eastry hd, 11b.
Robert the Latin (from bishop of Bayeux), 6 acres in Summerden hd, 11b.
Osbern (from bishop of Bayeux), 1½ sulungs in Eastry hd, 11b.
Ralf de Curbespine (from bishop of Bayeux), 40 acres in Bewsborough hd, 11b. D.M. p. 101 shows this was near (*ibi prope*) Boswell Banks.
Abbey of St Augustine, 12 sulungs in Chislet, 12. Excerpta (A. Ballard, p. 17) shows that 6 of these sulungs were at Margate.
Abbey of St Augustine, 3 virgates in Eastry hd, 12b.
Hugh de Montfort, one yoke in Romney Marsh in Newchurch hd, 13.
Hugh de Montfort, half a yoke in Newchurch hd, 13.
Hugh de Montfort, one sulung less half a virgate in Romney Marsh in Worth hd, 13.
Roger (from Hugh de Montfort), one yoke in Romney Marsh in Worth hd, 13.
Robert (from Hugh de Montfort), ⅙ yoke in Romney Marsh in Worth hd, 13.
Hugh de Montfort, half a sulung in Hayne hd, 13.
Hugh de Montfort, one sulung in Newchurch hd, 13.
Hugh de Montfort, half a sulung in Romney Marsh in Newchurch hd, 13.
Hugh de Montfort, one yoke in Romney Marsh in Aloesbridge hd, 13.
Hugh de Montfort, half a yoke in Blackburn hd, 13.
Hugh de Montfort, 3½ virgates in *Limowart* lathe, 13b.
Ansfrid (from Hugh de Montfort), one yoke in Street hd, 13b.
Robert the cook (from Hugh de Montfort), one yoke in Street hd, 13b.
Gilbert (from Hugh de Montfort), one yoke in Longbridge hd, 13b.
One sokeman (from Hugh de Montfort), 16 acres in Bewsborough hd, 13b.
Fulbert (from Hugh de Montfort), one mill in Bewsborough hd, 13b.
A certain woman (from Hugh de Montfort), one virgate in Chart hd, 13b.
Herald (from Hugh de Montfort), half a sulung less one virgate in Blackburn and Newchurch hds, 14.
Haimo the sheriff (from the king), 2½ sulungs in Wye hd, 14.

LANCASHIRE

Inter Ripam et Mersham, folios 269b–270
Yorkshire folios 301b, 302, 327b, 332

MAPS 28–29

Abram	Not in D.B.
Accrington	Not in D.B.
Achetun	See Aughton
Acrer	See Altcar
Actun	See Aighton
Adlington	Not in D.B.
Aighton, F. 6	*Actun* 301b
Ainsdale, B. 9	*Einuluesdel* 269b
Ainsworth	Not in D.B.
Aintree	Not in D.B.
Aldcliffe, D. 3	*Aldeclif* 301b
Aldeclif	See Aldcliffe
Aldingham, A. 2	*Aldingham* 302
Alia Eglestun	See Little Eccleston
Alia Lies	See Leece
Alia Rodeclif	See Middle Rawcliff
Allerton, C. 11	*Alretune* 269b
Alretune	See Allerton
Alston	Not in D.B.
Alt	Not in D.B.
Altcar, B. 9	*Acrer* 269b
Altham	Not in D.B.
Anderton	Not in D.B.
Angerton	Not in D.B.
Anglezarke	Not in D.B.
Argarmelys, B. 8	*Erengermeles* 269b
Arkholme, E. 2	*Ergune* 301b
Aschebi, D. 6	Lost in Myerscough, 301b
Ashton (near Lancaster), D. 4	*Estun* 332
Ashton in Makerfield	Not in D.B.
Ashton on Ribble, D. 7	*Estun* 301b
Ashton under Lyne	Not in D.B.
Aspull	Not in D.B.

Astley	Not in D.B.
Atherton	Not in D.B.
Audenshaw	Not in D.B.
Aughton, C. 9	*Achetun* 269b
Bacup	Not in D.B.
Baguley, G. 11	*Bagelei* 268, Ches.
Balderstone	Not in D.B.
Bardsea, B. 2	*Berretseige* 301b
Bardsley	Not in D.B.
Bare, C. 2	*Bare* 301b
Barnacre	Not in D.B.
Barrowford	Not in D.B.
Barrow in Furness	Not in D.B.
Barton (in Downholland), B. 9	*Bartune* 269b
Barton (near Preston), D. 6	*Bartun* 301b
Barton Moss	Not in D.B.
Bartun	See Barton (near Preston)
Bartune	See Barton (in Downholland)
Berewic	See Borwick
Berretseige	See Bardsea
Bickerstaffe	Not in D.B.
Bileuurde	See Dilworth
Billington	Not in D.B.
Bilsborrow	Not in D.B.
Birkby, C. 2	*Bretebi* 327b
Birtle	Not in D.B.
Biscopham	See Bispham (in Blackpool)
Bispham (in Blackpool), B. 6	*Biscopham* 301b
Bispham (near Ormskirk)	Not in D.B.
Blacheburne	See Blackburn
Blackburn, F. 7	*Blacheburne* 270
Blackpool	Not in D.B.
Blackrod	Not in D.B.

Blawith	Not in D.B.
Bleasdale	Not in D.B.
Bodeltone	See Bolton le Sands
Bodetun	See Bolton (in Urswick)
Bold	Not in D.B.
Boltelai	See Bootle
Bolton (near Manchester)	Not in D.B.
Bolton (in Urswick), A. 2	*Bodeltun* 302
Bolton le Sands, D. 3	*Bodeltone* 301b
Bootle, B. 11	*Boltelai* 269b
Borch	See Broughton in Furness, Burrow
Borwick, D. 2	*Berewic* 332
Bretebi	See Birkby
Bretherton	Not in D.B.
Brierfield	Not in D.B.
Brindle	Not in D.B.
Broctun	See Broughton (near Preston)
Broughton (near Preston), D. 6	*Broctun* 301b
Broughton East	Not in D.B.
Broughton in Furness, G. 3	*Borch* 301b 2nd entry
Brune	See Burn
Burn, B. 5	*Brune* 301b
Burnley	Not in D.B.
Burrow, Nether and Over, E. 2	*Borch* 301b *bis* 1st and 3rd entries
Burscough	Not in D.B.
Burtonwood	Not in D.B.
Bury	Not in D.B.
Cabus	Not in D.B.
Cantesfelt	See Cantsfield
Cantsfield, E. 2	*Cantesfelt* 301b
Carlentun	See Carleton
Carleton, B. 6	*Carlentun* 301b
Carnforth, D. 2	*Chreneforde* 301b
Cartmel, C. 1	*Cherchebi* 302
Caton, D. 3	*Catun* 301b
Catrehala	See Catterall
Catterall, D. 5	*Catrehala* 301b
Catun	See Caton

Chadderton	Not in D.B.
Charnock Richard	Not in D.B.
Chatburn	Not in D.B.
Chellet	See Kellet
Chenulueslei	See Knowsley
Chercaloncastre	See Kirk Lancaster
Cherchebi	See Cartmel, Kirkby
Cherestanc	See Garstang
Chicheham	See Kirkham
Childwall, C. 11	*Cildeuuelle* 269b
Chilvestreuic	See Killerwick
Chipinden	See Chipping
Chipping, E. 5	*Chipinden* 301b
Chirchedele	See Kirkdale
Chorley	Not in D.B.
Chreneforde	See Carnforth
Church	Not in D.B.
Cildeuuelle	See Childwall
Clactun	See Claughton (near Lancaster)
Clactune	See Claughton (near Garstang)
Claife	Not in D.B.
Claughton (near Garstang), D. 5	*Clactune* 301b
Claughton (near Lancaster), E. 3	*Clactun* 301b
Clayton le Dale	Not in D.B.
Clayton le Moors	Not in D.B.
Clayton le Woods	Not in D.B.
Cleveley	Not in D.B.
Clifton (near Preston), D. 7	*Clistun* 301b
Clifton (near Prestwich)	Not in D.B.
Clistun	See Clifton (near Preston)
Clitheroe	Not in D.B.
Clivertun	See Crivelton
Cliviger	Not in D.B.
Cochreham	See Cockerham
Cockerham, D. 4	*Cochreham* 332
Colne	Not in D.B.
Colton	Not in D.B.
Coniston	Not in D.B.
Coppull	Not in D.B.
Crimbles, C. 4	*Crimeles* 301b
Crimeles	See Crimbles

Crivelton, A. 2	*Clivertun* 301b
Crompton	Not in D.B.
Cronton	Not in D.B.
Crosby, Great and Little, B. 10	*Crosebi* 269b *bis*
Crosebi	See Crosby
Croston	Not in D.B.
Cuerdale	Not in D.B.
Cuerden	Not in D.B.
Cuerdley	Not in D.B.
Culcheth	Not in D.B.
Dalton (near Wigan), D. 9	*Daltone* 269b
Daltone	See Dalton (near Wigan)
Dalton in Furness, A. 2	*Daltune* 301b
Daltune	See Dalton in Furness
Darwen	Not in D.B.
Davyhulme	Not in D.B.
Dendron, A. 2	*Dene* 302
Dene	See Dendron
Denton	Not in D.B.
Derbei, *-berie*	See West Derby
Dilworth, E. 6	*Bileuurde* 301b
Dinkley	Not in D.B.
Downham	Not in D.B.
Downholland, B. 9	*Holand* 269b
Down Litherland, B. 10	*Liderlant* 269b
Droylsden	Not in D.B.
Dunnerdale	Not in D.B.
Dunnockshaw	Not in D.B.
Dutton	Not in D.B.
Duxbury	Not in D.B.
Eccles	Not in D.B.
Eccleshill	Not in D.B.
Eccleston (near Chorley)	Not in D.B.
Eccleston (near Prescot)	Not in D.B.
Edelesuuic	See Elswick
Eglestun	See Great Eccleston
Eglestun, Alia	See Little Eccleston

Egton	Not in D.B.
Einuluesdel	See Ainsdale
Ellel, D. 4	*Ellhale* 332
Ellhale	See Ellel
Elston	Not in D.B.
Elswick, C. 6	*Edelesuuic* 301b
Erengermeles	See Argarmelys
Ergune	See Arkholme
Esmedune	See Smithdown
Estun	See Ashton (near Lancaster), Ashton on Ribble
Euxton	Not in D.B.
Failsworth	Not in D.B.
Fareltun	See Farleton
Farington	Not in D.B.
Farleton, E. 3	*Fareltun* 301b
Farnworth	Not in D.B.
Field Plumpton, C. 6	*Pluntun* 301b 1st entry
Fiscuic	See Fishwick
Fishwick, E. 7	*Fiscuic* 301b
Fleetwood	Not in D.B.
Flixton	Not in D.B.
Ford	Not in D.B.
Fordbootle, A. 2	*Fordebodele* 301b
Fordebodele	See Fordbootle
Formby, B. 9	*Fornebei* 269b
Fornebei	See Formby
Forton, D. 4	*Fortune* 301b
Fortune	See Forton
Foulridge	Not in D.B.
Frecheltun	See Freckleton
Freckleton, C. 7	*Frecheltun* 301b
Fulwood	Not in D.B.
Garstang, D. 5	*Cherestanc* 301b
Gerleworle	See Kirkby Ireleth
Ghersinctune	See Gressingham
Glassertun	See Gleaston
Gleaston, A. 2	*Glassertun* 301b
Golborne	Not in D.B.
Goldshaw	Not in D.B.
Goosnargh, E. 6	*Gusansarghe* 301b
Grange	Not in D.B.
Great Crosby	See Crosby

Place	Domesday form
Great Eccleston, C. 6	*Eglestun* 301b
Great Harwood	Not in D.B.
Great Marton	See Marton
Great Sankey	Not in D.B.
Greenhalgh, C. 6	*Greneholf* 301b
Greneholf	See Greenhalgh
Gressingham, E. 2	*Ghersinctune* 301b
Grimesarge	See Grimsargh
Grimsargh, E. 6	*Grimesarge* 301b
Gusansarghe	See Goosnargh
Haigh	Not in D.B.
Haighton, E. 6	*Halctun* 301b
Halctun	See Haighton
Hale	Not in D.B.
Halewood	Not in D.B.
Halsall, C. 9	*Heleshale* 269b *Herleshala* 269b
Halton, D. 3	*Haltun(e)* 301b
Haltun(e)	See Halton
Hambleton, C. 5	*Hameltune* 301b
Hameltune	See Hambleton
Hapton	Not in D.B.
Hardhorn	Not in D.B.
Hart, A. 2	*Hert* 301b
Hartshead	Not in D.B.
Haslingden	Not in D.B.
Haverthwaite	Not in D.B.
Hawkshead	Not in D.B.
Haydock	Not in D.B.
Heapey	Not in D.B.
Heaton (in Dalton in Furness), A. 2	*Hietun* 301b
Heaton (near Lancaster), C. 3	*Hietune* 301b
Heaton Norris	Not in D.B.
Heleshale, Herleshala	See Halsall
Hert	See Hart
Hesketh	Not in D.B.
Heskin	Not in D.B.
Hessam	See Heysham
Heysham, C. 3	*Hessam* 301b
Heywood	Not in D.B.
Hietun	See Heaton (in Dalton in Furness)
Hietune	See Heaton (near Lancaster)

Place	Domesday form
Higham	Not in D.B.
Hillham, C. 4	*Hillun* 301b
Hillun	See Hillham
Hindley	Not in D.B.
Hinne	See Ince Blundell
Hir(l)etun	See Hurlston
Hitune	See Huyton
Hoghton	Not in D.B.
Hoiland	See Upholland
Holand	See Downholland
Holecher	See Holker
Holker, B. 2	*Holecher* 327b
Holleth	Not in D.B.
Hornby, E. 2	*Hornebi* 301b
Hornebi	See Hornby
Horwick	Not in D.B.
Hothersall	Not in D.B.
Hotun	See Hutton (in Lancaster)
Hotune	See Priest Hutton
Houghton Middleton	Not in D.B.
Howick	Not in D.B.
Huncoat, G. 7	*Hunnicot* 270
Hunnicot	See Huncoat
Hurlston, C. 9	*Hir(l)etun* 269b *bis*
Hurst	Not in D.B.
Hutton (in Lancaster), D. 3	*Hotun* 301b 1st entry
Hutton (near Preston)	Not in D.B.
Huyton, C. 11	*Hitune* 269b
Ince Blundell, B. 10	*Hinne* 269b
Ince in Makerfield	Not in D.B.
Inscip	See Inskip
Inskip, C. 6	*Inscip* 301b
Irebi	See Ireby
Ireby, F. 2	*Irebi* 301b
Irlam	Not in D.B.
Jalant	See Yealand
Kearsley	Not in D.B.
Kellet, Nether and Over, D. 2, D. 3	*Chellet* 301b
Kenyon	Not in D.B.
Killerwick, A. 1	*Chilvestreuic* 301b

Kirkby (near Liverpool), C. 10	*Cherchebi* 269b
Kirkby Ireleth, A. 1	*Gerleworde* 301b
Kirkdale, B. 11	*Chirchedele* 269b
Kirkham, C. 7	*Chicheham* 301b
Kirk Lancaster, D. 3	*Chercaloncastre* 301b
Kirkland	Not in D.B.
Knowsley, C. 11	*Chenulueslei* 269b
Lailand	See Leyland
Lancaster, D. 3	*Loncastre* 301b
Lanesdale	See Lonsdale (near Cockerham)
Lathom, D. 9	*Latune* 269b
Latun	See Layton
Latune	See Lathom
Layton, B. 6	*Latun* 301b
Lea, D. 7	*Lea* 301b
Leagram	Not in D.B.
Lech	See Leck
Leck, F. 2	*Lech* 301b
Leece, A. 2	*Lies*, *Alia Lies* 301b *bis*
Lees	Not in D.B.
Leiate	See Lydiate
Leigh	Not in D.B.
Leyland, D. 8	*Lailand* 270
Liderlant	See Down Litherland
Lidun	See Lytham
Lies, *Alia Lies*	See Leece
Literland	See Up Litherland
Littleborough	Not in D.B.
Little Bowland	Not in D.B.
Little Crosby	See Crosby
Little Eccleston, C. 6	*Alia Eglestun* 301b
Little Hoole	Not in D.B.
Little Hulton	Not in D.B.
Little Marton	See Marton
Little Woolton	See Woolton
Liverpool	Not in D.B.
Livesey	Not in D.B.
Loncastre	See Lancaster
Longton	Not in D.B.
Lonsdale (near Cockerham), C. 4	*Lanesdale* 332
Lower Allithwaite	Not in D.B.
Lowick	Not in D.B.
Lowton	Not in D.B.
Lunt	Not in D.B.
Lydiate, B. 9	*Leiate* 269b
Lytham, B. 7	*Lidun* 301b
Magele	See Maghull
Maghull, C. 10	*Magele* 269b
Mamecestre	See Manchester
Manchester, H. 10	*Mamecestre* 270
Mansriggs	Not in D.B.
Martin, A. 2	*Meretun* 301b 2nd entry
Marton (in Burscough), C. 9	*Merretun* 269b
Marton, Great and Little, B. 6	*Meretun* 301b 1st entry
Mawdesley	Not in D.B.
Mearley	Not in D.B.
Medlar	Not in D.B.
Mele	See Raven Meols
Melinge	See Melling (near Liverpool)
Melling (near Lancaster), E. 2	*Mellinge* 301b
Melling (near Liverpool), C. 10	*Melinge* 269b
Mellinge	See Melling (near Lancaster)
Mellor	Not in D.B.
Meretun	See Martin; Marton, Great and Little
Merretun	See Marton (in Burscough)
Michelescherche	See St Michael on Wyre
Middeltun	See Middleton (near Lancaster)
Middle Rawcliff, C. 5	*Alia Rodeclif* 301b
Middleton (near Lancaster), C. 4	*Middeltun* 301b
Middleton (near Oldham)	Not in D.B.
Midehope	See Mythop
Milnrow	Not in D.B.

Moore	Not in D.B.
Mossley	Not in D.B.
Much Hoole	Not in D.B.
Much Woolton	See Woolton
Myerscough	Not in D.B.
Mythop	*Midehope* 301b
Nateby	Not in D.B.
Nelson	Not in D.B.
Nether Burrow	See Burrow
Nether Kellet	See Kellet
Netherton	Not in D.B.
Neuhuse	See Newsham (near Preston), Newsham (in Skerton)
Neutun	See Newton (in Cartmel), Newton (in Lancaster)
Neutune	See Newton (near Preston), Newton (in Whittington)
Neweton	See Newton-in-Makerfield
Newsham (near Preston), D. 6	*Neuhuse* 301b 1st entry
Newsham (in Skerton), D. 3	*Neuhuse* 301b 2nd entry
Newton (in Cartmel), C. 1	*Neutun* 301b 2nd entry
Newton (in Lancaster), D. 3	*Neutun* 301b 1st entry
Newton (near Preston), C. 7	*Neutune* 301b 1st entry
Newton (in Whittington), E. 2	*Neutune* 301b 2nd entry
Newton-in-Makerfield, E. 10	*Neweton* 269b
Norden	Not in D.B.
Northenden, H. 11	*Norwordine* 268, Ches.
North Meols, B. 8	*Otegrimele* 269b *Otringemele* 269b
Northtown	Not in D.B.
Oldham	Not in D.B.
Orgrave, A. 2	*Ouregrave* 301b
Ormskirk	Not in D.B.

Orrell (near Bootle)	Not in D.B.
Orrell (near Wigan)	Not in D.B.
Osbaldeston	Not in D.B.
Osmotherley	Not in D.B.
Oswaldtwistle	Not in D.B.
Otegrimele, Otringemele	See North Meols
Ouregrave	See Orgrave
Ouretun	See Overton
Out Rawcliffe, C. 5	*Tercia Rodeclif* 301b
Outwood	Not in D.B.
Over Burrow	See Burrow
Over Kellet	See Kellet
Overton, C. 4	*Ouretun* 301b
Oxcliffe, C. 3	*Oxeneclif* 301b
Oxeneclif	See Oxcliffe
Padiham	Not in D.B.
Pendlebury	Not in D.B.
Pendleton, G. 6	*Peniltune* 270
Peneverdant	See Penwortham
Peniltune	See Pendleton
Penketh	Not in D.B.
Pennigetun	See Pennington
Pennington, A. 1	*Pennigetun* 301b
Penwortham, D. 7	*Peneverdant* 270
Pilling	Not in D.B.
Pleasington	Not in D.B.
Pluntun	See Field Plumpton, Woodplumpton
Poltun	See Poulton-le-Fylde
Poltune	See Poulton-le-Sands
Poulton (near Warrington)	Not in D.B.
Poulton-le-Fylde, B. 6	*Poltun* 301b
Poulton-le-Sands, C. 3	*Poltune* 301b
Preesall, B. 5	*Pressouede* 301b
Preese, C. 6	*Pres* 301b
Pres	See Preese
Prescot	Not in D.B.
Pressouede	See Preesall

Preston, D. 7	*Prestune* 301b
Prestune	See Preston
Prestwich	Not in D.B.
Priest Hutton, D. 2	*Hotune* 301b
Quernmore	Not in D.B.
Rabil	See Roby
Radcliffe, G. 9	*Radecliue* 270
Radecliue	See Radcliffe
Rainford	Not in D.B.
Rainhill	Not in D.B.
Ramsbottom	Not in D.B.
Ramsgreave	Not in D.B.
Raven Meols, B. 9	*Mele* 269b
Rawtenstall	Not in D.B.
Read	Not in D.B.
Recedham	See Rochdale
Reddish	Not in D.B.
Ribby, C. 7	*Rigbi* 301b
Ribchester, F. 6	*Ribelcastre* 301b
Ribelcastre	See Ribchester
Rigbi	See Ribby
Rishton	Not in D.B.
Rivington	Not in D.B.
Rixton	Not in D.B.
Roby, C. 11	*Rabil* 269b
Rochdale, H. 9	*Recedham* 270
Rodeclif	See Upper Rawcliffe
Rodeclif, Alia	See Middle Rawcliffe
Rodeclif, Tercia	See Out Rawcliffe
Roose, A. 2	*Rosse* 301b
Rossall, B. 5	*Rushale* 301b
Rosse	See Roose
Royton	Not in D.B.
Rufford	Not in D.B.
Rushale	See Rossall
Sabden	Not in D.B.
St Helens	Not in D.B.
St Michael on Wyre, D. 6	*Michelescherche* 301b
Salesbury	Not in D.B.
Saleuuic	See Salwick
Salford, H. 10	*Salford* 270

Salwick, D. 6	*Saleuuic* 301b
Samlesbury	Not in D.B.
Satterthwaite	Not in D.B.
Scarisbrick	Not in D.B.
Schelmeresdele	See Skelmersdale
Schertune	See Skerton
Scotforth, D. 3	*Scozforde* 332
Scozforde	See Scotforth
Seaforth	Not in D.B.
Sefton, B. 10	*Sextone* 269b
Sextone	See Sefton
Shevington	Not in D.B.
Singleton, C. 6	*Singletun* 301b
Singletun	See Singleton
Silverdale	Not in D.B.
Simonstone	Not in D.B.
Simonswood	Not in D.B.
Skelmersdale, D. 9	*Schelmeresdele* 269b
Skelwith	Not in D.B.
Skerton, D. 3	*Schertune* 301b
Sline	See Slyne
Slyne, D. 3	*Sline* 301b
Smithdown, C. 11	*Esmedune* 269b
Sorbi	See Sowerby (near Preston)
Sourebi	See Sowerby (in Dalton in Furness)
Southport	Not in D.B.
Southworth	Not in D.B.
Sowerby (in Dalton in Furness), A. 2	*Sourebi* 301b
Sowerby (near Preston), D. 6	*Sorbi* 301b
Spec	See Speke
Speke, C. 12	*Spec* 269b
Staining, B. 6	*Staininghe* 301b
Staininghe	See Staining
Stainton, A. 2	*Steintun* 301b
Stalmine, C. 5	*Stalmine* 301b
Standish	Not in D.B.
Stapleton Terne, D. 3	*Stopeltierne* 301b
Staveley	Not in D.B.
Steintun	See Stainton
Stochestede	See Toxeth
Stockport	Not in D.B.

Stopeltierne	See Stapleton Terne
Stretford	Not in D.B.
Subberthwaite	Not in D.B.
Suenesat	See Swainseat
Suntun, A. 2	Lost in Barrow in Furness, 301b
Swainseat, D. 4	*Suenesat* 301b
Swinton	Not in D.B.
Tarbock, D. 11	*Torboc* 269b
Tarleton	Not in D.B.
Tathaim	See Tatham
Tatham, E. 2	*Tathaim* 301b
Tercia Rodeclif	See Out Rawcliffe
Thirnby, E. 2	*Tiernebi* 301b
Thornton (near Fleetwood), B. 5	*Torentun* 301b
Thornton (near Liverpool), B. 10	*Torentun* 269b
Threfall, D. 6	*Trelefelt* 301b
Thurnham, D. 4	*Tiernun* 301b
Tiernebi	See Thirnby
Tiernun	See Thurnham
Tockholes	Not in D.B.
Torboc	See Tarbock
Toredholme	See Torisholme
Torentun	See Thornton (near Fleetwood), Thornton (near Liverpool)
Torisholme, C. 3	*Toredholme* 301b
Torver	Not in D.B.
Tottington	Not in D.B.
Toxeth, B. 11	*Stochestede* 269b *bis*
Treales, C. 6	*Treueles* 301b
Trelefelt	See Threfall
Treueles	See Treales
Tunestalle	See Tunstall
Tunstall, E. 2	*Tunestalle* 301b
Turton	Not in D.B.
Twiston	Not in D.B.
Tyldesley	Not in D.B.
Ulnes Walton	Not in D.B.
Ulventune	See Woolton
Ulverston, B. 1	*Ulvrestun* 302
Ulvrestun	See Ulverston
Unsworth	Not in D.B.
Upholland, D. 9	*Hoiland* 269b
Up Litherland, C. 9	*Literland* 269b
Upper Allithwaite	Not in D.B.
Upper Rawcliffe, C. 5	*Rodeclif* 301b
Urmston	Not in D.B.
Urswick	Not in D.B.
Uuetone	See Woolton
Waletone	See Walton on the Hill
Waletune	See Walton le Dale
Walintune	See Warrington
Wallei	See Whalley
Walletun	See Walton (in Cartmel)
Walmersley	Not in D.B.
Walton (in Cartmel), B. 1	*Walletun* 301b
Walton (near Warrington)	Not in D.B.
Walton le Dale, E. 7	*Waletune* 270
Walton on the Hill, B. 11	*Waletone* 269b *bis*
Wardle	Not in D.B.
Warrington, E. 11	*Walintune* 269b
Wart, A. 2	*Warte* 301b
Warte	See Wart
Warton (near Carnforth), D. 2	*Wartun* 301b 2nd entry
Warton (near Preston), C. 7	*Wartun* 301b 1st entry
Wartun	See Warton (near Carnforth), Warton (near Preston)
Watelei	See Wheatley
Wauretreu	See Wavertree
Wavertree, C. 11	*Wauretreu* 269b
Weeton, C. 6	*Widetun* 301b
Welch Whittle	Not in D.B.
Wennigetun	See Wennington
Wennington, E. 2	*Wennigetun* 301b *Wininctune* 301b
Westbi	See Westby
Westby, C. 7	*Westbi* 301b

West Derby, C. 11	*Derbei*, *-berie* 269b *quater*
Westhoughton	Not in D.B.
Whalley, G. 6	*Wallei* 270
Wheatley, E. 6	*Watelei* 301b
Wheelton	Not in D.B.
Whiston	Not in D.B.
Whitefield	Not in D.B.
Whittingham, E. 6	*Witingheham* 301b
Whittington, E. 2	*Witetune* 301b
Whittle le Woods	Not in D.B.
Whitworth	Not in D.B.
Wibaldeslei, C. 11	Lost in Much Woolton, 269b
Widetun	See Weeton
Widnes	Not in D.B.
Wigan	Not in D.B.
Wilpshire	Not in D.B.
Windle	Not in D.B.
Wininctune	See Wennington
Winstanley	Not in D.B.
Winwick	Not in D.B.
Wiswell	Not in D.B.
Witetune	See Whittington
Withnell	Not in D.B.
Witingheham	See Whittingham
Witton	Not in D.B.
Woodplumpton, D. 6	*Pluntun* 301b 2nd entry
Woolston	Not in D.B.
Woolton, Little and Much, C. 11, C. 12	*Ulventune* 269b *Uuetone* 269b
Worsley	Not in D.B.
Worsthorne	Not in D.B.
Worston	Not in D.B.
Worthington	Not in D.B.
Wrightlington	Not in D.B.
Wyresdale	Not in D.B.
Yealand, D. 2	*Jalant* 332

ANONYMOUS HOLDINGS

None.

LEICESTERSHIRE—*LEDECESTRESCIRE*

Folios 230–237

MAP 25

Abegrave	See Prestgrave
Ab Kettleby, F. 2	*Chetelbi* 234b
Actorp	See Othorpe
Adelachestone	See Allexton
Aileston(e)	See Aylestone
Alctone	See Hallaton
Alebi(e)	See Welby
Alia Merdefelde	See South Marefield
Alia Petlinge	See Peatling Parva
Alia Scela	See Seal, Derby.
Allexton, G. 4	*Adelachestone* 230b, 236b *bis*
Alton, B. 3	*Heletone* 233
Andretesbie	See Enderby
Anelepe	See Wanlip
Anstey, D. 3	*Anstige* 232 *Hanstigie* 230
Anstige	See Anstey
Apleberie, *Aplebi*	See Appleby
Appleby Magna and Parva, A. 3	*Apleberie*, *Aplebi* 231b, 233b *Apleby* 274, Derby.
Arnesby, E. 5	*Erendesberie* 231 *Erendesbi* 235
Ascbi	See Ashby Folville
Ascebi	See Ashby de la Zouch
Asfordby, F. 2	*Esseberie* 236b *Osferdebie* 230b
Ashby de la Zouch, B. 2	*Ascebi* 233

Ashby Folville, F. 3	*Ascbi* 233, 236b
Ashby Magna, D. 5	*Essebi* 235, 236
Ashby Parva, D. 6	*Parva Essebi* 234
Aston Flamville	Not in D.B.
Atterton	Not in D.B.
Avederne	See Hathern
Avintone	See Evington
Aylestone, D. 4	*Aileston(e)* 231b *bis*, 237 *bis*
Badegrave	See Baggrave
Bageworde	See Bagworth
Baggrave, F. 3	*Badegrave* 230b
Bagworth, C. 3	*Bageworde* 237
Barcheberie, *Barchebi*	See Barkby
Barchestone	See Barkestone
Bardon	Not in D.B.
Bareswerde, *-worde*	See Husbands Bosworth
Barewelle	See Barwell
Barhou	See Barrow upon Soar
Barkby, E. 3	*Barcheberie* 233b *Barchebi* 236b
Barkestone, I. 2	*Barchestone* 233b
Barlestone, B. 4	*Berulvestone* 232b, 234
Barnesbi	See Barsby
Barrehorde	See Husbands Bosworth
Barrow upon Soar, D. 2	*Barhou* 230, 237
Barsby, F. 3	*Barnesbi* 230b, 236
Bartone	See Barton in the Beans
Barton in the Beans, B. 3	*Bartone* 233
Barwell, C. 4	*Barewelle* 231
Basurde	See Husbands Bosworth
Bebi	See Beeby
Beeby, E. 3	*Bebi* 231
Belgrave, D. 3	*Merdegrave* 230, 232, 236b
Belton	Not in D.B.
Belvoir	Not in D.B.
Berulvestone	See Barlestone
Bescaby	Not in D.B.
Betmeswel(le)	See Bitteswell
Bichesbie	See Bittesby
Bildestone	See Bilstone
Billesdon, F. 4	*Billesdone* 235b
Billesdone	See Billesdon
Bilstone, B. 4	*Bildestone* 231b
Birstall, D. 3	*Burstel(l)e* 230, 232, 232b
Bittesby, C. 6	*Bichesbie* 230b
Bitteswell, D. 6	*Betmeswel(le)* 231b, 235b
Blaby, D. 4	*Bladi* 237
Blackfordby	Not in D.B.
Bladestone	See Blaston
Bladi	See Blaby
Blaston, G. 5	*Bladestone* 236b *Bla(ue)stone* 230b, 233b
Bla(ue)stone	See Blaston
Boothorpe, A. 2	*Bortrod* 233b
Bortone	See Burton on the Wolds
Bortrod	See Boothorpe
Boseworde	See Market Bosworth
Bot(h)esford	See Bottesford
Bottesford, I. 1	*Bot(h)esford* 233b *bis*, 234 *Holesford* 234
Brandestorp, *Brandinestor*	See Bromkinsthorpe
Branston, G. 1	*Brantestone* 231
Brantestone	See Branston, Braunstone
Brascote, C. 4	*Brocardescote* 232
Braunstone, D. 4	*Brantestone* 232, 232b
Bredon on the Hill	Not in D.B.
Bringhurst	Not in D.B.
Brocardescote	See Brascote
Brochesbi	See Brooksby
Broctone	See Broughton Astley, Nether Broughton
Brohtone	See Broughton Astley

Bromkinsthorpe, D. 4	*Brandestorp* 235 *Brandinestor* 237 *Brunechinestorp* 232
Brooksby, E. 2	*Brochesbi* 236b, 237
Bro(s)tone	See Broughton Astley
Broughton Astley, D. 5	*Broctone* 236 *Brohtone* 230 *Bro(s)tone* 231b, 232b
Brunechinestorp	See Bromkinsthorpe
Brunestanestorp, *Brunestinestorp*	See Bruntingthorpe
Bruntingthorpe, D.5	*Brunestanestorp* 232 *Brunestinestorp* 230
Bucheminstre	See Buckminster
Buckminster, H. 2	*Bucheminstre* 231
Bugedone	See Great Bowden
Burbage, C. 5	*Burbece* 231
Burbece	See Burbage
Burc, *Burg*	See Burrough on the Hill
Burgo, G. 4	Lost in Launde, 230b, 235b
Burrough on the Hill, F. 3	*Burc*, *Burg* 233b, 236b *bis*
Burstel(l)e	See Birstall
Burtone	See Burton Lazars, Burton on the Wolds, Burton Overy
Burton Lazars, F. 2	*Burtone* 233b, 234b, 235b 1st entry
Burton on the Wolds, D. 2	*Bortone* 237 *Burtone* 235b 2nd entry, 236, 237
Burton Overy, E. 4	*Burtone* 230, 232
Bushby	Not in D.B.
Cacheuuorde	See Kegworth
Cadeby, B. 4	*Catebi* 232b
Caiham	See Keyham
Caitorp	See Keythorpe
Caldeuuelle	See Chadwell
Carbi	See Kirby Muxloe
Carletone, *Carlintone*	See Carlton Curlieu
Carlton (near Market Bosworth)	Not in D.B.
Carlton Curlieu, E. 5	*Carletone* 230b *Carlintone* 232
Castle Donington, C. 1	*Duni(n)tone* 231b, 237
Castone	See Coston
Catebi	See Cadeby
Catthorpe, D. 6	*Torp* 236
Cernelega	See Charley
Chadwell, F. 1	*Caldeuuelle* 230b
Charley, C. 3	*Cernelega* 237
Cheitorp	See Keythorpe
Chenemundescote	See Kimcote
Cherchebi	See Kirby Bellars, Kirby Muxloe, Kirkby Mallory
Cherebi	See Kirkby Mallory
Cherlintone	See Tur Langton
Chetelbi	See Ab Kettleby
Chiborne, *-burde*	See Kibworth
Chilcote, A. 3	*Cildecote* 272b, Derby.
Chirchebi	See Kirby Bellars
Chitebie	See Eye Kettleby
Chivelesworde	See Kilworth
Cilebi	See Kilby
Clachestone	See Long Clawson
Claibroc	See Claybrooke
Clanefelde	See Glenfield
Claybrooke Magna and Parva, C. 6	*Claibroc* 237
Cleveliorde	See Kilworth
Cliborne	See Kibworth
Closintone	See Knossington
Cnapetot	See Knaptoft
Cnihtetone	See Knighton
Cnip(e)tone	See Knipton
Cogeworde	See Kegworth
Cold Newton, F. 3	*Niwetone* 235b, 236b
Cold Overton, G. 3	*Ovretone* 236
Coleorton, B. 2	*Ovretone* 233b *bis*, 234b

Congerstone, B. 4	*Cuningestone* 233, 234b
Cosbi	See Cosby
Cosby, D. 5	*Cos(se)bi* 231b, 234, 236
Cosintone	See Cossington
Cossebi	See Cosby
Cossington, D. 3	*Cosintone* 237
Coston, G. 2	*Castone* 233
Cotes	Not in D.B.
Cotesbach, D. 6	*Cotesbece* 232b
Cotesbece	See Cotesbach
Cotes-de-Val, D. 6	*Toniscote* 231
Countesthorpe	Not in D.B.
Cranoe, F. 5	*Craueho* 230b *Craweho* 236b
Craueho, *Craweho*	See Cranoe
Crebre, *Crec*	See Croft
Crochestone	See South Croxton
Croft, C. 5	*Crebre* 231b *Crec* 232b
Crohtone	See Croxton Kerrial
Cropston	Not in D.B.
Croptone	See South Croxton
Croxton Kerrial, G. 1	*Crohtone* 230
Cuinburg	See Queniborough
Cuningestone	See Congerstone
Dadlington	Not in D.B.
Dalbi	See Dalby, Old Dalby
Dalby, Great and Little, F. 3	*Dalbi* 230, 231, 233b, 234b, 235b *bis*, 236
Dedigworde	See Thedding-worth
Deresford	See Desford
Desford, C. 4	*Deresford* 232 *bis* *Diresford* 230
Dexleia	See Dishley
Diresford	See Desford
Diseworth, C. 1	*Diwort* 235b
Dishley, C. 2	*Dexleia* 237 *Dislea* 230b
Dislea	See Dishley
Diwort	See Diseworth
Donington le Heath, B. 3	*Duntone* 236
Donisthorpe, A. 3	*Durandestorp* 233b, Leics.; 278, Derby.
Donitone	See Dunton Bassett
Draitone	See Fenny Drayton
Drayton (near Medbourne)	Not in D.B.
Duni(n)tone	See Castle Donington
Dunton Bassett, D. 5	*Donitone* 234
Duntone	See Donington le Heath
Durandestorp	See Donisthorpe
Earl Shilton, C. 4	*Sceltone* 230, 232 *bis*
East Langton	See Langton
East Norton, G. 4	*Nortone* 235, 235b
Eastwell, F. 1	*Est(e)welle* 235b, 236b
Eaton	Not in D.B.
Edmerestorp	See Edmondthorpe
Edmondthorpe, G. 2	*Edmerestorp* 233
Elmesthorpe	Not in D.B.
Elstede	See Halstead
Elvelege	Unid., 236
Elvestone	See Illston on the Hill
Enderby, D. 4	*Andretesbie* 230 *Endrebie* 232b
Endrebie	See Enderby
Erendesberie, *Erendesbi*	See Arnesby
Esmeditone	See Smeeton Westerby
Esseberie	See Asfordby
Essebi	See Ashby Magna
Essebi, *Parva*	See Ashby Parva
Estewelle	See Eastwell
Estone	See Great Easton
Estwelle	See Eastwell
Evington, E. 4	*Avintone* 232b, 234
Eye Kettleby, F. 2	*Chitebie* 235b
Fenny Drayton, B. 5	*Draitone* 231b

Flechenie, -nio	See Fleckney
Fleckney, E. 5	*Flechenie, -nio* 234b *bis*
Foston, D. 5	*Fostone* 235
Fostone	See Foston
Foxestone	See Foxton
Foxton, F. 5	*Fox(es)tone* 230b, 236
Foxtone	See Foxton
Fredebi	See Freeby
Freeby, G. 2	*Fredebi* 235b
Frel(l)esworde	See Frolesworth
Frisby (near Billesdon), F. 4	*Frisebi* 232b
Frisby on the Wreak, E. 2	*Frisebi(e)* 230b, 237 *bis*
Frisebi	See Frisby (near Billesdon), Frisby on the Wreak
Frisebie	See Frisby on the Wreak
Frolesworth, C. 5	*Frel(l)esworde* 231b, 232, 234, 236
Gaddesby, E. 3	*Gadesbi(e)* 230b, 236b *bis*, 237
Gadesbi(e)	See Gaddesby
Galbi	See Galby
Galby, E. 4	*Galbi* 230b, 232b
Garendon	Not in D.B.
Gerberie	See Ingarsby
Gilmorton, D. 6	*Mortone* 234
Glen	See Great Glen
Glenfield, D. 3	*Clanefelde* 232, 232b
Glooston, F. 5	*Glorstone* 236b
Glorstone	See Glooston
Glowesbi	See Lowesby
Gniptone	See Knipton
Goadby, F. 4	*Goutebi* 235b 1st entry
Goadby Marwood, F. 1	*Goltebi* 234b *Goutebi* 235b 2nd entry
Godmundelai	See Gumley
Godtorp	Unid., 235b
Goldsmith Grange formerly Ringoldthorpe, F. 1	*Ricoltorp* 236, 236b
Goltebi	See Goadby Marwood
Gopeshille	See Gopsall
Gopsall, B. 3	*Gopeshille* 233
Goutebi	See Goadby, Goadby Marwood
Great Bowden, F. 5	*Bugedone* 230b *bis*, 235b, 236
Great Dalby	See Dalby
Great Easton, G. 5	*Estone* 231
Great Glen, E. 4	*Glen* 232b
Great Stretton	See Stretton
Grimestone	See Grimston
Grimston, E. 2	*Grimestone* 230b, 234b
Grobi	See Groby
Groby, D. 3	*Grobi* 232
Gumley, E. 5	*Godmundelai* 234 *Gutmundeslea* 236
Gutmundeslea	See Gumley
Hadre	See Heather
Haliach	See Holyoaks
Hallaton, G. 5	*Alctone* 235b
Halstead, F. 4	*Elstede* 230b
Hanstigie	See Anstey
Harby, F. 1	*Herdebi* 233b *Hertebi* 234b
Harston, G. 1	*Herstan* 230
Hathern, C. 2	*Avederne* 237
Heather, B. 3	*Hadre* 236
Heletone	See Alton
Hemington	Not in D.B.
Herdebi	See Harby
Herstan	See Harston
Hertebi	See Harby
Higham on the Hill	Not in D.B.
Hinchelie	See Hinckley
Hinckley, B. 4	*Hinchelie* 231b
Hobie	See Hoby
Hoby, E. 2	*Hobie* 236
Hoches	See Hose
Hohtone	See Hoton, Houghton on the Hill

Holesford	See Bottesford
Holetone	See Hoton
Holewelle	See Holwell
Holwell, F. 1	*Holewelle* 231, 234b
Holyoaks, G. 5	*Haliach* 231
Horninghold, G. 4	*Horniwale* 233b
Horniwale	See Horninghold
Hose, F. 1	*Hoches* 233b
	Howes 235 *bis*, 237 *bis*
Hoton, D. 2	*Hohtone* 237
	Holetone 236b
Houghton on the Hill, E. 4	*Hohtone* 233
Howes	See Hose
Hugglescote	Not in D.B.
Humberstone, E. 3	*Humerstane* 232
Humerstane	See Humberstone
Huncote, C. 4	*Hunecote* 231b *bis*
Hunecote	See Huncote
Hungerton, E. 3	*Hungretone* 233b
Hungretone	See Hungerton
Husbands Bosworth, E. 6	*Bareswerde*, *-worde* 234, 235, 236
	Barrehorde 235
	Basurde 234
Ibestoche	See Ibstock
Ibstock, B. 3	*Ibestoche* 237
Illston on the Hill, F. 4	*Elvestone* 231, 232
	Nelvestone 230b, 234
Ingarsby, E. 4	*Gerberie* 232b
	Inuuaresbie 230
Inuuaresbie	See Ingarsby
Isley Walton	Not in D.B.
Kegworth, C. 1	*Cacheuuorde* 230
	Cogeworde 237
Keyham, E. 3	*Caiham* 230b
Keythorpe, F. 4	*Caitorp* 230b
	Cheitorp 235b
Kibworth Beauchamp and Harcourt, E. 5	*Chiborne* 230
	Chiburde 234b, 235
	Cliborne 234
Kilby, E. 5	*Cilebi* 236

Kilworth, North and South, D. 6, E. 6	*Chiveleswordc* 237
	Cleveliorde 234, 235
Kimcote, D. 6	*Chenemundescote* 231
King's Norton, E. 4	*Nortone* 230b
Kirby Bellars, F. 2	*Cherchebi* 235b
	Chirchebi 235b
Kirby Muxloe, C. 4	*Carbi* 235
	Cherchebi 231
Kirkby Mallory, C. 4	*Cher(ch)ebi* 232 *bis*, 232b
Knaptoft, E. 5	*Cnapetot* 231b
Knighton, D. 4	*Cnihtetone* 231
Knipton, G. 1	*Cnipetone* 230
	Gniptone 233b
Knossington, G. 3	*Closintone* 234b
	Nossitone 230b
Lachestone	See Laughton
Lagintone, *Langetone*	See Langton
Langley Priory	Not in D.B.
Langton, East and West, F. 5	*Lagintone* 230b
	Lang(e)tone 231, 232b
Langtone	See Langton
Laughton, E. 5	*Lachestone* 233b
Launde	Not in D.B.
Ledecestre	See Leicester
Leesthorpe, G. 3	*Luvestorp* 235b
Legham	Unid., 230
Legre	See Leire
Leicester, D. 4	*Ledecestre* 230, 230b, 232, 235
Leire, D. 5	*Legre* 231, 234, 234b
Lestone, *Letitone*	See Thurlaston
Lilinge	Unid., 235b
Lintone	See Linton, Derby.
Little Bowden, F. 6	*Bugedone* 223, N'hants.
Little Dalby	See Dalby
Little Stretton	See Stretton
Little Thorpe, D. 5	*Torp* 231b
Lobenho	See Lubenham
Lockington	Not in D.B.

Locteburne	See Loughborough
Loddington, G. 4	*Ludintone* 234b
Long Clawson, F. 1	*Clachestone* 233b, 235 *bis*, 237
Long Whatton	Not in D.B.
Loughborough, D. 2	*Locte-*, *Lucteburne* 230, 237 *bis*
Lowesby, F. 3	*Glowesbi* 236b
Lubanham	See Lubenham
Lubbesthorpe, D. 4	*Lupestorp* 235 *bis*
Lubeham	See Lubenham
Lubenham, F. 6	*Lobenho* 236 *Lubanham* 230b *Lubeham* 233b
Lucteburne	See Loughborough
Ludintone	See Loddington
Lupestorp	See Lubbesthorpe
Lutresurde	See Lutterworth
Lutterworth, D. 6	*Lutresurde* 236
Luvestorp	Sec Leesthorpe
Market Bosworth, B. 4	*Boseworde* 231b, 233
Market Harborough	Not in D.B.
Markfield, C. 3	*Merchenefeld* 236
Measham, A. 3	*Messeham* 272b, Derby.
Medbournc, G. 5	*Medburne* 230b *Metorne* 233b
Medburne	See Medbourne
Medeltone	See Melton Mowbray
Melton Mowbray, F. 2	*Medeltone* 235b *ter*
Menstretone	See Misterton
Merchenefeld	See Markfield
Merdefelde	See North Marefield
Merdefelde, Alia	See South Marefield
Merdegrave	See Belgrave
Mersitone	See Potters Marston
Metorne	See Medbourne
Ministone, *Minstretone*	See Misterton
Misterton, D. 6	*Menstretone* 235 *Ministone* 231 *Minstretone* 236
Mortone	See Gilmorton
Mountsorrel	Not in D.B.
Mowsley, E. 6	*Muselai* 235b, 236
Muselai	See Mowsley
Muston	Not in D.B.
Nailstone, B. 3	*Neulebi* 232b
Nanpanton	Not in D.B.
Narborough	Not in D.B.
Nelvestone	See Illston on the Hill
Nether Broughton, E. 1	*Broctone* 230
Netone	Unid., 236b
Neubold	See Newbold Saucey
Neulebi	See Nailstone
Neutone	See Newton Burgoland, Newton Harcourt
Nevill Holt	Not in D.B.
Newbold (near Knossington)	Not in D.B.
Newbold Folville, F. 3	*Niwebold* 233 2nd entry, 236b
Newbold Saucey, F. 3	*Neubold* 233b
Newbold Verdon, C. 4	*Niwebold* 232, 233 1st entry
Newton Burgoland, B. 3	*Neutone* 233b
Newton Harcourt, E. 5	*Neutone* 234 *Niwetone* 230
Newton Linford	Not in D.B.
Niwebold	See Newbold Folville, Newbold Verdon
Niwetone	See Cold Newton, Newton Harcourt
North Kilworth	See Kilworth
North Marefield, F. 3	*Merdefelde* 230b
Nortone	See East Norton, King's Norton, Norton-juxta-Twycross

Norton-juxta-Twycross, A. 3	*Nortone* 231b
Noseley, F. 4	*Noveslei* 232
Nossitone	See Knossington
Noveslei	See Noseley
Oadby, E. 4	*Oldebi* 232b, 236, 236b
Oakthorpe, A. 3	*Achetorp* 278, Derby.
Ocheham	See Oakham, Rutland
Odestone	See Odstone
Odstone, B. 3	*Odestone* 234b
Old Dalby, E. 1	*Dalbi* 235
Oldebi	See Oadby
Orton on the Hill, A. 4	*Wortone* 233
Osbaston, B. 4	*Sbernestun* 235
Osferdebie	See Asfordby
Osgathorpe, B. 2	*Osgodtorp* 233b
Osgodtorp	See Osgathorpe
Osulvestone	See Owston
Othorpe, F. 5	*Actorp* 236
Ovretone	See Cold Overton, Coleorton
Owston, F. 3	*Osulvestone* 236b
Pachintone	See Packington
Packington, B. 3	*Pachintone* 231
Parva Essebi	See Ashby Parva
Peatling Magna, D. 5	*Petlinge* 231, 234, 236, 237
Peatling Parva, D. 5	*Alia Petlinge* 232b, 236b
Pechintone	See Peckleton
Peckleton, C. 4	*Pechintone* 232
Petlinge	See Peatling Magna
Petlinge, Alia	See Peatling Parva
Pichewelle	See Pickwell
Pickwell, G. 3	*Pichewelle* 230, 235b *quater*
Plotelei	Unid., 237
Plungar	Not in D.B.
Pontenei	See Poultney
Potters Marston, C. 5	*Mersitone* 231
Poultney, D. 6	*Pontenei* 231
Prestewald, -wolde	See Prestwold
Prestgrave, G. 5	*Abegrave* 230b
Prestwold, D. 2	*Prestewald, -wolde* 236, 237
Primethorpe, C. 5	*Torp* 234b
Quenby, F. 3	*Queneberie* 233b
Queneberie	See Quenby
Queniborough, E. 3	*Cuinburg* 235b
Quorndon	Not in D.B.
Radeclive	See Ratcliffe on the Wreak
Ragdale, E. 2	*Ragendel(e)* 234b *bis*
Ragendel(e)	See Ragdale
Ratby, C. 4	*Rotebie* 232
Ratcliffe Culey, A. 4	*Redeclive* 234b
Ratcliffe on the Wreak, E. 3	*Radeclive* 234b
Ravenestorp	See Ravenstone
Ravenstone, B. 3	*Ravenestorp* 235 *Ravenestun* 278, Derby.
Rearsby, E. 3	*Re(d)resbi* 234b, 236, 237
Redebi	See Rotherby
Redeclive	See Ratcliffe Culey
Redmelde	See Redmile
Redmile, I. 2	*Redmelde* 233b
Re(d)resbi	See Rearsby
Ricoltorp	See Goldsmith Grange formerly Ringoldthorpe
Rodolei	See Rothley
Rolleston, F. 4	*Rovestone* 235b
Rotebie	See Ratby
Rotherby, E. 2	*Redebi* 237
Rothley, D. 3	*Rodolei* 230
Rovestone	See Rolleston
Sacrestone	See Shackerstone
Saddington, E. 5	*Sadin-, Setintone* 230, 230b
Sadintone	See Saddington
Saltby, G. 1	*Saltebi* 234b
Saltebi	See Saltby

San(c)tone	See Shangton
Sapcote, C. 5	*Sape-*, *Scepecote* 231b, 232, 232b
Sapecote	See Sapcote
Satgrave	See Seagrave
Sawelle	See Shawell
Saxby, G. 2	*Saxebi* 233, 236b
Saxebi	See Saxby
Saxelbie	See Saxelby
Saxelby, F. 2	*Saxelbie* 230b
Sbernestun	See Osbaston
Scaldeford	See Scalford
Scalford, F. 1	*Scaldeford* 234b, 236b
Scela, *Alia Scela*	See Seal, Derby.
Sceltone	See Earl Shilton
Sceneford	See Sharnford
Scenton	See Shenton
Scepa	See Sheepy
Scepecote	See Sapcote
Scepehe	See Sheepy
Scepe(s)hefde	See Shepshed
Scerneford(e)	See Sharnford
Sciftitone	See Skeffington
Scopestone	See Swepstone
Scrapentot	See Scraptoft
Scraptoft, E. 4	*Scrapentot* 231
Seagrave, E. 2	*Satgrave* 233 *Se(t)grave* 230b, 234b, 237
Seglebi	See Sileby
Segrave	See Seagrave
Sela	See Seal, Derby.
Seoldesberie	See Shoby
Setgrave	See Seagrave
Setintone	See Saddington
Seuesbi	See Shearsby
Sewesten	See Sewstern
Sewstern, H. 2	*Sewesten* 235b
Shackerstone, B. 3	*Sacrestone* 234b
Shangton, F. 5	*San(c)tone* 230b, 232b, 234
Sharnford, C. 5	*Sceneford* 231 *Scerneford(e)* 231, 232, 236, 236b
Shawell, D. 6	*Sawelle* 237
Shearsby, E. 5	*Seuesbi* 232b *Sue(ue)sbi* 231, 231b
Sheepy Magna and Parva, A. 4	*Scepa* 233 *Scepehe* 232b
Shenton, B. 4	*Scentone* 231b, 233, 234
Shepshed, C. 2	*Scepe(s)hefde* 230, 230b, 233
Shoby, E. 2	*Seoldesberie* 231b
Sibetesdone	See Sibson
Sibson, B. 4	*Sibetesdone* 231b
Siglebi, *Siglesbie*	See Sileby
Sileby, D. 2	*Seglebi* 230b *Siglebi* 233, 237 *Siglesbie* 230
Sistenebi	See Sysonby
Sitestone	See Syston
Sixtenebi	See Sysonby
Skeffington, F. 4	*Sciftitone* 230b
Slachestone, *Slagestone*	See Slawston
Slawston, F. 5	*Slachestone* 234 *Slagestone* 234
Smeeton Westerby, E. 5	*Esmeditone* 234b *Smi(te)tone* 230b, 232 *bis*
Smi(te)tone	See Smeeton Westerby
Smockington, C. 5	*Snochantone* 233
Snarchetone	See Snarestone
Snarestone, A. 3	*Snarchetone* 234b
Snochantone	See Smockington
Somerby, F. 3	*Sumerdeberie* 235 *Sumerlidebie* 230b *Summerdebi(e)* 233b, 235b
South Croxton, E. 3	*Crochestone* 231 *Croptone* 233b
South Kilworth	See Kilworth
South Marefield, F. 3	*Alia Merdefelde* 230b
Sprotone	See Sproxton
Sproxton, G. 1	*Sprotone* 235, 235b, 236b
Stachedirne, *Stachetone*	See Stathern
Stanford	See Stanford on Avon, N'hants.
Stantone	See Stanton under Bardon, Staunton Harold,

Stantone cont.	Stoney Stanton, Stonton Wyville
Stanton under Bardon, C. 3	*Stantone* 235b
Stapeford	See Stapleford
Stapleford, G. 2	*Stapeford* 233 *bis*
Stapleton, C. 4	*Stapletone* 231 *bis*, 232
Stapletone	See Stapleton
Stathern, F. 1	*Stachedirne* 234 *Stachetone* 235b
Staunton Harold, B. 2	*Stantone* 233
Stockerston, G. 4	*Stoctone* 232, 236b *Stoctun* 291b, Notts.
Stoctone	See Stockerston, Stoughton
Stoke Golding	Not in D.B.
Stonesby, G. 1	*Stovenebi* 235
Stoney Stanton, C. 5	*Stantone* 234b
Stonton Wyville, F. 5	*Stantone* 232b, 236b
Stormeorde, *Stormode*	See Stormsworth
Stormsworth, D. 6	*Stormeorde* 235 *Stormode* 235b
Stotone	See Stoughton
Stoughton, E. 4	*Sto(c)tone* 230, 232b
Stovenebi	See Stonesby
Stratone	See Stretton, Great and Little
Stretone	See Stretton en le Field
Stretton, Great and Little, E. 4	*Stratone* 230b
Stretton en le Field, A. 3	*Stretone* 233b *Streitun* 274, Derby.
Sue(ue)sbi	See Shearsby
Suine(s)ford, *Suinford*	See Swinford
Sumerdeberie, *Sumerlidebie*, *Summerdebi(e)*	See Somerby
Sutone	See Sutton Cheney, Sutton in the Elms

Sutton Cheney, B. 4	*Sutone* 231 1st entry, 232b
Sutton in the Elms, C. 5	*Sutone* 231 2nd entry, 231b, 234b
Swannington	Not in D.B.
Swepstone, B. 3	*Scopestone* 233b
Swinford, D. 6	*Suine(s)ford* 231, 234 *Suinford* 231, 231b, 232, 234, 235b
Swithland	Not in D.B.
Sysonby, F. 2	*Sist-*, *Sixtenebi* 235b *bis*, 236
Syston, E. 3	*Sitestone* 232b
Taiworde	See Twyford
Tedi(nges)worde	See Theddingworth
Terlintone	See Tur Langton
Tevlingorde	See Theddingworth
Theddingworth, E. 6	*Dedigworde* 236b *Tedi(nges)worde* 235b, 237 *Tevlingorde* 231b *bis*
Thornton	Not in D.B.
Thorpe Acre, C. 2	*Torp* 230, 230b
Thorpe Arnold, F. 2	*Torp* 233
Thorpe Langton, F. 5	*Torp* 232, 234 *bis*
Thorpe Satchville	Not in D.B.
Thringstone, B. 2	*Trangesbi*, *-by* 272b, 278, Derby.
Thrussington, E. 2	*Turstanestone* 235
Thurcaston, D. 3	*Turchi(te)lestone* 230, 232, 235b *ter*
Thurlaston, C. 4	*Lestone* 232 *Letitone* 230
Thurmaston, E. 3	*Turmodestone* 232, 232b
Thurnby	Not in D.B.
Tiletone, *Tillintone*	See Tilton
Tilton, F. 4	*Tiletone* 230b, 235 *Tillintone* 230b
Tochebi	See Tugby
Tonge, B. 2	*Tunge* 233
Toniscote	See Cotes-de-Val

Torp	See Catthorpe, Little Thorpe, Primethorpe, Thorpe Acre, Thorpe Arnold, Thorpe Langton
Tugby, F. 4	*Tochebi* 230b
Tuicros	See Twycross
Tuiuorde	See Twyford
Tunge	See Tonge
Turchi(te)lestone	See Thurcaston
Tur Langton, F. 5	*Cherlintone* 230 *Terlintone* 230b
Turmodestone	See Thurmaston
Turstanestone	See Thrussington
Twycross, A. 4	*Tuicros* 233
Twyford, F. 3	*Taiworde* 232b *Tuiuorde* 230b
Udecote	See Woodcote
Ulestorp	See Ullesthorpe
Ullesthorpe, C. 6	*Ulestorp* 235b
Ulverscroft	Not in D.B.
Upton	Not in D.B.
Wadford	See Watford, N'hants.
Walcote, D. 6	*Walecote* 231, 234
Walecote	See Walcote
Wal(end)eham	See Welham
Waletone	See Walton on the Wolds
Waltham on the Wolds, G. 1	*Waltham* 233, 235
Walton (near Kimcote), D. 6	*Waltone* 231b
Waltone	See Walton (near Kimcote)
Walton on the Wolds, D. 2	*Waletone* 231b
Wanlip, D. 3	*Anelepe* 231b
Wartnaby, F. 2	*Worcnodebie* 230b
Welby, F. 2	*Alebi(e)* 235b, 236, 236b *bis*
Weleham	See Welham
Welham, F. 5	*Waleham* 230b *Walendeham* 234 *Weleham* 236b
Werdebi	See Wyfordby
Werditone	See Worthington
Westham	See Whetstone
West Langton	See Langton
Weston, A. 4	*Westone* 235
Westone	See Weston
Wetberga, *Wetberge*	See Whatborough
Whatborough, F. 3	*Wetberga*, *Wetberge* 230b *bis*
Whetstone, D. 4	*Westham* 237
Whitwick, C. 2	*Witewic* 233
Wicestan	See Wigston Parva
Wiche	See Wycomb
Wichingestone	See Wigston Magna
Wicoc, *Wicote*	See Withcote
Wigston Magna, E. 4	*Wichingestone* 230, 232, 236b
Wigston Parva, C. 5	*Wicestan* 231
Wil(ech)ebi	See Willoughby Waterless
Wilges	See Willowes
Willesley, A. 3	*Wiuleslei(e)* 272b, 274, Derby.
Willoughby Waterless, D. 5	*Wil(ech)ebi* 232b, 236
Willowes, E. 2	*Wilges* 234b
Wimundesham	See Wymondham
Wimundeswald, *-wal(l)e*	See Wymeswold
Windesers	Unid., 233b
Wistanestou	See Wistow
Wistow, E. 5	*Wistanestou* 234b *Witenesto* 235
Witenesto	See Wistow
Witewic	See Whitwick
Withcote, G. 4	*Wicoc* 235b *Wicote* 235
Witherley	Not in D.B.
Witmeham	See Wymondham
Wivordebie	See Wyfordby
Woodcote, B. 2	*Udecote* 233b
Woodhouse	Not in D.B.
Woodthorpe	Not in D.B.
Worcnodebie	See Wartnaby
Wordebi	See Wyfordby
Worthington, B. 2	*Werditone* 233

Wortone	See Orton on the Hill
Wycomb, F. 1	*Wiche* 230b
Wyfordby, G. 2	*Werdebi* 233 *Wivordebie* 234b *Wordebi* 235b
Wymeswold, D. 1	*Wimundeswald* 234b *Wimindeswal(l)e* 232b, 236, 236b
Wymondham, G. 2	*Wimundesham* 234b *Witmeham* 233

ANONYMOUS HOLDINGS

No place-names appear in the following five entries, and it is possible that some (or even all) of these refer to holdings at places not named elsewhere in Domesday Book:

Osmund and Roger (from Robert de Todeni), 4 carucates in Framland wapentake, 234.
Hugh (from Robert de Buci), 3½ carucates less one virgate in Guthlaxton wapentake, 234.
Lanbert (from Robert de Buci), 3 carucates and ¼ virgate in Guthlaxton wapentake, 234.
Alsi (from Robert de Buci), 1½ carucates and ¼ virgate in Guthlaxton wapentake, 234.
Roger Busli (from Earl Hugh), one carucate in ? Guthlaxton wapentake, 237.

LINCOLNSHIRE — *LINCOLESCIRE*

Folios 336–371b, 375–377b

MAPS 30–31, 32

Abi	See Aby
Aburne	See Aubourn, Habrough
Aby, I. 7	*Abi* 343 *bis*, 349
Achelei	See Eagle
Achesbi	See Ashby (near Fenby)
Acheseia	See Haxey
Aclei, -ley	See Eagle
Addlethorpe, K. 8	*Ardulvetorp* 370b *Hardetorp* 348b *Herde(r)torp* 339b, 348b, 355, 360 *ter*, 363b *Heretorp* 341
Adelinctune, Adelingetone	See Allington
Adewelle, E. 14	Lost in Manthorpe 345b
Adredebi	See Bag Enderby
Adulvesbi	See Autby
Aestorp	See Aisthorpe
Agetorne	See Hackthorn
Agetorp	See Authorpe
Aig(he)lestorp	See Elsthorpe
Ailby, I. 7	*Alebi* 343 *Halebi* 339b
Aisby (in Corringham), C. 5	*Asebi, -by* 338, 338b
Aisby (in Heydour), E. 11	*Asebi* 357b
Aisthorpe, D. 6	*Aestorp* 354b *Estorp* 371
Akeley	See Eagle
Alchebarge	See Alkborough
Alchinton	See Elkington
Aldulvebi	See Audleby, Autby
Alebi	See Ailby

Alesbi	See Aylesby
Aletorp	See Althorpe
Alfgare	See Algarkirk
Alford, J. 7	*Alforde* 355b, 370
Alforde	See Alford
Algarkirk, H. 12	*Alfgare* 346b, 348b
Alia Pamtone	See Little Ponton
Alia Tisteltune	See Thistleton, Rutland
Alkborough, C. 2	*Alchebarge* 346, 350b
Allington, C. 11	*Adelinctune* 353b, 368 *Adelingetone* 353b
Altera Brune	See Burnham, High and Low
Altera Lund	See Craizelound and Eastlound
Altera Rase	See Rasen, Market, Middle and West
Altera Ravenedale	See Ravendale
Altera Rosbi	See Rauceby
Altera Torp	See Southorpe (in Northorpe)
Althorpe, C. 3	*Aletorp* 369
Alving(e)ham	See Alvingham
Alvingham, I. 5	*Alving(e)ham* 339, 343, 358 *bis*, 364
Alwolde(s)bi	See Autby
Amcotts, C. 3	*Amecotes* 369b, 376b
Amecotes	See Amcotts
Amuinc	See Anwick
Ancaster	Not in D.B.
Anderby	Not in D.B.
Andrebi	See Bag Enderby
Anwick, F. 10	*Amuinc* 369b *Haniuuic* 360b
Apelei(a)	See Apley
Aplebi	See Appleby
Apley, F. 7	*Apelei(a)* 354, 375b
Appleby, D. 2	*Aplebi* 346, 352b, 354b
Archintone	See Elkington
Ardulvetorp	See Addlethorpe
Aresbi	See Owersby
Aschebi	See Ashby (in Bottesford), Ashby (near Fenby), Ashby by Partney, Ashby de la Launde, Ashby Puerorum, West Ashby
Asebi	See Aisby (in Corringham), Aisby (in Heydour)
Aseby	See Aisby (in Corringham)
Asedebi	See Oasby
Asgarby (near Sleaford)	Not in D.B.
Asgarby (near Spilsby), H. 8	*Asgerebi* 351
Asgerebi	See Asgarby (near Spilsby)
Ashby (in Bottesford), D. 3	*Aschebi* 338 *bis*, 338b *bis*, 346
Ashby (near Fenby), G. 4	*Achesbi* 367 *Aschebi* 343 *bis* 3rd and 4th entries, 347
Ashby by Partney, I. 8	*Aschebi* 341, 349, 375b
Ashby de la Launde, E. 9	*Aschebi* 357b, 363
Ashby Puerorum, H. 7	*Aschebi* 343 *bis* 1st and 2nd entries, 359b
Aslachebi	See Aslackby
Aslackby, F. 12	*Aslachebi* 353 *bis*, 356, 364b, 376b
Asterby, H. 7	*Estrebi* 351
Asuuardebi	See Aswarby
Aswarby, E. 11	*Asuuardebi* 356, 367b *Wardebi* 355b
Aswardby	Not in D.B.
Atterby	Not in D.B.
Aubourn, D. 8	*Aburne* 353, 353b
Audleby, F. 4	*Aldulvebi* 342 *bis*, 352
Aunby	Not in D.B.
Aunsby, E. 11	*Ounesbi* 363b
Autby, H. 4	*Adulvesbi* 365 *bis* *Aldulvebi* 357b *Alwolde(s)bi* 342, 342b, 356

Place	Domesday Book form and folio
Boothby Graffoe, D. 9	*Bodebi* 337b, 358b
Boothby Pagnall, D. 12	*Bodebi* 355b, 368
Borotona, *Bortone*	See Gate Burton
Boston	Not in D.B.
Bottesford, D. 3	*Bu(d)lesforde* 338, 338b, 359
Boultham, D. 8	*Buletham* 368b
Bourne, F. 13	*Brune* 351b, 358b *bis*, 364b *ter*, 368b, 370, 377
Bowthorpe, E. 14	*Bergestorp* 345b *Bredestorp* 360b
Braceborough, F. 14	*Braseborg* 355 *Breseburc*, *-burg* 353, 368b
Bracebridge, D. 8	*Brachebrige* 343b *Bragebruge* 352b
Braceby, E. 12	*Bre(i)zbi* 337b, 338, 341, 351b
Brachebrige	See Bracebridge
Brachelesbi	See Brocklesby
Brachenberg	See Brackenborough
Brackenborough, H. 5	*Brachenberg* 358
Bradley, G. 3	*Bredelou* 343
Bragebruge	See Bracebridge
Brampton, C. 6	*Brantune* 344 *bis*
Brandon, D. 10	*Brandune* 356, 363
Brandune	See Brandon
Bransby, D. 7	*Branzbi* 352b *bis*
Branston, E. 8	*Branztone*, *-tun(e)* 361 *ter*, 376b
Brant Broughton, D. 9	*Burtune* 347b
Brantune	See Brampton
Branzbi	See Bransby
Branzewelle	See Brauncewell
Branztone, *-tun(e)*	See Branston
Branzuic	Unid., 352b
Braseborg	See Braceborough
Brattleby, D. 6	*Brotulbi* 340b, 354b, 356b
Bratoft, J. 8	*Bre(ie)toft* 349, 370b
Brauncewell, E. 10	*Branzewelle* 358b, 369b

Place	Domesday Book form and folio
Bredelou	See Bradley
Bredestorp	See Bowthorpe
Breietoft	See Bratoft
Breizbi	See Braceby
Breseburc, *-burg*	See Braceborough
Bretoft	See Bratoft
Brezbi	See Braceby
Brige(s)lai	See Brigsley
Brigg	Not in D.B.
Brigsley, G. 4	*Brige(s)lai* 343, 347b, 367
Brincle	See Brinkhill
Brinkhill, I. 7	*Brincle* 349
Brochelesbi	See Brocklesby
Brocklesby, F. 3	*Brachelesbi* 340b *Brochelesbi* 350b, 358b, 361b, 362, 375b
Broctone	See Broughton
Brotulbi	See Brattleby
Broughton, D. 3	*Bertone* 362b, 365 *Broctone* 376
Broxholme, D. 7	*Broxholme* 352b
Brumby, C. 3	*Brunebi* 338, 338b
Brune	See Bourne; Burnham (in Thornton Curtis); Burnham, High and Low
Brune, *Altera*	See Burnham, High and Low
Brunebi	See Brumby
Brunetorp	See Bonthorpe
Buchehale	See Bucknall
Buckland formerly Langton Thorpe, G. 8	*Torp* 339, 342b, 375
Bucknall, G. 8	*Buchehale* 346b, 349b, 356b
Budlesforde	See Bottesford
Bulby, E. 13	*Bolebi* 358, 368
Bulesforde	See Bottesford
Buletham	See Boultham
Bullington, F. 7	*Bolintone* 340b, 349b, 351, 354, 375b
Bundebi	See Bonby
Burch	See Burgh in the Marsh

Burg	See Burgh (in Evedon), Burgh in the Marsh, Burgh on Bain. See also Peterborough, N'hants.
Burgelai	See Burley, Rutland
Burgh (in Evedon), F. 10	*Burg* 370 *ter*, 371
Burgh in the Marsh, J. 8	*Burch* 348b *Burg* 355, 359b, 360 *quin*, 363b
Burgh on Bain, G. 6	*Burg* 362b
Burgrede	See Burreth
Burnham (in Thornton Curtis), E. 2	*Brune* 354, 362
Burnham, High and Low, B. 4	*Altera Brune* 369 *Brune* 369
Burreth, F. 8	*Burgrede* 342b, 351, 364b
Burringham	Not in D.B.
Burtoft, H. 12	*Burtoft* 346b
Burton	See Burton (near Lincoln), Burton Pedwardine
Burton (near Lincoln), D. 7	*Burton(e)* 344, 352b, 354b, 368b, 370b, 376
Burton Coggles, D. 13	*Bertone, -tune* 351b, 357b, 361, 362b, 376b
Burtone	See Burton (near Lincoln), Burton upon Stather
Burton Pedwardine, F. 11	*Burton, -tun* 356, 367b
Burton upon Stather, C. 2	*Burtone* 338b
Burtun	See Burton Pedwardine
Burtune	See Brant Broughton
Buruelle	See Burwell
Burwell, I. 7	*Buruelle* 366b, 375
Buslingthorpe, E. 6	*Esetorp* 352b
Butiate	See Butyate

Butrewic	See West Butterwick
Butruic	See Butterwick (near Freiston)
Butterwick (near Freiston), I. 10	*Butruic* 367b
Butyate, F. 7	*Butiate* 363b
Bytham, Castle and Little, E. 14	*Bi(n)tham* 345b, 360b, 366, 368b, 376b *bis* *Westbitham* 360b *bis*, 366
Cabourne, F. 4	*Caburne* 350b, 353b *bis*, 356 *ter*, 357b, 358, 365
Caburne	See Cabourne
Cadebi	See North Cadeby
Cadinton(e), Caditon	See Keddington
Cadney, E. 4	*Catenai* 338b, 352 *Catenase* 347 *bis*
Caenby, E. 5	*Couenebi* 344
Caistor, F. 4	*Castre* 338b, 357b, 375b
Calceby, I. 7	*Calesbi* 341b, 349 *bis*
Calcethorpe, G. 5	*Torp* 358 *bis*
Calchewelle	See Cawkwell
Caldecote	See Collow formerly Calcote
Cale	See West Keal
Calesbi	See Calceby
Caletorp	See Cawthorpe
Calnodesbi	See Candlesby
Came(s)lingeham	See Cammeringham
Cammeringham, D. 6	*Came(s)lingeham* 356b, 365
Candlesby, J. 8	*Calnodesbi* 348b, 355, 360, 370b
Can(eu)uic	See Canwick
Canwick, D. 8	*Can(eu)uic* 343b *bis*, 344b, 352b, 362, 370b, 377
Carlby, E. 14	*Carlebi* 344b, 355, 368b
Carlebi	See Carlby
Carlentone, -tun	See Carlton, Middle and South
Carleton	See Little Carlton

Carletone	See Carlton, Middle and South; Little Carlton
Carletun	See Carlton Scroop
Carletune	See Carlton, Middle and South; Carlton le Moorland, Carlton Scroop
Carlton, Middle and South, D. 7	*Carlentone*, *-tun* 342, 357 *Carletone*, *-tune* 354b, 362, 370b, 376
Carlton le Moorland, D. 9	*Carletune* 360b
Carlton Scroop, D. 11	*Carletun(e)* 347b, 351b, 377 *bis*
Carltorp	See Caythorpe
Carrington	Not in D.B.
Caschingetorp	See Casthorpe
Casewick, F. 15	*Casuic* 355, 358, 366b, 376b
Casthorpe, C. 12	*Caschingetorp* 368 *Chaschin(ge)torp* 368, 368b, 377 *bis* *Kaschingetorp* 343b
Castle Bytham	See Bytham
Castlethorpe, D. 3	*Castorp* 365
Castorp	See Castlethorpe
Castre	See Caistor
Casuic	See Casewick
Catebi	See South Cadeby
Catenai, *Catenase*	See Cadney
Catorp	See Caythorpe
Cawkwell, H. 6	*Calchewelle* 350b, 361b
Cawthorpe, F. 13	*Caletorp* 364b *bis*
Caythorpe, D. 10	*Ca(rl)torp* 363 *bis*, 377
Ceila	See Cheal
Chaschin(ge)torp	See Casthorpe
Cheal, G. 12	*Ceila* 344b
Checftesbi	See Kexby
Cheilestorne	See Kelstern
Chelebi	See Keelby, Kelby
Chelestorne, *-turne*	See Kelstern
Chelsi	See North Kelsey

Chelvingeholm, *Chelvingehou*, *Chelvingholme*	See Killingholme
Chenebi	See Kingerby
Cheneide	See Knaith
Cherchebi	See East Kirkby, Kirkby Green, Kirkby la Thorpe, Kirkby on Bain, Kirkby Underwood
Cherchetune	See Kirton (in Holland)
Chernitone	See Kirmington
Cherry Willingham, E. 7	*Gullingham* 345 *Ulingeham* 344b *Wilingeham* 354b *ter*
Chetelbi	See Kettleby
Chetelesbi	See Ketsby
Cheuremont	See Kirmond le Mire
Chevelestune	See Gelston
Chilebi	See Keelby
Chillebi	See Kelby
Chime	See South Kyme
Chinetorp	See Kingthorpe
Chirchebi	See Kirkby la Thorpe, Kirkby on Bain
Chircheton(e)	See Kirton in Lindsey
Chirchetune	See Kirton (in Holland)
Chisebi	See Keisby
Circeton	See Kirton in Lindsey
Clachesbi	See Claxby (near Normanby le Wold), Claxby (near Welton le Marsh), Claxby Pluckacre
Clactorp	See Claythorpe
Claipol	See Claypole
Clasbi	See Claxby Pluckacre
Claxby (near Normanby le Wold), F. 5	*Clachesbi* 348b, 351b, 355 *bis*, 356b

Claxby (near Welton le Marsh), J. 7	*Clachesbi* 350 *bis*, 359, 360b, 361b, 365, 376
Claxby Pluckacre, H. 8	*Clachesbi* 349, 359b *Clasbi* 359b
Claypole, C. 10	*Claipol* 343b, 370
Claythorpe, I. 7	*Clactorp* 349, 375
Cleatham, D. 4	*Cletham* 342, 346 *ter*, 359, 371
Clee, H. 3	*Cleia* 339b, 362b *bis*, 343, 350
Cleia	See Clee
Cletham	See Cleatham
Clisbi	See Clixby
Clixby, F. 4	*Clisbi* 338b
Coates (near Stow), D. 6	*Cotes* 342, 344, 352b, 357, 359
Cockerington, North and South, I. 5	*Cocrinton(e)* 343 *bis*, 357, 358, 364 *bis* *Crochinton* 341
Cocrinton(e)	See Cockerington
Colchesbi	See Goulceby
Cold Hanworth, E. 6	*Haneurde* 352b, 356b *Haneworde* 359
Colebi	See Coleby (near Boothby Graffoe), Coleby (in West Halton)
Coleby (near Boothby Graffoe), D. 9	*Colebi, -by* 337b *bis*, 362, 367
Coleby (in West Halton), D. 2	*Colebi* 349, 362b
Colesi	See South Kelsey
Colsterworth, D. 13	*Colsteuorde* 371 *Colstewrde* 340
Colsteuorde, Colstewrde	See Colsterworth
Collow formerly Calcote, F. 6	*Caldecote* 362b
Combreuorde	See Cumberworth
Conesby, North and South, C. 3	*Cunesbi* 349, 362 *bis*
Coningsby, G. 9	*Cuningesbi* 339, 349b, 360b, 363b, 370b, 375b
Conisholme	Not in D.B.
Copelade, Copolade	See Whaplode
Corbi, -by	See Corby
Corby, E. 13	*Corbi, -by* 344b *bis*, 371
Coring(e)ham	See Corringham
Corninctone, -tun(e), Cornintone	See Quarrington
Corringham, C. 5	*Coring(e)ham* 338 *bis*, 338b *bis*, 352b
Coteland, F. 10	*Coteland* 346b, 369b
Cotes	See Coates (near Stow), Coton, Great Coates
Coton, F. 3	*Cotes* 360 *ter*
Couenebi	See Caenby
Counthorpe, E. 13	*Cudetorp* 360b, 368b
Covenham St Bartholomew, St Mary, H. 5	*Covenham* 340b *ter*, 354 *bis*
Cowbit	Not in D.B.
Craiselound and Eastlound, B. 4	*Altera Lund* 369 *Lund* 369
Cranewelle	See Cranwell
Cranwell, E. 10	*Cranewelle* 346b, 355, 355b
Creeton, E. 13	*Cretone, -tun(e)* 358, 366, 368b *ter*, 371
Cretone, -tun(e)	See Creeton
Crocestone, Crochestone, Crochestune	See Croxton
Crochinton	See Cockerington
Crocsbi	See Croxby
Croft, J. 8	*Croft* 355b
Croiland	See Crowland
Cropesbi	See Crosby
Crosbi	See Croxby
Crosby, C. 3	*Cropesbi* 349, 362
Crowland, G. 15	*Croiland* 346b
Crowle, B. 3	*Crul(e)* 350b, 369b *ter*
Croxby, G. 4	*Cro(c)sbi* 350, 353, 361b *bis*, 366 *bis*, 376
Croxton, F. 3	*Crocestone* 352b, 356 *bis*

/over

Croxton cont.	*Crochestone, -tune* 338b, 344
Crul(e)	See Crowle
Cucualt	See Cuxwold
Cudetorp	See Counthorpe
Culverthorpe, E. 11	*Torp* 355
Cumberworth, J. 7	*Combreuorde* 348b, 364, 375
Cunesbi	See Conesby
Cuningesbi	See Coningsby
Cuxwold, G. 4	*Cucualt* 339b, 350b, 353b, 356, 357b *bis*, 358, 365, 371, 376 *bis*
Dalbi	See Dalby
Dalby, I. 8	*Dalbi* 349 *bis*
Dalderby	Not in D.B.
Darby, C. 2	*Derbi* 338b
Deeping St James, F. 15	*Depinge* 366 *Estdeping(e)* 358, 366, 376b
Delbebi, Dembelbi	See Dembleby
Dembleby, E. 11	*Delbebi* 357 *Dembelbi* 367b *Denbelbi* 355b
Denbelbi	See Dembleby
Denton, C. 12	*Dentone, -tune* 337b, 338, 353, 368b
Dentone, -tune	See Denton
Depinge	See Deeping St James
Derbi	See Darby
Derintone	See Dorrington
Dexthorpe, I. 7	*Dr(e)istorp* 349, 360
Dic	See Dyke
Dicbi	See Digby
Digby, F. 9	*Dicbi* 369b
Doddington, D. 8	*Dodinctone* 346, 377 *bis* *Dodintune* 370 *bis*, 377 *bis*
Dodinctone	See Doddington
Dodintone	See Dry Doddington
Dodintune	See Doddington, Dry Doddington

Donington, G. 12	*Donninctune* 348 *bis* *Duninctune* 345b
Donington on Bain, G. 6	*Duninctune* 350b
Donninctune	See Donington
Dorchesyg	See Torksey
Dorrington, F. 10	*Derintone* 369b
Dowdyke, H. 12	*Dwedic* 346b *bis*
Dowsby, F. 12	*Dusebi* 340, 367, 370b, 377b
Draitone	See Drayton
Drayton, G. 11	*Draitone* 346b, 348 *tredeciens*, 348b *octiens*, 368, 370b *bis*, 377b *bis*
Dreistorp	See Dexthorpe
Dreuistorp	See Trusthorpe
Dribi	See Driby
Driby, I. 7	*Dribi* 355b
Dristorp	See Dexthorpe
Druistorp	See Trusthorpe
Dry Doddington, C. 10	*Dodintone, -tune* 343b, 357, 370
Dunebi	See Owmby (near Fillingham)
Duneham	See Dunholme
Dunesbi	See Dunsby (near Hacconby)
Dunestune	See Dunston
Dunetorp	See Dunsthorpe
Dunholme, E. 7	*Duneham* 338, 353b, 362b, 366
Duninctune	See Donington, Donington on Bain
Dunnesbi	See Dunsby (in Brauncewell)
Dunsby (in Brauncewell), E. 10	*Dunnesbi* 346b, 369b
Dunsby (near Hacconby), F. 13	*Dunesbi* 344b *bis*, 377
Dunstall, C. 5	*Tonestale, -tele* 350, 352
Dunsthorpe, D. 12	*Dunetorp* 337b, 338
Dunston, E. 8	*Dunestune* 362
Dusebi	See Dowsby
Dwedic	See Dowdyke

Dyke, F. 13	*Dic* 364b *bis*, 369, 377
Eagle, C. 8	*Ac(he)lei* 352b, 366, 377
	Acley, *Akeley* 367 *ter*
	Aycle 365
East Barkwith	See Barkwith
East Firsby	See Firsby
East Graby	See Graby
East Halton, F. 2	*Haltune* 350b
East Keal, I. 8	*Estrecale* 340b *bis*, 341 *bis*, 351, 359b
East Kirkby, H. 8	*Cherchebi* 351b
Eastlound	See Craiselound
Eastoft	Not in D.B.
Easton, D. 13	*Estone* 340
East Ravendale	See Ravendale
East Torrington	See Torrington
East Wykeham	See Wykeham, East and West
Echintune	See Heckington
Ed(en)eham	See Edenham
Edenham, E. 13	*Ed(en)eham* 354b *bis*, 355b, 364b *bis*, 376b
Edlington, G. 7	*Ellingetone* 351, 354b, 375b
Ele(s)ham	See Elsham
Elgelo	See Belleau
Elkington, North and South, H. 5	*Alchinton* 354
	Archintone 351b
Ellingetone	See Edlington
Elsham, E. 3	*Ele(s)ham* 342, 344, 352, 370
Elsthorpe, E. 13	*Aig(he)lestorp* 358, 368
Endrebi	See Mavis Enderby, Wood Enderby
Endretorp	See Woodthorpe
Englebi	See Ingleby
Epeurde	See Epworth
Epworth, B. 4	*Epeurde* 369 *ter*
Eresby, I. 8	*Iresbi* 340b
Erforde	See Orford
Esbernebi	See Osbournby
Escumetorp	See Scunthorpe
Esetorp	See Buslingthorpe

Eslaforde	See Old Sleaford
Esnelent	See Snelland
Esnetrebi	See Snitterby
Estdeping(e)	See Deeping St James
Estone	See Easton
Estorp	See Aisthorpe
Estou	See Stowe
Estrebi	See Asterby
Estrecale	See East Keal
Eteleham	See Nettleham
Evedon, F. 10	*Evedune* 337b, 341 *bis*, 344b, 357b, 369b, 370
Evedune	See Evedon
Ewerby, F. 10	*Geresbi* 344b
	Grene(s)bi 365, 377
	Ieresbi 355, 370
Ewerby Thorpe, F. 10	*Oustorp* 337b, 355, 357, 365, 377
Exentune	See Exton, Rutland
Exewelle	See Ashwell, Rutland
Falding(e)urde	See Faldingworth
Faldingworth, E. 6	*Falding(e)urde* 356b, 366, 366b
	Falingeurde 356b
Falingeurde	See Faldingworth
Farforde	See Farforth
Farforth, H. 7	*Farforde* 349b *bis*
Farlesthorpe	Not in D.B.
Felingeham	See Fillingham
Fenby, G. 4	*Fendebi* 347b
Fendebi	See Fenby
Fenton (near Grantham)	Not in D.B.
Fenton (near Torksey)	Not in D.B.
Ferebi	See South Ferriby
Fi(ge)lingeham	See Fillingham
Fillingham, D. 6	*Felingeham* 356b
	Fi(ge)lingeham 352b, 356b, 357, 371
Firsby (near Spilsby)	Not in D.B.
Firsby, East and West, E. 6	*Frisebi* 342 *bis*

Fiscartone, -tune	See Fiskerton
Fishtoft, I. 11	*Toft* 348, 367b
Fiskerton, E. 7	*Fiscartone, -tune* 345b, 356b
Flec	See Fleet
Fleet, I. 13	*Flec* 348b *Fleot* 338
Fleot	See Fleet
Flichesburg	See Flixborough
Flixborough, C. 2	*Flichesburg* 361b
Fodrebi	See Fotherby
Folching(e)ham	See Folkingham
Folesbi	See Fulsby
Folkingham, E. 12	*Folching(e)ham* 345b, 355b, 367b *Fulchingeham* 353
Fonaby, F. 4	*Fuldenebi* 338b
Fordington, I. 7	*Fortintone* 349
Forebi	See Fotherby
Fortintone	See Fordington
Foston, C. 11	*Foztun(e)* 348 *bis*
Fotherby, H. 5	*Fo(d)rebi* 340b, 353, 354, 376
Foztun(e)	See Foston
Frampton, H. 11	*Franetone* 348 *Frantune* 367b
Franetone, Frantune	See Frampton
Freiston, I. 11	*Fristune* 367b
Friesthorpe, E. 6	*Frisetorp* 356b
Frieston, D. 10	*Fristun* 363
Frischenei	See Friskney
Frisebi	See Firsby, East and West
Frisetorp	See Friesthorpe
Friskney, J. 9	*Frischenei* 370b
Fristun	See Frieston
Fristune	See Freiston
Frithville	Not in D.B.
Fugelestou	See Fulstow
Fulbeck, D. 10	*Fulebec* 347b
Fulchingeham	See Folkingham
Fuldenebi	See Fonaby
Fulebec	See Fulbeck
Fulletby, H. 7	*Fullobi* 341b, 349b
Fullobi	See Fulletby
Fulnedebi	See Fulnetby
Fulnetby, F. 7	*Fulnedebi* 362b
Fulsby, G. 9	*Folesbi* 339 *bis*
Fulstow, H. 5	*Fugelestou* 340b, 347, 349, 363b, 376
Gadenai, -nay	See Gedney
Gainesburg	See Gainsborough
Gainsborough, C. 5	*Gainesburg* 369
Gainsthorpe, D. 4	*Gamelstorp* 350b
Gaintone	See Hainton
Gamelstorp	See Gainsthorpe
Ganthorpe or Ganthrops, D. 12	*Germuntorp* 366b
Garthorpe, C. 2	*Gerulftorp* 369b *ter*
Gate Burton, C. 6	*Borotona* 376 *Bortone* 347
Gautby	Not in D.B.
Gayton le Marsh	Not in D.B.
Gayton le Wold, G. 6	*Gedtune, Gettune* 338b, 375
Gedney, I. 13	*Gadenai, -nay* 338, 348b, 377b
Gedtune	See Gayton le Wold
Gelston, D. 10	*Chevelestune* 347b
Gereburg	See Yarburgh
Geresbi	See Ewerby
Germund(s)torp	See Grainthorpe
Germuntorp	See Ganthorpe
Gerneham	See Irnham
Gerulftorp	See Garthorpe
Gettune	See Gayton le Wold
Girsby, G. 6	*Grisebi* 339b, 362b
Glandham, Glantham	See Glentham
Glenteu(u)rde	See Glentworth
Glentham, E. 5	*Glandham, Glantham* 342 *bis*, 350 *Glentham* 344
Glentworth, D. 5	*Glenteu(u)rde* 338, 338b, 342, 359, 365, 366
Goldesbi	See Ingoldsby
Golsa, Golse	See Goxhill
Goltho	Not in D.B.
Gonerby, Great and Little, D. 11	*Gouerdebi* 377 *bis* *Gunfordebi* 337b, 341, 343b, 361, 367b *Gunnewordebi* 370b

Gosberton, G. 12	*Gosebertcherche*, *-bertechirche* 348b, 377b *Gozeberdecherca* 344b *bis*
Gosebertcherche, *-bertechirche*	See Gosberton
Gouerdebi	See Gonerby
Goulceby, H. 7	*Colchesbi* 350b
Goxhill, F. 2	*Golsa*, *Golse* 344, 357b, 360, 362, 371, 375b
Gozeberdecherca	See Gosberton
Graby, East and West, F. 12	*Greibi* 340, 353
Graham	See Grantham
Graingeham	See Grayingham
Grainsby, H. 4	*Grenesbi* 347
Grainthorpe, I. 5	*Germund(s)torp* 338b, 340b, 354
Grandham	See Grantham, Greetham
Grangeham	See Grayingham
Gran(t)ham	See Grantham
Grantham, D. 12	*Graham* 360b *Grandham* 337b, 377b *Granham* 337b *quin*, 338 *ter*, 370b *Grantham* 337b, 343b, 353, 368b, 377 *bis*
Grasby, F. 4	*Gros(e)bi* 338b, 342b, 370b
Grayingham, D. 5	*Gra(i)ngeham* 338, 338b *bis*, 344, 362b
Great Coates, G. 3	*Cotes* 342b, 347, 357b *bis*, 361b, 365, 375b
Greatford, F. 14	*Greteford* 368b *Griteford(e)* 353, 354b, 366
Great Gonerby	See Gonerby
Great Grimsby, H. 3	*Grimesbi* 343 *bis*, 360, 363, 376 *bis*
Great Hale	See Hale
Great Limber	See Limber
Great Ponton, D. 12	*Magna Panptune* 337b *Magna Pantone* 366b *Pamptune* 377 *Pamtone* 360b
Great Steeping	See Steeping
Great Sturton, G. 7	*Stratone* 342b, 364b
Grebby, J. 8	*Gredbi* 340b *Greibi* 341
Gredbi	See Grebby
Greetham, H. 8	*Grandham* 349 *bis* *Gretham* 355, 375 *ter*, 375b
Greetwell, E. 7	*Grentewelle* 352b
Greibi	See Graby, Grebby
Grenebi	See Ewerby
Greneham	See Irnham
Grenesbi	See Ewerby, Grainsby
Grentewelle	See Greetwell
Greteford	See Greatford
Gretham	See Greetham
Grimalbi	See Grimoldby
Grimblethorpe	Not in D.B.
Grimesbi	See Great Grimsby, Little Grimsby
Grimoldbi	See Grimoldby
Grimoldby, I. 5	*Grimalbi* 338b *Grimoldbi* 358
Grisebi	See Girsby
Griteford(e)	See Greatford
Gros(e)bi	See Grasby
Guinness	Not in D.B.
Guldelsmere	See Ingoldmells
Gullingham	See Cherry Willingham
Gunby (near Candlesby), J. 8	*Gunnebi* 360
Gunby (near North Witham), D. 13	*Gunnebi* 369
Gunfordebi	See Gonerby
Gunnebi	See Gunby (near Candlesby), Gunby (near North Witham)
Gunnerby, G. 4	*Gunresbi* 347b

Gunnewordebi	See Gonerby
Gunresbi	See Gunnerby
Haberdingham	See Hagworthingham
Habrough, F. 3	*Aburne* 353b *Haburne* 338b, 349, 350b, 357b, 358b, 361b, 362
Haburne	See Habrough
Hacam	See Hougham
Hacberdincham, -*ingam*, -*ing*(*e*)*ham*	See Hagworthingham
Hacconby, F. 13	*Hacone*(*s*)*bi* 364b *ter*, 368b, 369, 377 *bis* *Hacunesbi* 344b, 364b, 377
Haceby, E. 12	*Haȝebi* 355b, 357b, 365 *bis*, 365b, 367b *bis*
Hach	See Hough on the Hill
Hacham	See Hougham
Hache	See Hough on the Hill
Hackthorn, E. 6	*Agetorne* 339b *Hagetone* 352 *Hagetorn*(*e*) 356b, 357, 359, 365, 365b
Hacone(*s*)*bi*, *Hacunesbi*	See Hacconby
Haddington, D. 8	*Hadinctone*, -*tune* 353b, 370, 377
Hadeclive	See Hatcliffe
Hadinctone, -*tune*	See Haddington
Hag	See Hough on the Hill
Hage	See Haugh
Hagenebi	See Hagnaby
Hagetone, -*torn*(*e*)	See Hackthorn
Haghe	See Haugh
Hagnaby, I. 8	*Hagenebi* 351b, 359b
Hagworthingham, H. 8	*Haberdingham* 355 *bis* *Hacberdincham* 349 *Hacberdingam* 360b *Hacberding*(*e*)*ham* 348b *ter*, 359b, 360b
Haidure	See Heydour
Hainton, G. 6	*Gaintone* 375 *Haintone*, -*tun*(*e*) 340, 342b *bis*, 352 *quater*, 358, 364, 375
Haintone, -*tun*(*e*)	See Hainton
Hale, Great and Little, F. 11	*Hale* 355
Halebi	See Ailby
Halintun	See Hallington
Hallington, H. 6	*Halintun* 349b
Haltham, G. 8	*Holtham* 339, 363b
Haltone	See West Halton
Halton Holegate, I. 8	*Haltun* 347b, 351
Haltun	See Halton Holegate
Haltune	See East Halton
Hameringam	See Hameringham
Hameringham, H. 8	*Hameringam* 359b
Hamingebi	See Hemingby
Hanby, J. 8	*Humbi* 375 *Hunbia* 351b *Hundebi* 351b
Haneurde	See Cold Hanworth
Haneworde	See Cold Hanworth, Potter Hanworth
Haniuuic	See Anwick
Hannah	Not in D.B.
Hanthorpe, F. 13	*Hermodestorp* 355b, 364b, 369, 377
Hardetorp	See Addlethorpe
Harduic	See Hardwick (in Panton), Hardwick (near Torksey)
Hardwic	See Hardwick (in Panton)
Hardwick (in Panton), F. 7	*Harduic* 362b *Hardwic* 340b
Hardwick (near Torksey), C. 7	*Harduic* 337, 376b

Harebi	See Hareby
Hareby, H. 8	*Harebi* 351
Harlaxton, C. 12	*Herlavestune* 337b
Harmston, D. 9	*Hermestune* 362 *Hermodestone, -tune* 349b, 363
Haroldestorp	See Hasthorpe
Harpswell, D. 5	*Herpeswelle* 338, 338b, 340, 359 *bis*
Harrington	Not in D.B.
Harrowby, D. 12	*Herigerbi* 337b, 338, 348, 367b
Hasthorpe, J. 8	*Haroldestorp* 355
Hastinges	See Hastings, Sx.
Hatcliffe, G. 4	*Hadeclive* 347b
Hatton, G. 7	*Hatune* 362b
Hatune	See Hatton
Haugh, I. 7	*Hag(h)e* 341b, 349 *bis*
Haugham, H. 6	*Hecham* 349b, 375
Hawardebi	See Hawerby
Hawerby, H. 4	*Hawardebi* 347b
Hawthorpe, E. 13	*Awartorp* 358
Haxey, B. 4	*Acheseia* 369, 376b
Haythby, D. 2	*Hedebi* 345b, 346, 349, 361b
Haʒebi	See Haceby
Healing, G. 3	*Hechelinge* 357b *Heg(h)elinge* 339b, 342b
Heapham, C. 5	*Iopeham* 338, 338b, 347
Hecham	See Haugham
Hechelinge	See Healing
Hechintone, -tune	See Heckington
Heckington, F. 11	*Echintune* 344b, 370 *Hechintone, -tune* 337b, 355, 357, 363, 367b, 377
Hedebi	See Haythby
Heg(h)elinge	See Healing
Heidure	See Heydour
Heighington	Not in D.B.
Helmeswelle	See Hemswell
Helperi(n)cham	See Helpringham
Helpringham, F. 11	*Helperi(n)cham* 351b, 356, 357, 363, 366
Hemeldune	See Hambleton, Rutland
Hemingby, G. 7	*Hamingebi* 349b, 350b, 356b
Hemswell, D. 5	*Helmeswelle* 338, 338b, 342, 365
Herde(r)torp	See Addlethorpe
Heresbi	See Orby
Heretorp	See Addlethorpe
Herigerbi	See Harrowby
Herlavestune	See Harlaxton
Hermestune, Hermodestone	See Harmston
Hermodestorp	See Hanthorpe
Hermodestune	See Harmston
Herpeswelle	See Harpswell
Heydour, E. 11	*Hai-, Heidure* 357b, 367b
Hibaldstow, D. 4	*Hiboldeston(e)* 338, 338b *bis* *Hi(l)boldestou* 346, 350b *bis*, 357, 371
Hiboldeston(e), Hiboldestou	See Hibaldstow
Hicham	See South Hykeham
High Burnham	See Burnham, High and Low
High Toynton	See Toynton, High and Low
Hilboldestou	See Hibaldstow
Hochtune	See Houghton
Hoctun	See Holton le Moor
Hoctune	See Holton le Moor, Houghton
Hogetune	See Houghton
Hogsthorpe	Not in D.B.
Hogtone	See Houghton
Holbeach, I. 13	*Holebech, Holeben* 338 *bis*, 346b *Holobec(h)* 348b, 368, 377b
Holdingham	Not in D.B.
Holebech, -ben	See Holbeach
Holm	See Holme (in Beckingham), Holme (near Bottesford)

Holme	See Holme (in Sudbrooke)
Holme (in Beckingham), C. 10	*Holm* 355b
Holme (near Bottesford), D. 3	*Holm* 346
Holme (in Sudbrooke), E. 7	*Holme* 345b, 356b
Holobec(h)	See Holbeach
Holtham	See Haltham
Holtham, F. 6	*Houten* 354, 364
Holton (near Beckering), F. 6	*Houtone, -tune* 339b, 359b
Holtone	See Holton le Clay
Holton le Clay, H. 4	*Holtone, -tun* 347, 350, 364
Holton le Moor, F. 4	*Hoctun(e)* 338b, 350b, 352
Holtun	See Holton le Clay
Holywell	Not in D.B.
Hondintone	See Honington
Honington, D. 11	*Hondintone* 355b *Hundindune* 351b *Hundinton(e)* 351b *bis*, 377b
Horbelinge	See Horbling
Horbling, F. 12	*Horbelinge* 340, 348, 357b, 367b *Orbelinge* 348, 365
Horchetou	See Horkstow
Horkstow, D. 2	*Horchetou* 354b
Horncastle, H. 8	*Hornecastre* 339
Hornecastre	See Horncastle
Horsington, G. 8	*Horsi(n)tone* 349b, 351, 356b
Horsi(n)tone	See Horsington
Hoto(f)t	See Huttoft
Houflet, G. 3	*Wenflet* 342b
Hougham, C. 11	*Hac(h)am* 345, 357 *bis*, 366b
Hough on the Hill, D. 10	*Hach(e)* 347b *ter* *Hag* 356
Houghton, D. 12	*Hoc(h)tune* 345b, 370b *Hogetune* 361 *Hogtone* 368 *bis*
Houten	See Holtham
Houtone, -tune	See Holton

Howell, F. 10	*Huuelle* 355, 357 *Welle* 337b, 344b, 370
Howsham, E. 4	*Usun* 338b, 347 *bis*
Hubaldestorp	See Upperthorpe
Humberston, H. 4	*Humbrestone* 350
Humbi	See Hanby, Humby
Humbrestone	See Humberston
Humby, E. 12	*Humbi* 361
Humendone	See Hundon
Hunbia, Hundebi	See Hanby
Hundelbi	See Hundleby
Hundindune, Hundinton(e)	See Honington
Hundleby, I. 8	*Hundelbi* 340b, 351
Hundon, F. 4	*Humendone* 338b *Hunidune* 375b
Hungerton, C. 12	*Hungretune* 353
Hungretune	See Hungerton
Hunidune	See Hundon
Huttoft, J. 7	*Hoto(f)t* 349, 358b 370b, 375
Huuelle	See Howell, Wyville
Iadulf(es)torp	See Yaddlethorpe
Ieresbi	See Ewerby
Immingham, G. 2	*Imungeham* 353b *Mingeham* 361b
Imungeham	See Immingham
Ingeham	See Ingham
Ingham, D. 6	*Ingeham* 342, 344, 352b *bis*, 356b *bis*, 357, 359 *bis*, 364, 371 *Lageham* 356b
Ingleby, C. 7	*Englebi* 342, 352b, 354
Ingoldesbi	See Ingoldsby
Ingoldmells, K. 8	*Guldelsmere* 363b
Ingoldsby, E. 12	*Goldesbi* 356, 361, 370 *Ingoldesbi* 368, 377
Iole(s)torp	See Yawthorpe
Iopeham	See Heapham
Irby in the Marsh	Not in D.B.
Irby upon Humber, G. 4	*Irebi* 349 *Iribi* 350b, 365

Irebi	See Irby upon Humber
Iresbi	See Eresby
Iribi	See Irby upon Humber
Irnham, E. 13	*Gerneham* 363, 376b *Greneham* 358
Itrebi	See Itterby
Itterby, H. 3	*Itrebi* 342b, 343, 360, 365b
Kaschingetorp	See Casthorpe
Keadby	Not in D.B.
Keddington, I. 5	*Cadinton(e)* 364, 375 *Caditon* 341
Keelby, F. 3	*Chelebi* 338b, 339b, 342b, 344b, 350b, 360, 361b *bis*, 375b *Chilebi* 365b
Keisby, E. 12	*Chisebi* 368, 371 See also anon. holdings on p. 259
Kelby, E. 11	*Chelebi* 341 *Chillebi* 367b
Kelstern, G. 5	*Cheilestorne* 365b *Chelestorne*, *-turne* 349b, 358
Ketsby, I. 7	*Chetelesbi* 349b
Kettleby, E. 3	*Chetelbi* 360, 362, 370
Kettleby Thorpe, E. 3	*Torp* 356b
Kettlethorpe	Not in D.B.
Kexby, C. 6	*Cheftesbi* 344, 357, 371
Killingholme, North and South, F. 2	*Chelvingeholm* 347, 361b *Chelvingehou* 350b *Chelvingholme* 360
Kingerby, E. 5	*Chenebi* 342, 345
Kingthorpe, F. 7	*Chinetorp* 351, 351b, 362b, 364
Kirkby Green, F. 9	*Cherchebi* 361, 361b, 369, 376b
Kirkby la Thorpe, F. 10	*Cherchebi* 337b, 341, 357, 357b, 377 1st entry *Chirchebi* 341, 356
Kirkby on Bain, G. 8	*Cherchebi* 340b *bis*, 359b *Chirchebi* 340b, 343, 359b *bis*
Kirkby Underwood, E. 13	*Cherchebi* 348, 353, 358b, 377 2nd entry
Kirkstead	Not in D.B.
Kirmington, F. 3	*Chernitone* 338b, 347, 356, 360
Kirmond le Mire, G. 5	*Cheuremont* 354
Kirton (in Holland), H. 11	*Cher-*, *Chirchetune* 348, 348b, 367b
Kirton in Lindsey, D. 4	*Chircheton(e)* 338, 338b, 376b, Lincs.; 293, Notts. *Circeton* 281b, Notts.
Knaith, C. 6	*Cheneide* 344
Laceby, G. 3	*Lenesbi* 353b *Levesbi* 343, 360
Lac(es)tone	See Laughton (near Blyton)
Lageham	See Ingham
Lagesbi	See Legsby
Langene, J. 8	Lost in Irby in the Marsh, 349
Langetof	See Langtoft
Langetone	See Langton (near Horncastle), Langton by Wragby
Langetune	See Langton (near Spilsby)
Langriville	Not in D.B.
Langtoft, F. 14	*Langetof* 346b
Langton (near Horncastle), G. 8	*Langetone* 339, 342b, 360b
Langton (near Spilsby), I. 8	*Langetune* 349
Langton by Wragby, F. 7	*Langetone* 340b, 354b, 362b, 363b, 365b, 375 *bis*
Lanun	See Laneham, Notts.
Lastone	See Laughton (near Blyton)

Ludesforde	See Ludford
Ludford Magna and Parva, G. 5	*Lude(s)forde* 351, 354, 356b, 364
Ludintone	See Luddington
Lund	See Lound (in Toft), Craiselound and Eastlound
Lund, Altera	See Craiselound and Eastlound
Lunde(r)torp	See Londonthorpe
Lusby, H. 8	*Luzebi* 354b, 355 *bis*
Lutton, I. 13	*Luctone* 338
Luzebi	See Lusby
Mablethorpe, J. 6	*Malbertorp* 349 *Mal(te)torp* 355b, 364, 375
Machetone	See Muckton
Magna Panptune, Magna Pantone	See Great Ponton
Maidenwell, H. 7	*Welle* 349b, 375 1st entry
Malbertorp	See Mablethorpe
Malmetune	See Manton
Maltby (in Raithby), H. 6	*Maltebi* 349b
Maltby le Marsh, J. 6	*Maltebi, -by* 348b, 356b, 359b *Maltesbi* 355b
Maltebi	See Maltby (in Raithby), Maltby le Marsh
Malteby, Maltesbi	See Maltby le Marsh
Mal(te)torp	See Mablethorpe
Mameltune	See Manton
Manby (in Broughton), D. 3	*Mannebi* 365
Manby (near Stewton), I. 6	*Mannebi* 338b
Mannebi	See Manby (in Broughton), Manby (near Stewton)
Mannetor(p)	See Manthorpe (near Witham on the Hill)

Manthorpe (near Grantham)	Not in D.B.
Manthorpe (near Witham on the Hill), E. 14	*Mannetor(p)* 345b, 346, 355
Manton, D. 4	*Malmetune* 376b *Mameltune* 346
Marae, C. 2	Lost in Luddington, 369b
Marche(s)bi	See Markby
Mare	See Mere Haven
Mareham (in Burton Pedwardine), F. 11	*Marram* 367b
Mareham le Fen, H. 9	*Marun* 339
Mareham on the Hill, H. 8	*Meringhe* 363b
Markby, J. 7	*Marche(s)bi* 343, 349, 359b
Market Rasen	See Rasen
Market Stainton, G. 6	*Staintone* 364b
Marram	See Mareham (in Burton Pedwardine)
Marsh Chapel	Not in D.B.
Marston, D. 11	*Mereston(e), -tune* 347b, 357 *ter*, 358b, 366b, 367b, 377 *bis*, 377b
Martin (near Horncastle), G. 8	*Martone* 340b, 359b
Martin (near Timberland)	Not in D.B.
Marton, C. 6	*Martone* 347
Martone	See Martin (near Horncastle), Marton
Marun	See Mareham le Fen
Mavis Enderby, I. 8	*Endrebi* 340b, 351, 360
Medeltone	See Melton Ross
Medric(h)esham	See Metheringham
Melingesbi	See Miningsby
Melton Ross, E. 3	*Medeltone* 362
Mentinges, Duo Mentinghes	See Minting and Little Minting

Mere (near Lincoln)	Not in D.B.
Mere Haven, J. 5	*Mare* 375b
Mereston(e), *-tune*	See Marston
Meringhe	See Mareham on the Hill
Messingeham	See Messingham
Messingham, C. 4	*Messingeham* 344, 346, 362
Metheringham, E. 9	*Medric(h)esham* 349b, 361, 368b, 370b
Middle Carlton	See Carlton, Middle and South
Middle Rasen	See Rasen
Mingeham	See Immingham
Miningsby, H. 8	*Melingesbi* 351
Minting and Little Minting, F. 7, G. 7	*Duo Mentinghes* 351 *Mentinges* 367
Moorby, H. 8	*Morebi* 339
Morebi	See Moorby
Morton (near Gainsborough), C. 5	*Mortum* 338 *Mortune* 350
Morton (near Hanthorpe), F. 13	*Mortun(e)* 355b, 364b *quater*, 369, 377 *bis*
Morton (near Lincoln)	Not in D.B.
Mortum	See Morton (near Gainsborough)
Mortun	See Morton (near Hanthorpe)
Mortune	See Morton (near Gainsborough), Morton (near Hanthorpe)
Moulton, H. 13	*Multune* 351b, 368
Muckton, I. 6	*Machetone* 366b
Multune	See Moulton
Mumby, J. 7	*Mund(e)bi* 348b *ter*, 355, 360, 375
Mund(e)bi	See Mumby
Muscham	See South Muskham, Notts.
Navenby, E. 9	*Navenebi* 365 *bis*, 376b
Navenebi	See Navenby
Netelham	See Nettleham
Neteltone	See Nettleton
Nettleham, E. 7	*Eteleham* 366 *Netelham* 338 *bis*, 354b, 376
Nettleton, F. 4	*Neteltone* 342, 352b, 362, 365, 371b
Neuberie	See Newball
Neuhuse	See Newsham
Neutone	See Newton (near Folkingham), Newton (near Toft), Newton upon Trent, Wold Newton
Newball, E. 7	*Neuberie* 349b
Newsham, F. 3	*Neuhuse* 338b, 350b, 358b *bis*, 362
Newstead	Not in D.B.
Newton (near Folkingham), E. 12	*Neutone* 341, 341b, 357 *bis*, 365b *ter*, 370
Newton (near Toft), E. 6	*Neutone* 342 *bis*, 364, 371
Newton upon Trent, C. 7	*Neutone* 340
Nochetune	See Nocton
Nocton, E. 8	*Nochetune* 362 *bis*
Nongetune, *Nongtone*	See Spittlegate
Norchelsei	See North Kelsey
Normanby (in Burton upon Stather), C. 2	*Normanebi* 360 *bis*, 367, 376b
Normanby (near Fillingham), E. 6	*Normanebi* 350, 359 *Normanestou* 342
Normanby (in Stow), C. 6	*Normanebi* 344
Normanby le Wold, F. 5	*Normane(s)bi* 350, 359, 360b
Normanebi	See Normanby (in Burton upon Stather), Normanby (near Fillingham),

Osgotebi	See Osgodby (in Bardney), Osgodby (in Lenton), Osgodby (near West Rasen)
Osgotesbi	See Osgodby (near West Rasen)
Ostone	See Owston
Otby, F. 5	*Ote(s)bi* 350, 352
Ote(s)bi	See Otby
Ounebi	See Owmby (near Fillingham)
Ounesbi	See Aunsby, Owmby (near Fillingham)
Ouseby, F. 12	*Ulvesbi* 357 *bis*, 370b
	Uuesbi 365b
Oustorp	See Ewerby Thorpe
Overtune, *Ovretone*	See Market Overton, Rutland
Owersby, North and South, E. 5	*Aresbi* 343, 344b, 371
	Oresbi 352, 353b *bis*, 361b, 376
Owmby (near Fillingham), E. 6	*Dunebi* 359
	Oune(s)bi 343b, 344, 350, 359, 376
Owmby (in Searby), E. 4	*Odenebi* 338b, 347, 354
Owston, C. 4	*Ostone* 369, 369b
Oxcombe, H. 7	*Oxecumbe* 349b
	Oxetune 341b
Oxecumbe, *Oxetune*	See Oxcombe
Pamptune	See Great Ponton, Little Ponton
Pamtone, *Magna Panptune*	See Great Ponton
Panton, G. 7	*Pantone* 339b, 362b
Pantone	See Panton
Pantone, *Magna*	See Great Ponton
Pantone, *Parva*	See Little Ponton
Partenai, *Partene*	See Partney
Partney, I. 8	*Partenai*, *Partene* 355, 363b

Parva Lavintune	See Little Lavington
Parva Pantone	See Little Ponton
Picebech	See Pinchbeck
Picheu(o)rde, *Picheworde*	See Pickworth
Pickworth, E. 12	*Picheu(o)rde*, *Picheworde* 341, 355b, 357b *bis*, 377b
Pileham	See Pilham
Pilham, C. 5	*Pileham* 338, 338b
Pincebec	See Pinchbeck
Pinchbeck, G. 13	*Picebech* 351b
	Pincebec 368
Pochinton(e), *Podintone*	See Pointon
Pointon, F. 12	*Pochinton(e)* 348, 356, 366b, 367
	Podintone 357
Potter Hanworth, E. 8	*Haneworde* 361, 376b
Quadheueringe	See Quadring
Quadring, G. 12	*Quadheueringe* 344b *bis*
	Quedhaueringe 348b, 377b
Quedhaueringe	See Quadring
Quarrington, E. 11	*Corninctone*, *-tune(e)* 344b, 346b, 364b, 377 *bis*
	Cornintone 337b
Radburne	See Redbourne
Radebi	See Raithby (near Hundleby)
Radresbi	See Raithby (near Louth)
Ragenaltorp, *Rageneltorp*	See Raventhorpe
Raithby (near Hundleby), I. 8	*Radebi* 340b, 351, 360
Raithby (near Louth), H. 6	*Radresbi* 349b
Ranby, G. 7	*Randebi* 342b, 364b
Rand, F. 7	*Rande* 362b
Rande	See Rand

Ruskington, F. 10	*Reschintone* 369b *quater* *Rischintone* 360b
Salebi, *-by*	See Saleby
Saleby, J. 7	*Salebi*, *-by* 355b, 356b
Saleclif	See Sawcliffe
Salflatebi	See Saltfleetby
Salfluet	See Saltfleet
Salmonby, H. 7	*Salmundebi* 349
Salmundebi	See Salmonby
Saltfleet, J. 5	*Salfluet* 375b *bis*
Saltfleetby All Saints, St Clements, St Peter, J. 5	*Salflatebi* 338b, 341 *bis*, 358, 364, 366
Sanctone	See Santon
Santon, D. 3	*San(c)tone* 352b, 354b, 367
Santone	See Santon
Sapperton, E. 12	*Sapretone* 337b, 338, 351b
Sapretone	See Sapperton
Sassebi	See Saxby (near Fillingham)
Sausthorpe	Not in D.B.
Sawcliffe, D. 2	*Saleclif* 346, 352b, 354b
Saxby (near Fillingham), E. 6	*Sassebi* 338, 338b, 360
Saxby All Saints, E. 2	*Saxebi* 350b
Saxebi	See Saxby All Saints
Saxilby, C. 7	*Saxebi* 291b, Notts.
Scache(r)torp	See Scottlethorpe
Scal(l)ebi	See Scawby
Scaltorp	See Scotterthorpe
Scamblesby, H. 7	*Scamelesbi* 350b
Scamelesbi	See Scamblesby
Scampton, D. 7	*Scanton(e)*, *-tune* 354b *quater*, 368b, 376
Scanton(e), *-tune*	See Scampton
Scap(e)uic, *Scapewic*	See Scopwick
Scarhou	See Scartho
Scartho, H. 3	*Scarhou* 343
Scawby, D. 4	*Scal(l)ebi* 350b, 357 *bis*, 359, 363, 364 *bis*, 365, 365b *bis*
Scheldinchope, *Schellingop*	See Skellingthorpe
Schellintune	See Skillington
Scheueldebi	See Skendleby
Schillintone, *-tune*	See Skillington
Schinende	See Skinnand
Schirebec	See Skirbeck
Schitebroc	See Skidbrooke
Scirebec	See Skirbeck
Scitebroc	See Skidbrooke
Scoltorne	See Scothern
Scopwick, E. 9	*Scap(e)uic* 361, 361b, 369 *bis* *Scapewic* 376b
Scotere	See Scotter
Scothern, E. 7	*Sco(l)torne* 345b, 353b, 364b *Scotstorne* 356b, 362, 376
Scotone	See Scotton
Scotorne	See Scothern
Scotre	See Scotter
Scotstorne	See Scothern
Scotter, C. 4	*Scot(e)re* 345b, 376b
Scotterthorpe, C. 4	*Scaltorp* 345b
Scottlethorpe, E. 13	*Scache(r)torp* 353, 367
Scotton, C. 4	*Scotone*, *-tune* 345b, 350, 352, 367, 376b
Scott Willoughby, E. 11	*Wilgebi* 355b, 363b, 367b
Scotune	See Scotton
Scrafield	Not in D.B.
Scredinctun	See Scredington
Scredington, F. 11	*Scredinctun*, *-intune* 356, 368b
Scredintune	See Scredington
Scremby, J. 8	*Screnbi* 341 *bis*, 355, 359b, 375b *bis*
Screnbi	See Scremby
Scrivelesbi	See Scrivelsby
Scrivelsby, H. 8	*Scriv(v)elesbi* 339, 363b *bis*

South Stoke, D. 13	*Sudstoches* 337b
South Thoresby, I. 7	*Toresbi* 349
Southwell, E. 13	*Sudwelle* 361 *bis*
South Willingham, G. 6	*Ulingeham* 339b, 343, 364, 375b *bis*
South Witham	See Witham, North and South
Spalding, G. 13	*Spallinge* 346b, 351b *bis*, 368
Spallinge	See Spalding
Spanby, F. 11	*Spane(s)bi* 357, 364b
Spane(s)bi	See Spanby
Sperlin(c)tone	See Spridlington
Spilesbi	See Spilsby
Spilsby, I. 8	*Spilesbi* 340b *bis*, 351
Spingeham	See Sempringham
Spittlegate, D. 12	*Nongetune* 343b *Nongtone* 337b
Spredelintone	See Spridlington
Spridlington, E. 6	*Sperlin(c)tone* 356b, 357 *Spredelintone* 347b
Springetorp	See Springthorpe
Springthorpe, C. 5	*Springetorp* 338, 338b *bis*
Stainby, D. 13	*Stigandebi* 358
Stainfelde	See Stainfield (near Lincoln)
Stainfield (in Hacconby), F. 13	*Steintone* 364b *Stentuith* 369
Stainfield (near Lincoln), F. 7	*Stain-*, *Steinfelde* 353b, 375b
Stainton	See Stainton le Vale
Stainton (near Lincoln), E. 7	*Staintune* 349b
Stainton (in Waddingham), D. 5	*Sta(i)ntone* 338, 338b, 342, 352, 359, 369
Staintone	See Market Stainton, Stainton (in Waddingham), Stainton le Vale
Stainton le Vale, G. 5	*Stainton(e)* 354, 356, 360b, 364
Staintune	See Stainton (near Lincoln)

Stalin(ge)burg	See Stallingborough
Stallingborough, G. 3	*Stalin(ge)burg* 339b, 340, 342b, 356, 361b, 375b *Stalingeburg* 375b
Stamford, E. 15	*Stanford* 336b, 358
Stanford	See Stamford
Stangehou	See Stenigot
Stanlingeburg	See Stallingborough
Stantone	See Stainton (in Waddingham)
Stanwald, *-walt*	See Stenwith
Stapleford, C. 9	*Stapleforde* 343b, 366b
Stapleforde	See Stapleford
Steeping, Great and Little, J. 8	*Stepi(nge)* 347b, 351, 355, 363b
Steinfelde	See Stainfield (near Lincoln)
Steintone	See Stainfield (in Hacconby)
Stenigot, G. 6	*Stangehou* 350b
Stenning, G. 11	*Steveninge* 348b, 363, 377b
Stentuith	See Stainfield (in Hacconby)
Stenwith, C. 12	*Stanwald*, *-walt* 368, 377
Stepi(nge)	See Steeping
Stepingeham	See Sempringham
Steveninge	See Stenning
Stewton, I. 6	*Stiveton(e)* 343, 358, 375
Stichenai	See Stickney
Stichesforde	See Stickford
Stickford, I. 9	*Stichesforde* 351
Stickney, H. 9	*Stichenai* 351
Stigandebi	See Stainby
Stigeswald(e), *-walt*	See Stixwold
Stimblebi, *Stinblebi*	See Thimbleby
Stith	See Tydd St Mary
Stiveton(e)	See Stewton
Stixwold, G. 8	*Stigeswald(e)*, *-walt* 351, 358, 365
Stobetun	See Stubton

Stoche(s)	See Stoke Rochford
Stockwith	Not in D.B.
Stoke Rochford, D. 12	*Stoche(s)* 348b, 360b, 377
Stou	See Stow (in Threekingham), Stow (near Torksey)
Stow (in Threekingham), F. 12	*Stou* 356
Stow (near Torksey), C. 6	*Stou* 344 *sexiens*, 345, 347b, 353b, 354b, 359, 363
Stowe, F. 14	*Estou* 346 *bis*, 355, 358, 366
Stragglethorpe	Not in D.B.
Straitone	See Sturton (in Scawby)
Stratone	See Great Sturton, Little Sturton, Sturton (in Scawby), Sturton (near Torksey). See also Stretton, Rutland
Strobi	See Strubby (near Maltby le Marsh)
Stroustune	See Stroxton
Stroxton, D. 12	*Stroustune* 360b
Strubby (in Langton by Wragby), F. 7	*Strubi* 342b, 351, 352, 364
Strubby (near Maltby le Marsh), J. 6	*Strobi* 343, 348b, 355b, 356b
Strubi	See Strubby (in Langton by Wragby)
Stubetune	See Stubton
Stubton, C. 10	*Stobetun* 369b *Stubetune* 361b
Sturton (in Scawby), D. 4	*Stra(i)tone* 350b, 357, 359, 363
Sturton (near Torksey), C. 6	*Stratone* 342, 376
Suabi	See Swaby
Suafeld	See Swayfield
Sualun	See Swallow
Suamestede	See Swinstead
Suardesforde	See Snarford
Suarrebi	See Swarby
Suavetone, *Suavi(n)tone*	See Swaton
Sudborc	See Sudbrooke
Sudbrooke, E. 7	*Sudborc* 356b *Sutbroc* 345b
Sudcotes	See South Coates
Sudstoches	See South Stoke
Sudtone	See Long Sutton, Sutton (in Great Sturton), Sutton le Marsh
Sudtorp	See Southorpe (in Edenham)
Sudtrie	See Southrey
Sudtune	See Sutton le Marsh
Sudwelle	See Southwell
Suerefelt	See Surfleet
Suindrebi	See Swinderby
Suine	See Swine
Suinham(stede)	See Swinstead
Suinhope	See Swinhope
Sumerdebi	See Old Somerby, Somerby (in Corringham)
Sumertebi	See Somerby (near Howsham)
Summercotes	See Somercotes
Summerdebi	See Old Somerby, Somerby (in Corringham), Somersby
Summerlede	See Osgodby (near West Rasen)
Summertebi	See Somerby (in Corringham), Somerby (near Howsham)
Summertune	See Somerton
Sunderby	See Swinderby
Surfleet, G. 12	*Suerefelt* 369
Sutbroc	See Sudbrooke
Sutrebi	See Sutterby
Sutrei(e)	See Southrey
Sutterby, I. 7	*Sutrebi* 349

Sutterton	Not in D.B.
Sutton (in Great Sturton), G. 7	*Sudtone* 354b, 359b 1st entry
Sutton le Marsh, J. 6	*Sudtone* 348b, 359b 2nd entry, 370b *Su(d)tune* 339b, 349, 375
Sutune	See Sutton le Marsh
Swaby, I. 7	*Suabi* 349, 375
Swallow, G. 4	*Sualun* 339b, 342b, 347 *bis*, 352, 357b, 363, 375b
Swarby, E. 11	*Suarrebi* 366, 367b
Swaton, F. 11	*Suavetone* 357b *Suavi(n)tone* 363, 367b
Swayfield, E. 13	*Suafeld* 344b
Swinderby, C. 8	*Suindrebi* 370b *Sunderby* 367
Swine, I. 4	*Suine* 375b
Swineshead	Not in D.B.
Swinhope, G. 5	*Suinhope* 347b, 361b, 365b
Swinstead, E. 13	*Suamestede* 361 *Suinham(stede)* 344b, 362b, 366b, 371
Swinthorpe (near Lincoln)	Not in D.B.
Swinthorpe (in Snelland), E. 6	*Sonetorp* 338, 339b, 359
Syston, D. 11	*Sidestan* 351b, 377b *Sidestham* 363b
Tadewelle	See Tathwell
Talintone, *-tune*	See Tallington
Tallington, F. 15	*Talintone*, *-tune* 353, 358, 376b
Tatebi, I. 7	Lost in Ulceby, 339b
Tatenai	See Tetney
Tateshale	See Tattershall
Tathwell, H. 6	*Tadewelle* 349b, 363b, 375
Tattershall, G. 9	*Tateshale* 360
Tattershall Thorpe, G. 9	*Torp* 340b 1st entry, 341, 343, 359b, 360 *bis*
Tavel(s)bi	See Tealby
Tealby, F. 5	*Tavele(s)bi* 342b, 350, 352, 357b, 359, 362b *bis*, 364, 376
Tedforde	See Tetford
Tedintone	See Toynton, High and Low
Tedlagestorp	See Theddlethorpe
Tedlintune	See Toynton, High and Low
Tedul(f)bi	See Thealby
Telagestorp	See Theddlethorpe
Terintone	See Torrington
Ternesco(e), *Ternesc(r)ou*	See Thrunscoe
Tesforde	See Tetford
Tetford, H. 7	*Tedforde*, *Tesforde* 339b, 349, 359b
Tetney, H. 4	*Tatenai* 350 *bis*
Thealby, C. 2	*Tedul(f)bi* 338b, 349, 360, 361b, 376b
Theddlethorpe All Saints, St Helen, J. 5	*Te(d)lagestorp* 348b, 349, 358b, 370b, 375
Thimbleby, G. 8	*Stimblebi*, *Stinblebi* 339, 343, 360b
Thonock, C. 5	*Tunec* 352
Thoresthorpe, J. 7	*Thuorstorp* 356b
Thoresway, G. 5	*Toreswe* 350, 357b
Thorganby, G. 4	*Torgre(m)bi* 343, 350, 361b, 365b *bis*, 366 *Turgrebi* 353 *Turgrimbi* 340b
Thorley, F. 7	*Turlai* 351
Thornton (near Horncastle), G. 8	*Torintune* 363b
Thornton Curtis, F. 2	*Torentone*, *-tune* 362, 363
Thornton le Fen	Not in D.B.
Thornton le Moor, E. 5	*Torentone*, *-tun(e)* 352, 353b *bis*
Thorpe in the Fallows, D. 6	*Torp* 354b *bis*, 371

Thorpe on the Hill, D. 8	*Torp* 338 1st entry, 346, 377
Thorpe St Peter, J. 9	*Torp* 340b 2nd entry, 351
Thorpe Tilney	Not in D.B.
Threekingham, F. 12	*Triching(e)ham* 346b, 356, 365b, 367b, 370 *Trichingheham* 341b *Trinchigeham* 357
Thrunscoe, H. 3	*Ternesco(e)* 339b, 342b *Ternesc(r)ou* 343, 350
Thuorstorp	See Thoresthorpe
Thurlby (near Bourne), F. 14	*Torulfbi* 358b *Turolvebi* 345b, 346, 368b
Thurlby (near Cumberworth), J. 7	*Torulvesbi* 349
Thurlby (near Norton Disney), D. 9	*Turolfbi* 366 *Turolve(s)bi* 377 *bis* *Turulfbi* 367
Tid	See Tydd St Mary
Timberland, F. 9	*Timberlunt* 361, 361b, 369 *Timbrelund* 349b
Timberlunt, Timbrelund	See Timberland
Tisteltone, -tune, Tistertune	See Thistleton, Rutland
Tite	See Tydd St Mary
Todetorp	See Towthorpe
Todintune	See Toynton, High and Low
Toft	See Fishtoft, Toft (near Bourne)
Toft (near Bourne), E. 14	*Toft* 345b, 346, 355
Tofte	See Toft next Newton
Toft next Newton, E. 6	*Tofte* 342b
Tonestale	See Dunstall
Torchesey, -seyg, -sig, -siy, -syg	See Torksey
Torentone	See Thornton Curtis, Thornton le Moor
Torentun	See Thornton le Moor
Torentune	See Thornton Curtis, Thornton le Moor
Toresbi	See North Thoresby, South Thoresby
Toreswe	See Thoresway
Torgre(m)bi	See Thorganby
Torintune	See Thornton (near Horncastle)
Torksey, C. 7	*Dorchesyg, Torchesey, -seyg, -sig, -siy, -syg* 337
Torp	See Bassingthorpe, Buckland, formerly Langton Thorpe, Calcethorpe, Culverthorpe, Kettleby Thorpe, Northorpe, Tattershall Thorpe, Thorpe in the Fallows, Thorpe on the Hill, Thorpe St Peter
Torp	Unid., 340
Torp, Altera	See Southorpe (in Northorpe)
Torrington, East and West, F. 6	*Terintone* 352, 358, 362b
Torulfbi	See Thurlby (near Bourne)
Torulvesbi	See Thurlby (near Cumberworth)
Totele	See Tothill
Tothby, J. 7	*Touedebi* 343
Tothill, I. 6	*Totele* 349
Totintun(e)	See Toynton All Saints
Touedebi	See Tothby
Towthorpe, D. 11	*Tode-, Tudetorp* 367b, 368, 377b *Twetorp* 370b

Waletone, -tune	See Welton le Marsh
Walkerith	Not in D.B.
Walmesgar	See Walmsgate
Walmsgate, I. 7	*Walmesgar* 349b
Waltham, H. 4	*Waltham* 347, 347b *bis*
Waragebi	See Wragby, Wrawby
Wardebi	See Aswarby
Warton	See Wharton
Washingborough, E. 8	*Washingeburg* 337b *bis*
Washingeburg	See Washingborough
Waterton, C. 2	*Watretone* 369b
Watretone	See Waterton
Weelsby, H. 3	*Wivelesbi* 360
Welbourn, D. 9	*Wellebrune* 368
Welby, D. 11	*Wellebi* 337b, 338, 367b, 377b
Welingeham	See Willingham (near Torksey)
Welingoure	See Wellingore
Well, J. 7	*Welle* 343, 355b, 375 2nd entry
Welle	See Howell, Maidenwell, Well
Wellebi	See Welby
Wellebrune	See Welbourn
Welletone	See Welton (near Lincoln), Welton le Wold
Welletune	See Welton le Wold
Wellingore, D. 9	*Wel(l)ingoure* 337b, 365
Wellingoure	See Wellingore
Welton (near Lincoln), E. 6	*Welletone* 344
Welton le Marsh, J. 8	*Waletone, -tune* 351b, 355, 359b
Welton le Wold, H. 6	*Welletone, -tune* 339, 341b, 347b, 352b, 366b
Wemflet	See Wainfleet
Wenflet	See Houflet, Wainfleet
Weranghe, Werangle	See Wrangle
West Ashby, H. 7	*Aschebi* 339, 355b, 370, 370b
West Barkwith	See Barkwith
Westbi	See Westby
Westbitham	See Bytham
Westborough, C. 11	*Westburg* 369b *bis*
Westburg	See Westborough
West Butterwick, C. 3	*Butrewic* 369b
Westby, D. 12	*Westbi* 348, 357b, 371
West Deeping, F. 15	*Westdepinge* 366
Westdepinge	See West Deeping
West Firsby	See Firsby, East and West
West Graby	See Graby
West Halton, D. 2	*Haltone* 349
Westhorpe, D. 12	*West(t)orp* 361 *bis*, 377b
West Keal, I. 8	*Cale* 360 *bis*, 370b *bis*
	Westrecale 351b, 359b
Westlaby, F. 6	*Westledebi* 350b, 353b
Westledebi	See Westlaby
Weston, H. 13	*Westune* 351b, 368
Westorp	See Westhorpe
West Rasen	See Rasen
West Ravendale	See Ravendale
Westrecale	See West Keal
Westtorp	See Westhorpe
West Torrington	See Torrington
Westude	See Westwood
Westune	See Weston
West Willoughby, D. 11	*Wilgebi* 363
Westwood, B. 4	*Westude* 369b
West Wykeham	See Wykeham, East and West
Whaplode, H. 13	*Copelade, Copolade* 338, 346b, 348b, 368
Wharton, C. 5	*Warton* 352
Whisby, D. 8	*Wizebi* 370, 377
Whitton, D. 1	*Witenai* 353b
Wibertone, -tune	See Wyberton

Wizebi	See Whisby, Winceby
Wlurice(s)bi	See Worlaby (near Tetford)
Wold Newton, G. 5	*Neutone* 340b, 347b *bis*, 376
Wood Enderby, H. 8	*Endrebi* 339, 363b
Woodhall	Not in D.B.
Woodthorpe, J. 6	*Endretorp* 356b
Woolsthorpe, C. 12	*Ulestane(s)torp* 353, 377
Wootton, F. 2	*Udetone* 344, 361b, 363
Worlaby (near Elsham), E. 3	*Uluricebi* 344, 356 *Wirichebi* 349
Worlaby (near Tetford), H. 7	*Wlurice(s)bi* 340, 341b
Wragby, F. 7	*Waragebi* 354, 362, 362b, 365b *bis*, 375
Wrangle, I. 10	*Weranghe*, *Werangle* 348, 367b
Wrawby, E. 3	*Waragebi* 370 *bis*
Wroot	Not in D.B.
Wyberton, H. 11	*Wibertone*, *-tune* 348 *bis*, 367b
Wyham, H. 5	*Widun* 344, 351
Wykeham (in Nettleton), F. 4	*Wiham* 365
Wykeham, East and West, G. 7	*Wicham* 352b, 356b, 358 *bis*, 364 *bis*
Wyville, C. 12	*Huuelle* 353
Yaddlethorpe, C. 3	*Iadulf(es)torp* 338, 338b, 371
Yarburgh, I. 5	*Gereburg* 338b, 375
Yawthorpe, D. 5	*Iole(s)torp* 345b, 352, 369

ANONYMOUS HOLDINGS

No place-name appears in the following entry:

Offran (from Gilbert of Ghent), $3\frac{1}{2}$ carucates, 354b. Domesday says 'In Offran', but Offran was a landholder and it is likely that the entry refers to a holding in Keisby.

MIDDLESEX—*MIDELSEXE*

Folios 126b–130b

MAP 33

Acton	Not in D.B.
Æcclesia Sancti Petri Westmonasterii	See Westminster
Adelmetone	See Edmonton
Ashford, B. 6	*Exeforde* 129
Bedefunde, *-funt*	See East Bedfont
Bethnall Green	Not in D.B.
Bishopsgate, E. 5	*Porta Episcopi* 128
Brentford	Not in D.B.
Cercehede	See Chelsea
Cerdentone	See Charlton
Charlton, B. 6	*Cerdentone* 130b
Chelched	See Chelsea
Chelsea, D. 5	*Cercehede*, *Chelched* 130b
Chenesit'	See Kensington
Chenetone	See Kempton
Chingesberie	See Kingsbury
Chiswick	Not in D.B.
Coleham	See Colham
Colham, B. 5	*Coleham* 129 *quin*
Covelie	See Cowley
Cowley, B. 5	*Covelie* 128b
Cranford, B. 5	*Cranforde* 130b
Cranforde	See Cranford

Dallega	See Dawley
Dawley, B. 5	*Dallega* 129
Draitone	See Drayton
Drayton, B. 5	*Draitone* 128
Ealing	Not in D.B.
East Bedfont, B. 6	*Bedefunde*, *-funt* 129, 130
Ebury, E. 5	*Eia* 129b
Edgeware	Not in D.B.
Edmonton, E. 4	*Adelmetone* 129b
Eia	See Ebury
Enefelde	See Enfield
Enfield, E. 3	*Enefelde* 129b
Exeforde	See Ashford
Felteham	See Feltham
Feltham, B. 6	*Felteham* 129 *bis*
Finchley	Not in D.B.
Finsbury	Not in D.B.
Friern Barnet	Not in D.B.
Fuleham	See Fulham
Fulham, D. 5	*Fuleham* 127b
Gistelesworde	See Isleworth
Great Stanmore	See Stanmore
Greenford, C. 5	*Greneforde* 128b, 129b, 130b
Greneforde	See Greenford
Hackney	Not in D.B.
Haggerston, E. 5	*Hergotestane* 130
Haitone	See Hatton
Hamestede	See Hampstead
Hammersmith	Not in D.B.
Hamntone	See Hampton
Hampstead, D. 4	*Hamestede* 128
Hampton, C. 6	*Hamntone* 130
Handone	See Hendon
Hanewelle	See Hanwell
Haneworde	See Hanworth
Hanwell, C. 5	*Hanewelle* 128b
Hanworth, C. 6	*Haneworde* 129
Harefield, B. 4	*Herefelle* 130
Harlesdon, D. 5	*Herulvestune* 127b
Harlington, B. 5	*Herdintone* 129
Harmondsworth, B. 5	*Hermodesworde* 128b, 129
Harrow, C. 4	*Herges* 127
Hatone	See Hatton
Hatton, B. 6	*Ha(i)tone* 129, 130
Hayes, B. 5	*Hesa* 127
Hendon, D. 4	*Handone* 128b
Herdintone	See Harlington
Herefelle	See Harefield
Herges	See Harrow
Hergotestane	See Haggerston
Hermodesworde	See Harmondsworth
Herulvestune	See Harlesdon
Hesa	See Hayes
Heston	Not in D.B.
Hillendone	See Hillingdon
Hillingdon, B. 5	*Hillendone* 129
Hochestone	See Hoxton
Holborn, E. 5	*Holeburne* 127
Holeburne	See Holborn
Hornsey	Not in D.B.
Hoxton, E. 5	*Hochestone* 128 *bis*
Ickenham, B. 4	*Ticheham* 129, 129b, 130
Iseldone, *Isendone*	See Islington
Isleworth, C. 5	*Gistelesworde* 130
Islington, E. 5	*Iseldone* 130b *Isendone* 128, 129b
Kempton, B. 6	*Chenetone* 129 *bis*
Kensington, D. 5	*Chenesit'* 130b
Kingsbury, D. 4	*Chingesberie* 128b, 129b
Laleham, B. 6	*Leleham* 129, 130b
Leleham	See Laleham
Lilestone	See Lisson
Lisson, D. 5	*Lilestone* 130b
Little Stanmore	See Stanmore
London, E. 5	*Lundonia* 127b, Mdlx. *Lond-*, *Lundonia* 30, 30b, 31b, 34 *bis*, 34b *ter*, 36b, Surrey; 100, Devon; L.D.B. 15b, 17b, 59, 63, Ess.; Exon D.B. 88, Devon
Lundonia	See London

Mimes	See South Mimms
Neutone	See Newington
Newington, E. 4	*Neutone* 128
Northala	See Northolt
Northolt, B. 5	*Northala* 129b
Norwood	Not in D.B.
Paddington	Not in D.B.
Pinner	Not in D.B.
Poplar	Not in D.B.
Porta Episcopi	See Bishopsgate
Rislepe	See Ruislip
Rugemere	See Rug Moor
Rug Moor, D. 5	*Rugemere* 127b
Ruislip, B. 4	*Rislepe* 129b
St Pancras, E. 5	*Sanctus Pancratius* 128 *bis*
Sanctus Pancratius	See St Pancras
Scepertone	See Shepperton
Shepperton, B. 7	*Scepertone* 128b
Shoreditch	Not in D.B.
South Mimms, D. 3	*Mimes* 129b
Staines, B. 6	*Stanes* 128, 129 *bis*, 130b *bis*, Mdlx.; 145b, Bucks.
Stanes	See Staines
Stanestaple	Unid., 128
Stanmera, -mere	See Stanmore
Stanmore, Great and Little, C. 4	*Stanmera, -mere* 129b, 130b
Stanwell, B. 6	*Stanwelle* 130 *bis*
Stanwelle	See Stanwell

Stepney, E. 5	*Stibenhed(e)* 127, 127b, 130, 130b
Stibenhed(e)	See Stepney
Sunbury, B. 6	*Suneberie* 128b
Suneberie	See Sunbury
Teddington	Not in D.B.
Tiburne	See Tyburn
Ticheham	See Ickenham
Tolentone	See Tollington
Tollington, E. 4	*Tolentone* 130b
Toteham	See Tottenham
Totehele	See Tottenham Court
Tottenham, E. 4	*Toteham* 130b
Tottenham Court, E. 5	*Totehele* 128
Tueverde	See Twyford
Twickenham	Not in D.B.
Twyford, C. 5	*Tueverde* 127b
Tyburn, D. 5	*Tiburne* 128b
Uxbridge	Not in D.B.
Wellesdone	See Willesden
Wembley	Not in D.B.
Westbedefund	See West Bedfont
West Bedfont, B. 6	*Westbedefund* 130
Westminster, E. 5	*Æcclesia Sancti Petri Westmonasterii* 128
Willesden, D. 5	*Wellesdone* 127b
Yiewsley	Not in D.B.

ANONYMOUS HOLDINGS

No place-names appear in the following seven entries, and it is possible that some (or even all) of these refer to holdings at places not named elsewhere in Domesday Book:

The king, $12\frac{1}{2}$ acres of Nomansland (*de nanesmaneslande*) in Ossulstone hd, 127.
The king, 30 cottars in Ossulstone hd, 127.
Geoffrey de Mandeville (from archbishop of Canterbury), 2 hides in Elthorne hd, 127.
Hertald, *S. Trinitatis* interlined (from the king), one hide in Spelthorne hd, 128b.
Ralf (from Geoffrey de Mandeville), $1\frac{1}{2}$ hides in Ossulstone hd, 129b.
Nigel (from Robert Gernon), 2 hides in Elthorne hd, 130.
Ælveve, wife of Wateman of London (from the king), half a hide and one third of half a hide in Spelthorne hd, 130b.

NORFOLK — *NORDFOLC*

Little Domesday Book, folios 109–280b

MAPS 34–35

Acle, K. 5	*Acle* 128b
Acra	See Acre, Castle and West; South Acre
Acre, Castle and West, D. 5, E. 5	*Acra* 167, 213, 236 *Acre* 160b, 236 *bis*
Ælsaham	See Aylsham
Ahincham	See Hingham
Aietona, -*tuna*	See Eaton
Ailesham, *Ailessam*	See Aylsham
Ailincham	See Little Ellingham
Ailuertuna, *Ailunituna*	See Yelverton
Alabei	See Alby
Alatorp	See Alethorpe
Alburgh, J. 8	*Aldeberga* 125b, 138b, 149b, 246
Alby, I. 2	*Alabei*, *Alebei* 179b, 186b
Alcmuntona, *Altmuntona*	Unid., 204 *bis*
Aldborough, I. 2	*Aldebur(c)*, -*burg* 171b *bis*, 179b, 184b, 185
Aldeberga	See Alburgh
Aldebur(c), -*burg*	See Aldborough
Aldebury	See Aldeby
Aldeby, L. 7	*Aldebury* 230
Alderford	Not in D.B.
Alebei	See Alby
Alethorpe, F. 3	*Alatorp* 111
Algamundestuna	Unid., 177
Alia Atleburc	See Attleborough
Alia Lopham	See North Lopham
Alia Sculdeham	See Shouldham
Alia Snarshella	See Little Snarehill
Alia Walsingaham	See Walsingham, Great and Little
Alia Wer(e)tham	See Wretham
Almartune, *Almertuna*	See Aylmerton
Alpington, J. 6	*Appletona*, -*tuna* 177b, 203
Altera Pichenham	See Pickenham
Altera Scotessam	See Shottisham
Altmuntona	See *Alcmuntona*
Aluertuna, *Aluntuna*	See Yelverton
Anamere, *Anemere*	See Anmer
Anmer, D. 3	*Anamere*, *Anemere* 151, 161b
Antigeham	See Antingham
Antingham, I. 3	*Antigeham* 184b *bis* *Antingham* 187 *Attinga* 216
Apletuna	See Appleton
Appet(h)orp	Unid., 145b, 269
Appetuna	See Hapton
Appleton, C. 3	*Ap(p)letuna* 173b, 256
Appletona	See Alpington
Appletuna	See Alpington, Appleton
Arminghall, I. 6	*Hameringahala* 138
Ascebei	See Ashby St Mary
Aschebei	See Ashby (near Acle)
Asebei	See Ashby St Mary
Ashby (near Acle), K. 5	*Aschebei* 200b, 224b *Asseby* 216b
Ashby (in Snetterton), G. 7	*Essebei* 127
Ashby St Mary, J. 6	*Ascebei* 203b *As(s)ebei* 177, 177b *ter*, 203b
Ashill, E. 6	*Asscelea* 268 *Essalai* 232b
Ashmanhaugh	Not in D.B.
Ashwellthorpe, H. 7	*Torp* 151b
Ashwicken, C. 4	*Wica* 149 *Wiche* 231b

Becheam	See East Beckham
Bechesuuella	See Beechamwell, Bexwell
Beck, G. 4	*Bec* 147, 147b
Bedingaham	See Bedingham
Bedingham, J. 7	*Bedingaham* 130b, 131 *Bethingaham* 186
Beechamwell, D. 6	*Bechesuuella* 251b *Bicham* 231 *Bycham* 149, 190b *Hekesuuella* 251b
Beeston (near East Dereham)	Not in D.B.
Beeston Regis, H. 1	*Besentuna* 223b *Besetuna*, *-tune* 224, 237b
Beeston St Andrew, I. 5	*Beofetuna* 155b *Bes(e)tuna* 132 *ter*, 204, 229
Beeston St Lawrence, J. 4	*Besetuna* 219b
Beetley, F. 4	*Betellea* 191b
Begetona, *-tuna*	See Beighton
Beighton, K. 5	*Begetona*, *-tuna* 194b, 264
Bekesuuella	See Bexwell
Belaga	See Belaugh
Belaugh, J. 4	*Belaga* 133, 140b, 218b, 229b *ter*
Belega	See Bylaugh
Belingesfort	See Billingford (near East Dereham)
Benelai	See West Bilney
Benemara	See Barmer
Benham	See Banham
Benincham	See Binham
Beofetuna	See Beeston St Andrew
Berc	See Bergh Apton, Southburgh
Berch	See Southburgh
Bereforda, *-fort*	See Barford
Bereuucia	See Barwick
Berham	See Barnham Broom
Bergh Apton, J. 6	*Berc* 215

Berlei	See Barney
Berlingaham	See North Burlingham, South Burlingham
Berlingeham, *Berlungeham*	See North Burlingham
Berneia	See Barney
Berneswrde	See Little Barningham
Bernham	See Barnham Broom
Bernigeham	See North Barningham
Bermincham	See Little Barningham
Berningeham	See North Barningham, North Burlingham
Bertuna	See Barton Bendish, Barton Turf
Besentuna	See Beeston Regis
Besethorp	See Besthorpe
Besetuna	See Beeston Regis, Beeston St Andrew, Beeston St Lawrence
Besetune	See Beeston Regis
Bessingham, H. 2	*Basingeham* 247
Besthorpe, G. 7	*Besethorp* 183, 183b
Bestuna	See Beeston St Andrew
Betellea	See Beetley
Bethingaham	See Bedingham
Bexwell, B. 6	*Beches-*, *Bekesuuella* 190, 212b, 274, 276
Bicham	See Beechamwell
Bicherstuna	See Bickerston
Bichesle	See Bixley
Bickerston, H. 5	*Bicherstuna* 275
Bilenei	See West Bilney
Billingeforda	See Billingford (near East Dereham)
Billingford (near Diss), I. 9	*P(re)lestuna* 139b, 214b, 263

Billingford (near East Dereham), G. 4	*Billingeforda* 147b, 254, 262b
	Belingesfort 436, Suff.
Billockby, K. 5	*Bit(h)lakebei* 174b, 201, 217, 272b
Binctre	See Bintree
Bineham	See Binham
Binelai	See West Bilney
Binham, F. 2	*Benincham* 278b *bis*
	Bin(n)eham 257b *bis*
Binneham	See Binham
Binnetre	See Bintree
Bintree, G. 4	*Binctre* 204
	Binnetre 240b, 269b
Bircham Newton, D. 2	*Niwetuna* 225b
Bircham Tofts, D. 3	*Stofsta* 143
Bischelai, *Biskele*	See Bixley
Bit(h)lakebei	See Billockby
Bittering, F. 4	*Britringa* 121, 137
Bixley, I. 6	*Bichesle* 277b
	Bischelai 182b
	Biskele 176, 176b
	Fiskele 176
Blafelda	See Blofield
Blakeney formerly Snitterley, G. 1	*Esnuterle(a)* 111b, 242b
	Snuterlea 198
Blauuefelda	See Blofield
Blickling, I. 3	*Bliclinga* 196b
	Blikelinga, *-inges* 115, 198
Bliclinga, *Blikelinga*, *Blikelinges*	See Blickling
Blofield, J. 5	*Bla(uue)felda* 192b, 194b, 228b
Blo Norton, G. 9	*Nortuna* 164b, 178b *bis*, 209b, 214
Bodeneia	See Bodney
Bod(en)ham	See Bodham
Bodham, H. 2	*Bod(en)ham* 239, 242b
	Botham 279
Bodney, E. 7	*Bod-*, *Budeneia* 168, 235b, 237
Boethorp	See Bowthorpe
Boielund	See Boyland
Booton, H. 4	*Botuna* 261b
Borstuna	See Burston
Botham	See Bodham
Botuna	See Booton
Boughton, C. 6	*Buchetuna* 231 *bis*, 251
Boweseia	See Bawsey
Bowethorp	See Bowthorpe
Bowthorpe, H. 5	*Bo(w)ethorp* 121, 135
Boyland, I. 7	*Boielund* 249
Braccas, *Braccles*	See Bracon Ash
Bracon Ash, I. 6	*Braccas* 187b
	Braccles 187b
Brade(n)ham	See Bradenham
Bradenham, East and West, F. 5	*Brade(n)ham* 167b, 235, 252, 276b
	Brehendam 252b
Bradeston, J. 5	*Bregestuna* 200
	Breiestuna 200
Bradfield	Not in D.B.
Bramb(r)etuna	See Bramerton
Bramerton, J. 6	*Bramb(r)etuna* 124b, 143b, 175, 176b, 185b, 203, 277b
Brampton, I. 4	*Brantuna* 158b, 229b *bis*
Brancaster, D. 1	*Broncestra* 215b
Brandim	See Brandon Parva
Brandiston, H. 4	*Brantestuna* 114b
Brandon Parva, G. 5	*Brandim* 145
Brant	Unid., 224b
Brantestuna	See Brandiston
Brantuna	See Brampton
Brasincham	See Bressingham
Brecc(h)les, *Breces*	See Breckles
Brecham	See Great Bircham
Breckles, F. 7	*Brecc(h)les* 110, 110b *bis*, 126b, 236b
	Brec(l)es 110b, 183
Brecles	See Breckles

Bregestuna	See Bradeston
Breham	See Brettenham
Brehendam	See Bradenham
Breiestuna	See Bradeston
Bresing(a)ham	See Bressingham
Bressingham, G. 9	*Brasincham* 275b *Bresing(a)ham* 130b, 211 *bis*, 211b
Bretham	See Brettenham
Brettenham, F. 8	*Bre(t)ham* 183b, 213b, 239b, 266
Bridgham, F. 8	*Brugam* 213b
Briningham, G. 2	*Bruningaham* 146, 198 *Burningaham* 198
Brinton, G. 2	*Bruntuna* 192
Brisley	Not in D.B.
Briston, G. 3	*Burstuna* 112, 170
Britringa	See Bittering
Broc	See Brooke
Brockdish, I. 9	*Brodise*, *Brodiso* 139, 210b
Brodise, *Brodiso*	See Brockdish
Brom, *Bron*	See Broome
Broncestra	See Brancaster
Brooke, J. 6	*Broc* 210 *quater*, 210b, 212
Broome, J. 7	*Brom*, *Bron* 186b, 211b, 259b
Broomsthorpe, E. 3	*Brunestor* 214b
Brugam	See Bridgham
Brumeham	See Burnham Overy
Brumestada	See Brumstead
Brumstead, K. 3	*Brume-*, *Brunestada* 179b, 187b
Brunaham	See Burnham Norton etc.
Brundala	See Brundall
Brundall, J. 5	*Brundala* 132, 200, 200b, 268b
Bruneham	See Burnham Norton etc.
Brunehamtorp	See Burnham Thorpe
Brunestada	See Brumstead
Brunestor	See Broomsthorpe
Bruningaham	See Briningham
Bruntuna	See Brinton
Buc	See Burgh next Aylsham
Bucanaham	See Buckenham (near Acle)
Buccham	See Buckenham (near Attleborough)
Bucham	See Buckenham (near Acle), Buckenham (near Attleborough)
Buchanaham	See Buckenham (near Acle)
Bucheham	See Buckenham (near Attleborough)
Buchenham	See Buckenham Tofts
Buchestuna	See Buxton
Buchetuna	See Boughton
Buckenham	See Buckenham Tofts
Buckenham (near Acle), J. 6	*Bucanaham* 123b *Buc(hana)ham* 200, 209b
Buckenham (near Attleborough), G. 7	*Buccham* 209 *Buc(he)ham* 126b, 149b, 152, 164 *bis*, 164b *bis*, 183b *quin*, 223, 226, 239b *quater*, 266 *bis*, 268b, 270b, 271, 274b, 277b *bis*, 278b
Buckenham Tofts, E. 7	*Buchenham*, *Buckenham* 238b, 266b
Budeneia	See Bodney
Bukestuna	See Buxton
Bunwell	Not in D.B.
Burc	See Burgh next Aylsham, Burgh St Margaret, Southburgh
Burgh next Aylsham, I. 3	*Bu(r)c* 186b, 247b

Place	Domesday form and folios
Burgh St Margaret, K. 5	*Burc* 129b, 174b, 185, 217 *bis*, 272 *bis* *Burh* 201
Burgh St Peter	Not in D.B.
Burh	See Burgh St Margaret
Burnham Deepdale, D. 1	*Depedala* 184
Burnham Norton, Sutton, Ulph and Westgate, E. 1, E. 2	*Brunaham*, *Bruneham* 170b, 179, 183b, 215b, 237
Burnham Overy, E. 1	*Brumeham* 128
Burnham Thorpe, E. 2	*Brunehamtorp* 169, 262
Burningaham	See Briningham
Burston, H. 8	*Borstuna* 114, 130 *bis*, 130b *ter*, 154, 154b, 155, 211b
Burstuna	See Briston
Buxton, I. 4	*Buchestuna*, *Bukestuna* 229, 229b
Bycham	See Beechamwell
Bylaugh, G. 4	*Belega* 147
Caister, L. 5	*Castra*, *Castre*, *Castro* 129b *bis*, 134, 221
Caistor St Edmunds, I. 6	*Castra*, *Castru* 210, 228b *bis*
Caituna	See Catton (in Postwick)
Calatorp	See Calthorpe
Calda(n)chota	See Caldecote
Caldecote, D. 6	*Calda(n)chota* 231b, 235
Caletorp	See Calthorpe
Calthorpe, I. 3	*Calatorp*, *Caletorp* 179b, 218, 261b
Caluestune	See Cawston
Calvely, G. 6	*Cauelea* 214b
Cantelai	See Cantley
Cantley, K. 6	*Cantelai* 122b
Carboistorp	See Shouldham Thorpe
Carbrooke, F. 6	*Cherebroc* 235b, 265b, 266
Carleton Forehoe, H. 6	*Carletuna* 145b, 216 *Karletuna* 121
Carleton Rode, H. 7	*Carletuna* 135b, 150b, 159b, 189 *bis*, 189b, 246b *bis*
Carleton St Peter, J. 6	*Carletuna* 177 *Karlentona* 177b, 186b, 203b, 233b, 253b
Carletuna	See Carleton Forehoe, Carleton Rode, Carleton St Peter, East Carleton
Caste(s)tuna	See Caston
Castle Acre	See Acre
Castle Rising, C. 4	*Risinga* 142b
Caston, F. 7	*Caste(s)tuna* 110, 110b *Catestuna* 163b *Katestuna* 111b, 126
Castona	See Cawston
Castra	See Caister, Caistor St Edmunds
Castre, *Castro*	See Caister
Castru	See Caistor St Edmunds
Castune	See Cawston
Cate(s)felda	See Catfield
Catestuna	See Caston
Catetuna	See Catton (near Norwich)
Catfield, K. 4	*Cate(s)felda* 150, 179b
Catton (near Norwich), I. 5	*Cat(e)tuna* 131b, 140b
Catton (in Postwick), J. 6	*Caituna* 200 *Ca(t)tuna* 200, 240
Cattuna	See Catton (near Norwich), Catton (in Postwick)
Catuna	See Catton (in Postwick)

Cauelea	See Calvely
Cauestuna, *Caupstuna*, *Caustituna*, *Caustona*, *-tuna*	See Cawston
Cawston, H. 4	*Caluestune* 272 *Castona*, *-tune* 112b, 114b *Cauestuna* 114b *Caupstuna* 158b *Caustituna* 114b *Caustona*, *-tuna* 114b *bis*, 115 *bis*, 115b *bis*, 133, 158b, 193, 234b *bis*, 261b *Gaustuna* 115
Challinga	See Kelling
Chedgrave, K. 6	*Scatagraua* 253 *bis*
Chenighehala, *Chenikehala*, *Cheninchala*, *Cheninghala*, *Cheninkehala*	See Kenninghall
Cherebroc	See Carbrooke
Chesewic	See Keswick
Chineburlai	See Kimberley
Chiptena	See Kipton
Choseley	Not in D.B.
Cidesterna	See Syderstone
Claia	See Cley next the Sea, Cockley Cley
Clakestona	See Claxton
Clareia	Unid., 144
Clarestona	See Claxton
Claxton, J. 6	*Clakestona* 177b, 203b *Clarestuna* 177 *bis*, 203b
Cleia	See Cockley Cley
Cleietorpa	See Cleythorpe
Clenchwarton, B. 4	*Ecleuuartuna* 221b
Clepebei, *Clepesbe*(*i*)	See Clippesby
Cley next the Sea, G. 1	*Claia* 111b, 112
Cleythorpe, D. 6	*Cleietorpa* 232
Clipesby	See Clippesby
Clipestuna	See Clipstone

Clippesby, K. 5	*Clepebei* 272 *Clepesbe*(*i*) 113b *bis*, 129b, 174b, 201b *Clipesby* 217
Clipstone, F. 3	*Clipestuna* 168b
Cockley Cley, D. 6	*Claia* 167b, 276b *Cleia* 120, 167b
Cockthorpe, F. 2	*Torp* 192b, 198b
Cokereshala, *Coketeshala*	See Coltishall
Colby, I. 3	*Colebei* 115b
Colceteshala	See Coltishall
Colebei	See Colby
Colechirca, *Colekirka*	See Colkirk
Coleneia, *Coleneii*	See Colney
Coletuna	See Colton
Colkirk, F. 3	*Colechirca* 191b *Colekirka* 197b
Colney, I. 5	*Coleneia*, *Coleneii* 188b, 204b, 225b
Coltishall, J. 4	*Cokereshala* 158 *Coketeshala* 244 *Colceteshala* 159
Colton, H. 5	*Coletuna* 166
Colveston, D. 7	*Covestuna* 162b
Concham	See Congham
Congham, C. 4	*Concham* 267b *Congheham*, *Congreham* 161 *bis*
Congheham, *Congreham*	See Congham
Congrethorp	See Crownthorpe
Corpestig, *-stih*, *Corpsty*	See Corpusty
Corpusty, H. 3	*Corpestig*, *-stih* 158b, 225 *Corpsty* 193
Costesei(*a*)	See Costessey
Costessey, I. 5	*Costesei*(*a*) 145, 145b *ter*, 147, 147b, 150b *bis* *Coteseia* 144b, 145b
Coston	Not in D.B.
Coteseia	See Costessey
Covestuna	See Colveston
Crachefort	See Crackford

Crackford, I. 3	*Crachefort* 133 *Crakeforda* 158b
Crakeforda	See Crackford
Cranaworda	See Cranworth
Cranewisse	See Cranwich
Craneworda	See Cranworth
Cranwich, D. 7	*Cranewisse* 163
Cranworth, F. 6	*Cranaworda*, *Craneworda* 121b, 122
Creake, North and South, E. 2	*Crehic* 179 *Creic(h)* 168b, 179, 183b, 223b *Kreic(h)* 111, 179 *Suthcreich* 237
Crehic, *Creic(h)*	See Creake
Crep(e)lesham	See Crimplesham
Cresincghaham	See Great Cressingham
Cresingham, *Parva*	See Little Cressingham
Cressingaham	See Great Cressingham, Little Cressingham
Cressingaham, *Parva*	See Little Cressingham
Crimplesham, C. 6	*Crep(e)lesham* 230b *ter*
Cringaforda	See Cringleford
Cringleford, I. 6	*Cringaforda* 150b, 189 *Kiningaford* 143b *Kringelforda* 143b
Crokestona	See Croxton (near Fakenham)
Crokestuna	See Croxton (near Thetford)
Cromer	Not in D.B.
Cronkethor	See Crownthorpe
Crostueit	See Crostwick
Crostwick, I. 5	*Crostueit* 243b *bis* *Crotwit* 229
Crostwight, J. 3	*Crostwit* 248
Crostwit	See Crostwight
Crotwit	See Crostwick
Crownthorpe, G. 6	*Congrethorp* 121b *Cronkethor* 227b

Croxton (near Fakenham), F. 3	*Crokestona* 169
Croxton (near Thetford), E. 8	*Crokestuna* 136b
Cuidenham	See Quidenham
Culestorpa	See Custthorpe
Culver(s)testuna	See Kilverstone
Custthorpe, D. 5	*Culestorpa* 235b
Dalliga	See Field Dalling
Dallinga	See Field Dalling, Wood Dalling
Danefaela, *-fella*	See Denver
Denton, J. 8	*Dentuna* 138b, 139b, 246
Dentuna	See Denton
Denver, B. 6	*Danefaela*, *-fella* 160 *bis*
Deopham, G. 6	*D(i)epham* 166b, 227
Depedala	See Burnham Deepdale
Depham	See Deopham
Dereham	See West Dereham
Derham	See East Dereham, West Dereham
Dersincham	See Dersingham
Dersingham, C. 3	*Dersincham* 245b, 256, 256b, 278b
Dicclesburc	See Dickleburgh
Dice	See Diss
Dicingaham	See Ditchingham
Dickleburgh, H. 8	*Dicclesburc* 211
Didlington, D. 7	*Dudelingatuna* 167, 245
Diepham	See Deopham
Dilham, J. 3	*Dilham* 148, 156, 219b *Dillam* 187
Dillam	See Dilham
Diss, H. 9	*Dice* 114, 276b, Norf.; 282 *bis*, Suff.
Ditchingham, J. 7	*Dicingaham* 139b
Doching(h)e	See Docking
Docking, D. 2	*Doching(h)e* 143, 245b
Dodenham	See North Tuddenham

Dontuna	See Dunton
Downham Market, B. 6	*Dun(e)ham* 160, 190, 213 *bis*, 274, 275b
Draituna	See Drayton
Drayton, I. 5	*Draituna* 229
Dudelingatuna	See Didlington
Dumham	See Dunham
Duneham	See Downham Market
Dunestun(a)	See Dunston
Dunham	See Downham Market, Dunham
Dunham, Great and Little, E. 5	*Dumham*, *Dunham* 137, 235b, 264
Dunston, I. 6	*Dunestun(a)* 150, 188, 205, 230 *Dustuna* 273
Dunton, E. 3	*Dontuna* 111b
Dustuna	See Dunston
Dykebeck, H. 6	*Hidichetorp* 275 *Idikethorp* 253
Earlham, I. 5	*Erlham* 135 *bis*, 150b
Earsham, J. 8	*Ersam* 138b, 139, 139b, 140, 141, 141b, 186, 263b *Hersam* 138b, 139 *ter*, 139b *bis*, 140, 177b, 186, 210b *bis*, 246, 263b
East Barsham	See Barsham
East Beckham, H. 2	*Beccheham* 198b *Bech(e)am* 128, 185, 192
East Bilney	Not in D.B.
East Bradenham	See Bradenham
East Carleton, I. 6	*Carletuna* 187b, 229b, 254 *bis*, 273 *Karletuna* 180b
East Dereham, F. 5	*Derham* 214 *bis*, 227
East Harling	See Harling
East Lexham	See Lexham
Easton (near Norwich), H. 5	*Estuna* 145
Easton (in Scottow), J. 4	*Estuna* 217b, 219b
East Raynham	See Raynham
East Rudham	See Rudham
East Ruston, K. 3	*Ristuna* 248
East Somerton	See Somerton
East Tuddenham, G. 5	*Easttudenham* 228 *Toddenham* 208, 277 *Todeneham* 145b *Tudenham* 147
Easttudenham	See East Tuddenham
Eastuuininc	See East Winch
East Walton, D. 5	*Waltuna* 149, 149b, 173, 236
East Winch, C. 4	*Eastuuininc* 173 *Eastwninc* 125b, 190b *Estuunic*, *Estwnic* 236, 274b, 280
Eastwninc	See East Winch
East Wretham	See Wretham
Eaton, I. 6	*Aietona*, *-tuna* 124, 125 *Etona* 131 *Ettuna*, *Ettune* 123b *bis*, 132, 135
Eccles (near Attleborough), G. 8	*Eccles* 194
Eccles (in Hempstead), K. 3	*Eccles* 272b *Heccles* 220b
Echam	See Potter Heigham
Ecleuuartuna	See Clenchwarton
Edgamera	See Egmere
Edgefield, H. 2	*Edisfelda* 257b, 261
Edingthorpe	Not in D.B.
Edisfelda	See Edgefield
Egemere	See Egmere
Egmere, E. 2	*Edgamera* 192b *Egemere* 113 *Estgamera* 170b
Eia	See Eye, Suff.
Eilanda	See Nayland
Eilessam	See Aylsham
Ekincham	See Heckingham
Elesham	See Aylsham

Elincgham	See Little Ellingham
Elincham	See Ellingham (near Loddon), Great Ellingham
Ellingham	See Little Ellingham
Ellingham (near Loddon), K. 7	*Elincham* 141b
Elmenham	See North Elmham
Elsing, G. 4	*Helsinga* 157b
Emneth	Not in D.B.
Ennaham	See Hedenham
Erimestuna	See Grimston
Erlham	See Earlham
Erminclanda	See Irmingland
Erpincham	See Erpingham
Erpingham, I. 3	*Erpincham* 186b, 218, 247b, 260b *Herpincham* 279b
Ersam	See Earsham
Esco(u)	See Sco
Esingatuna	See Islington
Esnaringa	See Little Snoring
Esnuterle(a)	See Blakeney formerly Snitterly
Esparlai, *-le(a)*	See Sporle
Essalai	See Ashill
Essebei	See Ashby (in Snetterton)
Estanbyrda	See Stibbard
Estanforda	See Stanford
Esterestuna	See Sturston
Estgamera	See Egmere
Estodeia	See Stody
Estratuna	See Stratton St Mary, St Michael; Stratton Strawless
Estretona	See Testerton
Estuna	See Easton (near Norwich), Easton (in Scottow)
Estuunic, *Estwnic*	See East Winch
Eswinic	See West Winch
Etduuella	See Wells next the Sea
Etona, *Ettuna*, *Ettune*	See Eaton
Euincham	See Hevingham
Euluestorp	See Ingoldisthorpe
Fac(h)enham, *Fagan(a)ham*, *Fagenham*	See Fakenham
Fakenham, F. 3	*Fac(h)enham* 111, 111b *bis*, 112b, 113 *Fagan(a)ham* 113, 172b *Fagenham* 111b, 233 *Fangeham* 197b *Phacham* 110
Faltorp	See Felthorpe
Fangeham	See Fakenham
Fatwella	See Feltwell
Felbrigg, I. 2	*Felebruge* 184, 184b, 185b
Felebruge	See Felbrigg
Felethor(p), *-torp*	See Felthorpe
Felmi(n)cham	See Felmingham
Felmingham, I. 3	*Felmi(n)cham* 115b, 187, 219
Felthorpe, H. 4	*Faltorp* 234 *Felethor(p)*, *-torp* 114b, 147b, 229, 241b
Feltwell, C. 7	*Fatwella* 162 *bis* *Feltwella* 136, 213
Feltwella	See Feltwell
Ferseuella	See Fersfield
Fersfield, G. 8	*Ferseuella* 130 *bis*, 130b *ter* *Feru(ess)ella* 130b, 276b
Feru(ess)ella	See Fersfield
F..ham	See Fincham
Field Dalling, G. 2	*Dalli(n)ga* 113b, 146, 179, 262
Filby, L. 5	*Filebey* 180, 225b *Phileb(e)y* 159, 220b, 269b, 278
Filebey	See Filby
Fincham, C. 6	*F..ham* 160 *P(h)incham* 159b, 205b, 209, 212b, 230, 250b, 273b, 275, 276
Fiscele	See Fishley

Gadesthorp	See Gasthorpe
Gaituna	See Gayton
Gaiuude	See Gaywood
Galsingaham	See Walsingham, Great and Little
Garboldisham, G. 8	*Gerboldesham* 127b
Garveston, G. 5	*Gerolfestuna* 207b *Giro(l)festuna* 207b, 208
Gasthorpe, F. 9	*Gadesthorp* 209b *Gatesthor(p)* 127b, 128
Gatelea	See Gateley
Gateley, F. 4	*Gatelea* 197b, 239, 256b
Gatesthor(p)	See Gasthorpe
Gaustuna	See Cawston
Gayton, D. 4	*Gaituna* 160b *bis*, 221b, 222, 238b, 274b
Gayton Thorpe, D. 4	*T(h)orp* 142, 173, 207b, 236, 274b
Gaywood, C. 4	*Gaiuude* 191
Gegeseta, *-sete*	See Guist
Geg(h)estueit	See Guestwick
Geldeston	Not in D.B.
Gerboldesham	See Garboldisham
Gernemutha, *Gernemwa*	See Yarmouth
Gerolfestuna	See Garveston
Gersam	See Gresham
Gersinga, *Gessinga*	See Gissing
Gillingham, K. 7	*Kildincham* 116, 141b *Gillingaham* 283b, Suff.
Giming(e)ham	See Gimingham
Gimingham, J. 2	*Giming(e)ham* 170b *ter* *Gimingheham* 170b
Gimingheham	See Gimingham
Giro(l)festuna	See Garveston
Gissing, H. 8	*Gersinga*, *Gessinga* 130, 154, 155, 176b, 211, 211b *bis*, 276b
Glamforda	See Glandford
Glandford, G. 2	*Glamforda*, *Glanforda* 112, 242b
Glanforda	See Glandford
Glorestorp	See Glosthorpe
Glosthorpe, C. 4	*Glorestorp* 153b
Gnateshala	See Knettishall, Suff.
Gnatingdon, C. 2	*Nettinghetuna* 271b
Godestuna	See Gooderstone
Goduic	See Godwick
Godwick, E. 4	*Goduic* 235b
Golosa	See Ingloss
Gooderstone, D. 6	*Godestuna* 202, 202b
Gorleston, L. 6	*Gorlestuna* 116, Norf.; 283, 283b, 284b, Suff.
Gorlestuna	See Gorleston
Great Bircham, D. 3	*Brecham* 222, 222b, 226
Great Cressingham, E. 6	*Cresincghaham* 191 *Cressingaham* 144b, 197b, 235 *Gresingaham* 197b
Great Dunham	See Dunham
Great Ellingham, G. 7	*Elincham* 226 *Helincham*, *Helingham* 207, 274b
Great Fransham	See Fransham
Great Hautbois	See Hautbois
Great Massingham	See Massingham
Great Melton, H. 6	*In duabus Meltunis* 204b *Meltuna(na)* 204, 204b, 254b *bis*, 279b
Great Plumstead	See Plumstead
Great Ryburgh, F. 3	*Reieborh* 170 *Reienburh* 257 *bis*
Great Snarehill, E. 8	*Snareshella*, *-hul* 178, 209b, 277b *bis*
Great Snoring, F. 2	*Snaringa* 122b, 258
Great Walsingham	See Walsingham, Great and Little
Gregesete	See Guist

Herpincham	See Erpingham
Herringby, K. 5	*Haringebei* 273
Hersam	See Earsham
Hetella	See Hethel
Hethel, H. 6	*Hathella* 180b *Het(h)ella* 180, 180b, 263b
Hethella	See Hethel
Hethersett, H. 6	*Hederse(e)ta* 150, 204b, 205
Hethingham	See Heckingham
Heuincham	See Hevingham
Heuseda	See Bawsey
Heveringalanda	See Haveringland
Hevingham, I. 4	*Euincham* 241b *Heuincham* 133 *Strincham* 196b
Heydon	Not in D.B.
Hickling, K. 4	*Hikelinga* 148
Hidichetorp	See Dykebeck
Hidling(h)eia	See Hilgay
Hidolfestuna, *Hidolvestuna*	See Hindolveston
Hidringham	See Hindringham
Hierduic	See Hardwick
Hikelinga	See Hickling
Hilborough, E. 6	*Hildeburhwella* 167b
Hildeburhwella	See Hilborough
Hilgay, B. 7	*Halingheia* 136 *Hidling(h)eia* 159b, 209, 213, 215, 274 *Hulingheia* 190
Hillington, C. 3	*Helingetuna* 267b *Idlinghetuna* 245b *Nidlinghetuna* 161
Himcham	See Hingham
Hincham	See Hingham, Ingham
Hindolveston, G. 3	*Hidolfestuna* 192, 192b *Hidolvestuna* 193
Hindringaham	See Hindringham
Hindringham, F. 2	*Hidringham* 192b *Hindringaham* 113, 192, 198b *bis*, 202, 247 *Indregeham* 194b
Hingham, G. 6	*Ahincham* 179 *H(a)incham* 111, 166b, 227b *quin*, 253, 275 *Himcham* 110b *Hinham* 111
Hinham	See Hingham
Hobuisse, *Hobuist*	See Hautbois
Hoccham, *Hochaham*	See Holkham
Hocham	See Hockham, Holkham
Hocham, *Parva*	See Little Hockham
Hochelinga	See Hockering
Hockering, G. 5	*Hochelinga* 228 *Hokelinka* 227b
Hockham, F. 7	*Hocham* 178, 183, 277b
Hockwold, C. 8	*Hocwella* 162
Hocwella	See Hockwold
Hoe, F. 4	*Hou* 214
Hohttune	See Houghton St Giles
Hokelinka	See Hockering
Holcham	See Holkham
Holkham, E. 1	*Hoccham* 194b *Hoc(ha)ham* 192b, 258 *Holcham*, *Holkham* 113 *bis*, 146, 170b, 264b *Locham* 192b
Holm	See Holme Hale, Holme next the Sea
Holma	See Holme Hale
Holme Hale, E. 6	*Holm(a)* 120, 277
Holme next the Sea, C. 1	*Holm* 126, 222b
Holt, G. 2	*Holt* 111b, 112 *bis*, 112b *bis*, 113b *bis*
Holverston, J. 6	*Holvestuna* 124b, 143, 143b, 176, 203
Holvestuna	See Holverston
Honing, J. 3	*Haninga* 219b, 260b

Honingham, H. 5	*Huni(n)cham* 145, 145b
Honingham Thorpe, H. 5	*T(h)orp* 145 *bis*
Hornincgetoft	See Horningtoft
Horning, J. 4	*Horninga* 218b
Horninga	See Horning
Horninghetoft	See Horningtoft
Horningtoft, F. 4	*Hornincgetoft* 120b *Horninghetoft* 120b
Horseia	See Horsey
Horsey, L. 4	*Hors(h)eia* 180, 187b, 196b, 272b *bis*
Horsford, I. 5	*Hosforda* 155
Horsham, I. 5	*Horsham* 155b
Horsheia	See Horsey
Horstead, I. 4	*Ho(r)steda* 140, 140b *bis*
Horsteda	See Horstead
Hosforda	See Horsford
Hosteda	See Horstead
Hottune	Unid., 198b
Hou	See Hoe, Howe
Houby	See Oby
Houghton (near West Rudham), D. 3	*Houtuna* 169b *bis*
Houghton on the Hill, E. 6	*Houtuna* 232, 244b
Houghton St Giles, F. 2	*Hohttune* 113
Houtuna	See Houghton (near West Rudham), Houghton on the Hill
Hoveton St John, St Peter, J. 4	*Hovetuna* 158b, 217, 218, 218b *bis*, 229b, 244
Hovetuna	See Hoveton
Howa	See Howe
Howe, J. 6	*Hou* 123b *bis*, 210 *Howa* 135b
Hudeston, H. 7	*Hadestuna*, *Hatestuna* 181b, 249, 267b
Huerueles	See Quarles
Hulingheia	See Hilgay
Hunaworda	See Hunworth
Hunestanesteda, *Hunestanestuna*, *Hunes(ta)tuna*	See Hunstanton
Huneworda, *-worde*	See Hunworth
Huni(n)cham	See Honingham
Hunstanton, C. 2	*Hunestanesteda* 135b *Hunestanestuna* 197b, 265b *Hunes(ta)tuna* 173b, 183 *Huntanestuna* 215b
Huntanestuna	See Hunstanton
Hunworth, G. 2	*Hunaworda* 242 *Huneworda*, *-worde* 112, 146
Hwateaker	See Wheatacre
Hwimpwella	See Whimpwell
Iachesham, *Iakesham*	See Yaxham
Iarpestuna, *Ierpstuna*	Unid., 141b, 249b, 260
Ic(c)heburc, *Ic(c)heburna*	See Ickburgh
Ickburgh, E. 7	*Iccheburc*, *-burna* 242 *bis* *Icheburc*, *-burna* 236, 266b *Keburna* 162b
Idekethorp	See Dykebeck
Idlinghetuna	See Hillington
Ierpstuna	See *Iarpestuna*
Illington, F. 7	*Illinketuna* 164b
Illinketuna	See Illington
Ilsinghatuna, *Ilsinghetuna*	See Islington
Indregeham	See Hindringham
Ingewrda	See Ingworth
Ingham, K. 3	*Hincham* 148, 148b, 220b
Inghewurda	See Ingworth
Ingloss, J. 7	*Golosa* 259
Ingoldisthorpe, C. 3	*Euluestorp* 256b *Torp* 266b
Ingworth, I. 3	*Ingewrda* 179b *Inghewurda* 234b

Locham	See Holkham
Loddon, K. 7	*Lathaham* 255b *Lodna* 211b *Lodnes*, *Lodues* 212b, 255b *Lot(h)na* 203b, 255b, 259, 259b
Lodham	See Ludham
Lodna, *Lodnes*, *Lodues*	See Loddon
Longham, F. 4	*Lawingham* 274b
Lopham, North and South, G. 8	*Alia Lopham* 178b *Lopham* 178b *quin*, 183b
Losincham	See Lessingham
Lot(h)na	See Loddon
Ludham, K. 4	*Lodham* 220 *Ludham* 148, 150 *bis*, 220b, 272b
Lun	See Lynn
Lur(l)inga	See Larling
Lynford, E. 7	*Lineforda* 174, 242
Lyng, G. 4	*Ling* 147
Lynn, King's, North, South and West, B. 4	*Lena* 209, 236, 274b, 276 *Lun* 251b
Maeltuna	See Melton Constable
Maidestuna	See Mayton
Maltebei, *-bey*, *-by*	See Mautby
Manegrena	See Mangreen
Mangreen, I. 6	*Manegrena* 188
Mani(n)ctuna	See Mannington
Mannington, H. 3	*Mani(n)ctuna* 132b, 158
Manson, G. 6	*Mantatestona* 122
Mantatestona	See Manson
Marcham	See Martham
Mar(e)ham	See Marham
Marham, C. 5	*Mar(e)ham* 159b, 212b, 238 *Marsam* 205b
Maringatorp	See Morning Thorpe
Markeshalla	See Markshall
Markshall, I. 6	*Markeshalla* 230
Markshall cont.	*Merkeshala*, *Merkessal(l)e* 228b *bis*, 230
Marlingford, H. 5	*Marthingheforda* 209b *Merlingeforda* 145b
Marsam	See Marham, Marsham
Marsham, I. 4	*Marsam* 115, 196b *bis*, 229b, 241b
Marsincham, *Marsinghara*	See Massingham
Marstuna	See Morston
Martham, L. 4	*Marcham* 113b *Martham* 129b, 146b, 195, 195b, 200b, 217 *bis*, 272b
Marthingheforda	See Marlingford
Masin(i)cham, *Masing(h)eham*	See Massingham
Massingham, Great and Little, D. 4	*Marsincham* 161 *Marsinghara* 151 *Masincham* 109b, 151, 222 *bis*, 245b *Masing(h)eham* 173 *bis* *Masinicham* 231b
Matelasc, *-lesc*	See Matlask
Matelwalde	See Methwold
Mateshala	See Mattishall
Matingeles	See Matlask
Matlask, H. 2	*Matelasc*, *-lesc* 115b, 132b *bis*, 146b *Matingeles* 146
Mattishall, G. 5	*Mateshala* 166b, 214b, 228 *bis*, 275
Mautby, L. 5	*Maltebei*, *-bey*, *-by* 134b, 180, 225b
Mayton, I. 4	*Maidestuna* 243b *bis*
Mele(ha)m	See Mileham
Meltinga	See Mintlyn
Melton Constable, G. 3	*Maeltuna* 198
Meltuna(na)	See Great Melton
Meltunis, *In duabus*	See Great Melton, Little Melton

Mendaham	See Mendham
Mendham, I. 8	*Men(da)ham* 195b, 210b *ter*
Menham	See Mendham
Meretuna	See Merton
Merkeshala, *Merkessal(l)e*	See Markshall
Merlingeforda	See Marlingford
Merstona, *-tuna*	See Morston
Merton, F. 7	*Meretuna* 252
Methelwalde	See Methwold
Methwold, D. 7	*Matelwalde*, *Methelwalde* 136, 162
Metton, I. 2	*Hametuna* 184 *Metune* 184b
Metune	See Metton
Middeltuna	See Middleton (near King's Lynn)
Middleton (in Forncett), H. 7	*Mildeltuna* 150b
Middleton (near King's Lynn), C. 5	*Mid(d)eltuna* 209, 222 *bis*, 238 *Mildetuna* 149
Midelhale	See Mildenhall, Suff.
Mideltuna	See Middleton (near King's Lynn)
Mildeltuna	See Middleton (in Forncett)
Mildetuna	See Middleton (near King's Lynn)
Mileham, F. 4	*Mele(ha)m* 121, 136b, 138, 256b *Milham* 191b *Mulcham* 121 *Mul(e)ham* 137, 140b, 144b, 166 *bis*, 179, 197b, 207b, 214, 226b, 227, 232b, 252b *bis*, 256b, 274b, 275 *Mullam* 226b
Milham	See Mileham
Mintlyn, C. 4	*Meltinga* 197b
Modetuna	See Moulton St Mary
Molkeber(tes)tuna	See Mulbarton
Mondefort	See Mundford
Moor, K. 6	*Mora* 269b
Mora	See Moor
Morlea	See Morley
Morley St Botolph, St Peter, G. 6	*Morlea* 166b, 227b
Morning Thorpe, I. 7	*Maringatorp* 150b *Torp* 212 *ter*
Morston, G. 1	*Marstuna* 184 *Merstona*, *-tuna* 112b, 128
Mortofst	See Mortoft
Mortoft, H. 3	*Mortofst* 158
Morton on the Hill	Not in D.B.
Mothetuna	See Moulton St Mary
Moulton St Mary, K. 6	*Modetuna* 128b, 129b *bis* *Mothetuna* 113b
Moulton St Michael, H. 7	*Muletuna* 150b, 181, 189 *bis*, 189b, 190, 273
Mulbarton, I. 6	*Molkeber(tes)tuna* 188, 229b *bis*
Mulcham, *Muleham*	See Mileham
Muleslai	See Mundesley
Muletuna	See Moulton St Michael
Mulham, *Mullam*	See Mileham
Mundaham	See Mundham
Mundeforda	See Mundford
Mundesley, J. 2	*Muleslai* 171, 171b
Mundford, D. 7	*Mondefort* 162b, 213b *Mundeforda* 183
Mundhala	See Mundham
Mundham, J. 7	*Mundaham* 131, 140, 176b, 177 *bis*, 177b *bis*, 186b, 259, 259b *bis*, 264, 267, 270 *Mundhala* 211b
Murlai	Unid., 192b
Nache-, *Naketuna*	See Necton
Narborough, D. 5	*Nereburh* 177b

Narford, D. 5	*Nereforda* 144	*Norhrepes*	See Repps: Northrepps and Southrepps
Naruestuna	Unid., 255b		
Nayland, H. 7	*Eilanda* 153, 188		
	Neilanda 151b, 187b	*Norhwalde*	See Northwold
		Norrepes	See Repps: Northrepps and Southrepps
Neatishead, J. 4	*Snateshirda* 218b		
Nechetuna	See Necton		
Necton, E. 5	*Ketuna* 236	North Barningham, H. 2	*Berni(n)geham* 172, 184b *bis*, 185 *bis*, 198b, 242b, 247, 279
	Nache-, *Naketuna* 236 *ter*		
	Neche-, *Neketuna* 235, 235b *quin*, 236 *ter*, 236b *ter*	North Barsham, F. 2	*Norbarsam* 172b
		North Burlingham, K. 5	*Berlingaham*, *-ingeham* 123 *bis*, 200
Needham	Not in D.B.		
Neilanda	See Nayland		
Neketuna	See Necton		*Berlungeham* 199, 199b
Nereburh	See Narborough		
Nereforda	See Narford		*Berningeham* 224, 224b
Ness, L. 4	*Nessa* 180		
Nessa	See Ness	North Creake	See Creake
Nestesham	See Snettisham	North Elmham, F. 4	*Elmenham* 191b
Nettinghetuna	See Gnatingdon		
Neutuna, G.2	Lost near Holt, 112b	*North Langale*	See Langley
		North Lopham	See Lopham
Newotona	See Newton (near Norwich)	North Lynn	See Lynn
		North Pickenham	See Pickenham
Newton (near Castle Acre), E. 5	*Nieutuna* 120	Northrepps	See Repps: Northrepps and Southrepps
Newton (near Norwich), I. 5	*Newotona* 125		
		North Runcton, C. 5	*Runghetuna* 222
Newton Flotman, I. 7	*Niwe(s)tuna* 180b, 189, 265		*Rynghetona* 207
		North Tuddenham, G. 5	*Dodenham* 214b
Nidlinghetuna	See Hillington		*Nordtudenham* 275
Nieutuna	See Newton (near Castle Acre)		*Todden(c)ham* 228, 271b
Niuetuna	See West Newton		*Totdenham* 228
Niwestuna	See Newton Flotman		*Toteham* 275
		North Walsham, J. 3	*Walsam* 159, 218b, 219b
Niwetuna	See Bircham Newton, Newton Flotman	Northwold, D. 7	*Norhwalde*, *Nortwalde* 162, 213b
Norbarsam	See North Barsham		
Nordelph	Not in D.B.	Norton Subcourse, K. 7	*Norfen* 177
Nordtudenham	See North Tuddenham		*Nortuna* 182b, 203b, 205b, 212b, 230, 249b, 255b, 273
Norfen	See Norton Subcourse		

Nortuna	See Blo Norton, Norton Subcourse, Pudding Norton, Wood Norton
Nortwalde	See Northwold
Noruic, *-wic(i)*	See Norwich
Norwich, I. 5	*Noruic* 116 *Norwic(i)* 114, 117b, 118, 234b
Obuuessa	See Hautbois
Oby, K. 5	*Houby* 217 *Oebei* 174b *Orbi* 216b *Othebei* 174b
Ocselea	Unid., 111
Oebei	See Oby
Ohbouuessa	See Hautbois
Opetune, *Optuna*, *-tune*	See Upton
Orbeslei	See Ormesby
Orbi	See Oby
Ordesteda	See Worstead
Ormesbei, *-bey*, *-by*	See Ormesby
Ormesby St Margaret, St Michael, L. 5	*Orbeslei* 114 *Ormesbei*, *-bey*, *- by* 113b *bis*, 115b, 116, 174b, 273 *Osmesbei* 197
Oslactuna	See Aslacton
Osmesbei	See Ormesby
Osmondiston (now Scole), H. 9	*Osmundestuna* 176b, 263, 278
Osmundestuna	See Osmondiston
Ossuic	See Oxwick
Othebei	See Oby
Othestranda	See Overstrand
Otringheia, *Otrinkeehia*	See Ottering Hithe
Ottering Hithe, C. 7	*Otringheia* 162b *Otrinkeehia* 162b
Oulstuna	See Oulton
Oulton, H. 3	*Oulstuna* 115
Outwell, A. 6	*Utwella* 160 *Wtwella* 215b
Overstrand, I. 2	*Othestranda* 268
Ovington	Not in D.B.

Oxborough, D. 6	*Oxenbur(c)h* 202b, 245
Oxenbur(c)h	See Oxborough
Oxenedes	See Oxnead
Oxnead, I. 4	*Oxenedes* 271b
Oxwick, F. 3	*Ossuic* 214
Pag(g)rava	See Palgrave
Palgrave, E. 5	*Pag(g)rava* 119b *bis*, 144b, 167b
Palinga	See Palling
Palling, K. 3	*Pal(l)inga* 134, 150, 187
Pallinga	See Palling
Pancforda, *Pankesford(a)*	See Panxworth
Panworth, E. 6	*Pennewrde* 232
Panxworth, J. 5	*Pancforda* 148 *Pankesford(a)* 129 *bis*, 224
Parva Cresingham, *Parva Cressingaham*	See Little Cressingham
Parva Hocham	See Little Hockham
Parva Maltuna, *Parva Meltuna*	See Little Melton
Parva Reienburh	See Little Ryburgh
Paston, J. 2	*Pastuna* 158b, 219, 225
Pastuna	See Paston
Patesleia	See Pattesley
Pattesley, F. 4	*Patesleia* 256b
Penestorpa	See Pensthorpe
Pennewrde	See Panworth
Pensthorpe, F. 3	*Penestorpa* 232b
Penteleia	See Pentney
Pentney, C. 5	*Penteleia* 173
Phacham	See Fakenham
Phileb(e)y	See Filby
Phincham	See Fincham
Phlicham	See Flitcham
Phor(d)ham	See Fordham
Photestorp	See Fodderstone
Phuldona	See Foulden
Pichenham, *Altera Pichenham*	See Pickenham
Pickenham, North and South, E. 6	*Altera Pichenham* 144b

/over

Pickenham cont.	*Pichenham* 119b *bis*, 120, 168, 235, 276 *Pikeham* 268b *Pikenha(m)* 144b, 232 *Pinkenham* 232
Pikeham, *Pikenha(m)*	See Pickenham
Pincham	See Fincham
Pinkenham	See Pickenham
Pirenhou	See Pirnhow
Pirnhow, J. 7	*Pirenhou* 177b
Plestuna	See Billingford (near Diss)
Plic(e)ham	See Flitcham
Plumesteda	See Plumstead, Great and Little
Plumestede	See Plumstead (near Holt), Plumstead, Great and Little
Plummesteda, *-stede*	See Plumstead, Great and Little
Plumstead (near Holt), H. 2	*Plumestede* 172
Plumstead, Great and Little, J. 5	*Plumesteda*, *-stede* 123b, 199 *bis*, 224b, 269 *Plummesteda*, *-stede* 123b *bis*, 195, 199, 228b
Poringland, I. 6	*Porrikelanda* 203 *Porringalanda* 143, 186 *Porringelanda*, *-lant* 124, 210 *Porringhelanda* 182b, 278 *Porrinkelanda* 176, 186
Porrikelanda, *Porringalanda*, *Porringelanda*, *Porringelant*, *Porringhelanda*, *Porrinkelanda*	See Poringland
Possuic	See Postwick
Postwick, J. 5	*Possuic* 240, 279b

Potter Heigham, K. 4	*Echam* 272b
Prelestuna	See Billingford (near Diss)
Pudding Norton, F. 3	*Nortuna* 111b *bis*
Pulham St Mary Magdalene, St Mary the Virgin, I. 8	*Pul(la)ham* 139b, 214b
Pullaham	See Pulham
Quarles, E. 2	*Gueruelei* 179 *Huerueles* 113
Quidenham, G. 8	*Cuid-*, *Guidenham* 127b, 183b, 209b
Rachei(th)a	See Rackheath
Rackheath, J. 5	*Rachei(th)a* 132, 217b, 229
Rada(na)halla, *Radenhala*	See Redenhall
Ragadona, *Ragheduna*	See Roydon (near Diss)
Raimerestuna	See Reymerston
Rainestorp, *Rainiltorp*	See Rainthorpe
Rainthorpe, I. 7	*Rainestorp* 189 *Rainiltorp* 263b
Randuorda	See Ranworth
Ranworth, J. 5	*Randuorda* 129 *bis*
Ravelincham, *Ravenicham*	See Raveningham
Raveningham, K. 7	*Ravelincham* 267b *Ravenicham* 249 *Raverincham* 135b *Raveringham* 182 *Ravincham* 141b, 153, 197, 230, 249b *Ravingeham* 279 *Ruverincham* 273b
Raverincham, *Raveringham*, *Ravincham*, *Ravingeham*	See Raveningham
Raynham, East and West, E. 3	*Rein(e)ham* 122 *bis*, 184, 233, 237b
Redaham	See Reedham

Redanaha(lla)	See Redenhall
Redeham	See Reedham
Redelefuuorda	See Riddlesworth
Redenhall, I. 8	*Rada(na)halla* 125, 125b, 139b *Radenhala* 286 *Redanaha(lla)* 125b, 139, 139b
Reedham, K. 6	*Redaham*, *Redeham* 129b, 216 *bis*, 224
Reepham, H. 4	*Refham* 247b *bis*
Refham	See Reepham
Regadona, *Regedona*	See Roydon (near Diss)
Reiduna	See Roydon (near King's Lynn)
Reieborh	See Great Ryburgh
Reieburh	See Little Ryburgh
Reienburh	See Great Ryburgh
Reineburh, *Parva*	See Little Ryburgh
Rein(e)ham	See Raynham
Remingaland	See Ringland
Repes	See Repps (near Acle); Repps: Northrepps and Southrepps
Repps (near Acle), K. 4	*Repes* 146b, 174, 174b *bis*, 217, 224b, 272
Repps: Northrepps and Southrepps, I. 2	*Nor(h)repes* 171, 171b *Repes* 171, 216, 223b *Sutrepes* 171b
Reymerston, G. 6	*Raimerestuna* 275
Riddlesworth, F. 8	*Redelefuuorda* 262
Ridlington, J. 3	*Ridlinketuna* 260b
Ridlinketuna	See Ridlington
Rinc(s)teda	See Ringstead
Ringland, H. 5	*Remingaland* 241b
Ringstead, C. 2	*Rinc(s)teda* 173b, 215b, 222b, 226, 265b *bis*
Rippetuna	See Rippon
Rippon, I. 4	*Rippetuna* 241b
Riseurda	See Rushford
Rising (in Feltwell), C. 7	*Risinga* 162 *bis*
Risinga	See Castle Rising, Rising (in Feltwell), Woodrising
Ristuna	See East Ruston, Ryston, Sco Ruston
Riuessal(l)a	See Rushall
Rochelant	See Rockland All Saints
Rochesham	See Roxham
Rochinges	See Roding, Ess.
Rockland All Saints, St Andrew, F. 7, G. 7	*Rochelant* 183b *Rokelun(d)*, *-lunt* 164, 239b, 267
Rockland St Mary, J. 6	*Rokelonda*, *-lund(a)* 124 *bis*, 124b, 175 *bis*, 176, 176b, 185b, 195b, 203 *bis*
Rockland St Peter, F. 7	*Toftes* 163b
Roftuna	See Roughton
Rokelonda	See Rockland St Mary
Rokelun	See Rockland All Saints
Rokelund	See Rockland All Saints, Rockland St Mary
Rokelunda	See Rockland St Mary
Rokelunt	See Rockland All Saints
Rollesby, K. 5	*Roluesb(e)i* 201 *bis* *Rothbfuesbei* 272 *Rotholfuesbei*, *-by* 129b, 174, 216b *Thoroluesby* 217
Roluesb(e)i	See Rollesby
Romborc, *-boro*	See Rumburgh, Suff.
Romham, *Ronham*	See Runham
Rostuna	See Roughton
Rothbfuesbei, *Rotholfuesbei*, *-by*	See Rollesby
Roudham, F. 8	*Rudham* 127, 164b, 213b, 239b
Rougham, E. 4	*Ruhham* 120b, 165b, 207b

Roughton, I. 2	*Rof-*, *Ruftuna* 143b, 179b, 184b *Rugutune* 237b
Roxham, C. 6	*Rochesham* 275b
Roydon (near Diss), H. 9	*Ragheduna* 211 *Regadona*, *Regedona* 154b, 211b, 228b
Roydon (near King's Lynn), C. 4	*Reiduna* 142b
Rudeham	See Rudham
Rudham	See Roudham
Rudham, East and West, E. 3	*Rudeham* 146, 169, 169b *ter*, 257b
Ruftuna, *Rugutune*	See Roughton
Ruhham	See Rougham
Runcton Holme and South Runcton, B. 5	*Runghetuna* 209 *bis*, 275b
Runetune	See Runton
Runghetuna	See North Runcton; Runcton Holme and South Runcton
Runhal(a)	See Runhall
Runhall, G. 6	*Runhal(a)* 121b, 145
Runham, L. 5	*Romham*, *Ronham* 116, 134b, 180, 273
Runton, I. 2	*Runetune* 184b, 224
Rusceuuorda	See Rushford
Rushall, I. 8	*Riuessal(l)a* 139, 254b, 259
Rushford, F. 8	*Riseurda* 214 *bis* *Rusceuuorda* 270b
Rustuna	See Roughton
Ruverincham	See Raveningham
Rynghetona	See North Runcton
Ryston, B. 6	*Ristuna* 206b, 274, 276
Saham Toney, E. 6	*Saham* 110, 110b *ter*, 126, 126b, 183, 232b, 266, 277

Saiselingaham, *Saisselingham*	See Saxlingham Nethergate and Thorpe
Saleia	See Sloley
Salhouse	Not in D.B.
Salhus	See Salthouse
Sall, H. 3	*Salla* 131, 157b, 229, 270 *bis*
Salla	See Sall
Salthouse, G. 1	*Sal(t)hus* 171b, 223b, 279
Salthus	See Salthouse
Sandringham, C. 3	*Santdersincham* 258b
Santdersincham	See Sandringham
Santon, E. 8	*Santuna* 162b
Santuna	See Santon
Sasilingaham	See Saxilingham Nethergate and Thorpe
Sastorp	See Saxthorpe
Saxeling(h)aham, *Saxelingham*	See Saxlingham (near Holt)
Saxiorp	See Saxthorpe
Saxlingham (near Holt), G. 2	*Saxeling(h)aham* 191b, 257b *Saxelingham* 192 *Sexelingaham* 197b
Saxlingham Nethergate and Thorpe, I. 7	*Saiselingaham* 124b *Saisselingham* 217 *Sasilingaham* 125, 154, 185b, 243, 247, 258b, 266
Saxthorp	See Saxthorpe
Saxthorpe, H. 3	*Sastorp* 146b, 148 *Saxiorp* 146 *Saxthorp* 132b
Scarnetuna	See Sharrington
Scarning, F. 5	*Scernenga* 165b *Sc(h)erninga* 165, 252b, 275
Scartune	See Sharrington
Scatagraua	See Chedgrave
Scedgetuna	See Skeyton
Scelnangra	See Shelfanger
Sceltuna	See Shelton
Sceluagra(ua), *Sceluangra*	See Shelfanger
Scengutuna	See Skeyton

Scepedane	See Shipden
Scerepham	See Shropham
Scernebruna, -brune, -buna	See Shernborne
Scernenga, Scerninga	See Scarning
Scerpham	See Shropham
Scherninga	See Scarning
Scidesterna	See Syderstone
Scingham	See Shingham
Scipdham	See Shipdham
Scipedana	See Shipden, Shipdham
Scipedeham, Scippedana	See Shipdham
Sciraforda	See Shereford
Scisterna	See Syderstone
Sco, K. 4	*Esco(u)* 195b, 201
Scole	See Osmondiston
Sco Ruston, J. 4	*Ristuna* 159, 219b, 244b
Scotesham, Scotessa(m), Altera Scotessam	See Shotesham
Scothou	See Scottow
Scotoford	See Shotford
Scotoh(o)u	See Scottow
Scottow, I. 4	*Scothou* 234b *Scotoh(o)u* 133, 148, 217b, 219b, 229b *bis*, 234, 234b
Scoulton, F. 6	*Sculetuna* 164, 266b, 268
Scratby, L. 5	*Scroteby* 220b *Scroutebei, -bey* 197, 273
Scroteby	See Scratby
Scroutebei, -bey	See Scratby
Sculatorpa	See Sculthorpe
Sculdeham, Alia Sculdeham	See Shouldham
Sculetorpa	See Sculthorpe
Sculetuna	See Scoulton
Sculthorpe, E. 3	*Sculatorpa, Sculetorpa* 144b, 168
Scutherlingaham	See Surlingham
Scutreinaham	See South Raynham
Secesforda	See Sedgeford
Sedgeford, C. 2	*Secesforda, Sexforda* 193b, 278b
Seething, J. 7	*Silinga* 140, 264 *Sithinga, -inges* 152b, 175, 177, 177b *bis*, 186, 186b, 264b
Semera, Semere	See Semere
Semere, I. 8	*Semera, Semere* 155, 211b
Serlebruna	See Shernborne
Serpham	See Shropham
Setchey	Not in D.B.
Sexelingaham	See Saxlingham (near Holt)
Sexforda	See Sedgeford
Sharrington, G. 2	*Scarnetuna* 112b *Scartune* 112b
Shelfanger, H. 8	*Scelnangra* 272 *Sceluagra(ua)* 149b, 211, 211b, 275b *Sceluangra* 130, 149b, 150
Shelton, I. 7	*Sceltuna* 181, 189b *bis*, 259b
Shereford, E. 3	*Sciraforda* 170
Sheringham, H. 1	*Silingeham* 223b *bis*
Shernborne, C. 3	*Scernebruna, -brune, -buna* 142b, 167, 268, 278b *Serlebruna* 244b
Shimpling, H. 8	*Simplinga(ham)* 130, 130b, 154b, 176b, 211, 211b
Shingham, D. 6	*Scingham* 236
Shipden, I. 2	*Scepedane* 185, 194b *Scipedana* 216
Shipdham, F. 6	*Scipdham* 122, 166b *Scipedeham* 277 *Scip(p)edana* 132, 208

Spikeswrda	See Spixworth
Spixworth, I. 5	*Spikeswrda* 243b
Sporle, E. 5	*Esparlai, -le(a)* 121, 125b, 126, 126b *Sparle(a)* 119b *bis*, 126b
Spro(wes)tuna	See Sprowston
Sprowston, I. 5	*Spro(wes)tuna* 131b, 140b, 155b
Stabrige, -byrda	See Stibbard
Stalham, K. 3	*Stalham* 148b, 180, 187b, 220b, 272b *Stanham* 148
Stanfelda	See Stanfield
Stanfield, F. 4	*Stanfelda, Stanuelda* 144b, 166
Stanford, E. 7	*Estanforda* 197b, 231b, 238b *Stanforda* 183, 266b
Stanforda	See Stanford
Stanham	See Stalham
Stanho	See Stanhoe
Stanhoe, D. 2	*Stanho(u)* 110, 111, 143 *bis*, 167
Stanhou	See Stanhoe
Staningehalla	See Stanninghall
Stanninghall, I. 4	*Staningehalla* 140b
Stanuelda	See Stanfield
Starston, I. 8	*Sterestuna* 125b, 139, 186, 210b *bis*, 259, 263b
Steirtuna	See Sturston
Sterestuna	See Starston, Tharston
Sterstuna	See Tharston
Stibbard, F. 3	*Estanbyrda* 111 *Stabrige, -byrda* 111b, 169
Stiffkey, F. 1	*Stinekai* 113 *Stiuecai, Stiuekeia* 122, 122b, 128, 233
Stinekai	See Stiffkey
Stinetuna	See Stinton
Stinton, H. 3	*Stinetuna* 157
Stiuecai, Stiuekeia	See Stiffkey
Stoches	See Stoke Ferry, Stoke Holy Cross, Stokesby
Stockton, K. 7	*Stoutuna* 141, 141b *bis*
Stodeia	See Stody
Stody, G. 2	*Estodeia* 261 *Stodeia* 112
Stoffta	See West Tofts
Stofsta	See Bircham Tofts
Stoftes	See Toft Monks
Stohu	See Stow Bedon
Stoke	See Stoke Holy Cross
Stoke Ferry, C. 6	*Stoches* 149, 251, 275 *Stokes* 230b, 251b
Stoke Holy Cross, I. 6	*Stoches* 124, 124b *Stoke(s)* 125, 135, 175 *bis*, 176, 185b, 203, 243, 258b, 264b, 265
Stokes	See Stoke Ferry, Stoke Holy Cross
Stokesbei, -bey	See Stokesby
Stokesby, K. 5	*Stoches* 224 *Stokesbei, -bey* 224b *bis*, 225
Stou	See Stow Bardolph, Stow Bedon
Stoutuna	See Stockton
Stow Bardolph, B. 6	*Stou* 206, 206b, 274 *bis*
Stow Bedon, F. 7	*Sto(h)u* 110b, 122, 126, 126b, 162, 166 *Stuo* 126
Stradsett, C. 6	*Stra(te)seta* 190b, 206b
Stra(te)seta	See Stradsett
Stratton St Mary, St Michael, I. 7	*Estratuna* 150b *Stratuna, Stretuna* 151 *bis*, 181, 189b *bis*, 193, 197, 212, 215, 260
Stratton Strawless, I. 4	*Estratuna* 243b *Stratuna* 115b, 196b, 241b

Taseburc(h)	See Tasburgh
Taterforda	See Tatterford
Tatessete	See Tattersett
Tatituna	See Tuttington
Tatterford, E. 3	*Taterforda* 262b
Tattersett, E. 3	*Tatessete* 169b
Taverham, H. 5	*Taverham* 114b, 147b, 157b, 196, 201b *Tavresham* 229
Tavresham	See Taverham
Tedforda, -fort	See Thetford
Telve(n)tuna, *Telvetaham*	See Thelveton
Terna	See Thurne
Terrington St Clement, St John, A. 5, B. 4	*Tilinghetuna* 206b, 251b
Testerton, F. 3	*Estretona* 257b
Tetford	See Thetford
Teveteshala, *Tevetessalla*	See Tivetshall
Tharston, I. 7	*Ster(e)stuna* 181, 260 *Therstuna* 181
Thelveton, H. 8	*Telve(n)tuna* 154b, 215, 269 *Telvetaham* 154b
Themelthorpe	Not in D.B.
Therstuna	See Tharston
Thetford, E. 8	*Tedforda, -fort* 136, 137, 173 *Tetford* 118b *bis*
Thompson, F. 7	*Tomestuna* 164, 183, 264, 268 *Tumesteda* 277
Thornage, G. 2	*Tornedis* 192 *ter*
Thornham, D. 1	*Tornham* 191
Thoroluesby	See Rollesby
Thorp	See Gayton Thorpe, Honingham Thorpe, Shouldham Thorpe, Thorpe, Thorpe Abbots, Thorpe St Andrew
Thorpe next Haddiscoe	Not in D.B.

Thorpe (in Shipdham), F. 5	*Torp* 214, 214b
Thorpe Abbots, I. 9	*T(h)orp* 139, 139b, 210b
Thorpe Market, I. 2	*Torp* 171, 171b, 255b
Thorpe Parva, H. 9	*Torp* 154b *bis*
Thorpe St Andrew, I. 5	*T(h)orp* 117b, 137b, 138 *ter*, 140b *ter*, 279
Thorpland (near Downham Market), B. 6	*Torp* 209 *Torpelanda* 206, 273b
Thorpland (in Fakenham), F. 3	*Torpaland* 111
Threxton, E. 6	*Tre(c)stuna* 163b, 232b
Thrigby, L. 5	*Trikebei* 180, 197, 225b *Trukebei* 135
Thura	See Thurne
Thurgarton, I. 2	*Turgaitune* 179b *Turgartuna* 185, 216
Thurketeliart, L. 7	Lost in Aldeby, 230
Thurlton, K. 7	*T(h)uruertuna* 141b *bis*, 151, 182b, 225b, 250b, 267b, 273
Thurne, K. 5	*Terna* 216b, 277b *Thura* 174b
Thurning, G. 3	*Tirn-*, *Turn-*, *Tyrninga* 131b, 157b *bis*, 196, 270
Thursford, F. 3	*Tureforde*, *Turesfort* 122b *bis*
Thurstuna	See Thuxton
Thurton (in Witchingham), H. 4	*Tortuna* 225, 234b
Thurton (near Loddon), J. 6	*Tortuna* 177b *bis*, 215 *Turmentuna* 266
Thuruertuna	See Thurlton
Thustuna	See Thuxton

Thuxton, G. 6	*Thu(r)stuna* 121b, 183b *Toruestuna* 274b *Turestuna* 167 *Turs(tanes)tuna* 121b, 166b, 214b
Thwaite (near Erpingham), I. 3	*Tuit* 218
Thwaite (near Loddon)	Not in D.B.
Tibenham, H. 8	*Tib(en)ham* 150b, 181, 189b, 190 *bis*, 212, 246b, 280 *Tipham* 221 *Tybenham* 246
Tib(en)ham	See Tibenham
Tigeswella, *Tigeuuella*	See Titchwell
Tilinghetuna	See Terrington
Tilney All Saints, St Lawrence	Not in D.B.
Tipham	See Tibenham
Tirninga	See Thurning
Titchwell, D. 1	*Flicesuuella* 215b *Tigeswella* 109b *Tigeuuella* 183b
Titeshala	See Tittleshall
Tittleshall, E. 4	*Titeshala* 165b, 252b
Tivetessala	See Tivetshall
Tivetshall St Margaret, St Mary, H. 8	*Teveteshala* 210b, 215 *Tevetessalla* 201b *Tivetessala* 211 *Totessalla* 130
Tochestorp, *Toke(s)torp*	Unid., 145b, 166 *bis*, 202b
Toddencham	See North Tuddenham
Toddenham	See East Tuddenham, North Tuddenham
Todeneham	See East Tuddenham
Toffas	See Toftrees
Tofftes	See Rockland St Peter
Toft	See Toft Monks
Toftes	See Toft Monks, Toftrees
Toft Monks, K. 7	*Stoftes* 140 *Toft(es)* 140, 141, 141b, 230
Toftrees, E. 3	*Toffas* 168 *To(f)tes* 257, 257b
Toimere	See Toombers
Toke(s)torp	See *Tochestorp*
Tomestuna	See Thompson
Toombers, C. 6	*Toimere* 230b
Topcroft, I. 7	*Topecroft*, *-cropt* 211b, 246
Topecroft, *-cropt*	See Topcroft
Tornedis	See Thornage
Tornham	See Thornham
Torp	See Ashwellthorpe, Baconsthorpe (near Holt), Cockthorpe, Freethorpe, Gayton Thorpe, Honingham Thorpe, Ingoldisthorpe, Morning Thorpe, Swainsthorpe, Thorpe (in Shipdham), Thorpe Abbots, Thorpe Market, Thorpe Parva, Thorpe St Andrew, Thorpland (near Downham Market)
Torp (Loddon hd)	Unid., 204, 215
Torpaland	See Thorpland (in Fakenham)
Torpelanda	See Thorpland (near Downham Market)
Tortuna	See Thurton (in Great Witchingham), Thurton (near Loddon)

Toruestuna	See Thuxton
Totdenham, *Toteham*	See North Tuddenham
Totes	See Toftrees
Totessalla	See Tivetshall
Totintuna	See Tottington
Tottenhella	See Tottenhill
Tottenhill, C. 5	*Tottenhella* 251
Tottington, E. 7	*Totintuna* 174, 263
Tre(c)stuna	See Threxton
Treus(sa)	See Trowse
Trikebei	See Thrigby
Trimingham	Not in D.B.
Trowse, I. 6	*Treus(sa)* 114, 124b, 125, 185b
Truchet	See Trunch
Trukebei	See Thrigby
Trunch, J. 2	*Tru(n)chet* 171, 171b
Trunchet	See Trunch
Tuanatuna, *Tuane(s)tuna*	See Swanton (in Forncett)
Tudenham	See East Tuddenham
Tuit	See Thwaite (near Erpingham)
Tumesteda	See Thompson
Tunestalla, *-stalle*	See Tunstall
Tunesteda	See Tunstead
Tunstall, K. 5	*Tunestalla*, *-stalle* 228, 239b, 262, 268b
Tunstead, J. 4	*Tunesteda* 244
Tureforde, *Turesfort*	See Thursford
Turestuna	See Thuxton
Turgaitune, *-gartuna*	See Thurgarton
Turmentuna	See Thurton (near Loddon)
Turninga	See Thurning
Turs(tanes)tuna	See Thuxton
Turuertuna	See Thurlton
Tutincghetuna	See Tuttington
Tuttington, I. 3	*Tatituna* 158b *Tutincghetuna* 218
Twyford	Not in D.B.
Tybenham	See Tibenham
Tyby, G. 3	*Tytheby* 270
Tyrninga	See Thurning
Tytheby	See Tyby
Uidetuna	See Woodton
Ulterincham	See Itteringham
Ultertuna, *Ultretune*	See Wolterton
Upton, K. 5	*Op(e)tune* 129 *bis*, 202b *bis* *Optuna* 279 *Uptuna*, *-tune* 129, 216
Uptuna, *-tune*	See Upton
Upwell, A. 6	*Wella* 136, 206b, 230b, 231, 231b, 276
Urdestada	See Worstead
Urminclanda	See Irmingland
Urnincham	See Wreningham
Uroc(he)sham, *Uroscham*	See Wroxham
Utrincham	See Itteringham
Utwella	See Outwell
Wabrune, *Wabrunna*	See Weybourne
Wachetuna	See Wacton
Wacstanest, *Wacstenesham*, *Wactanesham*	See Waxham
Wacton, I. 7	*Wachetuna*, *Waketuna* 150b, 181, 189b *ter*
Wadetuna	See Watton
Waketuna	See Wacton
Walassam	See South Walsham
Walcheta	See Walcott
Walcott, K. 3	*Walcheta* 279b *Walecota* 260b
Walebruna	See Welborne
Walecota	See Walcott
Wales(h)am, *Walessam*	See South Walsham
Wal(l)inghetuna	See Wallington
Wallington, B. 5	*Wal(l)inghetuna* 190, 274
Walnccham	See Wellingham
Walpola	See Walpole

Walpole, A. 4 *Walpola* 266
Walsam See North Walsham, South Walsham
Walsincham See Walsingham (in East Carleton)
Walsingaham, *Alia Walsingaham*, *Walsingeham Magna* See Walsingham, Great and Little
Walsingham (in East Carleton), H. 6 *Wa(l)sincham* 187b, 254, 254b
Walsingham, Great and Little, F. 2 *Alia Walsingaham* 233; *Galsingaham* 113; *Walsingaham* 233; *Walsingeham Magna* 258
Walsocam See Walsoken
Walsoken, A. 5 *Walsocam* 215b
Waltuna See East Walton, West Walton
Waranpli(n)cham See Wramplingham
Warham All Saints, St Mary, F. 2 *Guarham* 113, 113b, 146; *Warham* 143, 192, 242b, 271 *bis*
Washingford, J. 6 *Wasingaford* 203b
Wasincham See Walsingham (in East Carleton)
Wasingaford See Washingford
Wateaker See Wheatacre
Waterden, E. 2 *Waterdenna* 168b
Waterdenna See Waterden
Watlingeseta, H. 9 Lost in Diss, 114
Watlington Not in D.B.
Watton, F. 6 *Wadetuna* 174
Waxham, K. 3 *Wacstanest* 148b; *Wacstenesham* 187; *Wactanesham* 149, 220, 272b
Wdetuna See Woodton, Wootton
Weasenham All Saints, St Peter, E. 4 *Wesenham* 121, 165
Weeting, D. 8 *Wetinga*, *-inge* 136, 162b
Welborne, G. 5 *Walebruna* 166
Well, C. 4 *Wella* 221b *ter*
Wella See Upwell, Well
Wellingham, E. 4 *Walnccham* 252b
Wells next the Sea, F. 1 *Etduuella* 258; *Gu(u)ella* 122b, 146, 192, 271 *ter*; *Guelle* 113
Welney Not in D.B.
Wendling, F. 5 *Wenlinga* 209b
Wenlinga See Wendling
Wereham, C. 6 *Wigreham* 203b *bis*
Wer(e)tham, *Alia* See Wretham
Wermegai See Wormegay
Wesbruge See West Briggs
Wesenham See Weasenham
Weskerebroc See West Carbrooke
West Acre See Acre, Castle and West
West Barsham See Barsham
West Beckham, H. 2 *Becham* 242
West Bilney, C. 5 *Benelai* 238; *Bilenei* 238b; *Binelai* 279
West Bradenham See Bradenham
West Briggs, C. 5 *Wesbruge* 206, 273b
West Carbrooke, F. 6 *Weskerebroc* 265b
West Dereham, C. 6 *Der(e)ham* 160, 190, 209, 215b, 251, 251b, 274, 275b
Westfelda See Westfield
Westfield, F. 5 *Westfelda* 145b
West Harling See Harling
West Lexham See Lexham
West Lynn See Lynn
West Newton, C. 3 *Niuetuna* 142b
Weston Longville, H. 5 *Westuna* 143b, 147, 225, 270
West Raynham See Raynham
West Rudham See Rudham
West Somerton See Somerton

West Tofts, E. 7	*Stoffta* 191
Westuna	See Weston Longville
West Walton, A. 5	*Waltuna* 160, 213, 226, 274b
Westwic	See Westwick
Westwick, J. 3	*Westwic* 244b
West Winch, B. 5	*Eswinic* 207
	Weswenic, -winic 231b, 274b, 276
West Wretham	See Wretham
Weswenic, -winic	See West Winch
Wetinga, -inge	See Weeting
Weybourne, H. 1	*Wabrune, -brunna* 152, 279 *bis*
Wheatacre, L. 7	*Hwateaker* 250
	Wateaker 250
Whimpwell, K. 3	*Hwimpwella* 220, 220b
Whinburgh, G. 5	*Wineberga* 207b, 208
Whissonsett, F. 4	*Witcingkeseta* 178b
Whitlingham, J. 6	*Wisinlingaham* 124b, 175b
	Wislingeham 124
Whitwell, H. 4	*Witewella* 114b, 233b
Wica	See Ashwicken, Wick
Wichamtuna	See Wickhampton
Wiche	See Ashwicken
Wichhamtun	See Wickhampton
Wicinghaham	See Witchingham
Wick, G. 8	*Wica* 164b, 202, 238b, 279
Wickhampton, K. 6	*Wichamtuna* 129b
	Wichhamtun 129b
Wicklewood, G. 6	*Wiclurde* 252b
	Wikelepuda 166
Wickmere, H. 3	*Wicmara, -mera* 115b, 143b, 158, 187, 218b
Wiclurde	See Wicklewood
Wicmara, -mera	See Wickmere
Widituna	See Witton (near North Walsham)
Widmundham	See Wymondham
Wiggenhall St Germans, St Mary Magdalen, St Mary the Virgin, St Peter, B. 5	*Wigghenham* 251
	Wigrehala 274b
Wigghenham	See Wiggenhall
Wighton, F. 2	*Guistune* 113b
	Wistune 112b, 113b
Wigrehala	See Wiggenhall
Wigreham	See Wereham
Wikelepuda	See Wicklewood
Wilby, G. 7	*Wilebey, Wilgeby* 183, 222b
	Willebeih 252
Wilebey, Wilgeby, Willebeih	See Wilby
Wilton, D. 8	*Wiltuna* 161b, 276b
Wiltuna	See Wilton
Wimbotsham, B. 6	*Winebotesham* 160, 206b, 215b, 274
Wimund(e)ham	See Wymondham
Wineberga	See Whinburgh
Winebotesham	See Wimbotsham
Wineferthinc	See Winfarthing
Winfarthing, H. 8	*Wineferthinc* 129b, 130 *bis*, 130b, 275b *bis*
Winterton, L. 4	*Wintretona, -tuna* 113b, 129b, 185b, 195b, 200b *bis*, 216b, 224b, 272b
Wintretona, -tuna	See Winterton
Wisinlingaham, Wislingeham	See Whitlingham
Wistune	See Wighton
Witchingham, H. 4	*Wicinghaham* 217b
	Witcincham 225
	Wit(t)cingeham 131b, 151b, 224b, 225, 241
	Witeingeham 233b
Witcincham, Witcingeham	See Witchingham
Witcingkeseta	See Whissonsett
Witeingeham	See Witchingham
Witewella	See Whitwell
Witona	See Witton (near Norwich)

Wittcingeham	See Witchingham
Witton (near North Walsham), J. 3	*Widituna* 219 *Wi(t)tuna* 133, 159
Witton (near Norwich), J. 5	*Witona* 123b, 200b *bis*, 270b
Wi(t)tuna	See Witton (near North Walsham)
Wiventona	See Wiveton
Wiveton, G. 1	*Wiventona*, *Wivetuna* 170, 233
Wivetuna	See Wiveton
Wodetona, *-tuna*	See Woodton
Wolferton	Not in D.B.
Wolterton, H. 3	*Ultertuna* 218b, 229b *Ultretune* 172
Woodbastwick, J. 5	*Bastu(u)ic* 113b, 129, 216 *bis*, 228, 228b, 278b, 279
Wood Dalling, H. 3	*Dallinga* 157b, 241, 258
Wood Norton, G. 3	*Nortuna* 192b, 234, 241, 270
Woodrising, F. 6	*Risinga* 111, 167
Woodton, J. 7	*Uidetuna* 131 *Wdetuna* 152b, 264 *Wodetona*, *-tuna* 131, 155, 177, 246b
Wootton, C. 4	*Wdetuna* 126
Wormegay, C. 5	*Wermegai* 206, 273b
Worstead, J. 3	*Ordesteda* 148 *Urdestada* 234b *Wrdesteda* 219
Worthing	Not in D.B.
Wortwell	Not in D.B.
Wramplingham, H. 6	*Waranpli(n)cham* 145b, 202b *bis* *Wranplincham* 145
Wranplincham	See Wramplingham
Wrdesteda	See Worstead
Wreningham, H. 6	*Urnincham* 187b, 208
Wretham, East and West, E. 7, F. 7	*Alia Wer(e)tham* 236b *bis* *Wretham* 236b
Wretton	Not in D.B.
Wrossham	See Wroxham
Wroxham, J. 4	*Grossa(ha)m* 228, 228b *Uroc(he)sham* 132, 217b, 228b *Uroscham* 229 *Wrossham* 228b *bis*
Wtwella	See Outwell
Wymondham, H. 6	*Widmundham* 166 *Wimund(e)ham* 137b, 141, 166b, 275
Yarmouth, L. 5	*Gernemutha* 283 *Gernemwa* 118 *Iernesmua* 371b, Suff.
Yaxham, G. 5	*Iachesham* 145b, 179, 214b *bis*, 232b, 275 *Iakesham* 208
Yelverton, J. 6	*Ailuertuna* 124, 176, 185b, 186, 203 *Ailunituna* 186 *Aluertuna* 143 *Aluntuna* 167

ANONYMOUS HOLDINGS

No place-names appear in the following three entries, and it is possible that some (or even all) of these refer to holdings at places not named elsewhere in Domesday Book:

Roger, 15 acres in North Erpingham hd, 182b.
Harold (from bishop of Thetford), 3½ carucates in South Erpingham hd, 196b.
One freeman (from Tovi), 5 acres in Henstead hd, 265.

NORTHAMPTONSHIRE
NORTHANTONESCIRE

Folios 219–229

MAPS 36–37

Abington, E. 6	*Abintone* 229
Abintone	See Abington
Abthorpe	Not in D.B.
Aceshille	See Ashton (near Towcester)
Achelau	See Oakley
Achurch	*Asechirce* 221b
Adelintone	See Elton, Hunts.
Adestanestone	See Easton Neston
Adstone, C. 7	*Atenestone* 219b *Etenestone* 222b, 224
Aienho	See Aynho
Ailsworth, H. 2	*Eglesworde* 221, 221b
Aldenesbi, *Aldenestone*	See Holdenby
Alderton, D. 8	*Aldritone* 223, 224
Aldevincle	See Aldwincle
Aldritone	See Alderton
Aldwincle All Saints, St Peter, G. 4	*Aldevincle* 227 *Eldewincle* 222
Alia Edintone	See Little Addington
Alia Hargindone	See Little Harrowden
Alidetorp	See Thorpe Malsor
Alio Cortenhalo	See Courteenhall
Altera Haiford	See Upper Heyford
Althorpe, D. 6	*Olletorp* 223, 225b
Apethorpe, G. 2	*Patorp* 220
Arintone	See Harrington
Armston, H. 3	*Mermeston* 221b
Arninguorde, *Arniworde*	See Arthingworth
Arthingworth, D. 4	*Arninguorde* 219b *Arniworde* 223 *Erniwade* 222 *Narninworde* 226
Asbi	See Mears Ashby

Asce	See Ashley, Ashton (near Towcester)
Ascebi	See Ashby St Ledgers, Canons Ashby
Ascele(i)	See Ashley
Ascetone	See Ashton (near Polebrook)
Asebi	See Castle Ashby
Asechirce	See Achurch
Ashby St Ledgers, B. 5	*Ascebi* 224b
Ashley, E. 3	*Asce* 225, 228 *Ascele(i)* 225 *bis* *Ascetone* 221b, 222
Ashton (near Polebrook), H. 3	
Ashton (near Towcester), D. 7	*Aceshille* 226 *Asce* 226b
Astcote, C. 7	*Aviescote* 226b
Aston le Walls, A. 7	*Estone* 227 3rd entry
Astwell, C. 7	*Estwelle* 227
Atenestone	See Adstone
Avelai	See Evenley
Aviescote	See Astcote
Aynho, B. 9	*Aienho* 227
Bachelintone	See Hackleton
Baculveslea	See Blakesley
Badby, B. 6	*Badebi* 222b
Badebi	See Badby
Bade-, *Baiebroc*	See Braybrooke
Bainton	Not in D.B.
Barby, B. 5	*Berchebi* 226
Barford, E. 4	*Bereford(e)* 220 *bis*
Barnack, H. 1	*Bernac* 226
Barnwell, H. 3	*Bernewelle* 220, 222
Barton Seagrave, F. 4	*Bertone* 220b
Bel(l)inge, *Bellica*	See Billing

Colleyweston, G. 1	*Westone* 225b
Collingtree, D. 7	*Colentreu* 227
Corb(e)i	See Corby
Corby, F. 3	*Corb(e)i* 219b, 220 *bis*, 229
Cortenhale, *-halo*, *Alio Cortenhalo*	See Courteenhall
Cosgrove, E. 8	*Covesgrave* 223 *bis*, 226b
Cota, *Cote*	See Coton
Cotesbroc	See Cottesbrooke
Cotesforde	See Cottisford, Oxon.
Cotingeham	See Cottingham
Coton, C. 5	*Cota*, *Cote* 226 *bis*
Cotterstock, H. 3	*Codestoche* 221b
Cottesbrooke, D. 5	*Codes-*, *Cotesbroc* 226b, 229
Cottingham, E. 3	*Cotingeham* 221
Courteenhall, D. 7	*Alio Cortenhalo* 226 *Cortenhale*, *-halo* 225b, 226
Covesgrave	See Cosgrove
Craneford	See Cranford
Craneslea, *-leg*	See Cransley
Cranford, F. 4	*Craneford* 220b, 222 *bis*, 227
Cransley, Great and Little, E. 4	*Craneslea*, *-leg* 219b, 227b, 228
Craptone	See Creaton
Creaton, Great and Little, D. 5	*Craptone* 227b *Cre(p)tone* 223, 223b, 225b
Crec	See Crick
Cre(p)tone	See Creaton
Creveltone	See Croughton
Crick, C. 5	*Crec* 227b
Criweltone	See Croughton
Croughton, B. 9	*Cliwetone* 227 *Creveltone* 221, 227 *Criweltone* 223b
Cugenho	See Cogenhoe
Culeorde	See Culworth
Culworth, B. 8	*Culeorde* 227b
Dailintone	See Dallington
Dallington, D. 6	*Dailintone* 222
Daventrei	See Daventry
Daventry, B. 6	*Daventrei* 228b
Deene, G. 3	*Dene* 222
Deenethorpe	Not in D.B.
Deisburg	See Desborough
Dene	See Deene
Deneforde	See Denford
Denford, G. 4	*Deneforde* 220b
Denton, E. 7	*Dodintone* 222, 228b
Dereburg	See Desborough
Desborough, E. 4	*De(i)sburg* 223, 225, 226 *Dereburg* 219b
Desburg	See Desborough
Dingle(i)	See Dingley
Dingley, D. 3	*Dingle(i)* 223, 225 *bis* *Tinglea* 228
Dodeforde	See Dodford
Dodford, C. 6	*Dodeforde* 223b
Dodintone	See Denton, Duddington, Great Doddington
Dotone	See Clapton
Dowthorpe, E. 6	*Widetorp* 229
Dractone	See Draughton
Draughton, D. 4	*Bracstone* 228 *Dractone* 219b, 228
Duddington, G. 2	*Dodintone* 219b
Duston, D. 6	*Dustone* 225b
Dustone	See Duston
Earls Barton, E. 6	*Burtone* 228 *bis* 2nd and 3rd entries
East Carlton, E. 3	*Carlintone* 223
East Farndon, D. 3	*Faredone* 223 *Ferendone* 222, 228b, 229
East Haddon, C. 5	*E(d)done* 223 *bis*, 223b, 224 *bis* *Hadone* 224
Easton Maudit, F. 6	*Estone* 225b, 229
Easton Neston, D. 8	*Adestanestone* 227b *Estanestone* 223b

Easton on the Hill, G. 1	*Estone* 227 *bis* 1st and 2nd entries, 227b
Ecdone	See West Haddon
Echentone	See Ecton
Ecton, E. 6	*Echentone* 225
Eddone	See East Haddon, West Haddon
Edgcote, B. 8	*Hocecote* 220b
Edintone	See Great Addington
Edintone, Alia	See Little Addington
Edone	See East Haddon, West Haddon
Egedone	See Eydon
Egforde	See Heyford, Oxon.
Eglesworde	See Ailsworth
Eldewincle	See Aldwincle
Elkington, C. 4	*Eltetone* 223b, 227 *Etendone* 227b
Elmedene	See Helmdon
Elmington, H. 3	*Elmintone* 222b *bis*
Elmintone	See Elmington
Eltetone	See Elkington
Epingeham	See Empingham, Rutland
Erdi(n)burne	See Irthlingborough
Erlestone	See Harlestone
Erniwade	See Arthingworth
Esbece	See Haselbech
Esindone	See Essindine, Rutland
Essebi	See Cold Ashby
Estanestone	See Easton Neston
Estone	See Aston le Walls, Easton Maudit, Easton on the Hill
Estwelle	See Astwell
Etendone	See Elkington
Etenestone	See Adstone
Etton	Not in D.B.
Evelai(a)	See Evenley
Evenley, B. 9	*Avelai* 223b *Evelai(a)* 223b, 224, 226b *ter*

Everdon, C. 7	*Everdone* 220
Everdone	See Everdon
Eydon, B. 7	*Egedone* 224b
Eye	Not in D.B.
Falelau, Falewesle, -lei, -leie	See Fawsley
Faredone	See East Farndon
Farnedis	See Farndish, Beds.
Farthingho, B. 9	*Ferningeho* 224
Farthingstone, C. 7	*Fordinestone* 223b, 224
Fawsley, B. 7	*Falelau* 219b *Falewesle, -lei, -leie* 220, 223, 223b *bis* *Feleslewe* 220 *Felewesleie* 224 *Felveslea* 222b
Faxton, E. 5	*Fextone* 219b
Feleslewe, Felewesleie, Felveslea	See Fawsley
Ferendon	See West Farndon
Ferendone	See East Farndon, West Farndon
Ferningeho	See Farthingho
Fextone	See Faxton
Finedon, F. 5	*Tingdene* 220, 220b
Finemere	See Finmere, Oxon.
Fineshade	Not in D.B.
Flora, Flore	See Flore
Flore, C. 6	*Flora, Flore* 223b, 225b *bis*, 227b *bis*
Fodringeia	See Fotheringhay
Fordinestone	See Farthingstone
Forho	See Furtho
Fotheringhay, H. 2	*Fodringeia* 228
Foxeslea	See Foxley
Foxley, C. 7	*Foxeslea* 223b
Furtho, E. 8	*Forho* 223, 223b
Gadintone	See Geddington
Gayton	Not in D.B.
Geddington, F. 4	*Gadintone* 222 *Geitentone* 219b

Harpole, D. 6	*Horpol* 226
Harrington, E. 4	*Arintone* 222b
Harringworth, F. 2	*Haringeworde* 228
Hartwell, E. 7	*Hertewelle* 220
Haselbech, D. 4	*Esbece* 223
Hasou	See Halse
Hecham	See Cold Higham, Higham Ferrers
Hedham	See Hethe, Oxon.
Heiford(e)	See Nether Heyford
Hellidon	Not in D.B.
Helmdon, C. 8	*Elmedene* 223
Helpston	Not in D.B.
Hemington, H. 3	*Hemintone* 222 *Hinintone* 221b
Hemintone	See Hemington
Herdewiche	See Hardwick
Herolvestone, *-tune*	See Harlestone
Hertewelle	See Hartwell
Higham Ferrers, G. 5	*Hecham* 225b, 226 *bis*
Hinintone	See Hemington
Hinton (in Woodford Halse), B. 7	*Hintone* 227
Hintone	See Hinton (in Woodford Halse), Hinton-in-the-Hedges
Hinton-in-the-Hedges, B. 9	*Hintone* 227b
Hirecestre	See Irchester
Hisham	See Isham
Hocecote	See Edgcote
Hohtone	See Hanging Houghton; Houghton, Great and Little
Holcot, E. 5	*Holecote* 219b, 228b
Holdenby, D. 5	*Aldenesbi* 224 *Aldenestone* 224
Holecote	See Holcot
Holewelle	See Hollowell
Hollowell, D. 5	*Holewelle* 221, 224 *bis*, 226, 229
Horne	See Horn, Rutland
Horpol	See Harpole
Horton, E. 7	*Hortone* 221 1st entry, 226b, 228b *bis*
Hortone	See Horton. See also Worton, Oxon.
Hothorpe, C. 3	*Udetorp* 222
Houghton, Great and Little, E. 6	*Hohtone* 220, 226, 229 *ter*
Hulcote, D. 7	*Hale-*, *Hulecote* 220, 227b
Hulecote	See Hulcote
Irchester, F. 6	*Hirecestre* 224 *Irencestre* 225b *bis*
Irencestre	See Irchester
Irthlingborough, G. 5	*Erdi(n)burne* 221b, 222
Isham, F. 5	*Hisham* 220b *Isham* 226b, 228
Islep	See Islip
Islip, G. 4	*Islep* 220b *Slepe* 219b *bis*
Keilmerse	See Kelmarsh
Kelmarsh, D. 4	*Cailmarc* 226 *Keilmerse* 219b
Kettering, F. 4	*Cateringe* 221b
Kilsby, B. 5	*Chidesbi* 222b
King's Cliffe, G. 2	*Clive* 220
King's Sutton, B. 9	*Su(d)tone* 219b, 220 *bis*, 222b, 223b *quater*, 224b *bis*
Kingsthorpe (in Northampton), D. 3	*Torp* 219b
Kingsthorpe (in Polebrook), H. 3	*Chingestorp* 221b
Kirby, F. 3	*Chercheberie* 229
Kislingbury, D. 6	*Ceselingeberie* 227b *Cifelingeberie* 223b
Knuston, F. 6	*Cnutestone* 225b, 227b
Lamport, D. 5	*Langeport* 222, 226b, 228
Langeport	See Lamport

Lastone	See Laxton
Laxton, F. 2	*Lastone* 229
Lepelie	See Lapley, Staffs.
Liceberge	See Litchborough
Lidentone	See Liddington, Rutland
Lidintone	See Lutton
Lilbourne, B. 4	*Lilleburne* 224 *Lineburne* 223b
Lilford, G. 3	*Lilleforde* 229
Lilleburne	See Lilbourne
Lilleforde	See Lilford
Lineburne	See Lilbourne
Litchborough, C. 7	*Liceberge* 222b
Little Addington, G. 5	*Alia Edintone* 220b
Little Billing	See Billing
Little Cransley	See Cransley
Little Creaton	See Creaton
Little Harrowden, F. 5	*Alia Hargindone* 220b
Little Houghton	See Houghton
Little Oakley	See Oakley
Little Oxendon	See Oxendon
Little Preston	See Preston Capes
Little Weldon, F. 3	*Parva Weledone* 224b
Loddington, E. 4	*Lodintone* 219b
Lodintone	See Loddington
Lower Boddington	See Boddington
Lowick, G. 4	*Ludewic* 228 *Luhwic* 220b
Luddington, H. 4	*Lullintone* 221b *Lolinctune* 206, Hunts.
Ludewic	See Lowick
Luditone	See Lutton
Lufenham	See Luffenham, Rutland
Luhwic	See Lowick
Lullintone	See Luddington
Lutton, H. 3	*Lidintone* 221b *Luditone* 222 *Lodintune* 204b, Hunts.
Maidford, C. 7	*Merdeford* 224b
Maidwell, D. 4	*Medewelle* 222, 222b, 228
Marholm	Not in D.B.
Marston St Lawrence, B. 8	*Merestone* 224b
Marston Trussell, D. 3	*Mersitone* 224b
Maxey	Not in D.B.
Mears Ashby, E. 6	*Asbi* 228
Medewelle	See Maidwell
Meletone	See Milton (in Castor)
Merdeford	See Maidford
Merestone	See Marston St Lawrence
Mermeston	See Armston
Mersetone	See Marston (in Church Eaton), Staffs.
Mersitone	See Marston Trussell
Middleton (near Cottingham)	Not in D.B.
Middleton Cheney, A. 8	*Mideltone* 223b, 224b *bis*
Mideltone	See Middleton Cheney, Milton (near Northampton)
Mildetone	See Milton (near Northampton)
Milton (in Castor), I. 2	*Meletone* 221b
Milton (near Northampton), D. 7	*Mideltone*, *Mildetone* 227 *bis*
Misecote	See Muscott
Molitone	See Mollington, Oxon.
Moltone	See Moulton
Morcote	See Morcott, Rutland
Moreton Pinkney, B. 8	*Mortone* 227
Mortone	See Moreton Pinkney
Moulton, E. 6	*Moltone* 225b *Mul(e)tone* 219b, 228b *ter*
Mul(e)tone	See Moulton
Muscott, C. 6	*Misecote* 223b

Narninworde	See Arthingworth
Naseby, D. 4	*Navesberie* 225b *bis*, 226
Nassington, H. 2	*Nassintone* 219b, 220
Nassintone	See Nassington
Navesberie	See Naseby
Nether Heyford, C. 6	*Haiford(e)* 224 *bis*, 227b *Heiford(e)* 220, 223b
Neubote	See Newbottle (in Harrington), Nobottle
Neutone	See Newton (near Geddington)
Newbottle (near Brackley), B. 9	*Niwebotle* 224b
Newbottle (in Harrington), E. 4	*Neubote* 222b
Newetone	See Newton (near Geddington)
Newnham	Not in D.B.
Newton (near Geddington), F. 4	*Neutone* 227b *Newentone* 228b *bis*
Newton Bromswold, G. 6	*Niwetone* 220b *Neuuentone* 210, Beds.
Niwebotle	See Newbottle (near Brackley)
Niwetone	See Newton Bromswold, Woodnewton
Nobottle, C. 6	*Neubote* 225b *bis*
Northampton, D. 6	*Hantone* 219 *Northantone* 219
Northantone	See Northampton
Northborough	Not in D.B.
Nortoft, C. 5	*Nortot* 224, 226
Norton (near Daventry), C. 6	*Nortone* 224 2nd entry
Nortone	See Greens Norton, Norton (near Daventry)
Nortot	See Nortoft
Oakley, Great and Little, F. 3	*Achelau* 228b
Ocedone	See Oxendon
Oitone	See Wootton, Oxon.
Old, E. 5	*Walda* 219b
Olletorp	See Althorpe
Optone	See Upton (near Northampton)
Ordinbaro	See Orlingbury
Orlingbury, E. 5	*Ordinbaro* 224
Orton, E. 4	*Overtone* 219b
Oundle, G. 3	*Undel(e)* 221, 221b *quater*
Overstone	Not in D.B.
Overtone	See Orton
Oxe(n)done	See Oxendon
Oxendon, Great and Little, D. 3, D. 4	*Ocedone* 228b *Oxe(n)done* 219b, 223
Parva Weledone	See Little Weldon
Pascelle	See Pattishall
Pas(s)eham	See Passenham
Passenham, E. 9	*Pas(s)eham* 222b, 223 *Passonham* 220
Passonham	See Passenham
Paston	Not in D.B.
Patorp	See Apethorpe
Pattishall, C. 7	*Pascelle* 226b *bis*
Paulerspury, D. 8	*Pirie* 226
Peakirk	Not in D.B.
Perie	See Potterspury
Peterborough, I. 2	*Burg* 220b, 221, N'hants:, 346, Lincs.
Picteslei	See Pytchley
Piddington, E. 7	*Pidentone* 229
Pidentone	See Piddington
Pidesford	See Pitsford
Pihteslea	See Pytchley
Pilchetone	See Pilton
Pillesgete	See Pilsgate
Pilsgate, H. 1	*Pillesgete* 221
Pilton, G. 3	*Pilchetone* 221b
Pipewell, E. 3	*Pipewelle* 223, 225, 226b
Pipewelle	See Pipewell
Pirie	See Paulerspury, Potterspury
Pitesford	See Pitsford

Piteslea	See Pytchley
Pitsford, D. 5	*Pidesford*, *Pitesford* 223, 226b
Plumpton, C. 8	*Pluntune* 226b
Pluntune	See Plumpton
Pochebroc	See Polebrook
Pocheslai, *-lei*	See Puxley
Polebrook, H. 3	*Pochebroc* 221b, 228
Potintone	See Podington, Beds.
Potterspury, D. 8	*Perie* 225 *Pirie* 229
Prestetone	See Preston Capes, Purston
Prestone	See Preston Deanery, Purston
Preston Capes and Little Preston, B. 7	*Prestetone* 224 *ter*
Preston Deanery, E. 7	*Prestone* 220b, 229
Purston, B. 9	*Pres(te)tone* 223b, 225
Puxley, D. 8	*Pocheslai*, *-lei* 220 *bis*
Pytchley, E. 5	*Picteslei* 224 *Pi(h)teslea* 222, 229
Quinton, E. 7	*Quintone* 228b, 229
Quintone	See Quinton
Radstone, C. 9	*Rodestone* 224b
Rande	See Raunds
Raunds, G. 5	*Rande* 220b, 225b *bis*
Ravenestorp	See Ravensthorpe
Ravensthorpe, C. 5	*Ravenestorp* 223, 226, 229
Ricsdone	See Rushton
Riehale	See Ryhall, Rutland
Ringstead	Not in D.B.
Ris(e)dene	See Rushden
Ris(e)tone	See Rushton
Roade, D. 7	*Rode* 220, 227b
Rochingeham	See Rockingham

Rockingham, F. 3	*Rochingeham* 220
Rode	See Roade
Rodestone	See Radstone
Rodewelle	See Rothwell
Rothersthorpe, D. 7	*Torp* 227 2nd entry, 227b
Rothwell, E. 4	*Rodewelle* 219b *bis*
Rushden, G. 6	*Ris(e)dene* 210, 212b, 225b *bis*
Rushton, E. 4	*Ricsdone* 220 *Ris(e)tone* 222b, 225, 225b, 228b
Salwebrige	See Sawbridge, Warw.
Scalde(s)welle	See Scaldwell
Scaldwell, D. 5	*Scalde(s)welle* 220b, 222, 228b
Scildeswelle	See Shelswell, Oxon.
Scipford	See Sibford, Oxon.
Sciptune	See Shipton on Cherwell, Oxon.
Sculetorp	See Sculthorpe, Rutland
Seawell, C. 7	*Sewelle* 225
Segentone, *Segestone*, *Seieton(e)*	See Seaton, Rutland
Selvestone	See Silverstone
Sewelle	See Seawell
Shutlanger	Not in D.B.
Sibbertoft, D. 4	*Sibertod* 223
Sibertod	See Sibbertoft
Sigre(s)ham	See Syresham
Silverstone, C. 8	*Sel-*, *Silvestone* 223b, 227, 227b
Silvestone	See Silverstone
Slapton, C. 8	*Slaptone* 224b
Slaptone	See Slapton
Slepe	See Islip
Slipton, G. 4	*Sliptone* 221b
Sliptone	See Slipton
Smelistone	See Snelston, Rutland
Snewelle	See Sywell
Snochescumbe	See Snorscomb

Snorscomb, C. 7	*Snochescumbe* 223b, 224
Solebi	See Sulby
Southorpe, H. 1	*Sudtorp* 221b
Southwick	Not in D.B.
Spratton, D. 5	*Spretone*, *Sprotone* 224, 225b, 229
Spretone, *Sprotone*	See Spratton
Stabintone	See Stibbington, Hunts.
Stane	See Steane
Stanere	See Stanion
Stanewiga	See Stanwick
Stanford	See Stanford on Avon
Stanford on Avon, C. 4	*Stanford* 226b, 227, N'hants.; 235 *bis*, Leics.
Stanion, F. 3	*Stanere* 219b, 220b
Stantone	See Stoneton, Warw.
Stanwick, G. 5	*Stanewiga* 210b *Stanwige* 221b
Stanwige	See Stanwick
Staverton, B. 6	*Stavertone* 223, 224b
Stavertone	See Staverton
Steane, B. 9	*Stane* 227
Stoche	See Stoke Albany, Stoke Bruerne, Stoke Doyle. See also Stoke Dry, Rutland
Stoke Albany, E. 3	*Stoche* 220, 225
Stoke Bruerne, D. 7	*Stoche* 228
Stoke Doyle, G. 3	*Stoche* 221, 221b
Stoteberie	See Stuchbury
Stowe, C. 7	*Stowe* 227b
Strixton	Not in D.B.
Stuchbury, B. 8	*Stoteberie* 227
Sudborough, G. 4	*Sutburg* 222
Sudtone	See King's Sutton
Sudtorp	See Southorpe
Sulby, C. 4	*Solebi* 227, 227b
Sulgrave, B. 8	*Sulgrave* 227
Sutburg	See Sudborough
Sutone	See King's Sutton, Sutton Bassett
Sutton (near Peterborough)	Not in D.B.
Sutton Bassett, D. 3	*Sutone* 225, 228
Syresham, C. 8	*Sigre(s)ham* 223b, 224 *bis*, 227
Sywell, E. 5	*Snewelle* 223
Taneford	See Thenford
Tanesovre	See Tansor
Tansor, H. 3	*Tanesovre* 220 *bis*
Teche	See Teeton
Tedinwelle	See Tinwell, Rutland
Teeton, D. 5	*Teche* 226
Teowelle	See Twywell
Terninge	See Thurning
Teworde	See Thenford
Thenford, B. 8	*Taneford* 228 *Teworde* 225
Thornby, C. 4	*Torneberie* 226 *bis*
Thornhaugh	Not in D.B.
Thorpe (in Peterborough), I. 2	*Torp* 221
Thorpe Lubbenham, D. 3	*Torp* 224b 1st entry
Thorpe Malsor, E. 4	*Alidetorp* 224
Thorpe Mandeville, B. 8	*Torp* 227 1st entry
Thrapston, G. 4	*Trapestone* 220b, 228
Thrupp Grounds, C. 6	*Torp* 223b, 224b 2nd entry, 228b
Thurning, H. 4	*Terninge* 221 *Torninge* 204, 206, Hunts.
Ticemerse	See Titchmarsh
Tichecote	See Tickencote, Rutland
Tichesovre	See Tixover, Rutland
Tifelde	See Tiffield
Tiffield, D. 7	*Tifelde* 223, 223b
Tingdene	See Finedon
Tinglea	See Dingley
Tircemesse	See Titchmarsh
Titchmarsh, G. 4	*Ticemerse* 225 *Tircemesse* 222

Toltorp	See Tolethorpe, Rutland
Torneberie	See Thornby
Torp	See Kingsthorpe (in Northampton), Rothersthorpe, Thorpe (in Peterborough), Thorpe Lubbenham, Thorpe Mandeville, Thrupp Grounds. See also Thorpe by Water, Rutland
Touecestre	See Towcester
Towcester, D. 8	*Touecestre* 219b, 223b
Trafford, B. 8	*Trapeford* 224b
Trapeford	See Trafford
Trapestone	See Thrapston
Tuiwella	See Twywell
Twywell, G. 4	*Teowelle* 228b *Tuiwella* 222b
Udetorp	See Hothorpe
Ufford	Not in D.B.
Undel(e)	See Oundle
Upper Boddington	See Boddington
Upper Heyford, C. 6	*Altera Haiford* 223
Upton (near Northampton), D. 6	*Optone* 219b
Upton (near Peterborough)	Not in D.B.
Wacafeld	See Wakefield
Wacherlei	See Wakerley
Wadenho	See Wadenhoe
Wadenhoe, G. 4	*Wadenho* 220b *bis*, 221b
Wakefield, D. 8	*Wacafeld* 224
Wakerley, G. 2	*Wacherlei* 227
Walda	See Old
Waldgrave	See Walgrave
Wale(s)done	See Great Weldon
Waletone	See Walton (near Peterborough), Walton Grounds, Welton
Walgrave, E. 5	*Waldgrave* 219b *Wold(e)grave* 224, 228b
Walton (near Peterborough), I. 1	*Waletone* 228b
Waltone	See Walton Grounds
Walton Grounds, B. 9	*Wal(e)tone* 220, 223b *bis*
Wansford	Not in D.B.
Wapeham	See Wappenham
Wappenham, C. 8	*Wapeham* 227
Waredone	See Chipping Warden
Warkton, F. 4	*Werchintone* 222
Warkworth	Not in D.B.
Warmington, H. 3	*War-*, *Wermintone* 221b *ter*
Warmintone	See Warmington
Watford, C. 5	*Watford* 229 *Wadford* 230, Leics.
Wavre	See Over, Warw.
Wedlingeberie	See Wellingborough
Wedone	See Weedon Beck, Weedon Lois
Weedon Beck, C. 6	*Wedone* 223, 224b
Weedon Lois, C. 8	*Wedone* 227
Weekley, F. 4	*Wiclei* 220
Weledene, *-done*	See Great Weldon
Weletone	See Welton
Welford, C. 4	*Wellesford* 227b
Welintone	See Welton
Wellesford	See Welford
Wellingborough, F. 5	*Wedlingeberie* 228b, 229 *Wendle(s)berie* 220b, 222b
Welton, B. 6	*Wale-*, *Weletone* 224, 228b *Welintone* 224b

Wendle(s)berie	See Wellingborough
Werchintone	See Warkton
Wermintone	See Warmington
Werrington, I. 1	*Widerintone* 221, 221b
West Farndon, B. 7	*Ferendon(e)* 223, 224b
West Haddon, C. 5	*Ecdone* 226 *E(d)done* 222b, 227b
Westhorp, B. 7	*Westorp* 227b
Weston by Welland, E. 3	*Westone* 222b, 225, 228
Westone	See Colleyweston, Weston by Welland, Weston Favell
Weston Favell, E. 6	*Westone* 219b, 223, 224, 227b
Westorp	See Westhorp
Whilton, C. 6	*Woltone* 223
Whiston, E. 6	*Wice(n)tone* 222, 222b, 228b
Whitfield, C. 9	*Witefelle* 219b
Whittlebury	Not in D.B.
Wice(n)tone	See Whiston
Wicford	See Whichford, Warw.
Wicha, *Wiche*	See Wicken
Wicken, D. 9	*Wicha*, *Wiche* 225, 228
Wiclei	See Weekley
Widerintone	See Werrington
Widetorp	See Dowthorpe
Widmale	See Wythemail
Wilavestone	See Wollaston
Wilbarston, E. 3	*Wilberdestone* 225 *Wilbertestone* 220
Wilberdestone, *Wilbertestone*	See Wilbarston
Wilby, F. 6	*Wilebi* 228
Wilebi	See Wilby
Winewic	See Winwick
Winewiche	See Winwick. See also Winwick, Hunts.
Winewincle	See Winwick, Hunts.
Winwick, C. 5	*Winewic(he)* 222b *ter*, 226
Witacre	See Whitacre, Warw.
Witefelle	See Whitfield
Wit(h)eringham	See Wittering
Witone	See Wootton
Wittering, H. 1	*Wit(h)eringham* 221b *bis*
Wodeford	See Woodford (near Denford), Woodford Halse
Wold(e)grave	See Walgrave
Wollaston, F. 6	*Wilavestone* 227b, 228b, 229
Woltone	See Whilton
Woodend	See Blakesley
Woodford (near Denford), G. 4	*Wodeford* 220b, 222
Woodford Halse, B. 7	*Wodeford* 224b
Woodnewton, G. 2	*Niwetone* 228
Wootton, D. 7	*Witone* 226b, 229
Wothorpe, G. 1	*Wri(d)torp* 221b, 222b
Wri(d)torp	See Wothorpe
Wythemail, E. 5	*Widmale* 226b
Yardley Gobion	Not in D.B.
Yardley Hastings, F. 7	*Gerdelai* 228, 229
Yarwell	Not in D.B.
Yelvertoft, C. 5	*Celvrecot* 223b *Gelvrecote* 223b *Givertost* 224b

ANONYMOUS HOLDINGS

/over

ANONYMOUS HOLDINGS

No place-names appear in the following nine entries. It is possible that some (or even all) of these refer to holdings at places not named elsewhere in Domesday Book:

Roger (from Ralf Pagenel), 2 hides in *Stoc* hd, 225b.
William Lovet, third of a virgate in *Stotfald* hd, 226.
Hugh (from Walter the Fleming), $1\frac{1}{2}$ hides and one fifth of half a hide in *Gravesend* hd, 226b.
Hugh (from Walter the Fleming), $3\frac{1}{5}$ hides in *Claile* hd, 226b.
Winemar, 2 hides and 3 virgates in *Hecham* hd, 226b.
Maialf (from Winemar) $2\frac{1}{2}$ virgates in *Claislund* hd, 226b.
Guy de Reinbuedcurt, 2 hides and 3 virgates in *Waredone* hd, 226b.
Gunfrid de Cioches, 2 hides and one virgate and half a hide of sokeland in *Gisleburg* hd, 227b.
Sigar de Cioches, 4 hides and four fifths of half a hide in *Touecestre* hd, 228.

NOTTINGHAMSHIRE—*SNOTINGHAMSCIRE*

Folios 280–293

MAP 38

Adbolton, C. 7	*Alboltune* 287, 288
Ættune	See Eaton
Agemuntone	See Egmanton
Aigrun	See Averham
Ailetone	See Elton
Alboltune	See Adbolton
Alia Marneham	See Low Marnham
Almentun(e), *Almuntone*	See Ompton
Alretun	See Ollerton
Altera Mortune	See North Morton
Alverton, E. 7	*Alvretun* 288b *Alvriton* 291, 291b
Alvretun, *Alvriton*	See Alverton
Alwoldestorp, D. 7	Lost in Caythorpe, 291
Aneslei	See Annesley
Annesley, B. 6	*Aneslei* 289b
Arnold, B. 7	*Ernehale* 281b *ter*, 293
Ascam	See Askham
Askham, D. 3	*Ascam* 283
Aslache(s)tone, *-tune*	See Aslockton
Aslockton, D. 7	*Aslache(s)tone*, *-tune* 281b, 288b, 291, 293 *Haslachestone* 290b
Averham, E. 6	*Aigrun* 291
Awsworth, A. 7	*Eldesuorde* 293 *Eldeurde* 288
Baburde	See Babworth
Babworth, D. 3	*Baburde* 281, 285
Badeleie	See Bathley
Balderton, E. 6	*Baldretone*, *-tune* 283b *bis*
Baldretone, *-tune*	See Balderton
Barnby in the Willows, F. 6	*Barnebi* 283b, 284
Barnby Moor, C. 2	*Barnebi* 281, 285b
Barnebi	See Barnby in the Willows, Barnby Moor
Barnstone, D. 8	*Bernestune* 288, 289
Bartone	See Barton in Fabis

Barton in Fabis, B. 8	*Bartone* 287, 289b *bis*, 292b
Baseford	See Basford
Basford, B. 7	*Baseford* 287b, 288, 292b, 293
Basin(g)felt	See Bassingfield
Bassingfield, C. 8	*Basin(g)felt* 286, 287
Bathley, E. 5	*Badeleie* 291b
Beching(e)ham	See Beckingham
Beckingham, E. 2	*Beching(e)ham* 283, 286b
Beeston, B. 8	*Bestune* 287b
Bernestune	See Barnstone
Bertune	See Burton Joyce
Besthorpe (in Caunton), D. 5	*Bestorp* 281 *bis*, 289
Besthorpe (near Sutton on Trent)	Not in D.B.
Bestorp	See Besthorpe (in Caunton)
Bestune	See Beeston
Bestwood Park	Not in D.B.
Bevercotes	Not in D.B.
Bilborough, B. 7	*Bileburch*, *-burg* 281b, 287b
Bilby, C. 2	*Billebi* 285
Bildestorp	See Bilsthorpe
Bileburch, *-burg*	See Bilborough
Billebi	See Bilby
Bilsthorpe, C. 5	*Bildestorp* 290b
Bingham, D. 7	*Bingheham* 286 *bis*
Bingheham	See Bingham
Bleasby	Not in D.B.
Blide	See Blyth
Blideworde	See Blidworth
Blidworth, B. 5	*Blideworde* 283 *bis*
Blyth, C. 2	*Blide* 285
Bodmescel(d)	See Bothamsall
Bole, E. 2	*Bolun* 283, 286b *bis*
Bolun	See Bole
Bonei	See Bunny
Bonnington, B. 9	*Bonniton(e)* 282b, 291b, 292b
Bonniton(e)	See Bonnington
Bothamsall, C. 3	*Bodmescel(d)* 281 *bis*, 285
Boughton, C. 4	*Buchetone*, *-tun* 284b, 290b

Brademere	See Bradmore
Bradmore, B. 8	*Brademere* 291b *bis*
Bramcote, B. 8	*Broncote* 281b *Brun(e)cote* 287b, 292
Brigeforde	See West Bridgford
Brinsley, A. 6	*Brunesleia* 287b
Broadholme, F. 3	*Brodeholm* 284b, 291b
Brochelestou	See Broxtowe
Brodeholm	See Broadholme
Broncote	See Bramcote
Brotone	See Upper Broughton
Broxtowe, B. 7	*Brochelestou* 281b, 287b, 292
Brugeford	See East Bridgford
Brun(e)cote	See Bramcote
Brunesleia	See Brinsley
Buchetone, *-tun*	See Boughton
Budby, C. 4	*Butebi* 281
Bulcote, C. 7	*Bulecote* 288b
Bulecote	See Bulcote
Bul(e)uuelle	See Bulwell
Bulwell, B. 7	*Bul(e)uuelle* 287b, 288 *bis*
Bunny, B. 9	*Bonei* 289b *bis*
Burtone	See West Burton
Burton Joyce, C. 7	*Bertune* 285b, 289
Butebi	See Budby
Caldecotes	See Oldcoates
Calnestone, *-tune*	See Caunton
Calun	See Kelham
Calverton, C. 6	*Calvretone* 283, 290, 292b
Calvretone	See Calverton
Carbertone	See Carburton
Carburton, C. 3	*Carbertone* 281
Car Colston, D. 7	*Colestone*, *-tune* 281b, 286b, 288b
Careltune	See Carlton (in Lindrick)
Carentune	See Carlton (near Nottingham), Carlton on Trent
Caretone	See Carlton (in Lindrick)

Carlentun(e), Carleton	See Carlton on Trent
Carletone	See Carlton (in Lindrick), Carlton on Trent
Carletun(e)	See Carlton on Trent
Carlton (in Lindrick), C. 2	*Careltune* 285 *Caretone* 281 *Carletone* 281 2nd entry
Carlton (near Nottingham), C. 7	*Carentune* 289
Carlton on Trent, E. 5	*Carentune* 281 *Carlentun(e)* 289b, 292b *Carleton(e)* 281 1st entry, 283 *Carletun(e)* 282b, 285b, 289 *bis*
Caunton, D. 5	*Calnestone, -tune* 283, 289
Cau(u)orde	See Keyworth
Caythorpe	Not in D.B.
Chelvinctune, Chelvintone, -tun	See Kilvington
Chena(pe)torp	See Knapthorpe
Cheneshale	See Kneesall
Cheniueton(e)	See Kneeton
Cherlinton	See Kirklington
Cherueshale	See Kersall
Chideuuelle	See Chilwell
Chilwell, B. 8	*Chideuuelle* 287b *Ciduuelle, Cilleuuelle* 289b *bis* *Cum duabus Ciluellis* 289b
Chineltone, -tune	See Kinoulton
Chinemarel(e)ie	See Kimberley
Chinestan	See Kingston on Soar
Chirchebi	See Kirkby in Ashfield
Chircheton	See Kirton in Lindsey, Lincs.
Ciduuelle, Cilleuuelle	See Chilwell
Ciluellis, Cum duabus	See Chilwell, East Chilwell
Circeton	See Kirton in Lindsey, Lincs.
Clarborough, D. 2	*Claueburch* 283 *Claureburg* 281b, 286b, 293 *bis*
Claueburch	See Clarborough
Clauorde	See Clayworth
Claureburg	See Clarborough
Clayworth, D. 2	*Clauorde* 281b, 286b
Cledretone	See Leverton
Clifton (near Nottingham), B. 8	*Cliftun(e)* 280b, 287 *bis*, 289b, 292b
Clifton, North and South, E. 4	*Cliftone, -tune* 283b, 284b *Cli(s)tone* 283b, 284b
Cliftone	See Clifton, North and South
Cliftun	See Clifton (near Nottingham)
Cliftune	See Clifton (near Nottingham); Clifton, North and South
Clipestune	See Clipston, Clipstone
Clipston, C. 8	*Clipestune* 286
Clipstone, C. 4	*Clipestune* 285
Cli(s)tone	See Clifton, North and South
Clown, B. 3	*Clune* 281
Clumber, C. 3	*Clumbre, Clunbre* 281, 285 *bis*
Clumbre, Clunbre	See Clumber
Clune	See Clown
Coddington, E. 6	*Cotintone, -tun* 283b *bis*, 284 *bis*
Colestone, -tune	See Car Colston
Coletone	See Colston Bassett
Coleuui(c)	See Colwick
Colingeham	See Collingham
Collingham, North and South, E. 5	*Colingeham* 284 *bis*, 289b

Colston Bassett, D. 8	*Coletone* 292 *bis*
Colui	See Colwick
Colwick, C. 7	*Coleuui(c)* 287, 289 *Colui* 292b
Cortingestoche(s)	See Costock
Cossall, A. 7	*Coteshale* 287b, 289b
Costock, B. 9	*Cortingestoche(s)* 288, 290 *Cotingestoche* 286, 287
Cotes	See Cotham
Coteshale	See Cossall
Cotgrove, C. 8	*Godegrave* 290 *ter*
Cotham, E. 6	*Cotes* 284, 288b *Cotun(e)* 283b, 284b
Cotingestoche	See Costock
Cotintone, -tun	See Coddington
Cottam	Not in D.B.
Cotun(e)	See Cotham
Creilege, C. 4	Lost in Wellow, 290b
Cromwell, E. 5	*Crunuuelle* 291, 292b
Crophelle, -hille	See Cropwell
Cropwell Bishop and Butler, D. 8	*Crophelle, -hille* 283, 289, 290, 291
Crunuuelle	See Cromwell
Cuchenai	See Cuckney
Cuckney, B. 4	*Cuchenai* 285, 291b
Dallintune, E. 7	Lost in Flawborough, 288b
Danethorpe, E. 5	*Dordentorp* 289b
Darlton, E. 3	*Derluuetun* 281
Derluuetun	See Darlton
Dordentorp	See Danethorpe
Draitone	See East Drayton, West Drayton
Draitun	See West Drayton
Dune(ham)	See Dunham
Dunham, E. 3	*Dune, Duneham* 281 *bis*
Eakring, D. 5	*Ec(he)ringhe* 281, 289, 290
East Bridgford, D. 7	*Brugeford* 286
East Chilwell, B. 8	*Estrecille(u)uelle* 289b, 293 *Cum duabus Ciluellis* 289b
East Drayton, E. 3	*Draitone* 281
East Leake, B. 9	*Lec(c)he* 282b, 286, 291b 1st entry, 292
East Markham, D. 4	*Marcham* 281, 284b *ter* *Mark* . . . 284b
East Retford	See Retford
East Stoke, D. 6	*Stochas, Stoches* 283b, 288b, 291 *bis*, 291b
Eastwood, A. 7	*Estewic* 287b
Eaton, D. 3	*Ættune* 284b *Ettone* 283, 284b *Etun(a)e* 284b *bis*, 285
Echelinge	See Hickling
Ec(he)ringhe	See Eakring
Eddingley	Not in D.B.
Edenestou	See Edwinstowe
Edwalton, C. 8	*Edwoltone, -tun* 290, 291b
Edwinstowe, C. 4	*Edenestou* 281 *bis*
Edwoltone, -tun	See Edwalton
Egmanton, D. 4	*Agemuntone* 284b *bis*
Elchesleie, -leig, -lie	See Elkesley
Elde(s)u(o)rde	See Awsworth
Elkesley, D. 3	*Elchesleie, -leig, -lie* 281, 285, 293
Elston, D. 6	*Eluestun(e)* 283b *bis*, 284b, 291 *bis*
Elton, E. 7	*Ailetone* 286b
Eluestun(e)	See Elston
Epperstone, C. 6	*Ep(re)stone* 285b, 289b
Ep(re)stone	See Epperstone
Ernehale	See Arnold
Escreventone	See Screveton
Estewic	See Eastwood
Estirape	See Styrrup
Estoches	See Stokeham

Place	Domesday form
Hawton, E. 6	*Holtone* 283b, 289b *Houtune* 288b
Hayton	Not in D.B.
Haywood Oaks	Not in D.B.
Headon, D. 3	*Hedune* 281, 284b *bis*
Hechelinge	See Hickling
Hedune	See Headon
Hegelinge	See Hickling
Hempshill, B. 7	*Hamessel* 288
Herd(r)ebi	See Harby
Hereuuelle	See Harwell
Hickling, D. 9	*Echelinge* 291 *Heche-*, *Hegelinge* 283, 289
High Marnham, E. 4	*Marneham* 285b
Hochehale, *-enale*	See Hucknall Torkard
Hoches(u)uorde	See Hawksworth
Hockerton, D. 5	*Hocretone*, *-tune* 285b, 288b *Ocretone* 283
Hocretone, *-tune*	See Hockerton
Hoctun	See Haughton
Hodsock, C. 2	*Odesach* 285
Holbeck	Not in D.B.
Holme	Not in D.B.
Holme Pierrepont, C. 7	*Holmo* 286 *bis*
Holmo	See Holme Pierrepont
Holtone	See Hawton
Horingeham	See Hoveringham
Horsepool, D. 6	*Horspol* 288b
Horspol	See Horsepool
Houtune	See Hawton
Hoveringham, D. 6	*Horingeham* 288b
Hucknall Torkard, B. 6	*Hochehale*, *-enale* 288, 290
Hucknall under Huthwaite	Not in D.B.
Inkersall formerly Winkerfield, C. 5	*Wirchenefeld* 290b
Kelham, E. 5	*Calun* 285b, 288b, 290, 291, 293
Kersall, D. 5	*Cherueshale* 290b
Keyworth, C. 8	*Cau(u)orde* 282b, 286 *bis*, 287, 289b
Kilvington, E. 7	*Chelvinctune* 291b *Chelvintone*, *-tun* 283b, 291
Kimberley, A. 7	*Chinemarel(e)ie* 288 *bis*
Kingston on Soar, A. 9	*Chinestan* 282b, 292b *bis*
Kinoulton, C. 8	*Chineltone*, *-tune* 289, 293
Kirkby in Ashfield, A. 5	*Chirchebi* 289b, 292b
Kirklington, D. 5	*Cherlinton* 290b
Kirton, D. 4	*Schidri(n)ctune* 289, 290b *Schidrinton*, *-tune* 281, 284b *Schitrintone* 281
Knapthorpe, D. 5	*Chena(pe)torp* 288b, 289, 289b, 292b
Kneesall, D. 4	*Cheneshale* 290b
Kneeton, D. 7	*Cheniueton(e)* 281b, 282b, 286, 286b
Lambecotes	See Lamcote
Lambeleia	See Lambley
Lambley, C. 7	*Lambeleia* 292b
Lamcote, C. 7	*Lambecotes* 293 *Lanbecote* 286, 290
Lanbecote	See Lamcote
Landeforde	See Langford
Laneham, E. 3	*Lanun* 283 *bis*, Notts.; 340, Lincs.
Langar, D. 8	*Langare* 288, 289
Langare	See Langar
Langford, E. 5	*Landeforde* 291
Lanun	See Laneham
Laxintune	See Laxton
Laxton, D. 4	*Laxintune* 289 *bis*
Lecche	See East Leake, West Leake
Leche	See East Leake
Legretone	See Leverton
Lenton, B. 7	*Lentone*, *-tune* 281b, 287b *bis*

Lentone, *-tune*	See Lenton
Leston	See Laughton (near Blyton), Lincs.
Leverton, North and South, E. 2, E. 3	*Cledretone* 281b, 282b, 287 *Legretone* 283
Lidebi	See Linby
Linby, B. 6	*Lidebi* 287b
Lindhurst	Not in D.B.
Litelburg	See Littleborough
Littleborough, E. 2	*Litelburg* 281b
Little Gringley, D. 3	*Grenelei(g)* 281b, 283 *Grenleige* 281
Lound, D. 2	*Lund* 281, 283, 285
Lowdham, C. 6	*Lud(e)ham* 283, 285b
Low Marnham, E. 4	*Alia Marneham* 285b
Lud(e)ham	See Lowdham
Lund	See Lound
Madressei(g)	See Mattersey
Mamesfeld(e), *Mammesfed*	See Mansfield
Mansfield, B. 5	*Mamesfeld(e)* 281 *ter*, 285 *Mammesfed* 281
Manton, C. 3	*Mennetune* 288
Mapelbec, *-berg*	See Maplebeck
Maplebeck, D. 5	*Mapelbec*, *-berg* 281 *bis* *Mapleberg* 290b
Mapleberg	See Maplebeck
Marcham, *Mark...*	See East Markham
Markham Clinton formerly West Markham, D. 4	*Westmarcham* 284b, 285
Marneham	See High Marnham
Marneham, *Alia*	See Low Marnham
Martin, C. 1	*Martune* 285b
Martune	See Martin
Mattersey, D. 2	*Madressei(g)* 281, 283, 287
Meering, E. 4	*Meringe* 281b
Mennetune	See Manton
Meringe	See Meering
Miletune	See Milton
Milton, D. 3	*Miletune* 287
Ministretone	See Misterton
Misna, *Misne*	See Misson
Misson, D. 1	*Misna*, *Misne* 281b, 284b, 293
Misterton, E. 1	*Ministretone* 281b, 286b *bis*
Morton (in Babworth), C. 3	*Mortune* 281
Morton (in Fiskerton), D. 6	*Mortun(e)* 288b, 289b
Morton (in Lenton), B. 8	*Mortune* 287b
Mortun	See Morton (in Fiskerton)
Mortune	See Morton (in Babworth), Morton (in Fiskerton), Morton (in Lenton)
Mortune, *Altera*	See North Morton
Muscham	See South Muskham
Nether Langwith	Not in D.B.
Neubold, D. 8	Lost in Kinoulton, 281b, 287b *bis*
Neutone	See Newton
Neutorp	See Newthorpe
Newark, E. 6	*Newerc(h)e* 283b *bis*, 291b
Newerc(h)e	See Newark
Newstead	Not in D.B.
Newthorpe, A. 7	*Neutorp* 282b, 287b, 288
Newton, D. 7	*Neutone* 289b *Niuuetune* 286
Niuuetune	See Newton
Nordermortune	See North Morton
Nordmuscham	See North Muskham
Normanton	See Normanton on Soar
Normanton (in Southwell), D. 6	*Normantun* 290b *Normentun* 292b
Normanton by Clumber, C. 3	*Normentone* 281

Normantone	See Normanton on Soar, Normanton on the Wolds
Normanton on Soar, B. 9	*Normanton* 282b *Normantone* 286 1st entry *Normantun(e)* 282b, 292b *ter*
Normanton on the Wolds, C. 8	*Normantone* 286 2nd entry *Normantun* 287
Normanton on Trent, E. 4	*Normentone*, *-tune* 284, 285b *bis*
Normantun	See Normanton (in Southwell), Normanton on Soar, Normanton on the Wolds
Normantune	See Normanton on Soar
Normentone	See Normanton by Clumber, Normanton on Trent
Normentun	See Normanton (in Southwell)
Normentune	See Normanton on Trent
North Clifton	See Clifton, North and South
North Collingham	See Collingham
North Leverton	See Leverton
North Morton (in Babworth), C. 3	*Altera Mortune* 281 *Nordermortune* 285 *Nortmortun* 293
North Muskham, E. 5	*Nordmuscham* 283, 284, 289, 292b
North Wheatley	See Wheatley
Nortmortun	See North Morton
Norton	Not in D.B.
Nortwelle	See Norwell
Norwell, E. 5	*Nortwelle* 283, 289b
Notintone	See Sneinton
Nottingham, B. 7	*Snoting(e)ham* 280 *quin*, 281
Nutehale	See Nuthall
Nuthall, B. 7	*Nutehale* 287b, 293

Obetorp	See Owthorpe
Ocretone	See Hockerton
Odesach	See Hodsock
Odestorp	Unid., 281, 285, 285b, 292b
Olavestone	See Wollaton
Oldcoates, C. 2	*Caldecotes* 285
Ollavestone	See Wollaton
Ollerton, C. 4	*Alretun* 284b, 290b
Ompton, D. 4	*Almentun(e)* 289, 290, 290b *Almuntone* 281
Opetone	See Upton (in Headon)
Ordeshale	See Ordsall
Ordsall, D. 3	*Ordeshale* 281 *bis*, 284b *bis*, 293
Orston, E. 7	*Oschintone* 281b
Osbernestune	See Osberton
Osberton, C. 3	*Osbernestune* 292b
Oschintone	See Orston, Ossington
Osmanthorpe, D. 5	*Osuuitorp* 283
Ossington, D. 4	*Oschintone* 290
Ostone, *Ostune*	See Oxton
Osuuitorp	See Osmanthorpe
Ovetorp	See Owthorpe
Owthorpe, C. 8	*Obetorp* 289b *Ovetorp* 286b, 291b
Oxton, C. 6	*Ostone*, *Ostune* 283, 285b, 288b
Papleuuic	See Papplewick
Papplewick, B. 6	*Papleuuic* 287b, 292b
Perlethorpe, C. 4	*Torp* 281 *ter*, 285
Plumtree, C. 8	*Pluntre* 286 *quater*
Pluntre	See Plumtree
Radcliffe on Trent, C. 7	*Radeclive* 288, 289
Radeclive	See Radcliffe on Trent, Ratcliffe on Soar
Radford, B. 7	*Redeford* 287
Ragenehil	See Ragnall
Ragnall, E. 3	*Ragenehil* 281
Rametone	See Rampton

Rampestone, *-tune*	See Rempstone
Rampton, E. 3	*Rametone* 287
Ranby, C. 3	*Rane(s)bi* 281 *ter*, 284b *bis*
Rane(s)bi	See Ranby
Ranskill, C. 2	*Raveschel* 283
Ratcliffe on Soar, A. 9	*Radeclive* 292b
Raveschel	See Ranskill
Rayton, C. 3	*Reneton* 281 *Rouuetone* 281
Redeford	See Radford
Redford(e)	See Retford
Rempstone, B. 9	*Rampestone*, *-tune* 288, 290 *Repestone* 286
Reneton	See Rayton
Repestone	See Rempstone
Retford, East and West, D. 3	*Redford(e)* 283, 285, 285b
Roddinton(e), *Rodintone*, *Rodintun*	See Ruddington
Roldestun	See Rolleston
Rolleston, D. 6	*Roldestun* 288b *Rollestone*, *-tune* 283, 284
Rollestone, *-tune*	See Rolleston
Rolvetune	See Roolton
Roolton, C. 3	*Rolvetune* 285
Rouuetone	See Rayton
Ruddington, B. 8	*Roddinton(e)* 286, 290b *Rodintone* 291b *Rodintun* 282b
Rufford, C. 5	*Rugforde* 290b
Rugforde	See Rufford
Salestune	See Selston
Salterford, C. 6	*Saltreford* 292
Saltreford	See Salterford
Sandebi	See Saundby
Sandiriaca	See Sandiacre, Derby.
Saundby, E. 2	*Sandebi* 281b, 283, 286b
Saxebi	See Saxilby, Lincs.
Saxeden	See Saxondale
Saxondale, D. 7	*Saxeden* 286
Scachebi	See Skegby (in Marnham)
Scafteorde	See Scaftworth
Scaftworth, C. 1	*Scafteorde* 283
Scarintone	See Scarrington
Scarrington, D. 7	*Scarintone* 281b
Scelford(e)	See Shelford
Sceltun(e)	See Shelton
Schegebi	See Skegby (in Sutton in Ashfield)
Schidri(n)ctune, *Schidrinton*, *-tune*, *Schitrintone*	See Kirton
Scofton, C. 3	*Scotebi* 281 *bis*
Scornelei	See South Scarle
Scotebi	See Scofton
Screveton, D. 7	*Escreventone* 286 *Screvetone*, *Screvintone* 281b, 284
Screvetone, *Screvintone*	See Screveton
Scrobi	See Scrooby
Scrooby, C. 1	*Scrobi* 283
Selston, A. 6	*Salestune* 288
Serlby, C. 2	*Serlebi* 285
Serlebi	See Serlby
Shelford, C. 7	*Scelford(e)* 286, 289
Shelton, E. 7	*Sceltun(e)* 284b, 289b, 291
Sibetorp	See Sibthorpe
Sibthorpe, E. 7	*Sibetorp* 282b, 287, 291
Simenton(e)	Unid., 281b, 283
Sirestun(e)	See Syerston
Skegby (in Marnham), E 4	*Scachebi* 285b
Skegby (in Sutton in Ashfield), A. 5	*Schegebi* 281
Sneinton, C. 7	*Notintone* 281b
Snoting(e)ham	See Nottingham
Sookholme	Not in D.B.
South Clifton	See Clifton, North and South
South Collingham	See Collingham
South Leverton	See Leverton

South Muskham, E. 5	*Muscham* 283, 293, Notts.; 376b, Lincs.
South Ordsall, D. 3	*Suderdeshale* 281
South Scarle, E. 5	*Scornelei* 283b
Southwell, D. 6	*Suduuelle*, *Sudwelle* 283 *quater*, 288b *ter*, 289b, 290b
South Wheatley	See Wheatley
Spaldesforde	See Spalford
Spalford, E. 4	*Spaldesforde* 283b, 284b
Stanford on Soar, B. 9	*Stanford* 286, 292 *bis*
Stanton on the Wolds, C. 8	*Stantun(e)* 282b *bis*, 286, 287 *bis*
Stantun(e)	See Stanton on the Wolds, Staunton
Stapleford, A. 8	*Stapleford* 287b
Startorp	See Staythorpe
Staunton, E. 7	*Stantun(e)* 281b, 288b
Staythorpe, D. 6	*Startorp* 291
Stochas	See East Stoke
Stoches	See East Stoke, Stoke Bardolph
Stockwith	Not in D.B.
Stoctun	See Stockerston, Leics.
Stoke Bardolph, C. 7	*Stoches* 289
Stokeham, E. 3	*Estoches* 284
Straelie, *Straleia*	See Strelley
Strelley, B. 7	*Straelie* 292b *Straleia* 287b
Sturton le Steeple, E. 2	*Estretone* 281b, 286b
Styrrup, C. 2	*Estirape* 285b
Suanesterne, E. 3	Lost in Dunham, 281
Suderdeshale	See South Ordsall
Sudtone	See Sutton (near East Retford), Sutton Bonnington, Sutton on Trent
Sudtune	See Sutton Passeys
Suduuelle, *Sudwelle*	See Southwell
Sutone	See Sutton Bonnington, Sutton in Ashfield, Sutton Passeys
Sutton (near East Retford), D. 2	*Sudtone* 283
Sutton Bonnington, B. 9	*Sudtone* 282b *bis* 2nd and 3rd entries *Sutone* 292b
Sutton in Ashfield, A. 5	*Sutone* 281
Sutton on Trent, E. 4	*Sudtone* 282b 1st entry, 285b *bis*
Sutton Passeys, B. 7	*Sudtune* 287b *Sutone* 293
Syerston, D. 6	*Sirestun(e)* 282b, 283b, 291b, 293
Teversal, A. 5	*Tevreshalt* 289b
Tevreshalt	See Teversal
Thoresby, C. 4	*Turesbi* 281
Thorney, F. 3	*Torneshaie* 283b
Thoroton, E. 7	*Toruentun* 291 *Toruertune* 281b
Thorpe by Newark, E. 6	*Torp* 289b
Thorpe in the Glebe, C. 9	*Torp* 281b, 286, 292b
Thrumpton, B. 8	*Turmodestun* 286, 287, 291b
Thurgarton, D. 6	*Turgarstune* 288b
Tiedebi	See Tithby
Tille	See Tiln
Tiln, D. 2	*Tille* 281b *Tilne* 281, 283 *bis*
Tilne	See Tiln
Tireswelle	See Treswell
Tithby, D. 8	*Tiedebi* 288, 288b
Tollerton, C. 8	*Troclavestune* 286
Toluestone	See Toton
Torneshaie	See Thorney
Torp	See Perlethorpe, Thorpe by Newark, Thorpe in the Glebe

Toruentun, *Toruertune*	See Thoroton
Torwalle	See Trowell
Torworth, C. 2	*Turdeworde* 285
Toton, B. 8	*Toluestone* 289b *Touetune* 287b
Touetune	See Toton
Treswell, E. 3	*Tireswelle* 282b, 287
Troclavestune	See Tollerton
Trouualle	See Trowell
Trowell, A. 7	*Torwalle* 292, 292b *Trouualle* 293
Turdeworde	See Torworth
Turesbi	See Thoresby
Turgarstune	See Thurgarton
Turmodestun	See Thrumpton
Tuxfarne	See Tuxford
Tuxford, D. 4	*Tuxfarne* 284b, 285
Ude(s)burg	See Woodborough
Upetone, *-tun(e)*	See Upton (in Headon)
Upper Broughton, D. 9	*Brotone* 281b
Upton (in Headon), D. 3	*Opetone* 284 *Upetone*, *-tun(e)* 281, 284b *bis*
Upton (near Southwell)	Not in D.B.
Wachering(e)ham	See Walkeringham
Walesbi	See Walesby
Walesby, D. 4	*Walesbi* 281, 284b, 289, 290
Waletone	See Wollaton
Walkeringham, E. 1	*Wachering(e)ham* 281b, 286b
Wallingwells	Not in D.B.
Wanddeslei	See Wansley
Wansley, A. 6	*Wanddeslei* 289b
Warberga, *Wareberg*, C. 8	Lost in Plumtree, 286, 290
Wares(h)ope	See Warsop
Warsop, B. 4	*Wares(h)ope* 281, 285, 293 *Warsope* 281
Warsope	See Warsop

Watelaie, *-leia*, *-leie*	See Wheatley
Watenot	See Watnall
Watnall, A. 7	*Watenot* 287b *quater*, 288
Watone	See Whatton
Welbeck	Not in D.B.
Welham, D. 2	*Wellon*, *Wellun* 281b, 283
Wellon	See Welham
Wellow	Not in D.B.
Wellun	See Welham
Werchesope	See Worksop
West Bridgford, B. 8	*Brigeforde* 287
West Burton, E. 2	*Burtone* 283, 286b
West Drayton, D. 3	*Draitone*, *-tun* 285 *bis*, 290
West Leake, B. 9	*Lecche* 291b 2nd entry
Westmarcham	See Markham Clinton formerly West Markham
Weston, E.4	*Westone* 285b
Westone	See Weston
West Retford	See Retford
Whatton, D. 7	*Watone* 290b
Wheatley, North and South, D. 2	*Watelaie*, *-leia*, *-leie* 281b, 283, 286b
Wicheburne	See Winkburn
Widmerpool, C. 9	*Wimarspol(d)* 289b, 293
Wigesleie	See Wigsley
Wigsley, F. 4	*Wigesleie* 283b
Wilesforde	See Wilford
Wilford, B. 8	*Wilesforde* 287
Wilgebi	See Willoughby (in Norwell), Willoughby (in Walesby), Willoughby on the Wolds
Willebi	See Willoughby on the Wolds
Willoughby (in Norwell), E. 5	*Wilgebi* 283, 289 2nd entry

Willoughby (in Walesby), D. 4	*Wilgebi* 281 *bis*, 289 1st entry, 290 2nd entry
Willoughby on the Wolds, C. 9	*Wilgebi* 286, 290 1st entry, 291b, 293
	Willebi 286, 287, 292b
Wimarspol(d)	See Widmerpool
Wimentun	See Wimpton
Wimpton, E. 3	*Wimentun* 281
Wimuntorp	See Winthorpe
Winkburn, D. 5	*Wicheburne* 291
Winthorpe, E. 5	*Wimuntorp* 283b
Wirchenefeld	See Inkersall formerly Winkerfield
Wiseton, D. 2	*Wisetone* 281b
Wisetone	See Wiseton
Wisoc	See Wysall
Wiverton, D. 8	*Wivretone*, *-tun(e)* 288 *bis*, 289 *bis*, 292
Wivretone, *-tun(e)*	See Wiverton
Wollaton, B. 7	*Ol(l)avestone* 287b, 293
	Waletone 281b
Woodborough, C. 6	*Ude(s)burg* 283, 285b, 289b, 292b *ter*
Woodhouse Hall	Not in D.B.
Worksop, B. 3	*Werchesope* 285
Wysall, C. 9	*Wisoc* 286 *bis*

ANONYMOUS HOLDINGS

None.

OXFORDSHIRE—*OXENEFORDSCIRE*

Folios 154–161

MAP 39

Ac(h)am	See Noke
Adderbury, East and West, C. 3	*Edburgberie* 154b, 155, 158
Adingeham	See Ingham
Adlach	Unid., 161
Aduelle	See Adwell
Adwell, F. 7	*Aduelle* 159b
Aieleforde	See Yelford
Albury, E. 6	*Aldeberie* 161
	Eldeberie 56, Berks.
Alcrintone	See Alkerton
Aldeberie	See Albury
Alia Ernicote	See Arncott
Alkerton, B. 2	*Alcrintone* 156b, 159b
Altera Cote	See Nethercote (in Lewknor)
Alvescot, A. 6	*Elfegescote* 160b
Alwoldesberie, A. 6	Lost in Alvescot, 160
Ambresdone	See Ambrosden
Ambrosden, E. 4	*Ambresdone* 157b
Amintone	See Emmington
Ardley, D. 3	*Ardulueslie* 157
Ardulueslie	See Ardley
Arncott, Lower and Upper, E. 4, E. 5	*Alia Ernicote* 156b
	Ernicote 160
Asce	Unid., 157b
Ascot D'Oily and Earl, A. 4	*Est(h)cote* 156b, 158b
Asterleigh	Not in D.B.
Asthall, A. 5	*Esthale* 158b
Aston, Middle, North and Steeple, C. 3, C. 4	*Estone* 156, 158 *bis*, 160, 160b
Aston Bampton	Not in D.B.
Aston Rowant, F. 7	*Estone* 159
Astrop, B. 6	*Estrope* 161

Badgemore, F. 8	*Begeurde* 157b
Baditone	See Bainton
Bainton, E. 3	*Baditone* 159b
Balde(n)done, *Baldentone*	See Baldon
Baldon, Marsh and Toot, D. 7	*Balde(n)done* 155b, 156, 157, 159b, 160 *Baldentone* 156
Balscott, B. 2	*Berescote* 156b
Bampton, B. 6	*Bentone* 154b, 155, 156, 158b
Banbury, C. 2	*Banesberie* 155, 155b
Banesberie	See Banbury
Barford St John, St Michael, C. 3	*Bereford* 156, 156b, 160
Barton, Sesswell, Steeple and Westcott, C. 4	*Bertone* 156, 156b, 159
Bechebroc	See Begbroke
Bechelie	See Beckley
Beckley, D. 5	*Bechelie* 158b
Begbroke, C. 5	*Bechebroc* 161
Begeurde	See Badgemore
Benson, E. 7	*Besintone* 154b, 160b *bis* *Besentone* 56, Berks.
Bentone	See Bampton
Bereford	See Barford
Berescote	See Balscott
Berewiche	See Berrick Salome
Bernecestre	See Bicester
Berrick Salome, E. 7	*Berewiche* 159b
Bertone	See Barton
Besintone	See Benson
Bicester, E. 4	*Bernecestre* 158
Bispesdone	Unid., 160
Bix, F. 8	*Bixa* 157b, 160b
Bixa	See Bix
Black Bourton, A. 6	*Bor-*, *Burtone* 160, 161 *bis*
Blackthorn	Not in D.B.
Blade	See Bladon
Bladon, C. 5	*Blade* 156
Blecesdone	See Bletchingdon

Bletchingdon, D. 5	*Blecesdone* 154 *Blicestone* 158b, 160b
Blicestone	See Bletchingdon
Blochesham	See Bloxham
Bloxham, C. 2	*Blochesham* 154, 154b *bis*
Bodicote, C. 2	*Bodicote* 157, 159
Boicote	See Boycott, Bucks.
Bollehede	See Bolney
Bolney, F. 9	*Bollehede* 161
Bortone	See Black Bourton
Bradewelle	See Broadwell
Bretewelle	See Brightwell Baldwin
Brighthampton, B. 6	*Bristelmestone* 156, 161
Brightwell Baldwin, E. 7	*Brete-*, *Britewelle* 155b, 160b
Bristelmestone	See Brighthampton
Britewelle	See Brightwell Baldwin
Britwell Salome, F. 7	*Brutuuelle* 159b
Brize Norton, A. 6	*Nortone* 158b, 160b *bis*
Broadwell, A. 6	*Bradewelle* 160
Brohtune	See Broughton (near Banbury)
Bromscott, A. 6	*Bumerescote* 158
Brotone	See Broughton Poggs
Broughton (near Banbury), C. 2	*Brohtune* 159
Broughton Poggs, A. 6	*Brotone* 160
Bruern	Not in D.B.
Brutuuelle	See Britwell Salome
Buchehelle	See Bucknell
Bucknell, D. 5	*Buchehelle* 158
Bumerescote	See Bromscott
Bureford	See Burford
Burford, A. 5	*Bureford* 154, 156
Burtone	See Black Bourton
Cadewelle	See Cadwell
Cadwell, E. 7	*Cadewelle* 157
Caningeham	See Kingham

Cassington, C. 5	*Cersetone*, *Cersitone* 156, 156b *Chersitone* 156
Caversfield, E. 4	*Cavrefelle* 148, Bucks.
Cavesham	See Caversham, Berks.
Cecadene	See Checkenden
Cedelintone	See Chadlington
Celelorde	See Chilworth
Celford	See Chalford
Celgraue	See Chalgrove
Cercelle	See Churchill
Cersetone, *Cersitone*	See Cassington
Certelintone	See Kirtlington
Cestitone	See Chastleton
Cestretone	See Chesterton
Chadlington, B. 4	*Cedelintone* 160b *bis*
Chalford, B. 4	*Celford* 157b *bis*
Chalgrove, E. 7	*Celgraue* 159, Oxon.; 56, Berks.
Charlbury	Not in D.B.
Charlton on Otmoor, D. 5	*Cerlentone* 224b, N'hants.
Chastleton, A. 3	*Cestitone* 156b, 157, 157b, 161
Checkenden, F. 8	*Cecadene* 160
Chedelintone	See Kidlington
Chenefelde	See Clanfield
Chenetone	See Kencott
Chenore	See Chinnor
Cherielintone	See Kirtlington
Chersitone	See Cassington
Chertelintone	See Kirtlington
Chesterton, D. 4	*Cestretone* 159b
Chidintone	See Kiddington
Chilson	Not in D.B.
Chilworth, E. 6	*Celelorde* 159b
Chingestone	See Kingston Blount
Chinnor, F. 6	*Chenore* 160b
Chippinghurst, E. 6	*Cibbaherste* 157
Chipping Norton, B. 3	*Nortone* 160
Churchill, A. 4	*Cercelle* 157
Cibbaherste	See Chippinghurst

Clanfield, A. 6	*Chenefelde* 159
Clattercote	Not in D.B.
Clawelle	See Crowell
Claydon	Not in D.B.
Claywell, A. 6	*Welde* 160b
Clifton Hampden	Not in D.B.
Codesdone	See Cuddesdon
Codeslam, *-laue*	See Cutslow
Coges	See Cogges
Cogges, B. 5	*Coges* 156
Combe, C. 5	*Cumbe* 155b
Cornbury, B. 4	*Corneberie* 154b
Corneberie	See Cornbury
Cornewelle	See Cornwell
Cornwell, A. 3	*Cornewelle* 161
Cortelintone	See Kirtlington
Cote, *Altera*	See Nethercote (in Lewknor)
Cottisford, E. 3	*Cotesforde* 224b, N'hants.
Covelie	See Cowley
Cowley, D. 6	*Covelie* 155b, 157b, 159b, 160b
Craumares	See Crowmarsh
Crawley	Not in D.B.
Cropelie	See Cropredy
Cropredy, C. 1	*Cropelie* 155, 155b
Crowell, F. 7	*Clawelle* 157b
Crowmarsh Gifford and Preston Crowmarsh, E. 8	*Craumares* 157, 157b *Crem* 56b, Berks.
Cuchesham	See Cuxham
Cuddesdon, E. 6	*Codesdone* 156b
Culham	Not in D.B.
Cumbe	See Combe
Curbridge	Not in D.B.
Cutslow, D. 5	*Codeslam*, *-laue* 157, 159
Cuxham, F. 7	*Cuchesham* 159b
Dadintone	See Deddington
Dean, B. 4	*Dene* 157b
Deddington, C. 3	*Dadintone* 155b
Dene	See Dean
Denton	Not in D.B.
Dochelintone	See Ducklington
Dorchecestre	See Dorchester

Dorchester, E. 7	*Dorchecestre* 155 *bis* *Dorkecestre* 56b, Berks.
Draicote	See Draycot
Draitone, A. 4	Lost in Bruern, 158
Draitone	See Drayton (near Wroxton)
Draycot, E. 6	*Draicote* 159b
Drayton (near Wroxton), C. 2	*Draitone* 160b *Draiton* 250, Staffs.
Drayton St Leonard	Not in D.B.
Duchitorp	See Tythorp, Bucks.
Ducklington, B. 6	*Dochelintone* 158b, 161
Dunesdene	See Dunsden
Dunetorp	See Dunthorp
Dunsden, F. 9	*Dunesdene* 155
Duns Tew, C. 3	*Teowe* 156 1st entry *Tewa* 156b 2nd entry, 158b *Twam* 158
Dunthorp, B. 3	*Dunetorp* 156b, 157
Easington, E. 7	*Esidone* 160b
East Adderbury	See Adderbury
Eaton, Water and Wood, D. 5	*Etone* 158, 158b
Ebestan	See Ibstone, Bucks.
Edburgberie	See Adderbury
Edrope	See Heythrop
Eglesham	See Eynsham
Elfegescote	See Alvescot
Elsfield, D. 5	*Esefelde* 158
Eltone	See Holton
Emmington, F. 6	*Amintone* 157b
Enstone, B. 4	*Henestan* 157
Epwell	Not in D.B.
Ernicote, *Alia Ernicote*	See Arncott
Esefelde	See Elsfield
Esidone	See Easington
Estcote	See Ascot
Esthale	See Asthall
Esthcote	See Ascot
Estone	See Aston, Middle, etc.; Aston Rowant
Estrope	See Astrop
Etone	See Eaton
Ewelme, E. 8	*Lau(u)elme* 157b, 159, 159b, 160b *Auuilma*, *-ilme* 56b *ter*, Berks.
Eynsham, C. 5	*Eglesham* 155
Fawler	Not in D.B.
Fencot	Not in D.B.
Feringeford	See Fringford
Fert(e)welle	See Fritwell
Fifhide	See Fifield
Fifield, A. 4	*Fifhide* 157b
Filkins	Not in D.B.
Finemere	See Finmere
Finmere, E. 3	*Finemere* 155b, Oxon.; 221, N'hants.
Finstock	Not in D.B.
Forest Hill, E. 6	*Fostel* 155b
Foscot, A. 4	*Foxcote* 159
Fostel	See Forest Hill
Foxcote	See Foscot
Fringford, E. 3	*Feringeford* 155b
Fritwell, D. 3	*Fert(e)welle* 155b, 161
Fulbrook, A. 5	*Fulebroc* 158b
Fulebroc	See Fulbrook
Fulewelle	See Fulwell
Fulwell, E. 3	*Fulewelle* 158
Gadintone	See Gatehampton
Galoberie	See Ilbury
Gangsdown, F. 8	*Ganguluesdene* 159b
Ganguluesdene	See Gangsdown
Garinges	See Goring
Garsington, E. 6	*Gersedune* 156b, 159b
Gatehampton, E. 9	*Gadintone* 157b, 159 *Gratentun* 61b, Berks.
Gersedune	See Garsington
Givetelei	See Iffley

Glympton, C. 4	*Glintone* 221 1st entry, N'hants.
Godendone	See Godington
Godington, E. 3	*Godendone* 159
Goring, E. 9	*Garinges* 158
Gosford	Not in D.B.
Grafton, A. 6	*Graptone* 157
Graptone	See Grafton
Great Bourton	Not in D.B.
Great Haseley	See Haseley
Great Milton	See Milton, Great and Little
Great Rollright	See Rollright
Great Tew	See Tew
Grimsbury, C. 2	*Grimberie* 227b, N'hants.
Haiforde	See Heyford
Hailey	Not in D.B.
Haliwelle	See Holywell
Hampton Gay and Poyle, D. 5	*Hamtone*, *Hantone* 154, 158b, 160b
Hamtone	See Hampton
Handborough, C. 5	*Haneberge* 159b
Haneberge	See Handborough
Hanewege	See Hanwell
Hansitone	See Hensington
Hantone	See Hampton
Hanwell, C. 1	*Hanewege* 160b
Hardewich	See Hardwick (near Stoke Lyne)
Hardintone	See Yarnton
Hardwick (near Stoke Lyne), E. 3	*Hardewich* 158
Hardwick (near Yelford)	Not in D.B.
Harpendene	See Harpsden
Harpsden, F. 9	*Harpendene* 159b
Haseley, Great and Little, E. 6	*Haselie* 155b, 159, Oxon.; 56, Berks.
Haselie	See Haseley
Headington, D. 6	*Hedintone* 154b
Hedintone	See Headington
Hegford	See Heyford
Hempton, C. 3	*Hentone* 157b, 160
Henestan	See Enstone
Henley on Thames	Not in D.B.
Hensington C. 5	*Hansitone* 156, 158b, 161
Henton, F. 6	*Hentone* 159b
Hentone	See Hempton, Henton
Hethe E. 3	*Hedham* 221, N'hants.
Heyford, Lower and Upper, D. 4	*Haiforde* 158 *Hegford* 159b *Egforde* 221, N'hants.
Heythrop, B. 3	*Edrope* 159b
Hidrecote	See Nethercott (in Tackley)
Hochenartone	See Hook Norton
Holton, E. 6	*Eltone* 158b
Holwell	Not in D.B.
Holywell, D. 6	*Haliwelle* 158b
Hook Norton, B. 3	*Hochenartone* 158
Horley, C. 2	*Hornelie* 157, 158, 159
Hornelie	See Horley
Hornton	Not in D.B.
Horspadan	See Horspath
Horspath, E. 6	*Horspadan* 158b
Horton	Not in D.B.
Hortone	See Worton, Nether and Over
Hucheuuode	See Wychwood
Hunesworde, E. 7	Lost in Stadhampton, 157b
Idbury, A. 4	*Ideberie* 159
Ideberi	See Idbury
Iffley, D. 6	*Givetelei* 157b
Ilbury, C. 3	*Galoberie* 158
Ingham, F. 7	*Adingeham* 161
Ipsden E. 8	*Yppesdene* 160b
Islip, D. 5	*Letelape* 160
Kelmscot	Not in D.B.
Kencott, A. 6	*Chenetone* 158b
Kiddington, C. 4	*Chidintone* 160, 161
Kidlington, D. 5	*Chedelintone* 158
Kingham, A. 4	*Caningeham* 159b
Kingston Blount, F. 7	*Chingestone* 159, 159b

Kirtlington, D. 4	*Certelintone* 158b *Cherielintone*, *Chertelintone* 154b 157 *Cortelintone* 161
Lachebroc	See Lashbrook
Langefort	See Langford
Langford, A. 6	*Langefort* 154b
Lantone	See Launton
Lashbrook, F. 9	*Lachebroc* 157b
Launton, E. 4	*Lantone* 154b
Lau(u)elme	See Ewelme
Leafield	Not in D.B.
Ledewelle	See Ledwell
Ledwell, C. 3	*Ledewelle* 154b
Lege	See North Leigh
Letelape	See Islip
Levec(h)anole	See Lewknor
Lew, B. 6	*Lewa* 157b, 160b
Lewa	See Lew
Lewknor, F. 7	*Levec(h)anole* 156b, 158
Lillingestan	See Lillingstone Lovell, Bucks.
Lineham	See Lyneham
Little Bourton	Not in D.B.
Little Haseley	See Haseley
Little Milton	See Milton, Great and Little
Little Minster	See Minster
Littlemore	Not in D.B.
Little Rollright	See Rollright
Little Stoke	See Stoke, Little etc.
Little Tew	See Tew
Lower Arncott	See Arncott
Lower Heyford	See Heyford
Ludewelle	See Ludwell
Ludwell, C. 4	*Ludewelle* 156, 158b, 160, 160b *bis*
Lyneham, A. 4	*Lineham* 156b
Malpedreham, *Mapeldreham*	See Mapledurham
Mapledurham, F. 9	*Malpedreham* 157b *Mapeldreham* 159

Marsh Baldon	See Baldon
Marston	Not in D.B.
Meretone	See Merton
Merton, E. 5	*Meretone* 160
Middeltone	See Milton, Great and Little
Middle Aston	See Aston, Middle, etc.
Middleton Stoney, D. 4	*Mideltone* 159
Midelcumbe	See Milcombe
Mideltone	See Middleton Stoney; Milton, Great and Little; Milton under Wychwood
Milcombe, C. 3	*Midelcumbe* 157, 161
Milton (near Bloxham)	Not in D.B.
Milton, Great and Little, E. 6	*Mid(d)eltone* 155, 155b
Milton under Wychwood, A. 4	*Mideltone* 157, 161
Minster Lovell and Little Minster, B. 5	*Minstre* 157b, 160b
Minstre	See Minster
Misseberie	See Mixbury
Mixbury, E. 3	*Misseberie* 158b
Mollington, C. 1	*Mollitone* 157, Oxon.; 244, Warw. *Molitone* 226, N'hants.
Mollitone	See Mollington
Mongewel	See Mongewell
Mongewell, E. 8	*Mongewel* 161
Murcot	Not in D.B.
Nethercote (in Lewknor), F. 7	*Altera Cote* 159, 159b
Nethercott (in Tackley), C. 4	*Hidrecote* 156
Nether Worton	See Worton, Nether and Over
Nettlebed	Not in D.B.
Neuham	See Nuneham Courtenay

Neutone	See Newington, South Newington
Newington, E. 7	*Neutone* 155 *Niwetune* 56b, Berks.
Newnham Murren, E. 8	*Niweham* 159b *Neuueham* 56, Berks.
Newton Purcell	Not in D.B.
Niweham	See Newnham Murren
Niwetone	See South Newington
Noke, D. 5	*Ac(h)am* 161 *bis*
Nor(t)broc	See Northbrook
North Aston	See Aston, Middle etc.
Northbrook, D. 4	*Nor(t)broc* 158, 158b, 159
North Leigh, B. 5	*Lege* 158b
Northmoor	Not in D.B.
North Newington	Not in D.B.
North Stoke	See Stoke, Little etc.
Nortone	See Brize Norton, Chipping Norton
Nuffield	Not in D.B.
Nuneham Courtenay, D. 7	*Neuham* 159
Oddington, D. 5	*Otendone* 160b
Optone	See Wootton
Otendone	See Oddington
Over Worton	See Worton, Nether and Over
Oxeneford	See Oxford
Oxford, D. 6	*Oxeneford* 154, 158 *juxta Oxeneford* 157 *juxta murum* 158, 160b *Oxene-*, *Oxineford* 56, 57b, 62, Berks.; 143b, Bucks.
Parva Rollandri	See Rollright
Pemscott, A. 6	*Pismanescote* 158
Peregie	See Woodperry
Pereio	Unid., 156
Pereiun	See Waterperry
Peritone	See Pyrton
Petintone	See Piddington
Piddington, E. 5	*Petintone* 160
Pishill	Not in D.B.
Pismanescote	See Pemscott
Prescote	Not in D.B.
Preston Crowmarsh	See Crowmarsh
Pyrton, F. 7	*Peritone* 157 *Piritune* 56b, Berks.
Radcot	Not in D.B.
Radeford	See Radford
Radford, C. 4	*Radeford* 161
Ramsden	Not in D.B.
Redrefeld	See Rotherfield
Reicote	See Rycote
Riseberge	See Risborough, Bucks.
Rocote	See Rycote
Rofford, E. 7	*Ropeford* 160b
Rollandri Majore, *Rollendri*	See Rollright
Rollright, Great and Little, A. 3, B. 3	*Parva Rollandri* 155 *Rollandri Majore* 160b *Rollendri* 158, 160b
Ropeford	See Rofford
Rotherfield Greys and Peppard, F. 9	*Redrefeld* 159, 161
Rousham, C. 4	*Rou(u)esham* 158b, 159
Rou(u)esham	See Rousham
Rycote, F. 6	*Reicote*, *Rocote* 157b, 159b, 160b
Salford, A. 3	*Salford*, *Salword* 156b, 161
Salword	See Salford
Sandford on Thames, D. 6	*Sanford* 156b *bis*, 2nd and 3rd entries
Sandford St Martin, C. 3	*Sanford* 156b 1st entry
Sanford	See Sandford on Thames, Sandford St Martin

Sarsden, A. 4	*Secendene* 159
Scipford	See Shifford, Sibford
Scipforde	See Sibford
Sciptone	See Shipton on Cherwell, Shipton under Wychwood
Scir(e)burne	See Shirburn
Scotorne	See Shotover
Secendene	See Sarsden
Sesswell Barton	See Barton
Sevewelle	See Showell
Sexintone, D. 4	Lost in Bucknell, 155b *bis*
Shelswell, E. 3	*Scildeswelle* 221, N'hants.
Shennington, B. 2	*Senendone* 163b, Gloucs.
Shifford, B. 6	*Scipford* 155
Shilton	Not in D.B.
Shiplake	Not in D.B.
Shipton on Cherwell, C. 5	*Sciptone* 156 *Sciptune* 224b, N'hants.
Shipton under Wychwood, A. 4	*Sciptone* 154, 154b *bis*, 160b *bis*
Shirburn, F. 7	*Scir(e)burne* 158, 158b *Sireburne* 56b, Berks.
Shorthampton	Not in D.B.
Shotover, D. 6	*Scotorne* 154b
Showell, B. 3	*Seve-*, *Sivewelle* 156b, 157
Shutford	Not in D.B.
Sibeford	See Sibford
Sibford Ferris and Gower, B. 2	*Scipforde* 157b *Scipford* 224b, N'hants. *Sibeford* 250, Staffs.
Sidreham	See Sydenham
Signet	Not in D.B.
Sivewelle	See Showell
Somerton, D. 3	*Sumertone* 155b, 159b *bis*
Souldern	Not in D.B.
South Newington, C. 3	*Neutone* 161 *Niwetone* 156
South Stoke	See Stoke, Little etc.
South Weston, F. 7	*Westone* 157 *Westune* 56b, Berks.
Spelsbury, B. 4	*Spelesberie* 238b Warw.
Stadhampton	Not in D.B.
Standlake	Not in D.B.
Stantone	See Stanton Harcourt, Stanton St John
Stanton Harcourt, C. 6	*Stantone* 155b
Stanton St John, E. 5	*Stantone* 156 *bis*, 156b
Stauuorde	See Stowford
Steeple Aston	See Aston, Middle etc.
Steeple Barton	See Barton
Stoch	See Stoke, Little etc; Waterstock
Stochelie	See Stockley
Stoches	See Stoke, Little etc; Stoke Lyne, Stoke Talmage
Stockley, A. 5	*Stochelie* 154b
Stoke, Little, North and South, E. 8	*Stoches* 155, 159 2nd entry, 160 *Estoche* 56, Berks.
Stoke Lyne, D. 3	*Stoches* 157b *bis*
Stoke Talmage, F. 7	*Stoches* 159 1st entry
Stonesfield, C. 5	*Stuntesfeld* 158
Stoner	Not in D.B.
Stowford, D. 6	*Stauuorde* 154b
Stowood	Not in D.B.
Stratone	See Stratton Audley
Stratton Audley, E. 4	*Stratone* 158
Studley	Not in D.B.
Stuntesfeld	See Stonesfield
Suinbroc	See Swinbrook
Suinecumbe	See Swyncombe
Sumertone	See Somerton
Surford	See Swerford
Swalecliffe	Not in D.B.
Swerford, B. 3	*Surford* 161

Swinbrook, A. 5	*Suinbroc* 160b
Swyncombe, F. 8	*Suinecumbe* 159b
Sydenham, F. 6	*Sidreham* 161
Tachelie	See Tackley
Tackley, C. 4	*Tachelie* 157
Tademertone	See Tadmarton
Tadmarton, B. 2	*Tademertone* 156b
Tame	See Thame
Taynton, A. 5	*Teigtone* 157
	Tentone 154
Teigtone, *Tentone*	See Taynton
Teova	See Tew
Teowe	See Duns Tew; Tew, Great and Little
Tetsworth	Not in D.B.
Tew, Great and Little, B. 3	*Teova* 156b
	Teowa 156 2nd entry
	Tewa 155b, 156b 1st entry
	Tewe 156
Tewa	See Duns Tew; Tew, Great and Little
Tewe	See Tew, Great and Little
Thame, F. 6	*Tame* 155, 155b
Thomley, E. 5	*Tobelie* 159b
	Tumbeleia 156
Thrupp, C. 5	*Trop* 159
Tiddington, E. 6	*Titendone* 160b
Titendone	See Tiddington
Tobelie	See Thomley
Toot Baldon	See Baldon
Toresmere	See Tusmore
Towersey, F. 6	*Eie* 151b, Bucks.
Trop	See Thrupp
Tuiforde	See Twyford, Bucks.
Tumbeleia	See Thomley
Tusmore, D. 3	*Toresmere* 157b
Twam	See Duns Tew
Ulfgarcote	See Wolvercot
Upper Arncott	See Arncott
Upper Heyford	See Heyford
Upton	Not in D.B.

Verneveld	Unid., 154b
Wainhill, F. 6	*Winehel(l)e* 159b, 161
Walton, D. 6	*Waltone* 159
Waltone	See Walton
Wandesberie	See Wendlebury
Warborough	Not in D.B.
Wardington	Not in D.B.
Warpsgrove, E. 7	*Werplesgrave* 156b
Watcombe, F. 7	*Watecumbe* 159b, 161
Watecumbe	See Watcombe
Watelintone	See Watlington
Water Eaton	See Eaton
Waterperry, E. 6	*Pereiun* 158b
	Perie 56b, Berks.
Waterstock, E. 6	*Stoch* 155b
Watlington, F. 7	*Watelintone* 157, 158, 161
	Watelintune 56b, Berks.
Welde	See Claywell
Wendlebury, D. 4	*Wandesberie* 159b
Werochestan	See Wroxton
Werplesgrave	See Warpsgrove
West Adderbury	See Adderbury
Westcott Barton	See Barton
Westone	See South Weston, Weston on the Green
Weston on the Green, D. 4	*Westone* 158b
Westwell, A. 5	*Westwelle* 160
Westwelle	See Westwell
Wheatfield, F. 7	*Witefelle* 158
Wheatley	Not in D.B.
Whitchurch, E. 9	*Witecerce* 159
Whitehill, C. 4	*Wistelle* 156, 158b
Wic(h)	See Droitwich, Worcs.
Wicham	See Wykeham
Widelicote	See Wilcote
Widelie	See Woodleys
Widford, A. 5	*Widiforde* 164b, Gloucs.
Wigentone	See Wigginton
Wigginton, B. 3	*Wigentone* 160
Wilcote, B. 5	*Widelicote* 156

Winehel(l)e	See Wainhill
Wistelle	See Whitehill
Witecerce	See Whitchurch
Witefelle	See Wheatfield
Witenie	See Witney
Witney, B. 5	*Witenie* 155
Wodestoch	See Woodstock
Wolvercot, D. 5	*Ulfgarcote* 159
Wood Eaton	See Eaton
Woodleys, C. 4	*Widelie* 161
Woodperry, E. 5	*Peregie* 156
Woodstock, C. 4	*Wodestoch* 154b
Wootton, C. 4	*Optone* 154b *Oitone* 221, N'hants.
Worton (in Cassington), C. 5	*Wrtone* 161
Worton, Nether and Over, C. 3	*Hortone* 156b, 161, Oxon.; 221 2nd entry, N'hants.
Wroxton, C. 2	*Werochestan* 159b
Wrtone	See Worton (in Cassington)
Wychwood, B. 5	*Hucheuuode* 154b
Wykeham, C. 2	*Wicham* 155b
Yarnton, C. 5	*Hardintone* 155b, 156
Yelford, B. 6	*Aieleforde* 160
Ypestan	See Ibstone, Bucks,
Yppesdene	See Ipsden

ANONYMOUS HOLDINGS

No place-names appear in the following five entries, and it is possible that some (or even all) of these refer to holdings at places not named elsewhere in Domesday Book:

Canons of St Frideswide, 4 hides *juxta* Oxford, 157. Counted with Oxford.
Walter Gifard, 2 hides less half a virgate, 157b.
Hugh (from Roger d'Ivry), $7\frac{1}{2}$ hides, 158b.
William Levric, 3 hides and $1\frac{2}{3}$ virgates, 160.
Sawold (from the king), 2 mills. They are close to the wall (*juxta murum*), 160b. Counted with Oxford.

RUTLAND—*ROTELAND*

Folios 293b–294

MAP 37

Alestanestorp	See Awsthorp
Ashwell, J. 6	*Exwelle* 293b *Exewelle* 349b, Lincs.
Awsthorp, J. 7	*Alestanestorp* 293b
Ayston	Not in D.B.
Barleythorpe	Not in D.B.
Barrow	Not in D.B.
Barrowden, K. 8	*Berchedone* 219, 225, N'hants.
Belmesthorpe, L. 7	*Belmestorp* 228, N'hants.; 366b, 376b, Lincs.
Belton	Not in D.B.
Bisbrooke, J. 8	*Bitlesbroch* 219, 228b, N'hants.
Braunston	Not in D.B.
Brooke	Not in D.B.
Burgelai	See Burley
Burley, J. 7	*Burgelai* 293b, Rutland; 355b, Lincs.
Caldecott, J. 9	*Caldecote* 221, N'hants.
Casterton, Great and Little, K. 7	*Castretone* 219b, 229, N'hants.

Clipsham	Not in D.B.
Cotesmore	See Cottesmore
Cottesmore, J. 6	*Cotesmore* 293b
Edith Weston	Not in D.B.
Egleston	Not in D.B.
Empingham, K. 7	*Epingeham* 226, 227b, N'hants.
Essindine, L. 7	*Esindone* 221, N'hants.
Exentune	See Exton
Exton, K. 7	*Exentune* 293b, Rutland; 367, Lincs.
Exwelle	See Ashwell
Glaston, J. 8	*Gladestone* 219, 228b, N'hants.
Great Casterton	See Casterton
Greetham, K. 6	*Gretham* 293b
Gretham	See Greetham
Gunthorpe	Not in D.B.
Hambleton, J. 7	*Hameldun(e)* 293b, 294 *Hemeldune* 336b, Lincs.
Hameldun(e)	See Hambleton
Horn, K. 7	*Horne* 220, 228b, N'hants.
Ketton, K. 7	*Chetene* 219, N'hants.
Langham	Not in D.B.
Leighfield	Not in D.B.
Liddington, J. 8	*Lidentone* 221, N'hants.
Little Casterton	See Casterton
Luffenham, North and South, K. 8	*Lufenham* 219 *bis*, 228b, N'hants.
Lyndon	Not in D.B.
Manton	Not in D.B.
Market Overton, J. 6	*Overtune* 293b, Rutland; 366b, Lincs. *Ovretone* 367, Lincs.
Martinsthorpe	Not in D.B.
Morcott, K. 8	*Morcote* 219, N'hants.
Normanton	Not in D.B.
North Luffenham	See Luffenham
Oakham, J. 7	*Ocheham* 293b, 294, Rutland; 230b, Leics.
Ocheham	See Oakham
Overtune	See Market Overton
Pickworth	Not in D.B.
Pilton	Not in D.B.
Preston	Not in D.B.
Redlinctune	See Ridlington
Ridlington, J. 8	*Redlinctune* 293b
Ryhall, L. 7	*Riehale* 228, N'hants.
Sculthorp, K. 8	*Sculetorp* 219, N'hants.
Seaton, J. 8	*Segentone*, *Segestone* 225, 228b, N'hants. *Seieton(e)* 219 *bis*, N'hants.
Snelston, J. 9	*Smelistone* 221, N'hants.
South Luffenham	See Luffenham
Stoke Dry, J. 8	*Stoche* 221, N'hants.
Stratone, *-tune*	See Stretton
Stretton, K. 6	*Stratone*, *-tune* 293b *Stratone* 366b, Lincs.
Teigh, J. 6	*Tie* 293b
Thistleton, J. 6	*Tistertune* 293b, Rutland; 367, Lincs. *Alia Tisteltune* 358b, Lincs. *Tisteltone*, *-tune* 358b *bis*, 366, 367, Lincs.

Thorpe by Water, J. 8	*Torp* 219, 228b, N'hants.
Tickencote, K. 7	*Tichecote* 228b, N'hants.
Tie	See Teigh
Tinwell, K. 7	*Tedinwelle* 221b, N'hants.
Tistertune	See Thistleton
Tixover, K. 8	*Tichesovre* 219, N'hants.
Tolethorpe, L. 7	*Toltorp* 226, N'hants.
Uppingham	Not in D.B.
Wardley	Not in D.B.
Whissendine, J. 6	*Wichingedene* 293b, Rutland; 367, Lincs.
Whitwell, K. 7	*Witewelle* 293b, Rutland; 367, Lincs.
Wichingedene	See Whissendine
Wing	Not in D.B.
Witewelle	See Whitwell

ANONYMOUS HOLDINGS

No place-name appears in the following entry, and it is impossible to say whether or not it refers to a place named elsewhere in Domesday Book:

Albert the clerk, one bovate, plus 7 bovates, in Martinsley wapentake, 294.

SHROPSHIRE—*SCIROPESCIRE*

Folios 252–260b

MAPS 40–41

Abdon, F. 9	*Abetune* 254
Abetune	See Abdon
Abretone	See Albright Hussey
Achel	See Ackhill, Wales
Achelai	See Ackley, Wales
Achetone	See Acton Reynold
Achetune	See Acton Round
Acton Burnell and Pigott, E. 7	*A(e)ctune* 254b, 255b
Acton Reynold, E. 5	*Achetone* 255
Acton Round, F. 8	*Achetune* 254
Acton Scott, D. 8	*Actune* 259b
Actune	See Acton Burnell and Pigott; Acton Scott
Adderley, G. 3	*Eldredelei* 259
Adelestune	See Adley, Heref.
Aectune	See Acton Burnell and Pigott
Aelmundestune	See Alcaston
Aitone	See Eyton on Severn, Isle Farm
Aitone (*Mersete* hd)	Unid., 254b
Alberberie	See Alberbury
Alberbury, C. 5	*Alberberie* 253b
Albricstone	See Albrighton (near Shifnal)
Albright Hussey, E. 5	*Abretone* 255
	Etbretone 255
Albrightlee, E. 5	*Etbretelie* 253
Albrighton (near Shifnal), H. 7	*Albricstone* 259
Albrighton (near Shrewsbury), E. 5	*Etbritone* 255b
Alcaston, D. 8	*Aelmundestune* 258b
Alchetune	See Alkington
Aldeberie	See Oldbury
Aldon, D. 9	*Alledone* 260b
Alfertintune	See Adforton, Heref.

Alkington, E. 3	*Alchetune* 257
Alledone	See Aldon
All Stretton	See Stretton
Alretone	See Cause
Alveley, H. 9	*Alvidelege* 248, Staffs.
Amaston, D. 6	*Enbaldestune* 259b
Andre(s)lau(e)	See Onslow
Aneberie	See Onibury
Anelege	See Onneley
Arcalun	See Child's Ercall
Archelou	See Ercall Magna
Ardintone	See Eardington
Ashford Bowdler and Carbonell, E. 10	*Esseford* 260
Asnebruge	See Isombridge
Astley, E. 5	*Hesleie* 252b
Astley Abbots	Not in D.B.
Aston (in Munslow), E. 9	*Estune* 255
Aston (in Oswestry), C. 4	*Estone* 256, 259
Aston (in Wem), E. 4	*Estune* 257
Aston Botterell, F. 9	*Estone* 255 2nd entry
Aston Eyre, G. 8	*Estone* 255 1st entry
Atcham, E. 6	*Atingeham* 253
Atingeham	See Atcham
Audley, F. 3	*Lai* 256
Avochelie	See Hawksley
Badger, H. 7	*Beghesovre* 257b
Baitune	See Betton (in Norton-in-Hales)
Barbingi	See Baveney
Bardestune	See Bearstone
Barlow, D. 9	*Berlie* 258
Barrow	Not in D.B.
Bascherche	See Baschurch
Baschurch, D. 5	*Bascherche* 253
Battlefield	Not in D.B.
Baveney, G. 9	*Barbingi* 257
Bayston, E. 6	*Begestan* 257
Bearstone, G. 3	*Bardestune* 258
Becheberie	See Beckbury
Beckbury, H. 7	*Becheberie* 259
Bedstone, C. 10	*Betietetune* 258b
Begestan	See Bayston
Beghesovre	See Badger
Beldewes	See Buildwas
Beleslei	See Bausley, Wales
Belleurdine	See Belswardyne
Belswardyne, F. 7	*Belleurdine* 258b
Benehale	See Benthall
Benehale (*Witentreu* hd)	Unid., 254
Benthall, D. 6	*Benehale* 259b
Berewic	See Berwick (in Atcham), Berwick (in Shrewsbury)
Beritune	See Berrington
Berlie	See Barlow
Berrington, E. 6	*Beritune* 254b
Berwick (in Atcham), E. 6	*Berewic* 254b
Berwick (in Shrewsbury), E. 5	*Berewic* 253b
Besford, F. 4	*Betford* 259
Beslow, F. 6	*Beteslauue* 257b
Beteslauue	See Beslow
Betford	See Besford
Betietetune	See Bedstone
Betton (in Berrington), E. 6	*Betune* 252
Betton (in Norton-in-Hales), G. 3	*Baitune* 259
Bettws-y-Crwyn	Not in D.B.
Betune	See Betton (in Berrington)
Bichetone	See Bicton
Bicton, D. 5	*Bichetone* 253
Billingsley	Not in D.B.
Bishops Castle	Not in D.B.
Bishton, H. 7	*Bispetone* 259
Bispetone	See Bishton
Bitterley, F. 10	*Buterlie* 256b
Bolas	Not in D.B.
Bolebec, G. 8	Lost in Eardington, 254
Bolledone	See Bouldon
Boningale	Not in D.B.
Boraston	Not in D.B.
Boreton, E. 6	*Burtune* 252b 1st entry

Boscobel	Not in D.B.
Bosle	See Broseley
Botewde	See Leebotwood
Bouldon, E. 9	*Bolledone* 258b
Bourton, F. 7	*Burtune* 252b 2nd entry
Brame	See Broome
Brantune	See Brompton (in Berrington). See also Brampton Bryan, Heref.
Bratton, F. 6	*Brochetone* 257b
Brochetone	See Bratton, Brockton (in Longford)
Brockton (in Longford), H. 5	*Brochetone* 257, 259b
Brockton (in Sheriff Hales), H. 6	*Brotone* 250b
Brockton (in Stanton Long), F. 8	*Broctune* 254b
Brockton (in Sutton Maddock), G. 7	*Broctone* 257b
Broctone	See Brockton (in Sutton Maddock)
Broctune	See Brockton (in Stanton Long)
Brogyntyn, B. 4	*Burtone* 259b
Bromfield, E. 10	*Brunfelde* 252b
Brompton (in Berrington), E. 6	*Brantune* 256, 258
Brompton (near Chirbury)	Not in D.B.
Broom, D. 4	*Bruma* 259
Broome, E. 7	*Brame* 259b
Broseley, G. 7	*Bosle* 258b
Brotone	See Brockton (in Sheriff Hales)
Broughton, E. 4	*Burtone* 253 *Burtune* 252b 3rd entry
Bruma	See Broom
Brunfelde	See Bromfield
Buchehale, F. 8	Lost in Acton Round, 257b

Buchehalle	See Bucknell (near Clun)
Bucknell (near Clun), C. 10	*Buchehalle* 260b
Buctone	See Buckton, Heref.
Buildwas, F. 7	*Beldewes* 252
Bureford	See Burford
Burertone	See Burwarton
Burford, F. 11	*Bureford* 260
Burtone	See Brogyntyn, Broughton
Burtune	See Boreton, Bourton, Broughton
Burwarton, F. 9	*Burertone* 257
Buterei	See Buttery
Buterlie	See Bitterley
Buttery, G. 5	*Buterei* 257b
Caiham	See Caynham
Caluestone	Unid., Worcs.
Calverhall, F. 3	*Cavrahalle* 259
Cantelop	See Cantlop
Cantlop, E. 6	*Cantelop* 259
Cardeston, D. 6	*Cartistune* 255b
Cardington, E. 8	*Cardintune* 255
Cardintune	See Cardington
Cartistune	See Cardeston
Cascop	See Cascob, Wales
Cateschesleie	See Catsley
Catewinde	See Chetwynd
Catinton	See Chetton
Catsley, G. 9	*Cateschesleie* 257
Caurtune	Unid., 258
Cause, C. 6	*Alretone* 253b
Cautune	See Choulton
Cavrahalle	See Calverhall
Caynham, E. 10	*Caiham* 256b
Celmeres	See Chelmarsh
Cerlecote	See Charlcotte
Cerletone	See Charlton
Cerlintone	See Cherrington
Cerlitone	See Charlton
Cesdille	See Chesthill
Cestelop	See Castlewright, Wales
Cestulle	See Chesthill
Charlcotte, F. 9	*Cerlecote* 258b

Charlton, F. 5	*Cerletone*, *Cerlitone* 253, 255b
Chelmarsh, G. 8	*Celmeres* 257
Chelmick, E. 8	*Elmundewic* 258b
Chenardelei	See Kinnerley
Chenbritone	See Kemberton
Chenelie	See Kenley
Cheneltone	Unid., 259
Cheney Longville, D. 9	*Languefelle* 259b
Chenistetune	See Knighton, Wales
Chenpitune	See Kempton
Cherrington, G. 5	*Cerlintone* 258b
Chesthill, F. 4	*Cesdille* 252 *Cestulle* 258b
Cheswardine, G. 4	*Ciseworde* 248b, Staffs.
Chetton, G. 8	*Catinton* 254
Chetwynd, H. 5	*Catewinde* 257b
Chetwynd Aston	Not in D.B.
Child's Ercall, G. 4	*Arcalun* 254b
Chimerestun	See Kynaston
Chinardeseie	See Kinnersley
Chinbaldescote	Unid., 258
Chinlete	See Kinlet
Chipnall, G. 4	*Ceppecanole* 248b, Staffs.
Chirbury, B. 7	*Cireberie* 253b
Choulton, D. 8	*Cautune* 256
Church Aston	Not in D.B.
Church Preen, E. 7	*Prene* 258b
Church Pulverbatch, D. 7	*Polrebec* 259
Church Stretton	See Stretton
Cireberie	See Chirbury
Cirestoc	See Churchstoke, Wales
Claiberie	See Cleobury Mortimer, Cleobury North
Claverley, H. 8	*Claverlege* 248, Staffs.
Cleberie	See Cleobury Mortimer, Cleobury North

Clee	See Cleestanton
Clee St Margaret, F. 9	*Cleie* 258b
Cleestanton, F. 9	*Clee* 252b
Cleie	See Clee St Margaret
Cleobury Mortimer, G. 10	*Claiberie*, *Cleberie* 257, 260 *bis*
Cleobury North, F. 8	*Claiberie*, *Cleberie* 260b *bis*
Cleu	Unid., 260b
Clive	Not in D.B.
Clone	See Clungunford
Clun, C. 9	*Clune* 258
Clunbury, C. 9	*Cluneberie* 258
Clune	See Clun
Cluneberie	See Clunbury
Clungunford, D. 9	*Clone* 255, 258
Clunton, C. 9	*Clutune* 258
Clutune	See Clunton
Cockshutt	Not in D.B.
Cold Hatton	See Hatton, Cold and High
Cold Weston	Not in D.B.
Colemere, D. 3	*Colesmere* 259
Colesmere	See Colemere
Comintone	See Culmington
Condover, E. 6	*Conendovre* 253
Conendovre	See Condover
Coreley, F. 10	*Cornelie* 260
Corfan	See Corfham
Corfham, E. 9	*Corfan* 253b
Corfton, E. 9	*Cortune* 256b
Cornelie	See Coreley
Corselle	See Cross Hills
Cortune	See Corfton
Cosford, H. 7	*Costeford* 257
Costeford	See Cosford
Coston, D. 9	*Coȝetune* 258
Cotardicote	See Cothercott
Cote	See Coton (in Wem)
Cothercott, D. 7	*Cotardicote* 259b
Coton (in Wem), E. 3	*Cote* 257
Coton upon Tern, F. 4	*Ludecote* 259
Cound, F. 6	*Cuneet* 254b
Coȝetune	See Coston

Cressage, F. 7	*Cristesache* 256b
Cristesache	See Cressage
Cross Hills, G. 4	*Corselle* 257
Crudgington, F. 5	*Crugetone* 256
Crugetone	See Crudgington
Culmington, E. 9	*Comintone* 254
Cuneet	See Cound
Dalelie	See Dawley
Dawley Magna and Parva, G. 6	*Dalelie* 253b, 254b
Dehocsele	See Deuxhill
Derintune	See Dorrington
Detton, G. 9	*Dodintone* 255b
Deuxhill, G. 9	*Dehocsele* 252b
Diddlebury	Not in D.B.
Dinthill, D. 6	*Duntune* 253
Ditton Priors, F. 8	*Doden-*, *Dodintone* 253b, 260b
Doddington, E. 3	*Dodetune* 256
Dodefort	See Tugford
Dodentone	See Ditton Priors, Earlsditton
Dodetune	See Doddington
Dodintone	See Detton, Ditton Priors
Donitone	See Donnington
Donnington, H. 7	*Donitone* 253b
Dorrington, H. 3	*Derintune* 257b
Draitune	See Drayton
Drayton, Little and Market, G. 3	*Draitune* 257, 258
Dudestune	See Dudston
Dudston, B. 7	*Dudestune* 254
Duntune	See Dinthill
Eardington, G. 8	*Ardintone* 254
Earlsditton, F. 10	*Dodentone* 260
Easthope, F. 8	*Stope* 254
Eaton Constantine, F. 6	*Etune* 254b 2nd entry
Eaton Mascott, E. 6	*Etone* 253 *Etune* 254b 1st entry
Eaton under Heywood	Not in D.B.
Edbaldinesham	See Edgbold
Edelactune	See Adley, Heref.
Edenhope, B. 8	*Etenehop* 254

Edeslai	See Edgeley
Edgbold, D. 6	*Edbaldinesham* 260b
Edgeley, F. 3	*Edeslai* 256
Edgmond, G. 5	*Edmendune* 253b
Edgton, D. 9	*Egedune* 258
Edmendune	See Edgmond
Edretehope	See Hope Bendrid
Edritune	See Edderton, Wales
Edstaston, E. 4	*Stanestune* 257
Egedune	See Edgton
Eiminstre	See Emstrey
Elchitun	See Hockleton
Eldone	See Eudon Burnell and George
Eldredelei	See Adderley
Ellerdine, F. 5	*Elleurdine* 258b
Ellesmeles	See Ellesmere
Ellesmere, D. 3	*Ellesmeles* 253b
Elleurdine	See Ellerdine
Elmundewic	See Chelmick
Emstrey, E. 6	*Eiminstre* 252b
Enbaldestune	See Amaston
English Frankton, D. 4	*Franchetone* 255
Ercall Magna, F. 5	*Archelou* 253b
Eslepe	See Sleap
Esseford	See Ashford
Estone	See Aston (in Oswestry), Aston Botterell, Aston Eyre. See also Aston, Wales
Estune	See Aston (in Munslow), Aston (in Wem)
Etbretelie	See Albrightlee
Etbretone	See Albright Hussey
Etbritone	See Albrighton (near Shrewsbury)
Etenehop	See Edenhope
Etone	See Eaton Mascott, Eyton upon the Weald Moors, Hatton (in Shifnal)

Haughton, F. 5	*Haustone* 259
Haustone	See Haughton
Haustune	See Halston
Havretescote	See Harcourt (in Stottesdon)
Hawksley, E. 7	*Avochelie* 259
Heath	Not in D.B.
Heme	See Hem, Wales
Henley, E. 10	*Haneleu* 255
Hesleie	See Astley
Hetone	See Eyton (in Baschurch)
Hetune	See Hatton, Cold and High
Hibrihteselle	Unid., 258b
Higford, H. 7	*Huchefor* 256b
High Hatton	See Hatton, Cold and High
Highley, H. 9	*Hugelei* 257
Hinstock, G. 4	*Stoche* 257
Hockleton, B. 7	*Elchitun* 254
Hodnet, F. 4	*Odenet* 253
Holdgate	See Stanton Long
Hope	See Hopesay
Hope Bagot	Not in D.B.
Hope Bendrid, C. 10	*Edretehope* 258
Hope Bowdler, E. 8	*Fordritishope* 258b
Hopesay, D. 9	*Hope* 258
Hopton (in Hodnet), F. 4	*Hotune* 256b
Hopton Cangeford	Not in D.B.
Hopton Castle, C. 9	*Opetune* 258
Hoptone	See Hopton Wafers
Hopton Wafers, F. 10	*Hoptone* 260b
Hoptune	See Hopton, Wales
Hordelei	See Hordley
Hordley, D. 4	*Hordelei* 257b
Horseforde	Unid., Wales
Horton (in Hadley), G. 5	*Hortune* 257b
Horton (in Wem), E. 4	*Hortune* 257
Hortune	See Horton (in Hadley), Horton (in Wem)
Hotune	See Hopton (in Hodnet)
Howle, G. 4	*Hugle* 257b
Huchefor	See Higford
Huelbec	See Welbatch
Hugelei	See Highley
Hughley	Not in D.B.
Hugle	See Howle
Humet	Unid., 260
Hundeslit	See Stapleton
Huntington, E. 10	*Hantenetune* 256b
Iagedone	See Yagdon
Iartune	See Yorton
Ightfield, F. 3	*Istefelt* 259
Ingardine, F. 9	*Ingurdine* 257b
Ingurdine	See Ingardine
Ioclehuile	See Yockleton
Isle Farm, D. 5	*Aitone* 255
Isombridge, F. 6	*Asnebruge* 257
Istefelt	See Ightfield
Iteshale	See Shifnal
Kemberton, G. 7	*Chenbritone* 256b
Kempton, C. 9	*Chenpitune* 258
Kenley, F. 7	*Chenelie* 254b
Kingsnordley, H. 8	*Nordlege* 248, Staffs.
Kinlet, G. 9	*Chinlete* 260
Kinnerley, C. 5	*Chenardelei* 259
Kinnersley, G. 5	*Chinardeseie* 258b
Knockin	Not in D.B.
Kynaston, C. 5	*Chimerestun* 255
Lach	See Lack, Lacon
Lack, B. 8	*Lach* 259b
Lacon, E. 4	*Lach* 256b
Lai	See Audley
Langedune	See Longden
Langeford	See Longford
Langley, E. 7	*Languelege* 259b
Languedune	See Longdon upon Tern
Languefelle	See Cheney Longville
Languelege	See Langley
Languenare	See Longner
Lau	See Lowe
Lauelei, -lie	See Lawley

Membrefelde	See Morville
Menistrelie	See Minsterley
Meole Brace, E. 6	*Melam* 252, 252b, 260b
Meresberie	See Maesbury
Meresbroc	See Maesbrook
Meritune	See Marrington
Merrington, E. 5	*Gellidone* 258
Mersse	See Marsh
Merstun, E. 9	Lost in Diddlebury, 257b
Mertune	See Marton
Messe	See Marsh
Middeltone	See Middleton (in Bitterley), Middleton Scriven
Middlehope, E. 8	*Mildehope* 256b
Middleton (in Bitterley), E. 10	*Middeltone* 257b
Middleton (in Chirbury), C. 7	*Mildetune* 256, 259b
Middleton Scriven, G. 8	*Middeltone* 255
Mildehope	See Middlehope
Mildetune	See Middleton (in Chirbury)
Millichope, E. 8	*Melicope* 258b
Milson, G. 10	*Mulstone* 260
Minsterley, C. 6	*Menistrelie* 253b
Minton, D. 8	*Munetune* 258, 259b
Monkhopton	Not in D.B.
Montford, D. 5	*Maneford* 255b
Montgomeri	See Montgomery, Wales
More	Not in D.B.
Moreton Corbet, F. 5	*Mortone* 258
Moreton Say, F. 3	*Mortune* 256
Morton (in Oswestry), C. 4	*Mortune* 254b
Mortone	See Moreton Corbet
Mortune	See Moreton Say, Morton (in Oswestry)
Morville, G. 8	*Membrefelde* 253
Moston, F. 4	*Mostune* 259
Mostune	See Moston

Much Wenlock, F. 7	*Wenloch* 252b 1st entry
Muletune, *Mulitune*	See Mellington, Wales
Mulleht	See Myddle
Mulstone	See Milson
Munete	See Myndtown
Munetune	See Minton
Munslow	Not in D.B.
Muntgumeri	See Montgomery, Wales
Mutone	See Mytton
Myddle, E. 4	*Mulleht* 255
Myndtown, D. 8	*Munete* 258
Mytton, D. 5	*Mutone* 252b
Nash	Not in D.B.
Neen Savage, G. 10	*Nene* 260 *bis* 2nd and 3rd entries
Neen Solars, G. 10	*Nene* 260 1st entry
Neenton, G. 8	*Newentone* 257
Nene	See Neen Savage, Neen Solars
Ness, Great and Little, D. 5	*Nesse* 255 *Nessham* 253b
Nesse, *Nessham*	See Ness
Netelie	See Netley
Netley, E. 7	*Netelie* 259b
Newentone	See Neenton
Newetone	Unid., 259b
Newport	Not in D.B.
Norbury	Not in D.B.
Norton (in Aston Botterell), F. 9	*Nortone* 255b
Norton (in Condover), E. 6	*Nortune* 257
Nortone	See Norton (in Aston Botterell)
Norton-in-Hales, G. 3	*Nortune* 258b
Nortune	See Norton (in Condover), Norton-in-Hales. See also Norton, Wales
Oaks, D. 7	*Hach* 256
Obelie	See Obley
Obley, C. 9	*Obelie* 258

Odenet	See Hodnet
Ofitone	See Uffington
Oldbury, G. 8	*Aldeberie* 255
Onibury, D. 9	*Aneberie* 252
Onneley, H. 2	*Anelege* 257b
Onslow, D. 6	*Andrelau* 253 *Andreslaue* 256
Opetone	See Uppington
Opetune	See Hopton Castle
Osbaston, C. 5	*Sbernestune* 255
Osuluestune	See Woolston (in West Felton)
Oswestry, B. 4	*Luure* 253b
Overs, D. 7	*Ovre* 254, 259b
Overton, G. 9	*Ovretone* 257
Ovre	See Overs
Ovretone	See Overton
Oxenbold, F. 8	*Oxibola* 258b
Oxibola	See Oxenbold
Pantesberie	See Pontesbury
Papelau	See Peplow
Patintune	See Patton
Patton, F. 8	*Patintune* 256b
Pectone	See Petton
Pedewrde	See Pedwardine, Heref.
Peplow, G. 4	*Papelau* 257
Petelie	Unid., 252b
Petton, D. 4	*Pectone* 256
Peventone	See Poynton
Piceforde	See Pitchford
Pichetorne	See Pickthorn
Pickthorn, G. 9	*Pichetorne* 252b
Pitchford, E. 7	*Piceforde* 258
Plaish, E. 7	*Plesham* 256b
Plesham	See Plaish
Plivesdone	See Puleston
Pole	See Polmere
Polelie	See Pulley
Polmere, D. 6	*Pole* 259b
Polrebec	See Church Pulverbatch
Pontesbury, D. 6	*Pantesberie* 255b
Posenhall	Not in D.B.
Posselau	See Purslow
Possetorn(e)	See Poston
Poston, Greater and Lesser, E. 9	*Possetorn(e)* 252b, 258b

Poynton, F. 5	*Peventone* 259b
Prees, F. 3	*Pres* 252
Prene	See Church Preen
Pres	See Prees
Preston	See Preston Brockhurst
Preston Brockhurst, E. 4	*Preston(e)* 258, 259
Prestone	See Preston Brockhurst, Preston Gubbals, Preston Montford
Preston Gubbals, E. 5	*Prestone* 253
Preston Montford, D. 5	*Prestone*, *-tune* 253, 255b
Preston upon the Weald Moors, G. 5	*Prestune* 257
Prestune	See Preston Montford, Preston upon the Weald Moors
Priest Weston, C. 7	*Westune* 256
Puleston, H. 5	*Plivesdone* 257b
Pulley, E. 6	*Polelie* 259, 260b
Purslow, C. 9	*Posselau* 258
Quatford, H. 8	*Quatford* 254
Quatt, H. 8	*Quatone* 239, Warw.
Ratlinghope, D. 7	*Rotelingehope* 256
Recordine	See Wrockwardine
Rhiston, B. 8	*Ristune* 259b
Riseberie	See Rushbury
Ristune	See Rhiston
Rochecestre	See Wroxeter
Rodington, F. 5	*Rodintone* 254b
Rodintone	See Rodington
Rohalle	See Ruthall
Romsley, H. 9	*Rameslege* 239, Warw.
Roritune	See Rorrington
Rorrington, C. 7	*Roritune* 255b, 256
Rosela	See Rossall
Rossall, E. 5	*Rosela* 253, 255

Rotelingehope	See Ratlinghope
Routone	See Rowton (in Ercall Magna)
Rowton (in Alberbury), D. 6	*Rutune* 259b
Rowton (in Ercall Magna), F. 5	*Routone* 259b
Ruckley	Not in D.B.
Rudge, H. 7	*Rigge* 239, Warw.
Ruitone	See Ruyton of the Eleven Towns, Ryton
Rushbury, E. 8	*Riseberie* 256b
Ruthall, F. 8	*Rohalle* 259
Rutune	See Rowton (in Alberbury)
Ruyton of the Eleven Towns, D. 5	*Ruitone* 257b 2nd entry
Ryton, H. 7	*Ruitone* 257b 1st entry
St Martins	Not in D.B.
Saleurdine	See Shrawardine
Saltone	See Shelton
Sambrook, G. 4	*Semebre* 257b
Sandford, F. 3	*Sanford* 258b
Sanford	See Sandford
Savintune	See Shavington
Sawesberie	See Shawbury
Sbernestune	See Osbaston
Scentune	See Sheinton
Scevintone	See Steventon
Schentune	See Sheinton
Scipetune	See Shipton
Sciropesberie	See Shrewsbury
Selattyn	Not in D.B.
Semebre	See Sambrook
Setham	See Sheet
Shavington, F. 3	*Savintune* 259
Shawbury, F. 5	*Sawesberie* 258b
Sheet, E. 10	*Setham* 260
Sheinton, F. 7	*Sc(h)entune* 256b, 260b
Shelton, E. 6	*Saltone* 252
Shelve	Not in D.B.
Sheriff Hales, H. 6	*Halam*, *Halas* 246, 248, Staffs.
Shifnal, H. 6	*Iteshale* 256b

Shipley, H. 8	*Sciplei* 239, Warw.
Shipton, F. 8	*Scipetune* 252b
Shrawardine, D. 5	*Saleurdine* 255
Shrewsbury, E. 6	*Sciropesberie* 252 *ter*, 252b, 253, 254
Sibdon Carwood, D. 9	*Sibetune* 258
Sibetune	See Sibdon Carwood
Sidbury, G. 9	*Sudberie* 257
Siefton, E. 9	*Sireton* 254
Silvington	Not in D.B.
Sirelei	See Shirley, Heref.
Sireton	See Siefton
Slacheberie, D. 4	Lost in Ellesmere, 259
Sleap, E. 4	*Eslepe* 257b
Smerecote	See Smethcott
Smethcott, D. 7	*Smerecote* 259b
Soulton, E. 4	*Suletune* 252b
Sponelege	See Spoonley
Spoonley, G. 3	*Sponelege* 259
Stanege	See Stanage, Wales
Stanestune	See Edstaston
Stanewei	See Stanway, Heref.
Staneweie	See Stanway
Stantone	See Stanton Lacy
Stanton Lacy, E. 9	*Stantone* 260b
Stanton Long and Holdgate, F. 8	*Stantune* 256b, 258b *bis*
Stanton upon Hine Heath, F. 4	*Stantune* 254
Stantune	See Stanton Long, Stanton upon Hine Heath. See also Hyssington, Wales
Stanwardine, D. 4	*Staurdine* 256
Stanway, E. 8	*Staneweie* 254
Stapleton, E. 7	*Hundeslit* 255b, 259b
Staurdine	See Stanwardine
Staurecote	Unid., 254
Steel, E. 3	*Stile* 256
Steple	See Stepple
Stepple, G. 9	*Steple* 260
Steventon, E. 10	*Scevintone* 258b
Stile	See Steel

Stirchley	Not in D.B.
Stoche	See Hinstock, Stoke upon Tern
Stoches	See Stokesay, Stoke upon Tern
Stochetone	See Stockton
Stockton, H. 7	*Stochetone* 259
Stodesdone	See Stottesdon
Stoke St Milborough, F. 9	*Godestoch* 252b
Stokesay, D. 9	*Stoches* 260b
Stoke upon Tern, G. 4	*Stoche(s)* 256b *ter*
Stope	See Easthope
Stottesdon, G. 9	*Stodesdone* 254
Stow	Not in D.B.
Straford	See Strefford
Stratun(e)	See Stretton
Strefford, D. 9	*Straford* 255
Stretton, All, Church and Little, D. 8	*Stratun(e)* 254, 259b
Sudberie	See Sidbury
Sudtelch	Unid., 257b
Sudtone	See Sutton (near Shrewsbury); Sutton, Great and Little; Sutton Maddock; Sutton upon Tern
Suletune	See Soulton
Sutton (near Shrewsbury), E. 6	*Sudtone* 252b
Sutton, Great and Little, E. 9	*Sudtone* 257b, 258b
Sutton Maddock, G. 7	*Sudtone* 259
Sutton upon Tern, G. 3	*Sudtone* 256
Sychtyn	Not in D.B.
Tasley	Not in D.B.
Tedenesolle	See Tetstill
Tetbristone	See Tibberton
Tetstill, G. 10	*Tedenesolle* 260
Tibberton, G. 5	*Tetbristone* 256
Tibetune	Unid., 254b
Tichelevorde	See Ticklerton
Ticklerton, E. 8	*Tichelevorde* 252b
Tirelire	See Tyrley, Staffs.
Tittenley, G. 3	*Titesle* 265b, Ches.
Tong, H. 6	*Tuange* 253b
Torneberie	See Thornbury, Wales
Tuange	See Tong
Tugford, F. 8	*Dodefort* 254
Tumbelawe	Unid., 260
Tunestan	Unid., 259b
Uchintune	See Uckington
Uckington, F. 6	*Uchintune* 253
Udecote	See Woodcote (in Bicton), Woodcote (near Newport)
Udeford	Unid., 257b
Udetone	See Wootton
Udevertune	See Wotherton
Uffington, E. 6	*Ofitone* 258b
Ulestanesmude	See Wolston Mynd, Wales
Ulestanestune	See Woolstaston
Ultone	See Upton Cressett
Uluretone	See Wollerton
Ulwardelege	See Wolverley
Umbruntune	See Womerton
Uppington, F. 6	*Opetone* 258b
Upton Cressett, G. 8	*Ultone* 255
Uptone	See Waters Upton
Upton Magna, F. 6	*Uptune* 254b
Uptune	See Upton Magna
Urbetune	See Wropton, Wales
Wadelestun	See Woodluston, Wales
Walanceslau	See Longslow
Walcot, B. 7	*Walecote* 254
Walecote	See Walcot
Waleford	See Walford
Walford, D. 5	*Waleford* 256
Waliford(e)	See Walford, Heref.
Walitone	See Wellington
Walle	See Walltown
Walltown, G. 9	*Walle* 257
Waltham	See Wheathill

Worfield, H. 8	*Guruelde* 246, Staffs.
	Wrfeld 248b, Staffs.
Worthen, C. 7	*Wrdine* 255b
Wotherton, B. 7	*Udevertune* 259b
Wrdine	See Worthen
Wrentnall, D. 7	*Werentenehale* 259
Wrockwardine, F. 6	*Recordine* 253
Wroxeter, F. 6	*Rochecestre* 254b
Wykey, D. 4	*Wiche* 257b
Yagdon, D. 5	*Iagedone* 259b
Yockleton, D. 6	*Iochehuile* 255b
Yorton, E. 4	*Iartune* 253

ANONYMOUS HOLDINGS

No place-names appear in the following seven entries, and it is possible that some (or even all) of these refer to holdings at places not named elsewhere in Domesday Book:

Church of St Remy, one hide in Overs hd, 252.
Alvrics's son (from church of St Milburga), half a hide in Condover hd, 252b.
Rainald (from Earl Roger), 2$\frac{2}{3}$ hides in Wrockwardine hd, 254b.
One freeman (from Earl Roger), half a hide and $\frac{2}{3}$ virgate in Wrockwardine hd, 254b.
Earl Roger, half a hide in *Ruesset* hd, 255b.
Robert son of Tetbald (from Earl Roger), one virgate in Wrockwardine hd, 256b.
Richard, from Ralf de Mortemer (from Earl Roger), 1$\frac{1}{2}$ hides in *Culveston* hd, 256b.

SOMERSET
SUMMERSETE (SUMERSETA)

Exchequer Domesday Book, folios 86–99.
Exeter Domesday Book, folios 75–82b, 88b–91b, 103–107b, 113–116b, 136b–160b, 173b–175b, 185–193b, 196–198b, 265–283, 286b–287, 315–315b, 344, 350–355b, 356–365, 369–370, 371b–375, 380, 382b–386, 422–454, 462b–467, 473b, 477–480b, 490–493b, 508b–525.
Exeter Domesday names and folio references are given in brackets. An asterisk * indicates that the names in the Exeter D.B. and the Exchequer D.B. are the same.

MAPS 42–43

Abbas Combe	See Combe, Abbas and Temple
Abbot's Leigh, I. 1	*Lege* 91b (*Lega* 198)
(*Acca*)	See Oake
(*Accheleia*)	See Oakley
*Acha**, *Ache*	See Oake
*Achelai** (*-laia*)	See Oakley
Adelingi (*Adeliniensis*)	See Athelney
Adsborough, G. 6	*Tetesberge* 95b (*-berga* 356, *Tegesberia* 508b)
(*Aeford*)	See Ford
Algi (*Aili*)	See Aley
Aisecome (*-coma*)	See Ashcombe
(*Aiseforde*)	See Exford
Aiselle	See Ashill
Aisholt	Not in D.B.
Aissa	See Ash Priors

(*Aissa*)	See Ashbrittle, Ash Priors
Aisse	See Ashbrittle
Aissebrige	See Axbridge
Aissecote (*-cota*)	See Ashcott
Aisseford, *-forde* (*-forda*)	See Exford
Aisselle (*-ella*)	See Ashill
Aixa, *Aixe* (*Aisxa*)	See Ash Priors
Alcombe, C. 4	*Aucome* 95b (*-coma* 358)
*Aldedeford**	See Alford
Alduic (*-uica*)	See Aldwick
Aldwick, I. 3	*Alduic* 97b (*-uica* 452b, 519)
Alentone (*-tona*)	See Alhampton
(*Alesistuna*)	See Alstone
Aley, F. 5	*Ailgi* 95b (*Aili* 356b)
Alfagestone (*-tona*)	See Alfoxton
Alford, J. 6	*Aldedeford* 92b (*277b)
Alfoxton, E. 5	*Alfagestone* 97 (*-tona* 373b)
Alhampton, J. 6	*Alentone* 90b (*-tona* 170)
Aller (in Carhampton), C. 5	*Alre* 94 (*Alra* 430b, 512)
Aller (near Langport), H. 6	*Alre* 97 (*Alra* 464b)
Aller (in Sampford Brett), D. 5	*Alre* 91b (*Alra* 286b)
Allercott, C. 5	*Alurenecote* 96 (*Alueronecota* 360)
Allerford, B. 4	*Alresford* 97 (*-forda* 463, *Alrefort* 510)
(*Almondesford*)	See Ansford
Almsworthy, B. 5	*Edmundesworde* 94 (*-worda* 430)
Almundesford	See Ansford
Alnodestone (*-tona*, *-tuna*)	See Alston Sutton
Alre (*Alra*)	See Aller (in Carhampton), Aller (near Langport), Aller (in Sampford Brett)
(*Alrefort*)	See Allerford
Alresford (*-forda*)	See Allerford
Alsebruge (*-brugia*)	See Axbridge
Alsistune	See Alstone
Alstone, G. 4	*Alsistune* 95b (*Alesistuna* 355)
Alston Sutton, H. 4	*Alnodestone* 95 (*-tona*, *-tuna* 351b, 518)
Altone	See Holton
Alurenecote (*Alueronecota*)	See Allercott
Alwarditone (*-tona*)	See Chapel Allerton
Amelberge (*-berga*, *-beria*)	See Emborough
Andersey, I. 4	*Ederesige* 90 (*172)
Angersleigh	Not in D.B.
Animere (*-mera*)	See Enmore
Ansford, K. 6	*Almundesford* 95 (*Almondesford* 352b)
Apelie (*-leia*)	See Appley
Appelie (*-leia*)	See Appley
Appley, D. 7	*Ape-*, *Appelie* 92, 93 (*Ape-*, *Appeleia* 269b, 315b)
Are (*Ar*)	See Oare
*Ascwei**	See Ashway
Ash (near Martock)	Not in D.B.
Ashbrittle, D. 7	*Aisse* 92 *bis* (*Aissa* 269, 272b, 513b)
Ashcombe, G. 3	*Aisecome* 88 (*-coma* 140)
Ashcott, H. 5	*Aissecote* 90 *bis* (*-cota* 163b, 164b)
Ashill, G. 8	*Aiselle*, *Aisselle* 91, 92 (*Aissella* 191b, 268b, 513b, 524b)
Ashington, J. 7	*Essentone* 94 (*-tona* 435)
Ash Priors, E. 6	*Aissa* 89b (*160, 520b)

Ash Priors cont.	*Aixa*, *Aixe* 96b *bis* (*Aisxa* 443b *bis*)
Ashway, B. 6	*Ascwei* 93b (*428b)
Ashwick, J. 4	*Escewiche* 89b (*Escwica* 187)
Ateberie (*-beria*)	See Adber, Do.
Athelney, G. 6	*Adelingi* 91 (*Adeliniensis* 191)
Atigete	See Havyat
Atiltone (*-tona*)	See Ilton
(*Attigetta*)	See Havyat
Aucome (*-coma*)	See Alcombe
*Avena**	See Avill
Avill, C. 5	*Avena* 95b (*359)
Axbridge, H. 3	*Aissebrige* 87 (*Axebruge* 107b) *Alsebruge* 86 (*-brugia* 90)
(*Axebruge*)	See Axbridge
Babacha .. (*Babakari*, *Babbacari*)	See Babcary
(*Babbig-*, *Babbingtona*)	See Babington
Babcary, J. 6	*Babacha* .. 92b (*Babakari* 277b) *Babecari* 99 (*466, *Babbacari* 521b)
*Babecari**	See Babcary
Babington, K. 4	*Babingtone* 88b (*Babbig-*, *Babbingtona* 147, 519b)
Babingtone	See Babington
(*Bachia*)	See Hatch Beauchamp
Backwell, I. 2	*Bacoile* 88 (*Bacoila* 143)
Bacoile (*Bacoila*)	See Backwell
*Bada**, *Bade**	See Bath
Badeheltone (*-tona*)	See Bathealton
Badgeworth, H. 4	*Bagewerre* 95 (*-werra* 351)
(*Bagaberga*)	See Bagborough
(*Bagaleia*)	See Bagley (in Stoke Pero)
(*Bagatrepa*)	See Bawdrip
Bagborough, East and West, E. 6	*Bageberge* 96, 96b (*Bagaberga*, *Bageberga* 364, 464) *Baweberga* 87b (*Bagueberga* 174)
Bageberge (*-berga*)	See Bagborough
Bagelie	See Bagley (in Stoke Pero)
Bagetrepe	See Bawdrip
Bagewerre (*-werra*)	See Badgeworth
Bagley (in Stoke Pero), B. 5	*Bagelie* 94 (*Bagaleia* 430b)
Bagley (in Wedmore), I. 4	*Bodeslege* 90 (*-lega* 164)
(*Bagueberga*)	See Bagborough
Baltonsborough, I. 6	*Baltunesberge* 90b (*-berga* 167)
Baltunesberge (*-berga*)	See Baltonsborough
(*Banuella*)	See Banwell
Banwell, H. 3	*Banwelle* 89b (*Banuella* 157)
Banwelle	See Banwell
Barintone (*-tona*)	See Barrington
Barrington, H. 8	*Barintone* 94b (*-tona* 435b, 524b)
Barrow, North and South, J. 6	*Berrowene* 92b (*-ena* 277) *Berue* 95 (*Berua* 353)
Barrow Gurney, I. 2	*Berue* 88 (*Berua* 143)
Barton St David, I. 6	*Bertone*, *-tune* 94, 98b (*-tona*, *tuna* 434b *bis*, 480)
Barwick	Not in D.B.
Batcombe, K. 5	*Batecumbe* 90b (*-comba* 167b)
Batecumbe (*-comba*)	See Batcombe
Bath, L. 2	*Bada*, *Bade* 87 *quater*, 88, 89, 89b, 98 *bis* (*113b, 114, 114b, 115, 141b, 143, 151b, 185, 437, 448b, 518b) *Bade* 64b, Wilts.

Bathampton, L. 2	*Hantone* 89b (*Hamtona* 186)
Bathealton, D. 7	*Badeheltone* 96 (-*tona* 362b, 511b)
Batheaston, L. 2	*Estone* 87 *bis*, 89b, 99 (-*tona* 114, 114b, 186, 465)
Bathford, L. 2	*Forde* 89b (*Forda* 185b)
Bathwick	See Swainswick
Bawdrip, G. 5	*Bagetrepe* 95 (*Bagatrepa* 353)
Baweberga	See Bagborough
Bechintone (-*tona*)	See Beckington
Beckington, L. 4	*Bechintone* 94b (-*tona* 444b)
Beer Crocumbe, G. 7	*Bere* 92 (*Bera* 271)
Beere, F. 5	*Bera* 91b (*196)
Beiminstre	See Bedminster, Gloucs.
(*Bela*)	See Hele
Beletone, *Belgetone* (*Belgetona*)	See Belluton
Belluton, J. 2	*Beletone*, *Belgetone* 87, 91b (*Belgetona* 114, 282b)
Bera	See Beere
(*Bera*)	See Beer Crocumbe, Beere
Berchelei (-*lec*)	See Berkley
Bere	See Beer Crocumbe
Berkley, L. 4	*Berchelei* 94b (-*lec* 444b)
(*Bernet*)	See Burnett
Berrow	Not in D.B.
Berrowene (-*ena*)	See Barrow, North and South
Bertone, -*tune* (-*tona*, *tuna*)	See Barton St David
Berue (*Berua*)	See Barrow, North and South; Barrow Gurney
(*Betministra*, -*tre*)	See Bedminster, Gloucs.
Bichecome (-*comma*, -*cumma*)	See Bickham
Bichehalle (-*halda*)	See Bickenhall
Bicheurde	See Bishopsworth
Bickenhall, G. 7	*Bichehalle* 92 (-*halda* 270b, 514b)
Bickham, C. 5	*Bichecome* 95b (-*comma*, -*cumma* 358b, 511)
Bicknoller	Not in D.B.
Biddisham	Not in D.B.
(*Billa*)	See Hillfarance
Binegar	Not in D.B.
(*Bischeurda*)	See Bishopsworth
Biscopeston, -*tone* (*Bisobestona*), I. 8	Lost in Montacute, 93 (280)
Bishop's Hull	Not in D.B.
Bishop's Lydeard, E. 6	*Lediart* 89b (*Liediart* 160) *Lidegar* 89 (*157)
Bishopsworth, J. 2	*Bicheurde* 88 (*Bischeurda* 141b) *Biscopewrde* 88 (-*wrda* 141b)
(*Bisobestona*)	See *Biscopeston*
(*Blachafort*)	See Blackford (near Wincanton)
(*Blachamora*)	See Blackmoor
Blachedone (-*dona*)	See Blagdon
Blacheford	See Blackford (in Wedmore), Blackford (near Wincanton)
(*Blacheforda*)	See Blackford (in Wedmore)
Blachemore	See Blackmoor
Blacheshale (-*ssala*)	See Blaxhold
Blackford (in Wedmore), H. 4	*Blacheford* 90 (-*forda* 163)
Blackford (near Wincanton), K. 7	*Blacheford* 97b (*Blachafort* 383b)
Blackmoor, F. 5	*Blachemore* 93b (*Blachamora* 426, 510)
Blagdon, I. 3	*Blachedone* 97b (-*dona* 452)
Blaxhold, F. 6	*Blacheshale* 94 (-*ssala* 432b)
Bleadon, G. 3	*Bledone* 87b (-*dona* 173b) *Bledone* 145b *bis*,

Bleadon cont.	Bucks.; 210 *ter*, Beds.
Bledone (*-dona*)	See Bleadon
Bocheland	See Buckland St Mary
Bochelande (*-landa*)	See Buckland Dinham, Buckland St Mary
Bodechelie (*Bodecaleia*)	See Butleigh
Bodeslege (*-lega*)	See Bagley (in Wedmore)
Boduchelei (*Boduccheleia*)	See Butleigh
Bosintone, *-tune* (*-tona*, *tuna*)	See Bossington
Bossington, B. 4	*Bosintone*, *-tune* 91, 97 (*-tona*, *-tuna* 191b, 463b, 510, 524b)
Brade (*Brada*)	See Goosebradon
*Bradeford**, *-forde* (*-forda*)	See Bradford
(*Bradeuda*)	See Broadwood
*Bradewei**	See Broadway
Bradewrde	See Broadwood
Bradford, E. 7	*Bradeford*, *-forde* 87b, 92 (*-ford*, *-forda* 174, 273)
Bradney, G. 5	*Bredenie* 95 (*-neia* 353b)
Bratone (*-tona*)	See Bratton (in Minehead)
Bratton (in Minehead), C. 4	*Bratone* 96 (*-tona* 360)
Bratton Seymour, K. 6	*Broctune* 95 (*-tuna* 352)
Brauetone	See Bruton
Brean, G. 3	*Brien* 95 (*354)
Bredde, *Brede*	See North Bradon
*Bredene** (*Bredena*)	See South Bradon
Bredenie (*-neia*)	See Bradney
Brentemerse (*Brentamersa*)	See East Brent
(*Bretda*)	See North Bradon
Brewham, North and South, K. 5, K. 6	*Briweham* 94, 96b (*364b, 434b, 520)

(*Bricefort*)	See Brushford
Bridgwater, G. 5	*Brugie* 95 (*-ia* 353)
*Brien**	See Brean
Brigeford (*-fort*)	See Brushford
*Bristou**	See Bristol, Gloucs.
(*Briuetona*, *Briutona*)	See Bruton
*Briweham**	See Brewham
Briwetone, *-tune* (*-tona*, *-tuna*)	See Bruton
Broadway, G. 8	*Bradewei* 92 (*268b)
Broadwood, C. 5	*Bradewrde* 95b (*-euda* 358b)
Brochelie (*-leia*)	See Brockley
Brockley, I. 2	*Brochelie* 99 (*-leia* 466b)
Broctune (*-tuna*)	See Bratton Seymour
Broford, C. 6	*Broford* 93b *bis* (*-fort* 429 *bis*)
Broford (*-fort*)	See Broford
Brompton Ralph, D. 6	*Burnetone* 95b (*-tuna* 357, 509b)
Brompton Regis, C. 6	*Brunetone* 86b (*-tona* 103, 510b) *Burnetone* 92 (*-tona* 272b, 515)
Broom, C. 5	*Brune* 95b (*Bruna* 358)
Broomfield, F. 6	*Brunfelle* 96 (*-fella* 363b)
*Brucheford**	See Brushford
Brugie (*-ia*)	See Bridgwater
Brumetone	See Bruton
Brune (*Bruna*)	See Broom
Brunetone (*-tona*)	See Brompton Regis, Brympton
Brunfelle (*-fella*)	See Broomfield
Brushford, C. 7	*Brigeford* 86b (*-fort* 103b, *Bricefort* 511) *Brucheford* 92 (*268)
Bruton, K. 6	*Brauetone* 87 (*Briuetona*, *Briutona* 107b, 520)

/over

Bruton cont.	*Briweton*, *-tone* 94, 95, 97b (*-tona* 352b, 382b, 434b, 520, 523) *Brumetone* 86b (*Briwetona* 90b)
Brympton, I. 8	*Brunetone* 94b (*-tona* 435)
Buckland Dinham, L. 4	*Bochelande* 99 (*-landa* 492b)
Buckland St Mary, F. 8	*Bocheland*, *-lande* 98b *bis* (*-landa* 490, 492)
Budicome (*-coma*)	See Butcombe
(*Buducaleia*)	See Butleigh
*Bur**	See East Bower, West Bower
Bure	See West Bower
(*Burh*)	See East Bower
*Burneham**	See Burnham
Burnetone (*-tona*)	See Brompton Ralph, Brompton Regis
Burnett, K. 2	Unnamed holding of Uluuard's wife 87 (*Bernet* 114)
Burnham, G. 4	*Burneham* 95 (*354)
Burrington	Not in D.B.
Butcombe, I. 3	*Budicome* 88 (*-coma* 143)
Butleigh, I. 6	*Bodechelie* 91 (*Bodecaleia* 173) *Boduchelei* 90 (*Boduccheleia* 165b)
Cadeberie (*-beria*)	See North Cadbury
(*Cadicota*)	See Catcott
(*Cafecoma*)	See Chaffcombe
Caffecome (*-coma*)	See Chaffcombe
Cainesham (*-essam*)	See Keynsham
*Caivel**	See Keyford
Caldecote	See Catcott
Caluiche (*-uica*)	See Chelvey
*Camel**	See Queen Camel
Camelei (*-leia*)	See Cameley
Camelertone (*-tona*)	See Camerton
Cameley, J. 3	*Camelei* 89 (*-leia* 150b, 522b)
Camelle (*-ella*)	See West Camel
Camerton, K. 3	*Camelertone* 90b (*-tona* 170)
*Candel**	See Caundle, Do.
Candetone (*-tona*)	See Cannington
Cannington, F. 5	*Candetone* 86b, 98b, 99 (*-tona* 89, 478, 493b, *Cantocton*, *-tona* 89b, 524b) *Cantetone* 86b, 91b (*-tona* 104, 196b)
Canole (*-ola*)	See Knowle, Gloucs.
Cantetone (*-tona*)	See Cannington
Cantoche (*-toca*)	See Quantock
Cantocheheve, *-tocheve* (*Cantocheheva*)	See Quantoxhead
(*Cantocton*, *-tona*)	See Cannington
Capilande (*-landa*)	See Capland
Capintone (*-tona*)	See Capton
Capland, G. 7	*Capilande* 98b (*-landa* 491b, 517b)
Capton, D. 5	*Capintone* 86b (*-tona* 104)
Carentone, *Caretone* (*Carentona*, *-tuna*)	See Carhampton
Carhampton, D. 5	*Carentone*, *Caretone* 86b *bis*, 91b, 96b, 97 (*Carentona*, *-tuna* 89, 104, 196b, 344, 463, 509b, 510)
*Cari**	See Cary Fitzpaine and Lyte's Cary, Castle Cary
Carlingcott, K. 3	*Credelincote* 92b (*-cota* 276b)
Carme (*Carma*)	See Quarme
Cary Fitzpaine and Lyte's Cary, I. 7, J. 7	*Cari*, *Curi* 94b, 98b *bis* (*Cari* 443b, 479b *bis*, 515, *Kari* 517b *bis*)
Castle Cary, K. 6	*Cari* 95 (*352b)
Catcott, H. 5	*Caldecote* 90 (*Cadicota* 162b)

Cathanger, G. 7	*Cathangre* 91 (*188b, *-hangra* 512b)
*Cathangre** (*-hangra*)	See Cathanger
(*Ceadra*, *Ceddra*)	See Cheddar
*Ceder**	See Cheddar
Cedre (*Cedra*)	See Cheddar, Cheddon Fitzpaine
Celeworde (*-worda*)	See Chelwood
*Cellewert**	See Chelwood
(*Celuia*)	See Chelvey
Ceolseberge	See Chiselborough
(*Ceorlatona*)	See Charlton Adam and Mackrell
(*Ceoselbergon*)	See Chiselborough
Ceptone (*-tona*)	See Chilton upon Polden
Cerdesling (*-linc*)	See Charlynch
*Cerdre**	See Chard
Cerlecume (*Cerlacuma*)	See Charlcombe
(*Cerletona*)	See Charlton (in Shepton Mallet), Charlton Adam and Mackrell
Cerletone	See Charlton (in Shepton Mallet), Charlton Adam and Mackrell, Charlton Musgrove
(*Cerletone*)	See Charlton Musgrove
Cerletune	See Charlton Adam and Mackrell
(*Ceselberia*)	See Chiselborough
Chaffcombe, G. 8	*Caffecome* 87b (*-coma* 136b, *Cafecoma* 509)
Chaivert	See Keyford
Chapel Allerton, H. 4	*Alwarditone* 95 (*-tona* 351, 518)
Chard, G. 9	*Cerdre* 89 (*156)
Charlcombe, L. 2	*Cerlecume* 89b (*Cerlacuma* 186)
Charlton (in Shepton Mallet), J. 5	*Cerletone* 90b (*-tona* 167b)
Charlton Adam and Mackrell, I. 6	*Cerletone*, *-tune* 92b, 94b (*-tona* 443b, *Ceorlatona* 273b, 516b, 523b)
Charlton Musgrove, K. 6	*Cerletone* 97 (*436b)
Charlynch, F. 5	*Cerdesling* 93 (*-linc* 423)
Charterhouse	Not in D.B.
Cheddar, I. 3	*Ceder* 94 (*432b) *Cedre* 86 *bis* (*Ceadra*, *Ceddra*, *Cedra* 90 *bis*, 515b)
Cheddon Fitzpaine, F. 6	*Cedre* 94b (*Cedra* 444) *Succedene* 87b (*-dena* 174)
Chedesford (*-forda*)	See Kittisford
Chelmetone	See Kilmington, Wilts.
Chelvey, I. 2	*Caluiche* 98 (*-uica* 450, *Celuia* 518b)
Chelwood, J. 3	*Celeworde* 91b (*-worda* 282b) *Cellewert* 97 (*447b)
Chen	See Kenn
Chenemeresdone	See Kilmersdon
Chenolle (*-nolla*)	See Knowlepark, Knowle St Giles
(*Chent*)	See Kenn
Cherintone (*-tona*)	See Cheriton
Cheriton, North and South, K. 7	*Cherintone* 96b (*-tona* 386) *Ciretune*, *Eiretone* 96b, 97b (*Ciretona*, *-tuna* 364b, 384b)
Chetenore (*-nora*)	See Culbone formerly Kitnor
Chew Magna, J. 2	*Chiwe* 89b (*Chiu* 159)
Chew Stoke	See Stoke Villice
Chewton Mendip, J. 4	*Ciwetune* 87 (*-tuna* 114b)

(*Chigtona*)	See Keinton Mandeville
Chilcompton, K. 4	*Contone*, *-tune* 87b, 95b *bis* (*Contona*, *Comtuna*, *Cumtona* 154, 354b *bis*, 522)
Chillington	Not in D.B.
Chillyhill, J. 2	*Cilele* 97b (*-ela* 452b, 517b)
(*Chilmatona*)	See Kilmington, Wilts.
Chilthorne Domer, I. 7	*Cilterne* 93 *bis* (*-terna* 279b, 280)
Chilton Cantelo, J. 7	*Citerne* 96b (*-erna* 439)
Chilton Trinity, G. 5	*Cildetone* 98 (*-tona* 477)
	Cilletone 93 (*-tona* 423)
Chilton Trivett, F. 5	*Cildetone* 93b *bis* (*-tona* 424b, 425)
Chilton upon Polden, H. 5	*Ceptone* 90 (*-tona* 162)
Chilvetune (*-tun*)	See Kilton
(*Chinemeresdone*)	See Kilmersdon
Chingesberie	See Kingsbury Episcopi
(*Chingestana*)	See Kingstone
(*Chingestona*)	See Kingston Seymour
Chingestone	See Kingstone, Kingston Seymour
Chinnock, East and West, I. 8	*Cinioch* 92b *ter* (*-ioc* 274, 274b *bis*)
Chintone, *-tune* (*-tona*, *-tuna*)	See Keinton Mandeville
Chinwardestune	See Kingweston
Chipstable, D. 7	*Cipestaple* 91 (*-apula* 188)
Chiselborough, I. 8	*Ceolseberge* 92b (*Ceoselbergon* 274b, *Ceselberia* 517b)
Chiwe (*Chiu*)	See Chew Magna
Chiwestoch (*-stoc*)	See Kewstoke
(*Chori*)	See Curry Rivel

Christon	Not in D.B.
(*Chruca*)	See Crewkerne
Chubworthy, D. 7	*Cibewrde* 96 (*-wrda* 362, 511b)
Churchill	Not in D.B.
Churchstanton, F. 8	*Stantone* 115b (*Estantona* 382), Devon
*Churi**	See Curry Rivel
Cibewrde (*-wrda*)	See Chubworthy
Cildetone (*-tona*)	See Chilton Trinity, Chilton Trivett
Cilele (*-ela*)	See Chillyhill
Cilemetone (*Cile-*, *Cillemetona*)	See Kilmington, Wilts.
Cilletone (*-tona*)	See Chilton Trinity
Cilterne (*-terna*)	See Chilthorne Domer
(*Ciretona*)	See Cheriton
Cinioch (*-ioc*)	See Chinnock
Cipestaple (*-apula*)	See Chipstable
Ciretune (*-tona*, *-tuna*)	See Cheriton
Citerne (*-erna*)	See Chilton Cantelo
Ciwetune (*-tuna*)	See Chewton Mendip
(*Cladforda*)	See Cloford
Claford (*-forda*)	See Cloford
Claftertone (*-tona*)	See Claverton
Claihelle (*-hella*)	See Clayhill
Clapton (in Cucklington), L. 6	*Clopetone* 92b (*Clope-*, *Cloppetona* 278, 523b)
Clapton (in Mapperton), K. 6	*Cloptone* 97b (*Clop-*, *Clopptona* 383b, 521)
Clapton in Gordano, I. 1	*Clotune* 88 (*-tuna* 142b)
Clateurde (*-eurda*)	See Clatworthy
Clatworthy, D. 6	*Clateurde* 95b (*-eurda* 357)
(*Claveham*)	See Claverham
Claverham, H. 2	*Cliveham* 88 (*Claveham* 141)

Claverton, L. 2	*Claftertone* 99 (*-tona* 465)
Clayhill, F. 5	*Claihelle* 93 (*-hella* 422b)
Clevedon, H. 1	*Clivedone* 98 (*-dona* 450)
Clewer, H. 4	*Cliveware* 88 (*-wara* 141b)
Clive (*Cliva*)	See Kilve, Old Cleeve
Clivedone (*-dona*)	See Clevedon
Cliveham	See Claverham
Cliveware (*-wara*)	See Clewer
Cloford, K. 5	*Claford* 92b (*-forda* 275b, *Cladforda* 523b)
Clopetune (*Cloppetona*)	See Clapton (in Cucklington)
Cloptone (*Clopptona*)	See Clapton (in Mapperton)
Closworth, J. 8	*Clovewrde* 92b (*-eswrda* 275)
Clotune (*-tuna*)	See Clapton in Gordano
Clovewrde (*-eswrda*)	See Closworth
Clutone (*-tona*)	See Clutton
Clutton, J. 3	*Clutone* 88 (*-tona* 140)
Coarme (*Coarma*)	See Quarme
(*Cochra*)	See Coker
Cocintone (*-tona*)	See Cucklington
Cocre	See Coker
Coker, East and West, I. 8	*Cocre* 87 (*Cochra* 107)
Coleford, E. 6	*Coleford*, *Colforde* 93b, 96 (*Colforda* 361b, 427)
Coleford, *Colforde* (*Colforda*)	See Coleford
(*Coma*)	See Combe, Abbas and Temple
(*Comba*)	See Combe (in Withycombe); Combe, Abbas and Temple
Combe (in Bruton), K. 6	*Sindercome* 97b (*-coma* 383)

Combe (in Withycombe), D. 5	*Cumbe* 94 (*Comba* 430b)
Combe, Abbas and Temple, K. 7	*Come* 87b (*153b) *Cumbe* 91 (*Comba* 193b) (*Coma* 467, 523), not in Exch. D.B.
Combe Florey	Not in D.B.
Combe Hay, L. 3	*Cume* 99 (*Cuma* 492b)
Combe St Nicholas, G. 8	*Cumbe* 89 (*Cumba* 156)
Combe Sydenham, D. 5	*Come* 96 (*Comma* 362b)
Combwich, F. 5	*Comich* 97 (*462b) *Commiʒ* 91b (*Commit* 282)
Come	See Combe, Abbas and Temple; Combe Sydenham
(*Come*)	See Combe, Abbas and Temple
*Comich**	See Combwich
(*Comma*)	See Combe Sydenham
Commiʒ (*Commit*)	See Combwich
Compton (in Compton Dundon), I. 6	*Contone* 90 (*-tona* 163b)
Compton Bishop	Not in D.B.
Compton Dando, K. 2	*Contone* 88b (*Comtuna* 144b)
Compton Dundon	See Compton; see Dundon
Compton Durville, H. 8	*Contone* 87 (*-tona* 113b, *Cumtona* 516b) *Contune* 91b (*Comtuna* 265b)
Compton Martin, I. 3	*Contone* 98 (*Comtona* 453b)
Compton Pauncefoot, K. 7	*Contitone* 91b (*-tona* 283) *Cuntone* 97b (*Cumtona* 383b)
(*Comtona*)	See Compton Martin

(*Comtuna*)	See Chilcompton, Compton Dando, Compton Durville
Congresberie (*-beria*)	See Congresbury
Congresbury, H. 2	*Con-*, *Cungresberie* 87, 89b (*Con-*, *Cungresberia* 106, 159b, 517, 518)
Contitone (*-tona*)	See Compton Pauncefoot
(*Contona*)	See Chilcompton, Compton (in Compton Dundon), Compton Durville
Contone	See Chilcompton, Compton (in Compton Dundon), Compton Dando, Compton Durville, Compton Martin
Contune	See Chilcompton, Compton Durville
Corfe	Not in D.B.
Corfetone (*-tona*)	See Corton Denham
(*Cori*)	See Curry Rivel
Coristone (*Coriscoma*)	See Croscombe
Corston, K. 2	*Corstune* 89b (*-tuna* 186b)
Corstune (*-tuna*)	See Corston
Corton Denham, K. 7	*Corfetone* 87 (*-tona* 116)
Cosintone (*-tona*)	See Cossington
Cossington, G. 5	*Cosintone* 90 (*-tona* 162b)
Crandon, G. 5	*Grenedone* 99 (*-dona* 465b)
Cranmore, East and West, K. 5	*Crenemelle* 90b (*-mella* 170b, *Crenemere* 527)
Crawecumbe (*-coma*)	See Crowcombe
Credelincote (*-cota*)	See Carlingcott
Creech St Michael, G. 7	*Crice* 86b (*104b)
Crenemelle (*-mella*, *-mere*)	See Cranmore
Crewkerne, H. 8	*Cruche* 86b, 87b *bis*, 91, 92 (*Chruca*, *Cruca*, *Crucca*, *Crucche*, *Cruche* 105b, 154 *bis*, 197, 272, 513b, 514b)
*Crice**	See Creech St Michael
Cricket Malherbie, H. 8	*Cruchet* 92 (*272, 515)
Cricket St Thomas, H. 9	*Cruche* 86, 91b (*Cruca* 89, 265, 509b)
Croscombe, J. 5	*Coristone* 90 (*Coriscoma* 166)
Crosse, G. 6	*Cruce* 95 (*Cruca* 350)
Crowcombe, E. 5	*Crawecumbe* 91b (*-coma* 266, 510)
(*Cruca*)	See Crewkerne, Cricket St Thomas, Crosse
(*Crucca*, *Crucche*)	See Crewkerne
Cruce	See Crosse
Cruche	See Crewkerne, Cricket St Thomas
(*Cruche*)	See Crewkerne
*Cruchet**	See Cricket Malherbie
(*Cucintona*)	See Cucklington
Cucklington, L. 6	*Cocintone* 92b (*-tona* 277, *Cucintona* 521)
(*Cudeorda*)	See Cudworth
Cudeworde (*-worda*)	See Cudworth
Cudworth, H. 8	*Cudeworde* 94b (*-worda* 441b, *Cudeorda* 509b)
Culbone formerly Kitnor, B. 4	*Chetenore* 88 (*-nora* 139)
(*Cuma*)	See Combe Hay, Monkton Combe

(*Cumba*)	See Combe St Nicholas
Cumbe	See Combe (in Withycombe); Combe, Abbas and Temple; Combe St Nicholas
Cume	See Combe Hay, Monkton Combe
(*Cumtona*)	See Chilcompton, Compton Durville, Compton Pauncefoot
Cungresberie (*-beria*)	See Congresbury
Cuntone	See Compton Pauncefoot
Curi	See Cary Fitzpaine and Lyte's Cary, Curry Mallet, Curry Rivel
(*Curi*)	See Curry Mallet, Curry Rivel
*Curiepol**	See Currypool
Curland	Not in D.B.
Curry Mallet, G. 7	*Curi* 93 *bis* (*429 *bis*, 511b)
Currypool, F. 5	*Curiepol* 93 (*423)
Curry Rivel, H. 7	*Churi*, *Curi* 86 *bis*, 91b, 92 *septiens*, 98b (*Chori*, *Churi*, *Cori*, *Curi* 89 *bis*, 197b, 268, 268b *bis*, 269b, 270 *bis*, 270b, 271, 491b, 513 *bis*, 513b, 514 *ter*, 514b *bis*, 517b)
Cutcombe, C. 5	*Udecome* 95b (*-coma* 357b)
Deadman's Well, F. 6	*Denesmodeswelle* 86 (*-suella* 89b, *Denemodeswella* 515b)
(*Denemodeswella*)	See Deadman's Well
Denesmodeswelle (*-suella*)	See Deadman's Well
Dereberge (*-berga*)	See Durborough
Derlege (*-lega*)	See Durleigh
Destone (*Derstona*)	See Durston
*Dicesget**	See Ditcheat
(*Digenescova*)	See Discove
Dinder	Not in D.B.
Dinescove	See Discove
Dinnington, H. 8	*Dinnitone* 90b (*-tona* 172b, 524) *Dunintone* 99 (*-tona* 490b)
Dinnitone (*-tona*)	See Dinnington
Discove, K. 6	*Dinescove* 99 (*Digenescova* 493)
Ditcheat, J. 5	*Dicesget* 90b (*169b, 519, 522)
(*Diuetona*)	See Kilton
Dodington	See Nether Stowey
*Doltin**	See Doulting
Dolvertone, *-tune* (*-tona*)	See Dulverton
Dondeme (*Dondeina*)	See Dundon (in Compton Dundon)
*Doneham**	See Dunwear
Donescumbe (*-cumba*)	See Downscombe
(*Donieht*)	See Donyatt
*Doniet**	See Donyatt
Donyatt, G. 8	*Doniet* 92 (*270, *Donieht* 514)
Doules (*Douelis*)	See Dowlish
Doulting, K. 5	*Doltin* 90b (*167)
Doverhay, B. 4	*Dovri* 94 (*Doveri* 431)
Dovri (*Doveri*)	See Doverhay
Dowlish Wake and West Dowlish, H. 8	*Doules* 87b (*Douelis* 136b, *Duuelis* 509)
Downhead, K. 4	*Dunehefde* 90b (*171b)
Downscombe, B. 5	*Donescumbe* 94 (*-cumba* 430)
(*Draecota*)	See Draycott (in Limington)
(*Draecotta*)	See Draycott (in Rodney Stoke)

Draicote	See Draycott (in Limington), Draycott (in Rodney Stoke)
(*Draintuna*)	See Drayton
Draitune (*-tunna*)	See Drayton
Draycott (in Limington), J. 7	*Draicote* 92 (*Draecota* 267) *Dreicote* 91 (*Dreg-cota*, *Dregecota* 172b, 524)
Draycott (in Rodney Stoke), I. 4	*Draicote* 99 (*Draecotta* 492)
Drayton, H. 7	*Draitune* 91, 94 (*-tunna*, *Draintuna* 188b, 429b)
Dreicote (*Dregcota*, *Dregecota*)	See Draycott (in Limington)
*Dudesham**	Unid., 93b (424b, 509b)
Dulverton, C. 6	*Dolvertone*, *-tune* 86b, 98b (*Dol-*, *Dulvertona* 103b, 478b, 510b)
(*Dulvertona*)	See Dulverton
Duncretone (*-tona*, *-tun*)	See Dunkerton
Dundon (in Compton Dundon), I. 6	*Dondeme* 90 (*Dondeina* 164)
Dundry	Not in D.B.
*Dunehefde**	See Downhead
Dunintone (*-tona*)	See Dinnington
Dunkerton, K. 3	*Duncretone* 97b (*-tona*, *-tun* 384b, 523)
Dunster, C. 5	*Torre* 95b (*Torra* 359)
Dunwear, G. 5	*Doneham* 95 (*350)
Durborough, F. 5	*Dereberge* 90 (*-berga* 163)
Durleigh, G. 6	*Derlege* 98b (*-lega* 479)
Durston, G. 6	*Destone* 94b (*Derstona* 441)
(*Duuelis*)	See Dowlish
Dyche, E. 5	*Leding* 97 (*Ledich* 373b)
Earnshill, H. 7	*Ernesel* 98b (*478b) *Erneshele* 94 (*-helt* 431b)
East Bagborough	See Bagborough
East Bower, G. 5	*Bur* 97 (*371b, *Burh* 508b)
East Brent, G. 4	*Brentemerse* 90b (*Brentamersa* 170b)
East Chinnock	See Chinnock
East Coker	See Coker
East Cranmore	See Cranmore
Eastham, I. 8	*Estham* 87, 92 (*Esteha*, *-ham* 105b, 272, 514b)
East Harptree, J. 3	*Harpetreu* 88, 92 (*-threu*, *-treu* 139b, 272b, *Hapetreua* 515)
East Huntspill, G. 4	*Hunespil* 95b (*355)
East Lydford, J. 6	*Lideford* 90 (*-forda* 161b)
East Myne, C. 4	*Mene* 96 (*Mena* 360)
Easton in Gordano, I. 1	*Estone* 88 (*-tona* 142)
East Pennard	See Pennard
East Quantoxhead	See Quantoxhead
Eastrip, K. 6	*Estrope* 99 (*-ropa* 493b) *Storpe* 97b (*Estropa* 382b)
(*Eatona*)	See Yatton
(*Eattebera*)	See Adber, Do.
(*Ecchewica*)	See Eckweek
*Ecclesia S. Andreae**	See Ilchester
Ecewiche	See Eckweek, Wick
Ecferdintone	See Fairoak
Eckweek, K. 3	*Ecewiche* 92b (*Ecchewica* 276b)
*Ederesige**	See Andersey
Edeuestone (*-tona*)	See Idson
Edington, H. 5	*Edwinetone* 90 (*-tona* 162)
Edingworth, G. 3	*Lodenwrde* 90b (*Lodenawirda* 171)

Edmundesworde (*-worda*)	See Almsworthy
Edstock, F. 5	*Ichetoche* 93b (*-tocha* 426)
Edwinetone (*-tona*)	See Edington
Eford	See Ford
Eiretone	See Cheriton
Elborough, H. 3	*Eleberie* 91 (*Elleberia* 172b, 524) *Lilebere* 88 (*Illebera* 139b, 516)
Eleberie	See Elborough
Eleigh, G. 8	*Illege* 93b (*-lega* 426b, 510)
(*Elleberia*)	See Elborough
Elworthy, D. 6	*Elwrde* 96 (*-wrda* 361)
Elwrde (*-wrda*)	See Elworthy
Emble, E. 6	*Imele* 93b (*Imela* 79b, 428)
Emborough, J. 4	*Amelberge* 89 (*-berga*, *-beria* 150, 522)
Engliscome	See English Combe
English Combe, K. 2	*Engliscome* 88b (*Ingleliscuma* 146)
Enmore, F. 6	*Animere* 94 (*-mera* 432)
Epse (*Eppsa*)	See Rapps
*Ernesel**	See Earnshill
Erneshele (*-helt*)	See Earnshill
Ernole	See Knowle
Escewiche (*Escwica*)	See Ashwick
Eslide (*-lida*)	See Lyde
(*Espachestona*)	See Spaxton
(*Essatuna*)	See Exton
Essentone (*-tona*)	See Ashington
Essetune (*-tuna*)	See Exton
(*Estalrewicca*)	See Standerwick
(*Estalweia*)	See Nether Stowey
(*Estana*)	See Stone (in Exford)
(*Estantona*)	See Stanton Drew, Staunton
(*Estanwella*)	See Stowell
(*Estapla*)	See Staple Fitzpaine
(*Estaweia*)	See Stowey (in Oare)
(*Estaweit*)	See Old Stowey
(*Estawella*)	See Stawell
Estham (*Esteha*, *-ham*)	See Eastham
(*Esthoca*)	See Stoke Pero
(*Estoca*)	See Radstock, Stocklinch, Stoke St Mary, Stoney Stoke
(*Estocha*)	See Storgursey, Stoke sub Hamdon
(*Estochelanda*)	See Stockland Bristol
(*Estochet*)	See Stocklinch, Stoke sub Hamdon
(*Estona*)	See Batheaston, Easton in Gordano, Ston Easton
Estone	See Batheaston, Easton in Gordano, Stone (in Exford), Ston Easton
(*Estragella*)	See Stretcholt
(*Estrart*, *Estrat*)	See Street (in Winsham)
Estrope (*-ropa*)	See Eastrip
Estune (*Esttuna*)	See Long Ashton
*Esturt**	See Steart
Etesberie (*-beria*)	See Adber, Do.
Ettebere	See Adber, Do.
Euestie (*-tia*), K. 3	Lost in Dunkerton, 89b (186b)
Evercreech, K. 5	*Evrecriʒ* 89b (*Evercriʒ* 158)
Evrecriʒ (*Evercriʒ*)	See Evercreech
Exford, B. 5	*Aisseford*, *-forde* 94 *ter*, 95b *bis* (*Aise-*, *Aisseforda* 359b *bis*, 430 *bis*, 431b)
Exmoor	Not in D.B.

Exton, C. 6	*Essetune* 87b (*Essatuna*, *Essetuna* 139, 510b)
Fairoak, L. 4	*Ecferdintone* 94 (*Hecferdintona* 434)
Farleigh Hungerford, L. 3	*Ferlege* 94 (*-lega* 434)
Farmborough, K. 3	*Ferenberge* 88 *bis* (*-berga* 141 *bis*, *-beria* 518 *bis*)
Farrington Gurney, J. 3	*Ferentone* 89 (*-tona* 149b)
Fedintone	See Foddington
Ferenberge (*-berga*, *-beria*)	See Farmborough
Ferentone (*-tona*)	See Farrington Gurney
Ferlege (*-lega*)	See Farleigh Hungerford
Fescheforde (*-forda*)	See Vexford
Fiddington, F. 5	*Fitintone* 94b (*-tona* 441b)
Fifhide (*Fihida*)	See Fivehead
Firford (*-forda*)	See Freshford
Fitintone (*-tona*)	See Fiddington
Fitzhead	Not in D.B.
Fivehead, G. 7	*Fifhide* 94 (*Fihida* 431b)
Flax Bourton	Not in D.B.
Foddington, J. 6	*Fedintone* 92b (*Fodintona* 278) *Fodindone* 99 *bis* (*-dona* 466, 466b)
Fodindone (*-dona*, *-tona*)	See Foddington
Ford, F. 7	*Eford* 92b (*Aeford* 273b) *Laford* 87b (*Iafort* 174)
Forde (*Forda*)	See Bathford
Foxcote, K. 3	*Fuscote* 88b (*-cota* 145b)
Freshford, L. 3	*Firford* 88b (*-forda* 144)
Frome (*Froma*)	See Frome
Frome, L. 4	*Frome* 86b, 87, 91 (*Froma* 90b, 107b, 198)
Fuscote (*-cota*)	See Foxcote
*Gahers**	See Goathurst
Gatelme (*-elma*)	See Goathill, Do.
Gerlintune (*Gerlincgetuna*)	See Yarlington
Gernefelle (*-fella*)	See Yarnfield, Wilts.
Geveltone (*-tona*)	See Yeovilton
Gildenecote (*-cota*)	See Golsoncott
Giuelcestre, *Giuelecestre* (*Giuelcestra*, *Giulecestra*)	See Ilchester
Givele (*-ela*)	See Yeovil
(*Giveltona*)	See Yeovilton
Glastingberie (*Glaestingeberia*)	See Glastonbury
Glastonbury, I. 5	*Glastingberie* 90 (*Glaestingeberia* 172)
Goathurst, F. 6	*Gahers* 97b (*374)
Godelege (*-lega*)	See Gothelney
Golsoncott, D. 5	*Gildenecote* 94 (*-cota* 431)
Goosebradon, H. 7	*Brade* 98b (*Brada* 491b)
Gothelney, F. 5	*Godelege* 93 (*-lega* 423b)
Graintone (*-tona*)	See Greinton
Great Elm, L. 4	*Telwe* 98 (*Telma* 447)
Greenham, D. 7	*Grindeham* 92 (*269)
Greinton, H. 5	*Graintone* 90 (*-tona* 164b)
Grenedone (*-dona*)	See Crandon
*Grindeham**	See Greenham
(*Guiel-*, *Guilecestra*)	See Ilchester
Hache (*Hachia*)	See Hatch Beauchamp
Hadworthy, G. 6	*Hateware* 93 (*-wara* 422)
*Hafella**	See Heathfield
*Haia**	See Hay Street

Halberge (*-berga*)	See Haselbury Plunknett
Hallatrow, J. 3	*Helgetreu* 89 (*151, *Helegetriueia* 522b)
*Halsa**, *Halse*	See Halse
Halse, E. 6	*Halsa*, *Halse* 87b, 94b (*Halsa* 174, 442b)
Halsway, E. 5	*Halsweie* 93b (*-weia* 427)
Halsweie (*-weia*)	See Halsway
Halswell, F. 6	*Hasewelle* 94b (*-willa* 443)
(*Haltona*)	See Holton
(*Hama*)	See High Ham
Hame	See Hamp, High Ham
(*Hamet*)	See Hamp
Hamintone, *Hamitone* (*Hamintona*, *Hammingtona*)	See Hemington
Hamp, G. 6	*Hame* 91 (*Hamet* 191b)
(*Hamtona*)	See Bathampton
(*Hantona*)	See Hinton Blewitt, Hinton Charterhouse, Hinton St George
Hantone	See Bathampton, Hinton Blewitt, Hinton Charterhouse, Hinton St George
(*Hapetreua*)	See East Harptree
Hardington (near Frome), L. 4	*Hardintone* 88b, 93 (*Hardingtona*, *Hardintona* 147, 315b, 519b)
(*Hardingtona*)	See Hardington
Hardington Mandeville, I. 8	*Hardintone* 87 (*-tona* 107)
Hardintone (*-tona*)	See Hardington, Hardington Mandeville
*Haretreu**	See Hartrow
(*Harpethreu*)	See East Harptree
*Harpetreu**	See East Harptree, West Harptree
Hartrow, E. 6	*Haretreu* 96 (*362)
Hasecumbe (*Hasecomba*)	See Hiscombe
Haselbury Plucknett, I. 8	*Halberge* 99 (*-berga* 492)
Hasewelle (*-willa*)	See Halswell
(*Hassecomba*)	See Hiscombe
Hatch Beauchamp, G. 7	*Hache* 92 (*Hachia* 271, *Bachia* 514b)
Hateware (*-wara*)	See Hadworthy
Hauechewelle (*Hauekewella*)	See Hawkwell
Havyat, I. 3	*Atigete* 88 (*Attigetta* 142b)
Hawkridge	Not in D.B.
Hawkwell, B. 7	*Hauechewelle* 99 (*Hauekewella* 491)
Hay Street, J. 4	*Haia* 98b (*480)
Heathfield, E. 7	*Hafella* 87b (*174) *Herfeld* 96 (*-felt* 364)
(*Hecferdintona*)	See Fairoak
(*Hecuiwicca*)	See Wick
(*Hederneberia*)	See Honibere
*Hela**, *Hele*	See Hele (in Bradford)
Hele (in Bradford), F. 7	*Hela*, *Hele* 87b *bis*, 92b (*Bela* 174, *Hela* 174, 273, 516b)
(*Helegetriueia*)	See Hallatrow
*Helgetreu**	See Hallatrow
Hemington, K. 4	*Hamintone*, *Hamitone* 88b, 93 (*Hamintona*, *Hammingtona* 147, 315)
*Hengesterich**	See Henstridge
Henstridge, K. 7	*Hengesterich* 91b (*286b) *Hesterige* 87 (*107)
(*Heorleia*)	See Warleigh
Herdeneberie	See Honibere
Herfeld (*-felt*)	See Heathfield
Herlei	See Warleigh
(*Hernola*)	See Knowle
*Herpetreu**	See West Harptree

*Hesterige**	See Henstridge
Hetsecome (*-coma*)	See Hiscombe
*Hewis**	See Huish (in Nettlecombe)
Highbridge	Not in D.B.
High Ham, H. 6	*Hame* 90 (*Hama* 165)
High Littleton, K. 3	*Liteltone* 89 (*-tona* 151b)
Hill, E. 5	*Hille* 93b (*Hilla* 428, 510b)
Hilla	See Hillfarrance
Hille (*Hilla*)	See Hill, Hillfarrance
Hillfarrance, E. 7	*Hilla*, *Hille* 87b, *bis* 97b (*Billa* 174, *Hilla* 174, 374b)
(*Hiltona*)	See Ilton
Hinton Blewitt, J. 3	*Hantone* 96b (*-tona* 438b)
Hinton Charterhouse, L. 3	*Hantone* 98 (*-tona* 437)
Hinton St George, H. 8	*Hantone* 96b (*-tona* 438)
Hiscombe, I. 8	*Hasecumbe* 87b (*Hasce-*, *Hassecomba* 137, 510b)
	Hetsecome 91 (*-coma* 172b, 524b)
Hiwis	See Huish (in Burnham on Sea), Huish Champflower
(*Hiwis*)	See Huish (in Burnham on Sea)
(*Hiwys*)	See Huish Champflower
(*Hoctona*)	See Hutton
Holcombe (near Kilmersdon)	Not in D.B.
Holecumbe (*-cumba*), F. 6	Lost in Aisholt, 93b (424)
Holeford	See Holford, Riche's and Trebles; Holford St Mary
Holeforde (*-forda*, *-fort*)	See Holford, Riche's and Trebles
Holford, Riche's and Trebles, E. 6	*Holeford* 94 (*-fort* 433b)
	Holeforde 87b, 94 (*-forda* 174, 433b)
Holford St Mary, E. 5	*Holeford* 96 (*Hulofort* 362)
Holme (*Holma*)	See Hone
Holnicote, B. 4	*Hunecote* 94 (*Hunecota*, *Hunnecota* 431, 512)
Holton, K. 7	*Altone* 99 (*Haltona* 466)
Hone, C. 6	*Holme* 94 (*Holma* 431)
Honecote (*-cota*)	See Huntscott
Honibere, E. 5	*Herdeneberie* 98b (*Hederneberia* 478)
*Honspil**	See West Huntspill
Horblawetone (*-tona*)	See Hornblotton
Horcerlei (*Hordcerleia*)	See Orchardleigh
Hornblotton, J. 6	*Horblawetone* 90b (*-tona* 169b)
Horsey, G. 5	*Hursi* 95 (*353b)
Horsey Pignes, G. 5	*Pigens* 98b (*Peghenes* 477)
Horsington, K. 7	*Horstenetone* 96b (*Horsstenetona* 386)
Horstenetone (*Horsstenetona*)	See Horsington
Hotune (*-tuna*)	See Hutton
Houndstone, I. 8	*Hundestone* 93 (*-tona* 280b, 523b)
Huish (in Burnham on Sea), G. 4	*Hiwis* 95b *bis* (*355 *bis*)
Huish (in Nettlecombe), D. 5	*Hewis* 93b, 96b (*427b, 464)

Huish Champflower, D. 6	*Hiwis* 94b (*Hiwys* 442b)
Huish Episcopi	Not in D.B.
(*Hulofort*)	See Holford St Mary
Hundestone (*-tona*)	See Houndstone
Hunecote (*-cota*)	See Holnicote
*Hunespil**	See East Huntspill
Hunlavintone (*-tona*)	See Woolavington
(*Hunnecota*)	See Holnicote
Hunteworde (*-euorda*)	See Huntworth
Huntscott, C. 5	*Honecote* 91b (*-cota* 196b)
Huntstile, F. 6	*Hustille* 98b (*-illa* 479, 516)
Huntworth, G. 6	*Hunteworde* 97 (*-euorda* 371b)
*Hursi**	See Horsey
Hustille (*-illa*)	See Huntstile
Hutone (*-tona*)	See Hutton
Hutton, G. 3	*Hotune* 88 (*-tuna* 139b, *Hoctona* 516) *Hutone* 91 (*-tona* 172b, 524)
(*Iafort*)	See Ford
Iatune (*-tuna*)	See Yatton
Ichetoche (*-tocha*)	See Edstock
Idson, F. 5	*Edeuestone* 93b (*-tona* 425)
(*Ila*)	See Isle Abbots, Isle Brewers
Ilchester, I. 7	*Giuelcestre*, *Giuelecestre* 86b, 87, 91, 95 (*Giuel-*, *Giulecestra*, *Guielcestra*, *Guilecestra* 91b, 107b, 171b, 352b, 522) *Ecclesia S. Andreae* 91 *bis* (*171b, 197b, 522)
Ile	See Isle Abbots, Isle Brewers
Ileminstre (*-monstre*)	See Ilminster
(*Illebera*)	See Elborough
Illege (*-lega*)	See Eleigh
Ilminster, H. 8	*Ileminstre* 91 (*-monstre* 188)
Ilton, G. 8	*Atiltone* 91 (*-tona* 191, *Hiltona* 512)
Imele (*Imela*)	See Emble
(*Ingleliscuma*)	See English Combe
Isle (*Isla*)	See Isle Brewers
Isle Abbots, G. 7	*Ile* 91 *bis* (*Ila* 188, 188b, 512b *bis*)
Isle Brewers, H. 7	*Ile*, *Isle* 91b, 97 (*Ila*, *Isla* 266, 374)
Ivle (*Ivla*)	See Yeovil
(*Kaivert*)	See Keyford
(*Kari*)	See Cary Fitzpaine and Lyte's Cary
Keinton Mandeville, J. 6	*Chintone*, *-tune* 92b, 94 (*-tona*, *-tuna* 276b, 434b, *Chigtona* 519b)
Kelston	Not in D.B.
Kenn, H. 2	*Chen* 88 (*Chent* 143)
Kewstoke, G. 2	*Chiwestoch* 98 (*-stoc* 446)
Keyford, L. 4	*Caivel* 88b (*149) *Chaivert* 97b (*Kaivert* 384)
Keynsham, K. 2	*Cainesham* 87 (*-essam* 113b)
Kilmersdon, K. 4	*Chenemeresdone* 91b (*Chinemeresdone* 198b)
Kilton, E. 5	*Chilvetune* 96 (*-tun* 360b, *Diuetona* 511)
Kilve, E. 5	*Clive* 93b (*Cliva* 428, 510b)
(*Kingesberia*)	See Kingsbury Episcopi
Kingsbury Episcopi, H. 7	*Chingesberie* 89 (*Kingesberia* 156)

Kingsdon	Not in D.B.
Kingston (near Taunton)	Not in D.B.
Kingstone, H. 8	*Chingestone* 92 (*-stana* 266b)
Kingston Seymour, H. 2	*Chingestone* 89 *bis* (*-tona* 150b, 151, 522b)
Kingweston, I. 6	*Chinwardestune* 91b (*Kinuardestuna* 283)
(*Kinuardestuna*)	See Kingweston
Kittisford, D. 7	*Chedesford* 94b (*-forda* 443)
Knowle, C. 5	*Ernole* 96 (*Hernola* 360)
Knowlepark, K. 6	*Chenolle* 99 (*-nolla* 465b, 522b)
Knowle St Giles, G. 8	*Chenolle* 93b (*-nolla* 426b, 510 *bis*)
Laford	See Ford
*Lamieta** (*Lamigeta*)	See Lamyatt
*Lamore**	See Moortown
Lamyatt, K. 5	*Lamieta* 90b (*170, *Lamigeta* 519)
*Lancheris**	See Langridge
(*Langaham*)	See Langham
Langeford (*-fortda*)	See Langford Budville
Langeham	See Langham
Langeport	See Langport
Langford Budville, E. 7	*Langeford* 86b (*-fortda* 104)
Langham, C. 6	*Langeham* 95b (358, *Langaham* 511)
Langport, H. 7	*Langeport*, *Langporth*, *Lanport*, *Lanporth* 86, 86b 87, 92 (*Lanporda*, *-port*, *Lantporta* 89b, 105, 107b, 270b)

Langporth	See Langport
Langridge, L. 2	*Lancheris* 88b (*144)
*Lanport**, *-porth* (*-porda*, *Lantporta*)	See Langport
Lattiford, K. 6	*Lodreford* 90 (*-forda* 165b, *Lodereforda* 522)
Laverton, L. 4	*Lavretone* 96b (*-tona* 438b)
Lavretone (*-tona*)	See Laverton
Lecheswrde (*-surda*)	See Lexworthy
(*Ledforda*, *Letford*)	Unid. (79b, 509b), not in Exch. D.B.
Lediart	See Bishop's Lydeard
(*Lediart*)	See Lydeard St Lawrence
Leding (*Ledich*)	See Dyche
Lega	See Leigh (in Lydeard St Lawrence), Overleigh
(*Lega*)	See Abbot's Leigh, Leigh (in Lydeard St Lawrence), Leigh (in Milverton), Leigh (in Winsham), Lyng, Overleigh, Woodcocks Ley
Lege	See Abbot's Leigh, Leigh (in Milverton), Leigh (in Winsham), Lyng, Overleigh, Woodcocks Ley
Leigh (in Lydeard St Lawrence), E. 6	*Lega* 87b (*174, 175, 517)
Leigh (in Milverton), E. 7	*Lege* 96 (*Lega* 363)
Leigh (in Winsham), G. 9	*Lege* 95b (*Lega* 356b)
Leigh upon Mendip	Not in D.B.

(*Letford*)	See (*Ledforda*)
Lexworthy, F. 6	*Lecheswrde* 91b, 94 *bis* (*-surda* 282, 432, 432b)
Lideford	See East Lydford, West Lydford
(*Lideford*)	See West Lydford
(*Lideforda*)	See East Lydford
*Lidegar**	See Bishop's Lydeard
Lidiard (*Lidiarda*)	See Lydeard St Lawrence
(*Liediart*)	See Bishop's Lydeard
Lilebere	See Elborough
Lilstock, E. 5	*Lulestoch* 98b (*-stoc* 478b)
(*Limigtona*)	See Limington
Limington, I. 7	*Limingtone*, *Limintone* 91, 94 (*Limigtona*, *Limintona* 172b, 435, 524)
Limingtone, *Limintone* (*Limintona*)	See Limington
Lincume (*-cuma*)	See Lyncombe
Litelande	See Litnes Field
Liteltone (*-tona*)	See High Littleton, Littleton (in Compton Dundon), Stony Littleton
Litnes Field, H. 6	*Litelande* 89 (*Littelaneia* 156b)
(*Littelaneia*)	See Litnes Field
Littleton (in Compton Dundon), I. 6	*Liteltone* 94 (*-tona* 433b, 517b)
Litton, J. 3	*Litune* 89b (*-tuna* 160)
Litune (*-tuna*)	See Litton
Lochestone (*-tona*)	See Loxton
Lochetone	See Lufton
Lochintone (*-tona*)	See Luckington
Locking	Not in D.B.
Locumbe (*-cumba*)	See Luccombe
(*Locutona*)	See Lufton
Lodenwrde (*Lodenawirda*)	See Edingworth
(*Lodereforda*)	See Lattiford
Lodreford (*-forda*)	See Lattiford
Loligtone (*-tona*)	See Lullington
Lolochesberie (*-beria*)	See Luxborough
Long Ashton, I. 2	*Estune* 88b (*Esttuna* 143b)
Long Load	Not in D.B.
Long Sutton, I. 7	*Sutone*, *-tune* 91 *bis*, 94b 1st entry (*Sutona*, *-tuna*, *Suttona* 191, 191b, 435b, 515, 524b, 525)
Lopen, H. 8	*Lopen*, *Lopene*, *Loptone* 91b, 93b, 98b (*Lopen*, *Lopena* 266, 427, 490b)
*Lopen**, *Lopene* (*Lopena*)	See Lopen
Loptone	See Lopen
Lovington, J. 6	*Lovintune* 98 (*-tona* 453, 521)
Lovintune (*-tona*)	See Lovington
Loxton, H. 3	*Lochestone* 91b (*-tona* 282b)
Luccombe, B. 5	*Locumbe* 97, 98 (*-cumba* 380, 463)
Luckington, K. 4	*Lochintone* 97b (*-tona* 375)
Lufton, I. 8	*Lochetone* 93 (*Locutona* 280b)
Lulestoch (*-stoc*)	See Lilstock
Lullington, L. 4	*Loligtone* 88b (*-tona* 147b)
Luxborough, C. 5	*Lolochesberie* 96 *bis* (*-beria* 360b *bis*, 511)
Lyde, J. 8	*Eslide* 94b (*Eslida* 445, 523)
Lydeard St Lawrence, E. 6	*Lidiard* 87b, 96 (*Lediart*, *Lidiarda* 174, 175, 363b, 517)
Lympsham	Not in D.B.

Lyncombe, L. 2	*Lincume* 89b (*-cuma* 186)
Lyng, G. 6	*Lege* 91 (*Lega* 191b)
Lyte's Cary	See Cary Fitzpaine
(*Maertoc, -toca, -toch, -tocha*)	See Martock
Maidenbrook, F. 7	*Maidenobroche* 87b (*-broca* 174)
Maidenobroche (*-broca*)	See Maidenbrook
Malpertone (*Malperettona*)	See Maperton
*Malrige**	See Merridge
Maneheue (*-heua*)	See Minehead
Maneworde (*Maneurda*)	See Manworthy
Manworthy, D. 7	*Maneworde* 96 (*Maneurda* 362b)
Maperton, K. 7	*Malpertone* 97b (*Malperettona* 384)
Mark	Not in D.B.
Marksbury, K. 2	*Mercesberie* 90b (*-beria* 169b)
Marshmills, F. 5	*Mulselle* 97 (*-sella* 372b)
Marston Bigot, L. 4	*Mersitone* 94b (*-tona* 444b)
Marston Magna, J. 7	*Merstone* 93 *bis* (*-tona* 278b, 279, *Mersetona* 523 *bis*)
(*Martocha*)	See Martock
Martock, I. 7	*Mertoch* 87 (*Maertoch, -tocha, Mar-, Mertocha* 113, *Maertoc, -toca* 516b)
Meare, I. 5	*Mere* 90 (*Mera* 172)
Megele (*-ela*)	See Midgell
Melcombe, G. 6	*Melecome* 95, 98b (*-coma* 350b, 477b, 508b, 509)
Meleburne (*-borna, -burna*)	See Milborne Port
Melecome (*-coma*)	See Melcombe
Mells, K. 4	*Mulle* 90b (*Mulla* 168, 520)
(*Melvertona*)	See Milverton
Mene (*Mena*)	See East Myne
(*Mera*)	See Meare
Mercesberie (*-beria*)	See Marksbury
Mere	See Meare
*Meriet**	See Merriott
Merridge, F. 6	*Malrige* 97b (*374b)
Merriott, H. 8	*Meriet* 92, 98b (*271b, 491b, 514b)
(*Mersetona*)	See Marston Magna
Mersitone (*-tona*)	See Marston Bigot
Merstone (*-tona*)	See Marston Magna
Mertoch (*-tocha*)	See Martock
Michelenie (*-neia*)	See Muchelney
Michaeliscerce (*Michelescerca*)	See St Michael Church
(*Middeltona*)	See Milton Podimore
Middeltone	See Milton (in Weston super Mare)
Midelenie (*-neia*)	See Midelney
Midelney, H. 7	*Midelenie* 91 (*-neia* 189)
(*Mideltona*)	See Milton (in Weston super Mare)
Mideltone	See Milton (in Weston super Mare), Milton Podimore
Mideltune (*-tuna*)	See Milton Clevedon
Midgell, I. 2	*Megele* 89 (*-ela* 151b)
Midsomer Norton	Not in D.B.
Milborne Port, K. 7	*Meleburne* 86b, 87, 91, 93 (*-borna, -burna* 91b *bis*, 107b, 193b, 278b *bis*) *Mileburne* 86b (*-borna* 91) *Meleburne* 77, Do.

(*Mildeltuna*)	See Milton (in Weston super Mare)
Mildetune (*-tuna*)	See Milton (in Skilgate)
Mileburne (*-borna*)	See Milborne Port
Millescote (*-cota*), K. 4	Lost in Mells, 88b (147b, 519b)
Milton (in Skilgate), C. 6	*Mildetune* 94b (*-tuna* 442)
Milton (in Weston super Mare), G. 2	*Middeltone* 95 (*Mildeltuna* 350b) *Mideltone* 98b (*-tona* 479)
Milton Clevedon, K. 5	*Mideltune* 98 (*-tuna* 450)
Milton Podimore, I. 7	*Mideltone* 90 (*Middeltona* 161b)
Milverton, E. 7	*Milvertone*, *-tune* 86b, 87, 89b, 91b, 94 (*-tona*, *-tuna* 103, 113, 160, 197, *Melvertona* 433)
Milvertone, *-tune* (*-tona*, *-tuna*)	See Milverton
Minehead, C. 4	*Maneheue* 95b (*-heua* 358)
Misterton	Not in D.B.
(*Modiforda*)	See Mudford
Monechetone	See West Monkton
Monksilver, D. 5	*Selve*, *-vere*, *-vre* 86b, 93b *bis*, 97 (*Selva*, *-vera*, *-vra* 89b, 373, 427 *bis*, 509b)
Monkton Combe, L. 3	*Cume* 89b (*Cuma* 185b)
Montacute, I. 8	*Montagud* 93 (*-gut* 280b)
Montagud (*-gut*)	See Montacute
Moorlinch	Not in D.B.
Moortown, H. 7	*Lamore* 94 (*429b)
(*Morchetona*)	See West Monkton
Moreton, J. 3	*Mortone* 98 (*Morthona* 453b, 521b)
Mortone (*Morthona*)	See Moreton
Muchelney, H. 7	*Michelenie* 91 (*-neia* 189)
Mudford, J. 7	*Mudiford* 98 (*454, *-forda* 522b) *Mundiford* 87, 93 (*Modiforda*, *Mundiforda* 116, 280)
*Mudiford** (*Mudiforda*)	See Mudford
Mulle (*Mulla*)	See Mells
Mulselle (*-sella*)	See Marshmills
Mundiford (*-forda*)	See Mudford
Nailsea	Not in D.B.
Nempnett Thrubwell	Not in D.B.
Netecumbe (*-coba*, *-comba*)	See Nettlecombe
Netelcumbe (*-comba*)	See Nettlecombe
Nether Stowey and Dodington, E. 5, F. 5	*Stalwei* 97 *bis* (*Estalweia* 373 *bis*, 510) *Stawe* 99 (*491)
Nettlecombe, D. 5	*Netecumbe* 87b (*-coba* 139, *-comba* 510b) *Netelcumbe* 86b (*-comba* 104)
Neuhalle	See Newhall
Newentone (*-tona*, *-tuna*)	See Newton (in North Petherton)
(*Newetona*)	See Newton St Loe
Newetone, *-tune*	See Newton (in North Petherton)
Newhall, E. 5	*Neuhalle* 96b (*Newiahalla* 464)
(*Newiahalla*)	See Newhall
Newton (in Bicknoller), E. 5	*Niwetune* 96 (*Niuetuna* 361)
Newton (in North Petherton), G. 6	*Newentone* 91b (*-tona* 282) *Newetone*, *-tune* 94b, 98b *bis* (*Newentona*,

Newton (in North Petherton) cont.	*Newentuna* 441, 447, 477b) *Niwetone* 93 (*-tona* 422)
Newton St Loe, K. 2	*Niwetone* 89 (*Newe-*, *Niwetona* 149, 521b)
Nichehede (*Nichebede*)	See Nynehead
(*Niuetuna*)	See Newton (in Bicknoller)
Niwetone (*-tona*)	See Newton (in North Petherton), Newton St Loe
Niwetune	See Newton (in Bicknoller)
Noiun (*Nonin*)	See Nunney
Nortcuri (*Nordchori*, *Nortchori*)	See North Curry
Nordperet, *-pereth*	See North Petherton
North Barrow	See Barrow, North and South
North Bradon, H. 7	*Bredde*, *Brede* 92 *bis* (*Breda*, *Bretda* 268b, 269b, 513, 514)
North Brewham	See Brewham
North Cadbury, J. 6	*Cadeberie* 97b (*-beria* 383, 520b)
North Cheriton	See Cheriton
North Curry, G. 7	*Nortcuri* 86b (*Nordchori*, *Nortchori* 105, 515b)
North Perrott, I. 9	*Peret* 92b (*Peredt* 274)
North Petherton, G. 6	*Nordperet*, *-pereth* 86, 86b (*Nortperret*, *-petreta* 89, 104) *Nortperet* 86 (*Peret* 88b) *Peret* 97 *bis* (*Pedret*, *Petret* 371b *bis*, 508b *bis*) *Peretune* 91b (*-tuna* 196)
North Stoke	Not in D.B.
North Widcombe	Not in D.B.
North Wootton, J. 5	*Utone* 90b (*Utona* 166b)
Nortone (*-tona*)	See Norton Fitzwarren, Norton Hawkfield and Malreward, Norton sub Hamdon
Norton Fitzwarren, F. 7	*Nortone* 87b, 92b (*-tona* 174, 273b)
Norton Hawkfield and Malreward, J. 2	*Nortone* 88 (*-tona* 140b)
Norton St Philip, L. 3	*Nortune* 98 (*-tuna* 437)
Norton sub Hamdon, I. 8	*Nortone* 92b (*-tona* 275)
Nortperet (*-perret*, *-petreta*)	See North Petherton
Nortune (*-tuna*)	See Norton St Philip
Nunney, L. 4	*Noiun* 96b (*Nonin* 364)
Nyland	Not in D.B.
Nynehead, E. 7	*Nichehede* 87b (*Nichebede* 174)
Oake, E. 7	*Acha*, *Ache* 87b, 94 (*Acca*, *Acha* 174, 433)
Oakley, I. 7	Unnamed, 3 hides added to Martock 87 (*Accheleia* 113, 516b) *Achelai* 97b (*374b, *Achelaia* 517)
Oaktrow, C. 5	*Wochetreu* 96 (*359b)
Oare, A. 4	*Are* 96b (*Ar* 344, 509b)
(*Oda*)	See Woodadvent
Odcombe, I. 8	*Udecome* 92b (*Odecoma* 274)
(*Odecoma*)	See Odcombe
Old Cleeve, D. 5	*Clive* 86b (*Cliva* 103b)

Old Stowey, C. 5	*Staweit* 96 (*Estaweit* 359b)
Opecedre (*-cedra*)	See Upper Cheddon
Opetone (*-tona*)	See Upton Noble
Opopille (*-illa*)	See Uphill
(*Orcerdleia*)	See Orchardleigh
Orchardleigh, L. 4	*Horcerlei* 88b (*Hordcerleia* 146b, *Orcerleia* 520b)
Orchard Portman	Not in D.B.
(*Oterammatona*)	See Otterhampton
Othery	Not in D.B.
Otone	See Wootton Courtenay
Otramestone (*-tona*)	See Otterhampton
Otremetone (*Otrammetona*)	See Otterhampton
Otterford	Not in D.B.
Otterhampton, F. 5	*Otramestone* 93 (*-tona* 424) *Otremetone* 97, 99 (*Otrammetona* 372b, 493b, *Oterammatona* 524b)
(*Ottona*)	See Wootton Courtenay
Overleigh, I. 6	*Lega* 90 (*164b)
Over Stratton, H. 8	*Stratone* 86 (*-tona* 88b, 508b)
(*Padenaberia*)	See Panborough
Panborough, I. 4	*Wadeneberie* 90 (*Padenaberia* 172)
Panteshede (*-heda*), H. 3	Lost in Banwell, 94 (433)
Pardlestone, E. 5	*Plestone* 93b (*-tona* 428, 510b)
Pauelet (*Paulet*)	See Pawlett
Paulton	Not in D.B.
Pawlett, G. 5	*Pauelet* 95 (*Paulet* 353b)
Pedewelle (*-willa*)	See Pedwell
(*Pedret*)	See North Petherton
(*Pedri*)	See Perry
Pedwell, H. 5	*Pedewelle* 90 (*-willa* 164)

Pegens (*Peghenes*)	See Horsey Pignes
Pendomer, I. 8	*Penne* 92b (*Penna* 275)
(*Penna*)	See Pendomer, Penselwood
Pennard, East and West, J. 5	*Pennarminstre* 90b (*-ministra* 166b)
Pennarminstre (*-ministra*)	See Pennard
Penne	See Pendomer, Penselwood
Penselwood, L. 6	*Penne* 94b (*Penna* 445)
(*Peredt*)	See North Perrott
Peret	See North Perrott, North Petherton
(*Peret*)	See North Petherton
Peretune (*-tuna*)	See North Petherton
*Peri**	See Perry
Peritone (*-tona*)	See Puriton
*Perredeham**	See Petherham
Perry, G. 5	*Peri* 93 *bis*, 94b, 98b (*421, 422, 422b, 477, 509, *Pedri* 509)
Petenie (*-neia*)	See Pitney
Petherham, F. 5	*Perredeham* 93b (*424b)
(*Petret*)	See North Petherton
Picote (*-cota*, *Piccota*)	See Pitcott
Pidecome (*-coma*)	See Pitcombe
Pightley, F. 6	*Puchelege* 93 (*-lega* 423b)
Pille (*Pilla*)	See Pylle
Pilloch (*Pilloc*)	See Pillock's Orchard
Pillock's Orchard, F. 5	*Pilloch* 93b (*Pilloc* 425)
Pilton, J. 5	*Piltone* 90, 90b (*-tona* 165b, 166b)
Piltone (*-tona*)	See Pilton
Pipeminstre (*Pinpeministra*)	See Pitminster
(*Pirtochesworda*)	Unid., (79b), not in Exch. D.B.

Pitcombe, K. 6	*Pidecome* 97b (*-coma* 382b)
Pitcott, K. 4	*Picote* 88b, 98b (*-cota*, *Piccota* 146, 480, 519)
Pitminster, F. 7	*Pipeminstre* 87b (*Pinpeminstra* 173b)
Pitney, H. 6	*Petenie* 87 (*-neia* 116)
Pixton, C. 7	*Potesdone* 93b (*-dona* 429)
Plainsfield, F. 5	*Planesfelle* 97 (*-fella* 372b)
Planesfelle (*-fella*)	See Plainsfield
Plestone (*-tona*)	See Pardlestone
Pochintune (*Pochingtona*, *Pokintuna*)	See Puckington
Poleshill, D. 7	*Pouselle* 96 (*-ella* 363, 511b)
Ponditone (*-tona*)	See Poyntington, Do.
Porberie (*-beria*)	See Portbury
Porlock, B. 4	*Portloc* 93 (*315)
Portbury, I. 1	*Porberie* 88b (*-beria* 143b)
Porteshe (*-heue*)	See Portishead
Portishead, I. 1	*Porteshe* 88 (*-heue* 142)
*Portloc**	See Porlock
Potesdone (*-dona*)	See Pixton
Pouselle (*-ella*)	See Poleshill
Prestetone (*-tona*)	See Preston Bermondsey, Preston Bowyer
Prestetune, *Prestitone*	See Preston Bowyer
Preston Bermondsey, I. 8	*Prestetone* 99 (*-tona* 467)
Preston Bowyer, E. 7	*Prestetone*, *-tune*, *Prestitone* 86b, 92, 97 (*Prestetona* 103, 272, 374, 510b, 515)
Priddy	Not in D.B.
Prisctone (*-tona*)	See Priston
Priston, K. 3	*Prisctone* 89b (*-tona* 185)
Publow	Not in D.B.
Puchelege (*-lega*)	See Pightley
Puckington, H. 8	*Pochintune* 93b *bis* (*Pokintuna* 429b *bis*, *Pochingtona* 512)
Puriton, G. 5	*Peritone* 91 (*-tona* 197b)
Puxton	Not in D.B.
Pylle, J. 5	*Pille* 90b (*Pilla* 166b)
Quantock, F. 6	*Cantoche* 97b (*-toca* 374b)
Quantoxhead, East and West, E. 5	*Cantocheheve*, *-tocheve* 96, 96b (*Cantocheheva* 360b, 463b)
Quarme, C. 6	*Carme* 98 (*Carma* 473b) *Coarme* 95b (*Coarma* 358b)
Queen Camel, J. 7	*Camel* 87 (*106b)
Queen Charlton	Not in D.B.
Rachedeworde (*-worda*)	See Rexworthy
Raddington, D. 7	*Radingetune* 94b (*-tuna* 94b, *Radinghetona* 510b)
Radeflot, *-flote* (*-flota*)	See Radlet
*Radehewis**	See Rodhuish
Radingetune (*-tuna*, *Radinghetona*)	See Raddington
Radlet, F. 5	*Radeflot* 97 (*Ratdeflot* 372b) *Radeflote* 93b (*-flota* 425b)
Radstock, K. 3	*Stoche* 88b (*Estoca* 146b, 519)
*Ragiol**	See Ridgehill
Rapps, G. 8	*Epse* 97 (*Eppsa* 464)
(*Ratdeflot*)	See Radlet
Reddene (*-dena*)	See Rodden

(*Redlisc*)	See Redlynch
Redlynch, K. 6	Unnamed, 9 acres taken away from Bruton 86b (*Retlis* 91, *Redlisc* 520) *Roliz* 92b (*Reliz* 276)
(*Reliz*, *Retlis*)	See Redlynch
Rexworthy, F. 6	*Rachedeworde* 93 (-*worda* 423)
Ridgehill, I. 2	*Ragiol* 91b, 98 (*198, 452b *bis*, 519)
Rime (*Rima*)	Unid., 93 (423)
Rimpton, J. 7	*Rintone* 87b (-*tona* 173b)
Rintone (-*tona*)	See Rimpton
(*Roda*)	See Rode
Rodden, L. 4	*Reddene* 98 (-*dena* 448b)
Rode	See Rode
Rode, L. 3	*Rode* 88b, 99 (*Roda* 148, 466b, 521b)
Rodhuish, D. 5	*Radehewis* 97 (*373b)
Rodney Stoke, I. 4	*Stoches* 87b (*Stocca* 137)
Roliz	See Redlynch
Rowberrow	Not in D.B.
Ruishton	Not in D.B.
Runetone (-*tona*)	See Runnington
Runnington, E. 7	*Runetone* 96 (-*tona* 363, 511b)
St Michael Church, G. 6	*Michaeliscerce* 98b (*Michelescerca* 477b)
Saltford, K. 2	*Sanford* 88 (-*fort* 142)
Sampford Arundel, E. 7	*Sanford* 94 (-*forda* 431b)
Sampford Brett, D. 5	*Sanford* 91b (-*forda* 286b)
Sandford, F. 5	*Sanford* 94b (*Santfort* 441)
Sanford	See Saltford, Sampford Arundel, Sampford Brett, Sandford. See also Sandford Orcas, Do.
(*Sanforda*)	See Sampford Arundel, Sampford Brett. See also Sandford Orcas, Do.
(*Sanfort*)	See Saltford
(*Santfort*)	See Sandford
Sapeswich (*Sapaeswica*)	See Shapwick
Scepeworde (*Shepbwurda*)	Unid., 99 (493)
(*Sceptona*)	See Shepton Beauchamp
Sceptone	See Shepton Beauchamp, Shepton Montague
Scheligate (*Schiligata*)	See Skilgate
Scobindare (*Scobinalre*)	See Shopnoller
Seavington (in Stogursey), F. 5	*Sedtametone* 95b (*Sedtammetona* 356b, *Setametona* 509)
Seavington Abbots, St Mary, St Michael, H. 8	*Seovenamentone* 91 (-*metona* 191) *Sevenehantune* 91b (-*hamtuna* 256b, *Seovenhamtona* 512b) *Sevenemetone* 98b (*Sevenametona* 490b)
Sedtametone (*Sedtammetona*)	See Seavington (in Storgursey)
Seleurde (-*urda*)	See Selworthy
Selve, -*vere*, -*vre* (*Selva*, -*vera*, -*vra*)	See Monksilver
Selworthy, C. 4	*Seleurde* 97 (-*urda* 463)

Seovenamentone (*Seovenametona*, *Seovenhamtona*)	See Seavington Abbots, etc.
Sepetone (*-tona*)	See Shepton Mallet
(*Septona*)	See Shepton Montague
Seveberge (*-berga*)	See Seaborough, Do.
Sevenehantune (*-hamtuna*)	See Seavington Abbots, etc.
Sevenemetone (*Sevenametona*)	See Seavington Abbots, etc.
(*Sewebeorga*)	See Seaborough, Do.
Sewelle (*-ella*)	See Swell
(*Sewoberga*)	See Seaborough, Do.
Shapwick, H. 5	*Sapeswich* 90 (*Sapaeswica* 161b)
Sharpham	Not in D.B.
Shearston, G. 6	*Siredestone* 93 (*-tona* 422b)
(*Shepbwurda*)	See *Scepeworde*
Shepton Beauchamp, H. 8	*Sceptone* 91b (*-tona* 266)
Shepton Mallet, J. 5	*Sepetone* 90 (*-tona* 166)
Shepton Montague, K. 6	*Sceptone* 92b (*Sheptuna* 276, *Septona* 519b)
(*Sheptuna*)	See Shepton Montague
Shipham, H. 3	*Sipeham* 94 (*433)
Shopnoller, E. 6	*Scobindare* 87b (*Scobinalre* 174)
Shovel, G. 6	*Siwoldestone* 98b (*-tona* 477b, 509)
Shurton	See Stockland Bristol
*Sideham**	See Sydenham
Sindercome (*-coma*)	See Combe (in Bruton)
*Sipeham**	See Shipham
Siredestone (*-tona*)	See Shearston
Siwoldestone (*-tona*)	See Shovel
Skilgate, C. 7	*Scheligate* 94b (*Schiligata* 442)
(*Soca*)	See Sock Malherbie

(*Socca*)	See Sock Dennis
Soche	See Sock Dennis, Sock Malherbie
Sock Dennis, I. 7	*Soche* 93 (*Socca* 281, 523b)
Sock Malherbie, J. 7	*Soche* 94b (*Soca* 435)
Somerton, I. 6	*Sumer-*, *Summertone* 86 *bis*, 98b (*Sumertona* 89b, 90, 479, 515b *bis*, 516)
Sordemaneford (*-manneford*)	See Stelford
South Barrow	See Barrow, North and South
South Bradon, H. 7	*Bredene* 92 (*269b, *-dena* 514)
South Brewham	See Brewham
South Cadbury, J. 7	*Sudcadeberie* 97b (*Sutcadaberia*, *-deberia* 383b, 521)
South Cheriton	See Cheriton
South Petherton, H. 8	*Sudperet* 86 *bis*, 91b (*Sutpedret*, *-perret*, *-petret* 88b, 89, 265, 265b, 508b *bis*, 512b) *Sudperetone* 91b (*Sutperettona* 196b)
South Stoke	Not in D.B.
*Sowi**	See Westonzoyland
Spachestone	See Spaxton
(*Sparkeforda*)	See Sparkford
Sparkford, J. 7	*Spercheforde* 95 (*Sparkeforda* 352b)
Spaxton, F. 5	*Spachestone* 97 (*Espachestona* 372)
Spercheforde	See Sparkford
Stalrewiche	See Standerwick
Stalwei	See Nether Stowey
(*Stana*)	See Stone (in Mudford)

Standerwick, L. 4	*Stalrewiche* 94 (*Estalrewicca* 434)
Stane	See Stone (in East Pennard), Stone (in Mudford)
(*Stane*)	See Stone (in East Pennard)
(*Stantona*)	See Stanton Prior
Stanton Drew, J. 2	*Stantone* 87 (*Estantona* 113b)
Stantone	See Stanton Drew, Stanton Prior
Stanton Prior, K. 2	*Stantone* 89b (*-tona* 185)
(*Stantuna*)	See Whitestaunton
Stantune	See Staunton, Whitestaunton
Stanwelle	See Stowell
Staple	See Staple Fitzpaine
Staple Fitzpaine, F. 8	*Staple* 92 (*Estapla* 270, 514)
Staplegrove	Not in D.B.
Staunton, C. 5	*Stantune* 95b (*Estantona*, *-tuna* 359, 511)
*Stawe**	See Nether Stowey
Stawei	See Stawley, Stowey (in Oare)
(*Staweia*)	See Stawley
Staweit	See Old Stowey
Stawell, H. 5	*Stawelle* 90 (*Estawella* 163)
Stawelle	See Stawell
Stawley, D. 7	*Stawei* 97 (*-weia* 373b)
Steart, J. 6	*Esturt* 92 (*272b)
Stelford, E. 5	*Sordemaneford* 96 (*-manneford* 362b)
Steyning	See Stockland Bristol
Stoca	See Stoke sub Hamdon
(*Stoca*)	See Stoke St Mary, Stoke sub Hamdon, Stoke Trister, Stoke Villice and Chew Stoke
(*Stocca*)	See Rodney Stoke, Stoke Villice and Chew Stoke, Stoney Stoke
Stocha	See Stoke St Mary
Stoche	See Radstock, Stocklinch, Stogursey, Stoke Pero, Stoke St Mary, Stoke sub Hamdon, Stoke Trister Stoke Villice and Chew Stoke, Stoney Stoke
Stocheland, *-lande* (*-landa*)	See Stockland Bristol
Stoches	See Rodney Stoke
Stochet	See Stoke sub Hamdon
Stockland Bristol, Shurton and Steyning, F. 5	*Stocheland*, *-lande* 93b, 95b, 96b (*-landa* 462b, *Estochelanda* 356, 425, 509)
Stocklinch Ottersay and St Magdalen, H. 8	*Stoche* 96, 99 (*Estoca*, *Estochet* 363b, 491)
Stogumber, E. 5	*Warverdinestoch* 91 (*-stoc* 197)
Stogursey, F. 5	*Stoche* 96b (*Estocha* 369, 509)
Stoke Lane	Not in D.B.
Stoke Pero, B. 5	*Stoche* 94 (*Esthoca* 430b)
Stoke St Gregory	Not in D.B.
Stoke St Mary, F. 7	*Stocha*, *Stoche* 87b, 96 (*Estoca*, *Stoca* 174, 364)
Stoke sub Hamdon, I. 8	*Stoca* 91 (*172b, 524) *Stoche*, *Stochet* 92 *ter* (*Estocha*, *Estochet* 267, 267b *bis*, 513 *bis*)
Stoke Trister, L. 6	*Stoche* 92b (*Stoca* 277, 521)

Stoke Villice and Chew Stoke, J. 3	*Stoche* 97b *bis*, 99 (*Stocca* 452, 452b 492, *Stoca* 517b)
Stone (in East Pennard), J. 6	*Stane* 91 (*172b, 524)
Stone (in Exford), B. 5	*Estone* 94 (*Estana* 431b)
Stone (in Mudford), J. 7	*Stane* 98 (*Stana* 454, 522b)
Ston Easton, J. 3	*Estone* 89, 98, 98b (*Estona* 149b, 446, 480b, 522)
Stoney Stoke, K. 6	*Stoche* 92b (*Stocca* 276, *Estoca* 519b)
Stony Littleton, L. 3	*Liteltone* 89 (*-tona* 149)
Storpe	See Eastrip
Stowell, K. 7	*Stanwelle* 89 (*Estanwella* 152)
Stowey (near Bristol)	Not in D.B.
Stowey (in Oare), A. 4	*Stawei* 96b (*Estaweia* 344)
Stragelle	See Stretcholt
Strate	See Street (in Winsham)
Stratone (*-tona*)	See Over Stratton, Stratton on the Fosse
Stratton on the Fosse, K. 4	*Stratone*, *Stretone* 88b, 91 (*Stratona*, *Stretona* 145b, 173, 519, 524b)
Street (near Glastonbury)	Not in D.B.
Street (in Winsham), G. 9	*Strate* 95b (*Estrat* 357, *Estrart* 524b)
Strenegestone, *Strengestune* (*Strengestona*,*-tuna*)	See Stringston
Stretcholt, G. 5	*Stragelle* 95 *bis* (*Estragella* 350 *bis*)
Stretone (*-tona*)	See Stratton on the Fosse
Stringston, E. 5	*Strenegestone*, *Strengestune* 93b, 97 (*Strengestona*, *-tuna* 372, 426, 509)
Succedene (*-dena*)	See Cheddon Fitzpaine
Sudcadeberie	See South Cadbury
Sudperet, *-peretone*	See South Petherton
Sumer-, *Summertone* (*Sumertona*)	See Somerton
Suindune (*-duna*)	See Swang
(*Sutcadaberia*, *-deberia*)	See South Cadbury
(*Sutona*)	See Long Sutton, Sutton Bingham, Sutton Mallet
Sutone	See Long Sutton, Sutton Bingham, Sutton Mallet, Sutton Montis
(*Sutpedret*, *-perettona*, *-perret*)	See South Petherton
(*Suttona*)	See Long Sutton
Sutton Bingham, J. 8	*Sutone* 94b 2nd entry (*-tona* 444)
Sutton Mallet, H. 5	*Sutone* 90 (*-tona* 162)
Sutton Montis, J. 7	*Sutone* 92b (*-tuna* 276)
(*Sutuna*)	See Long Sutton, Sutton Montis
Sutune	See Long Sutton
Swainswick and Bathwick, L. 2	*Wiche* 88b *bis*, 99 (*Wica* 144b *bis*, 492b, 518b)
Swang, F. 5	*Suindune* 93b (*-duna* 425b)
Swell, H. 7	*Sewelle* 92 (*-ella* 268, 513)
Sydenham, G. 5	*Sideham* 94b (*443)
Tablesford (*-forda*)	See Tellisford
Tadwick, L. 2	*Tatewiche* 99 *bis* (*-wica* 461b, 465)
*Talanda**	See Tolland
Talham (*Talam*)	See Tolland
Tantone (*-tona*)	See Taunton

Tarnock, H. 4	*Ternoc* 95 *bis* (*351b *bis*)
Tatewiche (*-wica*)	See Tadwick
Taunton, F. 7	*Tantone* 87b, 92b (*-tona* 173b, 273, 516b, 517)
Tedintone (*-tona*)	See Tetton
(*Tegesberia*)	See Adsborough
Tellisford, L. 3	*Tablesford* 88b (*-forda* 148, 521)
Telwe (*Telma*)	See Great Elm
Temesbare (*-bara*)	See Timsbury
Temple Combe	See Combe, Abbas and Temple
*Ternoc**	See Tarnock
Tetesberge (*-berga*)	See Adsborough
Tetton, F. 6	*Tedintone* 91b (*-tona* 286b)
(*Themesbera*)	See Timsbury
Thorent, K. 7	*Tornie* 87b (*Turnie* 153b) (*Turnietta* 467, 523), not in Exch. D.B.
Thorne, I. 8	*Torne* 93 *bis* (*Torna* 279b *bis*, 523b)
Thorne St Margaret, E. 7	*Torne* 94 (*Torna* 432, *Tornet* 512)
Thorney, H. 7	*Torleie* 91 (*-leia* 189)
Thorn Falcon, G. 7	*Torne* 92 (*Torna* 271b)
Thurlbeare, F. 7	*Torlaberie* 92 (*-beria* 271b)
Thurloxton	Not in D.B.
*Ticheham** (*Ticaham*)	See Tickenham
Tickenham, H. 1	*Ticheham* 96b, 98 (*438b, 448b, *Ticaham* 518b)
Timberscombe, C. 5	*Timbrecumbe* 94b (*-racumba* 442b, 510)
Timbrecumbe (*-racumba*)	See Timberscombe
Timesberie (*-berua*)	See Timsbury
Timsbury, K. 3	*Temesbare* 88 (*-bara* 140b *bis*, *Themesbera* 518) *Timesberie* 99 (*-berua* 464b)
Tintehalle (*Tintehella*, *Tintenelle*)	See Tintinhull
Tintinhull, I. 7	*Tintehalle* 91b (*-ehella* 266b) *Tutenelle* 90b (*Tintenelle* 170, *Tuttehella* 512b)
Tocheswelle (*-willa*)	See Tuxwell
Tolland, E. 6	*Talanda* 87b (*174) *Talham* 94 (*Talam* 433)
Torlaberie (*-beria*)	See Thurlbeare
Torleie (*-leia*)	See Thorney
Torne (*Torna*)	See Thorne, Thorne St Margaret, Thorn Falcon
Tornecome (*-coma*)	See Thorncombe (near Seaborough), Do.
(*Tornet*)	See Thorne St Margaret
Tornie	See Thorent
Torre (*Torra*)	See Dunster
Torweston, D. 5	*Turvestone* 96 (*-tona* 361b)
Traberge (*-berga*)	See Treborough
Treborough, D. 5	*Traberge* 97 (*-berga* 463b)
Trente (*Trenta*)	See Trent, Do.
Trull	Not in D.B.
*Tumbeli**	See Ubley
(*Turnie*, *Turnietta*)	See Thorent
Turvestone (*-tona*)	See Torweston
Tutenelle (*Tuttehella*)	See Tintinhull
Tuxwell, F. 5	*Tocheswelle* 94b, 99 (*-willa* 441b, 490b)
Twerton, K. 2	*Twertone* 88b *bis* (*-tona* 146, 146b)
Twertone (*-tona*)	See Twerton

Ubcedene (*-dena*)	See Upper Cheddon
Ubley, I. 3	*Tumbeli* 98 (*446)
Udeberge (*-berga*)	See Woodborough
(*Udecoma*)	See Cutcombe
Udecome	See Cutcombe, Odcombe
(*Ufetona*)	See *Wltune*
Ufetone (*-tona*, *-tuna*)	See Woolston (in North Cadbury)
(*Ulfertuna*)	See Woolston (in Bicknoller)
(*Ulfetona*, *Ulftona*)	See Woolston (in North Cadbury)
Ulmerestone (*-tona*)	See Woolmersdon
Ultone	See Woolston (in North Cadbury)
(*Ulvererona*)	See Waldron
Ulveronetone (*-tona*)	See Waldron
Ulvretune	See Woolston (in Bicknoller)
Ulwardestone	See Woolstone
Uphill, G. 3	*Opopille* 97b (*-illa* 452)
Upper Cheddon, F. 6	*Opecedre* 94b (*-cedra* 444) *Ubcedene* 87b (*-dena* 174)
Upton (near Dulverton)	Not in D.B.
Upton Noble, K. 5	*Opetone* 89 (*-tona* 151b)
Utone (*Utona*)	See North Wootton
Vexford, E. 6	*Fescheforde* 93b *bis* (*-forda* 427b *bis*)
Vndewiche (*Wdewica*), L. 3	Lost in Freshford, 89b (186b)
*Wacet**	See Watchet
Wadenaberie	See Panborough
Wadmendune (*-duna*)	See Wembdon
Waicome (*Waiecoma*)	See Weacombe
Waimora	See Wemberham
*Waistou**	See Westowe
Waldron, G. 5	*Ulveronetone* 93 (*-tona* 422, *Ulvererona* 509)

Walintone (*-tona*)	See Wellington
Wallepille (*-pilla*)	See Walpole
Walpole, G. 5	*Wallepille* 95 (*-pilla* 350)
Walton (near Glastonbury), I. 5	*Waltone* 90 *bis* (*-tona* 163b, 164b)
Walton (in Kilmersdon), K. 4	*Waltune* 98b (*-tuna* 480)
Waltone (*-tona*)	See Walton (near Glastonbury), Walton in Gordano
Walton in Gordano, H. 1	*Waltone* 96b (*-tona* 447b)
Waltune (*-tuna*)	See Walton (in Kilmersdon)
Wambrook	Not in D.B.
*Wandestreu**	See Wenstrow
Wanstrow, K. 5	*Wandestreu* 89b, 97b (*160, 384)
Warleigh, L. 2	*Herlei* 99 (*Heorleia* 465)
Warne (*Warna*)	See Wearne
Warverdinestoch (*-stoc*)	See Stogumber
Watchet, D. 5	*Wacet* 96 (*361b)
Watehelle (*-hella*)	See Wheathill
Watelege (*-lega*)	See Whatley (in Winsham)
Watelei (*-leia*)	See Whatley (near Frome)
Wayford	Not in D.B.
(*Wdewica*)	See *Vndewiche*
Weacombe, E. 5	*Waicome* 93b (*Waiecoma* 428b, 510b)
Weare, H. 4	*Werre* 95 (*Werra* 350b)
Wearne, H. 6	*Warne* 98b (*Warna* 479b)
Wedmore (*Wedmor*, *-mora*)	See Wedmore
Wedmore, H. 4	*Wedmore* 89b (*Wedmor*, *-mora* 159b, 515b) *Wetmore* 86 (*-mora* 90)
(*Weimorham*)	See Wemberham

(*Welesforda*)	See Wellisford
(*Weleuue*)	See Wellow
Welle (*Wella*)	See Wells
Welletone, *-tune*	See Williton
Wellington, E. 7	*Walintone* 89 (*-tona* 156b, *Wellintona* 513b)
(*Wellintona*)	See Wellington
Wellisford, E. 7	*Wilesforde* 98b (*Welesforda* 478b, 515b)
Wellow, L. 3	(*Weleuue* 63b, 64b), not in Exch. D.B.
Wells, J. 4	*Welle* 89 (*Wella* 157b, 524)
Wembdon, G. 5	*Wadmendune* 95 (*-duna* 353)
Wemberham, H. 2	*Waimora* 89b (*Weimorham* 159b, 518)
Wenfre (*-fro*, *-frod*)	See Winford
Weregrave (*-grava*)	See Weathergrove, Do.
Weritone (*-tona*)	See Wrington
Werocosale	See Wraxall
Werre (*Werra*)	See Weare
(*Werregrave*)	See Weathergrove, Do.
West Bagborough	See Bagborough
Westberie (*-beria*)	See Westbury
West Bower, F. 5	*Bur*, *Bure* 95, 98b (*Bur* 350b, 477b, 508b, 509)
West Bradley	Not in D.B.
West Buckland	Not in D.B.
Westbury, I. 4	*Westberie* 89b (*-beria* 158b)
West Camel, J. 7	*Camelle* 91 (*-ella* 189)
West Chinnock	See Chinnock
West Coker	See Coker
Westcombe, K. 5	*Westcumbe* 90b (*Westecomba* 168)
(*Westecomba*)	See Westcombe
West Cranmore	See Cranmore
Westcumbe	See Westcombe
West Dowlish	See Dowlish
West Harptree, J. 3	*Har-*, *Herpetreu* 89, 95b (*150, 354b)
West Hatch	Not in D.B.
West Huntspill, G. 4	*Honspil* 95 (*354)
West Lydford, J. 6	*Lideford* 99 (*493)
West Monkton, F. 6	*Monechetone* 90b (*Morchetona* 169)
Weston (near Bath), L. 2	*Westone* 89b, 98 (*-tona* 185b, 448b)
Weston Bampfylde, J. 7	*Westone* 92b, 97b *bis* (*-tona* 278, 383 *bis*, 520b)
Westone (*-tona*)	See Weston (near Bath), Weston Bampfylde, Weston in Gordano
Weston in Gordano, H. 1	*Westone* 88 *bis* (*-tona* 141b, 142b)
Weston Super Mare	Not in D.B.
Westonzoyland, G. 6	*Sowi* 90 (*162b)
*Westou**	See Westowe
Westowe, E. 6	*Waistou* 86b (*89b, 509b) *Westou* 93b (*428b)
West Pennard	See Pennard
West Quantoxhead	See Quantoxhead
Wetmore (*-mora*)	See Wedmore
Whatley (near Frome), L. 4	*Watelei* 90b (*-leia* 168b)
Whatley (in Winsham), H. 9	*Watelege* 96b (*-lega* 438)
Wheathill, J. 6	*Watehelle* 98 (*-hella* 453)
Whitchurch	Not in D.B.
Whitcomb, J. 7	*Witecumbe* 87 (*-cumba* 116)
Whitelackington, H. 8	*Wislagetone* 94b (*Wyslagentona* 443)
White Ox Mead, K. 3	*Witochesmede* 94 (*-meda* 434, *Wittocesmeda* 520)

Whitestaunton, G. 8	*Stantune* 91b (-*tuna* 265b)
Wiche (*Wica*)	See Swainswick
Wick (in Brent Knoll), G. 3	*Ecewiche* 95b (*Hecuiwicca* 354b)
Wick St Lawrence	Not in D.B.
Widicumbe (-*comba*)	See Withycombe
Widiete (-*ieta*)	See Withiel
Widepolle (-*polla*)	See Withypool
Wigborough, H. 8	*Wincheberie* 98b (*Winchinberia* 478)
Wilege	See Woolley
Wilesforde	See Wellisford
(*Wiletona*)	See Williton
*Willet**	See Willett
Willetone (-*tona*)	See Williton
Willett, E. 6	*Willet* 96 (*361b)
(*Willetuna*)	See Williton
Williton, D. 5	*Welletone*, -*tune*, *Willetone* 86b *quater*, 96 (*Wile-*, *Willetona* 89, 89b *bis*, 104, 361, 509b *ter*)
Wilmersham, B. 5	*Winemeresham* 88 (*139)
Wilmington, K. 2	*Wimedone* 89b (*Wimmadona* 185)
Wimedone (*Wimmadona*)	See Wilmington
Wincaletone (*Wincalletona*)	See Wincanton
Wincanton, K. 6	*Wincaletone* 95 (*Wincalletona* 352, 520b)
Wincheberie (*Winchinberia*)	See Wigborough
*Winemeresham**	See Wilmersham
Winescome (-*coma*)	See Winscombe
(*Winescuma*)	See Winscombe, Winsford
Winesford (-*forda*)	See Winsford
*Winesham**	See Winsham
Winford, I. 2	*Wenfre* 88b (-*fro*, -*frod* 145, 518b)
Winscombe, H. 3	*Winesome* 90 (-*coma*, -*cuma* 161, 515b)
Winsford, B. 6	*Winesford* 86b, 98b (-*forda* 104b, 479, 513b, *Winescuma* 516)
Winsham, H. 9	*Winesham* 89b (*158b)
Winterhead, H. 3	*Wintreth* 88 (-*tret* 140)
Wintreth (-*tret*)	See Winterhead
Wislagetone	See Whitelackington
Witecumbe (-*cumba*)	See Whitcomb
*Witeham**	See Witham Friary
Witham Friary, L. 5	*Witeham* 94, 97b (*382b, 434b, 520b)
Withiel (in Cannington), F. 5	*Widiete* 93b (-*ieta* 426)
Withiel Florey	Not in D.B.
Withycombe, D. 5	*Widicumbe* 88 (-*comba* 139)
Withypool, B. 6	*Widepolle* 98b (-*polla* 479, 513b)
Witochesmede (-*meda*, *Wittocesmeda*)	See White Ox Mead
Wivelescome (-*coma*)	See Wiveliscombe
Wiveliscombe, D. 6	*Wivelescome* 89 (-*coma* 156b)
(*Wlega*, *Wllega*)	See Woolley
Wltune (*Wlftuna*, *Ufetona*)	Unid., 97b (382b, 520b)
(*Wlwardestona*)	See Woolstone
*Wochetreu**	See Oaktrow
Woodadvent, D. 5	(*Oda* 79b), not in Exch. D.B.
Woodborough, K. 3	*Udeberge* 98 (-*berga* 447)
Woodcocks Ley, B. 4	*Lege* 97 (*Lega* 373b, 510)
Woodspring, G. 2	*Worsprinc* 96b (-*princa* 369b, 516)
Wookey	Not in D.B.
Woolavington, G. 5	*Hunlavintone* 90 (-*tona* 162)

Woolley, L. 2	*Wilege* 88b (*Wlega*, *Wllega* 144b, 518b)
Woolmersdon, G. 6	*Ulmerestone* 97 (-*tona* 371b, 508b)
Woolston (in Bicknoller), E. 5	*Ulvretune* 96 (*Ulfertuna* 361)
Woolston (in North Cadbury), K. 6	*Ufetone* 92b (-*tona*, -*tuna* 275b, 519b)
	Ultone 97b (*Ulfetona*, *Ulftona* 383b, 521)
Woolstone, F. 5	*Ulwardestone* 93b (*Wlwardestona* 424)
Woolverton	Not in D.B.
Wootton Courtenay, C. 5	*Otone* 96b (*Ottona* 369)
Worle (*Worla*)	See Worle
Worle, G. 2	*Worle* 95 (*Worla* 350b)
Worde (*Worda*)	See Wreath
(*Worochesela*, *Worocosala*)	See Wraxall
Worsprinc (-*princa*)	See Woodspring
Wraxall, I. 1	*Werocasale* 88b (*Worocosala* 144b, *Worochesela* 518b)
Wreath, G. 9	*Worde* 93b (*Worda* 426b, 510)
Wrington, I. 2	*Weritone* 90b (-*tona* 169)
Writelinctone (-*tuna*)	See Writhlington
Writhlington, K. 3	*Writelinctone* 99 (-*tuna* 493)
(*Wyslagentona*)	See Whitelackington
Yarlington, K. 6	*Gerlintune* 92b (*Gerlincgetuna* 275b)
Yatton, H. 2	*Iatune* 89b (-*tuna* 159b, *Eatona* 518)
Yeovil, J. 8	*Givele* 93 (*Givela* 281, 523b)
	Ivle 96b (*Ivla* 439)
Yeovilton, J. 7	*Geveltone* 96b (-*tona* 438, *Giveltona* 516)

ANONYMOUS HOLDINGS

The following twelve entries involve anonymous holdings. The Exon D.B., however, enables us to assign three of the holdings to their respective localities. It is possible that some (or even all) of the others refer to holdings at places not named elsewhere in Domesday Book:

The king, 9 acres taken away from (*ablata*) Bruton, 86b. Exon D.B. shows this was at Redlynch (91, 520).

The king, 3 hides added to (*additae*) Martock, 87. Exon D.B. shows this was at Oakley (113, 516b).

Wife of Uluuard, one hide, 87. Exon D.B. shows this was at Burnett (114).

Hunfrid (from the king), half a hide combined with Pitney, 87. Exon D.B. describes this separately as *i mansio* (116).

Roger de Courseulles, 2 hides and 3 virgates *alibi*, combined with Charlton, 90b. Exon D.B. describes this separately as *i mansio* (167b).

Church of St Mary of Montebourg, 5 hides, 91 (198).

Edith the nun (from the king), 12 acres, 91b (196).

ANONYMOUS HOLDINGS (continued)

Geoffrey (from Roger de Courseulles), *terra Colgrini*, half a virgate, 93 (423b).
Anschitil (from Roger de Courseulles), *terra Alwini*, one virgate and one ferling, 93b (424b).
Herbert (from Roger de Courseulles), *terra Teodrici*, one virgate, 93b (425b).
Robert (from Roger de Courseulles), *terra Olta*, one virgate, 93b (426).
Robert son of Gerold, 10 hides, 97 (436b).

STAFFORDSHIRE—*STATFORDSCIRE*

Folios 246–250b

MAPS 44–45

Abbey Hulton, D. 4	*Heltone* 249
Abbot's Bromley, F. 6	*Brunlege* 247b
Abetone	See Apeton
Ache	See Oaken
Acle	See Oakley (in Croxall)
Aclei	See Oakley (in Mucklestone)
Acovre	See Okeover
Actone	See Acton Trussell
Acton Trussell, D. 7	*Actone* 247
Adbaston, B. 6	*Edboldestone* 247
Ænestanefelt	See Alstonfield
Agardsley, G. 6	*Edgareslege* 248b
Aldidelege	See Audley
Aldridge, F. 9	*Alrewic* 250
Alia Ernlege	See Lower Arley, Worcs.
Almentone	See Almington
Almington, B. 5	*Almentone* 248
Alrewas, G. 7	*Alrewas* 246
Alrewic	See Aldridge
Alstone, D. 7	*Aluerdestone* 248b *bis*
Alstonfield, G. 3	*Ænestanefelt* 248
Alton, F. 4	*Elvetone* 246b
Aluerdestone	See Alstone
Alvidelege	See Alveley, Salop.
Amblecote, D. 11	*Elmelecote* 249b
Anne	See Onn
Anslow	Not in D.B.
Apeton, C. 7	*Abetone* 248b
Armitage	Not in D.B.
Ashley, B. 5	*Esselie* 248
Aspley, C. 6	*Haspeleia* 247
Aston (in Seighford), D. 7	*Estone* 247
Aston (in Stone), D. 6	*Estone* 246b, 248b, 249
Audley, C. 4	*Aldidelege* 250b
Badehale	See Baden Hall
Baden Hall, C. 6	*Badehale* 247
Bagnall	Not in D.B.
Balterley, C. 4	*Baltredelege* 250b *bis*
Baltredelege	See Balterley
Barcardeslim	See Burslem
Barlaston, D. 5	*Bernulvestone* 249
Barra, *Barre*	See Great Barr
Barton (in Bradley), D. 7	*Bernertone* 248b
Barton under Needwood, G. 7	*Bertone* 246b
Basford, E. 4	*Bechesword* 248b
Baswich, E. 7	*Bercheswic* 247 *bis*
Bechesword	See Basford
Beddintone	See Pillaton
Bedehala	See Bednall
Bednall, E. 7	*Bedehala* 247
Beffcote, C. 7	*Beficote* 246

Beficote	See Beffcote
Beighterton, C. 8	*Bertone* 250b
Belintone	See Billington
Bercheswic	See Baswich
Bernertone	See Barton (in Bradley)
Bertone	See Barton under Needwood, Beighterton, Burton upon Trent
Bescot, E. 9	*Bresmundescote* 246
Betelege	See Betley
Betley, B. 4	*Betelege* 250b
Bickford, D. 8	*Bigeford* 250b
Biddulph, D. 3	*Bidolf* 246b
Bidolf	See Biddulph
Bigeford	See Bickford
Bilbrook, D. 9	*Bilrebroch* 247b
Billestune	See Bilston
Billington, D. 7	*Belintone* 248b
Bilrebroch	See Bilbrook
Bilston, E. 10	*Billestune* 246
Biscopesberie	See Bushbury
Bishop's Offley	See Offley
Bishton, E. 7	*Bispestone* 250b
Bispestone	See Bishton
Blidevelt	See Blithfield
Blithfield, F. 6	*Blidevelt* 248
Blocheswic	See Bloxwich
Blora	See Blore
Blore, G. 4	*Blora* 249
Bloxwich, E. 9	*Blocheswic* 246
Blymhill, C. 8	*Brumhelle* 249b
Bobbington, C. 10	*Bubintone* 249
Bradeleg	See Bradley (in Bilston)
Bradeley, D. 4	*Bradelie* 249
Bradelia	See Bradley (near Stafford)
Bradelie	See Bradeley, Bradley (near Stafford)
Bradley (in Bilston), E. 10	*Bradeleg* 250
Bradley (near Stafford), D. 7	*Bradelia, -lie* 246, 248b *ter*, 249b
Bradley in the Moors, F. 5	*Bretlei* 250b
Bradnop	Not in D.B.
Bramelie	See Gerrard's Bromley
Bramshall, F. 5	*Branselle* 249
Branselle	See Bramshall
Branston, H. 7	*Brantestone* 247b
Brantestone	See Branston
Brereton	Not in D.B.
Bresmundescote	See Bescot
Bretlei	See Bradley in the Moors
Breude	See Brewood
Brewood, D. 8	*Breude* 247
Bridgeford, D. 6	*Brigeford* 247
Brigeford	See Bridgeford
Brineton, C. 8	*Brunitone* 249b
Brockhurst, C. 8	*Ruscote* 249b
Brockton (in Eccleshall), C. 6	*Broctone* 247 2nd entry
Brocton (near Stafford), E. 7	*Broctone* 247 1st entry
Broctone	See Brockton (in Eccleshall), Brocton (near Stafford)
Bromelei	See King's Bromley
Brotone	See Brockton (in Sheriff Hales), Salop.
Brough Hall, C. 7	*Bughale* 248b
Broughton, C. 5	*Herebor gestone* 247
Brumhelle	See Blymhill
Brunitone	See Brineton
Brunlege	See Abbot's Bromley
Bubintone	See Bobbington
Buchenole	See Bucknall
Bucknall, D. 4	*Buchenole* 246b
Bughale	See Brough Hall
Burouestone, G. 9	Lost near Weeford, 247
Burslem, D. 4	*Barcardeslim* 249
Burton (in Castle Church), D. 7	*Burtone* 248b *bis* 2nd and 3rd entries
Burtone	See Burton (in Castle Church),

Burtone cont.	Burton upon Trent
Burton upon Trent, H. 7	*Bertone* 247b *Burtone* 248b 1st entry
Bushbury, D. 9	*Biscopesberie* 247b, 250 *bis*, Staffs.; 243, Warw.
Butterton	Not in D.B.
Caldone	See Cauldon
Calton	Not in D.B.
Calwich	Not in D.B.
Cannock, E. 8	*Chenet* 246b, 250b
Castle Church	Not in D.B.
Catspelle	See Chasepool
Cauldon, F. 4	*Caldone* 248b
Caverswall, E. 4	*Cavreswelle* 249
Cavreswelle	See Caverswall
Cawdry	Not in D.B.
Cebbesio	See Chebsey
Cedla	See Cheadle, Checkley
Celle	See Cheadle
Celtetone	See Cheddleton
Ceppecanole	See Chipnall, Salop.
Cerletone	See Chapel Chorlton
Certelie	See Chartley
Cerueledone	See Hill Chorlton
Ceruernest	See Charnes
Cesteforde	See Seighford
Ceteruille	See Chatcull
Chapel Chorlton, C. 5	*Cerletone* 247
Charnes, C. 5	*Ceruernest* 247
Chartley, E. 6	*Certelie* 246b
Chasepool, D. 10	*Catspelle* 249b
Chatcull, C. 5	*Ceteruille* 247
Cheadle, E. 4	*Cedla* 246b *Celle* 249
Chebsey, D. 6	*Cebbesio* 248b
Checkley, F. 5	*Cedla* 250b
Cheddleton, E. 3	*Celtetone* 248
Chell	Not in D.B.
Chenet	See Cannock
Chenevare	See Kinver
Chenistelei	See Knightley
Chenistetone	See Knighton (in Mucklestone)
Chenwardestone	See Kinvaston
Chesterton	Not in D.B.
Chillington, D. 8	*Cillentone* 243, Warw.
Chingeslei(a)	See Kingsley
Chnitestone	See Knighton (in Adbaston)
Chorley	Not in D.B.
Church Eaton, C. 7	*Eitone* 249b
Cippemore, C. 11	Lost in Kinver, 249b
Ciseworde	See Cheswardine, Salop.
Claitone	See Clayton
Claverlege	See Claverley, Salop.
Clayton, D. 4	*Claitone* 250b
Clifton Campville, H. 8	*Cliftone*, *Clistone* 246b, 250b *Cliftune* 272b, Derby.
Cliftone, *Clistone*	See Clifton Campville
Clotone	See Knutton
Cobintone	Unid., 248
Cocortone, *Cocretone*	See Crockington
Codeshale	See Codsall
Codeuualle	See Cotwalton
Codsall, D. 9	*Codeshale* 250b
Coldmeece	See Meece
Cold Norton	Not in D.B.
Coley, E. 7	*Scoteslei* 247
Colt, F. 7	Lost in Colton, 248
Colton, F. 7	*Coltone*, *-tune* 248 *bis*, 249
Coltone, *-tune*	See Colton
Colwick	Not in D.B.
Comegrave	See Congreve
Compton, D. 9	*Contone* 246
Congreve, D. 8	*Comegrave* 246
Consall, E. 4	*Cuneshala* 246b
Contone	See Compton
Cooksland, D. 6	*Cuchesland* 249

Copehale	See Coppenhall
Coppenhall, D. 7	*Copehale* 249b
Cota	See Cotes
Cote	See Coton (in Milwich), Coton (near Stafford), Coton Clanford, Trescott
Cotes, C. 5	*Cota* 247
Cotewoldestune	See Cotwalton
Coton (in Milwich), E. 6	*Cote* 246b
Coton (near Stafford), D. 6	*Cote* 248
Coton Clanford, D. 7	*Cote* 247
Cotton	Not in D.B.
Cotwalton, D. 5	*Codeuualle* 248 *Cotewoldestune* 246b
Cove	See Coven
Covelau	See Cowley
Coven, D. 8	*Cove* 249b
Cowley, C. 7	*Covelau* 246
Crachemers	See Crakemarsh
Crakemarsh, F. 5	*Crachemers* 246b
Cressvale	See Creswell
Creswell, D. 6	*Cressvale* 248
Crochesdene	See Croxden
Crochestone	See Croxton
Crockington, C. 10	*Cocortone*, *Cocretone* 246, 250
Crotewiche	See Gratwich
Croxall, G. 8	*Crocheshalle* 274, Derby.
Croxden, F. 5	*Crochesdene* 250b
Croxton, C. 6	*Crochestone* 247
Cuchesland	See Cooksland
Cuneshala	See Consall
Curborough	Not in D.B.
Darlaston, D. 5	*Derlavestone* 247b
Denestone	See Denstone
Denstone, F. 5	*Denestone* 246b
Derlavestone	See Darlaston
Derrington, D. 7	*Dodintone* 248
Dilhorne, E. 4	*Dulverne* 249
Dimsdale, C. 4	*Dulmesdene* 250b

Dochesig	See Doxey
Dodintone	See Derrington
Dorsley, C. 6	*Dorueslau* 247
Dorueslau	See Dorsley
Doxey, D. 7	*Dochesig* 247
Draicote	See Draycott in the Clay
Draiton	See Drayton (near Wroxton), Oxon.
Draitone	See Drayton (in Penkridge), Drayton Bassett
Draycott in the Clay, G. 6	*Draicote* 248b
Draycott in the Moors	Not in D.B.
Drayton (in Penkridge), D. 7	*Draitone* 246
Drayton Bassett, G. 9	*Draitone* 246b
Dregetone	See Drointon
Drointon, E. 6	*Dregetone* 247
Dulmesdene	See Dimsdale
Dulverne	See Dilhorne
Dunestone	See Dunston
Dunstall	Not in D.B.
Dunston, D. 7	*Dunestone* 246
Eccleshall, C. 6	*Echeselle* 247 *Ecleshelle* 247 *ter*
Echeselle, *Ecleshelle*	See Eccleshall
Edboldestone	See Adbaston
Edelachestone	See Ellastone
Edgareslege	See Agardsley
Edingale, H. 8	*Ednunghal(l)e* 274, 278, Derby.
Efnefeld	See Enville
Eitone	See Church Eaton
Elachestone	See Ellastone
Eleford	See Elford
Elford, G. 8	*Eleford* 246b
Elkstones	Not in D.B.
Ellastone, G. 4	*E(de)lachestone* 247, 249
Ellenhall, C. 6	*Linehalle* 247
Elmelecote	See Amblecote
Elmhurst	Not in D.B.
Elvetone	See Alton

Endon, D. 3	*Enedun* 246b
Enedun	See Endon
Enson, E. 6	*Hentone* 246b
Enville, C. 11	*Efnefeld* 249b
Erlide	See Yarlet
Ernlege	See Upper Arley, Worcs.
Ernlege, *Alia*	See Lower Arley, Worcs.
Eseningetone	See Essington
Esselie	See Ashley
Essington, E. 9	*Eseningetone* 250, Staffs.; 243, Warw.
Estendone	See Huntington
Estone	See Aston (in Seighford), Aston (in Stone)
Estretone	See Stretton (near Penkridge)
Etinghale	See Ettingshall
Etone	See Water Eaton
Ettingshall, D. 9	*Etinghale* 250
Farley, F. 4	*Fernelege* 246b
Fauld, G. 6	*Felede* 248b
Fawfieldhead	Not in D.B.
Featherstone, D. 9	*Ferdestan* 247b
Felede	See Fauld
Fenton, D. 4	*Fentone* 250b
Fentone	See Fenton
Ferdestan	See Featherstone
Fernelege	See Farley
Field	Not in D.B.
Fisherwick	Not in D.B.
Flashbrook, B. 6	*Fletesbroc* 247
Fletesbroc	See Flashbrook
Forsbrook, E. 5	*Fotesbroc* 246b
Forton	Not in D.B.
Fotesbroc	See Forsbrook
Fradswell, E. 6	*Frodeswelle* 247
Fraiforde	See Freeford
Freeford, G. 8	*Fraiforde* 247
Fricescote	See Syerscote
Frodeswelle	See Fradswell
Fuleford	See Fulford
Fulfen	Not in D.B.
Fulford, E 5	*Fuleford* 246b
Gailey, D. 8	*Gragelie* 249b
Gaitone	See Gayton
Gayton, E. 6	*Gaitone* 248
Geneshale	See Gnosall
Gerrard's Bromley, C. 5	*Bramelie* 247
Gestreon	See Ingestre
Gnosall, C. 7	*Geneshale* 247b
Goldenhill	Not in D.B.
Gragelie	See Gailey
Gratwich, F. 6	*Crotewiche* 249
Great Barr, F. 10	*Barra*, *Barre* 250 *bis*
Great Haywood	See Haywood
Great Saredon	See Saredon
Grendone	See Grindon
Grindon, F. 3	*Grendone* 248b
Guruelde	See Worfield, Salop.
Hadesacre	See Handsacre
Haiwoda, *-wode*	See Haywood
Halam, *Halas*	See Sheriff Hales, Salop.
Halstone	See Haughton
Haltone	See Haughton, Hilton (near Wednesfield)
Hammerwich, Nether and Over, F. 8	*Duae Humerwich* 247
Hamstall Ridware	See Ridware
Hanbury	Not in D.B.
Hancese	See Hanchurch
Hanchurch, C. 5	*Hancese* 250b
Handsacre, F. 7	*Hadesacre* 247
Hanford, D. 4	*Heneford* 250b
Hanley	Not in D.B.
Hantone	See Wolverhampton
Hargedone	See Hatherton
Harlaston, H. 8	*Horuluestone* 246b
Haselour	Not in D.B.
Haspeleia	See Aspley
Haswic, D. 10	Lost in Kingswinford, 247b
Hatherton, E. 8	*Hargedone* 247b
Hatton, C. 5	*Hetone* 246b

Haughton, D. 7	*Hal(s)tone* 248b, 249b
Haunton	Not in D.B.
Haywood, Great and Little, E. 7	*Haiwoda*, *-wode* 247 *quater*
Heathlee	Not in D.B.
Heaton	Not in D.B.
Heighley, C. 4	*Heolla* 246b
Helcote	See Hilcote
Helduluestone	See Hilderstone
Heltone	See Abbey Hulton
Heneford	See Hanford
Hentone	See Enson
Heolla	See Heighley
Hereborgestone	See Broughton
Hetone	See Hatton
High Offley	See Offley
High Onn	See Onn
Hilcote, C. 6	*Helcote* 246b
Hilderstone, E. 5	*Helduluestone* 249 *Hilduluestune* 246b
Hilduluestune	See Hilderstone
Hill Chorlton, C. 5	*Cerueledone* 247
Hilton (in Shenstone), F. 9	*Iltone* 247b
Hilton (near Wednesfield), E. 9	*Haltone* 247b
Himelei	See Himley
Himley, D. 10	*Himelei* 249b
Hintes	See Hints
Hints, G. 9	*Hintes* 247
Hixon, E. 6	*Hustedone* 247
Hocintune	See Ogley Hay
Hollinsclough	Not in D.B.
Honesworde	See Handsworth, Warw.
Hopton, E. 6	*Hotone* 248b
Hopwas, G. 9	*Opewas* 246b
Horeborne	See Harborne, Warw.
Horton (in Fisherwick), G. 8	*Hortone* 247
Horton (near Leek)	Not in D.B.
Hortone	See Horton (in Fisherwick)
Horuluestone	See Harlaston
Hotone	See Hopton
Humerwich, *Duae*	See Hammerwich
Huntington, E. 8	*Estendone* 250b
Hustedone	See Hixon
Ilam	Not in D.B.
Iltone	See Hilton (in Shenstone)
Ingestre, E. 6	*Gestreon* 249
Iocheslei	See Loxley
Ipstones	Not in D.B.
Keele	Not in D.B.
Kidsgrove	Not in D.B.
King's Bromley, G. 7	*Bromelei* 246
Kingsley, E. 4	*Chingeslei(a)* 250b *bis*
Kingston	Not in D.B.
Kingswinford, D. 10	*Suinesford* 246 *Suinesford(e)* 172b *ter*, Worcs.
Kinvaston, D. 8	*Chenwardestone* 247b
Kinver, C. 11	*Chenevare* 246b *Chenefare* 172b, Worcs.
Knightley, C. 7	*Chenistelei* 248
Knighton (in Adbaston), B. 6	*Chnitestone* 247
Knighton (in Mucklestone), B. 5	*Chenistetone* 250b
Knutton, C. 4	*Clotone* 250b
Lapley, D. 8	*Lepelie* 222b, N'hants.
Lec	See Leek
Lecefelle	See Lichfield
Leek, E. 3	*Lec* 246b
Lege	See Leigh
Leigh, E. 5	*Lege* 247b
Levedale, D. 7	*Levehale* 249b
Levehale	See Levedale
Levintone	See Loynton
Licefelle	See Lichfield
Lichfield, G. 8	*Lece-*, *Licefelle* 247 *bis*

Linehalle	See Ellenhall
Litelbech, G. 9	Lost near Weeford, 247
Little Haywood	See Haywood
Little Onn	See Onn
Little Sandon, D. 6	*Parva Sandone* 248b
Little Saredon	See Saredon
Little Stoke, D. 6	*Stoca* 248b
Littywood, D. 7	*Lutiude* 248b
Locheshale	See Yoxall
Longdon	Not in D.B.
Longenalre	See Longnor (in Lapley)
Longnor (in Lapley), D. 8	*Longenalre* 248b
Longnor (near Leek)	Not in D.B.
Longsdon	Not in D.B.
Longton	Not in D.B.
Lowe	Not in D.B.
Lower Penn	See Penn
Loxley, F. 6	*Locheslei* 248
Loynton, C. 6	*Levintone* 249b
Lufamesles	See Paynsley
Lutiude	See Littywood
Madeley (in Checkley), F. 5	*Madelie* 249 2nd entry
Madeley (near Stoke on Trent), C. 4	*Madelie* 249 1st entry
Madelie	See Madeley (in Checkley), Madeley (near Stoke on Trent)
Maer, C. 5	*Mere* 249
Marchington, G. 6	*Merchametone* 248b
Marston (in Church Eaton), C. 8	*Mersetone* 222b, N'hants.
Marston (near Stafford), D. 6	*Mer(se)tone* 248 *bis*
Mavesyn Ridware	See Ridware
Mayfield, G. 4	*Medevelde* 246b
Meaford, D. 5	*Mepford*, *Metford* 247b, 248
Medevelde	See Mayfield

Meece: Coldmeece and Millmeece, C. 5, C. 6	*Mess* 246b, 247
Melewich	See Milwich
Mepford	See Meaford
Merchametone	See Marchington
Mera	See Mere
Mere	See Maer
Mere, B. 7	*Mera* 246b
Mer(se)tone	See Marston (near Stafford)
Mess	See Meece
Metford	See Meaford
Millmeece	See Meece
Milton	Not in D.B.
Milwich, E. 6	*Melewich* 246b *Mulewiche* 249
Mitton, D. 7	*Mutone* 248b
Moclestone	See Mucklestone
Moddershall, D. 5	*Modredeshale* 248
Modredeshale	See Moddershall
Moleslei	See Moseley
Monetvile, D. 7	Lost in Castle Church, 249b
Moreton (in Colwick), E. 7	*Mortone* 247, 250b
Moreton (in Draycott in the Clay), G. 6	*Mortune* 248b
Moreton (in Gnosall), C. 7	*Mortone* 248
Morfe, C. 11	*Morve* 249b
Mortone	See Moreton (in Colwich), Moreton (in Gnosall)
Mortune	See Moreton (in Draycott in the Clay)
Morve	See Morfe
Moseley, D. 9	*Moleslei* 250
Mucklestone, B. 5	*Moclestone* 250b
Mulewiche	See Milwich
Musden, G. 3	*Musedene* 246b
Musedene	See Musden
Mutone	See Mitton
Nether Hammerwich	See Hammerwich
Newborough	Not in D.B.

Modern name	Domesday form
Newcastle under Lyme	Not in D.B.
Newton (in Blithfield), F. 6	*Niwetone* 250b
Newton (in Draycott in the Moors), E. 5	*Niwetone* 246b
Niwetone	See Newton (in Blithfield), Newton (in Draycott in the Moors)
Norbury, C. 7	*Northerie* 248
Nordlege	See Kingsnordley, Salop.
Normacot, D. 4	*Normanescote* 250b
Normanescote	See Normacot
Northerie	See Norbury
Norton Canes, E. 8	*Nortone* 247
Nortone	See Norton Canes, Norton in the Moors
Norton in the Moors, D. 4	*Nortone* 249
Oakamoor	Not in D.B.
Oaken, D. 9	*Ache* 249
Oakley (in Croxall), G. 8	*Acle* 249
Oakley (in Mucklestone), B. 5	*Aclei* 246b
Offeleia, *-lie*	See Offley
Offley, Bishop's and High, C. 6	*Offeleia*, *-lie* 247, 248b
Ogley Hay, F. 9	*Hocintune* 247b
Okeover, G. 4	*Acovre* 247b
Onecote	Not in D.B.
Onn, High and Little, C. 7	*Anne* 250b *Otne* 248
Opewas	See Hopwas
Orretone	See Otherton
Orton, D. 10	*Overtone* 249b
Otherton, D. 8	*Orretone* 249b
Otne	See Onn
Outwoods	Not in D.B.
Over Hammerwich	See Hammerwich
Overtone	See Orton
Oxelie	See Oxley
Oxley, D. 9	*Oxelie* 249b
Packington, G. 8	*Padin-*, *Pagintone* 247 *bis*
Padin-, *Pagintone*	See Packington
Pancriz	See Penkridge
Parva Sandone	See Little Sandon
Patingham	See Pattingham
Patshull, C. 9	*Pecleshella* 249
Pattingham, C. 9	*Patingham* 246b
Paynsley, E. 5	*Lufamesles* 246b
Pecleshella	See Patshull
Peleshale	See Pelsall
Pelsall, E. 9	*Peleshale* 247b
Pendeford, D. 9	*Pendeford* 250
Penkhull, D. 4	*Pinchetel* 246b
Penkridge, D. 8	*Pancriz* 246, 247b
Penn, Lower and Upper, D. 10	*Penna*, *Penne* 246, 249b *bis*
Penna, *Penne*	See Penn
Perton, D. 9	*Pertone* 247b
Pertone	See Perton
Pillaton, E. 8	*Beddintone* 247b
Pinchetel	See Penkhull
Pipe Ridware	See Ridware
Pirio	See Perry Barr, Warw.
Podemore	See Podmore
Podmore, C. 5	*Podemore* 247
Prestwood	Not in D.B.
Quarnford	Not in D.B.
Ramshorn	Not in D.B.
Ranton, D. 6	*Rantone* 249
Rantone	See Ranton
Redbaldestone	See Rodbaston
Ricardescote	See Rickerscote
Rickerscote, D. 7	*Ricardescote* 249b
Rid(e)ware, *Ridvare*	See Ridware
Ridware, Hamstall, Mavesyn and Pipe, F. 7	*Rid(e)ware* 247, 247b, 249b *Ridvare* 248 *bis*, 249b
Rigge	See Rudge, The
Rischale	See Rushall
Risctone	See Rushton (in Stoke on Trent)

Risetone	See Rushton (in Leek)
Rocester, F. 5	*Rowecestre* 246b *Rouecestre* 275 *bis*, Derby.
Rodbaston, D. 8	*Redbaldestone* 250b
Rolleston, H. 6	*Rolvestune* 248b
Rolvestune	See Rolleston
Rouueleia	See Rowley
Rowecestre	See Rocester
Rowley, G. 7	*Rouueleia* 247
Rownall, E. 4	*Rugehala* 246b
Rudge, The, B. 5	*Rigge* 248b
Rudierd	See Rudyard
Rudyard, E. 3	*Rudierd* 246b
Rugehala	See Rownall
Rugeley, F. 7	*Rugelie* 246b
Rugelie	See Rugeley
Ruscote	See Brockhurst
Rushall, F. 9	*Rischale* 250
Rushton (in Leek), D. 2	*Risetone* 246b
Rushton (in Stoke on Trent), D. 4	*Risctone* 249
Salt, E. 6	*Selte* 248b
Sandon, E. 6	*Scandone* 246
Sardone	See Saredon
Saredon, Great and Little, E. 8	*Sardone* 249b *Seresdone* 250b
Scandone	See Sandon
Scelfeld	See Shelfield
Scelfitone	See Shelton
Sceon	See Sheen
Sceotestan	See Shushions
Scoteslei	See Coley
Sedgley, D. 10	*Segleslei* 249b *bis*
Segleslei	See Sedgley
Seighford, D. 6	*Cesteforde* 247
Seisdon, C. 10	*Seisdone* 250
Seisdone	See Seisdon
Selchemore	See Silkmore
Selte	See Salt
Seneste	See Shenstone
Seresdone	See Saredon
Servesed	See Shareshill
Shareshill, E. 8	*Servesed* 249b
Sheen, F. 2	*Sceon* 246b
Shelfield, F. 9	*Scelfeld* 246

Shelton, C. 5	*Scelfitone* 246b
Shenstone, F. 9	*Seneste* 248b
Shushions, C. 8	*Sceotestan* 250b
Sibeford	See Sibford, Oxon.
Silkmore, D. 7	*Selchemore* 248b
Silverdale	Not in D.B.
Slindon, C. 6	*Slindone* 247
Slindone	See Slindon
Smedeuuich	See Smethwick
Smethwick, E. 10	*Smedeuuich* 247
Sotehelle	See Sugnall
Stadford	See Stafford
Stafford, D. 7	*Stadford* 246, 247b, 248 *bis*, 248b *Statford* 247b, 248b
Stagrigesholle	See Stramshall
Standon, C. 5	*Stantone* 248b
Stanesope	See Stanshope
Stanley	Not in D.B.
Stanshope, G. 3	*Stanesope* 246b
Stanton, G. 4	*Stantone* 246b
Stantone	See Standon, Stanton
Stapenhill, H. 7	*Stapenhille* 273, 278, Derby.
Statford	See Stafford
Stoca	See Little Stoke
Stoche	See Stoke on Trent
Stoke on Trent, D. 4	*Stoche* 249
Stone	Not in D.B.
Stowe	Not in D.B.
Stramshall, F. 5	*Stagrigesholle* 250b
Stratone	See Stretton (near Burton upon Trent)
Streethay	Not in D.B.
Stretton (near Burton upon Trent), H. 6	*Stratone* 247b
Stretton (near Penkridge), D. 8	*Estretone* 249b
Stychbrook, G. 8	*Tichebroc* 247
Suesneshed	See Swinchurch
Sugnall, C. 6	*Sotehelle* 247
Suinesford	See Kingswinford
Sulvertone	See Swynnerton

Swinchurch, C. 5	*Suesneshed* 247
Swynnerton, D. 5	*Sulvertone* 249
Syerscote, H. 8	*Fricescote* 249
Talc	See Talke
Talke, C. 3	*Talc* 250b
Tamahore	See Tamhorn
Tamhorn, G. 8	*Tamahore* 247
Tamuuorde	See Tamworth
Tamworth, H. 9	*Tamuuorde* 246, 246b
	Tameuuorde 238, Warw.
Tatenhill	Not in D.B.
Tean, E. 5	*Tene* 248b
Teddesley Hay	Not in D.B.
Tene	See Tean
Tettenhall, D. 9	*Totehala* 246 *ter*
	Totenhale 247b *bis*
Thorpe Constantine, H. 8	*Torp* 250b
Thursfield, D. 3	*Turvoldesfeld* 250b
Tibintone	See Tipton
Tichebroc	See Stychbrook
Ticheshale	See Tixall
Tillington, D. 6	*Tillintone* 248b
Tillintone	See Tillington
Timmor	See Tymmore
Tipton, E. 10	*Tibintone* 247
Titesoure	See Tittensor
Tittensor, D. 5	*Titesoure* 249
Tittesworth	Not in D.B.
Tixall, E. 7	*Ticheshale* 248, 249
Torp	See Thorpe Constantine
Toteberie	See Tutbury
Totehala, *Totenhale*	See Tettenhall
Trenham	See Trentham
Trentham, D. 5	*Trenham* 246
Trescott, C. 9	*Cote* 247b
Treslei	See Trysull
Trysull, D. 10	*Treslei* 250
Tunestal	See Tunstall (in Adbaston)
Tunstall (in Adbaston), C. 6	*Tunestal* 247
Tunstall (near Burslem)	Not in D.B.

Turgarestone	See Wolgarston
Turvoldesfeld	See Thursfield
Tutbury, H. 6	*Toteberie* 248b
Tymmore, G. 8	*Timmor* 247
Tyrley, B. 5	*Tirelire* 257, Salop.
Ullauestone	See Woolaston
Ulselei	See Wolseley
Upper Penn	See Penn
Uttoxeter, F. 5	*Wotocheshede* 246b
Wadnesberie	See Wednesbury
Waletone	See Walton (in Baswich), Walton (in Eccleshall), Walton (in Stone)
Walton (in Baswich), E. 7	*Waletone* 247 1st entry
Walton (in Eccleshall), D. 6	*Waletone* 247 2nd entry
Walton (in Gnosall), C. 7	*Waltone* 248
Walton (in Stone), D. 5	*Waletone* 248b
Waltone	See Walton (in Gnosall)
Wamburne	See Wombourn
Warslow, F. 3	*Wereslei* 248
Water Eaton, D. 8	*Etone* 249b
Waterfall	Not in D.B.
Wednesbury, E. 10	*Wadnesberie* 246
Wednesfield, E. 9	*Wodnesfelde* 247b
Weeford, G. 9	*Weforde* 247
Weforde	See Weeford
Wennitone	See Winnington
Wereleia	See Wyrley
Wereslei	See Warslow
West Bromwich, E. 10	*Bromwic* 226, N'hants.
Weston (in Standon), C. 5	*Westone* 248b
Weston Coyney, D. 4	*Westone* 249
Westone	See Weston (in Standon), Weston Coyney, Weston under Lizard, Weston upon Trent

Weston under Lizard, C. 8	*Westone* 250b 1st entry
Weston upon Trent, E. 6	*Westone* 250b 2nd entry
Wetmore, H. 6	*Witmere* 247b
Wetton	Not in D.B.
Whiston, D. 8	*Witestone* 247b
Whitgreave	Not in D.B.
Whitmore, C. 5	*Witemore* 250b
Whittington	Not in D.B.
Wicenore	See Wychnor
Wigetone	See Wigginton
Wigginton, H. 8	*Wigetone* 246
Wightwick, D. 9	*Wisteuuic* 246
Wilbrestone	See Wilbrighton
Wilbrighton, C. 7	*Wilbrestone* 249b
Willenhall, E. 9	*Winehala* 246 *Winenhale* 247b
Winehala, *Winenhale*	See Willenhall
Winnington, B. 5	*Wennitone* 250b
Winshill, H. 7	*Wineshalle* 273, Derby.
Wisteuuic	See Wightwick
Witemore	See Whitmore
Witestone	See Whiston
Witmere	See Wetmore
Wlstanetone	See Wolstanton
Wodestone	See Wootton (in Eccleshall)
Wodetone	See Wootton (near Uttoxeter)
Wodnesfelde	See Wednesfield
Wolgarston, D. 8	*Turgarestone* 246
Wolseley, E. 7	*Ulselei* 247
Wolstanton, D. 4	*Wlstanetone* 246b
Wolverhampton, D. 9	*Hantone* 247b *bis*, 249b
Wombourn, D. 10	*Wamburne* 249b
Woolaston, D. 7	*Ullauestone* 248b
Wootton (in Eccleshall), C. 6	*Wodestone* 247
Wootton (near Uttoxeter), F. 4	*Wodetone* 246b
Worston	Not in D.B.
Wotocheshede	See Uttoxeter
Wrfeld	See Worfield, Salop.
Wrotolei	See Wrottesley
Wrottesley, C. 9	*Wrotolei* 249
Wychnor, G. 7	*Wicenore* 249
Wyrley, E. 8	*Wereleia* 247
Yarlet, D. 6	*Erlide* 248
Yoxall, G. 7	*Iocheshale* 247

ANONYMOUS HOLDINGS

No place-name appears in the following entry, and it is impossible to say whether or not it refers to a place named elsewhere in Domesday Book:

Urfer (from Robert of Stafford), 2 hides in Cuttlestone hd, 249b.

SUFFOLK—*SUDFULC*

Little Domesday Book, folios 281–450

MAPS 46–47

Acheham	See Akenham
Achetuna	See Acton
Achre(h)am	See Akenham
Acle	See Oakley
Acolt	See Occold
Acreham	See Akenham
Acton, E. 8	*Achetuna* 416 *Aketona* 416 *Aratona* 416
Akenham, G. 7	*Acheham* 427b *Achre(h)am* 352b, 422b

Akenham cont.	*Acreham* 289, 352b, 426b
Akethorpe, L. 2	*Aketorp* 284b
Aketona	See Acton
Aketorp	See Akethorpe
Aldeburc	See Aldeburgh
Aldeburgh, K. 6	*Aldeburc* 316, 388b
Aldeham	See Aldham
Alderton, J. 8	*Al(r)etuna* 317, 317b *bis*, 318, 324b, 387
Aldham, F. 8	*Aldeham* 287b *Ealdham* 369 *Ialelham* 419
Aldringham, K. 6	*Alrincham* 310, 310b
Aletuna	See Alderton
Alia Boituna	See Boyton (in Stoke by Clare)
Almaham, *Almeham*	See South Elmham
Almelega	See Hemley
Alnesbourn, H. 8	*Aluesbrunna* 347
Alnet'ne	Unid., 385b
Alretuna	See Alderton
Alrincham	See Aldringham
Alsi(l)destuna	Unid., 378, 420
Alston, I. 9	*Alteinestuna* 292, 341, 341b, 342b
Alteinestuna	See Alston
Altera Walingafella	See Waldingfield
Aluenelega	See Aveley
Aluesbrunna	See Alnesbourn
Aluredestuna	Unid., 425
Alwartuna	See Erwarton
Ampton, D. 5	*Hametuna* 363
Ane(h)us, *An(u)hus*	See Onehouse
Aratona	See Acton
Asce	See Ash Street
Asetona	See Assington
Asfelda	See Ashfield
Ash, I. 7	*Esce* 326b, 327
Ashbocking, H. 7	*Ass(i)a* 394, 433b *Essa* 285 *Hassa* 383
Ashby	Not in D.B.
Ashfield, H. 6	*Asfelda* 298b, 376b, 377
Ashfield cont.	*Assafelda*, *Assefelda* 295, 299, 306 *bis*, 384, 434, 441
Ash Street, F. 8	*Asce* 292
Aspala	See Aspall
Aspall, H. 5	*Aspala*, *-pella* 418, 450 *Espala*, *-palle* 320b, 321, 322b, 378b
Aspella	See Aspall
Assa	See Ashbocking
Assafelda, *Assefelda*	See Ashfield
Assia	See Ashbocking
Assington, E. 8	*Asetona* 416
Auokeduna	See Hawkedon
Aveley, E. 8	*Aluenelega* 401b
Bachetuna	See Bacton
Bacton, F. 5	*Bachetuna* 426b *bis*
Badele(i)a	See Badley
Bademondes-, *Bademundesfelda*	See Badmondisfield
Badincham	See Badingham
Badingafelda, *Badingefelda*, *Badingelelda*	See Bedingfield
Badingham, I. 5	*Badincham* 328b *Hadincham* 309
Badinghefelda	See Bedingfield
Badley, F. 7	*Badele(i)a* 285, 383, 393
Badmondisfield, C. 6	*Bademondesfelda* 289b *Bademundesfelda* 438b
Badwell Ash	Not in D.B.
Balde(re)seia	See Bawdsey
Balesheia	See Lindsey
Ballingdon, D. 8	*Belindune* 79, Ess.
Barchestuna	See Barkestone
Bardwell, E. 5	*Beordewella* 366, 448b *Berdeuuella* 391
Barham, G. 7	*Bercham* 305, 352, 352b, 383, 383b
Barkestone, I. 8	*Barchestuna* 425b

Barking, G. 7	*Berchingas, -ingis* 382b, 383 *bis* *Berkinges* 382b
Barnardiston	Not in D.B.
Barnby, K. 3	*Barnebei, -by* 283, 302
Barnebei, -by	See Barnby
Barnham, D. 4	*Ber(n)ham* 299, 330b, 366b, 398b, 405b
Barningham, E. 4	*Berni(n)cham* 354, 421 *Berningham* 365b
Barro	See Barrow
Barrow, C. 6	*Barro* 289b
Barsham, J. 3	*Barsham, Bersham* 327b, 335, 335b, 379, 380b
Barton Mills, C. 4	*Bertona, -tunna* 391b, 392, 435b
Batingefelda	See Bedingfield
Battisford, F. 7	*Beteforda* 336b *Betes-, Botesfort* 291b, 410, 434b, 446
Bawdsey, J. 8	*Balde(re)seia* 317, 317b *bis*, 354, 387, 387b *bis*
Baylham, G. 7	*Bel(e)ham* 336, 336b, 337, 337b *bis*, 448b
Beccles, J. 3	*Becles* 283b *ter*, 369b
Becclinga	Unid., 338b
Beche-, Beketuna	Unid., 283, 407
Becles	See Beccles
Bedfield, H. 5	*Berdefelda* 328b
Bedingafelda, Bedingefelda	See Bedingfield
Bedingfield, H. 5	*Badingafelda, Badingefelda* 310, 310b *ter*, 330, 406 *bis*, 447b, 450 *Badingelelda* 379b *Badinghefelda* 323b *Batingefelda* 305b *Bedingafelda, Bedingefelda* 368, 428b
Begatona	See Beyton
Beketuna	See *Bechetuna*
Beleham	See Baylham
Belenei	Unid., 378
Belesteda	See Belstead
Beletuna	See Belton
Belham	See Baylham
Belinges	See Great Bealings
Belinges, Parua	See Little Bealings
Belingesfort	See Billingford, Norf.
Belstead, G. 8	*Bel(e)steda* 306, 378, 411b, 418b, 430b, 445b
Belsteda	See Belstead
Belton, K. 1	*Beletuna* 283b, 284b
Benacre, K. 3	*Benagra* 371b
Benagra	See Benacre
Benehal(l)a, Benenhala	See Benhall
Benetleia	See Bentley
Benga, Benges	See Bing
Benhala	See Benhall
Benhall, J. 6	*Benehal(l)a* 297b, 309, 345b *Ben(en)hala* 308b, 309, 344b, 345b
Bentley, G. 8	*Benetleia* 287, 287b, 295b *bis*
Beordewella	See Bardwell
Bercham	See Barham
Berchingas, -ingis	See Barking
Bercolt	See East Bergholt
Berdefelda	See Bedfield, Bredfield
Berdesfella	See Bredfield
Berdeuuella	See Bardwell
Berham	See Barnham
Beria	Unid., 295
Berkinges	See Barking
Bermesdena	Unid., 434
Bernham	See Barnham
Berni(n)cham, Berningham	See Barningham
Bersham	See Barsham
Bertona	See Barton Mills
Bertuna	See Great Barton
Bertunna	See Barton Mills
Besemera	See Bosmere

Beteforda, -esfort	See Battisford
Beuresham	See Beversham
Beversham, J. 6	*Beuresham* 441
Beyton, E. 6	*Begatona* 410
Bildeston, F. 7	*Bilestuna* 426
Bilestuna	See Bildeston
Bing, I. 7	*Benga, Benges* 319b, 324b
Binneuetuna	See Dennington
Bischelea	See Bixley
Bixley, H. 8	*Bischelea* 293, 386b, 406b
Blaccheshala, -essala	See Blaxhall
Blac(he)ham	See Blakenham
Blacheshala, -essala, Blactheshala	See Blaxhall
Blalsega	See Lindsey
Blakenham, Great and Little, G. 7	*Blac(he)ham* 281b, 285, 351b, 353, 383, 404b
Blaxhall, J. 6	*Blac(c)heshala, -essala* 296, 296b *bis*, 306b, 307 *quater*, 307b, 353, 384, 430 *Blactheshala* 344
Bledeburc, Blideburc, -burh, -buro	See Blythburgh
Blideforda	See Blyford
Blieburc	See Blythburgh
Blundeston, K. 2	*Dun(e)stuna* 294, 336
Blyford, J. 4	*Blideforda* 355b
Blythburgh, K. 4	*Bledeburc* 415 *Blideburc, -burh, -buro* 282 *bis*, 311, 312b *Blieburc* 312
Boesteda	See Boxted
Bohtuna	See Boyton (near Alderton)
Boituna	See Boynton, Boyton (near Alderton), Boyton (in Stoke by Clare)
Boituna, Alia	See Boyton (in Stoke by Clare)
Bongeia	See Bungay
Bosmere, G. 7	*Besemera* 385b
Botesdale	Not in D.B.
Botesfort	See Battisford
Boulge, I. 7	*Bulges* 293b, 319, 324b, 347b, 400b, 411b, 425, 431, 443
Boxford	Not in D.B.
Boxted, D. 7	*Boesteda* 349b, 350
Boynton, G. 9	*Boituna* 296, 378, 395, 445b
Boyton (near Alderton), J. 7	*Bohtuna* 316 *bis*, 316b *bis* *Boituna* 318b
Boyton (in Stoke by Clare), C. 8	*Alia Boituna* 396b *Boituna* 390b, 396b
Bradefelda, -fella	See Bradfield, Bredfield
Bradeleia	See Bradley
Bradfield Combust, St Clare, St George, E. 6	*Bradefelda, -fella* 291, 362, 362b
Bradley, Great and Little, B. 7	*Bradeleia* 371b, 396b, 397, 429, 447b
Bradwell	Not in D.B.
Braiseworth, G. 5	*Briseuolda* 323b *Briseworde, -wrda* 320b, 321, 323b *bis*
Brameswella	See Bromeswell
Bramfield, J. 4	*Bru(n)felda* 292b *bis*
Bramford, G. 8	*Bran-, Brunfort* 281b, 282, 289, 393
Brammeswella	See Bromeswell
Brampton, K. 4	*Bramtuna, Brantuna* 288, 331b, 414
Bramtuna	See Brampton
Brandeston (near Framlingham), H. 6	*Brandes-, Brantestuna* 388b, 431b
Brandeston (in Waldingfield), E. 8	*Brantestona* 373b

Name	Reference
Brandestuna	See Brandeston (near Framlingham)
Brandon, C. 3	*Brandona*, *Brantona* 381b, 403
Brandona	See Brandon
Branfort	See Bramford
Branham	See Brantham
Brantestona	See Brandeston (in Waldingfield)
Brantestuna	See Brandeston (near Framlingham), Brantham
Brantham, G. 9	*Branham* 425 *Brantestuna* 295b *Brantham* 296 *bis*, 306, 378, 419b, 420 *bis*
Brantona	See Brandon
Brantuna	See Brampton
Bredefeld(a), *-fella*	See Bredfield
Bredfield, I. 7	*Berdefelda*, *-esfella* 324b, 387b *bis*, 400b, 442b *Bradefelda*, *-fella* 293b *bis*, 387, 388 *Bredefeld(a)*, *-fella* 318, 319, 325, 343b, 387, 391, 443
Brent Eleigh	See Eleigh
Bretenhama, *Bretham*	See Brettenham
Brettenham, E. 7	*Bretenhama* 369 *Bret(t)ham* 291b, 397b
Brettham	See Brettenham
Bricett, Great and Little, F. 7	*Brieseta* 393b, 404b, 405b, 417, 422b, 448b
Brictesceseia	See Brightlingsea, Ess.
Bricticeshaga	Unid., 433b
Bridge, K. 5	*Briges* 336 *Bringas* 331
Brieseta	See Bricett
Briges	See Bridge
Brightwell, I. 8	*Brihtewella* 386
Brihtewella	See Brightwell
Brihtoluestuna	See *Bri(t)htoluestuna*
Bringas	See Bridge
Briseuolda, *Briseworde*, *-wrda*	See Braiseworth
Bri(t)htoluestuna	Unid., 406, 406b
Brocfort	See Brockford
Brochola	See Brockley (in Kedington)
Brockestuna	See Browston
Brockford, G. 5	*Brocfort* 361
Brockley (in Kedington), C. 7	*Brochola* 390b
Brockley (near Whepstead), D. 6	*Brocle(ga)* 349b, 358, 425b
Brocle(ga)	See Brockley (near Whepstead)
Brodertuna	Unid., 294, 326b
Brom	See Brome
Brome, G. 4	*Brom* 282, 310 *bis*, 339, 354b, 371, 381 *Brum* 321
Bromeswell, I. 7	*Bram(m)eswella* 318, 319 *bis*, 387 *Bromeswella* 293, 324b, 387b *Brumesuelle*, *-swella* 319b, 324, 387b, 388 *Brumfella* 294
Bromeswella	See Bromeswell
Browston, K. 1	*Brockestuna* 284
Brufelda	See Bramfield
Bruisyard, I. 5	*Buresiart* 297, 339, 345
Brum	See Brome
Brumesuelle, *-swella*, *Brumfella*	See Bromeswell
Brundish	Not in D.B.
Brundon, D. 8	*Branduna*, *Brumduna* 90, 90b, Ess.
Brunfelda	See Bramfield
Brunfort	See Bramford
Bruntuna	Unid., 427b

Brutge	Unid., 306, 441
Bucklesham, H. 8	*Buclesham* 386b *Bukelesham* 292
Buclesham, *Bukelesham*	See Bucklesham
Bukeshala, *-ssalla*	See Buxhall
Bulcamp, K. 4	*Bulecampa*, *-campe* 333, 356
Bulecampa, *-campe*	See Bulcamp
Bulges	See Boulge
Bungay, I. 3	*Bongeia* 288 *bis*, 301 *Bunghea* 300 *Burghea* 288
Bunghea	See Bungay
Bura	See Bures
Burc(g)	See Burgh (near Woodbridge)
Burch	See Burgh (in Walton), Burgh (near Woodbridge), Burgh Castle
Burch (Plomesgate hd)	Unid., 317
Bure	See Bures
Buregata	See Burgate (in Walton)
Bures, E. 9	*Bura*, *Bure* 360, 392 *bis*, 421b, 435b
Buresiart	See Bruisyard
Buressalla	See Buxhall
Burg	See Burgh (in Walton), Burgh (near Woodbridge)
Burgata	See Burgate (near Eye)
Burgate (near Eye), G. 4	*Burgata* 418b, 419
Burgate (in Walton), I. 9	*Buregata* 339b, 342
Burgesgata	Unid., 317
Burgestala	See Burstall
Burgh (in Walton), I. 9	*Burch* 314b, 340 *Burg* 423b
Burgh (near Woodbridge), H. 7	*Burc(g)* 293, 347, 412b
Burgh (near Woodbridge) cont.	*Burch* 315b *ter* *Burg* 406b, 413, 431, 433 *Burh(c)* 300, 386b, 400b
Burgh Castle, K. 1	*Burch* 445
Burghea	See Bungay
Burghestala	See Burstall
Burh(c)	See Burgh (near Woodbridge)
Burstall, G. 8	*Burg(h)estala* 375, 377, 395, 395b, 417
Bury St Edmunds, D. 6	*Villa Sancti Eadmundi* 372
Butelai, *-lea*	See Butley
Butley, J. 7	*Butelai*, *-lea* 294 *bis*, 327b, 348
Buxhall, F. 6	*Bukeshala*, *-ssalla* 303b, 336, 350, 355b, 382b *Buressalla* 398
Cadenham	See Coddenham (near Needham Market)
Caldecota(n), *-coten*, *Kaldecotes* (Hartismere hd)	Unid., 321b, 370b, 371, 408 *bis*, 426b
Caldecotan	See Caldecott (in Fritton)
Caldecott (in Fritton), K. 1	*Caldecotan* 445
Caluwetuna	See Kalweton
Cambas	See Combs
Campese(i)a	See Campsey
Campsey, I. 6	*Campese(i)a* 293b, 326b, 327, 443b *Capeseia* 388b
Canap(p)etuna, *Canepetuna*	Unid., 287b, 296, 418b
Canauatham	See Cavenham
Candelenta	See Candlet
Candlet, I. 9	*Candelenta* 341
Canepetuna	See *Canap(p)etuna*
Capeles	See Capel St Andrew
Capel St Andrew, J. 7	*Capeles* 293, 317, 318, 319, 343b, 387 *bis*

Cleopetona	See Clopton (near Woodbridge)
Cle'pham	Unid., 316b
Cleptuna	See Clopton (in Wickhambrook)
Clieham	See Great Glemham
Clopetona, -tuna	See Clopton (near Woodbridge)
Clopton (in Wickhambrook), C. 7	*Clep-, Cloptuna* 390 *bis*, 396, 396b, 399 *Copletuna* 384b
Clopton (near Woodbridge), H. 7	*Cleopetona* 349b *Clopetona, -tuna* 315b, 349b, 406b, 417b *bis*, 431 *Cloptuna* 346b, 431 *bis*, 431b *ter*, 433
Cloptuna	See Clopton (in Wickhambrook), Clopton (near Woodbridge)
Cnotesheala, -heale	See Knoddishall
Cockfield, E. 7	*Cothefelda* 359
Coclesworda	See Chamberlain's Hall
Coddenham (in Boxford), E. 8	*Kode(n)ham* 428b *bis*, 449
Coddenham (near Needham Market), G. 7	*Cadenham* 436 *Code(n)ham* 285, 294b, 304b, 338, 338b, 352, 352b, 375, 383, 417, 422, 422b, 423 *bis*, 434b, 436 *bis*, 447
Code(n)ham	See Coddenham (near Needham Market)
Codetuna	See Cotton
Cokel(e)i	See Cookley
Colacar	Unid., 314b
Colestuna	See Colston
Colston, I. 5	*Colestuna* 441
Combs, F. 6	*Cambas* 291, 291b
Coney Weston, E. 4	*Cunegestuna* 365, 365b *bis*, 366 *bis*
Cookley, J. 4	*Cokel(e)i* 333b, 353b
Copdock	Not in D.B.
Copletuna	See Clopton (in Wickhambrook)
Coresfella	Unid., 392b
Cornard, Great and Little, D. 8, E. 8	*Corn(i)erda* 286b, 360, 392, 428b, 448
Corn(i)erda	See Cornard
Corton, L. 2	*Care-, Karetuna* 283b, 445
Cotetuna	See Cotton
Cothefelda	See Cockfield
Coti(n)tuna	See Cotton
Cotton, F. 5	*Code-, Cotetuna* 286b, 309b, 322b, 391 *Coti(n)tuna* 371, 408 *Cottuna* 285b *bis*, 286 *Kodetun* 370b
Cottuna	See Cotton
Coua	See South Cove
Covehithe formerly North Hales, K. 3	*Nordhalla* 332 *Norhals* 400, 412b *Norhhala* 293, 333b *Northala, -hals* 288, 449
Cowlinge, C. 7	*Culinge* 292b
Craneforda, -fort, Cranesfod, -forda	See Cransford
Cranlea	See Cranley
Cranley, G. 5	*Cranlea* 429
Cransford, I. 5	*Craneforda, -fort* 298, 307b, 309, 344b *Cranesfod, -forda* 316, 316b, 444 *Crenefort* 308b
Cratafelda	See Cratfield
Cratfield, I. 4	*Cratafelda* 415
Cratinga	See Creeting All Saints etc., Creeting St Peter
Cratingas	See Creeting All Saints etc.
Cratingis	See Creeting All Saints etc., Creeting St Peter

Creeting All Saints, St Mary, St Olave, G. 6	*Cratinga(s)*, *-ingis* 291b, 304b, 374b, 389 *ter*, 432b, 446
	Gratingis 398b
Creeting St Peter, G. 6	*Cratinga*, *-ingis* 291b, 304, 350b, 374, 389b, 411, 432b *bis*
	Gratinga 350b
Crenefort	See Cransford
Cretingham, H. 6	*Gratingeham* 433b
	Gretingaham, *Gretingeham* 294, 300, 373b, 388b, 406b, 433
Crofelda	See Crowfield
Croscroft	Unid., 301b
Crowfield, G. 6	*Crofelda* 374, 421b
Culeforda	See Culford
Culeslea, I. 8	Lost in Alderton, 317b
Culfol(a), *-fole*	See Culpho
Culford, D. 5	*Culeforda* 364, 366b
Culinge	See Cowlinge
Culpho, H. 7	*Culfol(a)*, *-fole* 346 *ter*, 413
Culuerdestuna	Unid., 406
Cunegestuna	See Coney Weston
Cybenhalla	See Chippenhall
Dagawarda, *-worda*	See Dagworth
Dagworth, F. 6	*Dagawarda*, *-worda* 408b *bis*, 409b *bis*, 427
Dalham, C. 6	*Dalham* 390
Dal(l)ingahou, *Dalingehou*	See Dallinghoo
Dallinghoo, I. 7	*Dal(l)ingahou*, *Dalingehou* 294 *bis*, 325b, 327, 348, 388b *bis*
	Delingahou 444
Damar-, *Danar-*, *Danerdestuna*	See Denston
Darmsden, G. 7	*Dermodesduna* 285, 294b, 383, 410

Darsham, J. 5	*Ders(h)am* 282b, 292b, 310b, 313, 313b, 314, 336
	Diresham 334b
Debach, H. 7	*De(ben)beis* 343b, 373b
	Depebecs, *-bek*, *-bes* 293b, 347b, 400b, 411b, 417b, 431
De(ben)beis	See Debach
Debenham, H. 6	*Depbe(n)ham* 305, 305b *ter*, 376b
	Deph(e)am 376b, 417b
	Dephenham 378b
	Depleham 384
De(l)ham	See Denham (near Eye)
Delingahou	See Dallinghoo
Denham (near Bury St Edmunds), C. 6	*Denham* 390b
Denham (near Eye), H. 4	*De(l)ham* 288b, 331
	Denham 310, 379b
Dennington, I. 5	*Binneuetuna* 328
	Dingifetuna 325 *bis*
	Dingiuetona, *-tuna* 325b *bis*, 326 *ter*, 327
	Dinguiet' 316b
Denston, C. 7	*Damar-*, *Danar-*, *Danerdestuna* 390 *bis*, 438b
Depbe(n)ham	See Debenham
Depdana	See Depden
Depden, C. 6	*Depdana* 396, 398b
Depebecs, *-bek*, *-bes*	See Debach
Deph(e)am, *Dephenham*, *Depleham*	See Debenham
Dermodesduna	See Darmsden
Derneford	Unid., 442b
Ders(h)am	See Darsham
Deselinga, *Desilinges*	See Desning

Desning, C. 6	*Deselinga* 390, 391b, 392 *bis* *Desilinges* 392 *bis*
Dice	See Diss, Norf.
Dingifetuna, *Dingiuetona*, *-tuna*, *Dinguiet'*	See Dennington
Diresham	See Darsham
Dodnash, G. 9	*Todenes* 295b
Drencestuna, *Drincestona*	See Drinkstone
Drinkstone, E. 6	*Drencestuna* 362b *Drincestona* 381b *Rengestuna* 291
Dunestuna	See Blundeston
Duneuuic	See Dunwich
Dunham	See Santon Downham
Duniworda	See Dunningworth
Dunningworth, J. 6	*Duniworda* 345b
Dunstuna	See Blundeston
Dunwich, K. 5	*Duneuuic* 311b, 312, 312b, 331b, 334b, 385b
Ealdham	See Aldham
Earl Soham, H. 6	*Saham* 293, 293b, 294 *bis*, 327, 410
Earl Stonham	See Stonham, Earl and Little
Eascefelda	See Great Ashfield
East Bergholt, G. 9	*Bercolt* 287, 287b *quater*, 289b, 295, 295b, 296 *ter*, 303b *ter*, 377 *bis*, 377b *bis*, 378, 378b *bis*, 394b *bis*, 395 *sexiens*, 395b *bis*, 403, 411b *bis*, 418b *ter*, 423, 425b *bis*, 436b, 437, 445b *ter*
Easton, I. 6	*Estuna* 326, 347b
Easton Bavants, K. 4	*Estuna* 282, 423b, 444, 444b *bis*
Ecclingaham	See Icklingham
Eduardestuna	See Edwardstone
Eduinestuna	Unid., 395, 420b
Eduluestuna	Unid., 425
Edwardstone, E. 8	*Eduardestuna* 304
Eia	See Eye
Eilanda	See Nayland
Elcheteshala	See Ilketshall
Eleigh, Brent and Monks, E. 7	*Ilelega* 373b, 392b, 427b *Illeleia* 373 *Lelega* 359b
Elga	See Ellough
Eli	See Ely, Cambs.
Ella	Unid., 404b
Ellough, K. 3	*Elga* 283b, 335b *bis*
Elmeham	See South Elmham
Elmeseta	See Elmsett
Elmeswella	See Elmswell
Elmingheham	See Helmingham
Elmsett, F. 7	*Elmeseta* 405
Elmswell, E. 6	*Elmeswella* 364b
Eluedena	See Elvedon
Elvedon, D. 4	*Eluedena* 358b *Haluedona* 391b *Heluedana*, *-dona* 303, 398
Eriswell, C. 4	*Hereswella* 402b
Eruestuna	Unid., 409
Erwarton, H. 9	*Alwartuna* 394b *Eurewardestuna* 395
Escarletuna, *Escaruestuna*	See Sharpstone
Esce	See Ash
Escefella	See Great Ashfield
Espala, *Espalle*	See Aspall
Essa	See Ashbocking
Estena	See Stonham Aspal
Estuna	See Easton, Easton Bavants, Stonham Aspal
Estutestuna	See Stuston
Eteseta	See Hessett
Ethereg	Unid., 302b
Euestuna	See Euston
Eurewardestuna	See Erwarton
Euston, E. 4	*Eu(e)stuna* 367b, 444b

Eustuna	See Euston
Evelincham	See Heveningham
Exning, B. 5	*Essel(l)inge*, Exch. D.B., 189b, 195b, Cambs.
Eye, G. 4	*Eia* 156, 319b, 321, 379, 449b *Heia* 310, 379 *Eia* 156, Norf.
Eyke	Not in D.B.
Facheduna	Unid., 394, 446
Fachenham	See Great Fakenham
Fachenham, Litla	See Little Fakenham
Falkenham, I. 8	*Faltenham* 339b, 340b, 341, 423b
Faltenham	See Falkenham
Faraham	See Farnham
Farleia	See Farley
Farley, C. 7	*Farleia* 390b
Farnham, J. 6	*Faraham, Farnham* 308b, 316b *Ferneham* 344b
Fealsham	See Felsham
Felincham	See Finningham
Felixstowe	Not in D.B.
Felsham, E. 6	*Fealsham* 362b
Fenstead, C. 8	*Finesteda* 428
Ferneham	See Farnham
Fessefelda	See Fressingfield
Finborough, Great and Little, F. 6, F. 7	*Fineberga* 285, 303, 382b, 403b, 448b
Fineberga	See Finborough
Finesteda	See Fenstead
Finesford(a), Finlesford(a), H. 7	Lost in Witnesham, 387, 405, 413, 423b, 427b
Finingaham	See Finningham
Finningham, F. 5	*Felincham* 323b *Finingaham* 309b, 321, 370b *bis*, 440
Flemingtuna	See Flempton
Flempton, D. 5	*Flemingtuna* 357b
Flixton (near Bungay), I. 3	*Flixtuna* 380, 380b, 434b
Flixton (near Lowestoft), K. 2	*Flixtuna* 283b, 284, 381
Flixtuna	See Flixton (near Bungay), Flixton (near Lowestoft)
Flochetuna	See Flowton
Flowton, G. 7	*Flochetuna* 337b, 393b, 404
Fordley, J. 5	*Forle(a), -lei* 310b, 312, 314, 334, 334b
Forle(a), -lei	See Fordley
Fornham All Saints, D. 5	*Fornham* 357b
Fornham St Genevieve, D. 5	*Genonefae Forham* 362
Fornham St Martin, D. 5	*Fornham* 361b
Foxehola	See Foxhall
Foxhall, H. 8	*Foxehola* 386b
Frakenaham	See Freckenham
Framalingaham, Frameling(a)ham	See Framlingham
Framesdena	See Framsden
Framincham, Framlingaham	See Framlingham
Framlingham, I. 6	*Framalingaham* 325b, 380 *Frameling(a)ham* 302b, 325b, 429 *Framincham* 299 *bis* *Framlingaham* 327
Framsden, H. 6	*Framesdena* 298b
Frandestuna	See Thrandeston
Freckenham, B. 5	*Frakenaham* 381
Fresetuna	See Freston
Fressingfield, I. 4	*Fessefelda* 321
Freston, H. 8	*Frese-, Frisetuna* 395b, 402
Fridetuna	See Fritton
Frisetuna	See Freston
Friston	Not in D.B.
Fritton, K. 1	*Fridetuna* 284, 284b
Frondestuna	See Thrandeston
Frostenden, K. 4	*Froxedena* 414b
Froxedena	See Frostenden
Gabbatuna, Gabbetuna	See Gapton

Gapton, K. 1	*Gabbatuna*, *Gabbetuna* 283b, 284
Gatagraua, *Gategraua*	See Gedgrave
Gazeley	Not in D.B.
Gedding, E. 6	*Ge(l)dinga* 363, 398
Gedgrave, J. 7	*Gatagraua*, *Gategraua* 294 *bis*, 326b, 327, 343b
Ge(l)dinga	See Gedding
Genonefae Forham	See Fornham St Genevieve
Gepesuiz, *Gepeswic*	See Ipswich
Gernemutha	See Yarmouth, Norf.
Ghenetessala	See Knettishall
Gildincham	See Gislingham
Gillingaham	See Gillingham, Norf.
Gipeswic, *-wiz*, *Gipewid*, *-wiz*	See Ipswich
Gipping	Not in D.B.
Gisilincham	See Gislingham
Gisleham, K. 3	*Gisleham* 283, 302, 407b
Gislincham, *Gislingaham*, *Gislingeham*	See Gislingham
Gislingham, G. 5	*Gildincham* 324 *Gis(i)lincham* 440, 444b *Gislingaham*, *Gislingeham* 282, 286, 408, 419 *Gislingheham* 322, 361, 419 *Gissilincham* 320b
Gislingheham, *Gissilincham*	See Gislingham
Giswortha	See Ixworth
Glaimham, *Glemham*	See Great Glemham
Glemsford, D. 7	*Clamesford(a)* 382, 416b
Glereuinges	See Glevering
Glevering, I. 6	*Glereuinges* 444
Gliemham	See Great Glemham
Gliemham, Thieue	See Little Glemham
Gnedassala, *Gnedeshalla*	See Knettishall
Gokesford	See Yoxford
Gorlestuna	See Gorleston, Norf.
Gosbeck	Not in D.B.
Gratinga	See Creeting St Peter
Gratingeham	See Cretingham
Gratingis	See Creeting All Saints etc.
Great Ashfield, F. 5	*Eascefelda* 367, 439 *Escefella* 370b, 440
Great Barton, D. 5	*Bertuna* 361b
Great Bealings, H. 7	*Belinges* 315b, 441b
Great Blakenham	See Blakenham
Great Bradley	See Bradley
Great Bricett	See Bricett
Great Cornard	See Cornard
Great Fakenham, E. 4	*Fachenham* 367b, 420b
Great Finborough	See Finborough
Great Glemham, I. 6	*Cliemham* 308b *Glaimham* 308b *Gl(i)emham* 297, 298, 308, 308b, 309, 345, 345b, 353, 360b, 403, 430
Great Livermere, D. 5	*Liuelmera*, *Liuermera* 359, 363b, 382, 408
Great Saxham	See Saxham
Great Thurlow	See Thurlow
Great Waldingfield	See Waldingfield
Great Welnetham	See Welnetham
Great Wenham	See Wenham
Great Wratting	See Wratting
Grenewic	Unid., 347
Gressegraua	See Kesgrave
Gretingaham, *Gretingeham*	See Cretingham
Grimestuna	See Grimston

Grimston, I. 9	*Grimestuna* 292, 341b
Grotena	See Groton
Groton, E. 8	*Grotena* 287, 359b, 392b, 447b
Grundesbur, *-burc(h)*, *-burg(h)*, *-burh*	See Grundisburgh
Grundisburgh, H. 7	*Grundesbur* 423b *Grundesburc(h)* 346 *bis*, 386 *Grundesburg(h)* 386, 412b, 441b *Grundesburh* 300, 315b
Gulpelea	See Gulpher
Gulpher, I. 9	*Gulpelea* 340
Gusford, G. 8	*Gutthuluesforda* 431
Guthestuna, I. 8	Lost in Kirton, 340b
Gutthuluesforda	See Gusford
Gypeswiz	See Ipswich
Hacestuna	See Hacheston
Hacheston, I. 6	*Hacestuna* 293b *Hece(s)tuna* 286b, 326b, 369b *Hetcetuna* 325b
Hadincham	See Badingham
Hadleigh, F. 8	*Hetlega* 372b
Hagala	See Haughley
Haldsteda	See Hawstead
Halesuuorda	See Halesworth
Halesworth, J. 4	*Halesuuorda* 293 *Haleurda* 333 *Healesuuorda* 299
Haleurda	See Halesworth
Halgestou, I. 8	Lost in Shottisham, 318b
Halmeham	See South Elmham
Halmelega, *-leia*	See Hemley
Haluedona	See Elvedon
Hametuna	See Ampton
Hami(n)gestuna, *Haminghelanda*	See Hemingstone
Hanchet, B. 8	*Haningehest* 396
Haningehest	See Hanchet
Haragraua	See Hargrave
Hargrave, C. 6	*Haragraua* 435
Harkstead, H. 9	*Herchesteda* 286b, 420b, 430b, Suff.; 6, Ess.
Harleston, F. 6	*Heroluestuna* 360
Harpole, I. 6	*Holapola* 293b *Horapola* 388, 443 *Horepola*, *-polo* 294, 324b, 325 *bis*, 388, 443 *Horpola* 343b
Hartest, D. 7	*Herte(r)st* 382, 392b
Hasc(h)etuna, *Hashetuna*	See Hasketon
Hasketon, H. 7	*Hasc(h)etuna* 315, 315b, 346b, 347, 386 *Hashetuna* 413
Haspelega	See Haspley
Haspley, I. 8	*Haspelega* 424b, 425 *Hespelea* 369b
Hassa	See Ashbocking
Hastelea	See Hestley
Hatheburgfelda, *Hetheburgafella*	Unid., 301b, 407
Hauerha, *Hauerhella*, *-hol*	See Haverhill
Haughley, F. 6	*Hagala* 408b
Hauochenduna, *Hauokeduna*	See Hawkedon
Hauungestuna	See Hemingstone
Haverhill, B. 8	*Hauerha*, *Hauerhella*, *-hol* 371b, 373, 396, 397 *bis*, 428
Hawkedon, C. 7	*Auokeduna* 390b *bis* *Hauochenduna* 348b *Hauokeduna* 396b, 397
Hawstead, D. 6	*Haldsteda* 358 *Hersteda* 391b
Hazlewood	Not in D.B.
Healesuurda	See Halesworth
Hece(s)tuna	See Hacheston
Hecham	See Higham (near Brantham), Hitcham

Heia	See Eye
Hei(h)ham	See Higham (near Brantham)
Helmele(a)	See Hemley
Helmincham	See Helmingham
Helmingham, H. 6	*Elmingheham* 433b *Helmincham* 423 *Helmingh(e)am* 352b, 394b *H(el)mingheham* 291b, 299, 375b, 376
Helmingh(e)am, *Helmingheham*	See Helmingham
Heluedana, *-dona*	See Elvedon
Hemegretham	See Hengrave
Hemingstone, G. 7	*Hami(n)gestuna* 294b, 295, 304b, 338, 351b, 352 *bis*, 352b, 375b, 383 *bis*, 437b *bis*, 438, 440b, 446 *bis* *Haminghelanda* 282, 446 *Hauungestuna* 436
Hemley, I. 8	*Almelega* 425 *Halmelega*, *-leia* 349b, 424 *Helmele(a)* 340b, 431, 431b
Henestede	See Henstead
Hengrave, D. 5	*Hemegretham* 357b, 358
Henham, K. 4	*Henham* 414b
Henle(i)a, *-leie*	See Henley
Henley, G. 7	*Henle(i)a*, *-leie* 305b, 352b, 353, 384, 404b, 427, 437b
Henstead, K. 3	*Henestede* 399b
Hepworda	See Hepworth
Hepworth, F. 4	*Hepworda* 365b, 439b
Herchesteda	See Harkstead
Hereswella	See Eriswell
Heringaflet	See Herringfleet
Herni(n)gawella	See Herringswell
Heroluestuna	See Harleston
Herringfleet, K. 2	*Herlingaflet* 284b
Herringswell, C. 5	*Herni(n)gawella* 392, 398 *Hyrningwella* 358b
Hersteda	See Hawstead
Herte(r)st	See Hartest
Hespelea	See Haspley
Hessett, E. 6	*Eteseta* 362b *Heteseta* 355
Hestley, G. 5	*Hastelea* 429
Hetcetuna	See Hacheston
Hetcham	See Hitcham
Heteseta	See Hessett
Hetheburgafella	See *Hatheburgfelda*
Hetlega	See Hadleigh
Heveniggeham	See Heveningham
Heveningham, I. 5	*Evelincham* 332 *Heveniggeham* 334
Higham (near Brantham), F. 9	*Hecham* 378, 395b, 436b *Hei(h)ham* 303b, 423
Higham (near Bury St Edmunds)	Not in D.B.
Hilderclea	See Hinderclay
Hinderclay, F. 4	*Hilderclea* 364b
Hinetuna	See Hinton
Hintlesham, G. 8	*Hintlesham* 289, 295b
Hinton, K. 5	*Hinetuna* 331
Hitcham, F. 7	*He(t)cham* 384b, 385, 391, 397b
Hmingheham	See Helmingham
Hobbestuna	See *Hopestuna*
Hodiham	See Odiham, Hants.
Hoi	See Hoo (in Sutton)
Hoketona	See Houghton
Holapola	See Harpole
Holbrook, H. 9	*Holebroc* 295
Holebroc	See Holbrook
Holeslea	See Hollesley
Holetuna	See Holton (near Halesworth), Holton St Mary
Hollesley, J. 8	*Holeslea* 317 *ter*, 317b *ter*, 325, 327b

Holton (near Halesworth), J. 4	*Holetuna* 314, 331b, 333b, 355b, 356
Holton St Mary, F. 9	*Holetuna* 411
Homersfield, I. 3	*Humbresfelda* 379, 380
Honilega	Unid., 416
Honington, E. 4	*Hunegetuna* 366
Hoo (near Kettleburgh), I. 6	*Hou* 388
Hoo (in Sutton), I. 7	*Hoi* 387b
	Hou 317b
Hopestuna, *Hobbestuna*	Unid., 315, 413
Hopetuna	See Hopton (near Fakenham)
Hopewella	Unid., 314b
Hoppetuna, *Opituna*	Unid., 313b, 334
Hopton (near Fakenham), F. 4	*Hopetuna* 365b
Hopton (near Lowestoft), K. 1	*Hotuna* 284
Horam	See Horham
Horan(t)	See Horham
Horapola, *Horepola*, *-polo*	See Harpole
Horham, H. 5	*Horam* 329, 329b *bis*, 331
	Horan(t) 371b, 379b *bis*, 406, 438, 447
Hornes	Unid., 407b
Horningeserda, *-esworda*	See Horringer
Horpola	See Harpole
Horringer formerly Horningsheath, D. 6	*Horningeserda*, *-esworda* 356b, 391b
Horswalda	See Horswold
Horswold, G. 6	*Horswalda* 383, 404b
Hotuna	See Hopton (near Lowestoft)
Hou	See Hoo (near Kettleburgh), Hoo (in Sutton)
Houghton, D. 7	*Hoketona* 428 *bis*

Hox(a), *Hoxana*, *Hoxna*	See Hoxne
Hoxne, H. 4	*Hox(a)* 286, 288b, 310, 329 *bis*, 329b *bis*, 349 *bis*, 349b, 371b, 385, 429b, 438b, 447, 447b
	Hoxana 379
	Hoxna 379b
	Oxa 329b, 385b
Huelfiham	See Welnetham
Huepestede	See Whepstead
Hulferestuna	See Woolverstone
Humbresfelda	See Homersfield
Hundesthoft, *-tuf*, I. 7	Lost in Sutton, 324b, 387b
Hundon, C. 7	*Hune(n)dana* 389b, 390
Hunedana	See Hundon
Hunegetuna	See Honington
Hunendana	See Hundon
Hunston, E. 5	*Hunterstuna* 286, 367
Hunterstuna	See Hunston
Huntingafelda, *-felde*	See Huntingfield
Huntingfield, I. 4	*Huntingafelda*, *-felde* 311 *ter*
Hyrningwella	See Herringswell
Iachele(i)a, *Iacheslea*	See Yaxley
Ialelham	See Aldham
Icheburna	Unid., 327b
Icklingham, C. 5	*Ecclingaham* 288b, 416, 434
Ickworth, D. 6	*Ikewortha* 357b
Icsewrda	See Ixworth
Iernesmua	See Yarmouth, Norf.
Iken	Not in D.B.
Ikewortha	See Ickworth
Ilchet(el)eshala	See Ilketshall
Ilelega	See Eleigh
Ilketshall St Andrew, St John, St Lawrence, St Margaret, J. 3	*Elcheteshala* 301
	Ilchet(el)eshala 300b *bis*, 301 *ter*, 301b, 356
Illeleia	See Eleigh

Kirkley, L. 2	*Kirkelea* 283 *bis*, 407b
Kirkton, H. 9	*Cherchetuna* 395
Kirton, I. 8	*Kirketuna* 340b, 342b, 423b
Kislea	Unid., 283
Kitelbeornastuna	See Kettlebaston
Knettishall, E. 4	*Ghenetessala* 321
	Gnedassala 448b
	Gnedeshalla 367b
	Gnateshala 120, Norf.
Knoddishall, J. 6	*Chenotessala* 338b
	Cnotesheala, *-heale* 333b, 334
Kode(n)ham	See Coddenham (in Boxford)
Kodetun	See Cotton
Kuluertestuna	Unid., 342b
Kyngestuna	See Kingston
Lackford, C. 5	*Leacforda* 357, 358
Lafham (Cosford hd)	See Layham
Lafham (Risbridge hd)	Unid., 445b
Lakenheath, C. 3	*Lakingaheda*, *-hethe* 392, 403
	Laringahetha, *-geheta* 382 *bis*
Lakingaheda, *-hethe*	See Lakenheath
Laneburc, *-burh*, I. 8	Lost in Sutton, 317, 318b *bis*
Langer, I. 9	*Langestuna* 341b *bis*
Langestuna	See Langer
Langham, E. 5	*Langham* 367, 439b
Lang(h)edana, *-dena*	Unid., 285, 338, 352 *bis*, 404b, 422b
Laringahetha, *-geheta*	See Lakenheath
Latham	See Layham
Lauen(ham)	See Lavenham
Lavenham, E. 7	*Lauen(ham)* 355, 418, 449
Lawessela	See Lawshall
Lawshall, D. 7	*Lawessela* 378b
Laxefelda	See Laxfield
Laxfield, I. 5	*Laxefelda* 328b
Layham, F. 8	*Lafham*, *Latham* 288, 368b, 420b, 437
	Leiham 403b, 432
Leacforda	See Lackford
Ledestuna	See Leiston
Ledringaham	See Letheringham
Leestuna, *Lehtuna*	See Leiston
Leiham	See Layham
Leiston, K. 6	*Le(d)estuna* 310, 314, 316b
	Lehtuna 311
	Leistuna 310
Leistuna	See Leiston
Lelega	See Eleigh
Leofstanestuna, I. 8	Lost in Trimley, 341, 342 *bis*
Letheringaham	See Letheringham
Letheringham, I. 6	*Ledringaham* 348, 412
	Letheringaham 388b
Leuentona, *Leuetuna*	See Levington
Levington, H. 8	*Leuentona* 406
	Leuetuna 341, 342b
Lidgate, C. 6	*Litgata* 435, 445
Linburna	See Linburne
Linburne, I. 3	*Linburna* 370
Lindsey, F. 8	*Balesheia* 397b
	Blalsega 369
Linesteda, *-stede*	See Linstead
Linhou	Unid., 421b
Linstead Magna and Parva, I. 4	*Linesteda*, *-stede* 311, 314
Litelcros	See Littlecross
Litgata	See Lidgate
Litla Fachenham	See Little Fakenham
Litla Liuermera	See Little Livermere
Little Bealings, H. 7	*Parua Belinges* 373, 386b, 406b, 442
Little Blakenham	See Blakenham
Little Bradley	See Bradley

Merlesham	See Martlesham
Mertlega	See Martley
Metfield	Not in D.B.
Metingaham	See Mettingham
Metles	See Mellis
Mettingham, J. 3	*Metingaham* 300b, 301
Mickfield, G. 6	*Mucelfelda* 417 *Mulcelfel* 360b
Middeltuna	See Middleton
Middleton, J. 5	*Middeltuna* 312, 335 *Mi(l)deltuna* 292b, 299b, 334, 400
Mi(l)deltuna	See Middleton
Milden, E. 8	*Mellinga* 360, 427
Mildenhall, C. 4	*Mitdenehalla* 288b *Mudenehalla* 392 *Midelhale* 263, Norf.
Milsemere	See Minsmere
Minima Waldringafelda	See Waldringfield
Minsmere, K. 5	*Menesmara* 314 *Milsemere* 334
Mitdenehalla	See Mildenhall
Monewdon, H. 6	*Munegadena* 325b *Mungadena*, *Mungedena* 347b *bis*, 348, 388b, 431
Monks Eleigh	See Eleigh
Monk Soham, H. 5	*Saham* 368, 385, 405b
Morestona, *-tuna*	See Morston
Morston, I. 8	*Morestona*, *-tuna* 292, 385b, 423b *Mot(h)estuna* 340b, 342b, 424
Mosa	See Moze, Ess.
Mot(h)estuna	See Morston
Moulton, B. 6	*Muletuna* 372b
Mucelfelda	See Mickfield
Mudenehalla	See Mildenhall
Mulcelfel	See Mickfield
Muletuna	See Moulton
Mundlesham	See Mendlesham
Munegadena, *Mungadena*, *Mungedena*	See Monewdon
Munlesham	See Mendlesham
Mutford, K. 3	*Mutford* 283 *ter*, 335b
Mycelegata, I. 9	Lost in Trimley, 314b, 342
Nachetuna	See Nacton
Nacton, H. 8	*Nach-*, *Nechetuna* 406, 406b, 410
Naughton	Not in D.B.
Nayland, E. 9	*Eilanda* 401b
Nebrunna	See Newbourn
Nec(c)hemara, *Netkemara*	Unid., 315, 413, 442
Nechetuna	See Nacton
Nedesteda	See Nettlestead
Nedging, F. 7	*Niedinga* 385
Needham Market	Not in D.B.
Netkemara	See *Nec(c)hemara*
Netlesteda	See Nettlestead
Nettlestead, G. 7	*Nedesteda* 295 *Netlesteda* 294b
Neubrumna, *-brunna*	See Newbourn
Neutuna	See Newton (near Bury St Edmunds), Newton (near Lowestoft), Newton (in Swilland), Old Newton
Newbourn, I. 8	*Nebrunna* 347b, 424b *Neubrumna*, *-brunna* 369b, 386
Newetona	See Newton (near Sudbury), Old Newton
Newetuna	See Old Newton
Newmarket	Not in D.B.
Newton (near Bury St Edmunds), D. 6	*Neutuna* 357
Newton (near Lowestoft), L. 2	*Neutuna* 284b
Newton (near Sudbury), E. 8	*Newetona* 428b *Niwetuna* 360
Newton (in Swilland), H. 7	*Neutuna* 423b *bis* *Niwetuna* 423

Petehaga	See Pettaugh
Pettaugh, H. 6	*Pet(t)ehaga* 377b, 384, 440b
Pettehaga	See Pettaugh
Pettistree	Not in D.B.
Peyton, I. 8	*Peituna* 402b
Pileberga	Unid., 404
Pisehalla	See Peasenhall
Playford, H. 7	*Plegeforda* 314b
Plegeforda	See Playford
Plugeard, I. 9	Lost in Trimley, 340, 385b
Polesteda	See Polstead
Polstead, F. 9	*Polesteda* 401
Poslindewrda, *Poslingeorda*, *-ewrda*	See Poslingford
Poslingford, C. 7	*Poslindewrda* 371b *Poslingeorda*, *-ewrda* 396b, 397, 413b
Possefelda	Unid., 326b
Potesforda	See Potsford
Potsford, I. 6	*Potesforda* 443b
Prestetona	See Preston (near Lavenham)
Prestetuna (Carlford hd)	See Preston (in Martlesham)
Prestetuna (Plomesgate hd)	Unid., 317
Prestetune	See Preston (near Lavenham)
Preston (near Lavenham), E. 7	*Prestetona*, *-tune* 350, 359b
Preston (in Martlesham), H. 8	*Prestetuna* 424b
Purtepyt	Unid., 394b
Radenhala	See Redenhall, Norf.
Radinghefelda	See Redlingfield
Ramburc	See Rumburgh
Ram(m)esholt	See Ramsholt
Ramsholt, I. 8	*Ram(m)esholt* 318b, 354b
Rastedena, *Ratesdana*, *-dane*, *Rathestdena*, *Ratlesdena*	See Rattlesden
Rattlesden, E. 6	*Rastedena* 391 *Ratesdana*, *-dane* 303, 381b *bis*, 398 *Rathestdena* 291 *Ratlesdena* 363
Raydon, F. 8	*Reinduna*, *-dune* 303b, 377b, 378 *bis*, 395, 411, 437 *Rienduna* 403, 411b
Reda	See Rede
Rede, D. 7	*Re(o)da* 358, 381b, 391b *Riete* 401
Redgrave, F. 4	*Regraua* 360b
Redesham	See Redisham
Redisham, J. 3	*Redesham* 336
Redles	Unid., 438
Redlingfield, H. 5	*Radinghefelda* 320
Regraua	See Redgrave
Reinduna, *-dune*	See Raydon
Remlesham	See Rendlesham
Rendham, J. 5	*Rimdham* 307b *Rincham* 297b *Rind(e)ham* 344, 344b *Rinham* 345 *bis*
Rendlesham, I. 7	*Remlesham* 326, 326b *Ren(d)lesham* 293b, 326, 343b, 443b *Rennesham* 326 *Renslesham* 388b
Rengestuna	See Drinkstone
Renlesham, *Rennesham*, *Renslesham*	See Rendlesham
Reoda	See Rede
Rescebroc	See Rushbrooke (in Thorpe Morieux)
Resebi	See Risby
Reydon, K. 4	*Rienduna* 414
Richingehala	See Rickinghall Superior
Richingehalla	See Rickinghall Inferior

Rickinghall Inferior, F. 4	*Richingehalla* 364b, 365b *Rikinchala* 328
Rickinghall Superior, F. 4	*Richingehala* 361, 419 *Rikingahala* 309b, 370b
Rienduna	See Raydon, Reydon
Riete	See Rede
Righeshala	See Ringshall
Rigneseta	Unid., 393b
Rikinchala	See Rickinghall Inferior
Rikingahala	See Rickinghall Superior
Rimdham, *Rincham*, *Rind(e)ham*	See Rendham
Ringesfelda, *-fella*	See Ringsfield
Ringeshala, *Ringhesehla*, *Ringheshala*	See Ringshall
Ringsfield, J. 3	*Ringesfelda*, *-fella* 282b *bis*, 301, 335
Ringshall, F. 7	*Righeshala* 336 *Ringeshala* 405 *Ringhesehla* 291b *Ringheshala* 405b
Rinham	See Rendham
Risangra	See Rishangles
Risby, C. 5	*Resebi* 349b *Risebi*, *-by* 356b, 358
Riscemara	See Rushmere (in Friston), Rushmere (near Lowestoft), Rushmere St Andrew
Risebi	See Risby
Risebroc	See Rushbrooke (in Thorpe Morieux)
Riseburc	Unid., 282
Riseby	See Risby
Risemara	See Rushmere St Andrew
Riseurda	See Rushford

Rishangles, H. 5	*Risangra* 323
Rishemara, *Rissemera*	See Rushmere St Andrew
Rodeham	Unid., 374
Rodenhala	Unid., 302, 407b
Romburc	See Rumburgh
Rougham, E. 6	*Ruhham* 362, 362b, 363b
Ruhham	See Rougham
Rumburgh, J. 4	*Ram-*, *Romburc* 292b, 298 *Romborc*, *-boro* 149b, 177, Norf.
Rushbrooke (near Bury St Edmunds), E. 6	*Ryscebroc* 363b
Rushbrooke (in Thorpe Morieux), E. 7	*Rescebroc* 369 *Risebroc* 397b
Rushford, E. 4	*Riseurda* 421
Rushmere (in Friston), J. 6	*Riscemara* 316b
Rushmere (near Lowestoft), K. 3	*Riscemara* 283 *bis*, 407b *Ryscemara* 302
Rushmere St Andrew, H. 8	*Riscemara* 282b, 293, 347b, 442 *Ris(h)emara* 386b *bis* *Rissemera* 305b *Ryscemara* 293, 315, 315b
Ryscebroc	See Rushbrooke (near Bury St Edmunds)
Ryscemara	See Rushmere (near Lowestoft), Rushmere St Andrew
Saham	See Earl Soham, Monk Soham
Saibamus	Unid., 448
Samundeham	See Saxmundham
Sancti Eadmundi, *Villa*	See Bury St Edmunds
Santon Downham, D. 3	*Dunham* 359, 382
Sapestuna	See Sapiston

Sapiston, E. 4	*Sapestuna* 366, 421, 436b, 439b
Sasmunde(s)ham	See Saxmundham
Saxam	See Saxham
Saxham, Great and Little, C. 6	*Sax(h)am* 285, 391 *Sexham* 357, 357b
Saxmondeham	See Saxmundham
Saxmundham, J. 6	*Samundeham* 338b *Sasmunde(s)ham* 333b *bis* *Saxmondeham* 338b, 339
Saxtead, I. 5	*Saxteda* 299
Saxteda	See Saxtead
Scadena, *Scadenafella*	See Shadingfield
Scaruerstuna, *Scarue(s)tuna*	See Sharpstone
Scerdatra	See Chadacre
Sceueleia	See Shelley
Scipmedu, *Scipmetdua*	See Shipmeadow
Scoteleia	See Shotley
Scotesham	See Shottisham
Seamera	See Semer
Seckford, I. 7	*Sekeforda* 373
Sedestana	See Chediston
Seilam, *Seilanda*	See Syleham
Sekeforda	See Seckford
Sellanda	See Shelland
Semer, F. 8	*Seamera* 368b
Sexham	See Saxham
Shadingfield, K. 3	*Scadena* 336 *Scadenafella* 288b, 335b, 412, 415b
Sharpstone, G. 7	*Escarletuna* 383b *Escaruestuna* 376 *Scaruerstuna* 285 *Scarue(s)tuna* 295, 375b, 384
Shelland, F. 6	*Sellanda* 392b
Shelley, F. 8	*Sceueleia* 287, 287b
Shimpling, D. 7	*Simplinga* 415b, 430b
Shipmeadow, J. 3	*Scipmedu* 301 *bis* *Scipmetdua* 335b
Shotley, H. 9	*Scoteleia* 287, 287b, 394b

Shottisham, I. 8	*Scotesham* 318, 319, 324, 387, 388
Sib(b)etuna	See Sibton
Sibton, J. 5	*Sib(b)etuna* 292b, 312b, 313
Simplinga	See Shimpling
Snape, J. 6	*Snapes* 316 *bis*
Snapes	See Snape
Soches	See Stoke Ash
Sogenhoe, I. 7	*Suggenhou* 324b
Somerledetona, *-tuna*	See Somerton
Somerleyton, K. 2	*Sumerlede(s)tuna* 283b, 284 *bis*, 445
Somersham, G. 7	*Sumers(h)am* 281b, 337, 404, 404b, 437b, 448b
Somerton, D. 7	*Somerledetona*, *-tuna* 360, 425b *Sumerledetuna* 359b
Soterlega	See Sotterley
Sotherton, K. 4	*Sudretuna* 432
Sotterley, K. 3	*Soterlega* 301, 301b
South Cove, K. 4	*Coua* 293, 313b
South Elmham, All Saints, St Cross, St James, St Margaret, St Michael, St Nicholas, St Peter, I. 3, I. 4, J. 3	*Almaham*, *Almeham* 298, 356, 379, 380 *Elmeham* 327b *Halmeham* 380
Southolt	Not in D.B.
Southwold, K. 4	*Sudholda*, *Sudwolda* 371b *bis*
Spexhall	Not in D.B.
Sproughton	Not in D.B.
Staham, *Stalham*, *Stanaham*	See Stonham, Earl and Little
Stanesfelda	See Stanningfield, Stansfield
Stanesteda	See Stanstead
Stanestrada	See Stone Street (in Hadleigh)
Stanfelda	Unid., 303b
Stanfella	See Stanningfield
Stanham	See Stonham, Earl and Little

Thorpe (in Aldingham), K. 6	*Thorpe* 333b *Torp* 292b, 316b, 333
Thorpe (in Ashfield), H. 6	*Torp* 298b, 299, 305b, 306 *ter*, 360b, 384
Thorpe (in Dallinghoo), I. 7	*Torp* 412b
Thorpe (in Trimley), I. 9	*Torp(a)* 292, 341b, 342b
Thorpe Morieux, E. 7	*Torp(a)* 348b, 369, 369b
Thrandeston, G. 4	*Fran-*, *Frondestuna* 371, 432b *Strandestuna* 310, 321, 419 *Thrandestuna* 348, 371, 379b, 381 *Thraudestuna* 310 *Thrundestuna* 320b
Thrand-, *Thraudestuna*	See Thrandeston
Thrillauura	See Thurlow
Thrundestuna	See Thrandeston
Thurlow, Great and Little, B. 7	*Thrillauura* 371b *Tridlauua* 397 *bis* *Tritlawa* 286
Thurlston, G. 7	*Toroluestuna* 354, 394 *Turduestuna* 352b *Turlestuna* 352b *bis* *Turolu(u)estuna* 295, 394b, 426b, 446, 446b *Turuestuna* 290, 295, 446b
Thurstanestuna	See Thurston (in Hawkendon), *Turstanestuna* (lost in Bromeswell)
Thurston (near Bury St Edmunds), E. 5	*Thurstuna* 362 *Torstuna* 284b
Thurston (in Hawkendon), C. 7	*Thurstanestuna* 348b
Thurstuna	See Thurston (near Bury St Edmunds)
Thwaite	Not in D.B.
Timeworda	See Timworth
Timworth, D. 5	*Timeworda* 391 *Timwrtha* 363
Timwrtha	See Timworth
Toddenham	See Tuddenham (near Ipswich)
Todeham	See Tuddenham (near Mildenhall)
Todenes	See Dodnash
Todenham	See Tuddenham (near Ipswich), Tuddenham (near Mildenhall)
Toft	Unid., 378b, 395
Tonestala	See Tunstall (in Nettlestead)
Topesfelda	See Toppesfield
Toppesfield, F. 8	*Topesfelda* 372b *bis*
Torentuna	See Thorington (near Dunwich), Thorndon
Torham	See Thornham Magna
Torintuna	See Thorington (near Dunwich), Thorington (in Stoke by Nayland)
Tornai	See Thorney
Torn(e)duna	See Thorndon
Tornei(a)	See Thorney
Tornham	See Thornham Magna
Tornintuna	See Thorington (near Dunwich)
Toroluestuna	See Thurlston
Torp	See Ixworth Thorpe, Thorpe (in Aldingham), Thorpe (in Ashfield), Thorpe (in Dallinghoo), Thorpe (in Trimley), Thorpe Morieux
Torp (Sanford hd)	Unid., 394b

Torpa	See Ixworth Thorpe, Thorpe (in Trimley), Thorpe Morieux
Torpe (Stow hd)	Unid., 409
Torstanestuna	See *Turstanestuna* (lost in Bromeswell)
Torstuna (Thedwaste hd)	See Thurston (near Bury St Edmunds)
Torstuna (Stow hd)	Unid., 409
Tostock, E. 6	*Totestoc* 284b
	Totstocha 363b
Totdenham	See Tuddenham (near Ipswich)
Totenham	See Tuddenham (near Mildenhall)
Totestoc, *Totstocha*	See Tostock
Tremelaia, *Tremlega*	See Trimley
Tridlauua, *Trillauura*	See Thurlow
Trimley St Martin, St Mary, I. 9	*Tremelaia* 423b
	Tremlega 341, 342b, 385b
Tritlawa	See Thurlow
Troston, E. 5	*Trostuna* 366b
Trostuna	See Troston
Tuddenham (near Ipswich), H. 7	*Tod(d)enham* 386b, 423
	Totdenham 423
	Tude(n)ham 293, 315b, 346, 423b, 442
Tuddenham (near Mildenhall), C. 5	*Tode(n)ham* 355, 403
	Totenham 392
Tude(n)ham	See Tuddenham (near Ipswich)
Tunestal	See Tunstall (near Wickham Market)
Tunstall (in Nettlestead), G. 7	*Tonestala* 350b, 351b, 398b
Tunstall (near Wickham Market), J. 7	*Tunestal* 307
Turchetlestuna	Unid., 420
Turduestuna	See Thurlston
Turintuna	See Thorington (near Dunwich)
Turlestuna, *Turolu(u)estuna*	See Thurlston
Tur-, *Thur-*, *Torstanestuna*, I. 7	Lost in Bromeswell, 317, 354, 400b
Turstanestuna, I. 8	Lost in Trimley, 340
Turuestuna	See Thurlston
Tusemera	Unid., 418
Ubbeston, I. 5	*Upbestuna* 415
Udebriga, *-brige*, *-bryge*	See Woodbridge
Udeham, I. 8	Lost in Sutton, 388b
Uffeforda, *Uffeworda*	See Ufford
Ufford, I. 7	*Offeworda* 343b
	Uffeforda 371b
	Uffeworda 324, 324b
	Ufforda 325
	Usforda 388
Ufforda	See Ufford
Uggecehala	See Uggeshall
Uggeshall, K. 4	*Uggecehala* 444b
	Ugghecala 371b
	Uggiceheala 299b
	Ulkesala 331b
	Wggessala 449
Ugghecala, *Uggiceheala*	See Uggeshall
Uledana	See Olden
Ulkesala	See Uggeshall
Ultuna	Unid., 409
Uluerestuna	See Woolverstone
Uluestuna, *-tune*	See Ulverston
Ulverston, G. 6	*Oluestuna* 417
	Uluestuna, *-tune* 376b *bis*, 377b, 417b, 418
Undley, B. 4	*Lundale* 382
Upbestuna	See Ubbeston
Usforda	See Ufford
Uuarle	Unid., 356
Uuereteham	See Wrentham

Uuesdana	See Ousden
Uurab(r)etuna	See *Wrabetuna*
Vratinga	See Wratting
Vrdresfelda	See Withersfield
Wadgata	See Wadgate
Wadgate, I. 9	*Wadgata* 340, 342
Walberswick	Not in D.B.
Waldingafelda	See Waldringfield
Waldingafella, *Waldingefelda*	See Waldingfield
Waldingfield, Great and Little, E. 8	*Altera Walingafella* 416; *Waldingafella*, *-gefelda* 360, 392b; *Walingafella* 350, 392b, 416, 418b, 425
Waldringafelda, *Minima Waldringfelda*	See Waldringfield
Waldringfield, I. 8	*Minima Waldringafelda* 315; *Wald(r)ingafelda* 369b, 424b
Walepola	See Walpole
Walesam	See Walsham le Willow
Waletuna	See Walton
Walingafella, *Altera Walingafella*	See Waldingfield
Walpole, J. 4	*Walepola* 292b
Walsam	See Walsham le Willows
Walsham le Willows, F. 5	*Wal(e)sam* 327b, 439, 440 *bis*; *Washam* 367
Walton, I. 9	*Waletuna* 339b, 340, 343b, 385b, 406b
Wamforda	See Wangford (near Brandon)
Wangford (near Brandon), C. 3	*Wamforda* 358b, 392
Wangford (near Southwold), K. 4	*Wankeforda* 414b
Wankeforda	See Wangford (near Southwold)
Wantesdana, *-dena*	See Wantisden
Wantisden, J. 7	*Wantesdana*, *-dena* 296b, 306b, 307 *bis*, 344, 353, 384; *Wanttesdena* 296
Wanttesdena	See Wantisden
Warabetuna	See *Wrabetuna*
Waracatinge	See Wratting
Warlingaham	See Worlingham
Washam	See Walsham le Willows
Washbrook	Not in D.B.
Watdena	See Wetherden
Watefelda	See Wattisfield, Whatfield
Watefella	See Whatfield
Watesfelda	See Wattisfield, Whatfield
Watlesfelda	See Wattisfield
Wattisfield, F. 4	*Wate(s)felda* 299, 405b; *Watlesfelda* 365b
Wattisham, F. 7	*Wecesham* 391, 435
Wcibrada	See Weybread
Wdebride, *-brige*	See Woodbridge
Wecesham	See Wattisham
Wederdena	See Wetherden
Wederingaseta	See Wetheringsett
Wedresfelda	See Withersfield
Weibrada, *-brade*	See Weybread
Weledana	Unid., 427
Wellingaham	See Willingham
Welnetham, Great and Little, D. 6	*Huelfiham* 363; *Telueteham* 291
Wenadestuna	See Wenhaston
Wenham, Great and Little, G. 8	Wenham 295, 296, 377b *bis*, 425b *bis*
Wenhaston, J. 4	*Wenadestuna* 292b
Weresdel	See Withersdale
Weringheseta	See Wetheringsett
Werlingaham	See Worlingham
Weruest(ed)a	See Wherstead
Wesletuna	See Westleton
Westerfield, H. 7	*Westrefelda* 294b, 295 *bis*, 305b, 306, 352b *bis*, 383b, 410, 411, 422b,

Westerfield cont.	423, 426b *bis*, 446b *bis*
Westhall	Not in D.B.
Westhorpe, F. 5	*Westor(p)* 309b *bis*, 426b *Westtorp* 370b, 371, 421b, 434b, 440 *Westurp* 321
Westlea	See Westley
Westledestuna, *Westlentuna*	See Westleton
Westleton, K. 5	*Wesletuna* 313b, 314 *Westledestuna* 440 *Westlentuna* 312
Westley, D. 6	*Westlea* 358b, 391
Weston, J. 3	*Westuna* 282b, 283, 288b, 335b *bis*, 336, 407, 412b
Westor(p)	See Westhorpe
Westrefelda	See Westerfield
West Stow, D. 5	*Stowa* 364
Westtorp	See Westhorpe
Westuna	See Market Weston, Weston. See also Weston Colville, Cambs.
Westurp	See Westhorpe
Wetherden, F. 6	*Watdena* 409, 427 *Wederdena* 360
Wetheringsett, G. 5	*Wederingaseta* 370 *Weringheseta* 285b, 324, 371, 384b
Wettingaham	See Whittingham
Weybread, H. 4	*Wcibrada* 379 *Weibrada*, *-brede* 286, 329b *ter*, 349 *ter*, 368b
Wggessala	See Uggeshall
Whatfield, F. 8	*Watefelda*, *-fella* 292, 369 *bis*, 397b, 405, 417b, 426, 440 *Watesfelda* 330b
Whepstead, D. 6	*Huepestede* 356b
Wherstead, G. 8	*Weruest(ed)a* 295b *bis*, 402
Whittingham, I. 4	*Wettingaham* 349
Whitton, G. 7	*Widituna* 446b
Wica	See Wyken
Wiccham	See Wickham Skeith
Wicham	See Wickhambrook, Wickham Skeith
Wichedis	Unid., 412b
Wickhambrook, C. 7	*Wicham* 397
Wickham Market, I. 6	*Wik(h)am* 293b, 324b *bis*, 343b, 373b, 412, 443
Wickham Skeith, G. 5	*Wic(c)ham* 285b, 286, 323b, 370, 371 *Wik(h)am* 348 *bis*
Widituna	See Whitton
Wighefelda	See Wingfield
Wik(h)am	See Wickham Market, Wickham Skeith
Wilby, H. 5	*Wilebey*, *-bi* 329, 379, 379b *bis*
Wilebey, *-bi*	See Wilby
Wileford(a)	See Wilford
Wilford, I. 7	*Wileford(a)* 318b, 325, 343b
Willaluesham	See Willisham
Willingaham	See Willingham
Willingham, K. 3	*Well-*, *Willingaham* 283b, 335, 407 *bis*
Willisham, F. 7	*Willaluesham* 351
Wimundahala	Unid., 336, 407b
Wimundestuna	Unid., 391, 397
Wineberga	See Wingfield
Winestuna	See Winston
Wingfield, H. 4	*Wighefelda* 379b *Wineberga* 328b, 385
Winston, H. 6	*Winestuna* 298b *bis*, 305b, 377, 383b
Wirilintona	See Worlington
Wis(s)eta	See Wissett
Wissett, J. 4	*Wis(s)eta* 293 *bis*, 449
Witdesham	See Witnesham
Witeskeou	See Wixoe

Withermarsh, F. 9	*Withermers* 401
Withermers	See Withermarsh
Withersdale, I. 4	*Weresdel* 314
Withersfield, B. 7	*Vrdresfelda* 396b *Wedresfelda* 397, 398b
Witnesham, H. 7	*Witdesham* 427b
Wiuerdestuna, *Wiuert(h)estuna*	See Wyverstone
Wixoe, C. 8	*Witeskeou* 414
Wledana	See Olden
Wlfpeta	See Woolpit
Wluerthestuna	See Wyverstone
Woodbridge, I. 7	*Udebriga*, *-brige* 344, 388b *bis*, 412, 423b *Udebryge* 294 *Wdebride*, *-brige* 327b, 348 *Wudebrige*, *-bryge* 325b, 327
Woolpit, E. 6	*Wlfpeta* 362b
Woolverstone, H. 8	*Hulferestuna* 420 *Ulueres tuna* 295b
Word(h)am	See Wortham
Wordwell, D. 5	*Wridewella* 366b
Worlingham, K. 3	*War-*, *Werlingaham* 282b, 283, 301b, 370, 407
Worlington, B. 4	*Wirilintona* 355
Worlingworth, H. 5	*Wyrlingwortha* 368
Wortham, G. 4	*Word(h)am* 320b, 361, 419 *bis* *Wortham* 322b, 354b *bis*
Wrabbatuna	See *Wrabetuna*
Wrabetuna, *Uurab(r)etuna*, *Warabetuna*, *Wrabbatuna*	Unid., 293, 312b, 313b, 314, 332, 334
Wratinga	See Wratting
Wratting, Great and Little, B. 7, B. 8	*Vratinga* 396 *Waracatinge* 371b *Wratinga* 390b, 396b
Wrentham, K. 3	*Uuereteham* 399b, 400 *Wretham* 399
Wretham	See Wrentham
Wridewella	See Wordwell
Wudebrige, *-bryge*	See Woodbridge
Wyken, E. 5	*Wica* 421, 439b *bis*
Wyrlingwortha	See Worlingworth
Wyverstone, F. 5	*Wiuerdestuna* 371 *Wiuert(h)estuna* 286, 309, 321b, 370, 370b, 436, 440 *Wluerthestuna* 408
Yaxley, G. 4	*Iachele(i)a* 320b, 323b *Iacheslea* 379b, 381
Yoxford, J. 5	*Gokesford* 429b *Iokesfort* 333

ANONYMOUS HOLDINGS

No place-names appear in the following four entries, and it is possible that some (or even all) of these refer to holdings at places not named elsewhere in Domesday Book:

In Hundret de Colenes est quedam pastura communis omnibus hominibus de hundret, 339b.
Richard son of Count Gilbert, 33 acres in Sampford hd, 395.
Robert Grenon, 120 acres in Sampford hd, 420b.
William de Alno (from Robert Grenon), 2 acres in Colneis hd, 420b.

SURREY—*SUDRIE*

Folios 30–36b

MAP 50

Abinceborne	See Abinger
Abinger, E. 5	*Abinceborne* 36
Acstede	See Oxted
Addington, H. 3	*Ed(d)intone* 36b *bis*
Aissela, *-ele*	See Esher
Albury, D. 5	*Eldeberie* 35b
Alford	Not in D.B.
Antisbury, E. 5	*Hanstega* 36
App's Court, E. 2	*Ebsa* 35 *quater*
Arseste	See Hartshurst
Ash	Not in D.B.
Ashstead, F. 3	*Stede* 31b
Aultone	See Carshalton
Bagshot	Not in D.B.
Balham, G. 2	*Belgeham* 36
Banstead, F. 3	*Benestede* 31b
Barnes, F. 1	*Berne* 34
Battersea, G. 1	*Patricesy* 31b, 32
Becesworde	See East Betchworth, West Betchworth
Beddington, G. 2	*Beddinton(e)* 34b, 36b *bis*
Beddinton(e)	See Beddington
Belgeham	See Balham
Benestede	See Banstead
Berge	See Burgh
Bermondsey, G. 1	*Bermundesy(e)* 30, 34
Bermundesy(e)	See Bermondsey
Berne	See Barnes
Biflet	See Byfleet
Bisley	Not in D.B.
Blachingelei	See Bletchingley
Bletchingley, G. 4	*Blachingelei* 34b
Bocheham	See Bookham, Ockham
Bochelant	See Buckland
Bookham, Great and Little, E. 4	*Bocheham* 32b, 35b 2nd entry
Borham	See Burgham
Brameselle	Unid., 34
Bramley, D. 5	*Brolege* 31 *Bronlei* 30, 31b *Brunlege*, *-lei* 30, 30b, 31 *ter*, 32, 34
Brolege, *Bronlei*, *Brunlege*, *-lei*	See Bramley
Buckland, F. 4	*Bochelant* 34b
Burgh, F. 3	*Berge* 32
Burgham, D. 4	*Borham* 34b
Burstow	Not in D.B.
Byfleet, D. 3	*Biflet* 34
Calvedone	See Chaldon
Camberwell, G. 1	*Cambrewelle* 36b
Cambrewelle	See Camberwell
Capel	Not in D.B.
Carshalton, G. 3	*Aultone* 36
Caterham	Not in D.B.
Cebeham	See Chobham
Ceiham	See Cheam
Celeorde	See Chilworth
Celesham	See Chelsham
Certesi	See Chertsey
Chaldon, G. 4	*Calvedone* 31b
Charlwood	Not in D.B.
Cheam, F. 3	*Ceiham* 30b
Chelesham	See Chelsham
Chelsham, H. 3	*C(h)elesham* 34b *bis*
Chenintune	See Kennington
Cherchefelle	See Reigate
Chertsey, D. 2	*Certesi* 32
Chessington, F. 3	*Cisedune* 36b *Cisendone* 35
Chiddingfold	Not in D.B.
Chilworth, D. 4	*Celeorde* 31
Chingestone, *-tun(e)*	See Kingston upon Thames
Chipstead, G. 3	*Tepestede* 33, 34b
Chivington, G. 4	*Civentone* 34b
Chobham, C. 3	*Cebeham* 32b
Cisedune, *Cisendone*	See Chessington

Civentone	See Chivington
Claigate	See Claygate
Clandon, East and West, D. 4	*Clanedun* 34 *bis*, 36
Clanedun	See Clandon
Clapham, G. 1	*Clopeham* 36
Claygate, E. 3	*Claigate* 32
Clopeham	See Clapham
Cobham, E. 3	*Covenham* 32b
Codintone	See Cuddington
Colesdone	See Coulsdon
Compton, C. 5	*Contone* 36
Contone	See Compton. See also Compton (near Harting), Sx.
Coombe, F. 2	*Cumbe* 36b *bis*
Coulsdon, G. 3	*Colesdone* 32b
Covenham	See Cobham
Cranleigh	Not in D.B.
Croindene	See Croydon
Crowhurst	Not in D.B.
Croydon, G. 2	*Croindene* 30b
Cuddington, F. 2	*Codintone* 31b
Cumbe	See Coombe
Dirtham, E. 4	*Driteham* 35, 35b
Ditone	See Ditton
Ditton, Long and Thames, E. 2	*Ditone*, *-tune* 32, 35
Ditune	See Ditton
Dorchinges	See Dorking
Dorking, E. 4	*Dorchinges* 30b
Driteham	See Dirtham
Dunsfold	Not in D.B.
East Betchworth, F. 4	*Becesworde* 35b 1st entry
East Clandon	See Clandon
East Horsley	See Horsley
East Molesey	See Molesey
Ebsa	See App's Court
Ed(d)intone	See Addington
Effingham, E. 4	*Epingeham* 32b, 35b
Egeham	See Egham
Egham, D. 2	*Egeham* 32b
Eldeberie	See Albury
Elstead	Not in D.B.
Ember, E. 2	*Limeurde* 35
Epingeham	See Effingham
Epsom, F. 3	*Evesham* 32b
Esher, E. 3	*Aissela*, *-ele* 32, 32b *ter*, 34, 36b
Essira, *Essire*	See Shere
Estreham	See Ham (in Croydon), Ham (near Kingston), Streatham
Etwelle	See Ewell
Evesham	See Epsom
Ewell, F. 3	*Etwelle* 30b
Ewhurst	Not in D.B.
Farleigh, H. 3	*Ferlega* 34b
Farncombe, C. 5	*Fernecome* 31, 31b
Farnham, B. 5	*Ferneham* 31
Feceham	See Fetcham
Ferlega	See Farleigh
Fernecome	See Farncombe
Ferneham	See Farnham
Fetcham, E. 4	*Feceham* 30b, 31b, 36b
Frensham	Not in D.B.
Frimley	Not in D.B.
Gatone	See Gatton
Gatton, G. 4	*Gatone* 31b
Gelde-, *Gildeford*	See Guildford
Godalming, C. 5	*Godelminge* 30b *bis*
Godelminge	See Godalming
Godstone	Not in D.B.
Gomeselle	See Gomshall
Gomshall, E. 4	*Gomeselle* 30b *bis*
Great Bookham	See Bookham
Guildford, D. 4	*Gelde-*, *Gildeford* 30, 35b
Hacheham	See Hatcham
Hallega	See Headley
Ham (in Croydon), H. 2	*Estreham* 34
Ham (near Kingston), E. 2	*Estreham* 32b
Hambledon, C. 6	*Hameledone* 36
Hameledone	See Hambledon
Hanstega	See Antisbury
Hartshurst, E. 5	*Arseste* 35b

Hascombe	Not in D.B.
Haslemere	Not in D.B.
Hatcham, G. 1	*Hacheham* 31b
Headley, F. 4	*Hallega* 36b
Henlei	See Henley
Henley, C. 4	*Henlei* 34
Hoclei	See Ockley
Horley	Not in D.B.
Hormera	See Hurtmore
Horne	Not in D.B.
Horsell	Not in D.B.
Horslei	See Horsley
Horsley, East and West, D. 4, E. 4	*Horslei* 31 *Orselei* 36
Hurtmore, C. 5	*Hormera* 36
Kennington, G. 1	*Chenintune* 36b
Kingston upon Thames, F. 2	*Chingestone*, *-tun(e)* 30b *bis*, 32, 32b, 36
Kingswood	Not in D.B.
Lambeth, G. 1	*Lanchei* 34 *bis*
Lanchei	See Lambeth
Leatherhead, E. 4	*Leret* 30b
Leigh	Not in D.B.
Leret	See Leatherhead
Limenesfeld	See Limpsfield
Limeurde	See Ember
Limpsfield, H. 4	*Limenesfeld* 34
Lingfield	Not in D.B.
Litelfeld	Unid., 36
Liteltone	See Littleton
Little Bookham	See Bookham
Littleton, C. 4	*Liteltone* 36b
Lodesorde	See Lodsworth, Sx.
Long Ditton	See Ditton
Losele	See Loseley
Loseley, C. 4	*Losele* 34b
Lower Tooting	See Tooting
Lundonia	See London, Mdlx.
Malden, F. 2	*Meldone* 32b, 35 *bis*
Meldone	See Malden
Meretone	See Merton
Merrow	Not in D.B.
Merstan	See Merstham
Merstham, G. 4	*Merstan* 31
Merton, F. 2	*Meretone* 30
Michelham	See Mickleham, Mitcham
Mickleham, E. 4	*Michelham* 35 *Micleham* 32
Micleham	See Mickleham
Mideham	Unid., 35b
Mildetone	See Milton
Milton, E. 4	*Mildetone* 36
Mitcham, G. 2	*Michelham* 31b, 35b
Molesey, East and West, E. 2	*Molesham* 35 *bis*, 36b
Molesham	See Molesey
Morden, F. 2	*Mordone* 32
Mordone	See Morden
Mortelaga, *-lage*	See Mortlake
Mortlake, F. 1	*Mortelaga*, *-lage* 30b, 31, 34
Newdigate	Not in D.B.
Newington	Not in D.B.
North Tadworth	See Tadworth
Notfelle	See Nutfield
Nutfield, G. 4	*Notfelle* 34
Ockham, D. 3	*Bocheham* 35b 1st entry
Ockley, E. 5	*Hoclei* 35b *bis*
Odemerestor	See Woodmansterne
Odetone	See Wotton
Orde	See Worth (near Crawley), Sx.
Orselei	See Horsley
Oxted, H. 4	*Acstede* 34
Pachesham, E. 3	*Pachesham* 31b
Paddington, E. 5	*Padendene* 36
Padendene	See Paddington
Patricesham	See Petersham
Patricesy	See Battersea
Pecheham	See Peckham
Pechingeorde	Unid., 36b
Peckham, G. 1	*Pecheham* 31b
Peliforde	See Pyrford
Peper Harow, C. 5	*Pipereherge* 36
Petersham, F. 2	*Patricesham* 32b
Pipereherge	See Peper Harow

Pirbright	Not in D.B.
Putelei	See Putney
Putney, F. 1	*Putelei* 30b
Puttenham	Not in D.B.
Pyrford, D. 3	*Peliforde* 32
Reddesolham, *Redessolham*	See Rodsell
Reigate, F. 4	*Cherchefelle* 30
Richmond	Not in D.B.
Rodsell, C. 5	*Reddesolham* 31b *Redessolham* 31
Rotherhithe	Not in D.B.
St Martha's	Not in D.B.
Sande	See Send
Sanderstead, G. 3	*Sandestede* 32
Sandestede	See Sanderstead
Scaldefor	See Shalford
Seale	Not in D.B.
Send, D. 4	*Sande* 36b
Shalford, D. 5	*Scaldefor* 35b
Shere, D. 4	*Essira*, *Essire* 30b *bis*
South Tadworth	See Tadworth
Southwark, G. 4	*Sudwerc(h)a*, *-werche* 30, 30b, 31b, 32 *quin*, 34 *bis*, 34b *bis*, 35 *bis*, 36b
Stede	See Ashstead
Stochae	See Stoke next Guildford
Stoche	See Stoke D'Abernon
Stoke D'Abernon, E. 3	*Stoche* 35
Stoke next Guildford, C. 4	*Stochae* 30
Streatham, G. 2	*Estreham* 31b, 34b
Sudtone	See Sutton (in Shere), Sutton (near Wallington)
Sudtune	See Sutton (in Woking)
Sudwerc(h)a, *-werche*	See Southwark
Sutton (in Shere), E. 5	*Sudtone* 32
Sutton (near Wallington), F. 3	*Sudtone* 32b
Sutton (in Woking), D. 4	*Sudtune* 36b
Tadeorde, *Tadorne*	See Tadworth
Tadworth, North and South, F. 3	*Tadeorde* 31b *Tadorne* 35b
Taleorde	See Tolworth
Tandridge, H. 4	*Tenrige* 34b
Tatelefelle	See Tatsfield
Tatsfield, H. 3	*Tatelefelle* 31b
Tellingedone	See Tillingdown
Tenrige	See Tandridge
Tepestede	See Chipstead
Tetinges	See Tyting
Thames Ditton	See Ditton
Thorncroft, E. 4	*Tornecrosta* 35b *bis*
Thorpe, D. 2	*Torp* 32b
Thursley	Not in D.B.
Ticesei	See Titsey
Tillingdown, G. 4	*Tellingedone* 34b
Titsey, H. 4	*Ticesei* 36b
Tiwesle	See Tuesley
Tolworth, F. 2	*Taleorde* 35, 35b
Tooting, Lower and Upper, G. 2	*Totinges* 32, 33 *bis*, 34b
Tornecrosta	See Thorncroft
Torp	See Thorpe
Totinges	See Tooting
Tuesley, C. 5	*Tiwesle* 30b
Tyting, D. 4	*Tetinges* 31
Upper Tooting	See Tooting
Wachelestede	See Walkingstead
Waddington, G. 3	*Watendone* 32b
Waleorde	See Walworth
Waletone	See Wallington, Walton on Thames
Walkingstead, H. 4	*Wachelestede* 34
Wallingeham	See Woldingham
Wallington, G. 3	*Waletone* 30
Waltone	See Walton on the Hill
Walton on Thames, E. 2	*Waletone* 35 *ter*, 36
Walton on the Hill, F. 4	*Waltone* 35

Walworth, G. 1	*Waleorde* 31
Wanborough, C. 4	*Weneberge* 36
Wand(el)esorde	See Wandsworth
Wandsworth, F. 1	*Wand(el)esorde* 32, 34 *Wendelesorde* 35b
Warlingham	Not in D.B.
Watendone	See Waddington
Webrige, -bruge	See Weybridge
Wendelesorde	See Wandsworth
Weneberge	See Wanborough
Werpesdune	See Worplesdon
Wescote	See Westcott
West Betchworth, F. 4	*Becesworde* 35b 2nd entry
West Clandon	See Clandon
Westcott, E. 4	*Wescote* 36b
West Horsley	See Horsley
West Molesey	See Molesey
Westone	See Weston on the Green
Weston on the Green, E. 2	*Westone* 34
Weybridge, D. 3	*Webrige, -bruge* 32, 32b
Whitford, G. 2	*Witford* 31b, 35b
Wimbledon	Not in D.B.
Windesores	See Windsor, Berks.
Windlesham	Not in D.B.
Wiselei	See Wisley
Wisley, D. 3	*Wiselei* 36b
Witford	See Whitford
Witlei	See Witley
Witley, C. 5	*Witlei* 36
Wochinges	See Woking
Woking, D. 3	*Wochinges* 30, 31
Woldingham, H. 4	*Wallingeham* 34b
Wonersh	Not in D.B.
Woodmansterne, G. 3	*Odemerestor* 35
Worplesdon, C. 4	*Werpesdune* 34b
Wotton, E. 5	*Odetone* 36b
Wucha	See Wyke
Wyke, B. 4	*Wucha* 34b

ANONYMOUS HOLDINGS

No place-names appear in the following twenty-six entries, and it is possible that some (or even all) of these refer to holdings at places not named elsewhere in Domesday Book:

The king, one hide in Wotton hd, 30b.
The king, 3 virgates in Wotton hd, 30b.
Aldi (from the king), one virgate in Elmbridge hd, 30b.
Bishop of Bayeux, 3 hides in Blackheath hd, 31.
Bishop of Bayeux, land for one plough in Blackheath hd, 31.
Hugh (from bishop of Bayeux), 4 hides in Tandridge hd, 31b.
Ansgot (from bishop of Bayeux), half a hide in Wallington hd, 31b.
Rannulf (from bishop of Bayeux), one hide and one virgate in Copthorne hd, 31b.
Baingiard (from bishop of Bayeux), one hide in Copthorne hd, 31b.
Adam son of Hubert (from bishop of Bayeux), one hide in Wallington hd, 31b.
William (from Chertsey abbey), 2 hides in Tandridge hd, 32b.
Chertsey abbey, 3 virgates in Tandridge hd, 32b.
William de Wateville (from Chertsey abbey), 2 hides in Elmbridge hd, 32b.
Edric (from Chertsey abbey), half a hide in Kingston hd, 32b.
Haimo the sheriff (from Chertsey abbey), $1\frac{1}{2}$ hides in Wallington hd, 33.
Haimo the sheriff (from Chertsey abbey), half a hide in Wallington hd, 33.
Barking abbey, 2 hides in Wallington hd, 34.
Count of Mortain, 2 hides and one virgate in Wallington hd, 34.
Earl Roger, one hide in Wotton hd, 34.

ANONYMOUS HOLDINGS (continued)

Robert de Wateville (from Richard of Tonbridge), 14 hides in Tandridge hd, 34b.
Richard of Tonbridge, one hide in Elmbridge hd, 35.
Westminster abbey, 2 hides in Copthorne hd, 35b.
William son of Ansculf, 2 hides in Copthorne hd, 35b.
Baldwin (from William son of Ansculf), 2 hides in Copthorne hd, 36.
Walter de Douai, 2 hides in Wallington hd, 36.
Seman (from the king), one virgate in Copthorne hd, 36b.

SUSSEX—*SUDSEXE*

Folios 16–29b

MAPS 48–49

Acescome	See Ashcombe
Achiltone	See Eckington
Achingeworde	See Etchingwood
Achintone	See Eckington
Albourne	Not in D.B.
Alchin, K. 2	*Alsihorne* 16b
Alchitone	See Eckington
Alciston, K. 5	*Alsi(s)tone* 17b, 19 *bis*, 19b *ter*
Aldingbourne, D. 5	*Aldingeborne* 16b
Aldingeborne	See Aldingbourne
Aldrington, H. 5	*Eldretune* 26b
Alfriston, K. 5	*Alvricestone* 21b *bis*
Alintune, *Alitone*	See Allington
Allington, J. 4	*Alintune* 27b *Alitone* 22b
Alsihorne	See Alchin
Alsi(s)tone	See Alciston
Alvricestone	See Alfriston
Amberley, E. 4	*Ambrelie* 17
Ambersham	Not in D.B.
Ambrelie	See Amberley
Angemare	See Angmering
Angmering, F. 5	*Angemare* 24b *bis* *Langemare* 29
Annington, G. 4	*Haningedune* 28
Antone	See East Hampnett
Apedroc	See Parrock
Aplesham	See Applesham
Appledram	Not in D.B.
Applesham, G. 4	*Aplesham* 28b
Ardingly	Not in D.B.
Arlington, K. 5	*Herlintone* 19
Arundel, E. 5	*Harundel* 23
Ashburnham, M. 4	*Esseborne* 18
Ashcombe, J. 4	*Acescome* 27b
Ashington, G. 4	*Essingetune* 29
Ashurst	Not in D.B.
Babintone	See Bepton
Balcombe	Not in D.B.
Balmer, I. 4	*Berge-*, *Burgemere* 22b, 26b
Barcombe, J. 4	*Bercham* 27b
Barkham, J. 3	*Bercheham* 22b *bis*
Barlavington, E. 3	*Berleventone* 23b
Barnham, E. 5	*Berneham* 25
Basingeham	Unid., 20
Batailge, La	See Battle
Bathurst, N. 4	*Wasingate* 17b
Battle, N. 4	*La Batailge* 17b
Bece	See Beech (in Battle)
Beche	See Beech (in Whatlington)
Bechingetone	See Bechington
Bechington, K. 5	*Bechingetone* 22
Beckley	Not in D.B.

Beddinges	See Upper Beeding
Beddingham, J. 4	*Bed(d)ingham* 20b *bis* *Beling(e)ham* 18b, 19 *bis*
Bedinges	See Upper Beeding
Bedingham	See Beddingham
Beech (in Battle), M. 3	*Bece* 17b
Beech (in Whatlington), N. 3	*Beche* 18b
Beling(e)ham	See Beddingham
Bellest	See Bellhurst
Bellhurst, O. 2	*Bellest* 20
Benefeld, H. 3	*Benefelle* 27b *bis*
Benefelle	See Benefeld
Benestede	See Binsted
Bepton, D. 3	*Babintone* 23b
Bercham	See Barcombe
Bercheham	See Barkham, Burpham
Berchelie	See Burleigh
Berchinges	See Perching
Berewice	See Berwick
Bergemere	See Balmer
Berie	See Bury
Berleventone	See Barlavington
Berneham	See Barnham
Bersted	Not in D.B.
Berth, I. 3	*Berts* 28
Bertredtone	See Binderton
Berts	See Berth
Bervice	See Berwick
Berwick, K. 5	*Berewice* 19b *Bervice* 19b
Bevedene	See Bevendean
Bevendean, I. 5	*Bevedene* 22b, 26b
Beverington, L. 5	*Bevringetone* 20b *bis*
Bevringetone	See Beverington
Bexelei	See Bexhill
Bexhill, N. 4	*Bexelei* 18
Bigeneure	See Bignor
Bignor, E. 4	*Bigeneure* 25
Bilesham	See Bilsham
Billingshurst	Not in D.B.

Bilsham, E. 5	*Bilesham* 25
Binderton, C. 4	*Bertredtone* 23
Binsted, E. 5	*Benestede* 25
Biochest	See Brockhurst
Birchgrove, J. 2	*Bontegraue* 22b
Birdham, C. 5	*Brideham* 24
Biscopestone	See Bishopstone
Bishopstone, K. 5	*Biscopestone* 16b
Bocheham	See Uckham
Bodeham	See Bodiam
Bodiam, N. 2	*Bodeham* 20
Bogelie, L. 4	Lost in Hailsham, 22
Bognor	Not in D.B.
Bolintun	See Bollington
Bollington, N. 4	*Bol(l)intun* 17b, 18
Bollintun	See Bollington
Bolney	Not in D.B.
Bongetune	See Buncton
Bontegraue	See Birchgrove
Borham	Unid., 25
Borne	See Bourne, Eastbourne, Westbourne
Bortone	See Broughton
Boseham	See Bosham
Bosgrave	See Boxgrove
Bosham, C. 5	*Boseham* 16, 17, 17b, 27, Sx.; 43, Hants.
Botechitone	See Burton
Botintone	See Buddington
Botolphs	Not in D.B.
Bourne, N. 2	*Borne* 19b *Burne* 19b
Boxgrove, D. 4	*Bosgrave* 25b
Bradewatre	See Broadwater
Bramber, G. 4	*Brembre* 28
Brambletye, J. 1	*Branbertei* 22b
Branbertei	See Brambletye
Brede	Not in D.B.
Brembre	See Bramber
Brideham	See Birdham
Brightling, M. 3	*Brislinga* 18b
Brighton, I. 5	*Bristelme(s)tune* 26b *bis*
Brislinga	See Brightling
Bristelme(s)tune	See Brighton

Broadwater, G. 5	*Bradewatre* 26b, 28b, Sx.; 50b, Hants.
Brockhurst, J. 1	*Biochest* 22b
Broomham, M. 4	*Brunham* 18b
Broomhill	Not in D.B.
Broughton, L. 5	*Bortone* 19
Brunham	See Broomham
Buddington, D. 3	*Botintone* 23b
Buncton, G. 4	*Bongetune* 29
Burgeham	See Burgham
Burgelstaltone	Unid., 19b
Burgemere	See Balmer
Burgham, M. 2	*Burgeham* 19b
Burleigh, I. 1	*Berchelie* 22b
Burne	See Bourne, Eastbourne, Westbourne
Burpham, F. 4	*Bercheham* 24b
Burton, E. 3	*Botechitone* 23b
Burwash	Not in D.B.
Bury, E. 4	*Berie* 17
Buxted	Not in D.B.
Calvintone	See Chalvington
Calvrestot	See Shovelstrode
Catsfield, M. 4	*Cedesfeld*, *-felle* 17b, 18
Caveltone	See Chalvington
Cedesfeld, *-felle*	See Catsfield
Celrestuis	See Shovelstrode
Cengeltune	See Chancton
Cerletone	See Charlston
Cerlocestone	See Charleston
Cetelingei	See Chiddingley
Chailey	Not in D.B.
Chalvington, K. 4	*Calvintone* 20, 22 *bis* *Caveltone* 19
Chancton, G. 4	*Cengeltune* 28, 28b
Charleston, K. 4	*Cerlocestone* 20b
Charlston, K. 5	*Cerletone* 21
Checeham	See Kitchenham
Chemere	See Keymer
Chenenolle	Unid., 22
Chichester, D. 5	*Cicestre* 16, 16b *bis*, 17, 17b *ter*, 23 *septiens*, 23b *septiens*, 24 *octiens*, 25b *bis*

Chiddingley, K. 4	*Cetelingei* 22b
Chidham	Not in D.B.
Childe(l)tune	See East Chiltington
Chingestone, *-tune*	See Kingston by Sea
Chithurst, C. 3	*Titeherste* 23
Chollington, L. 6	*Clotintone* 20b
Cicestre	See Chichester
Cilletone, *-tune*	See West Chiltington
Claitune	See Clayton
Clapham, F. 5	*Clopeham* 28
Claveham	See Claverham
Claverham, K. 4	*Clave(s)ham* 20, 22 *bis* *Clavreham* 19b
Clavesham, *Clavreham*	See Claverham
Clayton, I. 4	*Claitune* 27
Clepinges	See Climping
Climping, E. 5	*Clepinges* 25
Cloninctune	See Donnington
Clopeham	See Clapham
Clotinga	See Glatting
Clotintone	See Chollington
Coates	Not in D.B.
Cocheham	See Cokeham
Cochinges	See Cocking
Cocking, D. 3	*Cochinges* 23
Codeham	See Cootham
Cokeham, G. 5	*Cocheham* 29 *bis*
Coldwaltham	Not in D.B.
Compton (near Harting), C. 4	*Contone* 24, Sx.; 34, Surrey
Compton (in West Firle), K. 4	*Contone* 21
Contone	See Compton (near Harting), Compton (in West Firle)
Coombes, G. 4	*Cumbe* 28b
Coonare, *-nore*	See Cudnor
Cootham, F. 4	*Codeham* 24b
Cortesley, N. 4	*Croteslei* 18b
Cowfold	Not in D.B.
Crawley	Not in D.B.
Crohe(r)st	See Crowhurst
Croteslei	See Cortesley

Crowborough	Not in D.B.
Crowhurst, N. 4	*Crohe(r)st* 17b, 18b
Cuckfield	Not in D.B.
Cudnor, L. 5	*Coonare* 22 *Coonore* 22
Cumbe	See Coombes
Dalintone	See Dallington
Dallington, M. 3	*Dalintone* 18b
Danehill	Not in D.B.
Dankton, G. 5	*Dentune* 29
Dean, East and West (near Eastbourne), K. 5, L. 6	*Dene* 19, 19b, 21 *bis* *Esdene* 19
Dene	See Dean
Denton	Not in D.B.
Dentune	See Dankton
Derentune	See Durrington
Dicelinges, *Diceninges*	See Ditchling
Didling	Not in D.B.
Ditchling, I. 4	*Dicelinges* 22b, 26 *Diceninges* 22b
Dodimere	See Udimore
Donechitone	See Duncton
Donnington, C. 5	*Cloninctune* 17b
Drigsell, N. 3	*Drisnesel* 19b
Drisnesel	See Drigsell
Duncton, E. 3	*Donechitone* 23b
Durrington, F. 5	*Derentune* 28b *bis*
Earnley	Not in D.B.
Eartham	Not in D.B.
East Blatchington	Not in D.B.
Eastbourne, L. 5	*Borne* 20b, 22 *bis* *Burne* 22
East Chiltington, I. 4	*Childe(l)tune* 27 *bis*
East Dean (near Eastbourne)	See Dean
East Dean (near Singleton)	Not in D.B.
Eastergate, E. 5	*Gate* 25b
East Grinstead	Not in D.B.
East Guldeford	Not in D.B.
East Hall, L. 5	*Eshalle* 20b *bis*
East Hampnett, D. 5	*Antone* 25b
East Harting	See Harting
East Hoathly	Not in D.B.
East Lavant	See Lavant
East Lavington, D. 3	*Levitone* 17b
East Marden	See Marden
East Preston, F. 5	*Prestetune* 24b
East Wittering	See Wittering
Eaton, G. 3	*Etune* 29
Echentone	See Eckington
Eckington, K. 4	*Achiltone* 22 *Achintone* 22 *Alchitone* 19b *Echentone* 19 *Eschintone* 19b *Hechestone* 19
Edburton	Not in D.B.
Egdean	Not in D.B.
Eldretune	See Aldrington
Ellede	See Eyelid
Elsted, C. 3	*Halestede* 17b
Epinges	See Iping
Eringeham	See Erringham
Erringham, G. 4	*Eringeham* 28
Eschintone	See Eckington
Esdene	See Dean
Eshalle	See East Hall
Eslede	See Eyelid
Eslindone	See Slindon
Esmerewic	Unid., 26b
Esseborne	See Ashburnham
Esserintone	See Sherrington
Essete	See Exceat
Essingetune	See Ashington
Estochingeham	See Stockingham
Estone	See South Heighton, Stoughton
Estorchetone	See Storrington
Estrat	See Streat
Etchingham	Not in D.B.
Etchingwood, K. 3	*Achingeworde* 19
Etune	See Eaton
Evebentone	Unid., 19b
Ewhurst, N. 3	*Werste* 20 *bis*
Exceat, K. 5	*Essete* 21 *bis*
Eyelid, N. 3	*Ellede*, *Eslede* 18b *ter*

Fairlight (in East Grinstead), J. 1	*Ferlega* 22b
Fairlight (near Hastings), O. 4	*Ferlang* 19b
Falcheham	See Felpham
Falemere	See Falmer
Falmer, I. 4	*Falemere* 26, 26b *bis*
Felesmere	Unid., 22b
Felpham, E. 5	*Falcheham* 17b
Feringes	See Ferring
Ferla	See West Firle
Ferlang	See Fairlight (near Hastings)
Ferle	See Frog Firle, West Firle
Ferlega	See Fairlight (in East Grinstead)
Ferles	See Frog Firle
Fernhurst	Not in D.B.
Ferring, F. 5	*Feringes* 16b
Filleicham	See Sidlesham
Filsham, N. 4	*Pilesham* 17b *Wilesham* 18
Findon, F. 4	*Findune*, *Fintune* 28 *bis*
Findune, *Fintune*	See Findon
Fiseborne	See Fishbourne
Fishbourne, C. 5	*Fiseborne* 24
Fittleworth	Not in D.B.
Flescinge(s)	See Fletching
Fletching, J. 3	*Flescinge(s)* 22b *bis*
Fochinges	See Fulking
Fochintone	See Folkington
Fodilant	See Footland
Folkington, L. 5	*Fochintone* 21b
Footland, N. 3	*Fodilant* 20
Ford	Not in D.B.
Francwelle	See Frankwell
Frankwell, M. 4	*Francwelle* 18
Frant	Not in D.B.
Friston	Not in D.B.
Frog Firle, K. 5	*Ferle(s)* 21b *bis*, 26b
Fulking, H. 4	*Fochinges* 26b
Funtington	Not in D.B.
Garinges	See Goring
Garnecampo	See Warningcamp
Gate	See Eastergate
Gestelinges	See Guestling
Glatting, E. 4	*Clotinga* 23b
Glesham	See Glossams
Glossams, O. 3	*Glesham* 20
Glynde	Not in D.B.
Gorde	See Worth (in Little Horsted)
Goring, F. 5	*Garinges* 24b *bis*, 25 *bis*, 28 *bis*, 28b
Graffham, D. 3	*Grafham* 23b
Grafham	See Graffham
Greatham, F. 4	*Gretham* 24b
Greteham	See Grittenham
Gretham	See Greatham
Grittenham, E. 3	*Greteham* 23b
Guestling, O. 4	*Gestelinges* 19b
Hadlow Down	Not in D.B.
Hailsham, L. 4	*Hamelesham* 22
Haingurge	See Hawkridge
Halestede	See Elsted
Halnaker, D. 4	*Helnache*, *-neche* 25b *bis*
Halseeldene	See Hazelden
Hame	See Hamsey
Hamelesham	See Hailsham
Hamfelde	See Henfield
Hamsey, J. 4	*Hame* 22b, 27b
Hangetone	See Hangleton
Hangleton, H. 5	*Hangetone* 26b
Haningedune	See Annington
Hankham, L. 5	*Henecham* 22 *bis*
Hantone	See Littlehampton
Hardham, F. 3	*Heriedeham* 25
Harditone	See Lordington
Harpingden, J. 5	*Herbertinges* 26
Hartfield, K. 1	*Hertevel* 21b
Harting, East, South, and West, C. 3	*Hertinges* 23 *bis*
Harundel	See Arundel
Haslesse	See Hazelhurst
Hastinges	See Hastings
Hastings, O. 4	*Hastinges* 17, 18, Sx.; 60b, Berks.; 375b, Lincs.
Hawkridge, L. 4	*Haingurge* 21b
Haywards Heath	Not in D.B.

Hazelden, I. 1	*Halseeldene* 22b
Hazelhurst, M. 2	*Haslesse* 19
Heathfield	Not in D.B.
Hechestone	See Eckington
Hectone	See South Heighton
Heene, G. 5	*Hene* 28b
Hellingly	Not in D.B.
Helnache, *-neche*	See Halnaker
Hendene	See Hendon
Hendon, L. 4	*Hendene* 21b
Hene	See Heene
Henecham	See Hankham
Henfield, H. 4	*Hamfelde* 16b
Hentone	See Westhampnett
Herbertinges	See Harpingden
Heriedeham	See Hardham
Herlintone	See Arlington
Herst	See Hurstpierpoint
Herste	See Hurst, Hurstmonceux
Hertevel	See Hartfield
Hertinges	See Harting
Heyshott	Not in D.B.
Higham, O. 3	*Hiham* 20
Hiham	See Higham
Hoecourt, G. 5	*How* 29
Hoingesdene	See Ovingdean
Holintun	See Hollington
Hollington, N. 4	*Holintun* 17b *Horintone* 18b
Hooe, M. 4	*Hou* 17b, 18, 22
Horintone	See Hollington
Horns, L. 5	*Orne* 22 *bis*
Horselie	See Horsey
Horsey, L. 5	*Horselie* 22
Horsham	Not in D.B.
Horstede	See Horsted Keynes, Little Horsted
Horsted Keynes, J. 2	*Horstede* 22b
Hou	See Hooe
Houghton	Not in D.B.
Hove	Not in D.B.
Hovingedene	See Ovingdean
How	See Hoecourt
Hunestan	See Hunston
Hunston, D. 5	*Hunestan* 24

Hurst, N. 3	*Herste* 20
Hurstmonceux, M. 4	*Herste* 18
Hurstpierpoint, H. 3	*Herst* 27, 29
Icenore	See West Itchenor
Icklesham	Not in D.B.
Iden, P. 3	*Idene* 20
Idene	See Iden
Ifelt	See Ifield
Ifield, H. 1	*Ifelt* 29
Iford, J. 4	*Niworde* 26
Iping, D. 3	*Epinges* 29b
Isfield	Not in D.B.
Itchingfield	Not in D.B.
Itford, J. 5	*Litelforde* 20b
Ivet	Unid., 19b, 20
Jevington, L. 5	*Lov(r)ingetone* 19, 21
Keymer, I. 4	*Chemere* 27
Kingston (near Lewes)	Not in D.B.
Kingston by Sea, H. 5	*Chingestone*, *-tune* 26b, 28b
Kirdford	Not in D.B.
Kitchenham, O. 2	*Checeham* 19b
La Batailge	See Battle
Lancing, G. 5	*Lancinges* 29 *bis*
Lancinges	See Lancing
Laneswice	See Orleswick
Langelie	See Langney
Langemare	See Angmering
Langney, L. 5	*Langelie* 22
Laughton, K. 4	*Lestone*, *-tun* 19 *ter*, 19b, 21, 22, 26
Lavant, East and Mid, C. 4, D. 4	*Loventone* 16b, 23 *Lovintune* 22b
Lestone, *-tun*	See Laughton
Levitone	See East Lavington
Lewes, J. 4	*Lewes* 16b *ter*, 17, 17b, 26 *septiens*, 26b *octiens*, 27 *undeciens*, 27b *ter* *Lau(u)es*, L.D.B. 163 *bis*, 163b *bis*, Norf.

Lince	See Linch (in Bepton)
Linch	Not in D.B.
Linch (in Bepton), C. 3	*Lince* 23
Linchmere	Not in D.B.
Lindfield	Not in D.B.
Litelforde	See Itford
Litlington	Not in D.B.
Littlehampton, E. 5	*Hantone* 25
Little Horsted, K. 3	*Horstede* 22
Lodintone-, Lodiutone	See Wootton (in Folkington)
Lodsworth, D. 3	*Lodesorde* 36b, Surrey
Lolinminstre	See Lyminster
Lordine, N. 3	*Lordistret* 20
Lordington, C. 4	*Harditone* 24
Lordistret	See Lordine
Loventone	See Lavant
Lovingetone	See Jevington
Lovintune	See Lavant
Lovringetone	See Jevington, Yeverington
Lower Beeding	Not in D.B.
Lullington	Not in D.B.
Lurgashall	Not in D.B.
Lyminster, E. 5	*Lolinminstre* 24b, 28
Madehurst	Not in D.B.
Marden, East, North, Up and West, C. 4	*Meredone* 24 *quin*
Maresfield, J. 3	*Mesewelle* 22b
Mayfield	Not in D.B.
Medehei	Unid., 18
Mellinges	See South Malling
Meredone	See Marden
Mersitone	See Merston
Merston, D. 5	*Mersitone* 25b
Mesewelle	See Maresfield
Middeltone	See Middleton on Sea
Middleton on Sea, E. 5	*Middeltone* 25
Midhurst	Not in D.B.

Mid Lavant	See Lavant
Moham	See Muntham
Molstan	See Moustone
Montifelle	See Mountfield
Mordinges	See Worthing
Morleia	See Morley
Morley, H. 3	*Morleia* 28b
Mountfield, N. 3	*Montifelle* 18b
Moustone, I. 4	*Molstan* 27b
Mundham, D. 5	*Mundreham* 24
Mundreham	See Mundham
Muntham, F. 4	*Moham* 29
Nedrefelle	See Netherfield
Nerewelle	See Ninfield
Netherfield, M. 3	*Nedrefelle* 18b, *Nirefeld* 17b
Newhaven	Not in D.B.
Newick	Not in D.B.
Newtimber, H. 4	*Niuembre* 27
Ninfield, M. 4	*Nerewelle* 18
Nirefeld	See Netherfield
Nitinbreham	See Nyetimber
Niuembre	See Newtimber
Niworde	See Iford
Nonneminstre	Unid., 24b
Nordborne	See Nutbourne
North Marden	See Marden
North Stoke, E. 4	*Stoches* 24b
Nutbourne, F. 3	*Nordborne* 24b
Nuthurst	Not in D.B.
Nyetimber, F. 3	*Nitinbreham* 24b
Ode	Unid., 22b
Odemanscote	See Woodmancote
Odetone, *Odintune*	See Wootton (in East Chiltington)
Offham, E. 4	*Offham* 25
Offington, G. 5	*Ofintune* 28b
Ofintune	See Offington
Ordinges	See Worthing
Ore	Not in D.B.
Orne	See Horns
Orleswick, J. 5	*Laneswice* 26
Ovelei	See Woolfly
Oving	Not in D.B.
Ovingdean, I. 5	*Hoingesdene* 27b, *Hovingedene* 26b

Pageham	See Pagham
Pagham, C. 6	*Pageham* 16b
Palinges	See Peelings
Pangdean, H. 4	*Pinhedene*, *Pinwedene* 27 *bis*
Parham, F. 4	*Perham* 17, 24b
Parrock, J. 1	*Apedroc* 21b
Patcham, I. 4	*Piceham* 26
Patching, F. 5	*Petchinges* 16b
Paveorne	See Paythorne
Paythorne, H. 4	*Paveorne* 26b
Peasemarsh	Not in D.B.
Peelings, L. 5	*Palinges*, *Pellinges* 22 *bis*
Pellinges	See Peelings
Penehest	See Penhurst
Pengest	Unid., 21b
Penhurst, M. 3	*Penehest* 17b
Perching, H. 4	*Berchinges* 26b *Percinges* 27
Percinges	See Perching
Perham	See Parham
Petchinges	See Patching
Peteorde	See Petworth
Petworth, E. 3	*Peteorde* 23b
Pevenesel	See Pevensey
Pevensey, M. 5	*Pevenesel* 20b
Piceham	See Patcham
Piddinghoe	Not in D.B.
Pilesham	See Filsham
Pinhedene, *Pinwedene*	See Pangdean
Playden, P. 3	*Pleidena* 19b
Pleidena	See Playden
Plumpton, I. 4	*Pluntune* 27
Pluntune	See Plumpton
Poleberge	See Pulborough
Poling	Not in D.B.
Poninges	See Poynings
Porteslage, *-lamhe*	See Portslade
Portslade, H. 5	*Porteslage*, *-lamhe* 26b *bis*
Poynings, H. 4	*Poninges* 27
Presteton	See Preston (in Binderton)
Prestetone	See Preston (in Beddingham), Preston (near Brighton)

Prestetune	See East Preston
Prestitone	See Preston (in Beddingham)
Preston (in Beddingham), J. 5	*Prestetone*, *Prestitone* 19, 20b
Preston (in Binderton), C. 4	*Presteton* 17b
Preston (near Brighton), I. 5	*Prestetone* 17
Pulborough, F. 3	*Poleberge* 24b
Pyecombe	Not in D.B.
Rachetone	See Racton
Rackham	Not in D.B.
Racton, C. 4	*Rachetone* 24
Radetone, *Radintone*	See Ratton
Ramelle	See Rodmell
Rameslie	See Rye
Ratendone	See Ratton
Ratton, L. 5	*Radetone*, *Radintone* 19 *quater*, 21 *quater* *Ratendone* 19b
Redmelle	See Rodmell
Remecinges	See Renching
Renching, L. 5	*Remecinges* 22
Reredfelle	See Rotherfield
Ringmer	Not in D.B.
Ripe, K. 4	*Ripe* 19 *quater*, 22
Rochintone	See Runcton
Rodmell, J. 5	*Ramelle* 21b, 26 *Redmelle* 28
Rogate	Not in D.B.
Rotherfield, L. 2	*Reredfelle* 16
Rotingedene	See Rottingdean
Rottingdean, I. 5	*Rotingedene* 26b
Rudgwick	Not in D.B.
Rumboldswyke, D. 5	*Wiche* 24
Runcton, D. 5	*Rochintone* 25b
Rusper	Not in D.B.
Rustington	Not in D.B.
Rye, P. 3	*Rameslie* 17
Sacheham	See Sakeham
Saddlescombe, H. 4	*Salescome* 27

Sakeham, H. 3	*Sacheham* 28b
Salehurst, N. 3	*Salhert* 19b
Salescome	See Saddlescombe, Sedlescombe
Salhert	See Salehurst
Salmonesberie	See Shermanbury
Sasingham	See Sessingham
Seaford	Not in D.B.
Sedlescombe, N. 3	*Sales-*, *Selescome* 20 *quater*
Segnescome	Unid., 19b
Seleham	See Selham
Seleisie	See Selsey
Selescome	See Sedlescombe
Selham, D. 3	*Seleham* 23b
Selmeston, K. 5	*S(i)elmestone* 19b, 21b
Selmestone	See Selmeston
Selsey, D. 6	*Seleisie* 17
Semlintun	See Sullington
Sepelei	See Shipley
Serintone	See Sherrington
Sesingeham	See Sessingham
Sessingham, K. 4	*Sasingham* 19 *Sesingeham* 21b
Sheffield, J. 3	*Sifelle* 22b
Shermanbury, H. 3	*Salmonesberie* 28b
Sherrington, K. 4	*Esserintone* 19 *Serin-*, *Sirintone* 19b, 20b
Shipley, G. 3	*Sepelei* 26b
Shoreham, H. 5	*Sore(s)ham* 28, 29
Shovelstrode, J. 1	*Calvrestot* 22b *Celrestuis* 22b
Sidenore, K. 4	Lost in Selmeston, 21b *bis*
Sidlesham, C. 5	*Filleicham* 17
Sielmestone	See Selmeston
Sifelle	See Sheffield
Silletone	See Singleton
Sillintone	See Sullington
Singleton, D. 4	*Silletone* 23
Sirintone	See Sherrington
Slaugham	Not in D.B.
Slindon, E. 4	*Eslindone* 25
Slinfold	Not in D.B.
Somerley, C. 6	*Summerlege* 24
Sompting, G. 5	*S(t)ultinges* 28b *bis*
Sore(s)ham	See Shoreham
Southease, J. 5	*Suesse* 17b
South Harting	See Harting
South Heighton, J. 5	*Estone* 21b *Hectone* 20 *ter*
South Malling, J. 4	*Mellinges* 16, 16b
Southover	Not in D.B.
South Stoke, E. 4	*Stoches* 25
Southwick	Not in D.B.
Sperchedene	Unid., 22b
Standen, J. 1	*Standene* 22b
Standene	See Standen
Staninges	See Steyning
Stanmer, I. 4	*Stanmere* 16b
Stanmere	See Stanmer
Stedeham	See Stedham
Stedham, D. 3	*Stedeham* 23
Steyning, G. 4	*Staninges* 17, 28
Stoches	See North Stoke, South Stoke
Stochingham	See Stockingham
Stockingham, K. 4	*Estochingeham* 22b *Stochingham* 19
Stoechestone	Unid., 24
Stopeham	See Stopham
Stopham, E. 3	*Stopeham* 23b
Storgetune	See Storrington
Storrington, F. 4	*Estorchetone* 24 *Storgetune* 29
Stoughton, C. 4	*Estone* 24 *bis*
Stratone	See Strettington
Streat, I. 4	*Estrat* 27
Strettington, D. 4	*Stratone* 25b *bis*
Stultinges	See Sompting
Sudtone	See Sutton
Suesse	See Southease
Sullington, F. 4	*Semlintun* 28 *Sillintone* 24b
Sultinges	See Sompting
Summerlege	See Somerley
Sutton, E. 4	*Sudtone* 23b
Taceham	See Thakeham
Tadeham	See Todham
Tangemere	See Tangmere
Tangmere, D. 5	*Tangemere* 16b
Taring Neville, J. 5	*Toringes* 21b, 22b

Telentone, *Telitone*	See Tilton
Telscombe	Not in D.B.
Terringes	See West Taring
Terwick	Not in D.B.
Thakeham, F. 3	*Taceham* 29
Ticehurst	Not in D.B.
Tillington, E. 3	*Tolintone* 23b
Tilton, K. 5	*Telentone*, *Tilitone* 19, 20b, 21
Titeherste	See Chithurst
Toddington, F. 5	*Totintone* 24b
Todham, D. 3	*Tadeham* 23b
Tolintone	See Tillington
Toringes	See Taring Neville
Tornei	See West Thorney
Tortington, E. 5	*Tortinton* 25
Tortinton	See Tortington
Totintone	See Toddington
Totintune	See Tottington
Tottington, H. 4	*Totintune* 28
Trailgi	See Truleigh
Traitone	See Trotton
Treverde	See Treyford
Treyford, C. 3	*Treverde* 23
Trotton, C. 3	*Traitone* 23 *bis*
Truleigh, H. 4	*Trailgi* 26b, 28
Twineham	Not in D.B.
Uckfield	Not in D.B.
Uckham, N. 3	*Bocheham* 17b
Udimore, O. 3	*Dodimere* 19b
Up Marden	See Marden
Upper Beeding, G. 4	*Bed(d)inges* 26b, 27b, 28
Up Waltham, D. 4	*Waltham* 25b *bis*
Venningore	See Warningore
Wadhurst	Not in D.B.
Walberton, E. 5	*Walburgetone* 25
Walburgetone	See Walberton
Waldere, *-drene*	See Waldron
Waldron, K. 3	*Waldere* 19 *Waldrene* 22
Waliland	See Wellhead
Walnoch	See Wannock
Waltham	See Up Waltham
Waningore	See Warningore
Wannock, L. 5	*Walnoch* 21
Wantelei	See Wantley
Wantley, H. 3	*Wantelei* 28b
Wapingetorne	See Wappingthorn
Wappingthorn, G. 4	*Wapingetorne* 28
Warbleton, L. 3	*Warborgetone* 18b
Warblitetone	See Warblington, Hants.
Warborgetone	See Warbleton
Warlege	Unid., 22b
Warminghurst	Not in D.B.
Warnecham	See Warningcamp
Warnham	Not in D.B.
Warningcamp, F. 4	*Garnecampo* 29 *Warnecham* 24b
Warningore, I. 4	*Venningore* 27b *Waningore* 22b
Wartling, M. 4	*Werlinges* 18
Washington, G. 4	*Wasingetune* 28, 29 *bis*
Wasingate	See Bathurst
Wasingetune	See Washington
Waslebie	See Whalesbeach
Watlingetone	See Whatlington
Welbedlinge	See Woolbeeding
Wellhead, N. 3	*Waliland* 20
Wepeham	See Wepham
Wepham, F. 4	*Wepeham* 25
Werlinges	See Wartling
Werste	See Ewhurst
Wesmestun	See Westmeston
West Blatchington	Not in D.B.
Westbortone	See Westburton
Westbourne, B. 4	*Borne* 23b *Burne* 24
Westburton, K. 6	*Westbortone* 21
West Chiltington, F. 3	*Cilletone*, *-tune* 24b, 29
West Dean (near Eastbourne)	See Dean
West Dean (near Singleton)	Not in D.B.
Westewelle	See Westfield
Westfield, N. 4	*Westewelle* 18b
West Firle, K. 5	*Ferla*, *Ferle* 19 *ter*, 19b *ter*, 21
West Grinstead	Not in D.B.

Westham	Not in D.B.
Westhampnett, D. 5	*Hentone* 25b
West Harting	See Harting
West Hoathly	Not in D.B.
West Itchenor, C. 5	*Icenore* 17b, 24
West Marden	See Marden
Westmeston, I. 4	*Wesmestun* 27
Westringes	See Wittering
West Stoke	Not in D.B.
West Taring, G. 5	*Terringes* 16b
West Thorney, B. 5	*Tornei* 17
West Wittering	See Wittering
Whalesbeach, J. 1	*Waslebie* 22b
Whatlington, N. 3	*Watlingetone* 18b
Wicham	See Wickham
Wiche	See Rumboldswyke
Wickham, I. 3	*Wicham* 27
Wigentone	See Winton
Wiggenholt	Not in D.B.
Wildene	Unid., 21b
Wildetone	Unid., 22b
Wilendone	See Willingdon
Wilesham	See Filsham
Wille(n)done	See Willingdon
Willingdon, L. 5	*Wilendone* 19, 19b *bis*, 21, 22 *Wille(n)done* 19 *bis*, 19b
Wilmington, K. 5	*Wilminte* 17b *Wineltone* 21b
Wilminte	See Wilmington
Wilting, N. 4	*Wiltingham* 18b *Witinges* 17b
Wiltingham	See Wilting
Winchelsea	Not in D.B.
Wineltone	See Wilmington
Winterbourne, J. 4	*Wintreburne* 26b
Winton, K. 5	*Wigentone* 19
Wintreburne	See Winterbourne
Wisborough Green	Not in D.B.
Wistanestun	See Wiston
Wiston, G. 4	*Wistanestun* 28
Withyham	Not in D.B.
Witinges	See Wilting
Wittering, East and West, C. 6	*Westringes* 17, 24
Wivelsfield	Not in D.B.
Woodmancote, H. 4	*Odemanscote* 28b
Woolbeeding, D. 3	*Welbedlinge* 29b
Woolfly, H. 3	*Ovelei* 28b
Wootton (in East Chiltington), J. 4	*Odetone* 22b *Odintune* 16b, 27b
Wootton (in Folkington), L. 5	*Lodintone*, *Lodiutone* 22 *bis*
Worth (near Crawley), I. 1	*Orde* 34b, Surrey
Worth (in Little Horsted), J. 3	*Gorde* 21b
Worthing, G. 5	*Mordinges* 28b *Ordinges* 28b
Yapton	Not in D.B.
Yeverington, L. 5	*Lovringetone* 20b

ANONYMOUS HOLDINGS

No place-names appear in the following fifty-two entries, and it is possible that some (or even all) of these refer to holdings at places not named elsewhere in Domesday Book:

Canons of Chichester, 16 hides, 17.
Battle abbey, 4 hides in Totnore hd, 17b.
Ingelrann (from Count of Eu), one hide in Foxearle hd, 18.
Olaf (from Count of Eu), one virgate in Foxearle hd, 18.
Osbern (from Count of Eu), 2 virgates in Bexhill hd, 18.
Ingelrann (from Count of Eu), 3 virgates in Baldslow hd, 18b.
Hugh (from Count of Eu), 1½ hides in *Hailesaltede* hd, 18b.
Hugh (from Count of Eu), one virgate in Staple hd, 18b.

ANONYMOUS HOLDINGS (continued)

William (from Count of Eu), 1½ virgates in Foxearle hd, 18b.
William (from Count of Eu), half a hide in Henhurst hd, 19b.
Reinbert (from Count of Eu), one hide in Henhurst hd, 19b.
Norman (from Count of Eu), half a hide in Henhurst hd, 19b.
Reinbert (from Count of Eu), one virgate in Henhurst hd, 19b.
Reinbert (from Count of Eu), half a hide and 1½ virgates in Henhurst hd, 19b.
Reinbert (from Count of Eu), half a hide in Henhurst hd, 19b.
Reinbert (from Count of Eu), one virgate in Henhurst hd, 19b.
Alwin (from Count of Eu), one virgate in Goldspur hd, 20.
Saswalo (from Count of Eu), one virgate in *Hailesaltede* hd, 20.
Rannulf (from Count of Mortain), one virgate in Totnore hd, 20b.
Count of Mortain, 8 hides in Totnore hd, 20b.
Ralf (from Count of Mortain), 4½ hides in Willingdon hd, 21.
Durand (from Count of Mortain), one hide in Flexborough hd, 21b.
Count of Mortain, 1½ hides in Hartfield hd, 21b.
Ralf (from Count of Mortain), one hide in Hartfield hd, 21b.
William (from Count of Mortain), one virgate in Framfield hd, 21b.
Ansfrid (from Count of Mortain), 2 hides less one virgate in East Grinstead hd, 22b.
Count of Mortain, 2 hides in Rotherfield hd, 22b.
Turchil (from Earl Roger), one virgate in Rotherbridge hd, 23b.
Hamelin (from Earl Roger), 1½ hides in Rotherbridge hd, 23b.
Morin (from Earl Roger), one hide in Rotherbridge hd, 23b.
Chetel (from Earl Roger), land for one plough in Stockbridge hd, 24.
Hugh (from Earl Roger), 3 hides in *Benestede* hd, 25.
Hugh (from Earl Roger), 8 hides in *Benestede* hd, 25.
William (from Earl Roger), 3 hides in *Benestede* hd, 25.
Warin (from Earl Roger), half a hide in *Benestede* hd, 25b.
Gondran (from Earl Roger), one hide in *Benestede* hd, 25b.
Acard (from Earl Roger), 2½ hides in *Benestede* hd, 25b.
Pagen (from Earl Roger), one virgate in *Benestede* hd, 25b.
William (from Earl Roger), half a hide and 2 virgates in *Benestede* hd, 25b.
Hugh (from Earl Roger), 5½ virgates in *Benestede* hd, 25b.
Roland (from Earl Roger), one hide in *Benestede* hd, 25b.
Wineman (from Earl Roger), one virgate in *Benestede* hd, 25b.
William (from Earl Roger), 3 hides in *Bosgrave* hd, 25b.
William (from Earl Roger), one hide in *Bosgrave* hd, 25b.
Siuuard (from Earl Roger), one hide in *Bosgrave* hd, 25b.
Rainald (from Earl Roger), half a hide in *Bosgrave* hd, 25b.
Eustace (from William de Warenne), one hide in Falmer hd, 26b.
William de Braiose, 8 hides in Burbeach hd, 28.
William de Braiose, 7 hides in Burbeach hd, 28.
Gilbert (from William de Braiose), land for 3 ploughs in Steyning hd, 28.
Morin (from William de Braiose), one hide in Easewrithe hd, 29.
Aluiet (from William de Braiose), land for one plough in Easewrithe hd, 29.

WARWICKSHIRE — *WARWICSCIRE*

Folios 238–244b

MAPS 52–53

Abbots Salford	See Salford
Aderestone	See Atherstone
Admington, D. 9	*Edelmintone* 165b, Gloucs.
Ailespede	See Alspath
Ailstone, D. 8	*Alnodestone* 244
Alcester	Not in D.B.
Alderminster, D. 9	*Sture* 175, Worcs.
Aldulvestreu	See Austrey
Alia Bichehelle	See Middle Bickenhill
Allesley	Not in D.B.
Alne	See Great Alne
Alnodestone	See Ailstone
Alspath, E. 5	*Ailespede* 239b
Altone	See Hatton
Alveston, D. 8	*Alvestone* 238b *bis*
Alvestone	See Alveston
Amington, E. 3	*Ermendone* 243
Anestie	See Ansty
Ansley, E. 4	*Hanslei* 239b
Ansty, F. 5	*Anestie* 239b
Apleford	See Hopsford
Ardens Grafton	See Grafton
Ardreshille	See Hartshill
Arlei	See Arley
Arlescote, F. 9	*Orlavescote* 240b
Arley, E. 4	*Arlei* 244
Arrow, C. 8	*Arue* 238b
Arue	See Arrow
Asceshot	See Ashow
Ashow, E. 6	*Asceshot* 241b
Astley, E. 4	*Estleia* 240
Aston (in Birmingham), C. 4	*Estone* 243
Aston Cantlow, C. 7	*Estone* 244
. . . *atercote*	See Whatcote
Atherstone, E. 3	*Aderestone* 239b
Atherstone on Stour, D. 8	*Edricestone* 238b
Austrey, E. 2	*Aldulvestreu* 239, 242, 244
Avon Dassett	See Dassett
Baddesley Clinton	Not in D.B.
Baddesley Ensor, E. 3	*Bedeslei* 241
Badechitone	See Baginton
Baginton, F. 6	*Badechitone* 241b
Balsall	Not in D.B.
Barcheston, E. 10	*Berricestone*, *-tune* 243, 244b
Barford, E. 7	*Bereford(e)* 243, 244
Barnacle, F. 5	*Bernhangre* 240b
Barston, D. 5	*Bercestone* 244b
	Bertanestone 241, 242b
Bartley Green, B. 5	*Berchelai* 177, Worcs.
Barton on the Heath, E. 10	*Bertone* 242b
Baxterley	Not in D.B.
Bearley, D. 7	*Burlei* 242b, 243
Beausale, E. 6	*Beoshelle* 238b
Bedeford	See Bidford on Avon
Bedeslei	See Baddesley Ensor
Bedewod	See Bedworth
Bedworth, F. 4	*Bedeword* 240b
Beltone	See Bilton
Benechelie	See Bentley
Beninton(e), *Benitone*	See Binton
Bentley, E. 3	*Benechelie* 243b
Bentone	See Bilton
Beoshelle	See Beausale
Bercestone	See Barston
Berchewelle	See Berkswell
Berdingeberie	See Birdingbury
Bereford(e)	See Barford
Bericote, F. 6	*Bericote* 241b

Berkswell, E. 5	*Berchewelle* 240, Warw.; 224, N'hants.
Bermingeham	See Birmingham
Bernhangre	See Barnacle
Berricestone, *-tune*	See Barcheston
Bertanestone	See Barston
Bertone	See Barton on the Heath
Bevington, B. 8	*Buintun* 175b, Worcs.
Bichehelle	See Bickenhill
Bichehelle, *Alia*	See Middle Bickenhill
Bichemerse	See Bickmarsh, Worcs.
Bickenhill, D. 5	*Bichehelle* 240b
Bidford on Avon, C. 8	*Bedeford* 238, 238b
Biggin Mills	See Holme
Billeslei	See Billesley
Billesley, D. 8	*Billeslei* 242
Bilnei	See Binley
Bilton, G. 6	*Beltone* 239 *Bentone* 241
Bilueie	See Binley
Binley, F. 5	*Bilnei* 241b *Bilueie* 238b
Binton, C. 8	*Beninton(e)* 243, 244 *Benitone* 243b *bis*
Birdingbury, G. 7	*Berdingeberie* 241 *Derbingerie* 238b
Birmingham, C. 4	*Bermingeham* 243
Biscopesberie	See Bushbury, Staffs.
Bishop's Itchington, F. 8	*Icetone* 239
Bishop's Tachbrook	See Tachbrook
Blackwell, E. 9	*Blachewelle* 173b, Worcs.
Bochintone	See Bulkington
Bortone	See Bourton on Dunsmore, Burton Hastings
Bourton on Dunsmore, G. 6	*Bortone* 240
Brailes, E. 10	*Brailes* 238

Bramcote, F. 4	*Brancote* 239b, 242b, 244b
Brancote	See Bramcote
Brandon, F. 6	*Brandune* 241b
Brandune	See Brandon
Branklow	Not in D.B.
Brome	See Broom
Broom, C. 8	*Brome* 238b
Brownsover	See Over
Bubbenhall, F. 6	*Bubenhalle* 242b
Bubenhalle	See Bubbenhall
Budbrooke, E. 7	*Budebroc* 243
Budebroc	See Budbrooke
Bulkington, F. 4	*Bochintone* 240
Burdintone	See Burmington
Burlei	See Bearley
Burmington, E. 10	*Burdintone* 242b
Burton Dassett	See Dassett
Burton Hastings, G. 4	*Bortone* 242
Butlers Marston, E. 9	*Mersetone* 242
Bushwood	Not in D.B.
Calcutt, G. 7	*Caldecote* 241 *ter*
Caldecote	See Calcutt, Caldecote
Caldecote, F. 4	*Caldecote* 238b
Calvestone	See Cawston
Castle Bromwich	Not in D.B.
Cawston, G. 6	*Calvestone* 241 *bis*
Cedeleshunte	See Chadshunt
Celboldestone	See Edgbaston
Celverdestoche	See Chilvers Coton
Cerlecote	See Charlecote
Cestedone	See Chesterton
Cesters Over	See Over
Cestreton(e)	See Chesterton
Cetitone	See Shuttington
Chadshunt, F. 8	*Cedeleshunte* 239
Charlecote, E. 8	*Cerlecote* 239b
Chenevertone	See Kinwarton
Cherrington	Not in D.B.
Chesterton, F. 8	*Cestedone* 242 *Cestreton(e)* 239, 241b *bis*, 244b
Chilvers Coton, F. 4	*Celverdestoche* 244
Chinesberie	See Kingsbury

Chinewrde	See Kenilworth
Chircheberie	See Monks Kirby
Church Lawford	See Lawford
Churchover	See Over
Cillentone	See Chillington, Staffs.
Cintone	See Kineton Green, Kington
Clavendone	See Claverdon
Claverdon, D. 7	*Clavendone* 240
Clifford Chambers, D. 8	*Clifort* 163b, Gloucs.
Cliforde	See Ruin Clifford
Clifton upon Dunsmore, H. 6	*Cliptone* 238b, 239b
Cliptone	See Clifton upon Dunsmore
Clopton (in Quinton), D. 9	*Cloptune* 167, Gloucs.
Clopton (in Stratford upon Avon), D. 8	*Clotone* 242b
Clotone	See Clopton (in Stratford upon Avon)
Cobintone	See Cubbington
Coctune	See Coughton
Coleshelle	See Coleshill
Coleshill, D. 4	*Coleshelle* 238
Combrook	Not in D.B.
Compton Scorpion, D. 10	*Parva Contone* 242b
Compton Verney, E. 8	*Contone* 239b, 241b 2nd entry
Compton Wyniate, F. 9	*Contone* 242b
Condelme, *Condone*	See Coundon
Contone	See Fenny Compton, Compton Verney, Compton Wyniate
Contone, *Parva*	See Compton Scorpion
Copston Magna and Parva	Not in D.B.
Corley, E. 5	*Cornelie* 244b
Cornelie	See Corley
Cosford	Not in D.B.

Cotes	See Coton
Coton, E. 7	*Cotes* 238
Coughton, C. 7	*Coctune* 241b
Coundon, E. 5	*Condelme* 243 *Condone* 238b
Coventreu	See Coventry
Coventry, F. 5	*Coventreu* 239b
Credeworde	See Curdworth
Cubbington, F. 7	*Cobintone* 238b *Cubi(n)tone* 240b, 242
Cubi(n)tone	See Cubbington
Cuntone	See Long Compton
Curdworth, D. 4	*Credeworde* 240b
Dassett, Avon and Burton, F. 8, G. 9	*Derceto(ne)* 239b, 244
Derbingerie	See Birdingbury
Dercelai	See Dosthill
Derceto(ne)	See Dassett
Dicforde	See Ditchford
Ditchford, E. 10	*Dicforde* 242b
Donecerce	See Dunchurch
Donnelie	Unid., 240
Dorsington, C. 9	*Dorsitone* 243b *Dorsintune* 168, Gloucs.
Dorsitone	See Dorsington
Dosthill, D. 3	*Dercelai* 241
Dunchurch, G. 6	*Donecerce* 244
Easenhall	Not in D.B.
Eathorpe	Not in D.B.
Eatington, Nether and Over, E. 9	*Ete(n)done* 241b, 242 *bis*, 244b
Ecleshelle	See Exhall (near Alcester)
Edburberie	See Harbury
Edelmitone	See Ilmington
Edgbaston, B. 5	*Celboldestone* 243
Edricestone	See Atherstone on Stour, Edstone
Edstone, D. 7	*Edricestone* 242b
Elmdon, D. 5	*Elmedone* 241
Elmedone	See Elmdon
Epeslei	See Ipsley, Worcs.
Eptone	See Napton on the Hill

Erbur(ge)berie	See Harbury
Erdington, C. 4	*Hardintone* 243
Ermendone	See Amington
Eseningetone	See Essington, Staffs.
Estleia	See Astley
Estone	See Aston (in Birmingham), Aston Cantlow
Etedone	See Eatington
Etelincote	See Idlicote
Etendone	See Eatington
Etone	See Nuneaton
Exhall (near Alcester), C. 8	*Ecleshelle* 243
Exhall (near Coventry)	Not in D.B.
Farnborough, G. 9	*Ferneberge* 238b
Felingelei	See Fillongley
Feniniwebold	See Newbold Revel
Fenny Compton, G. 8	*Contone* 240b, 241b 1st entry
Ferneberge	See Farnborough
Filingelei	See Fillongley
Fillongley, E. 4	*Fel-*, *Filingelei* 242b, 244b *Filungelei*, *Filunger* 238b *bis*
Filungelei, *Filunger*	See Fillongley
Flechenho, *Flechenoc*	See Flecknoe
Flecknoe, H. 7	*Flechenho* 238b, 241, 244b *bis* *Flechenoc* 241
Focheshelle	See Foleshill
Foleshill, F. 5	*Focheshelle* 239b
Franchetone	See Frankton
Frankton, G. 6	*Franchetone* 239, 240
Fulbrook, E. 7	*Fulebroc* 239b
Fulebroc	See Fulbrook
Fullready, E. 9	*Fulrei* 241b
Fulrei	See Fullready
Gaura	See Over
Gaydon	Not in D.B.
Grafton, Ardens and Temple, C. 8	*Graston(e)* 243, 244
Grandborough, G. 7	*Graneberge* 238b *Greneberge* 244b
Graneberge	See Grandborough
Graston(e)	See Grafton
Great Alne, C. 7	*Alne* 239
Great Wolford	See Wolford
Grendon, E. 3	*Grendone* 242
Grendone	See Grendon
Greneberge	See Grandborough
Halford	Not in D.B.
Hampton in Arden, D. 5	*Hantone* 243b
Hampton Lucy, E. 8	*Hantone* 238b
Handsworth, B. 4	*Honesworde* 250, Staffs.
Hanslei	See Ansley
Hantone	See Hampton in Arden, Hampton Lucy
Harborne, B. 5	*Horeborne* 247, Staffs.
Harborough Magna, G. 5	*Herdeberge* 244b *bis*
Harbury, F. 7	*Edburberie* 239 *Erbur(ge)berie* 239b, 241b, 242, 243b
Hardintone	See Erdington
Hartshill, E. 4	*Ardreshille* 239b
Haseleia	See Haseley
Haseley, D. 6	*Haseleia* 244
Haselor, C. 8	*Haseloue* 244
Haseloue	See Haselor
Hatton, D. 7	*Altone* 244
Herdeberge	See Harborough Magna
Herdewiche	See Priors Hardwick
Hildebereurde, *Hildeborde*	See Hillborough
Hill, G. 7	*Hille* 239
Hillborough, C. 8	*Hildebereurde*, *Hildeborde* 243b, 244
Hille	See Hill
Hillmorton, H. 6	*Mortone* 242, 244b

Hoden(h)elle	See Hodnell
Hodnell, G. 8	*Hoden(h)elle* 240, 241, 243
Holehale	See Ullenhall
Holme, now Biggin Mills, H. 5	*Holme* 241, 241b
Honiley	Not in D.B.
Honington, E. 9	*Hunitone* 239
Hopsford, G. 5	*Apleford* 243b
Huningeham	See Hunningham
Hunitone	See Honington
Hunningham, F. 7	*Huningeham* 243
Icentone	See Long Itchington
Icetone	See Bishop's Itchington
Idlicote, E. 9	*Etelincote* 242b
Illintone	See Lillington
Ilmedone	See Ilmington
Ilmington, D. 9	*Edelmitone* 242b *Ilmedone* 240, 240b
Kenilworth, E. 6	*Chinewrde* 238
Keresley	Not in D.B.
Kineton, F. 8	*Quintone* 238
Kineton Green, C. 5	*Cintone* 243
Kingsbury, D. 3	*Chinesberie* 239b
King's Newnham	Not in D.B.
King's Norton, B. 5	*Nortune* 172, Worcs.
Kington, D. 7	*Cintone* 240
Kinwarton, C. 8	*Chenevertone* 239
Knowle	Not in D.B.
Ladbroke, G. 8	*Lodbroc(h)* 240b, 241 *quater*, 242
Lamintone	See Leamington Spa
Langedone	See Longdon (in Solihull)
Langley, D. 7	*Longelei* 242b
Lapeforde	See Lapworth
Lapworth, D. 6	*Lapeforde* 242
Lark Stoke, D. 9	*Stoch* 166, Gloucs.
Lawford, Church, Little and Long, G. 6	*Leileforde* 239 *Lelle-*, *Lilleford* 241b, 243b
Lea (in Lea Marston), D. 4	*Leth* 242b
Lea Green, B. 5	*Lea* 172, Worcs.
Leamington Hastings, G. 7	*Lunnitone* 244
Leamington Spa, E. 7	*Lamintone* 239
Leek Wootton	Not in D.B.
Leileforde, *Lelleford*	See Lawford
Leth	See Lea (in Lea Marston)
Lighthorne, F. 8	*Listecorne* 243
Lilleford	See Lawford
Lillington, F. 7	*Illintone* 240b *Lillintone* 241b
Lillintone	See Lillington
Lindsworth, C. 5	*Lindeorde* 172, Worcs.
Listecorne	See Lighthorne
Little Compton, E. 11	*Contone* 166, Gloucs.
Little Lawford	See Lawford
Little Wolford	See Wolford
Lochesham, *Locheslei*	See Loxley
Lodbroc(h)	See Ladbroke
Long Compton, E. 10	*Cuntone* 243b
Longdon (in Solihull), D. 6	*Langedone* 241
Longdon (in Tredington), D. 9	*Longedun* 173b, Worcs.
Longelei	See Langley
Long Itchington, G. 7	*Icentone* 244
Long Lawford	See Lawford
Long Marston, D. 9	*Merestone* 166, Gloucs.
Lower Shuckburgh	See Shuckburgh
Loxley, E. 8	*Lochesham* 238b *Locheslei* 240b, 242
Luddington, D. 8	*Luditone* 240b
Luditone	See Luddington
Lunnitone	See Leamington Hastings
Machitone	See Mackadown
Mackadown, D. 5	*Machitone* 241
Malvertone	See Milverton
Mancetter	Not in D.B.

Mapelberge	See Mapleborough
Mapleborough, C. 7	*Mapelberge* 243
Marston (in Lea Marston), D. 4	*Merston(e)* 242, 242b
Marston (in Wolston), G. 6	*Merstone* 241b
Marston Green, D. 5	*Merstone* 241
Marston Jabbett, F. 4	*Merstone* 240b
Marton, F. 7	*Mortone* 240 *bis*
Maxstoke	Not in D.B.
Melecote	See Milcote
Meneworde	See Minworth
Meon, D. 9	*Mene* 163, Gloucs.
Merevale	Not in D.B.
Meriden	Not in D.B.
Mersetone	See Butlers Marston
Merston	See Marston (in Lea Marston)
Merstone	See Marston (in Lea Marston), Marston (in Wolston), Marston Green, Marston Jabbett
Middle Bickenhill, D. 5	*Alia Bichehelle* 240b
Middleton, D. 3	*Mideltone* 242 *Mildentone* 244b
Mideltone	See Middleton
Milcote, D. 8	*Melecote* 243b
Mildentone	See Middleton
Milverton, E. 7	*Malvertone* 239b
Minworth, D. 4	*Meneworde* 240b
Moitone	See Myton
Mollitone	See Mollington, Oxon.
Monks Kirby, G. 5	*Chircheberie* 243b
Moreton Morrell, E. 8	*Mortone* 239b
Morton Bagot, C. 7	*Mortone* 242b 1st entry
Mortone	See Hillmorton, Marton, Moreton Morrell, Morton Bagot, Norton Lindsey
Moseley, C. 5	*Museleie* 172, Worcs.
Muitone	See Myton
Myton, E. 7	*Moi-*, *Muitone* 239b, 241b *bis*
Napton on the Hill, G. 7	*Eptone* 241 *bis* *Neptone* 240
Neptone	See Napton on the Hill
Nether Eatington	See Eatington
Nether Whitacre	See Whitacre
Newbold Comyn, F. 7	*Niwebold* 239, 240b
Newbold on Avon, G. 6	*Newebold* 243b
Newbold Pacey, E. 8	*Niwebold* 244
Newbold Revel, G. 5	*Feniniwebold* 243b
Newebold	See Newbold on Avon
Neweham	See Newnham (in Aston Cantlow)
Newnham (in Aston Cantlow), D. 7	*Neweham* 239
Newnham Paddox, G. 5	*Niweham* 243b
Newton (near Rugby), H. 5	*Niwetone* 241 *ter*
Newton Regis	Not in D.B.
Niwebold	See Newbold Comyn, Newbold Pacey
Niweham	See Newnham Paddox
Niwetone	See Newton (near Rugby)
Northfield, B. 5	*Nordfeld* 177, Worcs.
Norton Lindsey, D. 7	*Mortone*(*sic*) 242b 2nd entry
Nuneaton, F. 4	*Etone* 239b, 241b
Nuthurst	Not in D.B.
Octeselve	See Oxhill
Offchurch	Not in D.B.
Offeworde	See Offord
Offord, D. 7	*Offeworde* 242b *bis*

Oldberrow, C. 7	*Oleberge* 175b, Worcs.
Optone	See Upton
Optone	Unid., 238
Orlavescote	See Arlescote
Over: Brownsover, Cesters Over and Churchover, H. 5	*Gaura* 243b *Wara* 242b, 243b *Wavra*, *Wavre* 239b, 241b *Wavre* 226, N'hants.
Over Eatington	See Eatington
Oversley, C. 8	*Oveslei* 240b
Over Whitacre	See Whitacre
Oveslei	See Oversley
Oxhill, E. 9	*Octeselve* 242
Packington, D. 5	*Patitone* 241
Packwood	Not in D.B.
Pailton	Not in D.B.
Parva Contone	See Compton Scorpion
Patitone	See Packington
Perry Barr, C. 4	*Pirio* 250, Staffs.
Pilardetone, *-tune*, *Pilardintone*	See Pillerton
Pillerton Hersey and Priors, E. 9	*Pilardetone*, *-tune* 239, 242 *bis* *Pilardintone* 238
Polesworth	Not in D.B.
Prestetone	See Preston Bagot
Preston Bagot, D. 7	*Prestetone* 240, 240b
Preston on Stour, D. 9	*Preston* 166, Gloucs.
Princethorpe	Not in D.B.
Priors Hardwick, G. 8	*Herdewiche* 239
Priors Marston	Not in D.B.
Quatone	See Quatt, Salop.
Quinton, D. 9	*Quenintune* 169 *bis*, Gloucs.
Quintone	See Kineton
Radbourn, G. 8	*Redborne* 241
Radford Semele, F. 7	*Redeford* 241b
Radway, F. 9	*Radwei(a)* 239, 244b *Rodewei* 239b
Radwei(a)	See Radway
Rameslege	See Romsley, Salop.
Ratley, F. 9	*Rotelei* 241b
Redborne	See Radbourn
Redeford	See Radford Semele
Rednal, B. 6	*Weredeshale* 172, Worcs.
Rietone	See Ryton on Dunsmore
Rigge	See Rudge, Salop.
Rincele	See Roundhills
Rocheberie	See Rugby
Rochintone	See Rowington
Rodewei	See Radway
Rotelei	See Ratley
Roundhills, E. 6	*Rincele* 239b
Rowington, D. 6	*Rochintone* 242
Rugby, H. 6	*Rocheberie* 241
Ruin Clifford, D. 8	*Cliforde* 242b
Ryton on Dunsmore, F. 6	*Rietone* 240b
Salford Priors and Abbots Salford, C. 8, C. 9	*Salford* 239, 244
Sambourn, B. 7	*Sandburne* 239
Sandburne	See Sambourn
Sawbridge, H. 7	*Salwebrige* 222b, N'hants.
Scelftone	See Shilton
Sciplei	See Shipley, Salop.
Scireburne	See Sherbourne
Scotescote	See Shustoke
Sec(h)intone	See Seckington
Seckington, E. 2	*Sec(h)intone* 240, 243
Selly Oak, B. 5	*Escelie* 177 *bis*, Worcs.
Seruelei	See Shrewley
Sheldon	Not in D.B.
Sherbourne, E. 7	*Scireburne* 239b
Shilton, F. 5	*Scelftone* 240b

Shipston on Stour, E. 10	*Scepwestun* 173b, Worcs.
Shotteswell	Not in D.B.
Shrewley, D. 7	*Seruelei* 242
Shuckburgh, Lower and Upper, G. 7, H. 7	*Socheberge* 240, 241, 244b
Shustoke, E. 4	*Scotescote* 243b
Shuttington, E. 2	*Cetitone* 240
Smeeton, G. 5	*Smitham* 239b
Smercote, F. 5	*Smerecote* 240b
Smerecote	See Smercote
Smitham	See Smeeton
Snitefeld	See Snitterfield
Snitterfield, D. 7	*Snitefeld* 240
Socheberge	See Shuckburgh
Sole End, F. 4	*Soulege* 240b
Solihull	Not in D.B.
Soulege	See Sole End
Southam, G. 7	*Sucham* 238b
Sowa	See Walsgrave on Sowe
Spelesberie	See Spelsbury, Oxon.
Spernall, C. 7	*Spernore* 243b
Spernore	See Spernall
Stanlei	See Stoneleigh
Stivichall	Not in D.B.
Stockton	Not in D.B.
Stodlei	See Studley
Stoke (near Coventry)	Not in D.B.
Stoneleigh, F. 6	*Stanlei* 238 *bis*, 240b
Stoneton, G. 8	*Stantone* 225, N'hants.
Stourton	Not in D.B.
Stradforde	See Stratford upon Avon
Stratford upon Avon, D. 8	*Stradforde* 238b
Stratone	See Stretton Baskerville, Stretton on Dunsmore, Stretton on Fosse
Stretton Baskerville, G. 4	*Stratone* 243
Stretton on Dunsmore, F. 6	*Stratone* 239

Stretton on Fosse, D. 10	*Stratone* 243b, 244
Stretton under Fosse	Not in D.B.
Studley, C. 7	*Stodlei* 243, 243b
Sucham	See Southam
Surland	Unid., 238b
Sutone	See Sutton Coldfield
Sutton Coldfield, C. 3	*Sutone* 238
Sutton under Brailes, E. 10	*Sudtune* 166, Gloucs.
Tacesbroc	See Tachbrook
Tachbrook Mallory and Bishop's Tachbrook, E. 7	*Tacesbroc* 240b *Taschebroc* 238b
Tameuuorde	See Tamworth, Staffs.
Tanworth	Not in D.B.
Taschebroc	See Tachbrook
Temple Grafton	See Grafton
Tessal, B. 5	*Thessale* 172, Worcs.
Thurlaston, G. 6	*Torlavestone* 240, 242
Tidmington, E. 10	*Tidelmintun* 173, Worcs.
Tiheshoche	See Tysoe
Torlavestone	See Thurlaston
Tredington, E. 9	*Tredinctun* 173, Worcs.
Tysoe, F. 9	*Tiheshoche* 242b
Ufton, F. 7	*Ulchetone* 239
Ulchetone	See Ufton
Ulfelmescote	See Wolfhamcote
Ullavintone	See Willington
Ullenhall, C. 7	*Holehale* 242b
Ulveia	See Wolvey
Ulverlei	See Ulverley
Ulverley, C. 5	*Ulverlei* 244
Ulvestone, *Ulvricetone*	See Wolston
Ulwarda	See Wolford
Ulwarditone	See Wolverton
Ulware	See Wolford

Upper Shuckburgh	See Shuckburgh
Upton, C. 8	*Optone* 243b
Volwarde	See Wolford
Walcote, H. 6	*Walecote* 241
Waleborne	See Wellesbourne
Walecote	See Walcote
Walsgrave on Sowe, F. 5	*Sowa* 239, 244b
Walton, E. 8	*Waltone* 239b *bis*
Waltone	See Walton
Wapeberie	See Wappenbury
Wappenbury, F. 6	*Wapeberie* 243b
Wara	See Over
Warmington, G. 9	*Warmintone* 239b, 240b
Warmintone	See Warmington
Waru(u)ic	See Warwick
Warwick, E. 7	*Waru(u)ic* 238 *ter*, 238b *bis*, 241b, 242 *ter*, 242b *bis*, 243 *ter*
Wasmertone	See Wasperton
Wasperton, E. 8	*Wasmertone* 239
Water Orton	Not in D.B.
Watitune	See Weddington
Wavra, *Wavre*	See Over
Weddington, F. 4	*Watitune* 240
Weethley, B. 8	*Wilelei* 239
Welei	See Willey
Welford on Avon, C. 8	*Welleford* 166, Gloucs.
Wellesbourne Hastings and Mountford, E. 8	*Waleborne* 238
Werlavescote	Unid., 240
Westone	See Weston in Arden, Weston under Wetherley
Weston in Arden, F. 4	*Westone* 240
Weston on Avon, D. 8	*Westone*, *-tune* 166, 169, Gloucs.
Weston under Wetherley, F. 6	*Westone* 240b, 241b, 243
Whatcote, E. 9	*...atercote* 242
Whichford, E. 10	*Wicford* 227b, N'hants.

Whitacre, Nether and Over, D. 4, E. 4	*Witacre* 242 *Witecore* 241, 242b *Witacre* 224, N'hants.
Whitchurch, D. 9	*Witecerce* 240, 240b
Whitley, D. 7	*Witeleia* 242b
Whitnash, F. 7	*Witenas* 244
Wibetot	See Wibtoft
Wibtoft, G. 4	*Wibetot* 240
Wich	See Droitwich, Worcs.
Widecote	See Woodcote
Wiggins Hill, D. 4	*Winchicelle* 241
Wilebec, *-bei*, *-bene*, *-bere*	See Willoughby
Wilelei	See Weethley
Willenhall	Not in D.B.
Willey, G. 5	*Welei* 240
Willicote, D. 9	*Wilcote* 169, Gloucs.
Willington, E. 10	*Ullavintone* 242b, 243b
Willoughby, H. 7	*Wilebec*, *-bei*, *-bene*, *-bere* 241 *ter*, 242
Wilmcote, D. 8	*Wilmecote* 244
Wilmecote	See Wilmcote
Wilmundecote	See Wilnecote
Wilnecote, D. 3	*Wilmundecote* 240
Wimeles-, *Wimenes-*, *Wimerestone*	See Wormleighton
Winchicelle	See Wiggins Hill
Wincot, D. 9	*Wenecote* 163b, 167, Gloucs.
Wishaw, D. 4	*Witscaga* 243
Witacre	See Whitacre
Witecerce	See Whitchurch
Witecore	See Whitacre
Witelavesford	See Wixford
Witeleia	See Whitley
Witenas	See Whitnash
Withybrook	Not in D.B.
Witone	See Witton
Witscaga	See Wishaw
Witton, C. 4	*Witone* 243
Wixford, C. 8	*Witelavesford* 239

Wlfesmescot	See Wolfhamcote
Wolfhamcote, G. 7	*Ulfelmescote* 240b *Wlfesmescot* 241
Wolford, Great and Little, E. 10	*Ulwarda*, *Ulware* 238b, 240b *Volwarde* 242b *Worwarde* 242b
Wolston, G. 6	*Ulvestone* 239 *Ulvricetone* 239
Wolverton, D. 7	*Ulwarditone* 242b, 243
Wolvey, G. 4	*Ulveia* 242b
Woodcote, E. 6	*Widecote* 239b, 240b
Wootton Wawen, D. 7	*Wotone* 242b
Wormleighton, G. 8	*Wimeles-*, *Wimenes-*, *Wimerestone* 240b, 241b, 243b
Worwarde	See Wolford
Wotone	See Wootton Wawen
Wroxall	Not in D.B.
Wyken	Not in D.B.
Yardley, C. 5	*Gerlei* 175, Worcs.

ANONYMOUS HOLDINGS

No place-name appears in the following entry, and it is impossible to say whether or not it refers to a place named elsewhere in Domesday Book:

Algar (from Turchil of Warwick), 1½ hides in Stoneleigh hd, 241b.

WESTMORLAND

Yorkshire folios 301b–302, 332

MAP 65

Barbon, H. 3	*Berebrune* 301b
Beetham, G. 4	*Biedun* 332
Berebrune	See Barbon
Biedun	See Beetham
Bodelforde, G. 2	Lost in Helsington, 302
Bortun	See Burton
Burton, G. 4	*Bortun* 301b, 302
Castleton, H. 3	*Castretune* 301b
Castretune	See Castleton
Cherchebi	See Kirkby Kendal, Kirkby Lonsdale
Dalton, G. 4	*Daltun* 302
Daltun	See Dalton
Eureshaim	See Heversham
Fareltun	See Farleton
Farleton, G. 3	*Fareltun* 332
Helsingetune	See Helsington
Helsington, G. 2	*Helsingetune* 302
Hennecastre	See Hincaster
Heversham, G. 3	*Eureshaim* 332
Hincaster, G. 3	*Hennecastre* 332
Holm, G. 4	*Holme* 301b
Holme	See Holm
Hotun	See Hutton Roof, Old Hutton
Hutton Roof, H. 4	*Hotun* 301b 2nd entry
Kirkby Kendal, G. 2	*Cherchebi* 302
Kirkby Lonsdale, H. 4	*Cherchebi* 301b 2nd entry
Lefuenes	See Levens
Levens, G. 3	*Lefuenes* 332
Lupetun	See Lupton
Lupton, H. 3	*Lupetun* 301b

Mansergh, H. 3	*Manzserge* 301b	Patton, H. 2	*Patun* 302
Manzserge	See Mansergh	*Patun*	See Patton
Middeltun	See Middleton in Lonsdale	Preston Patrick and Richard, G. 3	*Prestun* 301b, 302
Middleton in Lonsdale, H. 3	*Middeltun* 301b	*Prestun*	See Preston
Mimet	See Mint House	Stainton, G. 3	*Steintun* 302
Mint House, G. 2	*Mimet* 302	*Steintun*	See Stainton
		Stercaland	See Strickland
Old Hutton, H. 3	*Hotun* 302	Strickland, G. 1	*Stercaland* 302

WILTSHIRE—*WILTESCIRE*

Folios 64b–74b

MAPS 54–55

Ablington, F. 8	*Alboldintone* 69
Addeston	See Winterbourne (on R. Till)
Adelingtone	See Allington (near All Cannings)
Adhelmertone	See Hilmarton
Aisi	See Eisey
Aistone	See Ashton, Steeple and West
Alboldintone	See Ablington
Aldbourne, G. 4	*Aldeborne* 65
Aldeborne	See Aldbourne
Alderbury, F. 10	*Alwar(es)berie* 68b *bis*, 72, 74b
Alderton, C. 4	*Aldri(n)tone* 72b, 73
Aldri(n)tone	See Alderton
All Cannings, E. 6	*Caninge* 68
Al(l)entone	See Allington (near Amesbury)
Allington (near All Cannings), E. 6	*Adelingtone* 70
Allington (near Amesbury), G. 8	*Al(l)entone* 68b, 69
Alton (in Figheldean), F. 8	*Eltone* 74b
Alton Barnes and Priors, F. 6	*Aul-*, *Awltone* 65b, 69
Alvediston	Not in D.B.
Alvestone	Unid., 67b
Alwar(es)berie	See Alderbury
Ambles-, *Ambresberie*	See Amesbury
Amesbury, F. 8	*Amblesberie* 64b, Wilts. *Ambresberie* 69, 69b, Wilts.; 39, Hants.
Anestige	See Ansty
Ansty, D. 10	*Anestige* 72, 73b
Ardescote	See Earlscourt
Ashton, Steeple and West, C. 7	*Aistone* 68
Ashton Gifford, D. 8	*Schetone* 70b
Ashton Keynes, E. 2	*Essitone* 67b
Atworth	Not in D.B.
Aultone	See Alton Barnes and Priors
Avebury, E. 5	*Avreberie* 65b
Avreberie	See Avebury
Awltone	See Alton Barnes and Priors
Babestoche	See Baverstock
Bachentune	See Beckhampton
Badbury, G. 4	*Badeberie* 66b
Bade	See Bath, Som.
Badeberie	See Badbury
Bagshot, H. 6	*Bechesgete* 60b, Berks.

Ballochelie	See Baycliff
Barford (in Downton), F. 10	*Bereford* 72
Barford St Martin, E. 9	*Bereford* 72b, 74, 74b
Bathampton, E. 9	*Wili*, *Wilrenone* 71 *bis*
Baverstock, E. 9	*Babestoche* 68
Baycliff, B. 8	*Ballochelie* 69b
Baydon	Not in D.B.
Bechenehilde, *Bichenehilde*	Unid., 70 *bis*
Bechenhalle	See Bincknoll
Beckhampton, E. 5	*Bachentune* 71b
Bedesdene	See Biddesden
Bedestone	See Biddestone
Beduin(d)e	See Bedwyn
Bedwyn, H. 6	*Beduin(d)e* 64b, 65b, 72
Beechingstoke, E. 6	*Bichenestoch* 67b
Bemerton, F. 9	*Bermentone* 73 *Bimertone* 73b
Bereford	See Barford (in Downton), Barford St Martin
Bermentone	See Bemerton
Berrelege, B. 6	Lost in South Wraxall, 73b
Berwick Bassett	Not in D.B.
Berwick St James	See Winterbourne (on R. Till)
Berwick St John	Not in D.B.
Berwick St Leonard	Not in D.B.
Beversbrook, D. 5	*B(r)evresbroc* 71b, 73
Bevresbroc	See Beversbrook
Bichenehilde	See *Bechenehilde*
Bichenestoch	See Beechingstoke
Biddesden, H. 7	*Bedesdene* 72b
Biddestone, C. 5	*Bedestone* 71
Bimertone	See Bemerton
Bincknoll, F. 4	*Bechenhalle* 71
Biscopestreu	See Bishopstrow
Bishop's Cannings, E. 6	*Cainingham* 66
Bishopstone (near Ramsbury)	Not in D.B.
Bishopstone (near Wilton)	Not in D.B.
Bishopstrow, C. 8	*Biscopestreu* 69b
Blontesdone	See Blunsdon
Blunsdon St Andrew and Broad Blunsdon, F. 3	*Blont-*, *Bluntesdone* 69b, 70b, 74
Bluntesdone	See Blunsdon
Bodeberie	See Budbury
Bodenham	Not in D.B.
Boientone	See Boyton
Boltintone	See Bulford
Boscombe, G. 9	*Boscumbe* 68b, 71b
Boscumbe	See Boscombe
Bouecome	See Bowcombe, I.O.W.
Bower Chalke	See Chalke
Box	Not in D.B.
Boyton, D. 8	*Boientone* 69b
Bradefelde	See Bradfield
Bradeford	See Bradford on Avon
Bradelie	See Maiden Bradley
Bradenestoch	See Bradenstoke
Bradenstoke, D. 4	*Bradenestoch* 74b *Stoche* 69b, 74b
Bradfield, C. 4	*Bradefelde* 72
Bradford on Avon, B. 6	*Bradeford* 67b
Bramessage	See Bramshaw, Hants.
Bratton	Not in D.B.
Braydon	Not in D.B.
Brecheorde	See Brinkworth
Bredecumbe	See Burcombe
Bredford	See Britford
Breme	See Bremhill
Bremhill, D. 5	*Breme* 67
Brenchewrde	See Brinkworth
Bretford	See Britford
Brevresbroc	See Beversbrook
Brigmerston, F. 8	*Brismartone* 72b
Brinkworth, E. 4	*Brecheorde* 67 *Brenchewrde* 71
Brismartone	See Brigmerston
Britford, F. 10	*Bredford*, *Bretford* 65, 74 *ter*

Brixton Deverill	See Deverill, Brixton etc.
Broad Blunsdon	See Blunsdon
Broad Chalke	See Chalke
Broad Hinton, F. 4	*Han-*, *Hentone* 71b, 72b
Broad Town	Not in D.B.
Brocheneberge	See Brokenborough
Broctone, *-tune*	See Broughton Gifford
Brokenborough, C. 3	*Brocheneberge* 67
Bromham, D. 6	*Bromham* 65
Broughton Gifford, C. 6	*Broctone*, *-tune* 70b, 74
Buberge	See Burbage
Budbury, B. 6	*Bodeberie* 74
Bulford, F. 8	*Boltintone* 68b
Bulkington	Not in D.B.
Burbage, G. 6	*Buberge* 74b *Burbed*, *Burbetc(e)* 65b, 70b, 74b
Burbed, *Burbetc(e)*	See Burbage
Burcombe, E. 9	*Bredecumbe* 68, 68b
Butremare, *-mere*	See Buttermere
Buttermere, H. 6	*Butremare*, *-mere* 70, 72, 74b
Cadeham	See Cadenham
Cadenham, D. 4	*Cadeham* 69
Cainingham	See Bishop's Cannings
Calcutt, F. 2	*Colecote* 73b
Caldefelle	See Chalfield
Calestone	See Calstone Wellington
Calne, D. 5	*Calne* 70, 73 *Cauna*, *Caune* 64b, 66
Calstone Wellington, E. 5	*Calestone* 70, 73 *bis*
Caninge	See All Cannings
Castle Combe, C. 4	*Come* 71
Castle Eaton, F. 2	*Ettone* 68b
Cauna, *Caune*	See Calne
Celdewelle	Unid., 72

Celdretone, *Celdrintone*	See Cholderton
Celeorde	See Chelworth (in Crudwell)
Celewrde	See Chelworth (in Cricklade)
Ceritone	See Chirton
Cerletone	See Charlton (near Malmesbury). See also Charlton (near Hungerford), Berks.
Chaddenwick or Charnage, B. 9	*Chedelwich* 66
Chalfield, C. 6	*Caldefelle* 70
Chalke, Bower and Broad, E. 10	*Chelche* 68
Charlton (near Malmesbury), D. 3	*Cerletone* 67
Charlton (near Pewsey)	Not in D.B.
Charnage	See Chaddenwick
Chedelwich	See Chaddenwick
Chedglow, D. 3	*Chegeslei* 70b *Cheieslaue* 70 *Cheseslaue* 71 *Chigelei* 74
Chegeslei, *Cheieslaue*	See Chedglow
Chelche	See Chalke
Chelestanestone	See Choulston
Cheltre	See Chitterne
Chelworth (in Cricklade), E. 3	*Celewrde* 74b
Chelworth (in Crudwell), D. 2	*Celeorde* 67
Chemele	See Kemble, Gloucs.
Chenebuild	Unid., 70
Chenet(e)	See Kennett
Chenvel	See Knoyle
Chepeham	See Chippenham
Cherhill	Not in D.B.
Cheseberie	See Chisbury
Cheseslaue	See Chedglow
Chesigeberie	See Chisenbury
Chetre	See Chitterne

Cheverell, Great and Little, D. 7	*Chevrel* 64b, 70
Chevrel	See Cheverell
Chicklade	Not in D.B.
Chigelei	See Chedglow
Chilmark, D. 9	*Chilmerc* 67b
Chilmerc	See Chilmark
Chilton Foliat, H. 5	*Cilletone* 71
Chintone	See Kington St Michael
Chipeham	See Chippenham
Chippenham, C. 5	*Chepe-*, *Chipeham* 64b, 73
Chirton, E. 6	*Ceritone* 71b
Chisbury, H. 5	*Cheseberie* 71
Chiseldene	See Chisledon
Chisenbury, F. 7	*Chesigeberie* 73
Chisledon, G. 4	*Chiseldene* 67b
Chitterne All Saints, St Mary, D. 8	*Che(l)tre* 69, 69b *ter*
Chittoe	Not in D.B.
Chivele	See Keevil
Cholderton, G. 8	*Celdretone* 71b *Celdrintone* 70 *ter*
Choulston, F. 7	*Chelestanestone* 68b
Christian Malford, D. 4	*Cristemeleford(e)* 66b *bis*
Chute	Not in D.B.
Cilletone	See Chilton Foliat
Clarendon	Not in D.B.
Clatford, F. 5	*Clatford* 72
Cleverton	Not in D.B.
Clive	See Clyffe Pypard
Clyffe Pypard, E. 4	*Clive* 65b, 68b *bis*, 70b *ter*, 71 *ter*, 71b, 72, 73, 74, 74b *ter*
Codford St Mary, St Peter, D. 8	*Coteford* 71b, 72, 72b
Coleburne	See Collingbourne Kingston
Colecote	See Calcutt
Colerne, B. 5	*Colerne* 71
Coleselle	See Coleshill, Berks.
Colesfeld	See Cowesfield
Colingeburne (Exon D.B., *Colingeburna*)	See Collingbourne Ducis
Collingbourne Ducis, G. 7	*Colingeburne* 65 (*Colingeburna*, Exon D.B., 9b)
Collingbourne Kingston, G. 7	*Coleburne* 67
Come	See Castle Combe
Compton (in Enford), F. 7	*Contone* 69
Compton Bassett, E. 5	*Contone* 70b, 71b, 74
Compton Chamberlayne, E. 9	*Contone* 65
Conock, E. 7	*Cowic* 68b
Contone	See Compton (in Enford), Compton Bassett, Compton Chamberlayne
Coombe Bissett, F. 10	*Cumbe* 65
Corselie	See Corsley
Corsham, C. 5	*Cosseham* 65
Corsley, B. 8	*Corselie* 73b
Corston, D. 4	*Corstone* 67
Corstone	See Corston
Cortitone	See Corton
Corton, D. 8	*Cortitone* 73
Cosseham	See Corsham
Coteford	See Codford
Covelestone	See East Coulston
Cowesfield, G. 10	*Colesfeld* 73b
Cowic	See Conock
Credvelle	See Crudwell
Crichelade	See Cricklade
Cricklade, F. 2	*Crichelade* 64b, 65, 66, 66b, 67 *bis*, 67b *bis*, 70, 70b, 73b *bis*, 74b
Cristemeleford(e)	See Christian Malford
Cristesfeld	See Frustfield
Crofton, G. 6	*Crostone* 70
Crostone	See Crofton
Crudwell, D. 3	*Credvelle* 67
Cumbe	See Coombe Bissett
Cumberwell, B. 6	*Cumbrewelle* 70b
Cumbrewelle	See Cumberwell

Cunuche	See Knock
Cuvlestone	Unid., 73
Dantesie	See Dauntsey
Darneford	See Durnford
Dauntsey, D. 4	*Dantesie* 66b
Dechementune	See Ditchampton
Depeford	See Deptford
Deptford, D. 9	*Depeford* 69b
Derintone	See Durrington
Deverill, Brixton, Hill and Longbridge, C. 8	*Devrel* 66b 1st entry, 68b 1st entry, 69b, 70, 72b, 74, 74b
Deverill, Kingston and Monkton, C. 9	*Devrel* 66b 2nd entry, 68b 2nd entry
Devizes	Not in D.B.
Devrel	See Deverill, Brixton etc.; Deverill, Kingston etc.
Diarneford	See Durnford
Dicehantone	See Ditchampton
Digeric	See Ditteridge
Dilton	Not in D.B.
Dinton, D. 9	*Domnitone* 67b
Ditchampton, E. 9	*Dechementune* 66 *Dicehantone* 68
Ditteridge, B. 5	*Digeric* 71b
Dobreham	See Damerham, Hants.
Domnitone	See Dinton
Donhead, C. 10	*Duneheve* 67b
Downton, F. 10	*Duntone* 65b
Dracote	See Draycot Foliat
Draicote	See Draycot Cerne, Draycot Fitz Payne
Draycot Cerne, D. 4	*Draicote* 74b
Draycot Fitz Payne, F. 6	*Draicote* 66
Draycot Foliat, F. 4	*Dracote* 71
Duene	See West Dean
Duneheve	See Donhead
Duntone	See Downton
Durnford, F. 9	*D(i)arneford* 67b, 71b
Durrington, F. 8	*Derintone* 69
Earlscourt, G. 4	*Ardescote* 73b
East Coulston, D. 7	*Covelestone* 73b
Easterton	Not in D.B.
East Grimstead	See Grimstead
East Kennett	See Kennett
East Knoyle	See Knoyle
Easton	Not in D.B.
Easton Grey, C. 3	*Estone* 72b
Easton Piercy, C. 4	*Estone* 70, 73
East Overton	See Overton
East Tytherton	See Tytherton
Ebbesborne Wake, D. 10	*Eblesborne* 72b
Eblesborne	See Ebbesborne Wake
Ec(h)esatingetone	See Etchilhampton
Edendone	See Edington
Edington, D. 7	*Edendone* 68, 74b
Edintone	See Heddington
Eisey, F. 2	*Aisi* 68b
Elcombe, F. 4	*Elecome* 69
Elecome	See Elcombe
Elendune, F. 4	Lost in Wroughton, 65b
Elston	See Winterbourne (on R. Till)
Eltone	See Alton (in Figheldean)
Enedforde	See Enford
Enford, F. 7	*Enedforde* 65b
Erlestoke	Not in D.B.
Essage	See Shaw (in West Overton)
Esselie	See Ashley, Gloucs.
Essitone	See Ashton Keynes
Estone	See Easton Grey, Easton Piercy
Etchilhampton, E. 6	*Ec(h)esatingetone* 69, 70, 74
Etesberie	See Yatesbury
Etone	See Yatton Keynell
Ettone	See Castle Eaton
Etune	See Yatton Keynell
Eunestetone	See Idmiston

Everleigh	Not in D.B.
Farlege	See Monkton Farleigh
Farley	Not in D.B.
Febefonte	See Fovant
Ferstesfeld	See Frustfield
Fifhide	See Fifield (in Enford), Fifield Bavant
Fifield (in Enford), F. 7	*Fifhide* 65b
Fifield Bavant, E. 10	*Fifhide* 70b *bis*
Figheldean, F. 8	*Fisgledene* 74
Fiscartone	See Fisherton Anger
Fisertone	See Fisherton de la Mere
Fisgledene	See Figheldean
Fisherton Anger, F. 10	*Fiscartone* 69
Fisherton de la Mere, D. 9	*Fisertone* 72b
Fistesberie	See Fosbury
Fistesferie	See Frustfield
Fittleton, F. 7	*Viteletone* 72b
Fontel	See Fonthill
Fonthill Bishop and Gifford, D. 9	*Fontel* 65b, 72b
Fosbury, H. 6	*Fistesberie* 72b *Fostesberge* 72b
Fostesberge	See Fosbury
Fovant, D. 10	*Febefonte* 68
Foxelege	See Foxley
Foxley, C. 3	*Foxelege* 72b
Fristesfeld	See Frustfield
Froxfield	Not in D.B.
Frustfield, G. 10	*Cristesfeld* 74 *Ferstesfeld* 72b, 73b *Fistesferie* 71 *Fristesfeld* 74
Fyfield	Not in D.B.
Gardone	See Garsdon
Gare	See St Joan à Gore
Garsdon, D. 3	*Gardone* 67
Gategram	Unid., 74
Gelingeham	See Gillingham, Do.
Gessic	See Gussage St Michael, Do.
Getone	Unid., 71b
Gomeldon	See Winterbourne (on R. Bourne)
Grafton, G. 6	*Graftone* 71b *Grastone* 74b *ter*
Graftone	See Grafton
Gramestede	See Grimstead
Grastone	See Grafton
Great Cheverell	See Cheverell
Great Hinton	Not in D.B.
Great Somerford	See Somerford
Great Wishford	See Wishford
Gremestede	See Grimstead
Grendewelle	See Groundwell
Gretelintone	See Grittleton
Grimstead, East and West, G. 10	*Gram-*, *Gremestede* 72, 73b, 74
Grittleton, C. 4	*Gretelintone* 66b
Groundwell, F. 3	*Grendewelle* 70b
Grovely	See anon. holdings on p. 457
Guerminstre	See Warminster
Ham, H. 6	*Hame* 65b
Hame	See Ham
Hampton, G. 3	*Hantone* 71
Hanging Langford	See Langford
Hanindine	See Hannington
Hankerton	Not in D.B.
Hannington, F. 3	*Hanindone* 66b
Hantone	See Broad Hinton, Hampton
Hardenehus	See Hardenhuish
Hardenhuish, C. 5	*Hardenehus* 70
Hardicote	See Hurdcott (in Barford St Martin)
Harding, H. 6	*Haredone* 74b
Haredone	See Harding
Harnham	Not in D.B.
Hartham, C. 5	*He(o)rtham* 68b, 69b, 71, 74 *ter*
Haseberie	See Hazelbury
Hazelbury, B. 5	*Haseberie* 65b, 71, 73, 73b

Heddington, D. 6	*Edintone* 69
Helmerintone, *Helmertune*	See Hilmarton
Helperintone, *Helperitune*, *Helprintone*	See Hilperton
Hentone	See Broad Hinton
Heortham	See Hartham
Herdicote	See Hurdcott (in Winterbourne Earls)
Hertham	See Hartham
Hestrebe	See Heytesbury
Heytesbury, D. 8	*Hestrebe* 65b
Heywood	Not in D.B.
Highway, E. 5	*Hiw(e)i* 66b, 72
Highworth, G. 3	*Wrde* 65b
Hill Deverill	See Deverill, Brixton etc.
Hilmarton, E. 5	*Adhelmertone* 71b *Helmerintone* 70 *Helmertune* 73b
Hilperton, C. 6	*Helperintone*, *Helperitune* 74 *bis* *Helprintone* 73b *bis*
Hindon	Not in D.B.
Hiw(e)i	See Highway
Holt	Not in D.B.
Homington, F. 10	*Humitone* 73
Horning(es)ham	Sec Horningsham
Horningsham, B. 8	*Horning(es)ham* 68b, 70b
Huish, F. 6	*Iwis* 74b
Hullavington, C. 4	*Hunlavintone* 72
Humitone	See Homington
Hunlavintone	See Hullavington
Hurdcott (in Barford St Martin), E. 9	*Hardicote* 71
Hurdcott (in Winterbourne Earls), F. 9	*Herdicote* 72
Idmiston, G. 9	*Eunestetone* 66b
Ierchesfonte	See Urchfont
Imber, D. 7	*Imemerie* 72
Imemerie	See Imber
Inglesham	Not in D.B.
Iwis	See Huish

Keevil, C. 6	*Chivele* 69b
Kellaways	See Tytherton
Kennett, East and West, F. 5	*Chenet(e)* 70b, 72, 73
Kilmington, B. 9	*Chelmetone* 98, Som. *Cilemetone* 86b, Som. (*Chilmatona*, *Cil(l)emetona*, Exon D.B. 91, 453, 520, Som.)
Kingston Deverill	See Deverill, Kingston and Monkton
Kington Langley, D. 4	*Langhelei* 66b
Kington St Michael, C. 4	*Chintone* 72b
Knighton, F. 8	*Wenistetone* 74
Knock, D. 8	*Cunuche* 73b, 74
Knoyle, East and West, C. 9	*Chenvel* 65, 68
Lacham	See Lackham
Lackham, C. 5	*Lacham* 71b
Lacoc(h)	See Lacock
Lacock, C. 5	*Lacoc(h)* 69b, 70b
Landford, G. 11	*Langeford* 74 2nd entry
Langefel	See Langley Burrell
Langeford	See Landford, Langford, Longford
Langeforde	See Langford
Langford, Hanging, Little and Steeple, E. 9	*Langeford(e)* 66b, 68, 68b, 69b, 72 *bis*
Langhelei	See Kington Langley
Langley Burrell, D. 4	*Langefel* 69b
Latone	See Latton
Latton, E. 2	*Latone* 68b
Lauvrecestohes	See Laverstock
Laventone	See Lavington
Laverstock, F. 9	*Lauvrecestohes* 68 *Lavertestoche* 74

Place	Domesday form
Lavertestoche	See Laverstock
Lavington, Market and West, D. 7, E. 7	*Laventone* 73 *bis*
Lea	Not in D.B.
Ledentone	See Liddington
Lediar	See Lydiard Tregoze
Leigh (near Cricklade)	Not in D.B.
Leigh Delamere	Not in D.B.
Liddington, G. 4	*Ledentone* 67b
Lidiarde	See Lydiard Millicent
Limpley Stoke	Not in D.B.
Liteltone	See Littleton Drew, Littleton Pannell
Litlecote	See Littlecott
Litlegarsele	See Ludgershall
Little Cheverell	See Cheverell
Littlecott, E. 4	*Litlecote* 71
Little Hinton	Not in D.B.
Little Langford	See Langford
Little Somerford	See Somerford
Littleton Drew, B. 4	*Liteltone* 66, 66b
Littleton Pannell, D. 7	*Liteltone* 71b
Little Wishford	See Wishford
Locherige	See Lockeridge
Lochintone	See Luckington
Lockeridge, F. 5	*Locherige* 71b
Longbridge Deverill	See Deverill, Brixton etc.
Longford, F. 10	*Langeford* 74 1st entry
Luckington, B. 4	*Lochintone* 71b, 72b
Ludgershall, G. 7	*Litlegarsele* 69
Lus Hill, F. 2	*Rusteselle* 69, 70b
Lydiard Millicent, E. 3	*Lidiarde* 65
Lydiard Tregoze, F. 3	*Lidiar* 70
Lyneham	Not in D.B.
Maddington	See Winterbourne (on R. Till)
Maiden Bradley, B. 8	*Bradelie* 71b
Malmesberie	See Malmesbury
Malmesbury, D. 3	*Ma(l)mesberie* 64b *ter*, 66, 66b, 67, 69b *bis*, 70b *bis*, 71 *bis*, 72, 72b *bis*, 73, 73b
Mamesberie	See Malmesbury
Maneforde	See Manningford
Manetune	See Manton
Maniford	See Manningford
Manningford Abbots, Bohun and Bruce, F. 6	*Maneforde* 67 *Maniford* 73b, 74
Manton, F. 5	*Manetune* 71
Marden, E. 6	*Meresdene* 73
Market Lavington	See Lavington
Marlborough, G. 5	*Merleberge* 64b, 65b
Marston (near Potterne)	Not in D.B.
Marston Meysey	Not in D.B.
Marten, H. 6	*Mar-*, *Mertone* 74, 74b *bis*
Martone	See Marten
Melchesham	See Melksham
Meleford	See Milford
Melksham, C. 6	*Melchesham* 65, 74
Mera, *Mere*	See Mere
Mere, B. 9	*Mera*, *Mere* 74 *ter*
Meresdene	See Marden
Merleberge	See Marlborough
Mertone	See Marten
Middleton, C. 8	*Mideltone* 69b, 72b
Mideltone	See Middleton
Mildenhall, G. 5	*Mildenhalle* 66b
Mildenhalle	See Mildenhall
Mildestone	See Milston
Milford, F. 10	*Meleford* 71, 74
Milston, F. 8	*Mildestone* 68b, 72b
Milton Lilborne	Not in D.B.
Minety	Not in D.B.
Monkton Deverill	See Deverill, Kingston and Monkton
Monkton Farleigh, B. 6	*Farlege* 73b *bis*

Mordone	See Moredon
Moredon, F. 3	*Mordone* 70b, 72b *Mortune* 71b
Mortune	See Moredon
Nechendune	See Netton
Netheravon, F. 7	*Nigra avra* 74b *Nigravre* 65, 73 *bis*
Netherhampton	Not in D.B.
Nettleton, B. 4	*Niteletone* 66b
Netton, F. 9	*Nechendune* 68b
Newenton	See South Newton
Newentone	See Newton Tony, South Newton. See also Long Newnton, Gloucs.
Newetone	See North Newnton
Newton Tony, G. 8	*Newentone* 70
Nigra avra, *Nigravre*	See Netheravon
Niteletone	See Nettleton
North Bradley	Not in D.B.
North Newnton, F. 6	*Newetone* 67b
North Tidworth, G. 7	*Todew(o)rde* 66, 69, 74b *Todowrde* 69
North Wraxall, B. 5	*Werocheshalle* 69b
Norton, C. 4	*Nortone* 67
Norton Bavant, C. 8	*Nortone* 70b
Nortone	See Norton, Norton Bavant
Nunton	Not in D.B.
Oaksey, D. 3	*Wochesie* 73b
Ocheborne, *-burne*	See Ogbourne
Ocheforde	See Ugford
Odestoche	See Odstock
Odstock, F. 10	*Odestoche* 73b
Ogbourne St Andrew, St George, G. 5	*Ocheborne*, *-burne* 65b, 71, 74 *bis*
Ogeford	See Ugford
Opetone	See Upton Scudamore
Oppavrene	See Upavon
Orc(h)estone	See Orcheston
Orcheston St George, St Mary, E. 8	*Orc(h)estone* 69 *bis*, 72b *bis*
Otone	See Wootton Rivers
Overton, East and West, F. 5	*Ovretone* 65b, 68
Ovretone	See Overton
Patney	Not in D.B.
Paueshou	See Poulshot
Perteworde	See Pertwood
Pertwood, C. 9	*Perteworde* 66
Pevesei, *-sie*	See Pewsey
Pewsey, F. 6	*Pevesei*, *-sie* 65b, 67b, 70, 74
Pewsham	Not in D.B.
Piritone	See Purton
Pitton	Not in D.B.
Pleiteford	See Plaitford, Hants.
Poertone	See Porton
Pole	See Poole Keynes, Gloucs.
Poltone	See Poulton. See also Poulton, Gloucs.
Pomeroy, B. 7	*Ponberie* 73b
Ponberie	See Pomeroy
Porton, F. 9	*Po(e)rtone* 69b, 74
Portone	See Porton
Poterne	See Potterne
Potterne, D. 6	*Poterne* 66, 69b, 73b
Poulshot, D. 6	*Paueshou* 65
Poulton, G. 5	*Poltone* 71
Preshute	Not in D.B.
Purton, F. 3	*Piritone* 67
Quintone	Unid., 64b
Ramesberie	See Ramsbury
Ramsbury, H. 5	*Ramesberie* 66
Ratfyn, F. 8	*Rotefeld(e)* 69, 74b

Redborne	See Rodbourne Cheney
Redlynch	Not in D.B.
Retmore	See Roughmoor
Rochelie	See Rockley
Rockley, F. 5	*Rochelie* 69b, 70b
Rodbourne Cheney, F. 3	*Redborne* 71
Rode	See Rowde
Rolleston	See Winterbourne (on R. Till)
Rotefeld(e)	See Ratfyn
Roughmore, D. 6	*Retmore* 68b
Roundway	Not in D.B.
Rowde, D. 6	*Rode* 70
Rushall, F. 7	*Rusteselve* 65
Rusteselle	See Lus Hill
Rusteselve	See Rushall
St Joan à Gore, D. 7	*Gare* 73
Saldeborne	See Shalbourne
Salisbury, F. 9	*Sarisberie* 64b, 66
Salteharpe	See Salthrop
Salthrop, F. 4	*Salteharpe* 70b
Sarisberie	See Salisbury
Savernake	Not in D.B.
Scage	See Shaw (in Chute)
Scaldeburne	See Shalbourne
Scarentone	See Sherrington
Scepeleia	Unid., 66
Schernecote	See Shorncote, Gloucs.
Schetone	See Ashton Gifford
Sclive	Unid., 70
Seagry, D. 4	*Segrete* 71b *Segrie* 72b
Sedgehill	Not in D.B.
Seend	Not in D.B.
Segrete, *Segrie*	See Seagry
Sela, *Sele*	See Zeals
Semington	Not in D.B.
Semley	Not in D.B.
Sevamentone	See Sevington
Sevington, C. 4	*Sevamentone* 71b
Shalbourne, H. 6	*Saldeborne* 74b *Scaldeburne* 73, 74 *bis*
Shalbourne cont.	*Eseldeborne* 57b, Berks.
Shaw (in Chute), H. 7	*Scage* 72b
Shaw (in West Overton), F. 6	*Essage* 72
Sherrington, D. 9	*Scarentone* 72b *bis*
Sherston, C. 3	*Sorestone* 71 *Sorstain* 65b
Shrewton	See Winterbourne (on R. Till)
Sirendone	See Surrendell
Slaughterford	Not in D.B.
Smalebroc	See Smallbrook
Smallbrook, C. 8	*Smalebroc* 74b
Smitecote	See Smithcot
Smithcot, D. 4	*Smitecote* 70b
Somerford, Great and Little, D. 4	*Somreforde* 69b *Sumreford* 67, 70b *bis*, 73b
Somreforde	See Somerford
Sopeworde	See Sopworth
Sopworth, B. 3	*Sopeworde* 71b
Sorestone, *Sorstain*	See Sherston
South Marston	Not in D.B.
South Newton, E. 9	*Newenton(e)* 68 *bis*
Southwick	Not in D.B.
South Wraxall	Not in D.B.
Stamere	See Stanmore
Standen, H. 7	*Standone* 70
Standene	See Standen, Berks.
Standlynch, G. 10	*Staninges* 72 *bis*, 73b
Standone	See Standen
Staninges	See Standlynch
Stanlege	See Stanley
Stanley, D. 5	*Stanlege* 72
Stanmore, F. 5	*Stamere* 71b
Stantone	See Stanton Fitzwarren, Stanton St Bernard, Stanton St Quinton
Stanton Fitzwarren, F. 3	*Stantone* 74
Stanton St Bernard, E. 6	*Stantone* 67b

Stanton St Quinton, C. 4	*Stantone* 66b, 72b
Stapleford, E. 9	*Stapleford* 74
Staverton, C. 6	*Stavretone* 73b
Stavretone	See Staverton
Steeple Ashton	See Ashton, Steeple and West
Steeple Langford	See Langford
Stert, E. 6	*Sterte* 70b
Sterte	See Stert
Stitchcombe, G. 5	*Stotecome* 74
Stoche	See Bradenstoke
Stockton, D. 9	*Stottune* 65b
Stortone	See Stourton
Stotecome	See Stitchcombe
Stottune	See Stockton
Stourton, B. 9	*Stortone* 72
Straburg	See Trowbridge
Stradford	See Stratford Tony
Stratford-sub-Castle	Not in D.B.
Stratford Tony, E. 10	*Stradford* 69
Stratone	See Stratton St Margaret
Stratton St Margaret, F. 3	*Stratone* 73
Sudtone	See Sutton Mandeville, Sutton Veny
Suindone, *-dune*	See Swindon
Sumreford	See Somerford. See also Somerford Keynes, Gloucs.
Surrendell, C. 4	*Sirendone* 72b
Sutone (Exon D.B., *Sutona*)	See Sutton Veny
Sutton Benger	Not in D.B.
Sutton Mandeville, D. 10	*Sudtone* 72
Sutton Veny, C. 8	*Su(d)tone* 72 *bis*, 73 (*Sutona*, Exon D.B. 47)
Svaloclive	See Swallowcliffe
Swallowcliffe, D. 10	*Svaloclive* 67b, 73b *bis*
Swindon, F. 4	*Suindone*, *-dune* 64b, 66, 70b, 74 *bis*, 74b
Tedelintone	See Tytherton
Tedrintone	See Tytherington
Teffont Evias, D. 9	*Tefonte* 70
Tefonte	See Teffont Evias
Terintone	See Tytherton
Theodulveside	See Tilshead
Thickwood, B. 5	*Ticoode* 69b
Thornhill, E. 4	*Tornelle* 71 *Tornvele* 74
Ticoode	See Thickwood
Tidcombe, H. 6	*Titicome* 74
Tidulfhide	See Tilshead
Tilshead, E. 8	*Theodulveside* 65 *Tidulfhide* 73b *quater*
Tisbury, D. 10	*Tisseberie* 67b
Tisseberie	See Tisbury
Titicome	See Tidcombe
Tocheham	See Tockenham
Tockenham, E. 4	*Tocheham* 71b, 72, 73b *ter*
Todew(o)rde	See North Tidworth
Todowrde	See North Tidworth
Tollard Royal, D. 11	*Tollard* 69b, 71b, 73
Tornelle, *Tornvele*	See Thornhill
Troi	See Trow
Trole	See Trowle
Trow, D. 10	*Troi* 73
Trowbridge, C. 6	*Straburg* 73b
Trowle, C. 6	*Trole* 73b
Tuderlege	See Tytherley, Hants.
Tytherington, C. 8	*Tedrintone* 69
Tytherton Lucas, East Tytherton and Kellaways, D. 4, D. 5	*Tedelintone* 70b *Terintone* 69b, 72b
Ufecote	See Uffcott
Uffcott, F. 4	*U(l)fecote* 71b, 74

Ugford, E. 9	*Ocheforde* 68 *Ogeford* 72b
Ulfecote	See Uffcott
Ulfela	See Wolf Hall
Upavon, F. 7	*Oppavrene* 65b
Uptone	See Upton Lovell
Upton Lovell, D. 8	*Uptone* 68b
Upton Scudamore, C. 8	*Opetone* 70, 70b, 71b
Urchfont, E. 6	*Ierchesfonte* 68
Viteletone	See Fittleton
Wadhulle	See Woodhill
Wadone	See Whaddon (in Semington)
Waisel	See Washern
Walcot, F. 3	*Walecote* 71
Walecote	See Walcot
Wanborough, G. 4	*Wemberge* 65b
Wardour, D. 10	*Werdore* 68
Warminster, C. 8	*Guerminstre* 64b
Washern, F. 9	*Waisel* 68
Watedene	See Whaddon (in Alderbury)
Wemberge	See Wanborough
Wenistetone	See Knighton
Werdore	See Wardour
Werocheshalle	See North Wraxall
Wertune, *Wervetone*	See Wroughton
Wesberie	See Westbury
West Ashton	See Ashton, Steeple and West
Westberie	See Westbury
Westbury, C. 7	*Wes(t)berie* 65, 74b
West Dean, G. 10	*Duene* 72
West Grimstead	See Grimstead
West Kennett	See Kennett
West Kington	Not in D.B.
West Knoyle	See Knoyle
West Lavington	See Lavington
Westlecott, F. 4	*Wichelestote* 73
West Overton	See Overton
Westwode	See Westwood
Westwood, B. 6	*Westwode* 65b
Whaddon (in Alderbury), G. 10	*Watedene* 72 *bis*
Whaddon (in Semington), C. 6	*Wadone* 73b
Whitecliff, C. 9	*Witeclive* 74b
Whiteparish	Not in D.B.
Whitley, C. 6	*Witelie* 73
Wicheford	See Wishford
Wichelestote	See Westlecott
Widecome	See Witcomb
Widehille	See Widhill
Widetone	See Witherington
Widhill, F. 3	*Wi(l)dehille* 70b, 74b
Wiflesford(e)	See Wilsford (near Amesbury)
Wilcot, F. 6	*Wilcote* 69
Wilcote	See Wilcot
Wildehille	See Widhill
Wilgi	See Wylye
Wili, *Wilrenone*	See Bathampton
Wilsford (near Amesbury), F. 8	*Wiflesford(e)* 68b, 72b
Wilsford (near Pewsey), E. 7	*Wivlesford* 73b
Wilton, E. 9	*Wiltone*, *-tune* 64b, 65 *bis*, 66, 68, 69, 70b, 71, 71b, 72b, 73, 73b
Wiltone, *-tune*	See Wilton
Winefel	See Wingfield
Wingfield, B. 7	*Winefel* 66
Winsley	Not in D.B.
Winterbourne (on R. Bourne): Gomeldon, Winterbourne Dauntsey, Winterbourne Earls and Winterbourne Gunner, F. 9	*Wintreburne* 66, 66b, 69b 2nd entry, 70 2nd entry, 73 2nd entry, 73b 1st entry, 74
Winterbourne (on R. Till): Addeston, Berwick St James, Elston, Maddington, Rolleston and Shrewton, E. 8	*Wintreburne* 67b, 68b 2nd entry, 69 *bis*, 69b 1st entry, 70 1st entry, 72b *bis*, 73 1st entry, 73b 2nd entry

Winterbourne Bassett, F. 5	*Wintreburne* 68b 1st entry, 71
Winterbourne Dauntsey, Earls, Gunner	See Winterbourne (on R. Bourne)
Winterbourne Monkton, F. 5	*Wintreborne* 66b
Winterbourne Stoke, E. 8	*Wintreburne(stoch)* 65, 69
Winterslow, G. 9	*Wintreslei, -leu* 68b, 69, 74 *bis*
Wintreborne	See Winterbourne Monkton
Wintreburne	See Winterbourne (on R. Bourne), Winterbourne (on R. Till), Winterbourne Bassett, Winterbourne Stoke
Wintreburnestoch	See Winterbourne Stoke
Wintreslei, -leu	See Winterslow
Wishford, Great and Little, E. 9	*Wicheford* 68, 74b *Witford* 72
Witcomb, E. 4	*Widecome* 70
Witeberge	See Woodborough
Witeclive	See Whitecliff
Witelie	See Whitley
Witford	See Wishford
Withenham, B. 6	Lost in Wingfield, 66
Witherington, F. 10	*Widetone* 74
Wivlesford	See Wilsford (near Pewsey)
Wochesie	See Oaksey
Wodetone	See Wootton Bassett
Wolf Hall, G. 6	*Ulfela* 74b
Woodborough, F. 6	*Witeberge* 72b
Woodfalls	Not in D.B.
Woodford	Not in D.B.
Woodhill, E. 4	*Wadhulle* 66
Wootton Bassett, E. 4	*Wodetone* 71
Wootton Rivers, G. 6	*Otone* 65
Worton	Not in D.B.
Wrde	See Highworth
Wroughton, F. 4	*Wertune* 70b *Wervetone* 73b
Wylye, D. 9	*Wilgi* 68
Yarnfield, B. 9	*Gernefelle* 95, Som. (*Gernefella*, Exon D.B. 447, Som.)
Yatesbury, E. 5	*Etesberie* 73
Yatton Keynell, C. 4	*Etone*, *Etune* 66, 70, 73
Zeals, B. 9	*Sela*, *Sele* 73, 73b

ANONYMOUS HOLDINGS

No place-names appear in the following eleven entries, and it is possible that some (or even all) of these refer to holdings at places not named elsewhere in Domesday Book:

Bishop Osmund of Salisbury, half a church with half a hide, 65b.
Hubold (from Arnulf de Hesdin), one hide, 70.
Durand of Gloucester, half a virgate, 70b.
Durand of Gloucester, half a virgate, 71.
Godescal, half a hide, 73.
Stephen the carpenter (from the king), 3 hides, 73b.
Alvric, 2 hides less one virgate, 73b.
Edmund, one virgate, 74.
Saieva, one virgate, 74.
Rainburgis, 5 hides, 74.
King's foresters, 1½ hides *in foresta de Grauelinges* (Grovely Forest), 74.

WORCESTERSHIRE — *WIRECESTRESCIRE*

Folios 172–178

MAP 51

Abberley, A. 4	*Edboldelege* 176
Abberton, D. 6	*Edbretintune* 175 *Edbritone* 175
Abbots Lench, D. 6	*Abeleng* 173
Abbots Morton, E. 6	*Mortune* 175b, 176b
Abeleng	See Abbots Lench
Achelenz	See Atch Lench
Actune	See Acton Beauchamp, Heref.
Aelmeleia	See Elmley Lovett
Aichintune	See Eckington
Alcrintun	See Offerton
Aldington, E. 7	*Aldintone* 175b
Aldintone	See Aldington, Oldington
Alfrick	Not in D.B.
Alia Frenesse	See Franche
Alia Ribeford	See Ribbesford
Alretune	See Orleton
Alton, A. 4	*Alvintune* 176
Alvechurch, E. 4	*Alvievecherche* 174
Alvievecherche	See Alvechurch
Alvintune	See Alton
Ambreslege	See Ombersley
Ardolvestone	See Eardiston
Areley Kings	Not in D.B.
Ashborough, D. 4	*Asseberga* 172
Ashton under Hill, D. 8	*Es(se)tone* 163b, 164, Gloucs.
Asseberga	See Ashborough
Astley, B. 4	*Eslei* 176
Aston Fields, D. 4	*Estone* 174
Aston Somerville, E. 8	*Estune* 169b, Gloucs.
Atch Lench, E. 6	*Achelenz* 175b *Lenc* 174
Baddington, D. 4	*Bedindone* 174
Badesei	See Badsey
Badsey, E. 7	*Badesei* 175b
Baldehalle, B. 7	Lost in Hanley Castle, 180b, Heref.
Barley, C. 8	*Burgelege* 173
Bastwood, A. 4	*Bestewde* 176
Bayton, A. 4	*Betune* 176
Beckford, D. 8	*Beceford* 164, Gloucs.
Bedindone	See Baddington
Beford	See Besford
Belintones	See Bellington
Belbroughton, C. 3	*Brotune* 177b
Bellem	See Bell Hall
Bell Hall, D. 3	*Bellem* 177
Bellington, C. 3	*Belintones* 177
Beneslei	See Bentley Pauncefoot
Bengeworth, E. 7	*Beningeorde* 175b *Bennicworte* 174
Beningeorde, *Bennicworte*	See Bengeworth
Bentley Pauncefoot, D. 5	*Beneslei* 177b
Beolege	See Beoley
Beoley, E. 4	*Beolege* 175
Berchelai	See Bartley Green, Warw.
Bericote	See Burcot
Beritune	See Berrington
Berlingeham	See Birlingham
Berrington, A. 1	*Beritune* 176b
Berrow	Not in D.B.
Besford, C. 7	*Beford* 174b
Bestewde	See Bastwood
Betune	See Bayton
Bewdley	Not in D.B.
Bickmarsh, F. 7	*Bichemerse* 170b, Gloucs.; 244, Warw.
Birlingham, D. 7	*Berlingeham* 174b
Birtsmorton	Not in D.B.
Bisantune	See Bishampton

Biscopesleng	See Rous Lench
Biselege	See Bushley
Bishampton, D. 6	*Bisantune* 173
Blachewelle	See Blackwell, Warw.
Blochelei	See Blockley, Gloucs.
Bockleton, A. 2	*Boclintun* 174
Boclintun	See Bockleton
Bradecote	See Bredicot
Bradelege	See Bradley
Bradeweia	See Broadway
Bradewesham	See Broadwas
Bradley, D. 5	*Bradelege* 173
Bradnesforde	See Bransford
Bransford, B. 6	*Bradnesforde* 175b
Bratfortune	See Bretforton
Bredicot, C. 6	*Bradecote* 173b
Bredon, C. 8	*Breodun* 173
Bredons Norton, D. 8	*Nortune* 173
Bremesgrave	See Bromsgrove
Breodun	See Bredon
Bretforton, E. 7	*Bratfortune* 175b *bis*
Bricklehampton, D. 7	*Bricstelmestune* 174b
Bricstelmestune	See Bricklehampton
Bristitune	Unid., 172
Broad Marston, F. 7	*Merestune* 169, Gloucs.
Broadwas, B. 6	*Bradewesham* 173b
Broadway, E. 8	*Bradeweia* 175
Broc	Unid., 176b
Broctune	See Broughton Hackett, Drake's Broughton
Bromsgrove, D. 4	*Bremesgrave* 172
Brotune	See Belbroughton
Broughton Hackett, C. 6	*Broctune* 175 1st entry
Buintun	See Bevington, Warw.
Burcot, D. 4	*Bericote* 172
Burgelege	See Barley
Bushley, C. 8	*Biselege* 173 *Biselie* 180b *bis*, Heref.
Cakemore	Not in D.B.
Caldeslei	See Shelsley
Caluestone	Unid., 253, Salop.
Carletune	See Carton
Carton, A. 4	*Carletune* 176b
Castlemorton	Not in D.B.
Cedeslai	See Chaddesley Corbett
Celdeslai	See Shelsley
Celdu(u)ic	See Chadwick
Celvestune	See Chauson
Cercehalle	See Churchill (near Kidderminster)
Chaddesley Corbett, C. 4	*Cedeslai* 178
Chadwick, D. 4	*Celdu(u)ic* 172 *bis*
Charlton	Not in D.B.
Chauson, C. 5	*Celvestune* 177b
Checinwiche	See Kenswick
Chemesege	See Kempsey
Chenefare	See Kinver, Staffs.
Chevington, C. 7	*Civintone* 175
Chideminstre	See Kidderminster
Childs Wickham, E. 8	*Wicuene* 168, Gloucs. *Wiquenna* 166, Gloucs.
Chintune	See Kington
Church Honeybourne, F. 7	*Huniburne* 175b
Churchill (near Kidderminster), C. 3	*Cercehalle* 177
Churchill (near Worcester), C. 6	*Circehille* 173b
Church Lench, E. 6	*Circelenz* 175b
Chure	See Kyre
Circehille	See Churchill (near Worcester)
Circelenz	See Church Lench
Civintone	See Chevington
Cleeve Prior, E. 7	*Clive* 174
Clent, C. 3	*Clent* 172b *bis*
Clifton on Teme, A. 5	*Clistune* 176b
Clistune	See Clifton on Teme

Clive	See Cleeve Prior
Clopton, C. 6	*Cloptune* 172b
Cloptune	See Clopton
Cnihtewic	See Knightwick
Cnistetone	See Knighton on Teme
Cochehi, C. 3	Lost near Wolverley, 177b
Cochesei, *-sie*	See Cooksey
Codestune	See Cutsdean, Gloucs.
Codrie	See Cotheridge
Cofton Hackett, D. 4	*Costone* 174, 177b
Colingvic	See Conningswick
Comberton, Great and Little, D. 7	*Cumbrintune* 175 *bis* *Cumbritone* 175
Comble, D. 4	*Comble* 172
Conderton	Not in D.B.
Conningswick, A. 4	*Colingvic* 176b
Cooksey, C. 4	*Cochesei*, *-sie* 172, 177b
Costone	See Cofton Hackett
Cotheridge, B. 6	*Codrie* 172b
Cow Honeybourne, F. 7	*Heniberge* 165b, Gloucs.
Cradeleie	See Cradley
Cradley, D. 3	*Cradeleie* 177
Croelai, *Crohlea*	See Crowle
Croome D'Abitot and Earls Croome, C. 7	*Crumbe* 173 *bis*
Cropetorn	See Cropthorne
Cropthorne, D. 7	*Cropetorn* 174
Crowle, C. 6	*Croelai* 176b *Crohlea* 174
Crumbe	See Croome
Cudelei	See Cudley
Cudley, C. 6	*Cudelei* 173b
Cumbrintune, *-britone*	See Comberton
Cuer	See Kyre
Cunhille	See Queenhill
Defford, C. 7	*Depeforde* 174b
Depeforde	See Defford
Dicford	See Ditchford, Gloucs.
Doddenham, B. 6	*Dodeham* 176b
Dodderhill	Not in D.B.
Dodeham	See Doddenham
Dormestun	See Dormston
Dormston, D. 6	*Dormestun* 174b
Doverdale, C. 5	*Lunvredele* 177b
Drake's Broughton, D. 7	*Broctune* 175 *bis* 2nd and 3rd entries
Droitwich, C. 5	*Wic*, *Wich* 172 *quater*, 172b *ter*, 173, 173b *ter*, 174 *octiens*, 174b *bis*, 175, 175b, 176 *quin*, 176b *bis*, 177, 177b *septiens*, 178 *Wic*, *Wicg* 143b, Bucks.; 154b, Oxon. *Wich* 160b, Oxon.; 166, 168b, Gloucs.; 179b *bis*, 180 *bis*, 180b *bis*, 181b *bis*, 182 *quater*, 187, Heref.; 243b, Warw.; 253b *bis*, Salop. *Wicha*, *Wiche* 163, 163b *quater*, Gloucs.
Dudelei	See Dudley
Dudley, D. 2	*Dudelei* 177
Dunclent, C. 4	*Dunclent* 176
Eardiston, A. 4	*Ardolvestone* 174
Earls Croome	See Croome
Eastbury, B. 6	*Eresbyrie* 173b
Eastham, B. 1	*Estham* 176
Eckington, C. 7	*Aichintune* 174b
Edboldelege	See Abberley
Edbretintune, *Edbritone*	See Abberton
Edevent	See Edvin Loach, Heref.

Eilesford	See Daylesford, Gloucs.
Eldersfield, B. 9	*Edresfelle* 180b, Heref.
Elmbridge, C. 4	*Elmerige* 176b
Elmerige	See Elmbridge
Elmley Castle	Not in D.B.
Elmley Lovett, C. 4	*Aelmeleia* 176
Eresbyrie	See Eastbury
Escelie	See Selly Oak, Warw.
Eslei	See Astley
Estham	See Eastham
Estone	See Aston Fields
Estun	See White Ladies Aston
Eunilade	See Evenlode, Gloucs.
Evesham, E. 7	*Evesham* 175b
Fastochesfelde	Unid., 172
Fecheham	See Feckenham
Feckenham, D. 5	*Fe(c)cheham* 178, Worcs.; 180b *bis*, Heref.
Fepsetenatun	See Phepson
Fladbury, D. 7	*Fledebirie* 172b
Fledebirie	See Fladbury
Flyford Flavell	Not in D.B.
Focheberie	See Fockbury
Fockbury, D. 4	*Focheberie* 172
Franche, B. 3	*Alia Frenesse* 172 *Frenesse* 172
Franchelie	See Frankley
Frankley, D. 3	*Franchelie* 177
Frenesse, *Alia Frenesse*	See Franche
Garstune	See Grafton Flyford
Gerlei	See Yardley, Warw.
Glasshampton, B. 5	*Glese* 177
Glese	See Glasshampton
Glouuecestre	See Gloucester, Gloucs.
Grafton (near Bromsgrove), D. 4	*Grastone* 172
Grafton Flyford, D. 6	*Garstune* 175 *bis*
Grastune	See Grafton (near Bromsgrove)
Great Comberton	See Comberton
Great Hampton	See Hampton
Great Witley	See Witley
Greenhill, B. 5	*Gremanhil* 172b
Gremanhil	See Greenhill
Grimanleh	See Grimley
Grimley, B. 5	*Grimanleh* 173b
Guarlford	Not in D.B.
Gurbehale	See Wribbenhall
Habberley, B. 3	*Harburgelei* 172
Hadesore	See Hadzor
Hadzor, C. 5	*Hadesore* 177
Hageleia	See Hagley
Hagley, C. 3	*Hageleia* 177
Hala	See Halesowen
Halac	Unid., 176
Halesowen, D. 3	*Hala* 176
Halhegan	See Hallow
Hallow, B. 6	*Halhegan* 173b
Hambyrie	See Hanbury
Hamcastle, A. 5	*Hamme* 176b
Hamme	See Hamcastle
Hampton, Great and Little, E. 7	*Hantun(e)* 174, 175b
Hampton Lovett, C. 5	*Hamtune* 177b
Hamtune	See Hampton Lovett
Hanbury, D. 5	*Hambyrie* 174
Hanlege	See Hanley Child and William
Hanley Castle, C. 7	*Hanlege* 163b, Gloucs. *Hanlie* 180b *bis*, Heref.
Hanley Child and William, A. 5, B. 2	*Hanlege* 176b, 177
Hantun, *Hantune* (Oswaldslow hd)	See Hampton, Great and Little
Hantune (Clent hd)	Unid., 177b
Harburgelei	See Habberley

Hartlebury, C. 4	*Huerteberie* 174
Harvington, E. 7	*Herferthun* 173b
Hatete	Unid., 177b
Helperic	See Helpridge
Helpridge, C. 5	*Helperic* 172
Hereford	See Hereford, Heref.
Herferthun	See Harvington
Hilcrumbe	See Hill Croome
Hilhamatone	See Hillhampton
Hill (near Evesham), D. 7	*Hylle* 173
Hill Croome, C. 8	*Hilcrumbe* 173
Hillhampton, B. 5	*Hilhamatone* 178
Himbleton, D. 6	*Himeltun* 173b
Himeltun	See Himbleton
Hindelep	See Hindlip
Hindlip, C. 6	*Hindelep* 173b
Hinton on the Green, E. 8	*Hinetune* 165b, Gloucs.
Holdfast, C. 8	*Holefest* 173
Holefest	See Holdfast
Holim	See Hollin
Hollin, A. 4	*Holim* 177
Hollow Court, D. 6	*Holowei* 178 *Haloede* 180b, Heref.
Holowei	See Hollow Court
Holt, B. 5	*Holte* 172b
Holte	See Holt
Horton, C. 5	*Hortune* 177b
Hortune	See Horton
Houndsfield, E. 3	*Hundesfelde* 172
Huddington, D. 6	*Hudintune* 173b
Hudintune	See Huddington
Huerteberie	See Hartlebury
Hundesfelde	See Houndsfield
Huniburne	See Church Honeybourne
Hurcott, C. 3	*Worcote* 172
Husentre	See Martin Hussingtree
Hylle	See Hill (near Evesham)
Iacumbe	See Church Iccomb, Gloucs.
Ildeberga	See Idleberg, Gloucs.
Illey	Not in D.B.
Inkberrow, E. 6	*Inteberga*, *-berge* 173, 174
Inteberga, *-berge*	See Inkberrow
Ipsley, E. 5	*Epeslei* 244, Warw.
Kemerton, D. 8	*Caneberton* 166, Gloucs. *Chenemertone*, *-tune* 163b, 166, Gloucs. *Chinemertune* 166 *bis*, Gloucs.
Kempsey, C. 7	*Chemesege* 172b
Kenswick, B. 6	*Checinwiche* 172b
Kidderminster, B. 3	*Chideminstre* 172
Kington, D. 6	*Chintune* 176b
Knighton on Teme, B. 1	*Cnistetone* 174
Knightwick, A. 6	*Cnihtewic* 173b
Kyre Magna and Parva, B. 2	*Chure* 176b *Cuer* 174, 176b
Langedune	See Longdon
Lappewrte	See Leopard Grange
Laughern, B. 6	*Laure* 172b *bis*
Laure	See Laughern
Lea	See Lea Green, Warw.
Lege	See Leigh
Leigh, B. 6	*Lege* 175b
Lenc	See Atch Lench
Lenche	See Sheriffs Lench
Lenchewic	See Lenchwick
Lenchwick, E. 7	*Lenchewic* 175b
Leopard Grange, C. 6	*Lappewrte* 174
Linde	See Lindon
Lindon, A. 4	*Linde* 176
Lindridge	Not in D.B.
Lindeorde	See Lindsworth, Warw.
Liteltune	See Littleton
Little Comberton	See Comberton
Little Hampton	See Hampton, Great and Little

Littleton, North and Middle, South, E. 7	*Liteltune* 175b *bis*
Little Witley	See Witley
Longdon, C. 8	*Langedune* 174b *Longedune* 180b, Heref.
Longedun	See Longdon (in Tredington), Warw.
Lower Arley, B. 3	*Alia Ernlege* 247b, Staffs.
Lower Mitton	See Mitton, Lower and Upper
Lower Sapey, A. 5	*Sapie* 176b
Lower Wolverton	See Wolverton
Ludeleia	See Lutley
Lulsley	Not in D.B.
Lunvredele	See Doverdale
Lutley, D. 3	*Ludeleia* 176
Lye	Not in D.B.
Madresfield	Not in D.B.
Malferna	See Malvern
Malvern, B. 7	*Malferna* 173
Mamble, A. 4	*Mamele* 176b
Mamele	See Mamble
Martin Hussingtree, C. 5	*Husentre* 174b
Martley, B. 5	*Merlie* 176b, 177, Worcs.; 180b, Heref. *Mertelai* 178, Worcs.
Matma	See Mathon, Heref.
Merlie	See Martley
Mertelai	See Martley
Mettune	See Mitton, Lower and Upper
Middle Littleton	See Littleton
Middlewich, C. 5	*Midelwic* 172
Midelwic	See Middlewich
Mitton (in Bredon), C. 8	*Mitune* 173
Mitton, Lower and Upper, B. 4	*Mettune* 172
Mitune	See Mitton (in Bredon)
Moor (near Pershore), D. 7	*More* 173
Moor (in Rock), A. 4	*More* 176 *bis*
More	See Moor (near Pershore), Moor (in Rock)
Mortune	See Abbots Morton
Mucenhil	See Mucknell
Mucknell, C. 6	*Mucenhil* 172b
Museleie	See Moseley, Warw.
Nadford	See Nafford
Nafford, D. 7	*Nadford* 175
Naunton Beauchamp, D. 6	*Newentune* 175
Neotheretune	See Netherton
Netherton, D. 7	*Neotheretune* 174
Newentune	See Naunton Beauchamp
Nordfeld	See Northfield, Warw.
North Claines	Not in D.B.
North Littleton	See Littleton
North Piddle, D. 6	*Pidelet* 175 *bis*
Northwick, C. 6	*Norwiche* 173b
Norton (near Evesham), E. 7	*Nortune* 175b
Norton juxta Kempsey	Not in D.B.
Nortune	See Bredons Norton, Norton (near Evesham). See also King's Norton, Warw.
Norwiche	See Northwick
Oddingley, C. 5	*Oddunclei* 173b
Oddunclei	See Oddingley
Offenham, E. 7	*Offenham* 175b
Offerton, C. 6	*Alcrintun* 173b
Oldbury	Not in D.B.
Oldington, B. 4	*Aldintone* 172
Old Swinford, C. 3	*Suineforde* 177
Oleberge	See Oldberrow, Warw.

Ombersley, C. 5	*Ambreslege* 175b
Orleton, A. 5	*Alretune* 177
Osmerley, E. 4	*Osmerlie* 177b
Osmerlie	See Osmerley
Overbury, D. 8	*Ovreberie* 173b
Ovreberie	See Overbury
Ovretone	Unid., 174
Pebworth, F. 7	*Pebeworde* 167 *bis*, 169, Gloucs.
Pedmore, C. 3	*Pevemore* 177
Pendesham	See Pensham
Pendock, B. 8	*Pe(o)nedoc* 173, 173b
Penedoc	See Pendock
Pensax	Not in D.B.
Pensham, D. 7	*Pendesham* 174b
Peonedoc	See Pendock
Peopleton, D. 6	*Piplintune* 175
Peritune	See Pirton
Perry Wood, C. 6	*Pirian* 173b
Pershore, D. 7	*Persore* 174b, 175 *bis*
Persore	See Pershore
Pevemore	See Pedmore
Phepson, D. 5	*Fepsetenatun* 174
Pidele	See Wyre Piddle
Pidelet	See North Piddle
Pinvin	Not in D.B.
Piplintune	See Peopleton
Pirian	See Perry Wood
Pirton, C. 7	*Peritune* 175
Poiwic	See Powick
Powick, B. 6	*Poiwic* 174b
Pull Court, C. 8	*Lapule* 180b, Heref.
Queenhill, C. 8	*Cunhille* 173
	Chonhelme 180b, Heref.
Redditch	Not in D.B.
Redmarley, B. 5	*Redmerleie* 176b
	Ridmerlege 176
Redmerleie	See Redmarley
Ribbesford, B. 4	*Alia Ribeford* 172
	Ribeford 172
Ribeford, *Alia Ribeford*	See Ribbesford
Ridmerlege	See Redmarley. See also Redmarley D'Abitot, Gloucs.
Rippel	See Ripple
Ripple, C. 8	*Rippel* 173
Rochford, B. 1	*Recesford* 186b *bis*, Heref.
Rock	Not in D.B.
Rodeleah, C. 6	Lost in Worcester, 173b
Romsley	Not in D.B.
Rous Lench, D. 6	*Biscopesleng* 173
Rushock, C. 4	*Russococ* 177b
Russococ	See Rushock
Salewarpe	See Salwarpe
Salwarpe, C. 5	*Salewarpe* 174, 176
Sapie	See Lower Sapey
Scelves	See Shell
Scepwestun	See Shipston on Stour, Warw.
Sedgeberrow, E. 8	*Seggesbarue* 173b
Seggesbarue	See Sedgeberrow
Severn Stoke, C. 7	*Stoche* 175
Shell, D. 5	*Scelves* 176b
Shelsley Beauchamp and Walsh, A. 5	*Caldeslei* 176b
	Celdeslai 176
Sheriffs Lench, E. 7	*Lenche* 176
Shrawley	Not in D.B.
Shurvenhill, D. 4	*Suruehel* 172
Snodesbyrie	See Upton Snodsbury
Sodington, A. 4	*Sudtune* 176b
South Littleton	See Littleton
Speclea	See Spetchley
Spetchley, C. 6	*Speclea* 173b
Stanes	See Stone
Stanford	See Stanford on Teme
Stanford on Teme, A. 5	*Stanford* 176b *bis*
Stildon, A. 4	*Stilledune* 177
Stilledune	See Stildon
Stoche	See Severn Stoke, Stoke Prior
Stockton on Teme, A. 5	*Stotune* 176b

Stoke Bliss, B. 2	*Stoch* 187b, Heref.
Stoke Prior, D. 4	*Stoche* 174
Stoltun	See Stoulton
Stone, C. 4	*Stanes* 177b
Stotune	See Stockton on Teme
Stoulton, C. 7	*Stoltun* 172b
Stourbridge	Not in D.B.
Stourport	Not in D.B.
Strensham	Not in D.B.
Sture	See Alderminster, Warw.
Suchelei	See Suckley
Suckley, A. 6	*Suchelei* 172, 178 *Suchelie* 180b, Heref.
Sudtone	See Sutton
Sudtune	See Sodington
Suduuale	Unid., 172
Suineforde	See Old Swinford
Suinesford(e)	See Kingswinford, Staffs.
Suruehel	See Shurvenhill
Sutton, B. 4	*Sudtone* 172
Tame(t)deberie	See Tenbury
Tardebigge, D. 4	*Terde(s)berie* 172b *bis*
Tenbury, A. 1	*Tame(t)deberie* 174, 176b
Teotintune	See Teddington, Gloucs.
Terde(s)berie	See Tardebigge
Teulesberge	Unid., 172
Thessale	See Tessal, Warw.
Thickenappletree, C. 5	*Tichenapletreu* 177b
Throckmorton	Not in D.B.
Tibberton, C. 6	*Tidbertun* 173b
Tichenapletreu	See Thickenappletree
Tidbertun	See Tibberton
Tidelmintun	See Tidmington, Warw.
Timberhanger, C. 4	*Timbrehangre* 172
Timbrehangre	See Timberhanger
Tonge, E. 4	Lost in Alvechurch, 174
Tothehel	See Tutnall

Tredinctun	See Tredington, Warw.
Trimpley, B. 3	*Trinpelei* 172
Trinpelei	See Trimpley
Tuneslega	See Tynsall
Tutnall, D. 4	*Tothehel* 172
Tynsall, D. 4	*Tuneslega* 172
Udecote	See Woodcote
Ulfrintun	See Wolverton
Ullington, F. 7	*Wenitone* 167, Gloucs.
Ulwardelei	See Wolverley
Upeuuic	See Upwich
Upper Arley, B. 3	*Ernlege* 247b, Staffs.
Upper Mitton	See Mitton, Lower and Upper
Upper Wolverton	See Wolverton
Upton Snodsbury, D. 6	*Snodesbyrie* 174b
Upton upon Severn, C. 8	*Uptun* 173
Upton Warren, D. 4	*Uptune* 177b
Uptun	See Upton upon Severn
Uptune	See Upton Warren
Upwich, C. 5	*Upeuuic* 172
Wadberge	See Wadborough
Wadborough, C. 7	*Wadberge* 175 *ter*
Wannerton, C. 3	*Wenuertun* 172
Warley, D. 2	*Werwelie* 177
Warndon, C. 6	*Wermedun* 173b
Warstelle	See Wast Hills (or West Hill)
Warthuil	See Wythall
Waseburne	See Little Washbourne, Gloucs.
Wast Hills (or West Hill), E. 4	*Warstelle* 174
Webheath	Not in D.B.
Welingewiche	See Willingwick
Welland	Not in D.B.
Wenuertun	See Wannerton
Weredeshale	See Rednal, Warw.
Wermedun	See Warndon

Wermeslai	See Worsley
Werwelie	See Warley
Westmancote, D. 8	*Westmonecote* 173
Westmonecote	See Westmancote
Westwood	Not in D.B.
White Ladies Aston, C. 6	*Estun* 173b *bis*
Whittington, C. 6	*Widintun* 172b, 173b
Wiburgestoke, E. 7	Lost in Harvington, 173b
Wic	See Droitwich
Wicelbold	See Wychbold
Wicg, *Wich*	See Droitwich
Wicha	See Droitwich, Wick by Pershore
Wiche	See Droitwich, Wick by Pershore, Wick Episcopi
Wichenford	Not in D.B.
Wick by Pershore, D. 7	*Wicha*, *Wiche* 174b, 175
Wick Episcopi, B. 6	*Wiche* 172b
Wickhamford, E. 7	*Wiquene* 175b
Widintun	See Whittington
Willingewic	See Willingwick
Willingwick, D. 4	*Welingewiche* 177 *Willingewic* 172
Wiquene	See Wickhamford
Wirecestre	See Worcester
Witeurde	See Wythwood
Witlege	See Witley
Witley, Great and Little, B. 5	*Witlege* 172b
Witone	See Witton
Witton, C. 5	*Witone*, *-tune* 177b *bis*
Witune	See Witton
Wollaston	Not in D.B.
Wollescote	Not in D.B.
Wolverley, B. 3	*Ulwardelei* 174
Wolverton, Lower and Upper, C. 6, C. 7	*Ulfrintun* 172b *bis*
Woodcote, C. 4	*Udecote* 172, 177b
Worcester, C. 6	*Wirecestre* 172 *bis*, 173b *ter*, 175b, 176 *bis*, 177, 177b *ter*, 178, Worcs.; 180b *quater*, 182, Heref.
Worcote	See Hurcott
Worsley, B. 4	*Wermeslai* 176
Wribbenhall, B. 4	*Gurbehale* 172
Wychbold, D. 5	*Wicelbold* 176b
Wyre Piddle, D. 7	*Pidele* 173, 175
Wythall, E. 4	*Warthuil* 172
Wythwood, E. 4	*Witeurde* 172

ANONYMOUS HOLDINGS

No place-name appears in the following entry, and it is impossible to say whether or not it refers to a place named elsewhere in Domesday Book:

Robert (from Urse d'Abetot), one hide in Clent hd, 177b.

YORKSHIRE, EAST RIDING
EURUICSCIRE, ESTREDING

Folios 298–333, 373–374, 379–382

MAPS 56–57

Ach	See Aike
Achetorp	See Hagthorpe
Acklam, D. 3	*Aclun* 307, 331b, 382

Aclun	See Acklam
Actun	See Aughton
Aike, G. 5	*Ach* 302b, 306b, 381b
Aiul(f)torp	See Youlthorpe
Aldbrough, I. 6	*Aldenburg* 324, 382
Aldenburg	See Aldbrough
Alia Bouint'	See Boynton Hall
Alia Bretingham	See Brantingham Thorpe
Alia Caue	See North Cave
Alia Chelch	See Little Kelk
Alia Coteuuid	See West Cottingwith
Alia Eslerton	See West Heslerton
Alia Geuedale	See Little Givendale
Alia Heslertone	See West Heslerton
Alia Ledlinge	See Leavening
Alia Turgislebi	See Thirkleby
Allerthorpe, D. 5	*Aluuarestorp* 299b, 381b
Alrecher	See Ellerker
Aluengi	See Kirk Ella
Aluuardebi	See Ellerby
Aluuarestorp	See Allerthorpe
Aluuinton(e)	See Elvington
Alverdebi	See Ellerby
Andrebi, J. 7	Lost in Roos, 323b, 374, 382
Anlaby, G. 7	*Umlouebi*, *Unlouebi* 301, 306, 325, 326b, 330b, 381b
Ansgote(s)bi	See Osgodby
Argam, H. 2	*Ergone* 301, 382
Argun	See Arram
Arnestorp, I. 5	Lost in Hatfield, 323b, 382
Arpen	See Harpham
Arram, H. 5	*Argun* 324b, 382
Asch	See Eske
Ascheltorp	See Haisthorpe
Aschilebi	See Asselby
Aschiltorp	See Haisthorpe
Ascri	See Escrick
Asselby, C. 7	*Aschilebi* 304b *bis*, 306b, 381b *bis*
Asteneuuic	See Elstronwick
Atwick	Not in D.B.
Auburn, H. 3	*Eleburne* 301, 381b
Aughton, C. 6	*Actun* 306b *ter*, 373, 381b
Au(gu)stburne	See Eastburn
Babetorp	See Babthorpe
Babthorpe, C. 7	*Babetorp* 304b *bis*, 381b
Bagenton(e)	See Bainton
Bainton, F. 5	*Bagenton(e)* 307, 328, 381b
Balchetorp	See Belthorpe
Balkholme	Not in D.B.
Ballebi	See Belby
Barche(r)torp	See Barthorpe
Bardulbi	See Barlby
Barlby, B. 7	*Bardulbi* 304b, 325b, 381b *bis*
Barmby on the Marsh, C. 7	*Barnebi* 304b *bis*, 381b
Barmby on the Moor, D. 5	*Barnebi* 302b *Bernebi* 299b, 381b
Barmston, H. 4	*Benestone*, *-tun* 324, 382
Barnebi	See Barmby on the Marsh, Barmby on the Moor
Barnhill, C. 7	*Berneheld*, *-helt* 304b, 381b
Barthorpe, D. 4	*Barche(r)torp* 307, 329b, 382
Baseuuic, *-ewic*	See Beswick
Basing(h)ebi	See Bessingby
Beeford, H. 4	*Biuuorde* 324, 382
Begun	See Bewholme
Belby, D. 7	*Ballebi* 301, 304b *ter*, 373, 381b *bis* *Bellebi* 373
Belebi	See Bielby
Bellasize	Not in D.B.
Bellebi	See Belby
Belthorpe, D. 4	*Balchetorp* 303, 381b
Bempton, H. 2	*Bentone* 307, 381b
Benedlage	See Bentley
Benestone, *-tun*	See Barmston
Beni(n)col	See Benningholme
Benningholme, H. 6	*Beni(n)col* 324, 382

Bentley, G. 6	*Benedlage* 304, 305, 381b
Bentone	See Bempton
Berg(u)etorp	See Burythorpe
Bernebi	See Barmby on the Moor
Berneheld, *-helt*	See Barnhill
Bessingby, H. 3	*Basing(h)ebi* 299b, 381b
Beswick, G. 5	*Baseuuic*, *-ewic* 299b, 306b, 381b
Beureli	See Beverley
Beverley, G. 6	*Beureli* 304 *bis*, 373b, 381b
Bewholme, H. 5	*Begun* 324b, 382
Bewick, I. 6	*Biuinch* 324 *Biuuich* 382
Bielby, D. 6	*Belebi* 299b, 301, 381b
Bigneton	See Binnington
Bileton(e), *Billetone*	See Bilton
Bilton, H. 7	*Bileton(e)* 324b, 382 *Billetone* 304, 382
Binneton	See Binnington
Binnington, F. 2	*Bigneton* 307 *Binneton* 382
Birdsall, D. 3	*Brideshala* 332b *Briteshala*, *-hale* 303, 307, 331, 382
Birland	See Burland
Bishop Burton, F. 6	*Burtone* 304 1st entry, 381b
Bishop Wilton, D. 4	*Widton* 302b *Wilton(e)* 302b, 381b
Biuinch, *Biuuich*	See Bewick
Biuuorde	See Beeford
Blacktoft	Not in D.B.
Bocheton(e)	See Buckton, Buckton Holms
Bodelton	See Bolton
Boletorp	See Bowthorpe
Bolton, D. 5	*Bodelton* 302b, 330b, 381b
Bonnebi	See Gunby
Bonwick	Not in D.B.
Bortona	See Burton Agnes
Bortun	See Brandesburton, Burton Pidsea, Hornsea Burton
Bortune	See Burton Pidsea
Bouint', *Alia*	See Boynton Hall
Bouinton(e), *-torp*	See Boynton
Bowthorpe, C. 7	*Boletorp* 381b
Boynton, H. 3	*Bouinton(e)* 299b, 301, 307 *Bouintorp* 381b
Boynton Hall, H. 3	*Alia Bouint'* 299b
Boythorpe, F. 2	*Buitorp* 299b, 382
Brachen	See Bracken
Brachene(l)holm	See Brackenholme
Bracken, F. 5	*Brachen* 381b
Brackenholme, C. 7	*Brachene(l)holm* 381b *ter*
Brandesburton, H. 5	*Bortun* 382 *Brantisburtone*, *-tune* 304, 382 *Branzbortune* 374 *Burtun* 324b
Brantingham, F. 7	*Bre(n)dingham* 304b *bis*, 381b *Brenting(e)ham* 332b, 373, 381b *Bretingham* 306
Brantingham Thorpe, F. 7	*Alia Bretingham* 304b *Brentingham* 381b
Brantisburtone, *-tune*, *Branzbortune*	See Brandesburton
Bred(d)ale, *Bredhalle*	See Burdale
Bredingham	See Brantingham
Bredinton	See Bridlington
Breighton, C. 7	*Bricstune* 326b *Briston(e)*, *-tun* 325 *ter*, 381b
Brendingham	See Brantingham
Brenting(e)ham	See Brantingham, Brantingham Thorpe
Bretingham	See Brantingham
Bretingham, *Alia*	See Brantingham Thorpe
Bretlinton	See Bridlington

Bricstune	See Breighton
Brideshala	See Birdsall
Bridlington, H. 3	*Bredinton* 381b *Bretlinton* 299b, 301, 307
Brigham, G. 4	*Bringeham* 307, 382
Bringeham	See Brigham
Briston(e), *-tun*	See Breighton
Briteshala, *-hale*	See Birdsall
Brocstewic	See Burstwick
Broomfleet	Not in D.B.
Brostewic	See Burstwick
Brunebi	See Burnby
Bruneton(e)	See Potter Brompton
Brunham	See Nunburnholme
Bubuid	See Bubwith
Bubwith, C. 6	*Bubuid* 326b, 381b
Buchetorp	See Bugthorpe
Buckton, H. 2	*Bocheton(e)* 299b, 307, 382
Buckton Holms, E. 3	*Bocheton(e)* 314b, 328, 382
Bug(h)etorp	See Bugthorpe
Bugthorpe, D. 4	*Buchetorp* 329b *Bug(h)etorp* 303, 382
Buitorp	See Boythorpe
Burdale, E. 3	*Bred(d)ale* 328, 382 *Bredhalle* 301
Burland, D. 7	*Birland* 373, 381b
Burnby, E. 5	*Brunebi* 299b, 302, 320b, 322b *bis*, 381b
Burnous	See Kirkburn
Burstwick, I. 7	*Bro(c)stewic* 323b, 382
Burton	See Burton Agnes, Cherry Burton, North Burton
Burton Agnes, G. 3	*Bortona* 332b *Burton(e)* 299b, 382
Burton Constable, H. 6	*Santriburtone* 304, 382
Burtone	See Bishop Burton, Burton Agnes, Cherry Burton, North Burton
Burton Fleming	See North Burton
Burton Pidsea, I. 7	*Bortun(e)* 323b, 382
Burtun	See Brandesburton
Burtune	See Hornsea Burton
Burythorpe, D. 3	*Berg(u)etorp* 301, 314b, 332b, 382
Butruid	See Butterwick
Butterwick, F. 2	*Butruid* 382
Caingeham	See Keyingham
Calgestorp	See Kelleythorpe
Camerinton	See Camerton
Camerton, I. 8	*Camerinton* 323b, 382
Caretorp	See Caythorpe
Carle(n)tun	See West Carlton
Carnaby, H. 3	*Cherendebi* 331, 382
Catefos(s)	See Catfoss
Catfoss, H. 5	*Catefos(s)* 324b, 374
Catin(ge)uuic	See Catwick
Caton	See Catton
Catton, C. 4	*Caton*, *Cattune* 305, 381b
Cattune	See Catton
Catwick, H. 5	*Catin(ge)uuic* 304, 324b, 374, 382 *Cotingeuuic* 382
Caue	See North Cave, South Cave
Caue, *Alia*	See North Cave
Cavil, D. 7	*Cheuede* 304b, 381b
Caythorpe, H. 3	*Caretorp* 301, 303, 382
Chaingeham	See Keyingham
Chelc	See Great Kelk
Chelch, *Alia*	See Little Kelk
Chelche	See Great Kelk, Little Kelk
Chelchefeld, *-felt*	See Kelfield
Cheldal(e)	See Kendale
Chelinge	See Nunkeeling
Chelingewic	See Kilnwick Percy
Chelpin	See Kilpin
Chemelinge	See Gembling

Chenecol, *Chenucol*, *Chenuthesholm*, H. 6	Lost in Long Riston, 324b, 374, 382
Chercan	See Kirkham
Cherchebi	See Kirby Underdale
Cherendebi	See Carnaby
Cheretorp	See Kennythorpe
Cherry Burton, F. 6	*Burton(e)* 304 2nd entry, 307, 373, 381b
Chetelstorp, B. 6	Lost in Escrick, 313, 381b
Chetelstorp, C. 6	Lost in Storwood, 325
Cheuede	See Cavil
Chileuuic	See Kilnwick Percy
Chileuuid, *-uuit*	See Kilnwick
Chiling(h)e	See Nunkeeling
Chilleuuinc	See Kilnwick Percy
Chillon, *Chillun*	See Kilham
Chilnesse	See Kilnsea
Chirchebi	See Kirby Grindalythe, Kirby Underdale
C(h)rachetorp, G. 7	Lost in Hessle, 326b, 381b
Cleaving, E. 5	*Cleuinde*, *-inge* 301, 381b
Cledinton	See Knedlington
Cleeton, H. 4	*Cleton*, *-tun(e)* 323b, 325, 382
Cleton, *-tun(e)*	See Cleeton
Cleuinde, *-inge*	See Cleaving
Cliffe (near Hemingbrough), C. 7	*Cliue* 306b, 373, 381b
Climbi-, *Clinbicote*	See Kiplingcotes
Cliue	See Cliffe, North Cliffe, South Cliffe
Cnateton(e)	See Knapton
Cogrun	See Croom
Coiningesbi	See Coniston
Coldrid	See Wheldrake
Coldun	See Little Cowden
Coledun	See Great Cowden
Coletun, *Colnun*	See Cowlam
Coningesbi	See Coniston
Coniston, H. 6	*Co(i)ningesbi* 323b, 382
Cotes	See Cotness
Coteuuid	See East Cottingwith, West Cottingwith
Coteuuid, *Alia*	See West Cottingwith
Cotingeham	See Cottingham
Cotingeuuic	See Catwick
Cotingham	See Cottingham
Cotinuui	See West Cottingwith
Cotness, D. 8	*Cotes* 304b, 381b
Cottam, F. 3	*Cottun* 303, 382
Cottingham, G. 7	*Coting(e)ham* 298b, 328, 381b
Cottun	See Cottam
Cowlam, F. 3	*Coletun* 382 *Colnun* 301, 303, 314b, 382
Crachetorp	See *Chrachetorp*
Cransuuic	See Cranswick
Cranswick, G. 5	*Cransuuic* 299b *Cranzuic* 307, 328, 381b *bis*
Cranzuic	See Cranswick
Crogun	See Croom
Croom, F. 3	*Cogrun* 314b *Crogun* 301, 303, 307b, 373, 382
Dalton(e)	See North Dalton
Danetorp	See Danthorpe
Danthorpe, I. 7	*Danetorp* 304, 323b, 382 *ter*
Deighton, B. 5	*Diston(e)* 313, 381b
Delton	See South Dalton
Dic(he)	See Lelley Dyke
Difgelibi, *Dighelibi*	See Duggleby
Dimeltun	See Dimlington
Dimlington, K. 8	*Dimeltun* 324
Diston(e)	See Deighton
Dodintone	See Dunnington (in Bewholme)

Etton, F. 6	*Eton* 381b *bis* *Etton(e)* 304, 306b, 328
Etton(e)	See Etton
Euertorp	See Everthorpe
Euringham	See Everingham
Everingham, D. 6	*Euringham* 302b, 381b
Everthorpe, E. 7	*Euertorp* 381b
Fangfoss, D. 4	*Frangefos* 299b, 381b
Faxfleet	Not in D.B.
Ferebi	See North Ferriby
Fidlinge	See Fitling
Filey, H. 1	*Fiuelac* 299, 380b
Fimber	Not in D.B.
Firby, D. 3	*Friebia* 332b
Fitling, I. 7	*Fidlinge*, *Fitlinge* 323b, 382
Fitlinge	See Fitling
Fiuelac	See Filey
Flamborough, I. 2	*Flaneburc*, *-burg* 305, 330b, 381b
Flaneburc, *-burg*	See Flamborough
Flentun	See Flinton
Fleuston(e)	See Flixton
Flinton, I. 6	*Flentun* 323b, 382 *Flintone* 304, 382
Flintone	See Flinton
Flixton, G. 1	*Fleuston(e)* 299b, 301, 382
Flotemanebi	See Flotmanby
Flotmanby, G. 1	*Flotemanebi* 304, 326, 382
Fodstone	See Foston on the Wolds
Foggathorpe, D. 6	*Fulcartorp* 306b, 325, 326b, 381b
Foleforde	See Gate Fulford
Folkton, G. 1	*Fulcheton* 301, 382
Fordon, G. 2	*Fordun* 301, 382
Fordun	See Fordon
Fornetorp, G. 2	Lost in Thwing, 301, 382
Fosham, I. 6	*Fos(s)ham* 324, 382
Fos(s)ham	See Fosham
Foston on the Wolds, G. 4	*Fodstone* 322b, 382
Fostun(e), I. 6	Lost in Humbleton, 323b, 382
Fotingham	See North Frodingham
Foxele, *Foxhole*	See Foxholes
Foxholes, F. 2	*Foxele* 299b *Foxhole* 382 *Foxohole* 332b
Foxohole	See Foxholes
Fraisthorpe, H. 3	*Frestintorp* 307, 328, 331, 381b
Frangefos	See Fangfoss
Frestintorp	See Fraisthorpe
Fridag(s)torp, *Frida(r)storp*	See Fridaythorpe
Fridaythorpe, E. 4	*Fridag(s)torp* 301, 329b *bis*, 382 *Frida(r)storp* 302b *bis*
Friebia	See Firby
Frotingham	See North Frodingham
Fulcartorp	See Foggathorpe
Fulcheton	See Folkton
Fuleford(e)	See Gate Fulford, Water Fulford
Fuletorp	See Water Fulford
Gagenestad	See Ganstead
Galmeton	See Ganton
Ganstead, H. 7	*Gagenestad* 324b, 382
Ganton, F. 2	*Galmeton* 299b, 382
Gardham, F. 6	*Gerdene* 304b, 381b
Garrowby, D. 4	*Geruezbi* 332b *Gheruenzbi* 331, 382
Garton	See Garton (near Aldbrough), Garton on the Wolds
Garton (near Aldbrough), I. 6	*Garton*, *-tun* 324, 382
Garton on the Wolds, F. 4	*Garton*, *-tune* 304, 305, 307, 382
Gartun	See Garton (near Aldbrough)

Gartune	See Garton on the Wolds
Gate Fulford, B. 5	*Foleforde* 313 *Fuleford(e)* 298, 379
Geduualestorp	See Eddlethorpe
Gembling, H. 4	*Chemelinge* 382 *Ghemelinge* 304
Gerdene	See Gardham
Gerendele	See Grindale
Gerueʒbi	See Garrowby
Geuedale	See Great Givendale
Geuedale, Alia	See Little Givendale
Ghemelinge	See Gembling
Gheruenʒbi	See Garrowby
Gheuetorp	See Gowthorpe
Ghiuedale	See Great Givendale
Gilberdyke	Not in D.B.
Golse	See Goxhill
Goodmanham, E. 6	*Gudmundham* 299, 302b, 306b, 322b, 381b *bis*
Gowthorpe, D. 4	*G(he)uetorp* 302b, 381b
Goxhill, H. 5	*Golse* 323b
Gransmoor, H. 4	*Grentesmor(a)* 332b, 333 *Grenʒmore* 299b, 331, 382
Great Cowden, I. 6	*Coledun* 304, 382
Great Driffield, G. 4	*Drifeld, -felt* 299b *ter*, 306b *ter*, 373 *ter*, 381b *bis*
Great Givendale, D. 4	*Geuedale* 381b *Ghiuedale* 299b
Great Hatfield, H. 6	*Haiefelt* 324b *Haifeld, -felt* 323b, 382
Great Kelk, G. 4	*Chelc(he)* 304, 382
Greenwick, E. 4	*Greneuuic* 302b, 381b
Grendele	See Grindale
Greneuuic	See Greenwick
Grentesmor(a), Grenʒmore	See Gransmoor
Gribthorpe, D. 6	*Gripetorp* 325, 326b, 381b
Grimestona	See North Grimston
Grimeston(e)	See Grimston (in Dunnington), Grimston Garth, Hanging Grimston, North Grimston
Grimestun	See Grimston Garth
Grimston (in Dunnington), C. 5	*Grimeston(e)* 307, 322b, 373, 381b
Grimston Garth (in Garton), I. 6	*Grimeston(e), -tun* 304, 323b, 382 *bis*
Grimthorpe, D. 4	*Grimtorp, Grintorp* 299b, 381b
Grimtorp	See Grimthorpe
Grindale, H. 2	*G(e)rendele* 299b, 302b, 381b
Grintorp	See Grimthorpe
Gripetorp	See Gribthorpe
Gudmundham	See Goodmanham
Guduualestorp	See Eddlethorpe
Guetorp	See Gowthorpe
Gunby, C. 6	*Bonnebi* 326b, 381b
Hagthorpe, C. 7	*Achetorp* 381b *bis*
Haiefelt, Haifeld, -felt	See Great Hatfield
Haisthorpe, H. 3	*Aschel-, Aschiltorp* 299b, 304, 382 *Haschetorp* 332b
Haiton(e)	See Hayton
Halsam, -sem	See Halsham
Halsham, I. 7	*Halsam, -sem* 302, 324, 382 *Halsham* 382
Haltemprice	Not in D.B.
Hamiburg	See Hemingbrough
Hanging Grimston, D. 4	*Grimeston(e)* 329b, 331, 382
Harlthorpe	Not in D.B.
Harpein	See Harpham
Harpham, G. 3	*Arpen* 299b, 331, 382 *Harpein* 332b, 333

Harswell, D. 6	*Erseuuelle* 299, 381b
Haschetorp	See Haisthorpe
Hase	See Hessle
Haselintonis, In duabus	See East Heslerton, West Heslerton
Haslinton	See Heslington
Hawold, F. 4	*Holde* 301, 381b
Hayton, D. 5	*Haiton(e)* 299b, 322b, 381b
Hedon	Not in D.B.
Hei(e)feld	See Little Hatfield
Heldeuueston, Heldouestun	See Hilston
Helmesuuelle	See Elmswell
Helperthorpe, F. 2	*Elpetorp* 303, 382
Hemingbrough, C. 7	*Hamiburg* 299, 381b
Hempholme	Not in D.B.
Hesinton(e)	See Easington
Heslerton(e)	See East Heslerton
Heslertone, Alia	See West Heslerton
Heslington, B. 5	*Eslinton* 381b *Haslinton* 327b
Hessle, G. 7	*Hase* 325, 326b, 381b
Hidon	See Hive
Hilderthorpe, H. 3	*Hilgertorp, Hilgretorp* 299b, 331, 381b
Hilgertorp, Hilgretorp	See Hilderthorpe
Hilston, J. 7	*Heldeuueston* 382 *Heldouestun* 323b
Hive, D. 7	*Hidon* 304b, 381b
Hode, Hodhu'	See Hotham
Holam	See Hollym
Holde	See Hawold
Hollym, J. 8	*Holam, Holun* 323b, 382
Holm	See Paull Holme
Holme	See Holme upon Spalding Moor, Paull Holme
Holme on the Wolds, F. 5	*Hougon* 304b, 381b
Holmetone, -tune	See Holmpton
Holme upon Spalding Moor, D. 6	*Holme* 326b, 381b
Holmpton, J. 8	*Holmetone, -tune* 324, 374 *Ulmetun* 382
Holun	See Hollym
Hornesse(i)	See Hornsea
Hornsea, I. 5	*Hornesse(i)* 323b, 382
Hornsea Burton, I. 5	*Bortun* 382 *Burtune* 323b
Hosteuuic	See Owstwick
Hotham, E. 7	*Hode, Hodhu'* 299, 304b, 306b *bis*, 320b *bis*, 332b, 381b
Hotone, Hot(t)une	See Hutton
Houed', Houeden(e)	See Howden
Houeton(e), -tun	See Houghton
Houghton, E. 6	*Houeton(e), -tun* 299, 320b, 326b, 381b *Oueton* 381b
Hougon	See Holme on the Wolds
Howden, D. 7	*Houed'* 381b *Houeden(e)* 304b *bis*, 306b *quater*, 373, 381b
Howsham, D. 3	*Huson* 307 *quin*, 382
Huggate, E. 4	*Hughete* 301, 330b, 381b
Hughete	See Huggate
Humbleton, I. 7	*Humeltone* 323b *Umeltun* 382
Humeltone	See Humbleton
Hundemanebi	See Hunmanby
Hund(r)eslege	See Hunsley
Hunmanby, G. 2	*Hundemanebi* 326 *bis*, 382
Hunsley, F. 6	*Hund(r)eslege* 304b, 328, 381b
Huson	See Howsham
Hutton, G. 4	*Hotone, Hot(t)une* 307, 328, 381b
Ianulfestorp, C. 5	Lost in Dunnington, 322b, 373 *bis*, 381b

Iapun	See Yapham
Iucufled	See Yokefleet (in Blacktoft)
Iugufled	See Yokefleet (in Blacktoft), Yokefleet (in Gilberdyke)
Kelfield, B. 6	*Chelchefeld, -felt* 313, 328, 381b
Kelleythorpe, G. 4	*Calgestorp* 299b *bis*, 304, 381b
Kendale, G. 4	*Cheldal(e)* 299b, 381b
Kennythorpe, D. 3	*Cheretorp* 328, 382
Kettlethorpe, E. 7	*Torp* 320b, 381b
Keyingham, I. 8	*C(h)aingeham* 324, 374, 382
Kilham, G. 3	*Chillon, Chillun* 299b *bis*, 301, 329b, 331, 382
Kilnsea, K. 9	*Chilnesse* 323b, 382
Kilnwick, F. 5	*Chileuuid, -uuit* 299b, 306b, 381b
Kilnwick Percy, D. 5	*Chelingewic* 332b *Chileuuic* 381b *Chilleuuinc* 299b *bis*
Kilpin, D. 7	*Chelpin* 304b, 381b
Kingston upon Hull	Not in D.B.
Kiplingcotes, F. 5	*Climbi-, Clinbicote* 304, 306b, 322b, 381b
Kirby Grindalythe, E. 3	*Chirchebi* 301, 307, 382
Kirby Underdale, D. 4	*Cherchebi* 301 *Chirchebi* 331, 382
Kirkburn, F. 4	*Burnous* 332b *Westburne* 299b, 381b
Kirk Ella, G. 7	*Aluengi* 306b, 325, 326b, 328, 381b
Kirkham, D. 3	*Chercan* 307 *bis*, 382
Knapton, E. 2	*Cnateton(e)* 325b, 382
Knedlington, C. 7	*Cledinton* 304b *bis*, 381b

La'betorp	See Langthorpe
Lachinfeld, -felt	See Leconfield
Ladon(e)	See Laytham
Lambe-, Lanbetorp	See Langthorpe
Langetorp	See Lowthorpe
Lang(h)etou	See Langtoft
Langthorpe, H. 6	*La'be-, Lambe-, Lanbetorp* 324b, 374, 382
Langtoft, F. 3	*Lang(h)etou* 299b, 301, 303, 382
Langton, D. 3	*Lanton* 328, 382
Languelt	See Langwith
Langwith, C. 5	*Languelt* 313, 381b
Lanton	See Langton
Laxinton	See Laxton
Laxton, D. 8	*Laxinton* 304b, 381b
Laytham, D. 6	*Ladon(e)* 306b, 326b, 381b
Leavening, D. 3	*Alia Ledlinge* 382 *Ledling(h)e* 331b, 382
Lecheton	See Lockington
Leconfield, G. 6	*Lachinfeld, -felt* 304, 306b, 322b, 381b
Ledemare, G. 2	Lost in Fordon, 301, 382
Ledling(h)e, Alia Ledlinge	See Leavening
Lelley Dyke, I. 7	*Dic(he)* 323b, 382
Lepinton	See Leppington
Leppington, D. 4	*Lepinton* 382
Lessete	See Lissett
Leuene	See Leven
Leven, H. 5	*Leuene* 304, 382
Linton, E. 2	*Linton* 382
Lissett, H. 4	*Lessete* 324, 382
Little Cowden, I. 6	*Coldun* 323b, 382
Little Driffield, G. 4	*Drigelinghe* 299b
Little Givendale, D. 4	*Alia Geuedale* 381b
Little Hatfield, H. 6	*Hei(e)feld* 324b, 382
Little Kelk, G. 4	*Alia Chelch* 382 *Chelche* 301

Neswick, F. 4	*Nesseuuic* 381b *Nessuinc* 307
Neuhusa	See Newsholme
Neuhuson	See Newsome
Neuson, G. 5	Lost in Leconfield, 307, 381b
Neuton	See Newton (in Cherry Burton), Newton (in Wintringham), Wold Newton
Neutone	See Newton (in Cherry Burton), West Newton, Wold Newton
Neuuetone	See Newton (in Wintringham)
Newbald, North and South, E. 6	*Niuuebold* 381b *Niwebolt* 302b
Newsholme, C. 7	*Nesse* 381b *Neuhusa* 325
Newsome, J. 7	*Neuhuson* 382 *Niuuehusu'* 324
Newton (in Cherry Burton), F. 6	*Neuton(e)* 304b *bis*, 373, 381b *bis*
Newton (in Wintringham), E. 2	*Neuton* 382 *Neuuetone* 325b
Newton Garth, H. 7	*Nichuetun* 323b *Niuueton* 382
Nichuetun	See Newton Garth
Niuuebold	See Newbald
Niuuehusu'	See Newsome
Niuueton	See Newton Garth, Out Newton
Niuuetone	See East Newton, Out Newton
Niuuetun	See East Newton
Niwebolt	See Newbald
Nortdufelt	See North Duffield
North Burton or Burton Fleming, G. 2	*Burton(e)* 301 *bis*, 382
North Cave, E. 7	*Alia Caue* 320b, 381b *Caue* 302b, 306, 328, 332, 373

North Cliffe, E. 6	*Cliue* 299, 331, 381b *bis*
North Dalton, F. 5	*Dalton(e)* 307, 314, 330b, 373, 381b
North Duffield, C. 6	*Dufeld*, *-felt* 306b *bis*, 381b *Nortdufelt* 326b, 373
North Ferriby, F. 8	*Ferebi* 306, 325, 381b
North Frodingham, G. 4	*F(r)otingham* 324, 382
North Grimston, E. 3	*Grimestona*, *-ton(e)* 301, 303 *bis*, 328, 332b, 382
North Newbald	See Newbald
Northorpe, K. 8	*Torp* 324, 374, 382
North Skirlaugh, H. 6	*Schire(s)lai* 323b, 382 *Scirlai* 382
Norton, D. 2	*Norton(e)* 301 *bis*, 325, 328, 382
Norton(e)	See Norton
Not(h)ele	See Nuthill
Nunburnholme, E. 5	*Brunham* 299, 299b, 330b, 381b
Nunkeeling, H. 5	*Chelinge* 324, 382 *Chiling(h)e* 324b, 382
Nuthill, I. 7	*Not(h)ele* 323b, 382
Ocheton	See Octon
Octon, G. 3	*Ocheton* 301, 382
Osgodby, B. 7	*Ansgote(s)bi* 306b *bis*, 373, 381b
Osteuuic	See Owstwick
Otrege, *Otrengham*, *Otringeham*	See Ottringham
Ottringham, I. 8	*Otrege* 324 *Otrengham* 324, 382 *Otringeham* 304, 382 *bis*
Oubrough, H. 6	*Ule(n)burg* 324b, 382
Oueton	See Houghton

Ousethorpe, D. 5	*Torp* 299b, 381b
Out Newton, K. 8	*Niuueton(e)* 324, 382
Owsthorpe, D. 7	*Duuestorp* 304b, 381b
Owstwick, I. 7	*Hosteuuic* 323b *bis* *Osteuuic* 382
Owthorne, J. 7	*T(h)orne* 323b, 382
Pagele, *Paghel*	See Paull
Painsthorpe, D. 4	*Thorf* 331, 382 *Torfe* 301
Patrictone	See Patrington
Patrington, J. 8	*Patrictone* 302, 382
Paull, H. 7	*Pagele* 382 *Paghel* 323b
Paull Holme, H. 8	*Holm(e)* 323b *bis*, 382 *bis*
Persene, G. 5	Lost in Scorborough, 304b, 381b
Pileford	See Pillwoods
Pillwoods, G. 7	*Pileford* 328, 381b
Pochetorp	See Pockthorpe
Pocklington, D. 5	*Poclinton* 299b *bis*, 320b, 326b, 329b, 330b, 373, 381b
Pockthorpe, G. 3	*Pochetorp* 322b, 382
Poclinton	See Pocklington
Portington, D. 7	*Portiton* 304b, 381b
Portiton	See Portington
Potter Brompton, F. 2	*Bruneton(e)* 299b, 382
Preston, H. 7	*Preston(e)*, *-tune* 323b, 325, 374, 382 *bis*
Preston(e), *-tune*	See Preston
Rag(h)eneltorp	See Raventhorpe
Raisthorpe, E. 3	*Redrestorp* 301, 328, 329b, 382
Rasbi	See Risby
Raventhorpe, F. 6	*Rag(h)eneltorp* 304, 306b, 381b
Redeuuic, *-uuince*	See Etherdwick
Redlinton(e)	See Rillington
Redmære, *-mar(e)*	See Redmere
Redmere, J. 7	*Redmære* 374 *Redmar(e)* 324, 382 *bis* *Rotmare* 323b
Redrestorp	See Raisthorpe
Reighton, H. 2	*Ricton(e)* 301, 304, 381b
Renliton	See Rillington
Riccall, B. 6	*Richale* 302b, 304b, 381b *bis*
Richale	See Riccall
Ricstorp, H. 1	Lost in Muston, 326, 382
Ricton(e)	See Reighton
Rigeborch, *Righeborg*	See Ringbrough
Rillington, E. 2	*Redlinton(e)* 301 *bis*, 382 *Renliton* 307
Rimesuuelle	See Rimswell
Rimswell, J. 7	*Rimesuuelle* 324, 382
Ringbrough, I. 6	*Rigeborch* 382 *Righeborg* 323b *Ringeborg*, *-burg* 382 *bis* *Ringheborg*, *-burg* 324 *bis*
Ringeborg, *-burg*, *Ringheborg*, *-burg*	See Ringbrough
Ripingham	See Riplingham
Riplingham, F. 7	*Ripingham* 325, 381b
Risbi	See Risby
Risby, F. 6	*Rasbi* 381b *Risbi* 304, 373b
Rise, H. 6	*Rison* 304, 382 *bis* *Risun* 324b, 374
Rison	See Rise, Rysome Garth
Riston, *-tun(e)*	See Long Riston
Risun	See Rise
Rodesta(i)n, *-stein*	See Rudston
Roluestun, *Roolfestone*	See Rowlston
Roos, J. 7	*Rosse* 323b, 325, 382 *bis*
Roreston	See Ruston Parva
Rosse	See Roos

Rotesse	See Rotsea
Rotmare	See Redmere
Rotsea, G. 5	*Rotesse* 381b
Routh, G. 6	*Rute* 323b, 382 *Rutha* 304, 382
Rowley	Not in D.B.
Rowlston, I. 5	*Roluestun* 382 *Roolfestone* 323b
Rowton, H. 6	*Rug(h)eton* 324, 382
Rudetorp	See Thorpe le Street
Rudston, G. 3	*Rodesta(i)n, -stein* 307, 325b, 331, 332b, 382
Rudtorp	See Thorpe le Street
Rug(h)eton	See Rowton
Ruston Parva, G. 3	*Roreston* 301, 304, 382
Rute, Rutha	See Routh
Rysome Garth, J. 8	*Rison* 324, 382 *Utrisun* 374
Saltemersc	See Saltmarshe
Saltmarshe, D. 8	*Saltemersc* 304b, 381b
Sancton, E. 6	*Santun(e)* 320b, 326b, 373, 381b
Santriburtone	See Burton Constable
Santun(e)	See Sancton
Scachelinge	See Skeckling
Scachetorp	See Scagglethorpe
Scagglethorpe, E. 2	*Scachetorp* 307, 382
Scalby	Not in D.B.
Scameston(a)	See Scampston
Scampston, E. 2	*Scameston(a)* 301, 325b, 332b, 382
Scardiʒtorp	See *Scradiʒtorp*
Scarpenbec, -pinberg	See Skirpenbeck
Schereltun(e)	See Skirlington
Scherle	See South Skirlaugh
Schilton	See Skelton
Schipewic	See Skipwith
Schirelai	See North Skirlaugh, South Skirlaugh
Schiresbur(ne)	See Sherburn
Schireslai	See North Skirlaugh
Schirle	See South Skirlaugh
Schirne	See Skerne
Schitebi	See Skidby
Scilton	See Skelton
Sciresburne	See Sherburn
Scirlai	See North Skirlaugh
Scloftone	See *Scolfstona*
Scogerbud	See Scorborough
Scolfstona, Scloftone, G. 2	Lost in Muston, 326, 382
Scorborough, G. 5	*Scogerbud* 304b *bis*, 381b
Scoreby, C. 4	*Scornesbi* 322b, 373, 381b
Scornesbi	See Scoreby
Scradiʒ-, Scardiʒtorp, D. 4	Lost in Skirpenbeck, 329b, 373b, 382
Scrayingham, C. 4	*Escr(a)ingham* 327b *bis* *Screngham* 328, 382
Screngham	See Scrayingham
Seaton, H. 5	*Settun* 324b, 382
Seaton Ross, D. 6	*Seton, Setton(e)* 299, 306, 381b
Sendriton	See Settrington
Seton, Setton(e)	See Seaton Ross
Settrington, E. 2	*Sendriton* 314b, 382
Settun	See Seaton
Sewerby, I. 3	*Siuuar(d)bi* 305, 307, 331, 381b
Sherburn, F. 2	*Schiresbur(ne)* 328 *bis*, 382 *Sciresburne* 303
Shipton, E. 6	*Epton* 299, 381b
Sigglesthorne, H. 5	*Siglesto(r)ne* 304, 382
Siglesto(r)ne	See Sigglesthorne
Siuuarbi	See Sewerby
Siuuarbi, C. 7	Lost in Wressell, 326b
Siuuardbi	See Sewerby
Sixte(n)dale	See Thixendale

Skeckling, I. 7	*Scachelinge* 323b, 382
Skeffling	Not in D.B.
Skelton, D. 8	*Sc(h)ilton* 304b, 381b
Skerne, G. 4	*Schirne* 299b, 328, 381b *bis*
Skidby, G. 7	*Schitebi* 304, 381b
Skipsea	Not in D.B.
Skipwith, C. 6	*Schipewic* 328, 381b
Skirlington, H. 5	*Schereltun(e)* 323b, 382
Skirpenbeck, D. 4	*Scarpenbec* 329b, 382 *Scarpinberg* 373b
Sledmere, F. 3	*Slidemare* 307b, 330, 382
Slidemare	See Sledmere
Sotecote(s)	See Southcoates
Southburn, F. 4	*Sudburne* 299b, 381b
South Cave, E. 7	*Caue* 320b, 381b
South Cliffe, E. 6	*Cliue* 304b, 332b, 373, 381b
Southcoates, H. 7	*Sotecote(s)* 304, 325, 374, 382 *bis*
South Dalton, F. 5	*Delton* 304, 381b
South Duffield, C. 7	*Suddufel(d)*, *-felt* 306b *bis*, 373, 381b
South Frodingham	Not in D.B.
South Newbald	See Newbald
Southorpe, H. 5	*Torp* 323b, 382
South Skirlaugh, H. 6	*Scherle* 324 *Sc(h)irelai* 324, 382 *Schirle* 382
Spaldington, D. 7	*Spellinton* 306b, 325, 326b, 381b
Specton	See Speeton
Speeton, H. 2	*Specton* 307 *Spetton* 382 *Spretone* 299b
Spellinton	See Spaldington
Spetton, *Spretone*	See Speeton
Sproatley, I. 7	*Sprotelai*, *-l(i)e* 323b *bis*, 325, 374, 382 *quater*
Sprotelai, *-l(i)e*	See Sproatley
Stactone	See Staxton
Stamford Bridge East	Not in D.B.
Staxton, G. 1	*Stactone* 299b, 382 *Staxtun* 301
Staxtun	See Staxton
Steflinflet, *-ingefled*	See Stillingfleet
Stei(n)torp, F. 6	Lost in Etton, 306b, 381b
Stillingfleet, B. 6	*Steflinflet* 301 *Steflingefled* 313, 328, 328b, 381b
Storkhill, G. 6	*Estorch* 304, 382
Storwood	Not in D.B.
Suauetorp	See Swaythorpe
Sudburne	See Southburn
Sudcniton, *Sudnicton*, D. 3	Lost in Wistow, 307, 382
Suddufel(d), *-felt*	See South Duffield
Sudton	See Sutton (in Norton), Sutton upon Derwent
Sudtone	See Sutton (in Norton), Sutton on Hull, Sutton upon Derwent
Suine	See Swine
Sunderlandwick, G. 4	*Sundre(s)lanuuic* 301, 330, 381b
Sundre(s)lanuuic	See Sunderlandwick
Suton	See Sutton (in Norton)
Sutone	See Sutton on Hull
Sutton (in Norton), D. 2	*Sudton(e)* 301, 303, 325, 331, 382 *Suton* 382
Sutton on Hull, H. 7	*Su(d)tone* 304, 323b, 324b, 382 *ter*
Sutton upon Derwent, C. 5	*Sudton(e)* 307, 322b, 381b
Suuine	See Swine
Swanland	Not in D.B.
Swaythorpe, G. 3	*Suauetorp* 329b, 382
Swine, H. 6	*Su(u)ine* 302, 382

Tansterne, I. 6	*Tansterne* 323b, 382
Tharlesthorpe, I. 8	*Toruelestorp* 302, 382
Thearne	Not in D.B.
Thirkleby, F. 3	*Alia Turgislebi* 382 *Turgi(s)lebi* 303, 307, 325b, 382
Thirnon	See Thornholme
Thirtleby, H. 7	*Torchilebi* 323b, 382
Thixendale, E. 4	*Sixte(n)dale* 329b *bis*, 382 *Xixtendale* 307
Thoralby, D. 4	*Turalʒbi* 331, 382
Thorf	See Painsthorpe
Thorganby, C. 6	*Turgisbi* 325b, 381b
Thorne	See Owthorne
Thorngumbald, I. 7	*Torn(e)* 323b, 382
Thornholme, H. 3	*Thirnon* 299b, 382 *Tirnu'* 322b
Thornthorpe, D. 3	*Torgrimestorp* 332b
Thornton, D. 5	*Tornetun* 381b *Tortetun* 325
Thorpe (in Rudston), H. 3	*Torp* 382
Thorpe Bassett, E. 2	*Torp* 301 2nd entry, 382
Thorpe le Street, E. 5	*Rud(e)torp* 326b, 373b, 381b
Thorpe Lidget, D. 7	*Torp* 304b 1st entry, 381b
Thwing, G. 2	*Tu(u)enc* 299b, 301 *bis*, 332b, 382
Tibetorp	See Tibthorpe
Tibthorpe, F. 4	*Tibetorp* 299b, 301, 330b, 381b *bis* *Tipetorp* 332b
Tichetone	See Tickton
Tickton, G. 6	*Tichetone* 304, 382
Tipetorp	See Tibthorpe
Tirnu'	See Thornholme
Toletorp	See Towthorpe (in Londesborough)
Torchilebi	See Thirtleby
Torfe	See Painsthorpe
Torgrimestorp	See Thornthorpe
Torn	See Thorngumbald
Torne	See Owthorne, Thorngumbald
Tornetun	See Thornton
Torp	See Kettlethorpe (in South Cave), Northorpe, Ousethorpe, Southorpe, Thorpe (in Rudston), Thorpe Bassett, Thorpe Lidget, Welwick Thorpe
Torp, F. 5	Lost in Etton, 328, 381b
Torp, F. 4	Lost in Tibthorpe, 301, 381b
Torp(i), E. 6	Lost in Thorpe le Street, 299, 381b
Tortetun	See Thornton
Toruelestorp	See Tharlesthorpe
Toschetorp, F. 7	Lost in Brantingham, 306b
Totele	See Totleys
Totfled, G. 7	Lost in Hull, 325, 381b
Totleys, I. 7	*Totele* 324 *bis*, 382 *bis*
Touetorp	See Towthorpe (in Fimber)
Towthorpe (in Fimber), E. 3	*Touetorp* 301, 307, 382
Towthorpe (in Londesborough), E. 6	*Toletorp* 302b, 381b
Tuenc	See Thwing
Tunestal(e)	See Tunstall
Tunstall, J. 7	*Tunestal(e)* 323b *bis*, 382 *bis*
Turalʒbi	See Thoralby
Turgilebi	See Thirkleby
Turgisbi	See Thorganby
Turgislebi, Alia Turgislebi	See Thirkleby

Turodebi, E. 3	Lost in Kirby Grindalythe, 299, 382
Tuuenc	See Thwing
Uela	See Weel
Ulchiltorp, F. 3	Lost in West Lutton, 303
Ule(n)burg	See Oubrough
Ulfardun	See Wolfreton
Ulfram	See Ulrome
Ulmetun	See Holmpton
Ulreham	See Ulrome
Ulrome, H. 4	*Ulfram* 382 *Ulreham* 324b
Uluardune	See Wolfreton
Umeltun	See Humbleton
Umlouebi	See Anlaby
Unchel(f)sbi	See Uncleby
Uncleby, D. 4	*Unchel(f)sbi* 301, 382 *Unglesbi* 314b
Unglesbi	See Uncleby
Unlouebi	See Anlaby
Upton, H. 4	*Uptun* 323b
Uptun	See Upton
Utrison	See Rysome Garth
Wadsande	See Wassand
Wag(h)ene	See Wawne
Walbi	See Wauldby
Walcheton, *Walchinton(e)*	See Walkington
Walkington, F. 6	*Walcheton* 304b *Walchinton(e)* 302b, 331, 373b, 381b *ter*
Wallingfen	Not in D.B.
Wansford	Not in D.B.
Waplington, D. 5	*Waplinton* 299b, 381b
Waplinton	See Waplington
Warham	See Wharram le Street
Warran	See Wharram le Street, Wharram Percy
Warron	See Wharram Percy

Warte	See Warter
Warter, E. 5	*Warte* 306b, 322b *Wartre* 299, 322b, 381b
Wartre	See Warter
Washam	See Waxholme
Wassand, H. 5	*Wadsande* 324b, 382
Wassham, *Wassum*	See Waxholme
Water Fulford, B. 5	*Fuleforde* 313 *Fuletorp*(*sic*) 381b
Waton	See Watton
Watton, G. 5	*Waton* 331 *Wattune*, *Watun* 306b, 381b
Wattune, *Watun*	See Watton
Wauldby, F. 7	*Walbi* 302b, 325, 381b *bis*
Wawne, G. 6	*Wag(h)ene* 304, 324, 382 *bis*
Waxham	See Waxholme
Waxholme, J. 7	*Was(s)ham* 323b, 324, 382 *ter* *Wassum* 324 *Waxham* 374
Weaverthorpe, F. 2	*Wifretorp* 303, 382
Weel, G. 6	*Uela* 382 *Wela* 304
Weeton, J. 8	*Wideton* 304, 382
Wela	See Weel
Welham, D. 3	*Wellon*, *Wellun* 325 *bis*, 328, 382
Wellet', *Welleton(e)*	See Welton
Wellon, *Wellun*	See Welham
Welton, F. 7	*Wellet'* 320b *Welleton(e)* 304b *ter*, 306b *quater*, 307, 373 *bis*, 373b *bis*, 381b
Weluuic	See Welwick
Welwick, J. 8	*Weluuic* 304, 382
Welwick Thorpe, J. 8	*Torp* 302, 382
Wentrig(e)ham	See Wintringham
Weresa	See Wressell
Westburne	See Kirkburn
West Carlton, I. 6	*Carle(n)tun* 325, 382

West Cottingwith, C. 6	*Alia Coteuuid* 381b *Coteuuid* 306b 1st entry, 328b *Cotinuui* 325b, 381b
West Heslerton, E. 2	*Alia Eslerton* 382 *Alia Heslertone* 331 *In duabus Haselintonis* 332b
West Lutton	See Lutton
West Newton, I. 6	*Neutone* 304, 382
Westow	Not in D.B.
Wetwang, F. 4	*Wetwangham* 302b, 381b
Wetwangham	See Wetwang
Wharram le Street, E. 3	*Warham* 307 *Warran* 382
Wharram Percy, E. 3	*Warran* 301, 331 *Warron* 382
Wheldrake, C. 5	*Coldrid* 322b, 373b, 381b
Wicstun	See Market Weighton
Wideton	See Little Weighton, Weeton
Widetone	See Little Weighton
Widetun(e)	See Wyton
Widfornessei	See Withernsea
Widforneuui(n)c	See Withernwick
Widlafeston, *Widlaueston*	See Willerby (near Hunmanby)
Widton	See Bishop Wilton
Wifestad, -stede	See Winestead
Wiflestorp	See Wilsthorpe
Wifretorp	See Weaverthorpe
Wilberfoss	Not in D.B.
Wilgardi	See Willerby (near Hull)
Wilgetot	See Willitoft
Willerby (near Hull), G. 7	*Wilgardi* 381b
Willerby (near Hunmanby), F. 1	*Widlafeston* 299b *Widlaueston* 382
Willitoft, D. 7	*Wilgetot* 306b, 325, 326b, 381b
Wilsthorpe, H. 3	*Wiflestorp* 299b, 325 *Wiulestorp* 381b
Wilton(e)	See Bishop Wilton
Wincheton(e)	See Winkton
Winestead, J. 8	*Wifestad, -stede* 323b, 382 *Wistede* 302 *Wiuestad* 382
Winkton, H. 4	*Wincheton(e)* 324, 382
Wintringham, E. 2	*Wentrig(e)ham* 325, 382
Wistede	See Winstead
Witfornes	See Withernsea
Witforneuuinc	See Withernwick
Withernsea, J. 7	*Widfornessei* 382 *Witfornes* 323b
Withernwick, I. 6	*Widforneuui(n)c* 323b, 324b, 382 *bis* *Wit(h)forneuuinc* 304, 382
Withforneuuinc	See Withernwick
Wiuestad	See Winestead
Wiulestorp	See Wilsthorpe
Wold Newton, G. 2	*Neuton(e)* 301, 326, 382 *bis*
Wolfreton, G. 7	*Ulfardun* 381b *Uluardune* 325
Woodmansey	Not in D.B.
Wressell, C. 7	*Weresa* 325, 326b *bis*, 381b
Wyton, H. 7	*Widetun(e)* 323b, 382
Xistendale	See Thixendale
Yapham, D. 5	*Iapun* 301, 381b
Yedingham	Not in D.B.
Yokefleet (in Blacktoft), D. 8	*Iucufled* 304b *Iugufled* 381b
Yokefleet (in Gilberdyke), D. 7	*Iugufled* 304b, 320b, 381b
Youlthorpe, D. 4	*Aiul(f)torp* 302b, 329b, 381b

ANONYMOUS HOLDINGS

None.

YORKSHIRE, WEST RIDING
EURUICSCIRE, WESTREDING

Folios 298–333, 373–374, 379–382

MAPS 58–59, 60–61

Place	Domesday form
Aberford	Not in D.B.
Acaster Malbis, L. 9	*Acastra*, *-tre* 321, 379b
Acaster Selby, L. 9	*Acastra*, *-tre* 313, 328b, 331b, 374 *Alia Acastre* 379b *Altera Acastre* 321
Acastra, *-tre*	See Acaster Malbis, Acaster Selby
Acastre, *Alia*, *Altera*	See Acaster Selby
Aceuurde	See Ackworth
Acheburg	See Eggborough
Achum	See Acomb
Ackton, J. 11	*Aitone* 317 *Attone* 379b
Ackworth, J. 12	*Aceuurde* 316, 379b
Acomb, L. 8	*Ac(h)um* 303b, 330b *Acun* 379b
Actone	See Aughton
Acum, *Acun*	See Acomb
Acurde	See Oakworth
Addingham, F. 8	*Edi(d)ham* 301b, 326b, 380 *Odingeham*, *-hen* 301b, 380
Addlethorpe, I. 8	*A(r)dulfestorp* 301b, 330 *Arduluestorp* 380
Adel, H. 9	*Adele* 307b, 379
Adele	See Adel
Adelingesfluet	See Adlingfleet
Adeuuic	See Adwick le Street, Adwick upon Dearne
Adeuuinc	See Adwick le Street
Adlingfleet, O. 11	*Adelingesfluet* 326, 379b
Adulfestorp	See Addlethorpe
Adwick le Street, K. 13	*Adeuui(n)c* 308 *bis*, 320, 379, 379b *Hadeuuic* 373b
Adwick upon Dearne, K. 14	*Adeuuic* 379 *Hadeuuic* 319
Airton, D. 7	*Airtone* 332
Airtone	See Airton
Aismunderby, I. 6	*Asmundrebi* 322, 380
Aitone	See Ackton
Alceslei, *Alchelie*, *Alcheslei*	See Auckley
Aldborough, J. 6	*Burc*, *Burg* 299b, 301b, 326b, 328b, 329b, 330, 380
Aldefeld, *-felt*	See Aldfield
Aldeuuorde	See Holdworth
Aldfield, H. 6	*Aldefeld*, *-felt* 301b, 303b, 330, 380
Alia Acastre	See Acaster Selby
Alia Ambretone	See Green Hammerton
Alia Branuuat	See South Bramwith
Alia Cattala	See Little Cattal
Alia Eurebi	See Earby
Alia Hauochesord, *Alia Henochesuurde*	See Hawksworth Mill
Alia Popletone	See Nether Poppleton
Alia Useburne	See Little Ouseburn
Allerton (in Bradford), G. 10	*Alreton(e)*, *-tune* 318 *bis*, 379b
Allerton Bywater, J. 11	*Alretun(e)* 315, 379

Allerton Mauleverer, J. 7	*Aluertone* 330, 330b *Alureton(a)*, *-tone* 301b, 332b, 380
Almaneberie	See Almondbury
Almondbury, G. 12	*Almaneberie* 317b, 379b
Alreton(e)	See Allerton (in Bradford)
Alretun	See Allerton Bywater, Chapel Allerton
Alretune	See Allerton (in Bradford), Allerton Bywater
Alstaneslei(e)	See Austonley
Altera Acastre	See Acaster Selby
Altera Crosland	See South Crosland
Altera Hanbretone	See Green Hammerton
Altera Holne	See Yateholme
Altera Popletone	See Nether Poppleton
Altofts	Not in D.B.
Altone	See Halton East
Aluertone, *Alureton(a)*, *-tone*	See Allerton Mauleverer
Aluuoldelei	See Alwoodley
Alwoodley, I. 9	*Aluuoldelei* 301, 379
Ambretone	See Kirk Hammerton
Ambretone, Alia	See Green Hammerton
Amelai, *-leie*	See Emley
Anele	See Anley
Anesacre	See Onesacre
Anestan	See North Anston
Angram	Not in D.B.
Anlei(e)	See Anley
Anley, C. 7	*Anele* 332 *Anlei(e)* 301b, 380
Apeltone, *Apleton(e)*	See Appleton Roebuck
Apletreuuic	See Appletreewick
Appleton Roebuck, L. 9	*Apeltone* 374 *Apleton(e)* 329, 379b
Appletreewick, F. 7	*Apletreuuic* 331b *bis*

Archedene	See Arkendale
Archesei(a)	See Arksey
Ardinton	See Arthington
Ardsley (near Barnsley)	Not in D.B.
Ardsley East and West, H. 11, I. 11	*Erdeslau(ue)* 317b, 379b *bis*
Ardulfestorp, *Arduluestorp*	See Addlethorpe
Arduwic	See West Hardwick
Arghendene	See Arkendale
Arkendale, J. 7	*Archedene* 301b, 380 *Arghendene* 328b
Arksey, L. 13	*Archesei(a)* 319b, 379b
Armley, H. 10	*Ermelai* 317b, 379b
Armthorpe, L. 13	*Einuluestorp* 379 *Ernulfestorp* 330b
Arncliffe, E. 6	*Arneclif* 332
Arneclif	See Arncliffe
Arnford, D. 7	*Erneforde* 332
Arthington, H. 9	*Ardinton* 379 *Hardinctone* 307b
Asc(h)am	See Askam Bryan, Askam Richard
Ascuid	See Askwith
Asele	See Hessle
Aserla, *-le*	See Azerley
Askam Bryan, K. 8	*Asc(h)am* 313, 374 2nd entry, 379b
Askam Richard, K. 8	*Asc(h)am* 329, 374 1st entry, 379b
Askern	Not in D.B.
Askwith, G. 8	*Ascuid* 314b, 322, 330, 380
Asmundrebi	See Aismunderby
Asserle	See Azerley
Aston, K. 16	*Estone* 308, 321 *bis*, 379
Atecliue	See Attercliffe
Attercliffe, J. 15	*Atecliue* 320, 379b
Attone	See Ackton
Auckley, M. 14	*Alceslei* 379 *Alchelie*, *Alcheslei* 307b, 379
Aughton, J. 15	*Actone* 321 *bis* *Hac(s)tone* 308 *bis*, 379

Austerfield, M. 14	*Oustrefeld* 307b, 379
Austhorpe, J. 10	*Ossetorp* 315, 379
Austhu'	See Owston
Austonley, G. 13	*Alstaneslei(e)* 299b, 379b
Austun	See Owston
Austwick, C. 6	*Ousteuuic* 301b
Azerley, H. 5	*Aserla* 330b *As(s)erle* 330, 380 *Haserlai* 332b
Badesuu(o)rde	See Badsworth
Badetone	See Bolton Percy
Badetorp(es)	See Bishopthorpe
Badresbi	See Battersby
Badsworth, J. 12	*Badesuu(o)rde* 316, 379b
Baildon, G. 9	*Beldone*, *-dun(e)* 303b, 328b, 379 *bis*
Balby, L. 14	*Balle(s)bi* 307b, 319b, 379 *bis*
Balle(s)bi	See Balby
Balne	Not in D.B.
Bank Newton, D. 8	*Neutone*, *-tune* 314b, 332 2nd entry
Barchestun	See Barkston
Barden	Not in D.B.
Bardsey, I. 9	*Berdesei* 379 *Bereleseie* 301
Baretone	See Brearton
Barge Ford, B. 8	*Bogeuurde* 332
Barkisland	Not in D.B.
Barkston, K. 10	*Barchestun* 315b, 379
Barlow, L. 11	*Berlai* 325b, 379
Barnbrough, K. 13	*Barneburg* 321 *bis*, 373b, 379 *Berneborc*, *-burg* 319, 373b
Barnby (in Cawthorne), I. 13	*Barnebi* 316b, 379b
Barnby Dun, L. 13	*Barnebi* 307b, 319b, 321b, 379
Barnebi	See Barnby, Barnby Dun
Barneburg	See Barnbrough

Barnoldswick (in Burton in Lonsdale), B. 6	*Bernulfesuuic* 301b
Barnoldswick (near Gisburn), D. 8	*Bernulfesuuic* 332
Barnsley, I. 13	*Berneslai* 317, 379b
Barrowby, I. 8	*Berghebi* 322, 328b, 380
Barugh, I. 13	*Berg* 316b, 379b
Barwick in Elmet, J. 10	*Bereuuit(h)* 315, 379
Baschelf	See Bashall
Bashall, B. 9	*Baschelf* 332
Bateleia, *Bathelie*	See Batley
Batley, H. 11	*Bateleia* 318 *Bathelie* 379b
Battersby, B. 8	*Badresbi* 332
Bawtry	Not in D.B.
Beal, K. 11	*Begale* 316, 379b
Beamsley, F. 8	*Bedmeslei(a)* 301b, 380 *Bemeslai* 301b, 326b *Bomeslai* 328b, 380
Beauchief	Not in D.B.
Beckwith, I. 8	*Becui* 326b, 380
Becui	See Beckwith
Bedmeslei(a)	See Beamsley
Beeston, I. 10	*Bestone* 318 *bis*, 379b
Begale	See Beal
Beldone, *-dun(e)*	See Baildon
Bemeslai	See Beamsley
Benedleia, *Benelei*, *Beneslaie*, *-lei*	See Bentley
Benetain	See Bentham
Bentham, B. 6	*Benetain* 301b
Bentley, L. 13	*Benedleia* 308 *Benelei* 379 *Beneslaie*, *-lei* 320, 379b
Berceuuorde	See Ingbirchworth, Roughbirchworth
Bercewrde	See Roughbirchworth
Berchi(n)ge, *Berchine*	See Birkin
Berdesei, *Bereleseia*	See Bardsey

Bereuuit(h)	See Barwick in Elmet
Berg	See Barugh
Berghebi	See Barrowby
Beristade	See Birstwith
Berlai	See Barlow
Berneborc, -burg	See Barnbrough
Berneslai	See Barnsley
Bernulfesuuic	See Barnoldswick (in Burton in Lonsdale), Barnoldswick (near Gisburn)
Bertone	See Kirkburton
Bestha(i)m, H. 7	Lost in Fewston, 300 *bis*, 380
Bestone	See Beeston
.bet.es	See Wibsey
Beurelie	See Bewerley
Bewerley, G. 6	*Beurelie* 328b, 380
Bicher(t)un, H. 8	Lost in Newhall, 303b, 379
Bichretone	See Bickerton
Bickerton, J. 8	*Bic(h)retone* 330, 379b
Bicretone	See Bickerton
Bierley, G. 10	*Birle* 318, 379b
Biggin	Not in D.B.
Bilam, Bilan	See Bilham
Bilbrough, K. 8	*Mileburg* 327, 379b
Bil(e)ham	See Bilham
Biletone	See Bilton (in Harrogate), Bilton (near Wetherby)
Bilham, K. 13	*Bilam, Bilan* 321 *bis* *Bil(e)ham* 307b, 319, 379
Bilingelei(a), -lie	See Billingley
Billeton(e)	See Bilton (in Harrogate)
Billingley, J. 13	*Bilingelei(a), -lie* 319b, 330b, 379 *Bingelie* 379
Bilton (in Harrogate), I. 7	*Biletone* 326b *Billeton(e)* 331b, 380
Bilton (near Wetherby), K. 8	*Biletone* 329, 379b
Bingelei	See Bingley
Bingelie	See Billingley
Bingheleia	See Bingley
Bingley, G. 9	*Bingelei* 379 *Bingheleia* 328b
Birkby, I. 9	*Bretebi* 315, 379
Birkenshaw	Not in D.B.
Birkin, K. 11	*Berchi(n)ge* 315b, 379 *Berchine* 373b
Birle	See Bierley
Birnebeham	See Brimham
Birstall	Not in D.B.
Birstwith, H. 7	*Beristade* 301b, 330, 380
Bishop Monkton, I. 6	*Monucheton(e)* 303b *bis*, 380
Bishopside	Not in D.B.
Bishop Thornton, H. 6	*Torentone, -tune* 303b, 380
Bishopthorpe, L. 8	*Badetorp(es)* 301b, 328, 330b, 331b, 379b
Bithen, L. 8	Lost in Middlethorpe, 379b
Blackshaw	Not in D.B.
Blaxton	Not in D.B.
Blubberhouses	Not in D.B.
Bodeltone	See Bolton (in Bradford), Bolton Abbey, Bolton by Bowland, Bolton Percy, Bolton upon Dearne
Bodeltune	See Bolton Percy
Bodetone	See Bolton Percy, Bolton upon Dearne
Bogeuurde	See Barge Ford
Bollinc	See Bowling
Bolton (in Bradford), G. 10	*Bodeltone* 318, 379b
Bolton Abbey, F. 8	*Bodeltone* 301b, 380
Bolton by Bowland, C. 8	*Bodeltone* 322

Place	Domesday Book form
Bolton Percy, K. 9	*Badetone* 379b *Bode(l)tone*, *-tune* 321b, 374 *ter*
Bolton upon Dearne, J. 14	*Bode(l)tone* 319b, 321b, 379
Bomeslai	See Beamsley
Borctune	See Burton in Lonsdale
Bordley, E. 6	*Borelaie* 332
Borelaie	See Bordley
Boroughbridge	Not in D.B.
Boston Spa	Not in D.B.
Bowling, G. 10	*Bollinc* 318, 379b
Bracewell, D. 8	*Braisuelle* 332
Bradeford	See Bradford
Bradeforde	See West Bradford
Bradelei	See Bradley, High and Low
Bradeleia, *-lie*	See Bradley (in Huddersfield)
Bradeuuelle	See Braithwell
Bradfield	Not in D.B.
Bradford, G. 10	*Bradeford* 318, 379b
Bradley (in Huddersfield), G. 12	*Bradeleia*, *-lie* 317b, 379b
Bradley, High and Low, E. 8	*Bradelei* 301b
Braham	See Bramham
Brahop	See Bramhope
Braiseuelle	See Bracewell
Braithwell, K. 14	*Bradeuuelle* 321 *bis*, 321b, 379
Brameham	See Bramham
Bramelei	See Bramley (in Leeds), Bramley (near Rotherham)
Brameleia	See Bramley (in Grewelthorpe), Bramley (in Leeds)
Bramelie	See Bramley (in Grewelthorpe)
Bramham, J. 9	*Brameham* 373b *Bra(m)ham* 307b, 379
Bramhop	See Bramhope
Bramhope, H. 9	*Bra(m)hop* 326b, 379
Bramley (in Grewelthorpe), H. 5	*Brameleia*, *-lie* 330, 380
Bramley (in Leeds), H. 10	*Bramelei(a)* 318, 379b
Bramley (near Rotherham), K. 15	*Bramelei* 321 *bis*
Brampton Bierlow, J. 14	*Brantone* 330b, 379 *bis*
Brampton en le Morthen, K. 15	*Brantone* 308, 379
Branton (in Cantley), L. 14	*Brantone* 326, 379
Brantona	See Branton Green
Brantone	See Brampton Bierlow, Brampton en le Morthen, Branton (in Cantley)
Branton Green, J. 7	*Brantona* 332b *Brantun(e)* 301b, 328b, 331b, 379b
Brantun(e)	See Branton Green
Branuuat, *-uuet*, *-uuit(h)e*, *-uuode*	See Kirk Bramwith
Branuuat, *Alia*	See South Bramwith
Braretone	See Brearton
Brayton, L. 10	*Bretone* 315b *Brettan* 379
Brearton, I. 7	*B(r)aretone* 300, 380
Breselai, *-lie*	See Brierley
Bretebi	See Birkby
Bretone	See Brayton, Monk Bretton, West Bretton
Brettan	See Brayton
Brettone	See Monk Bretton
Bridge Hewick, I. 6	*Hadeuuic* 303b, 380
Brierley, J. 13	*Breselai*, *-lie* 316b, 379b
Brighouse	Not in D.B.
Brimham, H. 7	*Birnebeham* 326b, 328b, 330, 380

Brinesford	See Brinsworth
Brin(e)shale	See Burnsall
Brinsworth, J. 15	*Brinesford* 319, 321b, 379
Brochesuuorde	See Brodsworth
Broctune	See Broughton
Brodesuu(o)rde	See Brodsworth
Brodsworth, K. 13	*Brochesuuorde* 379 *Brodesuu(o)rde* 308, 319b
Brogden	Not in D.B.
Brotherton	Not in D.B.
Broughton, E. 8	*Broctune* 314b, 332
Buckden	Not in D.B.
Burc	See Aldborough
Burden, I. 9	*Burg(h)edurun* 307b, 379
Burg	See Aldborough, Burghwallis
Burgedurun	See Burden
Burgelei	See Burley
Burghedurun	See Burden
Burghelai	See Burley
Burghwallis, K. 12	*Burg* 315b, 379b
Burley, G. 8	*Burgelei* 379 *Burghelai* 303b
Burn	Not in D.B.
Burnsall, F. 7	*Brin(e)shale* 329b, 331b
Burton	See Burton Leonard
Burton (in Gateforth), L. 11	*Burtone, -tun* 315b, 379
Burtone	See Burton (in Gateforth), Burton Leonard
Burton in Lonsdale, B. 6	*Borctune* 301b
Burton Leonard, I. 6	*Burton(e)* 299b 2nd entry, 380
Burton Salmon	Not in D.B.
Burtun	See Burton (in Gateforth)
Byram	Not in D.B.
Cadeby, K. 14	*Catebi* 319b, 329b, 379
Cadretone, J. 7	Lost in Allerton Mauleverer, 330

Cadretone, -tune	See Catterton
Caldecotes	See Coldcotes
Caldeuuelle	See *Cradeuuelle*
Calton, D. 7	*Caltun* 332
Caltorn(e)	See Cawthorne
Caltun	See Calton
Calverley, H. 10	*Caverlei(a)* 318, 379b
Camblesforth, M. 11	*Camelesford(e)* 325b, 379 *Canbesford* 330b, 379 *Gamesford* 332b
Camelesford(e)	See Camblesforth
Campsall, K. 12	*Cansale* 315b *bis*, 379b
Canbesford	See Camblesforth
Cansale	See Campsall
Canteleia, -lie	See Cantley
Cantley, L. 14	*Canteleia, -lie* 326, 379 *Cathalai* 373b
Caretorp, C. 7	Lost in Wigglesworth, 332
Carlentone	See Carleton (near Skipton), Carlton (in Barnsley), Carlton (in Lofthouse)
Carlesmoor, H. 5	*Carlesmor(e)* 330, 380
Carlesmor(e)	See Carlesmoor
Carleton	See Carlton (in Barnsley)
Carleton (near Pontefract)	Not in D.B.
Carleton (near Skipton), E. 8	*Carlentone* 332
Carletone	See Carlton (near Snaith)
Carletun	See Carlton (near Otley), Carlton (near Snaith)
Carletune	See Carlton (near Otley)
Carlton (in Barnsley), I. 13	*Carlentone* 316b *Carleton* 379b

Carlton (in Lofthouse), I. 11	*Carlentone* 317b, 379b
Carlton (near Otley), H. 9	*Carletun(e)* 320b, 379
Carlton (near Snaith), M. 11	*Carletone*, *-tun* 330b, 332b, 379
Cartworth, G. 13	*Cheteruurde* 299b *Cheteuuorde* 379b
Castelai	See Castley
Castleford	Not in D.B.
Castley, H. 9	*Castelai* 301b, 380
Catale	See Cattal
Catebi	See Cadeby
Cathalai	See Cantley
Cathale	See Little Cattal
Cattal, J. 8	*Catale*, *Cattala* 329b, 380
Cattala	See Cattal
Cattala, *Alia*	See Little Cattal
Catterton, K. 9	*Cadretone*, *-tune* 329, 373b, 379b
Caverlei(a)	See Calverley
Cawood	Not in D.B.
Cawthorne, I. 13	*Caltorn(e)* 316b, 379b
Cayton, I. 7	*Chettone* 380 *Chetune* 300
Celeslau	See Chellow
Ceuet	See Chevet
Ceʒeburg	See Kexbrough
Chapel Allerton, I. 10	*Alretun* 315, 379
Chapel Haddlesey	Not in D.B.
Chelbroc	See Kelbrook
Chelchis, *Cheldis*, E. 9	Lost in Glusburn, 322, 327
Chelintune, *Chel(l)inctone*	See Kellington
Chellow, G. 10	*Celeslau* 318 *bis*, 379b
Chenaresburg	See Knaresborough
Chenaresford	See Knaresford
Chenehalle, *Chenihalle*	See Killinghall
Cherchebi	See Kirkby Overblow, South Kirkby
Cherebi	See Kearby
Chersintone	See Grassington
Chesinc, *-ing*	See East Keswick
Chesuic	See Dunkeswick
Cheteleuuelle	See Kettlewell
Cheteruurde	See Cartworth
Chetesmor	See Kex Moor
Cheteuuorde	See Cartworth
Chettone, *Chetune*	See Cayton
Cheuebroc	See Kelbrook
Chevet, I. 12	*Ceuet* 317, 379b
Chiberewor de	See Kimberworth
Chichelai	See Keighley
Chicheltone	See Hickleton
Chidal(e)	See Kiddal
Childeuuic	See Kildwick
Chileseie	See Kilnsey
Chilingale	See Killinghall
Chineslai, *-lei*	See Kinsley
Chipertun	See Gipton
Chipesch	See Kippax
Chipetun	See Gipton
Chirchebi	See Kirby Hall, Kirkby Malham, Kirkby Malzeard, Kirkby Overblow, Kirkby Wharfe, South Kirkby
Chiʒeburg	See Kexbrough
Church Fenton	See Fenton
Churwell	Not in D.B.
Cipetun	See Gipton
Ciuetone	See Kiveton
Clactone, H. 13	Lost in Oxspring, 316b
Claiton	See Clayton (near Bradford)
Claitone	See Clayton (near Bradford), Clayton (near Thurnscoe), Clayton West
Clapeham	See Clapham
Clapham, C. 6	*Clapeham* 301b
Clareton, J. 7	*Clareton(e)* 299b, 330, 380
Clareton(e)	See Clareton
Clayton (near Bradford), G. 10	*Claiton(e)* 318 *bis*, 379b
Clayton (near Thurnscoe), J. 13	*Claitone* 308, 379

Clayton West, H. 13	*Claitone* 317, 379b
Cleckheaton, H. 11	*Hetone*, *-tun* 318, 379b
Clifford, J. 9	*Cliford* 307b, 379
Cliford	See Clifford
Clifton	See Clifton (in Conisbrough)
Clifton (in Brighouse), G. 11	*Cliftone* 318, 379b
Clifton (in Conisbrough), K. 14	*Clifton(e)*, *-tune* 321 *bis*, 373b *bis*
Clifton (with Newhall), H. 8	*Cliftun* 303b, 379
Clifton (with Norwood), H. 8	*Cliftone* 300, 380
Cliftone	See Clifton (in Brighouse), Clifton (in Conisbrough), Clifton (with Norwood)
Cliftun	See Clifton (with Newhall)
Cliftune	See Clifton (in Conisbrough)
Clint	Not in D.B.
Clotherholme, I. 5	*Cludun* 322, 380
Cludun	See Clotherholme
Cnapetone	See Knapton
Coates	Not in D.B.
Coldcotes, I. 10	*Caldecotes* 315, 379
Cold Hiendley, J. 12	*Hindelei(a)* 317, 379b
Coletone	See Colton (near York)
Coletorp	See Cowthorpe
Coletun	See Colton (near Leeds)
Coletune	See Colton (near York)
Colingauuorde	See Cullingworth
Colletun	See Colton (near Leeds)
Collingham	Not in D.B.
Collinghe	See Cowling
Colton (near Leeds), I. 10	*Col(l)etun* 315 *bis*, 379 *bis*
Colton (near York), K. 9	*Coletone*, *-tune* 329, 373b, 374 *ter*, 379b
Combreuuorde	See Lower Cumberworth
Compton, J. 9	*Contone* 373b
Coneghestone	See Coniston Cold
Coneythorpe	Not in D.B.
Coningesborc, *-burg*	See Conisbrough
Coningeston	See Coniston Cold
Conisbrough, K. 14	*Coningesborc*, *-burg* 321, 373b *sexiens*, 379 *Cuningesburg* 373b *bis*
Coniston Cold, D. 8	*Coneghestone* 301b *Coningeston* 380 *Cuningestone* 322, 332
Conistone, E. 6	*Cunestune* 331b
Cononley, E. 8	*Cutnelai* 301b
Contone	See Compton
Cookridge, H. 9	*Cucheric* 307b, 379
Copegraue	See Copgrove
Copemantorp	See Copmanthorpe
Copgrove, I. 7	*Copegraue* 328b, 380
Copmanthorpe, L. 8	*Copemantorp* 328b, 379b
Copt Hewick, I. 6	*Hauui(n)c* 303b, 380
Corne(l)bi	See Quarmby
Cotesmore	See Kex Moor
Cotingelai, *-lei*	See Cottingley
Cottingley, G. 10	*Cotingelai*, *-lei* 328b *bis*, 379
Cowling, E. 9	*Collinghe* 332
Cowthorpe, J. 8	*Coletorp* 321b, 322, 379b, 380
Cowthwaite, J. 9	*Cu(d)ford* 315, 379
Cracoe	Not in D.B.
Cradeuuelle, *Caldeuuelle*, J. 8	Lost in Spofforth, 322, 380
Creuesford	See Keresforth
Cridling Stubbs	Not in D.B.
Crigest', *Crigeston(e)*	See Crigglestone
Crigglestone, I. 12	*Crigest'*, *Crigeston(e)* 299b *bis*, 379b

Drebley, F. 7	*Drebelaie* 329b
Dreslin(g)tone	See Drighlington
Drighlington, H. 11	*Dreslin(g)tone* 318, 379b
Dringhouses	Not in D.B.
Dunesford(e)	See Dunsforth
Dunintone	See Dinnington
Dunkeswick, I. 8	*Chesuic* 331b, 380
Dunnitone	See Dinnington
Dunsforth, Lower and Upper, J. 6	*Doneforde* 332b *Dunesford(e)* 328b, 331b, 379b
Earby, D. 8	*Alia Eurebi* 332 *Eurebi* 332
Earlsheaton, H. 11	*Et(t)one* 299b, 379b
Easington, B. 8	*Esintune* 332
Eastburn, F. 9	*Esebrune*, *Estbrune* 301b, 327
East Hardwick	Not in D.B.
East Keswick, I. 9	*Chesinc*, *-ing* 301, 379
East Marton	See Marton
Eastoft	Not in D.B.
East Stainley, I. 5	*Estanlai* 303b *Stanlai* 380
Eastwick, J. 6	*Estuinc* 303b *Estuuic* 380
Eavestone, H. 6	*Euestone* 303b, 380
Eburg	See Eggborough
Ecclesfield, I. 15	*Eclesfeld*, *-felt* 319, 379
Ecclesall	Not in D.B.
Eccleshill, G. 10	*Egleshil* 379b
Eccup, I. 9	*Echope* 307b, 379
Echope	See Eccup
Eclesfeld, *-felt*	See Ecclesfield
Ectone, *Estone*, H. 8	Lost in Lindley, 303b, 379
Edenthorpe	See Street Thorpe
Edeshale	See Hensall
Edi(d)ham	See Addingham
Edlington, K. 14	*Eilin-*, *Ellintone* 321b, 379
Eg(e)burg	See Eggborough
Egescop	See Hexthorpe
Eggborough, L. 11	*Acheburg* 316b *Eburg* 316b *Eg(e)burg* 379b *bis*

Egleshil	See Eccleshill
Eilintone	See Edlington
Einuluestorp	See Armthorpe
Eistop	See Walden Stubbs
Elant	See Elland
Eldeb'ge, J. 14	Lost in Brampton Bierlow, 379 *bis*
Eldwick, G. 9	*Helguic* 328b *Heluuic* 379
Eleslac	See Elslack
Elesuuorde	See Elsworth
Eleuuic	See Elwicks
Elgebi	See Hellaby
Elland, G. 11	*Elant*, *Elont* 318, 379b
Ellenthorpe, C. 8	*Eluuinetorp* 332 *Haluuidetorp* 322
Ellintone	See Edlington
Elont	See Elland
Elslack, E. 8	*Eleslac* 332
Elsworth, H. 8	*Elesuuorde* 380
Eluuinetorp	See Ellenthorpe
Elwicks, J. 7	*Eleuuic* 380
Embesie	See Embsay
Embsay, F. 8	*Embesie* 301b, 380
Emley, H. 12	*Amelai*, *-leie* 299b, 379b
Erdeslau(ue)	See Ardesley East and West
Erleshold, *-holt*	See Herleshow
Ermelai	See Armley
Ermenia, *-nie*	See Little Airmyn
Ermeshala	See North Elmsall
Ermeshale	See North Elmsall, South Elmsall
Erneforde	See Arnford
Ernulfestorp	See Armthorpe
Erringden	Not in D.B.
Escafeld	See Sheffield
Esdesai	See Hessay
Esebrune	See Eastburn
Eseleuuode	See Hazelwood
Esholt	Not in D.B.
Eshton, E. 7	*Estune* 332
Esintune	See Easington
Esneid, *Esnoid*, *Esnoit*	See Snaith
Estanlai	See East Stainley
Estbrune	See Eastburn

Estollaia	See Studley Roger
Estone	See Aston, *Ectone*
Estorp	See Hexthorpe
Estuinc	See Eastwick
Estune	See Eshton
Estuuic	See Eastwick
Et(t)one	See Earlsheaton
Etun	See Hanging Heaton
Euestone	See Eavestone
Eurebi, *Alia Eurebi*	See Earby
Fairburn, K. 11	*Fareburne* 315b, 379
Fareburne	See Fairburn
Farneham	See Farnham
Farnham, I. 7	*Farneham* 300, 330, 380
Farnhill, F. 9	*Fernehil* 301b
Farnley (in Leeds), H. 10	*Fernelei* 379b
Farnley (near Otley), H. 8	*Fernelai*, *-lie* 303b, 379
Farnley Tyas, G. 12	*Fereleia* 317b *Ferlei* 379b
Farsley, H. 10	*Fersellei(a)* 318, 379b
Featherstone, J. 11	*Ferestane* 316 *Fredestan* 379b
Fechesbi	See Fixby
Felgesclif	See Fellisclife
Felliscliffe, H. 7	*Felgesclif* 300, 380
Fenton, Church and Little, K. 10	*Fentun* 315b, 379
Fentun	See Fenton
Fenwick	Not in D.B.
Fereia	See Ferrybridge
Fereleia	See Farnley Tyas
Feresbi	See Ferrensby
Ferestane	See Featherstone
Ferie	See Ferrybridge
Ferlei	See Farnley Tyas
Fernehil	See Farnhill
Fernelai	See Farnley (near Otley)
Fernelei	See Farnley (in Leeds)
Fernelie	See Farnley (near Otley)
Ferrensby, I. 7	*Feresbi* 300 *bis*, 380
Ferrybridge, K. 11	*Fereia*, *Ferie* 316, 379b
Ferry Fryston	See Fryston
Fersellei(a)	See Farsley
Fewston, H. 8	*Fostun(e)* 300, 380
Firbeck	Not in D.B.
Fiscelac	See Fishlake
Fishlake, M. 12	*Fiscelac* 373b *Fixcale* 321b
Fixby, G. 12	*Fechesbi* 379b
Fixcale	See Fishlake
Flasby, E. 7	*Flatebi* 332
Flatebi	See Flasby
Flatesbi	See Flaxby
Flaxby, J. 7	*Flatesbi* 328b, 380
Flocheton(e)	See Flockton
Flockton, H. 12	*Flocheton(e)* 317b, 379b
Fockerby	Not in D.B.
Follifoot	Not in D.B.
Fostun(e)	See Fewston
Fredestan	See Featherstone
Freschefelt	See Threshfield
Fricelei(a), *Frichehale*, *Frichelie*	See Frickley
Frickley, K. 13	*Fricelei(a)* 319b, 379 *Frichehale* 315b *Frichelie* 379b
Fristone	See Fryston
Fryston, Ferry and Water, K. 11	*Fristone* 316, 379b
Fugelestun	See Fulstone
Fulstone, G. 13	*Fugelestun* 379b
Gamesford	See Camblesforth
Garforth, J. 10	*Gereford(e)* 315 *bis*, 379 *bis*
Gargrave, E. 8	*G(h)eregraue* 301b, 332 *bis*, 380
Garsdale	Not in D.B.
Gateforth	Not in D.B.
Gemunstorp	See Ingmanthorpe
Gereford(e)	See Garforth
Geregraue	See Gargrave
Germundstorp	See Ingmanthorpe
Gersebroc	See Greasbrough

Geureshale	See Loversall
Ghelintune	See Kellington
Gheregraue	See Gargrave
Gherindale	See Givendale
Ghersintone	See Grassington
Ghigelesuuic	See Giggleswick
Ghiseburne	See Gisburn
Giggleswick, C. 6	*Ghigelesuuic* 332
Gildersome	Not in D.B.
Gildingwells	Not in D.B.
Gipton, I. 10	*Chipertun* 315 *C(h)ipetun* 315, 379 *bis*
Gisburn, D. 8	*Ghiseburne* 322, 332
Gisele	See Guiseley
Givendale, I. 6	*Gherindale* 303b, 380
Glass Houghton, J. 11	*Hoctun* 316, 379b
Glusburn, E. 9	*Glusebrun* 322, 327
Glusebrun	See Glusburn
God(en)esburg	See Goldsborough
Godetorp	See Goldthorpe
Golcar, G. 12	*Gudlagesarc, -sargo* 317b, 379b
Goldetorp	See Goldthorpe
Goldsborough, J. 7	*God(en)esburg* 325b, 380
Goldthorpe, K. 13	*Go(l)detorp* 319b, 379 *Guldetorp* 301, 379
Gomersal, H. 11	*Gome(r)shale* 318, 379b
Gome(r)shale	See Gomersal
Goole	Not in D.B.
Gowdall	Not in D.B.
Grafton, J. 7	*Graftona, -tone, -tune* 301b, 303b, 328b, 331b, 332b, 379b
Graftona, -tone, -tune	See Grafton
Grantley, H. 6	*Grentelai(a)* 303b, 380
Grassington, E. 6	*Chersintone* 301b *Ghersintone* 327
Greasbrough, J. 14	*Gersebroc* 319 *Gres(s)eburg* 321 *bis*, 379
Great Braham, I. 8	*Michelbram, -bran* 322, 327, 328b, 380
Great Heck	Not in D.B.
Great Houghton, J. 13	*Haltun(e)* 308, 373b, 379
Great Mitton, B. 9	*Mitune* 332
Great Ouseburn, J. 7	*Usebruna* 332b *Useburne* 301b 1st entry, 379b
Great Preston	See Preston
Great Ribston	See Ribston
Great Timble, G. 8	*Timble* 300, 380
Green Hammerton, J. 7	*Alia Ambretone* 380 *Altera Hanbretone* 329b
Greland	See Greetland
Greetland, F. 11	*Greland* 379b
Grentelai(a)	See Grantley
Gres(s)eburg	See Greasbrough
Gretlintone	See Grindleton
Grewelthorpe, H. 5	*Torp* 330 2nd entry, 332b 2nd entry, 380 *bis*
Grimeshou, J. 14	Lost in Rawmarsh, 319, 379
Grimeston, -tun	See Grimston
Grimston, K. 9	*Grimeston, -tun* 315b, 379 *bis*
Grindleton, C. 9	*Gretlintone* 332 *bis*
Gudlagesarc, -sargo	See Golcar
Guiseley, H. 9	*Gisele* 303b, 379
Guldetorp	See Goldthorpe
Gunthwaite	Not in D.B.
Hac(s)tone	See Aughton
Hadeuuic	See Adwick le Street, Adwick upon Dearne, Bridge Hewick
Hælgefeld	See Hellifield
Hage(n)debi, Haghedenebi, K. 9	Lost in Tadcaster East, 321b, 374 *bis*, 379b
Hageneuuorde	See Hainworth
Haghedenebi	See *Hage(n)debi*
Hailaga	See Healaugh

Modern name	Domesday form
Hainworth, F. 9	*Hageneuuorde* 328b
Haldenby	Not in D.B.
Haldeuurde	See Holdworth
Halifax	Not in D.B.
Hallam, I. 15	*Hallun* 320 *bis*, 379b
Halletun(e)	See Halton
Hallun	See Hallam
Halton, I. 10	*Halletun(e)* 315, 379
Haltone	See Halton East, Little Houghton
Halton East, F. 8	*Altone* 301b *Haltone* 380
Halton Gill	Not in D.B.
Halton West	Not in D.B.
Haltun(e)	See Great Houghton
Haluuidetorp	See Ellenthorpe
Hambleton, K. 10	*Hameltun* 315b, 379
Hamelesuurde	See Hemsworth
Hameltun	See Hambleton
Hamereton	See Hammerton
Hammerton, B. 8	*Hamereton* 332
Hamphall Stubbs, K. 13	*Hanepol* 316, 379b
Hampole, K. 13	*Honepol* 319b, 379
Hampsthwaite	Not in D.B.
Hanbretone	See Kirk Hammerton
Hanbretone, Altera	See Green Hammerton
Handesuuord, -uurde	See Handsworth
Handsworth, J. 15	*Handesuuord, -uurde* 308, 379
Hanelei(a)	See Honley
Hanepol	See Hamphall Stubbs
Hangelif	See Hanlith
Hanging Heaton, H. 11	*Etun* 379b
Hanlith, D. 7	*Hangelif* 301b, 380
Hardinctone	See Arthington
Harduic	See West Hardwick
Hareuuode	See Harewood
Harewood, I. 9	*Hareuuode* 301, 379
Harrogate	Not in D.B.
Harthill, K. 16	*Hertil* 321 *bis*
Hartlington, F. 7	*Herlintone, -tun* 331b *bis*
Hartshead, G. 11	*Hortes(h)eue* 318, 379b
Hartwith	Not in D.B.
Hasele	See Hessle
Haserlai	See Azerley
Hashundebi, I. 6	Lost in Sharow, 303b, 380
Hatelton, -tun	See Hathelton
Hatfield, M. 13	*Hedfeld* 321 *bis*
Hathelton, G. 9	*Hatelton, -tun* 328b, 379
Hauocesorde	See Hawksworth
Hauochesord, Alia	See Hawksworth Mill
Hauui(n)c	See Copt Hewick
Havercroft	Not in D.B.
Hawkswick, E. 6	*Hochesuuic* 332
Hawksworth, G. 9	*Hauocesorde* 379 *Henochesuurde* 303b
Hawksworth Mill, G. 9	*Alia Hauochesord* 379 *Alia Henochesuurde* 303b
Haworth	Not in D.B.
Hazelwood, J. 9	*Eseleuuode* 321b *Heseleuuode* 373b *bis*, 379
Headingley, I. 10	*Hedingelei(a)* 315, 379
Healaugh, K. 8	*Hailaga* 321b *bis*, 326, 374 *ter*, 379b *bis* *Helage* 374
Heathfield, G. 6	*Higrefeld, -felt* 314b, 380
Hebden, F. 7	*Hebedene* 329b
Hebden Bridge	Not in D.B.
Hebedene	See Hebden
Heckmondwike	Not in D.B.
Hedfeld	See Hatfield
Hedingelei(a)	See Headingley
Helage	See Healaugh
Heldetone, F. 9	Lost in Bingley, 328b

Heldetune, C. 6	Lost in Austwick, 301b
Helgebi	See Hellaby
Helgefeld, *-felt*	See Hellifield
Helguic	See Eldwick
Hellaby, K. 15	*Elgebi* 379 *bis* *Helgebi* 319 *bis*
Hellifield, D. 7	*Hælgefeld* 380 *Helgefeld*, *-felt* 301b, 322, 332 *bis*
Heluuic	See Eldwick
Hemsworth, J. 12	*Hamelesuurde* 316b *Hilmeuuord* 379b
Henochesuurde	See Hawksworth
Henochesuurde, *Alia*	See Hawksworth Mill
Hensall, L. 11	*Edeshale* 299b, 331b, 379b
Heppeuuord	See Hepworth
Heptone	See Kirkheaton
Heptonstall, E. 11	*Crumbetonestun* 299b
Hepworth, G. 13	*Heppeuuord* 379b
Herleshow, H. 6	*Erleshold*, *-holt* 303b *bis*, 380
Herlintone, *-tun*	See Hartlington
Hertil	See Harthill
Hesdesai	See Hessay
Heseleuuode	See Hazelwood
Hessay, K. 8	*Esdesai* 327, 379b *Hesdesai* 329
Hessle, J. 12	*Asele* 379b *Hasele* 316
Hestorp	See Hexthorpe
Hetone	See Cleckheaton
Hetton, E. 7	*Hetune* 332
Hetun	See Cleckheaton
Hetune	See Hetton
Heuu(o)rde, E. 6	Lost in Conistone, 330, 331b
Hexthorpe, L. 14	*Egescop* 319b *Estorp* 307b, 373b *bis*, 379 *Hestorp* 373b
Hickleton, K. 13	*Chicheltone* 329b *Icheltone* 379
High Bradley	See Bradley, High and Low
High Hoyland, H. 13	*Holand* 379b *Holant* 316b 2nd entry
High Melton, K. 14	*Medeltone* 379 *Middeltun* 319b 2nd entry
Higrefeld, *-felt*	See Heathfield
Hillam	Not in D.B.
Hilmeuuord	See Hemsworth
Hilton, I. 7	*Hilton(e)* 299b, 380
Hilton(e)	See Hilton
Hindelei	See Cold Hiendley
Hindeleia	See Cold Hiendley, South Hiendley
Hipperholme, G. 11	*Huperun* 379b
Hirst Courtney	Not in D.B.
Hochesuuic	See Hawkswick
Hoctun	See Glass Houghton
Hoiland	See Hoyland Nether
Holan	See Hoyland Swaine
Holand	See High Hoyland, Hoyland Nether
Holande	See Hoyland Swaine
Holant	See High Hoyland, Hoyland Swaine
Holbeck	Not in D.B.
Holdworth, I. 15	*Aldeuuorde* 379 *Haldeuurde* 319b
Holedene, F. 7	Lost in Hartlington, 331b
Holme	See Holme (near Gargrave), Long Holme
Holme (near Gargrave), E. 8	*Holme* 301b, 380
Holme (near Holmfirth), G. 13	*In duabus Holne* 379b *Holne* 299b, 301
Holne	See Holme (near Holmfirth)
Holne, *Altera*	See Yateholme
Holne, *In duabus*	See Holme (near Holmfirth), Yateholme

Holsingoure	See Hunsingore
Hom(p)tone	See Hopperton
Honepol	See Hampole
Honley, G. 12	*Hanelei(a)* 317b, 379b
Hook	Not in D.B.
Hooton Levitt, K. 15	*Hotone* 307b 1st entry, 379
Hooton Pagnell, K. 13	*Hotone* 307b 2nd entry *Hotun* 379
Hooton Roberts, K. 14	*Hotun* 319, 379
Hopperton, J. 7	*Hom(p)tone* 301b, 328b, 329b, 380 *Hopretone* 332b
Hopretone	See Hopperton
Hoptone, *-tun*	See Upper Hopton
Horberie	See Horbury
Horbury, I. 12	*Horberie* 379b *Orberie* 299b *ter*
Horninctune	See Hornington
Hornington, K. 9	*Horninctune* 374 *Horni(n)tone* 321b, 329, 374, 379b
Horni(n)tone	See Hornington
Horseford(e)	See Horsforth
Horsforth, H. 9	*Horseford(e)* 301, 379 *Hoseforde* 332b
Hortes(h)eue	See Hartshead
Horton (near Bracewell), D. 8	*Hortone*, *-tun* 322, 332
Horton in Ribblesdale, C. 6	*Hortune* 332
Hortone, *-tun*	See Horton (near Bracewell)
Hortune	See Horton in Ribblesdale
Hoseforde	See Horsforth
Hotone	See Hooton Levitt, Hooton Pagnell, Slade Hooton
Hotun	See Hooton Pagnell, Hooton Roberts
Hoyland Nether, J. 14	*Ho(i)land* 319b, 321 *bis*, 379 *bis*

Hoyland Swaine, H. 13	*Holan(de)* 317, 379b *Holant* 316b 1st entry
Hubberholme, E. 5	*Huburgheham* 332
Huburgheham	See Hubberholme
Huddersfield, G. 12	*Oderesfelt* 317b *Odresfeld* 379b
Huddleston	Not in D.B.
Hulsingoure	See Hunsingore
Hunchilhuse(s), K. 10	Lost in Sherburn, 315b, 379
Hunescelf	See Hunshelf
Hunshelf, H. 14	*Hunescelf* 317, 379b
Hunsingore, J. 8	*Hol-*, *Hulsingoure* 328b *bis*, 380 *Ulsigouere* 308b
Hunslet, I. 10	*Hunslet* 318, 379b
Hunsworth	Not in D.B.
Huntwick	Not in D.B.
Huperun	See Hipperholme
Hutton Wandesley, K. 8	*Wandeslage* 329, 379b
Iadon, *Iadun*	See Yeadon
Icheltone	See Hickleton
Idle	Not in D.B.
Ilecliue	See Ilkley
Ilkley, G. 8	*Il(l)ecliue* 303b, 379 *Illiclei(a)* 321b, 379
Illecliue, *Illiclei(a)*	See Ilkley
Indelie	See South Hiendley
Ingbirchworth, H. 13	*Berceuuorde* 317, 379b
Ingerthorpe	Not in D.B.
Inglestune	See Ingleton
Ingleton, B. 5	*Inglestune* 301b
Ingmanthorpe, J. 8	*Gemunstorp* 308b, 328b *Germundstorp* 380
Ingthorpe, D. 8	*Ucnetorp* 332
Istop	See Walden Stubbs
Kearby, I. 8	*Cherebi* 322, 380
Keighley, F. 9	*Chichelai* 301b
Kelbrook, D. 9	*Chelbroc* 322 *Cheuebroc* 332

Kellington, K. 11	*Chel(l)inctone* 316, 316b
	Chelintune 379b
	Ghelintune 379b
Kenaresforde	See Knaresford
Keresforth, I. 13	*Creuesford* 317, 379b
Kettlewell, E. 6	*Cheteleuuelle* 332
Kexbrough, I. 13	*Ceȝeburg* 379b
	Chiȝeburg 316b
Kex Moor, H. 5	*Chetesmor* 380
	Cotesmore 330
Kiddal, J. 9	*Chidal(e)* 315 *bis*, 379 *bis*
Kildwick, F. 9	*Childeuuic* 301b
Kilingala	See Killinghall
Killinghall, I. 7	*Chenehalle*, *Chenihalle* 300, 380
	Chilingale 380
	Kilingala 303b
Kilnsey, E. 6	*Chileseie* 332
Kimberworth, J. 15	*Chibereworde* 319b, 379
Kinsley, J. 12	*Chineslai*, *-lei* 316b, 379b
Kippax, J. 10	*Chipesch* 315, 379
Kirby Hall, J. 7	*Chirchebi* 329b, 379b
Kirk Bramwith, L. 12	*Branuuat*, *-uuet* 319b, 379
	Branuuit(h)e 321 *bis*
	Branuuode 373b
Kirkburton, H. 12	*Bertone* 299b, 379b
Kirkby Malham, D. 7	*Chirchebi* 332
Kirkby Malzeard, H. 5	*Chirchebi* 330 1st entry, 380
Kirkby Overblow, I. 8	*Cherchebi* 322, 380
	Chirchebi 322
Kirkby Wharfe, K. 9	*Chirchebi* 315b, 379 *bis*
Kirkhamgate	Not in D.B.
Kirk Hammerton, K. 7	*Ambretone* 380
	Hanbretone 329b
Kirkheaton, G. 12	*Heptone* 317b, 379b
Kirk Sandall, L. 13	*Sandale* 321 *bis*, 373b
	Sandalia, *-lie* 308, 379
Kirk Smeaton	See Smeaton
Kiveton, K. 16	*Ciuetone* 321
Knapton, L. 8	*Cnapetone* 327, 329, 379b
Knaresborough, I. 7	*Chenaresburg* 300, 301b, 322, 328b *bis*, 380
Knaresford, H. 6	*Chenaresford* 380
	Kenaresforde 303b
	Neresford(e) 330, 380
Knottingley, K. 11	*Notingelai*, *-leia* 316, 379b
Lacoc	See Lacock
Lacock, F. 9	*Lacoc* 301b
Lanclif	See Langcliffe
Langcliffe, C. 6	*Lanclif* 332
Langefelt	See Longfield
Langetouet	See Langthwaite
Langsett	Not in D.B.
Langthwaite, L. 13	*Langetouet* 308 *bis*, 379
Lastone	See Laughton en le Morthen
Laughton en le Morthen, K. 15	*Lastone* 319, 379
Lauretona, *-ton(e)*	See Laverton
Laverton, H. 5	*Lauretona* 332b
	Laureton(e) 301b, 330, 330b, 380
Lawkland	Not in D.B.
Lead, K. 10	*Led(e)* 373b, 379
	Lied 315
Leathley, H. 8	*Ledelai* 301b, 322, 326b, 332b, 380
Led(e)	See Lead
Ledelai	See Leathley
Ledes	See Leeds
Ledesham	See Ledsham
Ledestun(e)	See Ledston
Ledsham, J. 10	*Ledesham* 315b, 379
Ledston, J. 11	*Ledestun(e)* 315, 379

Leeds, I. 10	*Ledes* 315, 379
Lepton, H. 12	*Leptone* 317b, 379b
Leptone	See Lepton
Letwell	Not in D.B.
Leuetat, E. 7	Lost in Winterburn, 332
Lied	See Lead
Lillai(a)	See Lindley
Lindley, G. 12	*Lillai(a)* 317b, 379b
Lindrick	Not in D.B.
Linlei(e)	See Old Lindley
Linthwaite	Not in D.B.
Linton (near Hebden), E. 7	*Lipton* 327
Linton (near Wetherby), J. 8	*Lintone* 322, 380
Lintone	See Linton (near Wetherby)
Lipton	See Linton (near Hebden)
Litelanstan, *Litelastone*	See South Anston
Litelbra(n)	See Little Braham
Litone	See Litton
Little Airmyn, M. 11	*Ermenia*, *-nie* 325b, 379
Little Braham, J. 8	*Litelbra(n)* 328b, 380
Little Cattal now Old Thornville, J. 8	*Alia Cattala* 380 *Cathale* 328b
Little Fenton	See Fenton
Little Houghton, J. 13	*Haltone* 319b, 379
Little Newton, D. 7	*Neutone* 332 1st entry
Little Ouseburn, J. 7	*Alia Useburne* 379b *Useburne* 301b 2nd entry, 330b
Little Preston	See Preston
Little Ribston	See Ribston
Little Smeaton	See Smeaton
Littlethorpe, I. 6	*Torp* 303b, 380
Little Timble, G. 8	*Timbe* 303b, 379
Littleworth formerly Shuttleworth, L. 14	*Scitelesuuorde* 307b, 379
Litton, D. 5	*Litone* 332
Liuresec(h)	See Liversedge
Liversedge, H. 11	*Liuresec(h)* 318, 379b
Lockwood	Not in D.B.
Locthuse	See Lofthouse (near Wakefield)
Locthusun	See Lofthouse (in Harewood), Loftus
Lodresdene	See Lothersdale
Lofthouse (in Harewood), I. 9	*Locthusun* 379 *Lofthuse* 301
Lofthouse (near Wakefield), I. 11	*Locthuse* 379b *Loftose* 317b
Lofthuse	See Lofthouse (in Harewood)
Loftose	See Lofthouse (near Wakefield)
Loftus, J. 7	*Locthusun* 380 *Lotes* 328b *Lothuse* 330b
Longfield, E. 11	*Langefelt* 299b
Long Holme, C. 8	*Holme* 322
Long Marston, K. 8	*Mers(e)tone* 329 *bis*, 379b
Long Preston, D. 7	*Prestune* 332
Long Sandall, L. 13	*Sandala* 307b *Sandal(i)e* 321, 379 *Sandela* 321
Longwood	Not in D.B.
Lotes	See Loftus
Lothersdale, E. 9	*Lodresdene* 332
Lotherton	Not in D.B.
Lothuse	See Loftus
Loureshale	See Loversall
Loversall, L. 14	*Geureshale* 307b *Loureshale* 373b *bis* *Luureshale* 379
Low Bradley	See Bradley, High and Low
Lower Cumberworth, H. 13	*Combre-*, *Cumbreuuorde* 317, 379b
Luddenden Foot	Not in D.B.
Lupset	Not in D.B.
Luureshale	See Loversall

Mainestune	See Manston
Malchetone	See Malkton
Malgon, -gun	See Malham
Malham, D. 7	*Malgon, -gun* 301b, 322, 380
Malkton, K. 9	*Malchetone* 321b, 379b
Maltby, K. 15	*Maltebi* 319 *bis*, 379
Maltebi	See Maltby
Manestorp	See Minsthorpe
Manestun	See Manston
Manston, J. 10	*Mainestune* 315 *Manestun* 379
Mardelei	See Marley
Markingfield, I. 6	*Merchefeld* 322, 380
Markington, I. 6	*Merchinton(e)* 303b *bis*, 380 *bis*
Marle	See Marr
Marley, F. 9	*Mardelei* 328b, 379 *Merdelai* 328b
Marr, K. 13	*Marle* 320 *Marra* 307b, 308, 319b, 379
Marra	See Marr
Marsden	Not in D.B.
Marton (near Boroughbridge), J. 7	*Martone* 330, 379b
Marton, East and West, D. 8	*Martun* 332
Martone	See Marton (near Boroughbridge)
Martun	See Marton, East and West
Mechesburg	See Mexborough
Medelai	See Methley
Medeltone	See High Melton, West Melton
Meltham, G. 13	*Meltham* 317b, 379b
Menston, G. 9	*Mersintone* 303b, 379
Menwith	Not in D.B.
Merchefeld	See Markingfield
Merchinton(e)	See Markington
Merdelai	See Marley
Merelton(e)	See West Melton
Mersetone	See Long Marston
Mersintone	See Menston
Merstone	See Long Marston
Methley, J. 11	*Medelai* 317, 379b
Mexborough, K. 14	*Mechesburg* 319, 379
Michelbram, -bran	See Great Braham
Micklefield	Not in D.B.
Micklethwaite (in Bingley), G. 9	*Muceltu(o)it* 328b, 379
Micklethwaite (near Tadcaster)	Not in D.B.
Micleie	See Midgeley
Middeltun	See High Melton, West Melton
Middeltune	See Middleton (near Ilkley)
Middlethorpe, L. 8	*Torp* 321, 327 1st entry, 379
Middleton (near Ilkley), G. 8	*Middeltune*, *Mideltun* 303b, 379
Middleton (in Leeds), I. 11	*Milde(n)tone* 317b, 379b
Middop, D. 9	*Mithope* 322
Mideltone	See West Melton
Mideltun	See Middleton (near Ilkley)
Midgeley, F. 11	*Micleie* 299b
Milde(n)tone	See Middleton (in Leeds)
Mileburg	See Bilbrough
Mileford(e)	See North Milford
Minescip	See Minskip
Minskip, J. 6	*Minescip* 301b, 380
Minsthorpe, K. 12	*Manestorp* 316b, 379b
Mirefeld, -felt	See Mirfield
Mirfield, H. 12	*Mirefeld, -felt* 318, 379b
Mithope	See Middop
Mitune	See Great Mitton
Monechet	See Monkton
Monechetone	See Moor Monkton, Nun Monkton
Monechetune	See Moor Monkton
Monk Bretton, I. 13	*Bret(t)one* 317, 379b

Monk Fryston	Not in D.B.
Monkton, J. 9	*Monechet* 307b *Monuchetone* 379
Monucheton	See Bishop Monkton
Monuchetone	See Bishop Monkton, Monkton, Nun Monkton
Moor Monkton, K. 7	*Monechetone*, *-tune* 327, 379b
Moorthorpe, K. 13	*Torp* 315b 2nd entry, 379b
Morelege, *-lei(a)*	See Morley
Morley, H. 11	*Morelege*, *-lei(a)* 317b, 373b, 379b
Morton (near Keighley), F. 9	*Mortun(e)* 301 1st entry, 379
Mortun(e)	See Morton (near Keighley)
Mortune, I. 9	Lost in East Keswick, 301 2nd entry
Moss	Not in D.B.
Muceltu(o)it	See Micklethwaite
Mulehale, *Mul(h)ede*, L. 8	Lost in Bishopthorpe, 330b, 374, 379b
Mytholmroyd	Not in D.B.
Nacefeld	See Nesfield
Napars	See Nappa
Nappa, D. 8	*Napars* 322
Neresford(e)	See Knaresford
Nesfield, F. 8	*Nacefeld* 322, 380
Nether Poppleton, L. 7	*Alia Popletone* 379b *Altera Popletone* 329 *In duabus Popletunis* 374
Nether Soothill	Not in D.B.
Netherthong	Not in D.B.
Neuhalle	See Newhall (in Thurcroft), Newhill
Neuhuse	See Newsham, Newsholme (near Gisburn), Newsholme (in Keighley)
Neuhuse, *Niuuehusum*, K. 9	Lost in Ulleskelf, 315b, 373b, 379
Neuhusum	See Temple Newsam
Neusone	See Newsome
Neuton	See Newton Kyme
Neutone	See Bank Newton, Little Newton, Newton Kyme, Newton on Hodder
Neutune	See Bank Newton
Neuuehalla	See Newhall (in Thurcroft)
Neuueton	See Newton Kyme
Neuuose	See Newsham
Newby	Not in D.B.
Newhall, K. 15	*Neuhalle* 379 *Neuuehalla* 319
Newhill, J. 14	*Neuhalle* 379 *Niwehalla* 319
Newland (near Drax)	Not in D.B.
Newland (near Wakefield)	Not in D.B.
Newsham, L. 12	*Neuhuse* 379b *Neuuose* 315b
Newsholme (near Gisburn), D. 8	*Neuhuse* 322, 332
Newsholme (in Keighley), F. 9	*Neuhuse* 301b
Newsome, J. 8	*Neusone* 328b, 380
Newton (in Ledsham), J. 11	*Niuueton*, *-tun* 315b, 379
Newton Kyme, K. 9	*Neuton(e)* 329b, 373b, 379 *Neuueton* 329b *Niuueton* 307b, 379 *bis*
Newton on Hodder, B. 8	*Neutone* 332 3rd entry
Nidd, I. 7	*Nit(h)* 303b, 380
Nit(h)	See Nidd
Niuuehal(l)e, I. 9	Lost in Harewood, 301, 379 *bis*
Niuuehusum	See *Neuhuse* (lost in Ulleskelf)

Niuueton	See Newton (in Ledsham), Newton Kyme
Niuuetun	See Newton (in Ledsham)
Niwehalla	See Newhill
Nonnewic	See Nunwick
Nordstanlai(a)	See North Stanley
Norland	Not in D.B.
Normanton, J. 11	*Normatone*, *-tune* 299b, 379b *Normetune* 301
Normatone, *-tune*, *Normetune*	See Normanton
Nortgrave	See Orgreave
North Anston, K. 16	*Anestan* 319, 321 *bis*, 379
North Crosland, G. 12	*Crosland* 299b, 379b
North Elmsall, K. 12	*Ermeshala*, *-hale* 316b, 379b
North Milford, K. 9	*Mileford(e)* 315b, 373b, 379
North Owram	See Owram
North Stainley, I. 5	*Nordstanlai(a)* 303b, 380 *Staneleia* 308b *Stanlei* 380
Norton (near Doncaster), K. 12	*Nortone* 315b, 379b
Norton (near Sheffield), I. 16	*Nortun(e)* 272, 278, Derby.
Norton	See Notton
Nortone	See Norton (near Doncaster)
Norwood	Not in D.B.
Norwood Green	Not in D.B.
Nostell, J. 12	*Os(e)le* 316, 379b
Notingelai, *-leia*	See Knottingley
Notone	See Notton
Notton, I. 12	*Norton* 379b *Notone* 317
Nun Monkton, K. 7	*Monechetone* 329, 374 *Monuchetone* 379b
Nunwick, I. 5	*Nonnewic* 303b, 380
Oakworth, F. 9	*Acurde* 301b, 327

Ocelestorp	See Oglethorpe
Oderesfelt	See Huddersfield
Odingeham, *-hen*	See Addingham
Odresfelt	See Huddersfield
Oglestorp	See Oglethorpe
Oglestun	See Toulston
Oglethorpe, J. 9	*Ocelestorp* 307b *Oglestorp* 329b, 373b, 379 *bis*
Old Lindley, F. 12	*Linlei(e)* 301, 379b
Oleschel, *Oleslec*	See Ulleskelf
Ollei(e)	See Ulley
Onesacre, I. 15	*Anesacre* 301
Orberie	See Horbury
Orgreave, J. 15	*Nortgrave* 319
Osele	See Nostell
Ositone	See Oxton
Osle	See Nostell
Osleset	See Ossett
Osmondthorpe	Not in D.B.
Osprinc, *-pring*	See Oxspring
Ossetone	See Oxton
Ossetorp	See Austhorpe
Ossett, I. 12	*Osleset* 299b *ter*, 379b
Ot(h)elai	See Otley
Otley, H. 9	*Ot(h)elai* 303b, 379 *bis*
Otreburne	See Otterburn
Otterburn, D. 7	*Otreburne* 301b, 332, 380
Oulton	Not in D.B.
Oure	See Owram
Ousefleet	Not in D.B.
Ousteuuic	See Austwick
Ouston, K. 9	*Ulsitone* 321b, 379b *Wlsintone* 374
Oustrefeld	See Austerfield
Outwood	Not in D.B.
Ovenden	Not in D.B.
Overe	See Owram
Owram, North and South, G. 11	*Oure* 379b *Overe* 318 *Ufrun* 379b
Owston, K. 13	*Austhu'* 379b *Austun* 315b
Oxenhope	Not in D.B.
Oxetone	See Oxton

Oxspring, H. 14	*Osprinc*, *-pring* 317, 379b
Oxton, K. 9	*Ositone*, *Ossetone* 329, 379b *Oxetone* 374
Padehale, *Paghenale*	See Painley
Painley, D. 8	*Padehale* 332 *Paghenale* 322
Pallathorpe, K. 9	*Torp* 308b, 321b, 329 1st entry, 374 *bis*, 379b
Pangeston	See Penistone
Pannal	Not in D.B.
Parlington, J. 10	*Perlinctune* 315 *Perlintun* 379 *Pertilin(c)tun* 315, 379
Pathorme, *Pathorp*	See Paythorne
Paythorne, D. 8	*Pathorme* 332 *Pathorp* 322
Pengeston(e)	See Penistone
Penistone, H. 13	*Pangeston* 316b *Pengeston(e)* 301, 379b
Perlinctune, *Perlintun*, *Pertilin(c)tun*	See Parlington
Picheburne	See Pickburn
Pickburn, K. 13	*Picheburne* 308, 379
Pillei	See Pilley
Pilley, I. 14	*Pillei* 308, 379b
Plompton, I. 8	*Plontone* 322, 327, 380
Plontone	See Plompton
Podechesai(e)	See Pudsey
Pollington	Not in D.B.
Pontefract	Not in D.B.
Pool, H. 9	*Pouele* 303b, 379
Popletone, G. 6	Lost in Fountains Earth, 301b, 330, 380
Popletone, *-tune*	See Upper Poppleton
Popletone, *Alia*, *Altera*	See Nether Poppleton
Popletunis, *In duabus*	See Nether Poppleton, Upper Poppleton
Potertun	See Potterton
Potter Newton	Not in D.B.
Potterton, J. 9	*Potertun* 315, 379
Pouele	See Pool
Preston, Great and Little, J. 10	*Prestun(e)* 315, 379
Preston(e)	See Purston Jaglin
Prestun	See Preston
Prestune	See Long Preston; Preston
Pudsey, H. 10	*Podechesai(e)* 317b, 379b
Purston Jaglin, J. 12	*Preston(e)* 316, 379b
Quarmby, G. 12	*Corne(l)bi* 317b, 379b
Queldale	See Wheldale
Quick, E. 13	*Thoac* 299b *Tohac* 379b
Radholme Laund, B. 9	*Radun* 332
Radun	See Radholme Laund
Raghil	See Raygill
Rastric	See Rastrick
Rastrick, G. 11	*Rastric* 301, 379b
Rathmell, C. 7	*Rodemare*, *Rodemele* 332 *bis*
Rauenesfeld	See Ravenfield
Ravenfield, K. 14	*Rauenesfeld* 321 *bis*
Rawcliffe	Not in D.B.
Rawdon, H. 9	*Rodum* 332b *Roudun* 301, 379
Rawmarsh, J. 14	*Rodemesc* 326b, 379
Raygill, C. 8	*Raghil* 322
Redelesden(e)	See Riddlesden
Reedness	Not in D.B.
Renitone	See Rimington
Ribston, Great and Little, J. 8	*Ripesta(i)n*, *-sten* 301b, 322, 325b, 328b, 380
Riddlesden, F. 9	*Redelesden(e)* 301, 379
Ridre, *Rie*	See Ryther

Rigton (near Bardsey), J. 9	*Riston* 373b *Ritone*, *Ritun* 330b, 379
Rigton (near Harrogate), I. 8	*Riston(e)* 326b, 331b, 380
Rihella, *Rihelle*	See Ryhill
Rilestun, *Rilistune*	See Rylstone
Rimington, C. 9	*Renitone* 322
Ripeleia, *-leie*, *-lie*	See Ripley
Ripesta(i)n, *-sten*	See Ribston
Ripley, I. 7	*Ripeleia*, *-leie*, *-lie* 326, 331b, 380
Ripon, I. 6	*Ripum*, *Ripun* 303b *quater*, 380
Ripum, *Ripun*	See Ripon
Rishworth	Not in D.B.
Riston, I. 10	*Riston(e)* 317b, 379b
Riston	See Rigton (near Bardsey), Rigton (near Harrogate), Riston
Ristone	See Rigton (near Harrogate), Riston
Ritone, *Ritun*	See Rigton (near Bardsey)
Roall, L. 11	*Ruhale* 316b, 379b
Rodemare, *Rodemele*	See Rathmell
Rodemesc	See Rawmarsh
Rodeuuelle, *Rodouuelle*	See Rothwell
Rodreham	See Rotherham
Rodum	See Rawdon
Rodun	See Rowden
Roecliffe	Not in D.B.
Rofellinton(e), *Rofellnton*	See Rudfarlington
Rogartorp	See Rogerthorpe
Rogerthorpe, K. 12	*Rogar-*, *Rugartorp* 316, 379b
Rorestone, *-tun*	See Royston
Rosert(e)	See Rossett
Rossett, I. 8	*Rosert(e)* 301b, 326b, 380
Rossington	Not in D.B.
Rotherham, J. 15	*Rodreham* 307b, 379
Rothwell, I. 11	*Rodeuuelle*, *Rodouuelle* 317b, 329, 379b
Roudun	See Rawdon
Roughbirchworth, H. 14	*Berceuuorde*, *Bercewrde* 317b, 379b
Roundhay	Not in D.B.
Rowden, H. 7	*Rodun* 301b, 380
Royston, I. 13	*Rorestone*, *-tun* 316b, 379b
Rudfarlington, I. 8	*Rofellinton(e)* 322, 380 *Rofellnton* 327
Rufforth, K. 8	*Ruford(e)*, *-fort* 327, 374, 379b
Ruford(e), *-fort*	See Rufforth
Rugartorp	See Rogerthorpe
Ruhale	See Roall
Ryhill, J. 12	*Rihella*, *Rihelle* 317, 379b
Rylstone, E. 7	*Rilestun*, *Rilistune* 331b *bis*
Ryther, L. 9	*Ridre* 373b *Rie* 315b, 379
Sacrof(f)t	See Seacroft
Sactun	See Santon
Saddleworth	Not in D.B.
Salebi	See Selby
Sallai(a)	See Sawley
Salterforth	Not in D.B.
Sandala	See Long Sandall, Sandal Magna
Sandale	See Kirk Sandall, Long Sandall, Sandal Magna
Sandalia	See Kirk Sandall
Sandalie	See Kirk Sandall, Long Sandall
Sandal Magna, I. 12	*Sandala*, *-dale* 299b, 379b
Sandela	See Long Sandall
Santon, I. 12	*Sactun* 379b *Santone* 299b
Santone	See Santon
Sawley, H. 6	*Sallai(a)* 303b, 380
Sax(e)hala, *Saxhalla*, K. 9	Lost in Lead, 321b, 373b, 379

Saxton, K. 10	*Saxtun* 315, 379
Saxtun	See Saxton
Scachertorp	See Scagglethorpe
Scadeuuelle	See Shadwell
Scafeld	See Sheffield
Scagglethorpe, K. 7	*Scachertorp* 374, 379b *Scarchetorp* 329
Scalchebi	See Scawsby
Scalebre, *-bro*	See Skelbrooke
Scammonden	Not in D.B.
Scanhalla, *-halle*	See Skellow
Scarchetorp	See Scagglethorpe
Scarcroft	Not in D.B.
Scawsby, K. 13	*Scalchebi* 320, 379b
Scelf	See Shelf
Scellintone	See Sitlington
Scelmertorp	See Skelmanthorpe
Scelneleie	See Shelley
Sceltun(e)	See Skelton (in Leeds)
Scemeltorp	See Skelmanthorpe
Sceptone, *-tun*	See Shafton
Sceuelt	See Waldershelfe
Scheldone	See Skelton (near Boroughbridge)
Schelintone	See Sitlington
Scheltone	See Skelton (near Boroughbridge)
Schibeden	See Skibeden
Scholes	Not in D.B.
Scinestorp, L. 13	Lost in Sprotbrough, 308, 379
Scipeden	See Skibeden
Scipelei	See Shepley, Shipley
Scipeleia	See Shipley
Scipene	See Shippen
Scipton(e)	See Skipton
Scireburne	See Sherburn in Elmet
Scirestorp	See Street Thorpe
Scitelesuuorde	See Littleworth formerly Shuttleworth
Sciuelei	See Shelley
Scleneforde, *Sclenneford*	See Sleningford
Scosthrop, D. 7	*Scotorp* 301b, 332, 380
Scotona, *-tone*	See Scotton
Scotorp	See Scosthrop
Scotton, I. 7	*Scotona*, *-tone* 326b, 330b, 332b, 380 *bis*
Scotton Thorpe, I. 7	*Torp* 330b, 332b 1st entry, 380
Scrauing(h)e	See Scriven
Scriven, I. 7	*Scrauing(h)e* 300, 380
Scroftune, *Scrotone*	See Crofton
Scusceuurde	See Cusworth
Seacroft, I. 10	*Sacrof(f)t* 315, 379
Sedbergt	See Sedbergh
Sedbergh, B. 3	*Sedbergt* 301b
Selby, L. 10	*Salebi* 302b
Selesat	See Selside
Selside, C. 5	*Selesat* 332
Seppeleie	See Shepley
Setel	See Settle
Settle, C. 7	*Setel* 332
Shadwell, I. 9	*Scadeuuelle* 301, 379
Shafton, J. 13	*Sceptone*, *-tun* 308, 316b, 317, 379b
Sharlston	Not in D.B.
Sharow	Not in D.B.
Sheffield, I. 15	*Escafeld* 320 *Scafeld* 379b
Shelf, G. 11	*Scelf* 379b
Shelley, H. 13	*Scelneleie* 299b *Sciuelei* 379b
Shepley, H. 13	*Scipelei* 379b *Seppeleie* 299b
Sherburn in Elmet, K. 10	*Scireburne* 302b, 379
Shipley, G. 9	*Scipelei(a)* 318, 379b
Shippen, J. 10	*Scipene* 315, 379
Sickinghall, I. 8	*Sidingal(e)* 301b, 380
Sidingal(e)	See Sickinghall
Siglesdene	See Silsden
Silchestone, *Silcston*	See Silkstone
Silkstone, I. 13	*Silchestone* 316b *bis*, 379b *Silcston* 379b
Silsden, F. 8	*Siglesdene* 329b

Stanburne	See Stainburn
Stanbury	Not in D.B.
Stancil, L. 14	*Steineshale* 373b
Staneleia	See North Stainley
Stanesfelt	See Stansfield
Stanlai	See East Stainley, South Stainley
Stanland	See Stainland
Stanlei	See North Stainley, South Stainley, Stanley, Staveley
Stanleia	See Staveley
Stanleie	See South Stainley, Stanley
Stanley, I. 12	*Stanlei(e)* 299b, 379b
Stansfield, E. 11	*Stanesfelt* 299b
Stantone	See Stainton (near Tickhill)
Stantun	See Stutton
Stapleton, K. 12	*Stapleton(e)* 316, 379b
Stapleton(e)	See Stapleton
Starbotton, E. 5	*Stamphotne* 332
Staveley, I. 7	*Stanlei(a)* 330, 380
Steeton (near Keighley), F. 9	*Stiuetune* 327
Steeton (near York), K. 9	*Stiueton(e), -tune* 321b, 329, 373b, 374 *bis*, 379b
Steineshale	See Stancil
Ste(i)nforde	See Stainforth (near Thorne)
Stirestorp	See Street Thorpe
Stirton	Not in D.B.
Stiueton(e)	See Steeton (near York)
Stiuetune	See Steeton (near Keighley), Steeton (near York)
Stoche	See Stock
Stochetun	See Stockton
Stock, D. 8	*Stoche* 332
Stockton, I. 9	*Stochetun* 301, 379
Sto(d)fald	See Stotfold
Stollai	See Studley Roger, Studley Royal

Stollei(a)	See Studley Royal
Stotfalde	See Stotfold
Stotfold, K. 13	*Sto(d)fald* 319b, 379 *bis* *Stotfalde* 308
Stouetun	See Stutton
Stranforde	See Stainforth (near Settle)
Stratesergum, C. 8	Lost in Gisburn, 322
Street Thorpe (now Edenthorpe), L. 13	*Scires-, Stirestorp* 321 *bis*, 373b
Stretun(e)	See Sturton Grange
Stube	See Stubham
Stubham, G. 8	*Stube* 303b, 379
Stub House, I. 9	*Stubus(h)un* 301, 379
Stubus(h)un	See Stub House
Studley Roger, I. 6	*Estollaia* 303b *Stollai* 380
Studley Royal, H. 6	*Stollai* 322, 331b *Stollei(a)* 330, 380
Sturton Grange, J. 10	*Stretun(e)* 315 *bis*, 379 *bis*
Stutone	See Stutton
Stutton, K. 9	*Stantun* 373b *Stouetun* 379 *Stutone, -tun(e)* 321b, 329b, 379
Stutun(e)	See Stutton
Sualun, Suatune	See Swetton
Sudton, Sudtunen	See Sutton Grange
Suillictun, -igtune, -intun	See Swillington
Suindene	See Swinden
Suintone	See Swinton
Susacres, I. 7	*Sosacra, -acre* 300, 329b, 380 *Sotesac* 332b
Suthauuic, Sutheuuic, I. 6	Lost in Bridge Hewick, 303b, 380
Sutone	See Sutton (in Norton)
Sutton (near Keighley), F. 9	*Sutun* 301b
Sutton (in Norton), K. 12	*Sutone* 315b, 379b

Sutton Grange, I. 5	*Sudton*, *Sudtunen* 303b, 380
Sutun	See Sutton (near Keighley)
Swetton, H. 5	*Sualun* 380 *Suatune* 330
Swillington, J. 10	*Suillictun*, *-igtune*, *-intun* 315 *bis*, 379 *bis*
Swinden, D. 8	*Suindene* 322
Swinefleet	Not in D.B.
Swinton, J. 14	*Sinitun* 326b, 379 *Suintone* 319b, 379
Sykehouse	Not in D.B.
Tadcaster, K. 9	*Tatecastre* 321b, 373b *bis*, 379
Tancreslei(a)	See Tankersley
Tankersley, I. 14	*Tancreslei(a)* 308b, 379b
Tanshelf, J. 11	*Tateshalla*, *-hal(l)e* 316b, 317 *septiens*, 379b *Tatessella* 317
Tatecastre	See Tadcaster
Tateshalla, *-hal(l)e*, *Tatessella*	See Tanshelf
Tateuuic	See Todwick
Temple Hirst	Not in D.B.
Temple Newsam, I. 10	*Neuhusum* 315, 379
Ternusc, *Ternusch(e)*	See Thurnscoe
Thoac	See Quick
Thorlby, E. 8	*Torederebi* 380 *Toreilderebi* 301b
Thornbrough, J. 7	*Torn(e)burne* 330, 379b
Thorne, M. 12	*Torne* 321 *bis*
Thorner, J. 9	*Torneure*, *Tornoure* 315, 373b, 379
Thornhill, H. 12	*Torni(l)* 317b, 379b
Thornthwaite	Not in D.B.
Thornton (near Bradford), G. 10	*Torenton(e)*, *-tune* 318 *bis*, 379b
Thornton in Craven, D. 8	*Torentun(e)* 322, 332
Thornton in Lonsdale, B. 5	*Tornetun* 301b
Thorp Arch, J. 9	*Torp* 329 2nd entry, 379b
Thorpe (near Hebden), F. 7	*Torp* 329b, 331b
Thorpe Audlin, K. 12	*Torp* 316, 379b
Thorpe Hesley, J. 14	*Tor(p)* 379 *bis*
Thorpe Hill, K. 7	*Torp* 330 1st entry, 379b
Thorpe on Balne	Not in D.B.
Thorpe on the Hill, I. 11	*Torp* 317b, 379b
Thorpe Salvin, K. 16	*Torp* 319, 379
Thorpe Stapleton, I. 10	*Torp* 315, 379
Thorpe Underwood, K. 7	*Tuadestorp* 326, 379b
Thorpe Willoughby, L. 10	*Torp* 315b 1st entry, 379
Threshfield, E. 7	*Freschefelt* 301b, 327
Throapham, K. 15	*Trapu'*, *Trapun* 319, 379
Thruscross	Not in D.B.
Thrybergh, K. 14	*Triberga*, *-berge* 321b, 379
Thurgoland, I. 14	*Turgesland* 317, 379b
Thurlstone, H. 13	*Turolueston* 379b *Turulfestune* 317
Thurnscoe, J. 13	*Dermescop* 319b, 379 *Ternusc*, *Ternusch(e)* 308, 321b, 379
Thurstonland, G. 13	*Tostenland* 379b
Tickhill	Not in D.B.
Tidover, I. 8	*Todoure* 322, 380
Timbe	See Little Timble
Timble	See Great Timble
Tineslauue	See Tinsley
Tinsley, J. 15	*Ti(r)neslauue* 319, 379

Tirneslauue	See Tinsley
Tockwith, K. 8	*Tocvi* 329
Tocvi	See Tockwith
Todmorden	Not in D.B.
Todoure	See Tidover
Todwick, K. 16	*Tateuuic* 308, 379
Toftes, J. 14	Lost in Wombwell, 319b, 326, 379
Togleston, *-tun*	See Toulston
Tohac	See Quick
Tong, H. 10	*Tuinc* 318, 379b
Tor	See Thorpe Hesley
Tore(il)derebi	See Thorlby
Torenton	See Thornton (near Bradford)
Torentone	See Bishop Thornton, Thornton (near Bradford)
Torentun	See Thornton in Craven
Torentune	See Bishop Thornton, Thornton (near Bradford), Thornton in Craven
Tornburne	See Thornbrough
Torne	See Thorne
Torneburne	See Thornbrough
Tornetun	See Thornton in Lonsdale
Torneure	See Thorner
Torni(l)	See Thornhill
Tornoure	See Thorner
Torp	See Grewelthorpe, Littlethorpe, Middlethorpe, Moorthorpe, Pallathorpe, Scotton Thorpe, Thorp Arch, Thorpe (near Hebden), Thorpe Audlin, Thorpe Hesley, Thorpe Hill, Thorpe on the Hill, Thorpe Salvin, Thorpe
Torp cont.	Stapleton, Thorpe Willoughby
Tosside	Not in D.B.
Tostenland	See Thurstonland
Totley, I. 16	*Totingelei* 278b, Derby.
Touetun	See Towton
Toulston, J. 9	*Oglestun* 329b *Togleston*, *-tun* 307b, 329b, 373b, 379 *bis*
Towton, K. 9	*Touetun* 379
Trapu', *Trapun*	See Throapham
Trectone	See Treeton
Treeton, J. 15	*Tre(c)tone* 308, 379
Tretone	See Treeton
Triberga, *-berge*	See Thrybergh
Tuadestorp	See Thorpe Underwood
Tudeforde, *Tudeuuorde*	See Tudworth
Tudworth, M. 13	*Tudeforde*, *Tudeuuorde* 321 *bis*, 373b
Tuinc	See Tong
Turgesland	See Thurgoland
Turolueston, *Turulfestune*	See Thurlstone
Ucnetorp	See Ingthorpe
Ufrun	See Owram
Ughil	See Ughill
Ughill, H. 15	*Ughil* 319b, 379b
Ulleskelf, K. 9	*Oleschel*, *Oleslec* 303b, 379
Ulley, K. 15	*Ollei(e)* 308, 379
Ulsigouere	See Hunsingore
Ulsitone	See Ouston
Ultone	See Upton
Uluedel	See Wooldale
Upper Cumberworth, H. 13	*Cumbreuu(o)rde* 299b, 379b
Upper Hopton, H. 12	*Hoptone*, *-tun* 317b, 379b
Upper Poppleton, L. 8	*In duabus Popletunis* 374 *Popletone*, *-tune* 303b, 329, 379b

Upper Soothill	Not in D.B.
Upperthong	Not in D.B.
Upton, K. 12	*Ultone* 316 *Uptone* 379b
Uptone	See Upton
Usebruna	See Great Ouseburn
Useburne	See Great Ouseburn, Little Ouseburn
Useburne, Alia	See Little Ouseburn
Utelai	See Utley
Utley, F. 9	*Utelai* 301b
Wachefeld, -felt, Wach'f'	See Wakefield
Waddington, B. 9	*Widitun* 332
Wade	See Wath upon Dearne
Wadelei, Wadesleia	See Wadsley
Wadsley, I. 15	*Wadelei* 379b *Wadesleia* 319b
Wadesuurde	See Wadsworth
Wadewrde	See Wadworth
Wadsworth, F. 11	*Wadesuurde* 299b
Wadworth, L. 14	*Wadewrde* 319, 373b *bis*, 379
Wakefield, I. 11	*Wachefeld, -felt* 299b *ter*, 301 *bis*, 373b, 379b *bis* *Wach'f'* 299b
Walching(e)ham	See Walkingham
Walden Stubbs, K. 12	*Eistop* 316 *Istop* 379b
Waldershelfe, H. 14	*Sceuelt* 301, 379b
Wales, K. 16	*Wales* 319, 379 *Walis(e)* 308, 379
Waleton	See Walton (near Wakefield)
Waletone, -tune	See Walton (near Wetherby)
Walis(e)	See Wales
Walitone	See Walton (near Wetherby)
Walkingham, I. 7	*Walching(e)ham* 300, 380
Walton (in Kirkby Overblow), I. 8	*Waltone* 322, 380
Walton (near Wakefield), I. 12	*Waleton* 379b
Walton (near Wetherby), J. 8	*Waletone, -tune* 329, 374 *bis* *Walitone* 379b
Waltone	See Walton (in Kirkby Overblow)
Wanbella, Wanbuelle	See Wombwell
Wandeslage	See Hutton Wandesley
Wardam	See Weardley
Warley, F. 11	*Werlafeslei* 299b
Warmfield, J. 11	*Warnesfeld* 303b, 379b
Warmsworth, K. 14	*Wemesford(e)* 321 *bis* *Wermesford* 307b, 379
Warnesfeld	See Warmfield
Warsill, H. 6	*Wifleshale* 303b *Wiueshale* 380
Wartle	See Weardley
Wat(e)	See Wath upon Dearne
Watecroft	See Wheatcroft
Watelag(e)	See Wheatley
Water Fryston	See Fryston
Wath upon Dearne, J. 14	*Wade* 319b, 379 *Wat(e)* 330b, 379
Weardley, I. 9	*Wardam* 373b *Wartle* 300, 379
Wedrebi	See Wetherby
Weeton, I. 8	*Widetone, -tun(e)* 301b, 330, 330b 2nd entry *Widitun* 380
Weldale	See Wheldale
Wemesford(e)	See Warmsworth
Wentworth, J. 14	*Winteuuord(e)* 319b, 379 *ter* *Wintreuuorde* 379
Werlafeslei	See Warley
Wermesford	See Warmsworth
West Bradford, C. 9	*Bradeforde* 332
West Bretton, I. 12	*Bretone* 299b *bis*, 379b

Westerby, J. 11	*Westrebi* 317, 379b
West Haddlesey	Not in D.B.
West Hardwick, J. 12	*Arduwic* 316 *Harduic* 379b
West Marton	See Marton
West Melton, J. 14	*Medeltone* 326, 330b *bis*, 379 *bis* *Merelton(e)* 330b, 379 *Middeltun* 319b 1st entry *Mideltone* 379
Weston, G. 8	*Westone* 314b, 380
Westone	See Weston
Westrebi	See Westerby
Westu(u)ic	See Westwick
Westwick, I. 6	*Westu(u)ic* 303b, 380
Wetherby, J. 8	*Wedrebi* 322, 328b, 380
Wheatcroft, I. 9	*Watecroft* 315, 379
Wheatley, L. 13	*Watelag(e)* 308 *ter*, 379
Wheldale, J. 11	*Queldale* 316 *Weldale* 379b
Whipley, H. 7	*Wipelei(e)*, *-lie* 300, 328b, 331b, 380
Whiston, J. 15	*Widest(h)an* 308, 379 *Witestan* 321 *bis*
Whitgift	Not in D.B.
Whitley, L. 11	*Witelai(e)* 330b, 379b
Whitley Lower, H. 12	*Witelaia*, *-lei* 317b, 379b
Whitwood, J. 11	*Witewde* 315b, 317b, 379b
Whixley, J. 7	*Crucheslaga* 322 *Cucheslage* 329b, 380 *Cuselade* 321b
Wibetese	See Wibsey
Wibsey, G. 10	*.bet.es* 318 *Wibetese* 318, 379b
Wic	See Wike
Wich	See Wike, Wyke
Wiche	See Wyke

Wicheles, *In duabus*	See Wighill and Wighill Park
Wichingeslei	See Winksley
Wickersley, K. 15	*Wicresleia* 319 *Wincreslei* 379
Wiclesforde	See Wigglesworth
Wicresleia	See Wickersley
Widdington, K. 7	*Widetona*, *-tone* 330b 1st entry, 332b, 379b
Widest(h)an	See Whiston
Widetona	See Widdington
Widetone	See Weeton, Widdington
Widetun(e)	See Weeton
Widitun	See Waddington, Weeton
Widuntorp	See Wildthorpe
Wifleshale	See Warsill
Wigglesworth, C. 7	*Wiclesforde* 332 *Winchelesuu(o)rde* 332 *bis*
Wighill and Wighill Park, K. 8	*In duabus Wicheles* 326, 379b
Wigton	Not in D.B.
Wihala, *Wihale*	See Worrall
Wike, I. 9	*Wic(h)* 301, 379
Wildthorpe, K. 14	*Widuntorp* 319b, 379
Wilestorp	See Wilstrop
Wilmereslege	See Womersley
Wilsden, F. 10	*Wilsedene* 301b
Wilsedene	See Wilsden
Wilseuuice	See Wilsic
Wilsic, L. 14	*Wilseuuice* 321b *Wiseleuuinc* 373b
Wilstrop, K. 7	*Wi(u)lestorp* 329, 379b
Wiluelai	See Woolley
Winchelesuu(o)rde	See Wigglesworth
Wincheslaie	See Winksley
Wincreslei	See Wickersley
Winksley, H. 6	*Wichingeslei* 380 *Wincheslaie* 330
Winterburn, E. 7	*Witreburne* 332
Wintersett	Not in D.B.
Winteuuord(e), *Wintreuuorde*	See Wentworth

Wipelei(e), *-lie*	See Whipley
Wircesburg	See Worsborough
Wirlei, *Wirtleie*	See Wortley
Wiseleuuinc	See Wilsic
Wistow	Not in D.B.
Witelai	See Whitley
Witelaia	See Whitley Lower
Witelaie	See Whitley
Witelei	See Whitley Lower
Witestan	See Whiston
Witewde	See Whitwood
Witreburne	See Winterburn
Wiueshale	See Warsill
Wiulestorp	See Wilstrop
Wlmeresleia	See Womersley
Wlsintone	See Ouston
Wodehuse, *-husum*	See Wothersome
Wombwell, J. 14	*Wanbella*, *Wanbuelle* 319b, 326, 330b, 379
Womersley, K. 12	*Wilmereslege* 379b *Wlmeresleia* 316
Woodsetts	Not in D.B.
Wooldale, G. 13	*Uluedel* 379b
Woolley, I. 12	*Wiluelai* 299b
Worrall, I. 15	*Wihala*, *Wihale* 319b, 379b
Worsborough, I. 14	*Wircesburg* 317, 379b
Wortley, I. 14	*Wirlei* 379b *bis* *Wirtleie* 331b *Wrleia* 308b
Wothersome, J. 9	*Wodehuse*, *-husum* 301, 379
Wrleia	See Wortley
Wyke, G. 11	*Wich(e)* 318, 379b
Yateholme, G. 13	*Altera Holne* 299b *In duabus Holne* 379b
Yeadon, H. 9	*Iadon*, *Iadun* 301, 373b, 379

ANONYMOUS HOLDINGS

None.

YORKSHIRE, NORTH RIDING
EURUICSCIRE, NORTREDING

Folios 298–333, 373–374, 379–382

MAPS 62–63, 64

Ab(b)etune	See Habton
Achebi, H. 6	Lost in Snape, 312, 381
Acheford(e)	See Hackforth
Achelu', *Aclum*, *Aclun*	See West Acklam
Aculestorp	See Agglethorpe
Adelingestorp	See Ellenthorpe
Adeuuerca	See Aldwark
Aestanesbi	See Asenby
Agglethorpe, G. 5	*Aculestorp* 311b, 381
Aiendrebi	See Ainderby Quernhow
Aimundrebi	See Amotherby
Ainderby Miers, H. 5	*Endrebi* 310b *bis*, 381 *bis*
Ainderby Quernhow, I. 6	*A(ie)ndrebi* 313, 381
Ainderby Steeple, I. 5	*Andrebi* 310 *Eindrebi* 299, 381 *bis*
Airy Holme, L. 2	*Ergun* 300, 380b
Aiskew, I. 5	*Echescol* 312, 381
Aislaby (near Pickering), N. 5	*Aslache(s)bi* 300, 380b
Aislaby (near Whitby), O. 3	*Asuluebi*, *-esby* 305, 380b

Akebar	Not in D.B.
Aldbrough, H. 2	*Aldeburne* 309b *bis*, 381
Aldbrough (in Bainbridge), E. 6	*Borch* 311 *Burg* 381
Aldeburne	See Aldbrough
Aldeuuerc	See Aldwark
Aldwark, K. 8	*Adeuuerca* 306 *Aldeuuerc* 381
Alia Atun	See Great Ayton
Alia Atune	See West Ayton
Alia Berg	See Little Barugh
Alia Bodelton	See West Bolton
Alia Broctun	See Great Broughton
Alia Buschebi	See Little Busby
Alia Cherchebi, *Alia Chirchebi*	See Kirby (in Kirby Misperton)
Alia Cudton(e)	See North Cowton
Alia Dalton, *Alia Daltun*	See Dalton (near Ravensworth)
Alia Edestun	See Little Edstone
Alia Hamelsech	See Gate Helmsley
Alia Hauoc(he)swelle	See West Hauxwell
Alia Herlesege	See East Harlsey
Alia Lentun(e), *Alia Leuetona*	See Castle Leavington
Alia Loctehusum	See Loftus
Alia Morehusum	See Little Moorsholm
Alia Silftune	See Nether Silton
Alia Stenweghe	See Stanwick
Alia Tanefeld	See West Tanfield
Alia Wendreslaga	See Wensley
Alia Wercesel	See Low Worsall
Alia Wich(e)	See Wykeham Hill (in Malton)
Allerston, O. 6	*Aluestun(e)* 299, 380b *Aluresta(i)n* 300, 380b
Allerthorpe, I. 5	*Erleuestorp* 381 *Herleuestorp* 313
Almeslai	See Helmsley
Alne, K. 8	*Alne* 303, 381
Alrebec	See Ellerbeck
Alreton	See Ellerton on Swale

Aluerton, *-tune*	See Northallerton
Aluestun(e), *Aluresta(i)n*	See Allerston
Aluretune	See Northallerton
Alwardebi	See Ellerby
Ambreforde	See Ampleforth
Amotherby, N. 7	*Aimundrebi* 327b *Andebi* 380b *bis* *Edmundrebia* 332b *Eindebi* 300b
Ampleforth, L. 6	*Ambre-*, *Ampreforde* 303 *bis*, 327, 380b
Ampreforde	See Ampleforth
Andebi	See Amotherby
Andrebi	See Ainderby Quernhow, Ainderby Steeple
Ansgotebi	See Osgoodby
Apelton	See East Appleton
Apeltona	See Appleton Wiske
Apeltun	See Appleton-le-Moors, Appleton-le-Street
Aplebi	See Eppleby
Apleton	See East Appleton
Apletun	See Appleton-le-Street, Appleton Wiske
Apletune	See Appleton Wiske
Appleton-le-Moors, N. 5	*Apeltun* 380b
Appleton-le-Street, N. 7	*Apeltun*, *Apletun* 300b, 380b
Appleton Wiske, J. 3	*Apeltona* 332b *Apletun(e)* 300b, 381
Arden, K. 5	*Ardene* 327
Ardene	See Arden
Argun	See Eryholme
Arncliffe, K. 4	*Ernecliue* 332b *Gerneclif* 300b *Lerneclif* 381
Arnodestorp, O. 2	Lost in Hinderwell, 322b, 380b
Ascam, G. 5	Lost in East Witton, 311b, 381

Aschelesmersc, *Aschilesmares*, O. 6	Lost in Pickering Marishes, 299, 380b
Aschilebi	See Exelby
Ascric	See Askrigg
Asebi, J. 6	Lost in Baldersby, 313, 381
Asebi	See Easby (near Richmond)
Asenby, J. 7	*Aestanesbi* 323
Asgozbi	See Osgodby
Aske	Not in D.B.
Askrigg, E. 6	*Ascric* 311, 381
Aslache(s)bi	See Aislaby (near Pickering)
Asmundrelac	See Osmotherley
Astun(e)	See Eston
Asuluebi, *-esby*	See Aislaby (near Whitby)
Atun	See East Ayton, Little Ayton
Atun, Alia	See Great Ayton
Atune	See East Ayton, West Ayton
Atune, Alia	See West Ayton
Aysgarth, F. 6	*Echescard* 311, 381
Bachesbi	See Baxby
Badresbi	See Battersby
Bagby, K. 6	*Bag(h)ebi* 327 *bis*
Bag(h)ebi	See Bagby
Bainbridge	Not in D.B.
Baldebi, P. 2	Lost in Whitby, 305, 380b
Baldersby, J. 6	*Baldrebi* 313, 381
Baldrebi	See Baldersby
Balk	Not in D.B.
Barden, G. 4	*Bernedan* 311b, 381
Barforth, G. 2	*Bereford* 309 *bis*, 381 *bis*
Barnaby, L. 2	*Bernodebi* 305b, 380b
Barnby (in Bossall), N. 8	*Barnebi* 327b
Barnby (near Whitby), O. 2	*Barnebi* 380b
Barnebi	See Barnby (in Bossall), Barnby (near Whitby)

Barningham, G. 3	*Berningham* 309 *bis*, 381 *bis*
Barton	See Barton (near Aldbrough)
Barton (near Aldbrough), H. 3	*Barton* 309, 381
Bartone	See Barton le Street
Barton le Street, N. 7	*Bartone*, *-tun(e)* 299 *bis*, 305b, 380b *ter*
Barton le Willows, M. 8	*Bartun* 306, 381
Bartun	See Barton le Street, Barton le Willows
Bartune	See Barton le Street
Barwick, J. 2	*Bereuuic* 380b *Englebi* 305 1st entry
Basche(s)bi, N. 5	Lost in Lastington, 300, 380b
Basche(s)bi	See Baxby
Battersby, L. 3	*Badresbi* 300, 380b
Baxby, K. 7	*Bachesbi* 303 *bis* *Basche(s)bi* 327, 381
Beadlam, M. 5	*Bodlum*, *-lun* 305b, 306, 380b
Bedale, I. 5	*Bedale* 312, 381
Begeland	See Old Byland
Belgebi	See Bellerby
Bellerby, G. 5	*Belgebi* 311b, 381
Beningbrough, K. 8	*Benniburg* 327b
Benniburg	See Beningbrough
Berch	See Great Barugh, Little Barugh
Bereford	See Barforth
Bereuuic	See Barwick
Berg	See Great Barugh
Berg, Alia	See Little Barugh
Bergebi	See *Berghebi*, Borrowby (near Loftus), Borrowby (near Northallerton)
Bergesbi	See Borrowby (near Loftus)

Berg(h)ebi, J. 6	Lost in Topcliffe, 323, 381
Bergolbi, *Berguluesbi*, K. 2	Lost in Seamer, 300, 332b, 380b
Bernebi, K. 6	Lost in Birdforth, 320b, 381
Bernedan	See Barden
Berningham	See Barningham
Bernodebi	See Barnaby
Bertone	See Constable Burton
Bertune	See Burton Dale
Bilsdale	Not in D.B.
Birdforth	Not in D.B.
Birkby, I. 3	*Bretebi* 299, 381
Blandebi	See Blansby
Blansby, O. 5	*Blandebi* 299, 380b
Blaten Carr, K. 3	*Blatun* 305b, 380b
Blatun	See Blaten Carr
Bodelton	See Castle Bolton
Bodelton, *Alia*	See West Bolton
Bodlum, *-lun*	See Beadlam
Boldron	Not in D.B.
Boleber	See Bulmer
Bolebi	See Old Boulby
Bolemere	See Bulmer
Boletone	See Bolton on Swale
Bollebi	See Old Boulby
Boltby, K. 5	*Boltebi* 327b *bis*
Boltebi	See Boltby, Holtby (near York)
Bolton on Swale, H. 4	*Boletone* 309b, 381
Borc	See Brough
Borch	See Aldbrough (in Bainbridge)
Bordalebi, *Bordelbia*	See Bordelby
Bordelby, now Mount Grace, K. 4	*Bordalebi*, *Bordelbia* 332b, 381 *Bordlebi* 380b
Bordlebi	See Bordelby
Borel	See Burrill
Borrowby (near Loftus), N. 2	*Berge(s)bi* 305, 380b
Borrowby (near Northallerton), J. 5	*Bergebi* 299, 381
Bortone	See Constable Burton
Bortun	See Burton Dale
Boscele, *Bosciale*	See Bossall
Bossall, N. 8	*Boscele* 327b *Bosciale* 381
Bowes	Not in D.B.
Bracheberc	See Breckenbrough
Bradfortone, *-tune*	See Brafferton
Brafferton, J. 7	*Bradfortone*, *-tune* 300b, 330, 381 *Bratfortune* 306
Bragebi	See Brawby
Brampton, J. 7	*Bran(s)tone* 301b, 308b, 380 *bis*
Brandsby, L. 7	*Branzbi* 327b
Bran(s)tone	See Brampton
Branzbi	See Brandsby
Bratfortune	See Brafferton
Brawby, N. 6	*Bragebi* 303, 380b
Brecca, *Breche*	See Breck
Breck, O. 3	*Brecca*, *Breche* 305, 380b
Breckenbrough, J. 6	*Bracheberc* 306, 381
Brennigston	See Burneston
Bretebi	See Birkby
Brignall, F. 4	*Bring(en)hale* 309, 381
Bring(en)hale	See Brignall
Brinitun, *Brinnistun*	See Burniston
Brinton	See Brompton (near Northallerton)
Broctun	See Broughton (near Malton), Great Broughton, Little Broughton
Broctun(e), G. 3	Lost in Newsham, 310, 381
Broctun, *Alia*, *Magna*	See Great Broughton
Broctune	See Brotton, Broughton (near Malton), Little Broughton

Brompton (near Northallerton), J. 4	*Brinton* 299 *Bruntone*, -*tun*(*e*) 304b, 381 *bis*
Brompton (near Scarborough), P. 6	*Brunetona* 332b *Bruntun*(*e*) 299, 300, 314, 380b
Brompton on Swale, H. 4	*Brunton* 309b, 381
Brostone	See Broughton (near Malton)
Brotton, M. 1	*Bro*(*c*)*tune* 305b, 380b
Brotune	See Brotton
Brough, H. 4	*Borc*, *Burg* 310b, 381
Broughton (near Malton), N. 7	*Broctun*(*e*) 300b, 314, 380b *Brostone* 327b
Brunetona	See Brompton (near Scarborough)
Brunton	See Brompton on Swale, Patrick Brompton
Bruntone	See Brompton (near Northallerton), Patrick Brompton
Bruntun(*e*)	See Brompton (near Northallerton), Brompton (near Scarborough)
Bulmer, M. 7	*Boleber* 306 *Bolemere* 306, 380b
Burg	See Aldbrough (in Bainbridge), Brough
Burneston, I. 5	*Brennigston* 313, 381
Burniston, Q. 4	*Brinitun* 380b *Brinnistun* 299
Burrill, H. 5	*Borel* 312, 381
Burton	See Humburton, High Burton, West Burton
Burton Dale, Q. 5	*Bertune* 299 *Bortun* 380b
Burtone	See Humburton, High Burton

Burtun	See Humburton
Buschebi; *Buschebi*, *In duabus*	See Great Busby, Little Busby
Buschebia, *Alia Buschebi*	See Little Busby
Butecram(*e*)	See Buttercrambe
Butruic	See Butterwick
Buttercrambe, N. 8	*Butecram*(*e*) 327b *ter*
Butterwick, N. 6	*Butruic* 327b
Byland Abbey	Not in D.B.
Cahosbi	See Cowesby
Caimtona, *Caitun*(*e*)	See Cayton
Caldbergh, G. 5	*Caldeber* 311b, 381
Caldeber	See Caldbergh
Caldenesche, L. 8	Lost in Huby, 300b
Caldeuuella, -*elle*, J. 7	Lost in Marton le Moor, 308b *bis*, 380
Caldeuuelle	See Caldwell (near Barforth)
Caldwell (near Barforth), G. 2	*Caldeuuelle* 309b, 381
Caltorn(*a*), -*torne*	See Cawthorn
Calvetone, -*tun*	See Cawton
Camisedale, L. 3	Lost in Ingleby Greenhow, 300, 327b, 328, 380b
Capuic	See Kepwick
Carebi	See Cold Kirby
Careltone, -*tun*	See Carlton (in Stockton on the Forest)
Caretorp	See Carthorpe
Carleton	See Carlton (near Middleham), Carlton Husthwaite, Carlton Miniott
Carletun	See Carlton (near Stokesley), Carlton Husthwaite, Carlton Miniott
Carlton (near Middleham), F. 7	*Carleton* 311b, 381

Carlton (in Stanwick), H. 2	*Cartun* 309, 309b, 381 *Cattune* 381
Carlton (in Stockton on the Forest), M. 9	*Careltone*, *-tun* 303, 381
Carlton (near Stokesley), K. 3	*Carletun* 305b, 380b
Carlton Husthwaite, K. 6	*Carleton*, *-tun* 303, 381
Carlton Miniott, J. 6	*Carleton*, *-tun* 300b, 327, 381
Carperby, F. 6	*Chirprebi* 311, 381
Carthorpe, I. 6	*Caretorp* 312b, 381
Cartun	See Carlton (in Stanwick)
Castle Bolton, F. 6	*Bodelton* 311, 381
Castle Leavington, K. 3	*Alia Lentun(e)* 300b, 381 *Alia Leuetona* 332b
Catrice	See Catterick
Catterick, H. 4	*Catrice* 310b, 381
Catton, J. 6	*Catune* 323, 381
Cattune	See Carlton (in Stanwick)
Catune	See Catton
Cawthorn, N. 5	*Caltorn(a)*, *-torne* 300, 332b, 380b
Cawton, M. 6	*Calvetone*, *-tun* 305b, 327, 380b
Cayton, Q. 6	*Caimtona* 333 *Caitun(e)* 300, 380b
Chelesterd, *Chelestuit*	See Kelsit
Chelvinctune, *-intun*	See North Kilvington
Chenetesbi	See Gatenby
Cheneuetone, *Cheniueton*, *-tune*, *Chennieton*	See Knayton
Cherchebi	See Kirby (in Kirby Misperton), Kirby (near Stokesley), Kirby Wiske, Kirkby (in Kirkby Fleetham)
Cherchebi, *Alia*	See Kirby (in Kirby Misperton)
Cherdinton	See Kirklington
Chetelestorp	See Kettlethorpe
Chigesburg	See Guisborough
Chigogemers, *Chigogesmersc*, *Chigomersc*, O. 6	Lost in Thornton Dale, 299, 305b, 380b
Childala, *-dale*	See Kildale
Chileburne	See Kilburn
Chilton, *-tun*	See Kilton
Chiluesmares, *-mersc*, O. 6	Lost in Pickering, 299, 380b
Chiluordebi	See Killerby (near Catterick)
Chilverte(s)bi	See Killerby (in Cayton)
Chinetorp	See Kingthorpe
Chipeling	See Kiplin
Chipuic	See Kepwick
Chirchebi	See Kirby (in Kirby Misperton), Kirby Hill, Kirby Wiske, Kirkby (in Kirkby Fleetham), Kirkby Knowle, Kirkby Moorside
Chirchebi, *Alia*	See Kirby (in Kirby Misperton)
Chirprebi	See Carperby
Claxton, M. 8	*Claxtorp* 300b, 306, 381
Claxtorp	See Claxton
Cleasby, H. 2	*Clesbi* 309b, 381
Clesbi	See Cleasby
Cliffe, H. 2	*Cliue* 309, 381
Clifton	See Clifton upon Ure
Clifton (near York), L. 9	*Cliftun(e)* 298b, 313 *ter*, 322b, 373b, 379
Clifton upon Ure, H. 6	*Clifton* 312, 381
Cliftun(e)	See Clifton (near York)
Cliue	See Cliffe
Cloctone, *-tune*	See Cloughton
Cloughton, Q. 4	*Cloctone*, *-tune* 299, 305b, 323, 380b
Codeschelf, *Codresche(l)f*	See Skutterskelfe

Danby (in Thornton Steward), G. 5	*Danebi* 311b, 381
Danby Wiske, I. 4	*Danebi* 310, 381
Danebi	See Danby (near Moorsholm); see Danby (in Thornton Steward), Danby Wiske
Danebia	See Danby (near Moorsholm)
Danefeld, *-felt*	See East Tanfield
Deepdale, Q. 5	*Depedale* 299, 380b
Deighton, J. 3	*Dictune* 304b, 381
Deltune	See Dalton (near Topcliffe)
Denton(e), E. 6	Lost in Low Abbotside, 311, 381
Depedale	See Deepdale
Dic(he), L. 8	Lost in Haxby, 300b, 381
Dictune	See Deighton
Didderston, H. 3	*Dird(r)eston* 310, 381
Di(g)neshale	See Over Dinsdale
Dird(r)eston	See Didderston
Dirneshala, *-hale*	See Over Dinsdale
Disforde	See Dishforth
Dishforth, J. 7	*Disforde* 322
Downholme, G. 4	*Dune* 311, 381
Dragmalebi	See Dromonby
Dromonby, K. 3	*Dragmalebi* 331, 380b
Dune	See Downholme
Dunesla, *-le*	See Dunsley
Dunsley, O. 2	*Dunesla*, *-le* 300, 380b
Earswick, L. 9	*Edresuuic*, *Edreȝuic* 303b, 381
Easby (near Ingleby Greenhow), L. 3	*Esebi* 300, 380b
Easby (near Richmond), H. 4	*Asebi* 309b, 381
Easington, N. 2	*Esingeton*, *-tun* 305 *bis*, 380b
Easingwold, K. 7	*Eisicewalt* 299 *Eisincewald* 381
East Appleton, H. 4	*Apelton*, *Apleton* 310b, 381
East Ayton, Q. 5	*Atun(e)* 314, 323, 380b
East Cowton, I. 3	*Corketune* 299 *Cottune*, *Cotun(e)* 310, 381 *bis*
East Harlsey, J. 4	*Alia Herlesege* 300b *In duabus Erleseie* 381 *Herlesia* 332b
East Hauxwell, G. 4	*Hauoc(he)swelle* 311b, 381
Easthorpe, N. 7	*Estorp* 299, 380b
East Layton, G. 3	*Latone*, *Latton* 309 *bis*, 381 *bis*
East Lilling, M. 8	*Lilinga*, *-inge* 300b, 306, 331, 381
East Newton, M. 6	*Neutone*, *-tun* 327b, 380b *Newentune* 300b *Neweton* 303
East Rounton, J. 3	*Rantune* 300 *Rontun* 380b
East Tanfield, I. 6	*Danefeld*, *-felt* 308b, 380 *Tanefeld* 312b, 381
East Witton, G. 5	*Witone*, *-tun(e)* 311, 311b, 312, 381
Ebberston, P. 6	*Edbriȝtun(e)* 299, 380b
Ebor-, *Eburacum*	See York
Echescard	See Aysgarth
Echescol	See Aiskew
Ecinton	See Eshingtons
Edbriȝtun(e)	See Ebberston
Edestun, *Alia*, *Parva*	See Little Edstone
Edmundrebia	See Amotherby
Edresuuic, *Edreȝuic*	See Earswick
Egetune	See Egton
Egglestone, F. 3	*Eghiston*, *-tun* 309, 381
Eghiston, *-tun*	See Egglestone

Modern name	Domesday form
Egton, O. 3	*Egetune* 305, 380b
Eiford	See Yafforth
Eindebi	See Amotherby
Eindrebi	See Ainderby Steeple
Eisicewalt, *Eisincewold*	See Easingwold
Ellenthorpe, J. 7	*Adelingestorp* 300, 380
Ellerbeck, J. 4	*Alre-*, *Elrebec* 300b, 327b, 381
Ellerburn, O. 5	*Elrebrune*, *-burne* 299, 300, 380b
Ellerby, N. 2	*Alwardebi* 380b *Elwordebi* 305
Ellerton Abbey, G. 4	*Elreton* 311, 381
Ellerton on Swale, H. 4	*Alreton* 309b *bis*, 310 *quater*, 381
Ellington, H. 6	*Ellintone* 311b, 381
Ellintone	See Ellington
Elmeslac	See Helmsley
Elrebec	See Ellerbeck
Elrebrune, *-burne*	See Ellerburn
Elreton	See Ellerton Abbey
Eltebi	See Holtby (near Kirkby Fleetham)
Elwordebi	See Ellerby
Endrebi	See Ainderby Miers
Englebi	See Barwick, Ingleby Arncliffe, Ingleby Greenhow, Ingleby Hill
Englebia	See Ingleby Arncliffe
Eppleby, H. 2	*Aplebi* 309, 381
Ergun	See Airy Holme
Erleseie, *In duabus*	See East Harlsey, West Harlsey
Erleuestorp	See Allerthorpe
Ernebi	See Harmby
Ernecliue	See Arncliffe
Eryholme, I. 3	*Argun* 309, 381
Eschalchedene	See Scackleton
Esebi	See Easby (near Ingleby Greenhow)

Modern name	Domesday form
Eshingtons, F. 7	*Ecinton* 311
Esingeton, *-tun*	See Easington
Eslingesbi	See Slingsby
Eslinton	See Hesselton
Esteintona	See Stainton (in Stanghow)
Estiresbi	See Stearsby
Eston, L. 2	*Astun(e)* 305b, 380b
Eston	See Theakston
Estorp	See Easthorpe
Eterstorp, R. 6	Lost in Gristhorpe, 299, 380b
Eureslage	See Yearsley
Everley, P. 5	*Evrelag*, *-lai* 323, 380b
Evrelag, *-lai*	See Everley
Exelby, I. 5	*Aschilebi* 313, 381
Faceby, K. 3	*Fe(i)ȝbi* 300, 380b *Foitesbi* 332b
Fademora, *-more*	See Fadmoor
Fadmoor, M. 5	*Fademora*, *-more* 305b, 380b
Falsgrave, Q. 5	*Wal(l)esgrif*, *-grip* 299, 305b, 323, 380b
Farlington, L. 7	*Far-*, *Ferlintun* 306, 381
Farlintun	See Farlington
Farmanby, O. 6	*Farmanesbi* 299, 380b
Farmanesbi	See Farmanby
Farndale	Not in D.B.
Fawdington	Not in D.B.
Fearby, H. 6	*Fedebi* 312, 381
Fedebi	See Fearby
Feiȝbi	See Faceby
Fencotes, *In duabus Fencotes*	See Great Fencote, Little Fencote
Ferlintun	See Farlington
Feȝbi	See Faceby
Figclinge, *Fig(e)linge*	See Fyling Old Hall
Finegal(a)	See Fingall
Fingall, H. 5	*Finegal(a)* 312, 381
Firby, I. 5	*Fredebi* 312, 381
Flastun	See Flaxton

Flaxton, M. 8	*Flastun*, *Flaxtun(e)* 300b, 303, 313, 327b, 381
Flaxtun(e)	See Flaxton
Fleteham	See Kirkby Fleetham
Flore, *Florun*	See Flowergate
Flowergate, O. 2	*Flore*, *Florun* 305, 380b
Foitesbi	See Faceby
Forcett, H. 2	*Forsed*, *-set* 309, 381
Fornetorp, L. 7	Lost in Farlington, 306, 314, 381
Fors Abbey, E. 6	*Fors* 311, 381
Forsed, *-set*	See Forcett
Foston, M. 8	*Fostun* 313, 381
Fostun	See Foston, Foxton (in Crathorne)
Fo(u)stune	See Foxton (in Thimbleby)
Foxton (in Crathorne), K. 3	*Fostun*, *Foxtun* 305b, 332b, 380b
Foxton (in Thimbleby), J. 4	*Fo(u)stune* 304b, 381
Foxtun	See Foxton (in Crathorne)
Fredebi	See Firby
Fremington, F. 5	*Fremin(g)ton* 311, 381
Fremin(g)ton	See Fremington
Fridebi, K. 5	Lost in Felixkirk, 327b
Frideton, *Fritun*	See Fryton
Fryton, M. 7	*Frideton*, *Fritun* 306, 327b, 380b
Fyling Old Hall, P. 3	*Figclinge* 322b *Fig(e)linge* 305, 373, 380b
Fyling Thorpe, P. 3	*Nortfigelinge* 305, 380b
Galmetona, *Gameltorp*	See Ganthorpe
Ganthorpe, M. 7	*Galmetona* 332b *Gameltorp* 300b, 306, 380b
Garriston, G. 5	*Gerdeston(e)* 311b, 381
Gate Helmsley, M. 9	*Alia Hamelsech* 381 *Hamelsec* 303
Gatenby, I. 5	*Chenetesbi* 381 *Ghetenesbi* 313
Gayles	Not in D.B.
Gedlingesmore	See Gillamoor
Gellinge	See Gilling East
Gellinges	See Gilling
Gerdeston(e)	See Garriston
Gerlinton	See Girlington
Gerneclif	See Arncliffe
Gernuic	See Yarnwick
Gerou	See Yarm
Ghellinge	See Gilling East
Ghelling(h)es	See Gilling
Ghetenesbi	See Gatenby
Ghigesborg, *-burg*	See Guisborough
Ghinipe	See Gnipe Howe
Gighesborc	See Guisborough
Gillamoor, M. 5	*Gedlingesmore* 327b
Gilling, H. 3	*Gellinges* 381 *Ghelling(h)es* 309 *bis*, 310
Gilling East, L. 6	*G(h)ellinge* 325b, 327b, 380b
Gilmonby	Not in D.B.
Girlington, G. 2	*Gerlinton* 309, 381
Girsby, J. 3	*Grisebi* 304b, 381
Giseborne	See Guisborough
Gnipe Howe, P. 3	*Ghinipe* 305, 380b
Goindel	See Cundall
Golborg, *Goldeburg*	See Goldsborough
Goldsborough, O. 2	*Golborg* 305 *Goldeburg* 380b
Goltona, *Gotun*	See Goulton
Goulton, K. 3	*Goltona* 332b *Go(u)tun* 300, 305b, 380b
Goutun	See Goulton
Gratorne	See Crathorne
Great Ayton, L. 2	*Alia Atun* 320b, 380b
Great Barugh, N. 6	*Berch* 327b *Berg* 300b, 303, 380b
Great Broughton, L. 3	*Alia Broctun* 380b *Broctun* 300, 327b *Magna Broctun* 305b

Great Busby, K. 3	*Buschebi* 300, 320b, 331 *In duabus Buschebi* 380b
Great Crakehall, H. 5	*Crachele* 312b, 381
Great Edstone, M. 6	*Micheledestun* 314, 380b
Great Fencote, I. 4	*In duabus Fencotes* 381 *Fencotes* 310b
Great Habton	See Habton
Great Langton, I. 4	*Langeton* 309, 381
Great Smeaton, I. 3	*Smet(t)on* 309, 381 *Smidetun(e)* 299, 381
Grif	See Griff, Mulgrave
Griff, L. 6	*Grif* 300b, 380b
Grimesbi, *Grimesdi*, N. 2	Lost in Borrowby, 305, 380b
Grimeston	See Grimston
Grimston, L. 7	*Grimeston* 327b
Grinton, F. 5	*Grinton* 311, 381
Grisebi	See Girsby
Grisetorp	See Gristhorpe
Gristhorpe, R. 6	*Grisetorp* 299, 380b
Gristorentun	See Thornton le Beans
Guisborough, L. 2	*Chigesburg* 300, 380b *Ghigesborg*, *-burg* 305b, 320b *Gighesborc* 305 *Giseborne* 332b
Habetun	See Habton
Habton, Great and Little, N. 6	*Ab(b)etune* 300, 380b *Habetun* 305b
Hackforth, H. 4	*Acheford(e)* 310b, 381
Hackness, P. 5	*Hagenesse* 323, 380b
Hagenesse	See Hackness
Hale	See Low Hail
Halm(e)bi	See Hawnby
Hamelsec	See Gate Helmsley, Upper Helmsley
Hamelsech	See Upper Helmsley
Hamelsech, *Alia*	See Gate Helmsley
Hanechetonis, *In duabus*	See Hangton and Hangton Hill
Hangton and Hangton Hill, N. 3	*In duabus Hanechetonis* 333
Harem	See Harome
Harmby, G. 5	*Ernebi* 381 *Hernebi* 311b
Harome, M. 6	*Harem* 327b *Harum*, *-un* 300b, 305b, 314b, 380b
Hartforth, H. 3	*Herford*, *-fort* 309, 381
Hartoft	Not in D.B.
Harton, M. 8	*Heretun(e)* 300b, 381
Harum, *-un*	See Harome
Harwood Dale	Not in D.B.
Has(s)e, I. 4	Lost in Kirkby Fleetham, 310b, 381
Hauoc(he)swelle	See East Hauxwell
Hauoc(he)swelle, *Alia*	See West Hauxwell
Hawade, M. 7	Lost in Wath, 327b
Hawes	Not in D.B.
Hawnby, L. 5	*Halm(e)bi* 301, 320b, 381
Hawsker	Not in D.B.
Haxby, L. 8	*Haxebi* 303, 381
Haxebi	See Haxby
Healey	Not in D.B.
Helmsley, L. 6	*Almeslai* 302 *Elmeslac* 303b, 306, 380b
Helperby, J. 7	*Hel-*, *Hilprebi* 303, 303b, 381 *Ilprebi* 381
Helprebi	See Helperby
Heltebi	See Holtby (near Kirkby Fleetham)
Hemlington, K. 2	*Himeligetun* 305 *Himelintun* 380b
Henderskelfe, N. 7	*Hildreschelf* 314 *Ilderschelf* 380b
Herelsaie	See West Harlsey

Heretun(e)	See Harton
Herford, -fort	See Hartforth
Herlesege	See West Harlsey
Herlesege, Alia; Herlesia	See East Harlsey
Herleuestorp	See Allerthorpe
Hernebi	See Harmby
Herselaige	See West Harlsey
Heslintone	See Hesselton
Hesselton, H. 5	*Eslinton* 381 *Heslintone* 312b
Hewarde, -worde	See Heworth
Heworth, L. 9	*Hewarde, -worde* 298, 328, 379
High Burton, H. 6	*Burton(e)* 312, 381
High Stakesby, O. 2	*Staxebi* 305, 380b
High Sutton, H. 6	*Sudton(e)* 312, 381 *Sutone* 381
High Worsall, J. 3	*In duabus Wirceshel* 381 *Wercesel* 300b
Hilchetun	See Ilton
Hildegrip	See Hill Grips
Hildenley, N. 7	*Hildingeslei* 300b *Ildingeslei* 381
Hildingeslei	See Hildenley
Hildreschelf	See Henderskelfe
Hildrewelle	See Hinderwell
Hill Grips, Q. 5	*Hildegrip* 323 *Ildegrip* 380b
Hilprebi	See Helperby
Hilton, K. 2	*Hiltona, -tun(e)* 300, 305b, 332b, 380b
Hiltona, -tun(e)	See Hilton
Himeligetun, Himelintun	See Hemlington
Hinderwell, N. 2	*Hildrewelle* 305, 322b *bis* *Ildrewelle* 380b
Hindrelag(he)	See Richmond
Hiplewelle	See Hipswell
Hipswell, H. 4	*Hiplewelle* 310b, 381
Hipton	See Shipton
Hobi	See Huby
Hogram, Hograve, Hogrem	See Howgrave
Holm(e)	See North Holme, South Holme
Holme (near Thirsk), J. 6	*Hulme* 304b, 380
Holtby (near Kirkby Fleetham), I. 5	*Eltebi* 381 *Heltebi* 310b
Holtby (near York), M. 9	*Boltebi* 300b *Holtebi* 381
Holtebi	See Holtby (near York)
Holtorp	See Howthorpe
Holwick	Not in D.B.
Hom	See North Holme
Hore(n)bodebi, K. 6	Lost in Hutton Sessay, 304b, 320b, 381
Hornby (near Appleton Wiske), J. 3	*Hornebia* 332b
Hornby (near Hackforth), H. 4	*Hornebi* 310b, 381
Hornebi	See Hornby (near Hackforth)
Hornebia	See Hornby (near Appleton Wiske)
Hoton	See Hutton Conyers
Hotone	See Hutton Conyers, Hutton Mulgrave, Sand Hutton (near York), Sheriff Hutton
Hottone	See Hutton Conyers
Hottun	See Hutton Magna
Hottune	See Sand Hutton (near Thirsk), Sand Hutton (near York)
Hotun	See Hutton Buscel, Hutton Hang, Hutton le Hole, Hutton Lowcross, Hutton Rudby, Low Hutton, Sand Hutton (near York), Sheriff Hutton

Hotune	See Hutton Bonville, Hutton Buscel, Hutton Hang, Hutton Magna, Hutton Mulgrave, Sand Hutton (near Thirsk), Sand Hutton (near York), Sheriff Hutton
Hou	See Howe
Houetune	See Hoveton
Hoveton, M. 5	*Houetune* 327b
Hovingham, M. 6	*Hovingham* 327b
Howe, J. 6	*Hou* 313, 381
Howgrave, I. 6	*Hogram*, *Hogrem* 303b, 304b, 380 *bis* *Hograve* 312b, 381
Howthorpe, M. 7	*Holtorp* 327b
Huby, L. 8	*Hobi* 299, 331, 381
Hudreswelle	See Hudswell
Hudswell, G. 4	*Hudreswelle* 311 *Udreswelle* 381
Hulme	See Holme (near Thirsk)
Humburton, J. 7	*Burton(e)*, *-tun* 330 *bis*, 380
Hunderthwaite, E. 3	*Hundredestoit(h)* 310, 381
Hundredestoit(h)	See Hunderthwaite
Hundulfthorpe, J. 5	*Hundulftorp* 306, 381
Hundulftorp	See Hundulfthorpe
Huntindune	See Huntington
Huntington, L. 9	*Huntindune* 300b, 306, 313, 381
Hunton, H. 5	*Hunton(e)* 312b, 381
Hunton(e)	See Hunton
Husthwaite	Not in D.B.
Hutton Bonville, I. 4	*Hotune* 300b, 381
Hutton Buscel, P. 6	*Hotun(e)* 299, 380b
Hutton Conyers, I. 7	*Hoton(e)*, *Hottone* 303b, 304b, 380 *ter*
Hutton Hang, G. 5	*Hotun(e)* 312, 381
Hutton le Hole, M. 5	*Hotun* 327b
Hutton Lowcross, L. 2	*Hotun* 305b, 380b
Hutton Magna, G. 2	*Hottun*, *Hotune* 309, 381
Hutton Mulgrave, O. 3	*Hotone*, *-tune* 305, 380b
Hutton Rudby, K. 3	*Hotun* 305b *bis*, 380b
Iaforbe, *Ia(i)forde*	See Yafforth
Iarun	See Yarm
Ilcheton	See Ilton
Ildegrip	See Hill Grips
Ilderschelf	See Henderskelfe
Ildingeslei	See Hildenley
Ildrewelle	See Hinderwell
Ilprebi	See Helperby
Ilton, H. 6	*Hilchetun* 312 *Ilcheton* 381
Indrelag(e)	See Richmond
Ingleby Arncliffe, K. 4	*Englebi(a)* 300b, 332b, 381
Ingleby Greenhow, L. 3	*Englebi* 331, 380b
Ingleby Hill, J. 2	*Englebi* 305 2nd and 3rd entries, 380b
Inglethwaite, L. 8	*Inguluestuet* 323, 381
Inguluestuet	See Inglethwaite
Ioletun(e)	See Youlton
Irby, J. 3	*Irebi* 299, 381
Irebi	See Irby
Iretone	See Irton (in Thornton on the Hill)
Iretune	See Irton (near Scarborough)
Irton (near Scarborough), Q. 6	*Iretune* 323, 380b
Irton (in Thornton on the Hill), K. 7	*Iretone* 327
Iselbec	See Islebeck
Islebeck, K. 6	*Iselbec* 327

Modern name	Domesday form
Kelsit, L. 8	*Chelesterd* 299 *Chelestuit* 381
Keneueton	See Knayton
Kepwick, K. 5	*Capuic* 301, 381 *Chipuic* 327
Kettlethorpe, O. 5	*Chetelestorp* 300, 380b
Kilburn, K. 6	*Chileburne* 327
Kildale, L. 3	*Childala*, *-dale* 331, 332b, 380b
Killerby (near Catterick), H. 4	*Chiluordebi* 310b, 381
Killerby (in Cayton), Q. 6	*Chilverte(s)bi* 323, 380b
Kilton, M. 2	*Chilton*, *-tun* 300, 305b, 380b
Kilton Thorpe, M. 2	*Torp* 300, 305b, 380b
Kingthorpe, O. 5	*Chinetorp* 299, 380b
Kiplin, I. 4	*Chipeling* 309b, 381
Kirby (in Kirby Misperton), N. 6	*Alia Cherchebi*, *Alia Chirchebi* 314, 380b *Cherchebi*, *Chirchebi* 314, 380b
Kirby (in Stokesley), L. 3	*Cherchebi* 331, 380b
Kirby Hill, J. 7	*Chirchebi* 301b, 330 2nd entry, 380
Kirby Wiske, J. 5	*Cherchebi*, *Chirchebi* 309b, 381 *Kirkebi* 299
Kirkby (in Kirkby Fleetham), I. 4	*Cherchebi*, *Chirchebi* 310b, 381
Kirkby Fleetham, I. 4	*Fleteham* 309b *ter*, 310b, 381
Kirkby Knowle, K. 5	*Chirchebi* 327
Kirkby Moorside, M. 5	*Chirchebi* 327b *bis*
Kirkebi	See Kirby Wiske
Kirkleatham, L. 1	*Weslide* 322b *Westlid(um)*, *-lidun* 305, 305b, 380b *Westude* 300
Kirk Leavington, J. 3	*Lentune* 300b, 381 *Leuetona* 332b
Kirklington, I. 6	*Cherdinton* 312b, 381
Knayton, J. 5	*Cheneuetone* 304b *Cheniueton*, *-tune* 381 *bis* *Chennieton* 299 *Keneueton* 299
Kneeton, H. 3	*Naton* 309, 381
Lach(en)ebi	See Lackenby
Lackenby, L. 1	*Lach(en)ebi* 305, 305b, 380b
Laclum	See Lealholme
Laisinbia	See Lazenby (near Guisborough)
Landemot	See Landmoth
Landmoth, J. 5	*Landemot* 299, 381
Langeton	See Great Langton, Little Langton
Langetorp	See Langthorne
Langthorne, H. 5	*Langetorp* 310b, 381
Langthorpe, J. 7	*Torp* 330 3rd entry, 380
Lartington, F. 3	*Lertinton* 310, 381
Lastingham, N. 5	*Lesting(e)ham* 314, 380b
Laston, *-tun*	See West Layton
Latone, *Latton*	See East Layton
Laysthorpe, M. 6	*Lechestorp* 327b
Lazenby (near Guisborough), L. 1	*Laisinbia* 332b *Leisingebi* 305 *Lesighebi* 331 *Lesingebi* 300, 380b
Lazenby (near Northallerton), I. 4	*Leisenchi* 299 *Leisenghi* 381
Leake, J. 5	*Lec(h)e* 299, 306, 381 *bis*
Lealholme, N. 3	*Laclum* 333 *Lelun* 327b, 328, 380b
Lebberston, Q. 6	*Ledbestun*, *Ledbeʒtun* 299, 380b
Leborne	See Leyburn
Lec(h)e	See Leake
Lechestorp	See Laysthorpe
Leckby, J. 7	*Ledebi* 308b, 380
Ledbestun, *Ledbeʒtun*	See Lebberston

Ledebi	See Leckby
Leidtorp, O. 6	Lost in Wilton, 314, 380b
Leisenchi	See Lazenby (near Northallerton)
Leisingebi	See Lazenby (near Guisborough)
Leisinghi	See Lazenby (near Northallerton)
Lelun	See Lealholme
Lentune	See Kirk Leavington
Lentun(e), *Alia*	See Castle Leavington
Lerneclif	See Arncliffe
Lertinton	See Lartington
Lesighebi, *Lesingebi*	See Lazenby (near Guisborough)
Lesting(e)ham	See Lastingham
Leuetona	See Kirk Leavington
Leuetona, *Alia*	See Castle Leavington
Leu(u)ecen	See Levisham
Levisham, O. 5	*Leu(u)ecen* 299, 380b
Leyburn, G. 5	*Leborne* 311b, 381
Lid	See Lythe
Lilinga, *-inge*	See East Lilling, West Lilling
Linton upon Ouse, K. 8	*Luctone* 306 *bis*
Little Ayton, L. 3	*Atun* 300 *ter*, 305b, 320b, 380b *bis*
Little Barugh, N. 6	*Alia Berg* 300b, 303, 380b *Berch* 327b
Little Broughton, L. 3	*Broctun(e)* 331, 380b
Little Busby, K. 3	*Alia Buschebi* 331 *Buschebia* 332b *In duabus Buschebi* 380b
Little Edstone, N. 5	*Alia Edestun*, *Parva Edestun* 314, 380b
Little Fencote, I. 5	*In duabus Fencotes* 381 *Fencotes* 310b
Little Habton	See Habton
Little Langton, I. 4	*Langeton* 309b, 381
Little Marish, P. 6	*Parva Mersc* 314, 380b
Little Moorsholm, M. 2	*Alia Morehusum* 305b, 380b
Little Smeaton, I. 3	*Smidetun(e)* 300b, 381 *bis* *Smitune* 299
Liuretun	See Liverton
Liverton, N. 2	*Liuretun* 305, 380b
Lochetun	See Lockton
Lockton, O. 5	*Lochetun* 300, 380b
Loctehusum	See South Loftus
Loctehusum, *Alia*	See Loftus
Loctemares, *-mersc*	See Loft Marishes
Loctushum	See South Loftus
Loctusum	See Loftus
Loft Marishes, O. 6	*Loctemares*, *-mersc* 300, 305b, 380b
Loftus, N. 2	*Alia Loctehusum* 380b *Loctusum* 300
Lonton, E. 2	*Lontone*, *-tune* 310, 381
Lontone, *-tune*	See Lonton
Low Hail, I. 3	*Hale* 309, 381
Low Hutton, N. 7	*Hotun* 300b, 314, 332b, 380b
Low Worsall, J. 3	*Alia Wercesel* 300b *In duabus Wirceshel* 381 *Wercheshala* 332b
Luctone	See Linton upon Ouse
Lythe, O. 2	*Lid* 305, 380b
Magna Broctun	See Great Broughton
Malmerbi	See Melmerby (near Hutton Conyers)
Malsenebi	See Melsonby
Maltby, K. 2	*Maltebi* 305, 380b
Maltebi	See Maltby
Maltun(e)	See Old Malton
Manefeld	See Manfield

Manfield, H. 2	*Manefeld*, *Mannefelt* 309, 381
Mange	See Marrick
Mannebi	See Maunby
Mannefelt	See Manfield
Mannesbi	See Maunby
Marderby, K. 6	*Martrebi* 327
Marrick, F. 5	*Mange* 311, 381
Marske (near Richmond)	Not in D.B.
Marske (near Saltburn), M. 1	*Mersc*, *Mersch*(*e*) 305, 305b, 322b, 323, 380b
Marton (near Middlesbrough), K. 2	*Martona*, *-tun*(*e*) 300, 320b *bis*, 331 *bis*, 332b, 380b
Marton (near Pickering), N. 6	*Martone*, *-tun* 314, 327b, 380b
Martona	See Marton (near Middlesbrough)
Martone	See Marton (near Pickering)
Marton in the Forest, L. 7	*Martun* 306, 381
Marton le Moor	Not in D.B.
Martrebi	See Marderby
Martun	See Marton (near Middlesbrough), Marton (near Pickering), Marton in the Forest
Martun(*e*), P. 6	Lost in Hutton Buscel, 299, 300, 380b
Martune	See Marton (near Middlesbrough)
Masham, H. 6	*Massan* 312 *ter*, 312b, 381
Massan	See Masham
Maunby, I. 5	*Manne*(*s*)*bi* 299, 309b, 381 *bis*
Maxudesmares, *-mersc*, O. 6	Lost in Pickering Marishes, 299, 380b
Medelai	See Middleham (near Leyburn)
Melmerbi	See Melmerby (near Middleham)

Melmerby (near Hutton Conyers), I. 6	*Malmerbi* 312b, 381
Melmerby (near Middleham), G. 5	*Melmerbi* 311b, 381
Melsonby, H. 3	*Malsenebi* 310, 381
Mersc, *Mersch*(*e*)	See Marske (near Saltburn)
Mersc, *Parva*	See Little Marish
Michelbi	See Mickleby
Micheledestun	See Great Edstone
Mickleby, O. 2	*Michelbi* 305, 380b
Mickleton, E. 2	*Micleton* 310, 381
Micleton	See Mickleton
Middelham, M. 6	Lost in Muscoates, 327b
Middelton	See Middleton upon Leven
Middeltone	See Middleton (near Guisborough)
Middeltun	See Middleton (in Appleton Wiske), Middleton (near Pickering), Middleton Quernhow, Middleton Tyas, Middleton upon Leven
Middleham (near Leyburn), G. 5	*Medelai* 311b, 381
Middlesbrough	Not in D.B.
Middleton (in Appleton Wiske), J. 3	*Middeltun* 330
Middleton (near Guisborough), L. 2	*Middeltone*, *Mideltune* 305b, 380b
Middleton (near Pickering), N. 5	*Mid*(*d*)*eltun* 299, 380b
Middleton Quernhow, I. 6	*Middeltun*, *Mideltune* 312b, 381
Middleton Tyas, H. 3	*Middeltun*, *Midelton* 309, 381
Middleton upon Leven, K. 3	*Middelton*, *-tun*, *Mideltun* 305b *bis*, 380b

Midelton	See Middleton Tyas
Mideltun	See Middleton (near Pickering), Middleton upon Leven
Mideltune	See Middleton (near Guisborough), Middleton Quernhow
Milby, J. 7	*Mildebi* 300, 380
Mildebi	See Milby
Misperton (in Kirby Misperton), N. 6	*Mispeton* 327b
Mispeton	See Misperton
Mitune	See Myton on Swale
Molscebi	See Moxby
Moltun	See Moulton
Molzbi	See Moxby
Moorsholm, M. 2	*Morehusum*, *-husun*, *Morhusum* 300, 305b, 332b, 380b
Morehusum, *-husun*, *Morhusum*	See Moorsholm
Morehusum, *Alia*	See Little Moorsholm
Mortham, G. 2	*Mortham* 309, 381
Morton (in East Harlsey), J. 4	*Mortona*, *-tune* 300b, 332b, 381
Morton (near Guisborough), L. 2	*Mortona*, *-tun* 300, 332b, 380b
Morton (in Skelton), L. 8	*Mortun* 298b, 379
Mortona	See Morton (in East Harlsey), Morton (near Guisborough)
Morton upon Swale, I. 5	*Mortun(e)* 309b *bis*, 381
Mortun	See Morton (near Guisborough), Morton (in Skelton), Morton upon Swale,

Mortun cont.	Murton (near Cold Kirby), Murton (in Sutton in the Forest), Murton (near York)
Mortune	See Morton (in East Harlsey), Morton upon Swale, Murton (in Sutton in the Forest), Murton (near York)
Moulton, H. 3	*Moltun* 309, 381
Mowthorpe, M. 7	*Muletorp* 381
Moxby, L. 7	*Molscebi* 381 *Molzbi* 299
Muker	Not in D.B.
Muletorp	See Mowthorpe
Mulgrave, O. 2	*Grif* 305, 380b
Murton (near Cold Kirby), K. 5	*Mortun* 320b, 381
Murton (in Sutton on the Forest), L. 8	*Mortun(e)* 299, 303, 381
Murton (near York), M. 9	*Mortun(e)* 298, 379
Muscoates	Not in D.B.
Myton on Swale, J. 8	*Mitune* 300b, 303, 306, 381 *bis*
Nageltone, *-tune*, *Naghelton*, *Nagletune*	See Nawton
Naton	See Kneeton
Nawton, M. 5	*Nageltone*, *-tune* 314b, 380b *Naghelton* 303 *Nagletune* 327b
Ne(i)sse	See Ness Hall
Ness Hall, M. 6	*Ne(i)sse* 325b, 327b, 380b
Nether Silton, K. 5	*Alia Silftune* 381
Neueham	See Newholme
Neuham	See Newham, Newholme
Neuhuse	See Newsham (in Amotherby), Newsham (in

Neuhuse cont.	Brompton), Newsham (near Kirby Wiske)
Neuhuson	See Newsham (near Hutton Magna)
Neuhusu	See Newsham (near Kirby Wiske)
Neuton	See Newton (near Levisham), Newton le Willows, Newton Morrell, Newton upon Ouse
Neutone, H. 4	Lost in Scorton, 309b, 381
Neutone	See East Newton, Newton Mulgrave, Newton Picot
Neutun	See East Newton
Neutune	See West Newton
Newbiggin	Not in D.B.
Newburgh	Not in D.B.
Neweham	See Newham
Newehusum	See Newsham (in Amotherby)
Newentune, *Neweton*	See East Newton
Newetone	See Newton (in West Ayton), Newton upon Ouse
Newetun	See Newton (near Guisborough), Newton (near Levisham), Newton (in West Ayton)
Newetune	See Newton (near Levisham), Newton Mulgrave, West Newton
Newham, K. 2	*Neuham* 380b *Neweham*, *Niu(u)eham* 300, 320b, 332b
Newholme, O. 2	*Neu(e)ham* 305, 380b
Newsham (in Amotherby), N. 6	*Neuhuse* 327b, 380b *Newe-*, *Niehusum* 300, 305b, 331, 332b
Newsham (in Brompton), J. 4	*Neuhuse* 299, 381
Newsham (near Hutton Magna), G. 3	*Neuhuson* 310, 381
Newsham (near Kirby Wiske), J. 5	*Neuhuse*, *-husu* 300b, 327, 381
Newton (near Guisborough), L. 2	*Newetun* 300, 380b *Nietona* 332b
Newton (near Levisham), O. 5	*Neuton* 380b *bis* *Newetun(e)* 299, 314
Newton (in West Ayton), P. 5	*Newetone*, *-tun* 299, 380b
Newton le Willows, H. 5	*Neuton* 312b, 381
Newton Morrell, H. 3	*Neuton* 309, 381
Newton Mulgrave, N. 2	*Neutone* 380b *Newetune* 305
Newton Picot, I. 5	*Neutone* 313, 381
Newton upon Ouse, K. 8	*Neuton* 381 *Newetone* 325b, 326
Niehusum	See Newsham (in Amotherby)
Nietona	See Newton (near Guisborough)
Niu(u)eham	See Newham
Noningtune, *Nonnin(c)tune*	See Nunnington
Nordfeld, *Norfel*	See Northfield
Normanby (near Eston), L. 2	*Normanebi* 305b, 320b, 323, 380b
Normanby (in Fylingdales), P. 3	*Normanebi* 300, 380b
Normanby (near Thornton Riseborough), N. 6	*Normanebi* 300b, 327b, 380b

Normanebi, I. 6	Lost in Carthorpe, 312b, 381
Normanebi	See Normanby (near Eston), Normanby (in Fylingdales), Normanby (near Thornton Riseborough)
Nortfigelinge	See Fyling Thorpe
Northallerton, J. 4	*Aluerton*, *-tune* 299, 309 *Aluretune* 381
North Cowton, I. 3	*Alia Cudton(e)* 309, 381
Northfield, P. 5	*Nordfeld*, *Norfel* 299, 380b
North Holme, M. 6	*Holm(e)* 300b, 380b *Hom* 314
North Kilvington, J. 5	*Chelvinctune* 306 *bis* *Chelvintun* 299, 381
North Otterington, J. 5	*Otrinctun*, *Otrintune* 299, 381
Norton	See Norton Conyers
Norton Conyers, I. 6	*Norton(e)* 304b, 380
Nortone	See Norton Conyers, Norton le Clay
Norton le Clay, J. 7	*Nortone* 308b, 380
Nunnigetune	See Nunnington
Nunnington, M. 6	*Noningtune*, *Nonnin(c)tune* 305b, 325b, 380b *Nunnigetune* 300b
Nunthorpe, L. 2	*Torp* 300, 332b, 380b
Odulfesmare, *Ouduluesmersc*, O. 6	Lost in Pickering Marishes, 299, 380b
Old Boulby, N. 2	*Bol(l)ebi* 300, 305, 380b
Old Byland, L. 5	*Begeland* 320b, 381
Old Malton, N. 7	*Maltun(e)* 300b *bis*, 303, 305b, 380b
Oldstead	Not in D.B.
Opetone, *-tune*, H. 6	Lost in Snape, 312, 381
Opsala	See Upsland
Ormesbi(a)	See Ormesby
Ormesby, K. 2	*Ormesbi(a)* 331 *bis* 332b, 380b
Osbaldwick, M. 9	*Osboldewic* 298, 303b, 379
Osboldewic	See Osbaldwick
Osgodby, Q. 5	*Asgozbi* 299, 380b
Osgoodby, K. 6	*Ansgotebi* 327
Osmotherley, K. 4	*Asmundrelac* 300b, 381
Ostrinctune	See South Otterington
Oswaldescherca, *-cherce*	See Oswaldkirk
Oswaldkirk, L. 6	*Oswaldescherca*, *-cherce* 305b, 314, 380b
Otrinctun	See North Otterington
Otrintona	See South Otterington
Otrintune	See North Otterington, South Otterington
Ouduluesmersc	See *Odulfesmare*
Oulston, L. 7	*Uluestone*, *-tun* 300b *bis*, 330, 381
Ounesbi, I. 5	Lost in Gatenby, 313, 381
Oustorp	See Pinchingthorpe
Over Dinsdale, I. 2	*Di(g)neshale* 299, 381 *Dirneshala*, *-hale* 309, 381
Over Silton, K. 4	*Silftune*, *Siluetune* 300b, 381
Overton, L. 9	*Overtun(e)* 298b *bis*, 379 *Ovretun* 313
Overtun(e)	See Overton
Ovington, G. 2	*Ulfeton* 309, 381
Ovretun	See Overton

Parva Edestun	See Little Edstone
Parva Mersc	See Little Marish
Patrick Brompton, H. 5	*Brunton(e)* 312b, 381
Picala, -le	See Pickhill
Picheringa, -inge	See Pickering
Pickering, N. 6	*Picheringa, -inge* 299, 380b
Pickhill, I. 6	*Picala, -le* 313, 381
Pinchingthorpe, L. 2	*Oustorp* 332b *Torp* 300, 320b, 380b
Pochelac, -laf	See Pockley
Pockley, M. 5	*Pochelac, -laf* 303, 305b, 380b
Potto	Not in D.B.
Prestby, P. 2	*Prestebi* 305 *bis*, 380b
Prestebi	See Prestby
Presteton, -tune	See Preston (in Hutton Buscel)
Preston	See Preston upon Scar
Preston (in Hutton Buscel), P. 5	*Presteton, -tune* 299, 380b
Preston upon Scar, F. 6	*Preston, -tun* 311, 381
Prestun	See Preston upon Scar
Quennebi	See Whenby
Raininchton, Rainingewat	See Rainton
Rainton, J. 7	*Rainingewat* 381 *Ranewat* (*Raininchton* superscribed) 323 *Reineton* 313, 381
Ranewat	See Rainton
Rantune	See East Rounton
Raschel	See Raskelf
Raskelf, K. 7	*Raschel* 300b, 381
Ravene(s)torp	See Ravensthorpe
Ravenesu(u)et	See Ravensworth
Ravensthorpe, K. 5	*Ravene(s)torp* 299, 327b *bis*, 381
Ravensworth, G. 3	*Ravenesu(u)et* 310, 381
Rawcliff Banks, M. 2	*Roudclive*, *Roudeclif* 305, 380b
Rawcliffe, L. 9	*Roudclif*, *Roudeclif(e)* 298b, 301, 379
Redmire, F. 6	*Ridemare* 311, 381
Reeth, F. 5	*Rie* 311, 381
Reineton	See Rainton
Ricalf	See Riccall
Riccall, M. 6	*Ricalf* 300b, 380b
Richmond, H. 4	*Hindrelag(he)* 309b, 311 *Indrelag(e)* 381 *bis*
Ridemare	See Redmire
Rie	See Reeth
Rievaulx	Not in D.B.
Risewic	See Ruswick
Ritone, -tun	See Ryton
Rochebi	See Rokeby
Rocuid	See Rockwith
Rodebestorp, *Roudeluestorp*, R. 6	Lost in Gristhorpe, 299, 380b
Rodebi	See Rudby
Rokeby, F. 4	*Rochebi* 310, 381
Romaldkirk, F. 3	*Rumoldesc(h)erce* 310, 381
Romanby, J. 4	*Romund(r)ebi* 299 *bis*, 300b, 381 *ter*
Romund(r)ebi	See Romanby
Rontun	See East Rounton
Rookwith, H. 5	*Rocuid* 312, 381
Roscebi	See Roxby (near Loftus)
Roscheltorp	See Roskelthorpe
Rosedale	Not in D.B.
Roskelthorpe, N. 2	*Roscheltorp* 305, 380b
Rostun(e)	See Ruston
Roudclif	See Rawcliffe
Roudclive	See Rawcliff Banks
Roudeclif	See Rawcliff Banks, Rawcliffe
Roudeclife	See Rawcliffe
Roudeluestorp	See *Rodebestorp*
Roxby (near Loftus), N. 2	*Roscebi* 305 *ter* *Rozebi* 300, 380b

Roxby (in Thornton Dale), O. 6	*Rozebi* 299, 380b
Rozebi	See Roxby (near Loftus), Roxby (in Thornton Dale)
Rudby, K. 3	*Rodebi* 305b
Rumoldesc(h)erce	See Romaldkirk
Runtune	See West Rounton
Ruston, P. 6	*Rostun(e)* 299, 380b
Ruswick, H. 5	*Risewic* 312b, 381
Ryton, N. 7	*Ritone*, *-tun* 300, 327b, 380b
Salescale, N. 6	Lost in Ryton, 380b
Saletun	See Salton
Saltburn by the Sea	Not in D.B.
Salton, N. 6	*Saletun* 303, 380b
Sambura, *-bure*	See Sandburn
Sandburn, M. 8	*Sambura*, *-bure* 298, 379
Sand Hutton (near Thirsk), J. 6	*Hot(t)une* 299, 381
Sand Hutton (near York), M. 8	*Hotone*, *Hotun(e)* 300b, 373, 381 *Hottune* 327b
Scachelden(e)	See Scackleton
Scackleton, M. 7	*Eschalchedene* 327b *Scachelden(e)* 300b, 305b, 380b
Scage(s)torp	See Scawthorpe
Scalby, Q. 5	*Scal(l)ebi* 299, 380b
Scalebi	See Scalby
Scalftun	See West Scrafton
Scallebi	See Scalby
Scaltun(e)	See Scawton
Scarborough	Not in D.B.
Scargill, F. 4	*Scracreghil* 309 *Seacreghil* 381
Scawthorpe, R. 6	*Scage(s)torp* 299, 380b
Scawton, L. 6	*Scaltun(e)* 305b, 320b, 380b
Sceltun	See Skelton (near Saltburn), Skelton (near York)
Scetun(e)	See Seaton
Scheltun	See Skelton (near Saltburn), Skelton (near York)
Schipetune	See Skipton on Swale
Schirebi	See Skeeby
Scorton, H. 4	*Scortone* 310, 381
Scortone	See Scorton
Scotton, H. 4	*Scot(t)une* 310b, 381
Scot(t)une	See Scotton
Scoxebi	See Skewsby
Scracreghil	See Scargill
Scraftun	See West Scrafton
Scruton, I. 5	*Scurueton(e)* 310b, 381
Scurueton(e)	See Scruton
Seacreghil	See Scargill
Seamer (near Scarborough), Q. 6	*Semær*, *Semer* 323, 380b
Seamer (near Stokesley), K. 3	*Semer(s)* 305b, 380b
Seaton, N. 2	*Scetun(e)* 305, 380b
Selungesbi	See Slingsby
Semær	See Semer (near Scarborough)
Semer	See Semer (near Scarborough), Semer (near Stokesley)
Semers	See Semer (near Stokesley)
Senerebi	See Sinderby
Sessay, K. 7	*Sezai* 304b *bis*, 381
Seuenetorp, I. 5	Lost in Swainby, 313, 381
Sevenictun	See Sinnington
Sexhow	Not in D.B.
Sezai	See Sessay
Sheriff Hutton, M. 8	*Hotone*, *-tun(e)* 300b, 306, 373, 380b

Shipton, L. 8	*Hipton* 381
Sig(h)estun	See Sigston
Sigston, J. 4	*Sig(h)estun* 299, 381
Silftune	See Over Silton
Silftune, Alia	See Nether Silton
Siluetune	See Over Silton
Sinderby, I. 6	*Senerebi* 313, 381
Sinnington, N. 5	*Sevenictun* 314
	Siveníntun 380b
	Siverinctun, -intune 314b, 380b
Sivenintun, Siverinctun, -intune	See Sinnington
Siwartorp	See Swarthorpe
Skeeby, H. 3	*Schirebi* 309b, 381
Skelton (near Saltburn), M. 2	*Sc(h)eltun* 305b, 380b
Skelton (near York), L. 9	*Sc(h)eltun* 298b, 301, 313, 379
Skewsby, M. 7	*Scoxebi* 306, 381
Skipton on Swale, J. 6	*Schipetune* 323
Skutterskelfe, K. 3	*Codeschelf* 331
	Codresche(l)f 300, 305b
Slingsby, M. 7	*Eslingesbi* 327b
	Selungesbi 305b, 380b
Smet(t)on	See Great Smeaton
Smidetun(e)	See Great Smeaton, Little Smeaton
Smitune	See Little Smeaton
Snainton, P. 6	*Snechintone, -tun(e)* 299, 314, 323, 330, 380b
Snape	Not in D.B.
Sneaton, O. 3	*Sneton, -tune* 305, 380b
Snechintone, -tun(e)	See Snainton
Sneton, -tune	See Sneaton
Snilesworth	Not in D.B.
Solberge, J. 5	*Solberge* 309b, 381
Sorebi	See Sowerby (near Thirsk)
Sourebi	See Sowerby (in Whitby), Sowerby under Cotcliffe

South Cowton, I. 3	*Cudton(e)* 309, 381
South Holme, M. 6	*Holm(e)* 325b, 327b, 380b
South Loftus, N. 2	*Loctehusum* 380b
	Loctushum 305
South Otterington, J. 5	*Ostrinctune* 300b
	Otrintona, -tune 332b, 381
Sowerby (near Thirsk), J. 6	*Sorebi* 299, 300b, 381
Sowerby (in Whitby), O. 3	*Sourebi* 305 *bis*, 380b
Sowerby under Cotcliffe, J. 4	*Sourebi* 299, 301, 381 *bis*
Spantun(e)	See Spaunton
Spaunton, N. 5	*Spantun(e)* 314, 380b
Speningetorp	See Spennithorne
Spennithorne, G. 5	*Speningetorp* 311b, 381
Sprostune	See Sproxton
Sproxton, L. 6	*Sprostune* 300b, 380b
Stainegrif	See Stonegrave
Stainsacre	Not in D.B.
Stainsby, K. 2	*Steinesbi* 305, 380b
Stainton (near Reeth)	Not in D.B.
Stainton (in Stanghow), M. 2	*Esteintona* 332b
	Steintun 300, 305 2nd entry, 380b
Stainton (near Thornaby on Tees), K. 2	*Steintun* 305 1st entry, 320b *bis*, 380b
Stainton Dales, P. 4	*Steintun* 299, 380b
Stanegrif	See Stonegrave
Stanwick, H. 2	*Alia Stenweghe* 309
	In duabus Steinueges 381
	Ste(i)nwege 309, 381
	Stenweghes 309
Staple(n)dun	See Stapleton
Stapleton, H. 2	*Staple(n)dun* 309 *bis*, 381 *bis*
Startforth, F. 3	*Stradford* 309b, 381

Thirn, H. 5	*Thirne* 312, 381
Thirne	See Thirn
Thirsk, J. 6	*Tresc*, *Tresch(e)* 300b, 327, 381
Tholthorpe, K. 7	*Turoluestorp* 381 *Turulfestorp* 303
Thoralby, F. 7	*Turo(l)desbi* 311, 381
Thoraldby, K. 3	*Tor-*, *Turoldesbi* 300, 331, 380b
Thoresby (near Castle Bolton), F. 6	*Toresbi* 311, 311b, 381 *bis*
Thormanby, K. 7	*Tor-*, *Turmozbi* 299, 320b, 381
Thornaby, K. 2	*Tormozbi(a)* 300, 305, 320b, 332b *Turmozbi* 380b
Thornbrough	Not in D.B.
Thornton (near Thornaby on Tees), K. 2	*Torentun* 305, 320b, 380b
Thornton (in Thornton Watlass), H. 5	*Torreton*, *-tun* 312, 381
Thornton Bridge, J. 7	*Torenton(e)* 330, 380
Thornton Dale, O. 6	*Torentona*, *-tun(e)* 299, 300, 314, 333, 380b
Thornton Fields, L. 2	*Tornetun* 300, 380b
Thornton le Beans, J. 5	*Gristorentun* 299, 381
Thornton le Clay, M. 8	*Torentun(e)* 306, 313, 320b, 381
Thornton le Moor, J. 5	*Torentone*, *-tune* 320b, 381
Thornton le Street, J. 5	*Torentun* 299, 381
Thornton on the Hill	Not in D.B.
Thornton Riseborough, N. 6	*Tornentun* 380b *Tornitun* 300
Thornton Rust, E. 6	*Tore(n)ton* 311, 381
Thornton Steward, H. 5	*Tornenton(e)* 311b, 381
Thornton Watlass	See Thornton; see Watlass
Thorpe (in Sutton on the Forest), L. 8	*Torp* 299, 381
Thorpe (near Wycliffe), G. 2	*Torp* 309, 381
Thorpefield (near Scarborough), Q. 5	*Torp* 323, 380b
Thorpefield (near Thirsk), J. 6	*Torp* 327 2nd entry
Thorpe Hill, N. 8	*Torp* 327b
Thorpe le Willows, L. 6	*Torp* 300b, 381
Thorpe Perrow, I. 5	*Torp* 312, 381
Thrintoft, I. 4	*Tirnecoste*, *-etoste* 309b, 381
Tilstun(e)	See Stiltons
Timbelbi, *-belli*	See Thimbleby
Tirnecoste, *-etoste*	See Thrintoft
Tocketts, M. 2	*Tocstune* 380b *Toscutun* 305b
Tocstune	See Tocketts
Tolentun	See Tollerton
Tolesbi	See Tollesby
Tollerton, K. 8	*Tolentun* 303 *Tolletune* 381
Tollesbi	See Tollesby
Tollesby, K. 2	*Tol(l)esbi* 300, 320b, 331, 332b, 380b
Tolletune	See Tollerton
Ton(n)estale	See Tunstall (near Stokesley)
Topcliffe, J. 6	*Topeclive* 323, 381
Topeclive	See Topcliffe
Torenton	See Thornton Bridge, Thornton Rust
Torentona	See Thornton Dale
Torentone	See Thornton Bridge, Thornton le Moor
Torentun	See Thornton (near Thornaby on Tees), Thornton Dale, Thornton le Clay, Thornton le Street

Torentune	See Thornton Dale, Thornton le Clay, Thornton le Moor
Toresbi	See Thoresby
Toresbi, K. 8	Lost in Newton upon Ouse, 325b, 381
Toreton	See Thornton Rust
Tormoȝbi	See Thormanby, Thornaby
Tormoȝbia	See Thornaby
Tornelai	See Thirley Cotes
Tornenton(e)	See Thornton Steward
Tornentun	See Thornton Riseborough
Torneslag	See Thirley Cotes
Torneton	See Cowling
Tornetun	See Thornton Fields
Tornitun	See Thornton Riseborough
Toroldesbi	See Thoraldby
Torp	See Kilton Thorpe, Langthorpe, Nunthorpe, Pinchingthorpe, Thorpe (in Sutton on the Forest), Thorpe (near Wycliffe), Thorpefield (near Scarborough), Thorpefield (near Thirsk), Thorpe Hill, Thorpe le Willows, Thorpe Perrow
Torp, H. 3	Lost in Croft, 309b, 381
Torp, J. 6	Lost in Pickhill, 304b, 380
Torreton, *-tun*	See Thornton (in Thornton Watlass)
Toscutun	See Tocketts
Touetorp	See Towthorpe
Towthorpe, M. 8	*Touetorp* 303b, 381

Tresc, *Tresch(e)*	See Thirsk
Troutsdale, P. 5	*Truȝstal* 300, 380b
Truȝstal	See Troutsdale
Tuislebroc	See Twislebrook
Tunestale	See Tunstall (near Catterick)
Tunstall (near Catterick), H. 4	*Tunestale* 310b *bis*, 381 *bis*
Tunstall (near Stokesley), K. 2	*Ton(n)estale* 300, 380b
Turchilebi	See Thirkleby
Turmoȝbi	See Thormanby, Thornaby
Turodesbi	See Thoralby
Turoldesbi	See Thoralby, Thoraldby
Turolues-, *Turulfestorp*	See Tholthorpe
Twislebrook, H. 6	*Tuislebroc* 312, 381
Uckerby	Not in D.B.
Udreswelle	See Hudswell
Ugetorp	See Ugthorpe
Ugglebarnby, O. 3	*Ugle-*, *Ulgeberdesbi* 305, 380b
Ughetorp	See Ugthorpe
Ugleberdesbi	See Ugglebarnby
Ugthorpe, N. 2	*Ug(h)etorp* 300, 380b
Ulfeton	See Ovington
Ulgeberdesbi	See Ugglebarnby
Uluestone, *-tun*	See Oulston
Upelider	See Upleatham
Upes(h)ale	See Upsall (near Eston)
Upleatham, M. 1	*Upelider* 305, 380b
Upper Helmsley, M. 9	*Hamelsec(h)* 306, 381
Upsale	See Upsall (near Kirkby Knowle), Upsland
Upsall (near Eston), L. 2	*Upes(h)ale* 300, 331, 332b, 380b
Upsall (near Kirkby Knowle), K. 5	*Upsale* 306 *bis*, 381
Upsland, I. 6	*Opsala* 312b *Upsale* 381

Wad	See Wath (near Hovingham)
Wadles	See Watlass
Walburn	Not in D.B.
Walesgrif, *-grip*	See Falsgrave
Waleton, *-tun(e)*	See Walton
Wallesgrif	See Falsgrave
Walton, M. 6	*Waleton*, *-tun(e)* 314b, 327b, 380b
Wardhilla, *Ward(h)ille*	See Warthill
Warlaby, I. 5	*Warlavesbi* 310, 381 *Wergelesbi* 299 *Werlegesbi* 381
Warlavesbi	See Warlaby
Warthill, M. 9	*Wardhilla*, *Ward(h)ille* 303, 306, 381
Waruelestorp, K. 8	Lost in Tollerton, 306
Wass	Not in D.B.
Wat	See Wath (near East Tanfield)
Wath (near East Tanfield), I. 6	*Wat* 312b, 381
Wath (near Hovingham), M. 7	*Wad* 327b
Watlass (in Thornton Watlass), H. 5	*Wadles* 312, 381
Welberga	See Welbury
Welburn (near Bulmer), N. 7	*Wellebrune* 306, 380b
Welburn (near Kirkby Moorside), M. 5	*Wellebrune* 300b, 314b, 327b, 380b
Welbury, J. 3	*Welberga* 332b *Welleberg(e)* 300b, 381
Well, I. 6	*Welle* 312 *bis*, 381
Welle	See Well
Welleberg(e)	See Welbury
Wellebrune	See Welburn (near Bulmer), Welburn (near Kirkby Moorside)
Wendreslaga, *Alia Wendreslaga*	See Wensley
Wensley, G. 5	*Alia Wendreslaga* 311b *In duabus Wentreslage* 381 *Wendreslaga* 311b
Wentreslage, *In duabus*	See Wensley
Wercesel	See High Worsall
Wercesel, *Alia*; *Wercheshala*	See Low Worsall
Wereltun	See Wrelton
Wergelesbi, *Werlegesbi*	See Warlaby
Werton	See Worton
Weslide	See Kirkleatham
West Acklam, K. 2	*Achelum* 332b *Aclum*, *Aclun* 300, 305, 320b, 380b
West Ayton, P. 5	*Alia Atune* 380b *Atune* 299
West Bolton, F. 6	*Alia Bodelton* 311, 381
West Burton, F. 7	*Burton* 311, 381
Westerdale	Not in D.B.
West Harlsey, J. 4	*In duabus Erleseie* 381 *Herelsaie* 299 *Herlesege* 300b *Herselaige* 381
West Hauxwell, G. 4	*Alia Hauoc(he)swelle* 311b, 381
Westhouse, J. 4	*Westhuse* 299, 381
Westhuse	See Westhouse
West Layton, G. 3	*Laston*, *-tun* 309, 381
Westlid(um), *-lidun*	See Kirkleatham
West Lilling, M. 8	*Lilinga*, *-inge* 300b, 306, 381
West Newton, M. 6	*Neutune*, *Newetune* 300b, 380b
West Rounton, J. 3	*Runtune* 299, 381
West Scrafton, F. 7	*Scalf-*, *Scraftun* 311b, 381
West Tanfield, I. 6	*Alia Tanefeld* 312b, 381
Westude	See Kirkleatham

West Witton, F. 6	*Witun* 311b, 381
Whashton	Not in D.B.
Whenby, M. 7	*Quennebi* 381
Whitby, P. 2	*Witebi* 305, 373, 380b
Whitwell	Not in D.B.
Whitwell on the Hill, N. 8	*Witeuella*, *-uuelle* 306, 381
Whorlton, K. 3	*Wirueltun(e)* 305b *bis*, 380b
Wibedstune	See Wide Open
Wicam	See Wykeham (near Scarborough)
Wich	See Wykeham (in Malton)
Wicham	See Wykeham (near Scarborough)
Wich(e), *Alia*	See Wykeham Hill
Wichingastorp	See Wigganthorpe
Wichintun, *-istun*	See Wigginton
Wichum	See Wykeham Hill
Wicum	See Wykeham (in Malton)
Wide Open, L. 9	*Wibedstune* 381 *Wipestune* 303
Widtune	See Wilton (near Eston)
Wigganthorpe, M. 7	*Wichingatorp* 300b, 306, 314, 380b
Wigginton, L. 8	*Wichintun*, *-istun* 298b, 379
Wilbetun	See Wombleton
Wildon, K. 6	*Wilema* 327
Wilema	See Wildon
Wilton (near Eston), L. 1	*Widtune*, *Wiltune* 305b, 331 *ter*, 380b
Wilton (near Pickering), O. 6	*Wiltune* 299, 380b
Wiltune	See Wilton (near Eston), Wilton (near Pickering)
Winbeltun	See Wombleton
Winetun(e)	See Winton
Winton, J. 4	*Winetun(e)* 304b, 381

Wipestune	See Wide Open
Wirceshel, *In duabus*	See High Worsall, Low Worsall
Wirueltun(e)	See Whorlton
Witclive	See Wycliffe
Witebi	See Whitby
Witeuella, *-uuelle*	See Whitwell on the Hill
Witone	See East Witton
Witun	See East Witton, West Witton
Witune	See East Witton
Wombleton, M. 6	*Wilbetun* 303 *Winbeltun* 380b
Worton, E. 6	*Werton* 311, 381
Wrelton, N. 5	*Wereltun* 300, 380b
Wycliffe, G. 2	*Witclive* 309, 381
Wykeham (in Malton), O. 7	*Wich*, *Wicum* 300b, 380b
Wykeham (near Scarborough), P. 6	*Wic(h)am* 299, 300, 333, 380b
Wykeham Hill (in Malton), O. 7	*Alia Wich(e)* 300b, 380b *Wichum* 303, 325b
Yafforth, I. 4	*Eiford* 310, 381 *Iaforbe* 299 *Ia(i)forde* 299, 381 *bis*
Yarm, J. 2	*Gerou* 332b *Iarun* 300b, 381
Yarnwick, I. 6	*Gernuic* 312b, 381
Yearsley, L. 7	*Eureslage* 327
York, L. 9	*Eboracum* 298, 327, 379, Yorks.; 100, Som. *juxta ciuitatem Eboraci* 327 *juxta ciuitatem* 302b, 379b *juxta urbem* 379b *Eburacum*, Exon D.B. 88, Som. *Eurewic*, L.D.B. 15, Ess.
Youlton, K. 8	*Ioletun(e)* 303, 381

ANONYMOUS HOLDINGS

No place-names appear in the following two entries. It is possible either of these (or even both) refer to holdings at places not named elsewhere in Domesday Book:

Archbishop of York, 15 carucates *juxta ciuitatem*, 312b, 379b. Counted with York.

Richard son of Erfast, half a carucate and 3 tofts *juxta ciuitatem Eboraci*, 327; *juxta urbem*, 379b. Counted with York.

PLACES IN WALES

CHESHIRE FOLIOS

MAP 6

Allington, D. 6	*Allentune* 266b
Aston, D. 5	*Estone* 268b
Axton, A. 4	*Asketone* 269
Bagillt, C. 4	*Bachelie* 268b
Bettisfield, E. 9	*Bed(d)esfeld* 263, 264
Bistre, C. 6	*Biscopestreu* 269 *ter*
Blorant, A. 4	*Blorat* 269
Bodeugan, A. 4	*Bodugan* 269
Boteuuarul	Unid., 269
Broncoed, C. 6	*Bruncot* 269
Broughton, D. 6	*Brochetone*, *-tune* 268b *ter*
Bryn, A. 2	*Bren* 269 *bis*
Brynford, B. 4	*Brunfor(d)* 269 *bis*
Bryngwyn, A. 4	*Brenuuen* 269
Bryn-hedydd, B. 4	*Brennehedui* 269
Bychton, B. 4	*Putecain* 269
Caerwys, B. 4	*Cairos* 269
Calcot, B. 4	*Caldecote* 269
Carn-y-chain, A. 4	*Cancarnacan* 269
Cefndy, A. 4	*Keuend* 269
Chespuic	Unid., 268
Cilowen, A. 4	*Chiluen* 269
Claitone	Unid., 268b
Coiwen	Unid., 269
Coleshill, C. 4	*Coleselt* 268b
Cwybr, A. 4	*Cauber* 269
Cwybr-bach, A. 4	*Parva Cauber* 269
Cyrchynan, A. 4	*Charcan* 269

Danfrond	Unid., 269
Dincolyn, A. 4	*Dicolin* 269
Dissaren	Unid., 269
Dyserth, A. 4	*Dissard* 269
Edritone	Unid., 268b
Erbistock, D. 8	*Erpestoch* 267b
Eyton, D. 8	*Eitune* 263, 266b
Fulbrook (now Greenfield), B. 4	*Folebroc* 269
Gellilyfdy, B. 4	*Cheslilaued* 269
Golden Grove formerly Gwlgrave, A. 3	*Uluesgraue* 269
Golftyn, C. 5	*Ulfemiltone* 268b
Gop, A. 4	*Rahop* 269
Gresford, D. 7	*Gretford* 267b, 268
Gronant, A. 3	*Gronant* 269
Gwaenysgor, A. 4	*Wenescol* 269
Gwespyr, B. 3	*Wesberie* 269
Gwysaney, C. 5	*Quisnan* 269
Halkyn, C. 5	*Alchene* 269
	Helchene 269
Hawarden, D. 5	*Haordine* 268b
Hendrebiffa, C. 6	*Hendrebifau* 269
Hiraddug, A. 4	*Raduch* 269
Hope, D. 6	*Hope* 267
Horsepol, Duae	Unid., 269
Hoseley, D. 7	*Odeslei* 263

Inglecroft	Unid., 269
Iscoyd, F. 8	*Burwardestone* 264
Kelston, A. 3	*Calstan* 269
Leadbrook, C. 5	*Latbroc* 268b
Legge	Unid., 269
Llewerllyd, A. 4	*Lauarludon* 269
	Leuuarludae 269
Llysdan Hunedd, B. 5	*Lesthunied* 269
Llys Edwin, C. 5	*Castretone* 268b
Llys y Coed, B. 5	*Lessecoit* 269
Maen-Efa, A. 4	*Maineual* 269
Mechlas, B. 5	*Moclitone* 269
Meincatis	Unid., 269
Melchanestone	Unid., 269
Meliden, A. 4	*Ruestoch* 269
Mertyn, B. 4	*Meretone* 269
Mostyn, B. 4	*Mostone* 269
Mulintone	Unid., 269 *bis*
Munentone	Unid., 269
Penegors	Unid., 269
Pengdeslion	Unid., 269
Pentre, A. 4	*Peintret* 269
Picton, B. 3	*Pichetone* 269
Prestatyn, A. 3	*Prestetone* 269
Radington, C. 5	*Radintone* 268b
Radnor (near Gresford), D. 6	*Radenoure* 268
Rhos Ithel, C. 6	*Risteselle* 269
Rhuddlan, A. 4	*Roelend*, *-lent* 269 *quin*
Rhydorddwy, A. 3	*Reuuordui* 269
Ruargor	Unid., 269
St Asaph (Llan Elwy), A. 4	*Lanuuile* 269
Soughton, C. 5	*Sutone* 268b
Sudfell	Unid., 269
Sutton, E. 7	*Sutone* 266b
Tredueng	Unid., 269
Trefraith, B. 4	*Treueri* 269
Trelawnyd, A. 4	*Riuelenoit* 269
Trellyniau, B. 5	*Treuelesneu* 269
Tremeirchion, A. 4	*Dinmersch* 269
Ulchenol	Unid., 269
Weltune	Unid., 269
Wenfesne	Unid., 269
Wepre, D. 5	*Wepre* 263b, 268b
Whitford, B. 4	*Widford* 269 *bis*
Widhulde	Unid., 269
Wiselei	Unid., 269
Witestan	Unid., 269
Worthenbury, E. 7	*Hurdingberie* 264
Ysceifiog, B. 5	*Schiuian* 269

ANONYMOUS HOLDINGS

Domesday Cheshire extended far to the west of the modern county, and it included the whole of what is now Flintshire and part of what is now Denbighshire. To the west (i.e. beyond the Clwyd) were two districts of Rhos and Rhufoniog (*Ros et Reweniou*) for which but few resources and no named settlements were entered in the Domesday folios. Farther west still, presumably beyond the Conway, was *Nortwales* which comprised the principality of Gwynedd. We also hear of the hundred of *Arvester* which has been identified with the district of Arwystli to the south of Gwynedd. These districts are mentioned at the foot of folio 269 but we are told nothing of their settlements.

GLOUCESTERSHIRE FOLIOS

MAP 18

Caerleon, A. 7 (see also under Heref.)	*Carleion* 162	Dinham, B. 7	*Dinan* 162
Caerwent, B. 7	*Caroen* 162 *bis*	Llanvair-Discoed, B. 7	*Lamecare* 162
Caldicot, B. 7	*Caldecote* 162		
Chepstow, C. 6	*Estrighoiel* 162 *Strigoielg* 162	Portskewett, B. 7	*Poteschiuet* 162

ANONYMOUS HOLDINGS

The somewhat anomalous description of the land beyond the present county of Gloucester (i.e. beyond the Wye) refers only sporadically to population and resources, and names only the seven places set out above. The rest of the description is couched in general terms, e.g. 'in Wales' or 'between the Usk and the Wye' or 'beyond the Usk'. Reference is made to 71 vills, 4 wasted vills, one *wasta terra*, and to 12 other holdings. These details are set out below in the order in which they occur on folio 162:

Under Waswic the reeve, 13 vills.
Under Elmui the reeve, 14 vills.
Under Bleio the reeve, 13 vills.
Under Idhel the reeve, 14 vills.
Under the same reeves, 4 wasted vills.
Walter the crossbowman, *una wasta terra.*
Berdic the king's jester, 3 vills.
Morinus, one vill.
Chenesis, one vill.
Son of Waswic, one vill.
Sessisbert, one vill.
Abraham the priest, 2 vills.
The king, one vill.
St Michael, one carucate.
St Dewin, one carucate.
Beluard of Caerwent, half a carucate.
Walter the crossbowman, 2 carucates.
Girard, 2 carucates.
Ovus the king's reeve, 2 carucates.
King's demesne, one carucate.
Bishop of Coutances (from the king), 5 carucates.
William of Eu, 32 carucates in Wales.
Turstin son of Rolf, *inter Huscham et Waiam*, 17 ploughlands
Turstin son of Rolf, *ultram Huscham*, 6 carucates.
Alvred de Hispaniensis, 2 carucates.
Alvred de Hispaniensis, 7 vills in Wales.

HEREFORDSHIRE FOLIOS

MAP 22

Burlingjobb, A. 3	*Berchelincope* 181	Harpton, A. 3	*Hertune* 186b *Ortune* 183b
Caerleon, Map 18, A. 7 (see also under Gloucs.)	*Carlion* 185b	Monmouth, D. 9	*Monemude* 180b
Cascob, A. 2 (see also under Salop.)	*Cascope* 186b	Old Radnor, A. 3	*Raddrenoue* 181
Clatterbrune, A. 3	*Clatretune* 186b	Pilleth on Lugg, A. 2	*Pelelei* 183b
Discoed, A. 3	*Discote* 186b	*Querentune*, A. 3	Lost in Presteigne, 186b

ANONYMOUS HOLDINGS

A possible anonymous holding is the eight carucates held by William de Scohies in the jurisdiction of Caerleon castle (*in castellaria de Carlion*), 185b.

SHROPSHIRE FOLIOS

MAPS 40–41

Ackhill, C. 11	*Achel* 260	Hyssington, C. 8	*Stantune* 254
Ackley, B. 7	*Achelai* 254 *ter*	Knighton, B. 10	*Chenistetune* 260b
Aston, C. 8	*Estone* 254	Leighton, B. 6	*Lestune* 255b
Bausley, C. 6	*Beleslei* 255b	Mellington, B. 8	*Muletune*, *Mulitune* 254, 259b
Cascob, C. 11 (see also under Heref.)	*Cascop* 260	Montgomery, B. 7	*Montgomeri* 253b *Muntgumeri* 254
Castlewright, B. 8	*Cestelop* 254	Norton, C. 11	*Nortune* 260b
Churchstoke, B. 8	*Cirestoc* 259b	Stanage, C. 10	*Stanege* 260
Edderton, B. 7	*Edritune* 254 *bis*	Thornbury, B. 7	*Torneberie* 254
Forden, B. 7	*Furtune* 254	Weston, B. 8	*Westune* 254
Goseford	Unid., 254	Wolston Mynd, B.7	*Ulestanesmude* 254
Hem, B. 7	*Heme* 254 *bis*	Woodluston, A. 7	*Wadelestun* 254
Hopton, B. 8	*Hoptune* 254	Wropton, B. 7	*Urbetune* 254
Horseforde	Unid., 254		

ANONYMOUS HOLDINGS

The Shropshire folios record 25 named places in that part of Wales to the west of the county; these are set out above. There are in addition four general references to districts in Wales and these do not specify individual vills or holdings. They are set out below in the order in which they occur in the folios for the county:

Tuder, a certain Welshman (from Earl Roger), a district of Welsh land (*fines terrae Walensis*), 253b. Possibly the Welsh commote of Nanheudwy in the Vale of Llangollen.

Earl Roger, a district of Wales (*de uno fine de Walis*), 253b. Probably the hundred of *Arvester* (Arwystli) mentioned in the Cheshire folios (269) – see p. 541.

Earl Hugh (from Earl Roger), in Wales the land of Ial or Yale (*in Walis terra de Gal*), 254.

Rainald the sheriff (from Earl Roger), in Wales two districts, Cynllaith and Edeyrnion (*duo fines Chenlei et Derniou in Walis*), 255.

KEY TO MAPS

The county boundaries are those of about 1900

Symbol	Example	Meaning
■	COLCHESTER	Domesday borough
●	Grantchester	Domesday vill
●	*Mycelegata*	Domesday vill of uncertain site (i.e. lost) but of known parish
○	Little Shelford	Adjoining places not separately distinguished in Domesday Book but having same basic name
●	(Ballingham)	Unnamed in Domesday Book but identified from associated documents

Height of land

Feet	Metres
800	245
400	122
200	61
0	0

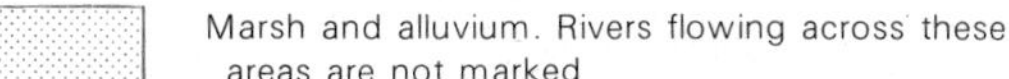

Marsh and alluvium. Rivers flowing across these areas are not marked

Scale: Six miles to one inch

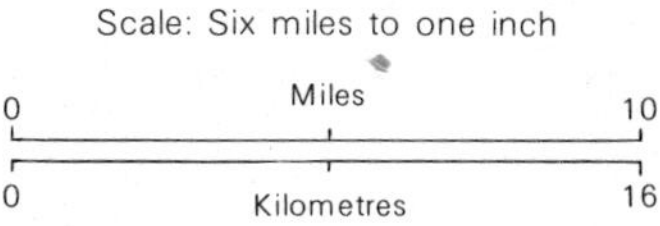

2 BEDFORDSHIRE

A B C D E F G H I

1 2 3 4 5 6

Wytham
Seacourt
Cumnor
Eaton
Bessels Leigh
Kennington
Bayworth
Sugworth
Sunningwell
Appleton
Dry Sandford
Tubney
Shippon
Barton
Abingdon
Marcham
Frilford
Kingston Bagpuize
Fyfield
Draycott
Duxford
Longworth
Hinton Waldrist
Garford
Drayton
Sutton Courtenay
Appleford
Long Wittenham
Little Wittenham
Milton
Steventon
Willington
Brightwell
Sotwell
Clapcot
WALLINGFORD
North Moreton
South Moreton
Cholsey
Aston Tirrold
Lollingdon
Blewbury
Hagbourne
East Hagbourne
Upton
Chilton
Harwell
Fulscot
East Hendred
West Hendred
Ardington
West Hagbourne
East Lockinge
Ginge
West Lockinge
Wantage
Charlton
Betterton
Letcombe Bassett
Letcombe Regis
East Hanney
West Hanney
Denchworth
Charney Bassett
Lyford
Goosey
Stanford in the Vale
East Challow
West Challow
Childrey
Sparsholt
Uffington
Woolstone
Compton Beauchamp
Odstone
Knighton
Ashbury
Shrivenham
Beckett
Watchfield
Great Coxwell
Little Coxwell
Coleshill
Eaton Hastings
Buscot
Great Faringdon
Shellingford
Hatford
Pusey
Littleworth
Buckland
Newton
Carswell
R. Ock
Farnborough
Fawley
Woolley
Whatcombe
Lambourn
Bockhampton
R. Lambourn
West Ilsley
Hodcott
East Ilsley
Catmore
Compton
Aldworth
Streatley
Ashridge
Beedon
Brightwalton
Chaddleworth
Peasemore
Leckhampstead
Hartridge
Hampstead Norris
Basildon
Pangbourne
Yattendon
Eling
Chieveley
Curridge
Frilsham
Wellhouse
Bradfield
Stanford Dingley
R. Pang
Bucklebury
West Shefford
East Shefford
Weston
Welford
Boxford
Winterbourne
Donnington
Shaw
Bagnor
Speen
Newbury
Greenham
Thatcham
Crookham
Midgham
Woolhampton
Brimpton
Wasing
Aldermaston
Padworth
Ufton Nervet
Hampstead Marshall
Enborne
Benham
Kintbury
Avington
Denford
Inglewood
Inkpen
Combe
Eddington
Leverton
Calcot
Standen
Charlton
R. Kennett
Purley
Sulham
Englefield
Sheffield
Southcot
Burghfield
Wokefield
Stratfield Mortimer
R. Thames
Caversham
READING
Earley
Whitley
Shinfield
Swallowfield
Sonning
R. Loddon
Whistley
Barkham
Finchampstead
Remenham
Wargrave
Hurley
Bisham
Cookham
Maidenhead
Bray
Shottesbrook
White Waltham
Waltham St Lawrence
Winkfield
Warfield
Easthampstead
Dedworth
Losfield
Clewer
WINDSOR

4 BUCKINGHAMSHIRE

A
B
C
D
E
F
1
2
3
4
5
6
7
8
9
Wisbech
Thorney
Whittlesey
March
Doddington
Chatteris
Littleport
Downham
Witcham
Ely
Sutton
Witchford
Wentworth
Stuntney
Little Thetford
Hill
Haddenham
Henny
Wilburton
Linden
Stretham
Isleham
Soham
Over
Willingham
Wicken
Badlingham
Fordham
Swavesey
Chippenham
Fen Drayton
Rampton
Kennett
Cottenham
Long Stanton All Saints
Burwell
Snailwell
Conington
Long Stanton St Michael
Papworth St Agnes
Westwick
Waterbeach
Boxworth
Landbeach
Graveley
Elsworth
Lolworth
Oakington
Swaffham Prior
Histon
Impington
Milton
Papworth Everard
Knapwell
Horningsea
Swaffham Bulbeck
Girton
Silverley
Childerley
Dry Drayton
Bottisham
Ashley
Cheveley
Eltisley
Madingley
Chesterton
Quy
Saxon Street
Croxton
(Stow)
Woodditton
Hardwick
Whitwell
CAMBRIDGE
Little Wilbraham
Stetchworth
Caxton
Teversham
Great Wilbraham
Dullingham
Caldecote
Bourn
Comberton
Cherry Hinton
Kirtling
Toft
Long Stowe
Westley Waterless
Grantchester
Fulbourn
Barton
Kingston
Trumpington
Burrough Green
Little Gransden
R. Cam
Great Eversden
Weston Colville
Gamlingay
Harlton
Great Shelford
Little Eversden
Carlton
Hatley St George
Wimpole
Haslingfield
Hauxton
Stapleford
West Wratting
Little Shelford
Arrington
Harston
Babraham
Balsham
East Hatley
Orwell
Barrington
Little Abington
Croydon
Wratworth
Sawston
West Wickham
Whittlesford
Hildersham
Clopton
Foxton
Great Abington
(Streetly)
Wendy
Tadlow
Pampisford
Shepreth
Little Linton
Shingay
Thriplow
Horseheath
Linton
Whaddon
Meldreth
Duxford
Barham
Fowlmere
Abington Pigotts
Hinxton
Shudy Camps
Guilden Morden
Melbourn
Bassingbourn
Ickleton
Steeple Morden
Castle Camps
Litlington
Heydon
Great Chishill
Little Chishill

6 CHESHIRE AND NORTH-EAST WALES

1 Cefndy
2 Bryn
3 Cwybr
4 Cwybr-bach
5 Pentre
6 Rhydorddwy
7 Llewerllyd
8 Dyserth
9 Dincolyn
10 Meliden
11 Gwaenysgor
12 Prestatyn
13 Gronant
14 Golden Grove
15 Carn-y-chain
16 Gop
17 Trelawnyd
18 Axton
19 Kelston
20 Gwespyr
21 Picton

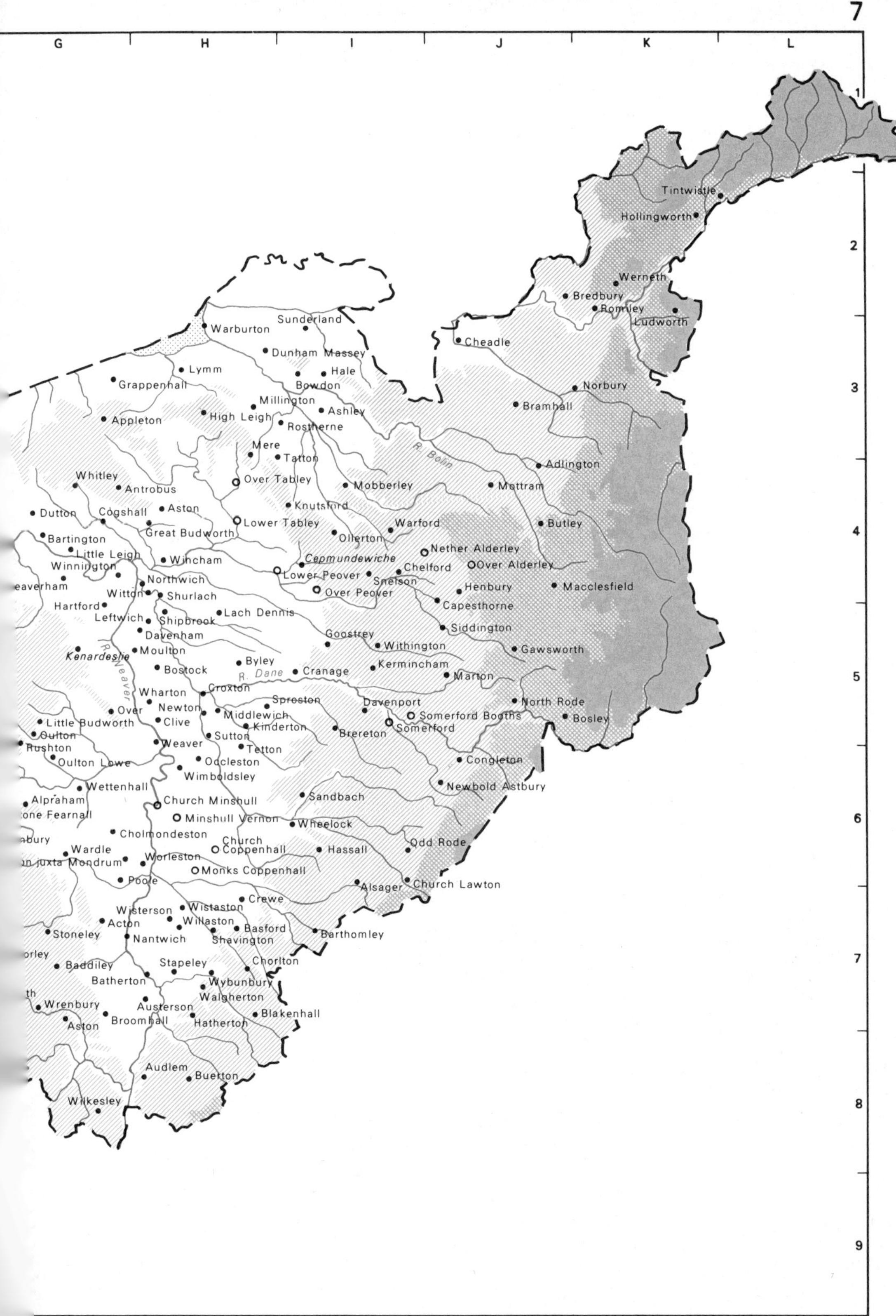
G
H
I
J
K
L
1
2
3
4
5
6
7
8
9
Tintwistle
Hollingworth
Werneth
Bredbury
Romiley
Ludworth
Cheadle
Norbury
Bramhall
Adlington
Mottram
Butley
Macclesfield
Warburton
Sunderland
Dunham Massey
Hale
Bowdon
Lymm
Grappenhall
Millington
Ashley
Appleton
High Leigh
Rostherne
Mere
Tatton
R. Bolin
Whitley
Antrobus
Over Tabley
Mobberley
Knutsford
Dutton
Cogshall
Aston
Lower Tabley
Warford
Great Budworth
Ollerton
Bartington
Little Leigh
Nether Alderley
Winnington
Wincham
Cepmundewiche
Chelford
Over Alderley
Lower Peover
Northwich
Snelson
Henbury
Over Peover
Witton
Shurlach
Capesthorne
Hartford
Leftwich
Shipbrook
Lach Dennis
Siddington
Davenham
Goostrey
Withington
Gawsworth
Kenardeslie
Moulton
R. Weaver
Byley
Kermincham
Bostock
R. Dane
Cranage
Marton
Wharton
Croxton
Sproston
Davenport
North Rode
Over
Newton
Middlewich
Somerford Booths
Bosley
Little Budworth
Clive
Kinderton
Somerford
Oulton
Sutton
Brereton
Rushton
Weaver
Tetton
Congleton
Oulton Lowe
Occleston
Wimboldsley
Newbold Astbury
Wettenhall
Sandbach
Alpraham
Church Minshull
Minshull Vernon
Wheelock
Cholmondeston
Church
Coppenhall
Odd Rode
Hassall
Wardle
Worleston
Monks Coppenhall
Poole
Alsager
Church Lawton
Crewe
Wisterson
Wistaston
Acton
Willaston
Basford
Barthomley
Stoneley
Nantwich
Shavington
Chorlton
Baddiley
Stapeley
Batherton
Wybunbury
Walgherton
Wrenbury
Austerson
Blakenhall
Broomhall
Hatherton
Audlem
Buerton
Wilkesley

8 CORNWALL

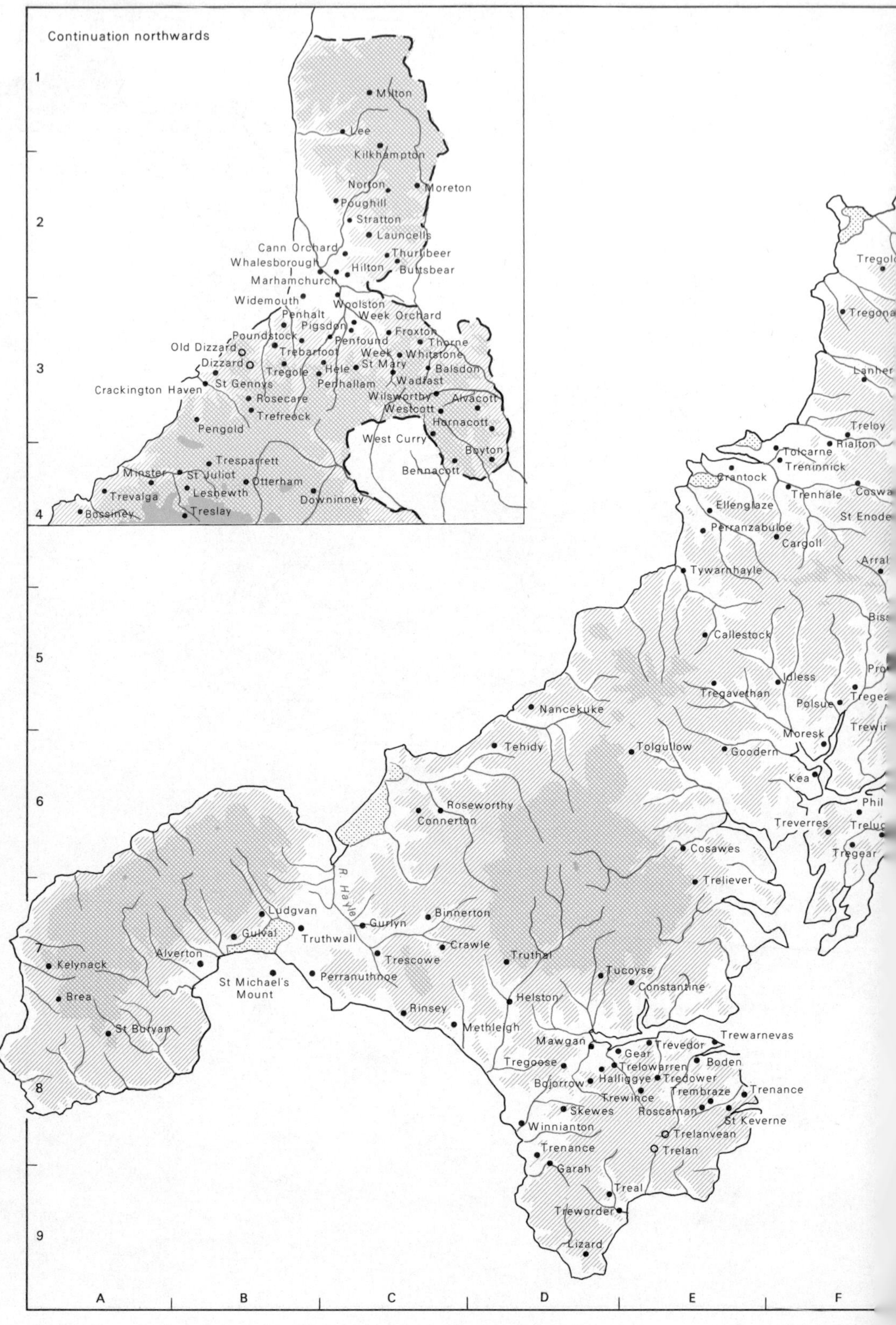
Continuation northwards
Milton
Lee
Kilkhampton
Norton
Moreton
Poughill
Stratton
Launcells
Cann Orchard
Thurlibeer
Whalesborough
Hilton
Buttsbear
Marhamchurch
Widemouth
Woolston
Penhalt
Week Orchard
Pigsdon
Poundstock
Penfound
Froxton
Thorne
Old Dizzard
Trebarfoot
Week
Whitstone
Dizzard
Tregole
Hele
St Mary
Balsdon
Crackington Haven
St Gennys
Penhallam
Wadfast
Rosecare
Wilsworthy
Alvacott
Trefreock
Westcott
Hornacott
Pengold
West Curry
Boyton
Tresparrett
Bennacott
Minster
St Juliot
Otterham
Trevalga
Lesnewth
Downinney
Bossiney
Treslay
Tregold
Tregona
Lanher
Treloy
Rialton
Tolcarne
Treninnick
Crantock
Trenhale
Cosway
Ellenglaze
St Enode
Perranzabuloe
Cargoll
Arral
Tywarnhayle
Biss
Callestock
Idless
Pro
Tregavethan
Polsue
Tregea
Nancekuke
Moresk
Trewin
Tehidy
Tolgullow
Goodern
Kea
Roseworthy
Connerton
Phil
Treverres
Treluc
Tregear
Cosawes
R. Hayle
Treliever
Ludgvan
Binnerton
Gulval
Truthwall
Gurlyn
Alverton
Crawle
Kelynack
Trescowe
Truthal
St Michael's Mount
Perranuthnoe
Tucoyse
Constantine
Brea
Helston
Rinsey
St Buryan
Methleigh
Mawgan
Trewarnevas
Gear
Trevedor
Tregoose
Trelowarren
Boden
Halliggye
Tredower
Bojorrow
Trembraze
Trenance
Trewince
Skewes
Roscarnan
St Keverne
Winnianton
Trelanvean
Trenance
Trelan
Garah
Treal
Treworder
Lizard
1
2
3
4
5
6
7
8
9
A
B
C
D
E
F

Treknow
Tremblary
Tremail
Worthyvale
Treglasta
Tredwen
Trenuth
Rosebenault
Penheale
St Stephens
Launceston
Delabole
Tregardock
Dannonchapel
Helstone
Bowithick
Landinner
Polyphant
Lawhitton
Trewethart
Roscarrock
Trefreock
Tredaule
Penpont
Trevell
Trewint
Trelaske
Trewanta
Trevague
Halvana
Hametethy
Polrode
Lamellen
Kilmarth
Carbihan
Lanow
Trewen
St Tudy
Tinten
Amble
Padstow
Trewornan
Trevisquite
Burniere
R. Allen
Trethevey
Tolcarne
Illand
Treveniel
Trebartha
R. Inny
Trefrize
Penhole
R. Tamar
Pengelly
Patrieda
Rillaton
Climsom
South Hill
Blisland
Pendavy
Pencarrow
Colquite
Pawton
R. Camel
Lancarffe
Trezance
BODMIN
West Draynes
Great Draynes
Caradon
Penharget
Woolston
Bicton
Callington
Calstock
Fawton
St Neot.
Tremar
Rosecraddock
Appledore
Ashton
Fursnewth
Penhawger
Trevallack
Trebeigh
Newton Ferrers
Withiel
Trevornick
Tremore
Cabilla
Glynn
Clinnick
Havet
Tregarrick
Liskeard
Trewolland
Hammett
Halton
Tremoan
R. Lynher
Bosent
Hagland
Boduel
Leigh
Pillaton
Tregrill
Cartuther
Penpoll
Ellbridge
Landulph
Braddock
Trevillis
Killigorrick
Trehawke
R. Fowey
Trevellion
Higher Polscoe
Dawna
Boconnoc
Lametton
Landrake
Tremoddrett
Bodardle
Botelet
Trevego
Bodbrane
Bonyalva
Tredinnick
Trewidland
Trelugan
Trematon
Lower Polscoe
Trecan
Arworgie
Domellick
Gothers
Bodiggo
Tremadart
Carsella
Langunnett
Tregarland
St Germans
Lantyan
St Winnow
Trerice
Lanwarnick
Torwell
Trelowia
Treverbyn
Burthy
Lanreath
Trenant
Bucklawren
Lanescot
Manely
Pelynt
Pendrim
Antony
Tywardreath
Trevelyan
Lancare
Sheviock
Trelawne
Trenance
Penventinue
Trenewan
Trenderway
Bodigga
Trethake
Trigamelling
Trewoon
Brannel
Tregantle
Lansallos
Porthallow
Trenant
Lantivet
Lannear
Maker
Trenowth
Trelowth
Raphael
Elland
Towan
Rame
Tybesta
Lanhadron
Trewithen
Pentewan
Tucoyse
Treworrick
Penpell
Lancallen
Goviley
Galowras
Bodrugan
Tretheake
St Goran
Veryan

1
2
3
4
5
6
7
8
9

G
H
I
J
K
L

10 DERBYSHIRE

A
B
C
D
E
F
G
H
I

1
2
3
4
5
6

Hadfield
Padfield
Glossop
Whitfield
Chunal
Dinting
Charlesworth
Chisworth
Kinder
Hayfield
Thornsett
Edale
Peak Cavern
Aston
Hope
Bamford
Hurst
Hathersage
Shatton
Offerton
Bradwell
Abney
Hazelbadge
Waterfield
Great Hucklow
Little Hucklow
Muchedeswelle
Tideswell
Litton
Wormhill
Stoke
Eyam
Stony Middleton
Calver
Rowland
Hassop
Bubnell
Baslow
Little Longstone
Great Longstone
Priestcliff
Blackwell
Taddington
Birchill
Ashford
Pilsley
Holme
Bakewell
Edensor
Chatsworth
Langley
Sheldon
Flagg
Monyash
Burton
Over Haddon
Nether Haddon
Rowsley
Beeley
Conkesbury
One Ash
Youlgreave
Harthill
Stanton in the Peak
Burley
Cotes
Darley
Cowley
Wensley
Farley
Middleton
Gratton
Birchover
Elton
Winster
Snitterton
Matlock Bridge
Matlock
Tansley
Ivonbrook
Bonsall
Ible
Cromford
Middleton
Lea
Soham
Pilsbury
Ludwell
Hartington
Coldeaton
Alsop le Dale
Holmesfield
Dronfield
Upton
Unstone
Coal Aston
Mosborough
Beighton
Killamarsh
Eckington
R. Rother
Handley
Ramshaw
Whittington
Barlow
Newbold
Brimington
Tapton
Chesterfield
Holme
Brampton
Wadshelf
Calow
Boythorpe
Staveley
Duckmanton
Walton
Temple Normanton
Wingerworth
Williamthorpe
Grevburst
Tupton
Egstow
Ashover
Handley
Stretton Hall
Stretton
Padleywood
Wingfield
North
Pilsley
Snodswick
Morton
Ogston
Shirland
Wessington
Uftonfields
Alfreton
Shuckstonefield
Tibshelf
Newton
South Normanton
Hardstoft
Bingsby
Rowthorne
Glapwell
Bramley
Stainsby
Heath
Lowne
Owlcotes
Sutton Scarsdale
Palterton
Scarcliffe
Stony Houghton
Bolsover
Elmton
Clowne
Whitwell
Barlborough

Bradbourne
Warrington
Pentrich
Tissington
Callow
Thorpe
Kniveton
Hognaston
Ripley
Broadlowash
Ferny Bentley
Kirk Ireton
Codnor
Offcote
Atlow
Wallstone
Smithycote
Mappleton
Langley
Ashbourne
Bradley
Hulland
Shottle
Bradley
Sturston
Hough
Holbrook
Denby
Heanor
Clifton
Fenton
Mugginton
Horsley
Kidsley
Snelston
Yeldersley
Weston Underwood
Milford
Mackeney
Smalley
Shipley
Osmaston
Coxbench
Mapperley
Edlaston
Duffield
Norbury
Wyaston
Ednaston
Mercaston
Little Eaton
Ilkeston
Shirley
Kedleston
West Hallam
Roston
Brailsford
Ireton
Quarndon
Morley
Yeaveley
Rodsley
Allestree
Breadsall
Stanley
Kirk Hallam
Hollington
Kirk Langley
Markeaton
Cubley
Hungry Bentley
Thurvaston
Stanton by Dale
Alkmonton
Little Chester
Sedsall
Mackworth
Sandiacre
Boyleston
Bupton
Osleston
Chaddesden
Hopwell
Eaton Dovedale
Radbourne
DERBY
Ulvritune
Potter Somersall
Barton Blount
Trusley
Litchurch
Spondon
Ockbrook
Risley
Sapperton
Dalbury
Mickleover
Osmaston
Draycott
Somersall Herbert
Sutton on the Hill
Littleover
Alvaston
Breaston
Church Broughton
Ash
Bearwardcote
Normanton
Doveridge
Boulton
Ambaston
Long Eaton
Sudbury
Etwall
Cottons
Chelton
Elvaston
Sawley
Foston
Hoon
Burnaston
Sinfin
Marsh
Thulston
Aston
Arleston
Hilton
Findern
Chellaston
Shardlow
Scropton
Hatton
Stenson
Aston upon Trent
Egginton
Twyford
Swarkeston
Marston on Dove
R. Trent
R. Dove
Willington
Potlock
Barrow upon Trent
Weston upon Trent
Derwent
Repton
Milton
Stanton by Bridge
Ingleby
Foremark
Newton Solney
Melbourne
Ticknall
Bretby
Hartshorne Hall
Stanton
Hartshorne
Drakelow
Swadlincote
Smisby
Hearthcote
Walton upon Trent
Caldwell
Rosliston
Linton
Over Seal
Catton
Coton in the Elms
Lullington
Nether Seal
7
8
9
10
11
12
A
B
C
D
E
F
G
H
I

12 DEVONSHIRE(NORTH)

G
H
I
J
K
L
1
2
3
4
5
6
7
8
9
Continuation eastwards
Chardstock
Deneord
Underleave
Smallridge
Weycroft
R. Axe
Axminster
Wyke
Forde
Uplyme
Bruckland
Combpyne
Charton
Rousdon
Down Ralph
Countisbury
Brendon
Lank Combe
Radworthy
Praunsley
Pulham
Ringdon
Molland
West Anstey
East Anstey
Wadham
Knowstone
Tapps
Highleigh
Morebath
Donningstone
Dipford
Clayhanger
Stallenge
Rose Ash
Woodburn
Mildon
Bampton
Yard
Oakford
Kerswell
Besley
Meshaw
Bickham
Spurway
Huntsham
Backstone
Creacombe
Worthy
Sydeham
Hockford Waters
Hockworthy
Little Rackenford
Warbrightsleigh
Holcombe Rogus
Rackenford
Stoodleigh
Coombe
Thorn
Rifton
Fenacre
Bradford
Bulworthy
Whitnole
Chieflowman
Murley
Canonsleigh
Queen Dart
Loxbeare
Whitnage
Essebeer
Washfield
Burlescombe
Coombe
Cheverthorne
Uplowman
Dart Raffe
Leigh
Bolham
Peadhill
Ayshford
Culm Davy
Clayhidon
Witheridge
Colston
West Worth
Kidwell
Boehill
Appledore
Culm Pyne
Middlewick
Bradley
Calverleigh
Chettiscombe
Drayford
Coombe
Great Bradley
Sellake
Sampford Peverell
Culmstock
Thelbridge
Craze Lowman
Halberton
Hemyock
Bolham Water
Washford Pyne
Cruwys Morchard
Tiverton
Uffculme
Pedley
Littleland
Manley
Muxbere
Puddington
Ruckham
Patcott
Ash Thomas
Dennington
Yowlestone
Hill
Leonard
Willand
Hole
Densham
Yedbury
Dart
Pirzwell
Blackborough
Gorwell
Woolfardisworthy
Coombe
Exworthy
Butterleigh
Sutton
Kingsford
Sheldon
Bywood
Yarcombe
Poughill
Hillersdon
Kentisbeare
Dunkeswell
Aller
Morchard Bishop
Coddiford
Cadeleigh
Cullompton
Orway
Upottery
Stockleigh English
Cheriton Fitzpaine
Bickleigh
Ponsford
Hays Park
Luppitt
Aller
Dunscombe
Colebrook
Kerswell
Mohun's Ottery
Shobrooke
Leigh
Greenway
Rawridge
Cadbury
Burn
Bradninch
Culm
Bulealler
Woodbeer
Chilton
Bowley
Chitterley
Broadhembury
Shapcombe
Stockland
Lower Credy
Stockleigh Pomeroy
Greenslinch
Langford
Hembury
Chaffcombe
Silverton
Hele
Clyst William
Combe Raleigh
Membury
West Raddon
Up Exe
Combe Sackville
Plymtree
Payhembury
Awliscombe
Cotleigh
R. Creedy
Raddon
Tale
Rudway
RYard
Clyst Hydon
Curscombe
Honiton
Wiburde
Shobrooke
Columbjohn
Aunk
Talaton
Cheriton
Waringstone
Crediton
Nether Exe
Ivelie
Clyst St Lawrence
Buckerell
Heathfield
Wilmington
Wyke
Rewe
Feniton
Offwell
Widworthy
Bramford Speke
Clyst Gerred
Deerpark
Colwell
Sutton
Kilmington
Newton St Cyres
Stoke Canon
Huxham
Clyst
Ashclyst
Larkbeare
Gittisham
Culbeer
Oldridge
Culm Vale
Broad Clyst
Whimple
Rapshays
Whitley
Brimley
Smallicombe
Bowlish
R. Exe
Poltimore
Strete Raleigh
Farway
Northleigh
Whitford
Cheriton Bishop
Tedburn St Mary
Pinhoe
Bluehayes
Ottery St Mary
Netherton
Farwood
Musbury
Upcott
Whitestone
Rockbeare
West Clyst
Great Huish
Polsloe
Exwick
Whipton
Bedricestan
Colyton
Crockernwell
Hackworthy
EXETER
Heavitree
Southleigh
Haccombe
Sowton
Melhuish
Halstow
Wonford
Holbrook
Aylesbeare
Radish
Stedcombe
Fulford
Holcombe Burnell
Cowick
Shyttenbrook
Sidbury
Combe
Farringdon
Axmouth
Clifford
Ide
St James Church
Creely
Gatcombe
Seaton
Alphington
R. Teign
Dunsford
Clyst St Mary
Beer
Matford
Clyst St George
Dotton
Salcombe Regis
Lowley
Shillingford
Peamore
Topsham
Sidmouth
Branscombe
Lowton
Exminster
Stowford
Dunchideock
Woodbury
Colaton Raleigh
Bridford
Doddiscombsleigh
Kenn
Nutwell
Bicton
Moretonhampstead
Wray
Ashton
Otterton
Bovey
Powderham
Lympstone
East Budleigh
George Teign
Elsford
Canonteign
Kenton
Trusham
Withycombe Raleigh
Hawkmoor
Mowlish
Littleham
Hennock
Bottor
Warmhill
Mamhead
Woolley
Bovey Tracey
Ashcombe
Southbrook

14 DEVONSHIRE (SOUTH)

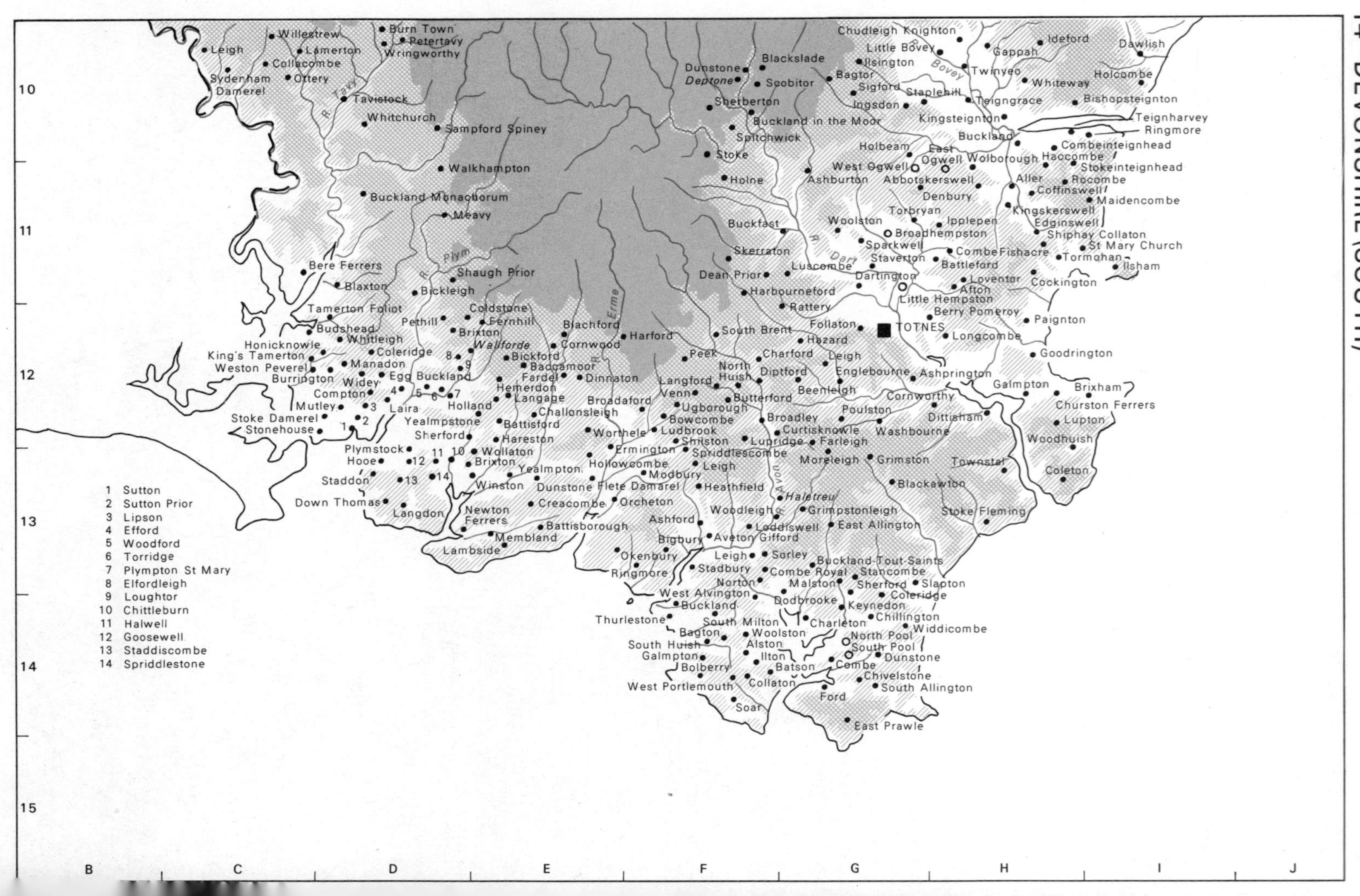

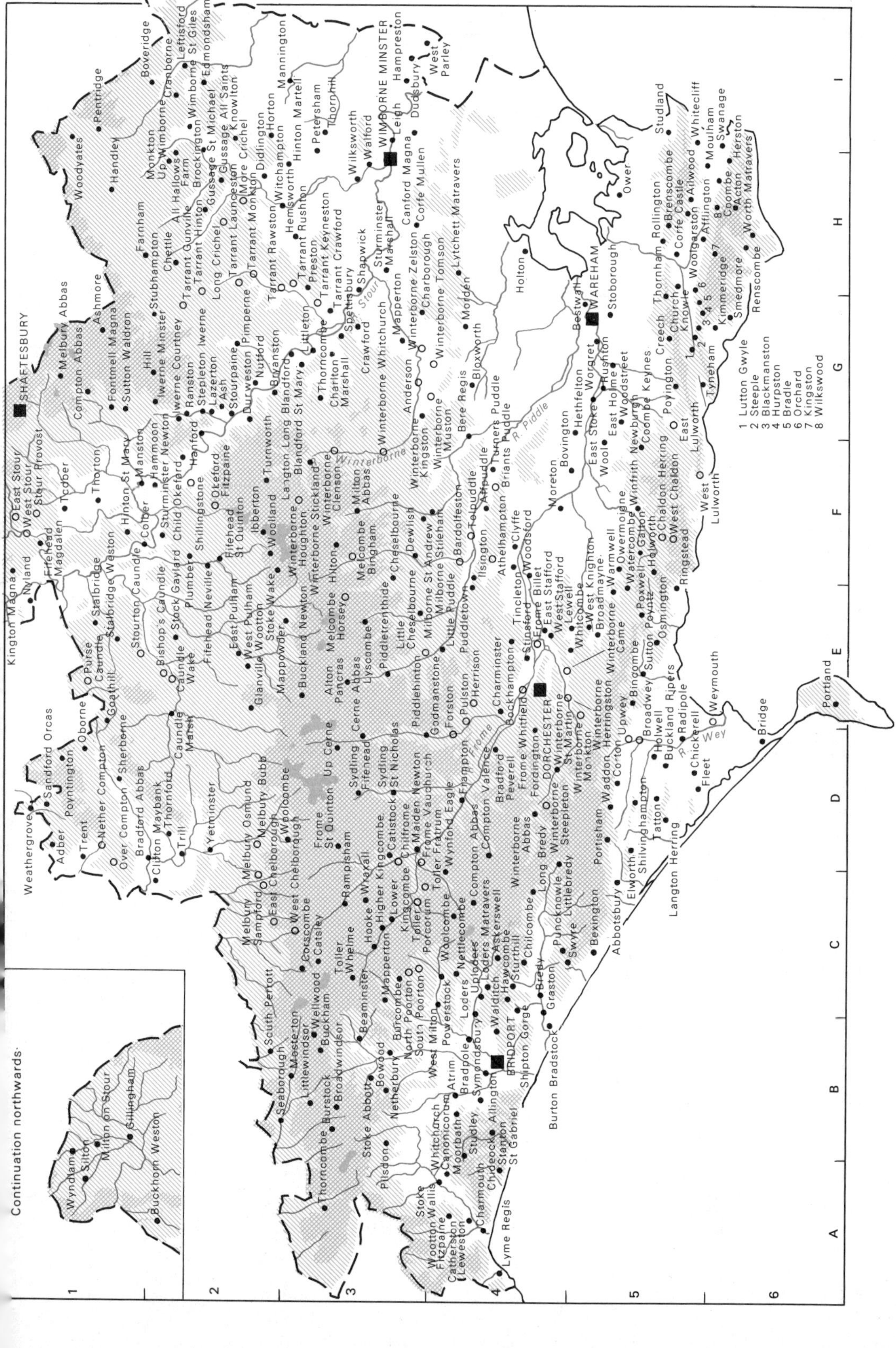
Continuation northwards
SHAFTESBURY
WIMBORNE MINSTER
WAREHAM
DORCHESTER
BRIDPORT
Lyme Regis
Weymouth
Portland
Swanage
Sherborne
Gillingham
R. Piddle
R. Wey
Frome
Stour
Winterborne
1
2
3
4
5
6
A
B
C
D
E
F
G
H
I
1 Lutton Gwyle
2 Steeple
3 Blackmanston
4 Hurpston
5 Bradle
6 Orchard
7 Kingston
8 Wilkswood

16 ESSEX

A
B
C
D
E
F
1
2
3
4
5
6
7
8
9
Hadstock
Coupals
Sturmer
Claret
Great Chesterford
Newnham
Stevington
Horseham
Baythorn
Ashen
Belchamp St Paul
Little Chesterford
Emanual Wood
Helions Bumpstead
Ovington
Ashdon
Steeple Bumpstead
Birdbrook
Ridgewell
Crawley
Strethall
Rothend
Tilbury
Elmdon
Littlebury
Bendysh
Stambourne
Little Yeldham
Chrishall
Wendens Lofts
Saffron Walden
Hempstead
Great Yeldham
Elmdon Lee
Radwinter
Chiswick
Cornish Hall
Toppesfield
Rockells
Wendens Ambo
Wimbish
Castle Hedingham
Thunderley
Smalton
Arkesden
Shortgrove
Great Sampford
Sible Hedingham
Chardwell
Newport
Little Sampford
Boyton
Bonhunt
Debden
Howe
Alderford
Wicken
Widdington
Yardley
Finchingfield
Clavering
Quendon
Amberden
Thaxted
Little Bardfield
Wethersfield
Rickling
Halstead
Berden
Great Bardfield
Ashwell
Ugley
Shalford
Peyton
Henham
Chaureth
Bollington
Chickney
Pinchpools
Lindsell
Pledgdon
Broxted
R. Pant
Manuden
Tilty
Lashley
Bardfield Saling
Bentfield
Elsenham
Great Easton
Great Saling
Panfield
Farnham
Stansted Mountfitchet
Bigods
Stebbing
Bocking
Little Easton
Braintree
Birchanger
Newton
Great Dunmow
Stebbingford
Rayne
Takeley
Little Dunmow
Little Canfield
Felsted
Black Notley
Great Slamseys
Great Hallingbury
Barnston
White
Moulsham
Great Canfield
Wallbury
Little Hallingbury
Lawn Hall
Little Leighs
High Roding
Fairstead
Ryes
Hatfield Broad Oak
Great Leighs
Ridley
Aythorpe Roding
Terling
Quickbury
High Easter
Chatham
Blunt's Hall
Leaden Roding
Little Waltham
Howbridge
Sheering
White Roding
R. Chelmer
Housham
Matching
Good Easter
Great Waltham
Margaret Roding
Mashbury
Hatfield Peverel
R. Lea
Harlow
Abbess Roding
Chignall
Walter
Little Parndon
Latton
Beauchamp Roding
Berners Roding
Broomfield
Belstead
Smallands
Roydon
Little Laver
Newland
Boreham
High Laver
Patching
Culverts
Great Parndon
Plesingho
Cuton
Little Baddow
Magdalen Laver
Shellow Bowells
Springfield
Curling Tye
Moreton
Willingale Doe
Chelmsford
Nazeing
Fyfield
Willingale Spain
Writtle
Woodham Walter
Bobbingworth
Shelley
Moulsham
Danbury
North Weald Bassett
Norton Mandeville
Great Baddow
High Ongar
Fingrith
Bensted
Paslow
Greensted
Chipping Ongar
Epping
East Hanningfield
Stanford Rivers
Margaretting
Waltham Holy Cross
Fristling
Theydon Garnon
Fryerning
West Hanningfield
Theydon Bois
Theydon Mount
Kelvedon Hatch
Ingatestone
Woodham Ferrers
Debden
Stapleford Tawney
Doddinghurst
Buttsbury
Loughton
Navestock
Alderton
Plunker's Green
South Hanningfield
Lambourne
Mountnessing
Stapleford Abbots
Rettendon
Woolston
Shenfield
Cowbridge
Ramsden Bellhouse
R. Roding
Runwell
Chigwell
South Weald
Hutton
Ramsden Crays
Chingford
Wickford
Havering-atte-Bower
Stanmer
Great Burstead
Fanton
Ingrave
Well
Cray's Hill
Woodford
Little Burstead
Nevendon
Little Warley
Fouchers
Higham
Basildon
Childerditch
Laindon
North Benfleet
Walthamstow
East Horndon
Barstable
Great Warley
Dunton
Lee Chapel
Pitsea
West Horndon
Wanstead
Upminster
Vange
Bowers Gifford
Langdon
Leyton
Ilford
Cranham
Bulphan
North Ockendon
West Ham
Barking
Horndon on the Hill
East Ham
South Ockendon
Fobbing
Hassenbrook
Corringham
Rainham
Kenningtons
Orsett
Wennington
Mucking
Aveley
Stifford
Chadwell
Grays Thurrock
West Tilbury
Little Thurrock
West Thurrock
East Tilbury
Gravesanda
R. Thames

G
H
I
J
K
L
1
2
3
4
5
6
7
8
9
Liston
Borley
Smeetham
Middleton
Little Henny
Great Henny
Lamarsh
Bures
R. Stour
Pebmarsh
Mount Bures
Wormingford
Eiland
Boxted
Langham
Dedham
Old Hall
Lawford
Mistley
Jacques
Wrabness
Dovercourt
Michaelstow
Cliff
Bradfield
Ramsey
Colne Engaine
White Colne
Wakes Colne
Crepping
Fordham
West Bergholt
Ardleigh
Dickley
Derleigh
Little Oakley
Foulton
Wix
Great Oakley
Little Bromley
Great Bromley
Moze
Great Tey
Aldham
COLCHESTER
Elmstead
Little Bentley
Beaumont
Marks Tey
Byrton
Lexden
Greenstead
R. Colne
Stanway
Tendring
Birch
Little Tey
Copford
Weeley
Kirby-le-Soken
Easthorpe
East Donyland
Wivenhoe
Frating
Great Bentley
Thorpe-le-Soken
Walton-le-Soken
Little Coggeshall
Bockingham
Feering
Little Birch
Alresford
Frinton
Prested
Great Birch
Thorrington
Great Holland
Abberton
Kelvedon
Messing
Layer de la Haye
Brightlingsea
Frowick
Little Clacton
Layer Breton
Langenhoe
Layer Marney
Peldon
Little Holland
Great Clacton
Great Wigborough
Sampsons
Barn Hall
St Osyth
Tolleshunt Knights
Little Wigborough
East Mersea
Virley
West Mersea
Little Braxted
Tolleshunt Major
Tolleshunt D'Arcy
Little Totham
Blatchams
Tollesbury
Goldhanger
Heybridge
Bradwell Quay
St Peter's Chapel
Osea Island
R. Blackwater
Down
Northey Island
Stanesgate
St Lawrence
Iltney
Tillingham
Mundon
Steeple
Dengie
Lawling
Asheldham
Cold Norton
Southminster
Latchingdon
Ulehams
North Fambridge
Creeksea
Burnham
R. Crouch
Pudsey
South Fambridge
Canewdon
Ashingdon
Paglesham
Little Stambridge
Great Stambridge
Barling
Sutton
Little Wakering
Shopland
Barrow
Great Wakering
Littlethorpe
Southchurch
North Shoebury
Milton
South Shoebury
Thorpehall

A B C D E F

1

2

Preston
Bromsberrow
Forthampton
Dymock
Redmarley D'Abitot
Ketford
Teling
Wightfi
Kempley
Pauntley
Oridge Street
Tirley
Carswall
Hasfield
Oxenhall
Upleaden
Newent
Leigh
Kilcot
Hayes
Ashleworth

3

Brawn
Morwent
Norto
Taynton
Sandhu
Tibberton
Down Hatherle
Rudford
Maisemore
Lassington
Highnam
Longhope
GLOUCEST
Huntley
Bulley
Mitcheldean
Morton
Wott
Churcham
Murcott
Ruardean
Barnwo
Hempsted
R. Severn
Barton
English Bicknor

4

Tuffley
Whittington
Upton St Leonards
Westbury on Severn
Whado
Stears
Staunton
Longney
Newnham
Rodley
Brooktho
Moreton Valence
Arlingham
Harescom
Haresfield
Wheatenhurst
Painswi
Bledisloe
Awre
Fretherne
Standish
Poulton
Frampton on Severn
Etloe

5

Wyegate
Purton
R. Frome
Stonehouse
Allaston
RIVER SEVERN
St Briavels
Alkerton
Lydney
Slimbridge
Frocester
Leonard Stanle
Hinton
Hurst
King's Stan
Newerne
Hewelsfield
Sharpness
Gossington
Woodches
Nass
Coaley
Alvington
R. Wye
Modesgate
Clingre
Nympsfield
Cam
Woolaston
Berkeley

6

Uley
Alkington
Dursley
Hors
Symond's Hall
Kingscote
Tidenham
Hill
Newington Bagpath
Beverst
Lashborough
Tortworth
Wotton under Edge
Chepstow
Ozleworth
Dinham
Rockhampton
Boxwell
Llanvair-Discoed
Caerleon
Caerwent
Charfield
Thornbury
Alderley
Littleton upon Severn
Cromhall
Wes
Caldicot

7

Aust
Hillsley
Elberton
Wickwar
Oldbury on the Hill
Portskewett
Tytherington
Alveston
Didmarton
Olveston
Itchington
Tockington
Redwick
Hawksbury
Horton
Earthcott
Almondsbury
Iron Acton
Little Sodbury
Yate
Chipping Sodbury
Great Badmi
Compton Greenfield
Old Sodbury
Frampton Cotterell

8

Winterbourne
Acton Turv
Dodington
Stoke Gifford
Wapley
Henbury
Hambrook
Tormarton
Weston
Westbury on Trym
Horfield
Pucklechurch
Mangotsfield
Stoke Bishop
Dyrham
Siston
Barton
R. Avon
Doynton
Marshfield
Clifton
BRISTOL
Cold Ashton

9

Hanham
Bedminster
Oldland
Knowle
Bitton

G
H
I
J
K
L
1
2
3
4
5
6
7
8
9
Mickleton
Norton
Hidcote Bartrim
Aston Subedge
Weston Subedge
Willersey
Ebrington
Chipping Campden
Charingworth
Saintbury
Todenham
Ditchford
Lemington
Blockley
Batsford
Twining
Saberton
Dumbleton
Wormington
Buckland
Aston on Carrant
Great Washbourne
Little Washbourne
Stanton
Pamington
Naunton
Alderton
Snowshill
TEWKESBURY
Teddington
Frampton
Toddington
Bourton on the Hill
Moreton in Marsh
Walton Cardiff
Natton
Oxenton
Stanway
Fiddington
Dixton
Littleworth
Taddington
Sezincote
Idleberg
Southwick
Woolstone
Hailes
Cutsdean
Longborough
Tredington
Stanley Pontlarge
Farmcote
Gotherington
Evenlode
WINCHCOMB
Pinnock
Condicott
Walton
Stoke Orchard
Broadwell
Temple Guiting
Hardwick
Bishop's Cleeve
Sudeley
Postlip
Upper Swell
Adlestrop
Elmstone
Castlett
Stow on the Wold
Oddington
Southam
Daylesford
Boddington
Eyford
Swindon
Roel
Lower Swell
Maugersbury
Uckington
Prestbury
Guiting Power
Charlton Abbots
Naunton
Upper Slaughter
Church Icomb
Staverton
Hawling
Harford
Lower Slaughter
Icomb
Bledington
Cheltenham
Aylworth
Sevenhampton
Westfield
Bourton on the Water
Wyck Rissington
Whittington
Hampen
Notgrove
Churchdown
Aston Blank
Little Rissington
Leckhampton
Dowdeswell
Salperton
Badgeworth
Shipton Oliffe
Clapton
Pegglesworth
Hazleton
Shipton Solars
Foxcote
Turkdean
Great Rissington
Brockworth
Compton Abdale
Hilcote
Coberley
Withington
Hampnett
Farmington
Cowley
Northleach
Sherborne
Yanworth
Great Barrington
Colesborne
Brimpsfield
Stowell
Windrush
Elkstone
Chedworth
Little Barrington
Coln St Dennis
Syde
Eycot
Calcot
Aldsworth
Winstone
Rendcomb
Miserden
Winson
North Cerney
Througham
R. Coln
Duntisbourne Abbots
Arlington
Bagendon
Bibury
Edgeworth
Coln St Aldwyn
Eastleach Turville
Bisley
Duntisbourne Rouse
Hatherop
Pinbury
Barnsley
Eastleach Martin
Baunton
Quenington
Sapperton
Stratton
Ampney Crucis
Ashbrook
Frampton Mansell
Norcott
Oakley
Ampney St Mary
Cirencester
Ampney St Peter
Fairford
Preston
Poulton
Harnhill
Lechlade
Hullasey
Siddington
Meysey Hampton
Trewsbury
Driffield
Tarlton
Hazleton
South Cerney
Down Ampney
Rodmarton
Avening
Kemble
Kempsford
R. Churn
Culkerton
Shorncote
R. Thames
Tetbury Upton
Poole Keynes
Somerford Keynes
Ashley
Tetbury
Long Newnton
Shipton Moyne
R. Windrush

20 HAMPSHIRE

Westbury
Otterbourne
Sherfield English
Plaitford
Romsey
Embley
East Wellow
West Wellow
North Charford
South Charford
Breamore
Rockbourne
Outwick
Rockstead
Burgate
Damerham
North Baddesley
Boyatt
Bishopstoke
Eastleigh
Chilworth
North Stoneham
Allington
South Stoneham
Lomer
Warnford
Exton
Corhampton
Meonstoke
Droxford
Bishop's Waltham
Soberton
Hoe
Hambledon
East Meon
Mapledurham
Sunwood
Chalton
Bramshaw
Ower
Nursling
Tatchbury
Testwood
Redbridge
Shirley
Millbrook
Hanger
Netley Marsh
Totton
Eling
Eyeworth
Canterton
Fordingbridge
Bickton
Midgham
Gorley
Harbridge
Ibsley
Ellingham
Rockford
Northam
SOUTHAMPTON
Woolston
Hound
Netley
Botley
R. Meon
Wickham
Minstead
Durley
Buckholt
Marchwood
Lyndhurst
Gritnam
Dibden
R. Avon
Ringwood
Crow
Bolderford
Hardley
Hartford
Fawley
Rollstone
Otterwood
Langley
Gatewood
Stanswood
Stone
Brookley
Brockenhurst
Hinchesiea
Beckley
Bisterne
Ripley
Avon
Wootton
Sway
Arnewood
Boldre
Battramsley
Pilley
Baddesley
Hurn
Sopley
Winkton
Beckley
Bashley
Fernhill
Hinton Admiral
Milton
Lymington
Walhampton
Hordle
Kinson
R. Stour
Holdenhurst
Burton
Hoburne
Ashley
Efford
Knapp
TWYNHAM
Barton
Stanpit
Milford
Funtley
Boarhunt
Segensworth
Fareham
Bedhampton
Havant
Newtimber
Porchester
Wymering
Cosham
Brockhampton
Hook
Titchfield
Brownwich
Crofton
Meon
Stubbington
Warblington
Copnor
Hayling Island
Buckland
Rowner
Fratton
Alverstoke
7
8
9
10
11
12
Whippingham
Sofleet
Wootton
R. Medina
Binstead
Puckpool
Barnsley
Nettlestone
Hamstead
Briddlesford
Little Whitefield
Whitefield
Eddington
Yarmouth
Thorley
Milford
Wilmingham
Shalfleet
Ningwood
Alvington
Haldley
Great Pan
Shide
Rowborough
Nunwell
Orham
Wellow
Bowcombe
Sullens
Standen
Down
Brading
Wolverton
Freshwater
Calbourne
Whitcombe
Arreton
Kern
Aviston
Hardley
Afton
Idlecombe
Perreton
Heasley
Yaverland
Shalcombe
Gatcombe
Compton
Sheat
Merstone
Hale
Borthwood
Lea
Sandown
Brook
Cheverton
Chillerton
Blackpan
Mottistone
Coombe
Downe
Chilton
Shorwell
Limerstone
Woolverton
Moor
Lessland
Scottlesford
Sandford
Shanklin
Dungewood
Kingston
Roud
Appleford
Wroxall
Luccombe
Atherfield
Gotten
Stenbury
Walpen
Bonchurch
Chale
Week
Niton
1
2
3
4
5
6
7
ISLE OF WIGHT
1 Watchingwell
2 Huffingford
3 Horringford
4 Knighton
5 Adgestone
6 Branstone
7 Bathingbourne
A
B
C
D
E
F
G
H
I

22 HEREFORDSHIRE

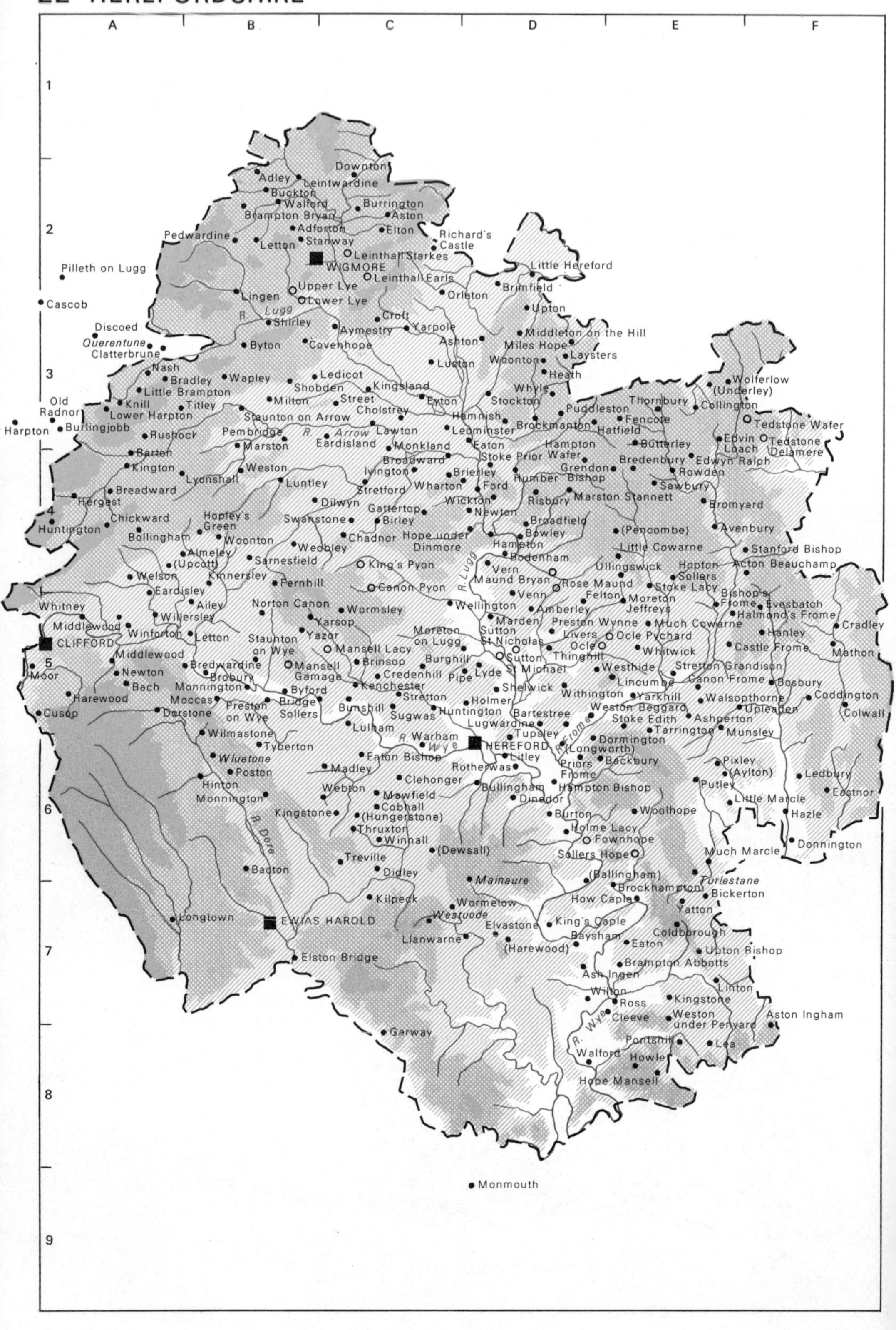

ASHWELL
HERTFORD
STANSTEAD ABBOTS
ST ALBANS
BERKHAMSTED
Hinxworth
Caldecote
Newnham
Bygrave
Radwell
Norton
Letchworth
Barley
Newsells
Cokenach
Barkway
Therfield
Kelshall
Reed
Orwell
Sandon
Buckland
Hodenhoe
Hyde Hall
Wyddial
Anstey
Meesden
Wallington
Rushden
Clothall
Broadfield
Throcking
Cottered
Cornbury
Beauchamps
Brent Pelham
Stocking Pelham
Great Hormead
Little Hormead
Furneaux Pelham
Hare Street
Stonebury
Bozen
Hixham
Patmore
Cockhampstead
Albury
Eckington
Alswick
Aspenden
Westmill
Berkesdon
Ardeley
Walkern
Wakeley
Braughing
Great Munden
Libury
Little Munden
Standon
Chaldean
Little Hadham
Much Hadham
Wickham
Bishop's Stortford
Thorley
Sawbridgeworth
Eastwick
Widford
Hunsdon
Thundridge
Ware
Great Amwell
Hadley
Rye
Broxbourne
Hoddesdon
Brickendon
Little Amwell
Bengeo
Sacombe
Watton
Bennington
Weston
Luffenhall
Willian
Great Wymondley
Graveley
Boxbury
Chells
Aston
Shephall
Stevenage
Almshoe
Woolwicks
Temple Dinsley
Minsden
Langley
Stagenhoe
King's Walden
St Paul's Walden
Knebworth
Datchworth
Mardleybury
Codicote
Oxwick
Welwyn
Digswell
Tewin
Bramfield
Sele
Epcombs
Hertingfordbury
Blackmore
Roxford
Bayford
Little Berkhamsted
Wormley
Cheshunt
Bishops Hatfield
North Mimms
Holwell
Hitchen
Charlton
Little Wymondley
Pirton
Wellbury
Little Offley
Great Offley
Wain Wood
Leygreen
Flexmore
Bendish
Wandon
Lilley
Hexton
Kimpton
Ayot St Lawrence
Ayot St Peter
Wheathampstead
Sandridge
Napsbury
Shenley
Theobald
Aldenham
Hanstead
Windridge
Abbots Langley
Bushey
Cassio
Rickmansworth
Kings Langley
Hemel Hempstead
Redbourn
Flamstead
Great Gaddesden
Little Gaddesden
Aldbury
Wiggington
Pendley
Dunsley
Tring
Miswell
Gubblecote
Tiscot
Boorscroft
Puttenham
R. Rib
R. Ash
R. Stort
R. Lea
R. Beane
R. Maran
R. Ver
R. Gade
R. Colne
A
B
C
D
E
F
G
H
I
1
2
3
4
5
6

A
B
C
D
E
F
1
2
3
4
5
6
7
8
9
Stibbington
Sibson
Water Newton
Botolph Bridge
Woodstone
Stanground
Fletton
Alwalton
Orton Waterville
Orton Longueville
Chesterton
Elton
Haddon
Yaxley
Morborne
Folkesworth
Washingley
Stilton
Caldecote
Denton
Glatton
Conington
Ramsey
Sawtry
Great Gidding
Little Gidding
Steeple Gidding
Wood Walton
Upwood
Wistow
Winwick
Coppingford
Hamerton
Warboys
Upton
Abbots Ripton
Broughton
Old Weston
Alconbury Weston
Somersham
Bythorn
Buckworth
Kings Ripton
Brington
Alconbury
Colne
Keyston
Molesworth
Leighton Bromswold
Little Stukeley
(Barham)
Woolley
Great Stukeley
Bluntisham
Catworth
Hartford
Spaldwick
Wyton
HUNTINGDON
Little Catworth
Houghton
Ellington
Botolph Bridge
Slepe
Holywell
(Long Stow)
Easton
Covington
Brampton
Hemingford Abbots
Godmanchester
Hemingford Grey
Tilbrook
Grafham
R. Ouse
Fen Stanton
Buckden
Kimbolton
Offord Cluny
Perry
Offord D'Arcy
Dillington
Diddington
Great Staughton
Southoe
Boughton
Cotton
Great Paxton
Little Paxton
Yelling
Hail Weston
Eynesbury
Gransden
Waresley
Everton

Continuation northwards
Bottesford
Redmile
Barkestone
Harston
Knipton
Branston
Croxton Kerrial
Stathern
Harby
Hose
Eastwell
Long Clawson
Nether Broughton
Goadby Marwood
Saltby
Waltham on the Wolds
Wycomb
Scalford
Chadwell
Stonesby
Sproxton
Buckminster
Folwel
Goldsmith Grange
Coston
Sewstern
Old Dalby
Wartnaby
Ab Kettleby
Grimston
Welby
Saxelby
Shoby
Sysonby
Thorpe Arnold
Freeby
Saxby
Wyfordby
Wymondham
Ragdale
Willowes
Wreak
Asfordby
Melton Mowbray
Stapleford
Edmondthorpe
Frisby on the Wreak
Kirby Bellars
Burton Lazars
Eye Kettleby
Hoby
Rotherby
Brooksby
Castle Donington
Kegworth
Diseworth
Tonge
Hathern
Dishley
Thorpe Acre
Loughborough
Wymeswold
Hoton
Prestwold
Burton on the Wolds
Walton on the Wolds
Staunton Harold
Worthington
Osgathorpe
Shepshed
Boothorpe
Woodcote
Thringstone
Coleorton
Ashby de la Zouch
Whitwick
Willesley
Alton
Charley
Donisthorpe
Packington
Ravenstone
Oakthorpe
Donington le Heath
Stretton en le Field
Measham
Swepstone
Chilcote
Appleby Magna
Heather
Snarestone
Ibstock
Stanton under Bardon
Markfield
Appleby Parva
Newton Burgoland
Odstone
Nailstone
Bagworth
Norton-juxta-Twycross
Shackerstone
Gopsall
Barton in the Beans
Bilstone
Congerstone
Barlestone
Twycross
Osbaston
Orton on the Hill
Weston
Newbold Verdon
Market Bosworth
Desford
Sheepy Parva
Cadeby
Brascote
Sheepy Magna
Sutton Cheney
Peckleton
Sibson
Shenton
Kirkby Mallory
Ratcliffe Culey
Stapleton
Fenny Drayton
Barwell
Earl Shilton
Potters Marston
Stoney Stanton
Hinckley
Sapcote
Burbage
Sharnford
Broughton Astley
Smockington
Frolesworth
Wigston Parva
Claybrooke Magna
Claybrooke Parva
Seagrave
Barrow upon Soar
Thrussington
Sileby
Rearsby
Ratcliffe on the Wreak
Great Dalby
Leesthorpe
Little Dalby
Cossington
Gaddesby
Newbold Folville
Rothley
Queniborough
Syston
Ashby Folville
Burrough on the Hill
Pickwell
Somerby
Cold Overton
Thurcaston
Wanlip
Barkby
Barsby
Twyford
Thurmaston
South Croxton
North Marefield
Knossington
Birstall
Beeby
Baggrave
Newbold
Saucey
Anstey
South Marefield
Lowesby
Owston
Groby
Hungerton
Keyham
Quenby
Whatborough
Glenfield
Belgrave
Humberstone
Tilton
Withcote
R. Soar
LEICESTER
Scraptoft
Ingarsby
Cold Newton
Ratby
Kirby Muxloe
Bromkinsthorpe
Halstead
Burgo
Evington
Houghton on the Hill
Billesdon
Loddington
Braunstone
Stoughton
Frisby
Skeffington
Lubbesthorpe
Knighton
Great Stretton
Galby
Tugby
East Norton
Aylestone
Oadby
Rolleston
Little Stretton
King's Norton
Keythorpe
Allexton
Enderby
Wigston Magna
Illston on the Hill
Goadby
Thurlaston
Noseley
Stockerston
Whetstone
Great Glen
Burton Overy
Hallaton
Huncote
Blaby
Newton Harcourt
Carlton Curlieu
Horninghold
Little Thorpe
Glooston
Croft
Kilby
Wistow
Shangton
Othorpe
Blaston
Holyoaks
Cosby
Foston
Stonton Wyville
Cranoe
Kibworth Harcourt
Tur Langton
Slawston
Great Easton
Sutton in the Elms
Kibworth Beauchamp
East Langton
Prestgrave
Primethorpe
Peatling Magna
Fleckney
West Langton
Welham
Medbourne
Smeeton Westerby
Thorpe Langton
Ashby Magna
Willoughby Waterless
Arnesby
Saddington
R. Welland
Shearsby
Gumley
Bruntingthorpe
Foxton
Dunton Bassett
Leire
Great Bowden
Peatling Parva
Knaptoft
Laughton
Cotes-de-Val
Mowsley
Ashby Parva
Gilmorton
Lubenham
Ullesthorpe
Little Bowden
Kimcote
Bitteswell
Walton
Theddingworth
Bittesby
Poultney
Husbands Bosworth
Lutterworth
Misterton
North Kilworth
Walcote
Cotesbach
South Kilworth
Shawell
Stormsworth
Swinford
Catthorpe

26 KENT

A
B
C
D
E
F
1
2
3
4
5
6
7
8
9
R. Thames
Woolwich
Plumstead
Charlton
Greenwich
Lessness
Howbury
Wricklesmarsh
Lee
Crayford
Stone
Northfleet
Gravesend
Cliffe
Cooling
Higham
Oakleigh
Stoke
Lewisham
Eltham
Bexley
Dartford
Swanscombe
Milton
Denton
Beckley
Chalk
R. Cray
North Cray
Foots Cray
Hawley
Darenth
Southfleet
Merston
Haven
Hoo
Ruxley
Pinden
Henhurst
Frindsbury
Bromley
Beckenham
St Pauls Cray
St Mary Cray
Horton Kirby
Longfield
Fawkham
Nurstead
ROCHESTER
Gillingham
Chatham
Sandlings
Crofton
Orpington
R. Darent
Farningham
Hartley
Meopham
Cuxton
Borstal
Delce
Nashenden
West Wickham
Keston
Eynsford
Lullingstone
Idleigh
Luddesdown
Newington
Chelsfield
Maplescombe
Ash
Ridley
R. Medway
Wouldham
Halling
Paddlesworth
Snodland
Burham
Trottiscliffe
Birling
Eccles
Tottington
Cudham
Otford
Wrotham
Ryarsh
Leybourne
Aylesford
Boxley
Addington
Siffleton
Ditton
Allington
Thurnham
Wrotham Heath
Seal
Offham
West Malling
East Malling
Penenden
Aldington
Brasted
Sundridge
Westerham
Maidstone
R. Len
West Barming
East Barming
Wateringbury
Teston
Otham
Mereworth
West Farleigh
East Farleigh
Leeds
Pimp's Court
West Peckham
Nettlestead
Stocking
Broomfield
Langley (Loose)
Yalding
Hadlow
East Peckham
Bensted
(Hunton)
East Sutton
Chart Sutton
R. Beult
R. Medway
Tonbridge
Tudeley
Benenden
Hawkhurst

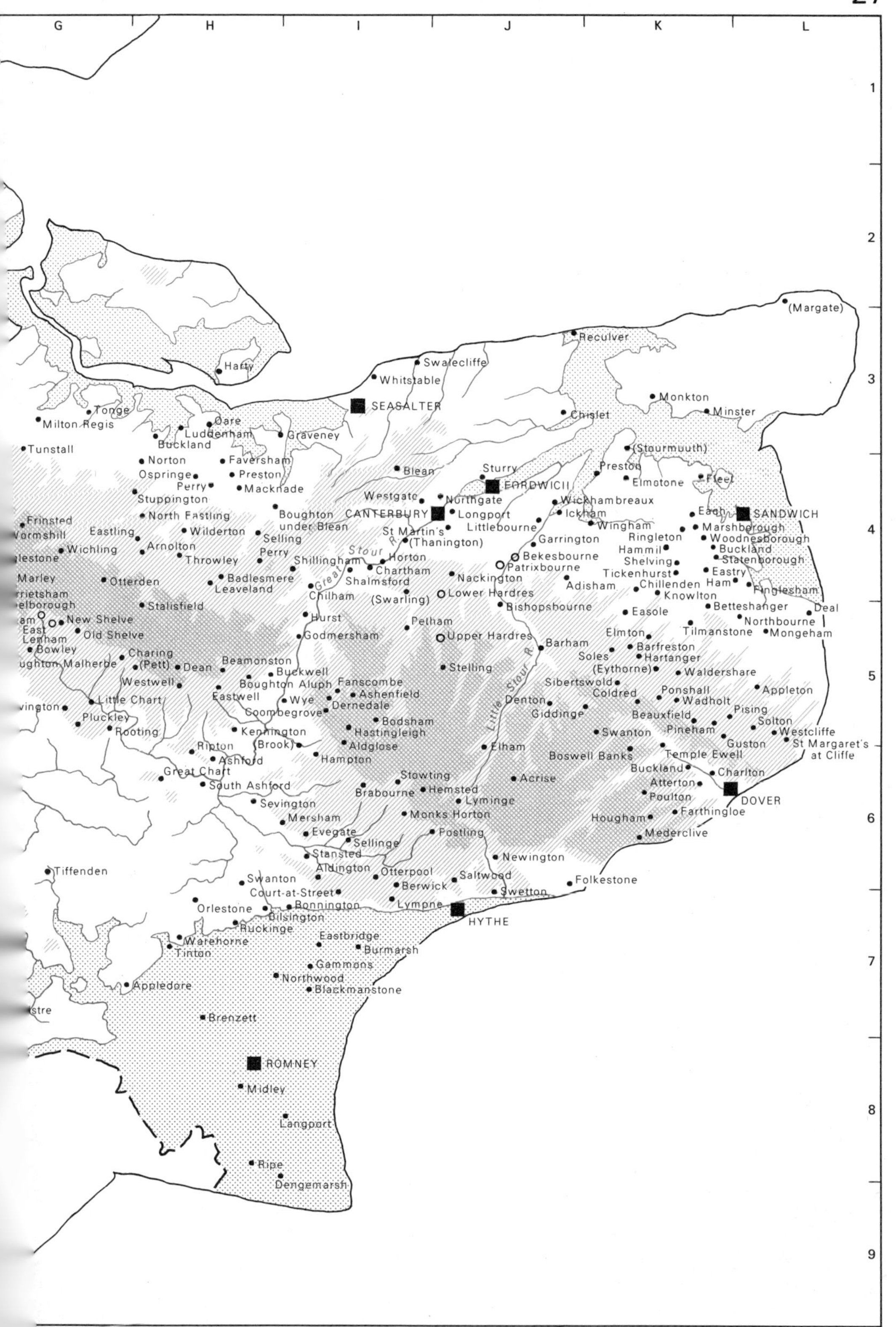
G
H
I
J
K
L
1
2
3
4
5
6
7
8
9
(Margate)
Reculver
Harty
Swalecliffe
Whitstable
SEASALTER
Monkton
Minster
Chislet
Tonge
Milton Regis
Oare
Luddenham
Buckland
Graveney
Tunstall
Norton
Faversham
(Stourmouth)
Preston
Elmstone
Fleet
Ospringe
Preston
Perry
Macknade
Blean
Sturry
FORDWICH
Stuppington
Westgate
Northgate
Wickhambreaux
North Eastling
Boughton under Blean
CANTERBURY
Longport
Ickham
Each
SANDWICH
Frinsted
Wormshill
Eastling
Wilderton
St Martin's
Littlebourne
Wingham
Marshborough
Selling
Woodnesborough
Wichling
Arnolton
(Thanington)
Garrington
Ringleton
Buckland
Hammil
Throwley
Perry
Shillingham
Horton
Bekesbourne
Shelving
Statenborough
Marley
Otterden
Badlesmere
Chartham
Patrixbourne
Tickenhurst
Eastry
Leaveland
Shalmsford
Nackington
Adisham
Chillenden
Ham
Finglesham
Chilham
(Swarling)
Lower Hardres
Knowlton
Stalisfield
Bishopsbourne
Betteshanger
Deal
New Shelve
Hurst
Easole
East Lenham
Old Shelve
Pelham
Northbourne
Godmersham
Upper Hardres
Elmton
Tilmanstone
Mongeham
Bowley
Charing
Barham
Barfreston
(Pett)
Dean
Beamonston
Soles
Hartanger
Buckwell
Stelling
(Eythorne)
Waldershare
Westwell
Boughton Aluph
Fanscombe
Sibertswold
Ashenfield
Ponshall
Appleton
Little Chart
Eastwell
Wye
Coldred
Dernedale
Denton
Wadholt
Pluckley
Coombegrove
Giddinge
Pising
Bodsham
Beauxfield
Solton
Rooting
Kennington
Swanton
Pineham
Westcliffe
Hastingleigh
(Brook)
Elham
Guston
St Margaret's at Cliffe
Ripton
Aldglose
Boswell Banks
Temple Ewell
Ashford
Hampton
Buckland
Great Chart
Charlton
Stowting
Acrise
South Ashford
Atterton
Brabourne
Hemsted
DOVER
Poulton
Sevington
Lyminge
Farthingloe
Mersham
Monks Horton
Hougham
Evegate
Postling
Sellinge
Mederclive
Stansted
Newington
Tiffenden
Aldington
Otterpool
Swanton
Saltwood
Folkestone
Court-at-Street
Berwick
Swetton
Orlestone
Bonnington
Lympne
Bilsington
HYTHE
Ruckinge
Eastbridge
Warehorne
Burmarsh
Tinton
Gammons
Appledore
Northwood
Blackmanstone
Brenzett
ROMNEY
Midley
Langport
Ripe
Dengemarsh
Great Stour R.
Little Stour R.

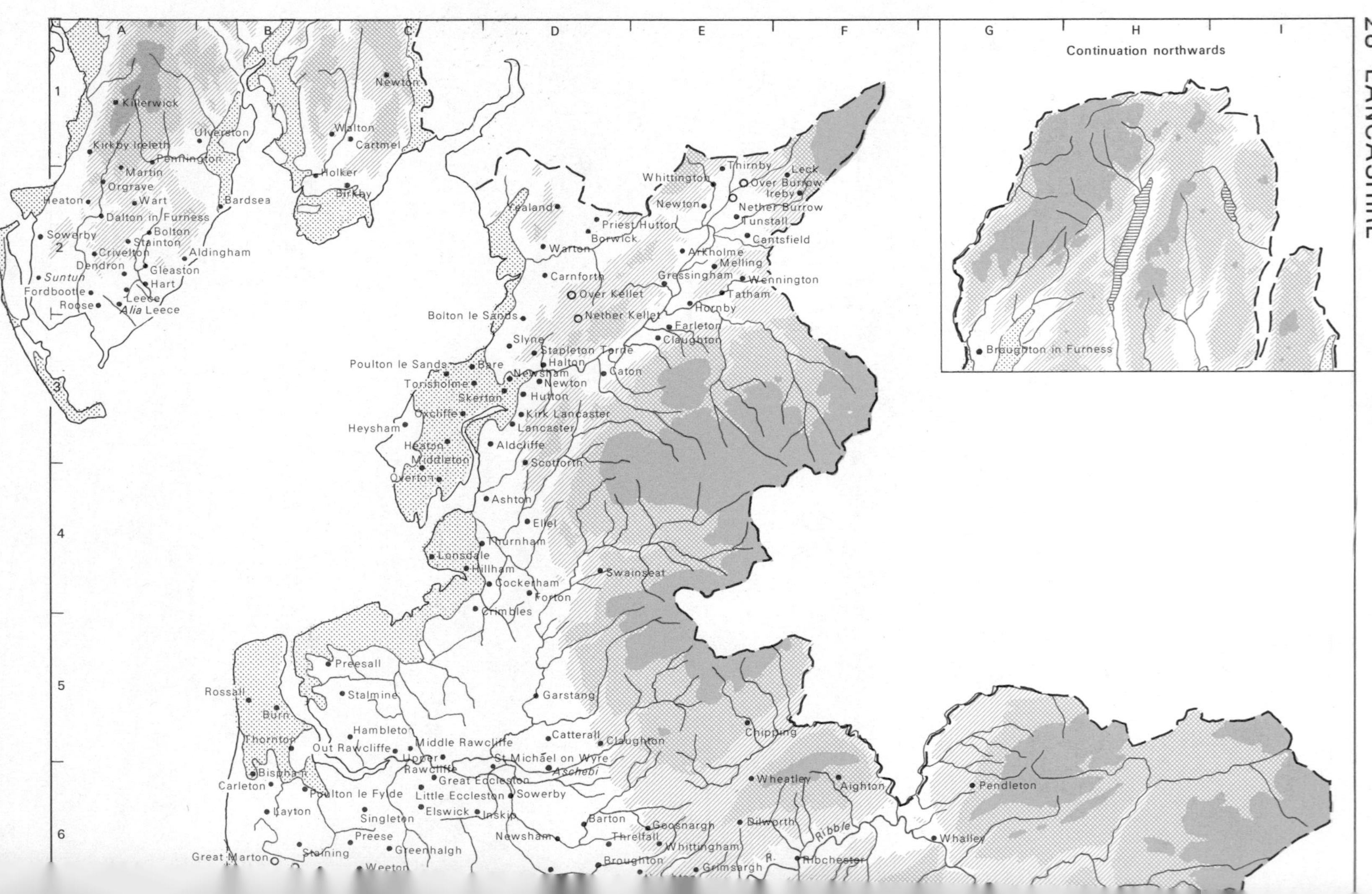

A
B
C
D
E
F
G
H
I
1
2
3
4
5
6
Continuation northwards
Broughton in Furness
Killerwick
Kirkby Ireleth
Ulverston
Pennington
Martin
Orgrave
Heaton
Wart
Bardsea
Dalton in Furness
Sowerby
Bolton
Stainton
Crivelton
Aldingham
Dendron
Gleaston
Suntun
Hart
Fordbootle
Leece
Roose
Alia Leece
Newton
Walton
Cartmel
Holker
Birkby
Yealand
Priest Hutton
Borwick
Warton
Carnforth
Over Kellet
Nether Kellet
Bolton le Sands
Whittington
Thirnby
Leck
Over Burrow
Ireby
Newton
Nether Burrow
Tunstall
Cantsfield
Arkholme
Melling
Gressingham
Wennington
Tatham
Hornby
Farleton
Claughton
Slyne
Stapleton Terne
Halton
Poulton le Sands
Bare
Newsham
Caton
Torrisholme
Newton
Skerton
Hutton
Oxcliffe
Kirk Lancaster
Heysham
Lancaster
Heaton
Aldcliffe
Middleton
Scotforth
Overton
Ashton
Ellel
Thurnham
Lonsdale
Hillham
Swainseat
Cockerham
Forton
Crimbles
Preesall
Rossall
Stalmine
Garstang
Burn
Hambleto
Thornton
Catterall
Claughton
Chipping
Out Rawcliffe
Middle Rawcliffe
Upper
Rawcliffe
St Michael on Wyre
Aschebi
Bispham
Great Eccleston
Wheatley
Aighton
Pendleton
Carleton
Poulton le Fylde
Little Eccleston
Sowerby
Layton
Elswick
Inskip
Singleton
Barton
Goosnargh
Dilworth
Ribble
Preese
Newsham
Threlfall
Whalley
Whittingham
Great Marton
Staining
Greenhalgh
Broughton
R.
Ribchester
Weeton
Grimsargh

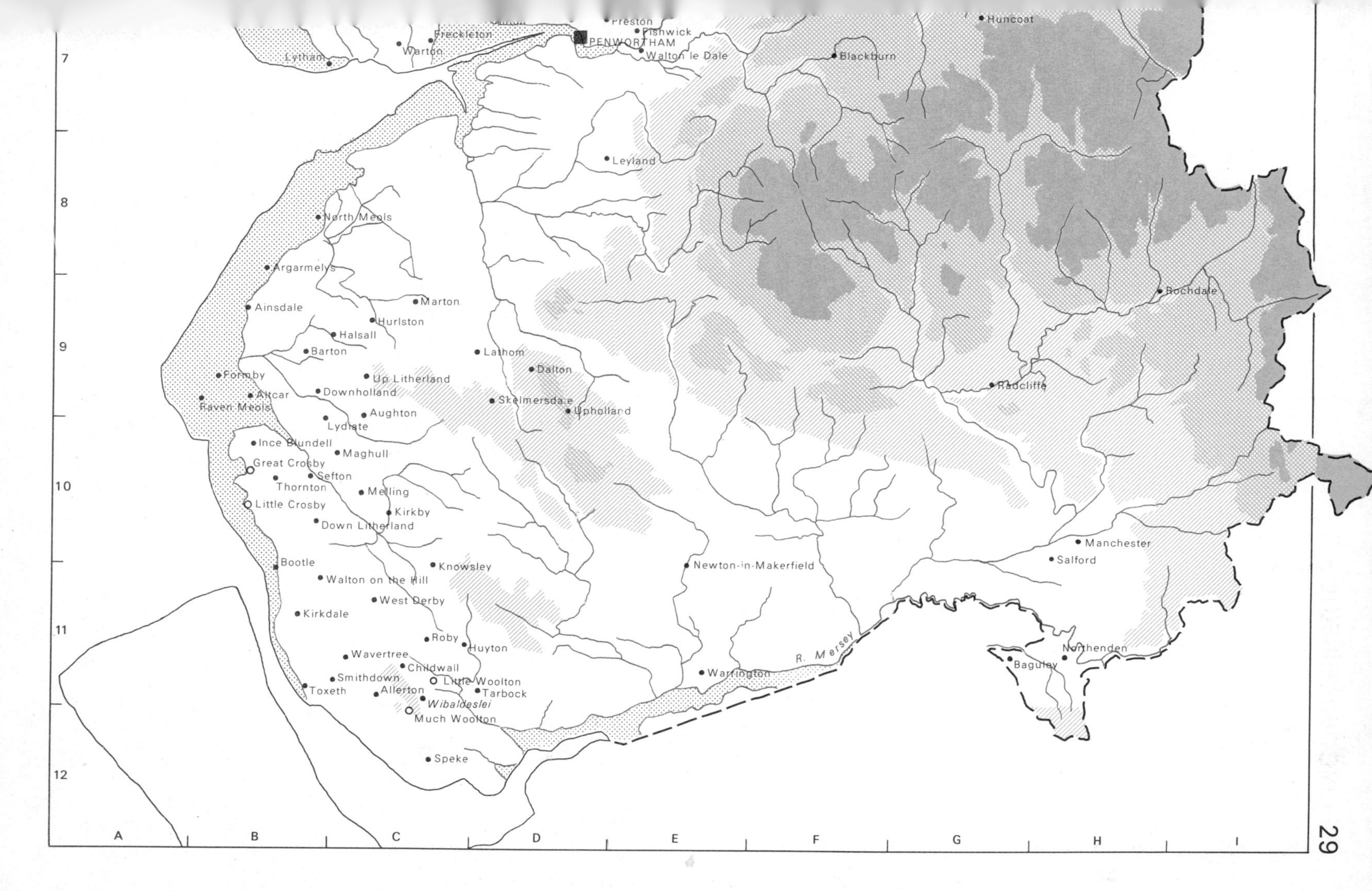
Freckleton
Preston
Fishwick
PENWORTHAM
Walton le Dale
Huncoat
Blackburn
Lytham
Warton
Leyland
North Meols
Argarmelys
Ainsdale
Marton
Hurlston
Halsall
Barton
Lathom
Dalton
Formby
Up Litherland
Altcar
Downholland
Raven Meols
Skelmersdale
Upholland
Aughton
Lydiate
Rochdale
Radcliffe
Ince Blundell
Maghull
Great Crosby
Sefton
Thornton
Melling
Little Crosby
Kirkby
Down Litherland
Bootle
Knowsley
Walton on the Hill
Newton-in-Makerfield
Manchester
Salford
West Derby
Kirkdale
Roby
Huyton
Wavertree
Childwall
Smithdown
Little Woolton
Toxeth
Allerton
Tarbock
Wibaldeslei
Much Woolton
Speke
R. Mersey
Warrington
Northenden
Baguley
7
8
9
10
11
12
A
B
C
D
E
F
G
H
I

30 LINCOLNSHIRE(NORTH)

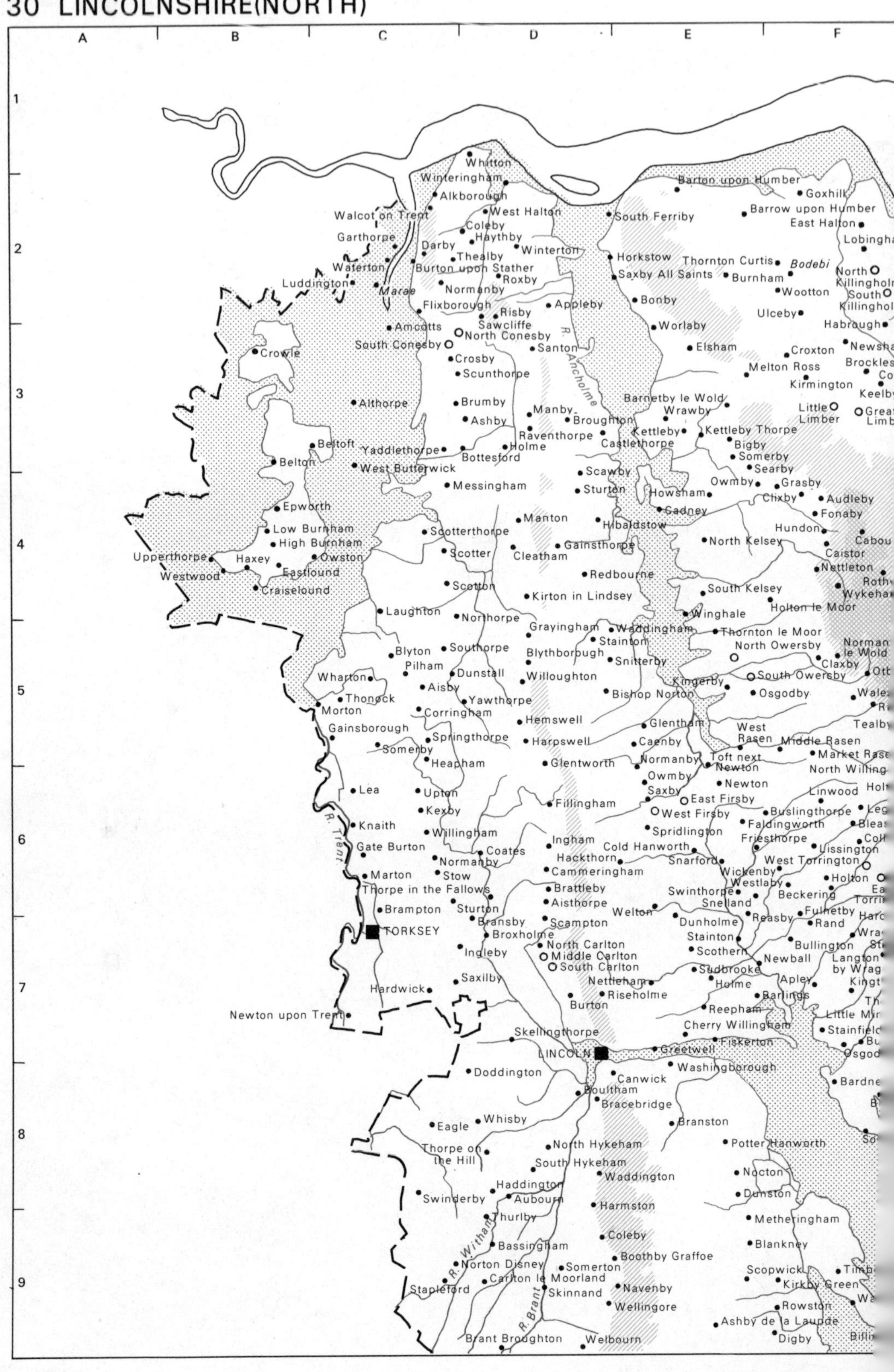

G
H
I
J
K
L
1
2
3
4
5
6
7
8
9
Houflet
Stallingborough
Healing
Great Grimsby
Great Coates
Little Coates
Clee
Itterby
Thrunscoe
Aylesby
Riby
Bradley
Weelsby
Laceby
Scartho
Irby upon Humber
Humberston
Waltham
Barnoldby le Beck
Holton le Clay
Beelsby
Brigsley
Hatcliffe
Ashby
Waithe
Tetney
Fenby
Grainsby
East Ravendale
North Thoresby
Swine
Thorganby
Hawerby
Wold Newton
Beesby
Autby
Fulstow
North Somercoates
Swinhope
North Cadeby
Grainthorpe
Ludborough
Covenham
Mere Haven
Orford
St Bartholomew
Wyham
Covenham St Mary
South
Somercoates
Binbrook
North Ormsby
Yarburgh
Skidbrooke
Saltfleet
Little
Grimsby
Alvingham
Saltfleetby St Clements
Fotherby
North Elkington
North Cockerington
Saltfleetby All Saints
Kelstern
Brackenborough
South
Cockerington
Saltfleetby
St Peter
Theddlethorpe St Helen
Ludford Magna
South
Calcethorpe
Elkington
Keddington
Grimoldby
Theddlethorpe All Saints
West
East Wykeham
LOUTH
Girsby
Welton le Wold
Stewton
Manby
South Cadeby
Gayton le Wold
Hallington
Little Carlton
Mablethorpe
Biscathorpe
Raithby
Legbourne
Maltby
South Willingham
Withcall
Reston
Trusthorpe
Donington on Bain
Tathwell
Withern
Strubby
Muckton
Maltby le Marsh
Benniworth
Stenigot
Haugham
Tothill
Woodthorpe
Sutton le Marsh
Cawkwell
Maidenwell
Authorpe
Beesby in the Marsh
Goulceby
Asterby
Farforth
Burwell
Claythorpe
Markby
Sotby
Ranby
Aby
Saleby
Scamblesby
Ruckland
Belleau
Thoresthorpe
Great Sturton
Oxcombe
Walmsgate
Swaby
Ailby
Tothby
Sutton
Worlaby
Ketsby
South
Thoresby
Bilsby
Huttoft
Belchford
South
Ormsby
Haugh
Alford
Thurlby
Little Sturton
Calceby
Rigsby
Hemingby
Tetford
Driby
Mumby
Baumber
Salmonby
Brinkhill
Well
Minting
Tatebi
Cumberworth
Fulletby
Somersby
Ulceby
Bonthorpe
West Ashby
Sutterby
Wispington
Bag Enderby
Fordington
Willoughby in the Marsh
Edlington
Low Toynton
Ashby Puerorum
Dexthorpe
Claxby
Sloothby
Thimbleby
Greetham
Langton
Dalby
Hasthorpe
High Toynton
Addlethorpe
Skendleby
Langton
Horncastle
Winceby
Hagworthingham
Hanby
Ingoldmells
Grebby
Welton le Marsh
Partney
Boothby
Horsington
Thornton
Lusby
Scremby
Candlesby
Mareham on the Hill
Raithby
Orby
Hameringham
Hundleby
Ashby by Partney
Gunby
Martin
Asgarby
Mavis
Enderby
Scrivelsby
Spilsby
Hareby
Halton Holegate
Burgh in the Marsh
Roughton
Claxby Pluckacre
Bolingbroke
Eresby
Bratoft
Moorby
Miningsby
East Keal
Great Steeping
Haltham
West Keal
Toynton St Peter
Wood Enderby
Skegness
Hagnaby
Toynton
Wilksby
East Kirkby
All Saints
Little Steeping
Croft
Kirkby on Bain
R. Bain
Revesby
Fulsby
Thorpe St Peter
Mareham le Fen
Stickford
Tumby
Wainfleet All Saints
Tattershall
Coningsby
Wainfleet St Mary
Stickney
Friskney

32 LINCOLNSHIRE(SOUTH)

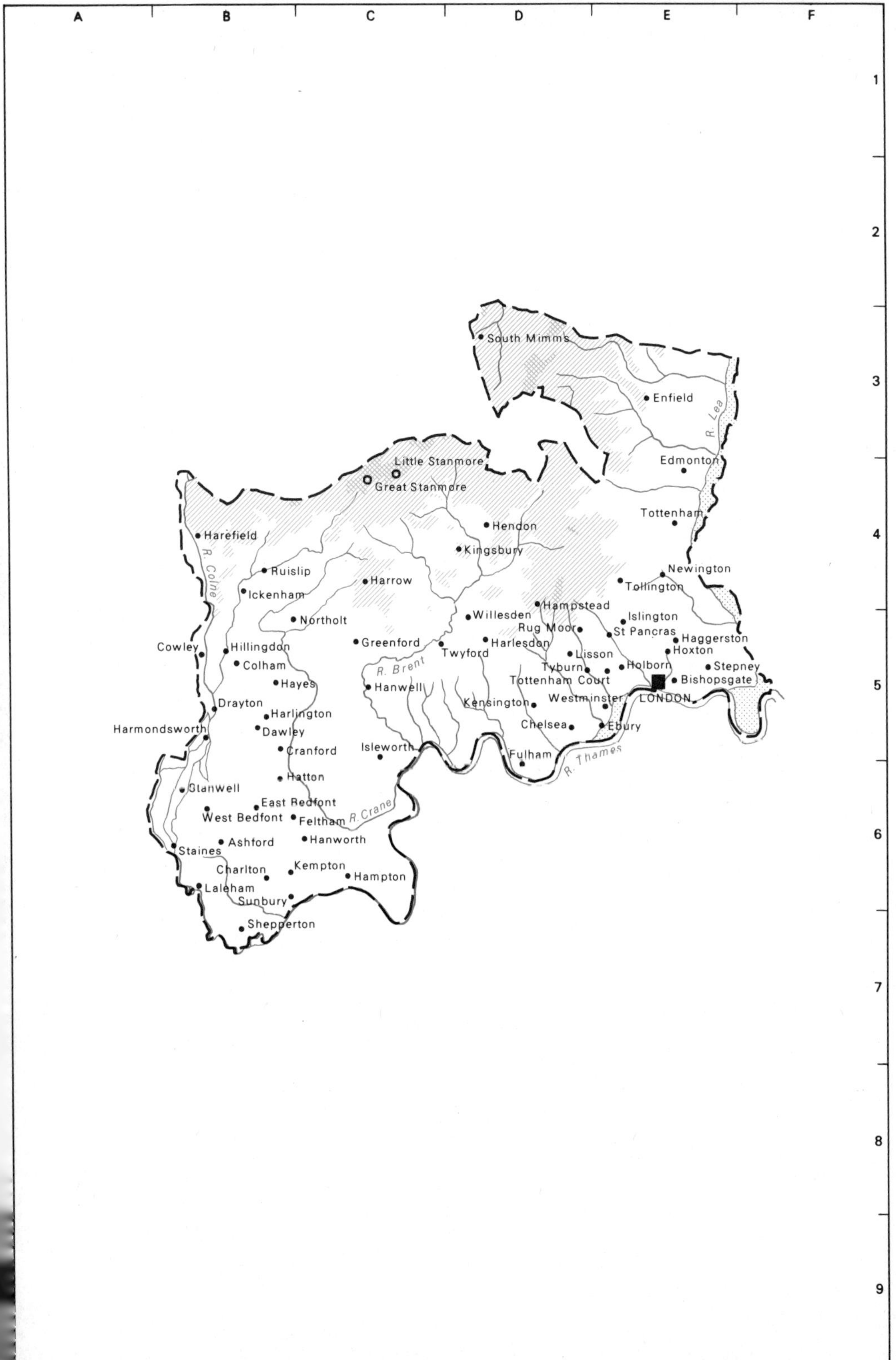
A
B
C
D
E
F
1
2
3
4
5
6
7
8
9
South Mimms
Enfield
R. Lea
Edmonton
Little Stanmore
Great Stanmore
Tottenham
Harefield
Hendon
Kingsbury
R. Colne
Ruislip
Ickenham
Harrow
Newington
Tollington
Northolt
Hampstead
Willesden
Islington
Rug Moor
St Pancras
Haggerston
Hoxton
Cowley
Hillingdon
Greenford
Twyford
Harlesdon
Lisson
Colham
R. Brent
Tyburn
Holborn
Stepney
Hayes
Hanwell
Tottenham Court
Bishopsgate
Drayton
Kensington
Westminster
LONDON
Harlington
Harmondsworth
Dawley
Chelsea
Ebury
Cranford
Isleworth
Fulham
R. Thames
Hatton
Stanwell
East Bedfont
West Bedfont
Feltham
R. Crane
Ashford
Hanworth
Staines
Charlton
Kempton
Hampton
Laleham
Sunbury
Shepperton

A
B
C
D
E
F
1
2
3
4
5
6
7
8
9
Brancaster
Burnham Deepdale
Holme next the Sea
Titchwell
B. Westgate
Burnham Norton
Wells next the Sea
Holkham
Thornham
Burnham Ulph
Burnham Overy
Hunstanton
Burnham Sutton
Warham St Mary
Burnham Thorpe
Warham All Saints
Ringstead
Gnatingdon
Wighton
Great Walsingham
Quarles
North Creake
Egmere
Heacham
Southmere
Docking
South Creake
Little Walsingham
Sedgeford
Stanhoe
Waterden
Barwick
Houghton St Giles
North Barsham
Fring
West Barsham
Snettisham
Bircham Newton
East Barsham
Thursford
Barmer
Ingoldisthorpe
Great Bircham
Syderstone
Little Snoring
Shernborne
Kettlestone
Bircham Tofts
Bagthorpe
Sculthorpe
Thorpland
Dersingham
Dunton
Alethorpe
Croxton
Anmer
Shereford
Fakenham
Tattersett
Sandringham
East Rudham
Broomsthorpe
Hempton
Houghton
Tatterford
Pudding Norton
West Newton
West Rudham
Appleton
Toftrees
Flitcham
Helhoughton
Babingley
Colkirk
Testerton
Hillington
Harpley
West Raynham
Oxwick
Castle Rising
East Raynham
Pattesley
Little Massingham
Congham
South Raynham
Whissonsett
Kipton
Roydon
Great Massingham
Wellingham
Horningtoft
Wootton
Weasenham St Peter
Godwick
Grimston
Terrington St Clement
Weasenham All Saints
North Elmham
North Lynn
Gaywood
Leziate
Well
Tittleshall
Stanfield
Clenchwarton
King's Lynn
Rougham
West Lynn
Bawsey
Gayton
Mileham
Mintlyn
Ashwicken
Sutton
South Lynn
Gayton Thorpe
Glosthorpe
West Lexham
Litcham
Bittering
Walpole
Islington
North Runcton
East Lexham
Longham
West Winch
East Winch
East Walton
Castle Acre
Kirtling
Terrington St John
Middleton
Kempstone
Newton
West Bilney
R. Nar
West Acre
Gressenhall
Wiggenhall St Mary the Virgin
South Acre
Great Dunham
Wiggenhall St Germans
Pentney
Custthorpe
Great Fransham
West Walton
Wiggenhall St Peter
Narford
Little Dunham
Wendling
Narborough
Scarning
Palgrave
Wormegay
Wiggenhall St Mary Magdalen
Little Fransham
West Briggs
Sporle
Walsoken
Tottenhill
Marham
West Bradenham
Runcton Holme
Fodderstone
Necton
Shouldham St Margaret
Swaffham
East Bradenham
South Runcton
Shouldham All Saints
Wallington
Shouldham Thorpe
Holme Hale
Thorpland
North Pickenham
Fincham
Toombers
Beechamwell
Houghton on the Hill
Stow Bardolph
Stradsett
Barton Bendish
Shingham
Panworth
Wimbotsham
Ashill
Cockley Cley
Cranworth
Downham Market
Crimplesham
South Pickenham
Outwell
Bexwell
Caldecote
Cleythorpe
Woodrising
West Dereham
R. Wissey
Saham Toney
Upwell
Boughton
Gooderstone
Denver
Wereham
Great Cressingham
Ryston
Oxborough
Watton
Roxham
Stoke Ferry
Little Cressingham
Hilborough
Threxton
Fordham
Foulden
Griston
Snore
Bodney
Merton
Caston
Hilgay
Northwold
Thompson
Didlington
Langford
Rockland All Saints
Colveston
Sturston
Southery
Methwold
Ickburgh
Cranwich
Stanford
Tottington
Ottering Hithe
Buckenham Tofts
Mundford
Lynford
West Tofts
Little Hockham
West Wretham
East Wretham
Feltwell
Rising
Weeting
Hockwold
Wilton
Santon
Croxton
Bridgham
Little Ouse R.
Kilverstone
Brettenham
THETFORD
Little Snarehill
Rushford
Great Snarehill

G
H
I
J
K
L
1
2
3
4
5
6
7
8
9
Cley next the Sea
Salthouse
Sheringham
Weybourne
Beeston Regis
Runton
Shipden
Wiveton
Glandford
Kelling
Overstrand
Langham
Bayfield
East Beckham
Saxlingham
Neutuna
West Beckham
Aylmerton
Sidestrand
Holt
Letheringsett
Bodham
Felbrigg
Northrepps
Field Dalling
Gresham
Hempstead
Sustead
Metton
Southrepps
Gimingham
Bale
Sharrington
Baconsthorpe
North Barningham
Mundesley
Roughton
Brinton
Thornage
Bessingham
Hanworth
Thorpe Market
Hunworth
Thurgarton
Trunch
Gunthorpe
Stody
Plumstead
Matlask
Alby
Gunton
Paston
Briningham
Wickmere
Edgefield
Aldborough
Antingham
Knapton
Bacton
Little Barningham
Thwaite
Swafield
Briston
Wolterton
Melton Constable
Mannington
Erpingham
Walcott
Witton
Calthorpe
Suffield
Happisburgh
Itteringham
Colby
Ridlington
North Walsham
Thurning
Saxthorpe
Banningham
Whimpwell
Corpusty
Ingworth
Crostwight
Felmingham
Hindolveston
Lessingham
Eccles
Irmingland
Blickling
Crackford
East Ruston
Oulton
Hempstead
Mortoft
Honing
Guestwick
Wood Norton
Tuttington
Brumstead
Palling
Wood Dalling
Aylsham
Swanton Abbot
Ingham
Burgh next Aylsham
Worstead
Waxham
Stinton
Skeyton
Foulsham
Sall
Westwick
Dilham
Stalham
Brampton
Hickling
Kerdiston
Marsham
Scottow
Oxnead
Sloley
Smallburgh
Bintree
Hackford
Reepham
Cawston
Rippon
Lamas
Easton
Tunstead
Sutton
Hevingham
Beeston St Lawrence
Foxley
Booton
Little Hautbois
Horsey
Barton Turf
Whitwell
Thurton
Brandiston
Sco Ruston
Catfield
Buxton
Great Hautbois
Ness
Bawdeswell
Beck
Haveringland
Neatishead
Guton
Stratton Strawless
Mayton
Potter Heigham
East Somerton
Billingford
Sparham
Witchingham
Coltishall
Hoveton St Peter
Winterton
Horstead
West Somerton
Belaugh
Bylaugh
Swannington
Ludham
Martham
Hainford
Sco
Lyng
Hoveton St John
Frettenham
Bastwick
Hemsby
Felthorpe
Swanton Morley
R. Wensum
Wroxham
Repps
Ormesby St Michael
Elsing
Attlebridge
Stanninghall
Horning
Thurne
Rollesby
Scratby
Helmingham
Horsford
Crostwick
Ashby
Weston Longville
Spixworth
Woodbastwick
Clippesby
Ormesby St Margaret
Ringland
Horsham
Ranworth
Oby
Drayton
Beeston St Andrew
Panxworth
Billockby
Burgh St Margaret
Filby
Hockering
Taverham
Rackheath
South Walsham
North Tuddenham
Honingham
Upton
Mautby
Costessey
Little Plumstead
Caister
Sprowston
Catton
Fishley
Thrigby
East Tuddenham
Honingham Thorpe
Hemblington
Stokesby
Runham
Mattishall
Easton
Hellesdon
Acle
Herringby
Yaxham
Welborne
Great Plumstead
Colton
North Burlingham
Whinburgh
Bickerston
Bowthorpe
NORWICH
Witton
Blofield
Heigham
Thorpe St Andrew
Bradeston
Tunstall
Brandon Parva
Marlingford
R. Yare
Bawburgh
Earlham
Newton
Postwick
Brundall
South Burlingham
YARMOUTH
Garveston
Barford
Little Melton
Colney
Whitlingham
Strumpshaw
Moor
Beighton
Yaxton
Runhall
Barnham Broom
Lakenham
Catton
Moulton St Mary
Halvergate
Reymerston
Great Melton
Eaton
Trowse
Surlingham
Buckenham
Freethorpe
Calvely
Wramplingham
Cringleford
Markshall
Kirby Bedon
Wickhampton
Flockthorpe
Carleton Forehoe
Bixley
Hassingham
Southwood
Kimberley
Hethersett
Keswick
Bramerton
Cantley
Gorleston
Intwood
Arminghall
Rockland St Mary
Manson
Crownthorpe
Caistor St Edmunds
Fram. Pigot
Claxton
Limpenhoe
Ketteringham
Mangreen
Framingham Earl
Hellington
Hackford
Wicklewood
East Carleton
Swardeston
Dunston
Holverston
Carleton St Peter
Reedham
Hingham
Wymondham
Walsingham
Poringland
Yelverton
Ashby St Mary
Mulbarton
Grensvill
Alpington
Langley
Hardley
Deopham
Dykebeck
Hethel
Swainsthorpe
Stoke
Howe
Brooke
Thurton
Morley St Botolph
Bracon Ash
Holy Cross
Washingford
Heckingham
Little Ellingham
Wreningham
Kenningham
Shotesham
Bergh Apton
Chedgrave
Norton Subcourse
Morley St Peter
Nayland
Newton Flotman
All Saints
Sisland
Loddon
Ashwellthorpe
Saxlingham Thorpe
Shotesham St Mary
Kirstead
Mundham
Thurlton
Great Ellingham
Fundenhall
Flordon
Rainthorpe
Saxlingham Nethergate
Langhale
Seething
Ingloss
Haddiscoe
Baconsthorpe
Tacolneston
Hapton
Hales
Raveningham
Besthorpe
Swanton
Toft Monks
Attleborough
Kettleton
Tharston
Tasburgh
Woodton
Stockton
Wheatacre
Attleborough Minor
Forncett St Peter
Stratton St Michael
Boyland
Hempnall
Bedingham
Kirby Cane
Aldeby
Forncett St Mary
Fritton
Topcroft
Hedenham
Gillingham
Thurketeliart
Hudeston
Middleton
Stratton St Mary
Morning Thorpe
Ditchingham
Ellingham
Hargham
Carleton Rode
Wacton
Shelton
Pirnhow
Broome
Buckenham
Moulton St Michael
Ashby
Aslacton
Hardwick
Eccles
Tibenham
Earsham
Banham
Denton
R. Waveney
Quidenham
Tivetshall St Margaret
Alburgh
Tivetshall St Mary
Pulham St Mary Magdalene
Kenninghall
Gissing
Pulham St Mary the Virgin
Winfarthing
Redenhall
North Lopham
Semere
Starston
Shelfanger
Burston
Harleston
Rushall
Mendham
Fersfield
Shimpling
Shotford
Dickleburgh
South Lopham
Bressingham
Thelveton
Roydon
Diss
Frenze
Thorpe Parva
Brockdish
Blo Norton
Watlingeseta
Thorpe Abbots
Osmondiston
Billingford

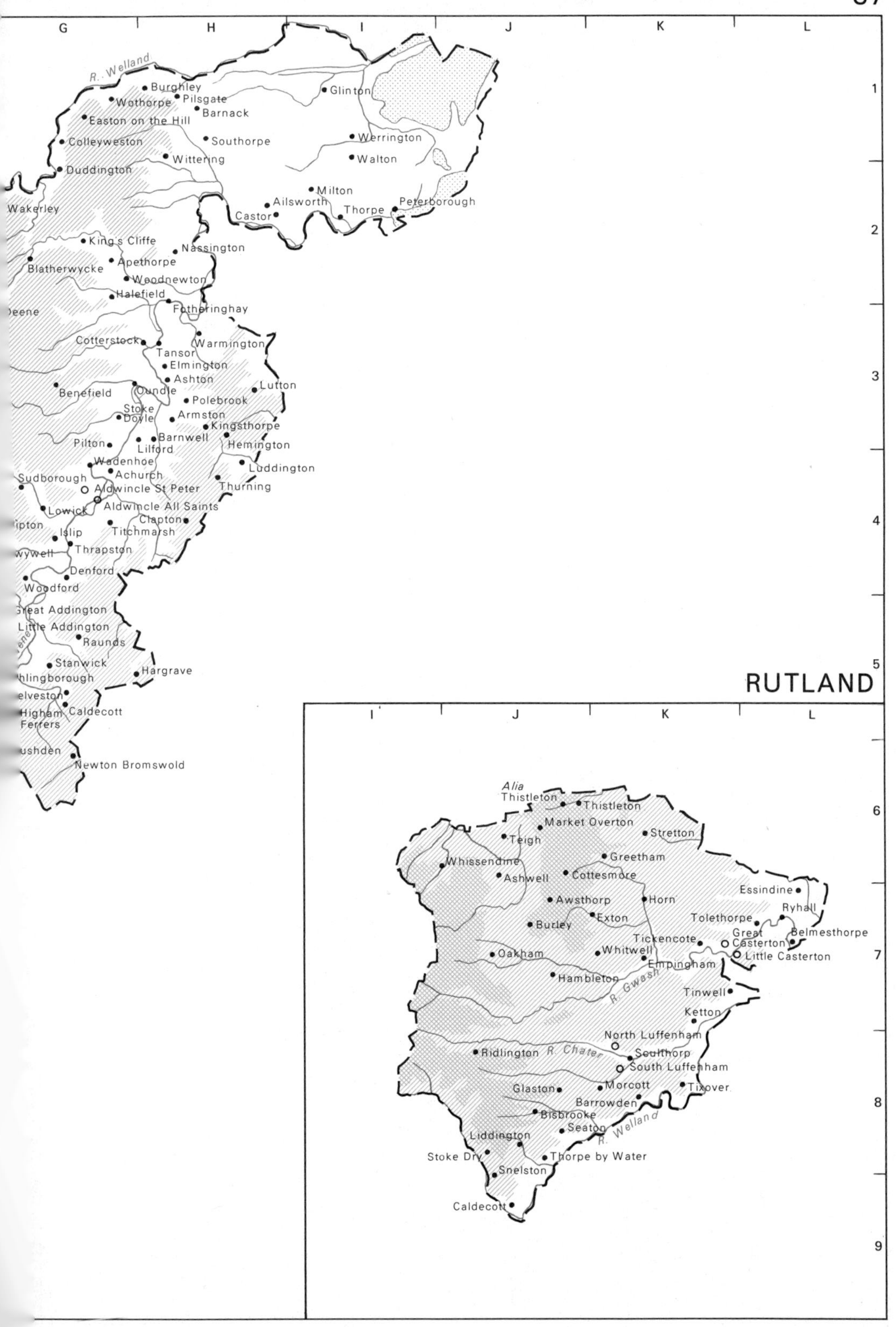
G
H
I
J
K
L
1
2
3
4
5
R. Welland
Burghley
Wothorpe
Pilsgate
Barnack
Easton on the Hill
Glinton
Colleyweston
Southorpe
Werrington
Wittering
Walton
Duddington
Milton
Ailsworth
Peterborough
Wakerley
Castor
Thorpe
King's Cliffe
Nassington
Blatherwycke
Apethorpe
Woodnewton
Halefield
Fotheringhay
Cotterstock
Warmington
Tansor
Elmington
Ashton
Lutton
Benefield
Oundle
Polebrook
Stoke Doyle
Armston
Kingsthorpe
Pilton
Barnwell
Hemington
Lilford
Wadenhoe
Luddington
Achurch
Sudborough
Aldwincle St Peter
Thurning
Lowick
Aldwincle All Saints
Clapton
Islip
Titchmarsh
Thrapston
Denford
Woodford
Little Addington
Raunds
Stanwick
Hargrave
Caldecott
Newton Bromswold
RUTLAND
I
J
K
L
6
7
8
9
Alia Thistleton
Thistleton
Market Overton
Stretton
Teigh
Greetham
Whissendine
Ashwell
Cottesmore
Essindine
Awsthorp
Horn
Ryhall
Exton
Tolethorpe
Burley
Great Casterton
Belmesthorpe
Tickencote
Oakham
Whitwell
Little Casterton
Empingham
Hambleton
R. Gwash
Tinwell
Ketton
North Luffenham
Ridlington
R. Chater
Sculthorp
South Luffenham
Glaston
Morcott
Tixover
Barrowden
Bisbrooke
Seaton
R. Welland
Liddington
Stoke Dry
Thorpe by Water
Snelston
Caldecott

38 NOTTINGHAMSHIRE

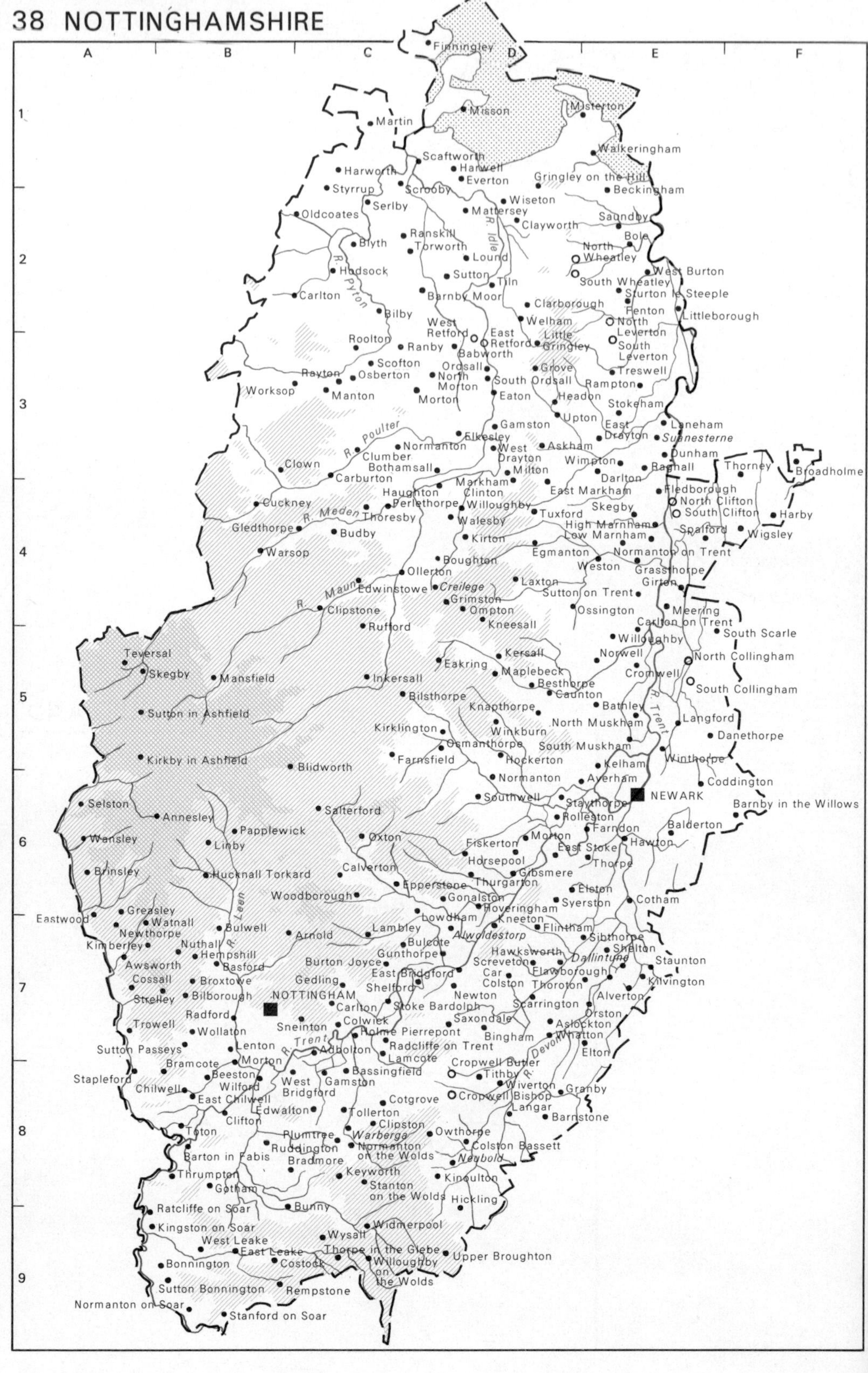

A
B
C
D
E
F
1
2
3
4
5
6
7
8
9
Mollington
Cropredy
Hanwell
Alkerton
Horley
Shennington
Wroxton
Grimsbury
Balscott
Drayton
Banbury
Broughton
Sibford Gower
Wykeham
Tadmarton
Bodicote
Sibford Ferris
Bloxham
East Adderbury
Milcombe
West Adderbury
Hook Norton
Wigginton
Barford St John
South Newington
Barford St Michael
Great Rollright
Hempton
Deddington
Swerford
Ilbury
Chastleton
Little Rollright
Nether Worton
Over Worton
Showell
Great Tew
North Aston
Fritwell
Dunthorp
Duns Tew
Somerton
Salford
Little Tew
Ledwell
Ardley
Cornwell
Heythrop
Sandford St Martin
Middle Aston
Upper Heyford
Chipping Norton
Chalford
Westcott Barton
Steeple Aston
Steeple Barton
Sesswell Barton
Lower Heyford
Kingham
Enstone
Rousham
Churchill
Radford
Kiddington
Dean
Sarsden
Chadlington
Ludwell
Northbrook
Foscot
Spelsbury
Glympton
Nethercott
Draitone
R. Glyme
R. Cherwell
Idbury
Lyneham
Wootton
Tackley
Fifield
Ascot D'Oily
Woodleys
Kirtlington
Milton under Wychwood
Ascot Earl
Cornbury
Whitehill
Shipton under Wychwood
Woodstock
Shipton on Cherwell
Wychwood
Stonesfield
Bletchingdon
Hensington
Hampton Gay
Combe
Hampton Poyle
Wilcote
Thrupp
Bladon
Kidlington
Evenlode
Taynton
North Leigh
Begbroke
Fulbrook
Handborough
Stockley
Yarnton
Burford
Swinbrook
Minster Lovell
Worton
Widford
Asthall
Cassington
Little Minster
Witney
Westwell
Eynsham
Cogges
Bromscott
Remscott
Astrop
Ducklington
Brize Norton
Lew
R. Windrush
Stanton Harcourt
Kendott
Black Bourton
Yelford
Alvescot
Broadwell
Bampton
Brighthampton
Langford
Claywell
Shifford
Clanfield
Grafton
Tusmore
Mixbury
Fulwell
Finmere
Cottisford
Shelswell
Hardwick
Hethe
Stoke Lyne
Fringford
Godington
Bainton
Saxintone
Stratton Audley
Bucknell
Caversfield
Middleton Stoney
Bicester
Launton
Chesterton
Wendlebury
Ambrosden
Weston on the Green
R. Ray
Upper Arncott
Merton
Lower Arncott
Piddington
Charlton on Otmoor
Oddington
Islip
Noke
Water Eaton
Wood Eaton
Beckley
Woodperry
Cutslow
Wolvercot
Elsfield
Stanton St John
Thomley
Stowford
Headington
Forest Hill
Walton
Holywell
Holton
OXFORD
Waterperry
Waterstock
Thame
Shotover
Draycot
Towersey
Iffley
Horspath
Rycote
Tiddington
Cowley
Chilworth
Albury
Cuddesdon
Emmington
Sandford on Thames
Great Milton
Henton
Garsington
Sydenham
Great Haseley
Wainhill
Chinnor
Chippinghurst
Little Milton
Little Haseley
Toot Baldon
Marsh Baldon
Adwell
Crowell
Stoke Talmage
Wheatfield
Hunesworde
Kingston Blount
Nuneham Courtenay
Nethercote
Rofford
Warpsgrove
S. Weston
Aston Rowant
Lewknor
Chalgrove
Easington
Newington
Cuxham
Shirburn
R. Thame
Cadwell
Pyrton
Brightwell Baldwin
Dorchester
Britwell Salome
Watlington
Berrick Salome
Ingham
Watcombe
R. Thames
Benson
Ewelme
Preston Crowmarsh
Swyncombe
Crowmarsh Gifford
Newnham Murren
Gangsdown
Mongewell
North Stoke
Bix
Ipsden
Little Stoke
Badgemore
South Stoke
Checkenden
Rotherfield Greys
Goring
Rotherfield Peppard
Harpsden
Gatehampton
Bolney
Lashbrook
Whitchurch
Mapledurham
Dunsden

A
B
C
D
E
F
G
H
I
1
2
3
4
5
6
Onneley
Gravenhunger
Woore
Dorrington
Bearstone
Norton in Hales
Adderley
Tittenley
Shavington
Whitchurch
Doddington
Edgeley
Alkington
Ightfield
Calverhall
Betton
Spoonley
Longslow
Market Drayton
Audley
Moreton Say
Sandford
Little Drayton
Chesthill
Steel
Coton
Prees
Whixall
Weston Rhyn
Welshampton
Ellesmere
Colemere
Slacheberie
Wolverley
Edstaston
Brogyntyn
Halston
Whittington
Broom
English Frankton
Horton
Lacon
Soulton
Wem
Aston
R. Roden
Weston under Redcastle
Marchamley
Wollerton
Sutton upon Tern
Chipnall
Cheswardine
Hodnet
Stoke upon Tern
Coton upon Tern
R. Tern
Hinstock
Oswestry
Weston Cotton
Wootton
Aston
Hordley
Loppington
Lee Brockhurst
Hopton
Petton
Sleap
Moston
Harcourt
High Hatton
Peplow
Cross Hills
Child's Ercall
Sambrook
Wykey
R. Perry
Maesbury
West Felton
Morton
Woolston
Stanwardine
Preston Brockhurst
Broughton
Besford
Stanton upon Hine Heath
Howle
Myddle
Yorton
Acton Reynold
Eyton
Fenemere
Grinshill
Moreton Corbet
Puleston
Osbaston
Ruyton of the Eleven Towns
Baschurch
Charlton
Cold Hatton
Maesbrook
Kinnerley
Walford
Merrington
Hadnall
Shawbury
Little Wytheford
Ellerdine
Rowton
Tibberton
Cherrington
Chetwynd
Kynaston
Little Ness
Great Ness
Yagdon
Preston Gubbals
Great Wytheford
Waters Upton
Edgmond
Astley
Felton Butler
Fitz
Mytton
Leaton
Albrighton
Albright Hussey
Poynton
Crudgington
Longford
Melverley
Isle Farm
Forton
Ercall Magna
Buttery
Brockton
Lilleshall
Kinnersley
Shrawardine
Loton
Bicton
Rossall
Albrightlee
Haughton
Preston upon the Weald Moors
Alberbury
Montford
Berwick
Longdon upon Tern
Eyton upon the Weald Moors
Woodcote
Bausley
Eyton
Benthall
Preston Montford
Severn
Rodington
Shelton
Uffington
Bratton
Hoxton
Wattlesborough
Ford
Rowton
Onslow
SHREWSBURY
Withington
Isombridge
Leegomery
Brockton
Wollaston
Cardeston
Dinthill
Woodcote
Upton Magna
Wrockwardine
Hadley
Wigmore
Amaston
Edgbold
Longner
Sheriff Hales
Wellington
Marsh
Yockleton
Meole Brace
Sutton
Berwick
Uckington
Westbury
Polmere
Hanwood
Emstrey
Atcham
Uppington
Lawley
Cause
Whitton
Pulley
Betton
Bayston
Brompton
Beslow
Wroxeter
Farley
Welbatch
Little Wenlock
Dawley Magna
Shifnal
Tong
Winsley
Norton
Boreton
Berrington
Eyton on Severn
Longden
Cantlop
Eaton Constantine
Dawley Parva

QUATFORD
R. Severn
R. Corve
R. Onny
Merstun
Bolebec
Buchehale
Albrighton
Cosford
Bishton
Ryton
Madeley
Brockton
Beckbury
Badger
Sutton Maddock
Higford
Stockton
Rudge
Shipley
Claverley
Worfield
Kingsnordley
Alveley
Romsley
Highley
Quatt
Eardington
Oldbury
Eudon Burnell
Chelmarsh
Glazeley
Middleton Scriven
Deuxhill
Kinlet
Catsley
Baveney
Walltown
Neen Savage
Cleobury Mortimer
Mawley
Neen Solars
Tetstill
Milson
Broseley
Willey
Much Wenlock
Sheinton
Belswardyne
Wigwig
Harley
Acton Round
Aston Eyre
Morville
Meadowley
Upton Cressett
Chetton
Eudon George
Faintree
Overton
Sidbury
Neenton
Ditton Priors
Charlcotte
Fulwardine
Burwarton
Aston Botterell
Pickthorn
Harcourt
Stottesdon
Walton
Detton
Stepple
Hopton Wafers
Earlsditton
Coreley
Norton
Wheathill
Farlow
Lowe
Stoke St Milborough
Ingardine
Cleestanton
Bitterley
Middleton
Henley
Caynham
Burford
Ashford Carbonell
Ashford Bowdler
Sheet
Steventon
Huntington
Ludford
Bromfield
Stanton Lacy
Ledwyche
Greater Poston
Lesser Poston
Great Sutton
Little Sutton
Culmington
Siefton
Corfton
Cortham
Clee St Margaret
Bouldon
Tugford
Abdon
Cleobury North
Holdgate
Ruthall
Stanton Long
Oxenbold
Shipton
Stanway
Rushbury
Millichope
Middlehope
Westhope
Aston
Brockton
Patton
Lutwyche
Easthope
Bourton
Gretton
Plaish
Golding
Acton Pigott
Acton Burnell
Kenley
Langley
Frodesley
Hawksley
Church Preen
Broome
Lydley Heys
Lee
Leebotwood
Cardington
All Stretton
Church Stretton
Hope Bowdler
Ticklerton
Chelmick
Little Stretton
Minton
Acton Scott
Whittingslow
Alcaston
Strefford
Cheney Longville
Sibdon Carwood
Stokesay
Aldon
Onibury
Clungunford
Hopton Castle
Bedstone
Bucknell
Stanage
Hope Bendrid
Obley
Clunbury
Purslow
Clunton
Kempton
Coston
Hopesay
Barlow
Edgton
Wistanstow
Woolston
Choulton
Myndtown
Wentnor
Lydham
Lydbury North
Clun
Llanvair Waterdine
Knighton
Norton
Ackhill
Cascob
Church Pulverbatch
Wilderley
Netley
Smethcott
Cothercott
Marsley
Womerton
Woolstaston
Ratlinghope
Overs
Hyssington
Priest Weston
Marton
Wotherton
Rorrington
Middleton
Hockleton
Walcot
Marrington
Chirbury
Dudston
Rhiston
Churchstoke
Lack
Mellington
Aston
Hopton
Castlewright
Edenhope
Ackley
Forden
Wropton
Hem
Thornbury
Montgomery
Weston
Woodluston
A
B
C
D
E
F
G
H
I
7
8
9
10
11
12

42 SOMERSET

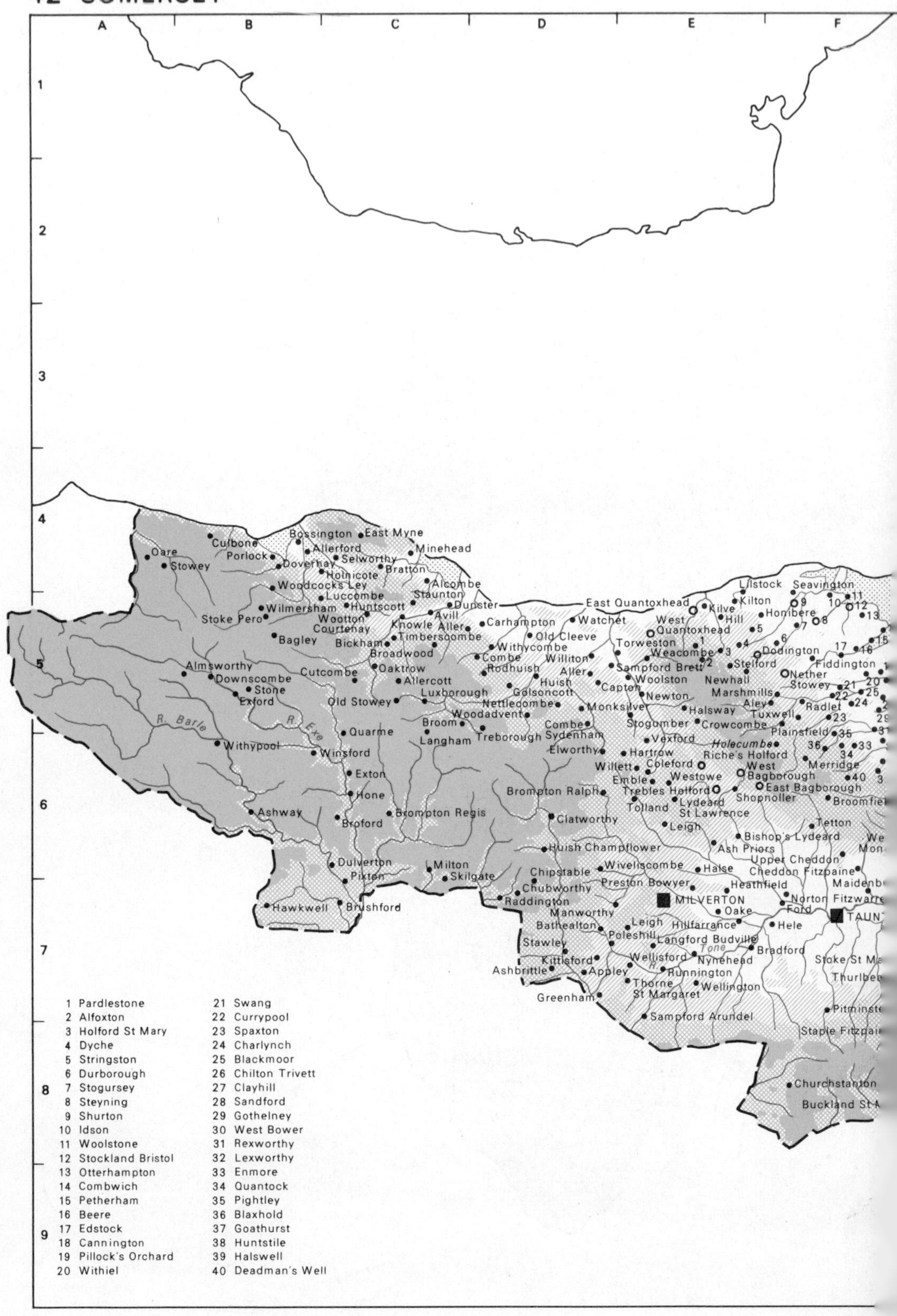
A
B
C
D
E
F
1
2
3
4
5
6
7
8
9
Bossington
East Myne
Culbone
Allerford
Minehead
Oare
Porlock
Selworthy
Stowey
Doverhay
Bratton
Holnicote
Alcombe
Woodcocks Ley
Luccombe
Staunton
Wilmersham
Huntscott
Dunster
Stoke Pero
Wootton Courtenay
Avill
Knowle
Aller
Carhampton
Watchet
East Quantoxhead
Kilve
Lilstock
Kilton
Seavington
Hill
Hombere
West Quantoxhead
Bagley
Bickham
Timberscombe
Old Cleeve
Withycombe
Torweston
Weacombe
Dodington
Broadwood
Combe
Williton
Sampford Brett
Stelford
Fiddington
Almsworthy
Oaktrow
Rodhuish
Aller
Woolston
Newhall
Nether Stowey
Downscombe
Cutcombe
Allercott
Huish
Capton
Marshmills
Stone
Luxborough
Golsoncott
Newton
Exford
Old Stowey
Nettlecombe
Monksilver
Halsway
Aley
Radlet
Woodadvent
Tuxwell
R. Barle
R. Exe
Broom
Combe Sydenham
Stogumber
Crowcombe
Plainsfield
Quarme
Treborough
Langham
Vexford
Holecumbe
Withypool
Winsford
Elworthy
Hartrow
Riche's Holford
Merridge
Willett
Coleford
West Bagborough
Exton
Emble
Westowe
Brompton Ralph
Trebles Holford
East Bagborough
Hone
Tolland
Lydeard St Lawrence
Shopnoller
Ashway
Brompton Regis
Clatworthy
Tetton
Broford
Leigh
Bishop's Lydeard
Ash Priors
Huish Champflower
Upper Cheddon
Dulverton
Milton
Wiveliscombe
Halse
Cheddon Fitzpaine
Chipstable
Pixton
Skilgate
Preston Bowyer
Heathfield
Chubworthy
Raddington
MILVERTON
Norton Ford
Hawkwell
Brushford
Manworthy
Oake
Bathealton
Leigh
Hillfarrance
Hele
Poleshill
Langford Budville
Stawley
Tone
Bradford
Wellisford
Nynehead
Kittisford
R.
Ashbrittle
Appley
Runnington
Thorne St Margaret
Wellington
Greenham
Sampford Arundel
Churchstanton
1 Pardlestone
2 Alfoxton
3 Holford St Mary
4 Dyche
5 Stringston
6 Durborough
7 Stogursey
8 Steyning
9 Shurton
10 Idson
11 Woolstone
12 Stockland Bristol
13 Otterhampton
14 Combwich
15 Petherham
16 Beere
17 Edstock
18 Cannington
19 Pillock's Orchard
20 Withiel
21 Swang
22 Currypool
23 Spaxton
24 Charlynch
25 Blackmoor
26 Chilton Trivett
27 Clayhill
28 Sandford
29 Gothelney
30 West Bower
31 Rexworthy
32 Lexworthy
33 Enmore
34 Quantock
35 Pightley
36 Blaxhold
37 Goathurst
38 Huntstile
39 Halswell
40 Deadman's Well

G
H
I
J
K
L
1
2
3
4
5
6
7
8
9
Portishead
Easton in Gordano
Portbury
Weston in Gordano
Abbot's Leigh
Clapton in Gordano
Walton in Gordano
R. Avon
Wraxall
Clevedon
Tickenham
Long Ashton
Bishopsworth
Kenn
Chelvey
Backwell
Midgell
Barrow Gurney
Keynsham
Kingston Seymour
Brockley
Claverham
Saltford
Woodspring
Yatton
Norton Malreward
Corston
Newton St Loe
Wemberham
Winford
Belluton
Burnett
Norton Hawkfield
Chew Magna
Compton Dando
Congresbury
Chillyhill
Stanton Drew
Stanton Prior
Kewstoke
Worle
Milton
Ashcombe
R. Yeo
Wrington
Ridgehill
Butcombe
Chew Stoke
Marksbury
Wilmington
Aldwick
Stoke Villice
Chelwood
Priston
Havyat
Farmborough
Euestia
Dunkerton
Pantesheda
Clutton
Timsbury
Carlingcott
Hutton
Elborough
Banwell
Blagdon
Moreton
Uphill
Ubley
Hinton Blewitt
Cameley
High Littleton
Camerton
Winterhead
Shipham
Compton Martin
West Harptree
Hallatrow
Bleadon
Winscombe
East Harptree
Woodborough
Brean
Loxton
Farrington Gurney
AXBRIDGE
Litton
Ston Easton
Radstock
Wick
Edingworth
Cheddar
Hay Street
Tarnock
Weare
Chewton Mendip
Chilcompton
Kilmersdon
Badgeworth
Alston Sutton
Walton
East Brent
Draycott
Emborough
Babington
Clewer
Stratton on the Fosse
Andersey
Chapel Allerton
Rodney Stoke
Luckington
Burnham
Pitcott
Wedmore
Westbury
Millescota
Ashwick
Huish
Blackford
Alstone
Bagley
Downhead
East Huntspill
Panborough
Wells
West Huntspill
Croscombe
Shepton Mallet
East Cranmore
Stretcholt
Charlton
West Cranmore
Pawlett
Doulting
Puriton
Woolavington
Meare
North Wootton
Walpole
Cossington
Chilton upon Polden
Pilton
Crandon
Horsey
Pignes
Bawdrip
Edington
Horsey
Bradney
Catcott
West Pennard
Glastonbury
Sydenham
Stawell
Shapwick
Pylle
Evercreech
East Bower
Sutton Mallet
Ashcott
East Pennard
Bridgwater
Dunwear
Pedwell
Walton
Hamp
Greinton
Overleigh
Ditcheat
Hadworthy
Westonzoyland
Baltonsborough
Stone
Huntworth
Butleigh
Alhampton
Hornblotton
North Petherton
Compton
West Lydford
Alford
Dundon
R. Brue
East Lydford
Shovel
Kingweston
Barton St David
Lovington
Melcombe
High Ham
Littleton
Wheathill
Foddington
St Michael Church
Keinton Mandeville
Somerton
R. Cary
Babcary
North Barrow
Lyng
Aller
Pitney
Charlton Mackrell
Charlton Adam
Durston
Wearne
Litnes Field
Steart
South Barrow
Crosse
Athelney
Cary Fitzpaine
R. Cam
LANGPORT
Lyte's Cary
Compton Pauncefoot
North Curry
Curry Rivel
Long Sutton
Sparkford
Drayton
Queen Camel
Muchelney
Milton Podimore
Thorn Falcon
West Camel
Weston Bampfylde
Swell
Moortown
Thorney
Cathanger
Fivehead
ILCHESTER
Yeovilton
Marston Magna
Isle Abbots
Earnshill
Midelney
Kingsbury Episcopi
Limington
Draycott
Rimpton
Curry Mallet
Isle Brewers
Sock Dennis
Ashington
Chilton Cantelo
Beer Crocumbe
Goosebradon
North Bradon
South Bradon
Oakley
Martock
Tintinhull
Mudford
R. Isle
R. Parrett
Capland
Puckington
Stoke sub Hamdon
Chilthorne Domer
Sock Malherbie
Stone
Thorne
Lyde
Ashill
Barrington
Ilton
Rapps
Lufton
Biscopeston
Montacute
Preston Bermondsey
Yeovil
Whitelackington
Houndstone
Norton sub Hamdon
Brympton
Broadway
Ilminster
Odcombe
Hiscombe
Chiselborough
Donyatt
Kingstone
Lopen
West Dowlish
Dowlish Wake
Dinnington
West Chinnock
East Chinnock
East Coker
Merriott
West Coker
Sutton Bingham
Cricket Malherbie
Hinton St George
Knowle St Giles
Cudworth
Eastham
Haselbury Plucknett
Hardington Mandeville
Pendomer
Chaffcombe
Crewkerne
North Perrott
Closworth
Chard
Cricket St Thomas
Wreath
Street
Whatley
Leigh
Winsham
Tadwick
Langridge
Woolley
Swainswick
Batheaston
Charlcombe
Bathwick
Weston
Bathford
Bathampton
BATH
Warleigh
Twerton
Lyncombe
Claverton
English Combe
Monkton Combe
Vndewiche
Combe Hay
Freshford
Wellow
Hinton Charterhouse
White Ox Mead
Eckweek
Farleigh Hungerford
Stony Littleton
Foxcote
Norton St Philip
Tellisford
Writhlington
Hemington
Laverton
Rode
Hardington
Lullington
Buckland Dinham
Beckington
Orchardleigh
Standerwick
Berkley
Great Elm
Mells
FROME
Fairoak
Whatley
Rodden
Keyford
Nunney
Marston Bigot
Cloford
Wanstrow
R. Frome
Witham Friary
Westcombe
Upton Noble
Batcombe
Milton Clevedon
Lamyatt
North Brewham
Eastrip
Combe
South Brewham
BRUTON
Discove
Ansford
Redlynch
Pitcombe
Stoney Stoke
Castle Cary
Shepton Montague
Knowlepark
Penselwood
Bratton Seymour
Charlton Musgrove
Yarlington
Stoke Trister
Clapton
Woolston
Wincanton
North Cadbury
Clapton
Lattiford
Cucklington
Holton
Maperton
Blackford
North Cheriton
South Cadbury
South Cheriton
Sutton Montis
Horsington
Whitcomb
Abbas Combe
Corton Denham
Stowell
Temple Combe
MILBORNE PORT
Henstridge
Thorent
1 Stocklinch St Magdalen
2 Stocklinch Ottersay
3 Shepton Beauchamp
4 Compton Durville
5 South Petherton
6 Seavington St Mary
7 Seavington Abbots
8 Seavington St Michael
9 Over Stratton
10 Wigborough

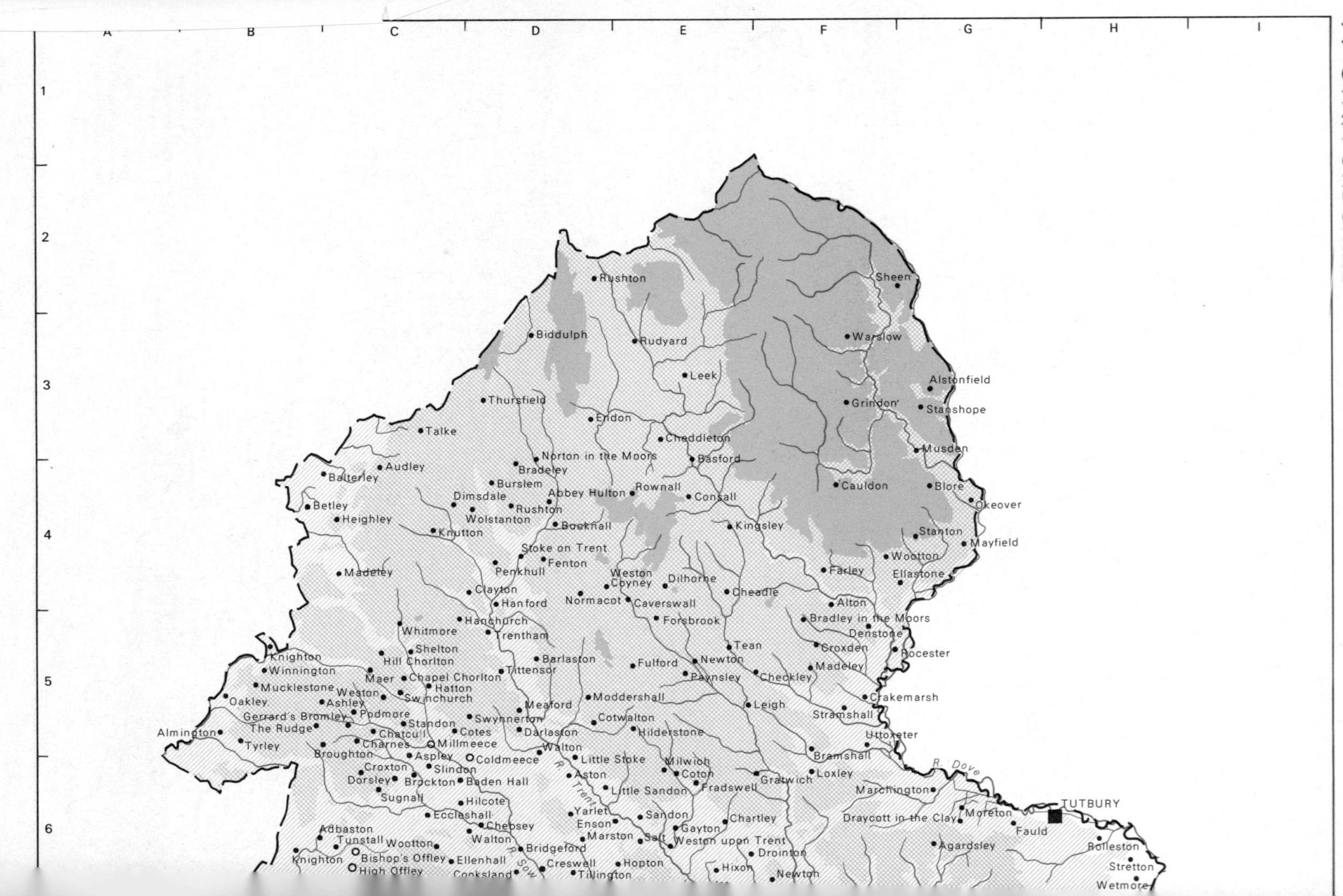
A
B
C
D
E
F
G
H
I
1
2
3
4
5
6
Rushton
Sheen
Biddulph
Rudyard
Warslow
Leek
Alstonfield
Thursfield
Grindon
Stanshope
Endon
Talke
Cheddleton
Musden
Norton in the Moors
Basford
Audley
Bradeley
Balterley
Burslem
Rownall
Cauldon
Blore
Dimsdale
Abbey Hulton
Consall
Okeover
Betley
Rushton
Wolstanton
Heighley
Bucknall
Kingsley
Stanton
Knutton
Mayfield
Stoke on Trent
Wootton
Fenton
Penkhull
Farley
Ellastone
Madeley
Weston Coyney
Dilhorne
Cheadle
Clayton
Normacot
Hanford
Caverswall
Alton
Forsbrook
Bradley in the Moors
Hanchurch
Denstone
Whitmore
Trentham
Tean
Croxden
Shelton
Rocester
Knighton
Hill Chorlton
Barlaston
Fulford
Newton
Madeley
Winnington
Maer
Chapel Chorlton
Tittensor
Paynsley
Checkley
Mucklestone
Weston
Hatton
Swinchurch
Moddershall
Crakemarsh
Oakley
Ashley
Meaford
Leigh
Gerrard's Bromley
Podmore
Swynnerton
Cotwalton
Stramshall
The Rudge
Standon
Almington
Chatcull
Cotes
Darlaston
Hilderstone
Uttoxeter
Tyrley
Charnes
Millmeece
Walton
Broughton
Aspley
Coldmeece
Little Stoke
Milwich
Bramshall
R. Dove
Croxton
Slindon
Aston
Coton
Gratwich
Loxley
Dorsley
Brockton
Baden Hall
R. Trent
Little Sandon
Fradswell
Marchington
Sugnall
Hilcote
Yarlet
Sandon
TUTBURY
Eccleshall
Enson
Chartley
Draycott in the Clay
Moreton
Adbaston
Chebsey
Gayton
Fauld
Tunstall
Wootton
Walton
Marston
Salt
Weston upon Trent
Agardsley
Bridgeford
Rolleston
Knighton
Bishop's Offley
Ellenhall
R. Sow
Creswell
Hopton
Drointon
High Offley
Cooksland
Tillington
Hixon
Newton
Stretton
Wetmore

Brough Hall
Derrington
Monetvile
Baswich
Coley
Little Haywood
Colt
Bishton
Colton
Wolseley
Rowley
Burton upon Trent
Stapenhill
Branston
Mere
Gnosall
Haughton
Billington
Burton
Silkmore
Walton
Rickerscote
Coppenhall
Brocton
Hamstall Ridware
Yoxall
Barton under Needwood
Cowley
Beffcote
Alstone
Littywood
Wilbrighton
Apeton
Walton
Moreton
Barton
Church Eaton
Bradley
Dunston
Bednall
Acton Trussell
Pipe Ridware
Rugeley
King's Bromley
Mavesyn Ridware
Handsacre
Wychnor
Alrewas
High Onn
Little Onn
Woolaston
Levedale
Drayton
Mitton
Shushions
Longnor
Penkridge
Marston
Bickford
Whiston
Wolgarston
Brineton
Blymhill
Lapley
Congreve
Pillaton
Huntington
Croxall
Oakley
Brockhurst
Kinvaston
Otherton
Rodbaston
Stychbrook
Edingale
Beighterton
Stretton
Water Eaton
Hatherton
Elford
Harlaston
Clifton Campville
Weston under Lizard
Penk
Gailey
Cannock
Lichfield
Horton
Thorpe Constantine
Brewood
Great Saredon
Nether Hammerwich
Tymmore
Syerscote
Little Saredon
Norton Canes
Freeford
Tamhorn
Over Hammerwich
Wyrley
Wigginton
Chillington
Coven
Shareshill
Ogley Hay
Packington
Featherstone
Hilton
Hopwas
Hilton
Shenstone
Codsall
Moseley
Essington
Burouestone
Weeford
TAMWORTH
R. Tame
Pendeford
Pelsall
Litelbech
Hints
Bilbrook
Bushbury
Shelfield
Oaken
Oxley
Bloxwich
Wrottesley
Rushall
Aldridge
Patshull
Wednesfield
Tettenhall
Drayton Bassett
Pattingham
Perton
Compton
Willenhall
Wightwick
Wolverhampton
Trescott
Ettingshall
Bescot
Bilston
Great Barr
Lower Penn
Seisdon
Upper Penn
Orton
Bradley
Wednesbury
Trysull
Crockington
Sedgley
Wombourn
Tipton
Himley
Bobbington
West Bromwich
Chasepool
Haswic
Kingswinford
Smethwick
Morfe
Enville
Amblecote
Cippemore
Kinver
7
8
9
10
11
12
A
B
C
D
E
F
G
H
I

46 SUFFOLK

A
B
C
D
E
F
1
2
3
4
5
6
7
8
9
Brandon
Santon Downham
Wangford
Lakenheath
Undley
Chamberlain's Hall
Eriswell
Elvedon
Little Ouse R.
Rushford
Knettishall
Euston
Barnham
Coney Weston
Hopton
Thelnetham
Market Weston
Little Fakenham
Barningham
Great Fakenham
Rickinghall Inferior
Sapiston
Hepworth
Honington
Stanton
Wattisfield
Bardwell
Ixworth Thorpe
Mildenhall
Worlington
Barton Mills
Icklingham
Little Livermere
Freckenham
Wordwell
Troston
Tuddenham
Ampton
Great Livermere
Wyken
Walsham le Willows
West Stow
Ingham
Lackford
Culford
Ixworth
Herringswell
Cavenham
Flempton
Timworth
Langham
Hengrave
Fornham St Genevieve
Stowlangtoft
Great Ashfield
Westhorpe
R. Lark
Fornham All Saints
Pakenham
Hunston
Bacton
Fornham St Martin
Risby
Norton
Great Barton
Exning
Thurston
Moulton
Westley
Desning
BURY ST EDMUNDS
Elmswell
Barrow
Little Saxham
Rougham
Tostock
Wetherden
Beyton
Great Saxham
Rushbrooke
Hessett
Woolpit
Dalham
Denham
Horringer
Drinkstone
Little Welnetham
Hargrave
Ickworth
Newton
Bradfield St George
Shelland
Harleston
Ousden
Chevington
Onehouse
Great Welnetham
Rattlesden
Hawstead
Stowmarket
Chedburgh
Whepstead
Bradfield St Clare
Gedding
Great Finborough
Lidgate
Buxhall
Manston
Bradfield Combust
Felsham
Depden
Brockley
Badmondisfield
Stanningfield
Rede
Clopton
Little Finborough
Cowlinge
Cockfield
Wickhambrook
Lawshall
Brettenham
Thorpe Morieux
Farley
Great Bradley
Denston
Somerton
Loose
Stradishall
Hartest
Manton
Little Bradley
Stansfield
Hawkedon
Rushbrooke
Chadacre
Wattisham
Little Thurlow
Thurston
Shimpling
Hitcham
Great Bricett
Great Thurlow
Boxted
Preston
Kettlebaston
Chilbourne
Stanstead
Little Bricett
Houghton
Lavenham
Bildeston
Hundon
Glemsford
Brent Eleigh
Nedging
Withersfield
Great Wratting
Poslingford
Kentwell
Monks Eleigh
Chelsworth
Brockley
Semer
Hanchet
Little Wratting
Kedington
Fenstead
Cavendish
Brandeston
Milden
Ash Street
CLARE
Long Melford
Little Waldingfield
R. Stour
Haverhill
alia Boyton
Acton
Lindsey
Boyton
Kersey
Stoke by Clare
Great Waldingfield
Stone Street
Wixoe
Brundon
Chilton
Edwardstone
SUDBURY
Groton
Newton
Ballingdon
Coddenham
Great Cornard
Aveley
Little Cornard
Assington
Polstead
Stoke by Nayland
Withermarsh
Bures
Thorington
Nayland
Stratford St Mary

G
H
I
J
K
L
1
2
3
4
5
6
7
8
9
Burgh Castle
Gapton
Belton
Browston
Caldecott
Hopton
Fritton
Lound
Herringfleet
Blundeston
Newton
Corton
Somerleyton
Flixton
Akethorpe
Lowestoft
Kirkley
Pakefield
Shipmeadow
BECCLES
Barnby
Carlton Colville
Bungay
Mettingham
Barsham
Worlingham
Ringsfield
Gisleham
Ilketshall St John
Ilketshall St Andrew
Weston
Mutford
Ellough
Rushmere
Flixton
Ilketshall St Lawrence
Kessingland
Homersfield
S.Elmham St Peter
Willingham
Henstead
Ilketshall St Margaret
Sotterley
Linburne
Redisham
Shadingfield
S.Elmham St Cross
S.Elmham St Michael
Benacre
South Elmham St Margaret
Wrentham
Mendham
S.Elmham All Saints
S.Elmham St Nicholas
Stone Street
Frostenden
Covehithe
Rumburgh
Stoven
Withersdale
Brampton
Instead
S.Elmham St James
South Cove
R. Waveney
Uggeshall
Weybread
Wissett
Sotherton
Wangford
Palgrave
Syleham
Easton Bavants
Stuston
Chediston
Halesworth
Henham
Oakley
Fressingfield
Whittingham
Holton
Reydon
Wortham
Hoxne
Linstead Parva
Blyford
Brome
Wingfield
Linstead Magna
Mells
Southwold
Thrandeston
Chickering
Burgate
Chippenhall
Cookley
Wenhaston
Bulcamp
Yaxley
Denham
Cratfield
Walpole
Blythburgh
EYE
Stradbroke
Huntingfield
Thorington
Parva
Cranley
Bramfield
Horham
Ubbeston
Braiseworth
Wilby
Heveningham
Hinton
Laxfield
Occold
Bridge
Magna
Stoke Ash
Redlingfield
Stickingland
DUNWICH
Thorndon
Peasenhall
Darsham
Hestley
Yoxford
Westleton
Wickham Skeith
Bedingfield
Worlingworth
Sibton
Rishangles
Badingham
Tannington
Middleton
Wetheringsett
Colston
Dennington
Fordley
Mendlesham
Kenton
Bedfield
Bruisyard
Theberton
Brockford
Aspall
Saxtead
Monk Soham
Cransford
Minsmere
Kelsale
Rendham
Ulverston
Carlton
Debenham
Earl Soham
Framlingham
Swefling
Ashfield
Saxmundham
Leiston
Thorpe
Great Glemham
Mickfield
Knoddishall
Winston
Sternfield
Little Stonham
Cretingham
Kettleburgh
Benhall
Aldringham
Parham
Pettaugh
Brandeston
Stratford St Andrew
Framsden
Thorpe
Stonham Aspal
Farnham
Hacheston
Snape
Hoo
Creeting
Easton
Little Glemham
Crowfield
Monewden
Martley
Beversham
Rushmere
St Olave
Helmingham
Letheringham
Marlesford
Dunningworth
Creeting
Potsford
Glevering
Blaxhall
Horswold
Charsfield
Aldeburgh
St Mary
Olden
Little Charsfield
Harpole
Wickham Market
Ashbocking
Thorpe
Campsey
Otley
Ash
Tunstall
Bosmere
Debach
Dallinghoo
Coddenham
Hemingstone
Kingsland
Bing
Loudham
Bredfield
Darmsden
Swilland
Clopton
Wantisden
Sogenhoe
Rendlesham
Boulge
Chillesford
Barham
Newton
Baylham
Henley
Burgh
Thistleton
Ufford
Sudbourne
Sharpstone
Grundisburgh
Bromeswell
Butley
Witnesham
Staverton
Claydon
Melton
Finlesforda
Hasketon
Turstanestuna
Culpho
Great
Akenham
Wilford
Tuddenham
Bealings
Gedgrave
Little
Woodbridge
Thurlston
Playford
Hundesthoft
Capel
Seckford
St Andrew
Blakenham
Little
Hoo
Whitton
Westerfield
Bealings
Stokerland
Kingston
Martlesham
Boyton
Rushmere
Sutton
Bramford
Preston
St Andrew
Laneburc
Barkestone
Kesgrave
Burstall
Littlecross
Gipping
Deben
Bixley
Shottisham
Waldringfield
Udeham
Hollesley
IPSWICH
Hintlesham
Stoke
Foxhall
Brightwell
Halgestou
Newbourn
Gusford
Isleton
Culeslea
Ramsholt
Hemley
Chattisham
Bucklesham
Alderton
Kembroke
Belstead
Wherstead
Haspley
Peyton
Alnesbourn
Guthestuna
Pannington
Nacton
Struestuna
Bawdsey
Freston
Levington
Kirton
R. Orwell
Woolverstone
Stratton
Falkenham
Bentley
Tattingstone
Shotley
Oxelanda
Boynton
Holbrook
Dodnash
Alston
Walton
Bergholt
Erwarton
Kirkton
Stutton
Burgh
Wadgate
Brantham
Harkstead
Kalweton
R. Stour
Langer
1 Leofstanestuna
2 Morston
3 Norton
4 Thorpe
5 Mycelegata
6 Turstanestuna
7 Trimley St Martin
8 Trimley St Mary
9 Grimston
10 Candlet
11 Plugeard
12 Burgate
13 Gulpher
14 Maistana

A
B
C
D
E
F
G
H
I
1
2
3
4
5
6
Burleigh
Hazelden
Worth
Ifield
Berth
East Chiltington
Warningore
Plumpton
Streat
Ditchling
Wickham
Hurstpierpoint
Keymer
Clayton
Westmeston
Newtimber
Pangdean
Saddlescombe
Poynings
Fulking
Woodmancote
Benefeld
Sakeham
Morley
Woolfly
Wantley
Henfield
Perching
Tottington
Paythorne
Truleigh
Upper Beeding
Annington
Erringham
Applesham
Shoreham
Kingston by Sea
Portslade
Hangleton
Aldrington
Preston
Brighton
Patcham
Moustone
Stanmer
Balmer
Falmer
Bevendean
Ovingdean
Rottingdean
Shermanbury
Eatton
Wappingthorn
Bramber
STEYNING
Wiston
Buncton
Ashington
Washington
Coombes
Lancing
Cokeham
Hoecourt
Sompting
Danktone
Broadwater
Worthing
West Tarring
Offington
Heene
Goring
Ferring
Findon
Muntham
Clapham
Durrington
Angmering
East Preston
Patching
Shipley
R. Adur
West Chiltington
Thakeham
Nyetimber
Nutbourne
Pulborough
Storrington
Chancton
Cootham
Sullington
Greatham
Parham
Hardham
Stopham
Amberley
North Stoke
South Stoke
Burpham
Wepham
Warningcamp
ARUNDEL
Lyminster
Toddington
Littlehampton
Tortington
Climping
Middleton on Sea
Bilsham
Binsted
Walberton
Offham
Bury
R. Arun
Bignor
Sutton
Glatting
Barlavington
Burton
Duncton
Petworth
Tillington
Grittenham
Lodsworth
Selham
Todham
Graffham
East Lavington
Up Waltham
Slindon
Eastergate
Barnham
Aldingbourne
Felpham
East Hampnett
Halnaker
Boxgrove
Tangmere
Rumboldswyke
Merston
Runcton
Mundham
Sidlesham
Pagham
Selsey
CHICHESTER
Strettington
Westhampnett
Mid Lavant
East Lavant
Singleton
Preston
Binderton
Cocking
Bepton
Linch
Buddington
Woolbeeding
Stedham
Iping
Chithurst
Trotton
R. Rother
Elsted
Treyford
East Harting
West Harting
South Harting
North Marden
East Marden
Up Marden
West Marden
Compton
Stoughton
Lordington
Racton
Westbourne
Fishbourne
Bosham
Donnington
Hunston
Birdham
Somerley
East Wittering
West Itchenor
West Wittering
West Thorney

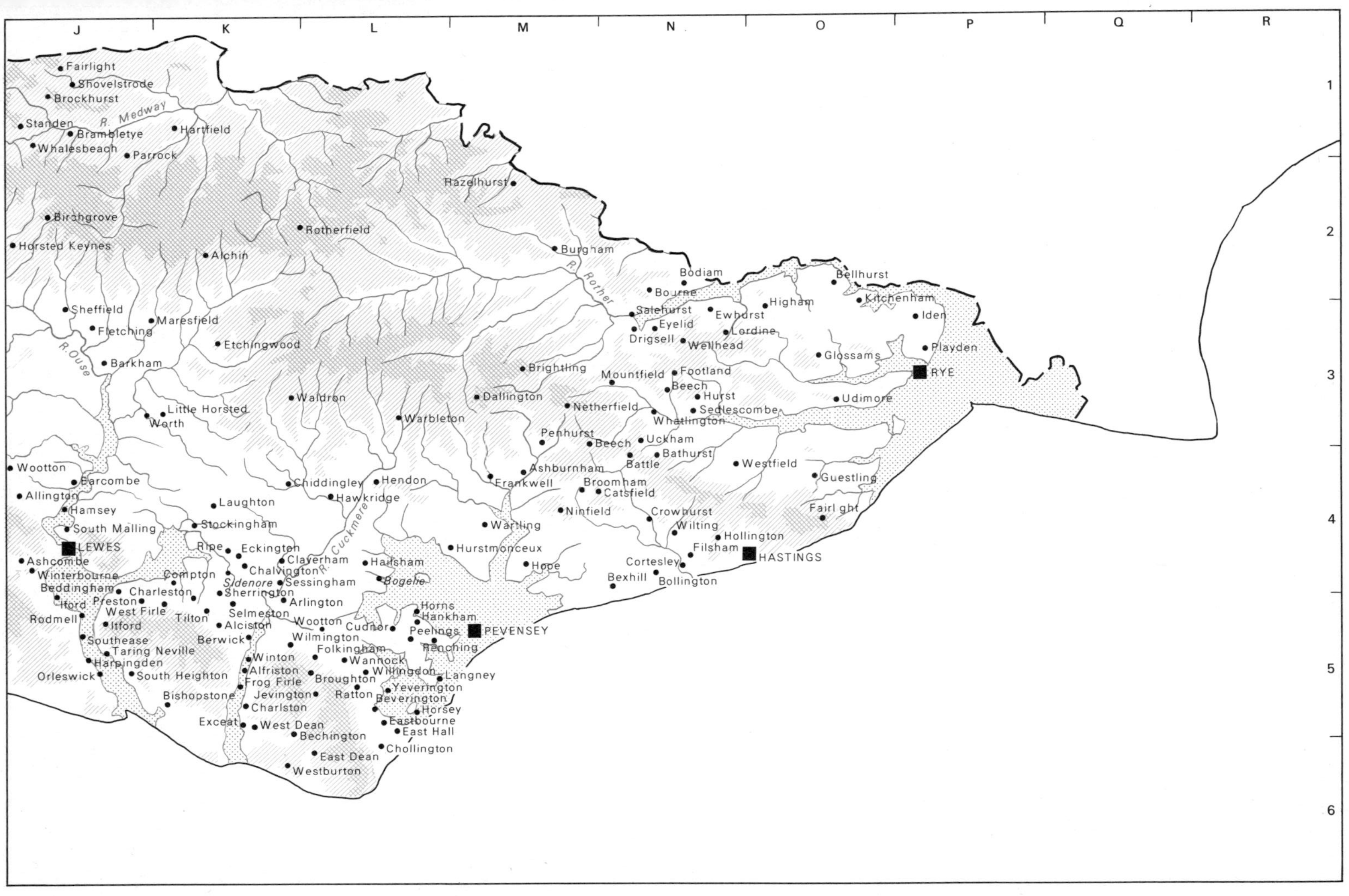

J
K
L
M
N
O
P
Q
R
1
2
3
4
5
6
Fairlight
Shovelstrode
Brockhurst
R. Medway
Standen
Brambletye
Hartfield
Whalesbeach
Parrock
Razelhurst
Birchgrove
Rotherfield
Horsted Keynes
Alchin
Burgham
R. Rother
Bodiam
Bellhurst
Bourne
Higham
Kitchenham
Sheffield
Maresfield
Salehurst
Ewhurst
Iden
Fletching
Eyelid
Lordine
Drigsell
Wellhead
Playden
Etchingwood
Glossams
R. Ouse
Barkham
Brightling
Mountfield
Footland
RYE
Beech
Waldron
Dallington
Hurst
Udimore
Little Horsted
Netherfield
Sedlescombe
Worth
Warbleton
Whatlington
Penhurst
Uckham
Beech
Bathurst
Battle
Westfield
Wootton
Ashburnham
Guestling
Barcombe
Chiddingley
Hendon
Frankwell
Broomham
Catsfield
Allington
Hawkridge
Laughton
Hamsey
Ninfield
Crowhurst
Fairl ght
R. Cuckmere
South Malling
Stockingham
Wartling
Wilting
Hollington
LEWES
Ripe
Eckington
Hurstmonceux
Filsham
HASTINGS
Ashcombe
Claverham
Hailsham
Cortesley
Hope
Winterbourne
Compton
Chalvington
Sidenore
Sessingham
Bogelie
Bexhill
Bollington
Beddingham
Charleston
Sherrington
Preston
Arlington
Iford
West Firle
Horns
Selmeston
Hankham
Rodmell
Tilton
Wootton
Cudnor
Alciston
Peelings
PEVENSEY
Itford
Wilmington
Southease
Berwick
Renching
Taring Neville
Folkingham
Winton
Harpingden
Wannock
Willingdon
Alfriston
Orleswick
South Heighton
Langney
Frog Firle
Broughton
Yeverington
Bishopstone
Jevington
Ratton
Beverington
Charlston
Horsey
Exceat
West Dean
Eastbourne
Bechington
East Hall
Chollington
East Dean
Westburton

50 SURREY

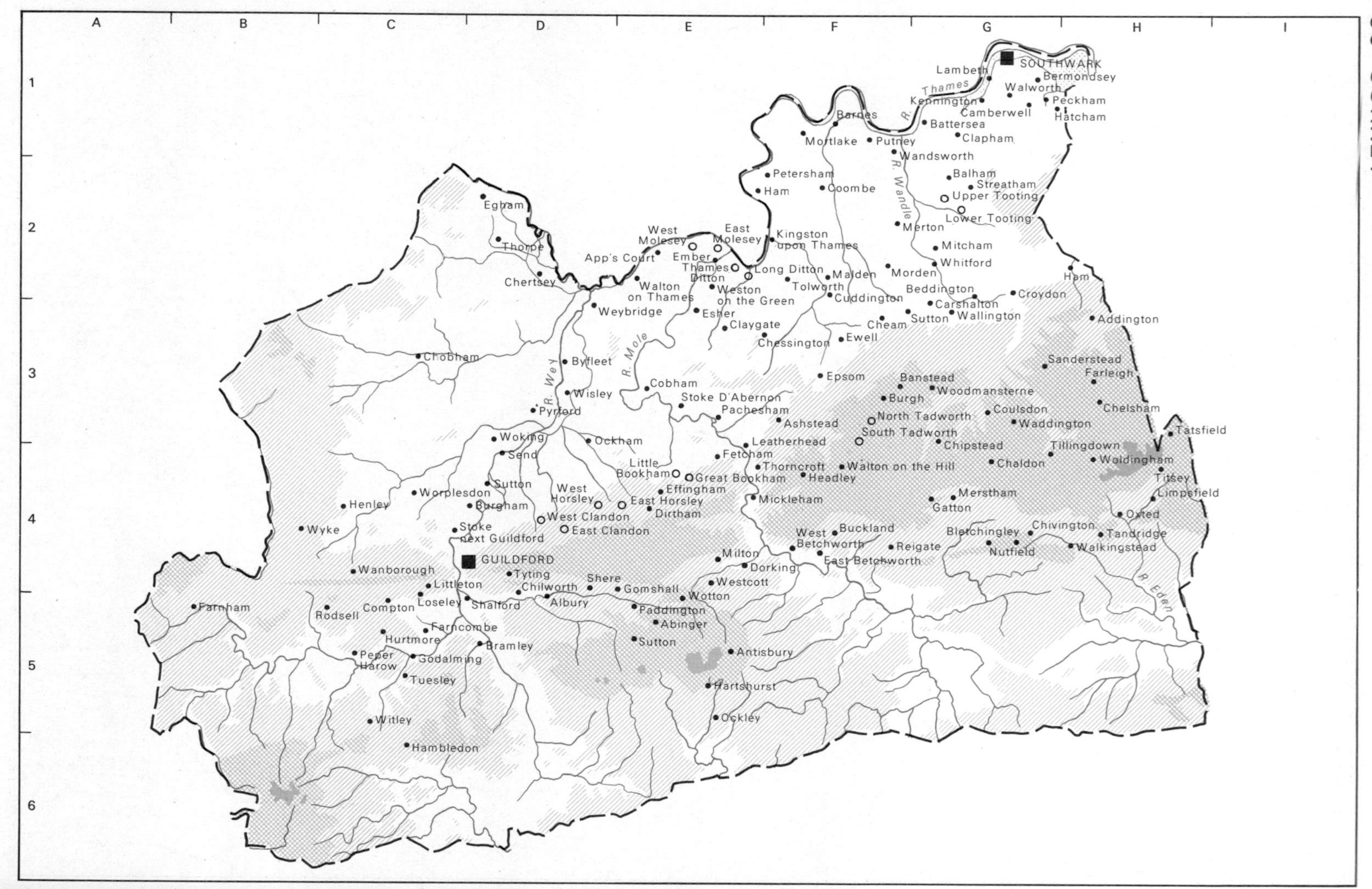
A
B
C
D
E
F
G
H
I
1
2
3
4
5
6
R. Thames
R. Wandle
R. Mole
R. Wey
R. Eden
SOUTHWARK
Lambeth
Bermondsey
Walworth
Kennington
Camberwell
Peckham
Hatcham
Barnes
Battersea
Mortlake
Putney
Clapham
Wandsworth
Petersham
Ham
Coombe
Balham
Streatham
Upper Tooting
Lower Tooting
Egham
Merton
Thorpe
West Molesey
East Molesey
Kingston upon Thames
Mitcham
App's Court
Ember
Thames Ditton
Long Ditton
Malden
Morden
Whitford
Chertsey
Walton on Thames
Weston on the Green
Tolworth
Cuddington
Beddington
Carshalton
Croydon
Ham
Weybridge
Esher
Claygate
Cheam
Sutton
Wallington
Addington
Chessington
Ewell
Chobham
Byfleet
Epsom
Banstead
Sanderstead
Farleigh
Cobham
Woodmansterne
Wisley
Stoke D'Abernon
Burgh
Pyrford
Pachesham
North Tadworth
Coulsdon
Chelsham
Ashstead
Waddington
Tatsfield
South Tadworth
Woking
Ockham
Leatherhead
Chipstead
Tillingdown
Send
Fetcham
Woldingham
Little Bookham
Thorncroft
Walton on the Hill
Chaldon
Great Bookham
Headley
Titsey
Sutton
Effingham
West Horsley
Henley
Worplesdon
East Horsley
Mickleham
Merstham
Limpsfield
Burgham
Dirtham
Gatton
Oxted
West Clandon
Stoke next Guildford
Wyke
East Clandon
West Betchworth
Buckland
Bletchingley
Chivington
Tandridge
Reigate
Nutfield
Walkingstead
GUILDFORD
Milton
Wanborough
Tyting
Dorking
East Betchworth
Littleton
Shere
Chilworth
Gomshall
Westcott
Farnham
Loseley
Wotton
Rodsell
Compton
Shalford
Albury
Paddington
Farncombe
Abinger
Hurtmore
Sutton
Bramley
Peper Harow
Godalming
Antisbury
Tuesley
Hartshurst
Witley
Ockley
Hambledon

A
B
C
D
E
F
1
2
3
4
5
6
7
8
9
Continuation westwards
Knighton on Teme
Eastham
Rochford
Tenbury
Berrington
Hanley Child
Kyre Magna
Kyre Parva
Bockleton
Stoke Bliss
Dudley
Warley
Cradley
Old Swinford
Halesowen
Lutley
Pedmore
Hagley
Clent
Frankley
Upper Arley
Lower Arley
R. Stour
Cochehi
Wolverley
Churchill
Trimpley
Franche
Wannerton
Habberley
Hurcott
Alia Franche
Bellington
Bell Hall
Belbroughton
Houndsfield
Kidderminster
Sutton
Dunclent
Chadwick
Cofton Hackett
Wythwood
Wribbenhall
Stone
Willingwick
Wythall
Ribbesford
Chaddesley Corbett
Shurvenhill
Tonge
Alton
Carton
Oldington
Comble
Alvechurch
Bayton
Alia Ribbesford
Ashborough
Osmerley
Upper Mitton
Woodcote
Mamble
Conningswick
Lower Mitton
Fockbury
Burcot
West Hill
Moor
Rushock
Sodington
Lindon
Hartlebury
Bromsgrove
Hollin
Elmley Lovett
Timberhanger
Tutnall
Beoley
Stildon
Worsley
Tynsall
Cooksey
Grafton
Aston Fields
Tardebigge
Eardiston
Abberley
Elmbridge
Upton Warren
Baddington
Bastwood
Astley
Stockton on Teme
Stoke Prior
Orleton
Glasshampton
Horton
Helpridge
Redmarley
Hanley William
Great Witley
Doverdale
Wychbold
Ipsley
Bentley Pauncefoot
Stanford on Teme
Hillhampton
Hampton Lovett
Thickenappletree
Hanbury
Shelsley Walsh
Little Witley
Ombersley
DROITWICH
Middlewich
Witton
Shelsley Beauchamp
Holt
Chauson
Hadzor
Hamcastle
Salwarpe
Clifton on Teme
Upwich
Feckenham
Grimley
Martin Hussingtree
Lower Sapey
Phepson
Shell
Bradley
Martley
Greenhill
Oddingley
Hindlip
Hollow Court
Kenswick
Hallow
Offerton
Himbleton
Dormston
Northwick
Tibberton
Inkberrow
Eastbury
Huddington
Doddenham
Warndon
Leopard
Crowle
Kington
Knightwick
Laughern
Bredicot
Broughton Hackett
Grafton Flyford
Cotheridge
Abbots Morton
Broadwas
WORCESTER
Perry
Cudley
North Piddle
R. Teme
Upton Snodsbury
Leigh
Rodeleah
Spetchley
Churchill
Abberton
Rous Lench
Wick Episcopi
Bransford
White Ladies Aston
Naunton Beauchamp
Clopton
Whittington
Abbots Lench
Suckley
Powick
Mucknell
Piddle
Bishampton
Church Lench
Sheriffs Lench
Atch Lench
Bickmarsh
Upper Wolverton
Peopleton
R. Severn
Stoulton
Lower Wolverton
Wiburgestoke
Cleeve Prior
Harvington
Drakes Broughton
Kempsey
Hill
North Littleton
Norton
Moor
Wadborough
Wyre Piddle
Ullington
Pebworth
R. Avon
Lenchwick
Pirton
Chevington
PERSHORE
Fladbury
Offenham
South Littleton
Broad Marston
Malvern
Croome D'Abitot
Besford
Wick
Cropthorne
Pensham
Evesham
Aldington
Bretforton
Church Honeybourne
Severn Stoke
Birlingham
Great Hampton
Bengeworth
Baldehalle
Defford
Little Comberton
Little Hampton
Badsey
Cow Honeybourne
Hanley Castle
Earls Croome
Nafford
Bricklehampton
Wickhamford
Great Comberton
Netherton
Eckington
Hill Croome
Hinton on the Green
Upton upon Severn
Bredons Norton
Sedgeberrow
Childs Wickham
Barley
Westmancote
Holdfast
Ripple
Aston Somerville
Overbury
Ashton under Hill
Queenhill
Broadway
Longdon
Bredon
Kemerton
Pull Court
Beckford
Bushley
Mitton
Pendock
Eldersfield

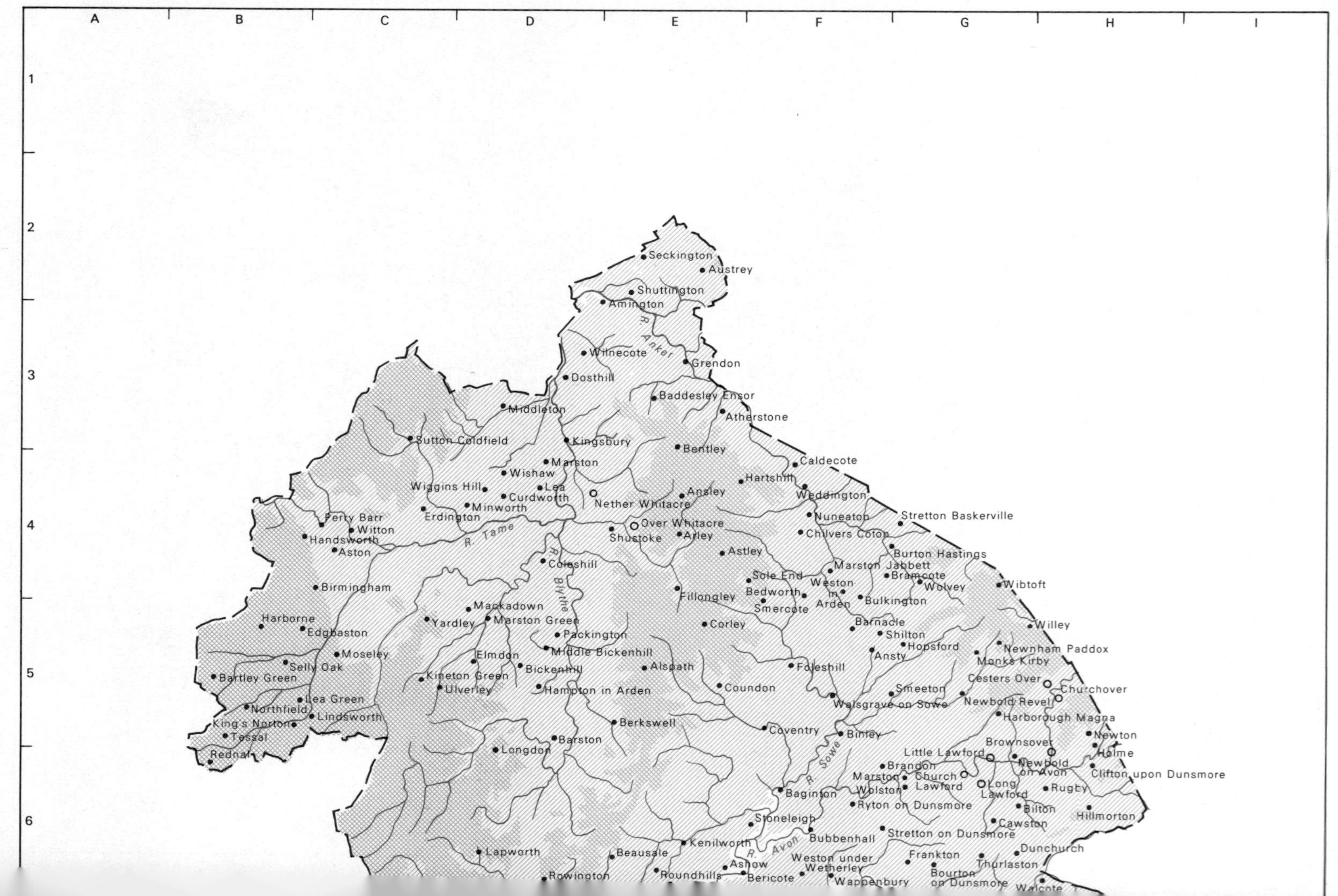
A
B
C
D
E
F
G
H
I
1
2
3
4
5
6
Seckington
Austrey
Shuttington
Amington
R. Anker
Wilnecote
Grendon
Dosthill
Baddesley Ensor
Atherstone
Middleton
Sutton Coldfield
Kingsbury
Bentley
Caldecote
Marston
Wishaw
Hartshill
Wiggins Hill
Lea
Curdworth
Minworth
Nether Whitacre
Ansley
Weddington
Perry Barr
Erdington
Witton
Handsworth
Aston
R. Tame
Over Whitacre
Shustoke
Arley
Nuneaton
Chilvers Coton
Stretton Baskerville
Astley
Burton Hastings
Coleshill
Marston Jabbett
Bramcote
Wolvey
Wibtoft
Sole End
Bedworth
Weston in Arden
Bulkington
Birmingham
Fillongley
Smercote
Mackadown
R. Blythe
Harborne
Yardley
Marston Green
Corley
Barnacle
Willey
Edgbaston
Packington
Shilton
Hopsford
Newnham Paddox
Moseley
Elmdon
Middle Bickenhill
Ansty
Monks Kirby
Selly Oak
Bickenhill
Alspath
Foleshill
Cesters Over
Bartley Green
Kineton Green
Churchover
Ulverley
Hampton in Arden
Coundon
Smeeton
Lea Green
Walsgrave on Sowe
Newbold Revel
Northfield
Lindsworth
Harborough Magna
King's Norton
Berkswell
Coventry
Tessal
Barston
Binley
Newton
Brownsover
Rednal
Longdon
Little Lawford
Holme
Newbold on Avon
Brandon
R. Sowe
Clifton upon Dunsmore
Marston
Church Lawford
Long Lawford
Rugby
Baginton
Wolston
Ryton on Dunsmore
Bilton
Hillmorton
Stoneleigh
Cawston
Bubbenhall
Stretton on Dunsmore
Kenilworth
Lapworth
Dunchurch
Beausale
R. Avon
Weston under Wetherley
Frankton
Ashow
Thurlaston
Rowington
Roundhills
Bericote
Wappenbury
Bourton on Dunsmore
Walcote

Mapleborough
Oldberrow
Whitley
Preston Bagot
Hatton
Milverton
Budbrooke
Coton
Lillington
R. Leam
Leamington
Hill
Willoughby
Grandborough
Sawbridge
Wolfhamcote
Flecknoe
Studley
Morton Bagot
Claverdon
WARWICK
Kington
Newbold Comyn
Leamington Spa
Myton
Radford Semele
Long Itchington
Calcutt
Wootton Wawen
Langley
Norton Lindsey
Whitnash
Ufton
R. Itchen
Lower Shuckburgh
Sperrnall
Sambourn
Offord
Wolverton
Sherbourne
Tachbrook Mallory
Bishop's Tachbrook
Southam
Napton on the Hill
Upper Shuckburgh
R. Arrow
R. Alne
Coughton
Great Alne
Edstone
Bearley
Newnham
Aston Cantlow
Barford
Fulbrook
Snitterfield
Harbury
Ladbroke
Kinwarton
Haselor
Upton
Wilmcote
Wasperton
Chesterton
Bishop's Itchington
Radbourn
Arrow
Oversley
Billesley
Clopton
R. Avon
Hampton Lucy
Charlecote
Newbold Pacey
Lighthorne
Hodnell
Priors Hardwick
Exhall
Weethley
Temple Grafton
Ardens Grafton
Stratford upon Avon
Alveston
Moreton Morrell
Wellesbourne Hastings
Wellesbourne Mountford
Stoneton
Wormleighton
Bevington
Wixford
Broom
Binton
Luddington
Milcote
Ruin Clifford
Clifford Chambers
Loxley
Compton Verney
Chadshunt
Walton
Bidford on Avon
Hillborough
Salford Priors
Welford on Avon
Weston on Avon
Alstone
Atherstone on Stour
Kineton
Fenny Compton
Burton Dassett
Avon Dassett
Farnborough
Abbots Salford
Dorsington
Preston on Stour
Alderminster
Over
Eatington
Butlers Marston
Pillerton Hersey
Arlescote
Willicote
Wincot
Long Marston
Nether Eatington
Whitchurch
Radway
Ratley
Warmington
Pillerton Priors
Quinton
R. Stour
Fulready
Meon
Oxhill
Admington
Clopton
Whatcote
Lark Stoke
Blackwell
Idlicote
Tysoe
Ilmington
Tredington
Honington
Compton Wyniate
Longdon
Shipston on Stour
Compton Scorpion
Barcheston
Ditchford
Willington
Brailes
Tidmington
Burmington
Stretton on Fosse
Sutton under Brailes
Little Wolford
Whichford
Great Wolford
Long Compton
Barton on the Heath
Little Compton
7
8
9
10
11
12
A
B
C
D
E
F
G
H
I

A
B
C
D
E
F
G
H
I
1
2
3
4
5
6
R. Thames
Latton
Castle Eaton
Eisey
Lus Hill
Ashton Keynes
CRICKLADE
Calcutt
Hannington
Highworth
Hampton
Chelworth
Widhill
Broad Blunsdon
Stanton Fitzwarren
Blunsdon St Andrew
Groundwell
Chelworth
Chedglow
Oaksey
Crudwell
Brokenborough
Charlton
Garsdon
MALMESBURY
Easton Grey
Sopworth
Sherston
Foxley
Purton
Moredon
Stratton St Margaret
Rodbourne Cheney
Lydiard Millicent
Lydiard Tregoze
Walcot
Swindon
Earlscourt
Elendune
Westlecott
Wanborough
Liddington
Luckington
Norton
Corston
Little Somerford
Brinkworth
Alderton
Bradfield
Great Somerford
Smithcot
Hullavington
Surrendell
Dauntsey
Seagry
Wootton Bassett
Elcombe
Wroughton
Badbury
Chisledon
Littleton Drew
Grittleton
Stanton St Quinton
Draycot
Cerne
Salthrop
Bincknoll
Tockenham
Bradenstoke
Christian Malford
Thornhill
Nettleton
Sevington
Easton Piercy
Kington St Michael
Castle Combe
Kington Langley
Cadenham
Littlecott
Clyffe Pypard
Uffcott
Draycot Foliat
Yatton Keynell
Kellaways
Woodhill
Broad Hinton
Langley Burrell
East Tytherton
Witcomb
Hilmarton
North Wraxall
Hardenhuish
Winterbourne Bassett
Aldbourne
Tytherton Lucas
Highway
Ogbourne St George
Biddestone
Chippenham
Beversbrook
Bremhill
Thickwood
Stanley
Compton Bassett
Winterbourne Monkton
Ogbourne St Andrew
Hartham
Rockley
Ramsbury
Colerne
Corsham
CALNE
Yatesbury
R. Kennet
Chilton Foliat
Poulton
Lackham
Avebury
Mildenhall
Ditteridge
Beckhampton
West Overton
Clatford
Stitchcombe
MARLBOROUGH
Calstone Wellington
Manton
Hazelbury
Lacock
West Kennett
Stanmore
East Kennett
East Overton
Lockeridge
R. Avon
Heddington
Chisbury
Whitley
Roughmore
Shaw
Monkton Farleigh
Bagshot
Bromham
Bishop's Cannings
BEDWYN
Chalfield
Melksham
Huish
Cumberwell
Allington
Alton Barnes
Wootton Rivers
Shalbourne
Broughton Gifford
Rowde
Stanton St Bernard
Draycot Fitz Payne
Crofton
Harding
Ham
Alton Priors
Berrelege
Budbury
Whaddon
All Cannings
Wolf Hall
Wilcot
Burbage
Buttermere
Staverton
Etchilhampton
Woodborough
Pewsey
BRADFORD ON AVON
Grafton
Marten
Westwood
Hilperton
Poulshot
Stert
Beechingstoke
Manningford Bruce
Withenham
Trowle
Potterne
Manningford Bohun
Manningford Abbots
Tidcombe
Fosbury

SALISBURY
WILTON
WARMINSTER
TILSHEAD
Collingbourne Kingston
Collingbourne Ducis
Shaw
Standen
Biddesden
Ludgershall
North Tidworth
Conock
Rushall
Upavon
Chisenbury
Compton
Enford
Fifield
Fittleton
Choulston
Netheravon
Figheldean
Ablington
Alton
Knighton
Brigmerston
Milston
Durrington
Bulford
Ratfyn
Amesbury
Cholderton
Newton Tony
Allington
Boscombe
Idmiston
Porton
Gomeldon
Winterbourne Gunner
Winterbourne Dauntsey
Winterslow
Hurdcott
Laverstock
Winterbourne Earls
Durnford
Wilsford
Netton
Winterbourne Stoke
Berwick St James
Little Wishford
Great Wishford
South Newton
Stapleford
Steeple Langford
Little Langford
Hanging Langford
Wylye
Bathampton
Deptford
Fisherton de la Mere
Codford St Mary
Codford St Peter
Stockton
Sherrington
Boyton
Ashton Gifford
Corton
Upton Lovell
Knock
Heytesbury
Norton Bavant
Bishopstrow
Middleton
Sutton Veny
Tytherington
Hill Deverill
Brixton Deverill
Whitecliff
Monkton Deverill
Kingston Deverill
Longbridge Deverill
Smallbrook
Upton Scudamore
Corsley
Horningsham
Baycliff
Maiden Bradley
Yarnfield
Kilmington
Stourton
Zeals
Mere
Chaddenwick
West Knoyle
East Knoyle
Pertwood
Fonthill Bishop
Fonthill Gifford
Chilmark
Baverstock
Dinton
Teffont Evias
Tisbury
Wardour
Swallowcliffe
Ansty
Donhead
Sutton Mandeville
Fovant
Compton Chamberlayne
Burcombe
Ugford
Barford St Martin
Ditchampton
Hurdcott
Washern
Bemerton
Fisherton Anger
Milford
Britford
Longford
Homington
Odstock
Coombe Bissett
Stratford Tony
Broad Chalke
Bower Chalke
Fifield Bavant
Ebbesborne Wake
Trow
Tollard Royal
Alderbury
East Grimstead
West Grimstead
West Dean
Whaddon
Witherington
Standlynch
Frustfield
Cowesfield
Barford
Downton
Landford
R. Avon
R. Wylye
R. Nadder
R. Ebble
R. Bourne
Edington
West Ashton
Great Cheverell
Little Cheverell
East Coulston
Littleton Pannell
Market Lavington
West Lavington
St Joan à Gore
Imber
Westbury
Orcheston St Mary
Orcheston St George
Elston
Chitterne All Saints
Chitterne St Mary
Addeston
Maddington
Shrewton
Rolleston
7
8
9
10
11
12
A
B
C
D
E
F
G
H
I

A B C D E F

1 2 3 4 5 6 7 8 9

Willerby
Binnington
East Heslerton
Ganton
Knapton
Sherburn
Potter Brompton
West Heslerton
Scampston
Rillington
Wintringham
Foxholes
Thorpe Bassett
Scagglethorpe
Newton
Boythorpe
Butterwick
Norton
Linton
Settrington
Weaverthorpe
Sutton
Thirkleby
Buckton Holms
Lutton
Helperthorpe
Welham
Alia Thirkleby
Ulchiltorp
Menethorpe
Thornthorpe
North Grimston
Turodebi
Langton
Kirby Grindalythe
Firby
Eddlethorpe
Duggleby
Mowthorpe
Langtoft
Kirkham
Kennythorpe
Croom
Wharram le Street
Cowlam
Birdsall
Sudcniton
Burythorpe
Sledmere
R. Derwent
Wharram Percy
Cottam
Leavening
Howsham
Alia Leavening
Towthorpe
Burdale
Acklam
Raisthorpe
Leppington
Thixendale
Scrayingham
Hanging Grimston
Garton on the Wolds
Barthorpe
Uncleby
Fridaythorpe
Wetwang
Thoralby
Kirby Underdale
Skirpenbeck
Bugthorpe
Painsthorpe
Elmswell
Scradiztorp
Garrowby
Greenwick
Torp
Youlthorpe
Eastburn
Scoreby
Gowthorpe
Bishop Wilton
Huggate
Tibthorpe
Catton
Belthorpe
Kirkburn
Great Givendale
Hawold
Fangfoss
Grimthorpe
Southburn
Meltonby
Neswick
Dunnington
Little Givendale
Bainton
Bolton
Millington
YORK
Yapham
Grimston
Ousethorpe
North Dalton
Ianulfestorp
Heslington
Warter
Bracken
Kilnwick Percy
Gate Fulford
Barmby on the Moor
Middleton on the Wolds
POCKLINGTON
Kilnwick
Langwith
Water Fulford
Elvington
Nunburnholme
Lund
Allerthorpe
Sutton upon Derwent
Lockington
Waplington
Burnby
Cleaving
Holme on the Wolds
Naburn
Hayton
Londesborough
South Dalton
Wheldrake
Thornton
Easthorpe
Kiplingcotes
Deighton
Thorpe le Street
Melbourne
Torp
Moreby
Towthorpe
Etton
Escrick
Chetelstorp
Bielby
Shipton
Goodmanham
Steintorp
Everingham
Raventhorpe
East Cottingwith
Torp
Market Weighton
Newton
West Cottingwith
Seaton Ross
Gardham
Cherry Burton
Chetelstorp
Thorganby
Harswell
Stillingfleet
Ellerton
Laytham
Bishop Burton
Sancton
Houghton
Kelfield
Skipwith
Aughton
Holme upon Spalding Moor
North Cliffe
Riccall
Foggathorpe
Walkington
North Duffield
North Newbald
Bubwith
South Cliffe
South Newbald
Gunby
Gribthorpe
Hunsley
Risby
Willitoft
Hotham
Barlby
Breighton
Kettlethorpe
Little Weighton
Osgodby
South Duffield
Lund
Spaldington
Drewton
Cliffe
Bowthorpe
North Cave
Yokefleet
Everthorpe
Riplingham
Wressell
Owsthorpe
Hemingbrough
Portington
South Cave
Hagthorpe
Cavil
Hive
Burland
Toschetorp
Babthorpe
Siuuarbi
Brantingham
Brackenholme
Thorpe Lidget
Wauldby
Newsholme
Ellerker
Eastrington
Barnhill
Brantingham Thorpe
Belby
Barmby on the Marsh
Howden
Elloughton
Asselby
Knedlington
Welton
Kilpin
R. Ouse
Laxton
North Ferriby
Skelton
Saltmarshe
Yokefleet
Cotness

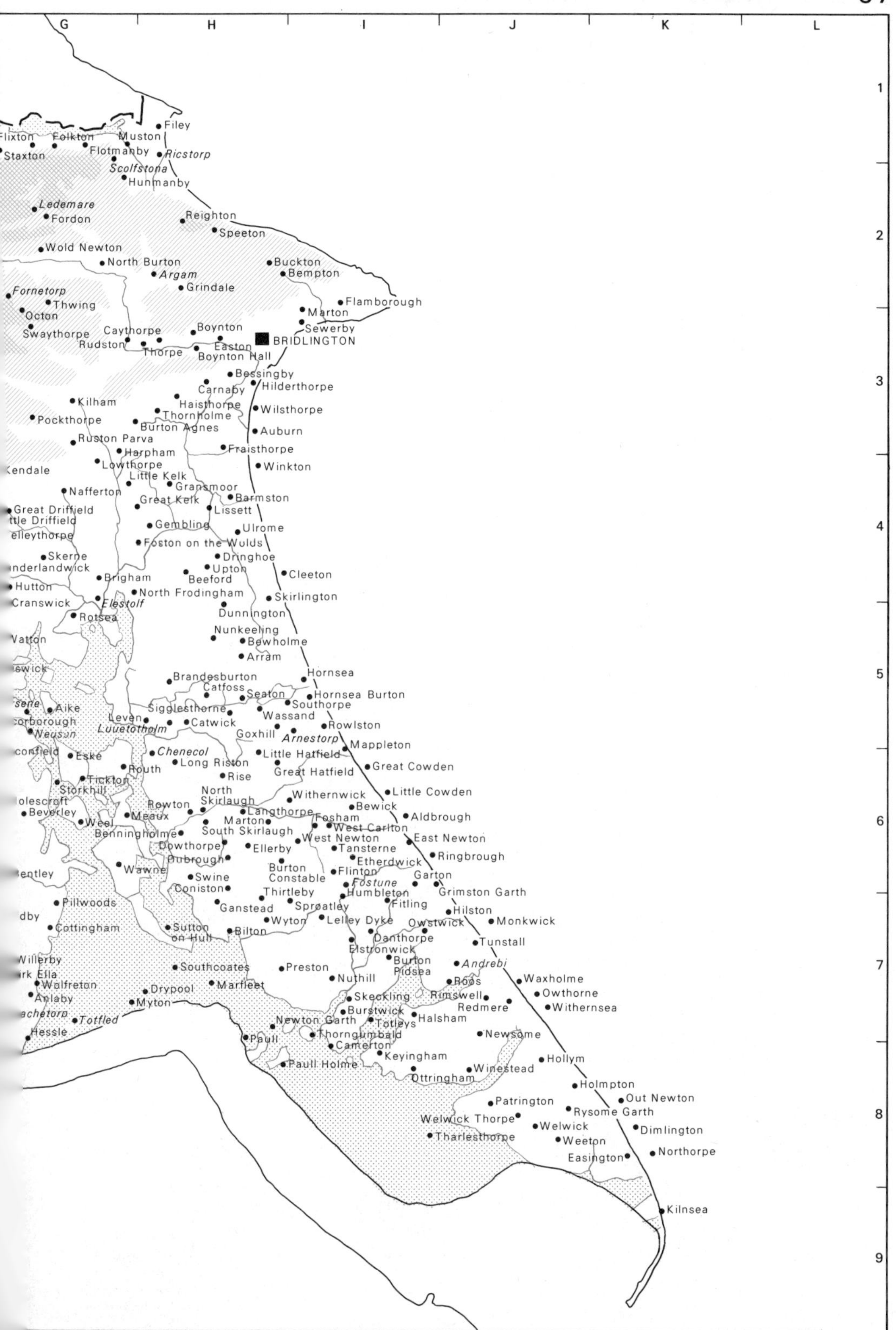
G
H
I
J
K
L
1
2
3
4
5
6
7
8
9
Filey
Muston
Flixton
Folkton
Staxton
Flotmanby
Ricstorp
Scolfstona
Hunmanby
Ledemare
Fordon
Reighton
Speeton
Wold Newton
North Burton
Buckton
Bempton
Argam
Grindale
Fornetorp
Thwing
Octon
Flamborough
Marton
Sewerby
Swaythorpe
Caythorpe
Boynton
Rudston
Thorpe
Easton
Boynton Hall
BRIDLINGTON
Bessingby
Carnaby
Hilderthorpe
Kilham
Haisthorpe
Thornholme
Wilsthorpe
Pockthorpe
Burton Agnes
Auburn
Ruston Parva
Harpham
Fraisthorpe
Lowthorpe
Winkton
Little Kelk
Gransmoor
Nafferton
Barmston
Great Kelk
Great Driffield
Lissett
Gembling
Ulrome
Foston on the Wolds
Skerne
Dringhoe
Upton
Cleeton
Brigham
Beeford
Hutton
North Frodingham
Skirlington
Cranswick
Elestolf
Rotsea
Dunnington
Nunkeeling
Watton
Bewholme
Arram
Hornsea
Brandesburton
Catfoss
Seaton
Hornsea Burton
Aike
Sigglesthorne
Southorpe
Wassand
Leven
Catwick
Rowlston
Luuetotholm
Goxhill
Arnestorp
Mappleton
Chenecol
Eske
Little Hatfield
Routh
Long Riston
Great Cowden
Great Hatfield
Tickton
Rise
Storkhill
North
Skirlaugh
Withernwick
Little Cowden
Rowton
Bewick
Beverley
Meaux
Langthorpe
Fosham
Aldbrough
Weel
Marton
West Carlton
Benningholme
South Skirlaugh
West Newton
East Newton
Dowthorpe
Ellerby
Tansterne
Oubrough
Etherdwick
Ringbrough
Wawne
Burton
Constable
Flinton
Garton
Swine
Fostune
Coniston
Thirtleby
Humbleton
Grimston Garth
Pillwoods
Ganstead
Sproatley
Fitling
Hilston
Wyton
Lelley Dyke
Owstwick
Monkwick
Cottingham
Sutton
on Hull
Bilton
Danthorpe
Tunstall
Elstronwick
Burton
Pidsea
Andrebi
Southcoates
Preston
Nuthill
Waxholme
Wolfreton
Marfleet
Roos
Drypool
Owthorne
Anlaby
Skeckling
Rimswell
Myton
Redmere
Withernsea
Totfled
Burstwick
Halsham
Hessle
Newton Garth
Totleys
Paull
Thorngumbald
Newsome
Camerton
Keyingham
Hollym
Paull Holme
Winestead
Ottringham
Holmpton
Patrington
Out Newton
Welwick Thorpe
Rysome Garth
Welwick
Dimlington
Tharlesthorpe
Weeton
Easington
Northorpe
Kilnsea

58 YORKSHIRE: WEST RIDING (NORTH)

A B C D E F

1 2 3 4 5 6 7 8 9

Sedbergh

Rubberholme
Selside
Starbotton
Thornton in Lonsdale
Litton
Ingleton
Horton in Ribblesdale
Kettlewell
Burton in Lonsdale
Arncliffe
Barnoldswick
Hawkswick
Bentham
Clapham
Kilnsey
Austwick
Conistone
Stainforth
Heldetune
Hequorde
Stackhouse
Langcliffe
Bordley
Grassington
Giggleswick
Threshfield
Settle
Hebden
Malham
Linton
Holedene
Anley
Thorpe
Hanlith
Burnsall
Kirkby Malham
Hartlington
Rathmell
Scosthrop
Appletree
Calton
Hetton
Little Newton
Drebley
Long Preston
Airton
Winterburn
Rylstone
Otterburn
Leuetat
Wigglesworth
Flasby
Hellifield
Caretorp
Eshton
Arnford
Coniston Cold
Swinden
Holme
Embsay
Gargrave
Halton E
Hammerton
Nappa
Bank Newton
Thorlby
Draughton
Slaidburn
Stainton
Skibeden
Battersby
Paythorne
Ingthorpe
Newsholme
Skipton
Newton on Hodder
Broughton
Horton
East Marton
Easington
Ellenthorpe
Crooks
West Marton
Snaygill
Addingham
Painley
Barge Ford
Bolton by Bowland
Raygill
Stock
Elslack
Carleton
High Bradley
Gisburn
Long Holme
Stratesergum
Bracewell
Thornton in Craven
Low Bradley
Alia Farby
Cononley
Barnoldswick
Earby
Farnhill
Silsden
Grindleton
Radholme Laund
Rimington
Lothersdale
Kildwick
Middop
Glusburn
Kelbrook
West Bradford
Steeton
Chelchis
Sotleie
Eastburn
Waddington
Sutton
Cowling
Utley
Bashall
Riddlesde
Lacock
Newsholme
Great Mitton
Oakworth
R. Ribble
R. Aire
Wharfe

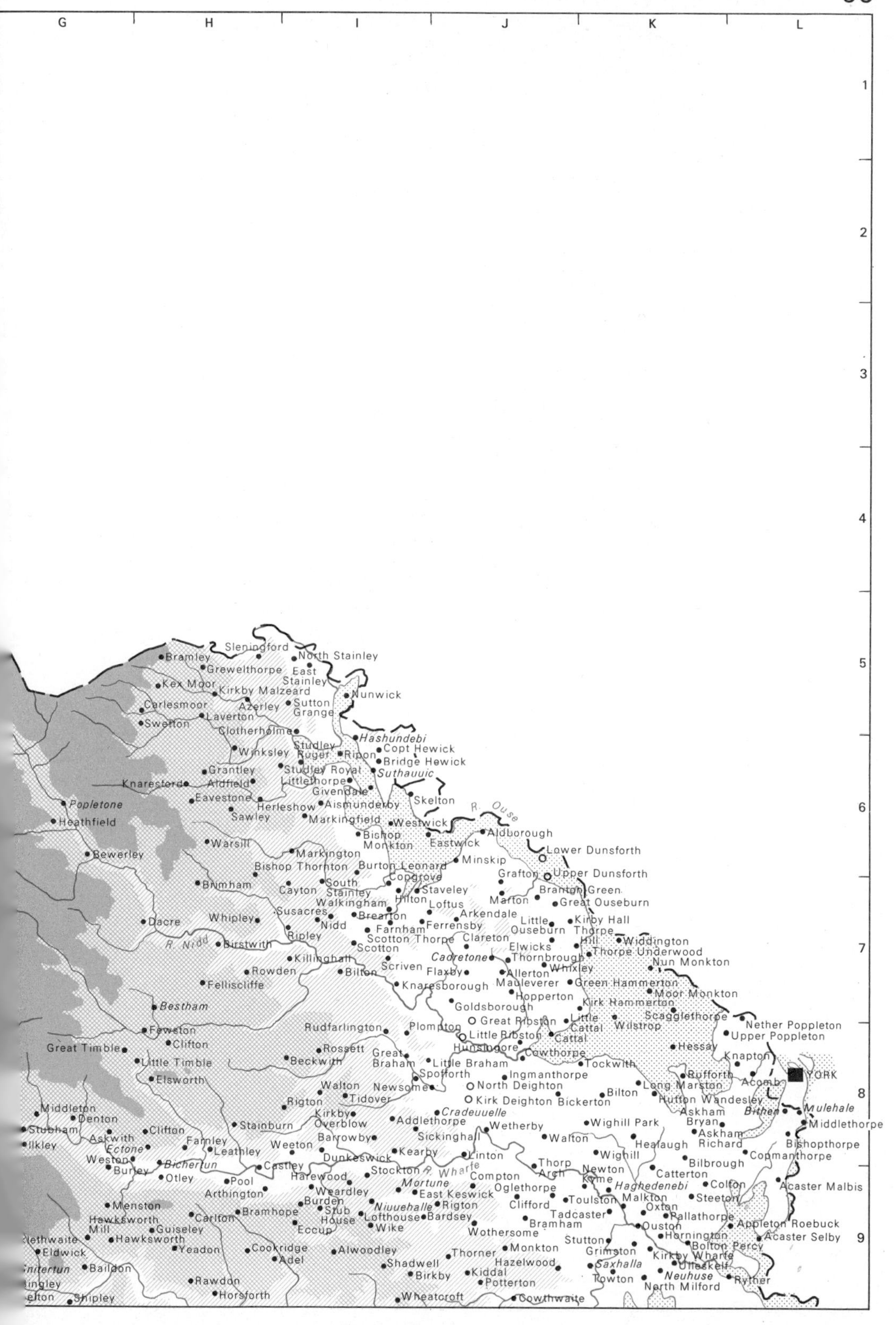
G
H
I
J
K
L
1
2
3
4
5
6
7
8
9
Sleningford
North Stainley
Bramley
Grewelthorpe
East
Stainley
Kex Moor
Kirkby Malzeard
Nunwick
Carlesmoor
Azerley
Sutton
Grange
Swetton
Laverton
Clotherholme
Hashundebi
Winksley
Studley
Roger
Ripon
Copt Hewick
Grantley
Studley Royal
Bridge Hewick
Suthauuic
Knaresford
Aldfield
Littlethorpe
Givendale
Eavestone
Skelton
Popletone
Herleshow
Aismunderby
Sawley
R. Ouse
Heathfield
Markingfield
Westwick
Bishop
Monkton
Eastwick
Aldborough
Warsill
Lower Dunsforth
Bewerley
Markington
Minskip
Bishop Thornton
Burton Leonard
Grafton
Upper Dunsforth
Brimham
Copgrove
South
Stainley
Cayton
Staveley
Branton Green
Hilton
Marton
Great Ouseburn
Walkingham
Loftus
Susacres
Arkendale
Dacre
Whipley
Brearton
Little
Ouseburn
Kirby Hall
Nidd
Farnham
Ferrensby
Thorpe
Ripley
Scotton Thorpe
Clareton
Hill
Widdington
R. Nidd
Birstwith
Scotton
Elwicks
Thorpe Underwood
Killinghall
Cadretone
Thornbrough
Nun Monkton
Rowden
Scriven
Bilton
Flaxby
Allerton
Whixley
Felliscliffe
Knaresborough
Mauleverer
Green Hammerton
Moor Monkton
Hopperton
Bestham
Goldsborough
Kirk Hammerton
Scagglethorpe
Rudfarlington
Plompton
Great Ribston
Little
Cattal
Wilstrop
Nether Poppleton
Fewston
Upper Poppleton
Clifton
Little Ribston
Cattal
Great Timble
Rossett
Hunsingore
Hessay
Great
Braham
Cowthorpe
Knapton
Little Timble
Beckwith
Little Braham
Tockwith
Spofforth
Rufforth
YORK
Elsworth
Ingmanthorpe
Acomb
Walton
Newsome
North Deighton
Long Marston
Tidover
Bilton
Hutton Wandesley
Rigton
Kirk Deighton
Bickerton
Middleton
Askham
Bithen
Mulehale
Denton
Kirkby
Overblow
Cradeuuelle
Bryan
Stubham
Stainburn
Addlethorpe
Wetherby
Wighill Park
Middlethorpe
Clifton
Askwith
Askham
Ilkley
Farnley
Sickinghall
Richard
Ectone
Weeton
Barrowby
Walton
Healaugh
Bishopthorpe
Leathley
Weston
Kearby
Wighill
Copmanthorpe
Burley
Bichertun
Dunkeswick
Linton
Bilbrough
Otley
Castley
Stockton
R. Wharfe
Thorp
Arch
Newton
Kyme
Catterton
Pool
Harewood
Compton
Acaster Malbis
Mortune
Haghedenebi
Colton
Weardley
Arthington
Oglethorpe
Menston
East Keswick
Toulston
Malkton
Steeton
Burden
Niuuehalle
Oxton
Stub
Rigton
Clifford
Hawksworth
Mill
Bramhope
Carlton
Lofthouse
Bardsey
Tadcaster
Pallathorpe
House
Bramham
Appleton Roebuck
Guiseley
Eccup
Wike
Ouston
Hawksworth
Wothersome
Acaster Selby
Eldwick
Yeadon
Cookridge
Alwoodley
Thorner
Monkton
Stutton
Hornington
Adel
Hazelwood
Grimston
Bolton Percy
Baildon
Shadwell
Kirkby Wharfe
Saxhalla
Ulleskelf
Birkby
Kiddal
Towton
Neuhuse
Ryther
Rawdon
Potterton
North Milford
Shipley
Horsforth
Wheatcroft
Cowthwaite

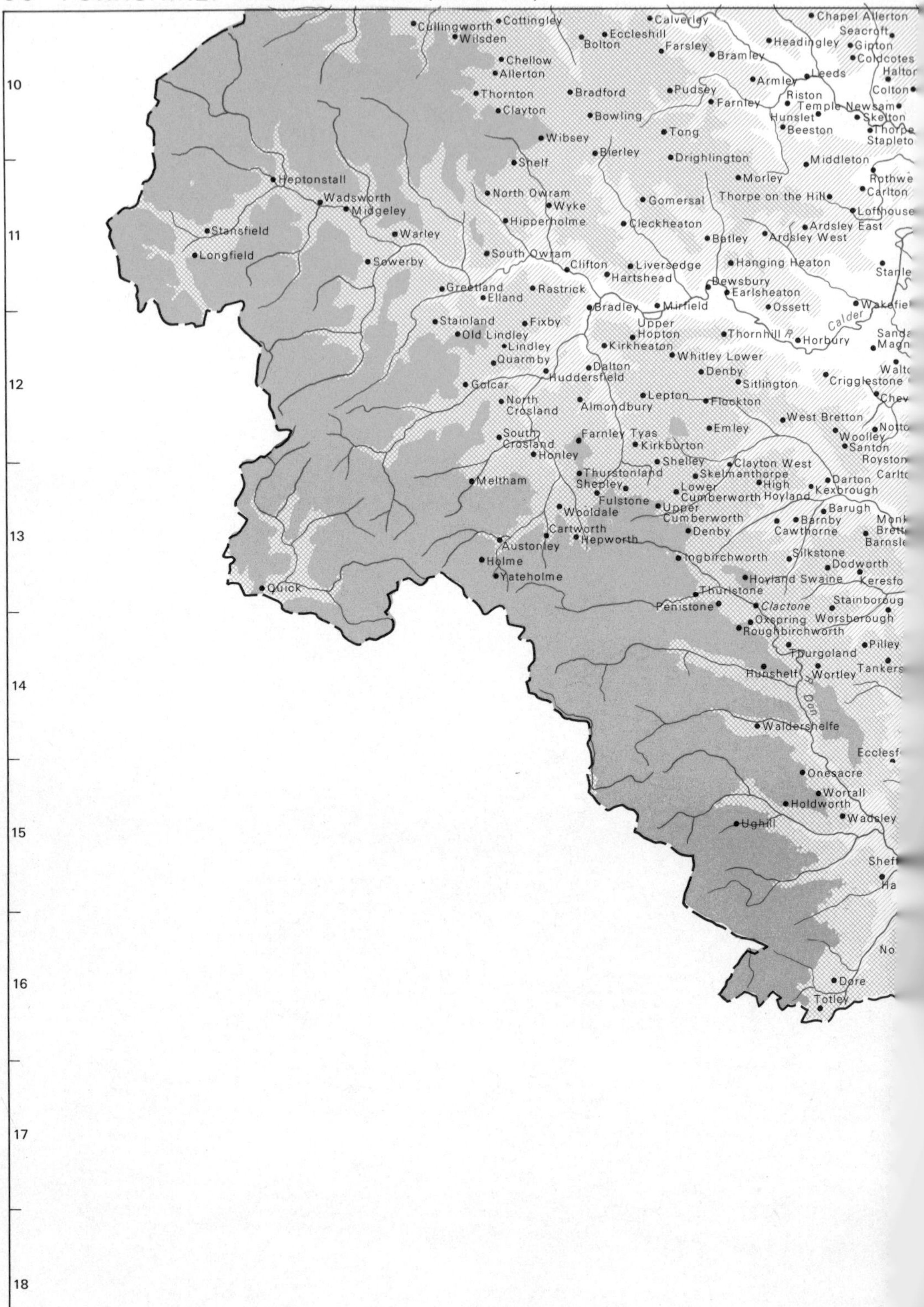

Cullingworth
Cottingley
Wilsden
Calverley
Eccleshill
Bolton
Farsley
Bramley
Chapel Allerton
Seacroft
Headingley
Gipton
Coldcotes
Chellow
Allerton
10
Thornton
Bradford
Pudsey
Armley
Leeds
Colton
Riston
Clayton
Farnley
Temple Newsam
Hunslet
Skelton
Bowling
Beeston
Tong
Wibsey
Bierley
Drighlington
Middleton
Shelf
Heptonstall
Morley
Wadsworth
North Owram
Thorpe on the Hill
Carlton
Midgeley
Gomersal
Wyke
Lofthouse
Hipperholme
Cleckheaton
Ardsley East
Stansfield
11
Warley
Batley
Ardsley West
Longfield
South Owram
Sowerby
Clifton
Liversedge
Hanging Heaton
Hartshead
Dewsbury
Greetland
Rastrick
Earlsheaton
Elland
Bradley
Mirfield
Ossett
Calder
Stainland
Fixby
Upper Hopton
Old Lindley
Thornhill
R.
Horbury
Lindley
Kirkheaton
Whitley Lower
Quarmby
Dalton
Denby
Huddersfield
12
Golcar
Sitlington
Criggleston
Lepton
North Crosland
Flockton
Almondbury
West Bretton
Emley
South Crosland
Farnley Tyas
Woolley
Kirkburton
Santon
Honley
Shelley
Clayton West
Thurstonland
Skelmanthorpe
Meltham
Shepley
Lower Cumberworth
High Hoyland
Darton
Kexbrough
Fulstone
Upper Cumberworth
Barugh
Wooldale
Barnby
13
Cartworth
Cawthorne
Denby
Austonley
Hepworth
Holme
Ingbirchworth
Silkstone
Dodworth
Yateholme
Hoyland Swaine
Quick
Thurlstone
Penistone
Clactone
Stainborough
Oxspring
Worsborough
Roughbirchworth
Pilley
Thurgoland
Hunshelf
Wortley
14
Don
Waldershelfe
Onesacre
Worrall
Holdworth
Wadsley
15
Ughill
16
Dore
Totley
17
18
D E F G H I

Barwick in Elmet
Saxton
Church Fenton
Lead
Parlington
Barkston
Little Fenton
Manston
Hunchilhuses
Shippen
Sturton Grange
Sherburn in Elmet
Garforth
Selby
Thorpe Willoughby
Swillington
Kippax
Hambleton
Brayton
Ledsham
Great Preston
R. Aire
Ledston
Burton
Barlow
Newton
Fairburn
R. Ouse
Allerton Bywater
Wheldale
Birkin
Drax
Methley
Water Fryston
Camblesforth
Little Airmyn
Ferry Fryston
Beal
Kellington
Roall
Whitwood
Ferrybridge
Carlton
Glass Houghton
Knottingley
Eggborough
Westerby
Hensall
Normanton
Featherstone
Snaith
Ackton
TANSHELF
Adlingfleet
Snydale
Whitley
Darrington
Purston Jaglin
Stapleton
Womersley
Crofton
West Hardwick
Ackworth
Walden Stubbs
Nostell
Little Smeaton
Hessle
Kirk Smeaton
Thorpe Audlin
Rogerthorpe
Norton
Ryhill
Kinsley
Badsworth
Campsall
Fishlake
Thorne
Hemsworth
Upton
Sutton
North Elmsall
Newsham
Kirk Bramwith
Minsthorpe
Skelbrooke
Burghwallis
Stainforth
Shafton
Moorthorpe
South Elmsall
Owston
South Bramwith
Tudworth
Brierley
South Kirkby
Hamphall Stubbs
Skellow
Hampole
Barnby Dun
Hatfield
Frickley
Adwick le Street
Hooton Pagnell
Kirk Sandall
Great Houghton
Clayton
Pickburn
Arksey
Deightonby
Brodsworth
Long Sandall
Little Houghton
Bilham
Langthwaite
Street Thorpe
Thurnscoe
Stotfold
Bentley
Marr
Hickleton
Scawsby
Wheatley
Darfield
Billingley
Goldthorpe
Cusworth
Armthorpe
Bolton upon Dearne
Barnbrough
Scinestorp
Doncaster
Wombwell
High Melton
Hexthorpe
Cantley
Tottes
Brampton Bierlow
West Melton
Adwick upon Dearne
Sprotbrough
Branton
Wildthorpe
Balby
Auckley
Wath upon Dearne
Newhill
Cadeby
Warmsworth
Mexborough
Eldeb'ge
Swinton
Denaby
Conisbrough
Loversall
Littleworth
Wentworth
Grimeshou
Edlington
Hooton Roberts
Wadworth
Rawmarsh
Clifton
Wilsic
Thryhergh
Stancil
Greasbrough
Ravenfield
R. Don
Braithwell
DADSLEY
Austerfield
Dalton
Stainton
Kimberworth
Rotherham
Hellaby
Wickersley
Bramley
Maltby
Hooton Levitt
Tinsley
Newhall
Whiston
Brinsworth
Slade Hooton
Attercliffe
Brampton en le Morthen
Treeton
Ulley
Laughton en le Morthen
Orgreave
Throapham
Aughton
Handsworth
Dinnington
Aston
Todwick
North Anston
South Anston
Wales
Kiveton
Harthill
Thorpe Salvin
10
11
12
13
14
15
16
17
18
J
K
L
M
N
O

62 YORKSHIRE: NORTH RIDING (EAST)

M
N
O
P
Q
R
1
2
3
4
5
6
7
8
9
Marske
Upleatham
Skelton
Brotton
Kilton
Loftus
Old Boulby
Easington
Seaton
Kilton Thorpe
South Loftus
Hinderwell
Rawcliff Banks
Little Moorsholm
Liverton
Roxby
Arnodestorp
Stainton
Borrowby
Newton Mulgrave
Moorsholm
Roskelthorpe
Ellerby
Goldsborough
Grimesbi
Mickleby
Lythe
Barnby
Mulgrave
Whitby
Ugthorpe
Dunsley
Flowergate
Prestby
Newholme
Baldebi
Hutton Mulgrave
Breck
High Stakesby
Sowerby
Aislaby
Gnipe Howe
Lealholme
Sneaton
Crunkly Gill
Danby
Hangton
Egton
R. Esk
Ugglebarnby
Hangton Hill
Normanby
Fyling Thorpe
Fyling Old Hall
Stainton Dales
Thirley Cotes
Cloughton
Burniston
Northfield
Hutton le Hole
Lastingham
Levisham
Hackness
Scalby
Gillamoor
Baschebi
Newton
Locton
Troutsdale
Suffield
Stemanesbi
Fadmoor
Spaunton
Cawthorn
Everley
Cropton
Appleton-le-Moors
Kettlethorpe
Falsgrave
Hoveton
Dalby
Kirkby Moorside
Wrelton
Blansby
Hill Grips
Burton Dale
Nawton
Sinnington
Aislaby
Kingthorpe
West Ayton
East Ayton
Deepdale
Welburn
Middleton
Little Edstone
Ellerburn
Preston
Thorpefield
Osgodby
Rodebestorp
Great Edstone
Farmanby
Wykeham
Newton
Irton
Cayton
Wombleton
Marton
Pickering
Thornton Dale
Ebberston
Martune
Hutton Buscel
Killerby
Eterstorp
Walton
Ruston
Seamer
Harome
Thornton Riseborough
Leidtorp
Wilton
Allerston
Snainton
Brompton
Lebberston
Scawthorpe
North Holme
Normanby
Gristhorpe
Riccall
Middelham
Little Barugh
Alia
Chiluesmersc
Nunnington
Salton
Kirby Misperton
Chigomersc
Little Marish
East Newton
Ness Hall
Loft Marishes
Great Barugh
Kirby
Aschelesmersc
Brawby
Maxudesmersc
Stonegrave
South Holme
Butterwick
Cawton
Little Habton
Ouduluesmersc
Great Habton
Salescale
Fryton
Newsham
Wykeham
Wath
Slingsby
Ryton
Wykeham Hill
Hawade
Barton-le-Street
Appleton-le-Street
Swinton
Amotherby
Broughton
Howthorpe
Old Malton
Wigganthorpe
Coneysthorpe
Terrington
Easthorpe
Ganthorpe
Hildenley
Henderskelfe
R. Derwent
Mowthorpe
Stittenham
Welburn
Bulmer
Low Hutton
Sheriff Hutton
West Lilling
Whitwell on the Hill
Foston
Thornton le Clay
Crambe
Flaxton
Barton-le-Willows
Harton
Barnby
Claxton
Bossall
Sandburn
Thorpe Hill
Sand Hutton
Buttercrambe
Carlton
Upper Helmsley
Stockton on the Forest
Gate Helmsley
Holtby
Murton

64 YORKSHIRE: NORTH RIDING (WEST)

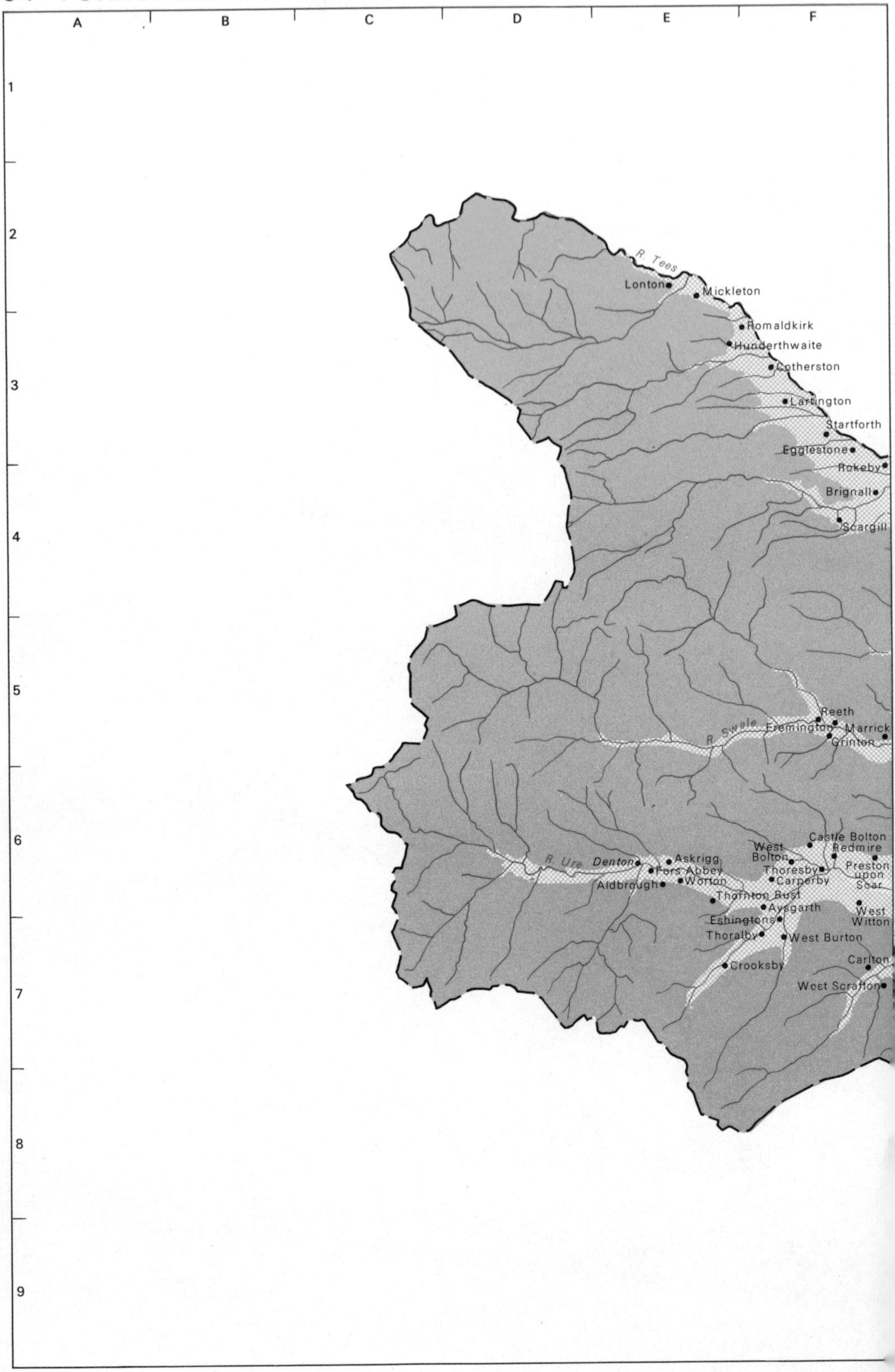

A
B
C
D
E
F
1
2
3
4
5
6
7
8
9
R. Tees
Lonton
Mickleton
Romaldkirk
Hunderthwaite
Cotherston
Lartington
Startforth
Egglestone
Rokeby
Brignall
Scargill
Reeth
R. Swale
Fremington
Marrick
Grinton
Castle Bolton
Redmire
West Bolton
Thoresby
Preston upon Scar
R. Ure
Denton
Askrigg
Fors Abbey
Worton
Aldbrough
Carperby
Thornton Rust
Aysgarth
West Witton
Eshingtons
Thoralby
West Burton
Crooksby
Carlton
West Scrafton